HARRAP'S
POCKET
ITALIAN
AND ENGLISH
DICTIONARY

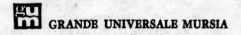
GRANDE UNIVERSALE MURSIA

HARRAP'S
POCKET
ITALIAN
AND ENGLISH
DICTIONARY

English-Italian/Italian-English

HARRAP

EDINBURGH
PARIS NEW YORK

Distributed in the United States by
PRENTICE HALL
New York

Hanno collaborato alla redazione del presente dizionario
Annamaria Fattore Maioechi e Ada Bichiacchi

First published as
Harrap's Compact Italian and English Dictionary
in 1968

First published in this edition in Great Britain 1988
by HARRAP BOOKS Ltd
43–45 Annadale Street, Edinburgh EH7 4AZ
© Copyright 1967 U. Mursia & Co., Milano, Via Tadimo 29

ISBN 0 245-54828-9

Reprinted 1990, 1991, 1993

In the United States, ISBN 0-13-383324-0

Library of Congress Cataloging-in-Publication Data

Harrap's pocket Italian-English dictionary : English-Italian/
Italian-English.
p.   cm.
"First published in this edition in Great Britain in 1988 by
Harrap Books Ltd." — T.p. verso.
ISBN 0-13-383324-0 : $10.00
1. Italian language — Dictionaries — English.
2. English language — Dictionaries — Italian.
PC1640.H344 1990   89-71137
453'.21 — dc20   CIP

Printed and bound in Great Britain by
Mackays of Chatham PLC, Chatham, Kent

NORME, REGOLE E INFORMAZIONI

NORME PER L'USO DEL DIZIONARIO

1. La parte iniziale del presente **Piccolo dizionario** comprende una serie di informazioni che valgono a completare l'opera, a facilitarne la consultazione o ad arricchire le conoscenze del lettore; tali si debbono considerare le **regole di pronuncia**, l'elenco dei **verbi irregolari inglesi**, la tabella di raffronto fra le **unità inglesi o americane e il sistema metrico**, le indicazioni relative al **sistema monetario inglese e americano**, l'elenco dei **numeri ordinali e cardinali** e, infine, l'**elenco delle abbreviazioni** usate nel dizionario stesso.

Inoltre comprende una serie di informazioni in inglese a facilitarne la consultazione per il lettore inglese.

2. La seconda parte comprende il **Compact English-Italian Dictionary** e reca in appendice un ampio elenco di **nomi propri, storici e geografici** (con la relativa traduzione in italiano), nonché l'elenco delle **sigle e abbreviazioni usate nei Paesi di lingua inglese** con l'indicazione dell'equivalente italiano.

3. La terza parte comprende il **Piccolo dizionario italiano-inglese** e reca in appendice un ampio elenco di **nomi propri, storici e geografici** (con la relativa traduzione in inglese), nonché l'elenco delle **sigle e abbreviazioni usate in Italia** con l'indicazione dell'equivalente inglese.

4. Nella parte **italiano-inglese**, i lemmi italiani non recano accento se si tratta di parole piane (es.: *violino, rosa, determinazione*); recano l'accento se si tratta di parole tronche (es.: *così, però, lassù*) o sdrucciole (es.: *richiùdere, rimpròvero, nàutico*) o bisdrucciole o terminanti in *ia, io* con l'accento sulla *i* (es.: *filosofìa, mormorìo*). Tali accenti sono tutti gravi, salvo nelle parole con accento su una *e*, nel qual caso ci si è attenuti a un criterio strettamente ortoepico (es.: *règola, desèrtico, maneggévole, pregévole*): si è, cioè, distinto fra accento grave (pronuncia aperta) e accento acuto (pronuncia chiusa).

5. Nel corpo delle singole voci sono stati ampiamente adottati, secondo la consuetudine generale dei grandi dizionari, i seguenti **segni grafici**:

a) la **doppia barra** (||) che sta a segnalare la peculiarità della fraseologia o una certa differenza di significato nell'ambito del lemma o il passaggio da un senso proprio a uno figurato o il passaggio dal significato corrente a uno più specialistico o, infine, l'inizio dell'elencazione di parole composte e di analoghe associazioni semantiche;

b) i **numeri arabi in neretto** (1., 2., 3. ecc.) che valgono ad attirare l'attenzione sui diversi significati in cui è stato possibile articolare una determinata voce del dizionario;

c) la **losanga nera** (♦) che sta a indicare il cambiamento di natura grammaticale che sopravviene internamente a due omonimi appartenenti a un medesimo gruppo etimologico (es.: passaggio da sostantivo maschile a sostantivo femminile; da sostantivo ad aggettivo; da aggettivo ad avverbio; da verbo transitivo a verbo riflessivo ecc.);

d) gli **esponenti in numeri arabi** (^{1}, ^{2}, ^{3} ecc.) che servono a distinguere parole omonime appartenenti però a gruppi etimologici diversi.

6. In entrambe le parti, nel caso di sostantivi che abbiano **numero diverso** nelle due lingue, si è data l'indicazione del numero stesso sùbito dopo il lemma. Es.: **fare** *sm.* manners (*pl.*) - **postage** *s.* spese postali (*pl.*) - **embers** *s. pl.* brace (*sing.*).

7. Per i **plurali irregolari inglesi** si sono usati i seguenti criteri:

a) nella parte **inglese-italiano** si è fatta seguire al lemma, fra parentesi, la forma plurale irregolare, per esteso - es.: **child** *s.* (*pl.* children) - nei casi generali o abbreviata - es.: **diagnosis** *s.* (*pl.* -ses) - nei casi di parole derivanti da altre lingue antiche o moderne. Nel primo caso i plurali sono stati elencati anche come voce a sé e con rimando: es.: **children** V. *child*;

b) nella parte **italiano-inglese** si è fatta seguire alla traduzione, fra parentesi, la forma plurale irregolare, per esteso - es.: **bambino** *sm.* child (*pl.* children) - nei casi generali o abbreviata - es.: **diàgnosi** *sf.* diagnosis (*pl.* -ses) - nei casi di parole derivanti da altre lingue antiche o moderne.

8. Per i **verbi irregolari inglesi** si sono usati i seguenti criteri:

a) nella parte **inglese-italiano** si è fatto seguire al lemma, fra parentesi, il paradigma: es.: to **bring (brought, brought)**. Le due forme del passato remoto e del participio passato sono state elencate anche come voce a sé e con rimando: es.: **brought** V. *to bring*;

b) nella parte **italiano-inglese** si è fatta seguire alla traduzione, fra parentesi, l'indicazione dell'irregolarità - es.: **costare** *vi.* to cost (*v. irr.*) - a meno che lo stesso verbo inglese ricorra più volte nell'ambito della stessa voce ed escludendo inoltre i due verbi ausiliari *to be* e *to have* (per i quali ultimi si suppone una costante attenzione del lettore circa l'irregolarità).

9. Per i **comparativi** e i **superlativi irregolari inglesi** sono stati seguiti analoghi criteri.

REGOLE DI PRONUNCIA

Alfabeto

L'alfabeto inglese è composto di 26 lettere, 5 in più dell'alfabeto italiano e precisamente: *j, k, w, x, y*. L'elenco completo delle lettere è il seguente:

a	(pron. *ei*)	**n**	(pron. *en*)
b	(pron. *bi*, con la *i* allungata)	**o**	(pron. *ou*)
c	(pron. *si*, con la *i* allungata e la *s* aspra, come in *sordo*)	**p**	(pron. *pi*, con la *i* allungata)
d	(pron. *di*, con la *i* allungata)	**q**	(pron. *chiù*)
e	(pron. *i*, con la *i* allungata)	**r**	(pron. *ar*, con la *a* allungata)
f	(pron. *ef*)	**s**	(pron. *es*, con la *s* aspra)
g	(pron. *gi*, con la *i* allungata)	**t**	(pron. *ti*, con la *i* allungata)
h	(pron. *eic*, con la *c* dolce)	**u**	(pron. *iù*)
i	(pron. *ai*)	**v**	(pron. *vi*, con la *i* allungata)
j	(pron. *gei*)	**w**	(pron. *dabliu*)
k	(pron. *kei*)	**x**	(pron. *ecs*)
l	(pron. *el*)	**y**	(pron. *uai*)
m	(pron. *em*)	**z**	(pron. *sed*, con la *s* dolce, come in *rosa*).

La pronuncia inglese è particolarmente difficile da apprendere ed è altresì difficile dare norme precise per l'apprendimento della stessa. Diamo comunque, qui di seguito, un elenco delle vocali, dei gruppi vocalici, delle consonanti e di alcuni gruppi consonantici con indicazioni approssimative sulla pronuncia.

Vocali

La vocale A ha vari suoni:

1. **ei** in sillaba tonica aperta come nella parola *tale* (racconto); nei gruppi **ange** e **aste** come nelle parole *danger* (pericolo) e *baste* (fretta);

2. **e** aperta in sillaba tonica chiusa come nella parola *cat* (gatto);

3. ha un suono incerto tra **e** aperta e **a** in sillabe atone iniziali o mediane come nelle parole *about* (circa) e *final* (finale);

4. **a** allungata quando è seguita da **r** finale (**r** muta) come nelle parole *car* (automobile) e *far* (lontano);

5. **ea** se è seguita da **re** finale (**e** aperta e **a** appena accennata) come nelle parole *care* (cura) e *dare* (sfida);

6. **o** breve in molti vocaboli che cominciano con il gruppo **qua** come in *quality* (qualità) e in *quantity* (quantità);

7. **o** aperta e prolungata se seguita da **l** o **ll** come in *all* (tutto), *tall* (alto);

nel gruppo a**lk** (l muta) come in *talk* (chiacchiera); preceduta da **w** (ma non seguita da **k** o **g**) come in *war* (guerra);

8. a allungata nei gruppi **ance, and, ant, ask, alf** (l muta), **ast, alm** (l muta), **aff, aft, asp** e **ath** quando la a è tonica;

9. i breve e velata nelle desinenze **age** e **ate** non accentate.

La vocale E ha vari suoni:

1. i allungata in sillaba tonica aperta come in *these* (questi) e nei monosillabi, come in *me* (me);

2. e aperta come nella parola italiana *bello*, in sillaba tonica chiusa, come in *let* (lasciare);

3. i come nella parola italiana *vita*, in sillaba atona, come in *repeat* (ripetere);

4. i brevissima quando è preceduta da **s, z, c, ch, sh, g** e seguita da **s** come in *roses* (rose) e quando è tra due dentali come in *rested* (riposato);

5. è muta in fine di parola come in *love* (amore) e nelle desinenze **es, ed,** come in *loves* (amori) e *loved* (amato);

6. eu francese quando è seguita da **r** in sillaba tonica, come in *term* (termine);

7. a gutturale quando è nel gruppo **er** in fine di parola, come in *letter* (lettera);

8. ia con la a appena accennata quando è seguita da **re** in fine di parola come in *severe* (severo) e in *mere* (semplice).

La vocale I ha vari suoni:

1. ai in sillaba tonica aperta, come in *fine* (bello) e in sillaba chiusa quando è seguita dai gruppi **gh** (muto), come in *high* (alto); **ght** (gh muto) come in *night* (notte); **gn** (g muta), come in *sign* (segno); **ld**, come in *child* (bambino) e **nd**, come in *mind* (mente);

2. i breve in sillaba tonica chiusa, come in *tin* (stagno);

3. eu francese, se seguita da **r** come in *fir* (abete);

4. aia, se seguita da **re** come in *fire* (fuoco).

La vocale O ha vari suoni:

1. ou (con la o chiusa) in sillaba tonica aperta, come in *home* (casa) e se seguita da **ld** come in *cold* (freddo);

2. o aperta e breve in sillaba tonica chiusa come in *not* (non);

3. o aperta e lunga se seguita da **r** come in *morning* (mattino);

4. oa se seguita da **re** in fine di parola come in *more* (più);

5. eu francese se preceduta da **w** e seguita da **r** come in *work* (lavoro);

6. u allungata nei seguenti vocaboli: *to do* (fare); *to move* (muovere); *to prove* (provare); *to lose* (perdere); *who* (chi); *two* (due); *tomb* (tomba); *womb* (grembo); *shoe* (scarpa); *wolf* (lupo); *woman* (donna);

7. **a** se preceduta da **w** e seguita da **n** come in *won* (vinto);
8. **ua** in *one* (uno).

La vocale **U** ha vari suoni:

1. **iù** in sillaba tonica aperta, come in *tune* (tono);
2. **a** in sillaba tonica chiusa, come in *but* (ma);
3. **u** allungata se preceduta da **l** o **r**, come in *Lucy* (Lucia) e *rule* (**regola**);
4. **u** breve, se preceduta da **b, f, p** e seguita da **l, ll, sh**, come in *bush* (cespuglio); *to push* (spingere); *bull* (toro); *full* (pieno); *to pull* (tirare);
5. **eu** francese se seguita da **r** in sillaba aperta, come in *fur* (pelliccia);
6. **iua** se seguita da **re** in fine di parola, come in *pure* (puro).

Gruppi vocalici

AI si pronuncia **ea** se seguito da **r**, come in *air* (aria).

AU, AW si pronunciano **o** allungata, come in *fraud* (frode) e *law* (legge).

EA si pronuncia **e** in circa 40 parole e loro composti; *bread* (pane); *dead* (morto); *death* (morte); *head* (testa); *heavy* (pesante) ecc.;
    i lunga in moltissime sillabe toniche: *beat* (calore); *meat* (carne);
    ei nelle seguenti parole: *great* (grande); *break* (rompere); *steak* (bistecca);
    eu francese se all'inizio di parola e seguito da **r** come in *earth* (terra);
    ea se in fine di parola seguito da **r**, come in *bear* (sopportare); in molte parole suona però **ia**, come in *tear* (lacrima), o **a** allungata, come in *heart* (cuore).

EE si pronuncia **i** allungata, come in *feeling* (sentimento).

EI si pronuncia **ei** in genere, come in *rein* (briglia);
    i se preceduto da sibilante, come in *ceiling* (soffitto).

EY si pronuncia **ei** in sillaba tonica, come in *prey* (preda);
    i in sillaba atona, come in *money* (denaro). L'eccezione più comune è *key* (chiave) che si pronuncia **ki**.

EU, EW si pronunciano **iù** come in *Europe* (Europa) e in *new* (nuovo).

IE si pronuncia **i** allungata come in *piece* (pezzo).

OI, OY si pronunciano **oi** come in *soil* (suolo) e *royal* (reale).

OA si pronuncia **ou** come in *boat* (barca).

OO si pronuncia **u** allungata come in *moon* (luna);
    u breve se seguita da **k** come in *book* (libro).
    Vi sono alcune eccezioni come *door* (porta) e *floor* (pavimento) dove il gruppo **oo** viene pronunciato **oa** e *blood* (sangue) e *flood* (alluvione) dove il gruppo **oo** viene pronunciato **a**.

OU, OW si pronunciano **au** come in *mouth* (bocca) e *now* (ora).

Consonanti

B è in generale pronunciata come in italiano; è però muta nei gruppi **bt** e **mb** in fine di parola, come in *debt* (debito) e *comb* (pettine).

C suona **s** aspra come nell'italiano *sordo* davanti a **e, i, y**, come in *cellar* (cantina), *city* (città) e *cyder* (sidro); suona **k** in fine di parola, come in *logic* (logico);
cce, cci, suonano **kse** e **ksi**;
ch suona **c** palatale come nell'italiano *città*, se seguito da vocale o in fine di parola; suona **k** in parole di origine greca o orientale. Suona **sc** come in italiano *sciare*, in parole di origine francese, come *machine* (macchina);
ck suona **k**;
tch suona **c** dolce.

G in fine di parola suona **g** gutturale come nell'italiano *gomma;*
ge, gi hanno suono palatale come nell'italiano *gesto, gita* in parole di origine latina; hanno suono gutturale in parole di origine germanica;
gh seguito da **t** o in fine di parola è muto;
gn ha la **g** muta quando le due lettere fanno parte della stessa sillaba, come in *sign* (segno); si pronunciano separate e la **g** ha suono gutturale quando le due lettere appartengono a due sillabe diverse, come in *signal* (segnale);
dge suona **g** palatale.

H è sempre aspirata tranne in *heir* (erede); *honest* (onesto); *honour* (onore) e *hour* (ora) e loro derivati.

J suona **g** palatale.

K è muta davanti a **n** come in *knee* (ginocchio).

L come in italiano.

M come in italiano.

N è nasale nei gruppi **ng** come in *ring* (anello) (la **g** è muta).

P suona **f** nei gruppi **ph**; è muta nel gruppo iniziale **psy**.

Q come in italiano.

R in genere, se mediana, non si pronuncia, ma allunga il suono della vocale che precede, come in *farm* (fattoria). Se è finale non si pronuncia.

S è in genere aspra all'inizio di parola o sillaba; è dolce se è posta tra due vocali;
sc suona **s** aspra se è seguita da **e, i, y**;
sh suona **sc** come nell'italiano *sciare.*
La **s** è muta in *aisle* (navata); *isle* e *island* (isola); *viscount* (visconte).

T ha due pronunce caratteristiche nel gruppo **th**:
a) un suono duro pronunciato con la lingua tra i denti, come in *thin* (sottile);
b) un suono dolce pronunciato con la lingua tra i denti, come in *this* (questo).

V come in italiano.

W in principio di parola suona **u** come in *west*; seguita da **r** è muta, come in *wrong* (sbagliato).

X finale ha il suono sordo **ks**; mediana può avere il suono sordo **ks** o il suono dolce **gs**; in principio di parola suona come la **s** dolce di *rosa.*

Y è semivocale; all'inizio di parola ha il suono consonantico **i**, come in *yes* (sì); ha tale suono anche in fine di polisillabi, come in *dignity* (dignità), e nel corpo della parola, come in *graveyard* (cimitero); in fine di monosillabi, invece, si pronuncia **ai**, come in *fly* (mosca) e in *cry* (grido).

Z s dolce di *rosa.*

Osservazioni

1. I gruppi finali **ble, cle, kle, gle** hanno la **l** appena accennata e le due consonanti vengono pronunciate staccate.

2. Nei gruppi **gua, gue, gui, build** e **cuit** finale la **u** è muta, come in *building* (fabbricato).

3. ough seguito da **t** si pronuncia **o** allungato, come in *thought* (pensiero); **ough** suona **of** in: *cough* (tosse) e *trough* (trogolo); suona **af** in: *enough* (abbastanza), *rough* (ruvido) e *tough* (duro); suona **au** in: *plough* (arare) e *bough* (ramo); suona **ou** in *though* (sebbene) e *dough* (pasta); suona **u** allungato in *through* (attraverso).

4. I gruppi **ci, sci, si, ti, xi** seguiti da vocale suonano **sc** come in *scelto*.

5. I gruppi finali **sten** e **stle** suonano rispettivamente **sn** e **sl**.

6. Il gruppo finale **sure** suona **ja** (**j** francese).

7. Il gruppo finale **ture** suona **cia** con la **a** allungata.

I SEGNI D'INTERPUNZIONE (PUNCTUATION MARKS)

,	*comma*	virgola
;	*semicolon*	punto e virgola
:	*colon*	due punti
.	*full stop*	punto
?	*question mark*	punto di domanda
!	*exclamation mark*	punto esclamativo
'	*apostrophe*	apostrofo
—	*dash*	lineetta
-	*hyphen*	trattino d'unione
« »	*quotation marks*	virgolette basse o quadre
' '	*inverted commas*	virgolette alte o inglesi
( )	*brackets*	parentesi rotonde
[ ]	*square brackets*	parentesi quadre
*	*asterisk*	asterisco
...	*dots*	puntini
	new paragraph	a capo
	full stop and new paragraph	punto e a capo
	capital letter	lettera maiuscola
	small letter	lettera minuscola

VERBI IRREGOLARI INGLESI [1]

Infinito	Passato	Participio passato	
to abide	abode	abode	dimorare
to arise	arose	arisen	sorgere
to awake*	awoke	awoke, awaked	svegliare, svegliarsi
to be	was	been	essere
to bear	bore	born, borne	sopportare, generare
to beat	beat	beaten, beat	battere
to become	became	become	diventare
to befall	befell	befallen	accadere
to beget	begot	begot, begotten	generare
to begin	began	begun	cominciare
to behold	beheld	beheld	mirare
to bend	bent	bent	piegare
to bereave*	bereft	bereft	orbare
to bet	bet	bet	scommettere
to bid	bade, bid	bidden, bid	ordinare
to bind	bound	bound	(ri)legare
to bite	bit	bitten, bit	mordere
to bleed	bled	bled	sanguinare
to blow	blew	blown	soffiare
to break	broke	broken	rompere
to breed	bred	bred	allevare
to bring	brought	brought	portare
to build	built	built	costruire
to burn*	burnt	burnt	bruciare
to burst	burst	burst	scoppiare
to buy	bought	bought	comperare
to cast	cast	cast	gettare, fondere
to catch	caught	caught	prendere, acchiappare
to chide*	chid	chid	sgridare
to choose	chose	chosen	scegliere
to cleave	cleft	cleft	fendere
to cling	clung	clung	attaccarsi
to come	came	come	venire
to cost	cost	cost	costare
to creep	crept	crept	strisciare
to cut	cut	cut	tagliare
to deal	dealt	dealt	trattare, commerciare
to dig*	dug	dug	scavare
to do	did	done	fare
to draw	drew	drawn	tirare, disegnare
to dream*	dreamt	dreamt	sognare
to drink	drank	drunk	bere
to drive	drove	driven	guidare
to dwell*	dwelt	dwelt	dimorare

[1] L'elenco, compilato per comodità del lettore, comprende i verbi di uso più comune. L'asterisco apposto accanto a un verbo indica l'esistenza, per il verbo stesso, di forme anche regolari.

to eat	ate, eat	eaten	mangiare
to fall	fell	fallen	cadere
to feed	fed	fed	nutrire
to feel	felt	felt	sentire, tastare
to fight	fought	fought	combattere
to find	found	found	trovare
to flee	fled	fled	fuggire
to fling	flung	flung	scagliare
to fly	flew	flown	volare
to forbid	forbade	forbidden	proibire
to forecast	forecast	forecast	predire
to forget	forgot	forgotten	dimenticare
to forgive	forgave	forgiven	perdonare
to forsake	forsook	forsaken	abbandonare
to freeze	froze	frozen	gelare
to get	got	got, gotten	ottenere, diventare
to gird	girt	girt	cingere
to give	gave	given	dare
to go	went	gone	andare
to grind	ground	ground	macinare
to grow	grew	grown	crescere, coltivare
to hang	hung	hung, hanged	appendere
to have	had	had	avere
to hear	heard	heard	udire
to hew*	hewed	hewn	recidere
to hide	hid	hidden, hid	nascondere
to hit	hit	hit	colpire
to hold	held	held	tenere, trattenere
to hurt	hurt	hurt	far male, ferire
to keep	kept	kept	tenere, conservare
to kneel*	knelt	knelt	inginocchiarsi
to knit*	knit	knit	lavorare a maglia
to know*	knew	known	conoscere, sapere
to lay	laid	laid	deporre, posare
to lead	led	led	condurre, guidare
to lean	leant	leant	appoggiarsi, inclinarsi
to leap	leapt	leapt	saltare
to learn*	learnt	learnt	imparare
to leave	left	left	lasciare, partire
to lend	lent	lent	prestare
to let	let	let	lasciare
to lie	lay	lain	giacere, trovarsi
to light*	lit	lit	accendere
to lose	lost	lost	perdere
to make	made	made	fare
to mean	meant	meant	intendere, significare
to meet	met	met	incontrare
to mislay	mislaid	mislaid	smarrire
to mislead	misled	misled	sviare
to mistake	mistook	mistaken	sbagliare
to mow*	mowed	mown	falciare
to pay	paid	paid	pagare
to put	put	put	mettere

to read	read	read	leggere
to rend	rent	rent	strappare
to ride	rode	ridden	cavalcare
to ring	rang	rung	suonare
to rise	rose	risen	alzarsi, sorgere
to run	ran	run	correre
to saw	sawed	sawn	segare
to say	said	said	dire
to see	saw	seen	vedere
to seek	sought	sought	cercare
to sell	sold	sold	vendere
to send	sent	sent	mandare
to set	set	set	porre
to sew	sewed	sewn	cucire
to shake	shook	shaken	scuotere, tremare
to shear*	sheared	shorn	tosare
to shed	shed	shed	spargere
to shine	shone	shone	brillare, splendere
to shoe	shod	shod	calzare
to shoot	shot	shot	sparare
to show	showed	shown	mostrare
to shred	shred	shred	tagliuzzare
to shrink	shrank, shrunk	shrunk, shrunken	restringersi
to shut	shut	shut	chiudere
to sing	sang	sung	cantare
to sink	sank, sunk	sunk	affondare
to sit	sat	sat	sedere
to slay	slew	slain	trucidare
to sleep	slept	slept	dormire
to slink	slunk	slunk	svignarsela
to smell*	smelt	smelt	fiutare, odorare
to sow*	sowed	sown	seminare
to speak	spoke	spoken	parlare
to spell	spelt	spelt	compitare
to spend	spent	spent	spendere
to spill*	spilt	spilt	spandere, versare
to spin	spun, span	spun	filare
to spit	spat, spit	spat, spit	sputare
to split	split	split	spaccare
to spoil	spoilt	spoilt	guastare, viziare
to spread	spread	spread	diffondere, stendere
to spring	sprang	sprung	saltare
to stand	stood	stood	stare (in piedi)
to steal	stole	stolen	rubare
to stick	stuck	stuck	appiccicare
to sting	stung	stung	pungere
to stink	stank, stunk	stunk	puzzare
to strike	struck	struck	battere, colpire
to strive	strove	striven	sforzarsi
to swear	swore	sworn	giurare
to sweat*	sweat	sweat	sudare
to sweep	swept	swept	spazzare
to swell*	swelled	swollen	gonfiare
to swim	swam	swum	nuotare
to swing	swung	swung	dondolare
to take	took	taken	prendere

to teach	taught	taught	insegnare
to tear	tore	torn	lacerare
to tell	told	told	dire, raccontare
to think	thought	thought	pensare
to thrive	throve	thriven	prosperare
to throw	threw	thrown	gettare
to thrust	thrust	thrust	spingere, gettare
to tread	trode	trod, trodden	calpestare
to understand	understood	understood	capire
to upset	upset	upset	capovolgere
to wake	woke	woke, woken	svegliare, svegliarsi
to wear	wore	worn	indossare, logorare
to weave	wove	woven	intrecciare, tessere
to weep	wept	wept	piangere
to win	won	won	vincere
to wind	wound	wound	serpeggiare
to withdraw	withdrew	withdrawn	ritirare, ritirarsi
to wring	wrung	wrung	torcere
to write	wrote	written	scrivere

TABELLA DI RAFFRONTO
FRA LE UNITÀ INGLESI O AMERICANE
E IL SISTEMA METRICO

	denominazione delle unità inglesi o americane	valore	equivalenza col sistema metrico *	equivalenza del sistema metrico con le unità inglesi **
misure lineari	pollice (inch - in)	—	2,54 cm	0,3937 (cm)
	piede (foot - ft)	12 in	0,304 m	3,28 (m)
	yarda (yard - yd)	3 ft	0,914 m	1,09 (m)
	fathom	6 ft	1,828 m	0,546 (m)
	miglio terrestre (statute mile)	5280 ft	1,609 km	0,621 (km)
	miglio inglese	5000 ft	1,523 km	0,656 (km)
	nodo (nautical mile)	6080 ft	1,853 km	0,539 (km)
superfici	pollice quadr. (square inch - sq.in)	—	6,45 cm²	0,155 (cm²)
	piede quadr. (square foot - sq.ft)	144 sq.in	829 cm²	10,76 (m²)
	yarda quadr. (square yard - sq.yd)	1296 sq.in	0,836 m²	1,196 (m²)
	miglio quadr. (square mile)	—	2,59 km²	0,386 (km²)
volumi e capacità	pollice cubo (cubic inch - cu.in)	—	16,38 cm³	0,061 (cm³)
	piede cubo (cubic foot - cu.ft)	1728 cu.in	28,32 dm³	0,0353 (dm³)
	yarda cubica (cubic yard - cu.yd)	27 cu.ft	0,764 m³	1,308 (m³)
	register ton	100 cu.ft	2,832 m³	0,353 (m³)
	oncia fluida americana (U.S. fl.oz)	1,8 cu.in	29,57 cm³	0,0338 (cm³)
	oncia fluida inglese (imp. fl.oz)	1,73 cu.in	28,4 cm³	0,0353 (cm³)
	bushel	8 gals	28,3 l	0,035 (l)
	gallone americano (U.S. gal)	231 cu.in	3,78 l	0,26 (l)
	gallone inglese (imp. gal)	277 cu.in	4,54 l	0,22 (l)
	pinta (pint)	1/8 gal	0,47 l	2,11 (l)
pesi	oncia avoirdupois (ounce - oz)	—	28,35 g	0,0352 (g)
	oncia troy (ounce troy - oz)	—	31,1 g	0,0321 (g)
	libbra avoirdupois (pound - lb)	16 oz.a.d.p.	453 g	2,204 (kg)
	libbra troy (pound - lb)	12 oz.t.	373 g	2,679 (kg)
	tonnellata americana (short ton - ton)	2000 lbs	907 kg	0,102 (t)
	tonnellata ingl. (long ton - ton)	2240 lbs	1016 kg	0,984 (t)

Con la graduale introduzione del sistema metrico, le unità di misura inglesi e americane diventeranno progressivamente meno diffuse.

* Coefficiente per il quale si deve moltiplicare il valore della grandezza per ottenere la misura nel sistema metrico.

** Coefficiente per il quale si deve moltiplicare il valore espresso nell'unità metrica segnato tra parentesi per ottenere la misura nel sistema inglese.

SISTEMA MONETARIO INGLESE
(Denaro circolante)
Unità base = **pound**, sterlina.

Monete (coins)

½p piece (half-penny), duecentesima parte della sterlina;
1p piece (one penny), centesima parte sterlina;
2p piece (two pence), cinquantesima parte della sterlina;
5p piece (five pence), ventesima parte della sterlina;
10p piece (ten pence), decima parte della sterlina;
50p piece (fifty pence), metà della sterlina.

Banconote (banknotes)

pound note (£1), sterlina carta;
five-pound note (£5), cinque sterline;
ten-pound note (£10), dieci sterline;
twenty-pound note (£20), venti sterline.

Monete nominali (nominal coins – usate nelle parcelle dei professionisti, prezzi par articoli di lusso, per libri, ecc.)

guinea (£1.05, 105p), ghinea, centocinque pence;
half (a) guinea (52 ½p), mezza ghinea, cinquantadue pence e mezzo.

SISTEMA MONETARIO AMERICANO
(Denaro circolante)
Unità base = **dollar**, dollaro.

Rame (copper):
cent o penny (1 c.), un centesimo di dollaro.

Lega di rame e nichel (copper and nickel alloy):
nickel o five cents (5 c.), cinque centesimi di dollaro.

Argento (silver):
dime (10 c.), dieci centesimi di dollaro;
quarter (25 c.), un quarto di dollaro;
half-dollar (50 c.), mezzo dollaro, cinquanta centesimi;
dollar ($ 1), dollaro (generalmente in banconota).

Banconote (bills):
si hanno tagli da $ 1, 2, 5, 10, 20, 50, 100, 500.
Esistono inoltre, sebbene non in circolazione normale, banconote da $ 1,000, 5,000 e 10,000.

I NUMERI

CARDINALI	ORDINALI
1 one	1° - 1st - the first
2 two	2° - 2nd - the second
3 three	3° - 3rd - the third
4 four	4° - 4th - the fourth
5 five	5° - 5th - the fifth
6 six	6° - 6th - the sixth
7 seven	7° - 7th - the seventh
8 eight	8° - 8th - the eighth
9 nine	9° - 9th - the ninth
10 ten	10° - 10th - the tenth
11 eleven	11° - 11th - the eleventh
12 twelve	12° - 12th - the twelfth
13 thirteen	13° - 13th - the thirteenth
14 fourteen	14° - 14th - the fourteenth
15 fifteen	15° - 15th - the fifteenth
16 sixteen	16° - 16th - the sixteenth
17 seventeen	17° - 17th - the seventeenth
18 eighteen	18° - 18th - the eighteenth
19 nineteen	19° - 19th - the nineteenth
20 twenty	20° - 20th - the twentieth
21 twenty-one	21° - 21st - the twenty-first
22 twenty-two	22° - 22nd - the twenty-second
30 thirty	30° - 30th - the thirtieth
40 forty	40° - 40th - the fortieth
50 fifty	50° - 50th - the fiftieth
60 sixty	60° - 60th - the sixtieth
70 seventy	70° - 70th - the seventieth
80 eighty	80° - 80th - the eightieth
90 ninety	90° - 90th - the ninetieth
100 one hundred	100° - 100th - the (one) hundredth
101 one hundred and one	101° - 101st - the one hundred and first
200 two hundred	200° - 200th - the two hundredth
1.000 one thousand	1.000° - 1,000th - the (one) thousandth
1.001 one thousand and one	1.001° - 1,001st - the one thousand and first
1.010 one thousand and ten	1.010° - 1,010th - the one thousand and tenth
10.009 ten thousand	10.000° - 10,000 the ten thousandth
100.000 one hundred thousand	100.000° - 100,000 the one hundred thousandth
200.000 two hundred thousand	200.000° - 200,000 the two hundred thousandth
1.000.000 one million	1.000.000° - 1,000,000 the one millionth

ELENCO DELLE ABBREVIAZIONI

abbr.	abbreviazione	*gen.*	genitivo
(aer.)	aeronautica	*general.*	generalmente
agg.	aggettivo	*(geogr.)*	geografia
(agr.)	agricoltura	*(geol.)*	geologia
(amer.)	americano, americanismo	*(geom.)*	geometria
		ger.	gerundio
amm.	amministrativo, amministrazione	*(gergo)*	gergo, gergale
		(giorn.)	giornalismo, giornalistico
(anat.)	anatomia		
(ant.)	anticamente, antiquato	*(giur.)*	giuridico
(arch.)	architettura	*(gramm.)*	grammatica
art.	articolo	*i.*	intransitivo
(arte)	arte, artistico	*id.*	idem
assol.	assoluto	*imp.*	impersonale
(astr.)	astronomia	*imperat.*	imperativo
attr.	attributo, attributivo	*ind.*	indicativo
aus.	ausiliare	*indef.*	indefinito
(auto)	automobilismo	*inf.*	infinito
avv.	avverbio	*int.*	interrogativo
(bot.)	botanica	*inter.*	interiezione, interiettivo
(biol.)	biologia	*(iron.)*	ironico
(chim.)	chimica	*irr.*	irregolare
(chir.)	chirurgia	*(itt.)*	ittiologia
(cine)	cinematografia	*(lat.)*	latino, latinismo
coll.	collettivo	*loc. avv.*	locuzione avverbiale
(comm.)	commercio, commerciale	*loc. cong.*	locuzione congiuntiva
comp.	comparativo	*loc. prep.*	locuzione prepositiva
compl.	complemento	*(lett.)*	letteratura, letterario
condiz.	condizionale	*m.*	maschile
cong.	congiunzione	*(mar.)*	marina, marittimo, marinaresco
(costr.)	costruzioni		
(cuc.)	cucina	*(mat.)*	matematica
(dial.)	dialettale	*(mecc.)*	meccanica
dif.	difettivo	*(med.)*	medicina
dim.	diminutivo	*(metal.)*	metallurgia
dimostr.	dimostrativo	*(mil.)*	militare
ecc., etc.	eccetera	*(min.)*	mineralogia, minerario
(eccl.)	ecclesiastico	*(mit.)*	mitologia
(econ.)	economia	*(mus.)*	musica
(edil.)	edilizia	*neg.*	negazione, negativo
(elettr.)	elettricità, elettrotecnica	*(neol.)*	neologismo
escl.	esclamativo, in esclamazione	*ogg.*	oggetto
		(ott.)	ottica
f.	femminile	*p.*	participio
(fam.)	familiare	*pass.*	passato
(farm.)	farmacia, farmaceutico	*pers.*	persona, personale
(ferr.)	ferrovia	*(pitt.)*	pittura
(fig.)	figurato	*pl.*	plurale
(fil.)	filosofia	*(poet.)*	poetico
(fis.)	fisica	*(pol.)*	politica
(foto)	fotografia	*(pop.)*	popolare
fut.	futuro	*poss.*	possessivo

pp.	participio passato	*sost.*	sostantivato
prep.	preposizione	*spec.*	specialmente
pred.	predicato, predicativo	*(sport)*	sport, sportivo
pres.	presente	*(spreg.)*	spregiativo
pron.	pronome, pronominale	*sthg.*	something
prov.	proverbio, proverbiale	*(stor.)*	storia
(psicol.)	psicologia	*superl.*	superlativo
qc.	qualcosa	*t.*	transitivo
qu.	qualcuno	*(teat.)*	teatro
r.	riflessivo	*(tec.)*	tecnica
(radio)	radiofonia	*(tel.)*	telefonia, telefono
rec.	reciproco	*(teol.)*	teologia
reg.	regolare	*(tip.)*	tipografia
rel.	relativo	*(tv.)*	televisione
(relig.)	religione	*(us.)*	uso, usato
s.	(dall'inglese) sostantivo	*v.*	verbo
s.	(dall'italiano) sostantivo maschile e femminile	*V.*	vedi
		(vezz.)	vezzeggiativo
semidif.	semidifettivo	*v. dif.*	verbo difettivo
sf.	sostantivo femminile	*vi.*	verbo intransitivo
sm.	sostantivo maschile	*(v. irr.)*	verbo irregolare
(scherz.)	scherzoso	*(volg.)*	volgare
(scol.)	scolastico	*vr.*	verbo riflessivo
(scult.)	scultura	*v. semidif.*	verbo semidifettivo
sing.	singolare	*vt.*	verbo transitivo
so.	someone	*(zool.)*	zoologia
sogg.	soggetto		

INGLESE-ITALIANO

A

a *art.* **1.** un, uno, una **2.** un certo || *once a week*, una volta alla settimana.

A *s.* (*mus.*) la.

aback *avv.* alla sprovvista.

abacus *s.* **1.** abaco **2.** pallottoliere.

abandon *s.* abbandono.

to abandon *vt.* abbandonare.

to abase *vt.* abbassare, umiliare.

abasement *s.* umiliazione.

to abash *vt.* confondere.

abashment *s.* confusione.

to abate *vt.* diminuire. ♦ **to abate** *vi.* placarsi (*di tempo atmosferico*).

abatement *s.* diminuzione.

abbess *s.* badessa.

abbey *s.* abbazia.

abbot *s.* abate.

abbreviation *s.* abbreviazione.

to abdicate *vt.* e *vi.* **1.** abdicare a **2.** dimettersi.

abdication *s.* abdicazione.

abdomen *s.* addome.

abdominal *agg.* addominale.

to abduct *vt.* rapire.

abduction *s.* rapimento.

abductor *s.* **1.** rapitore **2.** (*anat.*) abduttore.

aberration *s.* aberrazione.

abetter *s.* fautore.

abeyance *s.* sospensione.

to abhor *vt.* aborrire.

abhorrence *s.* aborrimento.

to abide (abode, abode) *vi.* abitare || *to — by*, conformarsi a.

ability *s.* abilità, capacità.

abject *agg.* abietto.

abjection *s.* abiezione.

abjuration *s.* abiura.

to abjure *vt.* abiurare.

ablation *s.* ablazione.

ablative *agg.* e *s.* ablativo.

able *agg.* capace || *to be — to*, essere in grado di, potere.

ablution *s.* abluzione.

abnegation *s.* **1.** abnegazione **2.** rinuncia.

abnormal *agg.* anormale.

aboard *avv.* e *prep.* a bordo.

abode V. *to abide.* ♦ **abode** *s.* dimora.

to abolish *vt.* abolire.

abolishment, abolition *s.* abolizione.

abolitionism *s.* abolizionismo.

abolitionist *agg.* e *s.* abolizionista.

abominable *agg.* abominevole.

to abominate *vt.* detestare.

abomination *s.* abominazione.

aboriginal *agg.* e *s.* aborigeno.

to abort *vi.* abortire.

abortion *s.* aborto.

abortive *agg.* abortivo.

to abound *vi.* abbondare.

about *avv.* **1.** circa **2.** intorno || *to be —*, stare per. ♦ **about** *prep.* **1.** intorno a **2.** presso di **3.** riguardo a.

above *prep.* **1.** al di sopra di **2.** più di || *— mentioned*, suddetto. ♦ **above** *avv.* in alto, sopra.

abrasion *s.* abrasione.

to abridge *vt.* **1.** abbreviare **2.** privare di.

abridg(e)ment *s.* **1.** abbreviazione, sommario **2.** privazione.

abroad *avv.* **1.** all'estero **2.** fuori.

to abrogate *vt.* abrogare.

abrogation *s.* abrogazione.

abrupt *agg.* **1.** scosceso **2.** brusco **3.** inaspettato.

abruptness *s.* **1.** ripidezza **2.** rudezza **3.** precipitazione.

abscess *s.* ascesso.

abscissa *s.* ascissa.

absence *s.* assenza.

absent *agg.* assente || *— -minded*, distratto; *— -mindedness*, distrazione.

to absent *vt.* *to — oneself*, assentarsi.

absenteeism *s.* assenteismo.

absinth(e) *s.* assenzio.

absolute *agg.* e *s.* assoluto.

absolution *s.* assoluzione.

absolutism *s.* assolutismo.

absolutist *agg.* e *s.* assolutista.

to absolve *vt.* assolvere.

to absorb *vt.* assorbire.

absorbent *agg.* e *s.* assorbente.

absorption *s.* assorbimento.

to abstain *vi.* astenersi.

abstemious *agg.* sobrio.

abstention *s.* astensione.

abstentionist *s.* astensionista.

abstinence *s.* astinenza.

abstract *agg.* astratto. ♦ **abstract** *s.* **1.** astrazione **2.** estratto.

to abstract *vt.* **1.** astrarre **2.** estrarre **3.** sottrarre **4.** riassumere.

abstraction *s.* **1.** astrazione **2.** distrazione **3.** furto.

abstractly *avv.* astrattamente.

abstruse *agg.* astruso.

abstruseness *s.* astrusità.

absurd *agg.* assurdo.
absurdity *s.* assurdità.
absurdly *avv.* assurdamente.
abundance *s.* abbondanza.
abundant *agg.* abbondante.
abuse *s.* 1. abuso 2. ingiuria.
to **abuse** *vt.* 1. abusare 2. ingiuriare.
abusive *agg.* 1. abusivo 2. ingiurioso.
abysm, abyss *s.* abisso.
abysmal, abyssal *agg.* abissale.
academic *agg. e s.* accademico.
academician *s.* accademico.
academy *s.* accademia: — *of music,* conservatorio.
acanthus *s.* acanto.
acarus *s.* (*pl.* -ri) acaro.
to **accelerate** *vt.* accelerare.
acceleration *s.* accelerazione.
accelerative *agg.* accelerativo.
accelerator *s.* acceleratore.
accent *s.* accento.
to **accent** *vt.* 1. accentare 2. accentuare.
to **accentuate** V. *to accent.*
accentuation *s.* accentuazione.
to **accept** *vt.* accettare, approvare.
acceptable *agg.* accettabile.
acceptance *s.* 1. accettazione 2. consenso.
acceptation *s.* accezione, significato.
access *s.* accesso.
accessible *agg.* accessibile.
accession *s.* 1. assunzione (*al trono*) 2. adesione 3. aggiunta.
accessory *agg. e s.* 1. accessorio 2. complice.
accident *s.* 1. caso: *by —,* per caso 2. incidente 3. irregolarità.
accidental *agg.* accidentale.
to **acclaim** *vt.* acclamare.
acclamation *s.* acclamazione.
acclimation, acclimatization *s.* acclimazione, acclimatazione.
to **acclimate,** to **acclimatize** *vt.* acclimatare. ♦ to **acclimate,** to **acclimatize** *vi.* acclimatarsi.
to **accommodate** *vt.* 1. adattare 2. ospitare 3. fornire.
accommodating *agg.* accomodante.
accommodation *s.* 1. accomodamento 2. comodità 3. alloggio 4. (*comm.*) facilitazione.
accompaniment *s.* accompagnamento.
accompanist *s.* (*mus.*) accompagnatore.
to **accompany** *vt.* accompagnare

(*anche mus.*).
accomplice *s.* complice.
to **accomplish** *vt.* compiere, realizzare.
accomplishment *s.* 1. compimento 2. compitezza 3. dote.
accord *s.* accordo.
to **accord** *vt.* accordare. ♦ to **accord** *vi.* accordarsi.
accordance *s.* accordo.
accordant *agg.* concorde, conforme.
according *agg.* 1. concordante, conforme 2. armonioso. ♦ **according** *avv.* — *as,* secondo che; — *to,* secondo.
accordingly *avv.* 1. in conseguenza 2. conformemente.
accordion *s.* fisarmonica.
accordionist *s.* fisarmonicista.
account *s.* 1. (*comm.*) conto 2. (*comm.*) acconto 3. valore 4. resoconto || *to take into —,* prendere in considerazione; *on — of,* a causa di.
to **account** *vt.* considerare || *to — for,* essere responsabile di.
accountable *agg.* responsabile.
accountancy *s.* ragioneria.
accountant *s.* contabile || *chartered —,* ragioniere.
to **accredit** *vt.* accreditare.
to **accrue** *vi.* 1. derivare 2. accumularsi.
to **accumulate** *vt.* accumulare. ♦ to **accumulate** *vi.* accumularsi.
accumulation *s.* accumulazione.
accumulative *agg.* accumulativo.
accumulator *s.* accumulatore.
accuracy *s.* esattezza.
accurate *agg.* esatto.
accusation *s.* accusa.
accusative *agg. e s.* accusativo.
to **accuse** *vt.* accusare.
accused *s.* accusato.
accuser *s.* accusatore.
to **accustom** *vt.* abituare.
accustomed *agg.* 1. abituale 2. abituato.
ace *s.* asso.
acetone *s.* acetone.
acetylene *s.* acetilene.
ache *s.* dolore.
to **ache** *vi.* far male: *my head aches,* mi fa male la testa.
to **achieve** *vt.* 1. compiere 2. ottenere.
achievement *s.* 1. compimento 2. conseguimento 3. gesta.
aching *agg.* 1. doloroso 2. afflitto.

♦ **aching** s. dolore.
acid agg. e s. acido.
acidity s. acidità.
acidulous agg. acidulo.
to **acknowledge** vt. riconoscere || to — receipt of, accusare ricevuta di.
acknowledg(e)ment s. riconoscimento.
acolyte s. accolito.
acorn s. ghianda.
acoustic(al) agg. acustico.
acoustics s. acustica.
to **acquaint** vt. informare || to become acquainted with, fare la conoscenza di.
acquaintance s. conoscenza.
acquiescence s. acquiescenza.
to **acquire** vt. acquisire, acquistare.
acquisition s. acquisto.
to **acquit** vt. 1. pagare 2. liberare 3. assolvere.
acquittal s. (giur.) assoluzione.
acquittance s. 1. saldo 2. quietanza.
acrid agg. acre.
acridity s. asprezza.
acrimony s. acrimonia.
acrobat s. acrobata.
acrobatic(al) agg. acrobatico.
acrobatics s. pl. acrobazia (sing.).
acropolis s. acropoli.
across avv. per traverso. ♦ **across** prep. attraverso || to come —, incontrare.
act s. atto, legge.
to **act** vt. e vi. 1. agire, fare 2. (teat.) recitare.
acting agg. facente funzione di. ♦ **acting** s. 1. azione 2. (teat.) rappresentazione.
action s. 1. azione 2. (giur.) processo 3. (mecc.) funzionamento.
active agg. attivo.
activism s. attivismo.
activist s. attivista.
activity s. attività.
actor s. attore.
actress s. attrice.
actual agg. reale.
actuality s. realtà.
actually avv. realmente.
to **actuate** vt. mettere in moto.
acuminate agg. acuminato.
acute agg. acuto.
ad s. V. advertisement.
adamantine agg. adamantino.
to **adapt** vt. adattare.
adaptable agg. adattabile.
adaptation s. adattamento.

to **add** vt. aggiungere || to — up, fare una somma.
addendum s. (pl. -da) aggiunta.
adder s. vipera.
addict s. tossicomane.
addition s. 1. (mat.) addizione 2. aggiunta.
additional agg. supplementare.
address s. 1. indirizzo 2. abilità. ♦ **addresses** s. pl. omaggi.
to **address** vt. e vi. indirizzare, arringare. ♦ to **address** vi. rivolgersi.
addressee s. destinatario.
addresser s. mittente.
to **adduce** vt. addurre.
adenoids s. pl. adenoidi.
adept agg. e s. perito, esperto.
adequate agg. adeguato.
to **adhere** vi. aderire.
adherence s. aderenza, adesione.
adherent agg. e s. aderente.
adhesion s. V. adherence.
adhesive agg. e s. adesivo.
adipose agg. adiposo.
adjacent agg. adiacente.
adjective agg. 1. aggettivale 2. addizionale. ♦ **adjective** s. aggettivo.
to **adjoin** vt. 1. aggiungere 2. essere contiguo.
adjoining agg. adiacente.
to **adjourn** vt. aggiornare.
adjournment s. aggiornamento.
adjunct s. 1. aggiunta 2. aggiunto 3. (gramm.) complemento.
adjuration s. implorazione.
to **adjust** vt. 1. aggiustare 2. adattare 3. regolare.
adjustment s. 1. adattamento, compromesso 2. (comm.) liquidazione.
adjutant s. aiutante.
to **administer** vt. 1. amministrare 2. fornire. ♦ to **administer** vi. contribuire.
administration s. 1. amministrazione 2. somministrazione.
administrative agg. amministrativo.
administrator s. amministratore.
admirable agg. ammirabile.
admiral s. ammiraglio.
admiralty s. ammiragliato.
admiration s. ammirazione.
to **admire** vt. ammirare.
admirer s. ammiratore.
admiringly avv. con ammirazione.
admissible agg. ammissibile.
admission s. 1. ammissione 2. con-

fessione.

to admit *vt.* **1.** ammettere **2.** contenere.

admittance *s.* ammissione, ingresso.

to admonish *vt.* ammonire.

admonition *s.* ammonimento.

ado *s.* **1.** fatica **2.** confusione.

adolescence *s.* adolescenza.

adolescent *agg.* e *s.* adolescente.

to adopt *vt.* adottare.

adoption *s.* adozione.

adoptive *agg.* adottivo.

adorable · *agg.* adorabile.

adoration *s.* adorazione.

to adore *vt.* adorare.

to adorn *vt.* adornare.

adornment *s.* ornamento.

adrenalin *s.* adrenalina.

adrift *avv.* alla deriva.

to adulate *vt.* adulare.

adulation *s.* adulazione.

adulator *s.* adulatore.

adult *agg.* e *s.* adulto.

to adulterate *vt.* adulterare.

adulteration *s.* adulterazione.

adulterer *s.* adultero.

adulteress *s.* adultera.

adulterine *agg.* adulterino.

adultery *s.* adulterio.

advance *s.* **1.** avanzamento **2.** anticipo **3.** approccio.

to advance *vt.* **1.** portar avanti **2.** anticipare (*denaro*) **3.** (*comm.*) aumentare. ♦ **to advance** *vi.* avanzare.

advancement *s.* **1.** avanzamento **2.** (*comm.*) rialzo.

advantage *s.* vantaggio || *to take —, of*, approfittare di.

to advantage *vt.* avvantaggiare.

advantageous *agg.* vantaggioso.

advent *s.* avvento.

adventure *s.* avventura.

to adventure *vt.* rischiare. ♦ **to adventure** *vi.* avventurarsi.

adventurer *s.* avventuriero.

adventurous *agg.* avventuroso.

adverb *s.* avverbio.

adverbial *agg.* avverbiale.

adversary *s.* avversario.

adverse *agg.* avverso.

adversity *s.* avversità.

to advert *vi.* alludere, riferirsi.

to advertise *vt.* e *vi.* fare pubblicità a, divulgare.

advertisement *s.* **1.** avviso **2.** cartellone pubblicitario **3.** inserzione.

advertiser *s.* inserzionista.

advertising *agg.* pubblicitario. ♦ **advertising** *s.* pubblicità.

advice *s.* **1.** consiglio **2.** notizia.

advisability *s.* opportunità.

advisable *agg.* consigliabile.

to advise *vt.* **1.** consigliare **2.** avvisare || *to — with so.*, consultarsi con qu.

advised *agg.* giudizioso.

adviser *s.* consigliere.

advocacy *s.* avvocatura.

advocate *s.* difensore.

aegis *s.* egida.

Aeolian *agg.* eolio.

to aerate *vt.* **1.** aerare **2.** gassare.

aeration *s.* **1.** aerazione **2.** (*chim.*) aggiunta di acido carbonico.

aerial *agg.* aereo. ♦ **aerial** *s.* (*radio*) antenna.

aerodrome *s.* aerodromo.

aerodynamics *s.* aerodinamica.

aeronaut *s.* aeronauta.

aeronautics *s.* aeronautica.

aeroplane *s.* aeroplano.

aerostat *s.* aerostato.

aerostatics *s.* aerostatica.

aesthete *s.* esteta.

aesthetic(al) *agg.* estetico.

aestheticism *s.* estetismo.

aesthetics *s.* estetica.

aestivation *s.* letargo estivo.

aether *s.* etere.

afar *avv.* lontano.

affability *s.* affabilità.

affable *agg.* affabile.

affair *s.* **1.** affare **2.** tresca.

to affect[1] *vt.* **1.** ostentare **2.** simulare.

to affect[2] *vt.* **1.** concernere **2.** commuovere **3.** (*med.*) intaccare.

affectation *s.* affettazione.

affected *agg.* **1.** affettato **2.** affetto **3.** commosso **4.** disposto.

affection *s.* **1.** affetto **2.** (*med.*) affezione.

affectionate *agg.* affezionato, affettuoso.

affective *agg.* affettivo.

to affiliate *vt.* affiliare. ♦ **to affiliate** *vi.* affiliarsi.

affiliation *s.* affiliazione.

affinity *s.* affinità, parentela.

to · affirm *vt.* **1.** affermare **2.** ratificare.

affirmation *s.* **1.** affermazione **2.** ratificazione.

affirmative *agg.* affermativo || *in the —*, affermativamente.

to affix *vt.* aggiungere, apporre.

to **afflict** *vt.* affliggere.
affliction *s.* afflizione.
affluence *s.* 1. affluenza 2. abbondanza.
affluent *agg.* ricco. ♦ **affluent** *s.* (*geogr.*) affluente.
afflux *s.* afflusso.
to **afford** *vt.* offrire || *can* —, potersi permettere.
to **afforest** *vt.* imboschire.
afforestation *s.* imboschimento.
affront *s.* affronto || *to take* — *at,* offendersi per.
to **affront** *vt.* 1. affrontare 2. insultare.
afloat *avv.* a galla. ♦ **afloat** *agg.* 1. galleggiante 2. in circolazione.
afore *avv.* precedentemente. ♦ **afore** *prep.* prima di.
aforementioned, aforesaid *agg.* predetto.
afraid *agg.* spaventato || *to be* —, temere.
African *agg.* e *s.* africano.
after *agg.* seguente. ♦ **after** *prep.* 1. dopo, dietro 2. secondo 3. alla maniera di. ♦ **after** *avv.* dopo. ♦ **after** *cong.* dopo che.
afternoon *s.* pomeriggio.
afterthought *s.* riflessione.
afterward(s) *avv.* poi.
again *avv.* ancora, di nuovo.
against *prep.* 1. contro 2. in previsione di.
agape *agg.* e *avv.* a bocca aperta.
age *s.* 1. età 2. secolo || *old* —, vecchiaia; *to be of* —, essere maggiorenne; *to be under* —, essere minorenne; *Middle Ages,* Medioevo.
to **age** *vt.* e *vi.* invecchiare.
aged *agg.* 1. vecchio 2. dell'età di.
agency *s.* 1. causa, azione 2. (*comm.*) agenzia, rappresentanza.
agent *s.* agente.
agglomerate *agg.* e *s.* agglomerato.
to **agglomerate** *vt.* agglomerare. ♦ to **agglomerate** *vi.* agglomerarsi.
agglomeration *s.* agglomerazione.
to **agglutinate** *vt.* agglutinare. ♦ to **agglutinate** *vi.* agglutinarsi.
to **aggravate** *vt.* 1. aggravare 2. irritare.
aggravation *s.* 1. aggravamento 2. esasperazione.
aggregate *agg.* e *s.* aggregato.
to **aggregate** *vt.* 1. aggregare 2. ammontare a. ♦ to **aggregate** *vi.* aggregarsi.

aggregation *s.* aggregazione.
aggression *s.* aggressione.
aggressive *agg.* aggressivo.
aggressiveness *s.* aggressività.
aggressor *s.* aggressore.
aghast *agg.* 1. atterrito 2. stupefatto.
agile *agg.* agile.
agility *s.* agilità.
to **agitate** *vt.* agitare.
agitation *s.* agitazione.
agitator *s.* agitatore.
agnostic *agg.* e *s.* agnostico.
ago *agg.* e *avv.* fa.
agonistic(al) *agg.* agonistico.
to **agonize** *vt.* tormentare. ♦ to **agonize** *vi.* 1. tormentarsi 2. agonizzare.
agony *s.* 1. agonia 2. dolore.
agrarian *agg.* e *s.* agrario.
to **agree** *vt.* e *vi.* 1. accordarsi 2. accettare 3. essere adatto.
agreeable *agg.* 1. gradevole 2. conforme.
agreement *s.* 1. accordo 2. conformità 3. consenso.
agricultural *agg.* agricolo.
agriculture *s.* agricoltura.
agronomist *s.* agronomo.
agronomy *s.* agronomia.
ague *s.* febbre malarica.
ahead *avv.* avanti.
aid *s.* aiuto.
to **aid** *vt.* aiutare, soccorrere.
to **ail** *vt.* affliggere. ♦ to **ail** *vi.* sentirsi male.
aileron *s.* alettone.
aim *s.* 1. mira 2. scopo.
to **aim** *vt.* e *vi.* 1. mirare 2. aspirare a.
aimless *agg.* senza scopo.
air *s.* aria || — *conditioning,* condizionamento d'aria; — *lift,* ponte aereo; —*line,* aviolinea; —*raid,* incursione aerea; — -*mail,* posta aerea.
to **air** *vt.* aerare.
aircraft *s.* aereo, aerei || — -*carrier,* portaerei.
airfield *s.* campo d'aviazione.
airiness *s.* leggerezza, disinvoltura.
airing *s.* 1. ventilazione 2. passeggiata.
to **air-mail** *vt.* trasportare per via aerea.
airman *s.* aviatore.
airport *s.* aeroporto.
airship *s.* aeronave.
airsickness *s.* mal d'aria.

airstrip s. pista (d'areoporto).
airtight agg. a tenuta d'aria.
airway s. via aerea.
airy agg. **1.** arioso **2.** aereo **3.** gaio.
aisle s. navata (laterale).
ajar avv. socchiuso.
akin agg. **1.** consanguineo **2.** simile.
alacrity s. alacrità.
alarm s. allarme || — -clock, sveglia; to take —, allarmarsi.
to alarm vt. allarmare.
alas inter. ahimè.
Albanian agg. e s. albanese.
albatross s. albatro.
albumen s. albume.
albumin s. albumina.
alchemist s. alchimista.
alchemy s. alchimia.
alcohol s. alcool: wood —, alcool metilico.
alcoholic agg. alcolico. ♦ **alcoholic** sm. alcolizzato.
alcoholism s. alcoolismo.
alcove s. alcova.
alder s. ontano.
alderman s. assessore.
ale s. birra || —house, birreria.
aleatory agg. aleatorio.
alembic s. alambicco.
alert agg. **1.** all'erta **2.** svelto. ♦ **alert** s. allarme.
algebraic(al) agg. algebrico.
alien agg. e s. **1.** estraneo **2.** straniero.
to alienate vt. alienare.
alienation s. alienazione.
alienist s. alienista.
alight agg. illuminato.
to alight vi. **1.** scendere **2.** posarsi, atterrare.
to align vt. allineare. ♦ **to align** vi. allinearsi.
alignment s. allineamento.
alike agg. simile. ♦ **alike** avv. similmente.
aliment s. alimento.
alimentary agg. alimentare.
alimentation s. alimentazione.
aliquot agg. e s. aliquota.
alive agg. **1.** vivo **2.** vivace **3.** sensibile.
alkaline agg. alcalino.
all agg. tutto, tutti, ogni || — the way, lungo tutto il cammino. ♦ **all** pron. tutto, tutti || not at —, niente affatto; — the better, tanto meglio || — of us, noi tutti; it is — up, tutto è finito. ♦ **all** avv. completamente, interamente || —

right, va bene; — but, quasi. ♦ **all** s. tutto, totalità.
to allege vt. adurre.
allegiance s. fedeltà.
allegoric(al) agg. allegorico.
allegory s. allegoria.
allergic agg. allergico.
allergy s. allergia.
to alleviate vt. alleviare.
alleviation s. alleviamento.
alley s. vialetto, vicolo.
alliance s. **1.** alleanza **2.** unione.
allied agg. alleato.
alligator s. alligatore.
alliteration s. allitterazione.
alliterative agg. allitterativo.
to allocate vt. assegnare, distribuire.
allocution s. allocuzione.
to allot vt. assegnare.
allotment s. **1.** distribuzione **2.** lotto (di terreno).
to allow vt. **1.** permettere **2.** riconoscere **3.** concedere.
allowance s. **1.** permesso **2.** assegno, indennità **3.** razione **4.** riconoscimento **5.** sconto.
alloy s. (metal.) lega.
to allude vi. alludere.
to allure vt. attrarre.
allurement s. allettamento.
allusion s. allusione.
allusive agg. allusivo.
alluvion s. alluvione.
ally s. alleato.
to ally vt. **1.** unire **2.** alleare. ♦ **to ally** vi. allearsi.
almanac s. almanacco.
almighty agg. onnipotente: the Almighty, l'Onnipotente.
almond s. mandorla || — -tree, mandorlo.
almost avv. quasi.
alms s. elemosina || — -house, ospizio per i poveri; — -man, accattone.
alone agg. e avv. solo.
along avv. e prep. **1.** lungo **2.** avanti.
alongside avv. (mar.) accanto, accosto. ♦ **alongside** prep. a fianco di, lungo.
aloof avv. a distanza. ♦ **aloof** agg. riservato, scontroso.
aloofness s. freddezza.
aloud avv. ad alta voce.
alp s. alpe.
alpha s. alfa.
alphabet s. alfabeto.
alphabetic(al) agg. alfabetico.

alpine *agg.* alpino.

already *avv.* già.

also *avv.* anche, inoltre.

altar *s.* altare || — *-boy,* chierichetto; — *-piece,* pala d'altare.

to **alter** *vt.* alterare. ♦ to **alter** *vi.* alterarsi, trasformarsi.

alteration *s.* alterazione.

altercation *s.* alterco.

alternacy *s.* alternanza.

alternate *agg.* alterno, alternato.

to **alternate** *vt.* alternare. ♦ to **alternate** *vi.* alternarsi.

alternation *s.* alternazione.

alternative *agg.* alternativo. ♦ **alternative** *s.* alternativa.

alternator *s.* (*elettr.*) alternatore.

although *cong.* benché.

altimeter *s.* altimetro.

altitude *s.* **1.** altitudine **2.** (*aer.*) quota.

altogether *avv.* interamente.

altruism *s.* altruismo.

altruist *s.* altruista.

altruistic *agg.* altruistico.

aluminium *s.* alluminio.

always *avv.* sempre.

amalgam *s.* amalgama.

to **amalgamate** *vt.* amalgamare. ♦ to **amalgamate** *vi.* amalgamarsi.

amalgamation *s.* amalgamazione.

amaranth *s.* amaranto.

to **amass** *vt.* ammucchiare.

amateur *agg.* e *s.* amatore, dilettante.

amateurism *s.* dilettantismo.

to **amaze** *vt.* stupire.

amazement *s.* sorpresa.

amazing *agg.* sorprendente.

Amazon *s.* amazzone.

ambages *s. pl.* ambagi.

ambassador *s.* ambasciatore.

amber *s.* ambra.

ambient *agg.* circostante. ♦ **ambient** *s.* ambiente.

ambiguity *s.* ambiguità.

ambiguous *agg.* ambiguo.

ambit *s.* ambito.

ambition *s.* ambizione.

ambitious *agg.* ambizioso.

ambivalence *s.* ambivalenza.

ambivalent *agg.* ambivalente.

amble *s.* ambio.

ambo *s.* ambone.

ambulance *s.* ambulanza.

ambush *s.* imboscata.

to **ambush** *vt.* e *vi.* tendere una imboscata (a).

to **ameliorate** *vt.* e *vi.* migliorare.

to **amend** *vt.* emendare. ♦ to **amend** *vi.* emendarsi.

amendment *s.* emendamento.

amends *s.* ammenda.

amenity *s.* amenità.

American *agg.* e *s.* americano.

Americanism *s.* americanismo.

amethyst *s.* ametista.

amiability *s.* amabilità.

amiable *agg.* amabile.

amiably *avv.* amabilmente.

amianthus *s.* amianto.

amicable *agg.* amichevole.

amid *prep.* in mezzo a, tra, fra.

amiss *avv.* a male; *to take sthg.* —, aversene a male. ♦ **amiss** *agg.* inopportuno, errato.

amity *s.* amicizia.

ammonia *s.* ammoniaca.

ammunition *s.* munizioni.

amnesty *s.* amnistia.

to **amnesty** *vt.* amnistiare.

amoeba *s.* ameba.

among(st) *prep.* tra, fra (*più di due*); in mezzo a.

amoral *agg.* amorale.

amorality *s.* amoralità.

amorous *agg.* amoroso.

amorphous *agg.* amorfo.

to **amortize** *vt.* (*comm.*) ammortizzare.

amount *s.* **1.** somma **2.** totale **3.** valore **4.** quantità.

to **amount** *vi.* **1.** ammontare **2.** equivalere.

amperometer *s.* amperometro.

amphibian *agg.* e *s.* anfibio.

amphibious *agg.* anfibio.

amphitheatre *s.* anfiteatro.

amphitryon *s.* anfitrione.

amphora *s.* anfora.

ample *agg.* ampio.

amplification *s.* amplificazione.

amplifier *s.* amplificatore.

to **amplify** *vt.* amplificare. ♦ to **amplify** *vi.* dilungarsi.

to **amputate** *vt.* amputare.

amputation *s.* amputazione.

amulet *s.* amuleto.

to **amuse** *vt.* divertire.

amusement *s.* divertimento.

an *art.* V. *a.*

anachronic *agg.* anacronistico.

anachronism *s.* anacronismo.

anachronistic(al) *agg.* anacronistico.

anaemia *s.* anemia.

anaemic *agg.* anemico.

anaesthesia *s.* anestesia.

anaesthetic *agg.* e *s.* anestetico.
anaesthetist *s.* anestesista.
to **anaesthetize** *vt.* anestetizzare.
anagram *s.* anagramma.
anal *agg.* anale.
analgesic *agg.* e *s.* analgesico.
analogic(al) *agg.* analogico.
analogous *agg.* analogo.
analogy *s.* analogia.
to **analyse** *vt.* analizzare.
analysis *s.* (*pl.* -ses) analisi.
analyst *s.* analista.
analytic(al) *agg.* analitico.
anarchic(al) *agg.* anarchico.
anarchism *s.* anarchia.
anarchist *s.* anarchico.
anarchy *s.* anarchia.
anathema *s.* anatema.
anatomic(al) *agg.* anatomico.
anatomist *s.* anatomista.
to **anatomize** *vt.* anatomizzare.
anatomy *s.* anatomia.
ancestor *s.* antenato.
ancestral *agg.* ancestrale.
ancestry *s.* stirpe.
anchor *s.* (*mar.*) ancora.
to **anchor** *vt.* ancorare. ♦ to **anchor** *vi.* ancorarsi.
anchorage *s.* ancoraggio.
anchoret *s.* anacoreta.
anchovy *s.* acciuga.
ancient *agg.* e *s.* antico.
and *cong.* e.
androgynous *agg.* androgino.
anecdote *s.* aneddoto.
anecdotic(al) *agg.* aneddotico.
anew *avv.* di nuovo.
anfractuosity *s.* anfrattuosità.
anfractuous *agg.* anfrattuoso.
angel *s.* angelo: *guardian* —, angelo custode.
angelic(al) *agg.* angelico.
anger *s.* collera.
to **anger** *vt.* irritare.
angle *s.* (*geom.*) angolo ‖ *at right angles*, perpendicolarmente.
to **angle** *vi.* **1.** pescare (*con l'amo*) **2.** *to* — *for*, andare in cerca di.
angler *s.* pescatore (*con l'amo*).
Anglican *agg.* e *s.* anglicano.
Anglo-Saxon *agg.* e *s.* anglosassone.
angrily *avv.* irosamente.
angry *agg.* irato, arrabbiato ‖ *to get* —, adirarsi.
anguish *s.* angoscia.
to **anguish** *vt.* angosciare. ♦ to **anguish** *vi.* angosciarsi.
angular *agg.* angolare.
anhydride *s.* anidride.

aniline *s.* anilina.
animadversion *s.* biasimo.
to **animadvert** *vi.* criticare: *to* — *on so., sthg.*, criticare qu., qc.
animal *agg.* e *s.* animale.
to **animate** *vt.* animare.
animatedly *avv.* animatamente.
animation *s.* animazione.
animator *s.* animatore.
animism *s.* animismo.
animosity *s.* animosità.
anise *s.* anice.
ankle *s.* caviglia.
ankylosis *s.* anchilosi.
annals *s. pl.* annali.
Annelida *s. pl.* anellidi.
to **annex** *vt.* annettere.
annexation *s.* annessione.
to **annihilate** *vt.* annichilire.
annihilation *s.* annichilimento.
anniversary *s.* anniversario.
to **annotate** *vt.* e *vi.* annotare.
annotation *s.* annotazione.
to **announce** *vt.* annunciare.
announcement *s.* annuncio.
announcer *s.* annunciatore.
to **annoy** *vt.* infastidire.
annoyance *s.* fastidio.
annoying *agg.* fastidioso.
annual *agg.* annuale. ♦ **annual** *s.* annuario.
annuity *s.* rendita annuale.
to **annul** *vt.* annullare.
annulment *s.* annullamento.
to **annunciate** *vt.* annunciare.
annunciation *s.* annuncio, annunciazione.
anode *s.* anodo.
anodyne *agg.* e *s.* anodino.
to **anoint** *vt.* ungere, consacrare.
anomalous *agg.* anomalo.
anomaly *s.* anomalia.
anonym *s.* anonimo.
anonymous *agg.* anonimo.
another *agg.* e *pron.* un altro ‖ *one* —, l'un l'altro.
answer *s.* risposta.
to **answer** *vt.* e *vi.* rispondere.
ant *s.* formica ‖ — *-bear*, formichiere.
antagonism *s.* antagonismo.
antagonist *s.* antagonista.
Antarctic *agg.* antartico.
antecedent *agg.* e *s.* antecedente. ♦ **antecedents** *s. pl.* antenati.
to **antedate** *vt.* **1.** antidatare **2.** anticipare.
antediluvian *agg.* e *s.* antidiluviano.

antelope s. antilope.

anteroom s. anticamera.

anthem s. inno.

anthological agg. antologico.

anthology s. antologia.

anthracite s. antracite.

anthropocentric agg. antropocentrico.

anthropologist s. antropologo.

anthropology s. antropologia.

anthropomorphic agg. antropomorfo.

anthropomorphism s. antropomorfismo.

anthropomorphous agg. antropomorfo.

anthropophagous agg. e s. (pl. -gi) antropofago.

anthropophagy s. antropofagia.

antiaesthetic agg. antiestetico.

anti-aircraft agg. antiaereo.

antibiotic agg. e s. antibiotico.

antibody s. anticorpo.

to **anticipate** vt. 1. anticipare 2. prevedere 3. pregustare.

anticipation s. 1. anticipo 2. previsione 3. pregustazione.

anticlerical agg. anticlericale.

anticlericalism s. anticlericalismo.

anticonceptive s. antifecondativo.

anticonstitutional agg. anticostituzionale.

anticyclone s. anticiclone.

anti-dazzle agg. antiabbagliante.

antidote s. antidoto.

anti-freeze s. anticongelante.

anti-gas agg. antigas.

antimilitarism s. antimilitarismo.

antimilitarist s. antimilitarista.

antimony s. antimonio.

antinomy s. antinomia.

antiparticle s. antiparticella.

antipathetic(al) agg. avverso.

antipathy s. antipatia.

antiphon(y) s. antifona.

antipodal agg. degli, agli antipodi.

antipode s. antipodo.

antiquarian agg. e s. antiquario.

antiquary s. antiquario.

antiquated agg. antiquato.

antique agg. antico. ♦ **antique** s. antichità || — dealer, antiquario.

antiquity s. antichità.

antirheumatic agg. antireumatico.

anti-rust agg. e s. antiruggine.

anti-Semite s. antisemita.

anti-Semitism s. antisemitismo.

antiseptic agg. e s. antisettico.

antisocial agg. antisociale.

antispasmodic agg. e s. antispasmodico.

anti-tank agg. anticarro.

antitetanic agg. antitetanico.

anti-theft agg. e s. antifurto.

antithesis s. (pl. -ses) antitesi.

antithetic(al) agg. antitetico.

antitoxic agg. antitossico.

anus s. ano.

anvil s. incudine.

anxiety s. ansietà.

anxious agg. ansioso.

any agg. 1. qualunque 2. (in frasi neg.; int.; dubitative) qualche, nessuno, del || at — rate, in ogni modo. ♦ **any** pron. 1. alcuno, nessuno 2. ne || have you — bread?, hai del pane?; I haven't —, non ne ho.

anybody pron. 1. chiunque 2. (in frasi neg.; int.; dubitative) qualcuno, nessuno.

anyhow avv. e cong. comunque.

anyone pron. V. anybody.

anything pron. 1. qualunque cosa 2. (in frasi neg.; int.; dubitative) qualche cosa, niente.

anyway avv. in ogni modo, comunque.

anywhere avv. dovunque.

apace avv. presto.

apanage s. appannaggio.

apart avv. 1. a parte 2. lontano.

apartheid s. discriminazione razziale.

apartment s. alloggio (in affitto).

apathy s. apatia.

ape s. scimmia.

to **ape** vt. scimmiottare.

aperitif s. aperitivo.

apex s. apice.

aphaeresis s. aferesi.

aphonia s. afonia.

aphorism s. aforisma.

aphrodisiac agg. e s. afrodisiaco.

aphtha s. afta.

apiece avv. a testa.

apish agg. scimmiesco.

apocalypse s. apocalisse.

apocalyptic(al) agg. apocalittico.

apocrypha s. pl. libri apocrifi.

apocryphal agg. apocrifo.

apogee s. apogeo.

apologetic(al) agg. apologetico.

apologist s. apologista.

to **apologize** vi. scusarsi.

apologue s. apologo.

apology s. scusa.

apoplexy s. apoplessia.

apostasy s. apostasia.
apostate agg. e s. apostata.
apostle s. apostolo.
apostolate s. apostolato.
apostolic(al) agg. apostolico.
apostrophe s. apostrofo.
to **apostrophize** vt. apostrofare.
apothecary s. farmacista.
apotheosis s. (pl. -ses) apoteosi.
to **appal** vt. spaventare.
appalling agg. spaventoso.
apparatus s. apparato.
apparent agg. 1. visibile, evidente 2. (giur.) legittimo.
apparition s. apparizione.
appeal s. 1. appello 2. attrattiva.
to **appeal** vi. 1. appellarsi 2. attrarre.
appealing agg. 1. supplichevole 2. attraente.
to **appear** vi. 1. apparire 2. sembrare.
appearance s. 1. apparenza, aspetto 2. apparizione.
to **appease** vt. placare.
appeasement s. pacificazione, tregua.
appellative agg. e s. appellativo.
appendicitis s. appendicite.
appendix s. appendice.
appetite s. appetito.
appetizer s. aperitivo.
appetizing agg. appetitoso.
to **applaud** vt. e vi. applaudire.
applauding agg. plaudente.
applause s. applauso.
apple s. mela || — -tree, melo.
appliance s. 1. applicazione 2. apparecchio.
applicant s. richiedente.
application s. 1. applicazione 2. domanda.
to **apply** vt. applicare. ♦ to **apply** vi. 1. applicarsi 2. rivolgersi.
to **appoint** vt. 1. fissare 2. nominare, assegnare.
appointee s. persona designata.
appointment s. 1. appuntamento 2. nomina 3. impiego.
apposition s. apposizione.
appraisal s. stima.
to **appraise** vt. stimare.
appreciable agg. apprezzabile.
to **appreciate** vt. 1. apprezzare 2. rendersi conto di. ♦ to **appreciate** vi. aumentare di valore.
appreciation s. 1. apprezzamento 2. aumento di valore.
to **apprehend** vt. assodare.

apprehension s. 1. apprensione 2. percezione 3. arresto.
apprehensive agg. 1. apprensivo 2. perspicace.
apprentice s. apprendista.
apprenticeship s. apprendistato.
approach s. 1. avvicinamento 2. approccio 3. impostazione (di una pratica ecc.).
to **approach** vt. avvicinare. ♦ to **approach** vi. avvicinarsi.
approachable agg. accessibile.
appropriate agg. appropriato.
to **appropriate** vt. 1. appropriarsi di 2. stanziare.
appropriation s. 1. appropriazione 2. stanziamento.
approval s. 1. approvazione 2. (comm.) prova: on —, in prova.
to **approve** vt. 1. approvare 2. mostrare.
approximate agg. approssimativo.
to **approximate** vt. approssimare. ♦ to **approximate** vi. approssimarsi.
approximation s. approssimazione.
approximative agg. approssimativo.
apricot s. albicocca || — -tree, albicocco.
April s. aprile.
apron s. 1. grembiale 2. riparo 3. (teat.) proscenio.
apse s. abside.
apt agg. 1. atto 2. intelligente 3. proclive.
aptitude, aptness s. 1. idoneità 2. intelligenza 3. proprietà (di vocabolo).
aqualung s. autorespiratore.
aquamarine s. acquamarina.
aquarium s. acquario.
aquatic(al) agg. acquatico.
aqueduct s. acquedotto.
aqueous agg. acqueo, acquoso.
Arab agg. e s. arabo.
arabesque s. arabesco.
Arabian agg. e s. arabo.
Arabic agg. arabico.
arable agg. arabile.
arbiter s. arbitro.
arbitrage s. arbitraggio.
arbitrary agg. arbitrario.
to **arbitrate** vt. e vi. arbitrare.
arbitrator s. (giur.) arbitro.
arboreal, arboreous agg. arboreo.
arboriculture s. arboricoltura.
arbour s. pergolato.
arc s. arco.
arcade s. galleria.

Arcadian *agg.* e *s.* arcadico.
arch *s.* arco.
to arch *vt.* **1.** fabbricare ad arco **2.** inarcare. ♦ **to arch** *vi.* inarcarsi.
archaeologic(al) *agg.* archeologico.
archaeologist *s.* archeologo.
archaeology *s.* archeologia
archaic(al) *agg.* arcaico.
archaism *s.* arcaismo.
archangel *s.* arcangelo.
archbishop *s.* arcivescovo
archduke *s.* arciduca.
archer *s.* arciere.
archetype *s.* archetipo.
archipelago *s.* arcipelago.
architect *s.* architetto.
architectonic, architectural *agg.* architettonico.
architecture *s.* architettura.
archive *s.* archivio.
archivist *s.* archivista.
Arctic *agg.* e *s.* artico.
ardent *agg.* ardente.
ardour *s.* ardore.
arduous *agg.* arduo.
area *s.* area.
arena *s.* (*arch.*) arena.
Areopagus *s.* areopago.
argent *s.* argenteo.
Argentine *agg.* e *s.* argentino.
argil *s.* argilla.
to argue *vi.* **1.** discutere **2.** ragionare. ♦ **to argue** *vt.* dimostrare.
argument *s.* **1.** discussione **2.** argomentazione.
arid *agg.* arido.
aridity *s.* aridità.
to arise (arose, arisen) *vi.* **1.** alzarsi **2.** (*fig.*) nascere.
aristocracy *s.* aristocrazia.
aristocrat *s.* aristocratico.
aristocratic(al) *agg.* aristocratico.
Aristotelian *agg.* e *s.* aristotelico.
arithmetic *s.* aritmetica.
arithmetic(al) *agg.* aritmetico.
arm[1] *s.* braccio || — -*in*- —, a braccetto.
arm[2] *s.* arma || *coat of arms*, stemma.
to arm *vt.* armare. ♦ **to arm** *vi.* armarsi.
armament *s.* armamento.
armchair *s.* poltrona.
armful *s.* bracciata.
armistice *s.* armistizio.
armless *agg.* inerme.
armlet *s.* braccialetto.
armour *s.* corazza.
to armour *vt.* corazzare || *armour-*

ed-car, autoblinda.
armoury *s.* **1.** arsenale **2.** armeria.
armpit *s.* ascella.
army *s.* esercito.
aromatic(al) *agg.* aromatico.
arose V. *to arise.*
around *avv.* intorno. ♦ **around** *prep.* **1.** intorno a **2.** circa.
to arouse *vt.* **1.** destare **2.** eccitare.
to arrange *vt.* **1.** accomodare **2.** predisporre **3.** (*mus.*) arrangiare.
arrangement *s.* **1.** accomodamento **2.** (*mus.*) arrangiamento **3.** dispositivo. ♦ **arrangements** *s. pl.* preparativi.
arras *s.* arazzo.
array *s.* **1.** apparato **2.** (*mil.*) spiegamento.
to array *vt.* **1.** ornare **2.** (*mil.*) schierare.
arrest *s.* arresto.
to arrest *vt.* arrestare.
arrival *s.* arrivo.
to arrive *vi.* arrivare.
arrogance *s.* arroganza.
arrogant *agg.* arrogante.
to arrogate *vt.* arrogarsi.
arrow *s.* freccia.
arsenal *s.* arsenale.
arsenic *s.* arsenico.
art *s.* arte.
arteriosclerosis *s.* arteriosclerosi.
artery *s.* arteria.
artesian *agg.* artesiano.
artful *agg.* **1.** abile **2.** artificioso **3.** astuto.
arthritic(al) *agg.* artritico.
arthritis *s.* artrite.
artichoke *s.* carciofo.
article *s.* articolo.
articulate *agg.* **1.** articolato **2.** chiaro.
to articulate *vt.* articolare. ♦ **to articulate** *vi.* articolarsi.
articulation *s.* articolazione.
artifice *s.* **1.** artificio **2.** abilità.
artificial *agg.* artificiale.
artificiality *s.* artificiosità.
artillery *s.* artiglieria.
artilleryman *s.* artigliere.
artist *s.* artista.
artistic(al) *agg.* artistico.
artistry *s.* abilità artistica.
artless *agg.* ingenuo.
Aryan *agg.* e *s.* ariano.
as *avv.* come || — ... —, tanto ... quanto; *so* — (*con infinito*), in modo da; — *for*, quanto a; — *far* —, sin dove, fino a; — *much*, al-

trettanto; — *well*, come pure. ♦ **as** *cong.* **1.** poiché **2.** mentre.

asbestos *s.* asbesto.

to **ascend** *vi.* ascendere. ♦ to **ascend** *vt.* risalire, scalare.

ascendancy *s.* ascendente.

ascendant *agg. e s.* ascendente.

ascension *s.* ascensione.

ascent *s.* ascesa.

to **ascertain** *vt.* accertarsi di.

ascertainment *s.* accertamento.

ascetic *s.* asceta.

ascetic(al) *agg.* ascetico.

asceticism *s.* ascetismo.

to **ascribe** *vt.* ascrivere.

asepsis *s.* asepsi.

aseptic *agg. e s.* asettico.

asexual *agg.* asessuale.

ash *s.* cenere || — *-tray*, portacenere.

ash(-tree) *s.* frassino.

ashamed *agg.* vergognoso || *to be* —, aver vergogna.

ashore *avv.* a terra.

ashy *agg.* cinereo.

Asiatic *agg. e s.* asiatico.

aside *avv.* a parte, da parte.

asininity *s.* asinità.

to **ask** *vt. e vi.* **1.** chiedere **2.** invitare || *to* — *so. for sthg.*, chiedere a qu. qc.; *to* — *for trouble*, cercar fastidi.

askance *avv.* di traverso.

asker *s.* interrogante.

asleep *agg.* addormentato.

asocial *agg.* asociale.

asp *s.* aspide.

asparagus *s. coll.* asparago, asparagi.

aspect *s.* aspetto.

aspen *s.* pioppo tremulo.

aspergillum *s.* aspersorio.

asperity *s.* **1.** asperità **2.** (*fig.*) asprezza.

aspersion *s.* **1.** aspersione **2.** calunnia.

asphalt *s.* asfalto.

asphyxia *s.* asfissia.

to **asphyxiate** *vt.* asfissiare.

aspirant *agg. e s.* aspirante.

to **aspirate** *vt.* aspirare.

aspiration *s.* aspirazione.

aspirator *s.* aspiratore.

to **aspire** *vi.* aspirare.

aspirin *s.* aspirina.

aspiring *agg.* ambizioso.

asquint *avv.* di traverso.

ass *s.* asino || *to make an* — *of oneself*, rendersi ridicolo.

to **assail** *vt.* assalire.

assailant, assailer *s.* assalitore.

assassin *s.* assassino.

to **assassinate** *vt.* assassinare.

assassination *s.* assassinio.

assault *s.* assalto, aggressione.

to **assault** *vt.* assalire.

assaulter *s.* assalitore.

to **assay** *vt.* saggiare.

assayer *s.* (as)saggiatore.

to **assemble** *vt.* riunire. ♦ to **assemble** *vi.* riunirsi.

assembly *s.* **1.** assemblea **2.** (*mil.*) adunata **3.** (*mecc.*) montaggio: — *line*, catena di montaggio.

assent *s.* consenso.

to **assent** *vt.* approvare.

to **assert** *vt.* asserire || *to* — *oneself*, farsi valere.

assertion *s.* asserzione.

assertor *s.* assertore.

to **assess** *vt.* **1.** tassare **2.** (*comm.*) ripartire.

assessment *s.* **1.** valutazione **2.** tassazione.

assessor *s.* agente delle tasse.

asset *s.* **1.** bene, vantaggio. ♦ **assets** *s. pl.* patrimonio, attività (*sing.*).

assiduity *s.* assiduità.

assiduous *agg.* assiduo.

to **assign** *vt.* **1.** assegnare **2.** trasferire **3.** designare.

assignation *s.* **1.** assegnazione **2.** (*giur.*) cessione **3.** appuntamento.

assignment *s.* **1.** assegnazione **2.** (*giur.*) cessione.

assimilable *agg.* assimilabile.

to **assimilate** *vt.* **1.** assimilare **2.** confrontare. ♦ to **assimilate** *vi.* assimilarsi.

assimilation *s.* **1.** assimilazione **2.** confronto.

to **assist** *vt. e vi.* assistere.

assistance *s.* assistenza.

assistant *agg. e s.* assistente || *shop* —, commesso.

assize *s.* **1.** (*giur.*) seduta. ♦ **Assizes** *s. pl.* Assise.

associate *agg. e s.* associato.

to **associate** *vt.* associare. ♦ to **associate** *vi.* associarsi.

association *s.* associazione.

assonance *s.* assonanza.

to **assort** *vt.* **1.** assortire **2.** classificare. ♦ to **assort** *vi.* **1.** armonizzarsi **2.** frequentare: *to* — *with so.*, frequentare qu.

to **assume** *vt.* **1.** assumere **2.** fingere **3.** presumere.

assuming agg. presuntuoso.
assumption s. 1. assunzione 2. finzione 3. supposizione 4. presunzione.
assurance s. 1. assicurazione 2. sicurezza 3. fiducia.
to **assure** vt. 1. assicurare 2. rassicurare.
assurer s. assicuratore.
asterisk s. asterisco.
astern avv. a poppa.
asteroid s. asteroide.
asthenia s. astenia.
asthma s. asma.
asthmatic agg. e s. asmatico.
astigmatic agg. astigmatico.
astigmatism s. astigmatismo.
astir agg. e avv. in moto.
to **astonish** vt. stupire.
astonishing agg. sorprendente
astonishment s. sorpresa.
to **astound** vt. sbalordire.
astragal(us) s. astragalo.
astrakhan s. astracan.
astral agg. astrale.
astray agg. e avv. fuori strada.
astride agg. e avv. a cavalcioni. ♦
  astride prep. a cavalcioni di.
astringent agg. e s. astringente
astrolabe s. astrolabio.
astrologer s. astrologo.
astrology s. astrologia.
astronaut s. astronauta.
astronautics s. astronautica.
astronomer s. astronomo.
astronomic(al) agg. astronomico.
astronomy s. astronomia.
astute agg. astuto.
asunder avv. 1. separatamente 2. in pezzi.
asylum s. 1. asilo, ricovero 2. manicomio.
asymmetric(al) agg. asimmetrico.
asymmetry s. asimmetria.
at prep. (stato, tempo, modo) a, da, in: to arrive — a place, arrivare in un luogo; — that time, in quel momento; — will, a volontà.
atavistic agg. atavico.
atavism s. atavismo.
ataxy s. atassia.
ate V. to eat.
atheism s. ateismo.
atheist s. ateo.
atheistic(al) agg. ateistico.
athlete s. atleta.
athletic agg. atletico.
athletics s. atletica.
atlas s. atlante.

atmosphere s. atmosfera.
atmospheric(al) agg. atmosferico.
atoll s. atollo.
atom s. atomo.
atomic(al) agg. atomico.
atomism s. atomismo.
to **atomize** vt. nebulizzare.
atomizer s. atomizzatore, nebulizzatore.
atomy s. atomo.
to **atone** vt. espiare.
atonement s. espiazione.
atonic agg. 1. atono 2. atonico.
atrocious agg. atroce.
atrocity s. atrocità.
atrophic agg. atrofico.
atrophy s. atrofia.
to **atrophy** vt. atrofizzare. ♦ to **atrophy** vi. atrofizzarsi.
atropin(e) s. atropina.
to **attach** vt. 1. attaccare, unire 2. attribuire 3. attrarre. ♦ to **attach** vi. attaccarsi.
attaché s. addetto.
attachment s. 1. attaccamento 2. (mecc.) accessorio.
attack s. attacco.
to **attack** vt. attaccare.
attacker s. assalitore.
to **attain** vt. raggiungere. ♦ to **attain** vi. giungere.
attainable agg. raggiungibile.
attainment s. 1. raggiungimento 2. cultura.
attempt s. 1. tentativo 2. attentato.
to **attempt** vt. 1. tentare 2. attentare a.
to **attend** vi. 1. badare a 2. obbedire ‖ to — on, essere al servizio di. ♦ to **attend** vt. 1. assistere 2. accompagnare 3. frequentare.
attendance s. 1. servizio 2. assistenza 3. frequenza.
attendant s. 1. servitore 2. assistente 3. assiduo frequentatore.
attention s. attenzione: to pay —, fare attenzione.
attentive agg. 1. attento 2. sollecito.
to **attenuate** vt. 1. assottigliare 2. attenuare. ♦ to **attenuate** vi. 1. assottigliarsi 2. attenuarsi.
attenuation s. 1. assottigliamento 2. attenuazione.
to **attest** vt. attestare.
attic agg. e s. attico.
to **attire** vt. vestire, agghindare. ♦ to **attire** vi. vestirsi.
attitude s. atteggiamento.

attorney s. 1. procura 2. procuratore ‖ — (-at-law), procuratore legale.

to **attract** vt. attrarre.

attraction s. 1. attrazione 2. attrattiva.

attractive agg attraente.

attribute s. attributo.

to **attribute** vt. attribuire.

attribution s. attribuzione.

attributive agg. attributivo. ♦ **attributive** s. attributo.

aubergine s. melanzana.

auction s. asta: — sale„ vendita all'asta.

to **auction** vt. vendere all'asta.

auctioneer s. banditore.

audible s. udibile.

audience s. 1. udienza 2. uditorio.

audiovisual agg. audiovisivo.

audit s. verifica, revisione.

audition s. audizione.

auditory agg. e s. uditorio.

auger s. trivella, succhiello.

to **augment** vt. aumentare. ♦ to **augment** vi. crescere.

augmentative agg. e s. accrescitivo.

to **augur** vt. e vi. predire.

august agg. augusto.

August s. agosto.

aunt s. zia ‖ great- —, prozia.

auricle s. 1. padiglione auricolare 2. (med.) orecchietta.

auricular agg. auricolare.

auriferous agg. aurifero.

to **auscultate** vt. auscultare.

auscultation s. auscultazione.

auscultator s. stetoscopio.

auspice s. auspicio.

auspicious agg. propizio.

austere agg. austero.

austerity s. austerità.

austral agg. australe.

Australian agg. e s. australiano.

Austrian agg. e s. austriaco.

autarky s. autarchia.

authentic(al) agg. autentico.

to **authenticate** vt. autenticare.

authentication s. autenticazione.

authenticity s. autenticità.

author s. autore.

authoress s. autrice.

authoritative agg. 1. autoritario 2. autorevole.

authoritativeness s. autorevolezza.

authority s. autorità.

authorization s. autorizzazione.

to **authorize** vt. autorizzare.

authorless agg. anonimo.

authorship s. paternità (di un libro).

autobiographic(al) agg. autobiografico.

autobiography s. autobiografia.

autochthon s. autoctono.

autochthonous agg. autoctono.

autocracy s. autocrazia.

autocrat s. autocrate.

autocriticism s. autocritica.

autoeducation s. autoeducazione.

autofinancing s. autofinanziamento.

autograph s. autografo.

autography s. autografia.

autolesion s. autolesione.

automatic agg. automatico. ♦ **automatic** s. arma automatica.

automation s. automazione.

automatism s. automatismo.

automaton s. automa.

autonomist s. autonomista.

autonomous agg. autonomo.

autonomy s. autonomia.

autopsy s. autopsia.

auto-suggestion s. autosuggestione.

autumn s. autunno.

autumnal agg. autunnale.

auxiliary agg. e s. ausiliare.

avail s. utilità.

to **avail** vt. e vi. servire a ‖ to — oneself of, approfittare di.

availability s. 1. disponibilità 2. validità.

available agg. 1. disponibile 2. valevole.

avalanche s. valanga.

avarice s. 1. avarizia 2. cupidigia.

avaricious agg. 1. avaro 2. cupido.

to **avenge** vt. vendicare.

avenger s. vendicatore.

avenue s. viale.

to **aver** vt. asserire, dichiarare.

average agg. medio. ♦ **average** s. 1. media 2. (comm.) avaria.

averse agg. avverso.

aversion s. avversione.

to **avert** vt. sviare.

aviary s. uccelliera.

aviation s. aviazione.

aviator s. aviatore.

avid agg. avido.

avidity s. avidità.

to **avoid** vt. 1. evitare 2. (giur.) annullare.

avoidable agg. 1. evitabile 2. (giur.) annullabile.

to **avow** vt. dichiarare, ammettere.

avowal s. dichiarazione, ammissione.

to **await** *vt.* attendere.

awake *agg.* **1.** sveglio **2.** conscio.

to **awake (awoke, awoke)** *vt.* svegliare. ♦ to **awake (awoke, awoke)** *vi.* svegliarsi.

to **awaken** *vt.* risvegliare, far aprire gli occhi. ♦ to **awaken** *vi.* risvegliarsi, aprire gli occhi.

awakening *s.* risveglio.

award *s.* **1.** sentenza **2.** ricompensa.

to **award** *vt.* aggiudicare.

aware *agg.* conscio.

away *avv.* via, lontano || *right* —, subito, seduta stante.

awe *s.* timore reverenziale.

awful *agg.* **1.** terribile **2.** imponente.

awkward *agg.* **1.** goffo, imbarazzato **2.** scomodo **3.** inopportuno **4.** delicato.

awkwardness *s.* **1.** goffaggine **2.** imbarazzo.

awl *s.* lesina.

awning *s.* tenda.

awoke V. *to awake.*

awry *agg.* **1.** storto **2.** bieco. ♦ **awry** *avv.* **1.** per traverso **2.** perversamente.

ax(e) *s.* scure.

axiom *s.* assioma.

axiomatic(al) *agg.* assiomatico.

axis *s.* (*pl.* axes) asse.

axle *s.* (*mecc.*) asse.

azimuth *s.* azimut.

azote *s.* azoto.

to **azotize** *vt.* azotare.

Aztec *agg.* e *s.* azteco.

azure *agg.* e *s.* azzurro.

B

b *s.* (*mus.*) si.

babble *s.* balbettio.

to **babble** *vi.* e *vt.* **1.** balbettare **2.** mormorare (*di acque*).

babe *s.* bambino.

babel *s.* babele.

baboon *s.* babbuino.

baby *s.* bimbo, neonato || — *-sitter,* chi accudisce i bambini.

babyhood *s.* infanzia.

babyish *agg.* infantile.

baccarat *s.* baccarà.

Bacchanal *s.* **1.** baccante **2.** baccanale (*anche fig.*).

Bacchante *s.* baccante.

bacchic(al) *agg.* bacchico.

bachelor *s.* scapolo || *Bachelor of Arts,* titolo universitario in lettere.

bachelorhood *s.* celibato.

bacillus *s.* (*pl.* -li) bacillo.

back[1] *agg.* posteriore. ♦ **back** *avv.* dietro, indietro || *to be* —, essere di ritorno; *to go, to come* —, ritornare.

back[2] *s.* **1.** dorso, schiena **2.** spalle **3.** rovescio **4.** schienale **5.** fondo.

to **back** *vt.* **1.** sostenere **2.** fare indietreggiare || *to* — *a bill,* avallare una cambiale. ♦ to **back** *vi.* indietreggiare || — *down,* abbandonare la contesa.

to **backbite** *vt.* denigrare.

backbiter *s.* calunniatore.

backbiting *agg.* maldicente. ♦ **backbiting** *s.* maldicenza.

backbone *s.* **1.** spina dorsale **2.** (*fig.*) fermezza.

backer *s.* **1.** scommettitore **2.** sostenitore.

backfire *s.* ritorno di fiamma.

background *s.* **1.** sfondo **2.** curriculum **3.** ambiente.

backing *s.* **1.** sostegno **2.** marcia indietro.

backlash *s.* rimbalzo.

backslider *s.* apostata.

backward *agg.* **1.** lento **2.** tardo.

backward(s) *avv.* indietro.

backwash *s.* risacca.

bacon *s.* lardo affumicato, pancetta.

bacterial *agg.* batterico.

bacteriology *s.* batteriologia.

bacterium *s.* (*pl.* -ia) batterio.

bad (worse, worst) *agg.* **1.** cattivo **2.** brutto. ♦ **bad** *s.* **1.** male **2.** rovina.

bade V. *to bid.*

badge *s.* insegna.

badger *s.* tasso.

badly *avv.* male, malamente.

badness *s.* **1.** cattiveria **2.** cattiva qualità.

baffle *s.* (*-plate*) deflettore, diaframma.

to **baffle** *vt.* **1.** eludere **2.** confondere.

bag *s.* **1.** sacco **2.** borsa || *sleeping-*—, sacco a pelo.

to **bag** *vt.* **1.** gonfiare **2.** rubare **3.** insaccare.

baggage *s.* bagaglio.

bagpipe *s.* cornamusa.

bail *s.* **1.** cauzione **2.** garante.

to **bail**[1] *vt.* **1.** dar garanzia per **2.**

affidare (*dietro cauzione*).

to **bail**[2] *vt.* e *vi.* (*mar.*) aggottare || *to — out*, lanciarsi col paracadute.

bailiff *s.* **1.** magistrato inquirente **2.** ufficiale fiscale.

bain-marie *s.* bagnomaria.

bait *s.* **1.** esca **2.** sosta (*per ristoro*).

to **bait** *vt.* **1.** adescare **2.** tormentare. ♦ to **bait** *vi.* fermarsi (*per prendere ristoro*).

to **bake** *vt.* e *vi.* cuocere al forno.

baker *s.* fornaio.

bakery *s.* forno.

baking *s.* cottura al forno.

balance *s.* **1.** bilancia **2.** bilanciere **3.** equilibrio **4.** bilancio.

to **balance** *vt.* **1.** pesare **2.** pareggiare. ♦ to **balance** *vi.* **1.** bilanciarsi **2.** oscillare.

balanced *agg.* equilibrato.

balancer *s.* acrobata.

balcony *s.* **1.** balcone **2.** (*teat.*).balconata.

bald *agg.* **1.** calvo, pelato **2.** povero, nudo.

baldness *s.* **1.** calvizie **2.** (*fig.*) nudità.

baldric *s.* bandoliera.

bale *s.* (*comm.*) balla.

Balkan *agg.* balcanico.

ball *s.* **1.** palla **2.** ballo || *— -bearing*, cuscinetto a sfere.

to **ball** *vt.* appallottolare. ♦ to **ball** *vi.* appallottolarsi.

ballad *s.* ballata.

ballast *s.* zavorra.

to **ballast** *vt.* zavorrare.

ballet *s.* balletto || *— -dancer*, ballerino classico.

ballistics *s.* balistica.

balloon *s.* **1.** pallone **2.** lambicco **3.** fumetto.

ballot *s.* **1.** pallina, scheda (*per votazione*) **2.** voto **3.** scrutinio || *— -box*, urna.

to **ballot** *vt.* mettere in ballottaggio.

balm *s.* balsamo.

balm-cricket *s.* (*zool.*) cicala.

balmy *agg.* balsamico.

Baltic *agg.* baltico.

balustrade *s.* balaustrata.

bamboo *s.* bambù.

ban *s.* bando.

to **ban** *vt.* proibire.

banal *agg.* banale.

banality *s.* banalità.

banana *s.* **1.** banana **2.** banano.

band *s.* **1.** legame **2.** benda **3.** nastro **4.** banda.

to **band** *vt.* **1.** legare **2.** bendare.

bandage *s.* bendaggio.

to **bandage** *vt.* bendare.

banderole *s.* banderuola.

bandit *s.* bandito.

bandmaster *s.* capobanda.

bandog *s.* cane da guardia.

bandsman *s.* bandista.

bane *s.* **1.** calamità **2.** veleno.

baneful *agg.* velenoso.

bang *s.* **1.** botta **2.** detonazione.

to **bang** *vt.* e *vi.* sbattere violentemente.

banging *s.* **1.** colpi violenti **2.** detonazioni.

to **banish** *vt.* bandire, esiliare.

banishment *s.* bando, esilio.

banister *s.* ringhiera (*di scala*).

bank *s.* **1.** banca **2.** banco **3.** argine **4.** terrapieno.

to **bank** *vt.* **1.** arginare **2.** depositare in banca || *to — upon*, contare su. ♦ to **bank** *vi.* gestire una banca.

bankbook *s.* libretto bancario.

banker *s.* banchiere.

banking *agg.* bancario. ♦ **banking** *s.* tecnica, professione bancaria.

bank note *s.* banconota.

bankrupt *agg.* e *s.* fallito || *to go —*, fallire.

bankruptcy *s.* fallimento.

banner *s.* vessillo.

banns *s. pl.* pubblicazioni matrimoniali.

banquet *s.* banchetto.

to **banquet** *vi.* banchettare.

banter *s.* scherzo, beffa.

to **banter** *vt.* canzonare.

baptism *s.* battesimo.

baptist(e)ry *s.* battistero.

to **baptize** *vt.* battezzare.

bar *s.* **1.** sbarra **2.** diga **3.** striscia **4.** ostacolo **5.** (*fig.*) tribunale **6.** bar **7.** (*mus.*) battuta.

to **bar** *vt.* **1.** sbarrare **2.** ostacolare **3.** proibire.

barbarian *agg.* e *s.* barbaro.

barbaric *agg.* barbarico.

barbarism *s.* **1.** barbarie **2.** (*gramm.*) barbarismo.

barbarous *agg.* barbaro.

barbarousness *s.* barbarie.

barbecue *s.* **1.** animale arrostito intero **2.** festa campestre.

to **barbecue** *vt.* arrostire un animale intero.

barbed *agg.* dentato.

barber *s.* barbiere.

barbiturate s. barbiturico.
bard s. bardo, trovatore.
bare agg. 1. nudo 2. logoro.
to **bare** vt. 1. denudare 2. snudare 3. smascherare.
barefoot agg. scalzo.
barehanded agg. e avv. 1. a mano nuda 2. senz'armi.
bareheaded agg. a capo scoperto.
barely avv. 1. apertamente 2. appena.
bargain s. affare.
to **bargain** vt. e vi. contrattare.
bargaining s. contrattazione.
barge s. chiatta.
baritone s. baritono.
bark[1] s. corteccia.
bark[2] s. latrato.
to **bark**[1] vt. scortecciare.
to **bark**[2] vi. latrare, abbaiare.
barking[1] s. scortecciamento.
barking[2] s. abbaiamento.
barley s. orzo.
barmaid s. barista (donna).
barman s. barista.
barn s. granaio.
barometer s. barometro.
barometric(al) agg. barometrico
baron s. barone.
baroness s. baronessa.
baroque agg. e s. barocco.
barracks s. pl. caserma (sing.).
barrage s. sbarramento.
barrel s. 1. barile 2. cilindro 3. canna (di arma da fuoco) || — -organ, organetto.
to **barrel** vt. mettere in barili.
barrelled agg. double- — gun, fucile a due canne.
barren agg. sterile.
barrenness s. sterilità.
barricade s. barricata.
to **barricade** vt. barricare.
barrier s. barriera || transonic —, muro del suono.
barrister s. avvocato (che può discutere cause nelle corti superiori).
barrow s. 1. barella 2. carriola.
bartender s. barista.
barter s. baratto.
to **barter** vt. e vi. barattare.
basal agg. basilare.
basalt s. basalto.
base[1] agg. basso, vile.
base[2] s. base.
to **base** vt. basare.
baseless agg. senza base.
basement s. 1. fondamento 2. seminterrato.

baseness s. bassezza.
to **bash** vt. colpire.
bashful agg. timido.
bashfulness s. timidezza.
basic agg. 1. fondamentale 2. (chim.) basico.
basil s. basilico.
basilar agg. basilare.
basilisk s. basilisco.
basin s. 1. bacino 2. catino, lavabo || sugar —, zuccheriera.
basis s. (pl. -ses) base.
to **bask** vi. crogiolarsi (al sole, al fuoco).
basket s. cesto || —ball, pallacanestro; — -chair, poltroncina di vimini.
Basque agg. e s. basco.
bas-relief s. bassorilievo.
bass agg. e s. (mus.) basso.
bass s. pesce persico.
bassoon s. (mus.) fagotto.
bastard agg. e s. bastardo.
to **baste** vt. imbastire.
basting s. imbastitura.
bastion s. bastione.
bat[1] s. pipistrello.
bat[2] s. (sport) mazza.
batch s. 1. infornata 2. gruppo.
to **bate** vt. ridurre.
bath s. bagno || — -robe, accappatoio; — -tub, vasca da bagno.
to **bath** vt. bagnare. ♦ to **bath** vi. bagnarsi, fare il bagno.
bathe s. bagno (in mare, lago ecc.).
to **bathe** vt. bagnare. ♦ to **bathe** vi. bagnarsi, fare il bagno (in mare, lago ecc.).
bather s. bagnante.
bathing s. il bagnarsi || — -suit, costume da bagno.
bathroom s. stanza da bagno.
bathysphere s. batisfera.
batiste s. batista.
batman s. attendente.
baton s. 1. bastone 2. bacchetta (di direttore d'orchestra).
batrachian s. batrace.
batsman s. (sport) battitore.
battalion s. battaglione.
to **batten** vt. (mar.) chiudere (i boccaporti).
batter s. (cuc.) pastella.
to **batter** vt. battere || to — down, abbattere; to — in, sfondare.
battering s. cannoneggiamento.
battery s. batteria || storage —, accumulatore.
battle s. battaglia.

to **battle** *vt.* e *vi.* combattere.

battledore *s.* racchetta di legno || — *and shuttlecock*, volano.

battlement *s.* (*arch.*) merlo.

battleship *s.* nave da guerra.

bauxite *s.* bauxite.

bawdiness *s.* oscenità.

bawdy *agg.* osceno || — *house*, bordello.

bawl *s.* grido.

to **bawl** *vt.* e *vi.* gridare, vociare.

bay[1] *s.* **1.** baia **2.** insenatura, recesso (*nelle montagne*).

bay[2] *s.* alloro || — -*tree*, lauro.

bay[3] *s.* **1.** rientranza **2.** campata || — -*window*, bovindo.

bay[4] *s.* latrato || *at* —, senza scampo.

bay[5] *agg.* e *s.* baio.

to **bay**[1] *vt.* arginare.

to **bay**[2] *vi.* latrare.

bayonet *s.* baionetta.

baza(a)r *s.* **1.** bazar **2.** vendita di beneficenza.

to **be (was, been)** *vi.* **1.** essere **2.** stare **3.** andare **4.** costare: *how much is it?*, quanto costa? **5.** dovere || *to — in*, essere in casa; *to — about*, stare per; *so be it*, così sia.

beach *s.* spiaggia.

beacon *s.* faro.

to **beacon** *vt.* guidare con segnalazioni luminose.

bead *s.* **1.** goccia **2.** perlina. ♦ **beads** *s. pl.* rosario (*sing.*).

to **bead** *vt.* imperlare. ♦ to **bead** *vi.* imperlarsi.

beak *s.* **1.** becco, rostro **2.** beccuccio.

to **beak** *vt.* beccare.

beaker *s.* boccale.

beam *s.* **1.** trave **2.** raggio **3.** asta (*di bilancia*) **4.** fiancata (*di nave*).

to **beam** *vi.* brillare. ♦ to **beam** *vt.* irradiare.

beaming *agg.* raggiante.

bean *s.* fagiolo || *French* —, fagiolino; *coffee* —, grano di caffè.

bear *s.* orso.

to **bear**[1] *vt.* e *vi.* speculare al ribasso (*in Borsa*).

to **bear**[2] **(bore, born(e))** *vt.* **1.** portare **2.** sopportare **3.** generare. ♦ to **bear (bore, borne)** *vi.* **1.** resistere **2.** appoggiarsi **3.** pazientare || *to — with*, aver pazienza con.

bearable *agg.* sopportabile.

beard *s.* **1.** barba **2.** chioma (*di cometa*).

to **beard** *vt.* affrontare, sfidare.

bearded *agg.* barbuto.

beardless *agg.* senza barba.

bearer *s.* portatore.

bearing *s.* **1.** sopportazione **2.** portamento **3.** condotta **4.** relazione **5.** sostegno **6.** raccolto || *to lose one's bearings*, perdere l'orientamento; *to take the bearings of a coast* (*mar.*), rilevare una costa.

beast *s.* bestia.

beastliness *s.* bestialità.

beastly *agg.* bestiale. ♦ **beastly** *avv.* bestialmente.

beat *s.* **1.** battito **2.** (*mus.*) battuta.

to **beat (beat, beat(en))** *vt.* e *vi.* battere || *to — down*, abbattere; *to — back*, respingere.

beaten *agg.* abbattuto, vinto.

beater *s.* battitore.

beatification *s.* beatificazione.

beating *s.* **1.** battito **2.** bastonatura **3.** sconfitta.

beatitude *s.* beatitudine.

beautiful *agg.* bello.

beautifully *avv.* magnificamente.

to **beautify** *vt.* abbellire. ♦ to **beautify** *vi.* abbellirsi.

beauty *s.* bellezza.

beaver *s.* castoro.

became V. *to become*.

because *cong.* perché || — *of*, a causa di.

beck[1] *s.* ruscello.

beck[2] *s.* cenno, gesto.

to **become (became, become)** *vi.* **1.** divenire **2.** avvenire. ♦ to **become (became, become)** *vt.* addirsi a.

becoming *agg.* adatto.

bed *s.* **1.** letto **2.** fondo **3.** (*geol.*) strato || *double* —, letto matrimoniale || *flower-* —, aiuola; — -*cover*, copriletto.

bedclothes *s. pl.* lenzuola.

bedlam *s.* manicomio.

bedouin *agg.* e *s.* beduino.

bedroom *s.* camera da letto.

bedside *s.* capezzale.

bedstead *s.* telaio del letto.

bedtime *s.* ora di andare a letto.

bee *s.* ape.

beech *s.* faggio || — -*marten*, faina.

beef *s.* manzo.

beefsteak *s.* bistecca.

beehive *s.* alveare.

beeline *s.* linea diretta, linea d'aria.

been V. *to be*.

beer *s.* birra.

beet s. barbabietola.
beetle s. coleottero, scarafaggio.
beetroot s. V. beet.
to befall (befell, befallen) vt. e vi. accadere.
before avv. prima, già || — -mentioned, già citato. ♦ before prep. 1. prima (di) 2. davanti a. ♦ before cong. 1. prima che 2. piuttosto che.
beforehand avv. anticipatamente.
to beg vt. e vi. 1. chiedere, pregare 2. elemosinare.
began V. to begin.
to beget (begot, begot(ten)) vt. generare.
beggar s. mendicante.
beggarly agg. misero. ♦ beggarly avv. miseramente.
beggary s. mendicità.
begging agg. mendicante. ♦ begging s. accattonaggio.
to begin (began, begun) vt. e vi. cominciare || to — with, in primo luogo, per cominciare.
beginner s. 1. iniziatore 2. principiante.
beginning s. inizio.
begot V. to beget.
begotten V. to beget.
to begrime vt. insudiciare.
begun V. to begin.
behalf s. profitto, favore: on — of, da parte di, a nome di.
to behave vi. comportarsi:- to — oneself, comportarsi bene || ill -behaved, maleducato.
behaviour s. comportamento, condotta.
to behead vt. decapitare.
beheld V. to behold.
behind avv. dietro, indietro. ♦ behind prep. dietro (a). ♦ behind s. parte posteriore.
to behold (beheld, beheld) vt. guardare.
beholder s. spettatore.
to behove vt. imp. convenire, essere doveroso.
being agg. presente. ♦ being s. 1. esistenza 2. essere vivente.
belch s. 1. rutto 2. eruzione.
to belch vi. ruttare. ♦ to belch vt. eruttare.
belfry s. campanile.
Belgian agg. e s. belga.
to belie vt. 1. smentire 2. deludere.
belief s. credenza, fede.
to believe vt. e vi. credere, aver fede.

believer s. credente.
to belittle vt. sminuire.
bell s. 1. campana 2. campanello || — -boy, fattorino d'albergo; — -ringer, campanaro; — -tower, campanile.
belligerency s. belligeranza.
belligerent agg. e s. belligerante.
bellow s. muggito.
to bellow vi. muggire.
bellows s. pl. mantice, soffietto (sing.).
belly s. ventre.
to belong vi. 1. appartenere 2. concernere.
belongings s. pl. proprietà (sing.).
beloved agg. e s. amato.
below avv. giù, al di sotto. ♦ below prep. sotto: — zero, sotto zero.
belt s. 1. cintura 2. zona.
to belt vt. 1. cingere 2. staffilare.
to bemire vt. infangare. ♦ to bemire vi. impantanarsi.
bench s. 1. panca 2. banco 3. seggio 4. corte giudiziaria.
bend s. 1. curva 2. curvatura 3. (mar.) nodo.
to bend (bent, bent) vt. 1. piegare 2. tendere. ♦ to bend (bent, bent) vi. piegarsi.
bending s. V. bend.
beneath avv. e prep. V. below.
benediction s. benedizione.
benefactor s. benefattore.
benefactress s. benefattrice.
benefice s. beneficio.
beneficence s. beneficenza.
beneficent agg. benefico.
beneficiary agg. e s. beneficiario.
benefit s. 1. vantaggio 2. indennità 3. (giur.) beneficio.
to benefit vt. giovare, beneficare. ♦ to benefit vi. approfittare.
benevolence s. benevolenza.
benevolent agg. benevolo.
Bengal-light s. bengala.
benign agg. benigno.
benignity s. benignità.
bent V. to bend. ♦ bent agg. risoluto. ♦ bent s. inclinazione.
to benumb vt. intorpidire.
benumbing s. intorpidimento.
benzol s. benzolo.
to bequeath vt. lasciare per testamento.
bequest s. lascito.
Berber agg. e s. berbero.

to bereave (bereaved, bereft) *vt.* privare.

bergamot *s.* bergamotto.

berlin(e) *s.* berlina.

berry *s.* bacca.

berth *s.* **1.** cuccetta **2.** (*mar.*) ancoraggio **3.** (*fig.*) posto.

to berth *vt.* ancorare.

beryllium *s.* berillio.

to beseech (besought, besought) *vt.* supplicare.

beseeching *s.* supplica.

to beseem *vt.* addirsi a.

beseeming *agg.* adatto.

beside *prep.* **1.** vicino a **2.** fuori di.

besides *avv.* inoltre. ♦ **besides** *prep.* oltre a.

to besiege *vt.* assediare.

besieger *s.* assediante.

besought V. *to beseech.*

to besprinkle *vt.* spruzzare.

best *agg.* (*superl. di* good) il migliore || — *-seller*, libro molto venduto. ♦ **best** *s.* il meglio. ♦ **best** *avv.* **1.** nel modo migliore **2.** maggiormente.

bestial *agg.* bestiale.

bestiality *s.* bestialità.

to bestialize *vt.* abbrutire.

to bestir *vt.* agitare.

to bestow *vt.* concedere.

bestowal *s.* conferimento.

to bestrew (bestrewed, bestrewn) *vt.* cospargere, disseminare.

bet *s.* scommessa.

to bet (bet, bet) *vt. e vi.* scommettere.

to betake (betook, betaken) *vr.* — *oneself*: dirigersi, recarsi.

to betray *vt.* tradire.

betrayal *s.* tradimento.

betrayer *s.* traditore.

betrothal *s.* fidanzamento.

betrothed *agg. e s.* fidanzato.

better¹ *s.* scommettitore.

better² *agg.* (*comp. di* good) migliore. ♦ **better** *avv.* meglio || *had* —, sarebbe meglio che; *all the* —, so much the —, tanto meglio. ♦ **better** *s.* **1.** il meglio **2.** superiore.

to better *vt. e vi.* migliorare.

between *avv.* in mezzo. ♦ **between** *prep.* tra, fra (*due cose, due persone*).

beverage *s.* bevanda.

bevy *s.* stormo, frotta.

to beware *vi.* guardarsi, diffidare.

to bewilder *vt.* sconcertare.

bewildering *agg.* sbalorditivo.

bewilderment *s.* confusione.

to bewitch *vt.* incantare.

bewitcher *s.* incantatore.

bewitching *agg.* affascinante.

beyond *avv.* più in là. ♦ **beyond** *prep.* al di là di. ♦ **beyond** *s.* l'al di là.

bias *s.* **1.** pregiudizio **2.** predisposizione.

to bias *vt.* influenzare.

bib *s.* bavaglino.

Bible *s.* Bibbia.

biblical *agg.* biblico.

bibliographic(al) *agg.* bibliografico.

bibliography *s.* bibliografia.

bicameral *agg.* bicamerale.

bicarbonate *s.* bicarbonato.

bicentennial *agg. e s.* bicentenario.

bicephalous *agg.* bicipite.

biceps *s.* bicipite.

to bicker *vi.* litigare.

bicoloured *agg.* bicolore.

biconcave *agg.* biconcavo.

bicycle *s.* bicicletta.

bid *s.* **1.** offerta (*a un'asta*) **2.** appalto.

to bid¹ (bid, bid) *vt.* offrire (*a un'asta*). ♦ **to bid (bid, bid)** *vi.* fare offerta di appalto.

to bid² (bade, bidden) *vt. e vi.* **1.** comandare **2.** dire || *to* — *good-bye*, accomiatarsi.

biennial *agg.* biennale.

biennium *s.* (*pl.* -biennia) biennio.

bier *s.* bara.

big *agg.* **1.** grosso **2.** gravido **3.** importante.

bigamous *agg.* bigamo.

bigamy *s.* bigamia.

bigness *s.* grossezza.

bigot *s.* bigotto.

bigoted *agg.* bigotto, fanatico.

bilateral *agg.* bilaterale.

bilberry *s.* mirtillo.

bile *s.* bile.

bilingual *agg.* bilingue.

bilious *agg.* **1.** biliare **2.** collerico.

bill¹ *s.* becco.

bill² *s.* **1.** progetto di legge **2.** certi- **5.** lista **6.** affisso || — *of lading*, polizza di carico; — *of rights*, dichiarazione dei diritti.

to bill *vt.* **1.** fatturare **2.** affiggere **3.** (*teat.*) mettere in programma.

billhook *s.* falcetto.

billiard *agg.* di, da bigliardo: —

-*cue*, stecca da bigliardo.

billiards *s. pl.* bigliardo (*sing.*).

billion *s.* **1.** bilione **2.** (*amer.*) miliardo.

billow *s.* onda.

bimestrial *agg.* bimestrale.

bimonthly *agg.* e *s.* bimestrale. ♦ **bimonthly** *avv.* bimestralmente.

bin *s.* recipiente || *dust-* —, bidone della spazzatura.

bind *s.* **1.** legame **2.** fascia.

to **bind** (**bound, bound**) *vt.* **1.** legare **2.** fasciare **3.** rilegare **4.** obbligare.

binder *s.* **1.** rilegatore **2.** (*mecc.*) legatrice.

binding *agg.* impegnativo. ♦ **binding** *s.* **1.** legame **2.** fasciatura **3.** rilegatura.

binocular *s.* binocolo.

binomial *s.* binomio.

biochemistry *s.* biochimica.

biographer *s.* biografo.

biographic(al) *agg.* biografico.

biography *s.* biografia.

biological *agg.* biologico.

biologist *s.* biologo.

biology *s.* biologia.

biophysics *s.* biofisica.

biosphere *s.* biosfera.

bipartite *agg.* bipartito.

bipartition *s.* bipartizione.

biped *agg.* e *s.* bipede.

biplane *s.* biplano.

bipolar *agg.* bipolare.

birch *s.* **1.** betulla **2.** verga.

bird *s.* uccello.

birdcage *s.* gabbia (*per uccelli*).

birdseed *s.* miglio.

birth *s.* **1.** nascita **2.** stirpe.

birthday *s.* compleanno.

birthmark *s.* voglia, segno caratteristico (*di persona*).

birthplace *s.* luogo di nascita.

biscuit *s.* biscotto.

bisection *s.* bisezione.

bisector *s.* bisettrice.

bisexual *agg.* ermafrodito.

bishop *s.* vescovo.

bishopric *s.* vescovato.

bismuth *s.* bismuto.

bison *s.* bisonte.

bistoury *s.* bisturi.

bistre *s.* bistro.

bit *s.* **1.** pezzettino **2.** un poco **3.** (*mecc.*) parte tagliente di un utensile **4.** morso (*del cavallo*).

bit V. *to bite*.

bitch *s.* cagna.

bite *s.* **1.** morso **2.** presa.

to **bite** (**bit, bit(ten)**) *vt.* mordere. ♦ to **bite** (**bit, bit(ten)**) *vi.* abboccare || *to* — *in*, corrodere.

biting *agg.* **1.** mordente **2.** mordace.

bitten V. *to bite*.

bitter *agg.* **1.** amaro **2.** aspro **3.** (*di clima*) rigido || — *-sweet*, agrodolce. ♦ **bitter** *s.* amaro.

bitterish *agg.* amarognolo.

bitterness *s.* **1.** amarezza **2.** rancore **3.** rigidità (*di clima*).

bitumen *s.* bitume.

bivalent *agg.* bivalente.

bivouac *s.* bivacco.

bi-weekly *agg.* e *s.* bisettimanale. ♦ **bi-weekly** *avv.* due volte alla settimana.

to **blab** *vt.* e *vi.* **1.** chiacchierare **2.** spifferare.

black *agg.* **1.** nero **2.** negro **3.** (*fig.*) malvagio, minaccioso. ♦ **black** *s.* **1.** colore nero **2.** negro.

to **black** *vt.* annerire. ♦ to **black** *vi.* annerirsi.

to **blackball** *vt.* votare contro, bocciare.

blackberry *s.* mora selvatica.

blackbird *s.* merlo.

blackboard *s* lavagna.

to **blacken** *vt.* **1.** annerire **2.** (*fig.*) diffamare. ♦ to **blacken** *vi.* diventare nero.

blackguard *s.* mascalzone.

blackish *agg.* nerastro.

blackleg *s.* **1.** truffatore **2.** crumiro.

blackmail *s.* ricatto.

to **blackmail** *vt.* ricattare.

blackmailer *s.* ricattatore.

blackness *s.* **1.** nerezza **2.** oscurità.

blackout *s.* oscuramento.

blacksmith *s.* fabbro ferraio.

bladder *s.* vescica.

blade *s.* **1.** stelo **2.** lama.

blamable *agg.* biasimevole.

blame *s.* **1.** biasimo **2.** colpa.

to **blame** *vt.* **1.** biasimare **2.** incolpare.

blameful *agg.* biasimevole.

blameless *agg.* irreprensibile.

bland *agg.* blando.

blandishment *s.* blandizie (*pl.*).

blandly *avv.* blandamente.

blank *agg.* **1.** vuoto **2.** in bianco || — *verse*, verso sciolto. ♦ **blank** *s.* **1.** vuoto **2.** spazio in bianco **3.** mira || *point-* —, di punto in bianco.

blanket *s.* coperta.

blankly *avv.* 1. senza espressione 2. decisamente.

blare *s.* squillo (*di tromba*).

to **blaspheme** *vt.* e *vi.* bestemmiare.

blasphemous *agg.* blasfemo.

blasphemously *avv.* empiamente.

blasphemy *s.* bestemmia, empietà.

blast *s.* 1. raffica 2. squillo 3. scoppio 4. flagello || — -*furnace*, altoforno.

to **blast** *vt.* 1. far esplodere 2. rovinare.

blaze *s.* 1. fiamma 2. scoppio.

to **blaze** *vi.* ardere. ♦ to **blaze** *vt.* 1. bruciare 2. divulgare.

blazer *s.* giacca sportiva.

blazing *s.* 1. fiamma 2. splendore 3. vanteria.

blazon *s.* 1. blasone 2. ostentazione.

bleach *s.* imbianchimento, candeggio.

to **bleach** *vt.* imbiancare, candeggiare. ♦ to **bleach** *vi.* imbiancarsi.

bleacher *s.* recipiente per candeggio.

bleaching *s.* V. *bleach.*

bleak *agg.* 1. brullo 2. desolato 3. incolore.

bleakness *s.* 1. freddezza 2. squallore.

blear *agg.* 1. cisposo 2. ottuso.

bleat *s.* belato.

to **bleat** *vi.* belare.

to **bleed (bled, bled)** *vi.* sanguinare. ♦ to **bleed (bled, bled)** *vt.* salassare.

bleeding *s.* 1. emorragia 2. salasso 3. fuga.

blemish *s.* difetto.

blend *s.* miscela.

to **blend** *vt.* mescolare. ♦ to **blend** *vi.* mescolarsi.

to **bless** *vt.* benedire.

blessed *agg.* beato, santo.

blessing *s.* benedizione.

blew V. to *blow.*

blind *agg.* cieco. ♦ **blind** *s.* 1. tenda 2. persiana 3. paraocchi 4. finzione.

to **blind** *vt.* 1. accecare 2. oscurare 3. nascondere.

blindness *s.* cecità.

to **blink** *vi.* 1. battere le palpebre 2. lampeggiare 3. (*fig.*) chiudere gli occhi.

blinker *s.* 1. lampeggiatore 2. paraocchi.

blinking *agg.* 1. ammiccante 2. scintillante. ♦ **blinking** *s.* ammicco.

bliss *s.* beatitudine.

blissful *agg.* 1. beato 2. delizioso.

blister *s.* bolla.

blithe *agg.* gaio.

blizzard *s.* tormenta (*di neve*).

block *s.* 1. ceppo 2. masso 3. isolato (*di case*) 4. ostacolo 5. persona stupida || — *letters*, stampatello.

to **block** *vt.* bloccare.

blockade *s.* blocco.

blockhead *s.* stupido.

blonde *s.* donna bionda.

blood *s.* sangue.

bloodhound *s.* segugio.

bloodless *agg.* 1. esangue 2. incruento 3. (*fig.*) insensibile.

bloodshed *s.* spargimento di sangue.

bloodshot *agg.* iniettato di sangue.

bloody *agg.* 1. sanguinante 2. sanguinoso 3. sanguinario 4. maledetto.

bloom *s.* 1. fiore 2. rossore.

to **bloom** *vi.* 1. fiorire 2. arrossire.

blossom *s.* fiore.

to **blossom** *vi.* 1. fiorire 2. diventare.

blot *s.* macchia.

to **blot** *vt.* 1. macchiare 2. assorbire.

blotch *s.* 1. macchia 2. pustola.

blotting *s.* 1. il macchiare 2. l'asciugare || — -*paper*, carta assorbente; — -*pad*, tampone di carta assorbente.

blouse *s.* camicetta.

blow *s.* 1. soffio 2. colpo 3. fioritura || *to come to blows*, venire alle mani.

to **blow (blew, blown)** *vt.* 1. soffiare 2. suonare (*strumenti a fiato*) || *to* — *up*, (far) saltare in aria. ♦ to **blow (blew, blown)** *vi.* sbocciare.

blower *s.* 1. soffiatore 2. sfiatatoio.

blown V. to *blow.*

blowpipe *s.* 1. cannello per soffiare 2. cerbottana.

blue *agg.* 1. azzurro, blu 2. livido 3. triste.

bluebell *s.* campanula.

bluebottle[1] *s.* fiordaliso.

bluebottle[2] *s.* tafano.

blueprint *s.* ciánografia.

bluff *s.* ripida scogliera.

bluish *agg.* bluastro.

blunder *s.* errore.

blunt *agg.* 1. smussato 2. ottuso 3. schietto.

blush *s.* rossore.

to **blush** *vi.* arrossire.
board *s.* **1.** asse, tavola **2.** vitto **3.** pensione **4.** consiglio, ministero **5.** (*mar.*) bordo || *on* —, a bordo; *full* —, pensione completa. ◆ **boards** *s. pl.* palcoscenico (*sing.*).
to **board** *vt.* **1.** fornire di assi **2.** prendere a pensione **3.** (*mar.*) abbordare. ◆ to **board** *vi.* **1.** essere a pensione **2.** imbarcarsi.
boarder *s.* pensionante.
boarding *s.* assito || — *-house*, pensione; — *-school*, collegio.
boast *s.* vanto.
to **boast** *vt.* vantare. ◆ to **boast** *vi.* vantarsi.
boaster *s.* spaccone.
boastful *agg.* vanaglorioso.
boastfulness *s.* millanteria.
boasting *s.* vanteria.
boat *s.* barca, battello || *flying-* —, idrovolante; *sauce-* —, salsiera; *ferry-* —, traghetto.
boating *s.* canottaggio.
boatman *s.* barcaiolo.
boatswain *s.* nostromo.
to **bob** *vi.* dondolarsi, oscillare || *to* — *up*, venire a galla.
bobbin *s.* bobina.
bobsled *s.* guidoslitta.
bodice *s.* busto.
bodkin *s.* punteruolo, stiletto.
body *s.* **1.** corpo **2.** corporazione, ente **3.** massa || — *belt*, panciera.
bodymaker *s.* carrozziere.
Boeotian *agg.* e *s.* beota.
bog *s.*
boggy *agg.* paludoso.
bogy *s.* spauracchio.
boil *s.* bollitura.
to **boil** *vt.* e *vi.* bollire, ribollire || *to* — *away*, consumarsi; *to* — *over*, traboccare bollendo.
boiler *s.* bollitore, caldaia.
boiling *agg.* bollente. ◆ **boiling** *s.* ebollizione.
boisterous *agg.* **1.** rumoroso **2.** violento.
boisterousness *s.* fracasso.
bold *agg.* **1.** audace **2.** sfacciato **3.** vigoroso || — *-face*, neretto.
boldness *s.* **1.** audacia **2.** sfacciataggine.
bolide *s.* bolide.
Bolshevism *s.* bolscevismo.
Bolshevist *agg.* e *s.* bolscevico.
bolster *s.* **1.** cuscino **2.** supporto.
bolt *s.* **1.** catenaccio **2.** bullone **3.** otturatore **4.** freccia **5.** fulmine.

to **bolt**[1] *vt.* **1.** sprangare **2.** imbullonare.
to **bolt**[2] *vt.* setacciare, vagliare.
bolter *s.* setaccio.
bomb *s.* bomba.
to **bomb** *vt.* bombardare.
to **bombard** *vt.* bombardare.
bombardier *s.* bombardiere.
bombardment *s.* bombardamento.
bombastic *agg.* ampolloso.
bomber *s.* bombardiere.
bond *s.* **1.** vincolo **2.** patto **3.** (*comm.*) titolo **4.** cauzione || — *-holder*, portatore di obbligazioni; *goods in* —, merci in attesa di sdoganamento.
bondage *s.* schiavitù.
bone *s.* **1.** osso **2.** lisca.
to **bone** *vt.* **1.** disossare **2.** spinare.
bonfire *s.* falò.
bonnet *s.* **1.** cuffia **2.** (*auto*) cofano.
bonus *s.* gratifica || *cost of living* —, carovita.
bony *agg.* **1.** osseo **2.** ossuto.
bonze *s.* bonzo.
booby *s.* sciocco.
book *s.* **1.** libro **2.** registro || *note-* —, taccuino; *copy-* —, quaderno.
to **book** *vt.* **1.** registrare **2.** prenotare.
bookbinding *s.* rilegatura.
bookcase *s.* libreria.
booking *s.* **1.** registrazione **2.** prenotazione || — *-office*, biglietteria.
bookish *agg.* **1.** studioso **2.** libresco.
bookkeeper *s.* contabile.
bookkeeping *s.* contabilità.
booklet *s.* libretto.
bookmaker *s.* allibratore.
bookseller *s.* libraio.
bookshelf *s.* (*pl.* *-lves*) scaffale.
bookshop *s.* libreria.
bookstall *s.* edicola, bancarella (*di libri*).
boom *s.* **1.** rombo **2.** periodo di prosperità.
to **boom** *vi.* **1.** rimbombare **2.** essere in periodo di prosperità.
boor *s.* persona zotica.
boorish *agg.* rustico.
boorishness *s.* rozzezza.
boot *s.* **1.** stivale, scarpa **2.** (*auto*) portabagagli.
bootblack *s.* lustrascarpe.
booth *s.* baracca || *telephone* —, cabina telefonica.
booty *s.* bottino.

border s. 1. orlo 2. frontiera.
to border vt. orlare || to — on, confinare con.
borderer s. abitante di confine.
bordering s. 1. il bordare 2. il confinare.
bore V. to bear.
bore[1] s. 1. buco 2. calibro (di arma).
bore[2] s. 1. seccatura 2. seccatore.
to bore[1] vt. forare.
to bore[2] vt. annoiare.
boreal agg. boreale.
boredom s. noia.
boric agg. borico.
boring[1] agg. noioso.
boring[2] s. perforazione || — test, sondaggio.
born V. to bear. ♦ **born** agg. nato, generato || to be —, nascere.
borne V. to bear.
borough s. 1. municipio 2. circoscrizione elettorale.
to borrow vt. prendere a prestito.
borrower s. chi prende a prestito.
bosom s. seno || — friend, amico intimo.
boss[1] s. 1. protuberanza 2. (arch.) bugna.
boss[2] s. capo, padrone.
bossy[1] agg. a bugnato.
bossy[2] agg. (gergo) prepotente.
botanist s. botanico.
botany s. botanica.
botch s. pasticcio.
to botch vt. 1. rattoppare 2. arruffare.
botcher s. pasticcione.
both agg. e pron. entrambi, tutti e due. ♦ **both** avv. nel medesimo tempo || — ... and, sia... sia, tanto... quanto.
bother s. seccatura.
to bother vt. infastidire. ♦ to **bother** vi. preoccuparsi.
bothersome agg. fastidioso.
bottle s. bottiglia || feeding- —, poppatoio; — -feeding, allattamento artificiale.
to bottle vt. imbottigliare.
bottling s. imbottigliamento.
bottom agg. 1. inferiore 2. basilare. ♦ **bottom** s. 1. fondo 2. fondamento 3. deretano 4. (mar.) chiglia.
to bottom vt. 1. mettere il fondo (a) 2. impagliare 3. capire. ♦ to **bottom** vi. posare, essere posato.
bottomless agg. 1. senza fondo 2.

senza fine.
bough s. ramo (d'albero).
bought V. to buy.
boulder s. macigno.
boulevard s. viale.
bounce s. 1. balzo 2. vanteria.
to bounce vt. far rimbalzare. ♦ to **bounce** vi. 1. rimbalzare 2. gloriarsi.
bouncer s. fanfarone.
bound[1] s. limite, confine.
bound[2] s. salto.
bound[3] V. to bind.
bound[4] agg. 1. destinato 2. diretto a 3. certo.
to bound[1] vt. confinare, limitare.
to bound[2] vi. balzare.
boundary s. limite, frontiera.
boundless agg. illimitato.
bounteous agg. generoso.
bounty s. generosità.
bourgeois agg. e s. borghese.
bourgeoisie s. borghesia.
bow[1] s. 1. arco 2. archetto 3. fiocco || -window, bovino.
bow[2] s. inchino.
bow[3] s. prua.
to bow vt. piegare. ♦ to **bow** vi. 1. piegarsi 2. inclinarsi.
bowels s. pl. viscere.
bower s. 1. pergolato 2. dimora.
bowl[1] s. ciotola.
bowl[2] s. boccia.
to bowl vt. far rotolare. ♦ to **bowl** vi. 1. rotolare 2. giocare a bocce.
bowler s. giocatore di bocce || — bat, bombetta.
bowling s. gioco delle bocce.
bowman s. arciere.
bowshot s. tiro d'arco.
box[1] s. 1. scatola 2. stanzetta 3. stalla 4. (teat.) palco 5. (giur.) banco || letter- —, buca per le lettere; money- —, salvadanaio; strong- —, cassaforte.
box[2] s. pugno, ceffone.
to box[1] vt. mettere in scatola.
to box[2] vt. schiaffeggiare. ♦ to **box** vi. fare del pugilato.
boxer s. pugile.
boxing s. pugilato.
boy s. ragazzo.
to boycott vt. boicottare.
boyhood s. fanciullezza.
boyish agg. fanciullesco.
bra s. reggipetto.
brace s. 1. sostegno 2. coppia, paio 3. (mar.) braccio. ♦ **braces** s. pl. bretelle.

to **brace** vt. 1. legare 2. fortificare.
bracelet s. braccialetto.
brachycardia s. brachicardia.
bracket s. 1. mensola, sostegno 2. parentesi.
brackish agg. salato, salso.
brag s. 1. millanteria 2. millantatore.
to **brag** vt. vantare. ♦ to **brag** vi. vantarsi.
braggart agg. e s. spaccone.
bragging s. millanteria.
braid s. 1. treccia 2. gallone.
to **braid** vt. 1. intrecciare 2. guarnire.
brain s. cervello.
brainless agg. scervellato.
brake[1] s. 1. felce 2. boschetto.
brake[2] s. freno.
to **brake** vt. frenare.
brakesman s. frenatore.
bramble s. rovo.
bran s. crusca.
branch s. 1. ramo 2. filiale.
to **branch** vt. ramificare. ♦ to **branch** vi. ramificarsi || to — out, estendersi (di attività commerciale, affari).
branching s. ramificazione.
brand s. 1. tizzone 2. marchio (a fuoco) 3. marca || — -new, nuovo fiammante.
to **brand** vt. 1. marchiare 2. stigmatizzare.
to **brandish** vt. brandire.
brass agg. 1. di ottone 2. (fig.) sfacciato. ♦ **brass** s. 1. ottone 2. (mecc.) bronzina 3. (fig.) sfacciataggine || — band, fanfara
brassy agg. V. brass.
bravado s. bravata.
brave agg. e s. prode, coraggioso.
bravely avv. coraggiosamente.
bravery s. 1. coraggio 2. splendore.
brawl s. rissa.
to **brawl** vi. rissare.
brawn s. muscolo, forza muscolare.
brawny agg. muscoloso.
bray s. raglio.
to **bray**[1] vi. 1. ragliare 2. (fig.) stonare.
to **bray**[2] vt. frantumare, sminuzzare.
brazen agg. V. brass.
brazier[1] s. calderaio.
brazier[2] s. braciere.
Brazilian agg. e s. brasiliar.).
breach s. 1. rottura 2. breccia 3. infrazione || — of promise, rottura di fidanzamento.

bread s. pane.
to **bread** vt. rimpanare.
breadth s. 1. larghezza 2. altezza (di stoffe).
breadthwise avv. in larghezza (di stoffe).
break s. 1. rottura 2. interruzione, intervallo 3. infrazione || — -up, collasso, smembramento, fine.
to **break** (broke, broken) vt. 1. rompere 2. interrompere 3. domare 4. rovinare. ♦ to **break** (broke, broken) vi. 1. rompersi 2. irrompere || to — down, demolire, (auto) restare in panne, esaurirsi; to — off, mandare a monte; to — up, fare a pezzi.
breakdown s. 1. collasso 2. rottura 3. dissesto || nervous —, esaurimento nervoso.
breaker s. 1. rompitore 2. violatore 3. domatore 4. (mecc.) macchina rompitrice 5. (mar.) frangente 6. (elett.) interruttore.
breakfast s. prima colazione.
to **breakfast** vi. fare la prima colazione.
breaking s. 1. rottura 2. (comm.) fallimento.
breakneck agg. a rotta di collo.
breakwater s. frangiflutti.
breast s. petto || — -bone, sterno.
breasted agg. dal petto || double- —, a doppio petto.
breath s. 1. soffio 2. respiro.
breathable agg. respirabile.
to **breathe** vi. 1. respirare 2. spirare. ♦ to **breathe** vt. 1. infondere 2. sussurrare.
breathing s. V. breath.
breathless agg. 1. ansante 2. esanime.
breathlessness s. affanno.
bred V. to breed. ♦ **bred** agg. ill- —, maleducato.
breech s. 1. parte posteriore 2. culatta (di arma).
breeches s. pl. calzoni.
breed s. razza.
to **breed** (bred, bred) vt. 1. generare 2. allevare. ♦ to **breed** (bred, bred) vi. nascere.
breeder s. 1. chi genera 2. allevatore.
breeding s. 1. generazione 2. allevamento 3. educazione.
breeze s. brezza.
breezy agg. 1. ventilato 2. cordiale.
brethren s. pl. confratelli.

breviary s. breviario.

brevity s. brevità.

brew s. 1. mistura 2. fermentazione (di birra).

to brew vt. 1. mescolare 2. (fig.) macchinare. ♦ **to brew** vi. fare la birra.

brewer s. birraio.

brewery s. fabbrica di birra.

bribe s. dono (a scopo di corruzione), allettamento.

to bribe vt. corrompere.

briber s. corruttore.

bribery s. corruzione.

brick s. mattone.

bricklayer s. muratore.

brickwork s. muratura in mattoni.

brickyard s. mattonaia.

bride s. sposa.

bridegroom s. sposo.

bridge s. ponte || swing- —; ponte girevole; toll- —, ponte a pedaggio; — -head, testa di ponte.

bridle s. briglia, freno.

to bridle vt. imbrigliare.

bridling s. imbrigliamento.

brief agg. breve. ♦ **brief** s. riassunto.

to brief vt. 1. riassumere 2. (giur.) nominare (il proprio avvocato) 3. dare istruzioni.

briefness s. brevità, concisione.

brier s. 1. rovo 2. rosa selvatica.

brig s. brigantino.

brigade s. brigata.

bright agg. 1. chiaro, splendente 2. vivace.

to brighten vt. 1. far brillare 2. animare. ♦ **to brighten** vi. 1. brillare 2. animarsi.

brightness s. 1. splendore 2. gaiezza.

brill s. (itt.) rombo.

brilliance, brilliancy s. brillantezza.

brilliant agg. e s. brillante.

brilliantine s. brillantina.

brim s. 1. orlo 2. ala (di cappello).

brimful agg. colmo.

brindled agg. pezzato.

brine s. acqua salata.

to bring (brought, brought) vt. 1. portare 2. indurre || to — about, causare; to — back, richiamare alla memoria; to — forth, dare alla luce; to — up, educare, allevare.

brink s. orlo.

brisk agg. 1. vivace 2. frizzante.

briskness s. vivacità.

bristle s. setola.

to bristle vi. essere irto di.

bristly agg. 1. setoloso 2. ruvido.

British agg. britannico.

Briton agg. e s. britanno.

broad agg. 1. ampio 2. chiaro 3. marcato 4. volgare || — daylight, pieno giorno. ♦ **broad** s. larghezza. ♦ **broad** avv. ampiamente.

broadcast s. 1. radiodiffusione 2. radiocomunicazione.

to broadcast (broadcast, broadcast) (anche reg.) vt. e vi. radiotrasmettere.

broadcaster s. trasmettitore.

broadcasting s. radiodiffusione.

to broaden vt. allargare. ♦ **to broaden** vi. allargarsi, estendersi.

broadness s. 1. larghezza 2. grossolanità.

broadside s. (mar.) 1. bordo, fiancata 2. bordata.

brocade s. broccato.

bro(c)coli s. broccolo.

broil s. rissa.

to broil vt. cuocere alla griglia. ♦ **to broil** vi. abbrustolirsi (al sole).

broke V. to break.

broken V. to break. ♦ **broken** agg. 1. variabile (di tempo) 2. accidentale (di terreno) 3. indebolito 4. avvilito 5. scorretto.

broker s. 1. (comm.) agente 2. mediatore.

bromide s. bromuro.

bromine s. bromo.

bronchial agg. bronchiale.

bronchia s. pl. bronchi.

bronchitis s. bronchite.

broncho-pneumonia s. broncopolmonite.

bronze s. bronzo.

to bronze vt. abbronzare. ♦ **to bronze** vi. abbronzarsi.

brooch s. spilla.

brood s. covata.

to brood vt. 1. covare 2. (fig.) rimuginare, meditare.

brooding s. 1. cova 2. meditazione.

brook s. ruscello.

to brook vt. sopportare, tollerare.

brooklet s. ruscelletto.

broom s. 1. ginestra 2. scopa.

broth s. brodo.

brothel s. bordello.

brother s. 1. fratello 2. collega || — -in-law, cognato; half- —, fratellastro.

brotherhood s. 1. fratellanza 2. confraternita.

brotherlike agg. fraterno.

brotherly agg. fraterno. ◆ **brotherly** avv. fraternamente.

brought V. to bring.

brow s. fronte. ◆ **brows** s. pl. sopracciglia.

brown agg. 1. bruno 2. marrone. ◆ **brown** s. marrone.

to **brown** vt. 1. rendere bruno 2. rosolare. ◆ to **brown** vi. 1. diventare bruno 2. abbronzarsi

to **browse** vt. e vi. brucare.

bruise s. contusione.

to **bruise** vt. ammaccare. ◆ to **bruise** vi. ammaccarsi.

bruiser s. 1. pugilatore 2. (fig.) gradasso.

brush s. 1. spazzola, spazzolino 2. spazzolata 3. pennello 4. rissa || — -up, ripasso.

to **brush** vt. 1. spazzolare 2. sfiorare || to — aside (fig.), ignorare; to — up, ripassare.

brushwood s. sottobosco.

brushy agg. 1. ispido 2. folto (di bosco).

brusque agg. brusco.

brutal agg. brutale.

brutality s. brutalità.

to **brutalize** vt. 1. abbrutire 2. maltrattare. ◆ to **brutalize** vi. abbrutirsi.

brute agg. brutale. ◆ **brute** s. bruto.

brutish agg. brutale, rozzo.

bubble s. 1. bolla 2. gorgoglio.

to **bubble** vi. gorgogliare || to — over, traboccare.

bubo s. bubbone.

bubonic agg. bubbonico.

buccaneer s. bucaniere.

buck s. 1. daino 2. maschio (di molti animali).

to **buck** vi. sgroppare.

bucket s. secchio.

buckle s. fibbia.

to **buckle** vt. 1. affibbiare 2. piegare. ◆ to **buckle** vi. piegarsi.

bucolic agg. bucolico.

bud s. 1. gemma 2. germe.

to **bud** vi. germogliare.

Buddhism s. buddismo.

Buddhist agg. e s. buddista.

budget s. 1. raccolta (di documenti) 2. bilancio.

buffalo s. bufalo.

buffer s. respingente.

buffet[1] s. schiaffo.

buffet[2] s. credenza.

to **buffet** vt. schiaffeggiare.

buffoon s. buffone.

bug s. 1. coleottero 2. cimice || big —, (gergo) pezzo grosso.

bugbear s. spauracchio.

bugger s. sodomita.

build s. costruzione, struttura.

to **build (built, built)** vt. costruire || to — up, murare.

builder s. costruttore.

building agg. edilizio. ◆ **building** s. edificio.

built V. to build.

bulb s. 1. bulbo 2. lampadina || — socket, portalampada.

Bulgarian agg. e s. bulgaro.

bulge s. gonfiore.

to **bulge** vi. gonfiarsi. ◆ to **bulge** vt. 1. sporgere 2. gonfiare.

bulgy agg. rigonfio.

bulk s. 1. massa 2. carico.

bulkhead s. paratia.

bulky agg. massiccio.

bull s. 1. toro 2. maschio (di alcuni mammiferi) || —'s eye, oblò.

bulldog s. mastino.

bullet s. pallottola.

bulletin s. bollettino || news —, giornale radio.

bullfight s. corrida.

bullfighter s. torero.

bullock s. torello.

bully agg. borioso.

to **bully** vt. e vi. fare il prepotente (verso).

bulwark s. 1. bastione 2. (mar.) parapetto.

bumble-bee s. calabrone.

bump s. 1. urto 2. bernoccolo.

to **bump** vt. e vi. urtare, andare a sbattere contro.

bumper s. 1. paraurti 2. respingente.

bun s. 1. focaccia 2. crocchia.

bunch s. 1. mazzo 2. grappolo.

bundle s. 1. fagotto 2. fascio.

to **bundle** vt. riunire in fascio, fare un involto.

bung s. tappo.

bungler agg. e s. confusionario.

bunny s. coniglietto.

buoy s. boa.

buoyancy s. 1. galleggiabilità 2. ottimismo.

buoyant agg. 1. galleggiante 2. ottimista.

burden s. 1. peso 2. tonnellaggio.

to **burden** vt. caricare.
burdensome agg. gravoso.
bureau s. (pl. bureaux) ufficio.
bureaucracy s. burocrazia.
bureaucrat s. burocrate.
bureaucratic agg. burocratico.
burglar s. scassinatore (notturno).
burglary s. furto (notturno) con scasso.
to **burgle** vt. e vi. svaligiare con scasso.
burgomaster s. borgomastro.
burial s. sepoltura || — -ground, cimitero; — -service, ufficio funebre.
burin s. bulino.
burly agg. corpulento.
burn s. ustione.
to **burn** (**burnt, burnt**) (anche reg.) vt. e vi. bruciare, ardere.
burner s. bruciatore.
burning s. 1. incendio 2. (metal.) fusione.
to **burnish** vt. lustrare.
burnt V. to burn.
burrow s. tana, buca.
bursar s. economo.
bursary s. 1. ufficio dell'economato 2. borsa di studio.
burst s. 1. scoppio 2. squarcio.
to **burst** (**burst, burst**) vt. 1. far esplodere 2. sfondare. ♦ to **burst** (**burst, burst**) vi. 1. scoppiare 2. irrompere.
bursting s. scoppio.
to **bury** vt. seppellire.
bus s. autobus.
busby s. colbac.
bush s. cespuglio.
bushel s. staio.
bushy agg. folto.
busily avv. attivamente.
business s. 1. affare 2. mestiere 3. ditta 4. scopo || — -man, uomo d'affari; — -like, metodico, sistematico.
bust s. busto.
bustle s. trambusto.
to **bustle** vi. agitarsi.
busy agg. occupato.
to **busy** vt. occupare.
busybody s. ficcanaso.
but cong. ma. ♦ **but** avv. solo. ♦ **but** prep. tranne || — for, se non fosse per; — that, se non; cannot —, non poter far a meno di; all —, pressoché.
butane s. butano.
butcher s. macellaio.
butchery s. macello.

butler s. maggiordomo.
butt[1] s. 1. calcio (di arma) 2. impugnatura (di utensile) 3. mozzicone.
butt[2] s. urto.
to **butt** vt. e vi. cozzare.
butter s. burro.
to **butter** vt. imburrare.
buttercup s. ranuncolo.
butterfly s. farfalla.
buttery agg. burroso.
buttock s. natica.
button s. bottone.
to **button** vt. abbottonare.
button-hole s. occhiello.
to **button-hole** vt. 1. fare asole a 2. (fig.) attaccar bottone.
button-holer s. attaccabottoni.
buttress s. contrafforte.
buxom agg. formoso, avvenente (di donna).
to **buy** (**bought, bought**) vt. comprare || — off, riscattare; to — up, accaparrare.
buyable agg. acquistabile.
buyer s. acquirente.
buzz s. ronzio.
buzzard s. poiana.
to **buzz** vi. e vt. ronzare, bisbigliare.
buzzer s. 1. insetto che ronza 2. cicala, segnale acustico.
by avv. 1. vicino 2. da parte, in disparte || — and —, fra poco; — and large, complessivamente. ♦ **by** prep. 1. (agente, causa, mezzo) per, da, con, di || a book (written) — Shakespeare, un libro di Shakespeare; to travel — train, viaggiare col treno 2. (tempo) entro, per, durante || day — day, di giorno in giorno; — night, di notte 3. (luogo) vicino a, a fianco di, attraverso || a house — the sea, una casa sul mare. ♦ **by** agg. secondario.
bye-bye inter. arrivederci.
bygone agg. e s. passato.
by-line s. (giorn.) firma.
byname s. soprannome.
by-pass s. 1. circonvallazione 2. deviazione.
by-product s. sottoprodotto.
byroad s. strada secondaria.
byssus s. bisso.
bystander s. spettatore.
bystreet s. viuzza.
byway s. via traversa.
byword s. proverbio, epiteto.
bywork s. lavoro supplementare (a tempo perso).
Byzantine agg. e s. bizantino.

C

C (*mus.*) do.
cab *s.* vettura di piazza.
cabal *s.* intrigo, cospirazione.
cabbage *s.* cavolo.
cab(b)ala *s.* cabala.
cab(b)alistic *agg.* cabalistico.
cabin *s.* **1.** capanna **2.** (*aer.; fer.; mar.*) cabina.
cabinet *s.* **1.** stanzino **2.** stipo, armadietto **3.** (*pol.*) gabinetto, consiglio dei ministri || — -*maker*, ebanista; — -*minister*, membro del gabinetto.
cable *s.* **1.** cavo **2.** cablogramma || — -*way*, teleferica.
to **cable** *vt.* e *vi.* **1.** fornire di cavo **2.** trasmettere un cablogramma.
cablegram *s.* cablogramma.
cabman *s.* tassista.
caboose (*mar.*) cambusa.
cabotage *s.* cabotaggio.
cacao *s.* cacao.
cacophony *s.* cacofonia.
cactus *s.* cactus.
cadaverous *agg.* **1.** cadaverico **2.** esangue.
cadence *s.* cadenza, ritmo.
cadet *s.* cadetto.
caducity *s.* caducità.
Caesarean *agg.* cesareo, imperiale || — *operation*, parto cesareo.
caesura *s.* cesura.
café *s.* caffè (*locale pubblico*).
caffeine *s.* caffeina.
cage *s.* **1.** gabbia **2.** impalcatura.
to **cage** *vt.* mettere in gabbia.
cake *s.* torta, focaccia.
calamary *s.* calamaro.
calamitous *agg.* calamitoso.
calamity *s.* calamità.
calcareous *agg.* calcareo.
calcification *s.* calcificazione.
to **calcify** *vt.* calcificare. ♦ to **calcify** *vi.* calcificarsi.
calcination *s.* calcinazione.
to **calcine** V. *to calcify.*
calcite *s.* calcite.
calcium *s.* calcio.
to **calculate** *vt.* **1.** calcolare **2.** contare. ♦ to **calculate** *vi.* fare affidamento.
calculated *agg.* **1.** calcolato **2.** premeditato **3.** (*fig.*) idoneo.
calculating *agg.* calcolatore || — *machine*, macchina calcolatrice.
calculation *s.* calcolo.

calculator *s.* calcolatore, calcolatrice.
calendar *s.* calendario, almanacco.
calf¹ *s.* (*pl.* calves) vitello.
calf² *s.* polpaccio.
to **calibrate** *vt.* **1.** calibrare **2.** (*mecc.*) tarare.
calibration *s.* calibratura, taratura.
calibre *s.* calibro.
calico *s.* calicò.
call *s.* **1.** richiamo, chiamata **2.** breve visita: *to pay* (*v. irr.*) *so. a —*, fare una breve visita a qu. **3.** (*giur.*) appello **4.** (*mil.*) adunata **5.** (*mar.*) scalo || — *bird*, uccello da richiamo; — *box*, cabina telefonica; — *up*, chiamata alle armi; *trunk —*, chiamata intercontinentale.
to **call** *vt.* e *vi.* **1.** chiamare, richiamare: *to — aside*, chiamare in disparte; *to — to arms*, chiamare alle armi; *to — to mind*, richiamare alla mente **2.** esortare, ordinare || *to — into being*, creare; *to — out*, chiamare ad alta voce, esclamare; *to — up*, telefonare; *to — at*, fare scalo a; *to — for*, passare a prendere; *to — on*, fare una breve visita a; *to — upon*, implorare, invocare.
caller *s.* visitatore, visitatrice.
calligrapher *s.* calligrafo.
calligraphic *agg.* calligrafico.
calling *s.* **1.** appello **2.** mestiere, professione **3.** vocazione.
callosity *s.* **1.** callosità **2.** (*fig.*) insensibilità.
callous *agg.* **1.** calloso **2.** (*fig.*) insensibile.
calm *agg.* calmo. ♦ **calm** *s.* calma.
to **calm** *vt.* calmare. ♦ to **calm** *vi.* to — *down*, calmarsi (*di tempesta ecc.*).
calming *agg.* calmante.
calmly *avv.* con calma.
calmness *s.* calma, tranquillità.
calorific *agg.* calorifico.
calorimeter *s.* calorimetro.
calory *s.* caloria.
to **calumniate** *vt.* calunniare.
Calvary *s.* Calvario.
calves V. *calf.*
Calvinism *s.* calvinismo.
Calvinist *agg.* e *s.* calvinista.
came V. *to come.*
camel *s.* cammello.
camellia *s.* camelia.
cameo *s.* cammeo.
camera *s.* **1.** (*foto*) macchina foto-

grafica 2. (*giur.*) Camera di Consiglio.

camisole *s.* corpetto, farsetto.

camouflage *s.* 1. mascheramento 2. (*mil.*) mimetizzazione.

to **camouflage** *vt.* 1. mascherare 2. (*mil.*) mimetizzare.

camp *s.* 1. (*mil.*) campo 2. campeggio || — -*bed*, brandina.

to **camp** *vt.* (*mil.*) accampare. ♦ to **camp** *vi.* 1. accamparsi 2. attendarsi.

campaign *s.* (*mil.*) campagna.

camper *s.* campeggiatore.

camphor *s.* canfora.

camping *s.* 1. (*mil.*) accampamento 2. campeggio.

can[1] *s.* recipiente di latta, bidone.

can[2] *v. dif.* (*ind. cong. pres.*) **could** (*ind. cong. pass. e condiz.*) potere, essere in grado di.

Canadian *agg. e s.* canadese.

canal *s.* canale.

canalization *s.* canalizzazione.

to **canalize** *vt.* canalizzare.

canary *agg.* giallo canarino. ♦ **canary** *s.* canarino.

to **cancel** *vt.* annullare, cancellare.

cancellation *s.* annullamento, cancellatura.

cancer *s.* cancro.

candid *agg.* sincero, candido.

candidate *s.* candidato.

candidature *s.* candidatura.

candidly *avv.* sinceramente, candidamente.

candied *agg.* candito.

candle *s.* candela || — -*end*, moccolo; — -*holder*, candelabro; *by* — -*light*, a lume di candela.

candlestick *s.* candeliere.

candour *s.* candore, ingenuità.

candy *s.* candito.

to **candy** *vt.* candire. ♦ to **candy** *vi.* cristallizzarsi (*di zucchero*).

cane *s.* 1. giunco, canna 2. bastone da passeggio.

to **cane** *vt.* bastonare (*con una canna*).

canine *s.* dente canino.

caning *s.* bastonatura.

canned *agg.* conservato in scatola.

cannibal *s.* cannibale.

cannibalism *s.* cannibalismo.

cannon *s.* 1. cannone 2. carambola (*al biliardo*).

to **cannon** *vi.* 1. cannoneggiare 2. far carambola.

canoe *s.* canoa.

canon *s.* 1. canone. 2. (*eccl.*) canonico: — *law*, diritto canonico.

canonical *agg.* canonico.

to **canonize** *vt.* canonizzare.

canopy *s.* 1. baldacchino 2. volta (*del cielo*).

cant *s.* 1. (*arch.*) angolo esterno 2. inclinazione 3. gergo.

canteen *s.* 1. (*mil.*) dispensa 2. mensa aziendale.

canvas *s.* 1. canovaccio 2. (*mar.*) velatura 3. tela 4. tendone.

canyon *s.* burrone.

cap *s.* 1. berretto 2. (*arch.*) capitello 3. (*mecc.; elettr.*) cappuccio, capsula.

capability *s.* capacità, abilità.

capable *agg.* abile, capace.

capacitor *s.* condensatore.

capacity *s.* 1. capacità 2. (*elettr.*) potenza (*di motore*).

cape[1] *s.* capo, promontorio.

cape[2] *s.* cappa.

caper[1] *s.* cappero.

caper[2] *s.* piroetta, capriola.

to **caper** *vi.* far capriole.

capercaillie *s.* gallo cedrone.

capillarity *s.* capillarità.

capillary *agg.* capillare. ♦ **capillary** *s.* (*anat.*) vaso capillare.

capital[1] *agg. e s.* capitale.

capital[2] *s.* (*arch.*) capitello.

capitalism *s.* capitalismo.

capitalist *s.* capitalista.

capitalistic *agg.* capitalistico.

to **capitalize** *vt.* capitalizzare.

capitular *agg.* capitolare.

capitulary *s.* capitolare.

to **capitulate** *vi.* capitolare.

capitulation *s.* capitolazione.

capon *s.* cappone.

caprice *s.* capriccio.

to **capsize** *vt.* capovolgere. ♦ to **capsize** *vi.* capovolgersi.

capstan *s.* argano.

capsule *s.* capsula.

to **capsule** *vt.* incapsulare.

captain *s.* 1. capitano 2. (*comm.*) magnate.

captious *agg.* capzioso.

to **captivate** *vt.* cattivare, ammaliare.

captivating *agg.* cattivante, ammaliante.

captive *s.* prigioniero: *to take* —, far prigioniero.

captivity *s.* prigionia, cattività.

capture *s.* cattura.

to **capture** *vt.* far prigioniero, prendere (*di città ecc.*).

Capuchin *s.* **1.** (*eccl.*) Cappuccino **2.** scimmia cappuccina.

car *s.* **1.** carro **2.** automobile **3.** (*ferr.*) vagone || — *-licence*, permesso di circolazione; *dining-* —, vagone ristorante; *sleeping-* —, vagone letto.

carabin *s.* carabina.

carabineer *s.* carabiniere.

to caracole *vi.* caracollare.

carafe *s.* caraffa.

caramel *s.* caramello.

carat *s.* carato.

caravan *s.* **1.** carovana **2.** carro (*di zingari ecc.*).

caravel *s.* caravella.

carbon *s.* carbonio || — *paper*, carta carbone.

carbonate *s.* carbonato.

carboniferous *agg.* carbonifero

to carbonize *vt.* carbonizzare.

carbuncle *s.* carbonchio.

carburation *s.* carburazione.

carburetter, carburettor *s.* carburatore.

carcase *s.* carcassa.

carcinogen *s.* sostanza cancerogena.

card *s.* **1.** cartoncino, biglietto **2.** carta da giuoco.

to card *vt.* schedare.

cardan *s.* cardano || — *joint*, giunto cardanico.

cardboard *s.* cartone.

cardiac *agg.* cardiaco.

cardigan *s.* giacca di lana

cardinal *agg.* e *s.* cardinale.

cardiogram *s.* cardiogramma

cardiologist *s.* cardiologo.

cardiopathy *s.* cardiopatia.

care *s.* **1.** cura, attenzione, protezione: *take* —!, attenzione!; *to take* — *of*, aver cura **2.** preoccupazione || — *-free*, senza pensieri; — *-worn*, pieno di pensieri.

to care *vi.* curarsi, interessarsi.

career *s.* **1.** carriera **2.** andatura veloce.

careful *agg.* **1.** accurato **2.** prudente.

carefully *avv.* **1.** accuratamente **2.** attentamente.

careless *agg.* noncurante.

carelessly *avv.* negligentemente.

carelessness *s.* trascuratezza.

caress *s.* carezza.

to caress *vt.* accarezzare.

caressing *agg.* carezzevole.

caretaker *s.* guardiano, custode.

caricature *s.* caricatura.

Carmelite *s.* carmelitano.

carmine *agg.* e *s.* carminio.

carnage *s.* carneficina; strage.

carnal *agg.* carnale, sensuale.

carnation *agg.* carnicino. ♦ **carnation** *s.* garofano.

carnival *s.* carnevale.

carnivore *s.* carnivoro.

carnivorous *agg.* carnivoro.

carol *s.* canto, inno.

carotid *s.* carotide.

carousel *s.* carosello.

carp *s.* carpa.

carpenter *s.* carpentiere, falegname.

carpet *s.* tappeto || *bedside* —, scendiletto.

carriage *s.* **1.** carrozza, vettura **2.** (*comm.*) trasporto.

carrier *s.* **1.** portatore, spedizioniere **2.** (*mecc.*) trasportatore **3.** supporto.

carrion *s.* carogna.

carrot *s.* carota.

carry *s.* portata (*di arma da fuoco ecc.*).

to carry *vt.* e *vi.* **1.** portare (*un peso*), trasportare **2.** trasmettere (*suoni*) || *to* — *about*, portare addosso; *to* — *on*, continuare; *to* — *out*, eseguire, realizzare, compiere; *to* — *through*, portare a buon fine.

carrying *s.* trasporto.

cart *s.* carro.

cartel *s.* (*econ.; pol.*) cartello.

cartilage *s.* cartilagine.

cartography *s.* cartografia.

cartomancy *s.* cartomanzia.

carton *s.* scatola di cartone.

cartoon *s.* **1.** vignetta **2.** (*cine*) disegno animato.

cartridge *s.* **1.** cartuccia **2.** (*foto*) rotolo.

to carve *vt.* e *vi.* scolpire, incidere, cesellare.

carver *s.* intagliatore, scultore (*in legno e avorio*).

carving *s.* scultura, intaglio (*in legno e avorio*).

caryatid *s.* cariatide.

cascade *s.* piccola cascata (*d'acqua*).

case[1] *s.* **1.** caso, avvenimento **2.** (*giur.*) causa.

case[2] *s.* **1.** astuccio **2.** cassa, cassetta.

to case *vt.* imballare.

casement *s.* telaio di finestra (*a due battenti*), finestra.

cash s. cassa, contanti || — on delivery, pagamento alla consegna; by ready —, in contanti.

to **cash** vt. incassare, riscuotere.

cashier s. cassiere.

to **cashier** vt. destituire.

casing s. involucro, copertura.

cask s. barile, botte.

casket s. scrigno.

cassation s. cassazione.

cassock s. tunica (del clero anglicano).

cast s. **1.** getto, lancio **2.** (metal.) gettata, stampo **3.** complesso (di attori) || — -iron, ghisa.

to **cast** (cast, cast) vt. e vi. **1.** gettare, lanciare **2.** (metal.) fondere (in stampo) || to — aside, gettare da parte; to — down, abbassare (gli occhi).

castanets s. pl. nacchere.

castaway agg. arenato, respinto. ♦ **castaway** s. naufrago, reprobo.

caste s. casta.

caster s. V. castor.

to **castigate** vt. castigare, punire.

casting s. **1.** il gettare **2.** (metal.) getto, colata **3.** distribuzione (delle parti agli attori).

castle s. castello.

castor s. **1.** pepaiuola, saliera **2.** rotella da mobili.

castor-oil s. olio di ricino.

to **castrate** vt. castrare.

casual agg. casuale, fortuito.

casually avv. per caso.

casualness s. irregolarità, noncuranza.

casualty s. **1.** infortunio **2.** infortunato.

casuistry s. casistica.

cat s. gatto.

cataclysm s. cataclisma.

catacomb s. catacomba.

catalepsy s. catalessi.

cataleptic agg. e s. catalettico.

catalogue s. catalogo.

to **catalogue** vt. e vi. catalogare.

catalyst s. catalizzatore.

cataplasm s. cataplasma.

catapult s. catapulta.

cataract s. cateratta.

catarrh s. catarro.

catastrophe s. catastrofe, calamità.

catastrophic(al) agg. catastrofico.

catch s. **1.** presa, cattura **2.** trappola || — -as- — -can, lotta libera.

to **catch** (caught, caught) vt. **1.** afferrare, acchiappare, prendere: to

— the train, prendere il treno **2.** pescare, sorprendere.

catching agg. **1.** attraente **2.** orecchiabile (di melodia) **3.** (med.) contagioso.

catchy agg. **1.** attraente **2.** orecchiabile (di melodia) **3.** insidioso.

catechism s. catechismo.

to **catechize** vt. catechizzare.

catechumen s. catecumeno.

categoric(al) agg. categorico.

category s. categoria.

to **cater** vi. **1.** provvedere cibo **2.** procurare svaghi.

caterpillar s. **1.** bruco **2.** (mecc.) cingolo **3.** trattore a cingoli.

catharsis s. catarsi.

cathartic agg. catartico.

cathedral s. cattedrale.

Catherine-wheel s. girandola.

cathode s. catodo.

cathodic agg. catodico.

catholic agg. e s. cattolico.

Catholicism s. cattolicesimo.

cation s. catione.

cattish agg. felino.

cattle s. bestiame, armenti || — -dealer, negoziante di bestiame; — -lifter, ladro di bestiame.

caught V. to catch.

cauldron s. caldaia.

cauliflower s. cavolfiore.

causal agg. causale.

causality s. causalità.

causative agg. causativo.

cause s. **1.** causa, ragione, motivo **2.** (giur.) processo, causa.

to **cause** vt. causare, cagionare.

causeway s. strada rialzata.

caustic agg. caustico (anche fig.).

caustically avv. causticamente (anche fig.).

causticity s. causticità (anche fig.).

cauterization s. cauterizzazione.

to **cauterize** vt. cauterizzare.

caution s. **1.** prudenza, cautela **2.** cauzione, garanzia || — -money, cauzione, pegno.

to **caution** vt. mettere in guardia.

cautious agg. cauto, prudente.

cautiously avv. cautamente.

cavalier s. cavaliere.

cavalry s. cavalleria.

cave s. caverna, spelonca.

to **cave** vt. e vi. scavare || to — in, sprofondare.

cavernous agg. cavernoso (anche fig.).

caviar(e) s. caviale.

cavil *s.* cavillo.
to **cavil** *vi.* cavillare.
cavity *s.* cavità.
cavy *s.* cavia.
cayman *s.* caimano.
to **cease** *vt.* e *vi.* cessare, finire.
cedar *s.* cedro.
cedilla *s.* cediglia.
ceiling *s.* soffitto.
to **celebrate** *vt.* e *vi.* celebráre, solennizzare.
celebrated *agg.* famoso.
celebration *s.* celebrazione.
celebrity *s.* celebrità, persona famosa.
celerity *s.* celerità.
celery *s.* sedano.
celestial *agg.* celestiale, paradisiaco.
celibacy *s.* celibato.
cell *s.* **1.** cella **2.** cellula.
cellar *s.* cantina.
cellarman *s.* cantiniere.
cellular *agg.* cellulare, alveolare.
cellulitis *s.* cellulite.
celluloid *agg.* e *s.* celluloide.
cellulose *s.* cellulosa.
Celt *s.* celta.
Celtic *agg.* celtico.
cement *s.* **1.** cemento **2.** stucco, mastice.
to **cement** *vt.* cementare (*anche fig.*).
cemetery *s.* cimitero.
to **cense** *vt.* incensare.
censer *s.* turibolo.
censor *s.* censore.
to **censor** *vt.* censurare.
censorial *agg.* censorio.
censorship *s.* censura, censorato.
censure *s.* censura.
to **censure** *vt.* censurare.
census *s.* censo.
cent *s.* centesimo (*di dollaro*).
centaur *s.* centauro.
centenarian *agg.* e *s.* centenario.
centenary *agg.* e *s.* centenario.
centennial *agg.* centennale.
centesimal *agg.* centesimale.
centigrade *agg.* centigrado.
centigramme *s.* centigrammo.
centilitre *s.* centilitro.
centimetre *s.* centimetro.
central *agg.* **1.** centrale **2.** fondamentale.
centralism *s.* accentramento.
centralization *s.* concentrazione (*di poteri*).
to **centralize** *vt.* e *vi.* accentrare.
centre *s.* centro, parte centrale, interno.

centrifugal *agg.* centrifugo.
centripetal *agg.* centripeto.
centrism *s.* centrismo.
to **centuplicate** *vt.* centuplicare.
centurion *s.* centurione.
century *s.* **1.** secolo **2.** (*stor.*) centuria.
cephalalgia *s.* cefalea.
ceramics *s.* (*arte della*) ceramica.
cereal *agg.* e *s.* cereale.
cerebral *agg.* cerebrale.
cerebro-spinal *agg.* cerebro-spinale.
cerebrum *s.* cervello.
ceremonial *agg.* da cerimonia. ♦ **ceremonial** *s.* cerimoniale.
ceremonious *agg.* cerimonioso.
ceremony *s.* cerimonia || *to stand on* —, far complimenti.
certain *agg.* **1.** certo, sicuro **2.** indeterminato, certo.
certainly *avv.* certamente.
certainty *s.* certezza.
certificate *s.* certificato.
to **certify** *vt.* certificare, attestare.
certitude *s.* certezza.
cervical *agg.* cervicale. ♦ **cervical** *s.* vertebra cervicale. ♦ **cervicals** *s. pl.* nervi cervicali.
cessation *s.* cessazione.
cession *s.* cessione.
cess-pit, cess-pool *s.* pozzo nero.
cetacean *agg.* di cetaceo. ♦ **cetacean** *s.* cetaceo.
to **chafe** *vt.* **1.** riscaldare **2.** irritare.
to **chafe** *vi.* **1.** strofinarsi **2.** irritarsi.
chaff *s.* **1.** pula, paglia trinciata **2.** (*fig.*) oggetto di nessun valore.
chaffer *s.* contrattazione, baratto.
chain *s.* **1.** catena **2.** serie, concatenamento.
to **chain** *vt.* **1.** incatenare **2.** (*fig.*) mettere in ceppi.
chain-stores *s. pl.* catene (*di negozi o grandi magazzini*).
chair *s.* **1.** sedia: *deck-* —, sedia a sdraio; *easy-* —, poltrona **2.** cattedra (*universitaria*).
chairman *s.* presidente (*di consiglio, assemblea ecc.*).
chalice *s.* calice.
chalk *s.* **1.** gesso **2.** (*min.*) calcare || — *-drawing*, disegno a pastello; — *-stone* (*pat.*), calcolo.
chalky *agg.* gessoso.
challenge *s.* **1.** sfida **2.** (*mil.*) intimazione.
to **challenge** *vt.* **1.** sfidare **2.** (*mil.*) intimare.

challenger s. sfidatore, sfidante.
chamber s. **1.** sala, aula **2.** (*pol.; comm.*) camera ǁ — -*music*, musica da camera; —*maid*, cameriera (*specialmente d'albergo*).
chamberlain s. **1.** ciambellano **2.** tesoriere.
chameleon s. camaleonte.
chamois s. camoscio.
champion s. **1.** campione **2.** difensore.
championship s. campionato.
chance s. **1.** avvenimento fortuito, caso **2.** occasione.
to **chance** vi. accadere.
chancellery s. cancelleria.
chancellor s. cancelliere.
chancery s. cancelleria.
chandelier s. candeliere, lampadario.
change s. **1.** cambio, mutamento ǁ — *for a* —, tanto per cambiare **2.** moneta spicciola.
to **change** vt. e vi. cambiare.
changeability s. mutabilità.
changeable agg. **1.** mutabile **2.** incostante (*di tempo*).
changing agg. cangiante, mutevole.
♦ **changing** s. cambio.
channel s. **1.** canale, stretto. ♦ **channels** s. pl. vie di comunicazione.
chant s. canto, cantilena.
to **channel** vt. **1.** fare canali **2.** incanalare.
chaos s. caos.
chap[1] s. (*fam.*) individuo, ragazzo.
chap[2] s. screpolatura.
chapel s. cappella.
chaplain s. cappellano.
chaplet s. ghirlanda, corona (*di fiori*).
chapter s. capitolo.
to **char** vt. carbonizzare. ♦ to **char** vi. carbonizzarsi.
character s. **1.** carattere, indole **2.** scrittura **3.** (*lett.*) personaggio.
characteristic agg. caratteristico.
♦ **characteristic** s. caratteristica.
characterization s. caratterizzazione.
to **characterize** vt. caratterizzare.
charade s. sciarada.
charcoal s. carbone di legna.
charge s. **1.** prezzo richiesto, spesa **2.** incarico, sorveglianza **3.** (*giur.*) accusa.
to **charge** vt. **1.** far pagare, addebitare **2.** incaricare **3.** accusare: to

— *so. with a crime*, accusare qu. di un delitto.
chargeable agg. **1.** a carico di, da addebitarsi a **2.** accusabile.
chariot s. cocchio.
charitable agg. caritatevole.
charitably avv. caritatevolmente.
charity s. **1.** carità, benevolenza **2.** istituzione benefica.
charlatan s. ciarlatano.
charm s. **1.** fascino **2.** incantesimo, malia.
to **charm** vt. **1.** affascinare **2.** sottoporre a magia.
charming agg. affascinante.
charmingly avv. in modo affascinante.
charnel(-house) s. ossario.
chart s. **1.** grafico **2.** carta marina.
charter s. **1.** licenza, brevetto **2.** carta costituzionale.
chartography s. cartografia.
charwoman s. domestica ad ore.
charwork s. lavoro di domestica ad ore.
chase s. **1.** inseguimento, caccia **2.** riserva di caccia, cacciagione.
to **chase**[1] vt. inseguire, cacciare.
to **chase**[2] vt. cesellare.
chaser[1] s. cacciatore, inseguitore.
chaser[2] s. cesellatore.
chasing s. **1.** cesellatura **2.** filettatura (*di una vite*).
chasm s. baratro, abisso.
chaste agg. casto, puro.
chastely avv. castamente, virtuosamente.
chastity s. castità.
chat s. chiacchiera.
to **chat** vi. chiacchierare.
chatter s. **1.** chiacchiera, chiacchierio **2.** il battere dei denti.
to **chatter** vi. **1.** chiacchierare **2.** battere i denti.
chatterbox s. chiacchierone, chiacchierona.
chattering s. **1.** chiacchierio **2.** il battere dei denti.
chauvinism s. sciovinismo.
chauvinist s. sciovinista.
cheap agg. e avv. a buon mercato.
cheaply avv. economicamente, in modo poco costoso.
cheat s. **1.** frode **2.** imbroglione.
to **cheat** vt. e vi. imbrogliare.
cheater s. truffatore, baro.
cheating s. inganno.
check[1] s. **1.** scacco **2.** controllo, verifica **3.** scontrino, contromarca.

check² s. disegno a scacchi.
to **check** vi. dare scacco. ♦ to
check vt. controllare, verificare.
checked agg. quadrettato.
checkmate s. scacco matto.
to **checkmate** vt. dare scacco matto.
cheek s. guancia.
cheekily avv. sfacciatamente.
cheeky agg. sfacciato.
to **cheer** vt. rallegrare, incoraggiare. ♦ to cheer vi. essere di buon
umore, rallegrarsi.
cheerful agg. di buon umore.
cheerfully avv. allegramente.
cheerfulness s. buon umore.
cheering agg. incoraggiante. ♦
cheering s. acclamazioni (pl.).
cheese s. formaggio.
cheetah s. ghepardo.
chemical agg. chimico.
chemically avv. chimicamente.
chemicals s. pl. prodotti chimici.
chemisette s. camicetta.
chemist s. 1. chimico 2. farmacista.
chemistry s. chimica.
cheque s. assegno: to cash a —,
cambiare un assegno; — -book,
libretto d'assegni; blank —, assegno in bianco; crossed —, assegno
sbarrato.
to **cherish** vt. 1. (fig.) nutrire 2.
curare teneramente, coccolare.
cherry s. ciliegia.
cherub s. cherubino.
chess s. giuoco degli scacchi || —
-board, scacchiera; — -men, pezzi degli scacchi.
chest s. 1. cassetta, cassone 2. torace.
chestnut agg. castano. ♦ chestnut
s. 1. castagno 2. castagna.
to **chew** vt. e vi. masticare.
chicanery s. cavillo (legale).
chick s. 1. pulcino 2. (fig.) bambino.
chicken s. gallinella, pollo.
chicory s. cicoria.
to **chide** (chid, chid) (anche reg.)
vt. e vi. redarguire, sgridare.
chief agg. principale. ♦ chief s.
capo, comandante.
chiefly avv. principalmente.
chieftain s. capo (di tribù, clan
ecc.).
chilblain s. gelone.
child s. (pl. children) 1. bambino,
bambina 2. figlio, figlia.
childhood s. infanzia.
childish agg. infantile.

childishness s. fanciullaggine, puerilità.
childless agg. senza figli.
childlike agg. infantile.
children V. child.
Chilean agg. e s. cileno.
chill s. 1. colpo di freddo 2. (metal.)
conchiglia.
to **chill** vt. 1. raffreddare, agghiacciare (anche fig.) 2. (metal.) fondere in conchiglia. ♦ to chill vi.
raffreddarsi.
chilled agg. 1. congelato 2. (metal.)
fuso in conchiglia.
chilliness s. 1. freddo 2. (fig.) freddezza.
chilly agg. 1. freddoloso (di persona)
2. fresco (di tempo).
chime s. scampanio.
to **chime** vt. e vi. scampanare, suonare a festa.
chiming s. lo scampanare.
chimney s. camino, comignolo || —
-sweeper, spazzacamino.
chimpanzee s. scimpanzè.
chin s. mento || — -strap, sottogola.
china s. 1. porcellana fine 2. (fam.)
stoviglie di porcellana.
chinchilla s. cincillà.
chine s. spina dorsale.
Chinese agg. e s. cinese.
chink s. fessura, crepa.
chip s. 1. scheggia 2. (cuc.) patatina fritta.
to **chip** vt. 1. scheggiare 2. rompere. ♦ to chip vi. scheggiarsi,
frantumarsi.
chiromancer s. chiromante.
chiromancy s. chiromanzia.
chiropodist s. pedicure.
chirp s. 1. cinguettio, pigolio 2.
stridio, il frinire (di cicale ecc.).
to **chirp** vi. 1. cinguettare, pigolare
2. frinire, stridere (di cicale ecc.).
chisel s. cesello.
to **chisel** vt. cesellare.
chiseller s. cesellatore.
chitterlings s. pl. trippa.
chivalrous agg. cavalleresco.
chivalry s. 1. cavalleria 2. condotta
cavalleresca.
chloride s. cloruro.
chlorine s. cloro.
chlorite s. clorito.
chloroform s. cloroformio.
chlorophyl(l) s. clorofilla.
chock s. 1. cuneo, bietta 2. (mar.)
passacavi.
chocolate agg. 1. di cioccolato 2.

color cioccolata. ♦ **chocolate** *s*. cioccolato: *cake of* —, tavoletta di cioccolato.

choice *agg*. di prima qualità, scelto. ♦ **choice** *s*. **1.** scelta **2.** la cosa scelta **3.** assortimento.

choir *s*. coro.

choke *s*. **1.** soffocamento **2.** strozzatura (*di tubo*).

to **choke** *vt*. **1.** soffocare (*anche fig.*) **2.** ingorgare. ♦ to **choke** *vi*. ostruirsi.

choker *s*. soffocatore.

cholera *s*. colera.

cholesterol *s*. colesterolo.

to **choose (chose, chosen)** *vt*. scegliere.

chooser *s*. chi sceglie.

chop *s*. **1.** (*cuc.*) braciola **2.** colpo (*di scure ecc.*).

to **chop** *vt*. e *vi*. **1.** fendere, tagliare **2.** (*cuc.*) tritare || *to — down*, abbattere (*alberi*); *to — off*, tagliar via.

chopper *s*. **1.** ascia **2.** chi taglia con l'ascia **3.** tagliatrice.

choppy *agg*. **1.** screpolato **2.** increspato (*del mare*).

choral *agg*. corale.

chord *s*. **1.** (*mus.; anat.; geom.*) corda **2.** (*mus.*) accordo.

choreographer *s*. coreografo.

choreographic *agg*. coreografico.

choreography *s*. coreografia.

chorus *s*. coro || *— -singer*, corista.

chose V. *to choose.*

chosen V. *to choose.*

chrism *s*. crisma.

to **christen** *vt*. battezzare.

Christendom *s*. cristianità.

christening *s*. battesimo.

Christian *agg*. e *s*. cristiano || *— name*, nome di battesimo.

Christianity *s*. cristianesimo.

to **christianize** *vt*. convertire al cristianesimo.

Christmas *s*. Natale.

chromatic *agg*. cromatico.

chromatically *avv*. cromaticamente.

chromatism *s*. cromatismo.

chromatography *s*. cromatografia.

chrome *s*. cromo.

to **chrome** *vt*. cromare.

chromium *s*. cromo || *— -plated*, cromato; *— -plating*, cromatura.

chromolithograph *s*. cromolitografia.

chromosome *s*. cromosoma.

chromosphere *s*. cromosfera.

chronic *agg*. cronico (*anche fig.*).

chronicle *s*. cronaca.

chronicler *s*. cronista.

chronologic(al) *agg*. cronologico.

chronologically *avv*. cronologicamente.

chronology *s*. cronologia.

chronometer *s*. cronometro.

chrysalid *s*. crisalide.

chrysanthemum *s*. crisantemo.

chubby *agg*. paffuto.

church *s*. **1.** chiesa **2.** comunità religiosa || *— -going*, assiduità ai servizi religiosi; *— -living*, beneficio ecclesiastico; *— -service*, funzione religiosa.

churchman *s*. **1.** ecclesiastico **2.** membro della chiesa anglicana.

churchy *agg*. bigotto.

churchyard *s*. cimitero.

chyle *s*. (*fisiol.*) chilo.

ciborium *s*. ciborio.

cicada *s*. cicala.

to **cicatrize** *vt*. cicatrizzare. ♦ to **cicatrize** *vi*. cicatrizzarsi.

cider *s*. sidro.

cigar *s*. sigaro || *— -case*, portasigari, *— -end*, mozzicone; *— -holder*, bocchino per sigari.

cigarette *s*. sigaretta || *— -case*, portasigarette, *— -end*, mozzicone, *— -holder*, bocchino; *— -paper*, cartina per sigaretta.

cilice *s*. cilicio.

cinder *s*. **1.** brace **2.** scoria.

cine-camera *s*. macchina da presa.

cinema *s*. cinematografo.

cinematograph *s*. **1.** proiettore cinematografico **2.** macchina da presa.

cinematographer *s*. **1.** operatore cinematografico **2.** cineasta.

cinematographic *agg*. cinematografico.

cinematography *s*. cinematografia.

cine-projector *s*. proiettore cinematografico.

cinerary *agg*. cinerario.

cinnabar *s*. cinabro.

cinnamon *s*. cannella.

cipher *s*. **1.** cifrario **2.** monogramma **3.** (*mat.; anche fig.*) zero, nullità.

to **cipher** *vt*. e *vi*. cifrare.

circle *s*. **1.** cerchio, circolo (*anche fig.*) **2.** orbita (*dei pianeti*) **3.** galleria (*di teatro*).

circlet *s*. cerchietto.

circuit s. **1.** cinta, circonvallazione **2.** rivoluzione, rotazione (di astri) **3.** (elettr.; sport) circuito.
circular agg. circolare. ♦ **circular** s. lettera circolare.
to **circulate** vt. mettere in circolazione, diffondere. ♦ to **circulate** vi. circolare.
circulating agg. circolante.
circulation s. **1.** circolazione **2.** diffusione **3.** (giorn.) tiratura.
circulatory agg. circolatorio.
to **circumcise** vt. circoncidere.
circumcision s. circoncisione.
circumference s. circonferenza.
circumflex agg. circonflesso.
circumlocution s. circonlocuzione.
to **circumnavigate** vt. circumnavigare.
circumnavigation s. circumnavigazione.
circumnavigator s. circumnavigatore.
to **circumscribe** vt. circoscrivere.
circumscription s. circoscrizione.
circumspect agg. circospetto.
circumspection s. circospezione.
circumstance s. circostanza.
circumstantial agg. **1.** circostanziale **2.** circostanziato.
circumstantiality s. abbondanza di particolari.
circumstantially avv. circostanziatamente.
to **circumvent** vt. circuire.
circumvention s. raggiro.
circumvolution s. circonvoluzione.
circus s. **1.** circo, arena **2.** piazza rotonda.
cirrhosis s. cirrosi.
cisalpine agg. cisalpino.
cistern s. cisterna.
citadel s. cittadella.
to **cite** vt. citare.
citizen s. cittadino.
citizenhood s. cittadinanza.
citizenship s. diritto di cittadinanza.
citrate s. citrato.
citric agg. citrico.
citron s. cedro.
city s. **1.** città (grande) **2.** centro di grande traffico di una città.
civic agg. civico.
civil agg. civile, cortese.
civilian agg. e s. civile, borghese.
civility s. civiltà, cortesia.
civilization s. civilizzazione, civiltà.
to **civilize** vt. civilizzare.

civilly avv. civilmente.
civism s. civismo.
claim s. **1.** richiesta **2.** (giur.) rivendicazione **3.** (comm.) reclamo.
to **claim** vt. **1.** esigere, chiedere **2.** (giur.) rivendicare **3.** (comm.) reclamare.
claimant s. **1.** rivendicatore **2.** richiedente.
clairvoyance s. chiaroveggenza.
clairvoyant agg. e s. chiaroveggente.
to **clamber** vi. arrampicarsi.
clammy agg. vischioso.
clamour s. clamore, vocio.
to **clamour** vt. e vi. vociferare.
clan s. gruppo familiare, tribù.
clandestine agg. clandestino.
to **clang** vi. emettere un suono, un grido. ♦ to **clang** vt. far risonare.
clangour s. fragore.
to **clank** vi. tintinnare. ♦ to **clank** vt. far tintinnare.
clap s. **1.** applauso **2.** rumore improvviso **3.** piccolo colpo (con la mano).
to **clap** vt. e vi. **1.** applaudire **2.** dare un colpo (con la mano) **3.** battere (le ali).
clapper s. **1.** battente (di porta) **2.** (teat.) membro della « claque ».
claret s. **1.** color rosso-violetto **2.** vino chiaretto.
clarification s. chiarificazione.
to **clarify** vt. chiarificare. ♦ to **clarify** vi. chiarificarsi.
clarinet s. clarinetto.
clarity s. chiarità.
clash s. **1.** cozzo, urto **2.** scontro (d'opinioni).
to **clash** vt. e vi. **1.** cozzare, far strepito **2.** scontrarsi (d'opinioni).
clasp s. fermaglio, fibbia.
to **clasp** vt. afferrare.
class s. **1.** classe, categoria **2.** (scol.) classe **3.** (fig.) distinzione.
classic agg. e s. classico.
classical agg. classico.
classically avv. classicamente.
classicism s. classicismo.
classification s. classificazione.
to **classify** vt. classificare.
classmate s. compagno di classe.
classroom s. aula.
classy agg. (fam.) di classe.
clatter s. fracasso.
to **clatter** vi. far fracasso.
clause s. clausola.
claustrophobia s. claustrofobia.

claw s. 1. artiglio, zampa con artigli 2. uncino 3. chela.

to **claw** vt. artigliare.

clawed agg. munito di artigli.

clay s. argilla: fire- —, argilla refrattaria || — pigeon, piattello.

clayey agg. argilloso.

clean agg. 1. pulito 2. netto, nitido 3. (fig.) puro, schietto.

to **clean** vt. pulire.

cleaner s. pulitore, pulitrice || dry- —, smacchiatore a secco.

cleaning s. pulitura.

cleanliness s. pulizia.

cleanly agg. pulito. ◆ **cleanly** avv. in modo pulito.

cleanness s. 1. pulizia (anche fig.) 2. nitidezza.

to **cleanse** vt. 1. pulire 2. purificare.

cleanser s. 1. pulitore 2. detersivo.

cleansing agg. purificante. ◆ **cleansing** s. 1. purificazione 2. depurazione.

clear agg. 1. chiaro, limpido 2. distinto, evidente || — -cut, nettamente stagliato; — -sighted, dalla vista buona.

to **clear** vt. 1. chiarire, schiarire 2. discolpare 3. (comm.) svincolare || to — away, sparecchiare, dissiparsi (di nebbia); to — up, rassettare (una stanza), chiarire (un malinteso). ◆ to **clear** vi. schiarirsi.

clearance s. 1. chiarificazione 2. sgombero 3. (comm.) sdoganamento.

clearing s. 1. chiarimento 2. rimozione.

clearly avv. chiaramente.

clearness s. 1. chiarezza 2. (fig.) limpidezza.

cleavage s. 1. spaccatura 2. (min.) clivaggio.

to **cleave** (**cleft**, **cleft**) vt. e vi. fendere, spaccare.

cleft s. fenditura.

clemency s. clemenza.

clement agg. 1. clemente 2. dolce, gentile (di carattere) 3. mite (di tempo).

to **clench** vt. 1. stringere (mani, denti ecc.) 2. ribadire.

clergy s. clero.

clergyman s. ecclesiastico.

clerical agg. 1. clericale 2. impiegatizio.

clericalism s. clericalismo.

clerk s. impiegato || chief —, ca- poufficio.

to **clerk** vi. lavorare come impiegato.

clever agg. intelligente, abile, ingegnoso.

cleverly avv. intelligentemente.

cleverness s. intelligenza, abilità, ingegnosità.

clew s. gomitolo (di filo).

click s. scatto, rumore secco.

client s. cliente.

cliff s. scogliera.

climate s. clima.

climatic agg. climatico.

climax s. apice, culmine.

climb s. 1. rampa 2. ascesa.

to **climb** vt. e vi. 1. arrampicarsi 2. scalare (anche fig.).

climber s. 1. scalatore 2. (fig.) arrivista 3. pianta rampicante.

climbing s. 1. scalata 2. (fig.) arrivismo. ◆ **climbing** agg. rampicante.

to **cling** (**clung**, **clung**) vi. attaccarsi, aggrapparsi (anche fig.): to — to a hope, aggrapparsi ad una speranza.

clinical agg. clinico.

clinician s. clinico.

clinking s. tintinnio.

clip s. 1. fermaglio, molletta || hair —, forcina per capelli 2. graffa (per ferite) 3. tosatura (di pecore).

to **clip** vt. 1. tenere insieme (con un fermaglio) 2. tosare (pecore ecc.).

clipper s. 1. tosatore 2. (mar.) "clipper". ◆ **clippers** s. pl. 1. forbici 2. macchinetta per tosare (sing.).

cloak s. 1. mantello 2. (fig.) manto, velo.

clock s. orologio (da muro, da tavolo) || alarm- —, sveglia.

clockwise agg. in senso orario || counter- —, in senso antiorario.

clockwork s. meccanismo a orologeria.

clod s. zolla.

clog s. 1. impedimento, intoppo 2. zoccolo.

to **clog** vt. ostruire, impedire (anche fig.). ◆ to **clog** vi. incepparsi.

cloister s. chiostro.

close agg. 1. chiuso 2. serrato: — combat, combattimento corpo a corpo 3. afoso, viziato (di aria) 4. intimo: — friend, amico intimo 5. accurato, attento || — -fitting, aderente (di vestiti); —

-*mouthed*, riservato; — -*shaven*, rasato con cura.

close *s.* **1.** spazio cintato **2.** fine, termine **3.** corpo a corpo.

close *avv.* vicino, presso.

to **close** *vt.* chiudere || *to* — -*up*, turare, sbarrare (*di strada*). ♦ to **close** *vi.* chiudersi || *to* — *in*, avvicinarsi, accorciarsi (*di giorni*); *to* — *with*, venire a un accordo.

closed *agg.* chiuso.

closely *avv.* **1.** da vicino **2.** attentamente.

closeness *s.* **1.** afa, mancanza d'aria **2.** compattezza **3.** intimità **4.** vicinanza **5.** accuratezza.

closet *s.* **1.** studio, salotto privato **2.** armadio a muro **3.** gabinetto.

close-up *s.* (*cine*) primo piano.

closing *s.* chiusura (*di negozi, teatri ecc.*).

clot *s.* grumo.

to **clot** *vt.* raggrumare, coagulare. ♦ to **clot** *vi.* raggrumarsi, coagularsi.

cloth *s.* tessuto, stoffa, tela || (*table-*) —, tovaglia.

to **clothe** *vt.* vestire.

clothes *s. pl.* abiti, indumenti || — -*hook*, attaccapanni; — -*line*, corda (*per stendere il bucato*); — -*peg*, molletta (*fermabucato*).

clothing *s.* **1.** vestiario **2.** copertura.

cloud *s.* **1.** nuvola, nube **2.** nugolo (*di insetti*).

to **cloud** *vt. e vi.* annuvolare, oscurare || *to* — (*up, over*), annuvolarsi.

clouded *agg.* **1.** coperto (*di nubi*) **2.** torbido (*di liquidi*).

cloudily *avv.* nebulosamente.

cloudy *agg.* **1.** nuvoloso **2.** torbido.

clover *s.* trifoglio.

clown *s.* pagliaccio.

clownish *agg.* pagliaccesco.

club *s.* **1.** mazza, randello **2.** circolo, associazione **3.** (*carte*) fiori.

clue *s.* **1.** indizio, traccia **2.** filo di un racconto.

clumsily *avv.* goffamente.

clumsiness *s.* goffaggine.

clumsy *agg.* goffo, senza grazia.

clung V. *to* cling.

cluster *s.* **1.** grappolo (*d'uva*), mazzo (*di fiori*), gruppo **2.** folla, capannello (*di gente*) **3.** sciame.

clutch *s.* **1.** stretta, grinfia **2.** (*auto*) frizione.

to **clutch** *vt. e vi.* afferrare, afferrarsi, agguantare.

coach *s.* **1.** carrozza, cocchio **2.** pullman **3.** carrozza ferroviaria **4.** (*sport*) allenatore, istruttore || — -*house*, rimessa; *mourning-* —, carro funebre; *stage-* —, diligenza.

coachman *s.* cocchiere.

coachwork *s.* carrozzeria.

coadjutor *s.* coadiutore.

coagulant *s.* sostanza coagulante.

to **coagulate** *vt.* coagulare. ♦ to **coagulate** *vi.* coagularsi.

coagulation *s.* coagulazione.

coagulator *s.* coagulante.

coal *s.* carbone: — -*bed*, bacino carbonifero; — -*black*, nero come il carbone; — -*fed*, alimentato a carbone; — -*mine*, miniera di carbone.

to **coalesce** *vi.* **1.** coalizzarsi, unirsi **2.** fondersi.

coalition *s.* coalizione.

coarse *agg.* **1.** grossolano, rozzo **2.** ruvido, grosso (*di materiale*).

coarsely *avv.* grossolanamente.

coarseness *s.* **1.** grossolanità **2.** ruvidezza (*di stoffe ecc.*).

coast *s.* costa || — -*guard*, polizia costiera.

coastal *agg.* costiero.

coaster *s.* **1.** nave cabotiera **2.** sottobicchiere.

coat *s.* **1.** giacca, soprabito **2.** manto (*anche fig.*), pelliccia (*di animale*) **3.** rivestimento, intonaco || — *of arms*, stemma.

to **coat** *vt.* rivestire, coprire.

coating *s.* rivestimento, mano di vernice.

to **coax** *vt.* blandire, circuire. ♦ to **coax** *vi.* far moine.

coaxial *agg* coassiale.

cobalt *s.* cobalto.

cobble *s.* ciottolo.

to **cobble** *vt.* **1.** pavimentare (*con ciottoli*) **2.** rappezzare (*scarpe*).

cobbler *s.* ciabattino.

cobra *s.* cobra.

cobweb *s.* ragnatela.

cocaine *s.* cocaina.

coccyx *s.* (*pl.* -cyges) coccige.

cock *s.* **1.** gallo **2.** cane di fucile.

cockade *s.* coccarda.

cockatoo *s.* cacatoa.

cockboat *s.* (*mar.*) lancia.

cockerel *s.* galletto.

cock-eyed *agg.* strabico.

cockish *agg.* sfrontato.

cockney *agg.* e *s.* dialetto londinese.

cockpit *s.* 1. arena (*per combattimento di galli*) 2. (*mar.*) castello di poppa.

cockroach *s.* scarafaggio.

cockscomb *s.* 1. cresta (*di gallo*) 2. (*fig.*) zerbinotto.

cocktail *s.* 1. cavallo con coda mozzata 2. cocktail.

cocoa *s.* cacao.

coconut *s.* noce di cocco.

cocoon *s.* bozzolo.

cod *s.* merluzzo.

code *s.* codice.

to **code** *vt.* 1. codificare 2. cifrare (*un dispaccio*).

codeine *s.* codeina.

codex *s.* codice, manoscritto antico.

codfish *s.* merluzzo.

codicil *s.* codicillo.

codification *s.* codificazione.

to **codify** *vt.* codificare.

co-director *s.* condirettore.

co-education *s.* istruzione nella scuola mista.

co-educational *agg.* (*scol.*) misto.

coefficient *agg.* e *s.* coefficiente.

coenobium *s.* cenobio.

coercible *agg.* coercibile.

coercion *s.* coercizione.

coercive *agg.* coercitivo.

coeval *agg.* e *s.* coevo.

to **coexist** *vi.* coesistere.

coexistence *s.* coesistenza.

coffee *s.* caffè: — *-bean*, chicco di caffè; — *-grounds*, fondi di caffè || — *-house*, caffè, bar; — *-mill*, macinino; — *-pot*, caffettiera.

coffer *s.* cassa, cofano.

coffin *s.* bara.

cog *s.* dente (*di ruota*).

cognate *agg.* e *s.* consanguineo, congiunto.

cognition *s.* cognizione.

cognitive *agg.* avente conoscenza.

cognizable *agg.* 1. conoscibile 2. (*giur.*) entro la giurisdizione di una corte.

to **cohabit** *vi.* coabitare.

cohabitation *s.* coabitazione.

coheir *s.* coerede.

coheiress *s.* (*donna*) coerede.

coherence *s.* 1. coerenza 2. aderenza.

coherent *agg.* 1. coerente 2. aderente.

coherently *avv.* coerentemente.

cohesion *s.* coesione.

cohesive *agg.* coesivo.

cohort *s.* coorte.

coil *s.* 1. rotolo, spira 2. (*elettr.; mecc.*) bobina.

coin *s.* moneta (*di metallo*).

to **coin** *vt.* coniare (*anche fig.*).

coinage *s.* conio.

to **coincide** *vi.* coincidere.

coincidence *s.* coincidenza.

coiner *s.* falsario.

colander *s.* colino.

cold *agg.* 1. freddo: *to be* —, aver freddo 2. freddo (*di carattere*), apatico: *in* — *blood*, a sangue freddo. ◆ **cold** *s.* 1. freddo 2. raffreddore: *to catch a* —, prendere il raffreddore.

coldness *s.* freddezza (*anche fig.*).

Coleoptera *s. pl.* coleotteri.

colic *s.* colica.

colitis *s.* colite.

to **collaborate** *vi.* collaborare.

collaboration *s.* collaborazione.

collaborationist *s.* collaborazionista.

collaborator *s.* collaboratore.

collapse *s.* 1. crollo (*anche fig.*) 2. collasso.

to **collapse** *vi.* crollare (*anche fig.*).

collar *s.* 1. colletto 2. collare.

to **collate** *vt.* 1. collezionare, confrontare 2. riordinare (*pagine di un'opera*).

collateral *agg.* collaterale.

colleague *s.* collega.

to **collect** *vt.* 1. riunire 2. incassare, riscuotere 3. fare una raccolta. ◆ to **collect** *vi.* 1. riunirsi 2. riscuotere.

collecting *s.* il raccogliere: *stamp* —, il raccogliere francobolli.

collection *s.* 1. raccolta, collezione 2. riunione di persone 3. questua, colletta.

collective *agg.* collettivo || — *title* (*tip.*), titolo generale.

collectivism *s.* collettivismo.

collectivity *s.* collettività.

collectivization *s.* collettivizzazione.

to **collectivize** *vt.* collettivizzare.

collector *s.* 1. collezionista 2. esattore.

college *s.* 1. collegio 2. scuola secondaria (*con internato*).

collegial *agg.* collegiale.

collier *s.* minatore.

colliery *s.* miniera di carbone.

collimator *s.* collimatore.

collision s. **1.** collisione **2.** urto, conflitto (*d'interessi*).

collocation s. collocazione.

colloidal agg. colloidale.

colloquial agg. d'uso corrente, familiare.

colloquialism s. espressione familiare.

colloquially avv. nella lingua parlata.

colloquy s. colloquio.

collusion s. collusione.

colon s. (*gramm.*) due punti.

colonel s. colonnello.

colonial agg. coloniale.

colonialism s. sistema coloniale.

colonialist s. colonialista.

colonist s. **1.** colono **2.** colonizzatore.

colonization s. colonizzazione.

to **colonize** vt. colonizzare. ◆ to **colonize** vi. stabilirsi in colonia.

colonizer s. colonizzatore.

colonnade s. colonnato.

colony s. colonia.

colossal agg. colossale.

colossus s. colosso.

colour s. **1.** colore **2.** colorito || — -bearer, portabandiera; — -blind, daltonico; — -print, stampa a colori. ◆ **colours** s. pl. bandiera (*sing.*) || with the —, sotto le armi.

to **colour** vt. colorare, tingere. ◆ to **colour** vi. colorirsi, prender colore.

colourable agg. verosimile.

colouration s. colorazione.

coloured agg. colorato, colorito (*anche fig.*).

colourful agg. colorito, pittoresco.

colouring s. **1.** colorante **2.** coloramento.

colourless agg. incolore.

colt s. **1.** puledro **2.** (*fig.*) novellino.

columbarium s. (*pl.* -ria) colombario.

column s. colonna (*anche fig.*).

columnist s. giornalista (*che cura una rubrica*).

coma s. coma.

comatose agg. comatoso.

comb s. **1.** pettine **2.** cresta (*gallo, onde ecc.*).

to **comb** vt. pettinare. ◆ to **comb** vi. frangersi (*di onde*) || to — one's hair, pettinarsi.

combat s. combattimento, lotta.

combination s. **1.** combinazione

2. associazione.

to **combine** vt. **1.** unire **2.** (*chim.*) combinare **3.** contribuire. ◆ to **combine** vi. **1.** unirsi **2.** combinarsi.

combing s. pettinata.

comb-out s. rastrellamento.

combustible agg. e s. combustibile.

combustion s. combustione.

to **come (came, come)** vi. venire, arrivare, giungere, provenire || to — about, accadere; to — across, incontrare per caso; to — along (*fam.*), capitare; to — back, ritornare; to — down, scendere; to — in, entrare, salire (*di marea*); to — on, avanzare, sopraggiungere (*di malattie, stagioni ecc.*), entrare in scena (*di attori*); to — through, superare; to — under, essere soggetti, essere catalogati; to — upon, trovare per caso.

comedian s. autore, attore di commedie.

comedy s. commedia.

comeliness s. avvenenza.

comely agg. avvenente.

comer s. chi viene.

comet s. cometa.

comfit s. confetto.

comfort s. **1.** conforto **2.** comodità.

to **comfort** vt. **1.** confortare **2.** ristorare.

comfortable agg. comodo, confortevole || to be —, sentirsi a proprio agio.

comfortably avv. comodamente.

comforting agg. confortante.

comic agg. comico, buffo. ◆ **comic** s. **1.** attore comico **2.** il ridicolo, il comico. ◆ **comics** s. pl. (*fam.*) fumetti.

comical agg. comico, buffo.

comicality s. comicità.

coming agg. prossimo, futuro. ◆ **coming** s. **1.** venuta, arrivo || — away, partenza; — back, ritorno; — down, discesa, calo (*dei prezzi*).

comity s. cortesia, gentilezza.

comma s. virgola || inverted commas, virgolette.

command s. **1.** comando, ordine **2.** padronanza.

to **command** vt. e vi. **1.** comandare **2.** dominare (*anche fig.*).

commandant s. comandante.

commander s. comandante.

commandership s. funzioni di comandante.

commandment *s.* comandamento.

to commemorate *vt.* commemorare.

commemoration *s.* commemorazione.

commemorative *agg.* commemorativo.

to commend *vt.* lodare, encomiare.

commendable *agg.* lodevole.

commendably *avv.* lodevolmente.

commendation *s.* elogio, lode.

commendatory *agg.* laudativo.

commensal *s.* commensale.

commensurability *s.* commensurabilità.

commensurable *agg.* commensurabile.

commensurate *agg.* proporzionato.

comment *s.* **1.** commento **2.** critica.

to comment *vt.* e *vi.* commentare: *to — up (on) a test*, commentare un testo.

commentary *s.* commentario.

commentation *s.* annotazione, commento.

commentator *s.* **1.** commentatore **2.** radiocronista.

commerce *s.* commercio.

commercial *agg.* commerciale.

commercialism *s.* mercantilismo.

commercialist *s.* commercialista.

to commercialize *vt.* rendere commerciabile.

commercially *avv.* commercialmente.

commination *s.* comminazione.

to commiserate *vt.* e *vi.* commiserare.

commissary *s.* commissario, delegato.

commissaryship *s.* commissariato.

commission *s.* **1.** commissione, comitato **2.** commissione, incarico || *— agent (o merchant)*, commissionario.

to commission *vt.* **1.** commissionare **2.** delegare.

commissioned *agg.* munito di autorità || *non- — officer*, sottufficiale.

commissioner *s.* (*pol.*) delegato.

to commit *vt.* **1.** affidare, rimettere: *to — one's soul to God*, rimettere la propria anima a Dio **2.** commettere.

commitment, committal *s.* **1.** consegna **2.** incarico.

committed *agg.* (*neol.*) impegnato.

committee *s.* comitato.

commodity *s.* merce, oggetto di prima necessità || *free commodities*, merci esenti da dogana.

common *agg.* **1.** comune **2.** solito, abituale || *— law*, legge consacrata dalla consuetudine.

commoner *s.* **1.** cittadino (*non nobile*) **2.** membro della Camera dei Comuni.

commonness *s.* **1.** banalità **2.** frequenza (*di un avvenimento*).

commonplace *s.* luogo comune.

commons *s. pl.* il popolo (*sing.*) || *the House of —*, la Camera dei Comuni.

commonwealth *s.* **1.** confederazione **2.** repubblica (*anche fig.*).

commotion *s.* **1.** agitazione, confusione **2.** insurrezione, tumulto.

communal *agg.* della comunità.

commune *s.* comune.

communicability *s.* comunicabilità.

communicable *agg.* comunicabile.

to communicate *vt.* comunicare, trasmettere (*malattie, calore ecc.*).

♦ to communicate *vi.* mettersi in comunicazione.

communication *s.* **1.** comunicazione, informazione **2.** relazione, rapporto.

communicative *agg.* comunicativo.

communicativeness *s.* comunicativa.

communion *s.* comunione, comunanza || *Holy Communion*, Eucarestia.

communism *s.* comunismo.

communist *s.* comunista.

communistic *agg.* comunista.

community *s.* **1.** comunanza (*di beni ecc.*) **2.** collettività, società **3.** (*eccl.*) comunità.

commutability *s.* permutabilità, commutabilità.

commutable *agg.* permutabile, commutabile.

commutative *agg.* commutativo.

commutator *s.* commutatore.

to commute *vt.* commutare.

compact[1] *s.* patto, contratto.

compact[2] *agg.* **1.** compatto **2.** ridotto.

compactness *s.* **1.** compattezza **2.** concisione (*di stile*).

companion[1] *s.* compagno.

companion[2] *s.* (*mar.*) boccaporto: *— -way*, scaletta (*di boccaporto*), scalandrone.

companionable *agg.* socievole.

companionship s. amicizia, cameratismo.

company s. **1.** compagnia **2.** comitiva **3.** (*comm.*) società.

comparable agg. paragonabile.

comparative agg. **1.** comparativo **2.** comparato. ♦ **comparative** s. (*gramm.*) comparativo.

comparatively avv. **1.** comparativamente **2.** relativamente.

to compare vt. paragonare, verificare. ♦ **to compare** vi. competere, rivaleggiare, reggere al confronto.

comparison s. **1.** paragone, confronto **2.** (*gramm.*) comparazione.

compartment s. compartimento, scompartimento.

compass s. **1.** circonferenza, spazio, estensione **2.** bussola. ♦ **compasses** s. pl. (*a pair of —*) compasso (*sing.*).

to compass vt. circondare.

compassion s. compassione: *out of —*, per compassione.

compassionate agg. compassionevole.

to compassionate vt. compassionare.

compassionately avv. con compassione.

compatibility s. compatibilità.

compatible agg. compatibile.

compatibly avv. compatibilmente.

to compel vt. costringere, obbligare.

compelling agg. irresistibile.

compendious agg. compendioso.

to compensate vt. ricompensare, risarcire. ♦ **to compensate** vi. supplire.

compensation s. **1.** compenso **2.** (*mecc.*) compensazione **3.** indennità, risarcimento.

compensator s. compensatore.

compensatory agg. compensativo.

to compete vi. competere, gareggiare.

competence s. **1.** competenza **2.** mezzi sufficienti per vivere (*pl.*).

competent agg. competente, abile.

competently avv. con competenza.

competition s. **1.** competizione, gara **2.** rivalità.

competitive agg. **1.** di competizione **2.** (*comm.*) di concorrenza.

competitively avv. per mezzo di concorso.

competitor s. concorrente, rivale.

compilation s. compilazione.

to compile vt. compilare.

compiler s. compilatore.

complacency s. **1.** soddisfazione **2.** compiacenza di sé.

complacent agg. **1.** compiacente **2.** soddisfatto di sé.

to complain vi. lagnarsi, dolersi.

complaint s. **1.** lamento **2.** reclamo.

complaisant agg. compiacente.

complement s. complemento.

complemental agg. complementare.

complementary agg. complementare.

complete agg. completo.

to complete vt. **1.** completare **2.** riempire (*moduli ecc.*).

completely avv. completamente.

completeness s. completezza.

completion s. compimento.

complex agg. **1.** complicato **2.** (*gramm.*) composto. ♦ **complex** s. complesso.

complexion s. carnagione, colorito.

complexity s. complessità.

compliance s. **1.** condiscendenza **2.** servilismo.

compliant agg. **1.** compiacente **2.** servile.

to complicate vt. complicare.

complicated agg. complicato.

complication s. complicazione.

complicity s. complicità.

compliment s. complimento: *to pay so. a —*, far un complimento a qu.

to compliment vt. complimentare, congratularsi con.

complimentary agg. **1.** complimentoso **2.** di favore: *— tickets*, biglietti di favore.

to comply vi. accondiscendere, conformarsi.

component agg. e s. componente.

to comport vi. comportarsi.

to compose vt. **1.** comporre, costituire **2.** (*mus.*) comporre || *to — a quarrel*, comporre una vertenza.

composed agg. **1.** composto **2.** calmo.

composer s. compositore.

composing agg. calmante. ♦ **composing** s. **1.** il comporre **2.** (*tip.*) composizione.

composite agg. composto.

composition s. **1.** composizione **2.** compromesso **3.** concordato, intesa.

compositor s. (*tip.*) compositore.

composure s. posatezza, sangue freddo.

compote *s.* conserva di frutta.
compound 1. miscela 2. (*chim.*) composto 3. (*gramm.*) parola composta.
to **compound** *vt.* e *vi.* 1. comporre, mescolare 2. combinare (*ingredienti, elementi ecc.*).
to **comprehend** *vt.* 1. contenere 2. capire.
comprehensibility *s.* comprensibilità.
comprehensible *agg.* 1. comprensibile 2. delinitato.
comprehension *s.* 1. comprensione 2. portata.
comprehensive *agg.* 1. di vasta portata 2. comprensivo.
comprehensively *avv.* comprensivamente.
compress *s.* compressa (*di garza*).
to **compress** *vt.* 1. comprimere 2. (*fig.*) condensare (*idee ecc.*).
compressibility *s.* compressibilità.
compression *s.* 1. compressione 2. (*fig.*) concentrazione.
to **comprise** *vt.* contenere, includere.
compromise *s.* compromesso.
to **compromise** *vt.* compromettere. ♦ to **compromise** *vi.* venire a un compromesso.
compromising *agg.* compromettente.
compulsion *s.* costrizione: *under* —, per costrizione.
compulsive *agg.* coercitivo.
compulsory *agg.* obbligatorio.
compunction *s.* compunzione.
computable *agg.* calcolabile.
computation *s.* calcolo.
to **compute** *vt.* computare, calcolare.
computer *s.* calcolatore.
comrade *s.* camerata, compagno.
comradeship *s.* cameratismo.
to **concatenate** *vt.* concatenare.
concatenation *s.* concatenazione.
concave *agg.* concavo.
to **conceal** *vt.* nascondere.
concealment *s.* 1. occultamento 2. nascondiglio.
conceit *s.* vanità, presunzione.
conceited *agg.* presuntuoso, vanitoso.
conceivability *s.* concepibilità.
conceivable *agg.* concepibile.
to **conceive** *vt.* 1. concepire, generare 2. immaginare, ide re.
to **concentrate** *vt.* 1. concentrare

2. convergere. ♦ to **concentrate** *vi.* concentrarsi.
concentration *s.* 1. concentrazione 2. concentramento.
concentric *agg.* concentrico.
concept *s.* concetto.
conception *s.* 1. concezione, concepimento 2. concetto.
conceptional *agg.* concezionale.
conceptual *agg.* concettuale.
conceptualism *s.* concettualismo.
concern *s.* 1. interesse, rapporto 2. affare 3. sollecitudine 4. (*comm.*) ditta, azienda.
to **concern** *vt.* concernere, riguardare.
concerned *agg.* 1. interessato 2. ansioso, preoccupato || *as far as I am* —, per quanto mi riguarda.
concerning *prep.* riguardo a, circa.
concert *s.* 1. concerto 2. accordo.
concerted *agg.* 1. (*mus.*) concertato 2. convenuto.
concession *s.* concessione.
concessionary *agg.* e *s.* concessionario.
concettism *s.* concettismo.
conch *s.* conchiglia, mollusco.
conchoid *s.* concoide.
conchoidal *agg.* concoidale.
conciliar *agg.* conciliare.
to **conciliate** *vt.* conciliare.
conciliation *s.* conciliazione.
conciliator *s.* conciliatore, conciliatrice.
conciliatory *agg.* conciliante.
concise *agg.* conciso, succinto.
concision *s.* concisione.
conclave *s.* conclave.
to **conclude** *vt.* terminare, concludere. ♦ to **conclude** *vi.* terminare, concludersi.
conclusion *s.* conclusione.
conclusive *agg.* conclusivo.
to **concoct** *vt.* 1. mescolare (*di ingredienti*) 2. preparare, tramare.
concomitance *s.* concomitanza.
concomitant *agg.* concomitante.
concomitantly *avv.* simultaneamente.
concord *s.* 1. concordia 2. (*mus.*) accordo 3. (*gramm.*) concordanza.
concordant *agg.* 1. concorde 2. (*mus.*) armonioso.
concordat *s.* concordato.
concourse *s.* concorso, affluenza (*di persone ecc.*).
concrete *agg.* concreto. ♦ **concrete** *s.* calcestruzzo.

concreteness *s.* concretezza.
concretion *s.* concrezione.
concubinage *s.* concubinato.
concubine *s.* concubina.
concupiscence *s.* concupiscenza.
to **concur** *vi.* concorrere, contribuire (*di cause, avvenimenti*).
concurrence *s.* 1. concorso (*di circostanze*) 2. cooperazione (*di persone*) 3. (*geom.*) convergenza.
concurrent *agg.* concorrente, simultaneo.
to **concuss** *vt.* 1. urtare 2. (*med.*) provocare un trauma 3. intimidire.
concussion *s.* 1. urto 2. (*med.*) commozione cerebrale, trauma.
to **condemn** *vt.* 1. condannare 2. biasimare, censurare.
condemnable *agg.* 1. condannabile 2. censurabile.
condemnation *s.* 1. condanna 2. biasimo, censura.
condensability *s.* condensabilità.
condensable *agg.* condensabile.
condensate *s.* (*fis.; chim.*) condensamento.
condensation *s.* condensazione.
to **condense** *vt.* condensare, abbreviare. ♦ to **condense** *vi.* condensarsi, concentrarsi.
condenser *s.* condensatore.
to **condescend** *vi.* accondiscendere.
condescending *agg.* condiscendente.
condescendingly *avv.* con condiscendenza.
condescension *s.* 1. condiscendenza 2. affabilità.
condition *s.* condizione, clausola: *on — that*, a condizione che.
to **condition** *vt.* condizionare.
conditional *agg.* e *s.* condizionale.
conditionally *avv.* condizionatamente.
conditioned *agg.* condizionato: — *air*, aria condizionata.
conditioning *s.* 1. condizionatura (*di tessili*) 2. condizionamento.
condolence *s.* condoglianza.
conduct *s.* 1. condotta, comportamento 2. metodo.
to **conduct** *vi.* 1. condurre, guidare, dirigere 2. (*fis.*) condurre, trasmettere. ♦ to **conduct** *vi.* 1. comportarsi 2. indicare la via.
conductibility *s.* conducibilità.
conductivity *s.* conducibilità.
conductor *s.* 1. guida (*di persone*) 2. (*mus.*) direttore 3. bigliettario.

conduit *s.* 1. conduttura 2. passaggio segreto.
cone *s.* 1. cono 2. pigna.
to **confabulate** *vi.* confabulare.
confectionary *agg.* di pasticceria.
confectioner *s.* pasticciere.
confectionery *s.* pasticceria.
confederate *agg.* confederato. ♦ **confederate** *s.* 1. confederato 2. complice.
to **confederate** *vt.* confederare. ♦ to **confederate** *vi.* confederarsi.
confederation *s.* confederazione.
to **confer** *vt.* conferire, dare. ♦ to **confer** *vi.* conferire, consultarsi.
conference *s.* 1. conferenza 2. congresso.
to **confess** *vt.* e *vi.* confessare, professare.
confessedly *avv.* apertamente, dichiaratamente.
confession *s.* confessione, professione: — *of faith*, professione di fede.
confessional *agg.* e *s.* confessionale.
confessionary *agg.* confessionale.
confessor *s.* 1. confessore 2. chi si confessa.
confetti *s. pl.* coriandoli.
confidant *s.* confidente.
to **confide** *vt.* confidare. ♦ to **confide** *vi.* confidarsi: *to — in so.*, confidarsi con qu.
confidence *s.* 1. fiducia 2. confidenza 3. sicurezza in se stessi.
confident *agg.* fiducioso.
confidential *agg.* confidenziale, riservato.
confidently *avv.* con sicurezza, con fiducia.
confiding *agg.* senza sospetti.
configuration *s.* configurazione.
to **configure** *vt.* configurare.
to **confine** *vt.* relegare, limitare. ♦ to **confine** *vi.* confinare, essere contiguo.
confinement *s.* 1. reclusione 2. limitazione 3. puerperio.
to **confirm** *vt.* 1. confermare 2. cresimare.
confirmation *s.* 1. conferma 2. cresima 3. (*pol.; giur.*) ratifica.
confirmatory *agg.* confermativo.
confiscable *agg.* confiscabile.
to **confiscate** *vt.* confiscare.
confiscation *s.* confisca.
conflagration *s.* conflagrazione.
conflict *s.* conflitto, contrasto.

confluence s. **1.** confluenza **2.** incrocio (di strade ecc.).

confluent agg. confluente.

to **conform** vt. conformare. ♦ to **conform** vi. conformarsi, ottemperare.

conformation s. **1.** conformazione **2.** adattamento.

conformist s. conformista.

conformity s. **1.** conformità **2.** conformismo.

to **confound** vt. **1.** confondere, disorientare **2.** sconvolgere.

confounded agg. attonito, confuso.

confraternity s. confraternita.

to **confront** vt. **1.** affrontare **2.** trovarsi di fronte a.

confrontation s. confronto.

Confucianism s. confucianesimo.

to **confuse** vt. **1.** disorientare, sconcertare **2.** confondere.

confusedly avv. confusamente.

confusion s. **1.** disordine, confusione **2.** turbamento.

confutation s. confutazione.

to **confute** vt. confutare.

to **congeal** vt. ghiacciare. ♦ to **congeal** vi. gelarsi.

congenial agg. **1.** congeniale, affine **2.** amabile, simpatico.

congeniality s. **1.** affinità **2.** carattere simpatico.

congenially avv. amabilmente.

congenital agg. congenito.

conger s. anguilla marina.

congeries s. congerie.

to **congest** vt. congestionare. ♦ to **congest** vi. congestionarsi.

congested agg. congestionato.

congestion s. congestione.

to **conglobate** vt. conglobare. ♦ to **conglobate** vi. conglobarsi.

conglobation s. conglobazione.

conglomerate agg. e s. conglomerato.

to **conglomerate** vt. conglomerare. ♦ to **conglomerate** vi. conglomerarsi.

conglomeration s. conglomerazione.

to **congratulate** vt. congratulare, congratularsi con.

congratulation s. congratulazione.

congratulatory agg. congratulatorio.

to **congregate** vt. adunare. ♦ to **congregate** vi. adunarsi.

congregation s. **1.** unione, adunata, assemblea **2.** (relig.) congregazione.

congregational agg. della congregazione.

congress s. congresso, riunione.

congressional agg. di congresso.

congruence s. congruenza.

congruent agg. congruente, conforme.

congruity s. conformità.

congruous agg. congruente, conforme.

conic(al) agg. conico.

conifer s. conifera.

coniferous agg. conifero.

conjecture s. congettura.

to **conjecture** vt. e vi. congetturare, ipotizzare.

conjointly avv. congiuntamente.

conjugal agg. coniugale.

conjugate agg. congiunto. ♦ **conjugate** s. **1.** (mat.) coniugato **2.** (biol.) fusione.

to **conjugate** vt. coniugare. ♦ to **conjugate** vi. coniugarsi.

conjugation s. coniugazione.

conjunction s. congiunzione.

conjunctiva s. (anat.) congiuntiva.

conjunctive agg. **1.** (biol.) connettivo **2.** (gramm.) congiuntivo. ♦ **conjunctive** s. congiuntivo.

conjunctivitis s. congiuntivite.

conjuncture s. congiuntura, circostanza.

conjuration s. **1.** incantesimo **2.** evocazione solenne.

to **conjure** vt. **1.** scongiurare **2.** evocare. ♦ to **conjure** vi. fare giochi di prestigio.

conjurer s. prestigiatore.

conjuring s. prestidigitazione.

connatural agg. connaturale.

to **connect** vt. **1.** connettere, collegare, unire **2.** associare (mentalmente). ♦ to **connect** vi. **1.** avere relazioni, collegarsi **2.** (ferr.) far coincidenza.

connecting agg. che connette. ♦ **connecting** s. (elettr.) collegamento.

connection s. **1.** collegamento, connessione **2.** relazione, parentela **3.** coincidenza **4.** (comm.) clientela.

connective agg. connettivo.

conning-tower s. (mar.) torretta di comando.

connivance s. connivenza.

to **connive** vi. essere connivente.

connotation s. significato implicito.

to **connote** vt. implicare, significare.

to **conquer** *vt.* conquistare.
conqueror *s.* conquistatore.
conquest *s.* conquista.
consanguine *agg.* consanguineo.
consanguinity *s.* consanguineità.
conscience *s.* coscienza: *for —'
sake*, per scrupolo di coscienza; *to
be — -stricken*, sentirsi rimordere
la coscienza.
conscienceless *agg.* senza scrupoli.
conscientious *agg.* scrupoloso || —
objector, obiettore di coscienza.
conscientiously *avv.* coscienziosamente.
conscious *agg.* consapevole, conscio.
consciousness *s.* coscienza, consapevolezza.
conscript *agg.* e *s.* coscritto.
conscription *s.* coscrizione.
to **consecrate** *vt.* consacrare, dedicare.
consecration *s.* consacrazione, dedizione.
consecutive *agg.* consecutivo.
consecutively *avv.* consecutiva-
mente.
consensual *agg.* consensuale.
consensus *s.* consenso, accordo ||
— *of opinion*, unanimità.
consent *s.* consenso, accordo || *by
mutual —*, amichevolmente.
to **consent** *vi.* acconsentire.
consequence *s.* 1. conseguenza, effetto 2. importanza.
consequent *agg.* conseguente, risultante.
consequential *agg.* consequenziale.
consequently *avv.* di conseguenza.
conservatism *s.* conservatorismo.
conservative *agg.* conservativo. ◆
Conservative *s.* conservatore.
conservator *s.* 1. conservatore 2.
sovrintendente (*di museo ecc.*).
conserve *s.* conserva di frutta.
to **consider** *vt.* considerare, riflettere, stimare.
considerable *agg.* considerevole,
importante.
considerate *agg.* rispettoso, pieno
di riguardi.
consideration *s.* 1. considerazione
2. rimunerazione 3. (*comm.*) provvigione.
considering *prep.* tenuto conto di,
considerando.
to **consign** *vt.* 1. (*comm.*) inviare,
consegnare 2. depositare (*soldi in
banca*).

consignation *s.* 1. (*comm.*) pagamento 2. consegna (*di merce*).
consignee *s.* consegnatario.
consigner *s.* mittente.
consignment *s.* 1. invio, spedizione
2. consegna, deposito.
to **consist** *vi.* consistere, essere composto.
consistence, consistency *s.* 1.
consistenza, compattezza 2. costanza.
consistent *agg.* coerente, logico.
consistently *avv.* coerentemente.
consistory *s.* concistoro.
consolation *s.* consolazione.
consolatory *agg.* consolante.
to **console** *vt.* consolare.
to **consolidate** *vt.* consolidare. ◆
to **consolidate** *vi.* consolidarsi.
consolidation *s.* consolidazione.
consoling *agg.* consolante.
consonance *s.* consonanza, accordo.
consonant *agg.* consono. ◆ **consonant** *s.* consonante.
consort *s.* 1. consorte 2. compagno,
collega.
to **consort** *vi.* associarsi, unirsi. ◆
to **consort** *vt.* associare, unire.
conspicuous *agg.* cospicuo, notevole.
conspicuousness *s.* cospicuità.
conspiracy *s.* congiura.
conspirator *s.* cospiratore.
to **conspire** *vt.* e *vi.* cospirare.
constable *s.* 1. agente di polizia 2.
conestabile.
constabulary *s.* corpo della polizia.
constancy *s.* costanza.
constant *agg.* costante, fedele. ◆
constant *s.* (*mat.*) costante.
constantly *agg.* costantemente.
constellation *s.* costellazione.
consternation *s.* costernazione.
constipation *s.* stitichezza.
constituency *s.* 1. gli elettori (*pl.*)
2. circoscrizione elettorale.
constituent *agg.* costituente. ◆
constituent *s.* 1. elemento costitutivo 2. (*pol.*) elettore.
to **constitute** *vt.* 1. costituire 2.
eleggere.
constitution *s.* 1. costituzione, statuto 2. costituzione, composizione
(*del corpo, dell'aria ecc.*).
constitutional *agg.* costituzionale.
constitutionalism *s.* costituzionalismo.
constitutionality *s.* costituzionalità.

constitutive *agg.* costitutivo.
to **constrain** *vt.* costringere.
constrained *agg.* costretto, forzato.
constraint *s.* **1.** costrizione **2.** imbarazzo.
to **constrict** *vt.* costringere.
constriction *s.* costrizione.
to **construct** *vt.* costruire (*anche fig.*).
construction *s.* **1.** costruzione **2.** (*giur.*) interpretazione.
constructive *agg.* costruttivo.
to **construe** *vt.* **1.** costruire grammaticalmente **2.** interpretare. ♦ to **construe** *vi.* fare l'analisi grammaticale.
consuetudinary *agg.* consuetudinario: — *law*, diritto consuetudinario.
consul *s.* console.
consular *agg.* consolare.
consulate *s.* consolato.
to **consult** *vt.* consultare. ♦ to **consult** *vi.* consultarsi.
consultation *s.* **1.** consultazione **2.** consulto.
consultative *agg.* consultativo.
consulting *agg.* consulente || — -*room*, ambulatorio.
to **consume** *vt.* consumare. ♦ to **consume** *vi.* consumarsi.
consumer *s.* consumatore, utente.
consummate *agg.* consumato, perfetto.
consumption *s.* **1.** consumo **2.** sciupio **3.** distruzione **4.** tubercolosi.
consumptive *s.* tisico, tubercolotico.
contact *s.* contatto, relazione.
to **contact** *vt.* e *vi.* mettere, mettersi in contatto con, prender contatto.
contagion *s.* contagio.
contagious *agg.* contagioso.
to **contain** *vt.* **1.** contenere, comprendere **2.** reprimere, frenare (*i sentimenti*).
contained *agg.* frenato, contenuto (*di comportamento*).
container *s.* recipiente.
contamination *s.* contaminazione.
to **contemplate** *vt.* e *vi.* contemplare, meditare.
contemplation *s.* contemplazione.
contemplative *agg.* contemplativo.
contemplator *s.* contemplatore.
contemporaneousness *s.* contemporaneità.
contemporary *agg.* e *s.* contemporaneo.

contempt *s.* disprezzo || — *of Court* (*giur.*), vilipendio della Corte.
contemptibility *s.* spregevolezza.
contemptible *agg.* spregevole.
contemptuous *agg.* sprezzante.
contemptuously *avv.* sprezzantemente.
to **contend** *vi.* **1.** contendere. ♦ to **contend** *vt.* sostenere, affermare.
contending *agg.* contendente, rivale.
content *s.* **1.** volume, capacità **2.** contenuto. ♦ **contents** *s. pl.* indice (*di libro*) (*sing.*). ♦ **content** *agg.* contento, soddisfatto.
to **content** *vt.* contentare, soddisfare.
contented *agg.* contento, pago.
contention *s.* **1.** contesa **2.** emulazione **3.** controversia.
contentious *agg.* litigioso.
contest *s.* contestazione, contesa.
to **contest** *vt.* contestare, contendere. ♦ to **contest** *vi.* competere, rivaleggiare.
context *s.* contesto.
contiguity *s.* contiguità.
continence *s.* continenza.
continent *agg.* continente. ♦ **continent** *s.* (*geogr.*) continente.
continental *agg.* e *s.* continentale.
contingency *s.* contingenza, caso.
contingent *agg.* eventuale, imprevisto.
continual *agg.* continuo.
continuation *s.* continuazione, seguito.
to **continue** *vt.* e *vi.* continuare, far continuare.
continuity *s.* **1.** continuità **2.** (*cine*) sceneggiatura.
continuous *agg.* continuo.
to **contort** *vt.* contorcere.
contortion *s.* contorsione.
contortionist *s.* contorsionista.
contour *s.* contorno, profilo.
contraband *s.* contrabbando.
contraceptive *s.* anticoncezionale.
contract *s.* contratto, patto.
to **contract** *vt.* **1.** contrarre (*matrimonio, amicizia ecc.*) **2.** (*comm.*) contrattare **3.** contrarre, restringere. ♦ to **contract** *vi.* contrarsi, restringersi.
contractile *agg.* contrattile.
contraction *s.* accorciamento.
contractor *s.* **1.** contraente **2.** appaltatore **3.** imprenditore.

contractual *agg.* contrattuale.
to **contradict** *vt.* contraddire.
contradiction *s.* contraddizione.
contradictory *agg.* contraddittorio.
to **contraindicate** *vt.* controindicare.
contraindication *s.* controindicazione.
contraposition *s.* opposizione, antitesi.
contrarily *avv.* contrariamente.
contrary *agg.* contrario, opposto. ♦ **contrary** *s.* il contrario: *on the* —, al contrario. ♦ **contrary** *avv.* contrariamente, all'opposto.
contrast *s.* contrasto, opposizione.
to **contrast** *vt.* e *vi.* far contrasto, mettere in contrasto.
to **contravene** *vt.* contravvenire.
to **contribute** *vt.* contribuire. ♦ to **contribute** *vi.* collaborare (*a un giornale*).
contribution *s.* 1. contributo 2. (*comm.*) apporto di capitale 3. collaborazione (*a un giornale*).
contributor *s.* 1. contributore 2. collaboratore (*di giornale ecc.*).
contrite *agg.* contrito.
contrition *s.* contrizione.
contrivance *s.* 1. espediente 2. apparato, congegno 3. invenzione.
to **contrive** *vt.* escogitare. ♦ to **contrive** *vi.* adoperarsi, riuscire.
control *s.* autorità, influenza, dominio, controllo || — *device* (*mecc.*), dispositivo di controllo; — *room*, camera di manovra; *birth-* —, limitazione delle nascite; *self-* —, autocontrollo. ♦ **controls** *s. pl.* (*mecc.*) comandi.
to **control** *vt.* controllare, dirigere.
controller *s.* controllore, sovrintendente.
controversial *agg.* controverso.
controversy *s.* controversia, polemica.
controvertible *agg.* controvertibile.
contumacious *agg.* 1. insubordinato 2. contumace.
contumacy *s.* 1. ribellione 2. contumacia.
contumely *s.* onta, contumelia.
contusion *s.* contusione.
contusive *agg.* contundente.
convalescence *s.* convalescenza.
convalescent *agg.* e *s.* convalescente.
to **convene** *vt.* 1. convocare, riunire 2. (*giur.*) citare. ♦ to **convene**

vi. riunirsi, incontrarsi.
convenience *s.* 1. comodo, vantaggio. ♦ **conveniences** *s. pl.* comodità.
convenient *agg.* conveniente, comodo, adatto.
convent *s.* convento.
conventicle *s.* conventicola.
convention *s.* 1. patto, convenzione 2. assemblea 3. regola (*di gioco*). ♦ **conventions** *s. pl.* convenzioni (*sociali*).
conventional *agg.* convenzionale, comune.
conventionality *s.* convenzionalità.
conventual *agg.* e *s.* conventuale.
to **converge** *vi.* convergere. ♦ to **converge** *vt.* far convergere.
convergence *s.* convergenza.
convergent *agg.* convergente.
conversation *s.* conversazione.
converse *agg.* e *s.* inverso, contrario.
conversely *avv.* viceversa.
conversion *s.* conversione, trasformazione.
convert *s.* convertito.
to **convert** *vt.* 1. convertire 2. trasformare.
converter *s.* 1. convertitore 2. (*elettr.; mecc.*) convertitore, trasformatore.
convertible *agg.* convertibile || — *car*, automobile decappottabile.
convex *agg.* convesso.
convexity *s.* convessità.
to **convey** *vt.* 1. trasportare, convogliare 2. trasmettere (*suoni, odori ecc.*) 3. dare l'idea, suggerire.
conveyable *agg.* trasportabile, trasmissibile.
conveyance *s.* 1. trasporto 2. trasmissione 3. convogliamento.
conveyancer *s.* notaio.
conveyer *s.* 1. trasportatore 2. trasmettitore 3. convogliatore.
convict *s.* condannato, forzato.
to **convict** *vt.* condannare, dichiarare colpevole.
conviction *s.* 1. (*giur.*) verdetto di colpevolezza, condanna 2. convinzione.
to **convince** *vt.* convincere.
convincing *agg.* convincente.
convincingly *avv.* in modo convincente.
convivial *agg.* allegro, conviviale, gioviale.
conviviality *s.* giovialità.

convivially *avv.* convivialmente.

to **convocate** *vt.* convocare.

convocation *s.* convocazione.

convolution *s.* circonvoluzione.

convoy *s.* 1. (*mar.; mil.*) convoglio 2. scorta.

to **convoy** *vt.* 1. (*mar.; mil.*) convogliare 2. scortare.

convulsion *s.* 1. convulsione 2. rivolgimento.

convulsive *agg.* convulso.

to **coo** *vi.* tubare.

cook *s.* cuoco, cuoca: *head* —, capocuoco.

to **cook** *vt.* e *vi.* cucinare, cuocere.

cookery *s.* arte culinaria, cucina.

cooking *s.* 1. cottura 2. arte culinaria, cucina.

cool *agg.* 1. fresco 2. leggero (*di abito*) 3. calmo 4. freddo, senza entusiasmo 5. sfacciato.

to **cool** *vt.* 1. rinfrescare 2. calmare. ♦ to **cool** *vi.* 1. rinfrescarsi 2. calmarsi.

cooling *agg.* rinfrescante. ♦ **cooling** *s.* abbassamento di temperatura.

coolness *s.* 1. frescura 2. freddezza, calma, sangue freddo.

coop *s.* stia.

to **coop** *vt.* mettere nella stia.

cooper *s.* bottaio.

to **co-operate** *vi.* cooperare.

co-operation *s.* cooperazione.

co-operative *agg.* cooperativo.

co-operator *s.* cooperatore.

to **co-opt** *vt.* eleggere membro (*di comitato*).

co-ordinate *agg.* 1. dello stesso rango 2. coordinato. ♦ **co-ordinate** *s.* (*mat.*) coordinata.

to **co-ordinate** *vt.* coordinare.

co-ordination *s.* coordinazione.

co-ordinative *agg.* coordinativo.

co-owner *s.* comproprietario.

co-ownership *s.* comproprietà.

cop[1] *s.* cima (*di collina ecc.*).

cop[2] *s.* (*gergo*) poliziotto.

copartnership *s.* società, associazione.

to **cope** *vi.* fronteggiare, tener testa.

co-pilot *s.* (*aer.*) secondo pilota.

copper *s.* 1. rame 2. moneta di rame.

to **copper** *vt.* rivestire di rame.

copperplate *s.* 1. lastra di rame (*per incisione*) 2. incisione in rame.

Coptic *agg.* copto.

copulation *s.* copulazione.

copulative *agg.* copulativo.

copy *s.* 1. copia, trascrizione 2. riproduzione 3. esemplare || — -*book*, quaderno; — -*reader*, revisore di stampa; *fair* —, bella copia; *rough* —, brutta copia.

to **copy** *vt.* 1. copiare 2. imitare.

copyist *s.* copista.

copyright *s.* diritto d'autore, proprietà letteraria.

coquetry *s.* civetteria.

coral *s.* corallo.

cord *s.* corda, spago || *spinal* —, midollo spinale.

cordage *s.* cordame.

cordial *agg.* cordiale. ♦ **cordial** *s.* (*bevanda*) cordiale.

cordiality *s.* cordialità.

cordially *avv.* cordialmente.

cordon *s.* cordone.

core *s.* 1. torsolo 2. centro, cuore.

co-respondent *s.* (*giur.*) correo (*in adulterio*).

coriaceous *agg.* coriaceo.

cork *s.* 1. sughero 2. tappo, turacciolo || — *jacket*, cintura di salvataggio.

corkscrew *s.* cavaturaccioli.

cormorant *s.* cormorano.

corn[1] *s.* 1. grano 2. cereale || *ear of* —, spiga di grano; — -*cob*, pannocchia.

corn[2] *s.* callo, durone.

cornea *s.* cornea.

corner *s.* 1. angolo 2. (*comm.*) accaparramento (*di merci*).

to **corner** *vt.* 1. mettere, spingere in un angolo 2. (*fig.*) mettere con le spalle al muro. ♦ to **corner** *vi.* formare un angolo.

cornet *s.* cornetta.

cornice *s.* cornicione.

corolla *s.* corolla.

corollary *s.* corollario.

coronary *agg.* coronario.

coronation *s.* incoronazione.

coroner *s.* magistrato inquirente.

corporal[1] *agg.* corporale.

corporal[2] *s.* caporale.

corporation *s.* 1. corporazione 2. azienda municipale.

corporative *agg.* corporativo: — *system*, sistema corporativo.

corporeal *agg.* corporeo.

corpse *s.* cadavere.

corpulent *agg.* corpulento.

corpuscle *s.* corpuscolo.

corral *s.* recinto (*per bestiame*).

correct *agg.* corretto.
to correct *vt.* correggere.
correction *s.* correzione, rettifica.
corrective *agg.* e *s.* correttivo.
correctness *s.* correttezza.
corrector *s.* correttore: — *of the press* (*tip.*), correttore di bozze.
to correlate *vt.* essere, mettere in correlazione. ♦ **to correlate** *vi.* essere in correlazione.
correlation *s.* correlazione.
correlative *agg.* correlativo.
to correspond *vi.* 1. corrispondere, essere in rapporti epistolari 2. rispondere a (*esigenze ecc.*) 3. equivalere.
correspondence 1. corrispondenza 2. accordo, rispondenza.
correspondent *s.* corrispondente.
corridor *s.* corridoio.
corroborant *agg.* corroborante.
corroboration *s.* conferma, convalida.
to corrode *vt.* corrodere. ♦ **to corrode** *vi.* corrodersi.
corrosion *s.* corrosione.
corrosive *agg.* e *s.* corrosivo.
to corrugate *vt.* corrugare.
corrugation *s.* corrugamento.
corrupt *agg.* corrotto, guasto, depravato.
to corrupt *vt.* corrompere, alterare. ♦ **to corrupt** *vi.* corrompersi, alterarsi.
corruption *s.* corruzione.
corsair *s.* corsaro.
corset *s.* corsetto.
cortisone *s.* cortisone.
corvette *s.* corvetta.
corvine *agg.* corvino.
coryphaeus *s.* (*pl.* -aei) corifeo.
cosecant *s.* cosecante.
cosily *avv.* comodamente.
cosine *s.* coseno.
cosmetic *agg.* e *s.* cosmetico.
cosmic(al) *agg.* cosmico.
cosmogony *s.* cosmogonia.
cosmographer *s.* cosmografo.
cosmography *s.* cosmografia.
cosmology *s.* cosmologia.
cosmopolitan *agg.* e *s.* cosmopolita.
cosmopolitanism *s.* cosmopolitismo.
cosmopolite *agg.* e *s.* cosmopolita.
cosmopolitism *s.* cosmopolitismo.
cosmos *s.* cosmo.
Cossack *s.* cosacco.
cost *s.* costo, prezzo || — *of living*, carovita; *at all costs*, ad ogni costo;

extra —, spesa supplementare.
to cost (cost, eost) *vt.* e *vi.* costare.
costal *agg.* costale.
coster, costermonger *s.* venditore ambulante (*di frutta, verdura ecc.*).
costly *agg.* costoso.
costume *s.* 1. costume 2. abito.
cosy *agg.* comodo, intimo.
cot[1] *s.* capanna.
cot[2] 1. (*mar.*) cuccetta 2. culla.
cotangent *s.* cotangente.
cotenant *s.* coaffittuario.
cothurnus *s.* (*pl.*-ni) coturno.
cottage *s.* villino.
cotton *s.* cotone || — *-mill*, cotonificio; — *-spinner*, operaio di filatura; — *-wool*, ovatta; — *-waste*, cascame.
couch *s.* divano.
cough *s.* tosse.
to cough *vt.* e *vi.* tossire.
could *v. can.*
council *s.* 1. consiglio (*adunanza di persone*) 2. (*eccl.*) concilio.
councillor *s.* consigliere.
counsel *s.* 1. consultazione 2. consiglio 3. legale.
to counsel *vt.* e *vi.* consigliare.
counsellor *s.* 1. consigliere 2. legale.
count[1] *s.* 1. conto, calcolo 2. (*pol.*) scrutinio 3. (*giur.*) capo d'accusa.
count[2] *s.* conte.
to count *vt.* e *vi.* 1. contare, calcolare 2. considerare, avere importanza.
countable *agg.* numerabile.
countenance *s.* espressione del volto, aria.
counter[1] *s.* calcolatore, contatore || *revolution* —, contagiri.
counter[2] *s.* volta di poppa.
counter[3] *s.* 1. banco, cassa (*di negozio*) 2. sportello 3. gettone (*da gioco*).
counter[4] *agg.* contrario, opposto || — *clockwise*, in senso antiorario; — *poison*, antidoto. ♦ **counter** *avv.* in senso ontrario.
to counteract *vt.* agir contro, contrapporsi a.
counter-attack *s.* contrattacco.
to counter-attack *vt.* e *vi.* contrattaccare.
counterbalance *s.* contrappeso.
to counterbalance *vt.* controbilanciare.
counterblow *s.* contraccolpo.

countercharge *s.* controaccusa.
counterfeit *agg.* contraffatto, simulato. ♦ **counterfeit** *s.* contraffazione, simulazione.
counterfeiter *s.* **1.** falsario **2.** simulatore.
counterfoil *s.* matrice.
countermand *s.* revoca, contrordine.
counterpane *s.* copriletto.
counterpart *s.* **1.** sostituto **2.** duplicato, sosia **3.** complemento.
counterpoint *s.* contrappunto.
countershaft *s.* contralbero.
countersign *s.* contrassegno.
counterweight *s.* contrappeso.
countess *s.* contessa.
countless *agg.* innumerevole.
countrified *agg.* campagnolo, rurale.
country *s.* **1.** paese, regione **2.** campagna **3.** patria **4.** nazione.
countryman *s.* **1.** compaesano, compatriota **2.** contadino.
countryside *s.* campagna.
countrywoman *s.* **1.** compaesana, compatriota **2.** contadina.
county *s.* contea, provincia.
coup *s.* **1.** colpo **2.** (*fig.*) impressione.
couple *s.* coppia, paio.
to **couple** *vt.* accoppiare. ♦ to **couple** *vi.* accoppiarsi.
coupling *s.* accoppiamento.
coupon *s.* cedola, tagliando.
courage *s.* coraggio, ardire.
courageous *agg.* coraggioso.
course *s.* **1.** corso (*del tempo*), corso (*di lezioni, conferenze*) **2.** serie **3.** portata (*dei pasti*) **4.** (*sport*) circuito || *of* —, naturalmente; *in due* — a tempo debito.
court *s.* **1.** corte, cortile **2.** (*giur.*) corte || *— of justice*, tribunale.
to **court** *vt.* corteggiare.
courtier *s.* cortigiano.
courting *s.* corteggiamento.
courtyard *s.* cortile.
courtship *s.* corteggiamento.
cousin *s.* cugino, cugina.
cove *s.* **1.** insenatura **2.** grotta.
covenant *s.* convenzione, patto.
cover *s.* **1.** coperta, copertura **2.** calotta **3.** copertina (*di libro*) **4.** riparo, ricovero **5.** coperto (*a tavola*).
to **cover** *vt.* **1.** coprire, ricoprire **2.** proteggere **3.** percorrere **4.** nascondere **5.** comprendere, includere.
covering *s.* copertura, rivestimento.

coverlet *s.* copriletto.
covert *s.* ricovero, rifugio.
covertly *avv.* nascostamente.
to **covet** *vt.* agognare.
covetousness *s.* cupidigia.
cow *s.* mucca, vacca || *— bell*, campanaccio; *— -grass*, trifoglio di campo; *— -shed*, stalla.
coward *s.* codardo, vile.
cowardice *s.* codardia, viltà.
cowardly *agg.* codardo. ♦ **cowardly** *avv.* vilmente.
cowboy *s.* bovaro.
cowherd *s.* vaccaro.
cowl *s.* **1.** cappuccio, tonaca (*di frate*) **2.** (*auto; aer.*) cofano del motore.
coxswain *s.* timoniere.
coy *agg.* timido, riservato.
crab *s.* granchio.
crabbed *agg.* sgarbato, bisbetico.
crack *s.* **1.** schianto, detonazione, schiocco **2.** incrinatura, rottura.
to **crack** *vt.* **1.** schiantare, rompere, incrinare **2.** schioccare. ♦ to **crack** *vi.* **1.** screpolarsi, spezzarsi **2.** scricchiolare.
cracked *agg.* **1.** incrinato **2.** fesso (*di voce*).
cracker *s.* petardo || *nut-crackers*, schiaccianoci; *— of jokes*, burlone.
crackle *s.* **1.** crepitio **2.** screpolatura, incrinatura.
to **crackle** *vi.* scoppiettare, scricchiolare. ♦ to **crackle** *vt.* screpolare.
crackling *s.* scoppiettio.
cradle *s.* culla (*anche fig.*).
craft *s.* **1.** abilità, mestiere, professione **2.** astuzia, inganno.
craftsman *s.* artigiano.
craftsmanship *s.* artigianato.
crafty *agg.* astuto, abile.
crag *s.* rupe, cresta.
to **cram** *vt.* riempire, stipare, rimpinzare. ♦ to **cram** *vi.* rimpinzarsi.
cramp *s.* crampo.
to **cramp** *vt.* (*fig.*) bloccare, paralizzare.
crane *s.* gru (*anche mecc.*).
to **crane** *vt.* e *vi.* **1.** sollevare o abbassare (*mediante una gru*) **2.** allungare (*il collo*).
cranium *s.* cranio.
crank[1] *s.* manovella, manubrio.
crank[2] *agg.* **1.** piegato **2.** disinnestato.

to **crank** vt. e vi. **1.** piegare a gomito **2.** mettere in moto (con manovella).

cranking s. avviamento (di motore).

crash s. **1.** strepito, fracasso **2.** caduta **3.** scontro, collisione **4.** rovina (anche morale).

to **crash** vt. e vi. **1.** abbattere, precipitare, crollare con grande rumore **2.** scontrare, scontrarsi.

crate s. cassa da imballaggio.

crater s. cratere.

to **crawl** vi. **1.** strisciare, andar carponi **2.** brulicare **3.** avere la pelle d'oca.

crawl s. **1.** strisciamento **2.** (nuoto) « crawl ».

crayfish s. gambero (d'acqua dolce).

craze s. mania, smania.

craziness s. pazzia, follia.

crazy agg. **1.** folle **2.** maniaco, entusiasta.

to **creak** vi. cigolare, stridere.

cream s. **1.** panna, crema **2.** ogni sostanza densa e untuosa.

creamery s. caseificio.

creamy agg. cremoso.

crease s. piega, grinza.

to **crease** vt. fare pieghe, sgualcire. ♦ to **crease** vi. sgualcirsi.

to **create** vt. **1.** creare, produrre, suscitare **2.** nominare.

creation s. **1.** creazione **2.** universo, natura, il creato.

creative agg. creativo.

creator s. creatore.

creature s. **1.** essere vivente **2.** creatura (anche fig.), favorito.

credence s. credenza, fede.

credentials s. pl. credenziali.

credibility s. credibilità.

credible agg. credibile.

credit s. **1.** fiducia **2.** credito, reputazione, autorità **3.** (comm.) fido, credito.

to **credit** vt. **1.** prestar fede **2.** attribuire **3.** (comm.) accreditare

creditor s. creditore.

credulity s. credulità.

credulous agg. credulo.

creed s. credo, credenza religiosa.

creek s. **1.** insenatura **2.** (amer.) torrente.

to **creep (crept, crept)** vi. **1.** strisciare, avanzare lentamente **2.** arrampicarsi (di piante) || to — along, avanzare strisciando; to — away, allontanarsi strisciando.

creeper s. **1.** rettile, verme **2.** persona strisciante **3.** pianta rampicante.

creepy agg. **1.** strisciante **2.** che dà i brividi.

to **cremate** vt. cremare.

cremation s. cremazione.

crematory s. crematoio.

creole agg. e s. creolo.

crept V. to creep.

crepuscular agg. crepuscolare.

crescent agg. **1.** crescente **2.** a mezzaluna. ♦ **crescent** s. **1.** luna crescente **2.** mezzaluna (emblema turco) **3.** strada a semicerchio.

cress s. crescione.

crest s. **1.** cresta **2.** ciuffo, pennacchio **3.** criniera.

to **crest** vt. ornare di pennacchio. ♦ to **crest** vi. incresparsi (di onde).

crevasse s. crepaccio.

crevice s. fessura.

crew[1] s. equipaggio, ciurma.

crew[2] V. to crow.

crib s. **1.** greppia **2.** presepio **3.** stalla, capanna.

crick s. crampo || a — in the neck, torcicollo.

cricket s. grillo.

crime s. delitto, crimine.

criminal agg. e s. criminale.

criminalist s. penalista.

criminality s. criminalità.

criminology s. criminologia.

crimson s. cremisi.

to **cringe** vi. (fig.) farsi piccolo, umiliarsi.

cripple agg. e s. storpio, zoppo.

to **cripple** vt. storpiare. ♦ to **cripple** vi. essere zoppo.

crisis s. crisi.

crisp agg. **1.** croccante **2.** crespo **3.** tonificante. ♦ **crisp** s. patatina fritta, croccante.

criss-cross agg. incrociato.

critic s. critico.

critical agg. critico.

criticism s. critica.

to **criticize** vt. criticare.

critique s. critica, recensione.

croak s. gracidamento.

to **croak** vt. e vi. **1.** gracidare **2.** (fig.) brontolare.

Croatian agg. e s. croato.

crochet s. lavoro all'uncinetto || —-hook (o — -pin), uncinetto.

crock[1] s. coccio, vaso di terracotta.

crock[2] s. **1.** ronzino **2.** persona vecchia e malandata.

crock³ s. fuliggine, sudiciume.

crockery s. terraglia.

crocodile s. coccodrillo.

croft s. piccolo podere, campicello.

crook s. 1. gancio, uncino 2. curva, flessione 3. (gergo) truffatore.

crookback s. gobba.

crooked agg. 1. curvo, storto, deforme 2. (fig.) perverso.

crookedly avv. 1. tortuosamente 2. indirettamente 3. perversamente.

crop s. 1. raccolto, messe 2. gozzo (di uccello) 3. (fig.) gruppo 4. rapata (di capelli).

to **crop** vt. 1. mietere 2. tosare.

cropper¹ s. mietitore.

cropper² s. (fam.) capitombolo.

cross agg. 1. obliquo, trasversale 2. adirato || — -bar, traversa; — -road, incrocio. ♦ **cross** s. 1. croce 2. tribolazione, pena.

to **cross** vt. e vi. 1. fare il segno della croce 2. attraversare 3. incrociare 4. cancellare || to — one's legs, accavallare le gambe.

crossbeam s. trave maestra.

crossbelt s. cartucciera a tracolla.

crossbow s. balestra.

crossbreed s. ibrido, incrocio.

cross-country agg. campestre.

cross-examination s. controinterrogatorio.

to **cross-examine** vt. controinterrogare.

cross-hatch s. tratteggio.

crossing s. 1. passaggio, traversata 2. incrocio || level —, passaggio a livello.

crossly avv. di malumore.

crosswise avv. 1. di traverso 2. a forma di croce.

crossword s. parole incrociate (pl.) || — puzzle, cruciverba.

crouch s. l'accovacciarsi.

to **crouch** vi. accovacciarsi, rannicchiarsi.

crow¹ s. corvo, cornacchia || a white —, una mosca bianca; to eat (v. irr.) a —, inghiottire un rospo.

crow² s. canto del gallo.

to **crow** (**crew, crowed**) vi. cantare (del gallo).

crowd s. folla, massa, moltitudine.

to **crowd** vt. affollare. ♦ to **crowd** vi. affollarsi, accalcarsi || to .— together, stringere insieme.

crown s. 1. corona 2. cocuzzolo 3. coronamento, successo 4. (moneta) corona: half a —, mezza corona.

to **crown** vt. 1. incoronare 2. coronare, ricompensare.

crowning s. 1. incoronazione 2. coronamento.

crucial agg. cruciale.

crucible s. 1. crogiuolo 2. (fig.) dura prova.

crucifix s. crocifisso.

crucifixion s. crocifissione.

to **crucify** vt. crocifiggere.

crude agg. grezzo, rozzo, primitivo.

crudity s. asprezza.

cruel agg. crudele.

cruelty s. crudeltà.

cruet s. ampolla.

cruise s. crociera: to go on a —, fare una crociera.

cruiser s. incrociatore.

cruising s. crociera.

crumb s. 1. briciola 2. mollica.

to **crumb** vt. 1. sbriciolare 2. impanare.

to **crumble** vt. sbriciolare. ♦ to **crumble** vi. sbriciolarsi.

crumbly agg. friabile.

to **crumple** vt. spiegazzare. ♦ to **crumple** vi. spiegazzarsi.

to **crunch** vt. e vi. sgranocchiare rumorosamente.

crusade s. crociata.

crusader s. crociato.

crush s. 1. folla, calca 2. frantumazione 3. (gergo) cotta.

to **crush** vt. 1. frantumare, torchiare 2. (fig.) annientare, sconfiggere. ♦ to **crush** vi. accalcarsi, affollarsi.

crushing agg. schiacciante (anche fig.).

crust s. 1. crosta 2. incrostazione.

Crustacea s. pl. crostacei.

crutch s. 1. gruccia, stampella 2. forcella (di ramo).

cry s. grido, lamento, pianto || within —, a portata di voce.

to **cry** vt. e vi. 1. gridare 2. piangere || to — out, alzare la voce, protestare.

crypt s. cripta.

cryptogam s. crittogama.

cryptogram s. crittogramma.

cryptography s. crittografia.

crystal agg. cristallino. ♦ **crystal** s. cristallo || — work, cristalleria.

crystalline agg. cristallino (anche fig.).

crystallization s. cristallizzazione.

to **crystallize** vt. cristallizzare. ♦ to **crystallize** vi. cristallizzarsi.

crystallography s. cristallografia.
cub s. 1. volpacchiotto 2. (fam.) ragazzaccio.
cubage s. cubatura.
Cuban agg. e s. cubano.
cubature s. cubatura.
cube s. cubo || — root, radice cubica.
cubic agg. cubico.
cubism s. cubismo.
cubit s. cubito.
cuckold s. becco, cornuto.
to cuckold vt. tradire (il marito).
cuckoo s. cuculo.
cucumber s. cetriolo.
cudgel s. randello.
to cudgel vt. randellare.
cuff s. polsino (di camicia).
cuirass s. corazza.
cuirassier s. corazziere.
culinary agg. culinario.
to cull vt. scegliere.
culminant agg. culminante.
to culminate vi. culminare, giungere al culmine.
culottes s. pl. gonna pantaloni.
culprit s. 1. colpevole 2. imputato.
cult s. culto.
cultivable agg. coltivabile.
to cultivate vt. coltivare (anche fig.).
cultivation s. coltivazione.
cultural agg. culturale.
culture s. 1. coltura, coltivazione 2. cultura.
cultured agg. colto, educato.
cumbersome agg. ingombrante.
cumulative agg. cumulativo.
cumulus s. (pl. -li) cumulo.
cuneiform agg. cuneiforme.
cunette s. cunetta (di trincea).
cunning agg. astuto, furbo. ♦ cunning s. astuzia.
cup s. 1. tazza 2. (sport) coppa, trofeo || — -bearer, coppiere; tea- —, tazza da tè.
cupboard s. credenza, armadio.
cupel s. coppella.
cupidity s. cupidigia.
cupreous agg. cupreo.
cupric agg. ramico.
cur s. 1. cane bastardo 2. mascalzone.
curable agg. curabile.
curacy s. vicariato, cura.
curare s. curaro.
curate s. curato, vicario.
curative agg. curativo.
curator s. direttore (di museo, istituto ecc.).

curb s. 1. cordone del marciapiede 2. freno (fig.) || — -bit, morso della briglia.
curd s. giuncata.
to curdle vt. cagliare, coagulare. ♦ to curdle vi. cagliarsi, coagularsi.
curdy agg. cagliato, coagulato.
cure s. 1. cura, rimedio: to take a —, fare una cura 2. (eccl.) cura 3. vulcanizzazione (di gomma).
to cure vt. 1. curare, rimediare 2. salare, affumicare (di cibi) 3. vulcanizzare (una gomma). ♦ to cure vi. curarsi.
cureless agg. incurabile.
curette s. (chir.) raschiatoio.
curfew s. coprifuoco.
curio s. oggetto raro.
curiosity s. curiosità: out of —, per curiosità.
curious agg. 1. curioso 2. strano, singolare.
curl s. 1. ricciolo 2. curva, spirale.
to curl vt. 1. arricciare 2. torcere. ♦ to curl vi. 1. arricciarsi 2. torcersi 3. sollevarsi in spire.
curler s. ferro per arricciare i capelli, bigodino.
curly agg. 1. ricciuto 2. a spirale.
currency s. 1. (comm.) circolazione monetaria 2. corso, credito, voga.
current agg. corrente. ♦ current s. corrente (anche fig.) || alternating —, corrente alternata; direct —, corrente continua.
currently avv. comunemente.
curriculum s. curriculum.
to curry vt. 1. strigliare 2. conciare (di cuoio).
curry-comb s. striglia.
curse s. maledizione, anatema: a — upon him!, sia maledetto!
to curse vt. 1. maledire 2. scomunicare. ♦ to curse vi. imprecare, pronunciare bestemmie.
cursed agg. maledetto.
cursive agg. e s. corsivo.
to curtail vt. accorciare, abbreviare.
curtain s. 1. tenda, tendina 2. cortina 3. sipario || — -call, chiamata alla ribalta.
curtain-raiser s. avanspettacolo.
curtly avv. brevemente, bruscamente.
curtsey s. riverenza, inchino (di donna).
curve s. curva, svolta.
to curve vt. curvare. ♦ to curve vi.

curvarsi.
curvet s. falcata.
curvilinear agg. curvilineo.
cushion s. cuscino.
cusp s. **1.** cuspide **2.** (geom.) vertice.
custard s. crema (di uova e latte).
custody s. **1.** custodia, vigilanza **2.** arresto, detenzione.
custom s. costume, consuetudine.
♦ **customs** s. pl. dogana (sing.) || — -house officer, doganiere.
customary agg. **1.** abituale, d'uso comune **2.** (giur.) consuetudinario.
customer s. cliènte, avventore.
cut s. **1.** taglio **2.** decurtazione **3.** (sport) colpo secco.
to cut (cut, cut) vt. e vi. **1.** tagliare, tagliarsi || to — a poor figure, fare una brutta figura **2.** (comm.) ridurre **3.** praticare un'apertura || to — down, abbattere; to — out, ritagliare; to — up, trinciare (il pollo), sradicare (alberi).
cutlet s. costoletta.
cut-off s. **1.** scorciatoia **2.** ritaglio di giornale.
cutter[1] s. **1.** tagliatore **2.** (mecc.) fresa.
cutter[2] s. (mar.) "cutter".
cut-throat agg. spietato. ♦ **cut-throat** s. tagliagole.
cutting agg. tagliente, sferzante. ♦ **cutting** s. **1.** taglio, incisione **2.** ritaglio, truciolo **3.** (comm.) riduzione.
cuttlefish s. seppia.
cyanide s. cianuro.
cybernetics s. cibernetica.
cycle s. ciclo.
cycling s. ciclismo.
cyclostyle s. ciclostile.
cyclotron s. ciclotrone.
cyclist s. ciclista.
cyclometer s. contachilometri.
cylinder s. **1.** cilindro **2.** rullo.
cylindrical agg. cilindrico.
cynic agg. e s. cinico.
cynicism s. cinismo.
cypress s. cipresso.
Cyprian agg. e s. cipriota.
Cyrillic agg. cirillico.
cyst s. cisti.
cystitis s. cistite.
cytology s. citologia.
Czar s. zar.
Czech agg. e s. ceco.
Czecho-Slovak agg. e s. cecoslovacco.

D

D s. (mus.) re.
dab s. **1.** colpo **2.** macchia.
to dab vt. **1.** sfiorare **2.** applicare.
to dabble vt. inumidire. ♦ **to dabble** vi. **1.** inumidirsi **2.** sguazzare || to — in (at), dilettarsi di.
dachshund s. cane bassotto.
dad(dy) s. (fam.) papà, babbo.
daffodil s. narciso selvatico.
daft agg. sciocco, pazzoide.
dagger s. **1.** pugnale **2.** (tip.) croce || at daggers drawn, ai ferri corti.
daguerreotype s. dagherrotipo.
daguerreotypy s. dagherrotipia.
dahlia s. dalia.
daily agg. quotidiano, giornaliero.
♦ **daily** s. (giornale) quotidiano.
♦ **daily** avv. ogni giorno.
daintily avv. delicatamente.
daintiness s. squisitezza.
dainty agg. **1.** squisito **2.** esigente **3.** raffinato (di gusti). ♦ **dainty** s. leccornia.
dairy s. latteria.
dairymaid s. lattaia.
dairyman s. lattaio.
dais s. piattaforma.
daisy s. margherita.
dalliance s. amoreggiamento.
to dally vi. gingillarsi, oziare.
Dalmatian agg. e s. dalmata.
daltonism s. daltonismo.
dam[1] s. diga, sbarramento.
dam[2] s. madre (di animali).
to dam vt. arginare.
damage s. danno. ♦ **damages** s. pl. (giur.) indennizzo, risarcimento (sing.).
to damage vt. danneggiare.
damaging agg. dannoso.
damask s. damasco.
to damask vt. damascare.
dame s. dama, gentildonna.
damn s. maledizione.
to damn vt. **1.** dannare **2.** (spesso scritto d-) maledire, mandare all'inferno.
damnation s. dannazione.
damnatory agg. compromettente (di prove).
damp agg. umido. ♦ **damp** s. **1.** umidità **2.** (fig.) depressione || fire—, grisù.
to damp vt. **1.** inumidire **2.** (fig.) deprimere, smorzare.

damper s. **1.** regolatore (*di stufa, fornace ecc.*) **2.** (*mus.*) sordina.

dampness s. umidità.

dance s. danza.

to **dance** vt. e vi. danzare || to — attendance on, essere a disposizione di.

dancer s. ballerino.

dancing s. danza.

dandelion s. (*bot.*) soffione.

dandruff s. forfora.

dandy agg. elegante, raffinato. ♦ **dandy** s. zerbinotto.

Dane s. danese.

danger s. pericolo.

dangerous agg. pericoloso.

to **dangle** vi. ciondolare, penzolare ♦ to **dangle** vt. far penzolare.

dangling agg. penzolante.

Danish agg. danese.

dank agg. umido.

Dantean, Dantesque agg. dantesco.

dapple s. macchia || — -grey, leardo pomellato.

to **dapple** vt. chiazzare.

dare (**dared, durst**) v. dif. osare.

to **dare** vt. **1.** affrontare **2.** sfidare.

daredevil s. scavezzacollo.

daring agg. audace. ♦ **daring** s. audacia.

dark agg. **1.** scuro **2.** triste **3.** segreto. ♦ **dark** s. **1.** oscurità **2.** (*fig.*) ignoranza.

to **darken** vt. oscurare. ♦ to **darken** vi. oscurarsi.

darkling agg. oscuro. ♦ **darkling** avv. nell'oscurità.

darkness s. oscurità.

darling agg. e s. caro.

darn s. rammendo.

to **darn** vt. rammendare.

darnel s. loglio.

darner s. rammendatrice.

darni... s. rammendo.

dart s. **1.** dardo **2.** slancio.

to **dart** vt. lanciare. ♦ to **dart** vi. lanciarsi (*in avanti*).

darting agg. dardeggiante.

Darwinism s. darwinismo.

dash s. **1.** slancio **2.** attacco **3.** tonfo **4.** spruzzo **5.** lineetta || — -board, cruscotto (*di automobili*).

to **dash** vt. **1.** frantumare **2.** macchiare. ♦ to **dash** vi. **1.** precipitarsi **2.** infrangersi.

dashing agg. impetuoso.

dastard s. vigliacco, furfante.

date[1] s. **1.** data **2.** appuntamento || up to —, aggiornato; out of —,

antiquato.

date[2] s. dattero.

to **date** vt. e vi. datare || to — a girl, dare un appuntamento a una ragazza.

dating s. datazione.

dative agg. e s. dativo.

datum s. (*pl.* data) dato, elemento.

to **daub** vt. **1.** intonacare **2.** impiastrare.

dauber s. imbrattatore.

daughter s. figlia || — -in-law, nuora; grand- — (*di nonni*), nipotina.

to **daunt** vt. spaventare, intimidire.

dauntless agg. intrepido.

to **dawdle** vi. oziare, bighellonare.

dawn s. alba.

to **dawn** vi. **1.** albeggiare **2.** apparire, balenare (*nella mente*).

day s. giorno || — labourer, lavoratore a giornata; the — after tomorrow, dopodomani; the — before yesterday, l'altro ieri; this — week, oggi a otto; — off, giorno di riposo; — out, giorno di libera uscita.

daybook s. (*comm.*) brogliaccio.

daybreak s. alba.

daydream s. fantasticheria.

to **daydream** vi. fantasticare.

daydreamer s. sognatore.

daylight s. luce del giorno.

daylong agg. che dura tutto il giorno. ♦ **daylong** avv. per tutto il giorno.

daytime s. giornata.

daze s. sbalordimento.

to **daze** vt. sbalordire.

dazzle s. abbagliamento || — lamps (*auto*), fari abbaglianti.

to **dazzle** vt. abbagliare.

deacon s. diacono.

dead agg. **1.** morto **2.** assoluto || — drunk, ubriaco fradicio. ♦ **dead** avv. assolutamente || — sure, arcisicuro.

to **deaden** vt. **1.** attutire **2.** isolare (*acusticamente*). ♦ to **deaden** vi. attutirsi.

deadening s. isolamento acustico.

deadline s. **1.** linea non superabile **2.** scadenza, termine massimo.

deadly agg. mortale. ♦ **deadly** avv. mortalmente.

deadness s. torpore.

deaf agg. sordo.

to **deafen** vt. assordare.

deaf-mute s. sordomuto.

deafness s. sordità.

deal s. 1. quantità 2. accordo 3. affare 4. mano (*del gioco delle carte*) || *a great.* —, moltissimo.

to **deal** (**dealt, dealt**) vt. distribuire, dare. ♦ to **deal** (**dealt, dealt**) vi. trattare, comportarsi || *to — in,* commerciare in.

dealer s. 1. commerciante 2. mazziere (*delle carte*).

dealing s. 1. commercio 2. distribuzione 3. relazione || *double-* —, slealtà.

dealt V. *to deal.*

deambulatory agg. deambulatorio.

dean s. 1. decano 2. preside (*di facoltà universitaria*).

dear agg. caro || *— me!,* povero me!

dearly avv. 1. caramente 2. a caro prezzo.

dearness s. amorevolezza.

dearth s. penuria.

death s. morte || *— -rattles,* rantoli dell'agonia; *— -warrant,* ordine di esecuzione capitale.

deathly agg. e avv. V. *deadly.*

to **debase** vt. 1. avvilire 2. svalutare.

to **debar** vt. escludere, privare.

to **debark** vt. e vi. sbarcare.

debate s. dibattito.

to **debate** vt. e vi. 1. discutere 2. ponderare.

debauch s. intemperanza, corruzione.

debauched agg. corrotto.

debauchery s. 1. corruzione 2. dissolutezza.

debenture s. (comm.) obbligazione.

debit s. debito.

to **debit** vt. addebitare.

to **debouch** vi. sfociare.

debris s. detriti (pl.).

debt s. debito.

debtor s. debitore.

début s. debutto.

decadence s. decadenza.

decadent agg. e s. decadente.

decagram(m)e s. decagrammo.

decahedron s. decaedro.

to **decalcify** vt. decalcificare.

decalitre s. decalitro.

decalogue s. decalogo.

decametre s. decametro.

to **decamp** vi. levare le tende.

to **decant** vt. travasare.

decantation s. decantazione.

decanter s. caraffa.

to **decapitate** vt. decapitare.

decasyllabic agg. decasillabico.

decay s. 1. decadimento 2. rovina 3. carie (*dei denti*).

to **decay** vt. 1. far decadere 2. mandare in rovina. ♦ to **decay** vi. 1. decadere 2. andare in rovina 3. cariarsi.

decayable agg. deperibile.

decease s. decesso.

to **decease** vi. morire.

deceit s. 1. inganno 2. falsità.

deceitful agg. 1. ingannevole 2. falso.

to **deceive** vt. ingannare.

deceiving agg. ingannatore.

to **decelerate** vt. e vi. rallentare.

deceleration s. rallentamento.

decelerator s. rallentatore.

December s. dicembre.

decency s. decenza. ♦ **decencies** s. pl. convenienze.

decennary agg. decennale. ♦ **decennary** s. decennio.

decennial agg. e s. decennale.

decent agg. decente || *a — fellow,* un buon diavolo.

decentralization s. decentramento.

to **decentralize** vt. decentrare.

deception s. inganno.

deceptive agg. ingannevole.

to **decide** vt. decidere. ♦ to **decide** vi. decidersi, pronunciarsi.

decigram(me) s. decigrammo.

decimal agg. e s. decimale.

to **decimate** vt. decimare.

decimation s. decimazione.

decimetre s. decimetro.

to **decipher** vt. decifrare.

deciphering s. decifrazione.

decision s. decisione.

decisive agg. 1. decisivo 2. deciso.

deck s. (mar.) ponte, coperta || *— -chair,* sedia a sdraio; *quarter-* —, cassero.

to **deck** vt. ornare.

decker s. double- —, autobus a due piani.

to **declaim** vt. e vi. declamare.

declaimer s. declamatore.

declamation s. declamazione.

declamatory agg. declamatorio.

declaration s. dichiarazione.

to **declare** vt. e vi. dichiarare.

declension s. 1. declino 2. (gramm.) declinazione.

declinable agg. declinabile.

declination s. 1. inclinazione 2. declino.

decline s. declino, deperimento.

to **decline** vt. e vi. declinare.
declining s. 1. declinazione 2. deperimento 3. rifiuto.
declivity s. declivio.
to **decode** vt. decifrare, tradurre (*testi in codice*).
decolorization s. decolorazione.
decoloration s. decolorazione.
to **decolour(ize)** vt. decolorare.
decomposable agg. scomponibile.
to **decompose** vt. 1. decomporre 2. scomporre. ♦ to **decompose** vi. 1. decomporsi 2. scomporsi.
decomposition s. decomposizione.
to **deconsecrate** vt. sconsacrare.
to **decorate** vt. decorare.
decoration s. decorazione.
decorative agg. decorativo.
decorator s. decoratore.
decorous agg. decoroso.
decoy s. esca, richiamo.
decrease s. diminuzione.
to **decrease** vt. e vi. diminuire.
decree s. decreto.
to **decree** vt. decretare.
decrepit agg. decrepito.
decrepitude s. decrepitezza.
to **decry** vt. stigmatizzare, denigrare.
to **decuple** vt. decuplicare.
to **dedicate** vt. dedicare.
dedicatee s. persona a cui è dedicato qc.
dedication s. 1. dedica 2. consacrazione.
dedicative, dedicatory agg. dedicatorio.
to **deduce** vt. 1. dedurre 2. derivare.
to **deduct** vt. detrarre.
deduction s. 1. deduzione 2. detrazione.
deductive agg. deduttivo.
deed s. atto, azione.
to **deem** vt. giudicare.
deep agg. 1. profondo 2. cupo || — -freeze, surgelamento; — *mourning*, lutto stretto. ♦ **dcep** s. abisso, profondità. ♦ **deep** avv. profondamente || — *into the night*, fino a notte tarda.
to **deepen** vt. 1. approfondire 2. incupire. ♦ to **deepen** vi. 1. approfondirsi 2. incupirsi.
deeply avv. profondamente.
deepness s. profondità.
deep-rooted agg. radicato.
deer s. cervo || (*fallow*) —, daino.
to **deface** vt. sfregiare.

defacement s. sfregio.
defamation s. diffamazione.
defamatory agg. diffamatorio.
to **defame** vt. diffamare.
defamer s. diffamatore.
default s. 1. mancanza 2. inadempienza 3. (*giur.*) contumacia: *judgement by* —, giudizio in contumacia.
defaulting agg. (*comm.*) insolvente.
defeat s. 1. sconfitta 2. fallimento.
to **defeat** vt. 1. sconfiggere 2. frustrare.
defeatism s. disfattismo.
defeatist agg. e s. disfattista.
to **defecate** vt. purificare. ♦ to **defecate** vi. defecare.
defect s. difetto.
defection s. defezione.
defective agg. 1. difettoso 2. (*gramm.*) difettivo. ♦ **defective** s. anormale.
defence s. difesa.
defenceless agg. indifeso.
to **defend** vt. difendere.
defendant s. imputato.
defender s. difensore.
defenestration s. defenestrazione.
defensible agg. difensibile.
defensive agg. difensivo. ♦ **defensive** s. difensiva.
to **defer**[1] vt. e vi. differire || *deferred payment*, pagamento a rate.
to **defer**[2] vt. rimettere. ♦ to **defer** vi. rimettersi.
deference s. deferenza.
deferential agg. deferente.
deferment s. differimento.
defiance s. sfida.
defiant agg. ardito.
deficiency s. 1. deficienza 2. disavanzo.
deficient agg. e s. deficiente.
deficit s. (*comm.*) disavanzo.
to **defile** vi. marciare in fila. ♦ to **defile** vt. 1. insozzare 2. profanare.
defilement s. 1. contaminazione 2. profanazione.
definable agg. definibile.
to **define** vt. definire.
definite agg. definito.
definitely avv. in modo preciso.
definiteness s. precisione.
definition s. 1. definizione 2. nitidezza.
definitive agg. definitivo.
to **deflagrate** vt. far deflagrare. ♦ to **deflagrate** vi. deflagrare.

deflagration s. deflagrazione.
to deflate vt. sgonfiare. ♦ to **deflate** vi. sgonfiarsi.
deflation s. 1. sgonfiamento 2. deflazione.
to deflect vt. e vi. deviare.
deflection s. deviazione.
defloration s. deflorazione.
to deflower vt. 1. deflorare 2. devastare 3. spogliare (dei fiori).
to deforest vt. diboscare.
deforestation s. diboscamento.
to deform vt. deformare. ♦ to **deform** vi. deformarsi.
deformation s. deformazione.
deformed agg. deforme.
deformity s. deformità.
to defraud vt. defraudare.
defrauder s. frodatore.
to defray vt. pagare, risarcire.
defrayal s. pagamento, risarcimento.
to defrost vt. sgelare.
defroster s. riscaldatore.
deft agg. abile, destro.
to defy vt. sfidare.
degenerate agg. e s. degenerato.
to degenerate vt. e vi. degenerare.
degeneration s. degenerazione.
degradation s. degradazione.
to degrade vt. degradare.
degree s. 1. grado 2. rango 3. laurea, diploma || by degrees, gradatamente.
to dehydrate vt. disidratare.
dehydration s. disidratazione.
to deify vt. deificare.
deism s. deismo.
deity s. divinità.
to deject vt. abbattere, scoraggiare.
dejected agg. triste, abbattuto.
dejectedly avv. con aria abbattuta.
dejection s. abbattimento.
delation s. delazione.
delator s. delatore.
delay s. 1. ritardo 2. proroga.
to delay vt. e vi. ritardare.
delegacy s. delegazione.
delegate s. delegato.
to delegate vt. delegare.
delegation s. delegazione.
to delete vt. cancellare (anche fig.).
deliberate agg. 1. deliberato 2. cauto.
to deliberate vt. e vi. deliberare.
deliberately avv. deliberatamente.
deliberation s. 1. deliberazione 2. ponderatezza.
delicacy s. 1. delicatezza 2. ghiottoneria.

delicate agg. 1. delicato 2. esigente.
delicatessen s. pl. 1. ghiottonerie 2. salumeria (sing.).
delicious agg. delizioso.
delict s. (giur.) delitto.
delight s. delizia, gioia.
to delight vt. deliziare. ♦ to **delight** vi. dilettarsi.
delighted agg. lietissimo, entusiasta.
delightful agg. delizioso.
to delimit(ate) vt. delimitare.
delimitation s. delimitazione.
to delineate vt. delineare.
delineation s. delineazione.
delinquency s. 1. delinquenza 2. colpevolezza.
delinquent agg. colpevole. ♦ **delinquent** s. delinquente.
delirious agg. delirante.
deliriously avv. in modo delirante.
delirium s. delirio, frenesia.
to deliver vt. 1. liberare 2. consegnare 3. partorire 4. pronunciare (un discorso).
deliverance s. liberazione.
delivery s. 1. liberazione 2. consegna 3. parto 4. resa 5. dizione, pronuncia || — -man, fattorino.
deltoid agg. triangolare.
to delude vt. ingannare.
deluge s. diluvio.
delusion s. illusione.
delusive agg. illusorio.
to delve vt. scavare, esumare. ♦ to **delve** vi. compiere ricerche, frugare.
demagnetization s. demagnetizzazione.
to demagnetize vt. demagnetizzare.
demagogic(al) agg. demagogico.
demagogue s. demagogo.
demagogy s. demagogia.
demand s. 1. domanda 2. esigenza || on —, a richiesta.
to demand vt. 1. domandare 2. esigere.
demarcation s. demarcazione.
demeanour s. contegno.
demerit s. demerito.
demesne s. dominio, proprietà terriera.
demigod s. semidio.
demijohn s. damigiana.
demilitarization s. smilitarizzazione.
to demilitarize vt. smilitarizzare.
demise s. 1. trapasso (di proprietà)

2. decesso.
demiurge s. demiurgo.
demobilization s. smobilitazione.
to **demobilize** vt. smobilitare.
democracy s. democrazia.
democrat s. democratico.
democratic(al) agg. democratico.
democratization s. democratizzazione.
to **democratize** vt. democratizzare.
demographic(al) agg. demografico.
demography s. demografia.
to **demolish** vt. demolire.
demolisher s. demolitore.
demolition s. demolizione.
demon s. demonio.
demoniac(al) agg. demoniaco.
demonology s. demonologia.
demonstrability s. dimostrabilità.
demonstrable agg. dimostrabile.
demonstrant s. dimostrante.
to **demonstrate** vt. e vi. dimostrare.
demonstration s. dimostrazione.
demonstrative agg. **1.** dimostrativo **2.** espansivo.
demonstrativeness s. **1.** dimostrazione **2.** espansività.
demonstrator s. **1.** dimostratore **2.** dimostrante.
demoralization s. **1.** depravazione **2.** demoralizzazione.
to **demoralize** vt. **1.** depravare **2.** demoralizzare.
to **demur** vi. titubare, esitare.
demure agg. riservato, pudico.
demureness s. riservatezza, pudore.
den s. tana.
to **denationalize** vt. snazionalizzare.
to **denature** vt. denaturare.
deniable agg. negabile.
denial s. rifiuto || self- —, abnegazione.
to **denigrate** vt. denigrare.
denigration s. denigrazione.
denigrator s. denigratore.
to **denominate** vt. denominare.
denomination s. **1.** denominazione **2.** setta **3.** valore (di monete).
denominational agg. confessionale.
denominative agg. denominativo.
denominator s. denominatore.
denotation s. **1.** indicazione **2.** significato.
to **denote** vt. denotare, indicare.
to **denounce** vt. denunciare.
dense agg. **1.** denso **2.** opaco **3.** stupido.
density s. **1.** densità **2.** opacità **3.**

stupidità.
dent s. incavo, tacca.
dental agg. e s. dentale.
dentary agg. dentario.
dentine s. dentina.
dentist s. dentista.
dentistry s. odontoiatria.
dentition s. dentizione.
denture s. dentiera.
denudation s. denudazione.
to **denude** vt. denudare.
denunciation s. denunzia.
to **deny** vt. negare, rifiutare.
deodorant agg. e s. deodorante.
to **deodorize** vt. deodorare.
deontology s. deontologia.
deoxidization s. disossidazione.
to **deoxidize** vt. disossidare.
to **depart** vi. partire, allontanarsi.
department s. **1.** reparto **2.** (amer.) ministero || — store, grande magazzino.
departure s. **1.** partenza **2.** allontanamento.
to **depend** vi. **1.** dipendere: it all depends on circumstances, tutto dipende dalle circostanze **2.** contare: — on so., contare su qu.
dependable agg. fidato.
dependant agg. e s. dipendente.
dependence s. **1.** dipendenza **2.** fiducia.
dependency s. territorio dipendente.
dependent agg. dipendente.
to **depict** vt. dipingere.
to **depilate** vt. depilare.
depilatory agg. e s. depilatorio.
to **deplete** vt. **1.** vuotare **2.** esaurire.
depletion s. esaurimento.
deplorable agg. deplorevole.
to **deplore** vt. deplorare.
to **deploy** vt. schierare, spiegare. ◆ to **deploy** vi. schierarsi (di truppe ecc.).
to **depone** vt. deporre (in un processo).
deponent s. testimone.
to **depopulate** vt. spopolare.
to **deport** vt. deportare || to — oneself, comportarsi.
deportation s. deportazione.
deportment s. atteggiamento.
deposal s. deposizione.
to **depose** vt. e vi. deporre.
deposit s. deposito.
to **deposit** vt. depositare.
deposition s. **1.** deposizione **2.** de-

posito.
depositor *s.* depositante.
depot *s.* deposito.
to **deprave** *vt.* depravare.
depravity *s.* depravazione.
deprecable *agg.* deprecabile.
to **deprecate** *vt.* disapprovare.
deprecation *s.* disapprovazione.
deprecative, deprecatory *agg.* disapprovante.
to **depreciate** *vt.* svalutare. ♦ to **depreciate** *vi.* svalutarsi.
depreciation *s.* 1. svalutazione 2. ammortamento: — *charge,* quota d'ammortamento.
depreciative, depreciatory *agg.* spregiativo.
depredation *s.* saccheggio.
depredatory *agg.* predatorio.
to **depress** *vt.* 1. deprimere 2. abbassare.
depression *s.* 1. depressione 2. (*econ.*) crisi.
depressor *s.* depressore.
deprivation *s.* privazione.
to **deprive** *vt.* privare.
depth *s.* 1. profondità 2. (*mar.*) fondale.
to **depurate** *vt.* depurare. ♦ to **depurate** *vi.* depurarsi.
depuration *s.* depurazione.
depurative *agg.* e *s.* depurativo.
depurator *s.* depuratore.
deputation *s.* delega.
to **depute** *vt.* deputare.
deputy *s.* 1. deputato 2. sostituto.
derailment *s.* deragliamento.
to **derange** *vt.* sconvolgere.
derangement *s.* sconvolgimento.
deratization *s.* derattizzazione.
to **deride** *vt.* deridere.
derision *s.* 1. derisione 2. zimbello.
derisive, derisory *agg.* derisorio.
derivable *agg.* derivabile.
derivation *s.* derivazione.
derivative *agg.* e *s.* derivato.
derivatively *avv.* per derivazione.
to **derive** *vt.* e *vi.* derivare.
derm *s.* derma.
dermatologist *s.* dermatologo.
dermatology *s.* dermatologia.
to **derogate** *vi.* derogare.
derogation *s.* deroga.
derogatory *agg.* derogatorio.
derrick *s.* 1. argano 2. torre di trivellazione.
descant *s.* 1. melodia 2. dissertazione.
to **descend** *vt.* e *vi.* (di)scendere ||

to — upon so., aggredire qu.
descendance *s.* discendenza.
descendant *s.* discendente.
descent *s.* 1. discesa 2. incursione 3. lignaggio 4. caduta.
describable *agg.* descrivibile.
to **describe** *vt.* descrivere.
description *s.* descrizione.
descriptive *agg.* descrittivo.
to **descry** *vt.* scoprire.
to **desecrate** *vt.* profanare.
desert[1] *agg.* deserto. ♦ **desert** *s.* deserto.
desert[2] *s.* 1. merito 2. compenso.
to **desert** *vt.* abbandonare. ♦ to **desert** *vi.* disertare.
deserted *agg.* deserto.
deserter *s.* disertore.
desertion *s.* 1. abbandono 2. diserzione.
to **deserve** *vt.* meritare.
deservedly *avv.* meritatamente.
deserving *agg.* meritevole.
design *s.* disegno.
to **design** *vt.* 1. destinare 2. progettare 3. disegnare.
designate *agg.* designato.
to **designate** *vt.* 1. designare 2. indicare.
designation *s.* designazione.
designer *s.* disegnatore.
designing *agg.* astuto. ♦ **designing** *s.* 1. disegno 2. complotto.
desirable *agg.* desiderabile.
desire *s.* desiderio.
to **desire** *vt.* 1. desiderare 2. domandare.
desirous *agg.* desideroso.
to **desist** *vi.* desistere.
desk *s.* 1. scrivania 2. cassa || *school- master's —,* cattedra (*di insegnante*).
desolate *agg.* desolato.
to **desolate** *vt.* 1. affliggere 2. devastare.
desolation *s.* desolazione.
despair *s.* disperazione.
to **despair** *vi.* disperare.
despairing *agg.* disperato.
desperate *agg.* disperato.
despicable *agg.* spregevole.
despicableness *s.* spregevolezza.
despisable *agg.* spregevole.
to **despise** *vt.* disprezzare.
despite *prep.* malgrado.
despiteful *agg.* maligno, dispettoso.
despondency *s.* scoraggiamento.
despondent *agg.* scoraggiato.
despot *s.* despota.

despotic(al) *agg.* dispotico.
despotism *s.* dispotismo.
destination *s.* destinazione.
to **destine** *vt.* destinare.
destiny *s.* destino.
destitute *agg.* 1. povero 2. privo.
destitution *s.* 1. povertà 2. privazione.
to **destroy** *vt.* distruggere.
destroyable *agg.* distruggibile.
destroyer *s.* 1. distruttore 2. cacciatorpediniere.
destroying *agg.* distruttore.
destruction *s.* distruzione, rovina.
destructive *agg.* distruttivo.
destructor *s.* distruttore.
desuetude *s.* disuso.
desultory *agg.* saltuario.
to **detach** *vt.* distaccare.
detachable *agg.* staccabile.
detached *agg.* 1. distaccato 2. isolato.
detachment *s.* 1. distacco 2. (*mil.*) distaccamento.
detail *s.* 1. dettaglio, particolare 2. pattuglia.
to **detail** *vt.* 1. dettagliare 2. (*mil.*) distaccare (*una pattuglia*).
to **detain** *vt.* 1. detenere 2. trattenere.
to **detect** *vt.* scoprire.
detectable *agg.* scopribile.
detection *s.* scoperta.
detective *s.* investigatore || — *novel,* romanzo poliziesco.
detector *s.* (*radio*) rivelatore.
detent *s.* (*mecc.*) arpione.
detention *s.* 1. detenzione 2. ritardo forzato.
to **deter** *vt.* trattenere.
to **deterge** *vt.* detergere.
detergent *agg.* e *s.* detergente, detersivo.
to **deteriorate** *vt.* deteriorare. ♦ to **deteriorate** *vi.* deteriorarsi.
deterioration *s.* deterioramento.
determinable *agg.* determinabile.
determinant *s.* causa determinante.
determinate *agg.* determinato.
determination *s.* determinazione.
determinative *agg.* determinativo.
to **determine** *vt.* determinare, decidere. ♦ to **determine** *vi.* risolversi || *to — on,* fissarsi su.
determined *agg.* deciso.
determinism *s.* determinismo.
determinist *agg.* e *s.* determinista.
deterrent *agg.* e *s.* (*neol.*) deterrente.

detersive *agg.* e *s.* detersivo.
to **detest** *vt.* detestare.
detestable *agg.* detestabile.
detestation *s.* 1. odio 2. esecrazione.
dethronement *s.* deposizione (*dal trono*).
to **detonate** *vt.* e *vi.* esplodere.
detonator *s.* detonatore.
detour *s.* deviazione, giravolta.
to **detract** *vt.* e *vi.* diminuire.
detraction *s.* detrazione.
detractor *s.* detrattore.
detriment *s.* detrimento.
detrimental *agg.* dannoso.
to **devaluate** *vt.* svalutare.
devaluation *s.* svalutazione.
to **devastate** *vt.* devastare.
devastation *s.* devastazione.
to **develop** *vt.* sviluppare. ♦ to **develop** *vi.* svilupparsi.
developer *s.* sviluppatore.
development *s.* sviluppo.
to **deviate** *vt.* e *vi.* deviare.
deviation *s.* deviazione.
deviationism *s.* deviazionismo.
device *s.* 1. trovata 2. dispositivo. ♦ **devices** *s. pl.* capriccio, inclinazione (*sing.*).
devil *s.* diavolo.
devilish *agg.* diabolico.
devious *agg.* 1. remoto 2. errante.
to **devise** *vt.* 1. escogitare 2. lasciare in eredità.
deviser *s.* inventore.
devising *s.* invenzione.
devoid *agg.* privo.
devolution *s.* 1. trasmissione (*di beni*) 2. degenerazione.
to **devolve** *vt.* trasmettere. ♦ to **devolve** *vi.* trasferirsi.
to **devote** *vt.* dedicare.
devoted *agg.* 1. devoto 2. votato.
devotion *s.* devozione.
devotional *agg.* devoto.
to **devour** *vt.* divorare.
devourer *s.* divoratore.
devout *agg.* devoto, pio, religioso.
dew *s.* rugiada.
dewy *agg.* rugiadoso.
dexterity *s.* destrezza.
dexterous *agg.* destro.
dextrin(e) *s.* destrina.
diabetes *s.* diabete.
diabetic *agg.* e *s.* diabetico.
diabolic(al) *agg.* diabolico.
diadem *s.* diadema.
to **diagnose** *vt.* diagnosticare.
diagnosis *s.* (*pl.* -ses*) diagnosi.

diagnostic agg. diagnostico.
diagonal agg. e s. diagonale.
diagram s. diagramma.
dial s. quadrante.
to **dial** vt. comporre (*un numero telefonico*) || to — so., telefonare a qu.
dialect s. dialetto.
dialectal agg. dialettale.
dialectic(al) agg. dialettico.
dialectics s. dialettica.
dialogue s. dialogo.
to **dialogue** vt. e vi. dialogare.
diameter s. diametro.
diametrically avv. diametralmente.
diamond s. 1. diamante 2. losanga.
diaper s. 1. arabesco 2. pannolino.
diaphanous agg. diafano.
diaphragm s. diaframma.
diapositive s. diapositiva.
diarchy s. diarchia.
diarist s. diarista.
diarrhoea s. diarrea.
diary s. diario.
diatribe s. diatriba.
dice V. **die**.
to **dice** vt. 1. giocare ai dadi 2. tagliare a dadi 3. quadrettare.
dictaphone s. dittafono.
dictate s. dettame.
to **dictate** vt. e vi. dettare.
dictation s. 1. dettato 2. dettame.
dictator s. dittatore.
dictatorial agg. dittatoriale.
dictatorship s. dittatura.
diction s. 1. stile 2. dizione.
dictionary s. dizionario.
dictograph s. dittografo.
did V. to **do**.
didactic agg. didattico.
didactics s. didattica.
die s. (pl. dice) dado.
to **die** vi. morire || to — away, svanire; to — out, estinguersi.
dielectric agg. e s. dielettrico.
diet s. dieta.
to **diet** vt. mettere a dieta. ♦ to **diet** vi. essere a dieta.
dietarian s. chi sta a dieta.
dietary agg. dietetico. ♦ **dietary** s. dieta.
dietetic(al) agg. dietetico.
to **differ** vi. differire.
difference s. 1. differenza 2. divergenza.
different agg. differente.
differential agg. e s. differenziale.
to **differentiate** vt. differenziare.
♦ to **differentiate** vi. differen-

ziarsi.
differentiation s. differenziazione.
differently avv. differentemente.
differing agg. 1. differente, discordante.
difficult agg. difficile.
difficulty s. difficoltà.
diffidence s. timidezza.
diffident agg. esitante.
diffraction s. diffrazione.
diffuse agg. diffuso.
to **diffuse** vt. diffondere. ♦ to **diffuse** vi. diffondersi.
diffusedly, diffusely avv. 1. diffusamente 2. ovunque.
diffuser s. (foto) diffusore.
diffusion s. 1. diffusione 2. prolissità.
diffusive agg. 1. diffusivo 2. prolisso.
diffusor s. diffusore.
to **dig** (dug, dug) vt. vangare, scavare || to — in, affondare; to — out, estrarre.
digest s. 1. sommario 2. condensato.
to **digest** vt. classificare, condensare, redigere. ♦ to **digest** vt. e vi. digerire.
digestibility s. digeribilità.
digestible agg. digeribile.
digestion s. digestione.
digestive agg. e s. digestivo.
digger s. 1. zappatore 2. scavatrice.
digging s. 1. scavo 2. miniera. ♦ **diggings** s. pl. (gergo) alloggio (sing.).
digital agg. digitale.
dignified agg. dignitoso.
to **dignify** vt. elevare, nobilitare.
dignitary s. dignitario.
dignity s. 1. dignità 2. dignitario.
digression s. digressione.
digressive agg. digressivo.
dike s. diga.
to **dike** vt. arginare.
to **dilapidate** vt. dilapidare. ♦ to **dilapidate** vi. andare in rovina.
dilatability s. dilatabilità.
dilatable agg. dilatabile.
dilatation s. dilatazione.
to **dilate** vt. dilatare. ♦ to **dilate** vi. dilatarsi.
dilatory agg. 1. dilatorio 2. lento.
diligence s. diligenza.
diligent agg. diligente.
diluent agg. e s. diluente.
to **dilute** vt. diluire.
dilution s. 1. diluzione 2. sostanza

diluita.
diluvial *agg.* diluviale.
dim *agg.* **1.** debole **2.** appannato **3.** oscuro.
to **dim** *vt.* **1.** indebolire **2.** oscurare.
♦ to **dim** *vi.* **1.** indebolirsi **2.** oscurarsi.
dime *s.* quarto di dollaro.
dimension *s.* dimensione.
dimeter *s.* dimetro.
to **diminish** *vt.* e *vi.* diminuire.
diminishable *agg.* diminuibile.
diminution *s.* diminuzione.
diminutive *agg.* minuscolo. ♦ **diminutive** *s.* diminutivo.
dimissory *agg.* dimissorio.
dimly *avv.* **1.** debolmente **2.** oscuramente.
dimness *s.* **1.** debolezza **2.** offuscamento (*di vista*).
dimple *s.* fossetta.
din *s.* baccano.
to **din** *vt.* e *vi.* rintronare.
to **dine** *vi.* pranzare.
diner *s.* commensale.
to **ding** *vt.* e *vi.* suonare, scampanellare.
dingy *agg.* scuro, sporco.
dining *s.* il pranzare || — -room, sala da pranzo.
dinner *s.* pranzo || — -wagon, carrello (*per i pasti*); — -car, vagone ristorante.
dinosaur *s.* dinosauro.
dint *s.* tacca || by — of, a forza di.
diocesan *agg.* e *s.* diocesano.
diocese *s.* diocesi.
diode *s.* diodo.
Dionysiac, Dionysian *agg.* dionisiaco.
diopter *s.* diottria.
dioptric *agg.* diottrico.
dioxid(e) *s.* biossido.
dip *s.* **1.** bagno **2.** inclinazione **3.** (*aer.*) picchiata **4.** tuffo.
to **dip** *vt.* **1.** imm~ ere **2.** abbassare. ♦ to **dip** *vi.* **1.** immergersi **2.** abbassarsi **3.** tuffarsi.
diphtheria *s.* difterite.
diphtheric *agg.* difterico.
diphthong *s.* dittongo.
diplomacy *s.* diplomazia.
diplomat *s.* diplomatico.
diplomatic *agg.* diplomatico.
diplomatically *avv.* diplomaticamente.
diplomatics *s.* diplomazia.
diplomatist *s.* diplomatico.
dipody *s.* dipodia.

dipper *s.* **1.** tuffatore **2.** mestolo || the Big —, l'Orsa Maggiore.
dipsomaniac *s.* dipsomane.
dipteral *agg.* dittero.
diptych *s.* dittico.
dire *agg.* terribile, orrendo.
direct *agg.* diretto.
to **direct** *vt.* **1.** dirigere **2.** ordinare.
direction *s.* **1.** direzione **2.** indicazione.
directional *agg.* direzionale.
directive *agg.* direttivo. ♦ **directive** *s.* direttiva.
directly *avv.* **1.** direttamente **2.** subito.
director *s.* **1.** direttore **2.** regista.
directorial *agg.* direttivo.
directory *agg.* direttivo. ♦ **directory** *s.* **1.** (*tel.*) guida **2.** (*amer.*) consiglio di amministrazione.
direful *agg.* orrendo.
dirge *s.* canto funebre.
diriment *agg.* dirimente.
dirt *s.* sporcizia.
dirtiness *s.* sozzura.
dirty *agg.* **1.** sporco **2.** brutto **3.** sboccato.
to **dirty** *vt.* sporcare. ♦ to **dirty** *vi.* sporcarsi.
disability *s.* **1.** incapacità **2.** invalidità.
to **disable** *vt.* rendere incapace, inabile.
to **disabuse** *vt.* disingannare.
to **disaccustom** *vt.* disabituare.
disadvantage *s.* svantaggio.
disadvantageous *agg.* svantaggioso.
to **disagree** *vi.* dissentire.
disagreeable *agg.* sgradevole.
disagreeableness *s.* sgradevolezza.
disagreement *s.* dissenso.
to **disappear** *vi.* scomparire.
disappearance *s.* sparizione.
to **disappoint** *vt.* deludere.
disappointingly *avv.* in modo deludente.
disappointment *s.* delusione.
disapprobation, disapproval *s.* disapprovazione.
to **disapprove** *vt.* e *vi.* disapprovare.
disapprovingly *avv.* con disapprovazione.
to **disarm** *vt.* e *vi.* disarmare.
disarmament *s.* disarmo.
to **disarrange** *vt.* scompigliare.
disarrangement *s.* scompiglio.
disarray *s.* scompiglio, confusione.

to **disassemble** *vt.* smontare.
disassembling *s.* smontaggio.
disaster *s.* disastro.
disastrous *agg.* disastroso.
to **disavow** *vt.* ripudiare.
to **disband** *vt.* sciogliere. ♦ to **disband** *vi.* sbandarsi.
disbelief *s.* incredulità.
to **disbelieve** *vt.* e *vi.* non credere.
disbeliever *s.* incredulo.
disbursement *s.* pagamento.
to **discard** *vt.* scartare.
to **discern** *vt.* discernere.
discernible *agg.* visibile.
discernment *s.* discernimento.
discharge *s.* 1. scarico 2. scarica 3. congedo 4. assoluzione 5. liberazione 6. pagamento.
to **discharge** *vt.* 1. scaricare 2. congedare 3. assolvere 4. liberare. ♦ to **discharge** *vi.* scaricarsi.
disciple *s.* discepolo.
disciplinable *agg.* disciplinabile.
disciplinary *agg.* disciplinare.
discipline *s.* disciplina.
to **disclaim** *vt.* rifiutare, declinare (*responsabilità*).
disclaimer *s.* rinuncia, rifiuto.
to **disclose** *vt.* svelare.
disclosure *s.* rivelazione.
discoid *agg.* e *s.* discoide.
to **discolour** *vt.* scolorire. ♦ to **discolour** *vi.* scolorirsi.
discolouration *s.* scoloramento.
to **discomfit** *vt.* 1. sconfiggere 2. disorientare.
to **discomfort** *vt.* mettere a disagio.
to **discompose** *vt.* agitare.
to **disconcert** *vt.* turbare.
to **disconnect** *vt.* separare, disunire.
disconnected *agg.* 1. sconnesso 2. disinnestato.
disconnectedness *s.* sconnessione.
disconsolate *agg.* sconsolato.
discontent *s.* scontento.
to **discontinue** *vt.* e *vi.* cessare.
discontinuity *s.* discontinuità.
discontinuous *agg.* discontinuo.
discord *s.* 1. discordia, dissenso 2. (*mus.*) dissonanza.
discordance *s.* 1. disaccordo 2. discordanza (*di suoni*).
discordant *agg.* discorde.
discordantly *avv.* in disaccordo.
discount *s.* sconto ‖ *at a —*, sottocosto.
to **discount** *vt.* 1. scontare 2. tenere in poco conto.

discountable *agg.* 1. scontabile 2. poco attendibile.
to **discourage** *vt.* scoraggiare.
discouragement *s.* scoraggiamento.
to **discover** *vt.* scoprire.
discoverer *s.* scopritore.
discovery *s.* scoperta.
discredit *s.* 1. discredito 2. dubbio.
to **discredit** *vt.* 1. screditare 2. mettere in dubbio.
discreditable *agg.* vergognoso, infamante.
discreet *agg.* prudente, discreto.
discrepancy *s.* disaccordo.
discrete *agg.* separato, distinto.
discretion *s.* 1. discrezione 2. saggezza.
discretionary *agg.* discrezionale.
discriminate *agg.* discriminato.
to **discriminate** *vt.* e *vi.* discriminare.
discriminating *agg.* 1. sagace 2. discriminante.
discrimination *s.* 1. discriminazione 2. discernimento.
discursive *agg.* divagante.
discus *s.* disco ‖ *— -thrower*, discobolo.
to **discuss** *vt.* discutere.
discussion *s.* discussione.
disdain *s.* sdegno.
to **disdain** *vt.* disdegnare.
disdainful *agg.* sdegnoso.
disease *s.* malattia.
to **disembark** *vt.* e *vi.* sbarcare.
to **disembarrass** *vt.* sbarazzare.
to **disembody** *vt.* 1. disincarnare 2. congedare.
to **disembowel** *vt.* sventrare.
disembowelment *s.* sventramento.
to **disenchant** *vt.* disincantare.
disenchantment *s.* disincanto.
to **disengage** *vt.* 1. disimpegnare 2. disinnestare. ♦ to **disengage** *vi.* liberarsi.
disengagement *s.* 1. liberazione 2. disinnesto.
to **disentangle** *vt.* districare. ♦ to **disentangle** *vi.* districarsi.
disentanglement *s.* districamento.
disesteem *s.* disistima.
to **disesteem** *vt.* disprezzare.
disfavour *s.* 1. disgrazia 2. disapprovazione.
to **disfigure** *vt.* sfigurare.
disfigurement *s.* deturpamento.
to **disfranchise** *vt.* privare dei diritti (*civili o di voto*).
to **disgorge** *vt.* 1. emettere 2. vomi-

tare (*anche fig.*).
disgrace *s.* 1. vergogna 2. disgrazia.
to **disgrace** *vt.* disonorare.
disgraceful *agg.* vergognoso.
disgregation *s.* disgregazione.
disguise *s.* travestimento || *in* —,
travestito, camuffato.
to **disguise** *vt.* mascherare.
disgust *s.* disgusto.
to **disgust** *vt.* disgustare.
disgustedly *avv.* con disgusto.
disgustful, disgusting *agg.* disgustoso.
dish *s.* 1. piatto 2. vivanda || —
-*washer*, lavapiatti.
to **dish** *vt.* servire || *to* — *up*, ser-
vire in tavola.
to **disharmonize** *vt.* disarmonizzare.
to **dishearten** *vt.* scoraggiare.
disheartenment *s.* scoraggiamento.
to **dishevel** *vt.* arruffare.
dishonest *agg.* disonesto.
dishonesty *s.* disonestà.
dishonour *s.* 1. disonore 2. mancato pagamento.
to **dishonour** *vt.* 1. disonorare 2.
rifiutare di pagare.
dishonourable *agg.* disonorevole.
dishonourableness *s.* disonorabi-
lità.
disillusion(ment) *s.* disillusion.
to **disinfect** *vt.* disinfettare.
disinfectant *s.* disinfettante.
disinfection *s.* disinfezione.
to **disinfest** *vt.* disinfestare.
disinfestation *s.* disinfestazione.
to **disinherit** *vt.* diseredare.
to **disintegrate** *vt.* disintegrare. ◆
to **disintegrate** *vi.* disintegrarsi.
disintegration *s.* disintegrazione.
disintegrator *s.* disintegratore.
to **disinter** *vt.* dissotterrare.
disinterested *agg.* disinteressato.
disinterment *s.* dissotterramento.
to **disjoin** *vt.* disgiungere. ◆ to
disjoin *vi.* disgiungersi.
to **disjoint** *vt.* 1. disgregare 2. disarticolare. ◆ to **disjoint** *vi.* di-
sgregarsi.
disjunction *s.* separazione.
disjunctive *agg.* disgiuntivo.
disjunctively *avv.* disgiuntamente.
disk *s.* disco.
dislike *s.* avversione.
to **dislike** *vt.* detestare, provar avversione per.
to **dislocate** *vt.* 1. spostare 2. slogare 3. disorganizzare.

dislocation *s.* 1. dislocazione 2.
slogatura 3. disorganizzazione.
to **dislodge** *vt.* sloggiare.
disloyal *agg.* sleale.
disloyalty *s.* slealtà.
dismal *agg.* tetro.
to **dismantle** *vt.* smantellare.
dismantlement *s.* smantellamento.
to **dismast** *vt.* (*mar.*) disalberare.
dismay *s.* costernazione.
to **dismay** *vt.* costernare.
to **dismember** *vt.* smembrare.
dismemberment *s.* smembramento.
to **dismiss** *vt.* 1. congedare 2. licenziare 3. bandire.
dismissal *s.* 1. congedo 2. licenziamento 3. destituzione 4. rigetto.
to **dismount** *vt.* e *vi.* smontare.
disobedience *s.* disubbidienza.
disobedient *agg.* disubbidiente.
to **disobey** *vt.* disubbidire.
to **disoblige** *vt.* essere scortese con.
disobliging *agg.* scortese.
disorder *s.* 1. disordine 2. disturbo.
to **disorder** *vt.* 1. scompigliare 2.
disturbare.
disorderly *agg.* 1. disordinato 2.
turbolento.
disorganization *s.* disorganizzazione.
to **disorganize** *vt.* disorganizzare.
to **disorient(ate)** *vt.* disorientare.
disorientation *s.* disorientamento.
to **disown** *vt.* rinnegare.
disowning *s.* rinnegamento.
to **disparage** *vt.* 1. deprezzare 2.
screditare.
disparagement *s.* 1. deprezzamento 2. denigrazione.
disparaging *agg.* 1. sprezzante 2.
denigratorio.
disparate *agg.* disparato.
disparity *s.* disparità.
dispassionate *agg.* spassionato.
dispatch *s.* 1. spedizione 2. dispaccio 3. disbrigo 4. celerità.
to **dispatch** *vt.* 1. spedire 2. sbrigare.
to **dispel** *vt.* dissipare.
dispensary *s.* dispensario.
dispensation *s.* 1. (*eccl.*) dispensa
2. distribuzione 3. beneficio.
to **dispense** *vt.* dispensare. ◆ to
dispense *vi.* fare a meno di: *to*
— *with so.*, fare a meno di qu.
dispersal *s.* dispersione.
to **disperse** *vt.* disperdere. ◆ to **disperse** *vi.* disperdersi.
dispersion *s.* dispersione.

dispersive *agg.* dispersivo.
dispirited *agg.* depresso.
to **displace** *vt.* 1. spostare 2. destituire.
displacement *s.* 1. spostamento 2. sostituzione 3. (*mar.*) dislocamento.
display *s.* mostra, esibizione.
to **display** *vt.* mostrare, esporre.
to **displease** *vt.* dispiacere.
displeasing *agg.* spiacevole.
displeasure *s.* dispiacere.
disposal *s.* 1. disposizione 2. cessione.
to **dispose** *vt. e vi.* disporre || *to — of*, disfarsi di, smerciare.
disposition *s.* 1. disposizione 2. indole.
to **dispossess** *vt.* spogliare.
dispossession *s.* 1. spoliazione 2. (*giur.*) esproprio.
disproportion *s.* sproporzione.
disproportionate, disproportioned *agg.* sproporzionato.
to **disprove** *vt.* 1. confutare 2. dimostrare la falsità di.
disputable *agg.* discutibile.
dispute *s.* controversia, disputa.
to **dispute** *vt.* 1. disputare 2. contestare.
disqualification *s.* 1. incapacità 2. (*giur.*) interdizione 3. squalifica.
to **disqualify** *vt.* 1. rendere incapace 2. (*giur.*) interdire 3. squalificare.
disquieting *agg.* inquietante.
disquisition *s.* 1. disquisizione 2. inchiesta.
disregard *s.* noncuranza.
to **disregard** *vt.* ignorare.
disreputable *agg.* 1. sconveniente 2. screditato.
disreputably *avv.* disonorevolmente.
disrepute *s.* discredito.
disrespectful *agg.* irrispettoso.
to **disrobe** *vt.* svestire. ♦ to **disrobe** *vi.* svestirsi.
disruption *s.* rottura.
disruptive *agg.* 1. che smembra 2. dirompente.
dissatisfaction *s.* insoddisfazione.
dissatisfactory *agg.* insoddisfacente.
dissatisfied *agg.* scontento.
to **dissatisfy** *vt.* scontentare.
to **dissect** *vt.* sezionare.
dissection *s.* 1. sezionamento 2. parte sezionata.
to **dissemble** *vt. e vi.* dissimulare,

ignorare.
dissembling *s.* dissimulazione. ♦ **dissembling** *agg.* ipocrita.
dissemblingly *avv.* ingannevolmente.
to **disseminate** *vt.* (dis)seminare.
dissemination *s.* disseminazione.
disseminator *s.* propagatore.
dissension *s.* divergenza.
dissent *s.* 1. dissenso 2. (*relig.*) separazione, scisma.
to **dissent** *vi.* dissentire.
dissenter *s.* dissidente.
dissenting *agg.* dissenziente.
to **dissertate** *vi.* dissertare.
dissertation *s.* dissertazione.
dissertator *s.* dissertatore.
disservice *s.* cattivo servizio.
to **dissever** *vt.* scindere. ♦ to **dissever** *vi.* scindersi.
dissidence *s.* dissidio.
dissident *agg. e s.* dissidente.
dissimilar *agg.* dissimile.
dissimilarity *s.* dissomiglianza.
dissimilation *s.* dissimilazione.
to **dissimulate** *vt. e vi.* dissimulare.
dissimulation *s.* dissimulazione.
dissimulator *s.* dissimulatore.
to **dissipate** *vt.* dissipare. ♦ to **dissipate** *vi.* dissiparsi.
dissipation *s.* dissipazione.
dissociable *agg.* 1. dissociabile 2. riservato.
to **dissociate** *vt.* dissociare. ♦ to **dissociate** *vi.* dissociarsi.
dissociation *s.* 1. dissociazione 2. sdoppiamento (*della personalità*).
dissolubility *s.* dissolubilità.
dissoluble *agg.* dissolubile.
dissolute *agg.* dissoluto.
dissoluteness *s.* dissolutezza.
dissolution *s.* dissoluzione.
to **dissolve** *vt.* dissolvere. ♦ to **dissolve** *vi.* dissolversi.
dissolvent *agg. e s.* dissolvente.
dissonance *s.* dissonanza.
dissonant *agg.* dissonante.
to **dissuade** *vt.* dissuadere.
dissuasion *s.* dissuasione.
dissyllabic *agg.* bisillabico.
dissyllable *s.* bisillabo.
dissymmetry *s.* asimmetria.
distaff *s.* conocchia.
distance *s.* distanza || *long- — call*, telefonata interurbana; *at a —*, da lontano.
distant *agg.* 1. lontano 2. riservato.
distantly *avv.* (da) lontano.
distaste *s.* ripugnanza.

distasteful *agg.* repellente.
distemper[1] *s.* **1.** turbamento fisico **2.** cimurro **3.** tumulto.
distemper[2] *s.* tempera.
to **distend** *vt.* distendere. ♦ to **distend** *vi.* distendersi.
to **distil(l)** *vt.* e *vi.* (di)stillare.
distillate *s.* distillato.
distillation *s.* distillazione.
distiller *s.* distillatore.
distillery *s.* distilleria.
distinct *agg.* distinto.
distinction *s.* distinzione.
distinctive *agg.* distintivo.
to **distinguish** *vt.* e *vi.* distinguere.
distinguished *agg.* **1.** distinto **2.** illustre.
to **distort** *vt.* distorcere.
distortion *s.* distorsione.
to **distract** *vt.* **1.** distrarre **2.** turbare, far impazzire.
distraction *s.* **1.** distrazione **2.** follia: *to love to —,* amare alla follia.
to **distrain** *vi.* sequestrare.
distrait *agg.* distratto, smarrito.
distraught *agg.* **1.** folle **2.** sconvolto.
distress *s.* **1.** angoscia **2.** pericolo **3.** sequestro.
to **distress** *vt.* **1.** affliggere **2.** sequestrare.
distressful *agg.* penoso.
distributable *agg.* distribuibile.
to **distribute** *vt.* distribuire.
distribution *s.* distribuzione.
distributive *agg.* distributivo.
distributor *s.* distributore.
district *s.* distretto.
distrust *s.* diffidenza.
to **distrust** *vt.* diffidare di.
distrustful *agg.* diffidente.
to **disturb** *vt.* **1.** disturbare **2.** turbare.
disturbance *s.* agitazione.
disturber *s.* disturbatore.
disunion *s.* separazione.
to **disunite** *vt.* disunire. ♦ to **disunite** *vi.* separarsi.
disunited *agg.* disunito.
disuse *s.* disuso.
disused *agg.* disusato.
ditch *s.* fosso || *to die in the last —,* resistere ad oltranza.
to **ditch** *vi.* scavare fossi.
dithyramb *s.* ditirambo.
dithyrambic *agg.* ditirambico.
ditty *s.* **1.** canzone **2.** poemetto.
diuretic *agg.* e *s.* diuretico.
diurnal *agg.* **1.** diurno **2.** quotidiano.

diuturnal *agg.* diuturno.
diuturnity *s.* diuturnità.
divan *s.* divano.
dive *s.* **1.** tuffo **2.** (*aer.*) picchiata.
to **dive** *vi.* **1.** tuffarsi **2.** (*aer.*) lanciarsi in picchiata.
diver *s.* **1.** tuffatore **2.** palombaro.
to **diverge** *vi.* divergere.
divergence *s.* divergenza.
divergent *agg.* divergente.
diverse *agg.* **1.** diverso **2.** mutevole.
to **diversify** *vt.* rendere diverso.
diversion *s.* **1.** diversione **2.** passatempo.
diversity *s.* diversità.
to **divert** *vt.* **1.** deviare **2.** divertire.
to **divest** *vt.* spogliare.
to **divide** *vt.* dividere. ♦ to **divide** *vi.* dividersi.
dividend *s.* dividendo.
dividing *s.* divisione.
divination *s.* divinazione.
divinatory *agg.* divinatorio.
divine *agg.* divino. ♦ **divine** *s.* (*eccl.*) teologo.
to **divine** *vt.* e *vi.* predire.
diviner *s.* indovino || *water —,* rabdomante.
diving *s.* tuffo || *— -bell,* campana subacquea; *— -board,* trampolino.
divining *s.* divinazione.
divinity *s.* **1.** divinità **2.** teologia.
divisibility *s.* divisibilità.
divisible *agg.* divisibile.
division *s.* divisione.
divisional *agg.* di divisione.
divisor *s.* divisore.
divorce *s.* divorzio.
to **divorce** *vt.* divorziare.
divulgation *s.* divulgazione.
to **divulge** *vt.* divulgare.
divulger *s.* divulgatore.
dizzily *avv.* vertiginosamente.
dizziness *s.* vertigine.
dizzy *agg.* **1.** vertiginoso **2.** preso da vertigine **3.** stordito.
to **do (did, done)** *vt.* e *vi.* **1.** (*v. aus. in frasi int., neg., int.-neg.*) *— you understand English?,* capisci l'inglese?; *I do not (I don't),* non capisco; *he does not (he doesn't) speak English,* non parla l'inglese **2.** (*uso enfatico*) *I do study!,* studio veramente! **3.** (*sostitutivo*) *he said he would come and he did,* disse che sarebbe venuto e venne **4.** fare (*in senso generale, astratto*) *what are you doing?,* che cosa stai facendo?; *to*

— *one's duty*, fare il proprio dovere 5. bastare: *that will do*, ciò basta 6. addirsi, convenire: *this house will do me*, questa casa mi va bene || *to — without*, fare a meno.

docile *agg.* docile.

docility *s.* docilità.

dock[1] *s.* bacino: *dry- —*, bacino di carenaggio || *— -master*, capitano di porto; *wet- —*, darsena.

dock[2] *s.* banco degli imputati (*in tribunale*).

docker *s.* scaricatore.

docket *s.* 1. (*giur.*) estratto verbale 2. etichetta.

dockyard *s.* cantiere.

doctor *s.* dottore.

doctoral *agg.* dottorale.

doctorate *s.* dottorato.

doctrinaire *agg.* e *s.* dottrinario.

doctrinal *agg.* dottrinale.

doctrine *s.* dottrina.

document *s.* documento.

to **document** *vt.* documentare.

documentary *agg.* e *s.* documentario.

documentation *s.* documentazione.

to **dodder** *vi.* tremare, vacillare.

dodecagon *s.* dodecagono.

dodecahedron *s.* dodecaedro.

dodge *s.* 1. schivata 2. balzo.

to **dodge** *vt.* schivare. ♦ to **dodge** *vi.* scansarsi.

doe *s.* femmina (*di daino, cervo ecc.*).

doer *s.* chi agisce, chi fa.

dog *s.* 1. cane 2. (*mecc.*) gancio || *— -cart*, calesse; *— catcher*, accalappiacani; *— -days*, giorni di canicola; *— -ear*, orecchia (*a una pagina*); *— -tired*, stanco morto.

to **dog** *vt.* inseguire.

dogged *agg.* ostinato.

doggerel *s.* filastrocca.

dogmatic(al) *agg.* dogmatico.

dogmatism *s.* dogmatismo.

doily *s.* tovagliolino.

doings *s. pl.* azioni, imprese.

dole *s.* 1. ripartizione 2. sussidio.

doleful *agg.* triste.

dolichocephalic *agg.* dolicocefalo.

doll *s.* bambola.

dollar *s.* dollaro.

dolly *s.* 1. bambola 2. (*cine*) carrello.

dolomitic *agg.* dolomitico.

dolphin *s.* 1. delfino 2. boa.

dolt *s.* stupido.

domain *s.* dominio.

dome *s.* cupola.

domestic *agg.* 1. domestico 2. nazionale. ♦ **domestic** *s.* domestico.

domicile *s.* domicilio.

domiciliary *agg.* domiciliare.

dominant *agg.* dominante.

to **dominate** *vt.* e *vi.* dominare.

domination *s.* dominazione.

domineering *agg.* dispotico.

Dominican *agg.* e *s.* domenicano.

dominion *s.* dominio, possedimento (*di territori*).

donation *s.* donazione.

donative *s.* dono.

done V. *to do* || *over- —*, troppo cotto; *under- —*, poco cotto.

donjon *s.* torrione.

donkey *s.* asino.

donor *s.* donatore.

doodle *s.* ghirigoro.

doom *s.* 1. destino 2. giudizio.

to **doom** *vt.* condannare.

doomsday *s.* giudizio universale.

door *s.* porta, portiera || *— -keeper*, portinaio; *— -post*, stipite; *— -way*, soglia.

dope *s.* 1. vernice 2. stupefacente.

to **dope** *vt.* 1. verniciare 2. drogare.

doping *s.* drogaggio.

Doric *agg.* dorico.

dormer (window) *s.* abbaino.

dormitory *s.* dormitorio.

dormouse *s.* (*pl.* dormice) ghiro.

dorsal *agg.* dorsale.

dosage *s.* dosaggio.

to **dose** *vt.* 1. dosare 2. adulterare.

dosimeter *s.* dosatore.

dossal *s.* dossale.

dossier *s.* incartamento.

dot *s.* punto, puntino.

to **dot** *vt.* punteggiare.

dotage *s.* 1. rimbambimento 2. infatuazione.

dotal *agg.* dotale.

doting *agg.* 1. senile 2. infatuato. ♦ **doting** *s.* senilità.

double *agg.* doppio. ♦ **double** *s.* 1. doppio 2. (*cine*) controfigura. ♦ **double** *avv.* 1. doppiamente 2. in due.

to **double** *vt.* 1. raddoppiare 2. doppiare 3. piegare. ♦ to **double** *vi.* 1. raddoppiarsi 2. piegarsi.

double-dealing *s.* imbroglio.

doubleness *s.* doppiezza.

doubling *s.* raddoppiamento.

doubly *avv.* doppiamente.

doubt *s.* dubbio || *no —*, indubbiamente.

to **doubt** *vt.* e *vi.* dubitare.

doubtful *agg.* incerto, dubbio.
doubtfulness *s.* dubbiosità.
doubtless *agg.* indubbio. ♦ **doubtless** *avv.* indubbiamente.
dough *s.* pasta.
dove *s.* colomba || — -*cot(e)*, colombaia.
dowdy *agg.* sciatto.
dower *s.* dote.
down[1] *s.* 1. duna 2. collina.
down[2] *s.* 1. piumino 2. lanugine.
down[3] *agg.* 1. diretto verso il basso 2. depresso.
down[4] *avv.* (in) giù || — *with!*, abbasso: — *with the tyrant!*, abbasso il tiranno! ♦ **down** *prep.* giù per.
to **down** *vt.* abbattere, rovesciare.
downcast *agg.* abbattuto.
downfall *s.* rovescio.
downhearted *agg.* scoraggiato.
downhill *agg.* discendente, inclinato. ♦ **downhill** *arv.* in discesa.
downpour *s.* acquazzone.
downright *agg.* vero, sincero. ♦ **downright** *avv.* completamente.
downstairs *avv.* giù. ♦ **downstairs** *agg.* dabbasso. ♦ **downstairs** *s.* pianterreno.
downtrodden *agg.* calpestato, oppresso.
downward *agg.* in giù, discendente.
downward(s) *avv.* in giù.
downy[1] *agg.* ondulato.
downy[2] *agg.* 1. lanuginoso 2. morbido.
dowry *s.* dote.
dowser *s.* rabdomante.
doze *s.* sonnellino.
to **doze** *vi.* sonnecchiare.
dozen *s.* dozzina.
drab *s.* 1. sciattona 2. sgualdrina.
draff *s.* feccia.
draft *s.* 1. tiro 2. sorso 3. abbozzo 4. corrente d'aria 5. (*comm.*) tratta 6. (*mar.*) pescaggio.
to **draft** *vt.* 1. tirare 2. abbozzare.
drag *s.* 1. erpice 2. (*mar.*) draga 3. ostacolo.
to **drag** *vt.* 1. trascinare 2. dragare. ♦ to **drag** *vi.* trascinarsi || *to — on*, tirare in lungo.
to **draggle** *vt.* inzaccherare. ♦ to **draggle** *vi.* inzaccherarsi.
dragon *s.* drago || — -*fly*, libellula.
drain *s.* 1. canale, fogna 2. fuga.
to **drain** *vt.* prosciugare. ♦ to **drain** *vi.* 1. prosciugarsi 2. defluire.
drainage *s.* 1. fognatura 2. drenaggio.

draining *s.* 1. scolatura 2. drenaggio.
dram *s.* dramma (*unità di peso*).
drama *s.* dramma.
dramatic(al) *agg.* drammatico.
dramatics *s. pl.* produzioni drammatiche (*di dilettanti*).
dramatist *s.* drammaturgo.
to **dramatize** *vt. e vi.* drammatizzare.
dramaturgy *s.* drammaturgia.
drank V. *to drink*.
to **drape** *vt.* drappeggiare.
draper *s.* negoziante di tessuti.
drapery *s.* 1. tessuti 2. drappeggi.
drastic *agg.* drastico.
draught *s.* V. *draft*. ♦ **draughts** *s. pl.* gioco della dama (*sing.*).
draught-board *s.* scacchiera.
draw *s.* 1. tiro 2. estrazione 3. attrazione.
to **draw** (**drew, drawn**) *vt.* 1. tirare 2. attirare 3. disegnare 4. estrarre 5. (*comm.*) emettere || *to — up*, compilare. ♦ to **draw** (**drew, drawn**) *vi.* tirarsi || *to — on*, avvicinarsi; *to — in*, ritirarsi; *to — up*, fermarsi.
drawback *s.* ostacolo.
drawbridge *s.* ponte levatoio.
drawer *s.* 1. estrattore 2. disegnatore 3. cassetto.
drawers *s. pl.* mutande.
drawing *s.* 1. disegno 2. estrazione 3. attrazione || — -*pen*, tiralinee; — -*pin*, puntina da disegno.
drawing-room *s.* salotto.
to **drawl** *vt.* strascicare la voce.
drawn V. *to draw*.
dread *s.* spavento.
dreadful *agg.* terribile.
dreadnought *s.* 1. impavido 2. (*mar.*) corazzata.
dream *s.* sogno.
to **dream** (**dreamt, dreamt**) (*anche reg.*) *vt. e vi.* sognare.
dreamer *s.* sognatore.
dreamt V. *to dream*.
dreamless *agg.* senza sogni.
dreamy *agg.* 1. sognante 2. vago.
dreariness *s.* tristezza.
dreary *agg.* tetro, squallido.
dredge *s.* draga.
to **dredge**[1] *vt. e vi.* dragare.
to **dredge**[2] *vt.* cospargere, spolverizzare.
dredger[1] *s.* draga.
dredger[2] *s.* spolverizzatore.
dredging *s.* dragaggio.

dregs *s. pl.* **1.** feccia (*sing.*) **2.** sedimento (*sing.*).

to **drench** *vt.* inzuppare || *to get drenched*, inzupparsi.

dress *s.* abito, abbigliamento.

to **dress** *vt.* **1.** vestire **2.** bendare **3.** condire, rifinire. ♦ to **dress** *vi.* vestirsi.

dressing *s.* **1.** abbigliamento **2.** medicazione **3.** condimento || —-*gown*, vestaglia; — -*table*, toletta.

dressmaker *s.* sarta.

dressmaking *s.* sartoria.

drew V. *to draw*.

dribble *s.* **1.** gocciolamento **2.** (*sport*) palleggio.

to **dribble** *vt. e vi.* **1.** stillare **2.** (*sport*) palleggiare.

dribbling *s.* V. *dribble*.

drier *s.* essiccatore.

drift *s.* **1.** spinta **2.** deriva **3.** raffica **4.** (*fig.*) significato.

to **drift** *vt.* sospingere. ♦ to **drift** *vi.* andare alla deriva, essere trascinato.

drill *s.* **1.** trapano, trivella **2.** esercitazione.

to **drill** *vt.* **1.** trapanare, trivellare **2.** esercitare.

drilling *s.* **1.** trapanazione, trivellazione **2.** esercitazione || — *machine*, trapano.

drink *s.* **1.** il bere **2.** bevanda.

to **drink (drank, drunk)** *vt. e vi.* bere.

drinkable *agg.* bevibile.

drinker *s.* bevitore.

drinking *s.* il bere.

drip *s.* gocciolamento.

to **drip** *vt. e vi.* gocciolare.

dripping *s.* gocciolio.

drive *s.* **1.** gita (*in auto*) **2.** viale (*carrozzabile*) **3.** spinta.

to **drive (drove, driven)** *vt.* **1.** condurre **2.** guidare **3.** azionare || *to — away*, scacciare; *to — in*, conficcare. ♦ to **drive (drove, driven)** *vi.* andare (*in veicolo*) || *to — off*, partire (*in veicolo*); *to — up*, arrivare (*in veicolo*).

drive-in *s.* cinema, banca ecc. in cui si entra in auto.

driver *s.* conducente.

driving *s* **1.** guida **2.** comando.

drizzle *s.* pioggerella.

to **drizzle** *vi.* piovigginare.

drizzly *agg.* piovigginoso.

droll *agg.* buffo.

drollery *s.* **1.** buffoneria **2.** scherzo.

dromedary *s.* dromedario.

drone *s.* **1.** fuco **2.** ronzio.

to **drone** *vt. e vi.* ronzare.

to **droop** *vt.* abbassare. ♦ to **droop** *vi.* afflosciarsi, languire.

drooping *agg.* **1.** pendente, abbassato **2.** abbattuto.

drop *s.* **1.** goccia **2.** caduta **3.** ribasso.

to **drop** *vt.* lasciar cadere. ♦ to **drop** *vi.* cadere || *to — in*, fare una visitina; *to — away*, scomparire.

dropper *s.* contagocce.

dropsical *agg.* idropico.

dropsy *s.* idropisia.

dross *s.* scoria.

drought *s.* siccità.

drove V. *to drive*.

to **drown** *vt.* **1.** annegare **2.** smorzare. ♦ to **drown** *vi.* annegare.

drowning *s.* annegamento.

to **drowse** *vi.* sonnecchiare, assopirsi.

drowsily *avv.* in modo sonnolento.

drowsiness *s.* sonnolenza.

drowsy *agg.* sonnolento.

to **drub** *vt.* percuotere, bastonare.

drudge *s.* sgobbone.

to **drudge** *vi.* sfacchinare.

drudgery *s.* lavoro faticoso.

drug *s.* **1.** medicina **2.** droga || —-*store*, farmacia (*in cui si vendono articoli vari*).

to **drug** *vt.* drogare.

druggist *s.* farmacista.

Druid *s.* druido.

drum *s.* **1.** tamburo **2.** timpano.

to **drum** *vi.* suonare il tamburo. ♦ to **drum** *vt.* (*fig.*) inculcare.

drummer *s.* tamburino.

drumming *s.* tambureggiamento.

drunk V. *to drink*. ♦ **drunk** *agg.* ubriaco.

drunkard *s.* ubriacone.

drunken *agg.* ubriaco.

drunkenness *s.* ubriachezza.

dry *agg.* asciutto, arido, secco || — *cleaning*, lavaggio a secco.

to **dry** *vt.* **1.** seccare **2.** asciugare. ♦ to **dry** *vi.* **1.** seccarsi **2.** asciugatsi || *to — up*, ammutolire.

dryad *s.* driade.

drying *agg.* essiccante. ♦ **drying** *s.* essiccamento.

dual *agg.* duplice.

dualism *s.* dualismo.

dualist *s.* dualista.

dualistic *agg.* dualistico.

duality s. dualità.

to dub[1] vt. creare cavaliere.

to dub[2] vt. (cine) doppiare.

dubbing s. doppiaggio.

dubious agg. 1. dubbio 2. dubbioso.

dubiousness s. dubbiosità.

dubitative agg. dubitativo.

ducal agg. ducale.

duchess s. duchessa.

duchy s. ducato.

duck[1] s. anitra.

duck[2] s. tela.

duck[3] s. tuffo.

to duck vt. 1. tuffare 2. piegare. ♦ to duck vi. 1. tuffarsi 2. piegarsi.

duckling s. anatroccolo.

duct s. condotto.

ductile agg. duttile.

ductility s. duttilità.

due agg. e s. dovuto || to be —, dover arrivare; to fall —, scadere.

duel s. duello.

to duel vi. duella.e.

duet s. duetto.

dug V. to dig.

duke s. duca.

dukedom s. ducato.

dull agg. 1. tardo, sciocco 2. sordo 3. triste 4. noioso 5. opaco.

to dull vt. 1. istupidire 2. intorpidire 3. smorzare. ♦ to dull vi. 1. istupidirsi 2. intorpidirsi 3. smorzarsi.

dullard s. imbecille.

dul(l)ness s. 1. lentezza 2. noia 3. opacità 4. ottusità.

dully avv. 1. ottusamente 2. lentamente 3. in modo noioso 4. debolmente.

duly avv. debitamente.

dumb agg. muto || — -show, pantomima.

to dumbfound vt. confondere.

dumbness s. mutismo.

dumb-waiter s. montavivande.

dummy agg. 1. muto 2. falso. ♦ dummy s. fantoccio.

dump s. 1. colpo sordo 2. ammasso.

dumping s. « dumping » (tipo di vendita concorrenziale sui mercati esteri).

dunce s. ignorante.

dune s. duna.

dung s. 1. sterco 2. letame.

dungarees s. pl. tuta (da lavoro) (sing.).

dungeon s. 1. torrione 2. prigione sotterranea.

dunghill s. letamaio.

to dunk vt. e vi. inzuppare.

duodenal agg. duodenale.

duodenum s. (pl. -na) duodeno.

dupe s. gonzo.

duplex agg. duplice.

duplicate agg. doppio. ♦ duplicate s. duplicato.

to duplicate vt. duplicare.

duplication s. 1. raddoppiamento 2. riproduzione.

duplicator s. copialettere.

duplicity s. doppiezza.

durability s. durata.

durable agg. durevole.

durallumin s. duralluminio.

duration s. durata.

duress s. 1. prigionia 2. coercizione.

during prep. durante.

durst V. dare.

dusk s. 1. oscurità 2. crepuscolo.

dusky agg. oscuro.

dust s. polvere || — -bin, pattumiera.

to dust vt. 1. impolverare 2. spolverare. ♦ to dust vi. impolverarsi.

duster s. 1. strofinaccio (per la polvere) 2. polverizzatore.

dustman s. spazzino.

dusty agg. polveroso.

Dutch agg. olandese.

Dutchman s. olandese.

dutiful agg. rispettoso.

duty s. 1. ubbidienza 2. dovere 3. tassa.

duumvirate s. duumvirato.

dwarf s. nano.

dwarfish agg. nano.

to dwell (dwelt, dwelt) vi. 1. abitare 2. fermarsi.

dweller s. abitatore.

dwelling s. abitazione.

dwelt V. to dwell.

dye s. tintura.

to dye vt. tingere. ♦ to dye vi. tingersi.

dyer s. tintore.

dyerworks s. pl. tintoria (sing.).

dying agg. morente.

dynamic(al) agg. dinamico.

dynamics s. dinamica.

dynamism s. dinamismo.

dynamite s. dinamite.

dynamiter s. dinamitardo.

dynamo s. dinamo.

dynamometer s. dinamometro.

dynast s. dinasta.

dynastic(al) agg. dinastico.

dynasty s. dinastia.

dyne s. dina.

dysenteric *agg.* dissenterico.
dysentery *s.* dissenteria.
dyspepsia *s.* dispepsia.
dyspeptic(al) *agg.* dispeptico.

E

E (*mus.*) mi.
each *agg.* ogni, ciascuno. ♦ **each** *pron.* ognuno, ciascuno || — *other,* l'un l'altro.
eager *agg.* 1. ardente, appassionato 2. avido, desideroso.
eagerly *avv.* 1. ardentemente 2. avidamente.
eagerness *s.* 1. ardore 2. impazienza, premura.
eagle *s.* aquila.
ear[1] orecchio || — *-ache* mal d'orecchi — *-drum;* timpano; — *-ring,* orecchino; — *-vax,* cerume; *within* — *-shot,* a portata di voce.
ear[2] *s.* spiga (*di grano*).
earl *s.* conte.
earldom *s.* 1. titolo di conte 2. contea.
early *agg.* 1. primo, il principio, la prima parte (*di qualsiasi tempo*) 2. mattiniero 3. prematuro 4. remoto || — *train,* treno del primo mattino.
early *avv.* 1. presto, di buon'ora, per tempo 2. al principio.
earmark *s.* 1. marchio, caratteristica 2. (*comm.*) contrassegno.
to **earn** *vt.* guadagnare, meritare.
earnest *agg.* 1. serio, zelante 2. ardente. ♦ **earnest** *s.* caparra, pegno.
earnestly *avv.* 1. seriamente 2. con ardore.
earnestness *s.* 1. serietà 2. ardore.
earnings *s. pl.* 1. guadagni 2. (*comm.*) utili.
earth *s.* 1. terra, mondo 2. terreno.
earth-bound *agg.* radicato, attaccato ai beni terreni.
earthen *agg.* di terra, di terracotta.
earthenware *s.* terraglia.
earthly *agg.* terrestre.
earthquake *s.* terremoto.
earthworm *s.* lombrico.
earthy *agg.* terroso, di terra.
ease *s.* 1. tranquillità (*di spirito*),

benessere 2. facilità, agevolezza 3. sollievo.
to **ease** *vt.* e *vi.* 1. alleviare, calmare 2. liberare, alleggerire.
easeful *agg.* tranquillo.
easel *s.* cavalletto, telaio.
easily *avv.* 1. facilmente 2. comodamente.
easiness *s.* 1. comodità, benessere 2. facilità.
east *s.* est, oriente: *the Far East,* l'Estremo Oriente. ♦ **east** *avv.* ad est, verso est.
Easter *s.* Pasqua.
easterly *agg.* dell'est, dall'est, orientale.
eastern *agg.* dell'est, orientale.
eastward *agg.* verso est.
easy *agg.* 1. facile 2. agiato, modo 3. piacevole.
easy *avv.* facilmente, comodamente.
easygoing *agg.* facilone, indolente.
to **eat** (**ate, eaten**) *vt.* e *vi.* 1. mangiare 2. rodere, corrodere.
eatable *agg.* mangiabile, commestibile.
eatables *s. pl.* vivande, viveri.
eaten V. to *eat.*
eater *s.* mangiatore.
eating *s.* il mangiare.
eaves *s. pl.* gronda, cornicione (*sing.*).
to **eavesdrop** *vi.* origliare.
ebb *s.* 1. riflusso, l'abbassarsi della marea 2. (*fig.*) decadenza || — *-tide,* bassa marea.
ebbing *agg.* 1. defluente 2. in declino.
ebonist *s.* ebanista.
ebonite *s.* ebanite.
ebony *s.* ebano.
ebullition *s.* ebollizione.
eccentric *agg.* e *s.* eccentrico (*anche fig.*).
eccentricity *s.* eccentricità.
ecclesiastic *agg.* e *s.* ecclesiastico.
ecclesiastical *agg.* ecclesiastico.
echelon *s.* scaglione.
echinoderm *s.* echinoderma.
echo *s.* eco.
to **echo** *vt.* e *vi.* 1. far eco (a) 2. echeggiare.
eclectic *agg.* e *s.* eclettico.
eclecticism *s.* eclettismo.
eclipse *s.* eclissi.
to **eclipse** *vt.* eclissare.
ecliptic *agg.* eclittico.
eclogue *s.* egloga.
ecology *s.* ecologia.

economic *agg.* economico.
economical *agg.* economico.
economics *s.* scienze economiche.
economist *s.* economista.
to **economize** *vt.* e *vi.* economizzare.
economy *s.* economia.
ecstasy *s.* estasi.
ecstatic *agg.* estatico.
ecstatically *avv.* estaticamente.
ecumenic(al) *agg.* ecumenico.
eczema *s.* eczema.
eddy *s.* 1. turbine d'aria, vortice 2. gorgo, risucchio.
edge *s.* 1. orlo, margine 2. ciglio, sponda 3. taglio (*di lama*) 4. spigolo.
to **edge** *vt.* e *vi.* 1. bordare, fare un bordo 2. affilare, arrotare, aguzzare (*anche fig.*).
edged *agg.* affilato, tagliente || *double- —*, a doppio taglio (*anche fig.*).
edgeless *agg.* 1. senza bordo 2. smussato, che non taglia.
edging *s.* orlatura, fettuccia.
edible *agg.* mangereccio.
edibles *s. pl.* commestibili.
edict *s.* editto.
edifice *s.* edificio (*anche fig.*).
edifying *agg.* edificante.
to **edit** *vt.* 1. pubblicare, curare (*un libro*) 2. redigere 3. (*cine*) montare.
editing *s.* 1. redazione, commento (*di un testo*) 2. direzione (*di un giornale, ecc.*).
edition *s.* edizione.
editor *s.* 1. commentatore, curatore (*di un testo*) 2. direttore, redattore (*di un giornale*).
editorial *s.* editoriale, articolo di fondo. ♦ **editorial** *agg.* editoriale.
editorship *s.* direzione, redazione (*di giornali*).
to **educate** *vt.* 1. istruire, educare 2. affinare, esercitare.
educated *agg.* 1. istruito, colto 2. addestrato (*di animali*).
education *s.* 1. cultura, educazione 2. istruzione, insegnamento.
educational *agg.* educativo.
educative *agg.* istruttivo.
educator *s.* educatore.
to **educe** *vt.* estrarre, sviluppare.
educible *agg.* che si può estrarre.
to **edulcorate** *vt.* dolcificare.
eel *s.* anguilla.
eerie, eery *agg.* irreale, sovrannatu-

rale.
to **efface** *vt.* cancellare, distruggere.
effect *s.* 1. effetto, risultato 2. impressione. ♦ **effects** *s. pl.* effetti personali.
to **effect** *vt.* effettuare, eseguire.
effective *agg.* 1. efficace 2. effettivo.
effectiveness *s.* efficacia.
effectual *agg.* efficace.
effectuality *s.* efficacia, validità.
effectuation *s.* effettuazione.
effeminacy *s.* effeminatezza.
effeminate *agg.* effeminato.
effervescence *s.* 1. effervescenza 2. (*fig.*) eccitamento.
effete *agg.* logoro, esaurito.
efficacious *agg.* efficace.
efficaciousness *s.* 1. efficacia 2. rendimento (*di una macchina*).
efficiency *s.* efficienza, rendimento.
efficient *agg.* 1. efficiente, di alto rendimento 2. abile, capace.
effigy *s.* effigie.
to **effloresce** *vi.* fiorire, germogliare.
effluent *agg.* defluente.
effort *s.* sforzo, fatica.
effortless *agg.* senza sforzo, facile.
effrontery *s.* sfrontatezza.
effulgence *s.* splendore.
effusion *s.* effusione, esuberanza.
effusive *agg.* espansivo, esuberante.
egg *s.* uovo || *boiled —*, uovo alla coque; *hard-boiled —*, uovo sodo.
to **egg** *vt. to — on so.*, istigare, incitare qu.
egocentric *agg.* egocentrico.
egocentrism *s.* egocentrismo.
egoism *s.* egoismo.
egoist *s.* egoista.
egoistic(al) *agg.* egoistico.
egotism *s.* egotismo.
egotist *s.* egotista.
egregious *agg.* insigne, eminente.
egress *s.* uscita.
Egyptian *agg.* e *s.* egiziano.
eider-down *s.* piumino (*da letto*).
eight *agg.* otto.
eighteen *agg.* diciotto.
eighteenth *agg.* diciottesimo.
eighth *agg.* ottavo.
eightieth *agg.* ottantesimo.
eighty *agg.* ottanta.
either *agg.* 1. l'uno o l'altro 2. ciascuno dei due, tutti e due. ♦ **either** *avv.* anche, pure. ♦ **either** *avv.* (*in frasi neg.*) neanche, neppure. ♦ **either** *cong.* (*seguito da or*) o, oppure.
to **ejaculate** *vt.* 1. eiaculare 2. e-

sclamare.

ejaculation s. **1.** eiaculazione **2.** esclamazione.

to eject vt. gettar fuori.

ejection s. **1.** espulsione **2.** (fig.) destituzione.

ejector s. espulsore.

elaborate agg. elaborato, accurato.

to elaborate vt. e vi. elaborare.

elaboration s. elaborazione.

to elapse vi. trascorrere, passare (del tempo).

elastic agg. elastico (anche fig.).

elasticity s. elasticità.

to elate vt. inebriare, esaltare.

elbow s. gomito.

to elbow vt. e vi. spingere con il gomito, andare avanti a gomitate.

elder agg. (comp. di old) maggiore, più vecchio (tra due persone). ◆ **elder** s. maggiore, più vecchio (fra due).

elderly agg. attempato.

eldest agg. (superl. di old) maggiore (tra fratelli), primogenito.

elect agg. eletto, scelto.

to elect vt. eleggere.

election s. **1.** elezione **2.** scelta.

elective agg. **1.** elettivo **2.** elettorale.

elector s. elettore.

electoral agg. elettorale.

electorate s. elettorato.

electric(al) agg. elettrico.

electrician s. elettricista.

electricity s. elettricità.

to electrify vt. **1.** elettrificare **2.** elettrizzare.

electrization s. elettrizzazione.

electrocardiogram s. elettrocardiogramma.

to electrocute vt. fulminare mediante elettricità.

electrocution s. elettroesecuzione.

electrode s. elettrodo.

electrodynamics s. elettrodinamica.

electrolysis s. elettrolisi.

electro-magnet s. elettromagnete.

electromagnetic agg. elettromagnetico.

electron s. elettrone.

electronic agg. elettronico.

electronics s. elettronica.

electrostatics s. elettrostatica.

elegance s. eleganza.

elegant agg. elegante, raffinato.

elegiac agg. elegiaco.

elegy s. elegia.

element s. **1.** elemento **2.** principio costitutivo.

elemental agg. **1.** dei quattro elementi **2.** elementare **3.** fondamentale.

elementary agg. elementare.

elephant s. elefante.

elephantiasis s. elefantiasi.

elephantine agg. elefantesco.

to elevate vt. innalzare, elevare (anche fig.).

elevated agg. **1.** elevato **2.** sopraelevato.

elevation s. **1.** elevazione **2.** collina, luogo alto.

elevator s. ascensore, montacarichi.

eleven agg. undici.

elevenses s. (fam.) spuntino a metà mattina.

eleventh agg. undicesimo.

elf s. (pl. elves) elfo, folletto.

elfish agg. **1.** incantato **2.** vivace.

to elicit vt. estrarre, strappare.

eligibility s. eleggibilità.

eligible agg. eleggibile.

to eliminate vt. eliminare.

elimination s. eliminazione.

elision s. elisione.

elixir s. elisir.

elk s. alce.

ellipse s. ellisse.

ellipsis s. ellissi.

elliptic(al) agg. ellittico.

elm s. olmo.

elocution s. **1.** elocuzione **2.** dizione.

to elope vi. fuggire (con un amante).

elopement s. fuga (con un amante).

eloquence s. eloquenza.

eloquent agg. eloquente (anche fig.).

else avv. (dopo avv. e pron. int., indef.) altro.

elsewhere avv. altrove.

to elude vt. eludere, schivare.

elusive agg. **1.** elusivo, ambiguo **2.** sfuggevole.

elytron s. (pl. elytra) elitra.

Elzevir agg. e s. elzeviro.

to emaciate vt. far deperire, far dimagrire.

emaciated agg. emaciato.

to emanate vi. emanare.

emanation s. emanazione.

to emancipate vt. emancipare.

emancipation s. emancipazione.

to embalm vt. **1.** imbalsamare **2.** profumare.

embalmer s. imbalsamatore.

embankment s. 1. argine, diga 2. alzaia.

embarcation s. imbarco.

embargo s. embargo, fermo.

to **embark** vt. imbarcare (truppe, merci). ♦ to **embark** vi. imbarcarsi.

embarkation s. imbarco.

to **embarrass** vt. mettere in imbarazzo.

embarrassing agg. imbarazzante.

embarrassment s. 1. imbarazzo 2. difficoltà.

embassy s. ambasciata.

to **embattle** vt. disporre in ordine di battaglia, fortificare.

to **embed** vt. incassare, conficcare.

to **embellish** vt. abbellire, ornare.

embellishment s. abbellimento, ornamento.

ember s. tizzone. ♦ **embers** s. pl. brace (sing.).

embezzler s. malversatore.

to **embitter** vt. 1. rendere amaro 2. (fig.) amareggiare.

embitterment s. amarezza, inasprimento.

to **emblazon** vt. 1. decorare 2. celebrare.

emblem s. emblema, simbolo (fig.).

emblematic(al) agg. emblematico.

embodiment s. 1. incarnazione 2. incorporamento.

to **embody** vt. 1. incarnare 2. personificare 3. incorporare.

to **embolden** vt. incoraggiare.

embolism s. embolia.

embolus s. (pl. -li) embolo.

to **emboss** vt. 1. scolpire 2. stampare in rilievo.

embossed agg. 1. sbalzato 2. fatto in rilievo.

embrace s. abbraccio, amplesso.

to **embrace** vt. abbracciare (anche fig.). ♦ to **embrace** vi. abbracciarsi.

embrasure s. 1. vano (di porta, finestra) 2. feritoia.

to **embroider** vt. ricamare.

embroiderer s. ricamatore.

embroidery s. ricamo.

to **embroil** vt. coinvolgere in una disputa.

embryo s. embrione.

embryonic agg. embrionale (anche fig.).

to **emend** vt. emendare.

emendation s. emendamento.

emerald s. smeraldo.

to **emerge** vi. 1. emergere, affiorare 2. (fig.) risultare.

emergency s. emergenza, caso imprevisto || — -door, uscita di sicurezza; — means, mezzi di fortuna.

emersion s. emersione.

emery s. smeriglio || — -paper, carta smerigliata.

emetic agg. e s. emetico.

emigrant agg. e s. emigrante.

to **emigrate** vi. emigrare.

emigration s. emigrazione.

eminence s. 1. luogo, parte eminente 2. (anat.) protuberanza 3. (fig.) eminenza, eccellenza.

eminent agg. eminente (anche fig.).

eminently avv. eminentemente.

emir s. emiro.

emissary s. emissario, agente segreto.

emission s. emissione.

to **emit** vt. 1. emettere 2. esalare.

emollient agg. e s. emolliente.

emolument s. remunerazione, salario.

emotion s. emozione, turbamento.

emotional agg. 1. emotivo, impressionabile 2. commovente.

emotionalism s. emotività.

emotionally avv. con emozione.

emotive agg. 1. commovente 2. emotivo.

emperor s. imperatore.

emphasis s. 1. accentuazione, rilievo 2. enfasi.

to **emphasize** vt. accentuare.

emphatic agg. 1. accentuato 2. enfatico.

emphysema s. enfisema.

emphyteusis s. enfiteusi.

empire s. impero.

empiric s. empirico.

empirical agg. empirico.

empiricism s. empirismo.

emplacement s. 1. collocazione 2. (mil.) piazzuola.

employ s. impiego: out of —, senza impiego.

to **employ** vt. 1. impiegare, adoperare 2. assumere.

employee s. impiegato.

employer s. datore di lavoro.

employment s. impiego, occupazione.

to **empoison** vt. avvelenare.

emporium s. 1. centro commerciale 2. emporio.

to **empower** vt. dare pieni poteri a.

emptiness s. **1.** vuoto **2.** vanità.
empty agg. **1.** vuoto **2.** vano **3.** vacante || — -handed, a mani vuote.
to **empty** vt. vuotare. ♦ to **empty** vi. vuotarsi.
to **emulate** vt. emulare.
emulation s. emulazione.
emulator s. emulatore.
emulous agg. emulo.
to **emulsify** vt. emulsionare.
emulsion s. emulsione.
emulsive agg. emulsivo.
to **enable** vt. mettere in grado.
to **enact** vt. decretare, emanare (una legge).
enactment s. **1.** promulgazione **2.** legge.
enamel s. smalto.
to **enamel** vt. smaltare.
to **encamp** vi. accamparsi.
encaustic agg. encaustico.
encephalic agg. encefalico.
encephalitis s. encefalite.
to **enchant** vt. incantare, affascinare.
enchanter s. incantatore, mago.
enchanting agg. incantevole.
enchantment s. incanto, incantesimo.
enchantress s. incantatrice.
to **encircle** vt. circondare, cingere.
enclitic agg. enclitico.
to **enclose** vt. **1.** racchiudere, cingere **2.** accludere.
enclosed agg. **1.** racchiuso, circondato **2.** accluso.
enclosure s. **1.** recinto, staccionata **2.** allegato.
encomiast s. encomiasta.
to **encompass** vt. circondare (anche fig.).
encore avv. (teat.) bis.
to **encore** vt. chiedere il bis.
encounter s. scontro.
to **encourage** vt. incoraggiare, animare.
encouragement s. incoraggiamento.
encouraging agg. incoraggiante.
to **encroach** vt. **1.** usurpare, invadere **2.** (giur.) ledere.
to **encrust** vt. incrostare.
to **encumber** vt. **1.** ingombrare, imbarazzare **2.** ostruire.
encumbrance s. ingombro, impedimento.
encyclic(al) agg. enciclico. ♦ **en-cyclic(al)** s. enciclica.
encyclop(a)edia s. enciclopedia.
encyclop(a)edic(al) agg. enciclo-

pedico.
end s. **1.** estremità, fine, termine **2.** scopo, mira **3.** morte.
to **end** vt. e vi. finire, concludere.
to **endanger** vt. mettere in pericolo, compromettere.
to **endear** vt. affezionare, rendere caro.
endearing agg. affettuoso, tenero.
endearment s. tenerezza. ♦ **en-dearments** s. pl. blandizie.
to **endeavo(u)r** vi. sforzarsi. ♦ to **endeavo(u)r** vt. tentare.
endemic agg. endemico.
ending agg. finale, ultimo. ♦ **end-ing** s. fine, conclusione.
endless agg. senza fine, eterno, continuo.
endocarditis s. endocardite.
endocardium s. endocardio.
endocarp s. endocarpo.
endocrine agg. endocrino.
endocrinology s. endocrinologia.
endogeny s. endogenesi.
to **endorse** vt. (comm.) girare, vistare.
endorsee s. (comm.) giratario.
endorsement s. (comm.) girata.
endorser s. (comm.) girante.
to **endow** vt. **1.** dotare **2.** fare una donazione.
endowment s. **1.** costituzione di dote, donazione **2.** (fig.) talento.
endurance s. **1.** resistenza, sopportazione **2.** durata.
to **endure** vt. tollerare, sopportare. ♦ to **endure** vi. resistere, durare.
enduring agg. **1.** tollerante, paziente **2.** durevole.
enema s. clistere.
enemy agg. e s. nemico.
energetic(al) agg. **1.** energico **2.** energetico.
to **energize** vt. infondere energia.
energumen s. energumeno.
energy s. energia, forza.
to **enervate** vt. snervare, indebolire.
enervation s. indebolimento.
to **enfeeble** vt. indebolire.
to **enfold** vt. **1.** avvolgere **2.** cingere.
to **enforce** vt. **1.** imporre, far rispettare **2.** mettere in vigore (una legge).
to **enframe** vt. incorniciare.
to **enfranchise** vt. affrancare, liberare.
enfranchisement s. affrancamento,

liberazione.

to **engage** vt. **1.** impegnare **2.** ingaggiare **3.** attrarre (l'attenzione). ♦ to **engage** vi. impegnarsi || to — in conversation, prendere parte alla conversazione.

engaged agg. **1.** impegnato **2.** fidanzato **3.** occupato, riservato.

engagement s. **1.** impegno **2.** fidanzamento **3.** assunzione, impiego.

engaging agg. attraente, avvincente.

engagingly avv. in modo attraente.

to **engender** vt. produrre, causare.

engine s. **1.** macchina, motore **2.** (ferr.) locomotrice || fire- —, autopompa.

engineer s. **1.** ingegnere **2.** tecnico.

engineering s. **1.** ingegneria **2.** costruzione meccanica.

English agg. inglese. ♦ **English** s. lingua inglese.

Englishman s. (uomo) inglese.

Englishwoman s. (donna) inglese.

to **engrave** vt. **1.** intagliare, incidere **2.** (fig.) imprimere.

engraver s. incisore.

engraving s. arte dell'incisione || wood- —, xilografia.

to **engross** vt. **1.** copiàre (un atto legale), redigere (un documento) **2.** assorbire (l'attenzione).

engrossment s. copiatura (di documento).

to **enhance** vt. accrescere.

enigma s. enigma.

enigmatic(al) agg. enigmatico.

to **enjoy** vt. **1.** gòdere, gioire **2.** gùstare, provar piacere di || to — oneself, divertirsi.

enjoyable agg. piacevole, gradevole.

enjoyably avv. piacevolmente.

enjoyment s. godimento, piacere.

to **enkindle** vt. infiammare, eccitare. ♦ to **enkindle** vi. infiammarsi, eccitarsi.

to **enlarge** vt. **1.** allargare, ampliare **2.** (foto) ingrandire. ♦ to **enlarge** vi. allargarsi, ampliarsi.

enlargement s. **1.** allargamento **2.** (foto) ingrandimento.

enlarger s. (foto) ingranditore.

to **enlighten** vt. rischiarare, illuminare (anche fig.).

enlightenment s. **1.** spiegazione, schiarimento **2.** (lett.) l'illuminismo.

to **enlist** vt. arruolare. ♦ to **enlist** vi. arruolarsi.

enlistment s. arruolamento, ingaggio.

to **enliven** vt. rianimare, ravvivare.

to **enmesh** vt. impegolare, irretire.

enmity s. ostilità, inimicizia.

to **ennoble** vt. nobilitare.

enormity s. mostruosità.

enormous agg. enorme, immenso.

enough avv. abbastanza, sufficientemente. ♦ **enough** agg. sufficiente. ♦ **enough** s. il necessario, quanto basta.

to **enrage** vt. far arrabbiare, esasperare.

to **enrapture** vt. rapire, estasiare.

to **enrich** vt. **1.** arricchire (anche fig.) **2.** abbellire.

enrichment s. **1.** arricchimento **2.** abbellimento.

to **enrol** vt. **1.** arruolare, ingaggiare **2.** iscrivere.

enrolment s. **1.** arruolamento, iscrizione **2.** (giur.) registrazione.

ensign s. **1.** bandiera, stendardo **2.** portabandiera.

to **enslave** vt. assoggettare, far schiavo (anche fig.).

enslavement s. asservimento, schiavitù (anche fig.).

to **ensnare** vt. adescare, intrappolare (anche fig.).

to **ensue** vt. e vi. seguire.

to **ensure** vt. assicurare, garantire.

entail s. eredità, ordine di successione (vincolato).

to **entangle** vt. impigliare, intralciare (anche fig.).

entanglement s. groviglio, impiccio.

to **enter** vt. e vi. **1.** entrare, penetrare **2.** iscrivere **3.** (comm.) registrare || to — upon, intraprendere (una carriera).

enteric agg. enterico.

enteritis s. enterite.

enterocolitis s. enterocolite.

enterogastritis s. gastroenterite.

enterprise s. **1.** impresa **2.** iniziativa, intraprendenza.

enterprising agg. intraprendente.

to **entertain** vt. **1.** ricevere, ospitare **2.** intrattenere, divertire **3.** carezzare (un'idea), nutrire (dubbi, speranze).

entertainer s. **1.** anfitrione, ospite **2.** comico.

entertaining agg. divertente.

entertainment s. **1.** trattenimento, spettacolo **2.** ricevimento, festa **3.** divertimento.

to **enthral** *vt.* (*fig.*) affascinare, incantare.

enthralment *s.* incanto, malia.

to **enthrone** *vt.* mettere sul trono.

enthronement *s.* investitura, intronizzazione.

enthusiasm *s.* entusiasmo.

enthusiast *s.* entusiasta.

enthusiastic(al) *agg.* entusiastico.

enthusiastically *avv.* entusiasticamente.

to **entice** *vt.* sedurre, allettare.

enticement *s.* 1. attrattiva 2. adescamento, istigazione.

enticing *agg.* seducente, attraente.

entire *agg.* intero, completo.

entirely *avv.* interamente, completamente.

to **entitle** *vt.* 1. intitolare (*un libro*) 2. dare un titolo.

entity *s.* entità, esistenza.

entomological *agg.* entomologico.

entomologist *s.* entomologo.

entomology *s.* entomologia.

entrails *s. pl.* intestino (*sing.*), visceri.

entrance *s.* 1. ingresso, entrata 2. ammissione || — *hall*, vestibolo.

to **entrap** *vt.* prendere in trappola, truffare.

to **entreat** *vt.* pregare, supplicare.

entreaty *s.* supplica, istanza.

to **entrench** *vt.* e *vi.* trincerare, fortificare (*anche fig.*) || *to* — *upon*, usurpare.

entrepreneur *s.* 1. (*teat.*) impresario 2. imprenditore.

to **entrust** *vt.* affidare, commettere.

entry *s.* 1. entrata 2. ingresso, passaggio 3. (*comm.*) registrazione.

to **entwine** *vt.* attorcigliare, intrecciare. ♦ to **entwine** *vi.* arrotolarsi.

to **enucleate** *vt.* spiegare, chiarire.

enucleation *s.* spiegazione, chiarimento.

to **enumerate** *vt.* enumerare.

enumeration *s.* enumerazione.

enumerator *s.* numeratore.

to **enunciate** *vt.* enunciare, proclamare.

enunciation *s.* enunciazione.

to **envelop** *vt.* avvolgere, avviluppare.

envelope *s.* busta, involucro.

envelopment *s.* avvolgimento.

enviable *agg.* invidiabile.

envious *agg.* invidioso.

to **environ** *vt.* circondare, accer-

chiare.

environment *s.* ambiente.

environs *s. pl.* dintorni.

envy *s.* invidia.

to **envy** *vt.* invidiare.

enzyme *s.* enzima.

epaulet(te) *s.* (*mil.*) spallina.

ephebe *s.* efebo.

ephemeral *agg.* effimero.

ephemeris *s.* (*pl.* -ides) effemeride.

epic *agg.* epico. ♦ **epic** *s.* poema epico.

epically *avv.* epicamente.

epicentre *s.* epicentro.

epicurean *agg.* e *s.* epicureo.

epidemic(al) *agg.* epidemico.

epidemically *avv.* epidemicamente.

epidermal *agg.* epidermico.

epidermis *s.* epidermide.

epigastric *agg.* epigastrico.

epigram *s.* epigramma.

epigrammatic *agg.* epigrammatico.

epigrammatist *s.* epigrammista.

epigraph *s.* epigrafe.

epigraphy *s.* epigrafia.

epilepsy *s.* epilessia.

epileptic *agg.* epilettico.

epilogue *s.* epilogo.

Epiphany *s.* Epifania.

episcopacy *s.* episcopato.

episcopal *agg.* episcopale.

episcopate *s.* episcopato.

episode *s.* episodio.

episodic(al) *agg.* episodico.

epistle *s.* epistola.

epistolary *agg.* epistolare.

epitaph *s.* epitaffio.

epithalamium *s.* epitalamio.

epithet *s.* epiteto.

epitome *s.* epitome, riassunto.

epoch *s.* epoca, età.

epopee *s.* epopea.

equability *s.* uguaglianza, uniformità.

equal *agg.* uguale, simile, stesso. ♦ **equal** *s.* pari (*di rango*).

equality *s.* uguaglianza, parità.

equalization *s.* eguagliamento.

to **equalize** *vt.* e *vi.* uguagliare.

equally *avv.* ugualmente, imparzialmente.

equanimity *s.* equanimità.

equanimous *agg.* equanime.

equation *s.* 1. equazione 2. pareggio.

equator *s.* equatore.

equatorial *agg.* equatoriale.

equestrian *agg.* equestre.

equidistant *agg.* equidistante.

equilateral *agg.* equilatero.

equine *agg.* equino.
equinoctial *agg.* equinoziale.
equinox *s.* equinozio.
to **equip** *vt.* 1. equipaggiare 2. fornire, arredare.
equipment *s.* 1. equipaggiamento 2. attrezzatura.
equipoise *s.* equilibrio.
equipollent *agg.* equipollente.
equitation *s.* equitazione.
equity *s.* giustizia, equità.
equivalence *s.* equivalenza.
equivalent *agg.* e *s.* equivalente.
equivocal *agg.* 1. ambiguo, equivoco 2. sospetto, losco.
equivocally *avv.* 1. ambiguamente 2. in modo losco.
to **equivocate** *vi.* equivocare, giocare sull'equivoco.
equivocation *s.* 1. l'equivocare 2. equivoco.
equivoke *s.* 1. gioco di parole 2. ambiguità (*d'espressione*).
era *s.* era, epoca.
eradicable *agg.* estirpabile.
to **eradicate** *vt.* sradicare, estirpare.
to **erase** *vt.* raschiare, cancellare.
eraser *s.* 1. raschietto 2. gomma per cancellare.
erasure *s.* raschiatura, cancellatura.
erect *agg.* diritto, ritto.
to **erect** *vt.* 1. raddrizzare 2. costruire.
erection *s.* 1. raddrizzamento 2. erezione.
eremite *s.* eremita.
ermine *s.* ermellino.
to **erode** *vt.* corrodere, logorare.
erosion *s.* erosione.
erosive *agg.* corrosivo.
erotic *agg.* erotico.
eroticism *s.* erotismo.
to **err** *vi.* 1. sbagliare 2. errare, vagabondare.
errand *s.* commissione || — *-boy,* fattorino.
errant *agg.* 1. errante 2. che sbaglia.
erratic *agg.* 1. erratico 2. irregolare.
erratically *avv.* 1. irregolarmente 2. eccentricamente.
erring *agg.* 1. errante 2. che sbaglia.
erroneous *agg.* erroneo.
error *s.* 1. errore 2. torto.
erudite *agg.* erudito.
erudition *s.* erudizione.
to **erupt** *vi.* eruttare.
eruption *s.* eruzione.
eruptive *agg.* eruttivo.
escalade *s.* scalata.

escalator *s.* scala mobile.
escape *s.* 1. fuga, evasione 2. scampo, salvezza.
to **escape** *vt.* e *vi.* 1. fuggire, evadere 2. scampare.
escapism *s.* evasione dalla realtà.
escapist *s.* chi cerca di evadere dalla realtà.
eschatology *s.* escatologia.
to **eschew** *vt.* evitare, astenersi da.
escort *s.* scorta.
to **escort** *vt.* scortare, accompagnare.
Eskimo *s.* esquimese.
esoteric *agg.* esoterico.
especial *agg.* speciale.
especially *avv.* specialmente.
espionage *s.* spionaggio.
esplanade *s.* spianata.
to **espy** *vt.* scorgere, avvistare.
esquire *s.* (*titolo di cortesia*) John Smith *Esq.*, egregio sig. John Smith.
essay *s.* 1. esperimento, prova 2. (*lett.*) saggio.
to **essay** *vt.* provare, mettere alla prova.
essayist *s.* saggista.
essence *s.* essenza.
essential *agg.* essenziale.
to **establish** *vt.* 1. affermare (*un diritto ecc.*) 2. instaurare 3. (*comm.*) fondare, costituire.
established *agg.* 1. stabilito, affermato 2. fondato.
establishment *s.* 1. affermazione, conferma 2. instaurazione 3. stabilimento, azienda.
estate *s.* 1. terra, proprietà (*terriera*) 2. stato, gruppo politico 3. condizione, classe sociale || — *agent,* mediatore.
esteem *s.* stima, considerazione.
to **esteem** *vt.* 1. stimare, tenere in gran conto 2. considerare.
estimable *agg.* degno di stima.
estimate *s.* 1. stima, giudizio 2. (*comm.*) preventivo.
to **estimate** *vt.* 1. stimare, valutare 2. preventivare.
estimator *s.* perito, stimatore.
to **estrange** *vt.* alienare, alienarsi, allontanare.
estrangement *s.* alienazione, allontanamento.
estuary *s.* estuario.
etching *s.* acquaforte.
eternal *agg.* eterno.
eternity *s.* eternità.

ether *s.* etere.
ethereal *agg.* etereo.
ethic(al) *agg.* etico.
ethics *s.* etica.
Ethiopian *agg.* etiopico. ♦ **Ethiopian** *s.* etiope.
Ethiopic *agg.* etiopico.
ethnic(al) *agg.* etnico.
ethnography *s.* etnografia.
ethnologist *s.* etnologo.
ethnology *s.* etnologia.
ethylene *s.* etilene.
ethylic *agg.* etilico.
etiquette *s.* 1. etichetta 2. cerimoniale.
Etrurian, Etruscan *agg. e s.* etrusco.
etymologic(al) *agg.* etimologico.
etymology *s.* etimologia.
eucalyptus *s.* eucalipto.
Eucharist *s.* Eucaristia.
eucharistic(al) *agg.* eucaristico.
eugenics *s.* eugenetica.
eulogist *s.* elogiatore.
to eulogize *vt.* elogiare.
eulogy *s.* elogio, panegirico.
eunuch *s.* eunuco.
euphemism *s.* eufemismo.
euphonic *agg.* eufonico.
euphony *s.* eufonia.
euphoria *s.* euforia.
euphuism *s.* eufuismo.
euphuist *s.* affettato.
euphuistic *agg.* affettato, ricercato (*di stile*).
European *agg. e s.* europeo.
Eurovision *s.* eurovisione.
euthanasia *s.* eutanasia.
to evacuate *vt. e vi.* evacuare, sfollare.
evacuation *s.* evacuazione, sfollamento.
to evade *vt.* evitare, schivare, eludere.
to evaluate *vt.* valutare.
evaluation *s.* valutazione.
evanescent *agg.* evanescente.
evangelic(al) *agg.* evangelico.
evangelist *s.* evangelista.
evangelistic *agg.* di un evangelista, missionario.
evangelization *s.* evangelizzazione.
to evangelize *vt.* evangelizzare.
to evaporate *vi.* evaporare. ♦ **to evaporate** *vt.* far evaporare.
evaporation *s.* evaporazione.
evasion *s.* 1. evasione, scappatoia 2. scusa, pretesto.
evasive *agg.* evasivo.

evasively *avv.* evasivamente.
evasiveness *s.* ambiguità.
eve *s.* vigilia.
even *agg.* 1. uguale, uniforme, costante, regolare 2. pari, equo. ♦ **even** *avv.* 1. ancora (*con comp.*) 2. persino, anche || — *as*, nel momento in cui.
evening *s.* 1. sera, serata 2. (*fig.*) declino, fine.
evenly *avv.* in modo uguale, uniformemente.
evensong *s.* vespro.
event *s.* 1. caso, eventualità 2. avvenimento 3. (*sport*) prova.
eventful *agg.* ricco di avvenimenti, movimentato.
eventual *agg.* finale, definitivo.
eventuality *s.* eventualità.
eventually *avv.* alla fine.
ever *avv.* 1. mai 2. sempre.
evergreen *s.* sempreverde.
everlasting *agg.* eterno.
everliving *agg.* immortale.
evermore *avv.* perpetuamente.
every *agg.* ogni, ciascuno, tutti.
everybody *pron. indef.* ognuno, tutti.
everyday *agg.* di tutti i giorni, quotidiano.
everyone *pron. indef.* V. everybody.
everything *pron. indef.* ogni cosa, tutto.
everywhere *avv.* ovunque.
to evict *vt.* sfrattare, espellere.
eviction *s.* sfratto.
evidence *s.* 1. evidenza 2. prova.
to evidence *vt.* provare, dimostrare.
evident *agg.* evidente, chiaro.
evil *agg.* cattivo, malvagio || — -*eye*, malocchio. ♦ **evil** *s.* male, peccato.
to evirate *vt.* evirare.
to evocate *vt.* evocare.
evocation *s.* evocazione.
evocative *agg.* evocatore.
to evoke *vt.* evocare.
evolution *s.* evoluzione.
evolutional *agg.* evolutivo.
evolutionism *s.* evoluzionismo.
to evolve *vt.* evolvere. ♦ **to evolve** *vi.* evolversi.
evolvement *s.* evoluzione, sviluppo.
ewe *s.* pecora (*femmina*).
to exacerbate *vt.* esacerbare, inasprire.
exacerbation *s.* esacerbazione, inasprimento.
exact *agg.* 1. esatto, giusto 2. puntuale, rigoroso.

to **exact** vt. 1. esigere 2. rendere necessario.

exacting agg. 1. esigente 2. impegnativo.

exaction s. esazione, estorsione.

exactitude s. esattezza, precisione.

exactly avv. esattamente.

exactness s. esattezza, precisione.

to **exaggerate** vt. esagerare, ingrandire.

exaggeration s. esagerazione.

to **exalt** vt. 1. innalzare, elevare 2. esaltare, lodare.

exaltation s. 1. innalzamento 2. esaltazione.

exalted agg. 1. elevato (di grado ecc.) 2. esaltato, eccitato.

examination s. 1. esame, ispezione 2. esame scolastico 3. (giur.) interrogatorio.

to **examine** vt. 1. verificare, ispezionare 2. esaminare 3. (giur.) istruire un processo.

examiner s. esaminatore.

example s. esempio.

to **exasperate** vt. 1. peggiorare, aggravare 2. esasperare.

exasperatingly avv. in modo esasperante.

exasperation s. esasperazione.

to **excavate** vt. scavare, fare scavi (archeologici).

excavation s. 1. scavo 2. fossa, buca.

excavator s. 1. operaio scavatore 2. (mecc.) escavatore.

to **exceed** vt. e vi. 1. eccedere, superare (i limiti) 2. essere superiore.

exceeding agg. esagerato.

exceedingly avv. eccessivamente, troppo.

to **excel** vt. superare. ♦ to **excel** vi. primeggiare.

excellence s. 1. eccellenza 2. pregio, superiorità.

Excellency s. (titolo) Eccellenza.

excellent agg. eccellente.

except prep. eccetto, tranne.

to **except** vt. eccettuare, escludere. ♦ to **except** vi. obiettare, sollevare eccezioni.

excepting prep. eccetto, tranne.

exception s. eccezione.

exceptional agg. eccezionale, straordinario.

excerpt s. brano scelto.

excess s. 1. eccesso, intemperanza 2. supplemento.

exchange s. 1. scambio 2. (finanza) cambio 3. borsa, mercato || bill of —, cambiale; — -broker, agente di cambio.

to **exchange** vt. cambiare, scambiare. ♦ to **exchange** vi. fare un cambio.

exchangeable agg. scambiabile.

exchanger s. cambiavalute.

exchequer s. Tesoro, Scacchiere, fisco.

excise s. imposta indiretta || — duty, dazio.

to **excise**[1] vt. tassare.

to **excise**[2] vt. estirpare, mutilare (un testo).

exciseman s. daziere, funzionario degli uffici delle imposte.

excision s. taglio, recisione.

excitability s. eccitabilità.

excitable agg. eccitabile.

excitant agg. e s. eccitante.

excitation s. eccitazione.

to **excite** vt. 1. provocare, far nascere (una rivolta, un sentimento ecc.) 2. eccitare, animare.

excited agg. eccitato.

excitement s. eccitazione.

to **exclaim** vt. e vi. esclamare.

exclamation s. esclamazione.

exclamatory agg. esclamativo.

to **exclude** vt. escludere.

exclusion s. esclusione.

exclusive agg. 1. altezzoso 2. chiuso, scelto (di ambiente) 3. esclusivo.

exclusiveness s. esclusività.

to **excogitate** vt. escogitare.

excommunicable agg. scomunicabile.

excommunicate agg. e s. scomunicato.

to **excommunicate** vt. scomunicare.

excommunication s. scomunica.

excrement s. escremento.

excrescence s. escrescenza, protuberanza.

excruciating agg. tormentoso, straziante.

to **exculpate** vt. giustificare, scolpare.

excursion s. 1. escursione, gita 2. (mil.) sortita.

excursionist s. escursionista, gitante.

excusable agg. scusabile.

excuse s. 1. scusa, giustificazione 2.

pretesto.

to **excuse** *vt.* scusare, giustificare.

execrable *agg.* escrabile.

to **execrate** *vt.* e *vi.* **1.** escrare, detestare **2.** maledire.

execration *s.* **1.** escrazione **2.** maledizione.

executant *s.* esecutore.

to **execute** *vt.* **1.** eseguire, mettere in esecuzione **2.** (*giur.*) convalidare **3.** giustiziare.

execution *s.* **1.** compimento, attuazione **2.** esecuzione.

executioner *s.* esecutore, boia.

executive *agg.* esecutivo.

executor *s.* esecutore.

exedra *s.* esedra.

exegesis *s.* (*pl.* -ses) esegesi.

exegete *s.* esegeta.

exemplary *agg.* esemplare.

exemplification *s.* esemplificazione.

to **exemplify** *vt.* esemplificare.

exempt *agg.* esente, esonerato.

to **exempt** *vt.* esentare, esonerare.

exemption *s.* esenzione, esonero.

exequies *s. pl.* esequie.

exercise *s.* esercizio, esercitazione || — *-book*, quaderno.

to **exercise** *vt.* esercitare, usare. ♦ to **exercise** *vi.* esercitarsi, allenarsi.

exercitation *s.* esercizio, uso (*di una facoltà*).

to **exert** *vt.* esercitare.

exertion *s.* **1.** esercizio (*di autorità*) **2.** sforzo.

exhalation *s.* esalazione.

to **exhale** *vt.* e *vi.* esalare, emettere.

exhaust *s.* **1.** (*mecc.*) scarico, scappamento **2.** apparato aspiratore.

to **exhaust** *vt.* e *vi.* **1.** aspirare (*aria, gas ecc.*) **2.** esaurire (*anche fig.*).

exhausted *agg.* **1.** aspirato **2.** esausto, spossato.

exhausting *agg.* che esaurisce.

exhaustion *s.* **1.** aspirazione **2.** esaurimento.

exhaustive *agg.* **1.** esauriente **2.** spossante.

exhibit *s.* **1.** insieme di oggetti in mostra **2.** (*giur.*) documento.

to **exhibit** *vt.* **1.** esibire, mostrare **2.** (*giur.*) produrre (*documenti ecc.*).

exhibition *s.* **1.** presentazione (*di documenti*) **2.** esposizione, mostra.

exhibitionism *s.* esibizionismo.

exhibitionist *s.* esibizionista.

exhibitor *s.* espositore.

to **exhilarate** *vt.* rallegrare, esilarare.

exhilarating *agg.* esilarante.

to **exhort** *vt.* esortare, ammonire.

exhortation *s.* esortazione.

exhortative *agg.* esortativo.

exhumation *s.* esumazione.

to **exhume** *vt.* esumare.

exigence *s.* **1.** esigenza, necessità **2.** situazione critica.

exigent *agg.* **1.** pressante, urgente **2.** esigente.

exigible *agg.* esigibile.

exiguity *s.* esiguità.

exiguous *agg.* esiguo.

exile *s.* **1.** esilio, bando **2.** esule.

to **exile** *vt.* esiliare.

to **exist** *vi.* esistere.

existence *s.* esistenza.

existent *agg.* esistente.

existential *agg.* esistenziale.

existentialism *s.* esistenzialismo.

existentialist *agg.* e *s.* esistenzialista.

existing *agg.* esistente, attuale.

exit *s.* uscita.

exode, exodus *s.* esodo.

exogenous *agg.* esogeno.

to **exonerate** *vt.* **1.** esonerare, dispensare **2.** giustificare.

exoneration *s.* **1.** dispensa, esonero **2.** giustificazione.

exorbitant *agg.* esorbitante.

to **exorcise** *vt.* esorcizzare.

exorciser *s.* esorcista.

exorcism *s.* esorcismo.

exorcist *s.* esorcista.

exothermic *agg.* esotermico.

exotic *agg.* esotico.

exoticism *s.* esotismo.

to **expand** *vt.* espandere, dilatare, allargare. ♦ to **expand** *vi.* espandersi, dilagare, dilatarsi, allargarsi, svilupparsi.

expanse *s.* distesa, estensione, spazio.

expansion *s.* espansione, dilatazione, allargamento.

expansionism *s.* espansionismo.

expansive *agg.* **1.** espansivo **2.** dilatabile.

to **expatiate** *vi.* **1.** errare, vagabondare **2.** parlare e scrivere diffusamente.

expatiation *s.* **1.** dissertazione **2.** prolissità.

expatriate *agg.* e *s.* espatriato.

to **expatriate** *vt.* esiliare. ♦ to

expatriate *vi.* espatriare.
expatriation *s.* espatrio.
to **expect** *vt.* 1. aspettare, aspettarsi 2. esigere, insistere 3. pensare, credere || *to — somebody to come*, prevedere la venuta di qu.
expectance *s.* aspettativa, attesa.
expectant *s.* 1. chi attende 2. candidato.
expectation *s.* attesa, aspettativa. ♦ **expectations** *s. pl.* speranze.
expectorant *agg. e s.* espettorante.
expectoration *s.* espettorazione.
expediency *s.* 1. convenienza 2. opportunismo.
expedient *s.* espediente, ripiego.
to **expedite** *vt.* affrettare.
expedition *s.* 1. spedizione 2. prontezza, celerità.
expeditious *s.* svelto, sbrigativo.
to **expel** *vt.* espellere, cacciare.
expense *s.* 1. spesa, sborso 2. (*fig.*) sacrificio, prezzo.
expensive *agg.* costoso, caro.
experience *s.* esperienza.
to **experience** *vt.* sperimentare, provare.
experienced *agg.* pratico, esperto.
experiment *s.* esperimento, prova.
experimental *agg.* sperimentale.
experimentation *s.* sperimentasmo.
experimentalist *s.* sperimentalista.
experimentation *s.* sperimentazione.
expert *agg.* esperto. ♦ **expert** *s.* esperto, perito, competente.
expertly *avv.* abilmente.
to **expiate** *vt.* espiare.
expiation *s.* espiazione.
expiatory *agg.* espiatorio.
expiration *s.* 1. fine, scadenza 2. espirazione.
expiratory *agg.* espiratorio.
to **expire** *vt. e vi.* 1. finire, scadere 2. spirare, morire.
expiring *agg.* 1. che scade 2. spirante, morente.
expiry *s.* fine, cessazione.
to **explain** *vt. e vi.* spiegare, chiarire.
explanation *s.* spiegazione, delucidazione.
expletive *agg.* espletivo, pleonastico. ♦ **expletive** *s.* 1. imprecazione 2. pleonasmo.
explicable *agg.* spiegabile.
to **explicate** *vt.* sviluppare (*un principio, un'idea ecc.*).
explication *s.* spiegazione, sviluppo.
explicit *agg.* esplicito, chiaro.
to **explode** *vt.* esplodere, far esplodere. ♦ to **explode** *vi.* scoppiare, esplodere.
to **exploit** *vt.* 1. utilizzare, sfruttare 2. approfittare di.
exploitation *s.* sfruttamento, utilizzazione.
exploiter *s.* 1. chi valorizza (*idea, invenzione ecc.*) 2. sfruttatore.
exploration *s.* esplorazione.
to **explore** *vt.* esplorare.
explorer *s.* esploratore, esploratrice.
explosion *s.* esplosione, scoppio.
explosive *agg. e s.* esplosivo.
exponent *s.* 1. divulgatore 2. esponente.
exponential *agg.* esponenziale.
export *s.* esportazione.
to **export** *vt.* esportare.
exportation *s.* esportazione.
exporter *s.* esportatore.
to **expose** *vt.* 1. esporre 2. (*foto*) impressionare.
exposé *s.* esposto, resoconto.
exposition *s.* 1. spiegazione, commento 2. mostra, esposizione.
expositive *agg.* espositivo.
expositor *s.* commentatore.
expository *agg.* esplicativo.
exposure *s.* 1. esposizione (*al freddo, al caldo ecc.*) 2. mostra 3. (*foto*) (tempo di) esposizione.
to **expound** *vt.* spiegare (*una teoria*).
express *agg.* 1. chiaro, preciso 2. espresso, diretto. ♦ **express** *s.* espresso, corriere || *— train*, direttissimo.
to **express** *vt.* esprimere, manifestare.
expression *s.* espressione.
expressionism *s.* espressionismo.
expressionist *s.* espressionista.
expressive *agg.* espressivo, significativo.
expressly *avv.* espressamente.
to **expropriate** *vt.* espropriare.
expropriation *s.* espropriazione.
expulsion *s.* espulsione.
expulsive *agg.* espulsivo.
expunction *s.* cancellatura.
to **expurgate** *vt.* espurgare (*uno scritto*).
expurgation *s.* espurgazione (*di uno scritto*).

exquisite *agg.* **1.** squisito **2.** fine, sensibile. ♦ **exquisite** *s.* raffinato.

exquisiteness *s.* squisitezza, finezza.

extant *agg.* ancora esistente.

extemporaneous, extempory *agg.* estemporaneo.

extempore *agg.* improvvisato.

extemporization *s.* improvvisazione.

to **extemporize** *vt.* e *vi.* improvvisare.

to **extend** *vt.* **1.** estendere, allungare, prolungare. ♦ to **extend** *vi.* estendersi, allungarsi, prolungarsi.

extendible *agg.* estendibile.

extensible *agg.* estensibile.

extension *s.* **1.** estensione, allungamento **2.** (*comm.*) proroga.

extensive *agg.* **1.** esteso, ampio **2.** estensivo.

extent *s.* **1.** estensione **2.** volume **3.** limite, grado.

to **extenuate** *vt.* attenuare.

extenuation *s.* attenuazione.

exterior *agg.* esterno, esteriore. ♦ **exterior** *s.* **1.** l'esterno **2.** esteriorità.

exteriority *s.* esteriorità.

exteriorization *s.* esteriorizzazione.

to **exteriorize** *vt.* esternare.

to **exterminate** *vt.* sterminare.

extermination *s.* sterminio.

external *agg.* esteriore, esterno.

externality *s.* superficialità.

to **externalize** *vt.* esternare.

externally *avv.* esternamente, esteriormente.

exterritorial *agg.* estraterritoriale.

extinct *agg.* **1.** estinto **2.** spento.

extinction *s.* estinzione.

to **extinguish** *vt.* **1.** estinguere, spegnere **2.** pagare, ammortizzare.

extinguisher *s.* spegnitore, estintore.

to **extirpate** *vt.* estirpare, sradicare.

extirpation *s.* estirpazione, sradicamento.

to **extol** *vt.* lodare, magnificare

to **extort** *vt.* estorcere, strappare.

extorter *s.* chi estorce.

extortion *s.* estorsione.

extortioner *s.* ricattatore.

extra *agg.* **1.** straordinario **2.** in più, extra. ♦ **extra** *s.* **1.** supplemento **2.** (*giorn.*) edizione straordinaria **3.** (*cine*) comparsa. ♦ **extra** *avv.* extra, di più, in più, insolitamente.

extract *s.* **1.** estratto **2.** citazione.

to **extract** *vt.* estrarre, togliere.

extractable *agg.* estraibile.

extraction *s.* **1.** estrazione **2.** origine, stirpe.

extractive *agg.* estrattivo.

extractor *s.* estrattore.

to **extradite** *vt.* estradare.

extradition *s.* estradizione.

extraneous *agg.* estraneo.

extraordinary *agg.* straordinario, eccezionale.

extraterritorial *agg.* estraterritoriale.

extraterritoriality *s.* estraterritorialità.

extravagance *s.* **1.** prodigalità, sperpero **2.** stravaganza.

extravagant *agg.* **1.** prodigo **2.** stravagante.

extreme *agg.* **1.** estremo, ultimo **2.** grave. ♦ **extreme** *s.* estremo, estremità.

extremely *avv.* estremamente.

extremism *s.* estremismo.

extremist *s.* estremista.

extremity *s.* estremità.

extrinsic(al) *agg.* estrinseco.

extrovert *s.* estroverso.

to **extrude** *vt.* estromettere.

exuberance *s.* esuberanza.

exuberant *agg.* **1.** copioso, abbondante **2.** esuberante, pieno di vita.

exudation *s.* essudazione.

to **exude** *vt.* e *vi.* trasudare.

to **exult** *vi.* gioire, esultare.

exultant *agg.* esultante.

exultation *s.* esultanza.

eye *s.* occhio.

eyeball *s.* bulbo oculare.

eyebrow *s.* sopracciglio.

eyeglass *s.* lente, monocolo.

eyehole *s.* orbita, occhiaia.

eyelash *s.* ciglio.

eyelet *s.* occhiello, asola.

eyelid *s.* palpebra.

eyesight *s.* vista.

eyesore *s.* cosa brutta e spiacevole.

eyewitness *s.* testimone oculare.

F

F *s.* (*mus.*) fa.

fable *s.* favola.

fabled *agg.* **1.** mitico **2.** inventato.

fabric *s.* **1.** tessuto **2.** manufatto **3.**

struttura **4.** fabbricazione.
to **fabricate** *vt.* **1.** fabbricare **2.** inventare.
fabrication *s.* **1.** fabbricazione **2.** invenzione.
fabulist *s.* **1.** favolista **2.** bugiardo.
fabulosity *s.* favolosità.
fabulous *agg.* favoloso.
façade *s.* facciata.
face *s.* **1.** faccia **2.** aspetto **3.** sfrontatezza **4.** facciata **5.** quadrante (*di orologio*) || *to pull faces*, fare boccacce || *— -powder*, cipria; — *value*, (*comm.*) valore nominale.
to **face** *vt.* **1.** fronteggiare **2.** affrontare **3.** ricoprire || *to — about*, fare dietro-front.
facet *s.* sfaccettatura.
facetious *agg.* faceto.
facetiousness *s.* lepidezza.
facial *agg.* facciale.
facile *agg.* **1.** facile **2.** pronto **3.** accomodante.
to **facilitate** *vt.* facilitare.
facilitation *s.* facilitazione.
facility *s.* facilità. ◆ **facilities** *s. pl.* facilitazioni.
facing *agg.* che sta di fronte. ◆ **facing** *s.* rivestimento. ◆ **facings** *s. pl.* mostrine.
fact *s.* **1.** fatto **2.** realtà || *in —*, infatti, di fatto; *as a matter of —*, effettivamente.
faction *s.* **1.** fazione **2.** faziosità.
factious *agg.* fazioso.
factiousness *s.* faziosità.
factitious *agg.* fittizio.
factitiousness *s.* artificiosità.
factor *s.* **1.** fattore **2.** agente.
factory *s.* fabbrica.
factual *agg.* effettivo.
facultative *agg.* **1.** facoltativo **2.** casuale.
faculty *s.* facoltà.
fad *s.* **1.** mania **2.** capriccio.
faddist *s.* maniaco.
faddy *agg.* capriccioso.
fade *s.* (*radio*) variazione graduale.
to **fade** *vi.* **1.** appassire **2.** sbiadire **3.** svanire || *to — in* (*cine*) aprire in dissolvenza; *to — out*, (*cine*) chiudere in dissolvenza. ◆ to **fade** *vt.* **1.** far sbiadire **2.** far svanire.
fading *s.* **1.** appassimento **2.** scolorimento **3.** affievolimento **4.** dissolvenza.
to **fag** *vt.* affaticare. ◆ to **fag** *vi.* **1.** affaticarsi **2.** sfacchinare.

fag(g)ot *s.* fascina.
faience *s.* terracotta.
fail *s.* fallo.
to **fail** *vi.* **1.** fallire **2.** mancare, venir meno **3.** indebolirsi **4.** esser bocciato. ◆ to **fail** *vt.* **1.** mancare di **2.** bocciare **3.** abbandonare.
failing[1] *agg.* debole. ◆ **failing** *s.* **1.** debolezza **2.** mancanza **3.** fallimento.
failing[2] *prep.* in mancanza di.
failure *s.* **1.** fallimento **2.** incapacità **3.** mancanza **4.** indebolimento **5.** guasto || *to be a —*, essere un fallito.
fain *agg.* contento, disposto. ◆ **fain** *avv.* volentieri || *I would — stay*, preferirei restare.
faint *agg.* **1.** debole **2.** timido **3.** vago.
faint *s.* svenimento || *— -hearted*, codardo.
to **faint** *vi.* svenire.
faintness *s.* **1.** debolezza **2.** timidezza.
fair[1] *agg.* **1.** onesto **2.** biondo **3.** gentile **4.** bello **5.** sereno (*di tempo*) **6.** (*comm.*) libero || *— -play*, comportamento leale. ◆ **fair** *avv.* **1.** con onestà **2.** con precisione.
fair[2] *s.* fiera || *fun —*, Luna Park.
fairly *avv.* **1.** onestamente **2.** abbastanza.
fairness *s.* **1.** bellezza **2.** onestà **3.** color biondo **4.** bianchezza (*di carnagione*).
fairway *s.* canale navigabile.
fairy *agg.* **1.** fatato **2.** immaginario. ◆ **fairy** *s.* fata || *— -tale*, fiaba.
fairyland *s.* paese delle fate.
fairylike *agg.* simile a fata.
faith *s.* **1.** fede **2.** promessa || *— -healer*, guaritore.
faithful *agg.* **1.** fedele **2.** degno di fiducia.
faithfulness *s.* fedeltà.
faithless *agg.* **1.** senza fede **2.** sleale.
to **fake** *vt.* (*gergo*) falsificare.
fakir *s.* fachiro.
falcon *s.* falcone.
falconry *s.* falconeria.
fall *s.* **1.** caduta, cascata **2.** (*amer.*) autunno.
to **fall** (**fell**, **fallen**) *vi.* **1.** cadere **2.** abbassarsi **3.** capitare in sorte **4.** dividersi || *to — back*, ritirarsi; *to — behind*, restare indietro; *to — in with*, imbattersi; *to — short*,

essere insufficiente; to — away, deperire; to — down, far fiasco; to — due, scadere.

fallacious agg. fallace.

fallaciousness s. fallacia.

fallacy s. 1. fallacia 2. errore 3. sofisma.

fallen V. to fall.

fallibility s. fallibilità.

fallible agg. fallibile.

falling agg. cadente. ♦ **falling** s. caduta || — back, ripiegamento; — off, diminuzione; — short, insufficienza.

fall-out s. pioggia radioattiva.

fallow agg. incolto.

false agg. 1. falso 2. stonato 3. ingannevole || — bottom, doppio fondo.

falsehood s. falsità.

falsely avv. falsamente.

falseness s. falsità.

falsifiable agg. falsificabile.

falsification s. falsificazione.

falsifier s. falsificatore.

to **falsify** vt. 1. falsificare 2. smentire.

falsity s. falsità.

to **falter** vi. vacillare. ♦ to **falter** vt. balbettare.

fame s. fama.

famed agg. celebre.

familiar agg. familiare. ♦ **familiar** s. amico intimo || to be — with, esser pratico di.

familiarity s. familiarità.

familiarization s. familiarità.

to **familiarize** vt. familiarizzare.

family s. famiglia.

famine s. carestia.

to **famish** vt. far morire di fame. ♦ to **famish** vi. morire di fame.

famous agg. famoso.

fan[1] s. 1. ventaglio 2. ventilatore 3. pala (d'elica).

fan[2] s. (gergo) tifoso, ammiratore.

to **fan** vt. 1. sventolare 2. (agr.) vagliare.

fanatic agg. e s. fanatico.

fanatical agg. fanatico.

fanaticism s. fanatismo.

to **fanaticize** vt. rendere fanatico. ♦ to **fanaticize** vi. agire da fanatico.

fanciful agg. 1. fantasioso 2. fantastico.

fancifulness s. 1. fantasia 2. capriccio.

fancy agg. 1. immaginario 2. stra-

vagante 3. decorato. ♦ **fancy** s. 1. fantasia 2. capriccio 3. inclinazione || — ball, ballo in costume; — -dress, costume.

to **fancy** vt. 1. immaginare 2. ritenere.

fang s. 1. zanna 2. dente (velenoso).

fanning s. ventilazione.

fantastic(al) agg. 1. immaginario 2. bizzarro.

to **fantasticate** vt. e vi. fantasticare.

fantasy s. 1. fantasia 2. capriccio.

far agg. (farther, farthest) (further, furthest) lontano. ♦ **far** avv. 1. lontano 2. di gran lunga || — away, — off, lontano; as — as, fino a, per quanto; so —, finora; — -gone, a uno stadio avanzato (di malattie).

farce s. farsa.

farcical agg. farsesco.

farcicality s. qualità farsesca.

fare s. 1. tariffa 2. vitto 3. passeggero || bill of —, lista delle vivande.

to **fare** vi. 1. andare 2. riuscire 3. nutrirsi || to — badly, andar male.

farewell s. congedo. ♦ **farewell** inter. addio.

farfetched agg. remoto.

farinaceous agg. farinaceo.

farinose agg. farinoso.

farm s. fattoria || — -yard, aia.

to **farm** vt. coltivare. ♦ to **farm** vi. fare l'agricoltore.

farmer s. agricoltore.

farmhouse s. casa colonica.

farming s. agricoltura.

farmstead s. cascina.

farraginous agg. farraginoso.

farrier s. maniscalco.

farsighted agg. e s. presbite.

farther agg. (comp. di far) più lontano, ulteriore. ♦ **farther** avv. 1. (di) più 2. più lontano 3. inoltre.

farthermost agg. il più lontano.

farthest agg. (superl. di far) il più lontano, estremo. ♦ **farthest** avv. (il) più lontano.

farthing s. "farthing" (moneta inglese: un quarto di penny).

fascicle s. fascicolo.

to **fascinate** vt. affascinare.

fascinating agg. affascinante.

fascination s. fascino.

fascinator s. affascinatore.

fascism s. fascismo.

fascist agg. e s. fascista.

fashion s. 1. modo 2. abitudine 3. moda ||.— -*plate*, figurino; *a man of* —, un uomo di mondo.
to fashion vt. foggiare.
fashionable agg. 1. alla moda 2. elegante.
fast agg. 1. fermo 2. fedele 3. inalterabile 4. rapido 5. (*fig.*) dissoluto 6. in anticipo (*di orologio*). ♦ **fast** avv. 1. fermamente 2. fortemente 3. velocemente 4. in modo dissoluto.
fast s. digiuno.
to fast vi. digiunare.
to fasten vt. 1. attaccare 2. allacciare 3. chiudere 4. fissare. ♦ **to fasten** vi. 1. allacciarsi 2. chiudersi 3. fissarsi.
fastener s. 1. fermaglio 2. legaccio, chiusura || *snap* —, automatico.
fastening s. 1. legatura 2. gancio, chiavistello.
faster s. digiunatore.
fastidious agg. schizzinoso.
fastidiousness s. schizzinosità.
fastness s. 1. velocità 2. fermezza 3. solidità 4. dissolutezza.
fat agg. 1. grasso 2. (*fig.*) proficuo. ♦ **fat** s. grasso || — -*head*, zuccone.
to fat V. *to fatten*.
fatal agg. fatale.
fatalism s. fatalismo.
fatalist s. fatalista.
fatalistic agg. fatalistico.
fatality s. 1. fatalità 2. fatalismo.
fatally avv. 1. in modo fatale 2. fatalmente.
fate s. fato.
father s. padre || — -*in-law*, suocero.
fatherhood s. paternità.
fatherland s. madrepatria.
fatherless agg. senza padre.
fatherlike agg. paterno. ♦ **fatherlike** avv. paternamente.
fatherly agg. e avv. V. *fatherlike*.
fathom s. (*mar.*) braccio (*misura di profondità*).
to fathom vt. scandagliare.
fathomless agg. 1. incommensurabile 2. incomprensibile.
fatidic(al) agg. fatidico.
fatigue s. fatica.
to fatigue vt. affaticare. ♦ **to fatigue** vi. affaticarsi.
fatness s. grassezza.
to fatten vt. ingrassare. ♦ **to fatten** vi. ingrassarsi.

fattener s. ingrassatore.
fattening s. ingrassamento.
fattiness s. grassezza.
fatty agg. grasso.
fatuity s. fatuità.
fatuous agg. fatuo.
fault s. 1. fallo 2. colpa 3. difetto || — -*finder*, criticone.
faultiness s. imperfezione.
faultless agg. 1. perfetto 2. irreprensibile.
faulty agg. difettoso.
faun s. fauno.
favour s. favore.
to favour vt. 1. favorire 2. sostenere 3. (*fam.*) assomigliare a.
favourable agg. favorevole.
favourite agg. e s. favorito.
favouritism s. favoritismo.
fawn s. cerbiatto.
to fawn vt. fare le feste || *to* — *on*, adulare.
fawner s. adulatore.
fawning s. servilismo.
fear s. paura, timore.
to fear vt. e vi. temere, aver paura.
fearful agg. 1. terribile 2. timoroso.
fearfulness s. 1. aspetto terribile 2. timore.
fearless agg. intrepido.
feasibility s. fattibilità.
feasible agg. fattibile.
feast s. 1. festa 2. banchetto.
to feast vt. 1. rallegrare 2. festeggiare. ♦ **to feast** vi. banchettare.
feaster s. convitato.
feat s. impresa, prodezza.
feather s. penna, piuma.
to feather vt. 1. coprire di penne, piume 2. (*mar.*) spalare.
feathered agg. 1. pennuto 2. (*fig.*) alato.
feathering s. piumaggio.
featherless agg. implume.
feature s. 1. lineamento 2. (*cine*) attrazione 3. caratteristica || — *film*, parte principale di un film.
to feature vt. 1. caratterizzare 2. (*teat.*) dare una parte importante a.
featureless agg. senza caratteristiche.
febrifuge s. febbrifugo.
febrile agg. febbrile.
February s. febbraio.
fecal agg. fecale.
fecund agg. fecondo.
to fecundate vt. fecondare.
fecundation s. fecondazione.

fecundity s. fecondità.
fed V. to feed.
federacy s. federazione.
federal agg. federale.
federalism s. federalismo.
federate agg. confederato.
to **federate** vt. confederare. ♦ to
federate vi. confederarsi.
federation s. (con)federazione.
federative agg. federativo.
fee s. 1. onorario 2. tassa 3. (giur.)
proprietà ereditaria.
feeble agg. debole.
feebleness s. debolezza.
feed s. 1. alimentazione 2. ascolo.
to **feed** (fed, fed) vt. 1. nutrire
2. pascere 3. rifornire || to be fed
up, essere stufo. ♦ to **feed** (fed,
fed) vi. nutrirsi || to — up, in-
grassare.
feeder s. 1. ciò che, chi nutre 2.
cavo di alimentazione 3. affluente
4. serbatoio.
feeding s. alimentazione.
feel s. tatto.
to **feel** (felt, felt) vt. 1. sentire
(col tatto o col sentimento) 2. tastare, sondare. ♦ to **feel** (felt,
felt) vi. 1. sentirsi 2. andare a tastoni.
feeling agg. sensibile. ♦ **feeling** s.
1. sentimento 2. sensibilità 3. sensazione.
feet V. foot.
to **feign** vt. 1. inventare 2. falsificare. ♦ to **feign** vi. fingersi.
feignedly avv. simulatamente.
feigner s. simulatore.
feint s. 1. finta 2. simulazione.
to **feint** vi. fare una finta.
feldspar s. feldspato.
to **felicitate** vt. felicitarsi con || to
— so. on sthg., felicitarsi con qu.
di qc.
felicitation s. felicitazione.
felicitous agg. appropriato.
feline agg. e s. felino.
fell[1] V. to fall.
fell[2] agg. 1. crudele 2. funesto.
to **fell** vt. abbattere.
felling s. taglio (di un bosco).
fellow s. 1. individuo 2. compagno,
collega || — -citizen, concittadi-
no; — -creature, simile; a good
—, un buon diavolo.
fellowship s. 1. amicizia 2. associazione.
felon agg. e s. criminale.
felony s. crimine, delitto.

felt[1] V. to feel.
felt[2] s. feltro.
to **felt** vt. feltrare.
felucca s. feluca.
female agg. 1. femminile 2. (mecc.)
femmina. ♦ **female** s. femmina.
feminine agg. e s. femminile.
femininity s. femminilità.
feminism s. femminismo.
femur s. femore.
fen s. palude || — -berry, mirtillo;
— -fire, fuoco fatuo.
fence s. 1. recinto 2. scherma 3.
(fam.) ricettatore.
to **fence** vt. cintare. ♦ to **fence** vi.
tirar di scherma.
fencer s. schermidore.
fencing s. 1, cinta 2. scherma.
fender s. 1. riparo 2. paraurti 3.
(mar.) parabordo.
fennel s. finocchio.
feracity s. feracità.
feral[1] agg. ferale, funesto.
feral[2] agg. ferino.
ferial agg. feriale.
ferine agg. ferino.
ferment s. fermento.
to **ferment** vi. 1. fermentare 2. agitarsi. ♦ to **ferment** vt. 1. far fermentare 2. eccitare.
fermentation s. 1. fermentazione 2.
fermento.
fermentative agg. fermentativo.
fern s. felce.
ferocious agg. feroce.
ferocity s. ferocia.
ferreous agg. 1. ferroso 2. ferreo.
ferret[1] s. furetto.
ferret[2] s. nastro, fettuccia.
ferro-concrete s. cemento armato.
ferrous agg. ferroso.
ferruginous agg. ferruginoso.
ferry s. traghetto.
to **ferry** vt. e vi. traghettare.
ferryman s. traghettatore.
fertile agg. fertile.
fertility s. fertilità.
fertilization s. fertilizzazione.
to **fertilize** vt. 1. fertilizzare 2. fecondare.
fertilizer s. fertilizzante.
fervency s. fervore.
fervent, fervid agg. ardente.
fervour s. ardore.
festal agg. festivo.
fester s. suppurazione, piaga.
to **fester** vi. suppurare (di ferita).
festival s. 1. festa 2. festival.
festive agg. 1. festivo 2. festoso.

festivity s. festività. ♦ **festivities** s. pl. festeggiamenti.

festoon s. festone.

to fetch vt. 1. andare a prendere 2. tirare 3. fruttare, rendere || to — back, riportare.

fetid agg. fetido.

fetish s. feticcio.

fetishism s. feticismo.'

fetishist s. feticista.

fetter s. ceppo, catena.

to fetter vt. incatenare.

fettle s. condizione || in fine —, in forma.

feud[1] s. ostilità.

feud[2] s. feudo.

feudal agg. feudale.

feudalism s. feudalesimo.

feudality s. 1. feudalesimo 2. feudo.

feudatory agg. e s. feudatario.

fever s. febbre || to be in a —, avere la febbre.

feverish agg. 1. febbricitante 2. febbrile.

few agg. e pron. pochi || a —, alcuni; quite a —, un numero considerevole; a good —, parecchi.

fewness s. scarsità, esiguità.

fiancé s. fidanzato.

fib s. fandonia.

to fib vi. dire fandonie.

fibre s. fibra.

fibroid, fibrous agg. fibroso.

fickle agg. incostante.

fickleness s. incostanza.

fictile agg. fittile.

fiction s. 1. narrativa 2. finzione.

fictional agg. immaginario.

fictitious agg. fittizio.

fiddle s. violino || fit as a —, in ottima salute.

to fiddle vi. 1. suonare il violino 2. gingillarsi.

fiddler s. violinista.

fiddlestick s. archetto. ♦ **fiddle-sticks** s. pl. sciocchezze.

fidelity s. fedeltà.

to fidget vt. agitare. ♦ **to fidget** vi. agitarsi.

fidgety agg. irrequieto.

fiduciary agg. e s. fiduciario.

field s. campo || —-glass, binocolo; — -day, giorno di esercitazioni; — -officer, ufficiale superiore.

fiend s. demonio.

fiendish agg. diabolico.

fierce agg. 1. fiero 2. selvaggio 3. ardente.

fierceness s. 1. ferocia 2. ardore.

fiery agg. 1. di fuoco 2. focoso 3. infiammabile.

fife s. piffero.

fifteen agg. e s. quindici.

fifteenth agg. e s. quindicesimo.

fifth agg. e s. quinto.

fiftieth agg. e s. cinquantesimo.

fifty agg. e s. cinquanta || — - —, a metà.

fig[1] s. fico.

fig[2] s. tenuta, vestiario.

fight s. 1. lotta 2. spirito combattivo.

to fight (fought, fought) vt. e vi. combattere || to — down, vincere; to — off, respingere; to — shy of, tenersi alla larga da.

fighter s. 1. combattente 2. (aer.) caccia.

fighting s. combattimento, rissa.

figuration s. figurazione.

figurative agg. 1. figurativo 2. figurato.

figure s. 1. figura, forma 2. cifra 3. diagramma.

to figure vt. raffigurare. ♦ **to figure** vi. 1. immaginarsi 2. passare per.

figurehead s. 1. prestanome 2. (mar.) polena.

filament s. filamento.

filamentary, filamentous agg. filamentoso.

filcher s. ladruncolo.

file[1] s. lima.

file[2] s. 1. schedario, archivio 2. fila 3. raccolta.

to file[1] vt. limare.

to file[2] vt. 1. archiviare 2. ordinare. ♦ **to file** vi. marciare in fila.

filial agg. filiale.

filiation s. filiazione.

filibuster s. filibustiere.

filigree s. filigrana.

filing[1] s. limatura.

filing[2] s. 1. archiviazione 2. sfilata.

fill s. sazietà.

to fill vt. 1. riempire 2. occupare 3. otturare (di denti) || to — in, to — up, riempire, compilare. ♦ **to fill** vi. riempirsi.

fillet s. 1. nastro 2. (cuc.) filetto.

filling s. 1. riempitura 2. otturazione 3. (cuc.) ripieno || — station, stazione di rifornimento.

fillip s. 1. schiocco (delle dita) 2. stimolo.

film s. 1. pellicola 2. velo 3. membrana.

to film vt. 1. coprire con una pellicola 2. filmare. ♦ to **film** vi. 1. coprirsi con una pellicola 2. girare un film.

filmy agg. velato.

filter s. filtro.

to **filter** vt. e vi. filtrare.

filth s. sozzura.

filthily avv. in modo sudicio.

filthiness s. 1. sozzura 2. corruzione morale.

filthy agg. 1. sozzo 2. corrotto.

filtration s. filtrazione.

fin s. 1. pinna 2. (mecc.) aletta.

final agg. e s. finale.

finalist s. finalista.

finality s. 1. finalità 2. carattere definitivo.

finally avv. alla fine.

finance s. finanza.

to **finance** vt. finanziare.

financial agg. finanziario.

financier s. 1. finanziere 2. finanziatore.

financing s. finanziamento.

finch s. fringuello.

find s. scoperta, ritrovamento.

to **find (found, found)** vt. 1. trovare 2. provvedere 3. ritenere || to — out, scoprire.

finding s. 1. scoperta 2. sentenza.

fine[1] agg. 1. bello 2. fine. ♦ **fine** avv. bene.

fine[2] s. multa.

to **fine**[1] vt. raffinare. ♦ to **fine** vi. raffinarsi.

to **fine**[2] vt. multare.

finely avv. 1. bene 2. finemente.

finger s. dito || — -print, impronta digitale; — -tip, punta delle dita; — -post, cartello segnavia.

to **finger** vt. 1. toccare con le dita 2. rubare || to be light-fingered (fig.), avere le mani lunghe.

finish s. 1. fine 2. finezza 3. finitura.

to **finish** vt. e vi. finire.

finished agg. (fig.) perfetto.

finishing agg. ultimo, conclusivo. ♦ **finishing** s. (ri)finitura.

finite agg. limitato.

Finn s. finlandese.

Finnic, Finnish agg. finlandese.

fir (-tree) s. abete || — -wood, abetaia.

fire s. 1. fuoco 2. incendio || on —, in fiamme; — -guard, parafuoco; — -plug, bocca da incendio; — station, caserma dei pompieri; — -works, fuochi d'artificio.

to **fire** vt. 1. dar fuoco 2. far fuoco

3. (fig.) infiammare. ♦ to **fire** vi. 1. prender fuoco 2. (fig.) infiammarsi.

firedamp s. grisù.

fire escape s. 1. scala di sicurezza 2. scala dei pompieri.

firefly s. lucciola.

fireman s. pompiere.

fireplace s. caminetto.

fireproof agg. incombustibile.

fireside s. angolo del focolare.

firewood s. legna da ardere.

firing s. 1. accensione 2. sparo 3. alimentazione (di un fuoco) || — squad, plotone d'esecuzione.

firm[1] agg. 1. fisso 2. solido 3. deciso.

firm[2] s. azienda, ditta.

firmament s. firmamento.

firmly avv. 1. fermamente 2. solidamente.

firmness s. 1. fermezza 2. stabilità.

first agg. primo || — -aid, pronto soccorso; — -born, primogenito; — -class, di prima qualità; — -name, nome di battesimo. ♦ **first** avv. 1. prima di tutto 2. per la prima volta || at —, sulle prime. ♦ **first** s. 1. primo 2. principio.

firth s. fiordo.

fiscal agg. fiscale.

fish s. pesce || — -hook, amo.

to **fish** vi. 1. pescare 2. cercare. ♦ to **fish** vt. pescare.

fisher s. pescatore.

fisherman s. pescatore.

fishery s. pesca.

fishing s. pesca || — -boat, peschereccio; — -line, lenza.

fishmonger s. pescivendolo.

fishy agg. 1. di pesce 2. pescoso 3. (fig.) equivoco.

fission s. fissione.

fist s. pugno.

fit[1] agg. 1. adatto 2. pronto.

fit[2] s. 1. giusta misura 2. attacco, accesso (di febbre, ira ecc.).

to **fit** vt. 1. adattare 2. andar bene a 3. provare || to — out, equipaggiare.

fitful agg. 1. irregolare 2. spasmodico.

fitfulness s. irregolarità.

fitness s. convenienza.

fitter s. 1. aggiustatore 2. montatore.

fitting agg. adatto, conveniente. ♦ **fitting** s. 1. adattamento, prova 2. equipaggiamento. ♦ **fittings**

s. pl. **1.** accessori **2.** arredamento (*sing.*).

five *agg.* e *s.* cinque.

fix *s.* **1.** difficoltà **2.** (*mar.*) punto.

to fix *vt.* fissare || *to — up*, sistemare, riparare. ♦ **to fix** *vi.* stabilirsi.

fixation *s.* fissazione.

fixed *agg.* **1.** fisso **2.** stabilito.

fixer *s.* **1.** montatore **2.** fissatore.

fixing *s.* **1.** collocamento **2.** messa in opera **3.** fissaggio.

fixity *s.* **1.** stabilità **2.** fissità.

fizz *s.* **1.** effervescenza **2.** bevanda effervescente.

to fizz *vi.* frizzare.

fjord *s.* fiordo.

flabbiness *s.* **1.** mollezza **2.** fiacchezza (*di carattere ecc.*).

flabby *agg.* **1.** floscio **2.** fiacco.

flaccid *agg.* flaccido.

flaccidness *s.* flaccidezza.

flag¹ *s.* bandiera || *— -ship*, nave ammiraglia.

flag² *s.* lastra di pietra (*per pavimentazione*).

to flag¹ *vt.* **1.** imbandierare **2.** pavesare. ♦ **to flag** *vi.* **1.** pendere **2.** avvizzire.

to flag² *vt.* lastricare.

to flagellate *vt.* flagellare.

flagellation *s.* flagellazione.

flagellator *s.* flagellatore.

flagrancy *s.* flagranza.

flagrant *agg.* flagrante.

flagstaff *s.* asta di bandiera.

flair *s.* fiuto, intuizione.

flake *s.* **1.** fiocco (*di neve, lana ecc.*) **2.** favilla **3.** lamina **4.** scaglia.

to flake *vt.* **1.** sfaldare **2.** squamare **3.** coprire di fiocchi. ♦ **to flake** *vi.* **1.** sfaldarsi **2.** squamarsi **3.** cadere in fiocchi.

flaky *agg.* **1.** a falde **2.** a lamine, a scaglie.

flame *s.* fiamma || *— -thrower*, lanciafiamme.

to flame *vi.* fiammeggiare.

flaming *agg.* ardente.

flange *s.* orlo, frangia.

flank *s.* fianco.

to flank *vt.* **1.** fiancheggiare **2.** (*mil.*) attaccare il fianco di.

flannel *s.* flanella. ♦ **flannels** *s. pl.* calzoni di flanella.

flap *s.* **1.** lembo, falda **2.** colpo, agitazione **3.** linguetta **4.** (*aer.*) alettone.

flare *s.* **1.** fiammata improvvisa **2.**

chiarore.

to flare *vi.* **1.** brillare (*di luce incerta*) **2.** agitarsi **3.** divampare.

flash *s.* **1.** lampo **2.** chiusa || *-back*, scena retrospettiva; *— -light*, lampo al magnesio.

to flash *vt.* **1.** proiettare **2.** diffondere. ♦ **to flash** *vi.* **1.** lampeggiare **2.** muoversi rapidamente.

flashing *agg.* risplendente. ♦ **flashing** *s.* splendore, scintillio.

flask *s.* fiasca.

flat¹ *agg.* **1.** piatto, piano **2.** disteso **3.** deciso **4.** sgonfio (*di pneumatico*).

flat² *s.* **1.** superficie piana **2.** pianura **3.** bassofondo **4.** chiatta **5.** appartamento **6.** (*mus.*) bemolle || *— -iron*, ferro da stiro.

flatly *avv.* **1.** pianamente **2.** scialbamente **3.** recisamente.

flatness *s.* **1.** piattezza **2.** decisione.

to flatten *vt.* **1.** appiattire **2.** smorzare. ♦ **to flatten** *vi.* **1.** appiattirsi **2.** indebolirsi.

to flatter *vt.* **1.** adulare **2.** illudere.

flatterer *s.* adulatore.

flattery *s.* adulazione.

flatulence, flatulency *s.* **1.** flatulenza **2.** vanità.

flatus *s.* flatulenza.

to flaunt *vt.* **1.** sventolare **2.** ostentare.

flavour *s.* gusto, aroma.

to flavour *vt.* aromatizzare, dare gusto a.

flavoured *agg.* **1.** profumato **2.** saporito.

flavouring *s.* **1.** aroma **2.** condimento.

flavourless *agg.* insipido.

flaw *s.* **1.** screpolatura **2.** falla, pecca.

flawless *agg.* perfetto.

flax *s.* lino.

flaxen *agg.* **1.** di lino **2.** biondo.

to flay *vt.* **1.** scorticare **2.** criticare aspramente.

flea *s.* pulce || *— -bite* (*fig.*), inezia.

fleck *s.* **1.** macchia **2.** scaglia.

to flee (**fled, fled**) *vt.* **1.** abbandonare **2.** evitare, schivare. ♦ **to flee** (**fled, fled**) *vi.* **1.** fuggire **2.** svanire.

fleece *s.* vello.

fleecy *agg.* lanoso.

to fleer *vt.* e *vi.* far beffe (a).

fleet *s.* flotta.

fleeting *agg.* fugace.

Flemish *agg.* fiammingo.

flesh *s.* carne || *to lose* —, dimagrire; *to put on* —, ingrassare.

fleshiness *s.* **1.** carnosità **2.** corpulenza.

fleshless *agg.* scarno.

fleshly *agg.* carnale, sensuale.

flew V. *to fly.*

to **flex** *vt.* flettere, piegare. ♦ to **flex** *vi.* flettersi.

flexibility *s.* **1.** flessibilità **2.** docilità.

flexible *agg.* **1.** flessibile **2.** docile.

flexion *s.* **1.** flessione **2.** curva.

flexuosity *s.* flessuosità.

flexuous *agg.* flessuoso.

flicker *s.* tremolio, bagliore.

to **flicker** *vi.* **1.** tremolare **2.** guizzare. ♦ to **flicker** *vt.* far tremolare.

flight[1] *s.* **1.** volo **2.** stormo **3.** rampa (*di scale*).

flight[2] *s.* fuga.

flimsiness *s.* leggerezza, frivolezza.

flimsy *agg.* leggero, sottile.

to **flinch** *vi.* indietreggiare, ritirarsi.

fling *s.* **1.** getto **2.** beffa **3.** tentativo.

to **fling (flung, flung)** *vt.* gettare. || *to* — *open,* spalancare. ♦ to **fling (flung, flung)** *vi.* gettarsi.

flint *s.* selce, pietra focaia.

to **flip** *vt.* **1.** far schioccare **2.** sbattere.

flippancy *s.* leggerezza.

flippant *agg.* leggero.

flipper *s.* pinna.

flirt *s.* **1.** movimento rapido **2.** amoreggiamento.

to **flirt** *vt.* muovere rapidamente. ♦ to **flirt** *vi.* amoreggiare.

flirtation *s.* amoreggiamento.

to **flit** *vi.* **1.** volare **2.** scorrere.

float *s.* galleggiante.

to **float** *vt.* **1.** trasportare **2.** inondare **3.** (*comm.*) varare (*un progetto ecc.*). ♦ to **float** *vi.* **1.** galleggiare **2.** spandersi.

floatage *s.* **1.** galleggiamento **2.** relitto.

floatation *s.* (*comm.*) varo.

floater *s.* galleggiante.

floating *agg.* **1.** galleggiante **2.** oscillante, fluttuante.

flock *s.* **1.** bioccolo **2.** gregge **3.** cascame.

to **flock** *vi.* affollarsi.

floe *s.* banchisa.

to **flog** *vt.* fustigare || *to* — *a dead horse,* fare una fatica inutile.

flogger *s.* fustigatore.

flood *s.* inondazione, diluvio.

to **flood** *vt.* inondare. ♦ to **flood** *vi.* straripare.

flooding *s.* **1.** inondazione **2.** emorragia.

floodlight *s.* illuminazione con riflettore.

flood tide *s.* flusso della marea.

floor *s.* **1.** pavimento **2.** piano || —-*lamp,* lampada a stelo.

to **floor** *vt.* pavimentare.

flooring *s.* impiantito.

flop *s.* **1.** tonfo **2.** insuccesso.

floral *agg.* floreale.

floriculture *s.* floricultura.

floriculturist *s.* floricultore.

florid *agg.* **1.** florido **2.** fiorito (*di stile*).

floridity *s.* floridezza.

florin *s.* fiorino.

florist *s.* fiorista.

flotilla *s.* flottiglia.

to **flounce** *vi.* agitarsi || *to* — *out,* andarsene furibondo.

flour *s.* farina || *potato-* —, fecola.

to **flour** *vt.* **1.** infarinare **2.** macinare.

flourish *s.* **1.** ornamento **2.** squillo di tromba.

to **flourish** *vi.* **1.** prosperare **2.** essere attivo.

flourishing *agg.* **1.** fiorente **2.** pomposo.

floury *agg.* **1.** farinoso **2.** infarinato.

flow *s.* corrente, flusso.

to **flow** *vi.* **1.** scorrere **2.** derivare da. ♦ to **flow** *vt.* inondare.

flower *s.* fiore || —-*bed,* aiuola; —-*bud,* bocciuolo.

to **flower** *vi.* fiorire. ♦ to **flower** *vt.* infiorare.

flowering *agg.* in fiore. ♦ **flowering** *s.* fioritura.

flowerless *agg.* senza fiori.

flowery *agg.* fiorito.

flowing *agg.* **1.** fluente **2.** fluido.

flown V. *to fly.*

flu *s.* influenza.

to **fluctuate** *vi.* **1.** fluttuare **2.** ondeggiare.

fluctuation *s.* oscillazione.

flue *s.* condotto per l'aria.

fluency *s.* **1.** fluidità **2.** scioltezza.

fluent *agg.* **1.** fluente **2.** dalla parola facile.

fluently *avv.* **1.** fluentemente **2.** speditamente.

fluff *s.* peluria.

fluffy *agg.* **1.** soffice, vaporoso **2.** coperto di peluria.
fluid *agg.* e *s.* fluido.
fluidity *s.* fluidità.
flung V. *to fling.*
fluorescence *s.* fluorescenza.
fluorescent *agg.* fluorescente.
fluoride *s.* fluoruro.
fluorine *s.* fluoro.
flurry *s.* **1.** ventata **2.** agitazione.
to flurry *vt.* agitare.
flush *agg.* **1.** abbondante **2.** pieno di vita **3.** a pari livello **4.** ben fornito. ◆ **flush** *s.* **1.** flusso **2.** vampata **3.** vigore.
to flush *vt.* **1.** lavare **2.** far scorrere **3.** rianimare. ◆ **to flush** *vi.* **1.** scorrere **2.** arrossire.
flute *s.* **1.** flauto **2.** increspatura.
fluted *agg.* **1.** flautato **2.** increspato.
flutter *s.* **1.** battito, movimento rapido **2.** eccitazione.
to flutter *vt.* agitare. ◆ **to flutter** *vi.* **1.** agitarsi **2.** battere le ali.
fluttering *agg.* **1.** svolazzante **2.** palpitante. ◆ **fluttering** *s.* **1.** svolazzamento **2.** palpitazione.
fluxion *s.* flusso.
fly¹ *s.* **1.** volo **2.** calesse **3.** (*mecc.*) volano.
fly² *s.* mosca.
to fly (flew, flown) *vi.* volare. ◆ **to fly (flew, flown)** *vt.* **1.** far volare **2.** sventolare || *to — about*, svolazzare; *to — away*, fuggire; *to off* (*aer.*), decollare.
flying *agg.* **1.** rapido **2.** sventolante || *—boat*, idrovolante.
flypaper *s.* carta moschicida.
foam *s.* schiuma || *— rubber* gommapiuma.
to foam *vi.* spumeggiare.
foamy *agg.* spumeggiante.
focal *agg.* focale.
focus *s.* **1.** fuoco **2.** focolaio.
to focus *vt.* mettere a fuoco.
fodder *s.* foraggio.
to fodder *vt.* foraggiare.
foe *s.* nemico.
foetus *s.* feto.
fog *s.* nebbia.
foggy *agg.* nebbioso (*anche fig.*).
foible *s.* debolezza.
foil¹ *s.* **1.** fioretto **2.** traccia.
foil² *s.* lamina.
fold¹ *s.* ovile.
fold² *s.* **1.** piega **2.** spira.
to fold¹ *vt.* **1.** piegare **2.** avvolgere **3.** abbracciare. ◆ **to fold** *vi.* piegarsi.
to fold² *vt.* chiudere nell'ovile.
folder *s.* **1.** volantino **2.** cartelletta.
folding *agg.* pieghevole. ◆ **folding** *s.* **1.** piega, piegatura **2.** avvolgimento **3.** abbraccio.
foliage *s.* fogliame.
folio *s.* (*tip.*) fo(g)lio.
folk *s.* gente, popolo.
folklore *s.* folclore.
folkloristic *agg.* folcloristico.
to follow *vt.* e *vi.* seguire.
follower *s.* seguace.
following *agg.* seguente. ◆ **following** *s.* seguito.
folly *s.* follia.
to foment *vt.* fomentare.
fomentation *s.* fomentazione.
fomenter *s.* fomentatore.
fond *agg.* **1.** amante **2.** affettuoso.
to fondle *vt.* vezzeggiare.
fondly *avv.* **1.** amorevolmente **2.** ingenuamente.
fondness *s.* tenerezza, amore.
font *s.* **1.** fonte battesimale **2.** acquasantiera.
food *s.* cibo.
foodstuff *s.* alimenti (*pl.*).
fool *s.* **1.** sciocco **2.** buffone || *to make a — of*, beffarsi di.
to fool *vt.* ingannare. ◆ **to fool** *vi.* fare lo sciocco || *to — away*, sperperare.
foolery *s.* follia.
foolhardiness *s.* folle temerarietà.
foolhardy *agg.* temerario.
foolish *agg.* sciocco.
foolishness *s.* sciocchezza.
foot *s.* (*pl.* feet) **1.** piede **2.** zampa || *on —*, a piedi.
football *s.* pallone.
footballer *s.* calciatore.
foot-bath *s.* pediluvio.
footboard *s.* predellino.
footbridge *s.* cavalcavia.
footfall *s.* passo.
footing *s.* punto d'appoggio.
footlights *s. pl.* luci della ribalta.
footman *s.* domestico.
footmark *s.* orma.
footnote *s.* poscritto.
footpath *s.* sentiero.
footprint, footstep *s.* orma.
footstool *s.* sgabello.
footway *s.* passaggio pedonale.
fop *s.* damerino.
foppery *s.* fatuità.
foppish *agg.* fatuo.
for¹ *prep.* per || *— all that*, ciò no-

nostante; *as* —, in quanto a.

for[2] *cong.* poiché.

forage *s.* foraggio.

foray *s.* incursione, saccheggio.

forbade V. *to forbid.*

to forbear (forbore, forborne) *vi.* 1. astenersi 2. essere paziente.

forbearance *s.* 1. astensione 2. pazienza.

forbearing *agg.* paziente.

to forbid (forbade, forbidden) *vt.* proibire, impedire.

forbidding *agg.* 1. severo 2. ripugnante.

forbore V. *to forbear.*

forborne V. *to forbear.*

force *s.* forza. ♦ **forces** *s. pl.* truppe || *the Armed Forces*, le Forze Armate.

to force *vt.* 1. forzare 2. costringere || *to* — *back*, respingere; *to* — *in*, sfondare; *to* — *on*, far avanzare.

forceful *agg.* forte.

forceps *s.* 1. forcipe 2. pinza.

forcible *agg.* 1. violento 2. potente.

ford *s.* guado.

to ford *vt.* guadare.

fordable *agg.* guadabile.

fore *agg.* anteriore. ♦ **fore** *s.* prua.

forearm *s.* avambraccio.

to forearm *vt.* premunire.

to forebode *vt.* presagire (*un male*).

foreboding *s.* presagio.

forecast *s.* previsione.

to forecast (forecast, forecast) *vt.* prevedere.

forecastle *s.* castello di prua.

forefather *s.* antenato.

forefinger *s.* indice.

foreground *s.* primo piano.

forehead *s.* fronte.

foreign *agg.* 1. straniero 2. estraneo || — *Office*, Ministero degli Esteri.

foreigner *s.* straniero.

forelock *s.* ciuffo.

foreman *s.* caposquadra, capereparto.

foremast *s.* albero di trinchetto.

forename *s.* nome di battesimo.

forensic(al) *agg.* forense.

to forerun (foreran, forerun) *vt.* precorrere.

forerunner *s.* 1. precursore 2. messaggero.

foresail *s.* vela di trinchetto.

to foresee (foresaw, foreseen) *vt.* prevedere.

foreseeable *agg.* prevedibile.

foreseeing *s.* previsione.

foreseen V. *to foresee.*

to foreshadow *vt.* adombrare.

foreshortening *s.* scorcio.

foresight *s.* 1. previsione 2. previdenza.

forest *s.* foresta.

forestal *agg.* forestale.

to forestall *vt.* 1. prevenire 2. accaparrare.

forestalling *s.* 1. anticipazione 2. accaparramento.

forester *s.* 1. guardia forestale 2. abitante di foreste.

forestry *s.* 1. foresta 2. silvicultura.

foretaste *s.* pregustazione.

to foretaste *vt.* pregustare.

to foretell (foretold, foretold) *vt.* predire.

forethought *agg.* premeditato. ♦ **forethought** *s.* 1. premeditazione 2. previdenza.

foretold V. *to foretell.*

forever *avv.* per sempre.

to forewarn *vt.* avvertire.

foreword *s.* prefazione.

forfeit *s.* 1. perdita 2. ammenda 3. penitenza.

forfeiture *s.* 1. multa 2. confisca.

to forgather *vi.* riunirsi, associarsi.

forgave V. *to forgive.*

forge *s.* fucina.

to forge *vt.* 1. foggiare, fabbricare 2. contraffare.

forger *s.* 1. fabbro 2. falsario.

forgery *s.* contraffazione.

to forget (forgot, forgotten) *vt.* e *vi.* dimenticare, dimenticarsi.

forgetful *agg.* 1. immemore 2. negligente.

forgetfulness *s.* 1. oblio 2. negligenza.

forget-me-not *s.* non-ti-scordar-di--me.

to forgive (forgave, forgiven) *vt.* perdonare.

forgiveness *s.* perdono.

forgot V. *to forget.*

forgotten V. *to forget.*

fork *s.* 1. forchetta 2. forca 3. forcella 4. biforcazione.

to fork *vi.* biforcarsi || *to* — *out*, (*gergo*) pagare. ♦ **to fork** *vt.* biforcare.

forked *agg.* biforcuto.

forlorn *agg.* abbandonato.

form *s.* 1. forma 2. modulo 3. banco.

to **form** *vt.* formare. ♦ to **form** *vi.* formarsi.

formal *agg.* formale || — *dress*, abito da cerimonia.

formalism *s.* formalismo.

formalist *s.* formalista.

formality *s.* formalità.

to **formalize** *vt.* **1.** formare **2.** formalizzare.

format *s.* formato.

formation *s.* formazione.

formative *agg.* formativo.

forme *s.* (*tip.*) forma di stampa.

former[1] *agg. e pron.* precedente, il primo (*fra due*).

former[2] *s.* **1.** artefice **2.** stampo.

formerly *avv.* precedentemente.

formic *agg.* formico.

formidable *agg.* **1.** formidabile **2.** spaventoso.

formless *agg.* informe.

formulary *s.* formulario.

to **formulate** *vt.* formulare.

formulation *s.* formulazione.

to **forsake (forsook, forsaken)** *vt.* abbandonare.

forsaking *s.* abbandono.

forsook V. *to forsake.*

to **forswear (forswore, forsworn)** *vt.* **1.** abiurare **2.** spergiurare.

fort *s.* (*mil.*) fortezza.

forth *avv.* **1.** avanti **2.** fuori || *and so* —, e così via.

forthcoming *agg.* prossimo.

fortieth *agg. e s.* quarantesimo.

fortification *s.* fortificazione.

to **fortify** *vt.* fortificare.

fortitude *s.* forza d'animo.

fortnight *s.* due settimane.

fortnightly *agg.* quindicinale. ♦ **fortnightly** *avv.* ogni due settimane.

fortress *s.* (*mil.*) fortezza.

fortuitous *agg.* fortuito.

fortunate *agg.* **1.** fortunato **2.** propizio.

fortune *s.* **1.** sorte: *to tell fortunes*, predire la sorte **2.** fortuna.

fortune-teller *s.* indovino.

forty *agg. e s.* quaranta.

forward *agg.* **1.** avanzato **2.** precoce **3.** pronto.

to **forward** *vt.* **1.** promuovere **2.** spedire.

forwarder *s.* spedizioniere.

forwarding *s.* spedizione.

forward(s) *avv.* avanti, in avanti.

fossil *agg. e s.* fossile.

fossilization *s.* fossilizzazione.

to **fossilize** *vt.* fossilizzare. ♦ to **fossilize** *vi.* fossilizzarsi.

to **foster** *vt.* **1.** favorire **2.** allevare, nutrire.

fought V. *to fight.*

foul *agg.* **1.** sporco **2.** tempestoso.

foulmouthed *agg.* sboccato.

to **foul** *vt.* **1.** sporcare **2.** urtare. ♦ to **foul** *vi.* **1.** sporcarsi **2.** urtarsi.

found V. *to find.*

to **found**[1] *vt.* fondare.

to **found**[2] *vt.* fondere.

foundation *s.* **1.** fondazione **2.** fondamenta **3.** fondamento.

founder[1] *s.* fondatore.

founder[2] *s.* fonditore.

to **founder** *vi.* crollare. ♦ to **founder** *vt.* affondare.

foundling *s.* trovatello || — *-hospital*, brefotrofio.

foundry *s.* fonderia.

fountain *s.* **1.** fontana **2.** sorgente || — *-pen*, penna stilografica.

four *agg. e s.* quattro || — *-handed*, quadrumane; — *-footed*, quadrupede.

fourscore *agg.* ottanta.

fourteen *agg. e s.* quattordici.

fourteenth *agg. e s.* quattordicesimo.

fourth *agg. e s.* quarto.

fowl *s.* pollo, pollame.

fox *s.* volpe: — *-hunt*, caccia alla volpe.

foxglove *s.* digitale.

foxy *agg.* **1.** volpino **2.** rossiccio **3.** scolorito **4.** aspro.

foyer *s.* ridotto.

fraction *s.* frazione.

fractional *agg.* frazionario.

to **fractionize** *vt.* frazionare.

fracture *s.* frattura.

to **fracture** *vt.* fratturare. ♦ to **fracture** *vi.* fratturarsi.

fragile *agg.* fragile.

fragility *s.* fragilità.

fragment *s.* frammento.

fragmentary *agg.* frammentario.

fragrance *s.* fragranza.

fragrant *agg.* fragrante.

frail *agg.* **1.** debole **2.** caduco.

frailness, frailty *s.* debolezza.

frame *s.* **1.** cornice **2.** struttura, intelaiatura.

to **frame** *vt.* **1.** incorniciare **2.** formare.

framework *s.* struttura.

framing *s.* incorniciatura.

franc s. franco.
franchise s. franchigia.
Franciscan agg. e s. francescano.
frank agg. franco.
frankness s. franchezza.
frantic agg. frenetico.
fraternal agg. fraterno.
fraternity s. 1. fraternità 2. confraternita.
fraternization s. affratellamento.
to **fraternize** vi. fraternizzare.
fratricidal agg. fratricida.
fratricide s. 1. fratricida 2. fratricidio.
fraud s. 1. frode 2. impostura 3. (fam.) impostore.
fraudulence s. frode.
fraudulent agg. fraudolento.
fray s. zuffa.
to **fray** vt. consumare. ◆ to **fray** vi. consumarsi.
freak s. 1. capriccio 2. macchiolina.
freakish, freaky agg. capriccioso.
freckle s. lentiggine.
freckled, freckly agg. lentigginoso.
free agg. 1. libero 2. (comm.) franco 3. abbondante 4. gratuito || — on board, franco porto. ◆ **free** avv. gratuitamente.
to **free** vt. liberare.
freedom s. libertà.
freely avv. 1. liberamente 2. gratuitamente.
freemason s. massone.
freemasonry s. massoneria.
freethinker s. libero pensatore.
freethinking s. libertà di pensiero.
freetrade s. libero scambio.
freetrader s. libero scambista.
freeze s. gelo, congelamento.
to **freeze (froze, frozen)** vt. e vi. 1. gelare 2. (imp.) far freddo.
freezer s. cella frigorifera.
freezing agg. glaciale, congelante. ◆ **freezing** s. congelamento.
freight s. 1. trasporto 2. nolo.
to **freight** vt. 1. trasportare 2. noleggiare 3. caricare.
French agg. francese. ◆ **French** s. lingua francese.
to **frenchify** vt. francesizzare. ◆ to **frenchify** vi. francesizzarsi.
Frenchman s. francese (uomo).
Frenchwoman s. francese (donna).
frenzied agg. frenetico.
frenzy s. frenesia, delirio.
frequency s. frequenza.
frequent agg. frequente.
to **frequent** vt. frequentare.

fresco s. affresco.
fresh agg. fresco, nuovo, puro || — water, acqua dolce. ◆ **fresh** s. sorgente.
fresh-water agg. d'acqua dolce.
to **freshen** vt. 1. rinfrescare 2. desalinizzare. ◆ to **freshen** vi. rinfrescarsi.
freshly avv. 1. in modo fresco 2. recentemente.
freshman s. matricola.
freshness s. 1. freschezza 2. inesperienza.
fret[1] s. agitazione.
fret[2] s. 1. fregio 2. traforo.
to **fret**[1] vt. rodere. ◆ to **fret** vi. 1. affliggersi 2. agitarsi.
to **fret**[2] vt. 1. ornare 2. traforare.
fretful agg. irritabile.
fretfully avv. con irritazione.
fretfulness s. irritabilità.
fretwork s. intaglio ornamentale.
friability s. friabilità.
friable agg. friabile.
friar s. frate || Black- —, domenicano; Grey- —, francescano; White- —, carmelitano.
friction s. frizione, attrito.
Friday s. venerdì: Good —, Venerdì Santo.
fried agg. fritto.
friend s. amico || to make friends, fare amicizia; the Society of Friends, i quaccheri.
friendless agg. senza amici.
friendliness s. cordialità.
friendly agg. amichevole. ◆ **friendly** avv. amichevolmente.
friendship s. amicizia.
frigate s. fregata.
fright s. spavento.
to **frighten** vt. spaventare.
frightful agg. spaventevole.
frightfulness s. spavento.
frigid agg. 1. glaciale 2. frigido.
frigidity s. 1. freddezza 2. frigidità.
frill s. 1. fronzolo 2. gala increspata.
to **frill** vt. ornare di gale.
fringe s. 1. frangia 2. bordo.
to **fringe** vt. orlare.
frippery s. cianfrusaglie (pl.).
to **frisk** vi. fare capriole.
frisky agg. gaio.
frivolity s. frivolezza.
frivolous agg. frivolo.
frizzly, frizzy agg. crespo.
frock s. 1. abito 2. tonaca.
frog[1] s. rana.

frog² s. alamaro.
frogman s. sommozzatore.
frolic s. scherzo.
frolicsome agg. scherzoso.
from prep. da, di.
front agg. anteriore. ♦ **front** s.
1. fronte 2. sfrontatezza.
to **front** vt. fronteggiare.
frontal agg. frontale.
frontier s. frontiera.
frontispiece s. frontespizio.
frost s. 1. gelo 2. brina || —bite,
congelamento; hoar- —, brinata.
to **frost** vt. 1. gelare 2. (cuc.) glassare 3. smerigliare.
frosty agg. 1. gelato 2. gelido 3.
canuto.
froth s. 1. schiuma 2. frivolezza.
to **froth** vi. far schiuma.
frothy agg. 1. schiumoso 2. leggero.
frown s. 1. l'aggrottare le ciglia 2.
cipiglio.
to **frown** vi. 1. aggrottare le ciglia
2. accigliarsi.
frowning agg. accigliato.
froze V. to freeze.
frozen V. to freeze.
fructiferous agg. fruttifero.
to **fructify** vi. fruttificare. ♦ to
fructify vt. fertilizzare.
frugal agg. frugale.
frugalist s. persona frugale.
frugality s. frugalità.
fruit s. 1. frutta 2. frutto.
fruiterer s. fruttivendolo.
fruitful agg. 1. fruttifero 2. fertile
3. redditizio.
fruitfulness s. 1. fertilità 2. vantaggio.
fruition s. 1. godimento 2. realizzazione.
fruitless agg. infruttuoso.
to **frustrate** vt. frustrare.
frustration s. frustrazione.
frustum s. (pl. -ta) (geom.) tronco.
fry s. fritto, frittura.
to **fry** vt. e vi. friggere.
fudge s. fandonia, sciocchezza.
to **fudge** vt. rattoppare.
fuel s. combustibile || — oil, nafta.
to **fuel** vt. alimentare di combustibile.
fugacity s. fugacità.
fugitive agg. 1. fuggitivo 2. effimero. ♦ **fugitive** s. 1. fuggitivo
2. rifugiato.
fugitiveness s. fuggevolezza.
fugue s. (mus.) fuga.
fulcrum s. (pl. fulcra) fulcro.

to **fulfil** vt. 1. compiere 2. adempiere, esaurire.
fulfilment s. 1. compimento 2.
adempimento, esaudimento.
fulgency s. fulgidezza.
fulgent agg. fulgente.
fulgid agg. fulgido.
fulguration s. folgorazione.
full agg. pieno || — up, completo;
— -stop, punto. ♦ **full** avv. interamente. ♦ **full** s. 1. intero 2.
massimo.
fullness s. pienezza.
fully avv. completamente.
fulminant agg. fulminante.
fulmination s. 1. fulminazione 2.
imprecazione.
fumarole s. fumarola.
to **fumble** vi. annaspare. ♦ to **fumble** vt. maneggiare goffamente.
fume s. 1. fumo 2. eccitazione.
to **fume** vi. 1. fumare 2. irritarsi.
fun s. 1. divertimento 2. facezia ||
to make — of so., canzonare qu.;
to have good —, divertirsi molto.
funambulism s. funambolismo.
funambulist s. funambolo.
function s. funzione.
to **function** vi. 1. funzionare 2.
fungere da.
functional agg. funzionale.
functionary s. funzionario.
fund s. fondo, riserva.
to **fund** vt. 1. accumulare 2. investire in obbligazioni.
fundament s. base.
fundamental agg. fondamentale. ♦
fundamental s. fondamento.
funeral agg. funebre. ♦ **funeral**
s. funerale.
funerary, funereal agg. funereo.
funicular agg. e s. funicolare.
funnel s. 1. imbuto 2. camino, ci-
miniera.
funny agg. 1. comico 2. strano.
fur s. 1. pelliccia 2. patina, rivestimento.
to **fur** vt. coprire con pelliccia.
furbelow s. falpalà.
furious agg. furioso.
to **furl** vt. 1. piegare, chiudere 2.
ammainare (vele ecc.). ♦ to **furl**
vi. piegarsi, chiudersi.
furnace s. fornace.
to **furnish** vt. 1. fornire 2. ammobiliare.
furnisher s. fornitore.
furnishings s. pl. arredamento
(sing.).

furniture s. **1.** mobilio **2.** contenuto.

furrier s. pellicciaio.

furriery s. pellicceria.

furrow s. **1.** solco **2.** scia.

to **furrow** vt. **1.** solcare **2.** arare.

further agg. (comp. di far) **1.** più lontano **2.** ulteriore. ♦ **further** avv. **1.** più in là **2.** ancora.

to **further** vt. favorire.

furthermore avv. inoltre.

furthermost agg. il più lontano.

furthest agg. (superl. di far) estremo. ♦ **furthest** avv. all'estremo limite.

furtive agg. furtivo.

furunculosis s. furuncolosi.

fury s. furia.

fuse s. **1.** valvola, fusibile **2.** spoletta **3.** miccia.

to **fuse** vt. **1.** fondere **2.** liquefare. ♦ to **fuse** vi. **1.** fondersi **2.** saltare (di valvola).

fuselage s. fusoliera.

fusible agg. fusibile.

fusion s. fusione.

fuss s. **1.** trambusto **2.** smancerie.

to **fuss** vi. far confusione. ♦ to **fuss** vt. irritare.

fussily avv. **1.** con inutile scalpore **2.** con esagerata importanza.

fussy agg. **1.** che fa confusione **2.** meticoloso.

fusty agg. stantio.

futility s. futilità.

future agg. e s. futuro.

futurism s. futurismo.

fuzz s. lanuggine.

fuzzily avv. confusamente.

fuzziness s. **1.** increspatura (di capelli) **2.** (foto) sfocatura.

fuzzy agg. **1.** lanuginoso **2.** confuso **3.** (foto) sfocato.

G

G s. (mus.) sol.

to **gabble** vt. e vi. parlare in modo confuso.

gabbler s. chiacchierone.

gable s. frontone.

gadfly s. **1.** tafano **2.** (fig.) persona irritante.

gadget s. aggeggio.

Gael s. gaelico.

Gaelic agg. e s. gaelico.

gaff s. uncino, rampone.

gag s. **1.** bavaglio **2.** improvvisazione **3.** trovata geniale.

to **gag** vt. imbavagliare. ♦ to **gag** vi. improvvisare (motti di spirito).

gage s. garanzia.

to **gage** vt. dare in pegno.

gaiety s. gaiezza. ♦ **gaieties** s. pl. divertimenti.

gaily avv. gaiamente.

gain s. **1.** guadagno **2.** aumento, miglioramento.

to **gain** vt. e vi. **1.** guadagnare **2.** aumentare || to — on, guadagnar terreno su.

gainer s. chi guadagna.

gainful agg. lucroso.

gainings s. pl. guadagni.

to **gainsay** vt. contraddire.

gainsaying s. contraddizione.

gait s. andatura.

gaiter s. ghetta.

galalith s. galalite.

galantine s. galantina.

galaxy s. galassia.

gale s. tempesta.

galenic agg. galenico.

Galilean agg. e s. galileo.

gall[1] s. bile, fiele || — -bladder, cistifellea.

gall[2] s. **1.** scorticatura **2.** irritazione.

to **gall** vt. irritare. ♦ to **gall** vi. irritarsi.

gallant agg. **1.** prode **2.** galante. ♦ **gallant** s. uomo di mondo.

gallantry s. **1.** galanteria **2.** coraggio **3.** atto, discorso amoroso.

galleon s. galeone.

gallery s. galleria || picture- —, pinacoteca.

galley s. **1.** (mar.) galea **2.** (mar.) cambusa **3.** (tip.) vantaggio || — proof (tip.), bozza in colonna; — slave, galeotto.

Gallic agg. e s. gallico.

gallicism s. francesismo.

gallinacean agg. e s. gallinaceo.

gallium s. gallio.

gallon s. gallone (misura).

galloon s. gallone (ornamento).

gallooned agg. gallonato.

gallop s. **1.** galoppo: at a —, al galoppo **2.** galoppata.

to **gallop** vt. far galoppare. ♦ to **gallop** vi. galoppare.

gallows s. pl. patibolo. (sing.)

galore s. abbondanza. ♦ **galore** avv. in abbondanza.

galosh(e) s. galoscia.

galvanic(al) *agg.* **1.** galvanico **2.** (*fig.*) galvanizzante.

galvanization *s.* galvanizzazione.

to galvanize *vt.* galvanizzare.

galvanometer *s.* galvanometro.

galvanoplastic *agg.* galvanoplastico.

gamble *s.* gioco d'azzardo.

to gamble *vt.* e *vi.* giocare (*d'azzardo*).

gambler *s.* giocatore d'azzardo.

gambling *s.* V. *gamble* || — *-house*, casa da gioco.

gambol *s.* piroetta.

game *agg.* risoluto. ♦ **game** *s.* **1.** gioco (*con regole*), mano (*in una partita*) **2.** (*fig.*) progetto **3.** selvaggina (*coll.*).

to game V. *to gamble*.

gamekeeper *s.* guardacaccia.

gamely *avv.* coraggiosamente.

gamesome *agg.* scherzoso.

gamester *s.* giocatore.

gammon *s.* (*mar.*) trinca di bompresso.

gang *s.* **1.** squadra **2.** banda.

to gang *vt.* e *vi.* formare una banda.

ganglion *s.* (*pl.* ganglia) ganglio.

gangrene *s.* cancrena.

to gangrene *vi.* andare in cancrena.

gangster *s.* bandito.

gangsterism *s.* banditismo.

gangway *s.* **1.** passaggio (*tra file di sedie ecc.*) **2.** (*mar.*) passerella.

gaol *s.* prigione.

to gaol *vt.* imprigionare.

gaoler *s.* carceriere.

gap *s.* **1.** apertura, breccia **2.** intervallo **3.** divergenza **4.** lacuna.

gape *s.* **1.** sbadiglio **2.** apertura **3.** stupore.

to gape *vi.* **1.** spalancare la bocca **2.** sbadigliare **3.** restare a bocca aperta.

gaping *agg.* **1.** aperto **2.** stupito.

garage *s.* autorimessa || — *keeper*, garagista.

garb *s.* costume.

garbage *s.* rifiuto.

garden *s.* giardino.

to garden *vi.* fare del giardinaggio.

gardener *s.* giardiniere.

gardening *s.* giardinaggio.

gargarism *s.* gargarismo.

gargle *s.* liquido per gargarismi.

to gargle *vt.* e *vi.* gargarizzare.

gargoyle *s.* doccione.

garish *agg.* **1.** abbagliante **2.** appariscente.

garland *s.* ghirlanda.

garlic *s.* aglio.

garment *s.* abito, indumento.

garnet[1] *s.* granato.

garnet[2] *s.* (*mar.*) paranco.

to garnish *vt.* guarnire.

garnish(ment) *s.* ornamento.

garret *s.* soffitta.

garrison *s.* guarnigione.

to garrison *vt.* presidiare.

garrulity *s.* garrulità.

garrulous *agg.* garrulo.

garter *s.* giarrettiera || *knight o, the Garter*, Cavaliere dell'Ordine della Giarrettiera.

gas *s.* gas || — *-fitter*, gassista; — *-mask*, maschera antigas; — *-meter*, contatore del gas.

to gas *vt.* **1.** fornire di gas **2.** asfissiare col gas.

Gascon *agg.* e *s.* guascone.

gasconade *s.* guasconata.

gaseous *agg.* gassoso.

gash *s.* sfregio.

to gash *vt.* sfregiare.

gas oil *s.* gasolio.

gasoline *s.* (*amer.*) benzina.

gasp *s.* respiro affannoso.

to gasp *vi.* **1.** ansare **2.** restare senza fiato **3.** parlare affannosamente.

gassy *agg.* gassoso.

gastric *agg.* gastrico.

gastritis *s.* gastrite.

gastroenteritis *s.* gastroenterite.

gastronome *s.* gastronomo.

gastronomic(al) *agg.* gastronomico.

gastronomy *s.* gastronomia.

gate *s.* cancello **2.** porta.

gatekeeper *s.* portiere, custode.

gateway *s.* portone, ingresso.

to gather *vt.* **1.** raccogliere **2.** acquistare **3.** dedurre. ♦ **to gather** *vi.* raccogliersi.

gathering *s.* **1.** raccolta **2.** (*med.*) ascesso.

gaud *s.* fronzolo.

gaudiness *s.* sfarzo.

gaudy *agg.* sfarzoso. ♦ **gaudy** *s.* festa (*universitaria*).

gauge *s.* **1.** misura **2.** calibro **3.** (*ferr.*) scartamento **4.** pescaggio || *narrow* —, scartamento ridotto.

to gauge *vt.* misurare.

gaunt *agg.* scarno.

gauze *s.* garza, velo, mussolina.

gauzy *agg.* trasparente.

gave V. *to give*.

gay *agg.* **1.** gaio **2.** licenzioso.

gayety *s.* gaiezza.

gaze *s.* sguardo fisso.
to gaze *vi.* fissare.
gazelle *s.* gazzella.
gazette *s.* gazzetta.
gazetteer *s.* **1.** giornalista **2.** dizionario geografico.
gear *s.* **1.** meccanismo **2.** (*auto*) marcia, cambio **3.** (*mecc.*) ingranaggio.
to gear *vt.* ingranare || *to — up, down,* aumentare, diminuire la velocità.
gearing *s.* ingranaggio, innesto.
geese V. *goose*.
gelatin(e) *s.* gelatina.
gelatinous *agg.* gelatinoso.
to geld *vt.* castrare.
gelid *agg.* gelido.
gem *s.* gemma.
gemmy *agg.* pieno di gemme.
gender *s.* genere.
genderless *agg.* di genere comune.
genealogical *agg.* genealogico.
genealogy *s.* genealogia.
generable *agg.* generabile.
general *agg.* e *s.* generale.
generality *s.* **1.** generalità **2.** maggioranza.
generalization *s.* generalizzazione.
to generalize *vt.* e *vi.* generalizzare.
generally *avv.* generalmente.
to generate *vt.* generare.
generation *s.* generazione.
generative *agg.* generativo.
generator *s.* generatore.
generic(al) *agg.* generico.
generosity *s.* generosità.
generous *agg.* **1.** generoso **2.** abbondante.
genesis *s.* (*pl.* -ses) genesi.
genetic(al) *agg.* genetico.
genetics *s.* genetica.
genial *agg.* **1.** gioviale **2.** geniale **3.** mite (*di clima*).
geniality *s.* **1.** giovialità **2.** mitezza (*di clima*).
genital *agg.* e *s.* genitale.
genitive *agg.* e *s.* genitivo.
genius *s.* genio.
genocide *s.* genocidio.
genre *s.* genere.
genteel *agg.* raffinato.
gentian *s.* genziana.
gentile *agg.* e *s.* pagano.
gentility *s.* signorilità.
gentle *agg.* **1.** nobile **2.** garbato **3.** moderato **4.** facile.
gentleman *s.* **1.** signore **2.** gentiluomo.
gentlemanlike, gentlemanly *agg.*

da gentiluomo.
gentleness *s.* gentilezza.
gentlewoman *s.* gentildonna.
gently *avv.* **1.** gentilmente, con delicatezza **2.** gradualmente.
gentry *s.* classe gentilizia.
to genuflect *vi.* genuflettersi.
genuflection *s.* genuflessione.
genuine *agg.* **1.** autentico **2.** sincero **3.** puro.
genuineness *s.* **1.** autenticità **2.** sincerità.
genus *s.* (*pl.* -nera) genere.
geodesy *s.* geodesia.
geographer *s.* geografo.
geographic(al) *agg.* geografico.
geography *s.* geografia.
geologic(al) *agg.* geologico.
geologist *s.* geologo.
geology *s.* geologia.
geometer *s.* geometra.
geometric(al) *agg.* geometrico.
geometrician *s.* geometra.
geometry *s.* geometria.
geophysics *s.* geofisica.
geopolitics *s.* geopolitica.
georgic *agg.* georgico.
geranium *s.* geranio.
gerent *s.* gerente.
germ *s.* germe.
german *agg.* germano.
German *agg.* e *s.* tedesco.
Germanic *agg.* germanico.
Germanism *s.* germanesimo.
Germanist *s.* germanista.
germanium *s.* germanio.
germinal *agg.* germinale.
to germinate *vt.* far germinare. ♦
to germinate *vi.* germinare.
germination *s.* germinazione.
gerontology *s.* gerontologia.
gerund *s.* gerundio.
gerundial *agg.* gerundivo.
gerundive *agg.* e *s.* gerundivo.
gestation *s.* gestazione.
to gesticulate *vi.* gesticolare.
gesticulation *s.* gesticolazione.
gesture *s.* **1.** gesto **2.** il gestire.
to gesture *vi.* far gesti.
to get (got, got) *vt.* **1.** ottenere, procurare **2.** prendere **3.** portare **4.** fare. ♦ **to get (got, got)** *vi.* **1.** andare **2.** divenire || *to — off,* scendere; *to — over,* scavalcare; *to — out,* (far) uscire; *to — up,* alzarsi; *to — married,* sposarsi; *to — hold of,* impossessarsi di.
getaway *s.* **1.** fuga **2.** (*sport*) partenza.

gettable *agg.* ottenibile.

get-up *s.* 1. equipaggiamento 2. presentazione (*di libro, giornale ecc.*).

geyser *s.* 1. geyser 2. scaldabagno.

ghastliness *s.* 1. aspetto spaventoso 2. pallore spettrale.

ghastly *agg.* 1. spaventoso 2. spettrale.

gherkin *s.* cetriolo.

Ghibelline *agg.* e *s.* ghibellino.

ghost *s.* 1. spirito 2. spettro || *to give up the* —, spirare.

ghostliness *s.* 1. l'essere spettrale 2. spiritualità.

ghostly *agg.* 1. spettrale 2. spirituale.

giant *s.* gigante.

giantism *s.* gigantismo.

gibbet *s.* patibolo.

to gibbet *vt.* 1. impiccare 2. (*fig.*) mettere alla berlina.

gibbosity *s.* gibbosità.

gibbous *agg.* gibboso.

gibe *s.* scherno.

to gibe *vt.* e *vi.* schernire.

giblets *s. pl.* regaglie.

giddily *avv.* vertiginosamente.

giddiness *s.* 1. capogiro 2. (*fig.*) frivolezza.

giddy *agg.* 1. stordito 2. vertiginoso 3. frivolo.

to giddy *vt.* stordire. ♦ **to giddy** *vi.* aver le vertigini.

gift *s.* 1. dono 2. dote.

to gift *vt.* dotare.

gig[1] *s.* 1. calessino 2. (*mar.*) iole.

gig[2] *s.* rampone, fiocina.

gigantean, gigantic *agg.* gigantesco.

giggle *s.* risatina.

to giggle *vi.* fare risatine.

to gild (gilt, gilt) (*anche reg.*) *vt.* (in)dorare.

gilder *s.* doratore.

gilding *s.* doratura.

gill *s.* 1. branchia 2. pappagorgia.

gilt V. *to gild.*

gilt *s.* doratura.

gimlet *s.* succhiello.

gin[1] *s.* "gin" (*liquore*).

gin[2] *s.* 1. elevatore 2. trappola (*per animali*).

ginger *s.* zenzero.

gingerly *agg.* cauto. ♦ **gingerly** *avv.* cautamente.

gipsy *s.* zingaro.

gipsydom *s.* gli zingari (*pl.*).

gipsyish *agg.* zingaresco.

giraffe *s.* giraffa.

to gird (girt, girt) (*anche reg.*) *vt.* cingere.

girder *s.* 1. trave maestra 2. sbarra.

girdle *s.* 1. cintura 2. reggicalze.

to girdle *vt.* cingere.

girl *s.* ragazza || *flower* —, fioraia.

girlhood *s.* adolescenza (*di ragazza*).

Girondist *agg.* e *s.* girondino.

girt V. *to gird.*

girth *s.* 1. circonferenza 2. cinghia.

to give (gave, given) *vt.* dare || *to* — *in*, cedere; *to* — *out*, annunciare, venir meno; *to* — *up*, smettere, abbandonare; *to* — *birth to*, generare; *to* — *oneself up*, costituirsi (*alla polizia*); *to* — *oneself up to*, dedicarsi (a); *to* — *off*, emettere (*luce ecc.*).

giver *s.* datore.

glacial *agg.* glaciale.

glaciation *s.* glaciazione.

glacier *s.* ghiacciaio.

glacis *s.* spalto.

glad *agg.* lieto.

to gladden *vt.* rallegrare. ♦ **to gladden** *vi.* rallegrarsi.

glade *s.* radura.

gladiator *s.* gladiatore.

gladiolus *s.* (*pl.* -li) gladiolo.

gladly *avv.* con piacere.

gladness *s.* contentezza.

glair *s.* albume.

gladsome *agg.* gioioso.

glair *s.* albume.

glamorous *agg.* affascinante.

glamour *s.* 1. fascino 2. incantesimo.

glance *s.* 1. occhiata 2. colpo obliquo.

to glance *vt.* e *vi.* 1. gettare uno sguardo 2. sfiorare 3. balenare || *to* — *off*, sorvolare su.

gland *s.* 1. ghiandola 2. ghianda.

glandiferous *agg.* ghiandifero.

glandular *agg.* glandolare.

glare *s.* 1. luce abbagliante 2. sguardo truce 3. abbagliamento.

to glare *vi.* 1. splendere 2. guardare torvamente.

glaring *agg.* 1. abbagliante 2. evidente.

glass *s.* 1. vetro 2. bicchiere 3. specchio || — *-ware*, articoli in vetro; — *-work*, fabbrica di vetro; — *-paper*, carta vetrata. ♦ **glasses** *s. pl.* occhiali, cannocchiale (*sing.*).

to glass *vt.* 1. specchiare 2. imbottigliare.

glassy *agg.* 1. vitreo 2. cristallino.

glaucous *agg.* glauco.

glaze *s.* superficie vetrosa.

to **glaze** *vt.* **1.** smaltare **2.** mettere vetri a. ◆ to **glaze** *vi.* diventare vitreo.

glazier *s.* vetraio.

glazy *agg.* vitreo.

gleam *s.* barlume.

to **gleam** *vi.* scintillare.

gleamy *agg.* scintillante.

to **glean** *vt.* e *vi.* spigolare.

gleaner *s.* spigolatore.

gleaning *s.* spigolatura.

glee *s.* allegria.

gleeful *agg.* allegro.

glib *agg.* **1.** liscio **2.** facondo **3.** sciolto.

glibness *s.* **1.** disinvoltura **2.** facondia.

glide *s.* scivolata.

to **glide** *vt.* **1.** far scorrere **2.** trascorrere. ◆ to **glide** *vi.* **1.** scivolare **2.** passare.

glider *s.* aliante.

gliding *agg.* scorrevole. ◆ **gliding** *s.* volo a vela.

glimmer *s.* barlume.

to **glimmer** *vi.* brillare.

glimpse *s.* **1.** visione **2.** occhiata **3.** vaga idea.

to **glimpse** *vt.* e *vi.* intravedere.

glitter *s.* scintillio.

to **glitter** *vi.* scintillare.

gloaming *s.* crepuscolo.

to **gloat** *vi.* fissare avidamente.

global *agg.* globale.

globe *s.* **1.** globo **2.** pianeta.

globous, globular *agg.* sferico.

globule *s.* globulo.

gloom *s.* **1.** oscurità **2.** tristezza.

to **gloom** *vt.* **1.** oscurare **2.** rattristare. ◆ to **gloom** *vi.* **1.** oscurarsi **2.** rattristarsi.

gloomy *agg.* cupo.

glorification *s.* glorificazione.

to **glorify** *vt.* glorificare.

glorious *agg.* **1.** glorioso **2.** splendido.

gloriousness *s.* V. *glory.*

glory *s.* **1.** gloria **2.** splendore.

to **glory** *vi.* vantarsi.

gloss *s.* **1.** glossa **2.** lucentezza **3.** apparenza.

glossarist *s.* glossatore.

glossary *s.* glossario.

glossy *agg.* lucido.

glottis *s.* glottide.

glottologist *s.* glottologo.

glottology *s.* glottologia.

glove *s.* guanto || *to be hand in — with,* essere molto intimo con.

gloved *agg.* inguantato.

glover *s.* guantaio.

glow *s.* **1.** calore **2.** splendore **3.** colorito || *—worm,* lucciola.

to **glow** *vi.* ardere.

glucose *s.* glucosio.

glue *s.* colla.

to **glue** *vt.* incollare.

glut *s.* **1.** scorpacciata **2.** saturazione.

to **glut** *vt.* **1.** saziare **2.** saturare. ◆ to **glut** *vi.* fare una scorpacciata.

gluten *s.* glutine.

gluteus *s.* (*pl.* glutei) gluteo.

glutton *s.* ghiottone.

gluttonous *agg.* ghiottone.

gluttony *s.* ghiottoneria.

glycerin(e) *s.* glicerina.

glycogen *s.* glicogeno.

gnarled *agg.* nodoso.

to **gnash** *vt.* e *vi.* digrignare.

gnat *s.* zanzara.

to **gnaw** *vt.* rodere.

gnawing *agg.* **1.** rosicante **2.** corrodente.

gnome[1] *s.* gnomo.

gnome[2] *s.* massima.

gnomic *agg.* gnomico.

gnosis *s.* gnosi.

gnostic *agg.* e *s.* gnostico.

gnosticism *s.* gnosticismo.

go *s.* **1.** movimento **2.** energia **3.** colpo || *— -between,* intermediario; *— -by,* evasione; *— -cart,* girello.

to **go (went, gone)** *vi.* **1.** andare **2.** divenire || *to — by,* passare; *to — for,* andare a cercare; *to — on,* continuare.

goad *s.* pungolo.

to **goad** *vt.* stimolare.

goal *s.* **1.** traguardo **2.** (*sport*) rete || *— -keeper,* portiere.

goat *s.* capra.

goatish *agg.* **1.** caprino **2.** lascivo.

to **gobble** *vt.* trangugiare, inghiottire.

goblin *s.* folletto.

god *s.* **1.** dio, divinità **2.** Dio.

godchild *s.* (*pl.* -children) figlioccio.

goddaughter *s.* figlioccia.

goddess *s.* dea.

godfather *s.* padrino.

godless *agg.* **1.** ateo **2.** empio.

godlike *agg.* divino.

godliness *s.* devozione.

godly *agg.* religioso.

godmother *s.* madrina.

godown s. deposito.
godsend s. dono del cielo.
godship s. divinità.
godson s. figlioccio.
goggle agg. **1.** stralunato **2.** sporgente (di occhi).
to **goggle** vt. stralunare. ♦ to **goggle** vi. essere sporgenti (di occhi).
goggles s. pl. occhiali di protezione.
going s. **1.** l'andare **2.** partenza.
goitre s. gozzo.
goitrous agg. gozzuto.
gold agg. d'oro. ♦ **gold** s. oro || — -field, zona aurifera; — -dig''', cercatore d'oro.
golden agg. dorato, d'oro.
goldfinch s. cardellino.
goldsmith s. orefice.
gone V. to go.
gonfalon s. gonfalone.
goniometer s. goniometro.
goniometry s. goniometria.
good (better, best) agg. **1.** buono **2.** bravo **3.** bello. ♦ **good** inter. bene!
good s. **1.** bene **2.** utilità || for —, per sempre.
good-bye inter. e s. addio, arrivederci.
good-for-nothing s. buono a nulla.
goodly agg. bello.
goodness s. **1.** bontà **2.** il meglio || my —!, Dio mio!
goods s. pl. merce (sing.).
goodwill s. **1.** buona volontà **2.** benevolenza.
goody agg. troppo buono. ♦ **goody** inter. bene!
goose s. (pl. geese) oca.
gooseberry s. uva spina.
goose-step s. passo dell'oca.
gore s. sangue rappreso.
gorge s. gola.
to **gorge** V. to glut.
gorgeous agg. magnifico.
gorgeousness s. magnificenza.
gospel s. vangelo.
gossamer s. ragnatela.
gossip s. **1.** pettegolezzo **2.** pettegolo.
to **gossip** vi. far pettegolezzi.
gossiper s. pettegolo.
gossipy agg. pettegolo.
got V. to get.
Gothic agg. e s. gotico.
gothicism s. **1.** stile gotico **2.** rozzezza.
gouache s. guazzo.
gouge s. sgorbia.

gourd s. zucca.
gourmand s. goloso.
gourmet s. buongustaio.
gout s. **1.** gotta **2.** goccia.
gouty agg. gottoso.
to **govern** vt. **1.** governare **2.** controllare **3.** (gramm.) reggere.
governable agg. docile.
governess s. istitutrice.
government s. governo.
governmental agg. governativo.
governor s. **1.** governatore **2.** regolatore.
gown s. **1.** veste **2.** toga || dressing- —, veste da camera; night- —, camicia da notte.
grab s. presa.
to **grab** vt. **1.** afferrare **2.** (mecc.) bloccare.
grace s. grazia.
to **grace** vt. adornare.
graceful agg. grazioso.
gracefulness s. grazia.
graceless agg. **1.** sgraziato **2.** depravato.
gracile agg. gracile.
gracility s. gracilità.
gracious agg. benigno || good —!, mio Dio!
gradation s. gradazione.
grade s. **1.** grado **2.** pendio.
to **grade** vt. **1.** graduare **2.** livellare.
gradient agg. che sale, scende gradatamente. ♦ **gradient** s. pendenza.
gradual agg. graduale.
graduality s. gradualità.
graduate s. laureato.
to **graduate** vt. **1.** graduare **2.** laureare. ♦ to **graduate** vi. laurearsi.
graduation s. **1.** graduazione **2.** laurea.
graft s. innesto.
to **graft** vt. innestare.
grain s. **1.** granaglie (pl.) **2.** chicco **3.** grano.
grainy agg. **1.** granuloso **2.** granoso.
gram s. grammo.
Gramineae s. pl. graminacee.
grammar s. grammatica.
grammarian s. grammatico.
grammatic(al) agg. grammaticale.
gramophone s. grammofono.
granary s. granaio.
grand agg. **1.** grande **2.** nobile || — -aunt, prozia; — -uncle, prozio; — -nephew, pronipote (maschio); — -niece, pronipote (femmina).

grandchild s. (pl. -children) nipote (di nonni).

granddaughter s. nipote (femmina) (di nonni).

grandeur s. grandiosità.

grandfather s. nonno.

grandiloquence s. magniloquenza.

grandiloquent agg. magniloquente.

grandiose agg. grandioso.

grandiosity s. grandiosità.

grandmother s. nonna.

grandmotherly agg. protettivo.

grandparents s. pl. nonni.

grandson s. nipote (maschio) (di nonni).

grange s. fattoria, casa colonica.

granite s. granito.

granitic agg. granitico.

granivorous agg. granivoro.

grant s. concessione.

to **grant** vt. concedere || to take for granted, dare per scontato.

granular agg. granulare.

granularity s. granulosità.

to **granulate** vt. granulare. ♦ to **granulate** vi. granularsi.

granulation s. granulazione.

granulous agg. granuloso.

grape s. 1. acino || — -shot, mitraglia. ♦ **grapes** s. pl. uva.

grapefruit s. pompelmo.

grapevine s. 1. vigna 2. (fam.) notizia ufficiosa.

graph s. grafico.

graphic(al) agg. 1. grafico 2. pittoresco.

graphite s. grafite.

graphologist s. grafologo.

graphology s. grafologia.

graphomania s. grafomania.

graphomaniac s. grafomane.

grapnel s. (mar.) grappino.

to **grapple** vt. afferrare. ♦ to **grapple** vi. lottare.

grappling s. (mar.) aggancio || — irons, grappini d'abbordaggio.

grasp s. 1. stretta 2. manico 3. potere.

to **grasp** vt. e vi. afferrare.

grasping agg. avido.

grass s. erba.

grasshopper s. cavalletta.

grass-widow s. donna separata dal marito.

grassy agg. erboso.

grate s. 1. grata 2. graticola.

to **grate** vt. 1. fornire di grata 2. grattugiare. ♦ to **grate** vi. stridere.

grateful agg. grato.

gratefulness s. gratitudine.

grater s. grattugia.

to **gratify** vt. 1. ricompensare 2. appagare.

gratifying agg. soddisfacente.

grating[1] agg. 1. irritante 2. stridente. ♦ **grating** s. stridore.

grating[2] s. 1. grata 2. (ott.) reticolo.

gratitude s. gratitudine.

gratuitous agg. gratuito.

gratuity s. mancia.

grave[1] agg. grave.

grave[2] s. tomba.

gravel s. ghiaia.

to **gravel** vt. inghiaiare.

gravelly agg. ghiaioso.

graven agg. intagliato.

graver s. 1. incisore 2. bulino.

gravestone s. pietra tombale.

graveyard s. cimitero.

gravid agg. gravido.

to **gravitate** vi. gravitare.

gravitation s. gravitazione.

gravitational agg. gravitazionale.

gravity s. gravità.

gravy s. sugo.

gray agg. e s. grigio.

graze s. 1. colpo di striscio 2. escoriazione.

to **graze**[1] vt. e vi. 1. graffiare 2. sfiorare.

to **graze**[2] vt. e vi. pascolare, condurre al pascolo.

grazier s. allevatore (di bestiame).

grazing[1] s. abrasione.

grazing[2] s. pascolo.

grease s. grasso.

to **grease** vt. ungere, lubrificare.

greaser s. ingrassatore.

greasiness s. untuosità.

greasy agg. 1. grasso 2. unto, untuoso 3. scivoloso.

great agg. grande || — -grandchild, pronipote (di nonni); — -grandfather, bisnonno; — -grandmother, bisnonna.

greatness s. grandezza.

Grecian agg. e s. greco.

greed(iness) s. avidità.

greedy agg. avido.

Greek agg. e s. greco.

green agg. 1. verde 2. inesperto 3. vigoroso 4. recente. ♦ **green** s. prato. ♦ **greens** s. pl. frasche, verdura (sing.).

greenery s. 1. vegetazione 2. serra.

greengrocer s. erbivendolo.

greenhouse s. serra.

greenish *agg.* verdastro.

greenness *s.* 1. color verde 2. acerbezza 3. ingenuità 4. vigore.

greenroom *s.* (*teat.*) camerino.

to **greet** *vt.* e *vi.* salutare.

greeting *s.* saluto.

Gregorian *agg.* gregoriano.

grenadier *s.* granatiere.

grenadine *s.* granatina.

grew V. *to grow.*

grey *agg.* e *s.* grigio.

greyhound *s.* levriere.

greyness *s.* grigiore.

grid *s.* griglia.

gridiron *s.* graticola.

grief *s.* 1. dolore 2. fallimento ||
to come to —, fare fiasco.

grievance *s.* 1. lagnanza 2. torto.

to **grieve** *vt.* affliggere. ♦ to **grieve**
vi. affliggersi.

grievous *agg.* 1. doloroso 2. grave.

griffon *s.* grifone.

grill *s.* 1. graticola 2. cibo ai ferri
|| *-room,* rosticceria.

to **grill** *vt.* e *vi.* arrostire (*alla graticola*).

grille *s.* inferriata.

grim *agg.* cupo.

grimace *s.* smorfia.

grime *s.* sudiciume.

to **grime** *vt.* insudiciare.

grimly *avv.* cupamente.

grimy *agg.* sudicio.

grin *s.* 1. largo sorriso 2. sogghigno.

to **grin** *vi.* 1. fare un largo sorriso
2. sogghignare.

to **grind** (**ground, ground**) *vt.* 1.
macinare 2. molare 3. digrignare
4. (*fig.*) opprimere.

grinder *s.* 1. mola 2. molare 3. arrotino || *organ- —,* suonatore di
organetto.

grinding *agg.* irritante. ♦ **grinding**
s. 1. macinatura 2. stridore 3. affilatura 4. (*fig.*) oppressione.

grindstone *s.* mola.

grip *s.* 1. stretta 2. manico 3. (*fig.*)
padronanza || *to lose one's grips,*
perdere le staffe.

to **grip** *vt.* e *vi.* afferrare.

gripe *s.* 1. presa 2. freno. ♦ **gripes**
s. pl. colica (*sing.*).

gripper *s.* pinza.

grist *s.* grano da macinare || *to
bring — to one's mill,* tirar l'acqua
al proprio mulino.

grit *s.* sabbia, arenaria.

grizzly *agg.* grigio. ♦ **grizzly** *s.*
orso grigio.

groan *s.* gemito.

to **groan** *vi.* gemere.

groaning *s.* gemito.

grocer *s.* droghiere.

grocery *s.* drogheria. ♦ **groceries**
s. pl. droghe e coloniali.

groggy *agg.* vacillante.

groin *s.* inguine.

groom *s.* stalliere.

to **groom** *vt.* strigliare.

groove *s.* solco.

to **grope** *vi.* brancolare.

gropingly *avv.* a tastoni.

gross *agg.* 1. grossolano 2. pesante
3. lussureggiante 4. (*comm.*) lordo.

grotesque *agg.* grottesco.

grotto *s.* grotta.

ground[1] V. *to grind.*

ground[2] *s.* 1. suolo, terreno 2. distanza, territorio 3. motivi, ragioni
(*general. pl.*) || *— -floor,* pianterreno.

to **ground** *vt.* fondare. ♦ to
ground *vi.* 1. fondarsi 2. arenarsi.

grounded *agg.* interrato.

groundless *agg.* infondato.

groundlessness *s.* infondatezza.

grounds *s. pl.* 1. fondi, sedimenti
2. parco (*sing.*).

group *s.* gruppo.

to **group** *vt.* raggruppare. ♦ to
group *vi.* raggrupparsi.

grouping *s.* raggruppamento.

grove *s.* boschetto || *olive —,* oliveto.

to **grovel** *vi.* 1. strisciare a terra 2.
(*fig.*) umiliarsi.

grovelling *s.* strisciamento. ♦ **grovelling** *agg.* 1. strisciante 2. (*fig.*)
abbietto.

to **grow** (**grew, grown**) *vi.* 1. crescere 2. diventare || *to — better,*
migliorare; *to — old,* invecchiare;
to — up, crescere, diventare maturo (*di persone*). ♦ to **grow**
(**grew, grown**) *vt.* coltivare.

grower *s.* coltivatore.

growing *s.* coltivazione.

growl *s.* brontolio.

to **growl** *vt.* e *vi.* brontolare.

growler *s.* brontolone.

grown V. *to grow.*

grown-up *agg.* e *s.* adulto.

growth *s.* 1. crescita 2. produzione.

grub *s.* 1. verme 2. larva.

to **grub** *vt.* e *vi.* scavare.

grubby *agg.* 1. bacato 2. sporco.

grudge *s.* malanimo || *to bear a —
against so.,* nutrire rancore verso

qu.

to **grudge** *vt.* **1.** dare a malincuore **2.** invidiare.

grudging *agg.* **1.** riluttante **2.** invidioso.

gruesome *agg.* raccapricciante.

gruff *agg.* burbero.

grumble *s.* brontolio.

to **grumble** *vt.* e *vi.* brontolare.

grumbler *s.* brontolone.

grumbling *s.* brontolio.

grumpy *agg.* burbero, tetro.

grunt *s.* grugnito.

to **grunt** *vt.* e *vi.* grugnire.

gruyère *s.* gruviera.

guarantee *s.* **1.** garanzia **2.** garante.

to **guarantee** *vt.* garantire.

guard *s.* **1.** guardia **2.** capotreno **3.** parapetto.

to **guard** *vt.* custodire.

guardian *s.* **1.** guardiano **2.** tutore.

guardianship *s.* **1.** protezione **2.** tutela.

guardless *agg.* indifeso.

guardrail *s.* **1.** spartitraffico **2.** corrimano (*di scala*).

Guelph *s.* guelfo.

guerrilla *s.* **1.** guerriglia **2.** guerrigliere.

guess *s.* supposizione.

to **guess** *vt.* e *vi.* **1.** supporre **2.** indovinare.

guess-work *s.* congettura.

guest *s.* ospite || — -*house*, pensione.

guffaw *s.* riso sguaiato.

guide *s.* guida.

to **guide** *vt.* guidare.

guild *s.* corporazione.

guile *s.* insidia.

guileful *agg.* insidioso.

guileless *agg.* sincero.

guillotine *s.* ghigliottina. ·

guilt *s.* colpa.

guiltiness *s.* colpevolezza.

guiltless *agg.* innocente.

guilty *agg.* colpevole.

guinea *s.* ghinea.

Guinea-pig *s.* cavia.

guise *s.* **1.** aspetto, apparenza **2.** falso aspetto.

guitar *s.* chitarra.

guitarist *s.* chitarrista.

gulf *s.* golfo.

gull[1] *s.* gabbiano.

gull[2] *s.* sciocco.

to **gull** *vt.* truffare.

gully *s.* condotto (*di scolo*) || —

-*hole*, tombino.

gulp *s.* **1.** boccone **2.** sorso.

to **gulp** *vt.* inghiottire.

gum[1] *s.* gengiva.

gum[2] *s.* gomma.

to **gum** *vt.* ingommare.

gummy *agg.* gommoso.

gun *s.* **1.** cannone **2.** fucile **3.** rivoltella, pistola || — -*barrel*, canna da fucile; — -*carriage*, affusto di cannone.

gunfire *s.* sparatoria.

gunner *s.* artigliere.

gunpowder *s.* polvere da sparo.

gun-room *s.* armeria.

gunshot *s.* colpo di arma da fuoco.

gunsmith *s.* armaiolo.

gurgle *s.* gorgoglic.

to **gurgle** *vi.* gorgogliare.

gush *s.* **1.** getto **2.** effusione.

to **gush** *vi.* **1.** sgorgare **2.** essere espansivo.

gusher *s.* pozzo petrolifero.

gushing *agg.* **1.** sgorgante **2.** esuberante.

gust *s.* **1.** raffica **2.** (*fig.*) impeto.

gustative, gustatory *agg.* gustativo.

gusty *agg.* ventoso. ·

gut *s.* budello.

to **gut** *vt.* sventrare.

gutter *s.* **1.** grondaia **2.** rigagnolo.

to **gutter** *vt.* scanalare. ♦ to **gutter** *vi.* colare.

guttural *agg.* e *s.* gutturale.

to **guzzle** *vt.* tracannare.

gymkhana *s.* gincana.

gymnasium *s.* palestra.

gymnast *s.* ginnasta.

gymnastic(al) *agg.* ginnastico.

gymnastics *s.* ginnastica.

gynaeceum *s.* (*pl.* -cea) gineçeo.

gynaecologic *agg.* ginecologico.

gynaecologist *s.* ginecologo.

gynaecology *s.* ginecologia.

gypsy *s.* V. *gipsy.*

to **gyrate** *vi.* girare.

gyroscope *s.* giroscopio.

gyves *s. pl.* ceppi, catene.

H

haberdasher *s.* merciaio.

haberdashery *s.* merceria.

habit *s.* **1.** abitudine **2.** temperamen-

to **3**. costume.
habitable *agg.* abitabile.
habitation *s.* abitazione.
habitual *agg.* abituale, consueto.
habitude *s.* abitudine.
hack[1] *s.* **1**. tacca, incisione **2**. piccone, mazza **3**. tosse secca.
hack[2] *s.* **1**. ronzino **2**. (*fig.*) scribacchino.
to **hack**[1] *vt.* sminuzzare. ♦ to **hack** *vi.* tossire a colpi secchi.
to **hack**[2] *vt.* e *vi.* **1**. adoperare cavalli da nolo **2**. adibire a un lavoro da scribacchino.
hackney *s.* **1**. cavallo da nolo **2**. vettura da nolo.
hacksaw *s.* seghetto.
had V. *to have*.
haematoma *s.* ematoma.
haemoglobin *s.* emoglobina.
haemophilia *s.* emofilia.
haemoptysis *s.* emottisi.
haemorrhage *s.* emorragia.
haemorrhoids *s. pl.* emorroidi.
haemostasia *s.* emostasi.
haemostatic *agg.* e *s.* emostatico.
haft *s.* manico, impugnatura.
hag *s.* **1**. strega, megera **2**. (*zool.*) lampreda.
haggard *agg.* sparuto, emaciato.
to **haggle** *vi.* mercanteggiare.
hagiographer *s.* agiografo.
hagiography *s.* agiografia.
hail[1] *s.* grandine || — -*stone*, chicco di grandine; — -*storm*, grandinata.
hail[2] *inter.* salve!, salute!
to **hail**[1] *vi.* grandinare.
to **hail**[2] *vt.* e *vi.* salutare, chiamare.
hair *s.* **1**. capelli, capigliatura **2**. pelo, crine, setola || — -*breadth*, spessore di un capello; — -*cut*, taglio dei capelli; — -*do*, acconciatura.
hairdresser *s.* parrucchiere.
hairiness *s.* pelosità.
hairless *agg.* senza capelli.
hairpin *s.* forcella (*per capelli*).
hairy *agg.* **1**. capelluto **2**. peloso.
halation *s.* alone.
halberd *s.* alabarda.
hale *agg.* robusto, gagliardo.
half *agg.* mezzo.
half *s.* (*pl.* halves) metà, mezzo. ♦ **half** *avv.* a mezzo, a metà || — -*brother*, fratellastro; — -*length*, di media lunghezza; — -*mast*, a mezz'asta; — -*pay*, stipendio ridotto; — -*processed*, semilavorato; — -*sister*, sorellastra; — -*year*, se-

mestre.
halfpenny *s.* mezzo penny.
halfway *agg.* e *avv.* a mezza strada.
hall *s.* **1**. sala, salone **2**. refettorio, sala di ritrovo.
hallo! *int.* pronto (*al telefono*).
to **hallow** *vt.* santificare.
to **hallucinate** *vt.* allucinare.
hallucination *s.* allucinazione.
halo *s.* alone, aureola.
to **halt**[1] *vt.* fermare. ♦ to **halt** *vi.* fermarsi.
to **halt**[2] *vi.* zoppicare.
halter *s.* **1**. capestro **2**. cavezza.
to **halve** *vt.* dividere a metà.
halyard *s.* (*mar.*) drizza.
ham *s.* **1**. prosciutto. ♦ **hams** *s. pl.* natiche.
hamlet *s.* piccolo villaggio.
hammer *s.* martello, martelletto: — -*blow*, colpo di martello, di maglio || to *bring under the* —, mettere all'asta.
to **hammer** *vt.* e *vi.* martellare.
hammering *s.* martellamento.
hammock *s.* amaca.
hamper[1] *s.* cesta.
hamper[2] *s.* impedimento.
to **hamper** *vt.* imbarazzare, ostacolare.
to **hamstring** *vt.* azzoppare.
hand *s.* **1**. mano: *hands off!*, via le mani!; *hands up!*, mani in alto! **2**. operaio, lavoratore **3**. calligrafia || *at* —, a portata di mano; *first-* —, di prima mano.
to **hand** *vt.* porgere, dare || *to* — *in*, consegnare; *to* — *out*, distribuire; *to* — *over*, rimettere.
handbag *s.* borsetta.
handbill *s.* volantino.
handbook *s.* manuale.
handcuffs *s. pl.* manette.
to **handcuff** *vt.* mettere le manette.
handful *s.* **1**. manciata **2**. piccolo numero (*di persone*).
handgrip *s.* stretta di mano, morsa della mano.
handicap *s.* svantaggio.
to **handicap** *vt.* svantaggiare, ostacolare.
handicraft *s.* **1**. lavoro manuale **2**. abilità manuale.
handicraftsman *s.* artigiano.
handily *avv.* **1**. abilmente **2**. a portata di mano.
handiwork *s.* lavoro fatto a mano.
handkerchief *s.* fazzoletto.
handle *s.* **1**. manico, impugnatura

2. (*fig.*) pretesto || — -*bar*, manubrio (*di bicicletta*).

to **handle** *vt.* **1.** maneggiare **2.** comportarsi verso.

handler *s.* manipolatore.

handling *s.* **1.** maneggiamento **2.** maniera di trattare.

handmade *agg.* fatto a mano.

handrail *s.* corrimano.

handshake *s.* stretta di mano.

handsome *agg.* bello, di bell'aspetto.

handwriting *s.* calligrafia.

handy *agg.* **1.** abile, destro **2.** a portata di mano || — -*man*, factotum.

hang *s.* inclinazione, pendio.

to **hang (hung, hung)** *vt.* appendere, attaccare.

to **hang (hung, hung)** *vi.* **1.** pendere **2.** appoggiarsi. ♦ to **hang** (*reg.*) *vt.* impiccare.

hanger *s.* gancio, uncino || — *on*, seguace, parassita; *dress*- —, attaccapanni; *paper*- —, tappezziere.

hanging *agg.* pendente, sospeso. ♦ **hanging** *s.* impiccagione.

hangman *s.* boia, carnefice.

hank *s.* matassa.

hapless *agg.* sfortunato.

to **happen** *vi.* avvenire, accadere.

happening *s.* avvenimento.

happily *avv.* felicemente.

happiness *s.* felicità.

happy *agg.* felice, contento.

harangue *s.* arringa.

to **harangue** *vt.* e *vi.* arringare, pronunciare un discorso solenne.

to **harass** *vt.* tormentare, molestare.

harbinger *s.* precursore.

harbour *s.* **1.** porto **2.** (*fig.*) rifugio.

to **harbour** *vt.* **1.** accogliere, dare asilo a **2.** nutrire (*pensieri ecc.*). ♦ to **harbour** *vi.* entrare in porto.

hard *agg.* **1.** duro **2.** severo, spietato **3.** difficile **4.** rigido (*di tempo*). ♦ **hard** *avv.* **1.** energicamente **2.** con difficoltà, duramente **3.** vicino, accanto || — -*boiled*, bollito fino a diventar duro; — -*headed*, ostinato; — -*set*, in bisogno.

to **harden** *vt.* indurire. ♦ to **harden** *vi.* indurirsi.

hardening *agg.* temprante. ♦ **hardening** *s.* tempra.

hardihood *s.* ardire, coraggio.

hardily *avv.* arditamente.

hardiness *s.* **1.** ardire **2.** robustezza.

hardly *avv.* **1.** a stento, a malapena **2.** quasi **3.** duramente, severamente.

hardness *s.* durezza (*anche fig.*).

hardship *s.* **1.** avversità **2.** stento.

hardware *s.* ferramenta.

hardy *agg.* ardito.

hare *s.* lepre || — -*brained*, scervellato; — -*lip*, labbro leporino.

to **hark** *vt.* e *vi.* ascoltare || *to* — *back*, risalire a (*col pensiero*).

harlequin *s.* arlecchino.

harlequinade *s.* arlecchinata.

harlot *s.* prostituta.

harm *s.* danno (*morale e fisico*) || *out of* — *'s way*, in salvo.

to **harm** *vt.* far male, far torto.

harmful *agg.* nocivo, dannoso.

harmfulness *s.* l'essere nocivo.

harmless *agg.* innocuo.

harmonic *agg.* **1.** armonico, armonioso **2.** (*mat.*) in progressione.

harmonious *agg.* armonioso.

harmonium *s.* armonium.

to **harmonize** *vt.* armonizzare. ♦ to **harmonize** *vi.* armonizzarsi.

harmony *s.* armonia, accordo.

harness *s.* finimenti (*pl.*).

to **harness** *vt.* bardare, mettere i finimenti a.

harp *s.* arpa.

harpist *s.* arpista.

harpoon *s.* rampone, fiocina.

harpsichord *s.* clavicembalo.

harrow *s.* erpice.

harsh *agg.* **1.** duro, ruvido **2.** aspro **3.** discordante (*di suono*).

harshness *s.* asprezza, durezza.

harvest *s.* raccolto, messe.

harvester *s.* **1.** mietitore **2.** mietitrice meccanica.

haste *s.* fretta, rapidità || *to make* —, far presto.

to **haste, to hasten** *vt.* affrettare. ♦ to **haste, to hasten** *vi.* affrettarsi.

hastily *avv.* **1.** frettolosamente **2.** precipitosamente.

hasty *agg.* **1.** frettoloso, affrettato **2.** avventato, impetuoso.

hat *s.* cappello.

hatch *s.* **1.** portello, mezza porta **2.** (*mar.*) boccaporto.

hatchet *s.* accetta.

hate *s.* odio.

to **hate** *vt.* odiare, avere in odio.

hateful *agg.* **1.** odioso **2.** pieno di odio.

hatred *s.* odio.

hatstand *s.* attaccapanni.

hatter *s.* cappellaio.

haughtily *avv.* altezzosamente.

haughtiness s. alterigia, boria.

haughty agg. altezzoso, arrogante.

haul s. 1. trazione, tiro 2. raccolta, retata.

to **haul** vt. tirare, trainare. ♦ to **haul** vi. cambiare (di vento).

haulage s. 1. trasporto 2. costo del trasporto.

haunt s. 1. ricovero, ritiro 2. covo, tana.

to **haunt** vt. 1. frequentare assiduamente 2. perseguitare (di ricordi, pensieri ecc.).

haunted agg. 1. frequentato 2. perseguitato.

haunting agg. che perseguita.

to **have (had, had)** vt. 1. (ausiliare) avere: I — gone, sono andato; I — not (I haven't) read the book, non ho letto il libro 2. avere, possedere || to — breakfast, far colazione 3. dovere: I — to go there, devo andarci 4. ricevere, ottenere || had better, sarebbe meglio che; I had rather, preferirei.

haven s. (fig.) porto, rifugio.

havoc s. strage, rovina.

hawk s. 1. falco, sparviero 2. (fig.) avvoltoio.

hawker[1] s. falconiere.

hawker[2] venditore ambulante.

hawser s. gomena.

hawthorn s. biancospino.

hay s. fieno, paglia || — -loft, fienile; — -making, falciatura.

haycock s. mucchio di fieno.

hayseed s. seme di erba.

haystack s. mucchio di fieno.

hazard s. 1. azzardo, rischio 2. giuoco di dadi.

to **hazard** vt. azzardare, arrischiare.

haze s. foschia, nebbia.

hazel s. nocciuolo || — -nut, nocciuola.

hazily avv. indistintamente.

haziness s. 1. foschia 2. (fig.) confusione.

hazy agg. 1. nebbioso 2. indistinto (anche fig.).

he pron. sogg. m. egli, lui, colui.

head s. 1. testa 2. capo, direttore 3. individuo 4. parte alta di una cosa 5. capo, unità di bestiame || — -first, a capofitto; — -master, direttore di una scuola; — -money, taglia; — -work, lavoro mentale.

to **head** vt. 1. colpire con la testa 2. dirigere, comandare 3. intestare. ♦ to **head** vi. dirigersi.

headache s. mal di testa.

headed agg. munito di testa || hot- —, esaltato; pig- —, ostinato; swollen- —, tronfio; wrong- —, caparbio.

heading s. 1. intestazione, titolo (di un capitolo) 2. (aer.) rotta.

headland s. promontorio.

headless agg. senza testa (anche fig.).

headlight s. faro anteriore.

headline s. intestazione di capitolo, articolo.

headlong avv. a capofitto, precipitosamente.

headquarters s. pl. quartier generale (sing.).

headstone s. pietra tombale.

to **heal** vt. 1. guarire, curare 2. (fig.) sanare. ♦ to **heal** vi. 1. guarire 2. sanarsi.

healer s. guaritore.

healing agg. salutare.

health s. 1. salute 2. salvezza divina.

healthful agg. salubre.

healthily avv. salubremente.

healthiness s. 1. salute 2. salubrità.

healthy agg. 1. sano, robusto 2. salutare.

heap s. mucchio, cumulo.

to **heap** vt. ammucchiare, accumulare.

to **hear (heard, heard)** vt. e vi. 1. sentire, udire 2. sentir dire, venire a sapere.

hearing s. 1. udito 2. udienza.

hearsay s. diceria, voce.

hearse s. carro funebre.

heart s. 1. cuore (anche fig.) 2. affetto, coraggio 3. centro, parte principale || — -beat, pulsazione; — -break, crepacuore; — -breaking, straziante; — -failure, collasso cardiaco; — -felt, sincero, di cuore.

heartache s. angoscia, angustia.

heartburn s. bruciore di stomaco.

hearted agg. dal cuore, di cuore || broken- —, desolato; chicken- —, pauroso; down- —, depresso; lion- —, dal cuore di leone; whole- —, generoso.

to **hearten** vt. incoraggiare. ♦ to **hearten** vi. prendere coraggio.

hearth s. 1. focolare (anche fig.) 2. (metal.) crogiuolo, letto di fusione.

heartily avv. cordialmente.

heartiness s. 1. cordialità.

heartless *agg.* senza cuore.
hearty *agg.* **1.** sincero, cordiale **2.** sano, robusto.
heat *s.* **1.** calore, caldo **2.** animosità || — -*stroke*, colpo di calore; — -*wave*, ondata di calore.
to **heat** *vt.* **1.** scaldare **2.** animare. ♦ to **heat** *vi.* **1.** scaldarsi **2.** animarsi.
heater *s.* bollitore, riscaldatore.
heath *s.* brughiera.
heathen *agg.* e *s.* pagano.
heather *s.* erica.
heating *s.* riscaldamento.
heave *s.* **1.** sforzo **2.** rigonfiamento (*di onde*) **3.** sollevamento.
heaven *s.* **1.** cielo, paradiso (*anche fig.*) **2.** stato di gioia.
heavenly *agg.* divino, celeste.
heavenward *agg.* rivolto al cielo.
heavily *avv.* pesantemente, gravemente.
heaviness *s.* pesantezza.
heavy *agg.* **1.** pesante **2.** violento, forte **3.** fangoso, pesante (*di terreno*).
Hebrew *agg.* e *s.* ebreo.
hecatomb *s.* ecatombe.
hectare *s.* ettaro.
hectic *agg.* **1.** tisico, etico **2.** febbricitante.
hectogram(me) *s.* ettogrammo.
hectolitre *s.* ettolitro.
hectometre *s.* ettometro.
hedge *s.* **1.** siepe **2.** barriera.
to **hedge** *vt.* circondare con una siepe. ♦ to **hedge** *vi.* essere evasivo.
hedgehog *s.* riccio, porcospino.
hedonism *s.* edonismo.
hedonist *s.* edonista.
heed *s.* attenzione, cura.
heedful *agg.* attento, vigile.
heedless *agg.* sventato.
heedlessness *s.* sventatezza, trascuratezza.
heel *s.* **1.** calcagno, tallone **2.** sperone (*di uccelli*).
Hegelian *agg.* hegeliano.
hegemony *s.* egemonia.
heifer *s.* giovenca.
heigh *inter.* ehi!
height *s.* **1.** altezza **2.** altitudine **3.** altura, collina **4.** sommità, il più alto grado.
to **heighten** *vt.* **1.** innalzare **2.** accrescere, intensificare. ♦ to **heighten** *vi.* innalzarsi.
heinous *agg.* atroce.

heir *s.* erede.
heiress *s.* ereditiera.
held V. to **hold**.
helicoid *agg.* elicoidale.
helicopter *s.* elicottero.
heliocentric(al) *agg.* eliocentrico.
heliotherapy *s.* elioterapia.
heliport *s.* eliporto.
helium *s.* elio.
hell *s.* inferno (*anche fig.*).
Hellenic *agg.* ellenico.
Hellenism *s.* ellenismo.
Hellenist *s.* ellenista.
hellish *agg.* infernale.
hello *inter.* salve!
helm[1] *s.* elmo, casco.
helm[2] *s.* timone (*anche fig.*).
helmet *s.* elmetto, casco.
helmsman *s.* timoniere.
help *s.* aiuto, soccorso.
to **help** *vt.* **1.** aiutare, soccorrere **2.** servire (*cibo*) || *cannot* —, non poter fare a meno di; *to* — *oneself to*, servirsi di (*cibo*).
helper *s.* aiutante.
helpful *agg.* utile, servizievole.
helpless *agg.* senza aiuto, indifeso.
helpmate *s.* collaboratore.
Helvetic *agg.* elvetico.
hem[1] *s.* orlo, bordo.
hem[2] *inter.* ehm!.
to **hem**[1] *vt.* orlare || *to* — *in*, circondare, accerchiare.
to **hem**[2] *vi.* schiarirsi la gola.
hemicycle *s.* emiciclo.
hemiplegia *s.* emiplegia.
hemisphere *s.* emisfero.
hemispheric(al) *agg.* emisferico.
hemlock *s.* cicuta.
hemp *s.* canapa.
hen *s.* **1.** gallina **2.** femmina (*di uccelli*) || — -*house*, pollaio.
hence *avv.* **1.** di qui, da questo momento **2.** donde.
henceforth *avv.* d'ora innanzi.
hendecasyllabic *agg.* endecasillabico.
hendecasyllable *s.* endecasillabo.
henna *s.* alcanna.
hepatic *agg.* epatico.
hepatitis *s.* epatite.
heptagon *s.* ettagono.
heptagonal *agg.* ettagonale.
her *agg. poss. f.* suo, sua, suoi, sue. ♦ **her** *pron. compl. f.* la, lei, le, colei.
herald *s.* **1.** araldo **2.** nunzio **3.** (*fig.*) precursore.

heraldic *agg.* araldico.
herb *s.* 1. erba 2. pianta medicinale.
herbaceous *agg.* erbaceo.
herbal *agg.* di erba.
herbarium *s.* erbario.
herbivorous *agg.* erbivoro.
herborist *s.* erborista.
Herculean *agg.* erculeo.
herd *s.* gregge, mandria.
herdsman *s.* mandriano.
here *avv.* qui, qua || — *I am*, eccomi.
hereabouts *avv.* qui intorno.
hereafter *avv.* d'ora innanzi.
hereby *avv.* 1. con questo mezzo 2. qui vicino.
hereditary *agg.* ereditario.
heredity *s.* (*biol.*) ereditarietà.
herein *avv.* 1. in questo 2. (*comm.*) nella presente.
heresiarch *s.* eresiarca.
heresy *s.* eresia.
heretic(al) *agg. e s.* eretico.
herewith *avv.* qui accluso.
heritable *agg.* ereditabile.
heritage *s.* eredità.
hermaphrodite *agg. e s.* ermafrodito.
hermeneutics *s.* ermeneutica.
hermetic(al) *agg.* ermetico.
hermetically *avv.* ermeticamente.
hermit *s.* eremita.
hermitage *s.* eremo, eremitaggio.
hernia *s.* ernia.
hernial *agg.* erniario.
hero *s.* eroe.
heroic(al) *agg.* eroico.
heroin *s.* (*chim.*) eroina.
heroine *s.* eroina.
heroism *s.* eroismo.
heron *s.* airone.
herpes *s.* erpete.
herring *s.* aringa || — *-bone*, spina di pesce (*nei tessuti ecc.*).
hers *pron. poss. f.* il suo, la sua, i suoi, le sue.
herself *pron. r. f.* 1. se stessa, sé, si 2. ella stessa.
hesitant *agg.* esitante.
to **hesitate** *vi.* esitare.
hesitatingly *avv.* con esitazione.
hesitation *s.* esitazione.
heteroclite *agg.* eteroclito.
heterodox *agg.* eterodosso.
heterodoxy *s.* eterodossia.
heterogeneity *s.* eterogeneità.
heterogeneous *agg.* eterogeneo.
to **hew** (hewed, hewn) *vt.* fendere, recidere || *to — down*, abbat-

tere.
hexagon *s.* esagono.
hexagonal *agg.* esagonale.
hexahedron *s.* esaedro.
hexameter *s.* esametro.
hiatus *s.* iato.
to **hibernate** *vi.* (*zool.*) cadere in letargo invernale.
hibernation *s.* 1. svernamento 2. ibernazione.
hiccough, hiccup *s.* singhiozzo, singulto.
hid V. *to hide*.
hidden V. *to hide*.
hide[1] *s.* pelle, cuoio.
hide[2] *s.* nascondiglio || — *-and-seek*, rimpiattino.
to **hide**[1] (hid, hidden) *vt.* nascondere, celare. ♦ to **hide** (hid, hidden) *vi.* nascondersi, celarsi.
to **hide**[2] *vt.* 1. spellare, scorticare 2. frustare.
hideous *agg.* orrendo, odioso.
hideousness *s.* odiosità, aspetto orribile.
hiding *s.* il nascondere.
hierarchy *s.* gerarchia.
hieratic *agg.* ieratico.
hieroglyph *s.* geroglifico.
hieroglyphic(al) *agg.* geroglifico.
high *agg.* 1. alto, elevato (*anche fig.*) 2. altezzoso 3. forte, intenso (*di luce, colori*) || — *-born*, di alto lignaggio; — *-class*, di prim'ordine; — *-coloured*, dal colore acceso; — *-hearted*, pieno di coraggio; — *-life*, vita di alta società; — *school*, scuola media; — *sea*, mare aperto; — *-speed*, ad alta velocità. ♦ **high** *avv.* 1. alto, in alto 2. fortemente.
highbrow *agg. e s.* intellettuale.
highland *s.* regione montuosa.
highlander *s.* montanaro.
highly *avv.* 1. molto, assai 2. altamente, nobilmente.
highness *s.* 1. altezza, elevatezza 2. eccellenza, valore.
highway *s.* strada maestra.
highwayman *s.* bandito, rapinatore.
hilarious *agg.* ilare.
hill *s.* collina, altura.
hillock *s.* collinetta.
hillside *s.* pendio.
hilltop *s.* sommità della collina.
hilly *agg.* collinoso.
hilt *s.* elsa.
him *pron. pers. m.* lo, lui, gli, colui, sé.
himself *pron. r. m.* 1. si, sé, se

stesso 2. egli stesso.

hind[1] *s.* cerva, daina.

hind[2] *s.* colono, fattore.

hind(er) *agg.* posteriore.

to **hinder** *vt.* e *vi.* 1. impedire, ostruire 2. imbarazzare.

hindrance *s.* ostacolo, impaccio.

Hindu *agg.* e *s.* indù.

hinge *s.* 1. cardine 2. (*fig.*) perno.

to **hinge** *vt.* munire di cardini. ♦ to **hinge** *vi.* 1. girare sui cardini 2. essere imperniato.

hint *s.* 1. cenno, allusione 2. consiglio.

to **hint** *vt.* e *vi.* alludere, accennare, suggerire.

hinterland *s.* retroterra.

hip *s.* anca, fianco.

hippocampus *s.* (*pl.* -pi.) ippocampo.

hippopotamus *s.* ippopotamo.

hire *s.* affitto, nolo.

to **hire** *vt.* prendere a servizio, noleggiare.

hireling *s.* mercenario.

his *agg. poss. m.* suo, sua, suoi, sue. ♦ **his** *pron. poss. m.* il suo, la sua, i suoi, le sue.

Hispanic *agg.* ispanico.

Hispanicism *s.* ispanismo.

Hispanist *s.* ispanista.

hispid *agg.* ispido.

hiss *s.* sibilo, fischio.

to **hiss** *vt.* e *vi.* 1. sibilare 2. fischiare.

histology *s.* istologia.

historian *s.* storico.

historic(al) *agg.* storico.

historicity *s.* storicità.

historiographer *s.* storiografo.

historiography *s.* storiografia.

history *s.* storia.

histrion *s.* istrione.

histrionic(al) *agg.* istrionico.

histrionism *s.* istrionismo.

hit *s.* 1. colpo, botta 2. osservazione sarcastica 3. caso fortunato 4. (*teat.*) successo.

to **hit** (hit, hit) *vt.* e *vi.* 1. battere, picchiare 2. urtare, venire a contatto 3. (*fig.*) toccare, colpire || to — the mark, colpire nel segno.

hitch *s.* 1. colpo, strattone, balzo repentino 2. nodo.

to **hitch** *vt.* 1. muovere a sbalzi 2. legare, attaccare. ♦ to **hitch** *vi.* muoversi a sbalzi.

to **hitchhike** *vi.* fare l'autostop.

hitchhiker *s.* autostoppista.

hitchhiking *s.* autostop.

hive *s.* 1. alveare, arnia 2. sciame (*anche fig.*).

hives *s. pl.* orticaria, eruzione cutanea.

hoar *s.* candore, vecchiaia || — -frost, brina.

hoard *s.* gruzzolo.

to **hoard** *vt.* ammassare, ammucchiare. ♦ to **hoard** *vi.* ammucchiarsi.

hoarder *s.* incettatore.

hoarding *s.* recinto provvisorio.

hoarse *agg.* rauco, fioco.

hoarseness *s.* raucedine.

hoary *agg.* 1. bianco, canuto 2. venerando.

hobble *s.* 1. zoppicamento 2. imbarazzo.

to **hobble** *vi.* zoppicare. ♦ to **hobble** *vt.* azzoppare.

hobby *s.* svago preferito, passatempo.

hobnail *s.* chiodo (*per scarponi*).

hobnailed *agg.* chiodato.

hodman *s.* manovale.

hoe *s.* zappa.

to **hoe** *vt.* zappare, estirpare le erbacce.

hog *s.* maiale.

hogshead *s.* barilotto (*per tabacco, zucchero*).

hoist *s.* montacarichi.

to **hoist** *vt.* alzare, sollevare.

hold[1] *s.* 1. presa 2. (*fig.*) ascendente.

hold[2] *s.* (*mar.*) stiva.

to **hold** (held, held) *vt.* e *vi.* 1. tenere, sostenere 2. contenere 3. ritenere, credere, pensare 4. occupare una carica, possedere 5. resistere, aggrapparsi || to — up, sollevare; to — back, esitare.

holder *s.* 1. possessore, detentore, proprietario 2. sostegno, supporto 3. dente canino.

holdings *s. pl.* beni, titoli.

hold-up *s.* intoppo nel traffico, panna di automobile.

hole *s.* 1. foro, apertura, buco 2. antro, tana.

holiday *s.* 1. festa, giorno festivo 2. vacanza.

holiness *s.* santità.

hollow *agg.* 1. concavo, infossato 2. cupo, cavernoso 3. (*fig.*) falso, irreale, vuoto.

to **hollow** *vt.* scavare, incavare.

hollow *avv.* (*fam.*) completamente.

hollowness *s.* 1. cavità 2. timbro

cavernoso (*di voce*).

holly *s.* agrifoglio.

holocaust *s.* olocausto.

holograph *agg.* e *s.* documento olografo.

holy *agg.* santo, sacro.

homage *s.* omaggio.

home[1] *s.* **1.** casa, focolare domestico **2.** patria **3.** rifugio, asilo, ospizio.

home[2] *agg.* domestico, casalingo.

home[3] *avv.* **1.** a casa, in patria **2.** direttamente, al segno || — -*born*, indigeno, locale; — -*bred*, allevato in casa; — -*made*, fatto in casa; — -*market*, mercato nazionale; — -*town*, città natia; — -*trade*, commercio interno

homeland *s.* patria.

homeless *agg.* senza casa.

homelike *agg.* domestico, familiare.

homely *agg.* **1.** semplice, modesto **2.** domestico.

homeopathic *agg.* omeopatico.

homeopathy *s.* omeopatia.

Homeric *agg.* omerico.

homesick *agg.* nostalgico.

homesickness *s.* nostalgia.

homeward *agg.* e *avv.* verso casa, verso la patria.

homework *s. coll.* compiti per casa.

homicidal *agg.* omicida.

homicide *s.* omicidio.

homily *s.* omelia.

homogeneity *s.* omogeneità.

homogeneous *agg.* omogeneo.

to **homogenize** *vt.* omogeneizzare.

to **homologate** *vt.* omologare.

homologation *s.* omologazione.

homologous *agg.* omologo.

homology *s.* omologia.

homonymous *agg.* omonimo.

homonymy *s.* omonimia.

homosexual *agg.* e *s.* omosessuale.

homosexuality *s.* omosessualità.

homy *agg.* casalingo.

honest *agg.* **1.** onesto, integro **2.** leale.

honesty *s.* **1.** onestà, probità **2.** lealtà.

honey *s.* miele.

honeycomb *s.* favo.

honeyed *agg.* **1.** coperto di miele **2.** (*fig.*) sdolcinato, adulatorio.

honeymoon *s.* luna di miele.

honeysuckle *s.* caprifoglio.

honorary *agg.* onorario, onorifico.

honorific *agg.* onorifico.

honour *s.* **1.** onore, reputazione **2.** stima, reverenza **3.** Eccellenza.

to **honour** *vt.* onorare, fare onore a.

honourable *agg.* stimato, onorevole.

honourableness *s.* onorabilità.

hood *s.* cappuccio.

to **hood** *vt.* incappucciare, fornire di cappuccio.

hoof *s.* zoccolo (*di animale*).

hook *s.* **1.** uncino, gancio **2.** amo **3.** tagliola **4.** falce per grano || *by* — *or by crook*, di riffa o di raffa.

to **hook** *vt.* agganciare. ♦ to **hook** *vi.* agganciarsi.

hooked *agg.* **1.** fornito di uncini **2.** adunco, uncinato.

hoop *s.* collare, cerchio (*di botte, ruota ecc.*).

to **hoop** *vt.* cerchiare (*una botte*).

to **hoot** *vt.* e *vi.* **1.** urlare, gridare **2.** suonare il clacson.

hop[1] *s.* salto (*su una gamba sola*).

hop[2] *s.* luppolo.

to **hop** *vt.* e *vi.* saltare su una gamba sola.

hope *s.* speranza.

to **hope** *vt.* e *vi.* sperare, essere fiducioso.

hopeful *agg.* pieno di speranza, fiducioso.

hopefulness *s.* fiducia, buona speranza.

hopeless *agg.* senza speranza, irrimediabile.

hopelessness *s.* disperazione.

hopper *s.* persona od insetto che saltella.

horde *s.* orda.

horizon *s.* orizzonte.

horizontal *agg.* orizzontale.

horizontally *avv.* orizzontalmente.

hormone *s.* ormone.

horn *s.* **1.** corno, tentacolo, antenna **2.** (*mus.*) corno, tromba.

to **horn** *vt.* **1.** fornire di corna **2.** ferire con le corna.

hornet *s.* vespa, calabrone.

hornpipe *s.* cornamusa.

horology *s.* orologeria.

horoscope *s.* oroscopo: *to cast a* —, fare un oroscopo.

horrible *agg.* **1.** orribile, orrendo **2.** (*fam.*) eccessivo.

horribly *avv.* orribilmente.

horrid *agg.* orrido, orrendo.

horrific *agg.* orribile, orripilante.

to **horrify** *vt.* **1.** atterrire, incutere timore **2.** scandalizzare.

horror *s.* **1.** orrore, spavento **2.** cosa orribile || — -*stricken*, atterrito.

hors-d'oeuvre *s.* antipasto.

horse *s.* cavallo || — *-bean*, fava; — *-boy*, mozzo di stalla; — *-chestnut*, ippocastano; — *-doctor*, veterinario; — *-race*, corsa ippica; — *-shoe*, ferro di cavallo.

horseback *s.* dorso di cavallo || *on* —, a cavallo.

horseman *s.* cavaliere.

horticultural *agg.* attinente all'orticultura.

horticulture *s.* orticultura.

hosanna *inter.* osanna.

hose *s.* 1. idrante 2. calze (*pl.*).

hosier *s.* commerciante in calze.

hosiery *s.* maglieria.

hospice *s.* alloggio, ospizio.

hospitable *agg.* ospitale.

hospital *s.* ospedale.

hospitality *s.* ospitalità.

host[1] *s.* folla, moltitudine.

host[2] *s.* ospite, anfitrione.

hostage *s.* ostaggio.

hostel *s.* pensionato (*per giovani, studenti, militari ecc.*).

hostess *s.* 1. ospite, padrona di casa 2. assistente di volo.

hostile *agg.* ostile, nemico.

hostility *s.* inimicizia, ostilità.

hot *agg.* 1. caldo, ardente 2. forte, piccante 3. violento, impetuoso || — *-headed*, scalmanato.

hotel *s.* albergo || — *-keeper*, albergatore.

hothead *s.* testa calda.

hothouse *s.* serra.

hotly *avv.* caldamente.

hotspur *s.* persona impulsiva.

hound *s.* bracco, segugio.

to hound *vt.* cacciare (*con bracchi*).

hour *s.* 1. ora 2. periodo. ♦ **hours** *s. pl.* orario (*sing.*).

hourly *agg.* 1. continuo 2. all'ora 3. ad ogni ora. ♦ **hourly** *avv.* 1. continuamente 2. ad ogni ora 3. d'ora in ora.

house *s.* 1. casa, abitazione 2. albergo, pensione 3. clinica 4. convento 5. casato, dinastia 6. teatro 7. (*comm.*) ditta 8. (*mar.*) tuga.

to house *vt.* 1. alloggiare, ricevere in casa 2. (*fig.*) offrire un rifugio. ♦ **to house** *vi.* 1. prendere alloggio 2. rifugiarsi.

housebreaker *s.* scassinatore.

housebreaking *s.* demolizione edilizia.

household *s.* famiglia: *Royal Household*, la famiglia reale.

householder *s.* capofamiglia.

housekeeper *s.* governante, domestica.

housekeeping *s.* il governo della casa.

houseless *agg.* senza casa.

housemaid *s.* domestica, cameriera.

housewife *s.* (*pl.* -wives) massaia, casalinga.

housework *s.* lavoro domestico.

housing *s.* 1. il ricevere, l'accogliere 2. alloggio, rifugio, riparo.

hovel *s.* 1. tana 2. baracca.

to hover *vi.* 1. librarsi, svolazzare 2. gironzolare.

how *avv.* come, in che modo.

however *avv.* 1. comunque 2. però, tuttavia.

howitzer *s.* obice.

howl *s.* urlo, grido.

to howl *vt.* e *vi.* urlare, ululare.

howling *agg.* urlante, ululante.

hub *s.* mozzo di ruota.

hubbub *s.* tumulto, fracasso.

huddle *s.* calca, folla.

to huddle *vt.* ammucchiare. ♦ **to huddle** *vi.* affollarsi, accalcarsi.

hue *s.* tinta, colore.

hug *s.* abbraccio.

to hug *vt.* abbracciare (*anche fig.*) || *to* — *oneself*, compiacersi.

huge *agg.* enorme, vasto.

hugeness *s.* grandezza, enormità.

hull *s.* scafo.

hullabaloo *s.* tumulto, fracasso.

hullo *inter.* 1. (*fam.*) salve 2. (*tel.*) pronto.

hum *s.* ronzio, mormorio.

to hum *vt.* e *vi.* 1. ronzare, mormorare 2. cantare a bocca chiusa.

human *agg.* 1. umano 2. sensibile.

humane *agg.* umano, compassionevole.

humaneness *s.* benevolenza, umanità.

humanism *s.* umanesimo.

humanist *s.* umanista.

humanistic *agg.* umanistico.

humanitarian *agg.* filantropico, umanitario.

humanity *s.* 1. umanità, il genere umano 2. bontà, benevolenza.

to humanize *vt.* 1. rendere umano 2. adattare alla natura umana. ♦ **to humanize** *vi.* acquisire sentimenti migliori.

humankind *s.* il genere umano.

humble *agg.* umile, modesto.

to humble *vt.* umiliare.

humbleness *s.* umiltà.

humbly *avv.* umilmente.

humbug *s.* frode, impostura.

humdrum *s.* monotonia, tedio. ♦ **humdrum** *agg.* monotono.

humeral *agg.* omerale.

humerus *s.* (*pl.* -ri) omero.

humid *agg.* umido.

humidity *s.* umidità.

to **humiliate** *vt.* umiliare, mortificare.

humiliation *s.* umiliazione.

humility *s.* umiltà.

humming *agg.* ronzante. ♦ **humming** *s.* ronzio.

humorist *s.* umorista.

humorous *agg.* arguto, dotato di senso dell'umorismo.

humour *s.* **1.** umorismo **2.** umore.

hump *s.* **1.** gobba, gibbosità **2.** collinetta, cresta.

humpback *s.* **1.** gobba **2.** gobbo.

hunch *s.* gobba, gibbosità.

hunchback *s.* persona gobba.

hundred *agg.* cento. ♦ **hundred** *s.* centinaio.

hundredth *agg.* centesimo.

hung V. *to hang.*

Hungarian *agg. e s.* ungherese.

hunger *s.* **1.** fame, appetito **2.** (*fig.*) ingordigia.

hungrily *avv.* **1.** con grande appetito **2.** avidamente.

hungry *agg.* **1.** affamato || *to be* —, aver fame **2.** (*fig.*) avido, bramoso.

hunt *s.* **1.** caccia **2.** ricerca, inseguimento.

to **hunt** *vt. e vi.* **1.** cacciare, andare a caccia **2.** cercare affannosamente.

hunter *s.* cacciatore (*anche fig.*).

hunting *s.* **1.** caccia **2.** ricerca.

huntsman *s.* cacciatore.

hurdle *s.* ostacolo (*anche fig.*).

hurl *s.* lancio violento.

to **hurl** *vt.* lanciare, scagliare (*anche fig.*).

hurrah *inter.* urrah!

hurricane *s.* uragano, ciclone (*anche fig.*).

hurried *agg.* affrettato, precipitoso.

hurry *s.* fretta, precipitazione: *to be in a* —, aver fretta.

to **hurry** *vt.* affrettare. ♦ to **hurry** *vi.* affrettarsi || — *up!*, fa presto!

hurt *s.* lesione, ferita (*anche fig.*).

to **hurt** (**hurt, hurt**) *vt. e vi.* **1.** dolere **2.** recar dolore, offendere.

hurtful *agg.* **1.** dannoso **2.** offensivo.

husband *s.* marito.

husbandry *s.* **1.** agricoltura **2.** amministrazione domestica.

hush *inter.* silenzio.

to **hush** *vt.* **1.** zittire, tacere **2.** (*fig.*) calmare.

husk *s.* **1.** guscio, baccello **2.** involucro **3.** (*pl.*) rifiuti.

to **husk** *vt.* sgusciare, sbucciare.

husky *agg.* rugoso, secco.

hussar *s.* ussaro.

hut *s.* **1.** capanna, casupola **2.** rifugio alpino.

hyacinth *s.* giacinto.

hybrid *agg. e s.* ibrido.

hybridism *s.* ibridismo.

hybridization *s.* ibridazione.

hydra *s.* idra.

hydrangea *s.* ortensia.

hydrant *s.* idrante.

hydrate *s.* idrato.

to **hydrate** *vt.* idratare.

hydraulic *agg.* idraulico.

hydraulics *s.* idraulica.

hydric *agg.* contenente idrogeno.

hydrocarbon *s.* idrocarburo.

hydrocephalus *s.* idrocefalo.

hydroelectric *agg.* idroelettrico.

hydrofluoric *agg.* fluoridrico.

hydrofoil boat *s.* aliscafo.

hydrogen *s.* idrogeno.

hydrology *s.* idrologia.

hydrolysis *s.* (*pl.* -ses) idrolisi.

hydrostatic(al) *agg.* idrostatico.

hyena *s.* iena.

hygiene *s.* igiene.

hygienics *s.* la scienza dell'igiene.

hygienist *s.* igienista.

hygrometry *s.* igrometria.

hymn *s.* inno.

hyperbole *s.* iperbole.

hyperbolic(al) *agg.* iperbolico.

hyperborean *agg. e s.* iperboreo.

hypercritical *agg.* ipercritico.

hypermetropy *s.* ipermetropia.

hypernutrition *s.* supernutrizione.

hypersensitive *agg.* ipersensibile.

hypersensitivity *s.* ipersensibilità.

hypertension *s.* ipertensione.

hypertrophy *s.* ipertrofia.

hyphen *s.* lineetta d'unione.

hypnosis *s.* (*pl.* -ses) ipnosi.

hypnotic *agg. e s.* ipnotico.

hypnotism *s.* ipnotismo.

to **hypnotize** *vt.* ipnotizzare.

hypochondria *s.* ipocondria.

hypochondriac *agg. e s.* ipocondriaco.

hypocrisy *s.* ipocrisia.

hypocrite s. ipocrita.
hypocritic(al) agg. ipocrita.
hypodermic agg. ipodermico.
hypodermoclysis s. ipodermoclisi.
hyposulphite s. iposolfito.
hypotenuse s. ipotenusa.
hypothecary agg. ipotecario.
to **hypothecate** vt. ipotecare.
hypothesis s. (pl. -ses) ipotesi.
to **hypothesize** vi. fare ipotesi.
hypothetic(al) agg. ipotetico.
hypothetically avv. ipoteticamente.
hysteria s. isterismo.
hysteric(al) agg. isterico.
hysterics s. attacco isterico.

I

I pron. pers. io.
iamb s. giambo.
iambic agg. giambico.
Iberian agg. e s. iberico.
ice s. ghiaccio || — -box, ghiacciaia;
— -breaker, rompighiaccio; —
-cream, gelato.
to **ice** vt. 1. ghiacciare 2. (cuc.) glassare.
iceboat s. nave rompighiaccio.
Icelander s. islandese.
Icelandic agg. islandese.
ichtyologist s. ittiologo.
ichthyology s. ittiologia.
icicle s. ghiacciuolo.
iciness s. gelo.
icing s. glassatura.
icon s. icona.
iconoclast s. iconoclasta.
iconoclastic agg. iconoclastico.
iconography s. iconografia.
icy agg. gelido, gelato.
idea s. idea.
ideal agg. e s. ideale.
idealism s. idealismo.
idealist s. idealista.
idealistic(al) agg. idealistico.
idealization s. idealizzazione.
to **idealize** vt. idealizzare.
ideally avv. idealmente.
to **ideate** vt. ideare.
ideation s. ideazione.
identic(al) agg. identico.
identifiable agg. identificabile.
identification s. identificazione.
to **identify** vt. identificare || to —
oneself with, immedesimarsi con.

identity s. identità.
ideogram s. ideogramma.
ideography s. ideografia.
ideologic(al) agg. ideologico.
ideologist s. ideologo.
ideology s. ideologia.
idiocy s. idiozia.
idiom s. 1. idioma 2. idiotismo.
idiomatic(al) agg. idiomatico.
idiosyncrasy s. idiosincrasia.
idiot s. idiota.
idiotic(al) agg. idiota.
idle agg. 1. ozioso 2. vano.
to **idle** vi. oziare.
idleness s. 1. ozio 2. futilità.
idler s. ozioso.
idly avv. oziosamente.
idol s. idolo.
idolater s. idolatra.
to **idolatrize** vt. idolatrare.
idolatrous agg. idolatrico.
idolatry, idolism s. idolatria.
idyl(l) s. idillio.
idyllic agg. idillico.
if cong. se || as —, come se.
igneous agg. igneo.
to **ignite** vt. accendere. ♦ to **ignite**
vi. accendersi.
ignition s. accensione || battery
coil —, spinterogeno.
ignobility s. ignobilità.
ignoble agg. ignobile.
ignominious agg. ignominioso.
ignominy, ignomy s. ignominia.
ignorance s. ignoranza.
ignorant agg. ignorante.
to **ignore** vt. ignorare.
ilex s. leccio.
iliac agg. iliaco.
ill (worse, worst) agg. 1. ammalato 2. cattivo. ♦ ill avv. male ||
— -advised, sconsiderato; — -disposed, malevolo; — -fated, sfortunato; — -mannered, maleducato.
♦ ill s. male.
illation s. illazione.
illegal agg. 1. illegale 2. illecito.
illegality s. illegalità.
illegible agg. illeggibile.
illegitimacy s. illegittimità.
illegitimate agg. illegittimo.
illiberal agg. 1. illiberale 2. meschino.
illiberality s. 1. illiberalità 2. meschinità.
illicit agg. illecito.
illimitable agg. illimitato.
illiteracy s. 1. analfabetismo 2. ignoranza.

illiterate *agg.* e *s.* **1.** analfabeta **2.** ignorante.
illness *s.* malattia.
illogical *agg.* illogico.
illogicality *s.* illogicità.
to ill-treat *vt.* maltrattare.
to illuminate *vt.* illuminare.
illumination *s.* illuminazione.
to illumine *vt.* illuminare.
illuminism *s.* illuminismo.
ill-usage *s.* maltrattamento.
to ill-use *vt.* maltrattare.
illusion *s.* illusione.
illusionism *s.* illusionismo.
illusionist *s.* illusionista.
illusive *agg.* illusorio.
illusiveness *s.* illusorietà.
illusory *agg.* illusorio.
to illustrate *vt.* illustrare.
illustration *s.* illustrazione.
illustrative *agg.* illustrativo.
illustrator *s.* illustratore.
illustrious *agg.* illustre.
ill-will *s.* malevolenza.
ill-wisher *s.* malevolo.
image *s.* immagine.
to image *vt.* **1.** immaginare **2.** descrivere **3.** riflettere.
imagery *s.* raffigurazione.
imaginable *agg.* immaginabile.
imaginary *agg.* immaginario.
imagination *s.* immaginazione.
imaginative *agg.* immaginativo.
to imagine *vt.* e *vi.* immaginare.
imagining *s.* immaginazione.
imbecile *agg.* e *s.* **1.** debole **2.** imbecille.
imbecility *s.* **1.** debolezza **2.** imbecillità.
to imbibe *vt.* assorbire. ♦ to imbibe *vi.* imbeversi.
to imbue *vt.* impregnare.
imitable *agg.* imitabile.
to imitate *vt.* imitare.
imitation *s.* imitazione.
imitative *agg.* imitativo.
imitator *s.* imitatore.
immaculate *agg.* immacolato.
immanence *s.* immanenza.
immanent *agg.* immanente.
immanentism *s.* immanentismo.
immaterial *agg.* **1.** immateriale **2.** irrilevante.
immaterialism *s.* immaterialismo.
immaterialist *s.* immaterialista.
immateriality *s.* immaterialità.
immature *agg.* immaturo.
immaturity *s.* immaturità.
immeasurability *s.* incommensura-

bilità.
immeasurable *agg.* incommensurabile.
immediacy *s.* **1.** immediatezza **2.** rapporto diretto.
immediate *agg.* **1.** immediato **2.** diretto.
immediateness *s.* V. *immediacy.*
immemorial *agg.* immemorabile.
immense *agg.* immenso.
immenseness, immensity *s.* immensità.
immensurability *s.* immensurabilità.
immensurable *agg.* immensurabile.
to immerge, to immerse *vt.* immergere. ♦ to immerge *vi.* immergersi.
immersion *s.* **1.** immersione **2.** eclisse.
immigrant *agg.* e *s.* immigrante.
to immigrate *vi.* immigrare.
immigration *s.* immigrazione.
imminence *s.* **1.** imminenza **2.** pericolo.
imminent *agg.* **1.** imminente **2.** sovrastante.
immobile *agg.* immobile.
immobility *s.* immobilità.
immobilization *s.* immobilizzazione.
to immobilize *vt.* immobilizzare.
immoderate *agg.* smodato.
immoderateness *s.* smoderatezza.
immodest *agg.* **1.** immodesto **2.** indecente.
immodesty *s.* **1.** immodestia **2.** indecenza.
to immolate *vt.* immolare.
immolation *s.* immolazione.
immolator *s.* immolatore.
immoral *agg.* immorale.
immorality *s.* immoralità.
immortal *agg.* e *s.* immortale.
immortality *s.* immortalità.
immortalization *s.* l'immortalare.
to immortalize *vt.* immortalare.
immovability *s.* **1.** immobilità **2.** inamovibilità.
immovable *agg.* **1.** immobile **2.** inamovibile.
immovables *s. pl.* beni immobili.
immune *agg.* **1.** immune **2.** esente.
immunity *s.* **1.** immunità **2.** esenzione.
immunization *s.* immunizzazione.
to immunize *vt.* immunizzare.
to immure *vt.* **1.** murare **2.** impri-

gionare **3.** chiudere fra mura.
immutability *s.* immutabilità.
immutable *agg.* immutabile.
imp *s.* diavoletto.
impact *s.* urto, collisione.
to **impact** *vt.* conficcare.
to **impair** *vt.* menomare.
impairment *s.* menomazione.
to **impale** *vt.* impalare.
impalpability *s.* impalpabilità.
impalpable *agg.* impalpabile.
imparity *s.* imparità.
to **impart** *vt.* **1.** impartire **2.** rivelare.
impartial *agg.* imparziale.
impartiality *s.* imparzialità.
impassable *agg.* invalicabile, impraticabile.
impassibility *s.* impassibilità.
impassible *agg.* impassibile.
to **impassion** *vt.* appassionare.
impassionate, impassioned *agg.*
eccitato, ardente.
impassive *agg.* impassibile.
impatience *s.* **1.** impazienza **2.** avversione.
impatient *agg.* **1.** impaziente **2.** intollerante.
impavid *agg.* impavido.
to **impeach** *vt.* **1.** imputare **2.** bia-
simare || *to — so. for high trea-
son,* accusare qu. di alto tradimento.
impeachable *agg.* accusabile.
impeacher *s.* accusatore.
impeachment *s.* accusa.
impeccability *s.* impeccabilità.
impeccable *agg.* impeccabile.
impecunious *agg.* povero.
to **impede** *vt.* **1.** impedire **2.** ostacolare.
impediment *s.* impedimento.
to **impel** *vt.* spingere, incitare.
impellent *agg.* impellente. ♦ **impellent** *s.* incentivo.
to **impend** *vi.* incombere.
impendence *s.* imminenza.
impendent *agg.* incombente.
impenetrability *s.* impenetrabilità.
impenetrable *agg.* impenetrabile.
impenitence *s.* impenitenza.
impenitent *agg.* impenitente.
imperative *agg. e s.* imperativo.
imperator *s.* imperatore.
imperceptibility *s.* impercettibilità.
imperceptible *agg.* impercettibile.
imperfect *agg.* **1.** imperfetto **2.** incompiuto.
imperfection *s.* **1.** imperfezione **2.**

incompiutezza.
imperial *agg.* imperiale.
imperialism *s.* imperialismo.
imperialist *s.* imperialista.
imperialistic *agg.* imperialistico.
to **imperil** *vt.* mettere in pericolo.
imperious *agg.* **1.** imperioso **2.** impellente.
imperiousness *s.* **1.** imperiosità **2.**
urgenza.
imperishability *s.* indistruttibilità.
imperishable *agg.* indistruttibile,
imperituro.
impermeability *s.* impermeabilità.
impermeable *agg.* impermeabile.
impersonal *agg.* impersonale.
impersonality *s.* l'essere impersonale.
to **impersonate** *vt.* impersonare.
impersonation *s.* personificazione.
impertinence *s.* **1.** impertinenza
2. non pertinenza.
impertinent *agg.* **1.** impertinente
2. non pertinente.
imperturbability *s.* imperturbabilità.
imperturbable *agg.* imperturbabile.
impervious *agg.* **1.** impervio **2.** impermeabile.
to **impetrate** *vt.* impetrare.
impetration *s.* impetrazione.
impetuosity *s.* impetuosità.
impetuous *agg.* impetuoso.
impetus *s.* impeto.
impiety *s.* empietà.
impious *agg.* empio.
impish *agg.* birichino.
implacability *s.* implacabilità.
implacable *agg.* implacabile.
to **implant** *vt.* **1.** impiantare **2.** inculcare.
implement *s.* utensile.
to **implement** *vt.* **1.** compiere **2.**
attrezzare.
to **implicate** *vt.* implicare.
implication *s.* implicazione.
implicit, implied *agg.* implicito.
to **implore** *vt.* implorare.
imploring *agg.* supplichevole.
to **imply** *vt.* implicare.
impolite *agg.* scortese.
impoliteness *s.* scortesia.
impolitic *agg.* impolitico.
imponderability *s.* imponderabilità.
imponderable *agg.* imponderabile.
import *s.* **1.** importanza **2.** significato **3.** (*comm.*) importazione.
to **import** *vt.* **1.** importare **2.** si-

gnificare **3.** (*comm.*) importare.
importance *s.* importanza.
important *agg.* importante.
importer *s.* importatore.
importunate, importune *agg.* urgente.
to **importune** *vt.* importunare.
importunity *s.* **1.** insistenza **2.** urgenza.
to **impose** *vt.* **1.** imporre **2.** (*tip.*) impaginare. ◆ to **impose** *vi.* imporsi || to — on, ingannare.
imposing *agg.* imponente.
imposition *s.* **1.** imposizione **2.** imposta **3.** inganno **4.** (*tip.*) messa in macchina.
impossibility *s.* impossibilità.
impossible *agg.* impossibile.
impostor *s.* impostore.
imposture *s.* impostura.
impotence *s.* impotenza.
impotent *agg.* impotente.
to **impoverish** *vt.* impoverire.
impoverishment *s.* impoverimento.
impracticability *s.* **1.** inattuabilità **2.** impraticabilità **3.** intrattabilità.
impracticable *agg.* **1.** inattuabile **2.** impraticabile **3.** intrattabile.
imprecation *s.* imprecazione.
imprecatory *agg.* imprecatorio.
impregnable *agg.* inespugnabile.
to **impregnate** *vt.* **1.** impregnare **2.** fecondare.
impregnation *s.* fecondazione.
to **impress** *vt.* **1.** imprimere, stampare **2.** impressionare.
impression *s.* **1.** impressione **2.** ristampa.
impressionability *s.* impressionabilità.
impressionable *agg.* impressionabile.
impressionism *s.* impressionismo.
impressionist *agg.* e *s.* impressionista.
impressive *agg.* impressionante.
imprint *s.* **1.** impronta **2.** stampa.
to **imprint** *vt.* **1.** imprimere **2.** stampare.
to **imprison** *vt.* imprigionare.
imprisonment *s.* prigionia.
improbability *s.* improbabilità.
improbable *agg.* improbabile.
improbably *avv.* improbabilmente.
impromptu *agg.* improvvisato. ◆
impromptu *s.* improvvisazione.
improper *agg.* **1.** erroneo **2.** inadatto **3.** sconveniente, irregolare.

impropriety *s.* **1.** scorrettezza **2.** sconvenienza.
to **improve** *vt.* **1.** migliorare **2.** valorizzare. ◆ to **improve** *vi.* migliorare, perfezionarsi.
improvement *s.* miglioramento.
improvidence *s.* imprevidenza.
improvident *agg.* imprevidente.
improvisation *s.* improvvisazione.
improvisator *s.* improvvisatore.
to **improvise** *vt.* e *vi.* improvvisare.
imprudence *s.* imprudenza.
imprudent *agg.* imprudente.
impudence *s.* impudenza.
impudent *agg.* impudente.
to **impugn** *vt.* (*giur.*) impugnare.
impugnable *agg.* (*giur.*) impugnabile.
impugner *s.* oppositore.
impulse, impulsion *s.* impulso.
impulsive *agg.* impulsivo.
impulsiveness, impulsivity *s.* impulsività.
impunity *s.* impunità.
impure *agg.* impuro.
impurity *s.* impurità.
imputable *agg.* imputabile.
imputation *s.* imputazione.
to **impute** *vt.* imputare.
in *avv.* e *prep.* a, in, dentro, entro, durante || to be — Paris, essere a Parigi; the best — the world, il migliore del mondo; — my opinion, secondo me; — all, in tutto; — that, in quanto che.
inability *s.* incapacità.
inaccessibility *s.* inaccessibilità.
inaccessible *agg.* inaccessibile.
inaccuracy *s.* inesattezza.
inaccurate *agg.* inesatto.
inaction *s.* inattività.
inactive *agg.* inattivo.
inactivity *s.* inattività.
inadaptability *s.* inadattabilità.
inadequacy *s.* inadeguatezza.
inadequate *agg.* inadeguato.
inadmissibility *s.* inammissibilità.
inadmissible *agg.* inammissibile.
inadvertence *s.* inavvertenza.
inadvertent *agg.* **1.** disattento **2.** involontario.
inalienability *s.* inalienabilità.
inalienable *agg.* inalienabile.
inalterability *s.* inalterabilità.
inalterable *agg.* inalterabile.
inane *agg.* e *s.* vuoto.
inanimate *agg.* **1.** inanimato **2.** fiacco.
inanity *s.* inanità.

inappeasable *agg.* implacabile.
inappellable *agg.* inappellabile.
inappetence *s.* inappetenza.
inapplicable *agg.* inapplicabile.
inappropriate *agg.* inadeguato.
inapt *agg.* **1.** inadatto **2.** inetto.
inarticulate *agg.* inarticolato.
inattention *s.* **1.** disattenzione **2.** negligenza.
inattentive *agg.* **1.** disattento **2.** negligente.
inaudible *agg.* impercettibile.
inaugural *agg.* inaugurale.
to **inaugurate** *vt.* inaugurare.
inauguration *s.* inaugurazione.
inboard *agg.* interno. ♦ **inboard** *avv.* internamente.
inborn, inbred *agg.* innato.
incalculable *agg.* **1.** incalcolabile **2.** incerto.
incandescence *s.* incandescenza.
incandescent *agg.* incandescente.
incantation *s.* incantesimo.
incapability *s.* incapacità.
incapable *agg.* incapace.
incapacity *s.* incapacità.
to **incarnate** *vt.* **1.** incarnare **2.** realizzare.
incarnation *s.* incarnazione.
incatenation *s.* incatenamento.
incautious *agg.* incauto.
incendiary *agg.* e *s.* **1.** incendiario **2.** sovversivo.
incensation *s.* incensamento.
incense *s.* incenso.
to **incense**[1] *vt.* incensare.
to **incense**[2] *vt.* provocare.
incensurable *agg.* incensurabile.
incentive *agg.* stimolante. ♦ **incentive** *s.* incentivo.
incertitude *s.* incertezza.
incessant *agg.* incessante.
incest *s.* incesto.
incestuous *agg.* incestuoso.
inch *s.* pollice (*misura*).
incidence *s.* incidenza.
incident *agg.* probabile. ♦ **incident** *s.* avvenimento.
incidental *agg.* fortuito. ♦ **incidental** *s.* caso.
incipient *agg.* incipiente.
to **incise** *vt.* incidere.
incisive *agg.* incisivo.
incisiveness *s.* incisività.
incisor *s.* incisivo.
incitation *s.* incitamento.
to **incite** *vt.* incitare.
incivility *s.* villania.
inclemency *s.* inclemenza.

inclement *agg.* inclemente.
inclinable *agg.* incline.
inclination *s.* inclinazione.
to **incline** *vt.* inclinare. ♦ to **incline** *vi.* propendere.
inclined *agg.* **1.** inclinato **2.** incline.
to **include** *vt.* includere.
included *agg.* incluso, compreso.
inclusion *s.* inclusione.
inclusive *agg.* compreso.
incoherence *s.* incoerenza.
incoherent *agg.* incoerente.
incombustible *agg.* incombustibile.
income *s.* rendita, reddito ‖ — -tax, imposta sul reddito.
incoming *s.* entrata. ♦ **incoming** *agg.* entrante.
incommensurability *s.* incommensurabilità.
incommensurable *agg.* incommensurabile.
incommensurate *agg.* **1.** inadeguato **2.** smisurato.
incommunicability *s.* incomunicabilità.
incommunicable *agg.* incomunicabile.
incommutable *agg.* incommutabile.
incomparable *agg.* incomparabile.
incompatibility *s.* incompatibilità.
incompatible *agg.* incompatibile.
incompetence *s.* incompetenza.
incompetent *agg.* e *s.* incompetente.
incomplete *agg.* incompleto.
incompleteness, incompletion *s.* incompletezza.
incomprehensibility *s.* incomprensibilità.
incomprehensible *agg.* incomprensibile.
incomprehension *s.* incomprensione.
inconceivability *s.* inconcepibilità.
inconceivable *agg.* inconcepibile.
inconclusive *agg.* inconcludente.
inconclusiveness *s.* inconcludenza.
incongruity *s.* incongruenza.
incongruous *agg.* incongruo.
inconsequence *s.* incongruenza.
inconsequent *agg.* incongruente.
inconsequential *agg.* **1.** incoerente **2.** irrilevante.
inconsiderate *agg.* sconsiderato.
inconsistence *s.* incoerenza.
inconsistent *agg.* incoerente.
inconsolable *agg.* inconsolabile.
inconstancy *s.* incostanza.
inconstant *agg.* incostante.

incontestability s. incontestabilità.

incontestable agg. incontestabile.

incontinence s. incontinenza.

incontinent agg. incontinente.

incontinently avv. smoderatamente.

incontrollable agg. incontrollabile.

incontrovertible agg. incontrovertibile.

inconvenience s. 1. disturbo 2. scomodità.

to **inconvenience** vt. scomodare. .

inconvenient agg. incomodo.

inconvertible agg. inconvertibile.

to **incorporate** vt. 1. incorporare 2. (comm.) costituire. ♦ to **incorporate** vi. incorporarsi.

incorporated agg. 1. (comm.) anonimo 2. incorporato.

incorporation s. 1. incorporazione 2. (comm.) costituzione.

incorporeal agg. incorporeo.

incorrect agg. scorretto.

incorrectness s. scorrettezza.

incorrigible agg. incorreggibile.

incorrupt agg. incorrotto.

incorruptibility s. incorruttibilità.

incorruptible agg. incorruttibile.

increase s. aumento.

to **increase** vt. e vi. aumentare.

increasing agg. crescente.

increasingly avv. sempre più.

incredibility s. incredibilità.

incredible agg. incredibile.

incredulity s. incredulità.

incredulous agg. incredulo.

increment s. incremento.

to **incriminate** vt. incriminare.

incrimination s. incriminazione.

incriminatory agg. incriminante.

incrustation s. incrostazione.

incubation s. incubazione.

incubator s. incubatrice.

to **inculcate** vt. inculcare.

inculcation s. inculcazione.

inculpable agg. innocente.

inculpation s. accusa.

incumbent agg. incombente.

to **incur** vt. incorrere in.

incurability s. incurabilità.

incurable agg. incurabile.

incursion s. incursione.

indebted agg. 1. indebitato 2. obbligato.

indecency s. indecenza.

indecent agg. indecente.

indecipherable agg. indecifrabile.

indecision s. indecisione.

indecisive agg 1. indeciso 2. non decisivo.

indeclinable agg. indeclinabile.

indecomposable agg. indecomponibile.

indecorous agg. indecoroso.

indeed avv. in verità, davvero.

indefatigable agg. infaticabile.

indefeasible agg. irrevocabile.

indefinable agg. indefinibile.

indefinite agg. indefinito.

indefiniteness s. indeterminatezza.

indelible agg. indelebile.

indelicacy s. 1. rozzezza 2. sconvenienza.

indelicate agg. 1. sgarbato 2. sconveniente.

to **indemnify** vt. 1. indennizzare 2. assicurare.

indemnity s. 1. indennità 2. assicurazione.

indemonstrable agg. indimostrabile.

indent s. 1. dentellatura 2. incavo 3. (comm.) ordinazione 4. (tip.) capoverso.

to **indent** vt. 1. dentellare, frastagliare 2. intagliare 3. (comm.) ordinare (merci).

indentation, **indention** s. 1. dentellatura 2. incisione.

indenture s. 1. dentellatura 2. contratto.

independence s. indipendenza.

independent agg. e s. indipendente.

indescribable agg. indescrivibile.

indestructibility s. indistruttibilità.

indestructible agg. indistruttibile.

indeterminable agg. indeterminabile.

indeterminate agg. indeterminato.

indetermination s. indeterminazione.

index s. indice.

Indian agg. e s. indiano.

to **indicate** vt. indicare.

indicating agg. indicatore.

indication s. 1. indicazione 2. segno.

indicative agg. e s. indicativo.

indicator s. indicatore.

to **indict** vt. accusare.

indictment s. (giur.) accusa.

indifference s. 1. indifferenza 2. imparzialità 3. mancanza di valore.

indifferent agg. 1. indifferente 2.

imparziale **3.** mediocre.
indifferentism s. indifferentismo.
indifferentist s. indifferentista.
indigence s. indigenza.
indigenous agg. indigeno.
indigent agg. indigente.
indigestible agg. indigesto.
indigestion s. dispepsia.
indignant agg. indignato.
indignation s. indignazione.
indignity s. **1.** indegnità **2.** offesa.
indigo s. indaco.
indirect agg. **1.** indiretto **2.** tortuoso.
indiscernible agg. indistinguibile.
indiscipline s. indisciplina.
indiscreet agg. **1.** sconsiderato **2.** indiscreto.
indiscrete agg. compatto.
indiscretion s. **1.** sconsideratezza **2.** indiscrezione.
indiscriminate agg. indiscriminato.
indispensable agg. indispensabile.
indisposed agg. indisposto.
indisposition s. **1.** avversione **2.** indisposizione.
indisputability s. indiscutibilità.
indisputable agg. indiscutibile.
indisputed agg. indiscusso.
indissolubility s. indissolubilità.
indissoluble agg. indissolubile.
indistinct agg. indistinto.
indistinguishable agg. indistinguibile.
individual agg. individuale. ♦ **individual** s. individuo.
individualism s. individualismo.
individualist agg. e s. individualista.
individualistic agg. individualistico.
individuality s. individualità.
individualization s. individualizzazione.
to individualize vt. individualizzare.
indivisibility s. indivisibilità.
indivisible agg. indivisibile.
indocility s. indocilità.
Indo-European agg. e s. indo-europeo.
indolence s. indolenza.
indolent agg. indolente.
indomitable agg. indomabile.
indoor agg. in casa.
indoors avv. in casa.
indraft, indraught s. risucchio, vortice.
indubitable agg. indubitabile.

to induce vt. indurre.
inducement s. **1.** allettamento **2.** movente.
induction s. **1.** induzione **2.** insediamento.
inductive agg. induttivo.
inductor s. induttore.
to indulge vt. essere indulgente verso. ♦ **to indulge** vi. indulgere.
indulgence s. **1.** indulgenza **2.** proroga.
indulgent agg. indulgente.
indult s. indulto.
industrial agg. industriale. ♦ **industrial** s. lavoratore dell'industria.
industrialism s. industrialismo.
industrialist s. industriale.
industrialization s. industrializzazione.
to industrialize vt. industrializzare.
industrious agg. industrioso.
industry s. **1.** industria **2.** operosità, diligenza.
inebriate agg. e s. ubriaco.
to inebriate vt. inebriare.
inedited agg. inedito.
ineffable agg. ineffabile.
ineffective agg. **1.** inefficace **2.** inefficiente.
ineffectiveness s. **1.** inefficacia **2.** inefficienza.
ineffectual agg. inutile.
inefficacy s. inefficacia.
inefficient agg. V. *ineffective.*
inelegance s. ineleganza.
inelegant agg. inelegante.
ineligibility s. ineleggibilità.
ineligible agg. ineleggibile.
ineluctable agg. ineluttabile.
inept agg. inadatto.
ineptitude, ineptness s. inettitudine.
inequality s. diseguaglianza.
inequity s. ingiustizia.
ineradicable agg. inestirpabile.
inerrability s. infallibilità.
inerrable agg. infallibile.
inert agg. inerte.
inertness s. inerzia.
inescapable agg. inevitabile.
inestimable agg. inestimabile.
inevitability s. inevitabilità.
inevitable agg. inevitabile.
inevitableness s. inevitabilità.
inexact agg. inesatto.
inexactitude s. inesattezza.
inexcusability s. inescusabilità.
inexcusable agg. imperdonabile.

inexecutable *agg.* ineseguibile.
inexhaustibility *s.* inesauribilità.
inexhaustible *agg.* inesauribile.
inexistence *s.* inesistenza.
inexistent *agg.* inesistente.
inexorability *s.* inesorabilità.
inexorable *agg.* inesorabile.
inexpedient *agg.* inopportuno.
inexpensive *agg.* poco costoso.
inexperience *s.* inesperienza.
inexperienced, inexpert *agg.* inesperto.
inexpiable *agg.* inespiabile.
inexplicable *agg.* inesplicabile.
inexplorable *agg.* inesplorabile.
inexpressible *agg.* inesprimibile.
inexpressive *agg.* inespressivo.
inexpressiveness *s.* inespressività.
inexpugnability *s.* inespugnabilità.
inexpugnable *agg.* inespugnabile.
inextinguishable *agg.* inestinguibile.
inextricable *agg.* inestricabile.
infallibility *s.* infallibilità.
infallible *agg.* infallibile.
infamous *agg.* infame.
infamy *s.* infamia.
infancy *s.* infanzia.
infant *agg.* infantile. ♦ **infant** *s.* 1. neonato 2. (*giur.*) minore.
infanticide *s.* 1. infanticida 2. infanticidio.
infantile *agg.* infantile.
infantilism *s.* infantilismo.
infantry *s.* fanteria || — -man, fante.
infarct *s.* infarto.
to **infatuate** *vt.* infatuare.
infatuation *s.* infatuazione.
to **infect** *vt.* contagiare.
infection *s.* contagio.
infectious *agg.* contagioso.
infective *agg.* infettivo.
infecund *agg.* infecondo.
infelicitous *agg.* infelice.
infelicity *s.* infelicità.
to **infer** *vt.* dedurre.
inferable *agg.* deducibile.
inference *s.* deduzione.
inferior *agg.* e *s.* inferiore.
inferiority *s.* inferiorità.
infernal *agg.* infernale.
to **infest** *vt.* infestare.
infestation *s.* infestamento.
infidel *agg.* e *s.* infedele.
infidelity *s.* 1. miscredenza 2. infedeltà.
to **infiltrate** *vt.* infiltrare. ♦ to **infiltrate** *vi.* infiltrarsi. ➤
infiltration *s.* infiltrazione.

infinite *agg.* e *s.* infinito.
infinitesimal *agg.* infinitesimale.
infinitive *agg.* e *s.* infinito.
infinitude *s.* infinità.
infinity *s.* infinità, infinito.
infirm *agg.* 1. infermo 2. irresoluto.
infirmary *s.* infermeria.
infirmity *s.* 1. infermità 2. irresolutezza.
to **inflame** *vt.* infiammare. ♦ to **inflame** *vi.* infiammarsi.
inflammability *s.* infiammabilità.
inflammable *agg.* infiammabile.
inflammation *s.* 1. l'infiammare, l'infiammarsi 2. infiammazione.
inflammatory *agg.* infiammatorio.
to **inflate** *vt.* gonfiare.
inflation *s.* 1. gonfiore, gonfiatura 2. (*comm.*) inflazione.
inflationary *agg.* inflazionistico.
to **inflect** *vt.* 1. flettere 2. modulare.
inflection *s.* 1. flessione 2. inflessione.
inflexibility *s.* inflessibilità.
inflexible *agg.* inflessibile.
to **inflict** *vt.* infliggere.
infliction *s.* 1. inflizione 2. pena.
inflorescence *s.* infiorescenza.
influence *s.* 1. influenza 2. (*elettr.*) induzione.
to **influence** *vt.* influenzare.
influential *agg.* influente.
influenza *s.* (*med.*) influenza.
influx *s.* 1. affluenza 2. sbocco (*di fiume*).
inform *agg.* informe.
to **inform** *vt.* 1. informare 2. dar forma a.
informal *agg.* non ufficiale.
informality *s.* assenza di formalità.
information *s.* (*solo sing.*) 1. informazione 2. sapere 3. accusa.
informative, informatory *agg.* informativo.
informed *agg.* istruito.
informer *s.* 1. informatore 2. accusatore.
infraction *s.* 1. infrazione 2. violazione.
infrangibility *s.* infrangibilità.
infrangible *agg.* 1. infrangibile 2. inviolabile.
infrared *agg.* infrarosso.
infrequent *agg.* raro.
to **infringe** *vt.* violare.
infringement *s.* violazione.
infringer *s.* trasgressore.
infructuous *agg.* infruttuoso.

to **infuse** *vt.* **1.** versare **2.** infondere **3.** mettere in infusione.

infusible *agg.* infusibile.

infusion *s.* **1.** infusione **2.** infuso.

ingenious *agg.* ingegnoso.

ingenuity *s.* ingegnosità.

ingenuous *agg.* **1.** ingenuo **2.** franco.

ingenuousness *s.* ingenuità.

to **ingest** *vt.* ingerire.

ingestion *s.* ingestione.

inglorious *agg.* inglorioso.

ingot *s.* lingotto.

ingratitude *s.* ingratitudine.

ingredient *s.* ingrediente.

inguen *s.* inguine.

inguinal *agg.* inguinale.

to **inhabit** *vt.* abitare.

inhabitable *agg.* abitabile.

inhabitancy *s.* domicilio.

inhabitant *s.* abitante.

inhalant *s.* **1.** inalatore **2.** sostanza da inalare.

inhalation *s.* inalazione.

to **inhale** *vt.* e *vi.* **1.** aspirare **2.** inalare.

inhaler *s.* inalatore.

inherent *agg.* inerente.

to **inherit** *vt.* e *vi.* ereditare.

inheritance *s.* eredità.

to **inhibit** *vt.* **1.** inibire **2.** interdire.

inhibition *s.* **1.** inibizione **2.** interdizione.

inhibitory *agg.* inibitorio.

inhospitable *agg.* inospitale.

inhospitality *s.* inospitalità.

inhuman *agg.* inumano.

inhumanity *s.* inumanità.

inhumation *s.* inumazione.

inimical *agg.* nemico.

inimitable *agg.* inimitabile.

iniquitous *agg.* iniquo.

iniquity *s.* iniquità.

initial *agg.* e *s.* iniziale.

to **initial** *vt.* siglare.

initiate *agg.* e *s.* iniziato.

to **initiate** *vt.* iniziare.

initiation *s.* **1.** inizio **2.** iniziazione.

initiative *agg.* introduttivo. ♦ **initiative** *s.* iniziativa.

initiator *s.* iniziatore.

to **inject** *vt.* iniettare.

injection *s.* iniezione.

injector *s.* iniettore.

injunction *s.* ingiunzione.

to **injure** *vt.* ledere, ferire.

injurer *s.* **1.** danneggiatore **2.** feritore.

injury *s.* **1.** torto, danno **2.** ferita.

injustice *s.* ingiustizia.

ink *s.* inchiostro || — -*pot*, calamaio.

inkholder *s.* calamaio.

inkling *s.* indizio.

inky *agg.* **1.** di, simile a inchiostro **2.** macchiato d'inchiostro.

inlaid V. *to inlay*.

inland *agg.* e *s.* interno. ♦ **inland** *avv.* all'interno.

inlay *s.* intarsio.

to **inlay (inlaid, inlaid)** *vt.* intarsiare.

inlet *s.* **1.** piccola insenatura **2.** apertura.

inmate *s.* **1.** inquilino **2.** ricoverato.

inmost *agg.* più interno.

inn *s.* locanda || — -*keeper*, locandiere; — *of court*, scuola di legge.

innate *agg.* innato.

innavigable *agg.* non navigabile.

inner *agg.* interno, intimo.

innermost *agg.* V. *inmost*.

innervation *s.* innervazione.

innocence *s.* innocenza.

innocent *agg.* e *s.* innocente.

innocuity *s.* innocuità.

innocuous *agg.* innocuo.

innominate *agg.* innominato.

to **innovate** *vt.* e *vi.* innovare.

innovation *s.* innovazione.

innovator *s.* innovatore.

innumerability *s.* innumerabilità.

innumerable *agg.* innumerevole.

inobservance *s.* **1.** inosservanza **2.** disattenzione.

inobservant *agg.* **1.** inosservante **2.** disattento.

to **inoculate** *vt.* **1.** inoculare **2.** inculcare.

inoculation *s.* inoculazione.

inodorous *agg.* inodoro.

inoffensive *agg.* inoffensivo.

inopportune *agg.* inopportuno.

inopportuneness *s.* inopportunità.

inordinate *agg.* smoderato.

inorganic *agg.* inorganico.

inoxidizable *agg.* inossidabile.

inpouring *agg.* affluente. ♦ **inpouring** *s.* afflusso.

input *s.* (*mecc.*; *elettr.*) alimentazione, entrata.

inquest *s.* **1.** inchiesta **2.** giuria.

inquietude *s.* inquietudine.

to **inquire** *vt.* e *vi.* chiedere || *to* — *after*, chiedere informazioni su; *to* — *into*, indagare su.

inquirer *s.* investigatore.

inquiring *agg.* **1.** indagatore **2.** curioso.

inquiry s. 1. ricerca 2. domanda 3. inchiesta.

inquisition s. 1. ricerca 2. inchiesta.

inquisitive agg. V. *inquiring*.

inquisitiveness s. curiosità

inrush s. irruzione.

insalubrity s. insalubrità.

insane agg. insano.

insanitary agg. malsano.

insanity s. insania.

insatiability s. insaziabilità.

insatiable, insatiate agg. insaziabile.

to **inscribe** vt. 1. iscrivere 2. scolpire 3. dedicare.

inscription s. 1. iscrizione 2. dedica.

inscrutability s. inscrutabilità.

inscrutable agg. inscrutabile.

inscrutableness s. inscrutabilità.

insect s. insetto.

insecticide s. insetticida.

insectivorous agg. insettivoro.

insecure agg. insicuro.

insecurity s. insicurezza.

insensate agg. 1. insensibile 2. insensato.

insensibility s. insensibilità.

insensible agg. 1. insensibile 2. inconscio.

insensitive agg. insensibile.

inseparable agg. inseparabile.

insert s. inserzione.

to **insert** vt. inserire.

insertion s. inserzione.

to **inset (inset, inset)** vt. inserire.

inside agg. e s. interno. ♦ **inside** avv. e prep. dentro.

insidious agg. insidioso.

insight s. 1. intuito 2. penetrazione.

insignificant agg. insignificante.

insincere agg. insincero.

insincerity s. falsità.

to **insinuate** vt. insinuare.

insinuation s. insinuazione.

insinuative agg. insinuante.

insipid agg. insipido.

insipidity, insipidness s. insipidezza.

insipience s. insipienza.

insipient agg. insipiente.

to **insist** vi. insistere.

insistence s. insistenza.

insistent agg. insistente.

insolation s. insolazione.

insolence s. insolenza.

insolent agg. e s. insolente.

insolubility s. insolubilità.

insoluble agg. insolubile.

insolvable agg. insolubile.

insolvency s. insolvenza.

insolvent agg. insolvente. ♦ **insolvent** s. debitore insolvente.

insomnia s. insonnia.

to **inspect** vt. ispezionare.

inspection s. ispezione.

inspector s. ispettore.

inspectoral agg. di ispettore, di ispezione.

inspectorate s. ispettorato.

inspiration s. 1. inspirazione 2. ispirazione.

to **inspire** vt. 1. inspirare 2. ispirare.

inspirer s. ispiratore.

inspiring agg. ispiratore.

instability s. instabilità.

to **install** vt. installare.

installation s. installazione.

instalment s. 1. rata 2. puntata.

instance s. 1. esempio 2. caso 3. istanza.

instancy s. 1. urgenza 2. insistenza.

instant agg. 1. urgente 2. corrente. ♦ **instant** s. istante.

instantaneous agg. istantaneo.

instantly avv. all'istante. ♦ **instantly** cong. non appena che.

instead avv. invece.

instep s. 1. collo del piede 2. collo di scarpa.

to **instigate** vt. istigare.

instigation s. istigazione.

instigator s. istigatore.

to **instil(l)** vt. instillare.

instinct agg. imbevuto. ♦ **instinct** s. istinto.

instinctive agg. istintivo.

institute s. istituto. ♦ **institutes** s. pl. istituzioni.

to **institute** vt. istituire.

institution s. istituto.

institutional agg. istituzionale.

institutor s. istitutore.

to **instruct** vt. 1. istruire 2. informare 3. ordinare.

instruction s. istruzione.

instructive agg. istruttivo.

instructor s. istruttore.

instrument s. 1. strumento 2. atto giuridico.

to **instrument** vt. 1. strumentare 2. redigere.

instrumental agg. 1. strumentale 2. utile.

instrumentation s. 1. orchestrazio-

ne **2.** uso di strumenti.
insubordinate *agg.* insubordinato.
insubordination *s.* insubordinazione.
insubstantial *agg.* incorporeo.
insufferable *agg.* insopportabile.
insufficiency *s.* insufficienza.
insufficient *agg.* insufficiente.
insular *agg.* **1.** insulare **2.** (*fig.*) di mentalità ristretta.
to **insulate** *vt.* isolare.
insulation *s.* isolamento.
insulator *s.* isolatore.
insulin *s.* insulina.
insult *s.* insulto.
to **insult** *vt.* insultare.
insuperable *agg.* insuperabile.
insuppressible *agg.* insopprimibile.
insurance *s.* assicurazione.
insurant *s.* assicurato.
to **insure** *vt.* assicurare.
insurer *s.* assicuratore.
insurgency *s.* insurrezione.
insurgent *agg. e s.* insorto.
insurmountable *agg.* insormontabile.
insurrection *s.* insurrezione.
insurrectional, insurrectionary *agg.* insurrezionale.
insurrectionist *s.* insorto.
intact *agg.* intatto.
intake *s.* **1.** presa **2.** energia assorbita.
intangible *agg.* intangibile.
integrable *agg.* integrabile.
integral *agg.* integrale.
integrant *agg.* integrante.
to **integrate** *vt.* integrare.
integration *s.* integrazione.
integrity *s.* integrità.
intellect *s.* intelletto.
intellective *agg.* intellettivo.
intellectual *agg. e s.* intellettuale.
intellectualism *s.* intellettualismo.
intelligence *s.* **1.** intelligenza **2.** informazioni (*pl.*).
intelligent *agg.* intelligente.
intelligibility *s.* intelligibilità.
intelligible *agg.* intelligibile.
intemperance *s.* intemperanza.
intemperate *agg.* **1.** smoderato **2.** rigido (*di clima*).
to **intend** *vt.* **1.** intendere **2.** destinare.
intendant *s.* intendente.
intended *agg.* progettato.
intense *agg.* intenso.
intensification *s.* intensificazione.
to **intensify** *vt.* intensificare. ♦ to

intensify *vi.* intensificarsi.
intensity *s.* **1.** intensità **2.** vigore.
intensive *agg.* intensivo, intenso.
intent *agg.* intento, dedito. ♦ **intent** *s.* intenzione, scopo.
intention *s.* intenzione.
intentional *agg.* intenzionale.
intently *avv.* intensamente.
to **inter** *vt.* seppellire.
to **intercalate** *vt.* intercalare.
to **intercede** *vi.* intercedere.
to **intercept** *vt.* intercettare.
interception *s.* intercettamento.
interceptor *s.* intercettatore.
intercession *s.* intercessione.
intercessor *s.* intercessore.
interchange *s.* scambio.
to **interchange** *vt.* scambiare. ♦ to **interchange** *vi.* scambiarsi.
interchangeable *agg.* scambievole.
intercom *s.* citofono.
intercommunication *s.* intercomunicazione.
intercontinental *agg.* intercontinentale.
intercostal *agg.* intercostale.
intercourse *s.* rapporto, relazione || *trade* —, scambi commerciali.
interdependence *s.* interdipendenza.
interdependent *agg.* interdipendente.
interdict *s.* **1.** interdizione **2.** interdetto **3.** proibizione.
to **interdict** *vt.* **1.** interdire **2.** proibire.
interdiction *s.* V. *interdict.*
interest *s.* interesse.
to **interest** *vt.* interessare.
interested *agg.* interessato || *those* —, gli interessati.
interesting *agg.* interessante.
to **interfere** *vi.* **1.** interferire **2.** scontrarsi.
interference *s.* **1.** interferenza **2.** collisione.
interior *agg. e s.* interno.
to **interject** *vt.* intromettere.
interjection *s.* intromissione.
to **interlace** *vt.* intrecciare. ♦ to **interlace** *vi.* intrecciarsi.
interlacing *s.* intreccio.
to **interline** *vt.* interlineare.
interlinear *agg.* interlineare.
interlineation *s.* interlineazione.
to **interlink** *vt.* concatenare.
to **interlock** *vt.* sincronizzare.
interlocution *s.* interlocuzione.
interlocutor *s.* interlocutore.

to **interlope** vi. immischiarsi.
interlude s. 1. intervallo 2. intermezzo.
intermarriage s. matrimonio tra membri di famiglie, razze diverse.
to **intermarry** vt. e vi. imparentarsi per mezzo di matrimonio.
to **intermeddle** vi. intromettersi.
intermeddler s. intrigante.
intermediary agg. intermedio, frapposto. ♦ **intermediary** s. 1. intermediario, mediatore 2. cosa intermedia.
intermediate agg. V. intermediary.
intermediation s. mediazione.
interment s. sepoltura.
interminable agg. interminabile.
to **intermingle** vt. mescolare. ♦ to **intermingle** vi. mescolarsi.
intermission s. sosta, pausa.
to **intermit** vt. interrompere. ♦ to **intermit** vi. interrompersi, essere intermittente.
intermittence s. intermittenza.
intermittent agg. intermittente.
to **intern** vt. internare.
internal agg. interno.
international agg. internazionale.
internationalism s. internazionalismo.
internationalist s. internazionalista.
to **internationalize** vt. internazionalizzare.
internment s. internamento.
to **interpellate** vt. interpellare.
interpellation s. interpellanza.
interphone s. citofono.
interplanetary agg. interplanetario.
interplay s. azione reciproca.
to **interpolate** vt. interpolare.
interpolation s. interpolazione.
to **interpose** vt. interporre. ♦ to **interpose** vi. interporsi.
interposition s. interposizione.
to **interpret** vt. interpretare. ♦ to **interpret** vi. fare l'interprete.
interpretation s. interpretazione.
interpretative agg. interpretativo.
interpreter s. interprete.
interpunction s. interpunzione.
interregnum s. 1. interregno 2. intervallo.
interrelation s. relazione.
interrelationship s. interdipendenza.
to **interrogate** vt. interrogare.
interrogation s. interrogazione || — -mark, punto interrogativo.

interrogative agg. e s. interrogativo.
interrogatory agg. interrogativo. ♦ **interrogatory** s. 1. interrogazione 2. interrogatorio.
to **interrupt** vt. e vi. interrompere.
interrupter s. interruttore.
interruption s. interruzione.
to **intersect** vt. intersecare. ♦ to **intersect** vi. intersecarsi.
intersection s. intersezione.
interspace s. intervallo, spazio.
to **intersperse** vt. cospargere.
interstice s. interstizio.
to **intertwine** vt. attorcigliare. ♦ to **intertwine** vi. attorcigliarsi.
interurban agg. interurbano.
interval s. intervallo.
to **intervene** vi. intervenire.
intervener s. chi interviene.
intervention s. intervento.
interventionist s. interventista.
interview s. intervista.
to **interview** vt. intervistare.
interviewer s. intervistatore.
to **interweave** (**interwove, interwoven**) vt. intessere, intrecciare.
intestinal agg. intestinale.
intestine agg. e s. intestino.
intimacy s. intimità.
intimate agg. intimo. ♦ **intimate** s. amico intimo.
to **intimate** vt. 1. intimare 2. accennare.
intimation s. 1. intimazione 2. preannunzio.
intimidation s. intimidazione.
intimidatory agg. intimidatorio.
into prep. in, dentro || to go — the, park, entrare nel parco; far — the night, fino a tarda notte.
intolerable agg. intollerabile.
intolerance s. intolleranza.
intolerant agg. e s. intollerante.
to **intonate** vt. intonare.
intonation s. intonazione.
to **intone** vt. intonare.
to **intoxicate** vt. inebriare.
intoxication s. ebbrezza.
intractable agg. intrattabile.
intramuscular agg. intramuscolare.
intransgressible agg. che non può essere trasgredito.
intransigence s. intransigenza.
intransigent agg. e s. intransigente.
intransitive agg. intransitivo.
intravenous agg. endovenoso.
intrepid agg. intrepido.

intrepidity s. intrepidezza.
intricacy s. complicazione.
intricate agg. intricato.
intrigant s. intrigante.
intrigue s. intrigo.
to **intrigue** vt. 1. ingannare 2. rendere perplesso 3. affascinare. ♦ to **intrigue** vi. avere una tresca.
intriguer s. intrigante.
intrinsic agg. intrinseco.
to **introduce** vt. 1. introdurre 2. presentare.
introduction s. 1. introduzione 2. presentazione.
introductive, introductory agg. introduttivo.
intromission s. interferenza.
to **intromit** vt. introdurre.
to **introspect** vi. autoesaminarsi.
introspection s. introspezione.
introspective agg. introspettivo.
introversion s. introversione.
introvert agg. e s. introverso.
to **intrude** vt. imporre. ♦ to **intrude** vi. intromettersi.
intruder s. 1. intruso 2. importuno.
intrusion s. intrusione.
intrusive agg. 1. intruso 2. importuno.
intrusiveness s. indiscrezione.
intuition s. intuizione.
intuitional agg. intuitivo.
intuitionism s. intuizionismo.
intuitive agg. intuitivo.
to **inundate** vt. inondare.
inundation s. inondazione.
inurbane agg. inurbano.
inurbanity s. inurbanità.
to **inure** vt. abituare.♦ to **inure** vi. venire in uso.
inurement s. abitudine.
inutility s. inutilità.
to **invade** vt. 1. invadere 2. violare.
invader s. invasore.
invalid agg. 1. invalido 2. nullo. ♦ **invalid** s. invalido.
to **invalid** vt. 1. rendere invalido 2. riformare.
to **invalidate** vt. invalidare.
invalidation s. invalidazione.
invalidity s. invalidità.
invaluable agg. inestimabile.
invariability s. invariabilità.
invariable agg. invariabile.
invasion s. invasione.
invective s. invettiva.
to **inveigh** vi. inveire.

to **invent** vt. inventare.
invention s. 1. invenzione 2. inventiva.
inventive agg. inventivo.
inventor s. inventore.
inventory s. inventario.
to **inventory** vt. fare l'inventario di.
inverse agg. e s. inverso.
inversion s. inversione.
invert agg. e s. invertito.
to **invert** vt. invertire.
invertebrate agg. e s. invertebrato.
invertible agg. invertibile.
to **invest** vt. 1. investire 2. rivestire.
to **investigate** vt. e vi. investigare.
investigation s. investigazione.
investigative agg. investigativo.
investigator s. investigatore.
investiture s. investitura.
investment s. investimento.
investor s. investitore.
inveterate agg. inveterato.
invidious agg. odioso.
invidiousness s. odiosità.
to **invigorate** vt. rinvigorire.
invigorative agg. rinforzante.
invincibility s. invincibilità.
invincible agg. invincibile.
inviolability s. inviolabilità.
inviolable agg. inviolabile.
inviolate agg. inviolato.
invisibility s. invisibilità.
invisible agg. invisibile.
invitation s. invito.
to **invite** vt. 1. invitare 2. provocare.
invocation s. invocazione.
invoice s. fattura.
to **invoice** vt. fatturare.
to **invoke** vt. 1. invocare 2. evocare.
involuntary s. involontario.
involute agg. 1. involuto 2. a spirale.
involution s. 1. involuzione 2. intrico 3. (mat.) elevazione a potenza.
to **involve** vt. 1. avvolgere 2. implicare 3. complicare.
invulnerability s. invulnerabilità.
invulnerable agg. invulnerabile.
inward agg. interiore.
inwardness s. interiorità.
inwards avv. internamente.
iodine s. iodio.
to **iodize** vt. iodare.
ion s. ione.
Ionic agg. ionico.

Ionization s. ionizzazione.
Ionosphere s. ionosfera.
Iranian agg. e s. iraniano.
Iraqi agg. e s. iracheno.
Irascibility s. irascibilità.
Irascible agg. irascibile.
Irate agg. adirato.
Ireful agg. irato.
Iridescence s. iridescenza.
Iridescent agg. iridescente.
Iris s. iride.
Irish agg. irlandese.
Irishman s. irlandese.
Irksome agg. noioso.
Iron agg. di ferro. ♦ **Iron** s. ferro
|| — -*foundry*, ferriera. ♦ **Irons**
s. pl. catene.
to **Iron** vt. 1. rivestire di ferro 2.
stirare.
Ironclad agg. corazzato. ♦ **Iron-
clad** s. corazzata.
Ironic(al) agg. ironico.
Ironing s. stiratura.
Ironmonger s. negoziante in ferra-
menta.
Ironsmith s. fabbro ferraio.
Ironware s. ferramenta.
Ironwork s. lavoro in ferro. ♦
ironworks s. pl. ferriera (sing.).
Irony s. ironia.
to **Irradiate** vt. irradiare. ♦ to **Ir-
radiate** vi. risplendere.
Irradiation s. 1. illuminazione 2.
irradiazione.
Irrational agg. irrazionale.
Irrationalism, irrationality s. ir-
razionalità.
Irrealizable agg. irrealizzabile.
Irreconcilability s. inconciliabilità.
Irreconcilable agg. irreconciliabile.
Irrecoverable agg. 1. irrecuperabi-
le 2. irrimediabile.
Irredentism s. irredentismo.
Irredentist s. irredentista.
Irreducible agg. irriducibile.
Irreflection s. irriflessione.
Irreflective agg. irriflessivo.
Irrefutable agg. irrefutabile.
Irregular agg. e s. irregolare.
Irregularity s. irregolarità.
Irrelevant agg. 1. non pertinente
2. insignificante.
Irreligious agg. irreligioso.
Irremediable agg. irrimediabile.
Irremissible agg. irremissibile.
Irremovability s. irremovibilità.
Irremovable agg. irremovibile.
Irreparable agg. irreparabile.
Irreplaceable agg. insostituibile.

Irreprehensible agg. irreprensibile.
Irrepressible agg. irrefrenabile.
Irrepressibleness s. irrefrenabilità.
Irreproachable agg. irreprensibile.
Irreprovable agg. irreprensibile.
Irresistible agg. irresistibile.
Irresolute agg. irresoluto.
Irresoluteness, irresolution s.
irresolutezza.
Irresolvable agg. insolubile.
Irrespective agg. noncurante.
Irresponsibility s. irresponsabilità.
Irresponsible agg. 1. irresponsabi-
le 2. insolvibile.
Irresponsive agg. che non risponde.
Irretrievable agg. irrecuperabile.
Irreverence s. irriverenza.
Irreverent agg. irriverente.
Irreversibility s. irreversibilità.
Irreversible agg. irreversibile.
Irrevocable agg. irrevocabile.
Irrigable agg. irrigabile.
to **Irrigate** vt. irrigare.
Irrigation s. irrigazione.
Irritability s. irritabilità.
Irritable agg. irritabile.
Irritant agg. e s. irritante.
to **Irritate** vt. irritare.
Irritation s. irritazione.
Irritative agg. irritante.
Irruption s. irruzione.
Islamic agg. islamico.
Islamism s. islamismo.
Island s. 1. isola 2. salvagente stra-
dale.
Islander s. isolano.
Isle s. piccola isola || *the British
Isles*, le isole britanniche.
Islet s. isolotto.
Isochronism s. isocronismo.
to **Isolate** vt. isolare.
Isolation s. isolamento.
Isolationism s. isolazionismo.
Isolationist s. isolazionista.
Isolator s. isolatore.
Isomorphism s. isomorfismo.
Isomorphous agg. isomorfo.
Isosceles agg. isoscele.
Isotherm s. isoterma.
Isothermal agg. isotermico.
Isotope s. isotopo.
Isotrope s. isotropo.
Israeli agg. e s. israeliano.
Israelite s. israelita.
Issue s. 1. uscita, sbocco, foce 2.
conclusione 3. prole, stirpe 4. pro-
blema 5. emissione, pubblicazione.
to **Issue** vt. 1. emettere, pubblicare
2. rilasciare. ♦ to **Issue** vi. 1.

uscire 2. risultare 3. discendere.
issueless *agg.* 1. senza sbocco 2. senza prole.
isthmus *s.* istmo.
it *pron. neutro* esso, essa, ciò, lo, gli, le, ne, sé || *I don't believe* —, non ci credo; — *is raining*, piove; — *is Sunday*, è domenica.
Italian *agg.* e *s.* italiano.
to **italicize** *vt.* e *vi.* 1. stampare in corsivo 2. sottolineare.
itch *s.* 1. prurito 2. scabbia.
to **itch** *vi.* 1. prudere 2. aver voglia di.
itching *s.* prurito.
item *s.* (*comm.*) voce.
to **itemize** *vt.* specificare, elencare.
to **iterate** *vt.* ripetere.
itincrant *agg.* ambulante.
itinerary *s.* itinerario.
its *agg.* e *pron. poss. neutro* suo, sua, suoi, sue.
itself *pron. r. neutro* esso stesso, essa stessa, sé, si || *by* —, da solo.
ivory *s.* avorio.
ivy *s.* edera.

J

Jesus — *maschu ituoi*

jab *s.* 1. stoccata 2. colpo improvviso.
jack *s.* 1. (*fam.*) marinaio 2. fante (*gioco delle carte*) 3. bandiera (*di nave*) 4. maschio (*di certi animali*) 5. uomo di fatica 6. (*mecc.*) cricco.
jackal *s.* sciacallo.
jackass *s.* somaro.
jackdaw *s.* cornacchia.
jacket *s.* 1. giacchetta 2. rivestimento protettivo, isolante.
Jacobin *s.* giacobino.
jade[1] *s.* giada.
jade[2] *s.* 1. cavallo, ronzino 2. megera.
to **jag** *vt.* frastagliare, dentellare.
jaguar *s.* giaguaro.
jail *s.* carcere.
to **jail** *vt.* incarcerare.
jailer *s.* carceriere.
to **jam** *vt.* premere, serrare, pigiare. ♦ to **jam** *vi.* bloccarsi, incepparsi.
jam[1] *s.* marmellata.
jam[2] *s.* 1. ammasso 2. compressione 3. ingorgo.
jamb *s.* stipite.

Jansenism *s.* giansenismo.
Jansenist *s.* giansenista.
January *s.* gennaio.
Japanese *agg.* e *s.* giapponese.
jar *s.* rumore aspro, stridio.
to **jar** *vi.* 1. discordare 2. stridere. ♦ to **jar** *vt.* 1. far discordare 2. far stridere.
jargon *s.* 1. gergo 2. linguaggio professionale.
jarring *agg.* discorde, stridente.
jasmin(e) *s.* gelsomino.
jasper *s.* diaspro.
jaundice *s.* itterizia.
javelin *s.* giavellotto.
jaw *s.* 1. mascella, mandibola 2. morsa, ganascia. ♦ **jaws** *s. pl.* stretta, gola.
jealous *agg.* geloso.
jealously *avv.* gelosamente.
jealousness, jealousy *s.* gelosia.
jeer *s.* beffa, scherno.
jelly *s.* gelatina (*anche di frutta*).
to **jeopardize** *vt.* mettere a repentaglio.
jeopardy *s.* rischio, pericolo.
jerk *s.* 1. scatto, strattone 2. spinta 3. sussulto, tic nervoso.
to **jerk** *vt.* dare uno strattone. ♦ to **jerk** *vi.* sobbalzare || *to* — *along*, avanzare a scatti.
jerky *agg.* 1. sussultante 2. convulso.
jersey *s.* camicetta a maglia con maniche.
jest *s.* facezia, scherzo.
to **jest** *vi.* scherzare, dire delle facezie.
jester *s.* burlone.
jestful *agg.* incline allo scherzo.
Jesuit *s.* gesuita.
Jesuitical *agg.* gesuitico.
jet[1] *agg.* nero lucido.
jet[2] *s.* 1. getto, spruzzo 2. spruzzatore || — *engine*, motore a reazione; — *plane*, aeroplano a reazione.
to **jet** *vt.* schizzare, sprizzare. ♦ to **jet** *vi.* slanciarsi.
jetty *s.* molo || *landing* —, imbarcadero.
Jew *s.* ebreo.
jewel *s.* gioiello.
jewelcase *s.* scrigno.
jeweller *s.* gioielliere.
jewellery *s.* 1. gioielli 2. commercio delle gemme.
Jewish *agg.* ebraico, ebreo.
to **jib** *vi.* recalcitrare, impuntarsi.
jig *s.* 1. giga 2. (*mecc.*) maschera.

jigsaw s. sega da traforo.
to **jingle** vt. far tintinnare. ♦ to **jingle** vi. tintinnare.
job s. 1. lavoro, impiego 2. (fam.) faccenda, situazione.
jobber s. 1. noleggiatore 2. lavoratore a cottimo 3. trafficante disonesto.
jockey s. fantino.
jocose agg. giocoso, allegro.
jocosity s. giocondità.
jocund agg. giocondo, gaio.
jocundity s. allegria, giocondità.
join s. giuntura.
to **join** vt. 1. unire 2. raggiungere. ♦ to **join** vi. 1. unirsi 2. essere contiguo.
joiner s. falegname.
joinery s. falegnameria.
joining s. congiunzione.
joint agg. unito, associato ‖ — account, conto di partecipazione; — -heir, coerede; — -stock, capitale sociale; — -tenant, comproprietario.
joint s. 1. giuntura, congiunzione 2. trancio di carne 3. articolazione.
jointer s. pialla.
jointly avv. unitamente.
joke s. scherzo, burla, facezia.
to **joke** vt. burlarsi di, canzonare. ♦ to **joke** vi. celiare.
joker s. tipo ameno, burlone.
jolly agg. gaio, vivace.
to **jolt** vt. far sobbalzare, scuotere. ♦ to **jolt** vi. traballare.
to **jostle** vt. spingere. ♦ to **jostle** vi. spingersi.
journal s. 1. giornale 2. diario.
journalism s. giornalismo.
journalist s. giornalista.
journalistic agg. giornalistico.
journey s. viaggio (general. per terra).
to **journey** vi. fare un viaggio.
journey-man s. operaio specializzato.
jovial agg. gioviale, allegro.
joviality s. giovialità.
jowl[1] s. 1. mascella 2. guancia.
jowl[2] s. gozzo.
joy s. gioia, contentezza.
joyful agg. giulivo, allegro.
joyfully avv. gaiamente, allegramente.
joyless agg. mesto, senza gioia.
joyous agg. gioioso, gaio.
joyously avv. gioiosamente.
jubilant agg. giubilante, trionfante.

to **jubilate** vi. esultare.
jubilation s. giubilo.
jubilee s. giubileo.
Judaic agg. giudaico.
Judaism s. giudaismo.
judge s. 1. giudice 2. intenditore.
to **judge** vt. e vi. 1. fare da giudice, giudicare 2. supporre, stimare.
judgement s. 1. giudizio 2. verdetto, sentenza 3. parere.
judicial agg. giudiziale, giudiziario.
judiciary agg. giudiziario. ♦ **judiciary** s. magistratura.
judicious agg. giudizioso.
jug s. 1. boccale 2. caraffa, bricco.
juggler s. 1. giocoliere 2. impostore.
jugular agg. e s. giugulare.
juice s. succo (di frutta ecc.).
juiciness s. succosità.
juicy agg. succoso.
jujube s. giuggiola.
Julian agg. giuliano.
July s. luglio.
jumble s. guazzabuglio.
jump s. salto, balzo: high — (sport), salto in alto.
to **jump** vt. 1. saltare, superare con un salto 2. mangiare (giuoco della dama). ♦ to **jump** vi. 1. saltare 2. trasalire.
jumper[1] s. saltatore.
jumper[2] s. maglione.
jumping agg. saltatore.
junction s. 1. congiunzione 2. nodo ferroviario.
juncture s. 1. articolazione 2. (fig.) congiuntura, momento critico.
June s. giugno.
jungle s. giungla.
junior agg. 1. minore, di secondaria importanza 2. il più giovane. ♦ **junior** s. 1. cadetto 2. minore.
juniper s. ginepro.
junk[1] s. 1. avanzo, rifiuto 2. gomena vecchia 3. carne salata.
junk[2] s. (mar.) giunca.
juridic(al) agg. giuridico.
jurisdiction s. giurisdizione.
jurisdictional agg. giurisdizionale.
jurisprudence s. giurisprudenza.
jurisprudent s. giurisprudente.
jurisprudential agg. legale.
jurist s. giurista.
jury s. giuria, giurì.
juryman s. giurato.
just agg. giusto, retto. ♦ **just** avv. appena, appunto, esattamente ‖ — now, proprio ora; — so, proprio così; — then, proprio allora.

justice s. giustizia, imparzialità.
justiciable agg. processabile.
justiciary agg. giudiziario.
justifiability s. legittimità di difesa.
justifiable agg. giustificabile, legittimo || — homicide, omicidio per legittima difesa.
justification s. giustificazione.
justificative agg. giustificativo.
to **justify** vt. 1. giustificare 2. difendere 3. perdonare.
justly avv. giustamente, esattamente.
jut s. sporgenza.
to **jut** vt. e vi. sporgere.
jute s. iuta.
juvenile agg. giovanile.
juxtaposition s. accostamento.

K

kaleidoscope s. caleidoscopio.
kalends s. pl. calende.
kangaroo s. canguro.
kaolin(e) s. caolino.
karting s. andare in « go-kart ».
kathode s. catodo.
keel s. 1. chiglia 2. chiatta (da carbone).
to **keel** vt. 1. rovesciare 2. (mar.) carenare.
keen agg. 1. aguzzo, affilato 2. pungente 3. forte 4. appassionato 5. acuto.
keenly avv. 1. in modo penetrante 2. dolorosamente 3. avidamente 4. (comm.) al minimo.
keenness s. 1. sottigliezza 2. intensità 3. ardore 4. acume.
keep s. 1. sostentamento 2. torrione.
to **keep (kept, kept)** vi. 1. restare 2. conservarsi || to — on, continuare; to — off, tenersi in disparte. ♦ to **keep (kept, kept)** vt. 1. tenere 2. mantenere 3. custodire 4. rispettare || to — back, dissimulare; to — up, tener alto, sostenere.
keeper s. guardiano.
keeping s. 1. sorveglianza 2. mantenimento 3. armonia.
keepsake s. oggetto ricordo.
keg s. barilotto.
kennel s. 1. canile 2. muta di cani 3. rigagnolo.

to **kennel** vt. tenere in un canile. ♦ to **kennel** vi. rintanarsi.
kepi s. chepì.
kept V. to keep.
kerbstone s. cordonatura (del marciapiede).
kerchief s. fazzoletto.
kernel s. 1. gheriglio 2. seme 3. (fig.) essenza.
kettle s. bollitore, bricco.
key s. 1. chiave 2. tasto || — -money, buonuscita.
to **key** vt. 1. (mecc.) inchiavettare 2. (mus.) accordare 3. chiudere a chiave || to — up (fig.), eccitare.
keyboard s. tastiera.
keyed agg. 1. munito di chiavi 2. (mus.) a tasti.
keyhole s. buco della serratura.
keyless agg. senza chiave.
keystone s. chiave di volta.
kick s. 1. calcio 2. rinculo || — -off (sport), calcio d'inizio.
to **kick** vt. prendere a calci. ♦ to **kick** vi. 1. tirar calci 2. rinculare (di armi) 3. recalcitrare.
kicker s. chi scalcia.
kid[1] s. 1. capretto 2. bimbo.
kid[2] s. tinozza.
to **kidnap** vt. rapire.
kidnapper s. rapitore.
kidnapping s. ratto.
kidney s. 1. rene 2. temperamento || stones in the kidneys, calcoli renali.
kier s. caldaia.
to **kill** vt. 1. uccidere 2. respingere 3. smorzare 4. fermare.
killer s. uccisore || lady- —, don-giovanni.
killing agg. mortale. ♦ **killing** s. uccisione.
killjoy s. guastafeste.
kiln s. fornace.
kilo, kilogram(me) s. chilo(grammo).
kilometer s. chilometro.
kilt s. gonnellino degli scozzesi.
kin agg. consanguineo, affine. ♦ **kin** s. parentela.
kind[1] agg. gentile || very — of you, molto gentile da parte tua.
kind[2] s. specie, tipo.
to **kindle** vt. accendere. ♦ to **kindle** vi. accendersi.
kindliness s. gentilezza.
kindling s. 1. accensione 2. legna facilmente infiammabile.
kindly agg. gentile. ♦ **kindly** avv.

gentilmente.

kindness s. gentilezza.

kindred agg. **1.** imparentato **2.** affine. ♦ **kindred** s. parentela.

kinematics s. cinematica.

kinetic agg. cinetico.

kinetics s. cinetica.

king s. re || king's English, la lingua inglese ufficiale.

kingdom s. regno.

kinghood s. regalità.

kingly agg. regale, regio.

kingship s. regalità.

kinless agg. senza parenti.

kinsfolk s. pl. parenti.

kinship s. parentela.

kinsman s. parente.

kinswoman s. parente (donna).

kiosk s. chiosco || newspaper —, edicola.

kipper s. aringa, salmone affumicato.

to **kipper** vt. affumicare (pesce).

kiss s. bacio.

to **kiss** vt. baciare || to — the dust, mordere la polvere.

kit s. **1.** cassetta **2.** equipaggiamento.

kitchen s. cucina || — garden, orto.

kitchener s. cuciniere.

kitchenette s. cucinino.

kitchenware s. batteria da cucina.

kite s. **1.** nibbio **2.** aquilone **3.** aliante.

kitten s. gattino.

kleptomania s. cleptomania.

kleptomaniac agg. e s. cleptomane.

knack s. **1.** abilità **2.** dispositivo ingegnoso.

knapsack s. zaino (per soldati).

knave s. furfante.

knavery s. disonestà.

knavish agg. disonesto.

to **knead** vt. impastare.

kneader s. **1.** chi impasta **2.** impastatrice.

kneading s. impasto || — trough, madia.

knee s. **1.** ginocchio **2.** tubo a gomito || — -cap, rotula, ginocchiera.

to **kneel (knelt, knelt)** vi. inginocchiarsi.

kneeler s. **1.** chi s'inginocchia **2.** inginocchiatoio.

knell s. rintocco funebre.

to **knell** vt. chiamare a raccolta. ♦ to **knell** vi. sonare a morto.

knelt V. to kneel.

knew V. to know.

knickerbockers s. pl. calzoni alla zuava.

knick-knack s. ninnolo.

knick-knackery s. cianfrusaglie.

knife s. (pl. knives) **1.** coltello **2.** bisturi || pen- —, temperino; pruning- —, falcetto || — -grinder, arrotino.

to **knife** vt. **1.** tagliare **2.** accoltellare.

knight s. cavaliere.

knighthood s. **1.** rango di cavaliere **2.** cavalleria.

knightliness s. cavalleria.

knightly agg. cavalleresco. ♦ **knightly** avv. cavallerescamente.

to **knit (knit, knit)** (anche reg.) vt. **1.** lavorare a maglia **2.** corrugare **3.** unire. ♦ to **knit (knit, knit)** (anche reg.) vi. unirsi, saldarsi.

knitter s. **1.** magliaia **2.** telaio per maglieria.

knitting s. lavoro a maglia.

knitwear s. maglieria.

knob s. **1.** protuberanza **2.** pomo, manopola.

knobby agg. nodoso.

knock s. **1.** colpo **2.** (mecc.) battito in testa.

to **knock** vt. urtare. ♦ to **knock** vi. **1.** bussare **2.** detonare || to — down, abbattere; to — out, sopraffare.

knocker s. battente.

knot s. **1.** nodo **2.** coccarda **3.** gruppo **4.** difficoltà.

to **knot** vt. annodare. ♦ to **knot** vi. annodarsi.

knottiness s. **1.** nodosità **2.** (fig.) difficoltà.

knotty agg. **1.** nodoso **2.** (fig.) difficile.

to **know (knew, known)** vt. **1.** conoscere **2.** sapere **3.** riconoscere || to — of, aver sentito parlare di; to — about, essere al corrente di.

knowable agg. **1.** comprensibile **2.** riconoscibile.

knowing agg. **1.** intelligente **2.** istruito.

knowledge s. conoscenza.

known V. to know.

knuckle s. articolazione, nocca || — -duster, pugno di ferro.

to **knuckle** vi. **1.** (fig.) cedere **2.** applicarsi || to — under, sottomettersi.

knurl s. zigrinatura.
to **knurl** vt. zigrinare.
Korean agg. e s. coreano.

L

la s. (mus.) la.
label s. etichetta.
to **label** vt. **1.** mettere l'etichetta a **2.** classificare.
labial agg. e s. labiale.
laboratory s. laboratorio.
laborious agg. laborioso.
laboriousness s. laboriosità.
labour s. **1.** lavoro, fatica **2.** mano d'opera **3.** doglie (pl.) || hard —, lavori forzati; — party, partito laborista.
to **labour** vi. **1.** lavorare, faticare **2.** avere le doglie. ◆ to **labour** vt. elaborare, sviluppare.
laboured agg. **1.** elaborato **2.** penoso.
labourer s. lavoratore.
labouring agg. laborioso.
labourism s. laburismo.
labourist s. laburista.
labyrinth s. labirinto.
lace s. **1.** laccio **2.** pizzo **3.** passamaneria.
to **lace** vt. **1.** allacciare **2.** guarnire con merletti, galloni.
to **lacerate** vt. lacerare.
lachrymal agg. lacrimale.
lachrymator s. gas lacrimogeno.
lack s. mancanza.
to **lack** vt. mancare di. ◆ to **lack** vi. mancare, scarseggiare.
lacker s. **1.** lacca **2.** oggetto laccato.
to **lacker** vt. laccare.
laconic(al) agg. laconico.
to **lacquer** V. to lacker.
lactation s. **1.** lattazione **2.** allattamento.
lacteal, lacteous agg. latteo.
lactose s. lattosio.
lacunar agg. lacunoso. ◆ **lacunar** s. soffitto a cassettoni.
lacustrine agg. lacustre.
lacy agg. simile a pizzo.
lad s. ragazzo.
ladder s. **1.** scala a pioli **2.** smagliatura.
to **ladder** vt. munire di scala. ◆ to

ladder vi. smagliarsi.
to **lade (laded, laden)** vt. caricare.
laden agg. (fig.) oppresso.
lading s. carico: bill of —, polizza di carico.
ladle s. mestolo.
to **ladle** vt. versare con un mestolo.
lady s. signora || Our Lady, la Madonna; — doctor, dottoressa.
ladybird s. coccinella.
ladykiller s. (fam.) dongiovanni.
ladylike agg. signorile, raffinato.
ladyship s. **1.** rango di nobildonna **2.** Signoria.
lag s. ritardo, rallentamento.
to **lag** vi. ritardare, restare indietro.
laggard agg. e s. pigro.
lagoon s. laguna.
to **laicize** vt. laicizzare.
laid V. to lay.
lain V. to lie.
lair s. tana.
laity s. **1.** i laici **2.** i profani.
lake s. lago.
laky agg. lacustre.
lamb s. agnello.
lambent agg. **1.** lambente **2.** scintillante.
lame agg. **1.** zoppo **2.** (fig.) debole (di argomenti).
to **lame** vt. storpiare.
lamellar agg. lamellare.
lameness s. **1.** zoppaggine **2.** imperfezione.
lament s. lamento.
to **lament** vt. lamentare. ◆ to **lament** vi. lamentarsi.
lamentable agg. lamentevole.
lamentation s. lamento.
lamented agg. **1.** deplorato **2.** compianto.
to **laminate** vt. laminare.
lamination s. **1.** laminazione **2.** lamina.
lamp s. lampada || — -black, nerofumo; — -shade, paralume.
lamplight s. luce artificiale.
lampoon s. libello.
lamprey s. lampreda.
lance s. **1.** lancia **2.** fiocina.
to **lance** vt. (med.) incidere.
lancer s. lanciere.
lancet s. bisturi.
land s. **1.** terra **2.** paese, contrada **3.** campagna, terreno || — -surveying, agrimensura; — surveyor, agrimensore.
to **land** vi. **1.** sbarcare **2.** atterrare. ◆ to **land** vt. **1.** sbarcare **2.** de-

porre **3.** prendere possesso di.
landed *agg.* fondiario.
landing *s.* **1.** sbarco **2.** atterraggio **3.** pianerottolo || — *-stage*, pontile di sbarco; — *-strip*, pista d'atterraggio.
landlady *s.* **1.** padrona di casa **2.** albergatrice.
landless *agg.* senza terreni.
landlord *s.* **1.** padrone di casa, di terra **2.** albergatore.
landmark *s.* **1.** punto di riferimento **2.** pietra miliare.
landowner *s.* proprietario terriero.
landscape *s.* paesaggio || — *-painter*, paesaggista.
landslide, landslip *s.* frana.
lane *s.* **1.** viottolo, vicolo **2.** (*mar.*) rotta **3.** corsia (*di strada*).
language *s.* linguaggio.
languid *agg.* languido.
languish *s.* languore.
to **languish** *vi.* languire.
languor *s.* languore.
languorous *agg.* languido.
lank *agg.* **1.** allampanato **2.** liscio (*di capelli*).
lanolin(e) *s.* lanolina.
lantern *s.* lanterna.
lap[1] *s.* **1.** grembo **2.** valletta **3.** lembo.
lap[2] *s.* **1.** sovrapposizione **2.** (*sport*) giro di pista.
to **lap** *vt*: **1.** piegare **2.** avvolgere **3.** lambire **4.** bere avidamente. ♦ to **lap** *vi.* ripiegarsi.
laparotomy *s.* laparatomia.
lapel *s.* risvolto (*di giacca, soprabito*).
lapidary *agg.* lapidario. ♦ **lapidary** *s.* tagliatore di pietre.
lapidation *s.* lapidazione.
Lapp *agg.* e *s.* lappone.
lappet *s.* **1.** falda **2.** lobo dell'orecchio.
lapse *s.* **1.** errore **2.** intervallo.
to **lapse** *vi.* **1.** errare **2.** scivolare.
larboard *s.* fiancata sinistra (*di nave*).
larceny *s.* furto.
larch *s.* larice.
lard *s.* lardo.
to **lard** *vt.* **1.** ungere con lardo **2.** lardellare.
larder *s.* dispensa.
large *agg.* **1.** largo **2.** grande, ampio **3.** generoso || *at* —, in genere; *to be at* —, essere in libertà.
largeness *s.* **1.** ampiezza, grandezza **2.** generosità.

lark *s.* allodola.
laryngitis *s.* laringite.
larynx *s.* laringe.
lascivious *agg.* lascivo.
lasciviousness *s.* lascivia.
lash *s.* **1.** frusta **2.** frustata **3.** (*eye*)-—, ciglio.
to **lash** *vt.* frustare || *to* — *at*, sferzare.
lashing *s.* **1.** frustata **2.** legatura.
lass, lassie *s.* ragazzina.
last *agg.* (*superl. di* late) **1.** ultimo **2.** scorso **3.** massimo || *the* — *but one*, il penultimo. ♦ **last** *s.* **1.** fine **2.** ultimo. ♦ **last** *avv.* **1.** ultimo **2.** l'ultima volta || *at* —, alla fine.
to **last** *vi.* durare.
lasting *agg.* durevole. ♦ **lasting** *s.* durata.
latch *s.* chiavistello.
late (**later, latter; latest, last**) *agg.* **1.** tardi **2.** in ritardo **3.** tardo **4.** precedente **5.** defunto. ♦ **late** *avv.* **1.** tardi **2.** in ritardo.
lately *avv.* recentemente.
latent *agg.* latente.
later *agg.* (*comp. di* late) posteriore. ♦ **later** *avv.* più tardi.
lateral *agg.* laterale.
latest *agg.* (*superl. di* late) ultimo, recentissimo || *at the* —, al più tardi.
latex *s.* lattice.
lathe *s.* tornio.
lather *s.* schiuma.
to **lather** *vt.* insaponare. ♦ to **lather** *vi.* schiumare.
Latin *agg.* e *s.* latino.
Latinism *s.* latinismo.
Latinist *s.* latinista.
Latinity *s.* latinità.
latitude *s.* **1.** latitudine **2.** ampiezza.
latter *agg.* (*comp. di* late) **1.** posteriore **2.** ultimo **3.** secondo.
latterly *avv.* recentemente.
lattice *s.* grata, traliccio.
latticed *agg.* munito di grata.
laudable *agg.* lodevole.
laudanum *s.* laudano.
laudatory *agg.* laudatorio.
laugh *s.* risata.
to **laugh** *vi.* ridere || *to* — *at*, deridere.
laughable *agg.* comico.
laughing *s.* risata || — *-stock*, zimbello.
laughter *s.* riso || *to burst into* —, scoppiare a ridere.

launch¹ s. varo.

launch² s. (mar.) lancia.

to launch vt. 1. lanciare 2. varare.

to launder vt. e vi. 1. fare il bucato 2. lavare e stirare.

launderette s. lavanderia con macchine automatiche.

laundress s. lavandaia.

laundry s. 1. lavanderia 2. bucato.

laureate agg. coronato d'alloro.

laurel s. lauro, alloro.

to laurel vt. coronare d'alloro.

lavatory s. gabinetto.

lavender s. lavanda.

lavish agg. prodigo.

to lavish vt. prodigare.

lavishness s. prodigalità.

law s. 1. legge 2. professione legale 3. processo, causa || — -court, tribunale; to go to —, ricorrere in giudizio.

lawful agg. 1. legale 2. legittimo.

lawfulness s. 1. legalità 2. legittimità.

lawgiver s. legislatore.

lawless agg. 1. illegale 2. sregolato.

lawn s. prato (rasato).

lawsuit s. (giur.) processo.

lawyer s. avvocato.

lax agg. allentato.

laxative agg. e s. lassativo.

laxity s. 1. negligenza 2. rilassatezza.

lay V. to lie.

lay agg. 1. laico 2. profano || — -brother, converso; — -sister, conversa. ♦ lay s. configurazione.

to lay (laid, laid) vt. 1. porre 2. deporre 3. preparare 4. calmare || to — aside, mettere da parte; to — out, stendere, spendere.

lay-by s. piazzola di sosta.

layer s. 1. strato 2. gallina che fa uova 3. (mil.) puntatore.

laying s. 1. posa 2. covata.

layoff s. stagione morta (di lavoro).

layout s. 1. esposizione 2. schema.

lazaret s. lazzaretto.

laziness s. pigrizia.

lazy agg. pigro.

lead¹ s. 1. piombo 2. grafite || red- —, minio; white- —, biacca.

lead² s. 1. comando 2. guinzaglio 3. mano (di carte).

to lead¹ vt. impiombare.

to lead² (led, led) vt. 1. condurre, capeggiare 2. indurre.

leaden agg. di piombo, plumbeo.

leader s. 1. capo 2. articolo di fondo.

leadership s. direzione.

leading¹ agg. 1. dominante 2. primo. ♦ leading s. guida.

leading² s. impiombatura.

leaf s. (pl. leaves) 1. foglia 2. foglio.

to leaf vt. sfogliare. ♦ to leaf vi. mettere le foglie.

leafless agg. senza foglie.

leaflet s. 1. fogliolina 2. volantino.

league s. lega.

to league vi. allearsi.

leak s. 1. fessura 2. (mar.) falla 3. perdita.

to leak vi. perdere || to — out, trapelare.

leakage s. 1. colatura 2. dispersione.

leaky agg. che cola, perde.

lean¹ agg. magro, esile.

lean² s. inclinazione.

to lean (leant, leant) (anche reg.) vt. e vi. 1. pendere 2. appoggiarsi 3. sporgersi 4. inclinare.

leaning s. 1. inclinazione 2. l'appoggiarsi.

leanness s. magrezza.

leant V. to lean.

leap s. salto || — -year, anno bisestile.

to leap (leapt, leapt) (anche reg.) vt. e vi. saltare.

to learn (learnt, learnt) (anche reg.) vt. e vi. imparare, apprendere.

learned agg. colto.

learner s. allievo.

learning s. cultura.

learnt V. to learn.

lease s. 1. contratto d'affitto 2. durata (di contratto) || on —, in affitto.

to lease vt. affittare.

leash s. guinzaglio.

to leash vt. tenere al guinzaglio.

least agg. (superl. di little) il minimo. ♦ least s. (il) meno. ♦ least avv. (il) meno.

leather s. 1. cuoio 2. oggetto in cuoio || patent —, vernice.

leathern agg. di cuoio.

leave s. 1. permesso 2. congedo.

to leave (left, left) vt. lasciare. ♦ to leave (left, left) vi. partire || to — off, smettere.

leaven s. 1. lievito 2. (fig.) fermento.

to leaven vt. far lievitare.

leaves V. *leaf.*
leaving s. partenza.
lecherous *agg.* lascivo.
lechery s. lascivia.
lecture s. **1.** conferenza **2.** lezione **3.** rimprovero.
to **lecture** *vt.* rimproverare. ♦ to **lecture** *vi.* fare una conferenza.
lecturer s. **1.** conferenziere **2.** lettore universitario.
led V. *to lead.*
ledger s. (*comm.*) libro mastro.
lee s. feccia.
leech s. sanguisuga (*anche fig.*).
to **leer** *vt.* e *vi.* guardare di sbieco.
leeward *agg.* e *avv.* sottovento.
leeway s. deriva.
left *agg.* sinistro. ♦ **left** s. sinistra || — *-handed*, mancino.
left V. *to leave.*
leftist s. (*pol.*) uomo di sinistra.
leg s. **1.** gamba **2.** (*cuc.*) cosciotto || *to pull so.'s* —, canzonare qu.
legacy s. legato.
legal *agg.* legale.
legality s. legalità.
legalization s. legalizzazione.
to **legalize** *vt.* legalizzare.
legatee s. legatario.
legation s. legazione.
legend s. leggenda.
legendary *agg.* leggendario.
leggins s. *pl.* gambali.
legible *agg.* leggibile.
legion s. legione.
legionary *agg.* e s. legionario.
to **legislate** *vi.* fare leggi. ♦ to **legislate** *vt.* trasformare per mezzo di leggi.
legislation s. legislazione.
legislative *agg.* legislativo.
legislator s. legislatore.
legislature s. **1.** legislatura **2.** corpo legislativo.
legitimacy s. legittimità.
legitimate *agg.* legittimo.
to **legitimate** *vt.* legittimare.
legitimation s. legittimazione.
legume s. legume.
leguminous *agg.* leguminoso.
leisure s. **1.** agio **2.** tempo libero.
leisurely *agg.* e *avv.* con comodo.
lemon s. limone.
lemonade s. limonata.
to **lend** (**lent, lent**) *vt.* prestare.
lender s. prestatore.
length s. **1.** lunghezza **2.** durata, spazio di tempo || *at* —, alla fine.
to **lengthen** *vt.* allungare. ♦ to

lengthen *vi.* allungarsi.
lengthy *agg.* lungo, prolisso.
lenient *agg.* **1.** emolliente **2.** mite.
lenitive *agg.* e s. calmante.
lens s. **1.** (*ott.*) lente **2.** (*foto*) obiettivo.
lent V. *to lend.*
Lent s. quaresima.
lentil s. lenticchia.
leonine *agg.* leonino.
leopard s. **1.** leopardo **2.** gattopardo.
leper s. lebbroso || — *hospital*, lebbrosario.
leporine *agg.* leporino.
leprosy s. lebbra.
leprous *agg.* lebbroso.
lesbian *agg.* e s. lesbica.
lesion s. lesione.
less *agg.* (*comp. di little*) minore, meno. ♦ **less** s. meno. ♦ **less** *avv.* meno. ♦ **less** *prep.* meno.
lessee s. affittuario.
to **lessen** *vt.* e *vi.* diminuire.
lesser *agg.* minore.
lesson s. lezione.
lest *cong.* per paura che.
to **let** (**let, let**) *vt.* **1.** lasciare, permettere **2.** affittare || *to* — *in*, far entrare; *to* — *off*, lasciar andare; *to* — *out*, lasciar uscire.
lethal *agg.* letale.
lethargy s. letargo.
letter s. lettera.
lettered *agg.* **1.** letterato **2.** intestato.
lettuce s. lattuga.
leucocyte s. leucocito.
leucocythaemia, leukemia s. leucemia.
levant s. levante.
level *agg.* **1.** livellato **2.** a livello **3.** regolato. ♦ **level** s. **1.** livello **2.** superficie piana **3.** livella || *on a* — *with*, sullo stesso piano di.
to **level** *vt.* **1.** livellare **2.** puntare (*un'arma*).
levelling s. **1.** livellamento **2.** puntamento (*di arma*).
lever s. **1.** manubrio **2.** leva.
to **lever** *vi.* far leva.
to **levigate** *vt.* **1.** levigare **2.** polverizzare.
levigation s. **1.** levigazione **2.** polverizzazione.
levity s. leggerezza.
levy s. **1.** leva **2.** imposta.
to **levy** *vt.* **1.** arruolare **2.** imporre (*di tasse*).

lewd *agg.* impudico.
lewdness *s.* impudicizia.
lexical *agg.* lessicale.
lexicographer *s.* lessicografo.
lexicography *s.* lessicografia.
lexicology *s.* lessicologia.
lexicon *s.* lessico.
liability *s.* 1. obbligo 2. tendenza 3. (*giur.*) responsabilità. ♦ **liabilities** *s. pl.* passività (*sing.*).
liable *agg.* 1. soggetto a 2. (*giur.*) responsabile.
liar *s.* bugiardo.
libation *s.* libagione.
libel *s.* 1. libello 2. (*giur.*) diffamazione.
to libel *vt.* 1. scrivere un libello contro 2. (*giur.*) sporgere querela.
liberal *agg.* 1. liberale 2. umanistico. ♦ **liberal** *s.* liberale.
liberalism *s.* liberalismo.
liberalist *s.* liberalista.
liberality *s.* liberalità.
to liberalize *vt.* rendere liberale.
to liberate *vt.* liberare.
liberation *s.* liberazione.
liberator *s.* liberatore.
liberticide *s.* 1. liberticida 2. liberticidio.
libertinage *s.* libertinaggio.
libertine *agg. e s.* libertino.
libertinism *s.* libertinaggio.
liberty *s.* libertà.
libidinous *agg.* libidinoso.
libido *s.* libidine.
librarian *s.* bibliotecario.
library *s.* biblioteca || *film* —, cineteca; *record* —, discoteca.
lice V. *louse.*
licence *s.* licenza || *driving* —, patente automobilistica.
to license *vt.* dare una licenza a.
licensed *agg.* autorizzato.
licentious *agg.* licenzioso.
licentiousness *s.* dissolutezza.
lichen *s.* lichene.
lick *s.* leccata.
to lick *vt.* 1. leccare 2. lambire.
lid *s.* coperchio.
lie[1] *s.* menzogna || *the* —, smentita.
lie[2] *s.* posizione.
to lie[1] *vi.* mentire.
to lie[2] **(lay, lain)** *vi.* giacere, trovarsi || *to* — *down*, coricarsi; *to* — *in*, partorire.
lieutenant *s.* tenente.
life *s.* (*pl.* lives) vita || — -*belt*, cintura di salvataggio; — *preserver*, salvagente.

lifeboat *s.* lancia di salvataggio.
lifeless *agg.* senza vita.
lifelike *agg.* vivido.
lift *s.* 1. ascensore 2. passaggio (*su un veicolo*) 3. sollevamento.
to lift *vt.* 1. alzare 2. rubare. ♦ **to lift** *vi.* alzarsi.
light[1] *agg.* 1. chiaro 2. biondo 3. leggero 4. agile 5. insignificante.
light[2] *s.* 1. luce 2. fuoco 3. lampada || *traffic lights*, semaforo.
to light (lit, lit) (*anche reg.*) *vt.* 1. accendere 2. illuminare. ♦ **to light (lit, lit)** (*anche reg.*) *vi.* 1. accendersi 2. illuminarsi 3. posarsi.
to lighten *vt.* 1. alleggerire, alleviare 2. illuminare. ♦ **to lighten** *vi.* 1. alleggerirsi 2. illuminarsi 3. (*imp.*) lampeggiare.
lighter *s.* 1. accenditore 2. (*mar.*) chiatta.
lighthouse *s.* faro.
lighting *s.* 1. accensione 2. luce (*di quadro*).
lightless *agg.* oscuro.
lightness *s.* 1. leggerezza 2. gaiezza 3. illuminazione.
lightning *s.* fulmine || — -*rod*, parafulmine.
Ligurian *agg. e s.* ligure.
like *agg.* 1. simile 2. caratteristico di. ♦ **like** *prep.* come || — *this*, — *that*, così; *to feel* —, aver voglia di; *to look* —, avere l'aria di.
like *s.* simile. ♦ **likes** *s. pl.* gusti.
to like *vt.* piacere. ♦ **to like** *vi.* volere.
likelihood *s.* probabilità.
likely *agg.* 1. probabile 2. adatto. ♦ **likely** *avv.* probabilmente.
likeness *s.* 1. somiglianza 2. immagine.
likewise *avv.* 1. allo stesso modo 2. anche.
liking *s.* 1. gusto 2. preferenza.
lilac *agg. e s.* lilla.
lily *agg.* bianco. ♦ **lily** *s.* giglio || *water*- —, ninfea.
limb *s.* 1. membro 2. ramo.
lime[1] *s.* 1. calce 2. pania.
lime[2] *s.* cedro.
lime[3] *s.* tiglio.
to lime *vt.* 1. cementare 2. invischiare.
limelight *s.* luce della ribalta.
limestone *s.* calcare.
limit *s.* limite.
to limit *vt.* limitare.

limitary *agg.* 1. limitato 2. limitativo 3. situato alla frontiera.
limitation *s.* limitazione.
limitative *agg.* limitativo.
limited *agg.* limitato || — *company*, società a responsabilità limitata; — *monarchy*, monarchia costituzionale.
limp *agg.* molle.
to **limp** *vi.* zoppicare.
limpid *agg.* limpido.
limpidity *s.* limpidezza.
limping *s.* zoppicamento.
line *s.* 1. linea, riga 2. ruga 3. discendenza 4. attività 5. verso 6. (*comm.*) articolo.
to **line** *vt.* 1. rigare 2. fiancheggiare 3. foderare || *to* — *up*, allineare, allinearsi.
lineage *s.* lignaggio.
lineal *agg.* in linea diretta.
lineament *s.* lineamento.
linear *agg.* lineare.
linen *agg.* di lino. ♦ **linen** *s.* 1. tela di lino 2. biancheria.
liner *s.* 1. transatlantico 2. aereo di linea.
to **linger** *vt.* e *vi.* indugiare.
linguist *s.* linguista.
linguistic(al) *agg.* linguistico.
linguistics *s.* linguistica.
liniment *s.* linimento.
lining *s.* 1. rigatura 2. allineamento 3. fodera 4. rivestimento.
link *s.* 1. anello 2. (*fig.*) legame || *cuff-links*, gemelli da polso.
to **link** *vt.* collegare. ♦ to **link** *vi.* collegarsi.
linotyping *s.* linotipia.
linotypist *s.* linotipista.
lint *s.* garza.
lintel *s.* architrave.
lion *s.* leone.
lioness *s.* leonessa.
lip *s.* 1. labbro 2. margine || —-*stick*, rossetto per labbra.
to **lip** *vt.* 1. toccare (*con le labbra*) 2. sussurrare.
liquefaction *s.* liquefazione.
to **liquefy** *vt.* liquefare. ♦ to **liquefy** *vi.* liquefarsi.
liqueur *s.* rosolio.
liquid *agg.* 1. liquido 2. chiaro 3. armonioso 4. instabile. ♦ **liquid** *s.* liquido.
to **liquidate** *vt.* liquidare.
liquidation *s.* liquidazione.
liquidator *s.* liquidatore.
liquor *s.* 1. liquido 2. bevanda alcolica.

liquorice *s.* liquirizia.
to **lisp** *vi.* parlare bleso.
lisping *agg.* bleso. ♦ **lisping** *s.* pronuncia blesa.
list[1] *s.* 1. lista 2. striscia 3. cimosa. ♦ **lists** *s. pl.* lizza (*sing.*).
list[2] *s.* (*mar.*) sbandamento.
to **list**[1] *vt.* elencare, catalogare.
to **list**[2] *vi.* (*mar.*) sbandare.
to **listen** *vi.* ascoltare: *to* — *to so.*, ascoltare qu.; *to* — *in*, ascoltare la radio.
listener *s.* ascoltatore.
listening *s.* ascolto.
listless *agg.* disattento.
lit *V. to light*.
litany *s.* litania.
literal *agg.* 1. letterale 2. prosaico 3. di lettera alfabetica.
literalism *s.* interpretazione letterale.
literary *agg.* letterario.
literate *agg.* e *s.* letterato.
literature *s.* letteratura.
lithe *agg.* agile.
lithograph *s.* litografia.
to **lithograph** *vt.* litografare.
lithographic(al) *agg.* litografico.
lithography *s.* (*arte della*) litografia.
litigant *s.* (*giur.*) contendente.
litmus *s.* tornasole.
litre *s.* litro.
litter *s.* 1. lettiga, barella 2. strame 3. rifiuti 4. figliata.
little (less, least) *agg.* 1. piccolo 2. breve 3. poco || *a* —, un po' di. ♦ **little** *s.* poco. ♦ **little** *avv.* poco || *a* —, piuttosto.
liturgic(al) *agg.* liturgico.
liturgy *s.* liturgia.
live *agg.* 1. vivo 2. ardente 3. carico (*di armi*).
to **live** *vi.* e *vt.* vivere, abitare.
livelihood *s.* mezzi di sussistenza.
liveliness *s.* vivacità.
lively *agg.* vivace.
liver *s.* fegato.
livery[1] *agg.* bilioso.
livery[2] *s.* 1. livrea 2. (*giur.*) passaggio di proprietà.
lives *V. life*.
livestock *s.* bestiame.
livid *agg.* livido.
living *agg.* 1. vivo 2. perfetto (*di somiglianza*). ♦ **living** *s.* 1. mezzo di mantenimento 2. vita || —-*room*, soggiorno.

lizard s. lucertola.
llama s. (zool.) lama.
load s. 1. carico, peso 2. (elettr.) carica, tensione.
to load vt. 1. caricare 2. adulterare.
loader s. caricatore.
loading s. caricamento.
loadstar s. stella polare.
loaf s. (pl. loaves) pagnotta || sugar- —, pan di zucchero.
to loaf vi. oziare.
loafer s. fannullone.
loan s. prestito: on —, a prestito.
to loan vt. prestare.
loath agg. riluttante.
to loathe vt. detestare.
loathing s. disgusto.
loathsome agg. 1. odioso 2. disgustoso.
loaves V. loaf.
lobby s. anticamera.
lobe s. lobo.
lobster s. aragosta.
local agg. e s. locale.
locality s. località.
to localize vt. localizzare.
to locate vt. 1. situare 2. individuare 3. indicare.
location s. 1. posizione 2. locazione.
lock¹ s. 1. ricciolo 2. fiocco.
lock² s. 1. serratura 2. diga 3. otturatore (di arma).
to lock vt. serrare. ♦ **to lock** vi. (mecc.) incepparsi.
locker s. armadio, bauletto a chiave.
locket s. medaglione.
lockout s. (econ.) serrata.
locomotion s. locomozione.
locomotive agg. locomotorio. ♦ **locomotive** s. locomotiva.
locust s. locusta || — -tree, carrubo, robinia.
locution s. locuzione.
lodge s. 1. loggia 2. padiglione.
to lodge vt. 1. alloggiare 2. collocare. ♦ **to lodge** vi. 1. alloggiare 2. entrare.
lodging s. alloggio, dimora.
loftiness s. 1. altezza 2. nobiltà.
lofty agg. 1. alto, elevato 2. orgoglioso, altero.
log s. ceppo || — -book, giornale di bordo.
logarithm s. logaritmo.
logic s. logica.
logical agg. logico.
logistic(al) agg. logistico.

logistics s. pl. (mil.) logistica (sing.).
logomachy s. logomachia.
loin s. lombo. ♦ **loins** s. pl. reni.
to loiter vt. sprecare (tempo ecc.). ♦ **to loiter** vi. bighellonare, oziare.
loitering s. il bighellonare, l'andare a zonzo.
Lombard agg. e s. lombardo.
Londoner s. londinese.
Londonese agg. londinese.
loneliness s. solitudine.
lonely, lonesome agg. solo, solitario.
long agg. lungo || — -distance call, telefonata interurbana. ♦ **long** s. molto tempo. ♦ **long** avv. a lungo || how —?, quanto tempo?; all day —, tutto il giorno; as — as, fino a, purché; so —!, arrivederci!; before —, tra poco.
to long vi. desiderare ardentemente: to — for sthg., desiderare ardentemente qc.
longanimity s. longanimità.
longboat s. lancia.
longevity s. longevità.
longevous agg. longevo.
longing agg. bramoso. ♦ **longing** s. brama.
longitude s. longitudine.
longitudinal agg. longitudinale.
long-sighted agg. 1. presbite 2. preveggente.
look s. sguardo. ♦ **looks** s. pl. aspetto (sing.).
to look vi. 1. sembrare 2. guardare || to — after, badare a; to — at, guardare; to — for, cercare; to — forward to, non veder l'ora di; to — like, somigliare; to — up, consultare (orario, dizionario ecc.); to — through, esaminare attentamente; to — up to, rispettare; to — down on, disprezzare.
looker-on s. spettatore.
looking-glass s. specchio.
lookout s. 1. guardia 2. vista panoramica 3. prospettiva.
loom s. telaio.
to loom vt. tessere. ♦ **to loom** vi. apparire indistintamente.
loop s. 1. cappio 2. gancio.
loophole s. feritoia.
loose agg. 1. sciolto 2. ampio 3. vago 4. licenzioso 5. allentato.
to loose vt. 1. sciogliere 2. liberare 3. lanciare.

to **loosen** *vt*. **1.** sciogliere **2.** allentare.

looseness *s*. **1.** scioltezza **2.** ampiezza **3.** libertinaggio **4.** imprecisione.

to **lop** *vt*. potare, mozzare.

loquacious *agg*. loquace.

loquacity *s*. loquacità.

lord *s*. **1.** signore **2.** Pari || — *Mayor*, sindaco.

to **lord** *vt*. dominare

lordly *agg*. **1.** fastoso, imponente **2.** altero.

lordship *s*. signoria, autorità.

lorry *s*. autocarro.

to **lose (lost, lost)** *vt*. e *vi*. perdere.

loser *s*. perdente.

losing, loss *s*. perdita.

lost V. *to lose*.

lot *s*. **1.** sorte **2.** parte **3.** lotto (*di terreno ecc.*) || *a — of*, una quantità di.

to **lot** *vt*. lottizzare.

lotion *s*. lozione.

lottery *s*. lotteria.

loud *agg*. forte, fragoroso, rumoroso || — *-speaker*, altoparlante. ♦ **loud(ly)** *avv*. ad alta voce.

lounge *s*. **1.** atrio (*di albergo, teat. ecc.*) **2.** lo stare in ozio.

to **lounge** *vi*. bighellonare.

lounger *s*. fannullone.

louse *s*. (*pl*. lice) pidocchio.

lousy *agg*. pidocchioso.

lovable *agg*. amabile.

love *s*. amore.

to **love** *vt*. amare.

loveless *agg*. senza amore.

loveliness *s*. bellezza.

lovely *agg*. bello.

lover *s*. amante, innamorato.

loving *agg*. amoroso.

lovingness *s*. affettuosità.

low[1] *agg*. **1.** basso **2.** debole || — *-spirited*, depresso. ♦ **low** *avv*. **1.** in basso **2.** a voce bassa **3.** a basso prezzo.

low[2] *s*. muggito.

to **low** *vi*. muggire.

to **lower** *vt*. **1.** abbassare **2.** abbattere. ♦ to **lower** *vi*. abbattersi.

lowering *s*. abbassamento.

lowland *s*. pianura.

lowly *agg*. **1.** basso **2.** umile. ♦ **lowly** *avv*. umilmente.

loyal *agg*. leale.

loyalty *s*. lealtà.

lozenge *s*. **1.** (*geom*.) rombo **2.** pastiglia.

lubber *s*. zoticone.

lubricant *agg*. e *s*. lubrificante.

to **lubricate** *vt*. lubrificare.

lubricating, lubrication *s*. lubrificazione.

lubricator *s*. lubrificatore.

lubricity *s*. **1.** viscosità **2.** (*fig*.) lascivia.

lubricous *agg*. lubrico.

lucent *agg*. lucente.

lucid *agg*. lucido, chiaro.

lucidity *s*. lucidità, chiarezza.

luck *s*. **1.** sorte **2.** fortuna || *to be in — , out of —*, essere fortunato, sfortunato.

luckily *avv*. fortunatamente.

luckless *agg*. sfortunato.

lucky *agg*. fortunato. •

lucrative *agg*. lucrativo.

to **lucubrate** *vi*. fare delle elucubrazioni.

lucubration *s*. elucubrazione.

ludicrous *agg*. ridicolo.

ludicrousness *s*. comicità.

luggage *s*. bagaglio.

lugubrious *agg*. lugubre.

lukewarm *agg*. tiepido, apatico.

to **lull** *vt*. **1.** cullare **2.** calmare.

lullaby *s*. ninna-nanna.

lumbago *s*. lombaggine.

lumbar *agg*. lombare.

lumber *s*. **1.** cianfrusaglie (*pl*.) **2.** legname || — *-room*, ripostiglio.

to **lumber** *vt*. **1.** ammucchiare **2.** ingombrare. ♦ to **lumber** *vi*. **1.** tagliare legname **2.** muoversi pesantemente e rumorosamente.

lumbering *s*. commercio di legname.

luminary *s*. **1.** corpo luminoso **2.** luminare.

luminous *agg*. luminoso.

luminousness *s*. luminosità.

lump *s*. **1.** mucchio **2.** gonfiore **3.** zolletta **4.** (*comm*.) blocco **5.** persona goffa.

to **lump** *vt*. ammassare. ♦ to **lump** *vi*. raggrumarsi.

lumpy *agg*. **1.** granuloso **2.** increspato (*di mare*) **3.** pesante.

lunacy *s*. pazzia.

lunar *agg*. lunare.

lunatic *agg*. e *s*. pazzo.

lunation *s*. lunazione.

lunch *s*. seconda colazione, pasto del mezzogiorno.

to **lunch** *vi*. fare la seconda colazione. ♦ to **lunch** *vt*. offrire la colazione a.

luncheon s. spuntino.
lunette s. (arch.) lunetta.
lung s. polmone: iron —, polmone d'acciaio.
lupine s. lupino.
lure s. esca.
to **lure** vt. adescare.
lurid agg. 1. spettrale 2. orribile.
lurk s. nascondiglio.
to **lurk** vi. nascondersi.
luscious agg. 1. dolce 2. sensuale.
lust s. 1. lussuria 2. brama.
to **lust** vi. bramare: to — for so., sthg., bramare qu., qc.
lustful agg. 1. sensuale 2. bramoso.
lustfulness s. 1. sensualità 2. brama.
lustral agg. lustrale.
lustre[1] s. lustro, splendore.
lustre[2] s. lustro, quinquennio.
lusty agg. vigoroso, gagliardo.
lute s. liuto.
Lutheran agg. e s. luterano.
Lutheranism s. luteranesimo.
to **luxate** vt. (med.) lussare.
luxation s. lussazione.
luxuriant agg. lussureggiante.
to **luxuriate** vi. lussureggiare || to — in, deliziarsi di.
luxurious agg. lussuoso, sontuoso.
luxury s. 1. lusso 2. oggetto di lusso.
lye s. lisciva.
lying[1] agg. bugiardo.
lying[2] agg. giacente, situato.
lymph s. linfa.
lymphatic agg. linfatico. ♦ **lymphatic** s. vaso linfatico.
to **lynch** vt. linciare.
lynch law s. linciaggio.
lynx s. lince.
lyre s. lira.
lyric(al) agg. lirico. ♦ **lyric** s. lirica.
lyricism, lyrism s. lirismo.
lyrist s. poeta lirico.

M

macabre agg. macabro.
macaroni s. maccheroni.
macaroon s. amaretto.
mace s. mazza || — -bearer, mazziere.
to **macerate** vt. macerare. ♦ to

macerate vi. macerarsi.
maceration s. macerazione.
Machiavellian agg. machiavellico.
Machiavellism s. machiavellismo.
to **machinate** vt. macchinare.
machination s. macchinazione.
machine s. macchina || sewing- —, macchina da cucire.
to **machine** vt. e vi. lavorare a macchina.
machine-gun s. mitragliatrice.
to **machine-gun** vt. mitragliare.
machine-gunner s. mitragliere.
machinery s. 1. macchinario 2. meccanismo.
machining s. lavorazione (a macchina).
machinist s. macchinista.
mackerel s. sgombro || — sky, cielo a pecorelle.
mackintosh s. impermeabile.
macrocephalic agg. macrocefalo.
macrocosm s. macrocosmo.
macrocosmic agg. macrocosmico.
macromulecule s. macromolecola.
macroscopic agg. macroscopico.
to **maculate** vt. maculare.
maculation s. maculamento.
mad agg. 1. pazzo 2. idrofobo || to go —, impazzire.
madam s. signora.
madcap s. scervellato.
to **madden** vt. far impazzire. ♦ to **madden** vi. diventare matto.
madding agg. folle.
made V. to make.
madhouse s. manicomio.
madly avv. pazzamente.
madman s. pazzo.
madness s. 1. pazzia 2. idrofobia.
madrepore s. madrepora.
madrigal s. madrigale.
Maecenas s. mecenate.
magazine s. 1. magazzino 2. rivista 3. arsenale.
maggot s. 1. bruco 2. (fig.) capriccio.
maggoty agg. 1. bacato 2. (fig.) capriccioso.
magic s. magia.
magic(al) agg. magico.
magician s. mago.
magisterial agg. 1. di magistrato 2. autoritario.
magistracy s. magistratura.
magistrate s. magistrato.
magistrature s. magistratura.
magnanimity s. magnanimità.
magnanimous agg. magnanimo.

magnesium *s.* magnesio.
magnet *s.* magnete, calamita.
magnetic(al) *agg.* magnetico.
magnetism *s.* magnetismo.
magnetization *s.* **1.** magnetizzazione **2.** forza d'attrazione.
to **magnetize** *vt.* magnetizzare.
magnetizer *s.* magnetizzatore.
magneto *s.* magnete.
magnetometer *s.* magnetometro.
magnification *s.* **1.** esaltazione **2.** ingrandimento.
magnificence *s.* magnificenza.
magnificent *agg.* magnifico.
magnifier *s.* **1.** esaltatore **2.** lente d'ingrandimento.
to **magnify** *vt.* **1.** esaltare **2.** ingrandire.
magniloquence *s.* magniloquenza.
magniloquent *agg.* magniloquente.
magnitude *s.* grandezza.
magpie *s.* gazza.
Magyar *agg.* e *s.* magiaro.
mahogany *s.* mogano.
maid *s.* **1.** fanciulla **2.** cameriera ‖ *old* —, zitella.
maiden[1] *agg.* **1.** vergine, puro **2.** esordiente.
maiden[2] *s.* fanciulla ‖ — *name*, nome da ragazza.
maidenhead, maidenhood *s.* verginità.
maidenliness *s.* modestia, verecondia.
maidenly *agg.* verginale.
maidservant *s.* cameriera.
maieutics *s.* maieutica.
maigre *agg.* magro.
mail *s.* posta ‖ — *-train*, treno postale.
to **mail** *vt.* mandare per posta.
to **maim** *vt.* storpiare.
main[1] *agg.* **1.** principale **2.** vigoroso ‖ — *road*, strada maestra.
main[2] *s.* **1.** alto mare **2.** l'essenziale **3.** condotto principale.
mainland *s.* terraferma.
mainly *avv.* principalmente.
mainmast *s.* (*mar.*) albero maestro.
mainsail *s.* vela maestra.
mainspring *s.* molla principale.
to **maintain** *vt.* **1.** mantenere **2.** asserire.
maintenance *s.* **1.** mantenimento **2.** manutenzione **3.** difesa.
maize *s.* granoturco.
majestic(al) *agg.* maestoso.
majesty *s.* maestà.
major *agg.* maggiore, principale. ♦

major *s.* **1.** maggiorenne **2.** (*mil.*) maggiore.
majority *s.* **1.** maggioranza **2.** maggiore età.
make *s.* **1.** fattura **2.** costituzione **3.** marca.
to **make (made, made)** *vt.* e *vi.* **1.** fare **2.** rendere **3.** fabbricare ‖ *to* — *for*, dirigersi; *to* — *up*, preparare, truccare; *to* — *up for*, compensare per ‖ *to* — *oneself understood*, farsi capire; *to* — *so. confess*, obbligare qu. a confessare; *to* — *so. do what one likes*, far fare a qu. ciò che si vuole.
make-believe *s.* finzione.
maker *s.* **1.** creatore **2.** costruttore ‖ — *-up*, truccatore.
makeshift *s.* espediente.
make-up *s.* **1.** composizione **2.** trucco **3.** (*tip.*) impaginazione.
making *s.* **1.** fattura **2.** formazione.
♦ **makings** *s. pl.* il necessario (*sing.*).
maladjusted *agg.* **1.** disadatto **2.** disadattato.
maladjustment *s.* inadattabilità.
maladministration *s.* cattiva amministrazione.
maladroit *agg.* maldestro.
malady *s.* malattia.
malaise *s.* malessere.
Malayan *agg.* e *s.* malese.
malcontent *agg.* e *s.* malcontento.
male *agg.* maschio, maschile. ♦ **male** *s.* maschio.
malediction *s.* maledizione.
malefactor *s.* malfattore.
malefic *agg.* malefico.
maleficence *s.* malvagità.
maleficent *agg.* malefico.
malevolence *s.* malevolenza.
malevolent *agg.* malevolo.
malformation *s.* malformazione.
malformed *agg.* malformato.
malice *s.* **1.** malignità **2.** astio: *to bear* — *to so.*, nutrire rancore verso qu.
malicious *agg.* **1.** maligno **2.** premeditato.
malign *agg.* maligno.
malignancy *s.* malignità.
malignant *agg.* maligno.
malignity *s.* V. *malignancy.*
malleability *s.* malleabilità.
malleable *agg.* malleabile.
mallet *s.* mazzuolo.
mallow *s.* malva.
malnutrition *s.* malnutrizione.

malpractice *s.* pratica illecita.
malt *s.* malto.
Malthusian *agg.* e *s.* maltusiano.
Malthusianism *s.* maltusianesimo.
maltose *s.* maltosio.
to **maltreat** *vt.* maltrattare.
maltreatment *s.* maltrattamento.
malversation *s.* malversazione.
mama *s.* mamma.
mamma[1] *s.* mamma.
mamma[2] *s.* mammella.
mammal *s.* mammifero.
mammalian *agg.* e *s.* mammifero.
mammiferous *agg.* mammifero.
mammoth *agg.* enorme. ♦ **mammoth** *s.* mammut.
mammy *s.* mammina.
man *s.* (*pl.* men) **1.** uomo **2.** marito
|| — *hour*, ora lavorativa; — *-of-
-war*, nave da guerra.
to **man** *vt.* munire, equipaggiare (*di uomini*).
manacle *s.* manetta.
to **manacle** *vt.* ammanettare.
to **manage** *vt.* **1.** dirigere **2.** maneggiare **3.** riuscire. ♦ to **manage** *vi.* destreggiarsi, cavarsela.
manageable *agg.* **1.** maneggevole **2.** fattibile.
management *s.* **1.** direzione, amministrazione **2.** abilità.
manager *s.* **1.** direttore **2.** amministratore **3.** impresario **4.** organizzatore.
manageress *s.* **1.** direttrice **2.** amministratrice.
managerial *agg.* direttivo.
managership *s.* **1.** direzione **2.** amministrazione.
managing *agg.* dirigente || — *director*, consigliere delegato.
mandarin *s.* mandarino.
mandatary *s.* mandatario.
mandate *s.* mandato.
mandator *s.* mandante.
mandatory *agg.* e *s.* mandatario.
mandible *s.* mandibola.
mandolin *s.* mandolino.
mandrake *s.* mandragora.
mandrel *s.* anima metallica.
mandrill *s.* mandrillo.
mane *s.* criniera.
manful *agg.* valoroso.
manganate *s.* manganato.
mange *s.* rogna.
manger *s.* mangiatoia.
to **mangle** *vt.* **1.** lacerare **2.** storpiare.
mangy *agg.* **1.** lacero **2.** rognoso **3.** spregevole.
to **manhandle** *vt.* manovrare (*a mano*).
manhole *s.* botola.
manhood *s.* **1.** virilità **2.** vigore **3.** genere umano.
maniac *agg.* e *s.* maniaco, pazzo.
Manich(a)eism *s.* manicheismo.
manicurist *s.* manicure.
manifest *agg.* manifesto.
to **manifest** *vt.* manifestare.
manifestant *s.* manifestante.
manifestation *s.* manifestazione.
manifold *agg.* molteplice.
manifoldness *s.* molteplicità.
manikin *s.* **1.** omiciattolo **2.** manichino.
maniple *s.* manipolo.
to **manipulate** *vt.* manipolare.
manipulation *s.* manipolazione.
manipulator *s.* manipolatore.
mankind *s.* umanità.
manlike *agg.* **1.** civile **2.** antropomorfo.
manliness *s.* virilità.
manly *agg.* maschio, virile.
manner *s.* **1.** maniera **2.** contegno. ♦ **manners** *s. pl.* **1.** modi **2.** usanze.
mannered *agg.* manierato || *ill-* —, maleducato.
mannerism *s.* manierismo.
mannerly *agg.* cortese.
manoeuvrable *agg.* manovrabile.
manoeuvre *s.* manovra.
to **manoeuvre** *vt.* manovrare. ♦ to **manoeuvre** *vi.* fare le manovre.
manoeuvrer *s.* stratega.
manometer *s.* manometro.
manor *s.* feudo || — *-house*, castello.
manorial *agg.* feudale.
mansard *s.* mansarda.
manservant *s.* domestico.
mansion *s.* palazzo.
manslaughter *s.* omicidio preterintenzionale.
mantelpiece, mantelshelf *s.* mensola di caminetto.
mantle *s.* manto, mantello.
to **mantle** *vt.* ammantare. ♦ to **mantle** *vi.* coprirsi.
manual *agg.* e *s.* manuale.
manufactory *s.* fabbrica.
manufacturable *agg.* fabbricabile.
manufacture *s.* **1.** manifattura **2.** manufatto.
to **manufacture** *vt.* fabbricare.
manufacturer *s.* fabbricante.

manufacturing *agg.* manifatturiero. ♦ **manufacturing** *s.* fabbricazione.

manure *s.* concime.

manuscript *agg.* e *s.* manoscritto.

many (more, most) *agg.* e *pron.* molti || — *a*, più di uno; — -*sided*, molteplice; *so* —, tanti; *too* —, troppi; *as* — *as*, tanti... quanti; *how* —*?*, quanti?

map *s.* carta geografica.

maple *s.* acero.

to **mar** *vt.* guastare.

marathon *s.* maratona.

to **maraud** *vt.* e *vi.* saccheggiare.

marauder *s.* predatore.

marble *s.* 1. marmo 2. biglia.

to **marble** *vt.* marmorizzare.

marble-cutter *s.* marmista.

March *s.* marzo.

march[1] *s.* confine.

march[2] *s.* marcia.

to **march** *vi.* 1. camminare 2. marciare || *to* — *in*, entrare marciando.

marching *agg.* in, di marcia.

marchioness *s.* marchesa.

mare *s.* cavalla.

margarine *s.* margarina.

margin *s.* margine.

marginal *agg.* marginale.

marine *agg.* marino, marittimo. ♦ **marine** *s.* 1. marina 2. fante di marina.

marital *agg.* maritale.

maritime *agg.* marittimo.

mark *s.* 1. segno 2. bersaglio 3. voto 4. marchio 5. importanza 6. marco || *question* —, punto interrogativo.

to **mark** *vt.* 1. segnare 2. dare i voti a 3. scegliere 4. osservare.

marked *agg.* notevole.

marker *s.* 1. chi segna 2. segnalibro.

market *s.* mercato.

to **market** *vt.* 1. vendere al mercato 2. introdurre sul mercato. ♦ to **market** *vi.* comprare, vendere sul mercato.

marketing *s.* 1. compra-vendita 2. « marketing » (*ricerche di mercato*).

marking *s.* segno.

marksman *s.* tiratore scelto.

marl *s.* marna.

marmalade *s.* marmellata (*d'arance*).

marmoreal *agg.* marmoreo.

marmot *s.* marmotta.

to **maroon** *vt.* abbandonare un luogo deserto.

marquee *s.* tendone.

marquess, marquis *s.* marchese.

marquise *s.* marchesa.

marriage *s.* matrimonio, unione.

married *agg.* 1. sposato 2. coniugale.

marrow *s.* midollo || (*vegetable*) —, zucca.

to **marry** *vt.* sposare. ♦ to **marry** *vi.* sposarsi.

marsh *s.* paludè || — -*fever*, malaria; — *gas*, metano.

marshal *s.* maresciallo.

to **marshal** *vt.* 1. schierare 2. introdurre.

marshy *agg.* paludoso.

marsupial *agg.* e *s.* marsupiale.

marten *s.* martora.

martial *agg.* 1. marziale 2. di Marte.

Martian *agg.* e *s.* marziano.

martyr *s.* martire.

martyrdom *s.* martirio.

to **martyrize** *vt.* martirizzare.

martyrology *s.* martirologio.

marvel *s.* meraviglia.

to **marvel** *vi.* meravigliarsi.

marvellous *agg.* meraviglioso.

Marxism *s.* marxismo.

Marxist *agg.* e *s.* marxista.

marzipan *s.* marzapane.

mascot(te) *s.* mascotte.

masculine *agg.* e *s.* maschile.

masculinity *s.* mascolinità.

mash *s.* 1. mistura 2. puré.

to **mash** *vt.* 1. mescolare 2. schiacciare.

mask *s.* maschera.

to **mask** *vt.* mascherare.

masking *s.* il mascherarsi.

masochism *s.* masochismo.

mason *s.* muratore || *Free Mason*, massone.

masonry *s.* 1. arte del muratore 2. costruzione in muratura 3. massoneria.

masquerade *s.* mascherata.

to **masquerade** *vi.* 1. mascherarsi 2. fingersi.

mass[1] *s.* messa.

mass[2] *s.* massa, ammasso.

to **mass** *vt.* ammassare. ♦ to **mass** *vi.* ammassarsi.

massacre *s.* massacro.

to **massacre** *vt.* massacrare.

massage *s.* massaggio.

to **massage** *vt.* massaggiare.

masseur s. massaggiatore.

masseuse s. massaggiatrice.

massif s. massiccio.

massive agg. **1.** massiccio **2.** potente.

massiveness s. compattezza.

to **mass-produce** vt. produrre in serie.

mass-producer s. produttore in serie.

mass-production s. produzione in serie.

massy agg. massiccio.

mast s. (mar.) albero.

to **mast** vt. (mar.) alberare.

master s. **1.** padrone **2.** maestro || — builder, capomastro; Master of Arts, laureato in lettere.

to **master** vt. **1.** conoscere a fondo **2.** dominare.

masterful agg. **1.** autoritario **2.** abile.

masterhood s. padronanza.

masterly agg. magistrale.

masterpiece s. capolavoro.

mastership s. **1.** autorità **2.** abilità.

masterstroke s. colpo magistrale.

mastery s. **1.** maestria **2.** signoria.

mastication s. masticazione.

mastiff s. mastino.

mastitis s. mastite.

mastodon s. mastodonte.

mastoid s. mastoide.

mastoiditis s. mastoidite.

masturbation s. masturbazione.

mat s. stuoia || door- —, zerbino.

to **mat** vt. **1.** intrecciare **2.** coprire con stuoie **3.** smerigliare.

match[1] s. **1.** gara, incontro **2.** avversario **3.** l'uguale **4.** matrimonio.

match[2] s. fiammifero.

to **match** vt. **1.** accoppiare, maritare **2.** uguagliare. ♦ to **match** vi. **1.** accoppiarsi **2.** accordarsi **3.** rivaleggiare.

matchless agg. impareggiabile.

mate s. **1.** compagno **2.** aiuto **3.** (mar.) ufficiale in seconda.

to **mate** vt. accoppiare. ♦ to **mate** vi. accoppiarsi.

material agg. **1.** materiale **2.** essenziale. ♦ **material** s. **1.** materia, materiale **2.** stoffa. ♦ **materials** s. pl. articoli || raw —, materie prime.

materialism s. materialismo.

materialist agg. e s. materialista.

materialistic agg. materialistico.

materialization s. materializzazione.

to **materialize** vt. materializzare. ♦ to **materialize** vi. **1.** materializzarsi **2.** avverarsi.

maternal agg. materno.

maternity s. maternità.

mathematic(al) agg. matematico.

mathematician s. matematico.

mathematics s. matematica.

matriarchy s. matriarcato.

matricidal agg. matricida.

matricide s. **1.** matricida **2.** matricidio.

to **matriculate** vt. immatricolare. ♦ to **matriculate** vi. immatricolarsi.

matriculation s. immatricolazione.

matrimonial agg. matrimoniale.

matrimony s. matrimonio.

matrix s. **1.** matrice **2.** (anat.) utero.

matron s. **1.** matrona **2.** direttrice **3.** governante.

matronal, matronly agg. matronale.

matter s. **1.** materia **2.** faccenda || what is the — with you?, che cosa vi succede?; what is the —?, che succede?

to **matter** vi. **1.** importare: it matters little, poco importa **2.** (med.) suppurare.

matter-of-fact agg. pratico.

matting s. stuoia.

mattock s. piccone.

mattress s. materasso.

to **maturate** vi. **1.** maturare **2.** suppurare.

maturation s. **1.** maturazione **2.** suppurazione.

mature agg. maturo.

to **mature** vt. e vi. maturare.

maturity s. **1.** maturità **2.** (comm.) scadenza.

matutine agg. mattutino.

maudlin agg. **1.** sdolcinato **2.** querulo.

to **maunder** vi. **1.** parlare a vanvera **2.** girovagare.

mausoleum s. mausoleo.

mawkish agg. **1.** nauseante **2.** sdolcinato.

mawkishness s. **1.** sapore nauseante **2.** sdolcinatezza.

maxim s. massima.

maximalist s. massimalista.

maximum agg. e s. massimo.

May s. maggio || — Day, primo maggio.

may (might) v. dif. potere (pres. ind. e congiuntivo) || — I go out?, posso uscire?; he — arrive to day, può darsi che arrivi oggi; — he live to repent it, possa egli vivere tanto da pentirsene

maybe avv. forse.

maybug s. maggiolino.

mayflower s. biancospino.

mayonnaise s. maionese.

mayor s. sindaco.

maze s. labirinto.

to **maze** vt. disorientare, confondere.

mazily avv. confusamente.

mazy agg. intricato.

me pron. pers. me, mi.

meadow s. prato.

meagre agg. **1.** magro **2.** scarso.

meal[1] s. farina.

meal[2] s. pasto.

mealy agg. **1.** farinoso **2.** infarinato **3.** pallido **4.** chiazzato.

mean[1] agg. **1.** meschino **2.** mediocre.

mean[2] s. punto medio, mezzo. ♦ **means** s. pl. mezzi || by no means, ben lungi da.

to **mean (meant, meant)** vt. e vi. **1.** intendere, significare **2.** destinare.

meander s. meandro.

to **meander** vi. serpeggiare.

meaning agg. **1.** disposto **2.** significativo. ♦ **meaning** s. **1.** significato **2.** idea.

meaningful agg. significativo.

meaningless agg. senza senso.

meanly avv. **1.** meschinamente **2.** umilmente.

meanness s. meschinità.

meant V. to mean.

meantime s. frattempo. ♦ **meantime** avv. frattanto.

meanwhile avv. frattanto.

measles s. morbillo || German —, rosolia.

measurable agg. misurabile.

measure s. **1.** misura **2.** ritmo.

to **measure** vt. e vi. misurare.

measureless agg. smisurato.

measurement s. misurazione.

measurer s. misuratore.

meat s. carne.

meaty agg. **1.** polposo **2.** sostanzioso.

mechanic s. meccanico.

mechanical agg. meccanico.

mechanics s. meccanica.

mechanism s. **1.** meccanismo **2.** tecnica.

mechanization s. meccanizzazione.

to **mechanize** vt. meccanizzare.

medal s. medaglia.

to **meddle** vi. immischiarsi.

meddler s. intrigante.

meddlesome agg. importuno.

medi(a)eval agg. medievale.

medi(a)evalism s. medievalismo.

medi(a)evalist s. medievalista.

medial agg. medio.

median agg. mediano.

mediate agg. mediato.

to **mediate** vt. conseguire con mediazione. ♦ to **mediate** vi. fare da intermediario.

mediation s. mediazione.

mediator s. mediatore.

medical agg. medico.

medicament s. medicamento.

medication s. medicazione.

medicative agg. curativo.

medicinal agg. medicinale.

medicine s. medicina || — -man, stregone.

mediocrity s. mediocrità.

to **meditate** vt. e vi. meditare.

meditation s. meditazione.

meditative agg. meditativo.

Mediterranean agg. mediterraneo.

medium agg. medio. ♦ **medium** s. mezzo.

mediumistic agg. medianico.

medlar s. nespola || — -tree, nespolo.

medley agg. misto. ♦ **medley** s. miscuglio.

medulla s. midollo.

medullar(y) agg. midollare.

meek agg. mite.

meekness s. mansuetudine.

to **meet (met, met)** vt. **1.** incontrare **2.** far fronte a. ♦ to **meet (met, met)** vi. incontrarsi || to — with, imbattersi in.

meeting s. **1.** incontro **2.** riunione || political —, comizio.

megalomaniac s. megalomane.

megaphone s. megafono.

melancholic agg. malinconico.

melancholy agg. malinconico. ♦ **melancholy** s. malinconia.

mellifluous agg. mellifluo.

mellow agg. **1.** maturo **2.** pastoso **3.** ubertoso.

to **mellow** vt. e vi. maturare.

mellowness s. **1.** maturità **2.** pastosità **3.** ubertosità.

melodic agg. melodico.

melodious *agg.* melodioso.
melodiousness *s.* melodiosità.
melodrama *s.* melodramma.
melodramatic *agg.* melodrammatico.
melody *s.* melodia.
melomaniac *s.* melomane.
melon *s.* melone || *water- —*, anguria.
melt *s.* fusione.
to **melt** *vt.* 1. sciogliere 2. intenerire. ♦ to **melt** *vi.* 1. sciogliersi 2. intenerirsi || *to — away*, svanire.
melter *s.* fonditore.
melting *s.* fusione || *— -pot*, crogiuolo.
meltingly *avv.* teneramente.
member *s.* membro.
membership *s.* 1. qualifica di membro 2. i membri.
membrane *s.* membrana.
memoirs *s. pl.* memorie.
memorable *agg.* memorabile.
memorandum *s.* (*pl.* -da) promemoria.
memorial *agg.* commemorativo. ♦ **memorial** *s.* 1. monumento 2. memoriale.
memorialist *s.* memorialista.
to **memorize** *vt.* imparare a memoria.
memory *s.* memoria.
men V. *man.*
menace *s.* minaccia.
to **menace** *vt.* e *vi.* minacciare.
menacing *agg.* minaccioso.
menagerie *s.* serraglio.
mend *s.* rattoppo.
to **mend** *vt.* 1. riparare 2. correggere. ♦ to **mend** *vi.* 1. correggersi 2. migliorare.
mendacious *agg.* mendace.
mendacity *s.* 1. abitudine di mentire 2. bugia.
mender *s.* 1. riparatore 2. rammendatrice.
mendicant *agg.* e *s.* mendicante.
mendicity *s.* mendicità.
mending *s.* 1. riparazione 2. rammendo.
menial *agg.* servile. ♦ **menial** *s.* servo.
meninx *s.* (*pl.* meninges) meninge.
meniscus *s.* menisco.
menopause *s.* menopausa.
menses *s. pl.* mestruazioni.
menstruation *s.* mestruazione.
mental *agg.* mentale || *— -hospi-*

tal, manicomio.
mentality *s.* 1. mentalità 2. intelligenza.
menthol *s.* mentolo.
mention *s.* menzione || *don't — it*, non c'è di che (*risposta a « grazie »*).
to **mention** *vt.* nominare.
mentionable *agg.* menzionabile.
mentor *s.* mentore.
mephitic *agg.* mefitico.
mercantile *agg.* mercantile.
mercantilism *s.* mercantilismo.
mercenary *agg.* e *s.* mercenario.
merchandise *s.* merce.
to **merchandise** *vt.* e *vi.* commerciare.
merchant *s.* mercante || *— ship*, nave mercantile.
merciful *agg.* pietoso.
merciless *agg.* spietato.
mercury *s.* mercurio.
mercy *s.* pietà, misericordia.
mere[1] *agg.* 1. mero 2. solo.
mere[2] *s.* confine.
mere[3] *s.* laghetto, stagno.
to **merge** *vt.* assorbire. ♦ to **merge** *vi.* 1. essere assortito 2. immergersi.
merger *s.* (*comm.*) fusione (*di società*).
meridian *agg.* 1. meridiano 2. culminante. ♦ **meridian** *s.* 1. meridiano 2. culmine.
meridional *agg.* e *s.* meridionale.
merit *s.* merito.
to **merit** *vt.* meritare.
meritorious *agg.* meritorio.
mermaid *s.* sirena.
merman *s.* tritone.
merrily *avv.* allegramente.
merry *agg.* gaio.
merry-go-round *s.* giostra.
merrymaking *s.* festa.
mesh *s.* maglia. ♦ **meshes** *s. pl.* reti.
mesocarp *s.* mesocarpo.
mesozoic *agg.* e *s.* mesozoico.
mess *s.* 1. mensa 2. confusione 3. pasticcio.
to **mess** *vt.* mettere in disordine || *to — up*, mettere a soqquadro.
message *s.* 1. messaggio 2. commissione.
messenger *s.* messaggero || *— -boy*, fattorino.
Messiah *s.* Messia.
Messianic *agg.* messianico.
mestizo *s.* meticcio.

met V. *to meet.*
metabolism *s.* metabolismo.
metal *s.* 1. metallo 2. pietrisco.
metallic *agg.* metallico.
metallization *s.* metallizzazione.
to **metallize** *vt.* metallizzare.
metalloid *s.* metalloide.
metallurgic(al) *agg.* metallurgico.
metallurgist *s.* metallurgico.
metallurgy *s.* metallurgia.
metamorphic *agg.* metamorfico.
metamorphism *s.* metamorfismo.
metamorphosis *s.* (*pl.* -ses) metamorfosi.
metaphor *s.* metafora.
metaphoric(al) *agg.* metaforico.
metaphysic(al) *agg.* metafisico.
metaphysics *s.* metafisica.
metapsychic(al) *agg.* metapsichico.
metapsychics *s.* metapsichica.
metastasis *s.* (*pl.* -ses) metastasi.
metayage *s.* mezzadria.
metayer *s.* mezzadro.
mete *s.* segno di confine || *metes and bounds* (*giur.*), limiti e confini.
metempsychosis *s.* metempsicosi.
meteor *s.* meteora.
meteoric *agg.* 1. meteorico 2. transitorio.
meteoroid *s.* meteorite.
meteorologic(al) *agg.* meteorologico.
meteorologist *s.* meteorologo.
meteorology *s.* meteorologia.
meter *s.* 1. contatore 2. tassametro.
methane *s.* metano.
method *s.* metodo.
methodic(al) *agg.* metodico.
methodist *s.* metodista.
methodological *agg.* metodologico.
methodology *s.* metodologia.
meticulosity *s.* meticolosità.
meticulous *agg.* meticoloso.
metre *s.* 1. metro 2. (*mus.*) tempo.
metrical *agg.* metrico.
metrics *s.* metrica.
metronome *s.* metronomo.
metropolis *s.* metropoli.
metropolitan *agg.* metropolitano.
   ♦ **metropolitan** *s.* abitante di una metropoli.
mettle *s.* tempra.
mettled, mettlesome *agg.* focoso.
mew[1] *s.* gabbiano.
mew[2] *s.* miagolio.
to **mew**[1] *vt.* rinchiudere in gabbia.
to **mew**[2] *vi.* miagolare.
to **mewl** *vi.* vagire.

Mexican *agg. e s.* messicano.
mezzanine *s.* mezzanino.
miaul *s.* miagolio.
mice V. *mouse.*
microbe *s.* microbo.
microbial *agg.* microbico.
microbiology *s.* microbiologia.
microcosm *s.* microcosmo.
micrometer *s.* micrometro.
micrometry *s.* micrometria.
micro-organism *s.* microorganismo.
microphone *s.* microfono.
microphotography *s.* microfotografia.
microscope *s.* microscopio.
microscopic(al) *agg.* microscopico.
microscopy *s.* microscopia.
mid *agg.* medio, mezzo.
midday *s.* mezzogiorno.
middle *agg.* medio || *Middle Ages,* medioevo; — *-aged,* di mezza età.
   ♦ **middle** *s.* 1. mezzo 2. cintola.
middle class *s.* borghesia.
middleman *s.* intermediario.
middling *agg.* medio.
midge *s.* moscerino.
midget *s.* nano.
midland *agg.* centrale. ♦ **midlands** *s. pl.* regione centrale (*sing.*).
midnight *s.* mezzanotte.
midriff *s.* 1. diaframma 2. costume da bagno a due pezzi.
midshipman *s.* guardiamarina.
midst *s.* mezzo.
midsummer *s.* solstizio d'estate.
midway *agg. e avv.* a mezza strada.
mid-week *agg.* di metà settimana.
midwife *s.* (*pl.* -wives) levatrice.
midwinter *s.* solstizio d'inverno.
mien *s.* portamento.
might *s.* potenza.
might V. *may.*
mighty *agg.* potente.
migrant *agg. e s.* migratore.
to **migrate** *vi.* (e)migrare.
migration *s.* (e)migrazione.
migratory *agg.* migratore.
milady *s.* nobildonna.
mild *agg.* dolce.
mildew *s.* muffa.
mildness *s.* dolcezza.
mile *s.* miglio.
milestone *s.* pietra miliare.
milfoil *s.* millefoglio.
miliary *agg.* migliare.
militant *agg.* militante. ♦ **militant** *s.* attivista.

militarily *avv.* militarmente.

militarism *s.* militarismo.

militarist *s.* militarista.

militarization *s.* militarizzazione.

to militarize *vt.* militarizzare.

military *agg. e s.* militare.

militiaman *s.* milite.

milk *s.* latte || — *-jug,* lattiera.

to milk *vt.* mungere. ♦ to milk *vi.* 1. produrre latte 2. mungere.

milker *s.* 1. mungitore 2. mucca da latte.

milking *s.* mungitura.

milkmaid *s.* mungitrice.

milkman *s.* lattaio.

milky *agg.* 1. latteo 2. (*fig.*) gentile || *the Milky Way,* la Via Lattea.

mill *s.* 1. mulino 2. macinino 3. fabbrica || *saw-* —, segheria.

to mill *vt.* 1. macinare 2. segare 3. frullare.

millenary *agg.* millenario. ♦ millenary *s.* 1. millennio 2. millenario.

millennium *s.* millennio.

millepede *s.* millepiedi.

miller *s.* 1. mugnaio 2. fresatore 3. fresa.

millet *s.* (*bot.*) miglio.

milliard *s.* 1. miliardo 2. (*amer.*) bilione.

milligram(me) *s.* milligrammo.

millimetre *s.* millimetro.

milliner *s.* modista.

millinery *s.* modisteria.

milling *s.* 1. macinatura 2. fresatura.

million *s.* milione.

millionaire *s.* milionario.

millstone *s.* macina.

mime *s.* mimo.

to mime *vi. e vt.* mimare.

to mimeograph *vt.* ciclostilare.

mimetic *agg.* mimetico.

mimic *agg.* imitativo || — *art,* mimica. ♦ mimic *s.* imitatore.

to mimic (mimicked, mimicked) *vt.* imitare.

mimicry *s.* 1. imitazione 2. mimetismo.

minaret *s.* minareto.

minatory *agg.* minatorio.

mince *s.* carne tritata.

to mince *vt.* 1. tritare 2. tagliuzzare 3. mitigare. ♦ to mince *vi.* camminare, parlare in modo affettato.

mincer *s.* tritacarne.

mincing *agg.* affettato.

mind *s.* 1. mente 2. opinione.

to mind *vt.* 1. badare a 2. spiacere || *never* —!, non importa!; *I do not* —, non mi preoccupo di.

minded *agg.* incline || *broad-* —, di larghe vedute; *narrow-* —, di idee ristrette || *if you are so* —, se la pensate così.

mindful *agg.* memore.

mindless *agg.* 1. disattento 2. stupido.

mine[1] *pron. poss.* il mio, la mia, i miei, le mie || *a friend of* —, un mio amico.

mine[2] *s.* 1. miniera 2. mina || *-sweeper,* dragamine.

to mine *vt.* 1. scavare 2. estrarre 3. minare.

miner *s.* minatore.

mineral *agg. e s.* minerale.

to mineralize *vt.* mineralizzare.

mineralogy *s.* mineralogia.

to mingle *vt.* mescolare. ♦ to mingle *vi.* mescolarsi.

miniature *agg.* in miniatura. ♦ miniature *s.* miniatura.

to miniature *vt. e vi.* fare miniature.

miniaturist *s.* miniaturista.

minim *s.* 1. (*mus.*) minima 2. quantità minima 3. inezia.

minimal *agg.* minimo.

to minimize *vt.* minimizzare.

minimum *s.* (*pl.* -ma) minimo.

mining *agg.* minerario. ♦ mining *s.* 1. scavo 2. estrazione 3. posa di mine.

minion *s.* favorito.

miniskirt *s.* minigonna.

minister *s.* ministro.

to minister *vi.* assistere.

ministerial *agg.* ministeriale.

ministry *s.* ministero.

mink *s.* visone.

minor *agg.* minore. ♦ minor *s.* minorenne.

minority *s.* 1. minoranza 2. età minore.

minstrel *s.* menestrello.

mint[1] *s.* zecca.

mint[2] *s.* menta.

to mint *vt.* coniare.

mintage *s.* conio.

minuend *s.* minuendo.

minuet *s.* minuetto.

minus *s. e prep.* meno.

minute *agg.* minuto, minuscolo.

minute *s.* 1. minuto 2. nota || — *-hand,* lancetta dei minuti.

minutely[1] *avv.* minutamente.
minutely[2] *avv.* di minuto in minuto.
minuteness *s.* **1.** minutezza **2.** minuziosità.
miracle *s.* miracolo.
miraculous *agg.* miracoloso.
mirage *s.* miraggio.
mire *s.* fango.
to **mire** *vt.* infangare. ♦ to **mire** *vi.* infangarsi.
mirror *s.* specchio || *driving- —*, specchietto retrovisore.
to **mirror** *vt.* rispecchiare.
mirth *s.* allegria.
mirthful *agg.* allegro.
mirthless *agg.* triste.
miry *agg.* fangoso.
misadventure *s.* disavventura.
misanthrope *s.* misantropo.
misanthropy *s.* misantropia.
misapplication *s.* applicazione erronea.
to **misapply** *vt.* applicare erroneamente.
misapprehension *s.* malinteso.
misbehaviour *s.* cattivo contegno.
misbelief *s.* falsa credenza.
to **misbelieve** *vi.* avere una falsa credenza.
misbeliever *s.* miscredente.
misbelieving *agg.* eretico.
to **miscalculate** *vt.* e *vi.* calcolare male.
miscarriage *s.* **1.** disguido **2.** fallimento **3.** aborto.
to **miscarry** *vi.* **1.** smarrirsi **2.** fallire **3.** abortire.
miscellaneous *agg.* miscellaneo.
miscellany *s.* miscellanea.
mischance *s.* sfortuna.
mischief *s.* **1.** danno, male **2.** malizia **3.** birichinata.
mischievous *agg.* **1.** nocivo **2.** malizioso.
misconduct *s.* cattiva condotta.
miscount *s.* conteggio errato.
misdeed *s.* misfatto.
misdemeanour *s.* misfatto.
to **misdirect** *vt.* mandare in direzione sbagliata.
misdirection *s.* indicazione sbagliata.
misdoing *s.* misfatto.
miser *s.* avaro.
miserable *agg.* **1.** triste **2.** miserabile.
miserliness *s.* avarizia.
miserly *agg.* avaro.

misery *s.* **1.** miseria **2.** sofferenza.
misfire *s.* cilecca.
misfit *s.* **1.** cosa che si adatta male **2.** (*fig.*) pesce fuor d'acqua.
misfortune *s.* sventura.
to **misgive (misgave, misgiven)** *vt.* preoccupare. ♦ to **misgive (misgave, misgiven)** *vi.* preoccuparsi.
misgiving *s.* **1.** presentimento **2.** timore.
to **misgovern** *vt.* governare male.
misgovernment *s.* malgoverno.
to **misguide** *vt.* **1.** guidare male **2.** traviare.
to **mishandle** *vt.* maltrattare.
mishap *s.* infortunio.
to **misinform** *vt.* informare male.
misinformation *s.* informazione sbagliata.
to **misinterpret** *vt.* interpretare male.
misinterpretation *s.* interpretazione errata.
to **misjudge** *vt.* giudicare male.
misjudgement *s.* giudizio erroneo.
to **mislay (mislaid, mislaid)** *vt.* smarrire.
to **mislead (misled, misled)** *vt.* **1.** traviare **2.** ingannare.
misogamy *s.* misogamia.
misogynist *s.* misogino.
misogyny *s.* misoginia.
misoneism *s.* misoneismo.
to **misplace** *vt.* collocare male, fuori posto.
misplacement *s.* spostamento.
misprint *s.* errore di stampa, refuso.
to **misprint** *vt.* stampare con errori.
to **mispronounce** *vt.* pronunciare male.
mispronunciation *s.* pronuncia scorretta.
misquotation *s.* citazione erronea.
to **misquote** *vt.* citare erroneamente.
to **misread (misread, misread)** *vt.* leggere erroneamente.
mesreading *s.* falsa interpretazione.
to **misrepresent** *vt.* travisare.
misrepresentation *s.* travisamento.
miss[1] *s.* **1.** colpo mancato **2.** difetto.
miss[2] *s.* signorina: *Miss Jane Smith*, la signorina Jane Smith.
to **miss** *vt.* **1.** mancare (*il colpo*) **2.** perdere **3.** notare, sentire la man-

canza di **4.** evitare.
missal *s.* messale.
missile *s.* missile.
missing *agg.* mancante || *the —,* i dispersi.
mission *s.* missione.
missionary *agg.* e *s.* missionario.
missioner *s.* missionario.
to **misspell** *vt.* sbagliare l'ortografia.
mist *s.* **1.** bruma **2.** pioggerella **3.** appannamento.
to **mist** *vt.* appannare. ♦ to **mist** *vi.* appannarsi.
mistakable *agg.* suscettibile d'errore.
mistake *s.* errore.
to **mistake** (**mistook, mistaken**) *vt.* **1.** sbagliare **2.** scambiare **3.** non capire.
mistaken *agg.* **1.** in errore **2.** erroneo.
mister *s.* signore: *Mr. Brown,* il signor Brown.
mistletoe *s.* vischio.
mistook V. *to mistake.*
mistral *s.* maestrale.
mistranslation *s.* traduzione errata.
mistress *s.* **1.** signora: *Mrs. Brown,* la signora Brown **2.** insegnante **3.** amante.
mistrust *s.* diffidenza.
to **mistrust** *vt.* e *vi.* diffidare di, sospettare.
mistrustful *agg.* diffidente.
misty *agg.* **1.** nebbioso **2.** confuso.
to **misunderstand** (**misunderstood, misunderstood**) *vt.* e *vi.* fraintendere.
misunderstanding *s.* **1.** malinteso **2.** disaccordo.
misunderstood V. *to misunderstand.*
misusage, misuse *s.* **1.** cattivo uso **2.** maltrattamento.
to **misuse** *vt.* **1.** usar male **2.** maltrattare.
to **miswrite** (**miswrote, miswritten**) *vt.* scrivere scorrettamente.
mithridatic *agg.* immunizzante (*contro veleni*).
mithridatism *s.* immunizzazione (*contro un veleno*).
to **mitigate** *vt.* mitigare.
mitigation *s.* mitigazione.
mitral *agg.* mitrale.
mitre *s.* **1.** (*eccl.*) mitra **2.** giunto ad angolo.

mitt(en) *s.* manopola, guantone.
to **mix** *vt.* mescolare || *to — up,* confondere. ♦ to **mix** *vi.* mescolarsi.
mixed *agg.* misto, eterogeneo.
mixer *s.* (*mecc.*) mescolatore.
mixing *s.* mescolanza.
mixture *s.* **1.** mescolanza **2.** miscela.
mizzen *s.* (*mar.*) mezzana.
mnemonic *agg.* mnemonico.
mnemonics *s.* mnemonica.
moan *s.* gemito.
to **moan** *vt.* e *vi.* gemere.
moanful *agg.* lamentoso.
moaning *s.* lamento.
moat *s.* fossato.
mob *s.* **1.** folla **2.** plebaglia.
to **mob** *vt.* **1.** assalire **2.** affollare.
mobile *agg.* **1.** mobile **2.** mutevole.
mobility *s.* **1.** mobilità **2.** mutevolezza.
mobilization *s.* mobilitazione.
to **mobilize** *vt.* mobilitare.
moccasin *s.* mocassino.
mock *agg.* **1.** ironico **2.** finto || *— -heroic,* eroicomico. ♦ **mock** *s.* **1.** derisione **2.** imitazione.
to **mock** *vt.* e *vi.* beffare, prendersi gioco di.
mocker *s.* burlone.
mockery *s.* **1.** derisione **2.** contraffazione.
mocking *agg.* beffardo.
modal *agg.* modale.
modality *s.* modalità.
model *agg.* modello. ♦ **model** *s.* **1.** modello **2.** copia.
to **model** *vt.* modellare.
modeller *s.* **1.** modellatore **2.** modellista.
modelling *s.* **1.** modellatura **2.** creazione di modelli.
moderate *agg.* e *s.* moderato.
to **moderate** *vt.* moderare. ♦ to **moderate** *vi.* moderarsi.
moderateness *s.* moderatezza.
moderation *s.* moderazione.
moderator *s.* moderatore.
modern *agg.* e *s.* moderno.
modernism *s.* modernismo.
modernist *s.* modernista.
modernity *s.* modernità.
modernization *s.* **1.** rimodernamento **2.** aggiornamento.
to **modernize** *vt.* modernizzare. ♦ to **modernize** *vi.* modernizzarsi.
modest *agg.* **1.** modesto **2.** pudico.

modesty s. 1. modestia 2. pudore.
modifiable agg. modificabile.
modification s. modificazione.
modifier s. modificatore.
to **modify** vt. modificare.
to **modulate** vt. e vi. modulare.
modulation s. modulazione.
modulator s. modulatore.
mofette s. mofeta.
Mohammedan agg. e s. maomettano.
moist agg. umido.
to **moisten** vt. inumidire. ♦ to
moisten vi. inumidirsi.
moistness s. umidità.
moisture s. vapore umido.
molar agg. e s. molare.
molasses s. melassa.
mole¹ s. neo.
mole² s. talpa.
mole³ s. molo.
molecular agg. molecolare.
molecule s. molecola.
moleskin s. 1. pelle di talpa 2. fustagno. ♦ **moleskins** s. pl. calzoni di fustagno.
to **molest** vt. molestare.
molestation s. molestia.
molester s. molestatore.
to **mollify** vt. addolcire.
mollusc s. mollusco.
molybdenum s. molibdeno.
moment s. 1. momento 2. importanza.
momentary agg. momentaneo.
momentous agg. importante.
monachal agg. monacale.
monad s. monade.
monarch s. monarca.
monarchic(al) agg. monarchico.
monarchist s. monarchico.
monarchy s. monarchia.
monastery s. monastero.
monastic(al) agg. monastico.
Monday s. lunedì.
monetary agg. monetario.
monetization s. monetazione.
to **monetize** vt. monetizzare.
money s. denaro || — -bag, porta-
monete; — -order, vaglia; earnest —, caparra; paper —, valuta
cartacea; ready —, contanti.
moneyed agg. 1. di, in denaro 2.
ricco.
moneyless agg. squattrinato.
monger s. mercante || fish —, pe-
scivendolo.
Mongolian agg. e s. mongolo.
mongolism s. mongolismo.

mongoloid agg. e s. mongoloide.
mongrel agg. misto. ♦ **mongrel**
s. 1. bastardo 2. incrocio.
monism s. monismo.
monition s. 1. ammonizione 2.
(giur.) citazione.
monitor s. 1. consigliere 2. capo-
classe 3. dispositivo di controllo.
monitory agg. ammonitore.
monk s. monaco.
monkey s. scimmia.
monkeyish agg. scimmiesco.
monkhood s. monacato.
monkish agg. monastico, manacale.
monochromatic agg. monocroma-
tico.
monochrome s. monocromia.
monocle s. monocolo.
monody s. monodia.
monogamist s. monogamo.
monogamy s. monogamia.
monogram s. monogramma.
monograph s. monografia.
monographic(al) agg. monogra-
fico.
monolith s. monolito.
monolithic agg. monolitico.
monologue s. monologo.
monometallic agg. monometallico.
monomial s. monomio.
monomolecular agg. monomoleco-
lare.
monoplane s. monoplano.
monopolist s. monopolista.
to **monopolize** vt. monopolizzare.
monopoly s. monopolio.
monorail s. monorotaia.
monosyllabic agg. monosillabico.
monosyllable s. monosillabo.
monotheism s. monoteismo.
monotheist s. monoteista.
monotheistic(al) agg. monoteistico.
monotone s. tono uniforme.
monotonous agg. monotono.
monotony s. 1. tono uniforme 2.
monotonia.
monotype s. monotipo.
monsoon s. monsone.
monster agg. colossale. ♦ **monster**
s. mostro.
monstrance s. ostensorio.
monstrosity s. mostruosità.
monstrous agg. mostruoso.
montage s. montaggio.
month s. mese.
monthly agg. e s. mensile. ♦
monthly avv. mensilmente.
monument s. monumento.
monumental agg. monumentale.

mood s. 1. umore 2. (*gramm.*) modo.
♦ **moods** s. pl. capricci.
moodily avv. di malumore.
moodiness s. malumore.
moody agg. di malumore.
moon s. luna.
to **moon** vi. 1. gingillarsi 2. allunare || to – about, bighellonare.
mooncalf s. (pl. -lves) idiota.
mooning s. vagabondaggio.
moonlight s. chiaro di luna.
moonlit agg. illuminato dalla luna.
moonshine s. V. *moonlight.*
moonshiny agg. V. *moonlit.*
moony agg. 1. lunare 2. distratto.
Moor s. moro.
moor s. brughiera.
to **moor** vt. e vi. ormeggiare.
moorage s. ormeggio. ♦ **moorings** s. pl. 1. gomena (*sing.*) 2. ormeggi.
mop[1] s. 1. scopa 2. zazzera.
mop[2] s. smorfia.
to **mop**[1] vt. 1. pulire 2. asciugare || to – up (*mil.*), rastrellare.
to **mop**[2] vi. fare smorfie.
mope s. 1. persona avvilita 2. tristezza.
to **mope** vt. avvilire. ♦ to **mope** vi. avvilirsi.
mopish agg. avvilito.
moraine s. morena.
moral agg., morale. ♦ **moral** s. 1. morale 2. principio morale. ♦ **morals** s. pl. costumi.
morale s. il morale.
moralism s. moralismo.
moralist s. moralista.
moralistic agg. moralistico.
morality s. moralità.
moralization s. moralizzazione.
to **moralize** vt. moralizzare. ♦ to **moralize** vi. trarre la morale.
morass s. palude.
moratory agg. moratorio.
moratorium s. (pl. -ria) moratoria.
moray s. murena.
morbid agg. 1. morboso 2. patologico.
morbidity s. 1. morbosità 2. stato patologico.
mordacity, mordancy s. mordacità.
mordant agg. e s. mordente.
more (*comp. di* much, many) agg., pron. e avv. più, di più, maggiormente || – and –, sempre più; once –, ancora una volta.
moreover avv. inoltre.

morganatic agg. morganatico.
morgue s. obitorio.
Mormon agg. e s. mormone.
morning s. mattino.
Moroccan agg. e s. marocchino.
moron s. deficiente.
morose agg. tetro.
morphia, morphine s. morfina.
morphinomaniac agg. e s. morfinomane.
morphologic(al) agg. morfologico.
morphology s. morfologia.
morsel s. boccone.
mortal agg. e s. mortale.
mortality s. mortalità.
mortally avv. mortalmente.
mortar[1] s. mortaio.
mortar[2] s. calcina.
mortgage s. ipoteca.
to **mortgage** vt. ipotecare.
mortgagee s. creditore ipotecario.
mortgager s. debitore ipotecario.
mortification s. mortificazione.
to **mortify** vt. 1. mortificare 2. incancrenire. ♦ to **mortify** vi. 1. mortificarsi 2. incancrenirsi.
mortuary agg. mortuario. ♦ **mortuary** s. camera mortuaria.
mosaic agg. musivo. ♦ **mosaic** s. mosaico.
Moslem agg. e s. mussulmano.
mosque s. moschea.
mosquito s. zanzara || – -net, zanzariera.
moss s. 1. acquitrino 2. muschio.
mossy agg. muscoso.
most agg. e pron. (*superl. di* much, many) il più, la maggior parte di, il massimo. ♦ **most** avv. 1. il più 2. molto 3. maggiormente.
mostly avv. per lo più.
mote s. particella.
moth s. 1. falena 2. tignola.
mother s. madre || – -country, madrepatria; – -in-law, suocera.
motherhood s. maternità.
motherless agg. senza madre.
motherly agg. materno.
mothproof agg. inattaccabile dalle tarme.
motif s. motivo.
motion s. 1. moto, movimento 2. mozione || – -picture, film.
motionless agg. immobile.
to **motivate** vt. 1. motivare 2. stimolare.
motivation s. 1. motivazione 2. stimolo.
motive agg. motore. ♦ **motive** s.

motivo, movente.

motley *agg.* **1.** screziato **2.** eterogeneo. ♦ **motley** *s.* miscuglio.

motor *agg.* e *s.* motore || — -*cycle*, motocicletta; — -*car*, automobile, — -*boat*, motobarca; — *ship*, motonave.

to **motor** *vi.* andare in automobile.

motoring *s.* automobilismo.

motorist *s.* automobilista.

motorization *s.* motorizzazione.

to **motorize** *vt.* motorizzare.

mottle *s.* chiazza.

to **mottle** *vt.* chiazzare.

moufflon *s.* muflone.

mould[1] *s.* stampo.

mould[2] *s.* muffa.

mould[3] *s.* terriccio.

to **mould**[1] *vt.* modellare.

to **mould**[2] *vi.* ammuffire.

moulding *s.* **1.** il modellare **2.** cornice **3.** fusione.

mouldy *agg.* ammuffito.

mound *s.* monticello.

mount[1] *s.* monte, montagna.

mount[2] **1.** cavalcatura **2.** intelaiatura **3.** affusto di cannone **4.** montatura.

to **mount** *vt.* salire. ♦ to **mount** *vi.* **1.** montare **2.** ammontare.

mountain *s.* montagna.

mountaineer *s.* **1.** montanaro **2.** alpinista.

mountaineering *s.* alpinismo.

mountainous *agg.* montuoso.

mountebank *s.* ciarlatano.

mounter *s.* montatore.

to **mourn** *vt.* e *vi.* piangere.

mourner *s.* chi è in lutto.

mournful *agg.* lugubre.

mourning *s.* **1.** dolore **2.** lutto: *to go into* —, mettere il lutto.

mouse *s.* (*pl.* mice) topo.

moustache *s.* baffi (*pl.*).

mouth *s.* bocca.

to **mouth** *vt.* declamare. ♦ to **mouth** *vi.* fare smorfie.

mouthful *s.* boccone.

mouthpiece *s.* **1.** bocchino **2.** portavoce.

movable *agg.* mobile.

movables *s. pl.* beni mobili.

move *s.* **1.** movimento **2.** mossa **3.** trasloco.

to **move** *vt.* **1.** muovere **2.** commuovere. ♦ to **move** *vi.* **1.** muoversi

movement *s.* **1.** movimento, moto. **2.** traslocare **3.** commuoversi.

mover *s.* promotore.

movie *s.* film. ♦ **movies** *s. pl.* cinema (*sing.*).

moving *s.* **1.** spostamento **2.** trasloco.

mow *s.* covone.

to **mow** (**mowed, mown**) *vt.* falciare.

mower *s.* falciatore.

mowing *s.* falciatura.

mown V. *to mow.*

much (**more, most**) *agg.*, *s.* e *avv.* molto || *so* —, tanto; *too* —, troppo; *as* — *as*, tanto quanto; *how* —?, quanto?

muck *s.* letame.

mucous *agg.* mucoso.

mucus *s.* muco.

mud *s.* fango || — -*guard*, parafango.

to **mud** *vt.* infangare.

muddle *s.* confusione, pasticcio.

to **muddle** *vt.* confondere.

muddleheaded *agg.* confusionario.

muddler *s.* confusionario.

muddy *agg.* **1.** fangoso **2.** torbido **3.** infangato.

to **muddy** *vt.* infangare.

muff[1] *s.* manicotto.

muff[2] *s.* **1.** colpo mancato **2.** babbeo.

to **muffle** *vt.* **1.** avvolgere **2.** smorzare.

muffler *s.* **1.** sciarpa **2.** guantone **3.** silenziatore.

mug *s.* (*fam.*) faccia || — *shot* (*tv*), primo piano.

mulberry *s.* mora || — (-*tree*) gelso.

mule *s.* mulo.

mulish *agg.* (*fig.*) testardo.

muller *s.* pestello.

multiform *agg.* multiforme.

multimillionaire *s.* multimilionario.

multiple *agg.* e *s.* multiplo.

multiplicable *agg.* moltiplicabile.

multiplicand *s.* moltiplicando.

multiplication *s.* moltiplicazione.

multiplicity *s.* molteplicità.

multiplier *s.* moltiplicatore.

to **multiply** *vt.* moltiplicare. ♦ to **multiply** *vi.* moltiplicarsi.

multitude *s.* moltitudine.

multitudinous *agg.* **1.** innumerevole **2.** vasto.

mumble *s.* borbottio.

to **mumble** *vt.* e *vi.* borbottare.

mumbling *s.* V. *mumble.*

mummer *s.* guitto.

mummification s. mummificazione.
to mummify vt. mummificare.
mummy¹ s. mummia.
mummy² s. mammina.
mumps s. pl. orecchioni.
to munch vt. e vi. biascicare.
municipal agg. municipale.
municipality s. municipalità.
municipalization s. municipalizzazione.
to municipalize vt. municipalizzare.
munificence s. munificenza.
munificent agg. munifico.
munitions s. pl. munizioni.
mural agg. murale. ♦ mural s. affresco.
murder s. assassinio.
to murder vt. assassinare.
murderer s. assassino.
murderous agg. omicida.
muriatic agg. muriatico.
murky agg. tenebroso.
murmur s. 1. mormorio 2. brontolio.
to murmur vt. mormorare. ♦ to
murmur vi. brontolare.
murmuring s. V. murmur.
muscat(el) s. moscato.
muscle s. muscolo.
muscled agg. muscoloso
muscular agg. 1. muscolare 2. muscoloso.
musculature s. muscolatura.
Muse s. musa.
to muse vi. meditare.
museum s. museo.
mushroom s. fungo.
mushy agg. infrollito.
music s. musica.
musical agg. 1. musicale 2. appassionato di musica.
musicality s. musicalità.
musician s. musicista || street —,
suonatore ambulante.
musicologist s. musicologo.
musicology s. musicologia.
musing agg. meditabondo. ♦ musing s. meditazione.
musk s. muschio.
musket s. moschetto.
musketeer s. moschettiere.
musky agg. muschiato.
Muslim agg. e s. mussulmano.
muslin s. mussola.
muss s. stato di confusione.
mussel s. mitilo.
must¹ s. mosto.
must² s. muffa.

must v. dif. (pres. ind.) dovere ||
he — return here, deve ritornare
qui, it — be true, deve essere vero;
you — know him!, non puoi non
conoscerlo!
mustard s. senape.
muster s. adunata.
to muster vt. adunare. ♦ to muster vi. adunarsi.
mutability s. mutabilità.
mutable agg. mutevole.
mutation s. cambiamento.
mute agg. muto. ♦ mute s. 1. muto 2. sordina.
to mutilate vt. mutilare.
mutilation s. mutilazione.
mutineer s. ammutinato.
mutinous agg. ammutinato, ribelle.
mutiny s. ammutinamento.
to mutiny vi. ammutinarsi.
mutism s. mutismo.
to mutter V. to murmur.
mutton s. montone.
mutual agg. 1. reciproco 2. comune.
muzzle s. 1. muso 2. museruola 3.
bocca (di arma).
to muzzle vt. mettere la museruola a.
my agg. poss. mio, mia, miei, mie,
mycosis s. (pl. -ses) micosi.
myocardial agg. miocardico.
myocarditis s. miocardite.
myocardium s. miocardio.
myopia s. miopia.
myopic agg. miope.
myosote s. miosotide.
myriad s. miriade.
myriagram s. miriagrammo.
myriametre s. miriametro.
Myriapoda s. pl. miriapodi.
myrrh s. mirra.
myrtle s. mirto.
myself pron. r. io stesso, me stesso,
mi.
mysterious agg. misterioso.
mystery s. mistero.
mystic agg. e s. mistico.
mystical agg. mistico.
mysticism s. misticismo.
mystification s. mistificazione.
mystifier s. mistificatore.
to mystify vt. 1. disorientare 2.
avvolgere nel mistero.
myth s. mito.
mythic(al) agg. mitico.
to mythicize vt. volgere in mito.
mythologic(al) agg. mitologico.
to mythologize vi. studiare i miti.
mythology s. mitologia.

mythomania *s.* mitomania.
mythomaniac *agg.* e *s.* mitomane.

N

nabob *s.* nababbo.
nacre *s.* madreperla.
to **nag** *vt.* e *vi.* brontolare.
naiad *s.* naiade.
nail *s.* **1.** unghia, artiglio **2.** chiodo.
to **nail** *vt.* **1.** inchiodare **2.** munire di chiodi.
nailer *s.* fabbricante di chiodi.
naïve *agg.* ingenuo, semplice.
naiveté *s.* ingenuità.
naked *agg.* **1.** nudo, spogliato **2.** spoglio, indifeso.
nakedness *s.* nudità.
name *s.* **1.** nome **2.** fama, reputazione || — *-day,* onomastico; *full* —, generalità.
to **name** *vt.* **1.** nominare, dare un nome **2.** designare.
nameless *agg.* **1.** senza nome **2.** innominabile.
namely *avv.* cioè.
nanny *s.* bambinaia, balia.
nap¹ *s.* siesta, sonnellino.
nap² *s.* pelo (*di stoffe*).
to **nap** *vi.* schiacciare un sonnellino, sonnecchiare.
nape *s.* nuca.
naphtha *s.* nafta.
napkin *s.* **1.** tovagliolo: — *-ring,* anello per tovagliolo **2.** pannolino.
narcissism *s.* narcisismo.
narcosis, narcotism *s.* narcosi.
narcotic *agg.* *s.* narcotico.
narcotization *s.* narcotizzazione.
to **narcotize** *vt.* narcotizzare.
to **narrate** *vt.* narrare.
narration *s.* narrazione, racconto.
narrative *agg.* narrativo. ♦ **narrative** *s.* resoconto, narrazione.
narrator *s.* narratore.
narrow *agg.* **1.** stretto, angusto, ristretto (*anche fig.*) **2.** esatto, minuzioso || *-minded,* di idee ristrette. ♦ **narrow** *s.* stretto, strettoia.
to **narrow** *vt.* stringere, ridurre. ♦ to **narrow** *vi.* stringersi, contrarsi.
narrowness *s.* strettezza, limitatezza.
narwhal *s.* narvalo.
nasal *agg.* nasale. ♦ **nasal** *s.* **1.**

suono nasale **2.** osso nasale.
nascent *agg.* nascente.
nastily *avv.* **1.** sgradevolmente **2.** con cattiveria.
nastiness *s.* **1.** cattivo gusto **2.** cattiveria.
nasty *agg.* **1.** sporco, sgradevole **2.** cattivo, tempestoso (*di tempo*).
natal *agg.* natale.
natality *s.* natalità.
natant *agg.* natante.
natation *s.* nuoto.
natatorial *agg.* natatorio.
nation *s.* nazione.
national *agg.* nazionale.
nationalism *s.* nazionalismo.
nationalist *s.* nazionalista.
nationality *s.* **1.** nazionalità **2.** patriottismo.
nationalization *s.* **1.** nazionalizzazione **2.** naturalizzazione.
to **nationalize** *vt.* **1.** nazionalizzare **2.** naturalizzare.
native *agg.* **1.** innato **2.** natio, indigeno. ♦ **native** *s.* indigeno, nativo.
nativity *s.* nascita, natività.
natural *agg.* **1.** naturale, fisico **2.** spontaneo **3.** istintivo, innato.
naturalism *s.* naturalismo.
naturalist *s.* naturalista.
naturalistic *agg.* naturalistico.
naturalization *s.* **1.** naturalizzazione **2.** acclimatamento.
to **naturalize** *vi.* **1.** naturalizzare **2.** acclimatare.
nature *s.* **1.** natura **2.** carattere, temperamento || *good* —, bontà.
natured *agg.* di natura, per natura || *good* —, buono, di buon carattere.
naturism *s.* naturismo, nudismo.
naturist *s.* naturista.
naughtily *avv.* con cattiveria.
naughtiness *s.* cattiveria.
naughty *agg.* cattivo, impertinente.
to **nauseate** *vt.* nauseare, disgustare. ♦ to **nauseate** *vi.* avere la nausea, disgustarsi.
nauseating *agg.* nauseabondo.
nautical *agg.* nautico.
naval *agg.* navale.
nave¹ *s.* mozzo di ruota.
nave² *s.* navata centrale (*di chiesa*).
navel *s.* **1.** ombelico **2.** (*fig.*) centro.
navigability *s.* navigabilità.
navigable *agg.* navigabile.
to **navigate** *vt.* e *vi.* **1.** navigare **2.** regolare la rotta.

navigation s. 1. navigazione 2. rotta.

navigator s. navigatore, ufficiale di rotta.

navvy s. sterratore.

navy s. marina da guerra, flotta.

nay avv. anzi, non solo.

Nazi agg. e s. nazista.

Neapolitan agg. e s. napoletano.

near agg. 1. vicino, prossimo 2. affine, intimo 3. fedele, esatto. ♦ **near** prep. vicino a, presso a. ♦ **near** avv. vicino, presso, accanto.

to **near** vt. e vi. avvicinarsi (a).

nearby agg. avv. prep. assai vicino.

nearly avv. quasi.

neat agg. 1. pulito, lindo 2. grazioso, di buon gusto 3. chiaro, conciso.

neatly avv. 1. lindamente, ordinatamente 2. con semplicità, con buon gusto 3. concisamente.

neatness s. 1. pulizia, ordine 2. grazia, armonia 3. semplicità 4. concisione.

nebula s. nebulosa.

nebular agg. nebulare.

nebulosity s. nebulosità.

nebulous agg. nebuloso, vago.

necessary agg. necessario.

to **necessitate** vt. 1. rendere necessario 2. obbligare.

necessity s. necessità.

neck s. collo || stiff —, torcicollo.

neckerchief s. fazzoletto da collo.

necklace s. collana, vezzo.

neckline s. scollatura.

necktie s. cravatta.

necrology s. necrologia.

necromancer s. negromante.

necromancy s. negromanzia.

necropolis s. necropoli.

necrosis s. (pl. -ses) necrosi.

nectar s. nettare.

need s. necessità, bisogno.

to **need** vt. e vi. essere necessario, occorrere, abbisognare, mancare di.

needful agg. necessario, indispensabile.

neediness s. bisogno, povertà.

needle s. 1. ago 2. puntina di grammofono.

to **needle** vt. 1. cucire, pungere (con un ago) 2. irritare.

needleful s. gugliata.

needless agg. inutile, superfluo.

needlewoman s. cucitrice.

needlework s. lavoro ad ago.

needs avv. necessariamente.

needy agg. povero, indigente.

ne'er avv. (contrazione di never) mai.

negation s. diniego.

negative agg. negativo. ♦ **negative** s. 1. negazione 2. qualità negativa.

neglect s. negligenza, trascuratezza.

to **neglect** vt. trascurare.

neglectful agg. negligente, noncurante.

negligence s. negligenza, trascuratezza.

negligent agg. negligente, trascurato.

negligible agg. trascurabile.

negotiable agg. negoziabile.

to **negotiate** vt. e vi. negoziare, trattare.

negotiation s. trattativa.

negress s. negra.

negro agg. e s. negro.

negroid agg. negroide.

neigh s. nitrito.

to **neigh** vi. nitrire.

neighbour s. vicino.

to **neighbour** vi. essere vicini di casa.

neighbourhood s. 1. i vicini, vicinato 2. paraggi, dintorni (pl.).

neighbouring agg. vicino, contiguo.

neither[1] agg. né l'uno né l'altro.

neither[2] avv. né, neppure, nemmeno: — ... nor, né ... né.

nemesis s. (pl. -ses) nemesi.

neo-classic(al) agg. neoclassico.

neo-classicism s. neoclassicismo.

neo-criticism s. neocriticismo.

neolithic agg. neolitico.

neologism s. neologismo.

neology s. neologia.

neon s. neon.

neophyte s. neofito.

neoplatonic agg. neoplatonico.

Neoplatonism s. neoplatonismo.

neopositivism s. neopositivismo.

neorealism s. neorealismo.

neorealist s. neorealista.

nephew s. nipote (di zio).

nephritic agg. nefritico.

nephrītis s. nefrite.

nepotism s. nepotismo.

nerve s. 1. nervo 2. nervatura 3. forza, energia, sangue freddo.

to **nerve** vt. tonificare, rinvigorire.

nerveless agg. snervato, inerte.

nervous agg. 1. nervoso 2. forte, vigoroso 3. timido, apprensivo.

nervously avv. 1. nervosamente 2.

timidamente.

nervousness s. 1. nervosismo, irritazione 2. timidezza.

nervy agg. 1. muscoloso, forte 2. nervoso.

nescient agg. ignorante.

nest s. 1. nido 2. (fig.) covo, tana 3. colonia (di vccelli, insetti ecc.).

to **nest** vi. fare il nido, nidificare.

to **nestle** vt. ospitare. ♦ to **nestle** vi. annidarsi, rifugiarsi.

nestling s. uccellino di nido.

net¹ agg. e s. netto.

net² s. 1. rete 2. (fig.) trappola.

to **net** vt. 1. coprire con reti 2. pescare con reti.

netful s. retata.

netting s. rete, reticolato.

nettle s. ortica || — rash, orticaria.

to **nettle** vt. pungere (di ortica).

network s. rete, reticolato.

neuralgia s. nevralgia.

neuralgic agg. nevralgico.

neurasthenia s. nevrastenia.

neurasthenic agg. nevrastenico.

neuritis s. nevrite.

neurologist s. neurologo.

neurology s. neurologia.

neuropathic agg. neuropatico.

neuropathology s. neuropatologia.

neurosis s. (pl. -ses) nevrosi.

neurotic agg. neuropatico.

neuter s. parola neutra, neutro.

neutral agg. neutrale.

neutralism s. neutralismo.

neutralist s. neutralista.

neutrality s. neutralità.

neutralization s. neutralizzazione.

to **neutralize** vt. neutralizzare.

neutron s. neutrone.

never avv. mai, giammai || — again, mai più; — mind, non importa; now or —, ora o mai più; — -ending, eterno.

nevermore avv. mai più.

nevertheless avv. nonostante, ciò nondimeno.

new agg. nuovo, recente || — -born, neonato; — -comer, nuovo venuto; — -made, appena fatto.

newish agg. piuttosto nuovo.

newly avv. recentemente.

news s. notizia, notizie || — -man, strillone (di giornali); — -reel, cinegiornale.

newsmonger s. persona pettegola e curiosa.

newspaper s. giornale, quotidiano.

New Zealander s. neozelandese.

next agg. 1. prossimo, vicino, il più vicino 2. futuro, venturo 3. primo, contiguo. ♦ **next** avv. dopo, in seguito, poi. ♦ **next** prep. presso, accanto.

nib s. pennino.

nibble s. morso.

to **nibble** vt. 1. mordicchiare, sgranocchiare 2. abboccare.

nibbler s. roditore.

nice agg. 1. piacevole, bello, simpatico 2. buono, gustoso 3. accurato, minuzioso.

nicely avv. 1. amabilmente, piacevolmente 2. esattamente.

nicety s. 1. finezza, precisione. ♦ **niceties** s. pl. minuzie.

niche s. nicchia.

nick s. tacca, intaccatura || in the — of time, al momento giusto.

to **nick** vt. 1. intaccare 2. colpire, afferrare al momento opportuno.

nickel s. nichel.

to **nickel** vt. nichelare.

nickname s. soprannome, nomignolo.

to **nickname** vt. soprannominare.

nicotine s. nicotina.

niece s. nipote (femmina) (di zio).

niggard agg. spilorcio.

niggardliness s. spilorceria.

niggardly agg. avaro, spilorcio.

nigger s. (spreg.) negro.

night s. 1. notte, sera 2. buio, oscurità || by —, di notte, good —, buona notte; — -bird, uccello notturno, nottambulo; — -dress, camicia da notte; — -shift, turno di notte.

nightcap s. berretto da notte.

nightfall s. tramonto.

nightingale s. usignolo.

nightly agg. notturno. ♦ **nightly** avv. di notte.

nightmare s. incubo.

nightpiece s. « notturno » (dipinto che rappresenta una scena notturna).

nihilism s. nichilismo.

nihilist s. nichilista.

nimble agg. 1. agile, leggero 2. acuto, sveglio.

nimbleness s. 1. agilità 2. prontezza, acutezza.

nimbly avv. 1. agilmente, leggermente 2. prontamente.

nine agg. nove.

ninepins s. pl. birilli.

nineteen agg. diciannove.

nineteenth *agg.* e *s.* diciannovesimo.

ninetieth *agg.* novantesimo.

ninety *agg.* novanta.

ninth *agg.* nono.

nip *s.* 1. pizzicotto, morso 2. stretta, presa 3. morso (*di freddo, gelo ecc.*).

to nip *vt.* 1. pizzicare, mordere (*anche di freddo ecc.*) 2. stroncare.

nipple *s.* capezzolo.

nitrate *s.* nitrato.

nitric *agg.* nitrico.

nitrite *s.* (*chim.*) nitrito.

nitroglicerin(e) *s.* nitroglicerina.

no *agg.* nessuno. ◆ **no** *avv.* 1. no 2. in nessun modo.

nobiliary *agg.* nobiliare.

nobility *s.* nobiltà (*anche fig.*).

noble *agg.* 1. nobile (*anche fig.*) 2. superbo, grandioso. ◆ **noble** *s.* nobile.

nobleman *s.* nobiluomo.

nobleness *s.* nobiltà (*anche fig.*).

noblewoman *s.* nobildonna.

nobly *avv.* nobilmente.

nobody *pron. indef.* nessuno.

nocturnal *agg.* notturno.

nocturne *s.* (*pitt.; mus.*) notturno.

nod *s.* 1. cenno del capo 2. ordine, comando.

to nod *vt.* e *vi.* 1. annuire col capo 2. assopirsi, chinare il capo dal sonno 3. inclinarsi (*di edifici ecc.*). ◆ **nodding** *agg.* chinato, incliato. ◆ **nodding** *s.* cenno del capo.

nodose *agg.* nodoso.

nodosity *s.* nodosità.

nodular *agg.* a forma di nodo.

nodule *s.* nodulo.

noise *s.* rumore, fragore, chiasso.

noiseless *agg.* senza rumore, silenzioso.

noisily *avv.* rumorosamente.

noisy *agg.* 1. rumoroso, turbolento 2. (*fig.*) vistoso, chiassoso.

nomad *agg.* e *s.* nomade.

nomadism *s.* nomadismo.

nomenclature *s.* nomenclatura.

nominal *agg.* nominale.

nominalism *s.* nominalismo.

nominalist *s.* nominalista.

nominalistic *agg.* nominalistico.

nominative *agg.* e *s.* nominativo.

nominator *s.* nominatore.

nonagenarian *agg.* e *s.* nonagenario.

non-aligned *agg.* non allineato.

non-alignment *s.* non allineamento.

non-appearance *s.* contumacia.

non-attendance *s.* assenza.

non-commital *agg.* evasivo.

non-conducting *agg.* isolante, non conduttore.

non-conductor *s.* isolante.

nonconformist *agg.* e *s.* anticonformista.

nonconformity *s.* anticonformismo.

non-delivery *s.* mancata consegna.

none *pron. sing.* e *pl.* nessuno, non uno. ◆ **none** *avv.* affatto, niente affatto.

nonentity *s.* 1. cosa o persona insignificante 2. inesistenza.

non-existence *s.* inesistenza.

non-resistance *s.* resistenza passiva.

nonsense *s.* assurdità, sciocchezza.

nonsensical *agg.* assurdo, sciocco.

non-stop *agg.* continuo, senza fermate. ◆ **non-stop** *avv.* di continuo, senza fermate.

non-transferable *agg.* non trasferibile.

noodle *agg.* sciocco, gonzo.

nook *s.* 1. cantuccio, angolo 2. ripostiglio.

noon *s.* mezzogiorno.

noose *s.* 1. nodo scorsoio 2. tranello.

nor *cong.* né, neppure ‖ *neither I — he*, né io né lui.

normal *agg.* 1. normale, regolare 2. perpendicolare.

normality *s.* normalità.

normalization *s.* normalizzazione.

to normalize *vt.* normalizzare.

Norman *agg.* e *s.* normanno.

normative *agg.* normativo.

north *s.* nord, settentrione ‖ *— wind*, vento di tramontana.

north-east *s.* nord-est.

northerly *agg.* del nord, settentrionale. ◆ **northerly** *avv.* verso il nord.

northern *agg.* nordico, settentrionale.

northerner *s.* abitante del nord.

northward(s) *agg.* e *avv.* verso nord.

Norwegian *agg.* e *s.* norvegese.

nose *s.* 1. naso 2. muso (*di animali*) 3. prua (*mar.*).

to nose *vt.* e *vi.* 1. fiutare 2. indagare 3. ficcare il naso.

nostril *s.* narice.

not *avv.* non ‖ *— at all*, niente affatto.

notability *s.* notabilità.
notable *agg.* degno di nota, notevole.
notarial *agg.* notarile.
notary *s.* notaio.
notation *s.* 1. (*mus.*) notazione 2. (*mat.*) numerazione.
notch *s.* tacca, dentellatura.
to notch *vt.* 1. intaccare 2. intagliare.
note *s.* 1. (*mus.*) nota, tono 2. marchio, segno 3. nota, appunto, commento 4. (*comm.*) cedola, acconto 5. banconota.
to note *vt.* notare.
notebook *s.* taccuino.
notehead *s.* intestazione.
noteless *agg.* privo di interesse.
noteworthiness *s.* importanza.
noteworthy *agg.* notevole.
nothing *pron. indef.* nulla, niente, nessuna cosa.
nothingness *s.* 1. il nulla 2. nullità.
notice *s.* 1. avviso, avvertimento 2. (*giur.*) intimazione 3. licenziamento 4. attenzione, cura 5. recensione || — *-board,* cartello pubblicitario, tabella.
to notice *vt.* 1. osservare, fare attenzione a 2. recensire.
noticeable *agg.* notevole.
notifiable *agg.* da denunciarsi.
notification *s.* notifica.
to notify *vt.* notificare; far sapere.
notion *s.* 1. nozione 2. idea, teoria.
notional *agg.* 1. immaginario 2. speculativo.
notoriety *s.* notorietà.
notorious *agg.* 1. noto, conosciuto 2. famigerato.
notoriously *avv.* notoriamente.
notwithstanding *prep.* nonostante, malgrado.
nougat *s.* torrone.
nought *s.* 1. nulla 2. (*mat.*) zero.
noumenon *s.* (*pl.* -ena) noumeno.
noun *s.* (*gramm.*) nome, sostantivo.
to nourish *vt.* nutrire (*anche fig.*).
nourishing *agg.* nutriente.
nourishment *s.* nutrimento.
novel *s.* romanzo.
novelist *s.* romanziere.
to novelize *vt.* romanzare.
novelty *s.* novità.
November *s.* novembre.
novice *s.* 1. (*eccl.*) novizio 2. apprendista.
novitiate *s.* noviziato.

now *avv.* 1. ora, adesso, subito, al presente 2. allora 3. a dire il vero. ♦ **now** *cong.* ora che. ♦ **now** *s.* ora, il presente.
nowadays *avv.* al giorno d'oggi.
nowhere *avv.* in nessun luogo.
noxious *agg.* nocivo, dannoso.
nozzle *s.* becco, beccuccio (*di teiera, pompa ecc.*).
nuclear *agg.* nucleare.
nuclein *s.* nucleina.
nucleonics *s. pl.* fisica nucleare.
nucleus *s.* (*pl.* -ei) 1. nucleo 2. nocciolo, centro.
nude *agg.* 1. nudo 2. (*fig.*) semplice. ♦ **nude** *s.* (*pitt.; scult.*) nudo.
nudism *s.* nudismo.
nudist *agg. e s.* nudista.
nugget *s.* pepita.
nuisance *s.* 1. noia, seccatura 2. danno.
null *agg.* nullo.
nullification *s.* annullamento.
to nullify *vt.* annullare.
nullity *s.* 1. nullità 2. il non essere valido.
numb *agg.* 1. intorpidito, intirizzito 2. tramortito, intontito.
to numb *vt.* 1. intorpidire, intirizzire 2. (*fig.*) istupidire.
number *s.* 1. numero, cifra 2. numero, quantità 3. numero di giornale.
to number *vt.* 1. contare, numerare 2. annoverare 3. ammontare.
numberless *agg.* innumerevole.
numbness *s.* torpore (*anche fig.*).
numerable *agg.* numerabile, calcolabile.
numeral *agg. e s.* numerale.
numerator *s.* numeratore.
numerical *agg.* numerico.
numerically *avv.* numericamente.
numerous *agg.* numeroso.
numismatic *agg.* numismatico.
numismatics *s.* numismatica.
numismatist *s.* numismatico.
numismatology *s.* numismatica.
nun *s.* 1. monaca, suora 2. piccione dal cappuccio.
nuncio *s.* (*eccl.*) nunzio.
nunnery *s.* convento (*di suore*).
nuptial *agg.* nuziale.
nuptials *s. pl.* nozze, sponsali.
nurse *s.* 1. nutrice, balia 2. infermiera.
to nurse *vt.* 1. allattare, nutrire 2. allevare 3. curare (*ammalati*).
nursling *s.* lattante.

nursery s. **1.** camera dei bambini **2.** scuola materna **3.** vivaio || — *rhyme,* filastrocca per bambini.

nursing agg. **1.** che allatta, nutre **2.** che cura || — *home,* casa di cura. ♦ **nursing** s. **1.** allattamento **2.** il curare **3.** professione di infermiera.

nurture s. vitto, nutrimento.

to **nurture** vt. nutrire, allevare.

nut s. **1.** noce **2.** (*mecc.*) dado.

nutcracker s. schiaccianoci.

nutmeg s. noce moscata.

nutrition s. nutrizione.

nutritive agg. nutritivo.

nutshell s. guscio di noce.

nylon s. nailon.

nymph s. ninfa.

O

oak s. quercia.

oakum s. stoppa.

oar s. remo || — *-blade,* pala di remo.

to **oar** vi. remare.

oarsman s. rematore.

oasis s. (*pl.* -ses) oasi.

oats s. *pl.* avena (*sing.*).

oath s. **1.** giuramento **2.** bestemmia.

obduracy s. **1.** inesorabilità **2.** ostinazione.

obdurate agg. **1.** inesorabile **2.** ostinato.

obedience s. ubbidienza.

obedient agg. ubbidiente.

obeisance s. riverenza.

obelisk s. obelisco.

obese agg. obeso.

obesity s. obesità.

to **obey** vt. e vi. ubbidire.

to **obfuscate** vt. **1.** offuscare **2.** confondere.

obituary s. necrologio.

object s. oggetto.

to **object** vt. e vi. obiettare.

objectification s. oggettivazione.

to **objectify** vt. oggettivare.

objection s. **1.** obiezione **2.** avversione.

objectionable agg. **1.** biasimevole **2.** sgradevole.

objective agg. oggettivo. ♦ **objective** s. obiettivo.

objectiveness s. oggettività.

objectivism s. oggettivismo.

objectivity s. oggettività.

objector s. oppositore || *conscientious* —, obiettore di coscienza.

obligation s. obbligo.

obligatoriness s. obbligatorietà.

obligatory agg. obbligatorio.

to **oblige** vt. **1.** obbligare **2.** fare un favore a.

obliging agg. cortese.

oblique agg. obliquo.

obliqueness, obliquity s. obliquità.

to **obliterate** vt. cancellare.

obliteration s. cancellatura.

oblivion s. oblio || *Act of* —, amnistia.

oblivious agg. dimentico.

oblong agg. **1.** oblungo **2.** rettangolare. ♦ **oblong** s. (*geom.*) rettangolo.

obnoxious agg. odioso.

obscene agg. osceno.

obscenity s. oscenità.

obscurantism s. oscurantismo.

obscurantist agg. e s. oscurantista.

obscuration s. oscuramento.

obscure agg. oscuro. ♦ **obscure** s. oscurità.

to **obscure** vt. oscurare.

obscurity s. oscurità.

obsecration s. supplica.

obsequies s. *pl.* esequie.

obsequious agg. ossequioso.

observable agg. **1.** visibile **2.** notevole.

observance s. **1.** osservanza **2.** (*relig.*) regola.

observant agg. osservante.

observation s. osservazione.

observatory s. osservatorio.

to **observe** vt. e vi. osservare.

observer s. osservatore.

observing agg. attento.

to **obsess** vt. ossessionare.

obsession s. ossessione.

obsessive agg. ossessivo.

obsolescence s. disuso.

obsolescent agg. che sta cadendo in disuso.

obsolete agg. **1.** antiquato **2.** scaduto (*di prezzi*).

obstacle s. ostacolo.

obstetric(al) agg. ostetrico.

obstetrician s. ostetrico.

obstetrics s. ostetricia.

obstinacy s. ostinazione.

obstinate agg. ostinato.

to **obstruct** vt. **1.** ostruire **2.** ri-

tardare **3.** intasare.
obstruction s. ostruzione, ostacolo.
obstructionism s. ostruzionismo.
obstructionist s. ostruzionista.
to **obtain** vt. ottenere. ♦ to **obtain** vi. prevalere.
obtainable agg. ottenibile.
to **obtrude** vt. imporre. ♦ to **obtrude** vi. **1.** imporsi **2.** intromettersi.
obtruder s. **1.** intruso **2.** importuno.
obtrusion s. intrusione.
obtrusive agg. **1.** intruso **2.** importuno.
obtrusiveness s. **1.** intrusione **2.** invadenza.
to **obtund** vt. ottundere.
obtundent agg. ottundente.
to **obturate** vt. otturare.
obturation s. otturazione.
obturator s. otturatore.
obtuse agg. **1.** ottuso **2.** sordo.
obtuseness s. ottusità.
to **obviate** vt. ovviare.
obvious agg. ovvio.
obviousness s. chiarezza.
occasion s. **1.** occasione **2.** motivo.
occasional agg. occasionale.
occident s. occidente.
occidental agg. occidentale.
occidentalism s. occidentalismo.
to **occidentalize** vt. occidentalizzare.
occidentally avv. all'occidentale.
occipital agg. occipitale.
occiput s. (pl. -pita) occipite.
to **occlude** vt. occludere.
occlusion s. occlusione.
occlusive agg. occlusivo.
occult agg. occulto.
to **occult** vt. occultare. ♦ to **occult** vi. occultarsi.
occultation s. occultamento.
occultism s. occultismo.
occultist s. occultista.
occupant s. occupante.
occupation s. occupazione.
occupational agg. professionale.
occupier s. occupante.
to **occupy** vt. occupare: to — oneself with, occuparsi di.
to **occur** vi. **1.** accadere **2.** venire in mente **3.** ricorrere.
occurrence s. avvenimento.
ocean s. oceano.
oceanic agg. oceanico.
oceanography s. oceanografia.
ocellus s. (pl. -li) ocello.

ochre s. ocra.
octagon s. ottagono.
octagonal agg. ottagonale.
octahedron s. ottaedro.
octane s. ottano.
octave s. ottava.
October s. ottobre.
octogenarian agg. e s. ottuagenario.
octonarian agg. e s. ottonario.
octonary agg. di otto in otto. ♦ **octonary** s. strofa di otto versi.
octopus s. (pl. -pi) polipo, piovra.
octosyllabic agg. ottosillabico.
octosyllable s. verso, parola di otto sillabe.
ocular agg. e s. oculare.
oculate(d) agg. maculato.
oculist s. oculista.
oculistic agg. oculistico.
odalisque s. odalisca.
odd agg. **1.** dispari **2.** scompagnato **3.** in più **4.** occasionale **5.** bizzarro. ♦ **odd** s. cosa extra.
oddity, oddness s. stranezza.
odds s. pl. **1.** differenza **2.** disaccordo **3.** pronostico || — and ends, rimanenze.
ode s. ode.
odious agg. odioso.
odontological agg. odontoiatrico.
odontologist s. odontoiatra.
odontology s. odontoiatria.
odoriferous agg. odorifero.
odorous agg. odoroso.
odour s. odore.
odourless agg. inodore.
oedema s. edema.
oenologist s. enologo.
oenology s. enologia.
oesophagus s. (pl. -gi) esofago.
of prep. **1.** di **2.** (tempo) a, in **3.** da parte di: very kind — you, molto gentile da parte vostra || — late, ultimamente.
off avv. **1.** lontano, via **2.** completamente | to be —, essere finito, fermo, in libertà. ♦ **off** prep. **1.** lontano, via da **2.** giù da. ♦ **off** agg. **1.** destro **2.** esterno **3.** lontano **4.** secondario **5.** libero || — day, giorno di libertà.
offence s. **1.** offesa **2.** colpa, delitto **3.** scandalo.
offenceless agg. **1.** inoffensivo **2.** innocente.
to **offend** vt. offendere. ♦ to **offend** vi. **1.** peccare **2.** violare la legge.
offender s. **1.** peccatore **2.** colpevole.

offensive *agg.* **1.** offensivo **2.** sgradevole. ♦ **offensive** *s.* offensiva.

offensiveness *s.* aggressività.

offer *s.* offerta.

to offer *vt.* offrire. ♦ **to offer** *vi.* offrirsi.

offerer *s.* offerente.

offering *s.* offerta.

offertory *s.* offertorio.

offhand *agg.* **1.** improvvisato **2.** spontaneo. ♦ **offhand** *avv.* lì per lì.

office *s.* ufficio, carica || *box-* —, botteghino.

officer *s.* ufficiale, funzionario || *non-commissioned* —, sottufficiale.

official *agg.* ufficiale. ♦ **official** *s.* funzionario.

officiant *s.* ufficiante.

to officiate *vi.* **1.** esercitare le funzioni di **2.** (*relig.*) ufficiare.

officious *agg.* **1.** ufficioso **2.** intrigante.

offing *s.* (*mar.*) largo.

offscourings *s. pl.* rifiuti, scarti.

offset *s.* **1.** compenso **2.** sperone (*di monte*) **3.** germoglio, progenie **4.** (*tip.*) fotolito.

offshoot *s.* **1.** germoglio **2.** ramo.

offshore *agg.* **1.** di terra **2.** lontano dalla costa. ♦ **offshore** *avv.* al largo.

offside *s.* (*sport*) fuori gioco.

offspring *s.* **1.** prole **2.** frutto.

often *avv.* spesso || *how* —?, quante volte?

ogive *s.* ogiva.

oil *s.* **1.** olio **2.** petrolio || — *cloth,* tela cerata; — *field,* giacimento petrolifero; — *-mill,* frantoio; — *paper,* carta oleata; — *pipeline,* oleodotto.

to oil *vt.* ungere, oliare.

oiler *s.* oliatore.

oily *agg.* oleoso, untuoso.

ointment *s.* unguento.

O.K. *avv.* bene: *to be* —, andar bene.

old (**elder, older; eldest, oldest**) *agg.* vecchio || *how* — *are you?,* quanti anni hai?; — *-fashioned,* antiquato. ♦ **old** *s.* passato.

oldish *agg.* attempato.

oleander *s.* oleandro.

oleograph *s.* oleografia.

oleographic *agg.* oleografico.

olfactory *agg.* olfattivo.

oligarch *s.* oligarchia.

oligarchic(al) *agg.* oligarchico.

oligarchy *s.* oligarchia.

olive *agg.* **1.** d'oliva **2.** olivastro. ♦ **olive** *s.* **1.** oliva **2.** (*-tree*) olivo.

Olympiad *s.* olimpiade.

Olympian *agg.* olimpico, olimpionico. ♦ **Olympian** *s.* olimpionico.

Olympic *agg.* V. *Olympian.*

omelet(te) *s.* frittata.

omen *s.* auspicio.

ominous *agg.* di cattivo augurio.

omission *s.* omissione.

to omit *vt.* omettere.

omnipotence *s.* onnipotenza.

omnipotent *agg.* e *s.* onnipotente.

omnipresent *agg.* onnipresente.

omniscience *s.* onniscienza.

omniscient *agg.* e *s.* onnisciente.

omnivorous *agg.* onnivoro.

on *prep.* **1.** su **2.** a, in, di, per || *on purpose,* apposta. ♦ **on** *avv.* **1.** su, indosso **2.** (in) avanti || *to be* —, essere in funzione, essere rappresentato; *and so* —, eccetera.

once *avv.* una volta || *at* —, subito; *all at* —, improvvisamente. ♦ **once** *cong.* una volta che.

on-coming *agg.* prossimo.

one *agg.* **1.** uno **2.** uno solo. ♦ **one** *pron.* **1.** (*dimostr.*) questo, quello **2.** (*indef.*) (l') uno || — *by* —, uno a uno. ♦ **one** *s.* uno || — *John Brown,* un certo John Brown.

one-eyed *agg.* guercio.

oneness *s.* unità, unicità.

onerous *agg.* oneroso.

oneself *pron. r.* se stesso.

one-sided *agg.* unilaterale.

one-sidely *avv.* unilateralmente.

oneway *agg.* a senso unico.

ongoings *s. pl.* avvenimenti.

onion *s.* cipolla || *spring-* —, cipollina.

onlooker *s.* spettatore.

only *agg.* e *avv.* solo.

onomastic *agg.* onomastico.

onomatopoeia *s.* onomatopeia.

onomatopoeic *agg.* onomatopeico.

onset *s.* **1.** attacco **2.** inizio.

onto *prep.* su, in cima a.

ontological *agg.* ontologico.

ontology *s.* ontologia.

onus *s.* onere.

onward *agg.* avanzato.

onward(s) *avv.* avanti.

onyx *s.* onice.

to ooze *vt.* e *vi.* stillare || *to* — *out,* trapelare.

oozy *agg.* melmoso.

opacity *s.* opacità.

opal s. opale.
opalescent agg. opalescente.
opaque agg. opaco.
open agg. aperto || wide —, spalancato; in the — air, all'aperto.
to **open** vt. aprire. ♦ to **open** vi. aprirsi.
open-handed agg. generoso.
opening s. 1. apertura 2. radura.
openly avv. apertamente.
open-minded agg. di larghe vedute.
open-mindedness s. larghezza di vedute.
openness s. 1. apertura 2. franchezza.
opera s. opera lirica || — -house, teatro dell'opera; — glass, binocolo.
to **operate** vt. 1. operare 2. far funzionare 3. gestire. ♦ to **operate** vi. 1. operare 2. funzionare.
operatic agg. di opera.
operation s. 1. operazione 2. funzionamento 3. azione.
operative agg. 1. attivo 2. operatono, operaio (meccanico). sentenza. ♦ **operative** s. artigianista, telegrafista.
operator s. 1. operatore 2. teleforio || — part, dispositivo di una
ophthalmia s. oftalmia.
ophthalmic agg. oftalmico.
ophthalmology s. oftalmologia, oculistica.
ophthalmoscopy s. oftalmoscopia.
opiate agg. 1. oppiato 2. soporifero. ♦ **opiate** s. narcotico.
opinion s. opinione.
opinionated, opinionative agg. ostinato.
opium s. oppio.
opponent s. avversario.
opportune agg. opportuno.
opportunism s. opportunismo.
opportunist s. opportunista.
opportunist(ic) agg. opportunistico.
opportunity s. occasione.
opposable agg. opponibile.
to **oppose** vt. opporre. ♦ to **oppose** vi. opporsi.
opposed agg. 1. opposto 2. ostile.
opposer s. oppositore.
opposite agg. e s. opposto. ♦ **opposite** avv. di fronte. ♦ **opposite** prep. di fronte a, dirimpetto a.
opposition s. opposizione.

to **oppress** vt. opprimere.
oppression s. oppressione.
oppressive agg. opprimente.
oppressor s. oppressore.
opprobrious agg. obbrobrioso.
to **opt** vi. optare.
optic(al) agg. ottico.
optician s. ottico.
optics s. ottica.
optimism s. ottimismo.
optimist agg. e s. ottimista.
optimistic(al) agg. ottimistico.
option s. opzione.
optional agg. facoltativo.
opulence s. opulenza.
opulent agg. opulento.
or cong. o, oppure || either... —, sia... sia.
oracle s. oracolo.
oracular agg. profetico.
oral agg. e s. orale.
orange s. 1. arancia 2. arancio.
orangeade s. aranciata.
orangery s. aranceto.
oration s. discorso.
orator s. oratore.
oratorical agg. oratorio.
oratory[1] s. oratorio.
oratory[2] agg. s. oratoria.
orb s. 1. cerchio 2. sfera.
orbit s. orbita.
orbital agg. orbitale.
orchard s. frutteto.
orchestra s. orchestra.
orchestral agg. orchestrale.
to **orchestrate** vt. orchestrare.
orchestration s. orchestrazione.
orchid, orchis s. orchidea.
to **ordain** vt. ordinare (anche eccl.).
ordeal s. 1. ordalia 2. dura prova.
order s. 1. ordine 2. classe || in — that, affinché; in — to, allo scopo di; postal —, vaglia postale; made to —, eseguito su ordinazione. ♦ **orders** s. pl. (relig.) ordini: to take —, farsi prete.
to **order** vt. 1. ordinare 2. riordinare.
ordering s. ordinamento.
orderly agg. ordinato. ♦ **orderly** s. 1. (mil.) ordinanza 2. (mil.) attendente.
ordinal agg. e s. ordinale.
ordinance s. 1. ordinanza 2. (relig.) rito.
ordinary agg. ordinario. ♦ **ordinary** s. 1. condizione ordinaria 2. pranzo a prezzo fisso.
ordinate s. ordinata.

ordination s. **1.** ordine **2.** (*relig.*) ordinazione.

ore s. minerale.

organ s. organo || *barrel-* —, organetto; *mouth-* —, armonica.

organic *agg.* organico.

organism s. organismo.

organist s. organista.

organizable *agg.* organizzabile.

organization s. organizzazione.

to organize *vt.* organizzare. ♦ **to organize** *vi.* organizzarsi.

organizer s. organizzatore.

organzine s. organzino.

orgasm s. orgasmo.

orgeat s. orzata.

orgiastic *agg.* orgiastico.

orgy s. orgia.

orient s. oriente.

to orient *vt.* **1.** orientare **2.** volgere verso oriente.

oriental *agg.* e s. orientale.

orientalist s. orientalista.

orientation s. orientamento.

orifice s. orifizio.

origan s. origano.

origin s. origine.

original *agg.* e s. originale.

originality s. originalità.

originally *avv.* **1.** originalmente **2.** originariamente.

to originate *vt.* dare origine. ♦ **to originate** *vi.* aver origine.

originator s. iniziatore.

ornament s. ornamento.

ornamental *agg.* ornamentale.

ornamentation s. decorazione.

ornate *agg.* ornato.

ornithological *agg.* ornitologico.

ornithologist s. ornitologo.

ornithology s. ornitologia.

orographic(al) *agg.* orografico.

orography s. orografia.

orphan *agg.* e s. orfano.

orphanage s. **1.** la condizione di orfano **2.** orfanotrofio.

orthodox *agg.* ortodosso.

orthodoxy s. ortodossia.

orthogonal *agg.* ortogonale.

orthographic(al) *agg.* **1.** ortografico **2.** ortogonale.

orthography s. **1.** ortografia **2.** (*geom.*) proiezione ortogonale.

orthop(a)edic(al) *agg.* ortopedico.

orthop(a)edics s. ortopedia.

orthop(a)edist s. ortopedico.

to oscillate *vi.* oscillare.

oscillation s. oscillazione.

oscillator s. oscillatore.

oscillatory *agg.* oscillatorio.

oscillograph s. oscillografo.

osier s. vimine.

osmose, osmosis s. osmosi.

osseous *agg.* osseo.

ossification s. ossificazione.

to ossify *vt.* ossificare. ♦ **to ossify** *vi.* ossificarsi.

ostensible *agg.* apparente.

ostensory s. ostensorio.

ostentation s. ostentazione.

ostentatious *agg.* ostentato.

osteological *agg.* osteologico.

osteology s. osteologia.

ostracism s. ostracismo.

to ostracize *vt.* dare l'ostracismo a.

ostrich s. struzzo.

other *agg.* e *pron.* altro || *each* —, l'un l'altro; *every* — *day*, un giorno sì e un giorno no. ♦ **others** *pron. pl.* altri || *some... —...*, gli uni... gli altri.

otherwise *agg.* diverso. ♦ **otherwise** *avv.* altrimenti.

otherworld s. mondo ultraterreno.

otitis s. otite.

otorhinolaryngologist s. otorinolaringoiatra.

otter s. lontra.

Ottoman *agg.* e s. ottomano.

ought s. zero.

ought *v. dif.* (*condiz.*) dovere: *you — to wait*, dovresti aspettare.

ounce s. oncia.

our *agg. poss.* nostro, nostra, nostri, nostre.

ours *pron. poss.* il nostro, la nostra, i nostri, le nostre.

ourselves *pron. r. pl.* noi stessi.

out *agg.* esterno. ♦ **out** *avv.* fuori. ♦ **out** (*of*) *prep.* **1.** fuori (*di*) **2.** senza **3.** per || — *-of-date*, fuori moda; — *-of-work*, disoccupato; — *-of-the-way*, remoto.

to outbid (outbade, outbidden) *vt.* offrire di più.

outboard *agg.* e *avv.* fuoribordo.

outbreak s. **1.** scoppio **2.** sommossa.

outburst s. scoppio.

outcast s. proscritto.

to outclass *vt.* surclassare.

outcome s. risultato.

outcry s. grido, scalpore.

outdid V. *to outdo*.

to outdistance *vt.* distanziare.

to outdo (outdid, outdone) *vt.* superare.

outdoor *agg.* all'aperto.

outdoors *avv.* all'aperto.

outer agg. esteriore.

outfit(ting) s. equipaggiamento.

to **outfit** vt. rifornire di equipaggiamento. ♦ to **outfit** vi. rifornirsi di equipaggiamento.

outfitter s. fornitore.

to **outfly (outflew, outflown)** vt. sorpassare nel volo.

outgone V. to outgo.

outgo s. uscita.

to **outgo (outwent, outgone)** vt. sorpassare.

outgoing agg. uscente, in partenza.

to **outgrow (outgrew, outgrown)** vt. **1.** diventare troppo grande per **2.** sorpassare (in statura).

outgrowth s. **1.** escrescenza **2.** risultato.

outhouse s. **1.** tettoia **2.** dipendenza.

outing s. escursione || — clothes, abiti sportivi.

outlandish agg. **1.** strano **2.** remoto.

outlaw s. fuorilegge.

outlawry s. (giur.) proscrizione.

outlay s. spesa.

outlet s. **1.** sbocco **2.** cortile.

outline s. **1.** contorno **2.** schema **3.** lineamento.

to **outline** vt. **1.** delineare **2.** abbozzare.

outliner s. bozzettista.

to **outlive** vt. sopravvivere a.

outlook s. **1.** veduta **2.** prospettiva **3.** vigilanza.

to **outnumber** vt. superare numericamente.

outpost s. avamposto.

outpour s. **1.** scroscio di pioggia **2.** (fig.) sfogo.

output s. produzione, rendimento.

outrage s. oltraggio.

to **outrage** vt. oltraggiare.

outrageous agg. **1.** oltraggioso **2.** violento.

outrageousness s. **1.** oltraggio **2.** violenza.

outran V. to outrun.

to **outrange** vt. avere una portata maggiore di.

to **outreach** vt. sorpassare.

outrider s. battistrada.

outright agg. **1.** franco **2.** completo. ♦ **outright** avv. **1.** francamente **2.** completamente.

outrightness s. **1.** immediatezza **2.** franchezza.

outroar s. fracasso.

to **outrun (outran, outrun)** vt. oltrepassare.

outrush s. fuga.

to **outsell (outsold, outsold)** vt. **1.** vendere in quantità superiore **2.** vendere a prezzo superiore.

outset s. esordio.

to **outshine (outshone, outshone)** vt. eclissare (anche fig.).

outside agg. e s. **1.** esterno **2.** massimo. ♦ **outside** avv. **1.** all'esterno **2.** all'aperto. ♦ **outside** prep. fuori di.

outsider s. **1.** profano **2.** estraneo **3.** (sport) non favorito.

outsize agg. fuori misura. ♦ **outsize** s. taglia fuori misura.

outskirt s. orlo. ♦ **outskirts** s. pl. periferia (sing.).

outsold V. to outsell.

outspoken agg. franco.

to **outspread (outspread, outspread)** vt. spiegare. ♦ to **outspread (outspread, outspread)** vi. spiegarsi.

outstanding agg. **1.** prominente **2.** resistente **3.** in sospeso.

to **outstretch** vt. distendere.

to **outstrip** vt. superare (in velocità).

outward agg. e s. esterno. ♦ **outward(s)** avv. esternamente.

outwent V. to outgo.

oval agg. e s. ovale.

ovary s. ovaia.

ovation s. ovazione.

oven s. forno.

over avv. **1.** di sopra **2.** eccessivamente || to be —, essere finito; — and — again, più e più volte. ♦ **over** prep. **1.** su **2.** più di **3.** durante || — there, dall'altra parte; — and above, oltre a.

overalls s. pl. tuta da lavoro (sing.).

overate V. to overeat.

to **overbear (overbore, overborne)** vt. dominare, sopraffare.

overbearing agg. imperioso.

overbearingness s. imperiosità.

overboard avv. in mare.

overbore V. to overbear.

overborne V. to overbear.

to **overburden** vt. sovraccaricare.

overcame V. to overcome.

overcast agg. scuro, nuvoloso.

to **overcast (overcast, overcast)** vt. oscurare. ♦ to **overcast (overcast, overcast)** vi. oscurarsi.

overcharge s. **1.** sovraccarico **2.** sovrapprezzo.

to **overcharge** vt. **1.** sovraccaricare **2.** far pagare troppo caro.

to **overcloud** vi. rannuvolarsi.

overcoat s. soprabito.

to **overcome** (**overcame, overcome**) vt. superare, vincere.

overcoming s. superamento, vittoria.

overconfident agg. troppo sicuro di sé.

overcredulity s. credulità eccessiva.

overcrowded agg. sovraffollato.

overcrowding s. sovraffollamento.

to **overdo** (**overdid, overdone**) vt. **1.** esagerare **2.** stancare.

overdone agg. troppo cotto.

overdose s. dose eccessiva.

overdrank V. to overdrink.

to **overdraw** (**overdrew, overdrawn**) vt. **1.** esagerare **2.** scoprire il conto in banca.

to **overdrink** (**overdrank, overdrunk**) vi. bere troppo.

overdue agg. scaduto.

to **overeat** (**overate, overeaten**) vi. mangiare troppo.

to **overestimate** vt. sopravvalutare.

overexcitability s. sovreccitabilità.

overexcitable agg. sovreccitabile.

to **overexcite** vt. sovreccitare.

overexcitement s. sovreccitazione.

to **overexert** vt. stancare.

to **overexpose** vt. sovresporre.

overfeeding s. superalimentazione.

overflew V. to overfly.

to **overflow** vt. inondare. ♦ to **overflow** vi. traboccare.

overflowing s. inondazione.

to **overfly** (**overflew, overflown**) vt. **1.** sorvolare **2.** superare in volo.

overfond agg. troppo appassionato.

to **overgrow** (**overgrew, overgrown**) vt. **1.** coprire **2.** superare. ♦ to **overgrow** (**overgrew, overgrown**) vi. **1.** coprirsi **2.** crescere troppo.

overgrowth s. **1.** crescita eccessiva **2.** vegetazione sovrabbondante.

overhang s. sporgenza, aggetto.

to **overhang** (**overhung, overhung**) vt. **1.** sovrastare **2.** ornare con tendaggi ecc.

to **overhaul** vt. **1.** revisionare **2.** sorpassare.

overhaul(ing) s. revisione.

overhead agg. **1.** alto **2.** (comm.) generale. ♦ **overhead** avv. in alto.

to **overhear** (**overheard, overheard**) vt. **1.** udire per caso **2.** origliare.

to **overheat** vt. surriscaldare. ♦ to **overheat** vi. surriscaldarsi.

overheating s. surriscaldamento.

overhung V. to overhang.

overindulgence s. eccessiva indulgenza.

overladen agg. sovraccarico.

overland avv. via terra.

overlap s. sovrapposizione.

overlay s. copertura.

to **overleap** vt. saltare di là da.

overload s. sovraccarico.

to **overload** vt. sovraccaricare.

to **overlook** vt. **1.** guardare dall'alto **2.** trascurare **3.** ispezionare.

overlooker s. ispettore.

overnight agg. **1.** compiuto durante la notte **2.** per una notte. ♦ **overnight** avv. durante la notte.

overpaid V. to overpay.

to **overpass** vt. **1.** attraversare **2.** sorpassare **3.** trasgredire.

overpast agg. passato.

to **overpay** (**overpaid, overpaid**) vt. pagare più del dovuto.

overpayment s. pagamento eccessivo.

overpeopled agg. sovrappopolato.

overplus s. sovrappiù.

overpopulated agg. sovrappopolato.

overpopulation s. sovrappopolazione.

to **overpower** V. to overbear.

overpowering agg. **1.** schiacciante **2.** prepotente.

overpressure s. sovrapressione.

to **overprint** vt. sovrastampare.

to **overprize** vt. sopravvalutare.

to **overproduce** vt. produrre in eccesso.

overproduction s. sovraproduzione.

overproud agg. troppo orgoglioso.

overran V. to overrun.

to **overrate** vt. sopravvalutare.

to **overreach** vt. **1.** oltrepassare **2.** imbrogliare.

to **overrule** vt. **1.** dirigere **2.** annullare **3.** dominare.

to **overrun** (**overran, overrun**) vt. **1.** invadere **2.** devastare **3.** oltrepassare.

oversaw V. *to oversee.*

oversea(s) *agg.* e *avv.* d'oltremare.

to **oversee** (**oversaw, overseen**) *vt.* ispezionare.

overseer *s.* **1.** ispettore **2.** capo squadra.

to **overset** (**overset, overset**) *vt.* rovesciare. ♦ to **overset** (**overset, overset**) *vi.* rovesciarsi.

to **overshadow** *vt.* **1.** ombreggiare **2.** adombrare **3.** proteggere.

overshoe *s.* soprascarpa.

to **overshoot** (**overshot, overshot**) *vt.* lanciare di là da || *to — the mark,* passare i limiti.

overside *avv.* lungo il fianco.

oversight *s.* **1.** svista **2.** sorveglianza.

to **oversleep** (**overslept, overslept**) *vi.* dormire oltre l'ora fissata.

to **overspread** (**overspread, overre.** ♦ to **overspread** (**overspread, overspread**) *vi.* spargersi.

to **overstate** *vt.* esagerare.

to **overtake** (**overtook, overtaken**) *vt.* **1.** cogliere **2.** superare.

overtaking *s.* sorpasso: *no —,* divieto di sorpasso.

overthrew V. *to overthrow.*

overthrow *s.* **1.** rovesciamento **2.** disfatta.

to **overthrow** (**overthrew, overthrown**) *vt.* **1.** rovesciare **2.** sconfiggere.

overtime *s.* straordinario (*orario di lavoro*).

overtook V. *to overtake.*

to **overturn** V. *to overthrow.*

overturnable *agg.* rovesciabile.

overturn(ing) *s.* rovesciamento.

overweary *agg.* stremato.

overweight *agg.* che supera il peso. ♦ **overweight** *s.* sovraccarico.

to **overwhelm** *vt.* **1.** sommergere **2.** sopraffare.

overwhelming *agg.* schiacciante.

overwork *s.* **1.** lavoro eccessivo **2.** straordinario.

to **overwork** *vt.* **1.** far lavorare troppo **2.** far eccessivo uso di. ♦ to **overwork** *vi.* lavorare troppo.

to **overwrite** (**overwrote, overwritten**) *vi.* scrivere troppo.

overwrought *agg.* **1.** esausto **2.** ricercato (*di stile*).

ovine *agg.* ovino.

oviparous *agg.* oviparo.

ovulation *s.* ovulazione.

ovule *s.* ovulo.

to **owe** *vt.* dovere, essere debitore di || *you must pay what is owing,* dovete pagare il vostro debito.

owing *agg.* dovuto.

owing to *prep.* a causa di.

owl *s.* gufo.

own *agg.* e *pron.* proprio.

to **own** *vt.* **1.** possedere **2.** ammettere || *to — to,* confessare.

owner *s.* proprietario || *shipowner,* armatore.

ownership *s.* proprietà.

ox (*pl.* oxen) *s.* bue.

oxidation *s.* ossidazione.

oxide *s.* ossido.

oxidizable *agg.* ossidabile.

to **oxidize** *vt.* ossidare. ♦ to **oxidize** *vi.* ossidarsi ||

oxygen *s.* ossigeno || *— tent,* tenda ad ossigeno.

to **oxygenate** *vt.* ossigenare.

oxygenation *s.* ossigenazione.

to **oxygenize** *vt.* ossigenare.

oxyhydrogen *agg.* ossidrico: *— blowpipe,* cannello ossidrico.

oyster *s.* **1.** ostrica **2.** persona silenziosa, riservata.

ozone *s.* ozono.

to **ozonize** *vt.* ozonizzare.

P

pace *s.* passo.

to **pace** *vi.* andare al passo. ♦ to **pace** *vt.* percorrere. ♦ to **pace** *vi.* andare al passo, marciare.

paced *agg.* misurato (*a passi*) || *slow- —,* a passi lenti.

pachyderm *s.* pachiderma.

pacific *agg.* pacifico.

to **pacificate** *vt.* pacificare.

pacification *s.* pacificazione.

pacificator, pacifier *s.* pacificatore.

pacificatory *agg.* conciliante.

pacifism *s.* pacifismo.

pacifist *agg.* e *s.* pacifista.

to **pacify** *vt.* pacificare.

pack *s.* **1.** pacco, balla, fagotto **2.** carico **3.** imballaggio **4.** muta (*di cani*) **5.** (*med.*) impacco || *— -ice,* banchisa; *— -saddle,* basto.

to **pack** *vt.* **1.** impacchettare **2.** im-

ballare 3. raggruppare. ♦ to **pack**
vi. raggrupparsi ‖ *to — up*, fare
i bagagli.
package *s.* 1. imballaggio 2. pacco.
to **package** *vt.* 1. imballare 2. impacchettare.
packer *s.* 1. imballatore 2. impacchettatrice (*macchina*).
packet *s.* 1. pacchetto 2. (*mar.*) —
(*-boat*), postale.
packing *s.* 1. imballaggio 2. (*mecc.*)
guarnizione 3. (*mar.*) baderna ‖
— -free, franco d'imballaggio.
pact *s.* patto.
pad[1] *s.* 1. imbottitura 2. zampa (*di cane, lupo, volpe*) 3. (*med.*) tampone.
pad[2] *s.* rumore sordo.
to **pad** *vt.* imbottire.
paddle *s.* 1. pala 2. pagaia.
to **paddle** *vi.* remare con pagaie.
paddy *s.* risaia.
padlock *s.* lucchetto.
to **padlock** *vt.* chiudere con lucchetto.
paediatric *agg.* pediatrico.
paediatrician *s.* pediatra.
paediatrics *s.* pediatria.
paediatrist *s.* pediatra.
pagan *agg. e s.* pagano.
paganism *s.* paganesimo.
page[1] *s.* paggio.
page[2] *s.* pagina.
to **page** *vt.* 1. (*tip.*) impaginare 2.
numerare le pagine.
pageant *s.* 1. (*teat.*) scena (*di sacra rappresentazione*) 2. parata, corteo.
pageantry *s.* 1. pompa, fasto 2.
ostentazione.
to **paginate** *vt.* V. *to page*.
pagination *s.* 1. paginatura 2. impaginazione.
paid V. *to pay*.
pail *s.* secchio.
paillasse *s.* pagliericcio.
pain *s.* 1. pena 2. dolore, sofferenza.
♦ **pains** *s. pl.* doglie.
to **pain** *vt.* far male, far soffrire.
painful *agg.* penoso.
painless *agg.* indolore.
painstaking *agg.* diligente. ♦
painstaking *s.* cura.
paint *s.* 1. pittura 2. belletto.
to **paint** *vt.* dipingere. ♦ to **paint**
vi. imbellettarsi.
painter *s.* 1. pittore 2. imbianchino.
painting *s.* 1. pittura 2. dipinto, quadro.

paintress *s.* pittrice.
pair *s.* paio, coppia.
to **pair** *vt.* accoppiare. ♦ to **pair**
vi. accoppiarsi.
palace *s.* palazzo.
paladin *s.* paladino.
palatable *agg.* 1. gustoso 2. (*fig.*)
gradevole.
palatal *agg. e s.* palatale.
palatalization *s.* palatalizzazione.
palate *s.* palato.
pale[1] *agg.* pallido.
pale[2] *s.* 1. palo 2. palizzata.
to **pale** *vt.* far impallidire. ♦ to
pale *vi.* impallidire.
paleness *s.* pallore.
paleochristian *agg.* paleocristiano.
paleographer *s.* paleografo.
paleography *s.* paleografia.
paleolithic *agg.* paleolitico.
paleologist *s.* paleologo.
paleology *s.* paleologia.
paleontologic(al) *agg.* paleontologico.
paleontologist *s.* paleontologo.
paleontology *s.* paleontologia.
paleozoic *agg.* paleozoico.
palette *s.* tavolozza.
palfrey *s.* palafreno.
palinode *s.* palinodia.
palisade *s.* palizzata.
pall *s.* 1. drappo funebre 2. (*eccl.*)
pallio.
to **pall**[1] *vt.* coprire con un drappo.
to **pall**[2] *vt.* saziare. ♦ to **pall** *vi.*
saziarsi.
pallet[1] *s.* pagliericcio.
pallet[2] *s.* 1. paletta 2. tavolozza.
to **palliate** *vt.* 1. attenuare 2. scusare.
palliation *s.* 1. attenuazione 2. scusante.
palliative *agg. e s.* palliativo.
pallid *agg.* pallido.
pallor *s.* pallore.
palm[1] *s.* palma (*anche fig.*).
palm[2] *s.* (*anat.*) palmo.
to **palm** *vt.* toccare con la mano.
palmaceous *agg.* (*bot.*) di palma.
palmar *agg.* palmare.
palmate, palmated, *agg.* palmato.
palmiped *agg. e s.* palmipede.
palmistry *s.* chiromanzia.
palmy *agg.* 1. coperto di palme 2.
prosperoso, vittorioso.
palpability *s.* palpabilità.
palpable *agg.* palpabile.
to **palpate** *vt.* palpare.
to **palpitate** *vi.* palpitare.

palpitation s. palpitazione.
palsy s. paralisi.
to palsy vt. paralizzare.
to palter vi. tergiversare.
paltriness s. meschinità.
paltry agg. meschino.
to pamper vt. viziare.
pamphlet s. opuscolo.
pamphleteer s. autore di opuscoli.
pan s. 1. padella 2. vaschetta 3. bacino 4. piatto di bilancia || baking- —, teglia.
pancake s. frittella.
panchromatic agg. pancromatico.
pancreatic agg. pancreatico.
pandemonium s. pandemonio.
pander s. mezzano, ruffiano.
to pander vi. fare il mezzano.
pane s. 1. lastra di vetro 2. (edil.) pannello 3. faccia (di brillante).
panegyric s. panegirico.
panegyric(al) agg. laudativo.
panel s. 1. pannello 2. (neol.) commissione, comitato 3. (giur.) lista di giurati.
pang s. 1. fitta 2. (fig.) stretta al cuore.
panic agg. e s. panico.
panicky agg. allarmato.
panicle s. pannocchia.
panification s. panificazione.
pannier s. paniere.
panoramic agg. panoramico.
pansy s. viola del pensiero.
pant s. 1. palpito 2. ansito.
to pant vi. 1. palpitare 2. ansimare.
pantagruelian agg. pantagruelico.
pantheism s. panteismo.
pantheist s. panteista.
pantheistic(al) agg. panteistico.
panther s. pantera.
panties s. pl. (fam.) mutandine.
panting s. 1. palpitazione 2. ansito 3. ansia.
pantograph s. pantografo.
pantomime s. pantomima.
pantry s. dispensa.
pants s. pl. (fam.) mutande.
pap s. pappa.
papacy s. papato.
papal agg. papale.
paper s. 1. carta 2. prova d'esame
paper s. 1. carta 2. certificato, documento 3. prova d'esame 4. giornale || — back, libro in brossura; — board, cartone; — hanger, tappezziere; — hanging, tappezzeria.
to paper vt. 1. incartare 2. tappezzare.

papery agg. cartaceo.
papillary agg. papillare.
papism s. papismo.
papist s. papista.
papyrology s. papirologia.
papyrus s. (pl. -ri) papiro.
parable s. parabola.
parabolic(al) agg. 1. parabolico 2. di parabola.
paraboloid s. paraboloide.
parachute s. paracadute.
to parachute vt. paracadutare. ♦
to parachute vi. paracadutarsi.
parachutism s. paracadutismo.
parachutist s. paracadutista.
parade s. 1. (mil.) parata 2. mostra, sfoggio 3. viale, passeggiata.
to parade vt. disporre in parata. ♦
to parade vi. marciare in parata.
paradigm s. paradigma.
paradisaic(al) agg. paradisiaco.
paradise s. paradiso.
paradisiac(al) agg. paradisiaco.
paradox s. paradosso.
paradoxical agg. paradossale.
paraffin s. paraffina.
paragon s. modello (di perfezione ecc.).
paragraph s. paragrafo.
to paragraph vt. dividere in paragrafi.
parallel agg. parallelo. ♦ parallel s. 1. parallelo 2. parallela.
to parallel vt. 1. mettere in posizione parallela 2. paragonare.
parallelepiped s. parallelepipedo.
parallelism s. parallelismo.
parallelogram s. parallelogramma.
paralogism s. paralogismo.
to paralyse vt. paralizzare.
paralysis s. (pl. -ses) paralisi.
paralytic agg. e s. paralitico.
parameter s. parametro.
paramount agg. supremo. ♦ paramount s. capo supremo.
paramour s. amante.
paranoia s. paranoia.
paranoiac agg. e s. paranoico.
paranymph s. paraninfo.
parapet s. parapetto.
paraphrase s. parafrasi.
to paraphrase vt. e vi. parafrasare.
parasite s. parassita.
parasitic(al) agg. parassitico.
parasitism s. parassitismo.
parasol s. parasole.
paratrooper s. paracadutista.
paratyphoid s. paratifo.

parcel s. **1.** pacco **2.** lotto, appezzamento di terreno **3.** gruppo.
to parcel vt. spartire.
parcelling s. spartizione.
parcener s. coerede.
to parch vt. **1.** arrostire **2.** disseccare. ♦ **to parch** vi. **1.** bruciarsi **2.** disseccarsi.
parchment s. pergamena.
pardon s. perdono.
to pardon vt. perdonare.
pardonable agg. perdonabile.
to pare vt. **1.** tagliare **2.** sbucciare.
parenchyma s. parenchima.
parent s. **1.** genitore **2.** causa, origine.
parentage s. **1.** discendenza **2.** nascita.
parental agg. paterno, materno.
parenthesis s. (pl. -ses) parentesi.
parenthetic(al) agg. parentetico.
parenthood s. paternità, maternità.
parentless agg. orfano.
paresis s. paresi.
pariah s. paria.
parietal agg. parietale.
parish s. parrocchia || — priest, parroco.
parishioner s. parrocchiano.
Parisian agg. e s. parigino.
parisyllabic agg. e s. parisillabo.
parity s. parità.
park s. **1.** parco **2.** posteggio.
to park vt. **1.** adibire a parco **2.** parcheggiare.
parking s. parcheggio || no —, divieto di sosta.
parkway s. (amer.) viale.
parley s. colloquio.
to parley vi. parlamentare.
parliament s. parlamento.
parliamentarian s. parlamentare.
parliamentarianism s. parlamentarismo.
parliamentary agg. parlamentare.
parlour s. **1.** salotto **2.** parlatorio || beauty —, istituto di bellezza.
Parmesan agg. parmigiano.
parochial agg. **1.** parrocchiale **2.** (fig.) ristretto.
parochialism s. ristrettezza di vedute.
parodist s. parodista.
parody s. parodia.
to parody vt. parodiare.
parole s. **1.** parola d'onore **2.** parola d'ordine.
paroxysm s. parossismo.
parricidal agg. parricida.

parricide s. **1.** parricidio **2.** parricida.
parrot s. pappagallo.
to parrot vt. ripetere pappagallescamente.
to parry vt. parare, schivare.
parsley s. prezzemolo.
parson s. parroco (anglicano).
parsonage s. (eccl.) canonica, parrocchia.
part s. parte.
to part vt. dividere. ♦ **to part** vi. dividersi.
to partake (partook, partaken) vi. partecipare, prendere parte.
parthenogenesis s. partenogenesi.
partial agg. parziale.
partiality s. parzialità.
partially avv. parzialmente.
participant agg. e s. partecipante.
to participate vi. **1.** partecipare **2.** condividere.
participation s. partecipazione.
participial agg. participiale.
participle s. participio.
particle s. particella (anche gramm.).
particular agg. **1.** particolare **2.** particolareggiato **3.** esigente. ♦ **particular** s. particolare.
particularism s. particolarismo.
particularist s. particolarista.
particularity s. **1.** particolarità **2.** meticolosità.
to particularize vt. e vi. dettagliare.
parting s. separazione.
partisan agg. e s. partigiano.
partition s. **1.** divisione **2.** tramezzo.
to partition vt. dividere.
partitive agg. e s. partitivo.
partly avv. in parte.
partner s. **1.** socio **2.** coniuge.
partnership s. **1.** associazione **2.** (comm.) società.
partook V. to partake.
partridge s. pernice.
parturient agg. partoriente.
parturition s. parto.
party s. **1.** parte **2.** partito **3.** brigata **4.** trattenimento **5.** pattuglia.
pasha s. pascià.
pass[1] s. passo, gola.
pass[2] s. **1.** passaggio **2.** trapasso **3.** promozione **4.** lasciapassare.
to pass vt. e vi. passare || to — away, sparire; to — by, passar oltre.

passable agg. passabile.
passage s. 1. passaggio 2. corridoio 3. brano.
passementerie s. passamaneria.
passenger s. passeggero.
passer s. — -by, passante.
passible agg. passibile.
passing agg. 1. passeggero 2. casuale. ♦ passing s. passaggio.
passion s. passione || — -flower, passiflora.
passional agg. passionale.
passionate agg. appassionato, passionale.
passionless agg. impassibile.
passive agg. e s. passivo.
passivism, passivity s. passività.
passport s. passaporto.
password s. parola d'ordine.
past agg. passato. ♦ past s. passato. ♦ past avv. vicino. ♦ past prep. al di là di.
paste s. pasta. || tooth —, dentifricio.
to paste vt. 1. incollare, appiccicare 2. (gergo) attaccare.
pasteboard agg. di cartone. ♦ pasteboard s. cartone.
pastel s. pastello.
pasteurization s. pastorizzazione.
to pasteurize vt. pastorizzare.
pastime s. passatempo.
pastoral agg. e s. pastorale.
pastry s. dolci (pl.).
pasture s. pascolo.
to pasture vt. e vi. pascolare.
pasty agg. pastoso. ♦ pasty s. (cuc.) pasticcio.
pat agg. adatto. ♦ pat avv. esattamente. ♦ pat s. 1. colpetto 2. panetto di burro.
to pat vt. battere leggermente.
patch s. 1. pezza, toppa 2. macchia.
to patch vt. aggiustare, rattoppare, raffazzonare.
patching s. rattoppo.
patchy agg. 1. rappezzato 2. a macchie.
patent agg. 1. chiaro, manifesto, evidente 2. brevettato. ♦ patent s. brevetto.
to patent vt. brevettare.
patentee s. detentore di brevetto.
paternal agg. paterno.
paternalism s paternalismo.
paternalistic agg. paternalistico.
paternity s. paternità.
path s. 1. sentiero 2. pista 3. per-

corso, traiettoria.
pathetic agg. patetico.
pathfinder s. esploratore.
pathless agg. 1. senza sentieri 2. inesplorato.
pathogenic agg. patogeno.
pathologic(al) agg. patologico.
pathologist s. patologo.
pathology s. patologia.
pathway s. sentiero.
patience s. pazienza.
patient agg. 1. paziente 2. suscettibile. ♦ patient s. paziente.
patriarch s. patriarca.
patriarchal agg. patriarcale.
patriarchate s. patriarcato.
patrician agg.. e s. patrizio.
patricide s. V. parricide.
patrimonial agg. patrimoniale.
patrimony s. patrimonio.
patriot s. patriota.
patriotic agg. patriottico.
patriotism s. patriottismo.
patrol s. pattuglia, ronda.
to patrol vt. e vi. pattugliare, fare la ronda.
patron s. patrono.
patronage s. patronato.
patronal agg. patronale.
patroness s. patronessa.
to patronize vt. 1. patrocinare 2. trattare con condiscendenza.
patronizing agg. 1. protettivo 2. condiscendente.
patter[1] s. gergo.
patter[2] s. picchiettio.
to patter vi. picchiettare.
pattern s. 1. modello, campione 2. disegno (di stoffa ecc.).
to pattern vt. modellare (su).
paunch s. pancia.
pauper s. povero.
pauperism s. povertà.
pause s. pausa.
to pause vi. 1. fare una pausa 2. esitare, indugiare.
pauseless agg. incessante.
to pave vt. 1. pavimentare 2. (fig.) appianare.
pavement s. 1. pavimentazione 2. marciapiede.
paver s. lastricatore.
pavilion s. padiglione.
paving s. pavimentazione.
paw s. zampa.
to paw vt. dare zampate. ♦ to paw vi. scalpitare (di cavalli).
pawn s. 1. pegno 2. pedina (di scacchi).

to **pawn** vt. impegnare (dare in pegno).
pawnbroker s. prestatore su pegno.
pawnbroking s. il prestare su pegno.
pawner s. chi dà qualcosa in pegno.
pawnshop s. agenzia di prestiti su pegno.
pay s. paga.
to **pay (paid, paid)** vt. e vi. 1. pagare 2. rendere, fruttare || to — off, liquidare.
payable agg. 1. pagabile 2. redditizio.
payee s. creditore.
payer s. pagatore.
paying out s. esborso.
payment s. pagamento.
payoff s. 1. giorno di paga 2. liquidazione.
payroll s. libro paga.
pea s. pisello || chick —, cece.
peace s. pace.
peaceable agg. pacifico.
peaceful s. pacifico, tranquillo.
peacefulness s. pace, calma.
peaceless agg. agitato.
peacemaker s. pacificatore.
peach s. (bot.) pesca.
peach-tree s. pesco.
peachy agg. simile a pesca.
peacock s. pavone.
to **peacock** vi. pavoneggiarsi.
peak s. 1. picco 2. punta 3. visiera.
peaky agg. appuntito.
peal s. 1. scampanio 2. scoppio, fragore, scroscio (di risa, applausi).
to **peal** vi. scampanare. ♦ to **peal** vt. far rimbombare.
peanut s. arachide.
pear s. pera.
pear-tree s. pero.
pearl s. perla.
to **pearl** vt. imperlare, ornare di perle. ♦ to **pearl** vi. imperlarsi.
pearly agg. 1. perlaceo 2. ricco di perle.
peasant s. contadino.
peasantry s. 1. condizione di contadino 2. i contadini (pl.).
peat s. torba || — -bog, torbiera.
pebble s. 1. ciottolo 2. cristallo di rocca.
to **pebble** vt. coprire con ciottoli.
peccary s. pecari.
peck s. beccata.
to **peck** vt. e vi. beccare.
pectoral agg. e s. pettorale.

peculation s. peculato.
peculiar agg. 1. particolare 2. strano.
peculiarity s. 1. particolarità 2. bizzarria, eccentricità.
pecuniary agg. pecuniario.
pedagogic(al) agg. pedagogico.
pedagogics s. pedagogia.
pedagogist s. pedagogista.
pedagogue s. pedagogo.
pedagogy s. pedagogia.
pedal s. pedale.
to **pedal** vt. e vi. pedalare.
pedant s. pedante.
pedantic agg. pedante.
pedantry s. pedanteria.
pedestal s. piedistallo.
pedestrian agg. pedestre. ♦ **pedestrian** s. pedone.
pediatrics ecc. V. paediatrics ecc.
pediment s. (arch.) frontone.
pedlar s. venditore ambulante.
peel s. buccia.
to **peel** vt. sbucciare. ♦ to **peel** vi. sbucciarsi.
peeling s. buccia.
peep[1] s. 1. sguardo furtivo 2. fessura.
peep[2] s. pigolio.
to **peep**[1] vi. 1. guardare furtivamente 2. far capolino.
to **peep**[2] vi. pigolare.
peeper[1] s. ficcanaso, persona curiosa.
peeper[2] s. piccioncino.
peer s. 1. pari 2. Pari, membro della Camera dei Lord.
to **peer** vt. uguagliare. ♦ to **peer** vi. 1. scrutare 2. far capolino.
peerage s. 1. i Pari 2. nobiltà.
peerless agg. senza pari.
peevish agg. irritabile.
peg s. piuolo.
to **peg** vt. fissare.
pejorative agg. e s. peggiorativo.
pelagic agg. oceanico.
pelican s. pellicano.
pellet s. 1. pallottolina (di carta ecc.) 2. pallottola 3. pillola.
pellucid agg. trasparente.
pelt[1] s. colpo (di proiettile ecc.).
pelt[2] s. pelle (di animale).
to **pelt** vt. colpire.
pelvic agg. pelvico.
pelvis s. bacino.
pen[1] s. penna || -nib, pennino; fountain- —, penna stilografica.
pen[2] s. recinto (per animali).
to **pen**[1] vt. scrivere.
to **pen**[2] vt. rinchiudere animali in un recinto.

penal *agg.* penale.
to **penalize** *vt.* (*sport.*) penalizzare.
penalty *s.* penalità, punizione.
penance *s.* penitenza.
pence *s.* V. *penny.*
pencil *s.* matita.
pendant, pendent *agg.* e *s.* pendente.
pending *prep.* **1.** durante **2.** fino a.
pendular *agg.* pendolare.
pendulous *agg.* pendulo.
pendulum *s.* pendolo || — *-clock,* pendola.
penetrable *agg.* penetrabile.
to **penetrate** *vt.* e *vi.* penetrare.
penetration *s.* penetrazione.
penetrative *agg.* penetrante.
penguin *s.* pinguino.
penicillin *s.* penicillina.
peninsula *s.* penisola.
peninsular *agg.* peninsulare.
penis *s.* pene.
penitence *s.* penitenza.
penitent *agg.* e *s.* penitente.
penitential *agg.* penitenziale.
penitentiary *agg.* penitenziale. ◆
   penitentiary *s.* (*eccl.*) penitenziere **2.** riformatorio **3.** (*amer.*) penitenziario.
penknife *s.* (*pl.* -knives) temperino.
pennant *s.* (*mar.*) pennone.
penniless *agg.* senza un soldo.
pennon *s.* pennone.
penny *s.* (*numero delle monete*), **pence** (*loro valore*) *s.* "penny".
pension *s.* pensione.
to **pension** *vt.* pensionare.
pensionable *agg.* pensionabile.
pensioner *s.* pensionato.
pensive *agg.* pensoso.
pent *agg.* chiuso.
pentagon *s.* pentagono.
pentagonal *agg.* pentagonale.
pentagram *s.* pentagono.
pentahedron *s.* pentaedro.
pentameter *s.* pentametro.
pentane *s.* pentano.
pentathlon *s.* pentatlon.
Pentecost *s.* Pentecoste.
Pentecostal *agg.* pentecostale.
penthouse *s.* tettoia.
pentode *s.* (*elettr.*) pentodo.
pentose *s.* pentosio.
penult(imate) *agg.* e *s.* penultimo.
penury *s.* povertà.
peony *s.* peonia.
people *s.* (*costruzione al pl.*) **1.** popolo **2.** gente **3.** folla.
to **people** *vt.* popolare.

pepper *s.* pepe || — *-mill,* macinapepe.
to **pepper** *vt.* condire con pepe.
peppercorn *s.* grano di pepe.
peppermint *s.* menta peperita.
peppery *agg.* **1.** pepato **2.** collerico.
pepsin(e) *s.* pepsina.
per *prep.* per: — *cent,* per cento.
peracid *s.* peracido.
to **perambulate** *vt.* **1.** attraversare **2.** ispezionare. ◆ to **perambulate** *vi.* passeggiare.
perambulation *s.* **1.** ispezione **2.** passeggiata.
perambulator *s.* carrozzella per bambini.
percale *s.* percalle.
perceivable *agg.* percettibile.
to **perceive** *vt.* percepire, scorgere.
   ◆ to **perceive** *vi.* accorgersi.
percentage *s.* percentuale.
perceptible *agg.* percettibile.
perception *s.* percezione.
perceptive *agg.* percettivo.
perch[1] *s.* gruccia.
perch[2] *s.* pesce persico.
to **perch** *vi.* appollaiarsi.
perchlorate *s.* perclorato.
percipience *s.* percezione.
to **percolate** *vt.* e *vi.* filtrare, colare.
percolator *s.* filtro.
percussion *s.* percussione || — *-pin,* percussore.
perdition *s.* perdizione.
perdurable *agg.* durevole.
to **peregrinate** *vi.* peregrinare.
peregrination *s.* peregrinazione.
peremptory *agg.* perentorio.
perennial *agg.* perenne.
perfect *agg.* perfetto.
to **perfect** *vt.* perfezionare.
perfectibility *s.* perfettibilità.
perfectible *agg.* perfettibile.
perfecting *s.* **1.** perfezionamento **2.** completamento.
perfection *s.* **1.** perfezione **2.** perfezionamento.
perfectionism *s.* perfezionismo.
perfectionist *s.* perfezionista.
perfectly *avv.* perfettamente.
perfidious *agg.* perfido, sleale.
perfidy *s.* perfidia, slealtà.
to **perforate** *vt.* perforare.
perforation *s.* perforazione.
to **perform** *vt.* **1.** eseguire **2.** (*teat.*) rappresentare.
performable *agg.* **1.** eseguibile **2.** rappresentabile.

performance s. **1.** esecuzione **2.** atto **3.** (teat.) rappresentazione.
performer s. **1** esecutore **2.** attore.
performing agg. ammaestrato.
perfume s. profumo.
to **perfume** vt. profumare.
perfumer s. profumiere.
perfumery s. **1.** profumeria **2.** profumi.
perfunctory agg. superficiale. ▸
to **perfuse** vt. aspergere.
perfusion s. aspersione.
perhaps avv. forse.
pericardium s. pericardio.
perigee s. perigeo.
peril s. pericolo.
perilous agg. pericoloso.
perimeter s. perimetro.
period s. **1.** periodo **2.** ora di lezione **3.** stadio, fase (di una malattia) **4.** (gramm.) punto.
periodic agg. periodico.
periodical agg. e s. periodico.
periodicity s. periodicità.
peripheral agg. periferico.
periphery s. **1.** perimetro **2.** superficie.
periphrase, periphrasis s. (pl. -ses) perifrasi.
periphrastic agg. perifrastico.
periscope s. periscopio.
to **perish** vi. perire.
perishable agg. **1.** deperibile **2.** mortale.
perishables s. pl. merci deteriorabili.
peristyle s. peristilio.
peritonitis s. peritonite.
periwig s. parrucca.
periwigged agg. imparruccato.
periwinkle s. pervinca.
to **perjure** vt. giurare falsamente.
perjurer, perjury s. spergiuro.
permanence s. permanenza.
permanent agg. permanente.
permanganate s. permanganato.
permeability s. permeabilità.
permeable agg. permeabile.
to **permeate** vt. permeare. ♦ to **permeate** vi. permearsi.
permission, permit s. permesso.
to **permit** vt. e vi. permettere.
to **permute** vt. permutare.
pernicious agg. pernicioso.
to **perorate** vi. perorare.
peroration s. perorazione.
peroxid(e) s. perossido || hydrogen —, acqua ossigenata.
to **peroxide** vt. ossigenare.

perpendicular agg. perpendicolare.
♦ **perpendicular** s. **1.** perpendicolare **2.** filo a piombo.
perpendicularity s. perpendicolarità.
to **perpetrate** vt. perpetrare.
perpetration s. perpetrazione.
perpetual agg. perpetuo.
to **perpetuate** vt. perpetuare.
perpetuity s. **1.** perpetuità **2.** rendita vitalizia.
to **perplex** vt. **1.** rendere perplesso **2.** complicare.
perplexed agg. perplesso.
perplexity s. **1.** perplessità **2.** complicazione.
to **persecute** vt. perseguitare.
persecution s. persecuzione.
persecutor s. persecutore.
perseverance s. perseveranza.
to **persevere** vi. perseverare.
Persian agg. e s. persiano.
persimmon s. (bot.) cachi.
to **persist** vi. persistere.
persistence s. persistenza.
persistent agg. persistente.
person s. persona.
personable agg. ben fatto.
personage s. personaggio.
personal agg. personale.
personality s. personalità.
personalization s. personificazione.
to **personalize** vt. personificare.
personally avv. personalmente.
personification s. personificazione.
to **personify** vt. personificare.
personnel s. personale.
perspective agg. prospettico. ♦ **perspective** s. prospettiva.
perspicacious agg. perspicace.
perspicacity s. perspicacia.
perspicuity s. perspicuità.
perspicuous agg. perspicuo.
perspiration s. traspirazione.
to **perspire** vt. e vi. sudare, trasudare.
to **persuade** vt. persuadere.
persuasion s. **1.** persuasione **2.** credenza.
persuasive agg. persuasivo.
pert agg. impertinente.
to **pertain** vi. appartenere.
pertinacious agg. pertinace.
pertinacy, pertinacity s. pertinacia.
pertinence s. pertinenza.
pertinent agg. pertinente.
pertly avv. insolentemente.
pertness s. insolenza.

to **perturb** vt. perturbare.
perturbation s. perturbazione.
perusal s. lettura attenta.
to **peruse** vt. leggere attentamente.
to **pervade** vt. pervadere.
pervasion s. penetrazione.
pervasive agg. penetrante.
perverse agg. **1.** perverso **2.** errato **3.** ostinato.
perversion s. perversione.
perversity s. perversità.
pervert s. **1.** pervertito **2.** apostata.
to **pervert** vt. pervertire.
pessimism s. pessimismo.
pessimist s. pessimista.
pessimistic agg. pessimistico.
pessimistically avv. in modo pessimistico.
pest s. peste (anche fig.).
to **pester** vt. importunare.
pestiferous agg. pestifero.
pestilence s. pestilenza.
pestilent agg. **1.** nocivo **2.** molesto.
pestilential agg. pestilenziale.
pestle s. pestello.
pet agg. e s. favorito || — name, vezzeggiativo.
to **pet** vt. vezzeggiare.
petal s. petalo.
petard s. petardo.
petition s. petizione, istanza.
to **petition** vt. e vi. fare una petizione (a).
petitioner s. postulante.
to **petrify** vt. pietrificare. ♦ to **petrify** vi. pietrificarsi.
petrography s. petrografia.
petrol s. benzina.
petticoat s. sottoveste.
pettifogger s. azzeccagarbugli.
petty agg. **1.** meschino **2.** subalterno.
petulant agg. petulante.
pew s. banco (di chiesa).
pewter s. peltro.
phagocyte s. fagocita.
phalanstery s. falansterio.
phalanx s. (pl. -ges) falange.
phallic agg. fallico.
phantasm s. fantasma.
phantasmagoria s. fantasmagoria.
phantasmagorial, phantasmagoric(al) agg. fantasmagorico.
phantom s. **1.** fantasma **2.** apparizione.
Pharaoh s. faraone.
Pharisee s. fariseo.
pharmaceutic(al) agg. farmaceutico.

pharmaceutics s. farmaceutica.
pharmacology s. farmacologia.
pharmacopoeia s. farmacopea.
pharmacy s. farmacia.
pharyngitis s. faringite.
pharynx s. (pl. -ges) faringe.
phase s. fase.
pheasant s. fagiano.
phenic agg. fenico.
phenol s. fenolo.
phenomenal agg. **1.** fenomenico **2.** fenomenale.
phenomenalism s. fenomenismo.
phenomenology s. fenomenologia.
phenomenon s. (pl. -na) fenomeno.
phial s. fiala.
to **philander** vi. fare il cascamorto.
philanderer s. cascamorto.
philanthrope s. filantropo.
philanthropic(al) agg. filantropico.
philanthropism s. filantropia.
philanthropist s. filantropo.
philanthropy s. filantropia.
philatelic(al) agg. filatelico.
philatelist s. filatelico.
philately s. filatelia.
philharmonic agg. filarmonico.
philippic s. filippica.
Philippine agg. filippino.
philologian, philologist s. filologo.
philology s. filologia.
philosopher s. filosofo.
philosophic(al) agg. filosofico.
philosophist s. pseudofilosofo.
to **philosophize** vi. filosofare.
philosophy s. filosofia.
phlebitis s. flebite.
phleboclysis s. fleboclisi.
phlegm s. flemma.
phlegmatic(al) agg. flemmatico.
phlegmon s. flemmone.
phlogistic agg. flogistico.
phobia s. fobia.
phoenix s. fenice.
phone s. V. telephone.
phones s. pl. cuffie.
phoneme s. fonema.
phonetics s. fonetica.
phonogram s. fonogramma.
phonograph s. fonografo.
phonology s. fonologia.
phosphate s. fosfato.
phosphor s. fosforo.
phosphorescence s. fosforescenza.
phosphorescent agg. fosforescente.
phosphoric agg. fosforico.
phosphorous agg. fosforoso.

PHOTO 204 **PILING**

photo s. foto.
photocell s. cellula fotoelettrica.
photocopy s. fotocopia.
photoelectric(al) agg. fotoelettrico.
photogenic agg. fotogenico.
photograph s. fotografia.
to **photograph** vt. fotografare.
photographer s. fotografo.
photography s. fotografia (come arte).
photometry s. fotometria.
photomontage s. fotomontaggio.
phrase s. 1. locuzione, frase 2. stile.
to **phrase** vt. esprimere.
phraseology s. fraseologia.
phrenetic(al) agg. frenetico.
phrenologist s. frenologo.
phrenology s. frenologia.
phthisiology s. tisiologia.
phthisis s. tisi.
phylloxera s. fillossera.
physic s. medicina.
physical agg. fisico.
physician s. medico.
physicist s. fisico.
physics s. fisica.
physiognomist s. fisionomista.
physiognomy s. fisionomia.
physiologic(al) agg. fisiologico.
physiologist s. fisiologo.
physiology s. fisiologia.
physiotherapy s. fisioterapia.
physique s. fisico.
pianist s. pianista.
picaresque agg. picaresco.
pick[1] s. 1. piccone 2. colpo di piccone || tooth —, stuzzicadenti.
pick[2] s. scelta, il meglio (di qc.).
to **pick** vt. 1. scavare 2. pulire 3. raccogliere 4. rubare.
pickax(e) s. piccone.
picker s. 1. piccone 2. zappatore 3. raccoglitore.
picket s. 1. piolo, palo 2. (mil.) picchetto.
pickle s. 1. salamoia 2. sottaceti (pl.).
to **pickle** vt. mettere in salamoia, sotto aceto.
picklock s. 1. scassinatore 2. grimaldello.
pickpocket s. borsaiolo.
pickup s. 1. raccolta 2. (mecc.) accelerazione 3. fonorivelatore.
pictorial agg. 1. illustrato 2. pittorico. ♦ **pictorial** s. giornale illustrato.
picture s. 1. quadro, dipinto, ritrat-

to 2. illustrazione. ♦ **pictures** s. pl. cinema (sing.) || — fook, libro illustrato.
to **picture** vt. dipingere || to — to oneself, immaginarsi, figurarsi.
picturesque agg. pittoresco.
pidgin agg. — English, inglese scorretto (usato tra cinesi ed europei).
pie[1] s. pica, gazza.
pie[2] s. torta, pasticcio.
pie[3] s. (tip.) refuso.
piece s. 1. pezzo 2. pezza (di tessuto) || by the —, a cottimo.
to **piece** vt. rappezzare, raggiustare.
piecemeal avv. pezzo per pezzo. ♦ **piecemeal** agg. frammentario.
piecework s. (lavoro a) cottimo.
pieceworker s. cottimista.
pied agg. screziato.
pier s. 1. molo 2. pilone || - -glass, specchiera.
to **pierce** vt. 1. forare 2. trafiggere.
piercer s. 1. punzone 2. punzonatore.
piercing agg. penetrante. ♦ **piercing** s. perforamento.
pietism s. pietismo.
piety s. pietà, reverenza.
pig s. 1. maiale 2. (metal.) lingotto.
pigeon s. piccione || — -house, piccionaia; carrier —, piccione viaggiatore.
pigeonhole s. 1. colombaia 2. casella 3. (giur.) casellario.
to **pigeonhole** vt. incasellare.
piggish agg. porcino.
pigheaded agg. testardo.
pigment s. pigmento.
pigmentation s. pigmentazione.
pigmy agg. e s. pigmeo.
pigsty s. porcile.
pike[1] s. picca.
pike[2] s. (amer.) pedaggio.
pilaster s. pilastro.
pile s. 1. mucchio 2. fabbricato 3. rogo 4. (elettr.) pila 5. (fig.) gruzzolo.
to **pile**[1] vt. ammucchiare. ♦ to **pile** vi. ammucchiarsi.
to **pile**[2] vt. conficcare pali in, fare palizzate.
piles s. pl. emorroidi.
to **pilfer** vt. e vi. rubacchiare.
pilferer s. ladruncolo.
pilgrim s. pellegrino.
pilgrimage s. pellegrinaggio.
piling[1] s. ammucchiamento.
piling[2] s. palificazione di sostegno.

pill *s.* pillola: *contraceptive (pill)*, pillola anticoncezionale.

pillage *s.* 1. saccheggio 2. bottino.

to pillage *vt.* saccheggiare.

pillar *s.* colonna, guanciale || — -*box*, cassetta delle lettere.

pillory *s.* berlina.

to pillory *vt.* mettere alla berlina.

pillow *s.* cuscino, guanciale || — -*case*, federa.

pilot *s.* pilota.

to pilot *vt.* pilotare.

pilotage *s.* pilotaggio.

pimple *s.* foruncolo.

pin *s.* 1. spillo 2. perno || *pins and needles*, formicolio.

to pin *vt.* 1. puntare 2. (*fig.*) inchiodare.

pinafore *s.* grembiulino.

pinaster *s.* pinastro.

to pincer *vt.* attanagliare.

pincers *s. pl.* tenaglie.

pinch *s.* 1. pizzico, pizzicotto 2. (*fig.*) angustia.

to pinch *vt.* 1. pizzicare 2. stringere 3. causare dolore. ♦ **to pinch** *vi.* essere avaro.

pinchbeck *s.* princisbecco.

pincushion *s.* puntaspilli.

Pindaric *agg.* pindarico.

pine *s.* pino || — -*apple*, ananasso; — -*cone*, pigna; — -*wood*, pineta.

to pine *vi.* struggersi.

pinion[1] *s.* penna remigante.

pinion[2] *s.* (*mecc.*) pignone.

to pinion *vt.* tarpare le ali a.

pink *agg.* rosa. ♦ **pink** *s.* 1. colore rosa 2. garofano 3. (*fig.*) quintessenza.

to pink *vt.* 1. traforare 2. trafiggere.

pinky *agg.* roseo.

pinnacle *s.* 1. pinnacolo 2. sommità.

pinpoint *s.* capocchia di spillo.

pint *s.* pinta.

pioneer *s.* pioniere.

pious *agg.* 1. pio 2. pietoso.

piousness *s.* pietà.

pip *s.* seme di frutto.

to pip *vi.* pigolare.

pipage *s.* 1. tubatura 2. trasporto per tubatura.

pipe *s.* 1. tubo 2. pipa 3. strumento a fiato 4. condotta.

to pipe *vi.* 1. suonare (*piffero ecc.*) 2. stridere. ♦ .**to pipe** *vt.* 1. suonare 2. trasportare con tubature 3.

fornire di tubature.

pipeline *s.* oleodotto.

piper *s.* pifferaio.

pipet(te) *s.* (*chim.*) pipetta.

piping *agg.* 1. flautato 2. acuto. ♦ **piping** *s.* 1. suono (*di piffero ecc.*) 2. suono acuto 3. tubatura.

piquancy *s.* gusto piccante.

piquant *agg.* piccante.

pique *s.* ripicco, risentimento.

piracy *s.* 1. pirateria 2. plagio.

pirate *s.* 1. pirata 2. plagiario.

pirogue *s.* piroga.

pirouette *s.* piroetta.

to pirouette *vi.* piroettare.

pistil *s.* pistillo.

pistol *s.* pistola.

piston *s.* pistone.

pit *s.* 1. fossa 2. cavità 3. platea.

to pit *vt.* 1. bucare 2. mettere in una fossa.

pitch[1] *s.* 1. lancio 2. beccheggio 3. (*mecc.*) passo 4. (*mus.*) intonazione 5. inclinazione.

pitch[2] *s.* pece, bitume || — -*dark*, nero come la pece.

to pitch[1] *vt.* 1. sistemare 2. gettare 3. intonare. ♦ **to pitch** *vi.* 1. beccheggiare 2. (*aer.*) picchiare.

to pitch[2] *vt.* impeciare.

pitcher *s.* brocca.

pitchfork *s.* forcone.

to pitchfork *vt.* 1. rimuovere 2. spingere (*col forcone*).

pitching *s.* beccheggio.

pitchy *agg.* 1. impeciato 2. simile a pece.

piteous *agg.* pietoso.

pitfall *s.* trappola.

pith *s.* 1. midollo 2. (*fig.*) essenza.

pithy *agg.* (*fig.*) vigoroso.

pitiable, pitiful *agg.* pietoso.

pitiless *agg.* spietato.

pittance *s.* poco denaro.

pitted *agg.* butterato.

pity *s.* pietà || *what a* —!, che peccato!

to pity *vt.* aver pietà di, compatire.

pitying *agg.* pietoso.

pivot *s.* cardine.

to pivot *vt.* montare su cardini. ♦ **to pivot** *vi.* girare su cardini.

placable *agg.* placabile.

placard *s.* manifesto.

to placate *vt.* placare.

placatory *agg.* conciliante.

place *s.* 1. posto 2. brano.|| *to take* —, aver luogo, accadere.

to **place** vt. mettere, porre, situare.
placement s. collocamento.
placid agg. placido.
placidity s. placidità.
placing s. sistemazione.
plagiarism s. plagio.
plagiarist s. plagiario.
to **plagiarize** vt. plagiare.
plagiary s. 1. plagio 2. plagiario.
plague s. peste.
to **plague** vt. affliggere.
plaguer s. tormentatore.
plaid s. 1. mantello scozzese 2. tessuto a quadri.
plain agg. 1. piano, chiaro, evidente 2. semplice 3. comune, scialbo. ♦ **plain** s.. pianura. ♦ **plain** avv. 1, chiaramente 2. semplicemente.
plain-clothes s. pl. abiti borghesi.
plainness s. 1. chiarezza 2. semplicità 3. aspetto scialbo.
plaint s. 1. lamento, lagnanza 2. (giur.) querela.
plaintiff s. (giur.) attore (nei processi civili).
plaintive agg. lamentoso.
plait s. 1. piega (di abiti) 2. treccia.
to **plait** vt. 1. pieghettare 2. intrecciare.
plan s. 1. piano, progetto 2. pianta (di una città).
to **plan** vt. progettare.
plane[1] agg. piano. ♦ **plane** s. 1. piano 2. aereo.
plane[2] s. pialla.
plane[3] s. — -tree, platano.
to **plane**[1] vi. volare.
to **plane**[2] vt. piallare.
planer s. (mecc.) piallatrice.
planet s. (astr.) pianeta.
planetary agg. planetario.
planimetric(al) agg. planimetrico.
planimetry s. planimetria.
planisphere s. planisfero.
plank s. tavola, asse.
to **plank** vt. coprire di tavole.
planking s. tavolato.
plankton s. plancton.
planner s. progettista.
planning s. progettazione.
plant s. 1. pianta 2. impianto, apparato 3. fabbrica, stabilimento.
to **plant** vt. (im)piantare.
plantation s. piantagione.
planter s. 1. piantatore 2. colonizzatore.
plantigrade agg. e s. plantigrado.
plaque s. placca.
plash s. pozzanghera.

plaster s. 1. cerotto 2. gesso 3. intonaco.
to **plaster** vt. 1. incerottare 2. ingessare 3. intonacare 4. ricoprire.
plastering s. 1. intonacatura 2. ingessatura.
plastic agg. plastico, malleabile.
plasticine s. plastilina.
plasticity s. plasticità.
to **plasticize** vt. rendere plastico.
plastics s. pl. materie plastiche.
plate s. 1. lastra, lamina 2. piatto 3. tavola fuori testo 4. targa 5. squama 6. vasellame.
to **plate** vt. 1. placcare 2. rivestire di piastre.
plateau s. altipiano.
platen s. 1. piastra metallica 2. rullo di macchina da scrivere.
platform s. 1. piattaforma 2. (ferr.) marciapiede 3. impalcatura 4. (amer.) programma politico.
plating s. 1. placcatura 2. rivestimento metallico.
to **platinize** vt. platinare.
platinum s. platino.
platitude s. banalità.
Platonic agg. platonico.
Platonism s. platonismo.
platoon s. plotone.
plausibility s. plausibilità.
plausible agg. plausibile.
play s. 1. gioco 2. dramma 3. (mus.) esecuzione 4. azione || — bill, cartellone teatrale; — -time, ricreazione.
to **play** vt. e vi. 1. giocare 2. recitare 3. agire 4. suonare || to — down, dare poca importanza a.
playboy s. (fam.) gaudente.
player s. 1. giocatore 2. attore 3. suonatore.
playful agg. giocoso.
playfulness s. allegria.
playground s. terreno di giochi.
playhouse s. teatro.
playing s. 1. gioco 2. rappresentazione 3. (mus.) esecuzione.
plaything s. giocattolo.
playwright, playwriter s. commediografo.
plea s. 1. giustificazione 2. (giur.) eccezione difensiva.
to **plead** vt. 1. patrocinare 2. addurre a pretesto 3. (giur.) perorare (una causa). ♦ to **plead** vi. 1. difendersi 2. supplicare.
pleader s. patrocinatore.
pleading agg. supplichevole. ♦

pleading s. difesa. ◆ **pleadings** s. pl. comparse.

pleasant agg. piacevole.

pleasantry s. piacevolezza.

to **please** vt. e vi. piacere (a) || — God, a Dio piacendo.

pleased agg. lieto.

pleasing agg. piacevole.

pleasure s. piacere.

pleat s. piega (di abiti ecc.).

to **pleat** vt. pieghettare.

plebeian agg. e s. plebeo.

plebiscitary agg. plebiscitario.

plebiscite s. plebiscito.

plectrum s. plettro.

pledge s. 1. pegno 2. promessa 3. brindisi.

to **pledge** vt. 1. impegnare 2. brindare a.

pledgee s. (giur.) creditore pignoratizio.

plenary agg. plenario || — session, seduta plenaria.

plenilune s. plenilunio.

plenipotentiary agg. e s. plenipotenziario.

plentiful agg. abbondante.

plenty s. abbondanza, quantità.

pleonasm s. pleonasma.

pleonastic agg. pleonastico.

plethora s. pletora.

plethoric agg. pletorico.

pleurisy s. pleurite.

plexus s. plesso.

pliability s. pieghevolezza.

pliable agg. pieghevole.

pliancy s. V. pliability.

pliant s. V. pliable.

pliers s. pl. pinze.

plight[1] s. situazione critica.

plight[2] s. impegno, promessa.

to **plight** vt. impegnare, promettere.

plod s. 1. passo pesante 2. lavoro faticoso.

to **plod** vt. e vi. 1. camminare faticosamente 2. sgobbare.

plodder s. 1. chi cammina faticosamente 2. sgobbone.

plot s. 1. appezzamento 2. trama 3. congiura.

to **plot** vt. e vi. 1. fare la pianta di 2. tramare.

plotter s. cospiratore.

plough s. aratro.

to **plough** vt. e vi. 1. arare 2. solcare.

ploughing s. aratura.

ploughman s. aratore.

ploughshare s. vomere.

plover s. piviere.

pluck s. 1. strappo 2. coraggio.

to **pluck** vt. 1. strappare 2. spennare 3. tirare || to — up, sradicare.

plucky agg. coraggioso.

plug s. 1. tappo (di lavandino ecc.) 2. (elettr.; tel.) spina || spark(ing)- — (mecc.), candela.

to **plug** vt. 1. tappare 2. tamponare || to — in, inserire la corrente; to — away, sgobbare.

plugging s. chiusura.

plum s. 1. prugna, susina 2. uva passa 3. (fig.) il meglio.

plumage s. piumaggio.

plumb agg. 1. a piombo 2. completo. ◆ **plumb** s. 1. filo a piombo 2. scandaglio. ◆ **plumb** avv. 1. a piombo 2. esattamente.

to **plumb** vt. 1. rendere verticale 2. scandagliare 3. impiombare.

plumber s. idraulico.

plumbery s. negozio di idraulico.

plumbing s. 1. piombatura 2. lavori idraulici.

plumbum s. piombo.

plume s. piuma, penna.

plummet s. piombino.

plump[1] agg. grassottello.

plump[2] agg. brusco, netto. ◆ **plump** avv. 1. improvvisamente 2. direttamente.

to **plump** vt. 1. ingrassare 2. far cadere. ◆ to **plump** vi. 1. ingrassare 2. cadere.

to **plunder** v. depredare.

plunderer s. saccheggiatore.

plunge s. tuffo.

to **plunge** vt. tuffare. ◆ to **plunge** vi. tuffarsi.

plunger s. 1. tuffatore 2. stantuffo.

plunk s. colpo metallico.

to **plunk** vt. far cadere pesantemente. ◆ to **plunk** vi. cadere pesantemente.

plural agg. e s. plurale.

pluralism s. pluralismo.

plurality s. pluralità.

plus agg. 1. in più 2. (elettr.) positivo || — value, plusvalore. ◆ **plus** s. 1. più 2. quantità positiva. ◆ **plus** prep. più.

plush s. « peluche », felpa.

plutocracy s. plutocrazia.

plutocrat s. plutocrate.

ply s. piega || — -wood, compensato.

to **ply** vt. 1. maneggiare 2. importunare. ◆ to **ply** vi. 1. lavorare assiduamente **2.** fare la spola.

pneumatic *agg.* e *s.* pneumatico.

pneumonia *s.* polmonite.

pneumothorax *s.* pneumotorace.

to **poach** *vt.* **1.** calpestare **2.** cacciare di frodo **3.** interferire.

poacher *s.* bracconiere.

poaching *s.* bracconaggio.

pocket *s.* **1.** tasca **2.** buca (*di biliardo*) || — *-book*, lib.o tascabile.

to **pocket** *vt.* **1.** intascare **2.** nascondere, soffocare (*sentimenti ecc.*).

pocketful *s.* tascata.

pod *s.* **1.** baccello **2.** gruppetto.

poem *s.* **1.** poesia **2.** poema.

poet *s.* poeta.

poetic(al) *agg.* poetico.

poetic(s) *s.* poetica.

poetry *s.* poesia.

pc:gnant *agg.* **1.** pungente **2.** commovente.

point *s.* **1.** punto **2.** punta, estremità **3.** caratteristica.

to **point** *vt.* **1.** indicare, segnare a dito **2.** appuntire **3.** dirigere || *to — out*, indicare, porre in rilievo.

pcint-blank *agg.* diretto. ♦ **point-blank** *avv.* direttamente.

pointed *agg.* **1.** appuntito **2.** mordace **3.** evidente.

pointer *s.* **1.** indicatore **2.** lancetta (*di orologio*).

pointless *agg.* **1.** spuntato **2.** inutile, senza scopo.

pointsman *s.* (*ferr.*) deviatore.

poise *s.* equilibrio.

to **poise** *vt.* bilanciare. ♦ to **poise** *vi.* bilanciarsi.

poison *s.* veleno.

to **poison** *vt.* avvelenare.

poisoning *agg.* velenoso. ♦ **poisoning** *s.* avvelenamento.

poisonous *agg.* velenoso (*anche fig.*).

poke *s.* spinta, urto.

to **poke** *vt.* e *vi.* **1.** spingere **2.** andare a tastoni.

poker *s.* attizzatoio.

poky *agg.* meschino.

polar *agg.* polare.

polarity *s.* polarità.

polarization *s.* polarizzazione.

to **polarize** *vt.* polarizzare.

pole[1] *s.* palo

pole[2] *s.* polo.

Pole[3] *s.* polacco.

polecat *s.* puzzola.

polemic *s.* **1.** polemica **2.** polemista.

polemic(al) *agg.* polemico.

polemi(ci)st *s.* polemista.

to **polemize** *vi.* polemizzare.

police *s.* polizia || — *-force*, corpo di polizia.

police court *s.* pretura.

policeman *s.* poliziotto.

policy[1] *s.* **1.** linea di condotta **2.** sagacia.

policy[2] *s.* polizza.

polio(myelitis) *s.* poliomielite.

Polish[1] *agg.* polacco.

polish[2] *s.* **1.** lucidatura **2.** lucido **3.** raffinatezza || *shoe* —, lucido per le scarpe.

to **polish** *vt.* **1.** lucidare **2.** raffinare. ♦ to **polish** *vi.* **1.** divenire lucido **2.** raffinarsi.

polisher *s.* **1.** lucidatore **2.** lucido.

polishing *s.* lucidatura.

polite *agg.* cortese.

politeness *s.* cortesia.

politic *agg.* abile.

political *agg.* politico.

politician *s.* uomo politico.

politics *s.* politica.

poll *s.* **1.** votazione, scrutinio **2.** referendum.

to **poll** *vt.* radere. ♦ to **poll** *vi.* votare, raccogliere voti.

pollen *s.* polline.

to **pollinate** *vt.* impollinare.

pollination *s.* impollinazione.

to **pollute** *vt.* contaminare.

pollution *s.* contaminazione.

polyandry *s.* poliandria.

polychrome *agg.* policromo.

polychromy *s.* policromia.

polyclinic *s.* policlinico.

polygamist *s.* poligamo.

polygamous *agg.* poligamo.

polygamy *s.* poligamia.

polyglot *agg.* e *s.* poliglotta.

polygon *s.* poligono.

polyhedral *agg.* poliedrico.

polyhedron *s.* poliedro.

polymerization *s.* polimerizzazione.

polymorphic *agg.* polimorfo.

polymorphism *s.* polimorfismo.

polyp *s.* polipo.

polyphonic *agg.* polifonico.

polyphony *s.* polifonia.

polysyllabic(al) *agg.* polisillabico.

polysyllable *s.* polisillabo.

polytechnic *agg.* e *s.* politecnico.

polytheism *s.* politeismo.

polytheist *s.* politeista.

polytheistic(al) *agg.* politeistico.

polyvalent *agg.* polivalente.

pomade *s.* pomata.

to pomade *vt.* impomatare.

pomegranate *s.* 1. melagrana 2. melograno.

pomp *s.* pompa, fasto.

pomposity *s.* pomposità.

pompous *agg.* pomposo.

pond *s.* stagno.

to pond *vt.* e *vi.* stagnare.

to ponder *vt.* e *vi.* ponderare.

ponderable *agg.* ponderabile.

ponderous *agg.* ponderoso.

pontiff *s.* pontefice.

pontifical *agg.* pontificio. ◆ pontifical *s.* pontificato.

pontificate *s.* pontificato.

to pontificate *vi.* pontificare.

pontoon *s.* pontone.

pony *s.* « pony », piccolo cavallo.

poodle *s.* barboncino.

pool[1] *s.* 1. stagno 2. pozza || *swimming* —, piscina.

pool[2] *s.* (*comm.*) 1. fondo comune 2. (*comm.*) consorzio, sindacato.

poor *agg.* povero.

poorly *avv.* male.

poorness *s.* povertà.

pop *s.* scoppio.

to pop *vi.* scoppiare. ◆ to pop *vt.* 1. far scoppiare 2. ficcare.

popcorn *s.* fiocco di granoturco.

pope *s.* papa.

popery *s.* papismo.

poplar *s.* pioppo.

poppied *agg.* coperto di papaveri.

poppy *s.* papavero.

populace *s.* plebaglia.

popular *agg.* popolare.

popularity *s.* popolarità.

popularization *s.* popolarizzazione.

to popularize *vt.* popolarizzare.

to populate *vt.* popolare.

population *s.* popolazione.

Populism *s.* populismo.

Populist *s.* populista.

populous *agg.* popoloso.

porch *s.* portico.

porcupine *s.* porcospino.

pore *s.* poro.

to pore *vi.* esaminare.

pork *s.* carne di maiale.

pornographic *agg.* pornografico.

pornography *s.* pornografia.

porosity *s.* porosità.

porous *agg.* poroso.

porphyry *s.* porfido.

port[1] *s.* porto.

port[2] *s.* 1. (*mecc.*) apertura, foro 2. (*mar.*) portello.

port[3] *s.* fianco sinistro di nave.

portable *agg.* portatile.

portal *s.* portale.

portcullis *s.* saracinesca (*di fortezza*).

to portend *vt.* preannunciare.

portent *s.* 1. presagio 2. portento.

portentous *agg.* 1. sinistro 2. portentoso.

porter[1] *s.* facchino.

porter[2] *s.* custode, portiere.

porter[3] *s.* birra scura.

portfolio *s.* 1. cartella, busta 2. (*pol.*) portafoglio.

porthole *s.* 1. (*mar.*) portello 2. feritoia.

portion *s.* porzione, parte.

to portion *vt.* dividere, distribuire.

portrait *s.* ritratto.

portraitist *s.* ritrattista.

to portray *vt.* ritrarre.

portrayal *s.* ritratto.

portrayer *s.* ritrattista.

Portuguese *agg.* e *s.* portoghese.

pose *s.* posa.

to pose[1] *vt.* proporre.

to pose[2] *vi.* posare.

poser *s.* posatore.

position *s.* posizione.

positive *agg.* 1. positivo 2. sicuro. ◆ positive *s.* 1. realtà 2. (*foto*) positiva.

positivism *s.* positivismo.

positivist *s.* positivista.

positivistic *agg.* positivistico.

posology *s.* posologia.

to possess *vt.* possedere.

possessed *agg.* indemoniato.

possession *s.* possesso.

possessive *agg.* possessivo.

possessor *s.* possessore.

possibility *s.* possibilità.

possible *agg.* possibile.

possibly *avv.* possibilmente.

post[1] *s.* posta, corrispondenza || — *card*, cartolina; *by return of* —, a giro di posta.

post[2] *s.* 1. palo, sostegno, puntello 2. stipite || *sign*- —, indicatore stradale.

to post[1] *vt.* imbucare, inviare per posta.

to post[2] *vt.* affiggere.

postage *s.* spese postali (*pl.*).

postage stamp *s.* francobollo.

postal *agg.* postale.

to postdate *vt.* posdatare.

poster *s.* 1. affisso 2. attacchino.

poste-restante *s.* fermo posta.

posterior *agg.* posteriore.
posterity *s.* posterità.
postern *s.* postierla.
post-free *agg.* franco di porto.
posthumous *agg.* postumo.
postil(l)ion *s.* postiglione.
postman *s.* postino.
postmark *s.* timbro postale.
postmaster *s.* direttore di ufficio postale.
to **postpone** *vt.* rimandare.
postponement *s.* rinvio.
to **post-score** *vt.* (*cine*) sonorizzare.
postscript *s.* poscritto.
postulate *s.* postulato.
to **postulate** *vt.* 1. porre come postulato 2. chiedere.
postulator *s.* postulante.
posture *s.* posizione.
to **posture** *vi.* assumere una posizione.
post-war *agg.* postbellico.
posy *s.* mazzolino di fiori.
pot *s.* 1. recipiente 2. pentola || —-bellied, panciuto.
to **pot** *vt.* conservare (*in vaso*).
potable *agg.* potabile.
potash *s.* potassa.
potassic *agg.* potassico.
potassium *s.* potassio.
potato *s.* patata.
potent *agg.* potente.
potential *agg.* e *s.* potenziale.
potentiality *s.* potenzialità.
potion *s.* pozione.
potter *s.* vasaio.
pottery *s.* 1. terraglie 2. fabbrica di terraglie.
pouch *s.* borsa.
to **pouch** *vt.* intascare.
poulterer *s.* pollivendolo.
poultry *s.* pollame.
pounce *s.* balzo.
to **pounce** *vi.* avventarsi su, contro.
pound[1] *s.* 1. libbra 2. sterlina.
pound[2] *s.* recinto.
to **pound**[1] *vt.* e *vi.* pestare.
to **pound**[2] *vt.* rinchiudere.
pour *s.* acquazzone.
to **pour** *vt.* versare. ♦ to **pour** *vi.* 1. versarsi 2. diluviare.
pout *s.* broncio.
to **pout** *vi.* fare il broncio.
poverty *s.* povertà.
powder *s.* 1. polvere 2. cipria, talco.
to **powder** *vt.* 1. polverizzare 2. incipriare. ♦ to **powder** *vi.* 1. polverizzarsi 2. incipriarsi.
powdery *agg.* 1. friabile 2. polveroso.
power *s.* potenza, potere || *horse* —, cavallo vapore; — -*station*, centrale elettrica.
to **power** *vt.* motorizzare.
powerful *agg.* potente.
powerless *agg.* debole.
pox *s.* sifilide || *chicken-* —, varicella, *small-* —, vaiolo.
practicability *s.* praticabilità.
practicable *agg.* 1. praticabile 2. fattibile.
practical *agg.* pratico.
practicality *s.* praticità.
practice *s.* 1. pratica 2. abitudine, regola 3. esercizio 4. professione 5. (*coll.*) clienti (*di medico ecc.*).
to **practise** *vt.* 1. praticare 2. esercitare. ♦ to **practise** *vi.* esercitarsi.
practitioner *s.* professionista.
praetorian *s.* pretoriano.
pragmatic(al) *agg.* prammatico.
pragmatism *s.* pragmatismo.
pragmatist *agg.* e *s.* pragmatista.
prairie *s.* prateria.
praise *s.* lode.
to **praise** *vt.* lodare.
praiser *s.* lodatore.
praiseworthy *agg.* lodevole.
prance *s.* impennata.
prank *s.* monelleria.
to **prank** *vt.* ornare, agghindare vistosamente. ♦ to **prank** *vi.* mettersi in mostra.
prate *s.* chiacchiera, sproloquio.
to **prate** *vi.* chiacchierare, proferire parole senza senso.
prattle *s.* balbettio.
to **prattle** *vt.* e *vi.* balbettare.
praxis *s.* prassi.
to **pray** *vt.* e *vi.* pregare.
prayer *s.* preghiera.
to **preach** *vt.* e *vi.* predicare.
preacher *s.* predicatore.
to **preachify** *vi.* predicare in modo noioso.
preaching *s.* predicazione.
preachy *agg.* (*fam.*) incline a far prediche.
to **pre-announce** *vt.* preannunziare.
to **prearrange** *vt.* predisporre.
prearrangement *s.* predisposizione.
prebend *s.* prebenda.
prebendary *s.* prebendario.
precarious *agg.* precario.

precariousness s. precarietà.
precatory agg. supplichevole.
precaution s. precauzione.
precautional agg. precauzionale.
to **precede** vt. e vi. precedere.
precedence s. precedenza.
precedent agg. e s. precedente.
preceding agg. precedente.
precept s. precetto.
preceptive agg. istruttivo
preceptor s. precettore.
precession s. precessione.
precinct s. 1. recinto 2. limiti 3. vicinanze (pl.).
preciosity s. preziosità.
precious agg. prezioso.
preciousness s. preziosità.
precipice s. precipizio.
precipitate agg. e s. precipitato.
to **precipitate** vt. e vi. precipitare.
precipitation s. precipitazione.
precipitous agg. ripido.
précis s. riassunto.
precise agg. preciso.
precision s. precisione.
to **preclude** vt. precludere.
precocious agg. precoce.
precociousness, precocity s. precocità.
preconceived agg. preconcetto.
precursor s. precursore, predecessore.
precursory agg. 1. preliminare 2. premonitore.
predaceous agg. rapace.
to **predate** vt. predatare.
predatory agg. rapace.
to **predecease** vt. premorire a.
predecessor s. predecessore.
to **predesignate** vt. predesignare.
predestination s. predestinazione.
to **predestine** vt. predestinare.
predetermination s. predeterminazione.
to **predetermine** vt. predeterminare.
predicable agg. asseribile.
predicament s. situazione scabrosa.
predicate agg. e s. predicato.
to **predicate** vt. 1. asserire 2. implicare.
predication s. affermazione.
predicative agg. 1. predicativo 2. affermativo.
predicatory agg. predicatorio.
to **predict** vt. e vi. predire.
prediction s. predizione.
predilection s. predilezione.

to **predispose** vt. predisporre.
predisposition s. predisposizione.
predominance s. predominanza.
to **predominate** vi. predominare.
pre-eminence s. preminenza.
pre-eminent agg. preminente.
pre-emption s. prelazione, priorità.
to **pre-engage** vt. impegnare in anticipo.
to **pre-establish** vt. prestabilire.
to **pre-exist** vi. preesistere.
pre-existence s. preesistenza.
to **prefabricate** vt. prefabbricare.
prefabricated agg. — house, casa prefabbricata.
preface s. prefazione.
to **preface** vt. 1. fare una prefazione a 2. iniziare.
prefatory agg. introduttivo.
prefect s. prefetto.
prefecture s. prefettura.
to **prefer** vt. 1. preferire 2. promuovere, elevare.
preferable agg. preferibile.
preference s. preferenza.
preferential agg. preferenziale.
preferment s. avanzamento, promozione.
prefiguration s. prefigurazione.
to **prefigure** vt. prefigurare.
prefix s. prefisso.
pregnancy s. 1. gravidanza 2. (fig.) significato, importanza.
pregnant agg. 1. incinta 2. significativo, importante 3. fecondo.
prehension s. 1. prensione 2. apprendimento.
prehistoric(al) agg. preistorico.
prehistory s. preistoria.
prejudice s. pregiudizio.
to **prejudice** vt. 1. pregiudicare 2. influenzare.
prejudicial agg. pregiudizievole.
prelate s. prelato.
prelatic(al) agg. prelatizio.
preliminary agg. preliminare. ◆ **preliminaries** s. pl. preliminari.
prelude s. preludio.
to **prelude** vt. preludere. ◆ to **prelude** vi. eseguire un preludio.
premature agg. prematuro.
to **premeditate** vt. premeditare.
premeditation s. premeditazione.
premier s. primo ministro.
premise s. 1. premessa 2. stabile con terreni annessi.
to **premise** vt. premettere.
premolar agg. e s. premolare.
premonitory agg. premonitore.

preoccupation *s.* preoccupazione.
to **preoccupy** *vt.* **1.** preoccupare **2.** occupare in precedenza.
preparation *s.* preparazione, preparativo.
preparative, preparatory *agg.* preparatorio.
to **prepare** *vt.* preparare. ♦ to **prepare** *vi.* prepararsi.
preponderance *s.* preponderanza.
preponderant *agg.* preponderante.
preposition *s.* preposizione.
prepositional *agg.* di preposizione.
to **prepossess** *vt.* **1.** occupare in precedenza **2.** influenzare.
prepossessing *agg.* attraente.
prepossession *s.* prevenzione.
preposterous *agg.* assurdo.
prepotence *s.* predominio.
prepotent *agg.* predominante.
Pre-Raphaeli(ti)sm *s.* preraffaellismo.
prerogative *agg.* privilegiato. ♦ **prerogative** *s.* prerogativa.
presage *s.* presagio.
presbyope *s.* presbite.
presbyopic *agg.* presbite.
Presbyterian *agg.* e *s.* presbiteriano.
Presbyterianism *s.* presbiterianismo.
presbytery *s.* presbiterio.
prescience *s.* prescienza.
to **prescribe** *vt.* prescrivere.
prescript *s.* ordinanza.
prescription *s.* prescrizione.
presence *s.* presenza.
present[1] *agg.* presente || — *-day,* contemporaneo. ♦ **present** *s.* presente, tempo presente || *at* —, attualmente. ♦ **presents** *s. pl.* (*giur.*) documento (*sing.*).
present[2] *s.* dono, regalo.
to **present** *vt.* **1.** presentare **2.** regalare.
presentable *agg.* presentabile.
presentation *s.* **1.** presentazione **2.** dono.
presenter *s.* **1.** presentatore **2.** donatore.
presentiment *s.* presentimento.
presently *avv.* presto, quanto prima.
presentment *s.* presentazione.
preservable *agg.* conservabile.
preservation *s.* conservazione.
preservative *agg.* e *s.* preservativo.
preserve *s.* **1.** riserva **2.** conserva (*di pomodoro, frutta ecc.*).
to **preserve** *vt.* **1.** preservare **2.** conservare **3.** mettere in conserva.

to **preside** *vi.* presiedere.
presidency *s.* presidenza.
president *s.* presidente.
presidential *agg.* presidenziale.
press *s.* **1.** stretta, pressione **2.** pressa **3.** (*fig.*) stampa **4.** calca, ressa || — *conference,* conferenza stampa.
to **press** *vt.* **1.** premere, comprimere **2.** costringere. ♦ to **press** *vi.* affollarsi.
pressing *agg.* **1.** urgente **2.** insistente.
pressman *s.* **1.** cronista (*di giornale*) **2.** (*tip.*) stampatore.
pressure *s.* pressione || — *-cooker,* pentola a pressione.
to **pressurize** *vt.* pressurizzare.
prestige *s.* prestigio.
presumable *agg.* presumibile.
to **presume** *vt.* e *vi.* **1.** presumere **2.** avere la presunzione di.
presuming *agg.* presuntuoso.
presumption *s.* **1.** presunzione **2.** supposizione.
presumptive *agg.* presunto.
presumptuous *agg.* presuntuoso.
presumptuousness *s.* presunzione.
to **presuppose** *vt.* presupporre.
presupposition *s.* presupposizione.
pretence *s.* **1.** pretesa **2.** pretesto **3.** simulazione.
to **pretend** *vi.* **1.** pretendere **2.** fingere.
pretender *s.* **1.** pretendente **2.** simulatore.
pretension *s.* **1.** pretesa **2.** presunzione.
pretentious *agg.* pretenzioso.
preternatural *agg.* soprannaturale.
pretext *s.* pretesto.
prettiness *s.* grazia.
pretty *agg.* grazioso. ♦ **pretty** *avv.* abbastanza.
to **prevail** *vi.* prevalere.
prevailing *agg.* **1.** prevalente **2.** efficace.
prevalence *s.* prevalenza.
to **prevaricate** *vi.* **1.** tergiversare **2.** mentire.
prevarication *s.* **1.** tergiversazione **2.** menzogna.
prevaricator *s.* **1.** chi tergiversa **2.** mentitore.
to **prevent** *vt.* impedire.
prevention *s.* **1.** impedimento **2.** prevenzione.
preventive *agg.* preventivo.

preview s. anteprima.
previous agg. precedente.
prevision s. previsione.
pre-war agg. prebellico.
prey s. preda.
to **prey** vi. 1. (de)predare 2. (fig.) consumare.
price s. prezzo, costo.
to **price** vt. fissare il prezzo di.
priceless agg. inestimabile.
prick s. 1. punta 2. puntura 3. (fig.) pungolo, rimorso.
to **prick** vt. 1. pungere 2. segnare 3. rizzare le orecchie. ♦ to **prick** vi. 1. formicolare 2. pungersi.
prickle s. 1. spina 2. pungiglione.
prickly agg. pungente.
pride s. orgoglio.
to **pride** vt. to — oneself upon, essere orgoglioso di.
priest s. prete.
priesthood s. 1. clero 2. sacerdozio.
prig s. presuntuoso.
prim agg. affettato.
primary agg. primo, primario.
primate s. (eccl.) primate.
prime agg. 1. primo 2. di prima qualità. ♦ **prime** s. 1. principio 2. (fig.) fiore.
to **prime** vt. caricare, innescare.
primer[1] s. sillabario.
primer[2] s. innesco.
primeval agg. primordiale.
primigenial agg. primigenio.
priming s. 1. innesco 2. prima mano (di vernice ecc.).
primitive agg. e s. primitivo.
primitiveness s. primitività.
primogeniture s. primogenitura.
primordial agg. primordiale.
primrose s. primula.
prince s. principe.
princely agg. principesco.
princess s. principessa.
principal agg. principale. ♦ **principal** s. 1. principale, direttore 2. (edil.) trave maestra 3. (comm.) mandante.
principality s. principato.
principle s. principio.
print s. 1. impronta 2. stampa 3. stampatello 4. (foto) copia.
to **print** vt. 1. stampare 2. scrivere a stampatello 3. imprimere.
printer s. 1. tipografo 2. (mecc.) stampatrice.
printing s. 1. stampa 2. tiratura || — -press, pressa tipografica.
prior agg. precedente. ♦ **prior** s.

priore. ♦ **prior** avv. prima.
priorate s. priorato.
prioress s. priora.
priority s. priorità.
prism s. prisma.
prismatic(al) agg. prismatico.
prison s. prigione.
prisoner s. prigioniero.
privacy s. 1. intimità 2. riserbo.
private agg. 1. privato 2. appartato 3. segreto, riservato, personale. ♦ **private** s. soldato semplice.
privation s. privazione.
privative agg. privativo.
privilege s. privilegio.
to **privilege** vt. privilegiare.
privy agg. 1. nascosto 2. al corrente di.*
prize s. premio.
to **prize** vt. stimare.
probabilism s. probabilismo.
probability s. probabilità.
probable agg. probabile.
probate s. omologazione.
probation s. prova.
probative agg. probativo.
probatory agg. probatorio.
probe s. sonda.
to **probe** vt. sondare.
probity s. probità.
problem s. problema.
problematic(al) agg. problematico.
procedural agg. procedurale.
procedure s. 1. procedimento 2. procedura.
to **proceed** vi. 1. procedere 2. provenire.
proceeding s. V. procedure.
proceeds s. pl. profitto (sing.).
process s. 1. procedimento 2. processo.
to **process** vt. 1. processare 2. (chim.) trattare.
procession s. processione.
processionary s. (zool.) processionaria.
proclaim s. proclama.
to **proclaim** vt. proclamare.
proclamation s. proclama(zione).
proconsul s. proconsole.
to **procrastinate** vt. e vi. procrastinare.
procrastination s. procrastinazione.
to **procreate** vt. procreare.
procreation s. procreazione.
procreator s. procreatore.
proctor s. 1. censore 2. (giur.) procuratore.

procurator *s.* procuratore.
to **procure** *vt.* 1. procurare, procurarsi 2. adescare.
procurer *s.* mezzano.
prod *s.* pungolo.
to **prod** *vt.* pungolare.
prodigal *agg.* e *s.* prodigo.
prodigality *s.* prodigalità.
prodigious *agg.* 1. prodigioso 2. enorme.
prodigiousness *s.* prodigiosità.
prodigy *s.* prodigio.
produce *s.* prodotto || *farm* ––, prodotto agricolo; *raw* —, materia prima.
to **produce** *vt.* 1. produrre 2. presentare.
producer *s.* 1. produttore 2. (*teat.*) regista.
product *s.* prodotto.
production *s.* 1. esibizione 2. produzione.
productive *agg.* produttivo.
productivity *s.* produttività.
proem *s.* proemio.
profanation *s.* profanazione.
profane *agg.* 1. profano 2. empio.
to **profane** *vt.* profanare.
profaner *s.* profanatore.
profanity *s.* 1. profanità 2. empietà.
to **profess** *vt.* 1. professare 2. pretendere.
profession *s.* professione.
professional *agg.* professionale || — *man*, professionista. ♦ **professional** *s.* professionista.
professionalism *s.* professionismo.
professor *s.* professore (*d'università*).
professorial *agg.* professorale.
proficiency *s.* competenza || — *in English*, buona conoscenza dell'inglese.
proficient *agg.* e *s.* esperto, competente.
profile *s.* profilo.
to **profile** *vt.* 1. profilare 2. tracciare il profilo di.
profit *s.* profitto, guadagno.
to **profit** *vt.* giovare. ♦ to **profit** *vi.* approfittare.
profitable *agg.* vantaggioso.
profiteer *s.* profittatore.
profligacy *s.* 1. sregolatezza 2. sperpero.
profligate *agg.* e *s.* 1. dissoluto 2. scialacquatore.
profound *agg.* profondo.

profuse *agg.* 1. abbondante 2. prodigo.
profusion *s.* 1. profusione 2. prodigalità.
progenitor *s.* progenitore.
progeny *s.* progenie.
prognathism *s.* prognatismo.
prognathous *agg.* prognato.
prognosis *s.* (*pl.* -ses) prognosi.
prognostic *agg.* rivelatore. ♦ **prognostic** *s.* 1. pronostico 2. sintomo.
prognostication *s.* 1. pronostico 2. prognosi.
program(me) *s.* programma.
to **program(me)** *vt.* programmare.
programming *s.* programmazione.
programmist *s.* programmista.
progress *s.* 1. progresso 2. avanzata 3. sviluppo 4. andamento, corso.
to **progress** *vi.* 1. progredire 2. avanzare 3. svilupparsi.
progression *s.* 1. progressione 2. avanzamento.
progressive *agg.* progressivo, progressista. ♦ **progressive** *s.* progressista.
to **prohibit** *vt.* proibire.
prohibition *s.* 1. proibizione 2. proibizionismo.
prohibitionist *s.* proibizionista.
prohibitive *agg.* proibitivo.
project *s.* progetto.
to **project** *vt.* 1. progettare 2. proiettare. ♦ to **project** *vi.* sporgere.
projectile *s.* proiettile.
projection *s.* 1. progetto 2. proiezione.
projector *s.* 1. progettista 2. proiettore.
proletarian *agg.* e *s.* proletario.
proletariat *s.* proletariato.
to **proliferate** *vt.* proliferare. ♦ to **proliferate** *vi.* moltiplicarsi.
proliferation *s.* proliferazione.
prolific *agg.* prolifico.
prolix *agg.* prolisso.
prolixity *s.* prolissità.
prologue *s.* prologo.
to **prolong** *vt.* 1. prolungare 2. (*comm.*) prorogare.
promenade *s.* passeggiata, passeggio pubblico, lungomare.
prominence *s.* prominenza.
prominent *agg.* prominente.
promiscuity *s.* promiscuità.
promiscuous *agg.* promiscuo.
promise *s.* promessa.
to **promise** *vt.* e *vi.* promettere.

promissory *agg.* contenente una promessa || — *note* (*comm.*), pagherò cambiario.

promontory *s.* promontorio.

to **promote** *vt.* 1. promuovere 2. dare impulso, favorire.

promoter *s.* promotore.

promotion *s.* 1. promozione 2. incoraggiamento.

prompt *agg.* 1. sollecito 2. (*comm.*) in contanti. ♦ **prompt** *s.* 1. (*comm.*) termine di pagamento 2. suggerimento.

to **prompt** *vt.* 1. spingere 2. suggerire.

prompter *s.* suggeritore.

promptness *s.* prontezza.

to **promulgate** *vt.* promulgare.

promulgation *s.* promulgazione.

promulgator *s.* promulgatore.

prone *agg.* prono.

prong *s.* 1. dente (*di forca*) 2. forca.

pronominal *agg.* pronominale.

pronoun *s.* pronome.

to **pronounce** *vt.* 1. pronunciare 2. dichiarare. ♦ to **pronounce** *vi.* pronunciarsi.

pronouncement *s.* dichiarazione.

pronouncing, pronunciation *s.* pronuncia.

proof *agg.* a prova di. ♦ **proof** *s.* 1. prova 2. bozza 3. gradazione alcoolica || — *-reader*, correttore di bozze; *burden of* — (*giur.*), onere della prova.

prop *s.* puntello.

to **prop** *vt.* 1. sostenere 2. appoggiare.

propaedeutic(al) *agg.* propedeutico.

propaedeutics *s.* propedeutica.

propagandist *s.* propagandista.

to **propagandize** *vt.* propagandare.

to **propagate** *vi.* propagare. ♦ to **propagate** *vi.* propagarsi.

propagation *s.* 1. propagazione 2. (*bot.; zool.*) riproduzione.

propagator *s.* propagatore.

propane *s.* propano.

to **propel** *vt.* spingere avanti.

propellent *agg.* e *s.* propulsore, propellente.

propeller *s.* propulsore || (*screw-*) —, elica.

propensity *s.* propensione.

proper *agg.* 1. proprio 2. adatto 3. corretto 4. propriamente detto.

property *s.* 1. proprietà 2. (*teat.*) costumi, arredi per la scena (*pl.*) ||

real —, beni immobili (*pl.*).

prophecy *s.* profezia.

to **prophesy** *vt.* e *vi.* profetizzare.

prophet *s.* profeta.

prophetic(al) *agg.* profetico.

prophylactic *agg.* e *s.* profilattico.

prophylaxis *s.* profilassi.

to **propitiate** *vt.* propiziare.

propitiation *s.* propiziazione.

propitiator *s.* propiziatore.

propitiatory *agg.* propiziatorio.

propitious *agg.* propizio.

proportion *s.* 1. proporzione 2. parte. ♦ **proportions** *s. pl.* dimensioni.

to **proportion** *vt.* 1. proporzionare 2. dividere in parti proporzionate.

proportional *agg.* proporzionale.

proportionality *s.* proporzionalità.

proportionate *agg.* proporzionato.

to **proportionate** V. to *proportion*.

proportioning *s.* proporzionamento.

proposal *s.* proposta.

to **propose** *vt.* proporre. ♦ to **propose** *vi.* 1. prefiggersi, intendere 2. fare richiesta di matrimonio || *to* — *the health of so.*, bere alla salute di qu.

proposition *s.* 1. proposta 2. proposizione 3. asserzione 4. problema.

proprietary *agg.* di proprietà. ♦ **proprietary** *s.* proprietario || — *rights*, diritti di proprietà.

proprietor *s.* proprietario.

propriety *s.* 1. proprietà 2. opportunità 3. decoro, decenza. ♦ **proprieties** *s. pl.* convenienze.

propulsion *s.* propulsione.

propulsive *agg.* propulsivo.

propylaeum *s.* (*pl.* -laea) propileo.

propylene *s.* propilene.

prosaic *agg.* prosaico.

prosaism *s.* prosaicità.

proscenium *s.* (*pl.* -nia) proscenio.

to **proscribe** *vt.* 1. bandire 2. vietare.

proscription *s.* 1. proscrizione 2. proibizione.

prose *s.* 1. prosa 2. prosaicità || — *writer*, prosatore.

prosecutable *agg.* perseguibile.

to **prosecute** *vt.* 1. proseguire 2. perseguire.

prosecution *s.* 1. proseguimento 2. processo 3. (*giur.*) accusa.

prosecutor *s.* 1. prosecutore 2. accusatore || *Public* — (*giur.*), l'accusa pubblica.

proselyte *s.* proselito.
proselytism *s.* proselitismo.
prosiness *s.* **1.** prosaicità **2.** banalità.
prosody *s.* prosodia.
prospect *s.* **1.** panorama **2.** prospettiva **3.** speranza, aspettativa.
to **prospect** *vt.* **1.** esplorare **2.** ricercare.
prospecting *s.* ricerca.
prospective *agg.* **1.** futuro **2.** eventuale.
to **prosper** *vt.* far prosperare. ♦ to **prosper** *vi.* prosperare.
prosperity *s.* prosperità.
prosperous *agg.* prospero.
prostate *s.* prostata.
prostatic *agg.* prostatico.
prosthesis *s.* (*med.*) protesi.
prostitute *s.* prostituta.
to **prostitute** *vt.* prostituire.
prostitution *s.* prostituzione.
prostrate *agg.* prostrato.
to **prostrate** *vt.* prostrare.
prostration *s.* **1.** prostrazione **2.** prosternazione.
prostyle *agg.* e *s.* prostilo.
prosy *agg.* **1.** prosaico **2.** noioso.
protagonist *s.* protagonista.
to **protect** *vt.* proteggere.
protection *s.* **1.** protezione **2.** salvacondotto.
protectionism *s.* protezionismo.
protectionist *s.* protezionista.
protective *agg.* protettivo.
protector *s.* protettore.
protectorate *s.* protettorato.
protectory *s.* patronato.
protein *s.* proteina.
protest *s.* **1.** protesta **2.** (*comm.*) protesto.
to **protest** *vt.* e *vi.* protestare.
protestant *agg.* e *s.* protestante.
Protestantism *s.* protestantesimo.
protestation *s.* dichiarazione.
protocol *s.* protocollo.
proton *s.* protone.
protoplasm *s.* protoplasma.
prototype *s.* prototipo.
Protozoa *s. pl.* protozoi.
to **protract** *vt.* **1.** protrarre **2.** rilevare.
protraction *s.* **1.** protrazione **2.** rilievo.
protractor *s.* **1.** protrattore **2.** goniometro.
to **protrude** *vt.* **1.** sporgere **2.** imporre. ♦ to **protrude** *vi.* **1.** sporgersi **2.** imporsi.

protrusion, protuberance *s.* protuberanza.
proud *agg.* orgoglioso, superbo.
to **prove** *vt.* **1.** provare, verificare **2.** omologare. ♦ to **prove** *vi.* risultare.
provender *s.* foraggio, biada.
proverb *s.* proverbio.
proverbial *agg.* proverbiale.
to **provide** *vi.* **1.** provvedere **2.** premunirsi **3.** stabilire (*di leggi*). ♦ to **provide** *vt.* **1.** procurare **2.** rifornire.
provided *cong.* purché, a patto che.
providence *s.* **1.** provvidenza **2.** previdenza.
provident *agg.* **1.** provvido **2.** previdente.
providential *agg.* provvidenziale.
province *s.* **1.** provincia **2.** (*fig.*) sfera, campo d'attività.
provincial *agg.* e *s.* provinciale.
provincialism *s.* provincialismo.
provision *s.* **1.** preparativo **2.** provvedimento **3.** clausola **4.** (*giur.*) disposizione. ♦ **provisions** *s. pl.* provviste.
to **provision** *vt.* approvvigionare.
provisional *agg.* provvisorio.
provisioning *s.* approvvigionamento.
provocation *s.* provocazione.
provocative *agg.* **1.** provocante **2.** stimolante.
provocativeness *s.* provocazione.
to **provoke** *vt.* **1.** provocare **2.** irritare.
provoker *s.* provocatore.
provost *s.* prevosto.
prow *s.* prora.
prowess *s.* prodezza, valore.
proximity *s.* prossimità.
proxy *s.* **1.** procura **2.** procuratore.
prude *s.* persona eccessivamente pudica.
prudence *s.* prudenza.
prudent *agg.* prudente.
prudential *agg.* prudénziale.
prudentials *s. pl.* provvedimenti precauzionali.
prudery *s.* ritrosia eccessiva.
prudish *agg.* pudibondo.
prune *s.* prugna secca.
to **prune** *vt.* potare.
pruner *s.* potatore.
pruning *s.* potatura || — *-book*, falcetto.
prussic *agg.* prussico.
pry[1] *s.* ficcanaso.

pry[2] s. leva.
to pry[1] vi. indagare.
to pry[2] vt. muovere con una leva.
psalm s. salmo.
psalmody s. salmodia.
pseudonym s. pseudonimo.
psyche s. psiche.
psychiatric(al) agg. psichiatrico.
psychiatrist s. psichiatra.
psychiatry s. psichiatria.
psychic s. 1. medium 2. psicologia.
psychic(al) agg. psichico.
psychoanalysis s. psicanalisi.
psychoanalyst s. psicanalista.
psychoanalytic(al) agg. psicana-
   litico.
to psychoanalyze vt. psicanalizzare.
psychologic(al) agg. psicologico.
psychologist s. psicologo.
psychology s. psicologia.
psychometry s. psicometria.
psychopathic agg. e s. psicopatico.
psychopathology s. psicopatologia.
psychopathy s. psicopatia.
psychosis s. psicosi.
psychotherapy s. psicoterapia.
ptisan s. tisana.
pub s. bar (in Gran Bretagna).
puberty s. pubertà.
pubis s. (pl. -bes) pube.
public agg. e s. pubblico || the read-
   ing —, i lettori (pl.).
publican s. 1. oste 2. (stor.) pubblicano.
publication s. pubblicazione.
publicity s. pubblicità.
to publish vt. 1. pubblicare 2. divulgare.
publishable agg. pubblicabile.
publisher s. editore.
pucker s. ruga, grinza.
to pucker vt. raggrinzare, corrugare. ♦ to pucker vi. raggrinzarsi,
   corrugarsi.
pudding s. 1. budino 2. pasticcio
   || black —, sanguinaccio.
puddle s. 1. pozzanghera 2. malta.
to puddle vt. 1. infangare 2. coprire
   di malta.
puerility s. puerilità.
Puerto Rican agg. e s. portoricano.
puff s. 1. soffio, sbuffo 2. piumino.
to puff vi. 1. sbuffare 2. gonfiarsi.
   ♦ to puff vt. 1. soffiare 2. gonfiare.
puffy agg. 1. gonfio 2. ansimante 3.
   paffuto, grasso.
pugilist s. pugile.

pugnacious agg. pugnace.
pugnacity s. combattività.
puke s. vomito.
to puke vt. e vi. vomitare.
pull s. 1. strappo 2. sforzo, tensione
   3. maniglia (di cassetto).
to pull vt. 1. tirare 2. strappare ||
   to — down, demolire. ♦ to pull
   vi. 1. trascinarsi 2. remare || to —
   back, ritirarsi; to — up, fermarsi.
puller s. (mecc.) estrattore.
pulley s. puleggia.
pulmonary agg. polmonare.
pulp s. polpa.
to pulp vt. ridurre in polpa. ♦ to
   pulp vi. diventare polposo.
pulpit s. pulpito.
pulpy agg. polposo.
pulsation s. pulsazione.
pulsatory agg. pulsante.
pulse s. 1. pulsazione, polso, battito
   2. (radio) impulso.
to pulse vi. pulsare.
to pulverize vt. polverizzare. ♦ to
   pulverize vi. polverizzarsi.
pumice s. pomice.
pump s. pompa || petrol —, distri-
   butore di benzina.
to pump vt. e vi. pompare || to —
   up, gonfiare.
pumpkin s. zucca.
pun s. gioco di parole.
punch[1] s. punzone.
punch[2] s. pugno.
punch[3] s. « punch » (bevanda alcoolica).
to punch[1] vt. (per)forare.
to punch[2] vt. prendere a pugni.
punching s. perforazione.
punctilio s. meticolosità.
punctilious agg. meticoloso.
punctual agg. puntuale.
punctuality s. puntualità.
punctually avv. puntualmente.
to punctuate vt. 1. punteggiare 2.
   (fig.) sottolineare.
punctuation s. punteggiatura.
puncture s. 1. puntura 2. foratura.
to puncture vt. 1. pungere 2. forare.
pungency s. 1. asprezza 2. acutezza (di dolore).
pungent agg. 1. pungente 2. acuto,
   cocente 3. piccante.
to punish vt. punire.
punishable agg. punibile.
punishment s. punizione.
punitive, punitory agg. punitivo.
punt s. chiatta.

punter s. puntatore (di corse ecc.).
puny agg. sparuto.
pup s. cucciolo.
pupil[1] s. 1. allievo 2. (giur.) pupillo.
pupil[2] s. pupilla.
pupil(l)age s. (giur.) minorità: child in —, bambino sotto tutela.
pupil(l)ary agg. (giur.) pupillare.
puppet s. burattino || — show, spettacolo di burattini; — player, burattinaio.
puppy s. cucciolo.
purchase s. acquisto.
to **purchase** vt. acquistare.
purchaser s. acquirente.
purchasing s. acquisto || — power, potere di acquisto.
pure agg. puro, schietto, casto.
purely avv. puramente, semplicemente.
purgative agg. purgativo. ♦ **purgative** s. purgante.
purgatory s. purgatorio.
purge s. 1. purga 2. epurazione.
to **purge** vt. 1. purgare 2. epurare. ♦ to **purge** vi. purgarsi.
purification s. purificazione.
purificatory agg. purificatore.
to **purify** vt. purificare.
purism s. purismo.
purist s. purista.
Puritan agg. e s. puritano.
Puritanism s. puritanismo.
purity s. purezza.
to **purloin** vt. rubare.
purloiner s. frodatore.
purple agg. 1. purpureo, paonazzo 2. ornato. ♦ **purple** s. porpora.
to **purple** vt. imporporare. ♦ to **purple** vi. imporporarsi.
purport s. significato.
to **purport** vt. 1. significare 2. pretendere.
purpose s. 1. intenzione, scopo 2. fermezza || on —, di proposito.
to **purpose** vi. proporsi (di).
purposeful agg. 1. premeditato 2. avveduto.
purposefully avv. intenzionalmente, espressamente.
purposeless agg. 1. inutile 2. senza intenzione.
purpurin s. porporina.
to **purr** vi. fare le fusa.
purse s. borsellino.
to **purse** vt. contrarre. ♦ to **purse** vi. incresparsi, contrarsi.
purser s. commissario di bordo.
pursuant agg. conforme.

to **pursue** vt. 1. (in)seguire 2. continuare.
pursuer s. 1. inseguitore 2. continuatore.
pursuit s. 1. inseguimento 2. occupazione, impiego.
purulence s. suppurazione.
purulent agg. purulento.
push s. 1. spinta, influenza, pressione 2. bisogno 3. (elettr.) pulsante.
to **push** vt. 1. spingere, incalzare, fare pressione 2. lanciare (una moda, un articolo ecc.) ♦ to **push** vi. spingersi.
pusher s. chi, ciò che spinge.
pusillanimity s. pusillanimità.
pusillanimous agg. pusillanime.
puss(y) s. micino.
pustule s. pustola.
to **put (put, put)** vt. 1. mettere, porre 2. esporre, sottoporre || to — off, rimandare, togliere (vestiti ecc.); to — on, indossare, accendere; to — through, mettere in comunicazione telefonica; to — up, alzare. ♦ to **put (put, put)** vi. dirigersi.
putative agg. putativo.
putrefaction s. putrefazione.
to **putrefy** vt. putrefare. ♦ to **putrefy** vi. putrefarsi.
putrescence s. putrescenza.
putrescible agg. putrescibile.
putrid agg. putrido.
putridness s. putridità.
puttees s. pl. mollettiere.
putty s. mastice, stucco.
puzzle s. 1. enigma 2. imbarazzo 3. intrigo.
to **puzzle** vt. imbarazzare. ♦ to **puzzle** vi. essere imbarazzato.
pygmy agg. e s. pigmeo.
pyjamas s. pl. pigiama (sing.).
pylon s. pilone || steel —, traliccio.
pylorus s. piloro.
pyorrh(o)ea s. piorrea.
pyramid s. piramide.
pyramidal agg. piramidale.
pyre s. pira.
pyrites s. pirite.
pyrography s. pirografia.
pyromancy s. piromanzia.
pyromaniac s. piromane.
pyrope s. piropo.
pyrotechnic(al) agg. pirotecnico.
pyrotechnics s. pirotecnica.
Pythagorean agg. e s. pitagorico.
python s. pitone.
pyx s. pisside.

Q

quack[1] s. ciarlatano.
quack[2] s. schiamazzare (di anitra).
to quack[1] vi. fare il ciarlatano.
to quack[2] vi. schiamazzare (di anitra).
quadrangle s. quadrangolo.
quadrangular agg. quadrangolare.
quadrant s. quadrante.
quadrennial agg. quadriennale.
quadrilateral agg. e s. quadrilatero.
quadrille s. quadriglia.
quadrumane s. quadrumane.
quadrumanous agg. quadrumane.
quadruped agg. e s. quadrupede.
quadruple agg. e s. quadruplo.
to quadruple vt. quadruplicare. ♦
to quadruple vi. quadruplicarsi.
quagmire s. pantano.
quail s. quaglia.
to quail vi. avvilirsi, sgomentarsi.
quaint agg. strano, bizzarro.
quake s. scossa, tremito.
to quake vi. 1. avere i brividi 2. tremare (anche di terra).
Quaker s. Quacchero.
quaky agg. tremante.
qualifiable agg. qualificabile.
qualification s. 1. qualificazione, capacità, requisito 2. condizione, riserva 3. qualifica.
qualified agg. 1. qualificato, competente 2. limitato || — acceptance (comm.), accettazione con riserva.
qualifier s. (gramm.) parola che modifica.
to qualify vt. 1. qualificare, definire 2. abilitare 3. (giur.) autorizzare.
♦ to qualify vi. 1. qualificarsi 2. abilitarsi.
qualitative agg. qualitativo.
quality s. qualità, caratteristica.
qualm s. 1. nausea 2. scrupolo.
qualmish agg. 1. soggetto a nausee 2. nauseante 3. scrupoloso.
quantitative agg. quantitativo.
quantity s. quantità.
quarantine s. quarantena.
quarrel s. lite, contesa.
to quarrel vi. litigare, venire a contesa.
quarreller s. attaccabrighe, contendente.
quarrelsome agg. attaccabrighe, rissoso.
quarry[1] s. 1. cava 2. (fig.) fonte d'informazione.

quarry[2] s. selvaggina, preda.
to quarry vt. 1. cavare (pietre, marmo ecc.) 2. ricavare informazioni da.
quarter s. 1. quarto: a — of an hour, un quarto d'ora 2. quartiere, rione. ♦ quarters s. pl. 1. alloggio 2. (mil.) acquartieramento.
to quarter vt. e vi. 1. dividere in quattro parti 2. alloggiare 3. (mil.) acquartierarsi.
quarterly agg. trimestrale. ♦ quarterly s. pubblicazione trimestrale.
♦ quarterly avv. trimestralmente.
quartermaster s. 1. commissario 2. quartiermastro.
quartet s. quartetto.
quartz s. quarzo.
to quash vt. (giur.) annullare.
quaternary agg. quaternario.
quatrain s. quartina.
quaver s. trillo, vibrazione.
to quaver vt. e vi. 1. vibrare, tremare (di voce) 2. gorgheggiare.
quay s. banchina, molo.
queasy agg. 1. nauseabondo 2. schizzinoso.
queen s. regina.
queenlike agg. regale.
queenly agg. regale, da regina.
queer agg. strano, eccentrico.
to queer vt. mettere in ridicolo.
queerly avv. stranamente.
to quench vt. 1. spegnere, estinguere 2. calmare.
quencher s. estintore.
quenchless agg. inestinguibile.
querulous agg. querulo, gemebondo.
query s. domanda, quesito.
to query vt. e vi. 1. chiedere, indagare 2. mettere in dubbio.
quest s. ricerca.
to quest vt. e vi. cercare, far ricerche.
question s. 1. domanda, interrogazione 2. dubbio, obiezione 3. questione, problema || — mark, punto interrogativo.
to question vt. 1. interrogare 2. mettere in dubbio.
questionable agg. incerto, discutibile.
questionably avv. discutibilmente.
questionary s. questionario.
queue s. 1. coda 2. fila di persone: to stand in a —, fare la coda.
to queue vt. e vi. fare la coda, mettere in coda.

quibble s. giuoco di parole, doppio senso.

to **quibble** vi. 1. fare giuochi di parole 2. cavillare.

quibbling agg. a doppio senso.

quick agg. 1. rapido, veloce 2. pronto, intelligente, acuto || — -eyed, dagli occhi penetranti; — -eared, dall'orecchio fino; — -lime, calce viva; — -sighted, dalla vista acuta; — -tempered, irascibile.

to **quicken** vt. 1. affrettare 2. animare. ♦ to **quicken** vi. 1. affrettarsi 2. animarsi.

quickly avv. rapidamente, prontamente.

quickness s. 1. rapidità 2. vivacità, acutezza.

quicksand s. sabbia mobile.

quickset s. siepe di sempreverdi.

quicksilver s. mercurio, argento vivo (anche fig.).

quickstep s. passo cadenzato.

quickthorn s. biancospino.

quiescence s. quiescenza.

quiescent agg. quiescente.

quiescently avv. tranquillamente.

quiet agg. 1. quieto, tranquillo 2. sobrio, tenue (di colore) 3. docile, dolce.

to **quiet** vt. acquietare. ♦ to **quiet** vi. acquietarsi.

quietism s. quietismo.

quietist s. quietista.

quietly avv. tranquillamente, con calma.

quietness s. quiete, tranquillità.

quill s. 1. penna, penna d'oca 2. piccolo galleggiante (per canna da pesca).

to **quill** vt. pieghettare, increspare.

quilt s. trapunta.

to **quilt** vt. trapuntare.

quince s. cotogna || — jam, marmellata di cotogne.

quinine s. chinino.

quinquennial agg. quinquennale.

quintal s. quintale.

quintessence s. quintessenza.

quintet s. quintetto.

quintuple agg. e s. quintuplo. ♦ to **quintuple** vi. quintuplicarsi.

quisling s. collaborazionista.

to **quit** vt. 1. abbandonare, lasciare 2. quietanzare, saldare.

quite avv. 1. completamente, interamente 2. piuttosto, abbastanza || — young, giovanissimo; to be

— well, stare proprio bene.

quiver s. fremito, brivido.

to **quiver** vt. e vi. 1. tremare, fremere 2. palpitare.

quivering agg. fremente, tremolante. ♦ **quivering** s. tremolio.

quixotic agg. donchisciottesco.

quiz s. (pl. quizzes) burlone.

to **quiz** vt. burlare.

quotation s. 1. citazione 2. (comm.) quotazione.

quote s. (fam.) citazione. ♦ **quotes** s. pl. virgolette.

to **quote** vt. 1. citare 2. (comm.) quotare (in borsa).

quotidian agg. quotidiano.

quotient s. quoziente.

R

rabbi s. rabbino.

rabbit s. coniglio.

rabble s. plebaglia.

to **rabble** vt. assaltare, linciare.

rabid agg. 1. rabbioso 2. irragionevole 3. idrofobo.

rabidity s. 1. rabbia 2. fanatismo.

rabies s. idrofobia.

race[1] s. 1. corso 2. corsa || — -meeting, concorso ippico.

race[2] s. razza.

to **race** vi. 1. correre 2. imballarsi (di motori) 3. prendere parte a una corsa 4. allevare cavalli da corsa.

racecourse s. ippodromo.

racehorse s. cavallo da corsa.

racer s. 1. corridore 2. cavallo da corsa 3. mezzo da corsa.

racial agg. razziale.

racialism s. razzismo.

racialist s. razzista.

racially avv. dal punto di vista razziale.

racily avv. vivacemente.

raciness s. vivacità.

racing s. corsa || — car, automobile da corsa.

racism s. razzismo.

racist s. razzista.

rack[1] s. 1. rastrelliera 2. reticella portabagagli 3. (mecc.) cremagliera || clothes —, attaccapanni.

rack[2] s. ruota, strumento di tortura.

rack[3] s. nembo, nuvolaglia.

rack[4] s. rovina, distruzione.

to **rack**[1] vt. **1.** torturare **2.** pretendere troppo.

to **rack**[2] vi. fuggire (di nubi).

racket[1] s. racchetta.

racket[2] s. **1.** fracasso **2.** baldoria **3.** (gergo) associazione a delinquere.

racy agg. **1.** genuino **2.** vivace, pungente.

radial agg. radiale.

radiance s. radiosità.

radiant agg. **1.** radiante **2.** raggiante.

to **radiate** vt. e vi. irradiare.

radiation s. (ir)radiazione.

radiator s. radiatore.

radical agg. e s. radicale.

radicalism s. radicalismo.

radio s. radio || — -beacon, radiofaro; — -control, radiocomando; — -operator, radiotelegrafista.

radioactive agg. radioattivo.

radioactivity s. radioattività.

radioengineering s. radiotecnica.

radiogoniometer s. radiogoniometro.

radiogram s. **1.** marconigramma **2.** radiogrammofono.

radiograph s. radiografia.

radiography s. radiografia.

radiologist s. radiologo.

radiology s. radiologia.

radioscopy s. radioscopia.

radiostatics s. pl. disturbi atmosferici.

radiotelegraphy s. radiotelegrafia.

radiotelephony s. radiotelefonia.

radiotherapeutics s. radioterapia.

radish s. ravanello.

radium s. radio.

radius s. raggio.

raffia s. rafia.

raft s. zattera || — -bridge, ponte di barche.

rag s. straccio.

ragamuffin s. pezzente.

rage s. **1.** furore **2.** passione.

to **rage** vi. infuriare || the plague raged, la peste infieriva.

ragged agg. **1.** lacero **2.** frastagliato **3.** spettinato **4.** rozzo.

raggedly avv. **1.** a brandelli **2.** in modo non uniforme.

raggedness s. **1.** cenciosità **2.** ineguaglianza.

raging agg. furioso.

raid s. incursione, scorreria.

to **raid** vt. e vi. fare un'incursione.

rail, railing s. **1.** sbarra **2.** ringhiera **3.** rotaia || to go by —, viaggiare per ferrovia.

raillery s. canzonatura.

railroad, railway s. ferrovia || — companies, società ferroviarie.

railwayman s. ferroviere.

rain s. pioggia || it looks like —, vuol piovere; to be drenched with —, essere inzuppato || — -glass, barometro.

to **rain** v. imp. piovere. ♦ to **rain** vt. far piovere.

rainbow s. arcobaleno.

raincoat s. impermeabile.

rainfall s. **1.** piovosità **2.** scroscio di pioggia.

rainproof agg. impermeabile.

rainy agg. piovoso.

raise s. aumento.

to **raise** vt. **1.** alzare **2.** innalzare **3.** allevare **4.** coltivare **5.** (mil.) arruolare.

raisin s. uva passa.

raising s. **1.** innalzamento **2.** aumento **3.** allevamento **4.** coltivazione **5.** educazione.

rake[1] s. rastrello.

rake[2] s. inclinazione.

rake[3] s. libertino.

to **rake**[1] vt. **1.** rastrellare **2.** raschiare || to — up, ammucchiare.

to **rake**[2] vi. essere inclinato.

rally[1] s. riunione, raduno.

rally[2] s. canzonatura.

to **rally**[1] vt. raccogliere. ♦ to **rally** vi. rianimarsi.

to **rally**[2] vt. canzonare.

ram s. **1.** ariete **2.** (mar.) sperone.

to **ram** vt. **1.** (mar.) speronare **2.** conficcare **3.** comprimere.

ramble s. vagabondaggio.

to **ramble** vi. **1.** vagare **2.** divagare.

rambler s. **1.** vagabondo **2.** rampicante.

rambling agg. **1.** errante **2.** sconnesso || — thoughts, divagazioni.

ramification s. ramificazione.

to **ramify** vt. ramificare. ♦ to **ramify** vi. ramificarsi.

rammer s. (mil.) pestello.

ramp[1] s. rampa.

ramp[2] s. (gergo) truffa.

rampage s. contegno iroso.

rampant agg. **1.** rampante **2.** violento **3.** predominante **4.** lussureggiante.

rampart s. bastione.

to **rampart** vt. fortificare.

ramshackle agg. sgangherato, che cade in rovina.

ran V. *to run.*
rancid *agg.* rancido.
rancour *s.* rancore.
rand *s.* soletta (*di scarpa*).
random *agg.* fatto a caso || *at* —, a casaccio.
rang V. *to ring.*
range *s.* 1. fila 2. catena (*di monti*) 3. spazio 4. sfera, raggio 5. gamma 6. fornello 7. (*aer.*) autonomia.
to range *vt.* 1. allineare 2. classificare 3. puntare. ♦ to range *vi.* 1. vagare 2. avere una portata di 3. oscillare (*di prezzi*).
ranger *s.* 1. guardia forestale 2. vagabondo.
rank *agg.* 1. rigoglioso 2. volgare 3. puzzolente. ♦ rank *s.* 1. fila 2. rango, grado 3. truppa.
to rank *vi.* 1. schierarsi 2. essere classificato.
to ransack *vt.* 1. frugare 2. saccheggiare.
ransom *s.* riscatto.
to ransom *vt.* riscattare.
to rant *vt.* e *vi.* declamare.
rap *s.* colpo.
to rap *vt.* e *vi.* 1. battere 2. bussare.
rapacious *agg.* rapace.
rapacity *s.* rapacità.
rape[1] *s.* violenza carnale.
rape[2] *s.* rapa.
to rape *vt.* violentare.
rapid *agg.* rapido. ♦ rapid *s.* rapida.
rapidity *s.* rapidità.
rapt *agg.* rapito.
raptorial *agg.* rapace.
rapture *s.* rapimento.
rare *agg.* 1. raro 2. rarefatto.
rarefaction *s.* rarefazione.
to rarefy *vt.* 1. rarefare 2. raffinare. ♦ to rarefy *vi.* rarefarsi.
rarely *avv.* 1. raramente 2. in modo eccellente.
rareness, rarity *s.* 1. rarità 2. rarefazione.
rascal *s.* furfante.
rascalism, rascality *s.* furfanteria.
rash *agg.* avventato. ♦ rash *s.* eruzione cutanea.
rashness *s.* avventatezza.
rasp *s.* 1. raspa 2. stridore.
to rasp *vt.* 1. raspare 2. irritare.
raspberry *s.* lampone.
rasping *agg.* stridente.
rat *s.* 1. topo 2. (*fig.*) traditore.
rate *s.* 1. tasso, quota 2. tassa 3. prezzo, tariffa 4. ritmo, andamento

|| first —, di prim'ordine; — of discount, tasso di sconto.
to rate[1] *vt.* 1. stimare 2. tassare 3. classificare.
to rate[2] *vt.* redarguire.
rateable *agg.* soggetto ad imposta.
ratepayer *s.* contribuente.
rather *avv.* piuttosto || I had —, preferirei; I would — not, non ci tengo.
ratification *s.* ratifica.
to ratify *vt.* ratificare.
rating[1] *s.* 1. stima 2. tassa 3. classificazione.
rating[2] *s.* sgridata.
ratio *s.* rapporto.
ration *s.* razione.
to ration *vt.* razionare.
rational *agg.* razionale.
rationalism *s.* razionalismo.
rationalist *s.* razionalista.
rationality *s.* razionalità.
to rationalize *vt.* 1. razionalizzare 2. spiegare razionalmente.
rationally *avv.* razionalmente.
rattle *s.* 1. sonaglio 2. rantolo 3. tintinnio.
to rattle *vt.* far risuonare. ♦ to rattle *vi.* 1. risuonare 2. cianciare.
rattling *agg.* 1. vivace 2. tintinnante.
ravage *s.* rovina.
to ravage *vt.* devastare.
rave *s.* delirio.
to rave *vt.* declamare. ♦ to rave *vi.* delirare || to — about sthg., andar pazzo per qc.
ravel *s.* 1. groviglio 2. lembo sfilacciato.
to ravel *vt.* ingarbugliare. ♦ to ravel *vi.* sfilacciarsi.
raven *s.* corvo.
to raven *vt.* e *vi.* saccheggiare.
ravenous *agg.* vorace.
ravine *s.* burrone.
raving *agg.* delirante. ♦ raving *s.* delirio.
to ravish *vt.* 1. rapire 2. violentare.
ravisher *s.* rapitore.
ravishing *agg.* (*fig.*) affascinante.
ravishment *s.* 1. rapimento 2. stupro.
raw *agg.* 1. crudo 2. greggio 3. inesperto 4. a nudo. ♦ raw *s.* punto vivo.
rawness *s.* 1. crudezza 2. rozzezza 3. inesperienza 4. escoriazione.
ray[1] *s.* 1. raggio 2. lampo.

ray[2] s. (zool.) razza.
to **ray** vt. irradiare. ♦ to **ray** vi. irradiarsi.
to **raze** vt. radere al suolo.
razor s. rasoio || — -blade, lametta.
to **reabsorb** vt. riassorbire.
reach s. 1. portata 2. penetrazione || beyond my —, irraggiungibile.
to **reach** vt. 1. raggiungere 2. porgere. ♦ to **reach** vi. estendersi.
to **react** vi. reagire.
reaction s. reazione.
reactionary agg. e s. reazionario.
reactive agg. reattivo.
read agg. colto. ♦ **read** s. lettura.
to **read** (read, read) vt. 1. leggere 2. interpretare 3. segnare || to — over, rileggere; to — through, esaminare.
readable agg. 1. leggibile 2. interessante.
reader s. 1. lettore 2. libro di lettura.
readily avv. prontamente.
readiness s. prontezza.
reading s. 1. lettura 2. interpretazione || — -desk, leggio.
to **readjust** vt. riaggiustare.
readjustment s. riordinamento.
to **readmit** vt. riammettere.
readmittance s. riammissione.
ready agg. pronto || — -made, confezionato; — money, contanti; — -made clothes, abito preconfezionato; — -built, prefabbricato.
to **ready** vt. preparare.
to **reaffirm** vt. riaffermare.
reafforestation s. rimboschimento.
reagent s. reagente.
real agg. e s. reale || — estate, beni immobili (pl.).
realism s. realismo.
realist s. realista.
realistic agg. realistico.
reality s. 1. realtà 2. realismo.
realizable agg. realizzabile.
realization s. 1. realizzazione 2. percezione.
to **realize** vt. 1. accorgersi di 2. realizzare 3. capire.
really avv. realmente.
realm s. reame.
realty s. beni immobili (pl.).
ream s. (tip.) risma.
to **reap** vt. 1. mietere 2. fare il raccolto (anche fig.).
reaper s. mietitore.
reaping s. mietitura.

to **reappear** vi. riapparire.
to **reappoint** vt. rinominare.
rear agg. posteriore. ♦ **rear** s. 1. retroguardia 2. retro.
to **rear** vt. 1. alzare, innalzare 2. allevare 3. coltivare.
to **rearm** vt. riarmare.
rearmament s. riarmo.
to **rearrange** vt. riordinare.
rearrangement s. riordinamento.
reason s. 1. ragione 2. causa, motivo 3. raziocinio.
to **reason** vt. e vi. 1. ragionare 2. persuadere || to — about a subject, discutere di un argomento.
reasonable agg. ragionevole.
reasonableness s. ragionevolezza.
reasonably avv. ragionevolmente.
reasoning s. ragionamento.
to **reassert** vt. riasserire.
reassurance s. rassicurazione.
to **reassure** vt. rassicurare.
to **reawaken** vt. risvegliare. ♦ to **reawaken** vi. risvegliarsi.
rebate s. riduzione, sconto.
rebel agg. e s. ribelle.
to **rebel** vi. ribellarsi.
rebellion s. ribellione.
rebellious agg. ribelle.
to **rebind** (rebound, rebound) vt. rilegare (un libro).
rebirth s. rinascita.
reborn agg. rinato.
rebound[1] V. to rebind.
rebound[2] s. rimbalzo.
to **rebound** vi. rimbalzare.
rebuff s. diniego, mortificazione.
to **rebuild** (rebuilt, rebuilt) vt. ricostruire.
rebuke s. rimprovero.
to **rebuke** vt. rimproverare.
to **rebut** vt. respingere, rifiutare.
recalcitrant agg. recalcitrante.
to **recalcitrate** vi. recalcitrare.
recall s. 1. richiamo 2. revoca.
to **recall** vt. 1. richiamare 2. rievocare, far tornare alla memoria.
to **recant** vt. e vi. ritrattare.
recantation s. ritrattazione.
to **recapitulate** vt. e vi. ricapitolare.
recapitulation s. ricapitolazione.
recapture s. riconquista.
to **recapture** vt. riconquistare.
recast s. nuova forma.
to **recast** (recast, recast) vt. 1. rifondere 2. rimaneggiare.
to **recede** vi. 1. indietreggiare 2. diminuire.

receding *agg.* **1.** rientrante **2.** sfuggente.

receipt *s.* **1.** ricevimento **2.** ricevuta **3.** ricetta.

to receipt *vt.* quietanzare.

to receive *vt.* **1.** ricevere **2.** accettare.

receiver *s.* **1.** ricevitore **2.** (*giur.*) ricettatore.

receiving *s.* ricezione.

recension *s.* revisione.

recent *agg.* recente.

receptacle *s.* ricettacolo.

reception *s.* **1.** ricevimento **2.** ricezione **3.** accoglienza.

receptive *agg.* ricettivo.

receptivity *s.* ricettività.

recess *s.* **1.** intervallo **2.** rientranza **3.** recesso.

recession *s.* **1.** ritiro **2.** recessione.

recessive *agg.* retrocedente.

recharge *s.* ricarica.

to recharge *vt.* ricaricare.

to rechristen *vt.* ribattezzare.

recidivism *s.* recidività.

recipe *s.* ricetta.

recipient *agg.* e *s.* ricevente.

reciprocal *agg.* reciproco. ♦ **reciprocal** *s.* (*mat.*) numero reciproco.

to reciprocate *vt.* **1.** contraccambiare **2.** muovere alternativamente. ♦ **to reciprocate** *vi.* muoversi alternativamente.

reciprocating *agg.* (*mecc.*) alternativo.

reciprocation *s.* **1.** moto alterno **2.** scambio.

reciprocity *s.* reciprocità.

recital *s.* **1.** relazione **2.** recitazione.

recitation *s.* **1.** recitazione **2.** recita **3.** narrazione.

recitative *agg.* e *s.* recitativo.

to recite *vt.* **1.** recitare **2.** riferire.

reckless *agg.* incurante.

recklessness *s.* noncuranza.

to reckon *vt.* **1.** contare, computare **2.** considerare.

reckoner *s.* calcolatore.

reckoning *s.* conto.

reclaim *s.* rivendicazione.

to reclaim *vt.* **1.** redimere **2.** bonificare **3.** rivendicare.

reclamation *s.* **1.** redenzione **2.** bonifica **3.** rivendicazione.

to recline *vt.* chinare. ♦ **to recline** *vi.* chinarsi.

reclining *agg.* chinato.

recluse *agg.* recluso. ♦ **recluse** *s.* eremita.

reclusion *s.* **1.** reclusione **2.** eremo.

recognition *s.* riconoscimento.

recognizable *agg.* riconoscibile.

to recognize *vt.* riconoscere.

recoil *s.* **1.** il ritrarsi **2.** rinculo.

to recoil *vi.* **1.** ritrarsi **2.** ricadere **3.** rinculare.

to recollect *vt.* **1.** raccogliere **2.** ricordare || *to* — *oneself*, riaversi.

recollection *s.* ricordo.

to recommence *vt.* e *vi.* ricominciare.

to recommend *vt.* raccomandare.

recommendation *s.* raccomandazione.

recommendatory *agg.* raccomandatorio.

recompense *s.* **1.** ricompensa **2.** risarcimento.

to recompense *vt.* **1.** ricompensare **2.** risarcire.

to recompose *vt.* ricomporre.

recomposition *s.* ricomposizione.

to reconcile *vt.* (ri)conciliare || *to* — *oneself*, rassegnarsi.

reconcilement *s.* **1.** riconciliazione **2.** rassegnazione.

reconnaissance *s.* ricognizione.

to reconnoitre *vt.* e *vi.* perlustrare.

to reconquer *vt.* riconquistare.

reconquest *s.* riconquista.

to reconsider *vt.* riconsiderare.

reconsideration *s.* revisione.

reconstitute *vt.* ricostituire.

to reconstruct *vt.* ricostruire.

reconstruction *s.* ricostruzione.

reconversion *s.* riconversione.

to reconvert *vt.* riconvertire.

record *s.* **1.** registrazione **2.** documento **3.** passato **4.** disco || — *player*, giradischi.

to record *vt.* registrare.

recorder *s.* **1.** cancelliere **2.** registratore **3.** archivista || *tape* —, magnetofono.

recording *s.* registrazione.

recordist *s.* (*cine*) tecnico del suono.

recourse *s.* ricorso.

to recover *vt.* ricuperare, riacquistare, riscoprire. ♦ **to recover** *vi.* ristabilirsi.

recoverable *agg.* **1.** ricuperabile **2.** guaribile.

recovery *s.* **1.** recupero **2.** guarigione **3.** (*giur.*) rivendicazione.

to recreate *vt.* divertire. ♦ **to recreate** *vi.* divertirsi.

to re-create *vt.* ricreare.

recreation *s.* ricreazione.

recreative agg. ricreativo.
to **recriminate** vi. recriminare.
recrimination s. recriminazione.
recrudescence s. recrudescenza.
recrudescent agg. che rincrudisce.
recruit s. recluta.
to **recruit** vt. **1.** reclutare **2.** rinforzare. ♦ to **recruit** vi. ristabilirsi.
recruitment s. reclutamento.
rectangle s. rettangolo.
rectangular agg. rettangolare.
rectification s. rettificazione.
rectifier s. (mecc.) rettificatrice.
to **rectify** vt. rettificare.
rectilineal agg. rettilineo.
rectitude s. rettitudine.
rector s. **1.** rettore **2.** parroco.
rectorate s. rettorato.
rectorship s. rettorato.
rectory s. **1.** presbiterio **2.** (eccl.) beneficio.
to **recur** vi. ritornare.
recurrence s. ricorso.
recurrent agg. ricorrente.
recusant agg. e s. dissidente.
red agg. e s. rosso || — -hot, rovente; — -lead, minio; — -letter day, giorno festivo. ♦ **Reds** s. pl. comunisti.
to **redact** vt. **1.** redigere **2.** revisionare.
redactor s. redattore.
to **redden** vt. arrossare. ♦ to **redden** vi. arrossire.
reddish agg. rossiccio.
to **redeem** vt. **1.** riscattare **2.** ricuperare **3.** estinguere: to — a mortgage, estinguere un'ipoteca.
redeemable agg. **1.** riscattabile **2.** ricuperabile.
redeemer s. redentore.
redemption s. **1.** redenzione **2.** (comm.) rimborso **3.** (giur.) riscatto.
redness s. rossore.
to **redouble** vt. e vi. raddoppiare.
redress s. riparazione.
to **redress** vt. riparare, rimediare.
redskin agg. e s. pellerossa.
to **reduce** vt. **1.** ridurre **2.** degradare.
reduced agg. ridotto.
reducer s. riduttore.
reduction s. **1.** riduzione **2.** degradazione.
redundance s. sovrabbondanza.
redundant agg. ridondante.
redwood s. sequoia.
to **re-echo** vt. e vi. riecheggiare.
reed s. canna || broken —, perso-

na infida; — -pipe, zampogna.
re-edification s. riedificazione.
to **re-edify** vt. riedificare.
to **re-educate** vt. rieducare.
reef s. secca || coral- —, banco di coralli.
to **reek** vi. puzzare. ♦ to **reek** vt. trasudare.
reel s. **1.** bobina **2.** giro vorticoso || news- —, cinegiornale.
to **reel** vt. avvolgere || to — off, snocciolare. ♦ to **reel** vi. girare.
to **re-elect** vt. rieleggere.
to **re-emerge** vi. riemergere.
to **re-enact** vt. richiamare in vigore (una legge).
to **re-enter** vt. rientrare.
re-entrance s. rientro.
re-entry s. **1.** rientro **2.** nuova registrazione.
to **re-establish** vt. ristabilire.
re-establishment s. ristabilimento.
re-examination s. riesame.
to **re-examine** vt. riesaminare.
refectory s. refettorio.
to **refer** vt. **1.** attribuire **2.** rimandare. ♦ to **refer** vi. **1.** riferirsi **2.** rivolgersi.
referable agg. riferibile.
referee s. arbitro.
to **referee** vt. e vi. arbitrare.
reference s. **1.** riferimento **2.** consultazione **3.** referenza **4.** (giur.) rinvio.
referential agg. riferentesi a.
refill s. ricambio.
to **refill** vt. riempire di nuovo.
to **refine** vt. raffinare. ♦ to **refine** vi. raffinarsi.
refined agg. **1.** raffinato **2.** colto.
refinement s. **1.** raffinamento **2.** raffinatezza.
refiner s. raffinatore.
refinery s. raffineria.
refit s. riparazione.
to **refit** vt. riparare.
to **reflect** vt. e vi **1.** riflettere **2.** meditare.
reflection s. **1.** riflessione, riflesso **2.** biasimo || to cast reflections on so., criticare qu.
reflective agg. riflessivo.
reflector s. riflettore.
reflex agg. e s. riflesso.
reflorescence s. rifioritura.
reflux s. riflusso.
reform s. riforma.
to **reform** vt. riformare.
reformation s. riforma.

reformational *agg.* di riforma.
reformatory *agg.* riformativo. ◆
reformatory *s.* riformatorio.
reformer *s.* riformatore.
to **refract** *vt.* rifrangere.
refraction *s.* rifrazione.
refractivity *s.* rifrangibilità.
refractor *s.* rifrattore.
refractory *agg.* **1.** refrattario **2.** ostinato.
refrain *s.* ritornello.
to **refrain** *vi.* trattenersi, astenersi.
to **refresh** *vt.* **1.** rinfrescare **2.** rinvigorire. ◆ to **refresh** *vi.* **1.** rinvigorirsi **2.** rifornirsi.
refreshment *s.* ristoro. ◆ **refreshments** *s. pl.* cibo, bevanda (*sing.*).
refrigerant *agg.* e *s.* refrigerante.
to **refrigerate** *vt.* refrigerare.
refrigeration *s.* refrigerazione.
refrigerator *s.* frigorifero.
refrigeratory *agg.* refrigerante.
to **refuel** *vt.* rifornire di carburante. ◆ to **refuel** *vi.* rifornirsi di carburante.
refuge *s.* rifugio.
refugee *s.* rifugiato, profugo.
refulgence *s.* fulgore.
refulgent *agg.* rifulgente.
refund *s.* rimborso.
to **refund** *vt.* rimborsare.
refusable *agg.* rifiutabile.
refusal *s.* **1.** rifiuto **2.** diritto di opzione.
refuse *s.* rifiuto.
to **refuse** *vt.* rifiutare. ◆ to **refuse** *vi.* rifiutarsi.
refuser *s.* ricusante.
refutal *s.* confutazione.
to **refute** *vt.* confutare.
to **regain** *vt.* riguadagnare.
regal *agg.* regale.
regality *s.* regalità.
regally *avv.* regalmente.
regard *s.* **1.** considerazione **2.** sguardo || *with — to*, riguardo a. ◆
regards *s. pl.* saluti.
to **regard** *vt.* **1.** considerare **2.** riguardare **3.** osservare.
regardful *agg.* **1.** attento **2.** rispettoso.
regardless *agg.* senza riguardo. ◆
regardless *avv.* senza riguardo a, senza badare a.
regatta *s.* regata.
regelation *s.* ricongelamento.
regency *s.* reggenza.
to **regenerate** *vt.* rigenerare. ◆ to
regenerate *vi.* rigenerarsi.

regeneration *s.* rigenerazione.
regenerative *agg.* rigeneratore.
regenerator *s.* rigeneratore.
regent *agg.* e *s.* reggente.
regicide *s.* **1.** regicida **2.** regicidio.
regimen *s.* regime.
regiment *s.* reggimento.
to **regiment** *vt.* **1.** irreggimentare **2.** disciplinare.
regimental *agg.* reggimentale.
regimentals *s. pl.* (*mil.*) uniforme (*sing.*).
region *s.* regione.
regional *agg.* regionale.
register *s.* registro.
to **register** *vt.* registrare, iscrivere. ◆ to **register** *vi.* iscriversi.
registrar *s.* **1.** segretario **2.** ufficiale di stato civile.
registration *s.* registrazione, iscrizione.
registry *s.* **1.** registrazione **2.** ufficio del Registro.
regnant *agg.* regnante.
regress *s.* retrocessione.
to **regress** *vi.* retrocedere.
regression *s.* regresso.
regressive *agg.* regressivo.
regret *s.* rammarico.
to **regret** *vt.* **1.** rimpiangere **2.** rammaricarsi di.
regretful *agg.* pieno di rammarico.
regular *agg.* e *s.* regolare.
regularity *s.* regolarità.
regularization *s.* regolarizzazione.
to **regularize** *vt.* regolarizzare.
regularly *avv.* regolarmente.
to **regulate** *vt.* regolare.
regulation *s.* **1.** regolamento **2.** regolazione.
regulative *agg.* e *s.* regolatore.
regulator *s.* regolatore.
to **rehabilitate** *vt.* **1.** riabilitare **2.** ripristinare.
rehabilitation *s.* **1.** riabilitazione **2.** ripristino.
rehearsal *s.* **1.** ripetizione **2.** (*teat.*) prova.
to **rehearse** *vt.* **1.** ripetere **2.** provare.
reign *s.* regno.
to **reign** *vi.* regnare.
to **reimburse** *vt.* rimborsare.
reimbursement *s.* rimborso.
rein *s.* redine.
to **rein** *vt.* tenere a freno.
to **reincarnate** *vt.* reincarnare.
reincarnation *s.* reincarnazione.
reindeer *s.* renna.

to **reinforce** vt. rinforzare.
reinforce(ment) s. rinforzo.
to **reinstate** vt. ristabilire.
to **reintegrate** vt. reintegrare.
reinvestment s. nuovo investimento.
to **reinvigorate** vt. rinvigorire.
reinvigoration s. rinvigorimento.
to **reiterate** vt. reiterare.
reiteration s. reiterazione.
reject s. persona, cosa rifiutata.
to **reject** vt. rifiutare.
rejection s. rifiuto.
to **rejoice** vt. rallegrare. ♦ to **rejoice** vi. rallegrarsi.
rejoicing s. 1. allegria 2. festa.
rejuvenation s. ringiovanimento.
relapse s. ricaduta.
to **relapse** vi. 1. ricadere 2. avere una ricaduta.
to **relate** vt. 1. narrare 2. mettere in relazione. ♦ to **relate** vi. aver rapporto con.
relater s. narratore.
relation s. 1. relazione 2. parente.
relationship s. 1. relazione 2. parentela.
relative agg. relativo. ♦ **relative** s. parente.
relativism s. relativismo.
relativity s. relatività.
to **relax** vt. 1. rilassare 2. allentare. ♦ to **relax** vi. rilassarsi.
relaxation s. 1. rilassamento 2. svago 3. mitigazione.
relay s. 1. turno 2. ricambio 3. (radio) collegamento.
to **relay** vt. (radio) collegare.
release s. 1. liberazione 2. quietanza 3. cessione 4. scarico.
to **release** vt. 1. liberare 2. cedere.
releasee s. cessionario.
to **relegate** vt. 1. relegare 2. rimettere.
relegation s. relegazione.
relentless agg. inflessibile.
to **relent** vi. impietosirsi.
relevance s. 1. relazione 2. pertinenza.
relevant agg. 1. relativo 2. pertinente.
reliability s. attendibilità.
reliable agg. attendibile, fidato.
reliance s. 1. fede 2. persona, cosa di fiducia.
relic s. reliquia.
relief[1] s. 1. sollievo 2. aiuto 3. esenzione 4. cambio.
relief[2] s. 1. rilievo 2. (pitt.) prospettiva.

to **relieve** vt. 1. alleviare, sollevare 2. aiutare 3. dare il cambio a 4. dare rilievo a.
reliever s. soccorritore.
relieving agg. 1. che allevia, soccorre 2. (mil.) che dà il cambio.
religion s. religione.
religiosity s. religiosità.
religious agg. e s. religioso.
to **relinquish** vt. abbandonare.
relinquishment s. abbandono.
reliquary s. reliquario.
reliques s. pl. resti.
relish s. 1. gusto 2. sapore, profumo, aroma 3. condimento.
to **relish** vt. 1. gustare 2. insaporire.
to **relive** vt. e vi. rivivere.
to **reload** vt. ricaricare.
to **reluct** vi. essere riluttante.
reluctance s. riluttanza.
reluctant agg. riluttante.
reluctantly avv. con riluttanza.
to **rely** vi. fidarsi.
remade V. to remake.
to **remain** vi. rimanere, restare.
remainder s. resto, avanzo, rimanenza.
remains s. pl. resti.
to **remake** (**remade, remade**) vt. rifare.
remark s. nota, osservazione, commento.
to **remark** vt. e vi. osservare.
remarkable agg. notevole.
remarkableness s. ragguardevolezza.
remarkably avv. notevolmente.
to **remarry** vt. risposare. ♦ to **remarry** vi. risposarsi.
remediable agg. rimediabile.
remedy s. rimedio, cura.
to **remedy** vt. rimediare.
to **remember** vt. ricordare. ♦ to **remember** vi. ricordarsi.
remembrance s. ricordo.
to **remind** vt. ricordare (qc. a qu.), far ricordare, rammentare.
reminder s. ricordo, promemoria.
remindful agg. 1. memore 2. che fa ricordare.
reminiscence s. ricordo.
reminiscent agg. che ricorda.
remise s. (giur.) cessione.
to **remise** vt. (giur.) rinunciare a, cedere (diritti ecc.).
remiss agg. negligente.
remissible agg. remissibile.

remission s. **1.** remissione **2.** esonero, annullamento **3.** (*med.*) remissione.

remissive agg. indulgente.

to **remit** vt. rimettere. ♦ to **remit** vi. diminuire, mitigarsi.

remittal s. (*giur.*) remissione (*condono*).

remittance s. rimessa (*di denaro*).

remittent agg. (*med.*) intermittente.

remnant agg. rimanente. ♦ **remnant** s. resto, rimanenza, avanzo.

to **remodel** vt. rimodellare.

remonstrance s. rimostranza.

to **remonstrate** vi. protestare.

remonstration s. rimostranza.

remorse s. rimorso.

remorseful agg. pieno di rimorso.

remorseless agg. senza rimorsi.

remote agg. remoto.

remoteness s. distanza, lontananza.

remotion s. rimozione, allontanamento.

remount s. rimonta (*di cavalli*).

to **remount** vt. e vi. **1.** rimontare (*a cavallo, in bicicletta*) **2.** risalire.

removable agg. rimovibile.

removal s. **1.** rimozione **2.** trasferimento, trasloco.

remove s. **1.** trasferimento **2.** grado (*di parentela*).

to **remove** vt. rimuovere. ♦ to **remove** vi. trasferirsi.

removed agg. lontano.

remover s. chi, ciò che toglie.

to **remunerate** vt. rimunerare.

remuneration s. rimunerazione.

remunerative agg. rimunerativo.

renaissance s. rinascimento.

renal agg. renale.

to **rename** vt. rinominare.

to **rend (rent, rent)** vt. lacerare. ♦ to **rend (rent, rent)** vi. lacerarsi.

to **render** vt. **1.** rendere **2.** consegnare.

rendering s. **1.** restituzione **2.** resa.

renegade s. rinnegato.

to **renew** vt. rinnovare. ♦ to **renew** vi. rinnovarsi.

renewable agg. rinnovabile.

renewal s. **1.** rinnovo **2.** ripresa.

renewer s. rinnovatore.

renitency s. riluttanza.

renitent agg. renitente, riluttante.

rennet s. ranetta.

to **renounce** vt. **1.** rinunciare a **2.** ripudiare.

renouncement s. rinuncia.

to **renovate** vt. rinnovare.

renown s. rinomanza, fama.

renowned agg. rinomato, famoso.

rent[1] s. affitto.

rent[2] s. **1.** strappo, squarcio **2.** spaccatura.

rent[3] V. to *rend*.

to **rent** vt. affittare. ♦ to **rent** vi. essere affittato.

rental s. affitto.

renunciation s. rinuncia.

to **reoccupy** vt. rioccupare.

to **reopen** vt. riaprire. ♦ to **reopen** vi. riaprirsi.

reopening s. riapertura.

reorganization s. riassetto, riorganizzazione.

repaid V. to *repay*.

repair s. **1.** riparazione, restaurazione **2.** stato, condizione.

to **repair** vt. riparare, restaurare.

repairer s. riparatore.

reparation s. riparazione.

repartee s. replica arguta.

repartition s. ripartizione.

to **repatriate** vt. e vi. rimpatriare.

repatriation s. rimpatrio.

to **repay (repaid, repaid)** vt. ripagare.

repayable agg. ripagabile.

repeal s. revoca.

to **repeal** vt. revocare.

repealer s. revocatore.

repeat s. ripetizione.

to **repeat** vt. ripetere. ♦ to **repeat** vi. ripetersi.

repeater s. **1.** ripetitore **2.** ripetente **3.** arma a ripetizione.

repeating agg. **1.** a ripetizione **2.** periodico (*di numero*).

to **repel** vt. respingere.

repellent agg. repellente.

to **repent** vt. e vi. pentirsi.

repentance s. pentimento.

repentant agg. pentito.

repenter s. penitente.

repercussion s. ripercussione.

repercussive agg. ripercussivo.

repertoire s. repertorio.

repertory s. **1.** repertorio **2.** raccolta.

repetition s. ripetizione.

to **repine** vi. lamentarsi.

to **replace** vt. **1.** ricollocare **2.** rimpiazzare, sostituire.

replaceable agg. sostituibile.

replacement s. **1.** ricollocamento **2.** sostituzione.

replete *agg.* pieno.
repletion *s.* pienezza.
replication *s.* replica.
reply *s.* risposta.
to **reply** *vi.* rispondere.
report *s.* 1. diceria 2. reputazione 3. rapporto 4. scoppio.
to **report** *vt.* riportare. ♦ to **report** *vi.* 1. stendere rapporto 2. fare il cronista 3. presentarsi.
reporter *s.* cronista (*di giornale*).
to **repose** *vt.* porre. ♦ to **repose** *vi.* riposare.
to **reprehend** *vt.* rimproverare.
reprehensible *agg.* biasimevole.
reprehension *s.* biasimo.
to **represent** *vt.* rappresentare, raffigurare.
representation *s.* 1. rappresentazione 2. rappresentanza.
representative *agg.* rappresentativo. ♦ **representative** *s.* rappresentante.
to **repress** *vt.* reprimere.
repressed *agg.* represso.
repressible *agg.* reprimibile.
repression *s.* repressione.
repressive *agg.* repressivo.
reprimand *s.* rimprovero.
reprint *s.* ristampa.
to **reprint** *vt.* ristampare.
reprisal *s.* rappresaglia.
reproach *s.* 1. rimprovero 2. discredito.
to **reproach** *vt.* 1. rimproverare 2. discreditare.
reproachable *agg.* riprovevole.
reproachful *agg.* di rimprovero.
reprobate *agg.* corrotto. ♦ **reprobate** *s.* reprobo.
to **reprobate** *vt.* 1. riprovare 2. dannare.
reprobation *s.* 1. riprovazione 2. dannazione.
to **reproduce** *vt.* riprodurre. ♦ to **reproduce** *vi.* riprodursi.
reproducer *s.* riproduttore.
reproducible *agg.* riproducibile.
reproduction *s.* riproduzione.
reproductive *agg.* riproduttivo.
reproof *s.* rimprovero.
to **reprove** *vt.* rimproverare.
reptile *agg.* strisciante. ♦ **reptile** *s.* rettile.
republic *s.* repubblica.
republican *agg. e s.* repubblicano.
republication *s.* ripubblicazione.
to **republish** *vt.* ripubblicare.
to **repudiate** *vt.* ripudiare.

repudiation *s.* ripudio.
repugnance *s.* 1. ripugnanza 2. incompatibilità.
repugnant *agg.* 1. ripugnante 2. incompatibile.
repulse *s.* ripulsa, rifiuto.
to **repulse** *vt.* respingere.
repulsion *s.* repulsione.
repulsive *agg.* ripulsivo.
reputable *agg.* onorato.
reputation *s.* reputazione.
repute *s.* fama.
to **repute** *vt.* reputare.
reputed *agg.* 1. supposto 2. putativo.
request *s.* richiesta.
to **request** *vt.* (ri)chiedere.
to **require** *vt.* 1. richiedere 2. ordinare, obbligare.
requirement *s.* 1. richiesta 2. requisito.
requisite *agg.* richiesto. ♦ **requisite** *s.* requisito.
requisition *s.* 1. richiesta 2. requisito 3. requisizione.
to **requisition** *vt.* requisire.
requital *s.* 1. contraccambio 2. ricompensa.
to **requite** *vt.* 1. ricompensare 2. contraccambiare.
to **reread (reread, reread)** *vt.* rileggere.
to **rescind** *vt.* rescindere.
rescission *s.* rescissione.
rescue *s.* 1. liberazione 2. soccorso.
to **rescue** *vt.* 1. liberare 2. riacquistare 3. soccorrere.
research *s.* ricerca || — *work*, lavoro di ricerca.
to **research** *vi.* fare ricerche.
researcher *s.* ricercatore.
to **resell (resold, resold)** *vt.* rivendere.
resemblance *s.* rassomiglianza.
to **resemble** *vt.* assomigliare a.
to **resent** *vt.* risentirsi di.
resentful *agg.* 1. risentito 2. permaloso.
resentment *s.* risentimento.
reservation *s.* 1. riserva 2. prenotazione.
reserve *s.* 1. riserva 2. riserbo.
to **reserve** *vt.* riservare.
reservoir *s.* serbatoio.
to **reset (reset, reset)** *vt.* 1. rimettere a posto 2. (*tip.*) ricomporre.
to **resettle** *vt.* risistemare. ♦ to **resettle** *vi.* risistemarsi.
resettlement *s.* risistemazione.

to **reshape** vt. dare nuova forma a.
to **reside** vi. risiedere.
residence s. residenza.
resident agg. e s. residente.
residential agg. residenziale.
residual agg. residuo. ♦ **residual**
s. **1.** residuo **2.** resto.
residue s. residuo, avanzo.
to **resign** vt. **1.** consegnare **2.** rinunciare ‖ *to — oneself*, rassegnarsi. ♦ to **resign** vi. dimettersi.
resignation s. **1.** dimissioni (pl.)
2. rinuncia **3.** rassegnazione.
resigned agg. rassegnato.
resilience, resiliency s. elasticità.
resilient agg. elastico.
resin s. resina.
resinous agg. resinoso.
resipiscence s. resipiscenza.
resipiscent agg. resipiscente.
resist s. sostanza protettiva.
to **resist** vt. e vi. resistere.
resistance s. resistenza.
resistant, resistent agg. resistente.
resistive agg. resistente.
resold V. *to resell*.
to **resole** vt. risolare.
resolubile agg. (ri)solubile.
resolute agg. risoluto.
resoluteness s. risolutezza.
resolution s. **1.** risolutezza **2.** risoluzione **3.** scissione.
resolutive agg. risolutivo.
resolvable agg. risolvibile.
resolve s. risoluzione.
to **resolve** vt. **1.** risolvere **2.** scindere. ♦ to **resolve** vi. risolversi.
resolvent agg. e s. solvente.
resonance s. risonanza.
resonant agg. risonante.
to **resorb** vt. riassorbire.
resorbent agg. riassorbente.
resort s. **1.** ricorso **2.** risorsa **3.** ritrovo **4.** luogo di soggiorno.
to **resort** vi. **1.** ricorrere **2.** recarsi.
to **resound** vi. risonare. ♦ to **resound** vt. proclamare.
resource s. risorsa.
resourceful agg. pieno di risorse.
resourceless agg. senza risorse.
respect s. **1.** rispetto, stima **2.** aspetto **3.** punto di vista.
to **respect** vt. rispettare.
respectability s. **1.** rispettabilità **2.**
convenzioni sociali (pl.).
respectable agg. rispettabile.
respectful agg. rispettoso.
respecting prep. rispetto a.
respective agg. rispettivo.

respiration s. respirazione.
respirator s. respiratore.
respiratory agg. respiratorio.
respite s. **1.** dilazione **2.** tregua.
to **respite** vt. concedere una dilazione, una tregua a.
resplendent agg. risplendente.
respond s. responsorio.
to **respond** vi. rispondere.
respondence s. rispondenza.
respondent agg. **1.** rispondente **2.**
sensibile. ♦ **respondent** s. (giur.)
convenuto.
response s. risposta.
responsibility s. responsabilità.
responsible agg. **1.** responsabile **2.**
di responsabilità.
responsive agg. rispondente.
responsory s. responsorio.
rest[1] s. **1.** riposo **2.** appoggio.
rest[2] s. resto, residuo.
to **rest** vt. **1.** riposare **2.** appoggiare.
♦ to **rest** vi. **1.** riposarsi **2.** appoggiarsi.
to **restate** vt. riesporre.
restaurant s. ristorante ‖ *— -car*,
vagone ristorante.
restful agg. tranquillo.
restfulness s. tranquillità.
resting-place s. luogo di riposo.
restitution s. restituzione.
restive agg. **1.** restio **2.** irrequieto.
restless agg. **1.** irrequieto **2.** incessante.
restlessness s. irrequietezza.
restorable agg. **1.** restituibile **2.** re-
staurabile.
restoration s. **1.** restituzione **2.** re-
stauro **3.** restaurazione **4.** ricostruzione.
to **restore** vt. **1.** restituire **2.** restaurare **3.** ricostruire **4.** ristabilire.
to **restrain** vt. **1.** trattenere **2.** confinare.
restrainable agg. reprimibile.
restraint s. **1.** freno **2.** detenzione.
to **restrict** vt. limitare.
restrictedly avv. limitatamente.
restriction s. restrizione.
restrictive agg. restrittivo.
result s. risultato.
to **result** vi. **1.** risultare **2.** risolversi.
resultant agg. e s. risultante.
resultful agg. utile, efficace.
resultless agg. inutile, inefficace.
to **resume** vt. riprendere.
resummons s. nuova convocazione.
resumption s. ripresa.

resurgent *agg.* risorgente.
to **resurrect** *vt.* (*fam.*) risuscitare.
resurrection *s.* risurrezione.
resurrectional *agg.* di risurrezione.
to **resuscitate** *vt.* e *vi.* risuscitare.
resuscitation *s.* risuscitamento.
to **ret** *vt.* macerare.
retail *s.* vendita al minuto ‖ *by* —, al minuto.
to **retail** *vt.* e *vi.* vendere al minuto.
retailer *s.* dettagliante.
to **retain** *vt.* trattenere, conservare.
retainable *agg.* trattenibile, conservabile.
retainer *s.* caparra, anticipo.
retaining *agg.* — **wall**, muro di sostegno.
retake *s.* (*cine*) replica di una ripresa.
to **retake** (**retook, retaken**) *vt.* **1.** riprendere **2.** (*cine*) ripetere una ripresa.
to **retaliate** *vi.* far rappresaglia.
retaliation *s.* rappresaglia.
retaliative, retaliatory *agg.* vendicativo.
retard *s.* ritardo.
to **retard** *vt.* e *vi.* ritardare.
to **retaste** *vt.* riassaggiare.
to **retch** *vi.* avere conati di vomito.
to **retell** (**retold, retold**) *vt.* ripetere.
retention *s.* **1.** ritenzione **2.** memoria.
retentive *agg.* **1.** che trattiene **2.** tenace (*di memoria*).
reticence, reticency *s.* reticenza.
reticent *agg.* reticente.
reticle *s.* (*ott.*) reticolo.
reticular *agg.* reticolare.
reticulate *agg.* reticolato.
reticulum *s.* (*pl.* -la) reticolo.
retinue *s.* seguito.
to **retire** *vt.* ritirare. ♦ to **retire** *vi.* ritirarsi.
retired *agg.* **1.** ritirato **2.** a riposo, in ritiro.
retirement *s.* **1.** ritiro **2.** collocamento a riposo **3.** (*mil.*) ritirata.
retiring *agg.* **1.** riservato **2.** che si ritira, uscente.
retold V. *to retell.*
retook V. *to retake.*
retorsion *s.* ritorsione.
retort *s.* storta.
to **retort** *vt.* ritorcere. ♦ to **retort** *vi.* ribattere.
retort(ion) *s.* ritorsione.
retouch *s.* ritocco.

to **retouch** *vt.* ritoccare.
to **retrace** *vt.* ripercorrere, risalire.
to **retract** *vt.* **1.** ritrarre **2.** ritrattare. ♦ to **retract** *vi.* ritrarsi.
retractable *agg.* ritraibile **2.** ritrattabile.
retractation *s.* ritrattazione.
retractile *agg.* retrattile.
retractor *s.* (*med.*) divaricatore.
to **retread** (**retrod, retrodden**) *vt.* ripercorrere.
retreat *s.* eremo, luogo appartato.
to **retreat** *vi.* ritirarsi, retrocedere.
retreating *agg.* sfuggente. ♦ **retreating** *s.* (*mil.*) ritirata.
retribution *s.* punizione.
retrievable *agg.* **1.** ricuperabile **2.** riparabile.
retrieval *s.* **1.** ricupero (*di beni*) **2.** riparazione.
to **retrieve** *vt.* **1.** ricuperare **2.** riparare.
retroaction *s.* **1.** reazione **2.** azione retroattiva.
retroactive *agg.* retroattivo.
to **retrocede**[1] *vi.* retrocedere.
to **retrocede**[2] *vt.* restituire.
retrocession[1] *s.* retrocessione.
retrocession[2] *s.* restituzione.
retrod V. *to retread.*
retrodden V. *to retread.*
retrospect(ion) *s.* sguardo retrospettivo.
retrospective *agg.* retrospettivo.
retroversion *s.* retroversione.
return *s.* **1.** ritorno **2.** restituzione **3.** guadagno, profitto **4.** relazione ‖ — **journey**, viaggio di ritorno; **election returns**, risultati elettorali.
to **return** *vi.* **1.** ritornare **2.** rispondere, ricambiare, replicare. ♦ to **return** *vt.* **1.** restituire, rimandare **2.** produrre, fruttare **3.** (*pol.*) eleggere.
reunion *s.* riunione.
to **reunite** *vt.* riunire. ♦ to **reunite** *vi.* riunirsi.
revaluation *s.* rivalutazione.
to **revalue** *vt.* rivalutare.
to **reveal** *vt.* rivelare.
revel *s.* baldoria.
to **revel** *vi.* far baldoria.
revelation *s.* rivelazione.
reveller *s.* chi fa baldoria.
revelry *s.* baldoria.
revenge *s.* vendetta.
to **revenge** *vt.* vendicare. ♦ to **revenge** *vi.* vendicarsi.
revengeful *agg.* vendicativo.

revenger *s.* vendicatore.
revenue *s.* **1.** entrata **2.** fisco.
to **reverberate** *vt.* e *vi.* riverberare.
reverberation *s.* riverberazione, riverbero.
to **revere** *vt.* riverire.
reverence *s.* riverenza.
to **reverence** *vt.* riverire.
reverend *agg.* reverendo.
reverent(ial) *agg.* riverente.
reverie *s.* fantasticheria.
reversal *s.* **1.** rovesciamento **2.** (*giur.*) annullamento.
reverse *agg.* e *s.* rovescio || — *gear*, retromarcia.
to **reverse** *vt.* rovesciare. ♦ to **reverse** *vi.* innestare la retromarcia.
reversibility *s.* reversibilità.
reversible *agg.* reversibile, rovesciabile.
reversion *s.* reversione.
to **revert** *vi.* ritornare.
review *s.* **1.** revisione **2.** recensione **3.** rivista, periodico **4.** (*mil.*) rivista.
to **review** *vt.* **1.** rivedere **2.** recensire **3.** (*mil.*) passare in rivista.
reviewal *s.* revisione, recensione.
reviewer *s.* recensore, revisore.
to **revile** *vt.* e *vi.* ingiuriare.
to **revise** *vt.* rivedere, modificare.
reviser *s.* revisore.
revision *s.* revisione, correzione.
revival *s.* **1.** ripristino **2.** ripresa **3.** rinascita.
to **revive** *vt.* e *vi.* resuscitare.
reviver *s.* chi, ciò che rinvigorisce.
revivification *s.* rinascita.
to **revivify** *vt.* ravvivare.
revocable *agg.* revocabile.
revocation *s.* revoca.
revocatory *agg.* revocatorio.
to **revoke** *vt.* revocare.
revolt *s.* rivolta.
to **revolt** *vt.* disgustare. ♦ to **revolt** *vi.* rivoltarsi.
revolution *s.* rivoluzione.
revolutionary *agg.* e *s.* rivoluzionario.
to **revolutionize** *vt.* rivoluzionare.
to **revolve** *vt.* meditare. ♦ to **revolve** *vi.* girare, rotare.
revolver *s.* rivoltella.
revolving *agg.* **1.** rotante **2.** rotativo.
revulsion *s.* **1.** revulsione **2.** mutamento.
revulsive *agg.* revulsivo.

reward *s.* ricompensa.
to **reward** *vt.* ricompensare.
rewarding *agg.* rimunerativo. ♦
rewarding *s.* rimunerazione.
to **rewrite (rewrote, rewritten)** *vt.* riscrivere.
rhagades *s. pl.* ragadi.
rhapsody *s.* rapsodia.
rheostat *s.* reostato.
rhetoric *s.* retorica.
rhetorical *agg.* retorico.
rhetorician *s.* retore.
rheumatic *agg.* e *s.* reumatico.
rheumatism *s.* reumatismo.
rhinitis *s.* rinite.
rhinoceros *s.* rinoceronte.
rhizome *s.* rizoma.
rhododendron *s.* rododendro.
rhomb *s.* rombo.
rhombic(al) *agg.* rombico.
rhombohedron *s.* (*pl.* -dra) romboedro.
rhomboid *agg.* e *s.* romboide.
rhubarb *s.* rabarbaro.
rhyme *s.* rima.
to **rhyme** *vt.* far rimare. ♦ to **rhyme** *vi.* rimare.
rhymer *s.* rimatore.
Rhynchota *s. pl.* rincoti.
rhythm *s.* ritmo.
rhythmic(al) *agg.* ritmico.
rib *s.* **1.** costola **2.** costa, nervatura **3.** stecca.
to **rib** *vt.* **1.** munire (*di coste ecc.*) **2.** scanalare.
ribbing *s.* **1.** nervatura **2.** rigatura.
ribbon *s.* nastro.
rice *s.* riso || — *-field* (o — *-swamp*), risaia.
rich *agg.* ricco.
richly *avv.* riccamente.
richness *s.* ricchezza.
rick *s.* bica.
ricket(s) *s.* rachitismo.
rickety *agg.* **1.** rachitico **2.** malsicuro.
to **rid (rid, rid)** *vt.* liberare || to *get — of*, sbarazzarsi di.
ridden V. to *ride*.
riddle[1] *s.* indovinello.
riddle[2] *s.* vaglio, crivello.
to **riddle[1]** *vt.* risolvere.
to **riddle[2]** *vt.* **1.** vagliare **2.** setacciare.
ride *s.* passeggiata, percorso (*a cavallo, su un veicolo*).
to **ride (rode, ridden)** *vt.* **1.** montare (*cavallo, bicicletta*) **2.** percorrere (*a cavallo, su un veicolo*) **3.**

(*fig.*) opprimere. ♦ to **ride (rode, ridden)** *vi.* andare (*a cavallo, su un veicolo*).

rider *s.* cavaliere, fantino.

ridge *s.* cresta, catena di monti.

ridicule *s.* ridicolo.

to **ridicule** *vt.* schernire.

ridiculous *agg.* ridicolo.

riding *s.* corsa (*a cavallo, in veicolo*).

rifle *s.* fucile.

rifleman *s.* fuciliere.

rift *s.* crepa.

rigging *s.* attrezzatura.

right[1] *agg.* 1. giusto 2. (*geom.*) retto 3. destro.

right[2] *s.* 1. il giusto, il bene 2. diritto 3. destra, mano destra, lato destro.

right[3] *avv.* 1. giustamente, bene 2. direttamente 3. proprio 4. a destra.

righteous *agg.* giusto.

righteousness *s.* rettitudine.

rightful *agg.* 1. legittimo 2. giusto.

rightly *avv.* 1. rettamente 2. esattamente.

rigid *agg.* rigido.

rigidity, rigor *s.* rigidità.

rigorism *s.* rigorismo.

rigorist *s.* rigorista.

rigorous *agg.* rigido.

rigour *s.* rigore.

rim *s.* bordo, orlo.

to **rim** *vt.* bordare, cerchiare.

rind *s.* 1. buccia 2. corteccia 3. crosta 4. cotenna.

to **rind** *vt.* 1. sbucciare 2. scortecciare.

ring[1] *s.* 1. anello, cerchio 2. pista.

ring[2] *s.* 1. scampanellata 2. (*fig.*) accento, tono.

to **ring**[1] *vt.* circondare.

to **ring**[2] **(rang, rung)** *vt.* suonare || *to* — *up*, telefonare. ♦ to **ring (rang, rung)** *vi.* risuonare.

ringleader *s.* capobanda.

rink *s.* pista di pattinaggio.

to **rinse** *vt.* sciacquare.

rinsing *s.* risciacquatura.

riot *s.* 1. rivolta 2. gazzarra.

to **riot** *vi.* 1. tumultuare 2. gozzovigliare.

rioter *s.* rivoltoso.

riotous *agg.* 1. tumultuante 2. sregolato.

rip *s.* lacerazione, scucitura, strappo.

to **rip** *vt.* lacerare. ♦ to **rip** *vi.* lacerarsi.

ripe *agg.* maturo.

to **ripen** *vt.* e *vi.* maturare.

ripeness *s.* maturità.

ripple *s.* 1. increspatura, ondulatura 2. gorgoglio.

to **ripple** *vt.* increspare, ondulare. ♦ to **ripple** *vi.* incresparsi, ondularsi.

rise *s.* 1. il sorgere 2. salita, ascesa 3. aumento 4. sorgente.

to **rise (rose, risen)** *vi.* 1. sorgere 2. aumentare.

riser *s.* chi si alza.

risible *agg.* risibile.

rising *s.* 1. sorgere 2. salita, ascesa 3. aumento 4. rivolta.

risk *s.* rischio.

to **risk** *vt.* rischiare.

risky *agg.* rischioso.

rissole *s.* polpetta.

rite *s.* rito.

ritual *agg.* e *s.* rituale.

rival *agg.* e *s.* rivale.

to **rival** *vt.* rivaleggiare.

rivality, rivalry *s.* rivalità.

river *s.* fiume.

riverside *s.* lungofiume.

to **rivet** *vt.* 1. ribadire 2. fissare.

rivulet *s.* fiumicello.

road *s.* strada || — *bed*, fondo stradale; — *sign*, cartello stradale.

roadstead *s.* (*mar.*) rada.

roadway *s.* carreggiata.

to **roam** *vt.* e *vi.* vagare (*per*).

roar *s.* 1. ruggito 2. rombo.

to **roar** *vt.* e *vi.* 1. ruggire 2. tuonare || *to* — *with laughter*, ridere fragorosamente.

roaring *agg.* 1. rumoroso 2. ruggente, mugghiante. ♦ **roaring** *s.* V. *roar*.

roast *agg.* e *s.* arrosto.

to **roast** *vt.* 1. arrostire 2. tostare. ♦ to **roast** *vi.* arrostirsi.

roasting *agg.* rovente. ♦ **roasting** *s.* 1. arrostimento 2. torrefazione.

to **rob** *vt.* derubare. ♦ to **rob** *vi.* rubare.

robber *s.* ladro.

robbery *s.* furto.

robe *s.* 1. toga 2. vestiti (*pl.*).

to **robe** *vt.* vestire. ♦ to **robe** *vi.* vestirsi.

robin *s.* pettirosso.

robust *agg.* 1. robusto 2. faticoso.

robustness *s.* robustezza.

rock[1] *s.* 1. roccia 2. rocca.

rock[2] *s.* dondolio.

to **rock** *vt.* cullare, dondolare. ♦

to **rock** *vi.* dondolarsi, oscillare, barcollare.

rocker *s.* 1. chi culla, dondola 2. dondolo (*di sedia ecc.*) 3. (*mecc.*) bilanciere.

rocket *s.* razzo.

rocking *agg.* 1. a dondolo 2. vacillante. ♦ **rocking** *s.* oscillazione, dondolio.

rocky *agg.* roccioso.

rod *s.* verga || *fishing*- —, canna da pesca.

rode V. *to ride.*

rodent *agg.* e *s.* roditore.

roe[1] *s.* capriolo maschio.

roe[2] *s.* uova di pesce.

rogue *s.* briccone.

roguery *s.* bricconeria.

roguish *agg.* bricconesco.

role *s.* 1. (*teat.*) ruolo, parte 2. funzione.

roll[1] *s.* 1. rotolo 2. elenco, lista 3. rullo, cilindro.

roll[2] *s.* 1. (*mar.; aer.*) rollio 2. rullo (*di tamburo*).

to **roll** *vt.* 1. far rotolare 2. arrotolare 3. spianare. ♦ to **roll** *vi.* 1. rotolare 2. arrotolarsi 3. ruotare 4. rollare 5. rullare.

roller *s.* 1. rullo, cilindro 2. cavallone || — *skates*, schettini.

rolling *s.* (ar)rotolamento || — *-mill*, laminatoio; — *pin*, matterello.

Roman *agg.* e *s.* romano.

Romance *agg.* romanzo, neolatino.

romance *s.* 1. poema cavalleresco, racconto fantastico 2. avventura romanzesca 3. idillio 4. poesia 5. (*mus.*) romanza.

Romanesque *agg.* e *s.* romanico.

Romanian *agg.* e *s.* romeno.

Romanic *agg.* romanico.

Romanist *s.* romanista.

Romansh *agg.* e *s.* ladino.

romantic *agg.* e *s.* romantico.

romanticism *s.* romanticismo.

to **romanticize** *vt.* romanzare.

to **romp** *vi.* giocare rumorosamente.

rompish *agg.* chiassoso.

rood *s.* croce.

roof *s.* tetto || — *-garden*, giardino pensile.

to **roof** *vt.* 1. coprire con un tetto 2. ospitare.

rook *s.* cornacchia.

room *s.* 1. stanza 2. spazio 3. possibilità.

to **room** *vt.* e *vi.* (*amer.*) alloggiare.

roomy *agg.* spazioso.

root *s.* radice.

to **root**[1] *vt.* piantare || to — *away*, *out*, *up*, sradicare. ♦ to **root** *vi.* mettere radice.

to **root**[2] *vt.* e *vi.* grufolare.

rope *s.* fune, corda || — *-dancer*, funambolo.

to **rope** *vt.* legare.

rosary *s.* 1. roseto 2. (*eccl.*) rosario.

rose *agg.* e *s.* rosa || — *-bush*, rosaio; — *-diamond*, rosetta; — *-window*, rosone.

rose V. *to rise.*

rosemary *s.* rosmarino.

roseola *s.* rosolia.

rosery *s.* roseto.

rosette *s.* 1. rosetta 2. (*arch.*) rosone 3. coccarda.

rosewood *s.* palissandro.

rosin *s.* pece greca.

rostrum *s.* (*pl.* rostra o rostrums) rostro.

rosy *agg.* roseo.

rot *s.* putrefazione.

to **rot** *vt.* e *vi.* imputridire.

rotary *agg.* rotante. ♦ **rotary** *s.* — (*press*), rotativa.

to **rotate** *vt.* e *vi.* rotare.

rotation *s.* rotazione.

rotative, rotatory *agg.* rotatorio.

rote *s.* abitudine, memoria meccanica.

rotogravure *s.* rotocalco.

rotor *s.* rotore.

rotten *agg.* marcio.

rottenness *s.* marciume.

rotund *agg.* 1. rotondo 2. enfatico.

rouble *s.* rublo.

rouge *agg.* rossetto.

rough *agg.* 1. irregolare, ruvido, scabro 2. tempestoso 3. rozzo.

to **rough** *vt.* irruvidire || to — *il* (*fam.*), vivere primitivamente.

to **roughen** *vt.* irruvidire. ♦ to **roughen** *vi.* irruvidirsi.

to **rough-hew** *vt.* abbozzare.

roughly *avv.* ruvidamente.

roughness *s.* 1. ruvidezza 2. rudezza 3. inclemenza (*di tempo*).

round *agg.* 1. rotondo 2. intero 3. franco 4. vigoroso 5. considerevole. ♦ **round** *s.* 1. cerchio 2. sfera 3. ciclo 4. giro, ronda.

round *avv.* intorno. ♦ **round** *prep.* intorno a.

to **round** *vt.* arrotondare. ♦ to **round** *vi.* 1. arrotondarsi 2. girare

3. svilupparsi.
roundabout *agg.* indiretto. ◆
roundabout *s.* giostra.
roundly *avv.* 1. vigorosamente 2.
francamente.
roundness *s.* 1. rotondità 2. scorrevolezza 3. franchezza.
to **rouse** *vt.* (ri)svegliare (*anche fig.*).
◆ to **rouse** *vi.* (ri)svegliarsi.
rouser *s.* ridestatore.
rousing *agg.* stimolante.
rout *s.* 1. plebaglia 2. tumulto 3.
rotta.
to **rout** *vt.* sconfiggere.
route *s.* via, rotta.
routinist *s.* abitudinario.
rove *s.* vagabondaggio.
to **rove** *vt.* e *vi.* vagare.
rover *s.* 1. vagabondo 2. pirata.
roving *s.* vagabondaggio.
row[1] *s.* fila.
row[2] *s.* remata, gita in barca.
to **row** *vt.* trasportare (*remando*). ◆
to **row** *vi.* remare.
rowdy *agg.* e *s.* turbolento.
rower *s.* rematore.
rowlock *s.* scalmo.
royal *agg.* regale, reale.
royalist *s.* realista.
royalty *s.* 1. regalità 2. i reali 3. diritto d'autore.
rub *s.* 1. fregata, grattata 2. ineguaglianza 3. ostacolo, difficoltà.
to **rub** *vt.* fregare. ◆ to **rub** *vi.* fregarsi.
rubber *s.* 1. massaggiatore 2. strofinaccio 3. gomma || *— -solution,*
mastice.
rubbish *s.* rifiuti (*pl.*).
rubble *s.* pietrisco.
ruby *s.* rubino.
rucksack *s.* zaino.
rudder *s.* timone.
ruddy *agg.* rosso, rubicondo.
rude *agg.* 1. rude, violento 2. rudimentale 3. grezzo.
rudeness *s.* 1. rozzezza 2. violenza.
rudiment *s.* rudimento.
rudimentary *agg.* rudimentale.
ruffian *agg.* brutale. ◆ **ruffian** *s.*
ribaldo.
ruffle *s.* 1. increspatura 2. sconvolgimento 3. tumulto.
to **ruffle** *vt.* 1. increspare 2. arruffare
3. agitare.
rug *s.* 1. coperta 2. tappetino.
rugged *agg.* 1. ruvido 2. scompigliato 3. austero 4. rozzo.
ruggedness *s.* 1. ruvidezza 2. auste

rità 3. rudezza.
ruin *s.* rovina.
to **ruin** *vt.* e *vi.* rovinare.
ruinous *agg.* 1. rovinoso 2. in rovina.
rule *s.* 1. regola 2. dominio 3. riga
da disegno.
to **rule** *vt.* 1. governare, dominare 2.
rigare.
ruler *s.* 1. dominatore 2. regolo.
ruling *s.* 1. governo 2. decisione.
Rumanian *agg.* e *s.* romeno.
rumble *s.* 1. rombo 2. brontolio.
to **rumble** *vt.* e *vi.* 1. rombare 2.
brontolare.
rumbling *s.* V. *rumble.*
rumen *s.* rumine.
ruminant *agg.* e *s.* ruminante.
to **ruminate** *vt* e *vi.* ruminare.
rummage *s.* ricerca, perquisizione.
to **rummage** *vt.* e *vi.* 1. rovistare
2. perquisire.
rumour *s.* diceria.
to **rumour** *vt.* far correre la voce.
rump *s.* 1. posteriore 2. resto.
to **rumple** *vt.* 1. spiegazzare 2. arruffare.
run *s.* 1. corsa 2. percorso, giro 3.
andamento 4. periodo 5. richiesta.
to **run (ran, run)** *vi.* 1. correre 2.
colare 3. diventare 4. estendersi 5.
essere in vigore, durare. ◆ to **run
(ran, run)** *vt.* 1. far funzionare
2. dirigere 3. seguire 4. passare ||
to — in, rodare; *to — over,* investire.
runaway *agg.* 1. fuggitivo 2. decisivo. ◆ **runaway** *s.* 1. fuggitivo
2. fuga.
rung[1] *s.* 1. piolo 2. raggio (*di
ruota*).
rung[2] V. to *ring.*
runnel *s.* ruscello.
runner *s.* 1. corridore 2. messo 3.
passatoia 4. pattino 5. carrello.
running *s.* 1. corsa 2. esercizio 3.
flusso || *— -in,* rodaggio.
runway *s.* pista.
rupture *s.* rottura.
rural *agg.* rurale.
rush[1] *s.* giunco.
rush[2] 1. attacco 2. impeto 3. afflusso || *— -hours,* ore di punta.
to **rush** *vt.* spingere. ◆ to **rush** *vi.*
precipitarsi.
rushy *agg.* 1. di giunchi 2. folto di
giunchi.
Russian *agg.* e *s.* russo.
rust *s.* ruggine.

to **rust** *vt.* arrugginire. ♦ to **rust** *vi.* arrugginirsi.

rustic(al) *agg.* rustico. ♦ **rustic(al)** *s.* campagnolo.

rustle *s.* fruscio, stormire (*di foglie*).

to **rustle** *vt.* far frusciare. ♦ to **rustle** *vi.* frusciare.

rusty *agg.* 1. rugginoso 2. (*fig.*) ombroso.

ruthless *agg.* spietato.

ruthlessness *s.* crudeltà.

rye *s.* segale.

S

Sabbath *s.* il giorno della settimana dedicato al riposo.

sable *s.* zibellino.

sabot *s.* zoccolo.

sabotage *s.* sabotaggio.

to **sabotage** *vt.* e *vi.* sabotare.

saboteur *s.* sabotatore.

sabre *s.* sciabola || — -*cut,* sciabolata.

to **sabre** *vt.* sciabolare.

saccharin(e) *s.* saccarina.

saccharose *s.* saccarosio.

sacerdotal *agg.* sacerdotale.

sack[1] *s.* 1. sacco 2. (*gergo*) licenziamento.

sack[2] *s.* (*mil.*) sacco, saccheggio.

sack[3] *s.* vino bianco delle Canarie.

to **sack**[1] *vt.* 1. insaccare 2. (*gergo*) licenziare.

to **sack**[2] *vt.* (*mil.*) saccheggiare.

sacking[1] *s.* tela da sacco.

sacking[2] *s.* saccheggio.

sacral[1] *agg.* (*anat.*) sacro.

sacral[2] *agg.* rituale.

sacrament *s.* sacramento.

sacramental *agg.* sacramentale.

sacred *agg.* 1. sacro, religioso 2. consacrato, dedicato.

sacrifice *s.* 1. sacrificio 2. abnegazione.

to **sacrifice** *vt.* e *vi.* 1. sacrificare, immolare 2. rinunziare.

sacrilege *s.* sacrilegio.

sacrist *s.* sagrestano.

sacristy *s.* sagrestia.

sacrosanct *agg.* sacrosanto.

sad *agg.* triste, mesto || *to make so.* —, rattristare qu.

to **sadden** *vt.* rattristare. ♦ to **sadden** *vi.* rattristarsi.

saddle *s.* 1. sella, sellino 2. giogaia.

to **saddle** *vt.* sellare, mettere in sella.

saddler *s.* sellaio.

sadism *s.* sadismo.

sadist *s.* sadico.

sadistic *agg.* sadico.

sadly *avv.* tristemente, mestamente.

sadness *s.* tristezza, mestizia.

safe *agg.* 1. sicuro, al riparo 2. salvo, intatto 3. innocuo || — *and sound,* sano e salvo; — -*conduct,* salvacondotto; — -*deposit,* cassetta di sicurezza. ♦ **safe** *s.* 1. cassaforte 2. sicura (*di armi*).

safeguard *s.* salvaguardia.

to **safeguard** *vt.* salvaguardare, difendere.

safekeeping *s.* custodia.

safety *s.* sicurezza, salvezza, scampo || — *belt,* cintura di sicurezza; — *device,* dispositivo di sicurezza; — -*pin,* spilla di sicurezza.

saffron *s.* zafferano.

sag *s.* 1. abbassamento, cedimento 2. (*mar.*) scarroccio.

sagacious *agg.* acuto, sagace.

sagaciousness, sagacity *s.* sagacia, perspicacia.

sage[1] *s.* salvia.

sage[2] *s.* saggio, dotto.

said V. *to say.*

sail[1] *s.* vela, velatura || *to set* (*v. irr.*) —, spiegare le vele, salpare; *to strike* (*v. irr.*) —, ammainare le vele.

sail[2] *s.* gita su imbarcazione a vela.

to **sail** *vt.* e *vi.* 1. veleggiare, navigare, costeggiare 2. salpare 3. volare, veleggiare (*di uccelli, nuvole ecc.*).

sailer *s.* veliero.

sailing *s.* 1. navigazione, traversata 2. partenza (*di navi*).

sailor *s.* marinaio.

sailplane *s.* veleggiatore.

saint *agg.* e *s.* santo.

to **saint** *vt.* canonizzare, santificare.

sainthood, saintliness *s.* santità.

saintly *agg.* santo, di santo.

sake *s.* 1. amore, interesse 2. riguardo, rispetto || *for God's* —, per l'amor di Dio.

salaam *s.* riverenza, salamelecco.

salacious *agg.* salace, lascivo.

salad *s.* insalata || *fruit* —, macedonia di frutta.

salamander *s.* salamandra.

salariat s. categorie salariate.

salary s. stipendio.

sale s. 1. vendita || *bill of* —, fattura; *on* —, in vendita 2. asta: — *by auction,* vendita all'asta 3. liquidazione, svendita.

sal(e)able agg. vendibile, commerciabile.

salesman s. venditore, commesso.

saleswoman s. venditrice, commessa.

salicylate s. salicilato.

salient agg. 1. sporgente, prominente 2. saliente, notevole.

saline agg. salino, salso.

salinity s. salsedine, salinità.

saliva s. saliva.

salivary agg. salivare.

salivation s. salivazione.

sallow agg. giallastro.

sally s. 1. (*mil.*) sortita 2. escursione.

to **sally** vi. fare una sortita || *to* — *forth,* uscire (*per una passeggiata*).

salmon s. salmone.

saloon s. salone || *dancing* —, sala da ballo.

salt s. sale. ◆ **salt** agg. 1. salato 2. sotto sale 3. (*fig.*) amaro, piccante || — *-cellar,* saliera; — *-mine,* salina.

to **salt** vt. 1. salare, cospargere di sale 2. rendere piccante (*anche fig.*).

salting s. palude costiera.

saltish agg. salmastro, salaticcio.

saltness s. salsedine.

saltpetre s. salnitro.

salty agg. 1. salato, salmastro 2. piccante (*anche fig.*).

salubrious agg. salubre.

salutary agg. salutare.

salutation s. saluto.

salute s. saluto, gesto di saluto || *to fire a* —, salutare a salve.

to **salute** vt. salutare, dare il benvenuto.

salvage s. salvataggio (*di navi, carico ecc.*).

salvation s. salvezza (*anche relig.*).

salve s. unguento, balsamo.

same agg. medesimo, stesso, uguale || *at the* — *time,* allo stesso tempo. ◆ **same** pron. lo stesso, il medesimo.

samely agg. monotono, uniforme.

sameness s. 1. somiglianza 2. monotonia.

sample s. campione, modello, esemplare || — *book,* campionario.

sanatorium s. sanatorio.

sanatory agg. curativo.

sanctification s. santificazione.

to **sanctify** vt. santificare.

sanction s. 1. autorizzazione, approvazione 2. (*giur.*) ratifica 3. sanzione.

to **sanction** vt. 1. autorizzare 2. (*giur.*) ratificare 3. aggiungere sanzioni penali (*ad una legge*).

sanctity s. santità.

sanctuary s. 1. santuario 2. asilo, rifugio.

sand s. sabbia, rena || — -*bath,* bagno di sabbia. ◆ **sands** s. *pl.* spiaggia (*sing.*).

to **sand** vt. 1. coprire di sabbia 2. arenare 3. smerigliare.

sandal s. sandalo.

sandpaper s. carta vetrata.

sandstone s. arenaria.

sandy agg. sabbioso.

sane agg. sano di mente, sensato.

saneness, sanity s. sanità (*di mente*), equilibrio.

sang V. *to sing.*

sanguinary agg. sanguinario, crudele.

sanguine agg. sanguigno.

sanguineous agg. del sangue, sanguigno.

sanitarian s. igienista. ◆ **sanitarian** agg. igienico.

sanitarist s. igienista.

sanitary agg. igienico, sanitario.

sanity s. V. *saneness.*

sank V. *to sink.*

Sanscrit, Sanskrit agg. e s. Sanscrito.

santon s. santone.

sap s. 1. linfa, succo 2. (*fig.*) vigore.

sapful agg. 1. succoso 2. vigoroso.

sapid agg. sapido, gustoso (*anche fig.*).

sapient agg. pedante.

sapless agg. 1. secco, avvizzito 2. fiacco.

saponification s. saponificazione.

to **saponify** vt. saponificare.

Sapphic agg. saffico.

sapphire s. zaffiro.

saraband s. sarabanda.

Saracen agg. e s. saraceno.

sarcasm s. sarcasmo.

sarcastic agg. sarcastico.

sarcophagus s. (*pl.* -gi) sarcofago.

sardine s. sardina.
sardonic agg. sardonico.
sash[1] s. fascia, cintura.
sash[2] s. telaio scorrevole (di finestra).
sat V. to sit.
satanic(al) agg. satanico.
satchel s. cartella (di scolaro).
to **sate** vt. saziare.
satellite s. satellite.
satiable agg. saziabile.
to **satiate** vt. saziare, satollare.
satiety s. sazietà.
satin s. raso.
satire s. satira.
satiric(al) agg. satirico.
satirist s. autore di satire.
to **satirize** vt. satireggiare.
satisfaction s. 1. soddisfazione 2. riparazione 3. (giur.) estinzione.
satisfactory agg. soddisfacente.
satisfiable agg. che può essere soddistatto.
to **satisfy** vt. soddisfare, appagare || to — a claim, accogliere un reclamo. ♦ to **satisfy** vi. fare ammenda.
satrap s. satrapo.
saturate agg. saturo.
to **saturate** vt. saturare, impregnare.
saturation s. saturazione.
Saturday s. sabato.
satyr s. satiro.
satyric agg. satiresco.
sauce s. salsa, intingolo.
saucepan s. casseruola.
saucer s. piattino, sottocoppa.
saucily avv. sfacciatamente.
saucy agg. sfacciato, insolente.
sauerkraut s. crauti.
to **saunter** vi. bighellonare.
saunterer s. bighellone.
sausage s. salsiccia, salame.
savage agg. 1. selvaggio, barbaro 2. feroce, crudele. ♦ **savage** s. selvaggio.
savagely avv. selvaggiamente, barbaramente.
savannah s. savana.
save prep. salvo, tranne, eccetto.
to **save** vt. e vi. 1. salvare, difendere 2. conservare, risparmiare.
saving s. liberazione, salvezza. ♦ **savings** s. pl. risparmi.
saviour s. salvatore, redentore.
to **savour** vi. aver sapore.
savoury agg. saporito, piccante.
saw s. sega || — -mill, segheria.
to **saw** (sawed, sawn) vt. e vi. segare.
saw V. to see.
sawdust s. segatura.
sawn V. to saw.
sawyer s. segatore.
Saxon agg. e s. sassone.
saxophone s. sassofono.
say s. il dire, detto, parola.
to **say** (said, said) vt. e vi. 1. dire, affermare 2. esprimere un'opinione || to — out, dire apertamente.
saying s. proverbio, massima: as the — goes, come dice il proverbio.
scabbard s. fodero.
scabby agg. coperto di croste.
scabies s. scabbia.
scaffold s. 1. impalcatura 2. patibolo, forca.
to **scaffold** vt. erigere impalcature.
scaffolding s. impalcatura.
scald s. scottatura.
to **scald** vt. 1. scottare 2. sterilizzare con acqua bollente. ♦ to **scald** vi. scottarsi.
scale[1] s. piatto (di bilancia). ♦ **scales** s. pl. bilancia (sing.).
scale[2] s. scaglia.
scale[3] s. scala, misura, gradazione.
to **scale**[1] vt. e vi. pesare.
to **scale**[2] vt. squamare, scrostare. ♦ to **scale** vi. squamarsi, scrostarsi.
to **scale**[3] vt. 1. scalare 2. graduare || to — down, diminuire; to — up, aumentare.
scalene agg. e s. scaleno.
scallop s. 1. conchiglia 2. dentellatura, festone, smerlo (di stoffa).
to **scallop** vt. 1. tagliare a festone 2. cuocere pesce in conchiglia.
scalp s. 1. cranio, cuoio capelluto 2. scalpo.
to **scalp** vt. 1. scalpare 2. criticare aspramente.
scalpel s. bisturi.
to **scan** vt. e vi. 1. scandire (versi) 2. esaminare, scrutare.
scandal s. 1. scandalo 2. maldicenza 3. (giur.) diffamazione.
to **scandalize** vt. scandalizzare.
scandalous agg. scandaloso.
Scandinavian agg. e s. scandinavo.
scanning s. 1. scansione (di versi) 2. osservazione || — -line, (tv), linea di scansione.
scansion s. scansione.
scantily avv. debolmente, scarsamente.
scantiness s. insufficienza, scarsezza.

scanty *agg.* **1.** scarso, insufficiente **2.** esiguo, angusto.

scapegoat *s.* capro espiatorio.

scapegrace *s.* **1.** scapestrato **2.** monello.

scapular *agg.* scapolare.

scar *s.* cicatrice, sfregio.

to **scar** *vt.* **1.** cicatrizzare **2.** sfregiare. ♦ to **scar** *vi.* cicatrizzarsi.

scarab *s.* scarabeo.

scarce *agg.* insufficiente, scarso.

scarcely *avv.* appena, a fatica, a malapena.

scare *s.* terrore, sgomento.

to **scare** *vt.* spaventare, sgomentare.

scarecrow *s.* **1.** spaventapasseri **2.** spauracchio.

scarf *s.* sciarpa, fascia.

to **scarify** *vt.* scarificare.

scarlet *agg.* scarlatto, porporino || — *-fever,* scarlattina.

scarp(e) *s.* scarpata.

to **scatter** *vt.* **1.** spargere **2.** mettere in fuga, disperdere. ♦ to **scatter** *vi.* spargersi, diffondersi.

scattered *agg.* sparso, disseminato.

scattering *s.* sparpagliamento, dispersione.

scenario *s.* sceneggiatura || — *writer,* sceneggiatore.

scene *s.* **1.** scena **2.** episodio **3.** scenario, quinta **4.** vista, panorama || — *-painter,* scenografo.

scenery *s.* **1.** scenario **2.** prospettiva, veduta.

scenographer *s.* scenografo.

scenographic *agg.* scenografico.

scenography *s.* scenografia.

scent *s.* **1.** odore, profumo **2.** traccia, pista (*anche fig.*).

to **scent** *vt.* **1.** fiutare, seguire la traccia **2.** profumare.

scented *agg.* profumato.

scentless *agg.* inodoro.

sceptical *agg.* scettico.

scepticism *s.* scetticismo.

sceptre *s.* scettro.

schedule *s.* **1.** catalogo, distinta, elenco **2.** (*amer.*) orario **3.** inventario.

to **schedule** *vt.* comporre una lista, un catalogo.

schematic(al) *agg.* schematico.

schematism *s.* schematismo.

scheme *s.* **1.** schema **2.** piano, progetto.

to **scheme** *vt.* e *vi.* **1.** progettare, fare un piano **2.** tramare.

schism *s.* scisma.

schismatic(al) *s.* scismatico.

schizophrenic *agg.* e *s.* schizofrenico.

scholar *s.* studioso, letterato.

scholarly *agg.* dotto, istruito.

scholarship *s.* **1.** dottrina, sapere **2.** borsa di studio.

scholastic *agg.* **1.** scolastico, pedante **2.** (*fil.*) scolastico.

scholastically *avv.* scolasticamente, secondo la scolastica.

scholasticism *s.* (*fil.*) scolastica.

school *s.* **1.** scuola, classe **2.** lezione, ora di lezione || — *-book,* libro di testo; — *-mate,* compagno di scuola; — *-report,* pagella; — *-term,* trimestre; — *-time,* periodo scolastico; *boarding-* —, collegio; *grammar-* —, ginnasio; *night-* —, serale.

to **school** *vt.* **1.** istruire **2.** controllare, disciplinare.

schoolboy *s.* scolaro.

schoolfellow *s.* compagno di scuola.

schoolmaster *s.* maestro, insegnante.

schoolmistress *s.* maestra, insegnante.

schoolroom *s.* aula scolastica.

schooner *s.* (*mar.*) goletta.

science *s.* scienza || — *fiction,* fantascienza; *man of* —, scienziato.

scientific *agg.* scientifico.

scientifically *avv.* scientificamente.

scientism *s.* scientismo.

scientist *s.* scienziato.

scimitar *s.* scimitarra.

scion *s.* **1.** germoglio **2.** rampollo, discendente.

scission *s.* scissione, divisione.

scissors *s. pl.* forbici, cesoie.

sclerosis *s.* (*pl.* -ses) sclerosi.

sclerotic *s.* sclerotico.

scoff *s.* derisione, scherno.

to **scoff** *vt.* e *vi.* deridere, schernire || *to* — *at so.,* farsi beffe di qu.

scold *s.* donna bisbetica.

to **scold** *vt.* sgridare, rimproverare. ♦ to **scold** *vi.* essere adirato.

scolding *s.* sgridata, rimprovero.

scoliosis *s.* scoliosi.

scooter *s.* **1.** monopattino **2.** motoretta.

scope *s.* **1.** portata, possibilità **2.** prospettiva, sfera, campo.

scorbutic *agg.* e *s.* scorbutico.

scorch *s.* bruciatura, scottatura.

to **scorch** *vt.* e *vi.* **1.** bruciacchiare **2.** inaridire (*di sole, gelo ecc.*).

scorching *agg.* **1.** bruciante, ardente **2.** (*fig.*) caustico, mordace.

score *s.* **1.** tacca, scanalatura **2.** linea, segno, linea di partenza, limite (*in corse, giuochi ecc.*) **3.** (*sport*) punteggio **4.** (*mus.*) spartito.

to score *vt. e vi.* **1.** intaccare, intagliare **2.** marcare, segnare **3.** (*sport*) segnare il punteggio **4.** (*mus.*) orchestrare || *to — up*, mettere in conto.

scorer *s.* (*sport*) marcatore.

scorn *s.* **1.** disprezzo, disdegno **2.** scherno.

to scorn *vt.* disprezzare, disdegnare.

scornful *agg.* sprezzante, sdegnoso.

scorpion *s.* scorpione || *— -fish,* scorfano.

Scot *s.* scozzese.

Scotch *agg.* scozzese.

Scotsman *s.* (*uomo*) scozzese.

Scottish *agg.* scozzese.

scoundrel *s.* furfante, farabutto.

scourge *s.* (*fig.*) flagello.

to scourge *vt.* sferzare, flagellare.

scout *s.* esploratore, ricognitore.

to scout *vi.* andare in esplorazione, in ricognizione. ♦ **to scout** *vt.* perlustrare.

scowl *s.* cipiglio, sguardo torvo.

to scowl *vt. e vi.* aggrottare le ciglia, guardare torvamente.

scramble *s.* **1.** arrampicata **2.** contesa, gara.

to scramble *vt.* **1.** arraffare **2.** mescolare alla rinfusa. ♦ **to scramble** *vi.* **1.** inerpicarsi **2.** gareggiare **3.** (*cuc.*) strapazzare (*le uova*).

scrap *s.* pezzetto, frammento || *— -heap,* mucchio di rifiuti. ♦ **scraps** *s. pl.* rimasugli, scarti.

scrape *s.* **1.** graffio, scalfittura **2.** raschio.

to scrape *vt. e vi.* **1.** raschiare, grattare **2.** levigare **3.** sfregare, strisciare || *to — a living,* sbarcare il lunario.

scraper *s.* **1.** raschietto **2.** strimpellatore.

scraping *s.* raschiatura.

scratch *s.* **1.** graffiatura, graffio **2.** grattata **3.** colpo fortunato (*al giuoco*).

to scratch *vt. e vi.* **1.** graffiare **2.** (*fig.*) scalfire **3.** grattare.

scrawl *s.* scarabocchio, sgorbio.

to scrawl *vt. e vi.* **1.** scarabocchiare **2.** scribacchiare.

scrawler *s.* chi scarabocchia.

scrawly *agg.* scarabocchiato || *— writing* (*fam.*), scritto a zampe di gallina.

scream *s.* grido acuto, strillo.

to scream *vt. e vi.* **1.** gridare, strillare **2.** fischiare (*di locomotiva*).

screamer *s.* strillone.

screaming *agg.* **1.** strillante, urlante **2.** sguaiato.

screech *s.* **1.** grido, strillo acuto **2.** stridore.

screen *s.* **1.** paravento **2.** (*cine; tv*) schermo **3.** (*mil.*) scorta.

to screen *vt. e vi.* **1.** riparare, schermare **2.** vagliare.

screenings *s. pl.* materiale vagliato (*sing.*).

screenplay *s.* (*cine*) sceneggiatura.

screenwriter *s.* sceneggiatore.

screw *s.* **1.** vite **2.** cavatappi, succhiello **3.** elica.

to screw *vt.* **1.** avvitare, stringere **2.** torcere. ♦ **to screw** *vi.* torcersi || *to — out,* svitare.

screwdriver *s.* cacciavite.

screwy *agg.* **1.** brillo **2.** tirchio, spilorcio.

scribble *s.* sgorbio, scarabocchio (*anche fig.*).

to scribble *vt. e vi.* scarabocchiare.

scribe *s.* copista.

scriber *s.* punta a tracciare.

scrip[1] *s.* **1.** pezzo di carta **2.** frammento di uno scritto.

scrip[2] *s.* certificato provvisorio, cedola.

scripture *s.* la sacra Scrittura.

to scrounge *vt. e vi.* rubacchiare.

scrounger *s.* ladruncolo, scroccone.

scrub *s.* **1.** boscaglia **2.** povero diavolo (*fam.*).

to scrub *vt. e vi.* sfregare.

scrubby *agg.* esile, debole.

scruff *s.* nuca, collottola.

scruple *s.* scrupolo.

scrupolosity *s.* scrupolosità.

scrupulous *agg.* scrupoloso.

to scrutinize *vt.* scrutinare, esaminare.

scrutiny *s.* **1.** esame minuzioso **2.** scrutinio **3.** esame (*di una legge*).

scuffle *s.* zuffa, tafferuglio.

to scuffle *vi.* azzuffarsi.

scullery *s.* retrocucina || *— -boy, -maid,* sguattero, sguattera.

sculptor *s.* scultore.

sculptress *s.* scultrice.

sculptural *agg.* scultorio, statuario.

sculpture s. scultura.

to **sculpture** vt. e vi. scolpire.

scum s. 1. schiuma, spuma 2. feccia (anche fig.).

to **scum** vt. e vi. 1. schiumare, far schiuma 2. produrre feccia.

scummer s. schiumarola.

scurf s. 1. squama, forfora 2. incrostazioni (pl.).

scurrility s. scurrilità, volgarità.

scurrilous agg. scurrile, triviale.

to **scurry** vi. precipitarsi.

scurvy agg. spregevole, meschino.

scuttle[1] s. recipiente per carbone.

scuttle[2] s. 1. (mar.) portellino 2. botola.

scuttle[3] s. fuga precipitosa.

to **scuttle**[1] vt. produrre falle (in una nave).

to **scuttle**[2] vi. correre via precipitosamente.

sea s. mare || — -bear, orso polare; — -biscuit, galletta; — calf, foca; — fight, battaglia navale; — food, frutti di mare; — front, lungomare; — quake, maremoto; — storm, mareggiata.

seacoast s. costa, spiaggia.

seafarer s. navigante, navigatore.

seafaring s. viaggi per mare.

seahorse s. ippocampo.

seal[1] s. foca.

seal[2] s. 1. sigillo, timbro 2. (fig.) suggello, vincolo.

to **seal**[1] vi. andare a caccia di foche.

to **seal**[2] vt. 1. sigillare 2. suggellare || to — one's fate, decidere la propria sorte.

sealing s. suggellamento || — -wax, ceralacca.

seam s. 1. cucitura 2. sutura.

to **seam** vt. 1. unire con cucitura 2. rigare, segnare.

seamen s. pl. equipaggio (di una nave).

seamanship s. arte della navigazione.

seamless agg. senza cucitura.

seamstress s. cucitrice.

seaplane s. idrovolante.

seaport s. porto marittimo.

search s. 1. ricerca, indagine 2. perquisizione, visita doganale || — warrant, mandato di perquisizione.

to **search** vt. e vi. cercare, perlustrare, perquisire || to — out, rinvenire, scovare.

searcher s. ricercatore.

searching agg. indagatore, inquisi-

torio. ♦ **searching** s. 1. ricerca, esame 2. sondaggio.

searchlight s. riflettore.

seashore s. spiaggia, lido.

seasickness s. mal di mare.

seaside s. spiaggia, riva.

season s. stagione, epoca || — bill (teat.), cartellone; — ticket, abbonamento stagionale.

to **season** vt. 1. stagionare 2. acclimatare 3. condire. ♦ to **season** vi. 1. stagionarsi 2. invecchiarsi (di vino).

seasonable agg. 1. di stagione 2. opportuno.

seasonal agg. stagionale.

seasoned agg. 1. stagionato 2. condito.

seasoning s. 1. stagionatura 2. condimento.

seat s. 1. sedile, posto 2. seggio 3. sede.

to **seat** vt. 1. mettere a sedere 2. insediare, collocare.

seaward agg. che va verso il mare.

seaweed s. alga marina.

sebaceous agg. sebaceo.

secant agg. e s. secante.

to **secede** vi. separarsi, ritirarsi.

seceder s. secessionista, separatista.

secession s. secessione, scissione.

secessionism s. secessionismo.

to **seclude** vt. 1. appartare, isolare 2. rinchiudere.

secluded agg. appartato, isolato, solitario.

seclusion s. 1. isolamento 2. solitudine.

seclusive agg. che serve ad isolare.

second[1] s. minuto secondo.

second[2] agg. secondo.

secondary agg. secondario.

secrecy s. 1. segretezza 2. riserbo.

secret agg. 1. segreto 2. nascosto, intimo. ♦ **secret** s. segreto.

secretariat(e) s. 1. segretariato 2. segreteria.

secretary s. 1. segretario 2. ministro (preposto ad un dicastero).

to **secrete**[1] vt. secernere.

to **secrete**[2] vt. occultare, nascondere.

secretion s. secrezione.

secretly avv. 1. segretamente 2. in modo reticente.

sect s. setta.

sectarian s. settario.

sectarianism s. spirito di setta.

sectary s. settario.

section *s.* **1.** sezione, parte **2.** paragrafo **3.** regione, quartiere.
to **section** *vt.* sezionare.
sectional *agg.* **1.** parziale, di classe **2.** a sezioni.
sector *s.* settore.
secular *agg.* **1.** secolare **2.** laico **3.** mondano, profano. ♦ **secular** *s.* laico.
secularism *s.* secolarismo.
secularist *agg.* e *s.* laico.
to **secularize** *vt.* laicizzare.
secure *agg.* **1.** sicuro, certo **2.** salvo.
to **secure** *vt.* **1.** assicurare, salvaguardare **2.** (*giur.; còmm.*) garantire **3.** mettere al sicuro.
security *s.* **1.** sicurezza, protezione **2.** certezza **3.** garanzia, cauzione. ♦ **securities** *s. pl.* titoli, valori.
sedan *s.* — (*-chair*), portantina.
sedate *agg.* **1.** posato, composto **2.** grave, serio.
sedative *agg.* e *s.* sedativo.
sedentary *agg.* e *s.* sedentario.
sediment *s.* sedimento.
sedimentary *agg.* sedimentario.
sedimentation *s.* sedimentazione.
sedition *s.* sedizione.
seditious *agg.* sedizioso.
to **seduce** *vt.* sedurre, corrompere.
seduction *s.* seduzione.
sedulous *agg.* assiduo.
to **see (saw, seen)** *vt.* e *vi.* **1.** vedere, scorgere **2.** capire, rendersi conto di **3.** esaminare, giudicare **4.** fare in modo che || *to — about,* assumersi l'incarico di; *to — off,* accompagnare (*alla partenza*); *to — over,* ispezionare; *to — through* (*fig.*), indovinare, penetrare.
see *s.* (*eccl.*) sede, diocesi.
seed *s.* **1.** seme, semenza **2.** (*fig.*) principio, germe **3.** stirpe.
seedy *agg.* pieno di semi.
to **seek (sought, sought)** *vt.* e *vi.* **1.** cercare, andare alla ricerca di **2.** ottenere **3.** chiedere, ricorrere a || *to — for sthg.,* ricercare qc.
seeker *s.* cercatore.
to **seem** *vi.* sembrare, apparire.
seeming *agg.* apparente, esteriore.
seemliness *s.* decenza, decoro.
seemly *agg.* decoroso, decente.
seen V. *to see.*
segment *s.* segmento, sezione.
segmentation *s.* segmentazione.
to **segregate** *vt.* segregare, separare. ♦ to **segregate** *vi.* separarsi, scindersi.

segregation *s.* segregazione.
seismograph *s.* sismografo.
seismologist *s.* sismologo.
seismology *s.* sismologia.
seizable *agg.* afferrabile.
to **seize** *vt.* e *vi.* **1.** afferrare, prendere **2.** capire, comprendere **3.** (*giur.*) avere in possesso, sequestrare.
seizing *s.* **1.** atto dell'afferrare **2.** conquista, cattura.
seizure *s.* **1.** (*giur.*) confisca, sequestro **2.** conquista, cattura.
seldom *avv.* raramente.
select *agg.* **1.** scelto, selezionato **2.** schizzinoso.
to **select** *vt.* selezionare.
selection *s.* selezione, scelta.
selective *agg.* selettivo.
selectivity *s.* selettività.
selector *s.* selettore.
self *s.* (*pl.* selves) l'io, l'individuo. ♦ **self** *agg.* **1.** della stessa materia **2.** uniforme.
self-conceit *s.* presunzione.
self-control *s.* autocontrollo.
self-defence *s.* legittima difesa.
self-denial *s.* abnegazione.
self-determination *s.* autodeterminazione.
self-educated *agg.* autodidatta.
self-examination *s.* esame di coscienza.
self-government *s.* (*pol.*) autogoverno.
self-help *s.* (*giur.*) legittima difesa.
selfish *agg.* egoistico.
selfishness *s.* egoismo.
self-portrait *s.* autoritratto.
sell *s.* (*fam.*) delusione.
to **sell (sold, sold)** *vt.* e *vi.* **1.** vendere **2.** (*fig.*) vendere, tradire || *to — off* (*comm.*), liquidare.
seller *s.* **1.** venditore **2.** articolo che si vende.
selling *s.* vendita, smercio || *— up,* vendita fallimentare.
selves V. *self.*
semantic *agg.* semantico.
semantics *s.* semantica.
semester *s.* semestre.
semi *prefisso* semi, mezzo, metà.
semicircle *s.* semicerchio.
semicircular *agg.* semicircolare.
semicolon *s.* punto e virgola.
semifinal *agg.* e *s.* semifinale.
seminar *s.* seminario (*d'università*).
seminarist *s.* seminarista.
seminary *s.* seminario.
semination *s.* semina.

Semite *agg.* e *s.* semita.
Semitic *agg.* semitico.
Semitism *s.* semitismo.
semitone *s.* semitono.
semivowel *s.* semivocale.
senate *s.* senato.
senator *s.* senatore.
senatorial *agg.* senatoriale.
to send (sent, sent) *vt.* e *vi.* mandare, inviare, spedire || *to — away,* congedare; *to — back,* rinviare; *to — for,* mandare a chiamare; *to — off,* inviare (*per lettera*); *to — out,* emettere.
sender *s.* **1.** mandante, mittente **2.** (*comm.*) spedizioniere **3.** (*radio, tv.*) emittente.
sending *s.* **1.** invio **2.** (*comm.*) spedizione **3.** (*radio, tv.*) trasmissione.
senescence *s.* senescenza.
senile *agg.* senile.
senility *s.* senilità.
senior *agg.* **1.** più vecchio, più anziano **2.** più ragguardevole, che ha più anzianità. ♦ **senior** *s.* **1.** decano, anziano **2.** il superiore.
seniority *s.* anzianità (*d'anni, di grado*).
sensation *s.* **1.** senso, sensazione **2.** colpo, impressione.
sensational *agg.* **1.** che dipende dai sensi **2.** sensazionale.
sense *s.* **1.** senso, sensazione, impressione **2.** conoscenza **3.** significato || *common —,* buon senso. ♦ **senses** *s. pl.* facoltà mentale (*sing.*).
senseful *agg.* significativo.
senseless *agg.* **1.** inanimato **2.** insensato.
sensibility *s.* **1.** sensibilità, sensitività **2.** emotività.
sensible *agg.* **1.** sensato, giudizioso **2.** percettibile **3.** notevole, considerevole **4.** consapevole.
sensibly *avv.* **1.** assennatamente **2.** percettibilmente.
sensism *s.* sensismo.
sensist *s.* sensista.
sensitive *agg.* **1.** sensitivo, sensibile **2.** suscettibile, impressionabile.
sensitively *avv.* sensibilmente.
sensitiveness *s.* **1.** sensibilità **2.** suscettibilità.
to sensitize *vt.* sensibilizzare.
sensitizer *s.* (*foto*) sensibilizzatore.
sensorial *agg.* sensorio.
sensory *agg.* sensoriale.
sensual *agg.* sensuale.

sensualism *s.* sensualismo.
sensuality *s.* sensualità.
sensually *avv.* sensualmente, voluttuosamente.
sensuous *agg.* sensoriale, voluttuoso.
sent V. *to send.*
sentence *s.* **1.** giudizio, sentenza **2.** (*gramm.*) frase || *to pass a —,* pronunciare una sentenza.
to sentence *vt.* giudicare, pronunciare una sentenza contro.
sententious *agg.* sentenzioso.
sententiously *avv.* sentenziosamente.
sentient *agg.* senziente, sensibile.
sentiment *s.* **1.** sentimento **2.** opinione, parere.
sentimental *agg.* sentimentale, romantico.
sentimentalism *s.* sentimentalismo.
sentimentalist *s.* persona sentimentale.
sentimentality *s.* sentimentalità.
sentinel *s.* sentinella, guardia.
sentry *s.* sentinella, guardia, scolta || *— box,* garitta.
separate *agg.* separato, staccato.
to separate *vt.* separare. ♦ **to separate** *vi.* separarsi.
separately *avv.* separatamente.
separation *s.* separazione, divisione.
separatism *s.* separatismo.
September *s.* settembre.
septicaemia *s.* setticemia.
septuagenarian *agg.* e *s.* settuagenario.
septuagenary *agg.* settuagenario.
septum *s.* (*pl.* -ta) diaframma.
sepulchral *agg.* sepolcrale.
sepulchre *s.* sepolcro.
sequacious *agg.* pedissequo, servile.
sequel *s.* **1.** conseguenza **2.** seguito.
sequence *s.* **1.** successione, sequela **2.** sequenza.
to sequestrate *vt.* sequestrare, confiscare.
sequestration *s.* sequestro, confisca.
sequin *s.* lustrino.
seraphic(al) *agg.* serafico.
serenade *s.* serenata.
serene *agg.* **1.** sereno, senza nubi **2.** calmo, tranquillo.
serenely *avv.* serenamente.
serenity *s.* **1.** serenità, limpidezza **2.** tranquillità.
sergeant *s.* **1.** sergente **2.** brigadiere.
serial *s.* romanzo a puntate, pubblicazione periodica.

serially avv. 1. in serie 2. periodicamente.
sericulture s. sericoltura.
sericulturist s. sericoltore.
series s. serie, successione.
serigraphy s. serigrafia.
serious agg. 1. serio, pensieroso 2. grave, importante.
seriousness s. 1. serietà 2. gravità.
sermon s. sermone, predica.
serotherapy s. sieroterapia.
serous agg. sieroso.
serpent s. serpente.
serum s. siero.
servant s. servo, servitore.
to **serve** vt. e vi. 1. servire, essere al servizio di 2. servire, essere utile 3. essere sotto le armi 4. (giur.) notificare (di atti) || to — out, distribuire.
server s. 1. chi serve 2. chierico 3. vassoio.
service s. 1. servizio (anche militare) 2. servigio, favore 3. funzione religiosa 4. (giur.) notifica. ◆ Services s. pl. forze armate.
serviceable agg. utile, pratico.
serviette s. tovagliolo.
servile agg. servile.
servilism s. servilismo.
servility s. servilità.
serving s. 1. il servire 2. servizio (di tavola).
servitude s. servitù, schiavitù.
session s. sessione, seduta. ◆ **sessions** s. pl. (giur.) udienze.
set[1] agg. 1. fermo, fisso 2. stabilito, prestabilito 3. studiato, preparato. ◆ set s. 1. il solidificarsi 2. forma, serie 3. gruppo 4. direzione, corso 5. (poet.) tramonto 6. serie completa, insieme: a — of teeth, una dentiera; the complete — of Shakespeare's works, la raccolta completa delle opere di Shakespeare.
to **set** (set, set) vt. e vi. 1. mettere, porre, collocare 2. sistemare, mettere a punto 3. tramontare (anche fig.) || to — about, accingersi; to — back, impedire; to — in, incominciare; to — out, esporre; to — up, fissare, installare; to — aside (giur.), annullare; to — off, compensare.
set-back s. contrattempo.
set-down s. rimprovero.
set-off s. 1. contrasto 2. compensazione.
setting s. 1. messa in opera, mon-

taggio 2. ambiente 3. scenario, messa in scena 4. incastonatura.
to **settle** vt. e vi. 1. fissare, decidere, determinare 2. saldare, liquidare (conti, questioni ecc.) 3. sistemare, sistemarsi 4. stabilire 5. calmare, calmarsi 6. depositare, depositarsi (di sedimenti ecc.) || to — down, stabilirsi (in un luogo).
settled agg. fissato, stabilito.
settlement s. 1. determinazione 2. saldo, liquidazione 3. sistemazione 4. lo stabilirsi (in un luogo) 5. colonia, distretto 6. (giur.) transazione || financial —, regolamento di conti.
settler s. 1. chi decide 2. colonizzatore.
settling s. 1. stabilizzazione 2. saldo, pagamento.
set-to s. zuffa.
setup s. disposizione, organizzazione.
seven agg. sette.
sevenfold agg. settuplo. ◆ **sevenfold** avv. sette volte tanto.
seventeen agg. diciassette.
seventeenth agg. diciassettesimo.
seventh agg. settimo.
seventieth agg. settantesimo.
seventy agg. settanta.
to **sever** vt. staccare, dividere. ◆ to **sever** vi. staccarsi, dividersi.
several agg. 1. parecchi, diversi (pl.) 2. separato, distinto. ◆ **several** pron. alcuni, diversi (pl.) || — of them, alcuni di loro.
severally avv. separatamente, individualmente.
severe agg. 1. severo, austero 2. violento, forte 3. rigido (di clima).
severely avv. 1. severamente 2. violentemente.
severity s. 1. severità, durezza 2. violenza.
to **sew** (sewed, sewn) vt. e vi. cucire.
sewage s. acque di scolatura.
sewer[1] s. chi cuce, cucitrice.
sewer[2] s. 1. canale artificiale di drenaggio 2. fogna.
sewing s. 1. il cucire 2. lavoro di cucito.
sewn V. to sew.
sex s. sesso.
sexagenarian agg. e s. sessagenario.
sextet(te) s. sestetto.
sexton s. sagrestano.
sextuple agg. e s. sestuplo.
sexual agg. sessuale.

shabbiness s. 1. l'essere male in arnese 2. meschinità.

shabby agg. 1. male in arnese, cencioso 2. meschino, gretto.

shackles s. pl. 1. manette, ceppi 2. (fig.) impedimenti.

shade s. 1. ombra (anche fig.) 2. sfumatura (di colore, significato ecc.) 3. spirito, ombra 4. schermo, riparo || eye- —, visiera.

to **shade** vt. e vi. 1. ombreggiare, riparare (da luce, calore) 2. velare, oscurare (anche fig.).

shadiness s. ombrosità.

shading s. 1. l'ombreggiare 2. ombreggiatura, sfumatura.

shadow s. ombra (anche fig.). ◆ **shadows** s. pl. oscurità.

to **shadow** vt. pedinare, seguire come un'ombra.

shadowy agg. 1. ombroso, ombreggiato 2. indistinto, vago.

shady agg. ombreggiato, all'ombra.

shaft[1] s. 1. lancia, giavellotto 2. fulmine 3. gambo, stelo 4. asta, bastone 5. (mecc.) albero.

shaft[2] s. sfiatatoio, condotto.

shaggy agg. 1. ispido, irsuto 2. peloso (di tessuto) 3. incolto.

Shah s. scià.

shake s. 1. scossa, scuotimento 2. tremore, tremito 3. frullato.

to **shake (shook, shaken)** vt. e vi. 1. scuotere, agitare (liquidi) 2. tremare, far tremare 3. turbare 4. indebolire.

shakily avv. instabilmente.

shaking agg. tremante, vacillante. ◆ **shaking** s. scossa, scuotimento.

shaky agg. 1. instabile, tremolante 2. malsicuro.

shall v. dif. 1. (aus. per le prime pers. del fut. predicente) I — go to England next summer, andrò in Inghilterra l'estate prossima; we — work next week, lavoreremo la prossima settimana 2. (aus. per le seconde e terze pers. del fut. volitivo) you — go to bed!, andrai a letto! 3. dovere: you — wait for me, devi aspettarmi.

shallow agg. 1. poco profondo, basso 2. (fig.) superficiale.

sham s. 1. finta, inganno 2. ipocrita.

shaman s. sciamano.

shambles s. pl. 1. mattatoio (sing.) 2. carneficina (sing.).

shame s. 1. vergogna, pudore 2. disonore.

to **shame** vt. 1. svergognare, far arrossire 2. disonorare.

shamefaced agg. 1. vergognoso 2. timido.

shameful agg. vergognoso, disonorevole.

shameless agg. svergognato, sfacciato.

shamelessly avv. sfacciatamente.

shank s. 1. gamba, stinco 2. gambo, stelo 3. fusto (di colonna) || — -bone, tibia.

shape s. forma, figura.

to **shape** vt. e vi. creare, dar forma a.

shapeless agg. informe.

shapely agg. ben fatto.

share s. 1. parte, porzione 2. (comm.) azione, titolo.

to **share** vt. dividere, spartire. ◆ to **share** vi. partecipare, condividere.

shareholder s. azionista.

share-out s. distribuzione.

shark s. 1. squalo, pescecane 2. (fig.) profittatore.

sharp agg. 1. tagliente, affilato 2. aguzzo 3. scosceso, ripido 4. netto, chiaro 5. intelligente, acuto.

sharp avv. puntualmente, in punto.

to **sharpen** vt. 1. affilare, aguzzare 2. (fig.) rendere più acuto.

sharper s. imbroglione.

sharply avv. acutamente.

sharpness s. 1. filo, affilatura 2. acutezza 3. vivacità, intelligenza.

sharp-sighted agg. dalla vista acuta.

to **shatter** vt. frantumare. ◆ to **shatter** vi. frantumarsi.

shattering s. disintegrazione.

shave[1] s. il radersi, rasatura.

shave[2] s. pialla.

to **shave**[1] vt. radere. ◆ to **shave** vi. radersi.

to **shave**[2] vt. piallare.

shaven agg. 1. rasato 2. (eccl.) tonsurato.

shaving s. 1. il radersi 2. truciolo.

shawl s. scialle.

she pron. pers. f. ella, lei, colei. ◆ **she** attr. indicante il sesso degli animali: a — -bear, un'orsa.

sheaf s. (pl. sheaves) 1. fascio, covone 2. (geom.) fascio (di rette ecc.).

to **shear (sheared, shorn)** vt. 1. cesoiare, tranciare 2. tosare.

shearing s. recisione, taglio.
shears s. pl. cesoie, forbici.
sheath s. guaina, fodero.
to **sheathe** vt. **1.** mettere nel fodero **2.** rivestire di.
sheaves V. sheaf.
to **shed (shed, shed)** vt. **1.** versare, spandere **2.** lasciar cadere.
shed s. tettoia, capannone.
shedding s. **1.** spargimento **2.** perdita, caduta (di foglie ecc.).
sheen s. splendore, lucentezza.
sheep s. (anche pl.) **1.** pecora, ovino **2.** (fig.) persona debole, timorosa.
sheepish agg. timido, impacciato.
sheepskin s. **1.** pelle di pecora **2.** cartapecora.
sheer[1] agg. **1.** puro, semplice, mero **2.** liscio, non diluito (di bevande).
sheer[2] s. virata, cambiamento di rotta.
sheet s. **1.** lenzuolo **2.** foglio **3.** lamina, lamiera.
sheik(h) s. sceicco.
shelf s. (pl. shelves) mensola, scaffale.
shell s. **1.** conchiglia, guscio **2.** involucro, carcassa **3.** bossolo (di cartuccia) **4.** (fig.) apparenza.
to **shell** vt. e vi. sgusciare, sgranare.
shelter s. **1.** riparo, rifugio **2.** pensilina.
to **shelter** vt. riparare. ♦ to **shelter** vi. ripararsi.
to **shelve** vt. **1.** provvedere di scaffali **2.** mettere negli scaffali.
shelves V. shelf.
shelving s. scaffalatura.
shepherd s. pastore, pecoraio.
sherbet s. sorbetto.
shield s. **1.** scudo **2.** (fig.) protezione.
to **shield** vt. proteggere, difendere.
shift s. **1.** cambiamento, sostituzione **2.** risorsa, espediente **3.** turno (di lavoro).
to **shift** vt. **1.** spostare **2.** cambiare. ♦ to **shift** vi. **1.** spostarsi **2.** arrangiarsi.
shilling s. scellino.
to **shilly-shally** vi. tentennare.
to **shimmer** vi. luccicare, mandare bagliori.
to **shine (shone, shone)** vt. e vi. **1.** splendere, brillare (anche fig.) **2.** essere brillante.
shine s. **1.** splendore, luminosità **2.** luce del sole.
Shintoist s. scintoista.

shiny agg. splendente, rilucente.
ship s. nave, bastimento || convoy- —, nave scorta; flag- —, nave ammiraglia; landing- —, nave da sbarco.
to **ship** vt. **1.** imbarcare **2.** (comm.) spedire. ♦ to **ship** vi. imbarcarsi.
shipboard s. bordo.
shipboy s. mozzo.
shipbuilder s. costruttore navale.
shipmate s. compagno di bordo.
shipment s. imbarco, spedizione di merci.
shipping s. **1.** forze navali (pl.) **2.** imbarco, spedizione.
shipwreck s. naufragio.
to **shipwreck** vi. naufragare.
shipyard s. cantiere navale.
shirker s. scansafatiche.
shirt s. camicia (da uomo).
shiver[1] s. scheggia.
shiver[2] s. brivido, fremito.
to **shiver**[1] vt. frantumare. ♦ to **shiver** vi. frantumarsi.
to **shiver**[2] vt. e vi. rabbrividire, tremare.
shivering s. V. shiver.
shivery agg. **1.** fragile **2.** tremante.
shoal[1] s. secca, bassofondo.
shoal[2] s. banco (di pesci).
shock s. **1.** urto, collisione **2.** forte impressione, violenta emozione.
to **shock** vt. **1.** colpire, disgustare **2.** provocare un collasso. ♦ to **shock** vi. **1.** scandalizzarsi **2.** scontrarsi.
shocking agg. **1.** che colpisce **2.** disgustoso.
shoe s. scarpa, calzatura || horse- —, ferro di cavallo.
shoeblack s. lustrascarpe.
shoemaker s. calzolaio.
shoe-string s. laccio (da scarpe).
shone V. to shine.
shook V. to shake.
shoot s. **1.** spedizione di caccia **2.** virgulto **3.** puntura, fitta.
to **shoot (shot, shot)** vt. e vi. **1.** lanciare **2.** sparare, uccidere sparando **3.** cacciare **4.** fare un'istantanea.
shooter s. cacciatore.
shooting s. **1.** tiro, sparo **2.** caccia **3.** il fotografare, il girare un film.
shop s. **1.** bottega, negozio **2.** officina, laboratorio || — -assistant, commesso; — -book, libro dei conti; — -lifter, taccheggiatore; — -window, vetrina.

shopkeeper s. negoziante.
shopman s. commesso di negozio.
shopping s. compere, acquisti (pl.).
shore s. spiaggia, lido.
shorn V. to shear.
short agg. 1. corto, breve 2. basso, piccolo (di statura) 3. conciso 4. brusco, rude. ♦ short s. 1. compendio 2. (cine) cortometraggio.
short avv. 1. bruscamente, improvvisamente 2. (comm.) allo scoperto.
shortage s. mancanza, carenza.
short-circuit s. corto circuito.
short-cut s. scorciatoia.
short-dated agg. (comm.) a breve scadenza.
to shorten vt. accorciare, abbreviare.
shortening s. accorciamento, abbreviazione.
shorthand s. stenografia.
shortly avv. 1. fra breve 2. brevemente.
shortness s. brevità.
short-sighted agg. miope.
shot¹ V. to shoot.
shot² s. 1. sparo, colpo 2. proiettile 3. ripresa cinematografica.
shotgun s. fucile da caccia.
should s. dif. 1. (aus. per le prime pers. del condiz.) I — be very happy, sarei felicissimo 2. dovere: it — be so, dovrebbe essere così.
shoulder s. spalla.
to shoulder vt. e vi. 1. spingere con le spalle 2. portare sulle spalle.
shout s. grido, chiasso.
to shout vt. e vi. gridare, urlare.
shove s. spinta, urto.
to shove vt. spingere. ♦ to shove vi. spingersi.
shovel s. pala.
to shovel vt. spalare.
shoveller s. spalatore.
show s. 1. mostra, esibizione 2. apparenza 2. pompa, ostentazione || — case, bacheca; — down, chiarificazione; — -off, esibizionismo.
to show (showed, shown) vt. e vi. 1. mostrare, far vedere 2. rappresentare, indicare 3. dimostrare, provare 4. apparire, farsi vedere || to — down, mettere le carte in tavola; to — off, darsi delle arie.
shower s. acquazzone, rovescio.
showman s. presentatore.
shown V. to show.

showy agg. fastoso, appariscente.
shrank V. to shrink.
shred s. brandello, frammento.
shrew s. bisbetica.
shrewd agg. sagace, accorto.
shrewdly avv. sagacemente.
shrewdness s. sagacia, accortezza.
shrewish agg. brontolone.
shriek s. grido, strillo, suono lacerante.
to shriek vt. e vi. gridare, stridere.
shrill agg. stridulo, acuto.
to shrill vt. e vi. strillare, stridere.
shrimp s. gamberetto.
shrine s. reliquiario.
shrink s. restringimento.
to shrink (shrank, shrunk) vt. e vi. 1. restringere, restringersi, contrarre 2. indietreggiare.
shrinkable agg. restringibile.
shrinkage s. 1. diminuzione, restringimento 2. (comm.) deprezzamento.
shrinking s. contrazione, ritiro.
shroud s. sudario.
shrub s. arbusto, cespuglio.
shrubbery s. boscaglia d'arbusti.
shrug s. spallucciata.
to shrug vi. alzare le spalle.
shrunk V. to shrink.
shudder s. brivido.
to shudder vi. rabbrividire.
shuffle s. 1. passo strascicato 2. scompiglio 3. il mescolare (le carte).
to shuffle vt. e vi. 1. muoversi a fatica 2. mescolare, scompigliare.
to shun vt. sfuggire, scansare.
shunt s. 1. (elett.) derivazione 2. (ferr.) scambio.
to shunt vt. e vi. 1. (elett.) inserire in derivazione 2. (ferr.) smistare, smistarsi.
shut agg. ben chiuso.
to shut (shut, shut) vt. e vi. chiudere, serrare || shut up!, taci!
shutter s. imposta, persiana.
shuttle s. spola, navetta.
shy agg. riservato, timido.
to shy vt. spaventare. ♦ to shy vi. scartare (di cavallo).
shyly avv. timidamente.
shyness s. timidezza, scontrosità.
Siberian agg. e s. siberiano.
sibilant agg. e s. sibilante.
Sibylline agg. sibillino.
Sicilian agg. e s. siciliano.
sick agg. 1. ammalato 2. nauseato || to fall —, ammalarsi.

to **sicken** vt. e vi. **1.** far ammalare, ammalarsi **2.** sfiorire **3.** sentir nausea.

sickening agg. nauseabondo, rivoltante.

sickle s. falce.

sickly agg. **1.** malaticcio **2.** pallido, debole **3.** nauseante.

sickness s. malattia.

side s. **1.** lato, fianco **2.** parte, partito, fazione **3.** discendenza || — -door, porta laterale; — -face, profilo; — -look, occhiata in tralice; — -note, nota marginale; — -post, stipite.

sideboard s. credenza.

sidecar s. motocarrozzetta.

sidelong agg. laterale, obliquo.

sidereal agg. sidereo.

sideways avv. lateralmente, obliquamente.

to **sidle** vi. camminare di fianco, andare a sghembo || to — up to so., avvicinarsi furtivamente a qu.

siege s. assedio.

sieve s. setaccio, crivello.

to **sieve** vt. setacciare, crivellare.

to **sift** vt. e vi. setacciare **2.** filtrare (di luce, polvere ecc.).

sigh s. sospiro.

to **sigh** vt. e vi. **1.** sospirare **2.** sibilare.

sight s. **1.** vista, visione **2.** veduta, panorama **3.** colpo d'occhio **4.** mirino.

to **sight** vt. e vi. **1.** avvistare **2.** prendere la mira.

sighted agg. **1.** fornito di vista || long- —, presbite; short- —, miope.

sightless agg. senza vista.

sign s. **1.** segno, cenno **2.** indicazione, traccia || traffic —, segnale stradale.

to **sign** vt. e vi. firmare, segnare, sottoscrivere.

signal s. segnale, segno.

to **signal** vt. segnalare. ♦ to **signal** vi. far segnali.

signalman s. segnalatore.

signatory s. firmatario.

signature s. **1.** firma, sigla **2.** (tip.) segnatura.

signboard s. insegna (di albergo, negozio ecc.).

significant agg. espressivo, significativo.

to **signify** vt. e vi. **1.** significare, voler dire **2.** denotare, indicare, presagire **3.** importare.

silence s. silenzio.

to **silence** vt. far tacere, imporre il silenzio.

silencer s. silenziatore.

silent agg. **1.** silenzioso, taciturno **2.** muto.

silently avv. silenziosamente.

silhouette s. profilo, contorno.

silica s. silice.

silicate s. silicato.

silicon s. silicio.

silicosis s. silicosi.

silk s. seta.

silken agg. serico, di seta.

silkworm s. baco da seta || — breeding, sericoltura.

silky agg. di seta, serico.

sill s. basamento, soglia.

silliness s. stupidità, sciocchezza.

silly agg. sciocco, stupido.

to **silo** vt. conservare, mettere in silo.

silt s. melma.

silver s. argento, argenteria || — -plate, argenteria; — -plating, argentatura || quick —, mercurio.

to **silver** vt. inargentare. ♦ to **silver** vi. inargentarsi.

silverware s. oggetti d'argento.

silvery agg. argenteo.

similar agg. simile, analogo.

similarity s. somiglianza, similitudine.

similitude s. **1.** similitudine **2.** somiglianza.

simoniac agg. e s. simoniaco.

simony s. simonia.

to **simper** vi. parlare in modo affettato.

simple agg. **1.** semplice, elementare **2.** sincero **3.** autentico.

simpleton s. sempliciotto.

simplicity s. semplicità, candore.

simplification s. semplificazione.

to **simplify** vt. semplificare.

simply avv. semplicemente.

simulation s. simulazione.

simulator s. simulatore.

simultaneity s. simultaneità.

simultaneous agg. simultaneo.

sin s. **1.** peccato, colpa **2.** offesa.

to **sin** vi. peccare.

since avv. da allora, da allora in poi || long —, molto tempo fa. ♦ **since** cong. **1.** da quando **2.** poiché. ♦ **since** prep. da, fin da.

sincere agg. sincero, schietto.

sincerely avv. sinceramente || yours —, cordialmente vostro (nelle lettere).

sincerity s. sincerità.
sinew s. 1. tendine, nervo 2. (fig.) vigore, nerbo.
sinful agg. peccaminoso, colpevole.
sinfully avv. peccaminosamente.
to **sing (sang, sung)** vt. e vi. cantare.
to **singe** vt. bruciacchiare, strinare (anche fig.). ♦ to **singe** vi. bruciarsi.
singer s. cantante.
singing s. 1. canto 2. fischio (del vento ecc.).
single agg. 1. solo, unico 2. individuale, particolare 3. celibe || every — day, tutti i giorni.
to **single** vt. distinguere, scegliere: to — out sthg., scegliere qc.
singleness s. 1. unicità 2. sincerità.
singly avv. 1. separatamente, ad uno ad uno 2. da solo, senza aiuto.
singsong s. cantilena, canto monotono.
singular agg. 1. singolare, solo 2. eccezionale 3. bizzarro, strano.
singularity s. 1. singolarità, rarità 2. particolarità 3. stranezza.
singularly avv. singolarmente.
sinister agg. sinistro, funesto, di cattivo augurio.
sink s. 1. lavandino, acquaio 2. scolo.
to **sink (sank, sunk)** vi. 1. affondare, andare a fondo 2. sprofondare 3. abbassare, abbassarsi, calare 4. cadere, cedere (di terreno, muro ecc.).
sinner s. peccatore.
sinuous agg. sinuoso.
sinus s. 1. cavità 2. seno.
sip s. sorso.
to **sip** vt. e vi. sorseggiare.
siphon s. sifone.
sir s. 1. (vocativo) signore 2. « sir » (titolo).
siren s. sirena.
siroc s. scirocco.
sirup s. sciroppo.
sister s. 1. sorella 2. suora || — -in--law, cognata.
sisterhood s. congregazione religiosa di suore.
sisterly avv. da sorella, amorevolmente.
to **sit (sat, sat)** vt. e vi. 1. sedere, stare seduto, far sedere 2. essere in seduta 3. appollaiarsi, posare 4. covare || to — out, rimanere fino alla fine; to — up, rimanere al-

zato.
site s. area fabbricabile.
sitting s. 1. posa, seduta 2. adunanza || -room, stanza di soggiorno. ♦ **sittings** s. pl. sessioni (di una Corte).
situated agg. 1. situato, collocato 2. in una certa situazione (di persona).
situation s. 1. situazione, posizione 2. stato, circostanza 3. posto, impiego: to apply for a —, fare una domanda di impiego.
six agg. sei.
sixfold agg. sestuplo. ♦ **sixfold** avv. sei volte tanto.
sixpence s. moneta da sei « pence », mezzo scellino.
sixpenny agg. del valore di sei « pence ».
sixteen agg. sedici.
sixteenth agg. sedicesimo.
sixth agg. sesto.
sixtieth agg. sessantesimo.
sixty agg. sessanta.
size s. 1. grandezza, misura, dimensione 2. formato, taglia 3. colla.
to **size** vt. allineare || to — up, valutare.
sizzle s. sfrigolio.
skate s. pattino || roller —, pattino a rotelle.
to **skate** vi. pattinare.
skating s. pattinaggio.
skein s. matassa.
skeleton s. scheletro (anche fig.).
to **skeletonize** vt. scheletrire. ♦ to **skeletonize** vi. scheletrirsi (anche fig.).
skeptic agg. e s. scettico.
skeptical agg. scettico.
skepticism s. scetticismo.
sketch s. 1. schizzo, abbozzo 2. scenetta.
to **sketch** vt. abbozzare, schizzare.
skewness s. asimmetria.
ski s. sci || — -lift, sciovia.
to **ski** vi. sciare.
skier s. sciatore.
skiff s. (mar.) schifo.
skilful agg. abile, esperto.
skilfully avv. abilmente.
skilfulness s. abilità.
skill s. abilità, destrezza.
skilled agg. esperto, abile, versato || — worker, operaio specializzato.
to **skim** vt. e vi. 1. schiumare, scremare 2. rasentare, sfiorare.
skimmer s. schiumarola.

skimming *s.* scrematura.

skin *s.* pelle, cute.

to **skin** *vt.* e *vi.* scuoiare || *to —
over,* rimarginarsi (*di ferite*).

skinny *agg.* magro, scarno.

to **skip** *vt.* e *vi.* fare un balzo, sal-
tare alla corda || *to — a few pages,*
saltare qualche pagina.

skirmish *s.* scaramuccia.

skirt *s.* **1.** sottana, gonna **2.** orlo,
lembo.

to **skirt** *vt.* e *vi.* orlare, costeggiare.

skittish *agg.* capriccioso, frivolo.

skittles *s. pl.* birilli.

skull *s.* cranio, teschio || *— -cap,*
papalina.

sky *s.* cielo, firmamento.

skylark *s.* allodola.

skylight *s.* lucernario.

skyline *s.* linea, profilo (*di montagne ecc.*).

skyman *s.* paracadutista.

skyscraper *s.* grattacielo.

skyward *agg.* e *avv.* verso il cielo.

slab *s.* **1.** lastra, piastra **2.** pezzo,
fetta.

slack *agg.* **1.** molle, allentato **2.** debole, fiacco **3.** (*comm.*) calmo, stagnante, debole. ♦ **slack** *s.* (*comm.*)
stagione morta.

to **slacken** *vt.* **1.** allentare, mollare
2. diminuire. ♦ to **slacken** *vi.*
1. allentarsi **2.** smorzarsi.

slacker *s.* fannullone.

slain V. *to slay.*

slam *s.* sbatacchiamento.

to **slam** *vt.* sbattere, chiudere violentemente. ♦ to **slam** *vi.* chiudersi violentemente.

slander *s.* **1.** calunnia **2.** (*giur.*) diffamazione.

to **slander** *vt.* **1.** calunniare **2.** (*giur.*)
diffamare.

slanderer *s.* **1.** calunniatore **2.**
(*giur.*) diffamatore.

slanderous *agg.* calunnioso, maldicente.

slang *s.* gergo.

slant *s.* pendenza, inclinazione.

to **slant** *vt.* e *vi.* essere in pendenza,
inclinare.

slanting *agg.* inclinato, obliquo,
sghembo.

slap *s.* schiaffo, ceffone.

to **slap** *vt.* **1.** schiaffeggiare **2.** sbattere.

slash *s.* **1.** taglio, sfregio **2.** frustata.

to **slash** *vt.* tagliare, fendere.

slate *s.* ardesia, tegola d'ardesia.

slaughter *s.* **1.** macello **2.** carneficina, massacro.

to **slaughter** *vt.* **1.** macellare **2.** massacrare.

slaughterer *s.* **1.** macellatore **2.**
massacratore.

slaughterhouse *s.* mattatoio.

Slav *agg.* e *s.* slavo.

slave *s.* schiavo.

slaver[1] *s.* schiavista.

slaver[2] *s.* saliva, bava.

slavery *s.* schiavitù.

to **slay** (**slew, slain**) *vt.* ammazzare.

sleek *agg.* lucido, levigato.

sleep *s.* sonno, dormita || *— walker,*
sonnambulo.

to **sleep** (**slept, slept**) *vt.* e *vi.* **1.**
dormire, riposare **2.** passare la
notte.

sleeper *s.* **1.** dormiente, dormiglione
2. (*ferr.*) traversina **3.** (*ferr.*) vettura letto.

sleepily *avv.* con aria assonnata.

sleeping *agg.* dormiente, addormen-
tato || *— bag,* sacco a pelo; *—
-berth,* cuccetta; *— -car,* vagone
letto; *— -draught,* sonnifero.

sleepless *agg.* insonne.

sleeplessness *s.* insonnia.

sleepy *agg.* assonnato, sonnolento.

sleet *s.* nevischio.

sleeve *s.* manica.

sleeved *agg.* con maniche.

sleigh *s.* slitta.

slender *agg.* **1.** magro, snello **2.** debole, fiacco.

slenderness *s.* **1.** snellezza, magrezza **2.** debolezza.

slept V. *to sleep.*

slew V. *to slay.*

slice *s.* pezzo, fetta, porzione.

to **slice** *vt.* affettare.

slicer *s.* affettatrice.

slid V. *to slide.*

slide *s.* **1.** scivolata **2.** pendenza **3.**
scivolo **4.** (*mecc.*) carrello, pattino.

to **slide** (**slid, slid**) *vt.* e *vi.* **1.**
scivolare, far scivolare, scorrere,
far scorrere **2.** sfuggire.

sliding *agg.* scorrevole.

slight *agg.* **1.** esile, minuto, magro
2. leggero, scarso.

slim *agg.* **1.** magro, sottile **2.** debole.

slime *s.* melma, limo.

slimy *agg.* fangoso, viscoso.

sling[1] *s.* fionda.

sling² s. cinghia.

to **sling¹** (slung, slung) vt. scagliare con la fionda.

to **sling²** vt. sospendere, appendere.

to **slink** (slunk, slunk) vi. sgattaiolare.

slip¹ s. **1.** innesto **2.** (tip.) bozza in colonna.

slip² s. **1.** scalo, molo **2.** guinzaglio **3.** sottoveste **4.** scivolone **5.** papera, lapsus.

to **slip** vt. e vi. **1.** scivolare, inciampare **2.** entrare, uscire furtivamente **3.** sgusciare, liberarsi || to — away, scorrere (di tempo).

slipper s. pantofola.

slippery agg. sdrucciolevole, viscido (anche fig.).

slipshod agg. **1.** scalcagnato **2.** trasandato.

slit s. fessura, fenditura.

to **slit** (slit, slit) vt. fendere.

slope s. pendenza, pendio.

to **slope** vi. essere in pendenza, inclinarsi.

sloping agg. inclinato, obliquo.

slot s. fessura, scanalatura || — -machine, distributore automatico a gettoni.

sloth s. pigrizia, indolenza.

slothful agg. pigro, indolente.

slouch s. andatura dinoccolata.

slouching agg. dinoccolato, goffo.

slovenliness s. sciatteria, sporcizia.

slovenly agg. sciatto, sudicio.

slow agg. **1.** lento **2.** tardo, ottuso || — -down, rallentamento; — -match, miccia.

to **slow** vt. e vi. to — up o down, rallentare.

slowly avv. lentamente.

slowness s. lentezza, pigrizia.

sluggish agg. pigro, tardo, indolente.

sluggishness s. pigrizia, indolenza.

slum s. vicolo, tugurio. ♦ **slums** s. pl. quartieri poveri (di una città).

slumber s. dormiveglia, assopimento.

to **slumber** vt. e vi. dormire, dormicchiare.

slung V. to sling.

slunk V. to slink.

slush s. poltiglia, fango.

sly agg. **1.** astuto, malizioso **2.** infido.

smack s. **1.** sapore, aroma **2.** schiocco **3.** schiaffo.

to **smack** vt. e vi. **1.** schioccare **2.** schioccare baci **3.** schiaffeggiare.

small agg. **1.** piccolo, minuto **2.** leggero, debole **3.** poco, scarso **4.** di poca importanza.

small-arms s. pl. armi portatili.

smallness s. piccolezza.

smallpox s. vaiolo.

smart agg. **1.** acuto, pungente **2.** vivace, sveglio **3.** elegante.

to **smarten** vt. e vi. abbellire || to — up, rianimarsi, farsi bello.

smartness s. **1.** acutezza, vivacità, brio **2.** eleganza.

smash s. **1.** urto, scontro **2.** rovina.

to **smash** vt. **1.** frantumare, fracassare **2.** sconfiggere; annientare. ♦ to **smash** vi. **1.** frantumarsi **2.** sfasciarsi **3.** crollare.

smasher s. **1.** chi frantuma **2.** (fam.) caso eccezionale.

smear s. macchia, imbrattatura.

to **smear** vt. macchiare, imbrattare.

smell s. **1.** odorato, olfatto **2.** odore.

to **smell** (smelt, smelt) vt. e vi. **1.** fiutare, sentire l'odore **2.** avere odore || to — of, sapere di; to — out, scovare.

smile s. sorriso.

to **smile** vt. e vi. sorridere || fortune smil'ed on you, la fortuna ti fu favorevole.

smiling agg. sorridente, sereno.

smirch s. onta, macchia.

to **smite** (smote, smitten) vt. e vi. **1.** colpire, percuotere **2.** sconfiggere, sgominare || to — down, abbattere.

smith s. fabbro.

smitten V. to smite.

smoke s. **1.** fumo **2.** fumata || — -stack, fumaiolo.

to **smoke** vt. e vi. **1.** fumare **2.** affumicare.

smoker s. fumatore, fumatrice.

smoking s. il fumare. ♦ **smoking** agg. fumante.

smoky agg. **1.** fumoso **2.** affumicato, annerito dal fumo **3.** che sa di fumo.

smooth agg. **1.** liscio, levigato **2.** omogeneo **3.** armonioso (di suono) **4.** mellifluo **5.** calmo, tranquillo (di mare).

to **smooth** vt. **1.** lisciare, spianare **2.** appianare.

smoothing s. lisciatura, spianatura.

smoothly avv. **1.** pianamente **2.** armonicamente **3.** in modo mellifluo.

smoothness s. **1.** levigatezza **2.** armonia (di verso, suono) **3.** affabilità.

smote V. *to* smite.

to **smother** *vt.* e *vi.* **1.** soffocare, opprimere **2.** ricoprire.

to **smoulder** *vi.* ardere sotto la cenere.

to **smuggle** *vt.* e *vi.* contrabbandare.

smuggler *s.* contrabbandiere.

smuggling *s.* contrabbando.

smut *s.* fuliggine.

snack *s.* **1.** boccone, porzione **2.** spuntino || — -*bar,* tavola calda.

snail *s.* chiocciola, lumaca.

snake *s.* serpente.

snakily *avv.* **1.** tortuosamente **2.** (*fig.*) slealmente.

snaky *agg.* serpentino.

snap *s.* **1.** colpo secco, morso, schiocco **2.** scatto **3.** fermaglio, fibbia.

to **snap** *vt.* e *vi.* **1.** schioccare, far schioccare **2.** aprirsi di colpo, spezzare con un colpo secco **3.** (*foto*) scattare un'istantanea.

snapshot *s.* (*foto*) istantanea.

snare *s.* **1.** trappola, rete **2.** insidia, tentazione.

to **snare** *vt.* prendere in trappola, al laccio (*anche fig.*).

snarl *s.* ringhio.

to **snarl** *vi.* ringhiare.

snatch *s.* **1.** strappo, strattone **2.** brano, frammento.

to **snatch** *vt.* e *vi.* afferrare, ghermire || *to* — *off,* strappare.

sneak *s.* persona malfida.

sneer *s.* sogghigno beffardo.

to **sneer** *vt.* e *vi.* sorridere beffardamente, schernire.

sneeze *s.* starnuto.

to **sneeze** *vi.* starnutire.

to **sniff** *vt.* e *vi.* fiutare || *to* — *at sthg.* annusare qc.

snip *s.* **1.** ritaglio, scampolo **2.** forbiciata.

to **snip** *vt.* tagliuzzare.

snobbery *s.* snobismo.

to **snore** *vi.* russare.

snort *s.* sbuffo, rumore sbuffante.

to **snort** *vt.* e *vi.* sbuffare.

snout *s.* muso, grugno.

snow *s.* neve, nevicata || — *plough,* spazzaneve; — -*slide,* valanga.

to **snow** *v. imp.* nevicare || *it is snowing,* nevica.

snowfall *s.* nevicata.

snowflake *s.* fiocco di neve.

snowy *agg.* **1.** nevoso, coperto di neve **2.** niveo.

snuff *s.* **1.** l'aspirare col naso **2.** tabacco da fiuto || — -*box,* tabacchiera.

to **snuff**[1] *vt.* e *vi.* **1.** annusare aspirando **2.** fiutare tabacco.

to **snuff**[2] *vt.* e *vi.* smoccolare (*una candela*).

to **snuffle** *vt.* e *vi.* pronunciare con tono nasale.

snug *agg.* **1.** comodo **2.** confortevole **3.** nascosto.

to **snuggle** *vi.* **1.** rannicchiarsi **2.** accoccolarsi.

so *avv.* così, tanto, talmente || — *far,* fino ad ora; — *long as,* a patto che; *if* —, in tal caso; *that being* —, stando così le cose.

to **soak** *vt.* **1.** immergere **2.** bagnare. ♦ to **soak** *vi.* **1.** inzupparsi, imbeversi **2.** bagnarsi.

soaking *agg.* **1.** che bagna, che inzuppa **2.** bagnato. ♦ **soaking** *s.* immersione, bagnatura.

soap *s.* sapone || — *dish,* portasapone.

to **soap** *vt.* insaponare. ♦ to **soap** *vi.* insaponarsi.

soapbox *s.* **1.** cassa per sapone **2.** (*fam.*) palco improvvisato per oratori (*da strada*).

soapsuds *s. pl.* saponata (*sing.*).

soapwort *s.* saponaria.

sob *s.* singhiozzo.

to **sob** *vt.* e *vi.* singhiozzare.

sober *agg.* **1.** sobrio (*nel bere*) **2.** calmo, composto.

sobriety *s.* **1.** sobrietà (*nel bere*) **2.** moderazione, calma.

so-called *agg.* cosiddetto.

sociability *s.* socievolezza.

sociable *agg.* socievole.

social *agg.* **1.** sociale **2.** socievole.

socialism *s.* socialismo.

socialist *s.* socialista.

sociality *s.* socievolezza.

to **socialize** *vt.* socializzare.

society *s.* **1.** società, compagnia **2.** strato sociale **3.** associazione.

sociological *agg.* sociologico.

sociologist *s.* sociologo.

sociology *s.* sociologia.

sock *s.* **1.** calzino, calza corta **2.** soletta.

socket *s.* **1.** cavità **2.** (*elett.*) presa di corrente, portalampada **3.** (*anat.*) orbita.

Socratic *agg.* e *s.* socratico.

sod *s.* zolla erbosa.

soda *s.* carbonato di sodio.

sodium *s.* sodio.
soft *agg.* **1.** molle, tenero **2.** liscio, morbido, soffice **3.** dolce, mite ‖ — *-boiled* (*egg*), uovo alla coque.
to soften *vt.* **1.** ammollire, ammorbidire **2.** calmare, raddolcire. ♦ **to soften** *vi.* **1.** ammorbidirsi **2.** intenerirsi.
softening *agg.* che rende molle. ♦ **softening** *s.* **1.** ammorbidimento **2.** intenerimento.
softly *avv.* **1.** teneramente **2.** sommessamente **3.** pian piano.
softness *s.* **1.** morbidezza **2.** dolcezza, mitezza.
soil *s.* **1.** suolo, terreno **2.** macchia (*anche fig.*).
to soil *vt.* macchiare. ♦ **to soil** *vi.* macchiarsi.
sojourn *s.* soggiorno.
to sojourn *vi.* soggiornare.
solace *s.* sollievo, conforto.
to solace *vt.* consolare.
solar *agg.* solare.
sold V. *to sell.*
solder *s.* lega per saldatura.
to solder *vt.* saldare.
soldering *s.* saldatura.
soldier *s.* **1.** soldato **2.** stratega ‖ *foot-* —, soldato di fanteria; *horse-* —, soldato di cavalleria.
soldierlike *agg.* militaresco.
soldiery *s.* *coll.* soldatesca, truppe.
sole[1] *agg.* solo, unico.
sole[2] *s.* suola, pianta del piede.
sole[3] *s.* sogliola.
solecism *s.* solecismo.
solely *avv.* solamente.
solemn *agg.* solenne, serio, grave.
solemnity *s.* solennità.
to solemnize *vt.* solennizzare.
solemnly *avv.* solennemente.
sol-fa *s.* solfeggio.
to sol-fa *vt. e vi.* solfeggiare.
to solicit *vt.* **1.** sollecitare **2.** adescare. ♦ **to solicit** *vi.* fare sollecitazioni.
solicitation *s.* **1.** sollecitazione **2.** invito, adescamento.
solicitor *s.* **1.** sollecitatore **2.** procuratore legale.
solicitous *agg.* **1.** sollecito **2.** ansioso, desideroso.
solid *agg.* **1.** solido, compatto **2.** reale, fondato. ♦ **solid** *s.* solido.
solidarity *s.* solidarietà.
solidary *agg.* solidale.
solidification *s.* solidificazione.
to solidify *vt.* solidificare. ♦ **to so-**

lidify *vi.* solidificarsi.
solidity *s.* **1.** solidità **2.** (*comm.*) solvenza.
solidly *avv.* **1.** solidamente **2.** all'unanimità.
soliloquy *s.* soliloquio.
solitaire *s.* solitario (*pietra preziosa e giuoco delle carte*).
solitary *agg.* **1.** solo, unico **2.** solitario **3.** isolato, romito.
solitude *s.* solitudine, isolamento.
soloist *s.* solista.
solstice *s.* solstizio.
solubility *s.* solubilità.
soluble *agg.* **1.** solubile **2.** scomponibile **3.** risolvibile.
solution *s.* **1.** (*chim.*) soluzione **2.** risoluzione.
solvability *s.* **1.** (*comm.*) solvibilità **2.** solubilità **3.** risolvibilità.
solvable *agg.* **1.** (*comm.*) solvibile **2.** solubile **3.** risolvibile.
to solve *vt.* risolvere, chiarire.
solvency *s.* (*comm.*) solvibilità.
solvent *agg.* **1.** (*comm.*) solvibile **2.** solvente. ♦ **solvent** *s.* solvente.
somatic(al) *agg.* somatico.
somatology *s.* somatologia.
sombre *agg.* **1.** fosco, scuro **2.** (*fig.*) tetro, triste.
some *agg.* **1.** qualche, alcuni, certi **2.** un certo, qualsiasi **3.** (*partitivo*) un po' di, del, della, dei, degli, delle. ♦ **some** *pron.* **1.** alcuni, alcune **2.** un po'. ♦ **some** *avv.* circa.
somebody *pron. indef.* qualcuno.
somehow *avv.* in qualche modo, in un modo o nell'altro.
someone *pron. indef.* qualcuno: — *else*, qualcun altro.
somersault *s.* **1.** salto mortale, capriola **2.** (*aer.*) capottamento **3.** (*auto*) ribaltamento.
to somersault, to somerset *vi.* **1.** fare salti mortali **2.** (*aer.*) capottare **3.** (*auto.*) ribaltare.
something *pron. indef.* qualche cosa.
sometime *avv.* **1.** un tempo **2.** presto o tardi, un giorno o l'altro.
sometimes *avv.* qualche volta, alcune volte.
someway *avv.* in un modo o nell'altro.
somewhat *pron. ind.* un poco.
somewhere *avv.* in qualche luogo.
somnambulism *s.* sonnambulismo.
somnambulist *s.* sonnambulo.

somnolent *agg.* **1.** sonnolento **2.** assopito.

son *s.* figlio, figliolo || — *-in-law,* genèro.

song *s.* canto, canzone.

songbook *s.* canzoniere.

songful *agg.* **1.** melodioso **2.** che ama cantare.

songster *s.* cantante (*uomo*).

sonnet *s.* sonetto.

sonority *s.* sonorità.

sonorous *agg.* sonoro, risonante.

sonorously *avv.* sonoramente.

soon (*comp. di* sooner) *avv.* presto, tra poco || *the sooner the better,* prima è meglio è; *sooner or later,* presto o tardi; *I had sooner,* preferirei; *as* — *as,* non appena.

soot *s.* fuliggine.

to **soot** *vt.* macchiare, sporcare di fuliggine.

to **soothe** *vt.* calmare, placare.

soothsayer *s.* indovino.

sooty *agg.* fuligginoso.

sophism *s.* sofisma.

sophist *s.* sofista (*anche fig.*).

sophistic(al) *agg.* sofistico, pedante.

sophisticated *agg.* **1.** sofisticato, raffinato **2.** adulterato.

sophistry *s.* sofisma.

sorcerer *s.* stregone, mago.

sorceress *s.* strega, maga.

sorcery *s.* stregoneria, sortilegio.

sordid *agg.* **1.** sordido, avaro **2.** vile, meschino.

sore *agg.* **1.** doloroso, dolorante, infiammato **2.** triste, addolorato **3.** estremo, intenso.

sorrel *s.* sauro.

sorrow *s.* **1.** dispiacere, dolore **2.** rincrescimento **3.** sventura.

to **sorrow** *vi.* affliggersi, addolorarsi.

sorrowful *agg.* **1.** triste, infelice **2.** penoso, doloroso.

sorry *agg.* spiacente, dolente || *sorry!,* scusate!; *to be* —, dispiacersi.

sort *s.* sorta, specie.

to **sort** *vt.* raggruppare, selezionare.

♦ to **sort** *vi.* accordarsi, adattarsi.

sought V. *to seek.*

soul *s.* **1.** anima, animo, spirito **2.** essenza, personificazione.

sound[1] *avv.* profondamente.

sound[2] *agg.* **1.** sano, intero, in buono stato **2.** buono, solido **3.** profondo, completo || — *-headed* equilibra-to, — *-minded,* di buon senso.

sound[3] *s.* suono, rumore || — *wave,* onda sonora.

sound[4] *s.* sondaggio.

sound[5] *s.* braccio di mare, stretto.

to **sound**[1] *vt. e vi.* **1.** suonare, risuonare **2.** sembrare, aver l'aria di.

to **sound**[2] *vt. e vi.* sondare, scandagliare.

sounding *agg.* sonoro, sonante, risonante.

soundless *agg.* muto, senza suono.

soundly *avv.* **1.** sanamente **2.** profondamente.

soundness *s.* **1.** buona condizione (*di salute*) **2.** solidità (*di argomento*).

soup *s.* zuppa, minestra.

sour *agg.* **1.** acido, aspro, acerbo **2.** bisbetico.

to **sour** *vt. e vi.* **1.** inacidire **2.** inasprire, esacerbare.

source *s.* **1.** fonte, sorgente **2.** origine.

sourdine *s.* (*mus.*) sordina.

sourish *agg.* acidulo.

sourness *s.* acidità.

south *s.* sud, mezzogiorno.

southern *agg.* del sud, meridionale.

southerner *s.* abitante del sud, meridionale.

southward *avv.* verso sud.

sovereign *s.* sovrano.

sovereignty *s.* sovranità.

sow *s.* scrofa.

to **sow** (**sowed, sown**) *vt. e vi.* seminare, piantare.

sowing *s.* seminagione.

sown V. *to sow.*

spa *s.* sorgente minerale.

space *s.* spazio || — *-ship,* astronave.

to **space** *vt.* spaziare, disporre ad intervalli.

spaceman *s.* astronauta.

spacesuit *s.* tuta spaziale.

spacial *agg.* spaziale.

spacing *s.* spaziatura, interlineatura.

spacious *agg.* spazioso, ampio.

spade *s.* vanga, badile.

span V. *to spin.*

span *s.* **1.** spanna, palmo **2.** breve spazio di tempo.

to **span** *vt.* **1.** misurare a spanne **2.** attraversare.

spangle *s.* lustrino.

Spaniard *s.* spagnolo.

Spanish *agg.* spagnolo.

to **spank** *vt.* (*fam.*) sculacciare.

spar¹ s. (*mar.*) antenna.

spar² s. incontro di pugilato.

spare agg. 1. parco, frugale 2. d'avanzo, disponibile, in più || — *room*, camera in più (*per gli ospiti*); — *time*, tempo disponibile; — *wheel*, ruota di scorta.

to **spare** vt. 1. economizzare, risparmiare 2. privarsi, fare a meno di. ♦ to **spare** vi. essere frugale.

sparing agg. 1. parco, frugale 2. limitato, .moderato.

spark s. 1. scintilla, favilla 2. (*fig.*) lampo, barlume.

to **spark** vi. scintillare, emettere scintille.

sparkle s. scintilla, favilla.

to **sparkle** vi. 1. emettere scintille (*di fuoco*) 2. sfavillare, brillare, risplendere (*anche fig.*).

sparkler s. stella filante.

sparkling agg. scintillante, vivace (*anche fig.*).

sparrow s. passero || — -*hawk*, sparviero.

Spartan agg. e s. spartano.

spasm s. 1. spasmo 2. attacco, spasimo (*anche fig.*).

spasmodic(al) agg. spasmodico.

spastic agg. spastico.

spat V. to *spit*.

spatial agg. spaziale.

spatiality s. spazialità.

spatter s. 1. schizzo 2. sgocciolio.

to **spatter** vt. e vi. 1. schizzare, inzaccherare 2. gocciolare.

to **speak (spoke, spoken)** vt. e vi. 1. parlare 2. esprimere, rivelare || *to — at*, alludere a; *to — out*, parlare francamente; *to — to*, garantire; *to — up*, alzare la voce.

speaker s. parlatore, oratore, annunciatore || *the — of the House of Commons*, il Presidente della Camera dei Comuni.

speaking agg. parlante, espressivo, eloquente. ♦ **speaking** s. 1. il parlare, discorso 2. eloquenza, declamazione.

spear s. 1. lancia, alabarda, asta 2. fiocina.

to **spear** vt. 1. trafiggere (*con lancia*) 2. fiocinare.

special agg. 1. speciale, particolare 2. eccezionale, straordinario.

specialist s. specialista.

speciality s. specialità, particolarità.

to **specialize** vt. specializzare. ♦ to

specialize vi. specializzarsi.

specially avv. specialmente, soprattutto.

specialty s. 1. (*comm.*) specialità 2. (*giur.*) contratto sigillato.

species s. 1. specie, classe 2. sorta, genere, tipo.

specific agg. specifico, particolare.

specification s. 1. specificazione 2. descrizione dettagliata.

to **specify** vt. specificare, precisare.

specimen s. modello, esemplare.

speck s. 1. macchiolina, punto 2. granello (*di polvere ecc.*).

speckled agg. macchiato, screziato.

speckless agg. senza macchia (*anche fig.*).

spectacle s. spettacolo, vista. ♦ **spectacles** s. pl. occhiali: *to put on one's* —, mettersi gli occhiali.

spectacled agg. che porta gli occhiali.

spectacular agg. spettacolare.

spectator s. spettatore.

spectral agg. spettrale.

spectre s. spettro, fantasma.

specular agg. speculare.

to **speculate** vt. e vi. 1. meditare, considerare 2. (*comm.*) speculare.

speculation s. 1. speculazione, meditazione 2. (*comm.*) speculazione.

speculative agg. contemplativo, speculativo (*anche comm.*).

speculator s. 1. spirito speculatore 2. (*comm.*) speculatore.

sped V. to *speed*.

speech s. 1. parola, favella 2. discorso, arringa 3. linguaggio.

speechless agg. senza parola, muto (*anche fig.*).

speed s. velocità, rapidità.

to **speed** vi. affrettarsi. ♦ to **speed (sped, sped)** vt. 1. aiutare 2. affrettare 3. regolare la velocità || *to — up the work*, affrettare i lavori.

speedometer s. tachimetro.

speedway s. pista, circuito (*di autodromo*).

speedy agg. rapido, pronto.

spell¹ s. incantesimo.

spell² s. 1. turno di lavoro 2. intervallo.

to **spell (spelt, spelt)** (*anche reg.*) vt. e vi. compitare, sillabare.

to **spellbind (spellbound, spellbound)** vt. incantare, affascinare.

spelling s. 1. compitazione 2. ortografia.

spelt V. *to spell*.

to **spend (spent, spent)** *vt. e vi.*
1. spendere, sborsare **2.** dedicare,
impiegare **3.** passare, trascorrere.

sperm *s.* sperma.

sphenoid *agg. e s.* sfenoide.

sphere *s.* sfera, globo.

spheric(al) *agg.* sferico.

sphericity *s.* sfericità.

sphincter *s.* sfintere.

Sphinx *s.* sfinge (*anche fig.*).

spice *s.* **1.** aroma **2.** (*fig.*) sapore,
gusto **3.** spezie (*pl.*).

to **spice** *vt.* **1.** condire con spezie
2. (*fig.*) dar gusto a, rendere interessante.

spicery *s.* spezie, aromi (*pl.*).

spicily *avv.* **1.** aromaticamente **2.**
(*fig.*) gustosamente.

spiciness *s.* **1.** aroma, profumo **2.**
(*fam.*) arguzia.

spick-and-span *agg.* (*fam.*) lindo,
lucente.

spicy *agg.* **1.** aromatico, piccante **2.**
(*fig.*) arguto, mordace.

spider *s.* ragno.

spidery *agg.* **1.** simile a ragno **2.**
infestato da ragni.

spike[1] *s.* punta, aculeo.

spike[2] *s.* spiga.

to **spike** *vt.* inchiodare || *to —
so.'s guns*, guastare i piani di qu.

to **spill (spilt, spilt)** *vt.* **1.** versare **2.** disarcionare. ♦ to **spill
(spilt, spilt)** *vi.* versarsi, traboccare.

spin *s.* (*aer.*) avvitamento.

to **spin (span, spun)** *vt. e vi.* **1.**
filare (*cotone ecc.*) **2.** (*mecc.*) lavorare al tornio **3.** girare, far girare.

spinach *s.* spinacio.

spinal *agg.* spinale.

spindle *s.* **1.** fuso, fusello **2.** (*mecc.*)
asse, mandrino.

spine *s.* **1.** spina, lisca **2.** spina dorsale.

spineless *agg.* **1.** senza spine **2.** senza spina dorsale **3.** (*fam.*) debole,
molle.

spinner *s.* **1.** ragno filatore **2.** (*aer.*)
ogiva **3.** filatore.

spinning *s.* **1.** filatura, filato **2.** mo-
vimento rotatorio || *— -mill*, fi-
landa.

spinster *s.* **1.** filatrice **2.** donna nu-
bile, zitella.

spiral *agg.* spirale, a spirale. ♦
spiral *s.* spirale.

spire[1] *s.* guglia, cuspide.

spire[2] *s.* spira, spirale.

spirit *s.* **1.** spirito, anima **2.** folletto, fantasma **3.** genio, intelletto
4. coraggio, vigore.

spirits[1] *s. pl.* umore, stato d'animo
(*sing.*).

spirits[2] *s. pl.* bevande fortemente
alcooliche.

spirited *agg.* brioso, vivace || *high-
- —*, fiero; *poor- —*, depresso.

spiritism *s.* spiritismo.

spiritual *agg.* spirituale.

spiritualism *s.* **1.** spiritualismo **2.**
spiritismo.

spiritualist *s.* **1.** spiritualista **2.** spiritista.

spirituality *s.* spiritualità.

spit *s.* sputo, saliva.

to **spit (spat, spat)** *vi.* sputare.

spite *s.* dispetto, ripicco: *out of
—*, per dispetto; *in — of*, a dispetto di.

spiteful *agg.* dispettoso.

spittle V. *spit*.

spittoon *s.* sputacchiera.

splash *s.* **1.** schizzo, spruzzo **2.** tonfo.

to **splash** *vt. e vi.* **1.** schizzare,
spruzzare **2.** inzaccherare, infangare. ♦ to **splash** *vi.* **1.** spruzzare
2. cadere con un tonfo.

splashy *agg.* bagnato, fangoso.

splay *agg.* largo e piatto. ♦ **splay**
s. (*arch.*) strombatura.

to **splay** *vt.* (*arch.*) strombare. ♦
to **splay** *vi.* essere in posizione
obliqua.

spleen *s.* **1.** milza **2.** (*fig.*) malumore, umore nero.

splendid *agg.* splendido, magnifico.

splendour *s.* splendore, lustro.

splenetic *agg. e s.* splenetico, bilioso.

splinter *s.* scheggia, frantume.

split *agg.* spaccato, diviso. ♦ **split**
s. **1.** fessura, crepaccio **2.** scissione.

to **split (split, split)** *vt.* **1.** fen-
dere **2.** spaccare, frazionare || *to
— hairs*, spaccare un capello in
quattro; *to — one's sides* (*with
laughing*), ridere a crepapelle. ♦
to **split (split, split)** *vi.* fen-
dersi.

splitting *agg.* che si fende, che fende. ♦ **splitting** *s.* fessura, spaccatura.

spoil(s) *s.* spoglia, preda.

to **spoil** (**spoilt, spoilt**) (*anche reg.*) *vt.* e *vi.* 1. rovinare, alterare, sciupare, viziare 2. saccheggiare, predare.

spoilt *agg.* 1. guasto, avariato 2. viziato.

spoke *s.* 1. raggio (*di ruota*) 2. piolo (*di scala*).

spoke V. *to speak.*

spoken V. *to speak.*

spokesman *s.* portavoce.

spoliation *s.* ruberia, saccheggio.

sponge *s.* spugna, colpo di spugna.

to **sponge** *vt.* 1. pulire, lavare con la spugna 2. fare spugnature 3. (*fig.; fam.*) scroccare.

sponger *s.* 1. pescatore di spugne 2. scroccone.

spongy *agg.* spugnoso, poroso.

sponsor *s.* 1. padrino, madrina 2. (*giur.*) garante, mallevadore.

to **sponsor** *vt.* 1. essere garante di 2. offrire (*programmi radio, tv*).

sponsorial *agg.* 1. di garanzia 2. di padrino, di madrina.

sponsorship *s.* 1. garanzia 2. qualità di padrino, di madrina.

spontaneity *s.* spontaneità.

spontaneous *agg.* spontaneo.

spontaneously *avv.* spontaneamente.

spool *s.* rocchetto, bobina.

spoon *s.* cucchiaio.

to **spoon** *vt.* prendere con un cucchiaio.

spoon-fed *agg.* coccolato, viziato.

spoonful *s.* cucchiaiata.

sporadic *agg.* sporadico, raro.

sport *s.* 1. giuoco, divertimento 2. scherzo 3. sport. ◆ **sports** *s. pl* gare, incontri.

to **sport** *vi.* 1. scherzare 2. giocare 3. fare dello sport.

sporting *agg.* sportivo.

sportive *agg.* 1. gioviale 2. sportivo.

sportsman *s.* 1. sportivo 2. uomo animato da spirito sportivo.

sportsmanlike *agg.* caratteristico di uno sportivo.

sportswoman *s.* donna sportiva.

spot *s.* 1. luogo, località 2. macchia (*anche fig.*) || *on the* —, sul colpo.

to **spot** *vt.* macchiare, punteggiare. ◆ to **spot** *vi.* macchiarsi.

spotless *agg.* senza macchia, immacolato (*anche fig.*).

spotlight *s.* riflettore, luce della ribalta.

spotty *agg.* macchiato, chiazzato.

spout *s.* 1. tubo di scarico, grondaia 2. getto, colonna (*d'acqua*).

to **spout** *vt.* scaricare, emettere. ◆ to **spout** *vi.* scaturire, zampillare.

sprain *s.* distorsione, strappo muscolare.

to **sprain** *vt.* storcere, slogare.

sprang V. *to spring.*

to **sprawl** *vi.* sdraiarsi in modo scomposto.

spray *s.* 1. spruzzo, schiuma 2. getto vaporizzato (*di acqua ecc.*) 3. spruzzatore.

to **spray** *vt.* 1. polverizzare, vaporizzare 2. aspergere, spruzzare.

sprayer *s.* spruzzatore.

spread *agg.* steso, aperto, spiegato.

to **spread** (**spread, spread**) *vt.* 1. stendere, spiegare, spalmare 2. (*fig.*) spargere, diffondere. ◆ to **spread** (**spread, spread**) *vi.* stendersi, spiegarsi.

spreader *s.* spruzzatore.

spreading *agg.* che si propaga. ◆ **spreading** *s.* (*fig.*) propagazione.

spree *s.* baldoria.

sprig *s.* 1. ramoscello 2. (*fig.*) rampollo.

spring *s.* 1. sorgente, fonte 2. primavera 3. salto, balzo 4. molla, elasticità || — *-board*, trampolino; — *-head*, fontana; — *-mattress*, materasso a molle.

to **spring** (**sprang, sprung**) *vi.* 1. nascere, discendere, scaturire (*di acqua*) 2. saltare 3. scattare || *to* — *up*, crescere (*di piante*). ◆ to **spring** (**sprang, sprung**) *vt.* 1. far scattare (*con una molla*) 2. far brillare (*una mina*) 3. saltare.

springiness *s.* elasticità.

springy *agg.* 1. pieno di sorgenti 2. elastico.

sprinkle *s.* aspersione, spruzzatina.

to **sprinkle** *vt.* e *vi.* spruzzare, aspergere.

sprinkler *s.* 1. spruzzatore, innaffiatoio 2. aspersorio.

sprint *s.* (*sport*) scatto finale.

to **sprout** *vi.* germogliare. ◆ to **sprout** *vt.* far germogliare.

to **spruce** *vt.* adornare, agghindare.

sprung V. *to spring.* ◆ **sprung** *agg.* 1. a molla 2. spaccato.

spun V. *to spin.*

spur *s.* 1. sperone 2. (*fig.*) sprone.

to **spur** *vt.* 1. spronare 2. (*fig.*) incitare.

to **spurn** vt. e vi. disdegnare, trattare con disprezzo.

spurt s. getto, vampata.

spy s. spia.

to **spy** vt. e vi. spiare, fare la spia.

squabble s. battibecco, lite.

to **squabble** vi. accapigliarsi, venire a parole.

squad s. squadra, one.

squalid agg. squallido, miserabile.

squall s. urlo, strepito.

squalor s. squallore.

to **squander** vt. sprecare, scialacquare.

squanderer s. sciupone, sperperatore.

square agg. 1. quadrato 2. robusto, massiccio 3. perpendicolare. ♦ **square** s. 1. quadrato 2. piazza 3. squadra || — -built, tarchiato; — -root, radice quadrata; — -shouldered, dalle spalle larghe e diritte. ♦ **square** avv. ad angolo retto, in squadra.

to **square** vt. e vi. 1. quadrare, squadrare 2. pareggiare un conto 3. elevare al quadrato.

squared agg. 1. squadrato, quadrato 2. elevato al quadrato.

squash s. 1. cosa schiacciata 2. spremuta (di frutta): orange- — spremuta d'arancio.

to **squash** vt. 1. schiacciare, spiaccicare 2. spremere.

squat agg. rannicchiato, accoccolato.

to **squat** vi. accovacciarsi, accoccolarsi.

squatter s. pioniere.

squeak s. 1. grido acuto 2. pigolio, squittio, guaito 3. cigolio.

to **squeak** vt. e vi. 1. strillare in tono acuto 2. squittire, guaire 3. cigolare.

squeaky agg. 1. che strilla 2. che guaisce, squittisce 3. cigolante.

squeamish agg. 1. soggetto a nausee 2. schizzinoso.

squeeze s. 1. compressione 2. spremitura 3. stretta, abbraccio.

to **squeeze** vt. 1. spremere 2. stringere, abbracciare. ♦ to **squeeze** vi. accalcarsi.

squeezer s. 1. ciò che preme 2. (mecc.) torchio.

squid s. seppia.

squint agg. strabico. ♦ **squint** s. strabismo.

to **squint** vi. essere strabico. ♦ to **squint** vt. guardare di traverso.

squire s. gentiluomo, nobiluomo (di campagna).

squirrel s. scoiattolo.

stab s. coltellata, pugnalata.

to **stab** vt. pugnalare, accoltellare.

to **stabilize** vt. stabilizzare.

stabilizer s. stabilizzatore.

stable[1] agg. stabile, permanente.

stable[2] s. scuderia, stalla.

stack s. mucchio, cumulo || chimney- —, ciminiera.

to **stack** vt. ammucchiare, accumulare.

staff s. 1. bastone, sostegno (anche fig.) 2. stato maggiore 3. personale (di ufficio ecc.) || editorial —, corpo redazionale; flag —, asta della bandiera.

stag s. cervo.

stage s. 1. piattaforma 2. palcoscenico 3. (fig.) campo d'azione, scena 4. stadio, grado 5. tappa || — -direction, didascalia; — -director, regista (teat.); — -effect, effetto scenico; — -name, nome d'arte; landing- — (mar.), pontile.

to **stage** vt. 1. mettere in scena 2. inscenare (una dimostrazione ecc.).

stagger s. barcollamento, andatura a zig-zag.

to **stagger** vi. 1. vacillare 2. dubitare, esitare. ♦ to **stagger** vt. far vacillare.

staginess s. teatralità.

staging s. 1. (teat.) messa in scena 2. (edil.) impalcatura.

stagnancy s. ristagno.

stagnant agg. stagnante.

to **stagnate** vi. ristagnare.

stagnation s. ristagno, stasi.

staid agg. posato, serio.

stain s. 1. scolorimento, macchia 2. (fig.) taccia, onta.

to **stain** vt. 1. macchiare 2. tingere. ♦ to **stain** vi. macchiarsi, sporcarsi.

stained agg. macchiato, sporco.

stainless agg. senza macchia.

stair s. scalino, gradino. ♦ **stairs** s. pl. scale || winding- —, scala a chiocciola; flight of —, rampa di scale.

staircase s. 1. scala, scalone 2. tromba delle scale.

stairway s. scalinata.

stake[1] s. 1. palo, paletto 2. piccola incudine.

stake[2] s. posta, scommessa || at —, in giuoco. ♦ **stakes** s. pl. (ippica) premio, corsa.

to **stake**[1] *vt.* cintare, chiudere (*con una palizzata*).

to **stake**[2] *vt.* mettere in giuoco, scommettere.

stale *agg.* **1.** vecchio, stantio **2.** (*fig.*) trito, caduto in disuso.

stalk[1] *s.* stelo, gambo.

stalk[2] *s.* andatura rigida e maestosa.

stall *s.* **1.** stalla **2.** bancarella, chiosco.

stammer *s.* balbuzie, balbettamento.

to **stammer** *vt.* e *vi.* **1.** balbettare **2.** farfugliare.

stammering *agg.* balbuziente. ♦ **stammering** *s.* balbuzie.

stamp *s.* **1.** impronta, segno **2.** francobollo, bollo **3.** stampo || — -*collector*, filatelico; — -*paper*, carta bollata.

to **stamp** *vt.* **1.** imprimere, incidere **2.** (*fig.*) dare l'impronta **3.** timbrare || *to — down*, calpestare. ♦ to **stamp** *vi.* battere i piedi.

stamping *s.* **1.** scalpitio **2.** timbratura.

stand *s.* **1.** pausa, fermata **2.** punto di vista **3.** posizione, luogo (*d'appostamento*) **4.** palco, tribuna **5.** bancarella, chiosco || *test*-—, banco di prova.

to **stand** (**stood, stood**) *vi.* **1.** essere, stare in piedi **2.** stare, trovarsi **3.** fermarsi, indugiare **4.** conservarsi, rimaner valido || *to — by*, stare accanto, restare fedele a; *to — for*, significare, implicare; *to — out*, resistere, tener duro, spiccare. ♦ to **stand** (**stood, stood**) *vt.* sopportare, resistere.

standard *s.* **1.** stendardo, bandiera **2.** modello, campione **3.** livello, qualità **4.** supporto, base **5.** tino.

standardization *s.* standardizzazione.

stand-by *s.* scorta, riserva.

standing *agg.* **1.** eretto, che sta in piedi **2.** fermo, inattivo **3.** fisso, immutabile. ♦ **standing** *s.* **1.** posizione eretta **2.** posizione, rango **3.** periodo di tempo.

standoffish *agg.* riservato, altezzoso.

standpoint *s.* **1.** luogo di osservazione **2.** punto di vista.

standstill *agg.* in riposo, fermo. ♦ **standstill** *s.* arresto, fermata.

stank V. *to stink*.

staple *s.* **1.** prodotto principale (*di un paese ecc.*) **2.** (*fig.*) argomento principale (*di una conversazione*).

star *s.* **1.** stella, astro **2.** (*fig.*) fortuna, destino **3.** (*tip.*) asterisco.

to **star** *vt.* **1.** costellare **2.** segnare con un asterisco. ♦ to **star** *vi.* (*cine, teat.*) avere il ruolo di protagonista.

starboard *agg.* di dritta. ♦ **starboard** *s.* (*mar.*) dritta.

starch *s.* **1.** amido **2.** (*fig.*) rigidezza, formalismo.

to **starch** *vt.* **1.** inamidare **2.** (*fig.*) rendere formale.

starchiness *s.* **1.** inamidatura **2.** (*fig.*) formalismo, rigidità.

stardom *s.* divismo.

stare *s.* sguardo fisso.

to **stare** *vt.* guardare intensamente, fissare. ♦ to **stare** *vi.* sgranare gli occhi.

starfish *s.* stella di mare.

staring *agg.* **1.** fisso, stupefatto **2.** sgargiante, vistoso.

staringly *avv.* fissamente, con occhi sbarrati.

stark *agg.* **1.** rigido, duro **2.** completo, vero e proprio.

starless *agg.* senza stelle.

starlet *s.* **1.** piccola stella **2.** (*cine*) stellina.

starlight *agg.* stellato, stellare. ♦ **starlight** *s.* luce stellare.

starlike *agg.* simile a stella.

starlit *agg.* illuminato dalle stelle.

starred *agg.* **1.** stellato, adorno di stelle **2.** a stella.

starry *agg.* stellato, trapunto di stelle, brillante come una stella.

start *s.* **1.** inizio, partenza **2.** soprassalto || *by fits and starts*, irregolarmente **3.** vantaggio dato all'inizio di una corsa **4.** (*mecc.*) avviamento.

to **start** *vi.* **1.** partire, mettersi in viaggio **2.** cominciare **3.** trasalire || *to — out*, aver intenzione di; *to — up*, spuntare all'improvviso. ♦ to **start** *vt.* **1.** cominciare **2.** far trasalire.

starter *s.* **1.** iniziatore, fondatore **2.** (*sport*) "starter", mossiere.

starting *s.* **1.** inizio, partenza **2.** debutto **3.** (*mecc.*) messa in moto, avviamento.

startle *s.* trasalimento.

to **startle** *vt.* spaventare, far trasalire. ♦ to **startle** *vi.* spaventarsi, trasalire.

startling *agg.* impressionante, sorprendente.

starvation *s.* inedia, fame.

to **starve** *vi.* **1.** morire di fame **2.** (*fig.*) bramare. ♦ to **starve** *vt.* far morire di fame.

state *s.* **1.** stato, condizione **2.** governo, nazione **3.** rango, dignità || — -*control*, statalizzazione; — -*documents*, documenti ufficiali; — -*prisoner*, prigioniero politico; — -*trial*, processo politico.

to **state** *vt.* **1.** affermare, dichiarare **2.** stabilire.

stateless *agg.* **1.** senza patria **2.** senza pompa **3.** apolide.

stately *agg.* nobile, signorile.

statement *s.* **1.** esposto, relazione **2.** asserzione, affermazione **3.** (*giur.*) deposizione, esposizione dei fatti.

statesman *s.* statista.

static(al) *agg.* statico.

statics *s.* statica.

station *s.* **1.** posto, luogo, base **2.** stazione **3.** condizione sociale || *petrol* —, stazione di rifornimento; *through* —, stazione di transito.

stationary *agg.* stazionario.

stationer *s.* cartolaio || —'*s* (*shop*), cartoleria.

stationery *s.* articoli di cancelleria.

station house *s.* guardina.

stationmaster *s.* capostazione.

statist *s.* statista.

statistic(al) *agg.* statistico.

statistically *avv.* statisticamente.

statistics *s.* **1.** scienza della statistica **2.** statistiche (*pl.*).

statuary *agg.* statuario, scultorio.

statue *s.* statua.

statuesque *agg.* statuario.

stature *s.* statura.

status *s.* **1.** stato, condizione sociale **2.** situazione.

statute *s.* statuto, regolamento.

statutory *agg.* statutario.

to **staunch** *vt.* **1.** arrestare **2.** stagnare. ♦ to **staunch** *vi.* stagnarsi.

stave *s.* **1.** doga (*di botte*) **2.** piolo (*di scala*) **3.** strofa.

stay[1] *s.* **1.** soggiorno **2.** pausa.

stay[2] *s.* **1.** sostegno, supporto **2.** (*mecc.*) puntello.

to **stay**[1] *vi.* **1.** fermarsi, sostare, soggiornare **2.** resistere || *to* — *away*, essere assente; *to* — *in*, stare in casa, (*mil.*) essere consegnato; *to*

— *up*, vegliare. ♦ to **stay** *vt.* **1.** arrestare, fermare **2.** resistere.

to **stay**[2] *vt.* (*mecc.*) puntellare.

steadfast *agg.* fermo, risoluto.

steadfastly *avv.* stabilmente, fermamente.

steadfastness *s.* fermezza, tenacia.

steadily *avv.* **1.** saldamente, fermamente **2.** costantemente.

steadiness *s.* **1.** fermezza, sicurezza **2.** assiduità, perseveranza.

steading *s.* tenuta agricola.

steady *agg.* **1.** fermo, saldo **2.** equilibrato **3.** continuo, regolare **4.** fedele, assiduo.

to **steady** *vt.* rafforzare, rendere fermo, equilibrato. ♦ to **steady** *vi.* rafforzarsi.

steak *s.* bistecca.

to **steal** (**stole**, **stolen**) *vt.* e *vi.* rubare || *to* — *along*, camminare furtivamente; *to* — *away*, svignarsela; *to* — *upon*, avvicinarsi pian piano.

stealing *s.* furto || *cattle* (*o horse*)- -—, abigeato.

stealthily *avv.* furtivamente.

stealthy *agg.* furtivo.

steam *s.* vapore: — -*engine*, macchina a vapore.

to **steam** *vt.* **1.** esporre al vapore **2.** cucinare al vapore. ♦ to **steam** *vi.* emettere vapore.

steamboat *s.* imbarcazione a vapore.

steamer *s.* nave a vapore.

steamship *s.* piroscafo.

steamtight *agg.* a tenuta di vapore.

steamy *agg.* **1.** che esala vapore **2.** appannato, umido.

stearic *agg.* stearico.

steel *s.* **1.** acciaio **2.** arma, spada **3.** acciarino || — *cap*, elmetto; — *company*, acciaieria || *stainless* —, acciaio inossidabile.

steelwork *s.* lavoro, struttura in acciaio.

steelwork *s. pl.* acciaieria (*sing.*).

steely *agg.* **1.** di acciaio, simile ad acciaio **2.** (*fig.*) severissimo.

steelyard *s.* stadera.

steep[1] *agg.* **1.** ripido, scosceso **2.** (*fig.*) ambizioso, arduo **3.** esorbitante (*di prezzi*).

steep[2] *s.* macerazione, l'inzuppare.

to **steep** *vt.* immergere (*anche fig.*), inzuppare.

steeple *s.* guglia, campanile.

steeplechase *s.* (*ippica*) corsa ad

ostacoli.

steer s. bue giovane, manzo.

to **steer** vt. **1.** governare, manovrare **2.** dirigere. ♦ to **steer** vi. **1.** dirigersi **2.** (auto) sterzare.

steering s. guida, governo (dello sterzo, del timone).

stem s. **1.** tronco, gambo, stelo **2.** cannello (di pipa) **3.** (mar.) prua.

to **stem** vt. arrestare, arginare.

stench s. puzzo, tanfo.

step s. **1.** passo (anche fig.), andatura **2.** orma, impronta **3.** provvedimento **4.** gradino || to be in — with so., tenere il passo con qu.; — by —, gradualmente; in — (elett.), in fase.

to **step** vi. camminare || to — aside, farsi da parte; to — forward, avanzare; to — in, montare (su un veicolo). ♦ to **step** vt. misurare a passi.

stepbrother s. fratellastro.

stepchild s. (pl. -children) figliastro.

stepdaughter s. figliastra.

stepfather s. patrigno.

stepmother s. matrigna.

stepsister s. sorellastra.

stepson s. figliastro.

stereophonic agg. stereofonico.

stereophony s. stereofonia.

stereoscope s. stereoscopio.

stereotype s. stereotipo.

sterile agg. sterile.

sterility s. sterilità.

to **sterilize** vt. rendere sterile, sterilizzare.

stern¹ agg. severo, austero.

stern² s. (mar.) poppa.

sternly avv. severamente.

sternness s. severità, austerità.

stethoscope s. stetoscopio.

stevedore s. scaricatore (di porto).

stew s. (cuc.) umido, stufato.

to **stew** vt. e vi. cuocere in umido.

steward s. **1.** amministratore, intendente **2.** (aer., mar.) cameriere di bordo.

stewardess s. **1.** dispensiere **2.** (aer., mar.) cameriera di bordo.

stick s. **1.** bastone **2.** bastoncino **3.** barra, stecca.

to **stick** (stuck, stuck) vt. **1.** ficcare, conficcare **2.** infilare **3.** incollare, appiccicare. ♦ to **stick** (stuck, stuck) vi. **1.** fissarsi, conficcarsi **2.** incollarsi.

stickiness s. viscosità, adesività.

sticky agg. **1.** appiccicaticcio, visco-

so **2.** poco accomodante.

stiff agg. **1.** rigido, duro **2.** (fig.) inflessibile **3.** indolenzito, intorpidito **4.** freddo, riservato || — collar, colletto duro; — -neck, torcicollo.

to **stiffen** vt. **1.** indurire **2.** indolenzire, intorpidire **3.** rassodare. ♦ to **stiffen** vi. **1.** indurirsi, irrigidirsi (anche fig.) **2.** rassodarsi.

stiffness s. **1.** durezza, rigidezza **2.** intorpidimento.

to **stifle** vt. **1.** soffocare **2.** (fig.) reprimere. ♦ to **stifle** vi. sentirsi soffocare.

stifling agg. soffocante.

to **stigmatize** vt. **1.** marchiare **2.** stigmatizzare.

stile s. scaletta.

still¹ agg. tranquillo, calmo, silenzioso || — -life (pitt.), natura morta.

still² avv. **1.** ancora, tuttora **2.** tuttavia, nondimeno.

still³ s. alambicco.

to **still** vt. acquietare, calmare. ♦ to **still** vi. acquietarsi, calmarsi.

stillness s. calma, quiete.

stilt s. trampolo.

stimulant s. **1.** stimolante **2.** bevanda alcolica.

to **stimulate** vt. stimolare, incitare.

stimulus s. (pl.- li) stimolo, incentivo.

sting s. **1.** pungiglione, aculeo **2.** puntura d'insetto **3.** dolore acuto **4.** pungolo, stimolo.

to **sting** (stung, stung) vt. e vi. **1.** pungere **2.** colpire, ferire (anche fig.).

stinginess s. avarizia, spilorceria.

stinging agg. pungente, mordace.

stingy agg. avaro, taccagno.

stink s. puzzo, fetore.

to **stink** (stank, stunk) vt. e vi. puzzare, riempire di puzzo.

stinking agg. puzzolente, fetido.

to **stipulate** vt. e vi. stipulare.

stipulation s. stipulazione, patto.

stir s. **1.** il rimescolare, l'attizzare || to give a —, dare una rimescolata **2.** animazione, tumulto.

to **stir** vt. **1.** rimescolare **2.** muovere, agitare. ♦ to **stir** vi. muoversi, agitarsi.

stirabout agg. indaffarato.

stirrer s. incitatore, istigatore.

stirring agg. eccitante.

stirrup s. staffa.

stitch s. **1.** punto **2.** maglia.

stock s. 1. rifornimento, provvista || to be out of —, essere sprovvisto 2. titoli, azioni (pl.) 3. tronco, ceppo 4. (fig.) stirpe.

to **stock** vt. 1. approvvigionare 2. tenere in magazzino.

stockbroker s. agente di cambio.

stockbroking s. professione dell'agente di cambio.

stock company s. società per azioni.

Stock Exchange s. Borsa valori.

stockfish s. stoccafisso.

stockholder s. azionista.

stocking s. calza lunga.

stoic agg. e s. stoico.

stoicism s. stoicismo.

stoker s. fuochista.

stole V. to steal.

stolen V. to steal.

stolid agg. 1. imperturbabile 2. sciocco.

stolidity s. flemma.

stomach s. stomaco: — -ache, mal di stomaco.

stomatitis s. stomatite.

stomatology s. stomatologia.

stone s. 1. pietra, ciottolo, sasso 2. nocciolo 3. (med.) calcolo || — -blind, completamente cieco; — -breaker, spaccapietre; — cutter, tagliapietre.

to **stone** vt. 1. lapidare 2. rivestire di pietra 3. snocciolare.

stoneless agg. senza nocciolo.

stoneware s. ceramica.

stony agg. 1. pietroso, sassoso 2. (fig.) duro, insensibile.

stood V. to stand.

stool s. sgabello, seggiolino.

stoop s. curvatura, inchino.

to **stoop** vi. 1. curvare, inchinarsi 2. (fig.) accondiscendere, abbassarsi.

stop s. 1. sosta, arresto 2. segno di punteggiatura || — watch, cronometro.

to **stop** vt. 1. fermare 2. turare, otturare 3. impedire. ♦ to **stop** vi. fermarsi.

stopper s. 1. tappo, turacciolo 2. otturatore.

stopping s. 1. otturazione 2. (comm.) cessazione, sospensione (di pagamenti ecc.).

storage s. 1. immagazzinamento 2. deposito, magazzino.

store s. 1. provvista, riserva 2. magazzino || — -keeper, magazzinie-

re; — -ship, nave da carico.

to **store** vt. 1. fornire, rifornire 2. immagazzinare, mettere da parte (anche fig.).

storehouse s. magazzino, deposito.

storey s. piano (di edificio).

stork s. cicogna.

storm s. 1. tempesta, temporale 2. tumulto, agitazione.

to **storm** vi. 1. infuriare, scatenarsi 2. (fam.) adirarsi. ♦ to **storm** vt. attaccare.

stormy agg. tempestoso, burrascoso.

story s. storia, racconto, novella, favola || to tell stories, contar frottole.

stoup s. acquasantiera.

stout agg. 1. forte, robusto, resistente 2. fermo, risoluto 3. grosso, tozzo.

stove s. 1. stufa 2. cucina economica: gas- —, cucina a gas.

to **stove** vt. mettere in forno, stufa.

to **stow** vt. stivare, riempire.

stowage s. (mar.) stivaggio.

straddle s. posizione a gambe divaricate, il mettersi a cavalcioni.

to **straddle** vt. stare a cavalcioni di. ♦ to **straddle** vi. mettersi a gambe divaricate.

straight[1] agg. 1. diritto, rettilineo 2. onesto, retto 3. ordinato || a — whisky, un whisky liscio.

straight[2] s. 1. posizione diritta 2. (fig.) condotta onesta.

straight[3] avv. 1. diritto, in linea retta 2. direttamente.

to **straighten** vt. raddrizzare. ♦ to **straighten** vi. raddrizzarsi.

straightforward agg. 1. diritto, diretto 2. schietto, leale.

straightforwardly avv. 1. in linea retta 2. francamente, schiettamente.

strain s. 1. tensione (anche fig.) 2. sforzo, fatica 3. distorsione, strappo muscolare.

to **strain** vt. 1. sottoporre a tensione 2. sforzare. ♦ to **strain** vi. sforzarsi.

strained agg. 1. teso 2. indebolito 3. non spontaneo, forzato.

strainer s. colino, filtro.

strait s. (geogr.) stretto. ♦ to **strand** vi. incagliarsi.

stranding s. incagliamento (di una nave).

strange agg. 1. strano, bizzarro 2. estraneo, sconosciuto.

stranger s. estraneo, sconosciuto, forestiero.

to **strangle** vt. strangolare.

strangling s. strangolamento.

strap s. **1.** cinghia, correggia **2.** maniglia a pendaglio (su tram ecc.).

to **strap** vt. legare con cinghia.

stratagem s. stratagemma.

strategic(al) agg. strategico.

strategist s. stratega.

strategy s. strategia.

stratification s. stratificazione.

to **stratify** vt. stratificare.

stratosphere s. stratosfera.

stratospheric agg. stratosferico.

stratum s. (pl. -ta) **1.** strato **2.** strato sociale.

straw s. **1.** paglia **2.** fuscello, cannuccia || — (-hat), paglietta; — -colour, giallo paglierino.

strawberry s. fragola.

stray agg. **1.** smarrito, randagio **2.** casuale. ♦ **stray** s. animale domestico smarrito.

to **stray** vi. vagare, vagabondare (anche fig.).

streak s. **1.** striscia, striatura **2.** vena (anche fig.).

to **streak** vt. **1.** striare **2.** venare.

stream s. **1.** corso d'acqua, ruscello **2.** flusso, fiotto **3.** corrente (anche fig.).

to **stream** vi. **1.** scorrere, fluire **2.** ondeggiare || to — out, effondersi. ♦ to **stream** vt. far scorrere.

street s. via, strada || one-way —, strada a senso unico.

streetwalker s. passeggiatrice.

strength s. **1.** forza, vigore **2.** solidità, tenacia.

to **strengthen** vt. rafforzare, irrobustire. ♦ to **strengthen** vi. rafforzarsi, irrobustirsi.

strengthening agg. fortificante.

strenuous agg. strenuo, energico.

strenuously avv. strenuamente.

strenuousness s. vigore.

streptococcus s. (pl. -cci) streptococco.

streptomycin s. streptomicina.

stress s. **1.** sforzo, pressione **2.** enfasi **3.** accento tonico.

to **stress** vt. **1.** forzare **2.** accentuare **3.** porre in rilievo.

stretch s. **1.** stiramento, tensione **2.** spazio di tempo **3.** distesa, estensione.

to **stretch** vt. tirare, tendere, stendere. ♦ to **stretch** vi. estendersi.

stretcher s. **1.** tenditore **2.** lettiga.

to **strew** (**strewed, strewn**) vt. spargere, sparpagliare.

strict agg. **1.** preciso, esatto **2.** (fig.) severo, rigido.

strictly avv. **1.** esattamente **2.** severamente.

stridden V. to stride.

stride s. passo lungo, andatura || to make great strides, avanzare a grandi passi.

to **stride** (**strode, stridden**) vi. camminare a grandi passi.

strident agg. stridente.

strife s. contesa, lotta.

strike s. **1.** sciopero **2.** scoperta (di giacimento) **3.** attacco aereo.

to **strike** (**struck, struck**) vt. e vi. **1.** battere, colpire **2.** (fig.) impressionare, colpire **3.** suonare le ore **4.** accendere (un fiammifero) **5.** scioperare || to — down, abbattere; to — in, frapporsi.

striker s. **1.** scioperante **2.** (mecc.) percussore.

striking agg. sorprendente.

string s. **1.** spago, cordicella **2.** laccio **3.** (mus.) corda.

to **string** (**strung, strung**) vt. e vi. **1.** legare con corde **2.** accordare (uno strumento) || to — up, impiccare.

strip s. striscia, nastro.

to **strip** vt. svestire. ♦ to **strip** vi. svestirsi.

stripe s. striscia, lista.

to **stripe** vt. rigare, listare.

striped agg. a righe, a strisce.

to **strive** (**strove, striven**) vi. sforzarsi.

strode V. to stride.

stroke s. **1.** colpo, percossa **2.** movimento **3.** bracciata (al nuoto), remata, battuta (al tennis) **4.** tratto (di penna ecc.) **5.** rintocco (d'orologio) **6.** (med.) colpo **7.** carezza.

to **stroke**[1] vi. vogare in cadenza.

to **stroke**[2] vt. accarezzare, lisciare.

stroll s. passeggiatina, quattro passi.

to **stroll** vi. gironzolare.

strolling agg. errante, girovago.

strong agg. forte, robusto, energico.

stronghold s. roccaforte.

strontium s. stronzio.

strove V. to strive.

struck V. to strike.

structural agg. strutturale.

structure s. **1.** struttura **2.** costruzione.

struggle s. **1.** lotta, combattimento **2.** sforzo || *hand-to-hand* —, lotta corpo a corpo.

to **struggle** vi. **1.** lottare, divincolarsi **2.** (fig.) sforzarsi.

struggler s. contendente, chi lotta.

to **strum** vt. e vi. strimpellare.

strumpet s. prostituta.

strung V. to string.

strut s. andatura solenne.

to **strut** vi. incedere con sussiego.

stub s. **1.** ceppo **2.** mozzicone.

stubble s. stoppia.

stubborn agg. ostinato, cocciuto, tenace, ribelle.

stubbornness s. caparbietà, tenacia.

to **stucco** vt. stuccare.

stuck V. to stick.

stud s. **1.** chiodo a capocchia larga **2.** bottoncino (da camicia).

to **stud** vt. guarnire di borchie.

student s. studente.

studentship s. borsa di studio.

studied agg. **1.** studiato, ricercato **2.** colto.

studio s. **1.** studio (d'artista) **2.** teatro di posa.

studious agg. studioso, diligente.

study s. **1.** studio **2.** esame attento, investigazione.

to **study** vt. e vi. **1.** studiare **2.** esaminare attentamente.

stuff s. **1.** sostanza, materia prima **2.** cosa, roba **3.** stoffa, tessuto.

to **stuff** vt. **1.** imbottire **2.** (cuc.) farcire **3.** rimpinzare.

stuffing s. **1.** imbottitura **2.** (cuc.) ripieno.

stuffy agg. afoso || — air, aria viziata.

to **stumble** vi. **1.** inciampare **2.** (fig.) fare passi falsi.

stump s. **1.** ceppo, tronco **2.** radice (di dente) **3.** piattaforma, podio.

to **stun** vt. stordire, tramortire.

stung V. to sting.

stunk V. to stink.

stunt s. (gergo) **1.** bravata, esibizione **2.** trovata pubblicitaria, notizia sensazionale.

stupefaction s. **1.** stupore **2.** torpore provocato da stupefacenti.

to **stupefy** vt. **1.** istupidire **2.** abbrutire. ♦ to **stupefy** vi. **1.** istupidirsi **2.** abbrutirsi.

stupendous agg. splendido, stupendo.

stupid agg. stupido, ottuso.

stupidity s. stupidità.

stupidly avv. stupidamente.

sturdy agg. **1.** vigoroso, forte **2.** risoluto.

to **stutter** vt. e vi. balbettare.

stuttering s. balbuzie.

sty s. porcile.

style s. **1.** stile (anche fig.) **2.** modello, genere **3.** moda.

to **style** vt. chiamare, denominare.

stylist s. stilista.

stylistic agg. stilistico.

stylization s. stilizzazione.

to **stylize** vt. stilizzare.

stylographic agg. stilografico.

stylus s. stilo.

subalpine agg. subalpino.

subaltern s. subalterno.

subaquatic agg. subacqueo.

subclass s. sottoclasse.

subcommission s. sottocommissione.

subcommissioner s. vice-commissario.

subcommittee s. sottocomitato.

subconscious agg. e s. subcosciente.

subcutaneous agg. sottocutaneo.

subdeacon s. suddiacono.

to **subdivide** vt. suddividere. ♦ to **subdivide** vi. suddividersi.

subdivisible agg. suddivisibile.

subdivision s. suddivisione.

subdual s. **1.** soggiogamento **2.** attenuazione.

to **subdue** vt. **1.** conquistare, soggiogare **2.** ridurre, attenuare.

subgovernor s. vicegovernatore.

subject[1] agg. **1.** soggetto, assoggettato **2.** sottoposto, esposto a.

subject[2] **1.** argomento, materia di studio **2.** (gramm.) soggetto **3.** suddito.

to **subject** vt. **1.** assoggettare **2.** esporre.

subjection s. **1.** assoggettamento **2.** dipendenza.

subjective agg. soggettivo.

subjectivism s. soggettivismo.

subjunctive s. congiuntivo.

sublease s. subaffitto.

to **sublease** vt. subaffittare.

tò **sublet (sublet, sublet)** vt. subaffittare.

sublieutenancy s. grado di sottotenente.

sublieutenant s. sottotenente.

sublimate agg. e s. sublimato.

to **sublimate** vt. sublimare.

sublime agg. e s. sublime.

sublimity s. sublimità.
submarine agg. subacqueo. ♦ **submarine** s. sommergibile.
submariner s. sommergibilista.
to **submerge** vt. immergere, sommergere. ♦ to **submerge** vi. immergersi.
submergence s. sommersione.
submersible agg. affondabile.
submersion s. immersione.
submission s. sottomissione, docilità.
submissive agg. remissivo, docile.
submissively avv. in modo remissivo.
submissiveness s. sottomissione.
to **submit** vt. sottomettere, sottoporre. ♦ to **submit** vi. sottomettersi, assoggettarsi.
submultiple agg. e s. sottomultiplo.
subnormal agg. al di sotto della norma.
subordinacy s. subordinazione.
subordinate agg. subordinato. ♦ **subordinate** s. subalterno, inferiore.
to **subordinate** vt. subordinare.
subordination s. subordinazione.
to **suborn** vt. subornare, corrompere.
subornation s. subornazione.
subplot s. trama secondaria.
to **subscribe** vt. e vi. 1. sottoscrivere, firmare 2. aderire, trovarsi d'accordo 3. abbonarsi.
subscriber s. 1. the —, il sottoscritto 2. abbonato.
subscription s. 1. sottoscrizione 2. abbonamento 3. consenso.
subsequence s. susseguenza.
subsequent agg. successivo, ulteriore.
subsequently avv. successivamente.
to **subside** vi. 1. calare, decrescere 2. quietarsi 3. cadere (sul fondo), depositare (di liquidi).
subsidiary agg. sussidiario, supplementare, ausiliario.
to **subsidize** vt. sussidiare.
subsidy s. sussidio.
to **subsist** vt. e vi. sussistere.
subsistence s. esistenza, sussistenza.
subsistent agg. sussistente.
subsoil s. sottosuolo.
subspecies s. sottospecie.
substance s. 1. sostanza, essenza 2. contenuto, l'essenziale 3. solidità, fondamento.
substantial agg. 1. sostanzioso, so-

lido 2. importante, notevole.
substantialism s. sostanzialismo.
substantiality s. 1. sostanzialità 2. concretezza.
substantially avv. sostanzialmente.
substantive agg. considerevole, reale. ♦ **substantive** s. (gramm.) sostantivo.
substitute s. 1. sostituto 2. surrogato, imitazione.
to **substitute** vt. e vi. sostituire.
substitution s. sostituzione.
substratum s. (pl. -ta) 1. sostrato (anche fig.).
subtenancy s. subaffitto.
subtenant s. subaffittuario.
subterfuge s. sotterfugio.
subterranean agg. sotterraneo.
sub-title s. sottotitolo, didascalia.
subtle agg. 1. penetrante, acuto, sottile 2. elusivo, indefinibile.
subtleness s. 1. sottigliezza, acutezza 2. carattere elusivo.
subtlety s. sottigliezza.
subtly avv. 1. acutamente, sottilmente 2. elusivamente.
to **subtract** vt. sottrarre, detrarre.
subtraction s. sottrazione.
subtractive agg. sottrattivo.
subtrahend s. sottraendo.
suburb s. sobborgo. ♦ **suburbs** s. pl. periferia (sing.).
suburban agg. suburbano, periferico.
subversion s. sovversione.
subversive agg. sovversivo.
to **subvert** vt. sovvertire.
subway s. 1. sottopassaggio 2. (amer.) metropolitana.
to **succeed** vt. succedere a, seguire, subentrare a. ♦ to **succeed** vi. 1. succedere, seguire 2. riuscire, aver successo.
success s. successo, riuscita.
successful agg. che ha successo.
successfully avv. con successo.
succession s. successione, serie.
successive agg. successivo, seguente.
successively avv. successivamente.
successor s. successore.
succint agg. succinto, conciso.
succulent agg. succulento.
to **succumb** vi. soccombere, soggiacere.
succursal s. succursale.
such agg. tale, simile: — that, — as, tale che, tale da. ♦ **such** pron. tale, tali, questo, quello, questa,

quella, questi, quelli, queste, quelle.

suchlike agg. simile, dello stesso genere.

suck s. succhiata, poppata.

to **suck** vt. e vi. 1. succhiare, poppare 2. assorbire.

sucker s. 1. (mecc.) pistone 2. ventosa.

to **suckle** vt. allattare.

suckling s. lattante.

sudden agg. improvviso, inaspettato.
♦ **sudden** s. evento improvviso.

suddenly avv. inaspettatamente.

suddenness s. subitaneità.

to **sue** vt. e vi. 1. ricorrere in giudizio 2. sollecitare.

to **suffer** vt. e vi. 1. subire, patire 2. tollerare 3. soffrire.

suffering s. 1. sofferenza, pena 2. tolleranza.

sufficiency s. sufficienza.

sufficient agg. sufficiente.

suffix s. (gramm.) suffisso.

to **suffocate** vt. e vi. soffocare.

suffocation s. soffocamento.

suffrage s. 1. suffragio, diritto di voto 2. preghiera.

to **suffuse** vt. coprire, cospargere.

sugar s. 1. zucchero 2. (fig.) atteggiamento mellifluo || — -beet, barbabietola da zucchero; — -cane, canna da zucchero; — -tongs, mollette per lo zucchero; lump —, zucchero in zollette.

to **sugar** vt. 1. inzuccherare 2. (fig.) addolcire, adulare.

sugariness s. 1. dolcezza 2. mellifluità.

sugary agg. 1. zuccheroso, zuccherino 2. (fig.) mellifluo.

to **suggest** vt. 1. suggerire 2. far nascere un'idea 3. insinuare.

suggestible agg. suggeribile, suggestionabile.

suggestion s. 1. suggerimento 2. suggestione 3. associazione di idee.

suggestive agg. stimolante, che ispira.

suggestiveness s. carattere allusivo.

suicidal agg. suicida, che ha tendenze al suicidio.

suicide s. 1. suicidio 2. suicida.

suit s. 1. domanda, preghiera 2. (giur.) causa 3. abito completo (da uomo) || — -case, valigia.

to **suit** vt. adattare, convenire a, far comodo a. ♦ to **suit** vi. essere conveniente, accordarsi, adattarsi.

suitability s. convenienza.

suitable agg. adatto, idoneo.

suitably avv. appropriatamente.

suite s. 1. seguito, corteo 2. serie.

suitor s. 1. postulante 2. corteggiatore.

sulkiness s. malumore.

sulks s. pl. malumore, broncio (sing.).

sulky[1] agg. 1. imbronciato, scontroso 2. tetro.

sulky[2] s. "sulky", sediolo.

sullen agg. 1. accigliato 2. tetro.

sullenly avv. accigliato, di malumore.

sulphate s. solfato.

sulphide s. solfuro.

sulphite s. solfito.

sulphonamide s. sulfamidico.

sulphur s. zolfo || — -mine (o — -pit), solfatara.

to **sulphur**, to **sulphurate** vt. solforare.

sulphuric agg. solforico.

sulphurous agg. solforoso.

sultan s. sultano.

sultanate s. sultanato.

sultriness s. afa, caldo soffocante.

sultry agg. afoso, soffocante.

sum s. 1. somma, quantità (di denaro) 2. addizione.

to **sum** vt. e vi. sommare, addizionare || to — up, riassumere.

summarily avv. sommariamente.

to **summarize** vt. e vi. riassumere.

summary s. sommario, ricapitolazione.

summer s. estate.

to **summer** vi. trascorrere l'estate.

summertime s. stagione estiva.

summit s. 1. cima, vetta 2. (fig.) culmine || at the — (pol.), al vertice.

to **summon** vt. 1. chiamare, mandare a chiamare 2. convocare 3. (giur.) citare.

summons s. 1. (giur.) citazione, ingiunzione 2. convocazione.

sumptuous agg. sontuoso.

sumptuously avv. sontuosamente.

sumptuousness s. sontuosità.

sun s. sole || — -bath, bagno di sole; — -glasses, occhiali da sole.

to **sun** vt. esporre al sole. ♦ to **sun** vi. esporsi al sole.

to **sun-bathe** vi. fare i bagni di sole.

sunbeam s. raggio di sole.

sunbow s. arcobaleno.

sunburn s. 1. abbronzatura 2. scottatura (solare).

sunburnt *agg*. 1. abbronzato 2. scottato dal sole.

sunburst *s*. sprazzo di sole.

Sunday *s*. domenica.

to **sunder** *vt*. separare, recidere. ♦
to **sunder** *vi*. separarsi, scindersi.

sundry *agg*. parecchi, vari.

sunflower *s*. girasole.

sung V. *to sing*.

sunk V. *to sink*.

sunlight *s*. luce del sole.

sunlit *agg*. soleggiato.

sunny *agg*. luminoso, soleggiato.

sunproof *agg*. inalterabile al sole.

sunrise *s*. il sorgere del sole.

sunset *s*. tramonto *(anche fig.)*.

sunshade *s*. parasole.

sunshine *s*. luce del sole.

sunspot *s*. macchia solare.

sunstroke *s*. insolazione.

sun-worship *s*. culto del Sole.

sup *s*. sorso, goccia.

to **sup¹** *vt*. e *vi*. sorseggiare.

to **sup²** *vi*. cenare.

superable *agg*. superabile.

to **superabound** *vi*. sovrabbondare.

superabundance *s*. sovrabbondanza.

superabundant *agg*. sovrabbondante.

superb *agg*. superbo, magnifico.

superciliary *agg*. sopracciliare.

supercilious *agg*. altero.

superelevation *s*. sopraelevazione.

superficial *agg*. superficiale, poco profondo.

superficiality *s*. superficialità.

superfluous *agg*. superfluo.

superhuman *agg*. sovrumano.

to **superimpose** *vt*. sovrapporre.

superintendence *s*. sovrintendenza.

superintendent *s*. sovrintendente.

superior *agg*. superiore.

superiority *s*. superiorità.

superlative *agg*. superlativo.

superman *s*. superuomo.

supermarket *s*. supermercato.

supermundane *agg*. ultraterreno.

supernatural *agg*. soprannaturale.

supernutrition *s*. supernutrizione.

to **supersede** *vt*. rimpiazzare.

supersensitive *agg*. ipersensibile.

supersensitiveness *s*. ipersensibilità.

supersession *s*. sostituzione.

supersonic *agg*. ultrasonoro, supersonico.

superstition *s*. superstizione.

superstitious *agg*. superstizioso.

superstructure *s*. sovrastruttura.

supertax *s*. soprattassa.

superterrestrial *agg*. ultraterreno.

to **supervise** *vt*. e *vi*. sovrintendere.

supervision *s*. sorveglianza, sovrintendenza.

supervisor *s*. sovrintendente.

supervisory *agg*. di controllo.

supine *agg*. supino *(anche fig.)*.

supinely *avv*. supinamente.

supper *s*. cena || to have —, cenare; — -*time*, ora di cena.

to **supplant** *vt*. soppiantare.

supple *agg*. 1. pieghevole, flessibile 2. elastico *(anche fig.)*.

supplement *s*. supplemento.

supplementary *agg*. supplementare.

suppliant *agg*. supplichevole. ♦
suppliant *s*. supplicante.

supply *s*. 1. rifornimento, approvvigionamento 2. *(comm.)* fornitura 3. sostituto, supplente.

to **supply** *vt*. fornire, rifornire. ♦
to **supply** *vi*. fare da sostituto.

support *s*. sostegno, appoggio || in — of, in favore di.

to **support** *vt*. 1. sostenere, reggere 2. dare appoggio a 3. mantenere.

supportable *agg*. sostenibile, sopportabile.

supporter *s*. 1. sostegno 2. fautore, sostenitore.

to **suppose** *vt*. supporre, presupporre, presumere.

supposed *agg*. presunto, supposto.

supposition *s*. supposizione, ipotesi.

suppository *s*. *(med.)* supposta.

to **suppress** *vt*. 1. sopprimere, reprimere 2. *(fig.)* soffocare, trattenere.

suppression *s*. 1. soppressione 2. il mettere a tacere.

to **suppurate** *vi*. suppurare.

suppuration *s*. suppurazione.

suprarenal *agg*. surrenale.

supremacy *s*. supremazia.

supreme *agg*. sommo, supremo.

surcharge *s*. 1. sovraccarico 2. soprattassa 3. sovrapprezzo.

sure *agg*. sicuro, certo, fidato.

surely *avv*. sicuramente, certamente.

surety *s*. garanzia, pegno.

suretyship *s*. garanzia.

surf *s*. 1. risacca 2. spuma dei marosi.

surface *s*. superficie *(anche fig.)*.

surfeit *s*. 1. eccesso 2. sazietà. ♦
to **surfeit** *vt*. saziare. ♦ to **sur-**

feit vi. saziarsi.
surge s. **1.** maroso, cavallone **2.** (fig.) impeto.
to **surge** vi. gonfiarsi, sollevarsi, tumultuare.
surgeon s. chirurgo.
surgery s. chirurgia.
surgical agg. chirurgico.
surlily avv. sgarbatamente.
surly agg. sgarbato.
to **surmount** vt. sormontare, superare.
surname s. **1.** cognome **2.** soprannome.
to **surname** vt. soprannominare.
to **surpass** vt. sorpassare, superare.
surpassing agg. superiore, eccellente.
surpassingly avv. straordinariamente.
surplus s. **1.** sovrappiù, eccedenza **2.** residuati di guerra.
surprise s. **1.** sorpresa **2.** stupore, meraviglia.
to **surprise** vt. **1.** sorprendere, cogliere all'improvviso **2.** stupire.
surprisedly avv. con sorpresa.
surprising agg. sorprendente.
surrealism s. surrealismo.
surrealist agg. e s. surrealista.
surrender s. **1.** resa, capitolazione **2.** abbandono, cessione.
to **surrender** vt. cedere, consegnare. ♦ to **surrender** vi. arrendersi.
surreptitious agg. clandestino, furtivo.
surrogate s. sostituto, supplente.
surround s. bordura, bordo.
to **surround** vt. **1.** circondare **2.** accerchiare.
surrounding agg. circostante. ♦ **surroundings** s. pl. dintorni.
survey s. esame, sguardo generale.
to **survey** vt. e vi. esaminare, fare rivelazioni.
surveyor s. ispettore.
survival s. **1.** sopravvivenza **2.** avanzo, reliquia.
to **survive** vi. sopravvivere. ♦ to **survive** vt. vivere più a lungo di.
survivor s. superstite.
susceptibility s. suscettibilità.
susceptible agg. **1.** suscettibile **2.** impressionabile.
suspect agg. sospetto. ♦ **suspect** s. persona sospetta.
to **suspect** vt. sospettare. ♦ to **suspect** vi. essere sospettoso.
to **suspend** vt. **1.** appendere, tenere

sospeso **2.** sospendere.
suspender s. giarrettiera, bretella.
suspense s. incertezza, attesa ansiosa.
suspension s. sospensione.
suspensive agg. sospensivo.
suspicion s. sospetto, dubbio.
suspicious agg. sospettoso, diffidente.
suspiciously avv. sospettosamente.
to **sustain** vt. **1.** mantenere, sostenere **2.** prolungare **3.** reggere.
sustainable agg. sostenibile.
sustenance s. mezzi di sussistenza (pl.).
suture s. sutura.
to **suture** vt. suturare.
swab s. **1.** strofinaccio **2.** (mar.) radazza **3.** (med.) tampone.
to **swab** vt. pulire, strofinare.
swag s. movimento ondeggiante.
swagger agg. sgargiante.
to **swagger** vi. **1.** pavoneggiarsi **2.** gloriarsi.
swallow[1] s. rondine.
swallow[2] s. **1.** baratro **2.** deglutizione.
to **swallow** vt. e vi. **1.** deglutire, inghiottire **2.** (fig.) ingoiare.
swam V. to swim.
swamp s. palude || — -fever, febbre malarica.
to **swamp** vt. inondare, inzuppare. ♦ to **swamp** vi. affondare (anche fig.).
swan s. cigno || — song, canto del cigno.
swarm s. sciame, folla.
to **swarm** vi. **1.** sciamare **2.** pullulare, brulicare, essere affollato.
swash s. **1.** sciacquio **2.** gradassata.
to **swash** vi. **1.** spruzzare, sguazzare **2.** turbinare, infrangersi. ♦ to **swash** vt. far sguazzare.
to **swat** vt. colpire, schiacciare (mosche ecc.).
swathe s. benda, fascia.
to **swathe** vt. bendare, fasciare.
sway s. **1.** oscillazione **2.** potere, potenza, preponderanza.
to **sway** vt. **1.** sballottolare **2.** dominare, influenzare **3.** maneggiare, impugnare **4.** (mar.) issare. ♦ to **sway** vi. **1.** ondeggiare **2.** propendere **3.** predominare.
swear s. bestemmia, imprecazione.
to **swear (swore, sworn)** vt. e vi. **1.** giurare, far giurare **2.** imprecare, bestemmiare.

sweat *s.* sudore, traspirazione.

to **sweat** *vt.* e *vi.* traspirare, sudare, sfacchinare.

sweater *s.* 1. chi suda 2. maglione di lana.

sweating *s.* sudore || — -*bath*, bagno turco.

sweaty *agg.* 1. sudato 2. che fa sudare.

Swede *s.* svedese.

Swedish *agg.* svedese.

sweep *s.* 1. scopata 2. movimento circolare 3. curva, distesa.

to **sweep (swept, swept)** *vi.* 1. spazzare, scopare 2. muoversi rapidamente 3. estendersi. ♦ to **sweep (swept, swept)** *vt.* 1. spazzare 2. sfiorare.

sweeping *agg.* 1. vasto 2. completo 3. rapido, impetuoso (*di corrente*). ♦ **sweepings** *s. pl.* rifiuti.

sweet *agg.* 1. dolce, amabile 2. piacevole, gentile. ♦ **sweet** *s.* 1. dolce, torta 2. caramella.

to **sweeten** *vt.* 1. zuccherare 2. addolcire. ♦ to **sweeten** *vi.* addolcirsi.

sweetening *s.* 1. addolcimento 2. sostanza che addolcisce.

sweetheart *s.* innamorato.

sweetly *avv.* dolcemente.

sweetmeat *s.* dolciumi, frutta candita.

sweetness *s.* 1. sapore dolce 2. dolcezza, amabilità.

swell *s.* 1. rigonfiamento 2. il gonfiarsi (*dell'acqua ecc.*).

to **swell (swelled, swollen)** *vi.* 1. gonfiarsi 2. crescere, aumentare. ♦ to **swell (swelled, swollen)** *vt.* gonfiare.

swelling *s.* rigonfiamento, ingrossamento.

swept V. *to sweep*.

to **swerve** *vt.* deviare. ♦ to **swerve** *vi.* fare uno scarto.

swift *agg.* rapido, veloce.

swim *s.* nuotata.

to **swim (swam, swum)** *vi.* nuotare. ♦ to **swim (swam, swum)** *vt.* attraversare a nuoto.

swimmer *s.* nuotatore.

swimming *s.* nuoto || — -*belt*, salvagente; — -*pool*, piscina.

swindle *s.* truffa, frode.

to **swindle** *vt.* e *vi.* truffare.

swindler *s.* truffatore.

swine *s.* maiale, porco || — -*herd*, porcaro.

swing *s.* 1. oscillazione 2. libertà d'azione 3. altalena.

to **swing (swung, swung)** *vt.* 1. dondolare, oscillare 2. ruotare 3. camminare dondolandosi. ♦ to **swing (swung, swung)** *vt.* 1. far dondolare 2. far ruotare.

swinging *s.* dondolio.

swish *s.* 1. sibilo 2. sferzata.

Swiss *agg.* svizzero.

switch *s.* 1. verga, frustino 2. (*elett.*) interruttore.

to **switch** *vt.* e *vi.* 1. colpire con un frustino 2. muovere bruscamente 3. (*ferr.*) smistare || *to* — *off*, spegnere (*la luce*); *to* — *on*, accendere (*la luce*).

swollen V. *to swell*.

swoon *s.* svenimento.

to **swoon** *vi.* svenire.

to **swoop** *vi.* calare improvvisamente, abbattersi.

sword *s.* spada.

swore V. *to swear*.

sworn V. *to swear*.

swum V. *to swim*.

swung V. *to swing*.

sycamore *s.* sicomoro.

syllable *s.* sillaba.

syllogism *s.* sillogismo.

syllogistic *agg.* sillogistico.

to **syllogize** *vt.* e *vi.* sillogizzare.

sylph *s.* silfo, silfide.

sylvan *agg.* silvano, silvestre.

symbiosis *s.* simbiosi.

symbol *s.* simbolo.

symbolic(al) *agg.* simbolico.

symbolism *s.* simbolismo.

to **symbolize** *vt.* simboleggiare.

symmetric(al) *agg.* simmetrico.

symmetry *s.* simmetria.

sympathetic *agg.* 1. sensibile, comprensivo 2. congeniale, adatto.

to **sympathize** *vi.* condividere i sentimenti altrui.

sympathizer *s.* 1. chi è comprensivo 2. simpatizzante (*di un partito ecc.*).

sympathy *s.* 1. comprensione, partecipazione 2. condoglianze (*pl.*).

symphonic *agg.* sinfonico.

symphony *s.* sinfonia.

symposium *s.* simposio, banchetto.

symptom *s.* sintomo.

symptomatic(al) *agg.* sintomatico.

synagogue *s.* sinagoga.

synchronism *s.* sincronismo.

synchronization *s.* sincronizza-

zione.
to **synchronize** *vt.* e *vi.* sincronizzare.
to **syncopate** *vt.* sincopare.
syncope *s.* sincope.
syndicalism *s.* sindacalismo.
syndicate *s.* sindacato.
synod *s.* sinodo.
synonym *s.* sinonimo.
synonymous *agg.* sinonimo.
synonymy *s.* sinonimia.
synovitis *s.* sinovite.
syntactic(al) *agg.* sintattico.
syntax *s.* sintassi.
synthesis *s.* (*pl.* -ses) sintesi.
to **synthesize** *vt.* sintetizzare.
synthetic(al) *agg.* sintetico.
syntony *s.* sintonia.
syphilis *s.* sifilide.
syphilitic *agg.* sifilitico.
Syrian *agg.* e *s.* siriano.
syringe *s.* siringa.
syrup *s.* sciroppo.
syrupy *agg.* sciropposo.
system *s.* **1.** sistema **2.** metodo || *railway* —, rete ferroviaria.
systematic(al) *agg.* sistematico, metodico.
systematically *avv.* sistematicamente, metodicamente.
systematization *s.* sistemazione.
to **systematize** *vt.* ridurre a sistema.

T

tab *s.* **1.** linguetta (*di scarpa*) **2.** (*mil.*) mostrina **3.** talloncino.
tabernacle *s.* **1.** tabernacolo **2.** tempio.
table *s.* **1.** tavola **2.** tavolata **3.** tabella || —*cloth*, tovaglia; *time-* —, orario.
tablet *s.* **1.** tavoletta **2.** pastiglia. compressa.
tabloid *s.* pasticca.
taboo *agg.* e *s.* tabù.
tabular *agg.* **1.** a forma di tabella **2.** catalogato **3.** piano, piatto.
tabulate *agg.* piano.
to **tabulate** *vt.* disporre in tabelle.
tabulation *s.* classificazione.
tabulator *s.* tabulatore.
tachometer *s.* tachimetro.
tachycardia *s.* tachicardia.

tacit *agg.* tacito.
taciturn *agg.* taciturno.
tack *s.* **1.** chiodo **2.** imbastitura **3.** bordata **4.** (*fig.*) linea di condotta.
to **tack** *vt.* **1.** inchiodare **2.** imbastire. ♦ to **tack** *vi.* **1.** bordeggiare **2.** virare.
tacking *s.* **1.** l'inchiodare **2.** imbastitura **3.** bordeggio.
tackle *s.* **1.** arnesi (*pl.*) **2.** (*mar.*) paranco.
to **tackle** *vt.* **1.** afferrare **2.** affrontare (*difficoltà ecc.*).
tacky *agg.* viscoso.
tact *s.* tatto.
tactful *agg.* pieno di tatto.
tactical *agg.* tattico.
tactician *s.* tattico.
tactics *s.* tattica.
tactile *agg.* **1.** tattile **2.** tangibile.
tactility *s.* **1.** tattilità **2.** tangibilità.
tactless *agg.* senza tatto.
tactlessness *s.* mancanza di tatto.
tactual *agg.* tattile.
tadpole *s.* (*zool.*) girino.
tag *s.* **1.** lembo pendente **2.** cartellino **3.** aggiunta **4.** luogo comune || *licence* —, bollo di circolazione.
to **tag** *vt.* mettere cartellini a.
tail *s.* coda || *-coat*, marsina.
to **tail** *vt.* munire di coda. ♦ to **tail** *vi.* **1.** essere in coda **2.** seguire da presso || *to* — *away*, affievolirsi.
tailor *s.* sarto || *-made costume*, tailleur.
to **tailor** *vi.* fare il sarto. ♦ to **tailor** *vt.* fare un abito.
taint *s.* **1.** infezione **2.** tara **3.** marchio.
to **taint** *vt.* guastare. ♦ to **taint** *vi.* guastarsi.
taintless *agg.* incontaminato.
take *s.* **1.** presa **2.** incasso **3.** (*cine*) ripresa.
to **take** (**took, taken**) *vt.* **1.** prendere **2.** portare **3.** accompagnare **4.** necessitare || *to* — *after*, assomigliare; *to* — *in*, ricevere, ridurre, capire; *to* — *off*, togliere, decollare; *to* — *on*, assumere; *to* — *to*, darsi a.
take-off *s.* (*aer.*) decollo.
taking *agg.* **1.** attraente **2.** contagioso. ♦ **taking** *s.* **1.** presa **2.** incasso.
talc(um) *s.* talco || *talcum powder*, talco in polvere.

tale s. racconto, storia novella.
talent s. talento.
talented agg. che ha talento.
talentless agg. senza talento.
tales s. pl. (giur.) giudici supplenti.
talisman s. talismano.
talk s. 1. conversazione 2. chiacchiera.
to talk vt. e vi. parlare, conversare, discutere || to — out, discutere a fondo.
talkative agg. loquace.
talkativeness s. loquacità.
talker s. 1. parlatore 2. chiacchierone.
talkies s. pl. (gergo) film sonoro (sing.).
talking s. conversazione.
talky agg. loquace.
tall agg. 1. alto 2. incredibile.
tallness s. altezza, statura.
tallow s. sego.
tally s. 1. tacca 2. cartellino, talloncino, etichetta.
to tally vt. registrare. ♦ to **tally** vi. combaciare.
tallyshop s. negozio che vende a rate.
talon s. 1. artiglio 2. (mecc.) dente 3. (comm.) matrice.
tamarind s. tamarindo.
tambourine s. tamburello.
tame agg. 1. addomesticato 2. mansueto 3. insipido, banale.
to tame vt. domare, addomesticare. ♦ to **tame** vi. ammansirsi.
tameable agg. addomesticabile.
tameless agg. indomito.
tamely avv. docilmente.
tameness s. 1. docilità 2. banalità.
tamer s. domatore.
taming s. addomesticamento.
to tamp vt. pigiare.
tamper s. pestello.
to tamper vi. 1. manomettere 2. immischiarsi: to — with, immischiarsi in 3. corrompere.
tamperer s. 1. falsificatore 2. corruttore 3. ficcanaso.
tampering s. 1. manomissione 2. corruzione.
tampon s. tampone.
tan agg. marrone rossiccio. ♦ **tan** s. 1. tannino 2. concia 3. abbronzatura.
to tan vt. 1. conciare 2. abbronzare. ♦ to **tan** vi. abbronzarsi.
tanning s. abbronzatura.

tang[1] s. 1. punta 2. odore, sapore penetrante.
tang[2] s. suono acuto.
to tang vt. far risuonare. ♦ to **tang** vi. risuonare.
tangency s. tangenza.
tangent agg. e s. tangente.
tangential agg. tangenziale.
tangerine s. mandarino.
tangibility s. tangibilità.
tangible agg. tangibile.
tangle s. groviglio.
to tangle vt. 1. aggrovigliare 2. intrappolare. ♦ to **tangle** vi. aggrovigliarsi.
tanglesome, tangly agg. ingarbugliato.
tank s. 1. serbatoio, cisterna 2. carro armato || — -truck, autobotte.
tankard s. boccale.
tanker s. nave cisterna || air —, aerocisterna; oil —, petroliera.
tanner s. conciatore.
tannery s. conceria.
tannin s. tannino.
tanning s. concia.
to tantalize vt. tormentare.
tantalizing agg. allettante.
tantamount agg. equivalente.
tap[1] rubinetto, spina.
tap[2] s. colpetto.
to tap[1] vt. 1. spillare 2. forare.
to tap[2] vt. battere leggermente.
tape s. nastro || — -recorder, magnetofono; recording —, nastro magnetico.
to tape vt. 1. legare con un nastro 2. misurare con un nastro 3. incidere su nastro magnetico.
taper agg. conico, rastremato ♦ **taper** s. 1. candela 2. conicità, rastremazione.
to taper vt. assottigliare. ♦ to **taper** vi. assottigliarsi, restringersi.
tapestry s. arazzo.
tapeworm s. tenia.
tapir s. tapiro.
tar s. catrame.
to tar vt. incatramare.
tardiness s. 1. lentezza 2. indolenza.
tardy agg. 1. lento 2. svogliato.
tare s. tara.
target s. bersaglio.
tariff s. tariffa.
tarnish s. 1. appannamento 2. macchia.
to tarnish vi. 1. appannarsi 2. macchiarsi. ♦ to **tarnish** vt. 1. mac-

chiare **2.** inquinare.
tarpaulin *s.* telone impermeabile.
tarry *agg.* **1.** catramato **2.** simile a
c⁻trame.
to **tarry** *vi.* indugiare.
tart *agg.* aspro.
tart *s.* torta di frutta, crostata.
tartan[1] *s.* tessuto scozzese.
tartan[2] *s.* (*mar.*) tartana.
tartar *agg.* e *s.* tartaro.
tartaric *agg.* tartarico.
tartlet *s.* pasticcino.
tartly *avv.* in modo acido.
task *s.* compito, dovere, impresa.
to **task** *vt.* **1.** assegnare un compito
a **2.** affaticare.
task-work *s.* lavoro a cottimo.
tassel *s.* **1.** nappa **2.** segnalibro.
to **tassel** *vt.* adornare di nappe.
taste *s.* **1.** gusto **2.** assaggio.
to **taste** *vt.* **1.** gustare **2.** assaggiare.
♦ to **taste** *vi.* sapere di.
tasteful *agg.* raffinato.
tastefulness *s.* buon gusto.
tasteless *agg.* **1.** insipido **2.** di cattivo gusto.
tastelessness *s.* **1.** scipitezza **2.**
mancanza di gusto.
taster *s.* assaggiatore.
tasty *agg.* **1.** saporito **2.** (*gergo*) di
buon gusto.
tatter *s.* cencio.
to **tatter** *vt.* stracciare. ♦ to **tatter**
vi. cadere a pezzi.
tattery *agg.* stracciato.
tattle *s.* chiacchiera.
to **tattle** *vi.* chiacchierare.
tattler *s.* chiacchierone.
tattoo[1] *s.* tatuaggio.
tattoo[2] *s.* (*mil.*) **1.** ritirata **2.** carosello militare.
to **tattoo**[1] *vt.* tatuare.
to **tattoo**[2] *vi.* tamburellare.
taught V. *to teach.*
taunt *s.* sarcasmo.
to **taunt** *vt.* **1.** rimproverare **2.** schernire.
taunting *agg.* beffardo. ♦ **taunting**
s. rimprovero sarcastico.
taut *agg.* **1.** teso **2.** in ordine.
to **tauten** *vt.* tendere. ♦ to **tauten**
vi. tendersi.
tautness *s.* tensione.
tautologic(al) *agg.* tautologico.
tautology *s.* tautologia.
tavern *s.* taverna || — -*keeper*, oste.
taw *s.* biglia.
tawdry *agg.* sgargiante.
tawny *agg.* bruno fulvo.

tax *s.* **1.** tassa **2.** peso || — -*payer*,
contribuente.
to **tax** *vt.* **1.** tassare **2.** accusare.
taxability *s.* tassabilità.
taxable *agg.* tassabile.
taxation *s.* tassazione.
taxi *s.* tassì || — -*driver*, tassista;
(*aer.*) — *track*, pista di rullaggio.
to **taxi** *vi.* (*aer.*) rullare.
taxicab *s.* autopubblica.
taximeter *s.* tassametro.
tea *s.* tè || — -*pot*, teiera; *high* —,
cena fredda; — -*set*, servizio da tè.
to **teach** (**taught, taught**) *vt.* insegnare.
teachable *agg.* **1.** che apprende facilmente **2.** che si insegna facilmente.
teacher *s.* insegnante.
teachership *s.* insegnamento.
tcaching *agg.* che insegna. ♦
teaching *s.* insegnamento.
teacup *s.* tazza da tè.
team *s.* **1.** squadra **2.** tiro (*di cavalli*).
to **team** *vt.* aggiogare, accoppiarsi,
raggrupparsi. ♦ to **team** *vi.* accoppiarsi, associarsi.
tear[1] *s.* **1.** lacrima **2.** goccia || —
-*gas*, gas lacrimogeno.
tear[2] *s.* strappo, lacerazione.
to **tear** (**tore, torn**) *vt.* strappare,
lacerare. ♦ to **tear** (**tore, torn**)
vi. strapparsi.
tearful *agg.* lacrimoso.
tearing *agg.* violento. ♦ **tearing** *s.*
strappo, lacerazione.
tear-off *s.* parte da staccare.
tease *s.* chi stuzzica.
to **tease** *vt.* **1.** stuzzicare **2.** cardare
(*lana ecc.*).
teaser *s.* **1.** seccatore **2.** cardatore
3. questione difficile.
teaspoon *s.* cucchiaino da tè.
technical *agg.* tecnico.
technicality *s.* tecnicismo.
technician *s.* tecnico.
technique *s.* tecnica.
technological *agg.* tecnologico.
technology *s.* tecnologia.
tectonics *s.* **1.** edilizia **2.** tettonica.
tedious *agg.* tedioso.
tediousness *s.* tedio.
to **teem** *vi.* brulicare.
teen-ager *s.* adolescente.
teens *s. pl.* età da tredici a diciannove anni.
teeth V. *tooth.*
teething *s.* dentizione.

teetotal(l)er s. astemio.

telecast s. teletrasmissione || — news, telegiornale.

to **telecast** (**telecast, telecast**) vt. teletrasmettere.

telecommunication s. telecomunicazione.

telecontrol s. telecomando.

telegram s. telegramma.

telegraph s. telegrafo.

to **telegraph** vt. e vi. telegrafare.

telegraphic agg. telegrafico.

telegraphist s. telegrafista.

telegraphy s. telegrafia.

telemeter s. telemetro.

telepathy s. telepatia.

telephone s. telefono || — booth, cabina telefonica; — -book, elenco telefonico.

to **telephone** vt. e vi. telefonare.

telephonist s. telefonista.

telephony s. telefonia.

telephoto s. telefoto.

telephotograph s. telefotografia.

telescope s. telescopio.

to **telescope** vi. incastrarsi.

teletype s. telescrivente.

teletyper s. telescriventista.

teletypewriter s. telescrivente.

to **teleview** vt. e vi. guardare la televisione.

televiewer s. telespettatore.

to **televise** vt. riprendere con la televisione.

television s. televisione || — set, televisore.

televisional agg. televisivo.

to **tell** (**told, told**) vt. e vi. 1. dire 2. raccontare 3. distinguere.

teller s. 1. narratore 2. (comm.) cassiere.

telling agg. efficace. ♦ **telling** s. 1. il raccontare 2. rivelazione.

telltale s. 1. chiacchierone 2. (tec.) controllore.

telluric agg. tellurico.

telpher s. cabina di funivia.

telpherage s. trasporto per teleferica.

temper s. 1. indole 2. umore 3. collera 4. moderazione.

to **temper** vt. temperare.

temperament s. temperamento.

temperamental agg. capriccioso.

temperance s. temperanza.

temperate agg. 1. temperato (di clima) 2. moderato.

temperature s. temperatura || to have a —, avere la febbre.

tempered agg. 1. temprato 2. moderato 3. di indole, umore || quick —, irritabile.

tempest s. tempesta.

temple[1] s. tempio.

temple[2] s. (anat.) tempia.

temporal agg. temporale.

temporariness s. temporaneità.

temporary agg. temporaneo.

temporization s. temporeggiamento.

to **temporize** vi. temporeggiare.

to **tempt** vt. tentare.

temptation s. tentazione.

tempter s. tentatore.

tempting agg. seducente.

ten agg. e s. dieci.

tenacious agg. 1. tenace 2. viscoso.

tenacity s. tenacia.

tenancy s. locazione.

tenant s. 1. proprietario 2. locatario.

to **tend**[1] vt. curare, badare a, custodire.

to **tend**[2] vi. tendere.

tendency s. tendenza.

tendential, tendentious agg. tendenzioso.

tender[1] agg. tenero || — of, sollecito verso.

tender[2] s. 1. guardiano, custode 2. nave di appoggio.

tender[3] s. offerta, proposta.

to **tender** vt. offrire, presentare.

tenderness s. 1. tenerezza 2. delicatezza.

tendon s. (anat.) tendine.

tendril s. viticcio.

tenebrous agg. tenebroso.

tenement s. 1. podere 2. abitazione.

tenor s. 1. tenore (di vita ecc.) 2. (giur.) copia esatta 3. (mus.) tenore.

tense[1] agg. teso.

tense[2] s. (gramm.) tempo.

to **tense** vt. tendere. ♦ to **tense** vi. tendersi.

tension s. tensione.

tent s. tenda.

tentacle s. tentacolo.

tentative agg. sperimentale. ♦ **tentative** s. tentativo, prova.

tenth agg. e s. decimo.

tenuity s. 1. tenuità 2. rarefazione 3. fluidità.

tenuous agg. 1. tenue 2. rarefatto 3. fluido.

tenure s. 1. possesso 2. gestione.

tepid *agg.* tiepido.
tepidity *s.* tepidezza.
tercet *s.* terzina.
tergal *agg.* dorsale.
to **tergiversate** *vi.* tergiversare.
tergiversation *s.* tergiversazione.
term *s.* 1. termine 2. (*scol.*) trimestre 3. (*giur.*) sessione 4. condizione. ♦ **terms** *s. pl.* rapporti.
to **term** *vt.* definire.
terminable *agg.* terminabile.
terminal *agg.* estremo. ♦ **terminal** *s.* 1. estremità 2. stazione di testa, capolinea 3. (*elettr.*) morsetto.
to **terminate** *vt.* 1. limitare 2. terminare. ♦ to **terminate** *vi.* 1. essere limitato 2. terminare.
termination *s.* 1. termine 2. (*gramm.*) desinenza.
terminator *s.* 1. chi termina 2. limite.
terminology *s.* terminologia.
terminus *s.* (*pl.* -ni) 1. capolinea 2. meta.
termite *s.* (*zool.*) termite.
tern *s.* terno.
ternary *agg.* ternario.
terrace *s.* 1. terrapieno 2. terrazzo (*sul tetto*) 3. fila di case.
terraqueous *agg.* terracqueo.
terrestrial *agg.* e *s.* terrestre.
terrible *agg.* terribile.
terrific *agg.* 1. spaventoso 2. (*fam.*) straordinario.
to **terrify** *vt.* atterrire.
territorial *agg.* territoriale.
territory *s.* territorio.
terror *s.* terrore.
terrorism *s.* terrorismo.
terrorist *s.* terrorista.
terroristic *agg.* terroristico.
to **terrorize** *vt.* terrorizzare.
terse *agg.* conciso.
terseness *s.* concisione.
tertiary *agg.* e *s.* terziario.
test *s.* 1. prova, esperimento, saggio 2. "test", reattivo psicologico || — *driver,* collaudatore; — *film,* provino; — *-tube,* provetta.
to **test** *vt.* 1. controllare 2. mettere alla prova 3. analizzare.
testament *s.* testamento.
testamentary *agg.* testamentario.
tester *s.* 1. collaudatore 2. apparecchio di misura 3. baldacchino.
testicle *s.* testicolo.
to **testify** *vt.* e *vi.* testimoniare.
testimonial *s.* 1. benservito 2. dono.
testimony *s.* testimonianza.

testing *s.* collaudo, prova.
tetanic(al) *agg.* tetanico.
tetanus *s.* tetano.
tetchy *agg.* stizzoso.
tetrahedron *s.* tetraedro.
tetralogy *s.* tetralogia.
Teutonic *agg.* teutonico.
text *s.* 1. testo 2. argomento.
textile *agg.* e *s.* tessile.
textual *agg.* testuale.
texture *s.* trama, tessuto.
thallium *s.* tallio.
than *cong.* che, di, di quello che (non), di quanto (non): *he is older — you,* è più vecchio di te.
to **thank** *vt.* ringraziare || — *you!,* grazie!
thankful *agg.* riconoscente.
thankfulness *s.* riconoscenza.
thankless *agg.* ingrato.
thanks *s. pl.* grazie, ringraziamenti.
thanksgiving *s.* ringraziamento.
that *agg.* (*pl.* those) quello, quella. ♦ **that** *pron. dimostr.* quello, questo, ciò. ♦ **that** *pron. rel.* che, il quale, la quale, i quali, le quali.
that *cong.* 1. che 2. affinché 3. purché.
thatch *s.* copertura di paglia (*per tetti*).
to **thatch** *vt.* coprire con paglia.
thaumaturge *s.* taumaturgo.
thaumaturgic(al) *agg.* taumaturgico.
thaw *s.* sgelo, disgelo.
to **thaw** *vt.* sgelare. ♦ to **thaw** *vi.* sgelarsi.
the *art.* il, lo, la, i, gli, le.
theatre *s.* teatro.
theatrical *agg.* teatrale.
theft *s.* furto.
their *agg. poss.* loro.
theirs *pron. poss.* il, la loro; i, le loro.
theism *s.* teismo.
them *pron.* loro, li, le, sé.
thematic *agg.* tematico.
theme *s.* tema.
themselves *pron. r.* 1. se stessi, se stesse, sé, si 2. essi stessi, esse stesse.
then *avv.* 1. allora 2. poi.
theocracy *s.* teocrazia.
theocratic(al) *agg.* teocratico.
theologian *s.* teologo.
theologic(al) *agg.* teologico.
theology *s.* teologia.
theorem *s.* teorema.

theoretic(al) *agg.* teorico.
theoretics *s.* teoretica.
theorist *s.* teorico.
to **theorize** *vi..* teorizzare.
theory *s.* teoria.
therapeutic(al) *agg.* terapeutico.
therapeutics *s.* terapeutica.
therapy *s.* terapia.
there *avv.* **1.** là; lì **2.** ci, vi **3.** in ciò. ♦ **there** *inter.* ecco! su!
thereabout(s) *avv.* **1.** là vicino **2.** all'incirca.
thereby *avv.* per mezzo di, perciò.
therefore *avv.* quindi, dunque.
thereupon *avv.* al che, tosto.
thermal *agg.* termico, termale.
thermic *agg.* termico.
thermionic *agg.* termoionico.
thermodynamics *s.* termodinamica.
thermoelectric *agg.* termoelettrico.
thermometer *s.* termometro.
thermonuclear *agg.* termonucleare.
thermostat *s.* termostato.
these (*pl. di* this), questi, queste.
thesis *s.* (*pl.* -ses) tesi, dissertazione.
thews *s. pl.* muscoli.
they *pron. pers.* **1.** essi, esse, loro **2.** (*in costruzioni impersonali*) si: — *say*, si dice.
thick *agg.* **1.** spesso, grosso: *a — book*, un grosso libro **2.** fitto, folto **3.** denso, torbido.
to **thicken** *vt.* ispessire, addensare. ♦ to **thicken** *vi.* ispessirsi, addensarsi.
thickening *s.* ispessimento.
thicket *s.* boschetto.
thickly *avv.* fittamente, densamente.
thickness *s.* **1.** spessore, grossezza **2.** densità **3.** strato.
thickset *agg.* **1.** fitto, spesso **2.** tarchiato.
thief *s.* (*pl.* thieves) ladro.
to **thieve** *vt.* e *vi.* rubare, essere ladro.
thievish *agg.* ladresco.
thigh *s.* coscia || — *bone*, femore.
thimble *s.* ditale.
thin *agg.* **1.** sottile **2.** magro, snello **3.** rado, raro **4.** fluido, rarefatto **5.** debole, fiacco.
to **thin** *vt.* e *vi.* **1.** assottigliare, assottigliarsi, dimagrire **2.** diradare, sfoltire. ♦ to **thin** *vt.* **1.** assottigliare **2.** diradare, sfoltire. ♦ to **thin** *vi.* **1.** assottigliarsi **2.** diradarsi.
thing *s.* **1.** cosa, oggetto **2.** argomen-

to, soggetto.
to **think** (**thought, thought**) *vt.* e *vi.* **1.** pensare, riflettere **2.** ritenere, considerare **3.** credere, aspettarsi || *to* — *of*, pensare, avere in animo di; *to* — *ill of so.*, avere una cattiva opinione di qu.; *to* — *out*, escogitare; *to* — *over*, riflettere.
thinkable *agg.* concepibile, immaginabile.
thinker *s.* pensatore.
thinking *agg.* pensante, ragionevole ♦ **thinking** *s.* pensiero, riflessione, opinione.
thinness *s.* sottigliezza, tenuità, magrezza, radezza.
third *agg.* e *s.* terzo.
thirdly *avv.* in terzo luogo.
third-rate *agg.* di terz'ordine.
thirst *s.* **1.** sete, arsura **2.** (*fig.*) avidità.
thirsty *agg.* assetato || *to be* —, aver sete; *to be* — *for* (*fig.*), bramare.
thirteen *agg.* tredici.
thirteenth *agg.* tredicesimo.
thirtieth *agg.* trentesimo.
thirty *agg.* trenta.
this *agg.* e *pron. dimostr.* (*pl.* these) questo, questa.
Thomism *s.* tomismo.
thomist *s.* tomista.
thorax *s.* torace.
thorn *s.* spina (*anche fig.*).
thorny *agg.* spinoso (*anche fig.*).
thorough *agg.* **1.** completo, totale **2.** perfetto, esperto **3.** meticoloso.
thoroughbred *agg.* **1.** purosangue (*di cavallo*) **2.** di antico lignaggio. ♦ **thoroughbred** *s.* purosangue.
thoroughfare *s.* arteria di grande traffico || *no* —, passaggio vietato.
those (*pl. di* that) quelli, quelle.
though *avv.* comunque, tuttavia. ♦ **though** *cong.* benché, sebbene.
thought V. *to think.*
thought *s.* **1.** pensiero, riflessione **2.** idea, parere **3.** concezione.
thoughtful *agg.* **1.** pensoso, pensieroso **2.** sollecito.
thoughtless *agg.* sconsiderato, sventato, negligente.
thoughtlessness *s* sconsideratezza, negligenza.
thousand *agg.* mille. ♦ **thousand** *s.* migliaio.
thrall *s.* schiavo.
to **thrash** *vt.* e *vi.* **1.** battere, sfer-

zare **2.** (*mar.*) navigare contro vento **3.** trebbiare **4.** bastonare || *to* — *out*, dibattere.

thrasher *s.* trebbiatore.

thrashing machine *s.* trebbiatrice.

thread *s.* **1.** filo (*anche fig.*) **2.** vena, filone.

to thread *vt.* **1.** infilare **2.** far passare attraverso.

threadbare *agg.* **1.** consumato, consunto **2.** (*fig.*) vieto, trito.

threading *s.* filettatura.

threadlike *agg.* filiforme.

threat *s.* minaccia.

to threaten *vt.* e *vi.* minacciare.

threatening *agg.* minaccioso.

three *agg.* e *s.* tre.

threescore *agg.* sessanta.

to thresh *vt.* e *vi.* trebbiare.

threshold *s.* **1.** soglia, limitare **2.** (*fig.*) esordio, inizio.

threw V. *to throw.*

thrice *avv.* tre volte.

thriftiness *s.* economia, parsimonia.

thrifty *agg.* frugale, economo.

thrill *s.* brivido, palpito.

to thrill *vt.* far fremere, elettrizzare. ◆ **to thrill** *vi.* fremere, vibrare, emozionarsi.

thriller *s.* (*gergo*) storia, film sensazionale, poliziesco.

thrilling *agg.* **1.** sensazionale, emozionante **2.** penetrante.

to thrive (throve, thriven) *vi.* **1.** prosperare, fiorire **2.** crescere vigorosamente.

thriving *agg.* **1.** prospero, fiorente **2.** rigoglioso.

throat *s.* gola || — *wash*, gargarismo; *sore* —, mal di gola.

throaty *agg.* gutturale.

throb *s.* battito, pulsazione, fremito.

to throb *vi.* battere, pulsare, fremere.

throbbing *agg.* palpitante, vibrante (*anche fig.*).

thrombosis *s.* trombosi.

throne *s.* trono.

throng *s.* folla, moltitudine.

to throng *vt.* affollare, stipare. ◆ **to throng** *vi.* affollarsi, affluire.

to throttle *vt.* strozzare, strangolare.

through *avv.* **1.** attraverso, da una parte all'altra **2.** (*ferr.*) direttamente || — *train*, treno diretto. ◆ **through** *prep.* **1.** attraverso, per **2.** durante, per tutta la durata di

3. per mezzo.

throughout *avv.* da un capo all'altro, dal principio alla fine. ◆ **throughout** *prep.* in ogni parte di, durante tutto il, dal principio alla fine di.

throve V. *to thrive.*

throw *s.* lancio, gittata (*di missile ecc.*), tiro.

to throw (threw, thrown) *vt.* e *vi.* **1.** gettare, scagliare, proiettare **2.** atterrare, rovesciare || *to* — *away*, buttar via; *to* — *off*, buttar fuori; *to* — *out* espellere.

throwback *s.* **1.** movimento brusco all'indietro **2.** ostacolo.

thrown V. *to throw.*

thrush *s.* tordo.

thrust *s.* **1.** colpo, botta **2.** colpo con arma appuntita.

to thrust (thrust, thrust) *vt.* e *vi.* **1.** spingere, ficcare **2.** frapporre **3.** forzare.

thud *s.* tonfo, rumore sordo.

to thud *vi.* fare un rumore sordo.

thumb *s.* pollice.

to thumb *vt.* **1.** lasciare ditate su (*un foglio ecc.*) **2.** strimpellare.

thump *s.* rumore sordo.

to thump *vt.* battere, percuotere, dar pugni.

thumping *agg.* pesante.

thunder *s.* **1.** tuono: *a peal of* —, un colpo di tuono **2.** scoppio, rombo **3.** fulmine (*anche fig.*).

to thunder *vt.* e *vi.* **1.** tuonare, rimbombare **2.** minacciare.

thunderbolt *s.* fulmine, saetta (*anche fig.*).

thundering *agg.* **1.** tonante, fulminante **2.** (*fam.*) straordinario.

thundery *agg.* minaccioso.

Thursday *s.* giovedì.

thus *avv.* così, in questo modo.

to thwart *vt.* opporsi a, ostacolare.

thyme *s.* timo.

thyroid *s.* tiroide.

tibia *s.* tibia.

tick *s.* tic-tac, ticchettio (*di orologio*).

to tick *vt.* e *vi.* ticchettare.

ticket *s.* **1.** biglietto, tessera, scontrino **2.** (*mil.*) congedo || — *-collector*, bigliettaio; — *-inspector*, controllore; *single* —, biglietto di andata.

to ticket *vt.* **1.** mettere il cartellino del prezzo a **2.** fornire di biglietto.

ticking s. traliccio.

tickle s. solletico.

to **tickle** vt. fare il solletico, solleticare (anche fig.). ♦ to **tickle** vi. prudere.

tickler s. **1.** chi solletica **2.** questione delicata.

ticklish agg. **1.** sensibile al solletico **2.** scabroso.

tide s. **1.** marea **2.** (fig.) corrente, corso ‖ — -gauge, mareografo.

to **tide** vi. salire, crescere come la marea.

tidily avv. lindamente.

tidings s. pl. novità.

tidy agg. ordinato, preciso, pulito.

to **tidy** vt. riordinare, mettere in ordine.

tie s. **1.** laccio, legaccio **2.** cravatta **3.** (fig.) legame **4.** (ferr.) traversina.

to **tie** vt. **1.** legare, allacciare, congiungere (anche fig.) **2.** annodare.

tied agg. vincolato, schiavo.

tier s. ordine, fila (di posti).

to **tier** vt. allineare.

tiff s. stizza, bisticcio ‖ to be in a —, essere in collera.

to **tiff** vi. essere stizzito.

tiger s. tigre.

tight agg. **1.** impermeabile, a perfetta tenuta **2.** teso, tirato **3.** stretto, aderente, attillato **4.** scarso, a corto di denaro **5.** (gergo) ubriaco. ♦ **tight** avv. **1.** ermeticamente **2.** in maniera tesa.

to **tighten** vt. **1.** serrare **2.** tirare, tendere. ♦ to **tighten** vi. **1.** serrarsi **2.** tendersi.

tightly avv. ermeticamente, strettamente.

tightness s. **1.** impermeabilità, tenuta **2.** tensione **3.** (gergo) ubriachezza.

tights s. pl. calzamaglia.

tigress s. tigre (femmina).

tile s. **1.** tegola, mattonella, piastrella **2.** (fam.) cappello a cilindro.

to **tile** vt. coprire di tegole, piastrelle.

tilemaking s. fabbricazione di tegole.

tilery s. fabbrica di tegole.

tiling s. tegolato, piastrellatura.

till[1] prep. fino a: — now, fino ad ora. ♦ **till** cong. finché, fino al momento in cui.

till[2] s. cassetto in cui si custodisce il denaro.

to **till** vt. dissodare, arare.

tillage s. **1.** dissodamento, aratura **2.** terreno coltivato.

tiller s. **1.** aratore **2.** (mar.) barra del timone.

tilt[1] s. tenda, tendone.

tilt[2] s. **1.** torneo, giostra **2.** contesa, disputa **3.** inclinazione, pendenza.

to **tilt** vt. **1.** inclinare **2.** rovesciare. ♦ to **tilt** vi. **1.** oscillare **2.** (mar.) beccheggiare.

timber s. **1.** legname da costruzione **2.** bosco con alberi d'alto fusto **3.** trave **4.** (fig.) tempra, carattere **5.** (mar.) costola ‖ — -work, costruzione in legno.

to **timber** vt. rivestire di legno.

timbre s. timbro (di suoni).

time s. **1.** tempo, periodo di tempo, circostanza, epoca, età **2.** volta, volte **3.** orario, ora ‖ with —, col passar del tempo; from — to —, di tanto in tanto; as times go, coi tempi che corrono; at times, a volte; in good —, per tempo; what — is it?, che ore sono?

to **time** vt. fissare l'orario di. ♦ to **time** vi. tenere il tempo.

timekeeper s. **1.** cronometro **2.** cronometrista.

timeliness s. tempestività.

timely agg. opportuno, tempestivo.

timepiece s. orologio (da tavolo).

timer s. cronometrista.

time-study agg. — engineer, analista tempi.

timid agg. timido.

timidity s. timidezza.

timing s. **1.** calcolo del tempo (di pose fotografiche ecc.) **2.** (mecc.) messa in fase.

timorous agg. timoroso.

tin s. **1.** stagno, latta **2.** recipiente.

to **tin** vt. **1.** stagnare **2.** conservare in scatola.

tincture s. **1.** (chim.) tintura, soluzione alcoolica **2.** tinta **3.** sfumatura, traccia **4.** gusto, aroma.

to **tincture** vt. **1.** tingere, colorare **2.** aromatizzare.

tinder s. esca (per fuoco).

tinge s. **1.** sfumatura, tocco **2.** (fig.) pizzico.

to **tinge** vt. dare una sfumatura a (anche fig.).

to **tingle** vt. **1.** pizzicare **2.** far tintinnare. ♦ to **tingle** vi. arrossire (di guance).

tink s. tintinnio.

tinker *s.* calderaio (*ambulante*), stagnino.

to **tinker** *vt.* rabberciare, riparare.

tinkle *s.* tintinnio.

to **tinkle** *vt.* far tintinnare. ♦ to **tinkle** *vi.* tintinnare.

tinkling *s.* tintinnio.

tinsel *agg.* vistoso, sgargiante. ♦ **tinsel** *s.* orpello (*anche fig.*).

tint *s.* tinta, colore delicato, sfumatura.

to **tint** *vt.* colorire, tinteggiare.

tiny *agg.* minuscolo.

tip¹ *s.* **1.** pùnta, cima **2.** puntale.

tip² *s.* **1.** immondezzaio **2.** inclinazione.

tip³ *s.* mancia.

to **tip¹** *vt.* toccare, battere leggermente.

to **tip²** *vt.* **1.** rovesciare **2.** inclinare. ♦ to **tip** *vi.* **1.** rovesciarsi **2.** inclinarsi.

to **tip³** *vt.* e *vi.* **1.** dare la mancia **2.** (*gergo*) dare, passare.

tippet *s.* mantellina.

tipsy *agg.* ubriaco.

tiptoe *s.* punta dei piedi: *on* —, in punta di piedi.

to **tiptoe** *vi.* camminare in punta di piedi.

tire *s.* **1.** cerchione di ruota **2.** pneumatico || *flat* —, gomma a terra.

to **tire¹** *vt.* stancare, annoiare. ♦ to **tire** *vi.* stancarsi, annoiarsi.

to **tire²** *vt.* fornire di cerchione, di pneumatico.

tired *agg.* stanco, affaticato, esausto || *to be* — *out*, essere stanco morto.

tireless *agg.* instancabile.

tiresome *agg.* faticoso, stancante, noioso.

tissue *s.* tessuto || — *paper*, carta velina.

Titan *s.* titano, gigante.

titanic *agg.* titanico (*anche fig.*).

title *s.* **1.** titolo **2.** titolo, grado, qualifica.

to **title** *vt.* **1.** intitolare, intestare **2.** conferire un titolo.

titular *s.* titolare.

to *prep.* **1.** (*con verbo di moto*) a, in, da **2.** verso, per **3.** (*di tempo*) fino a **4.** (*paragone, rapporto*) contro a **5.** riguardo a || — *all appearances*, stando alle apparenze; — *my despair*, con mia disperazione; — *this end*, a questo scopo.

toad *s.* rospo.

toady *s.* adulatore.

to **toady** *vt.* adulare, comportarsi servilmente.

toast¹ *s.* pane abbrustolito, crostino.

toast² *s.* brindisi.

to **toast¹** *vt.* abbrustolire, tostare.

to **toast²** *vt.* e *vi.* fare un brindisi.

toaster *s.* tostapane.

tobacco *s.* tabacco || — *-box*, tabacchiera.

tobacconist *s.* tabaccaio || —*'s shop*, tabaccheria.

tocsin *s.* segnale d'allarme.

today *s.* oggi. ♦ **today** *avv.* oggigiorno.

toddle *s.* andatura incerta, vacillante.

to **toddle** *vi.* camminare a passi incerti, passeggiare.

toe *s.* dito del piede.

together *avv.* assieme, insieme, unitamente.

toil¹ *s.* fatica, duro lavoro || — *-worn*, sfinito dalla fatica.

toil² *s.* laccio, trappola (*anche fig.*).

to **toil¹** *vi.* faticare, lavorare duramente.

to **toil²** *vt.* prendere in trappola (*anche fig.*).

toilet *s.* **1.** toletta, pulizia **2.** abbigliamento **3.** bagno, gabinetto || — *-paper*, carta igienica.

toilsome *agg.* faticoso, laborioso.

token *s.* **1.** segno, simbolo **2.** prova, pegno, ricordo.

tolerable *agg.* **1.** tollerabile **2.** discreto.

tolerance *s.* tolleranza.

tolerant *agg.* tollerante.

to **tolerate** *vt.* tollerare, sopportare.

toleration *s.* tolleranza

toll¹ *s.* pedaggio, dazio, gabella.

toll² *s.* rintocco (*di campana*).

to **toll** *vt.* suonare. ♦ to **toll** *vi.* rintoccare.

tomato *s.* pomodoro.

tomb *s.* tomba.

tomboy *s.* ragazza indiavolata.

tome *s.* tomo, volume.

tomfool *agg.* e *s.* sciocco, banale.

tommy *s.* **1.** pane, pagnotta **2.** provviste (*che l'operaio porta da casa*) (*pl.*).

tommy-gun *s.* fucile mitragliatore, mitra.

tomorrow *s.* e *avv.* domani.

ton *s.* tonnellata.

tonality *s.* tonalità.

tone *s.* tono, timbro, accento.

to **tone** vt. e vi. **1.** (mus.) dare il tono, intonare, accordare **2.** (pitt.) sfumare.

toneless agg. inespressivo, privo di colore, senza vigore.

tongs s. pl. pinze, molle, tenaglie.

tongue s. **1.** lingua **2.** lingua, linguaggio **3.** lingua (di terra, fuoco) || — -tied, muto, taciturno; — -twister, scioglilingua.

to **tongue** vt. leccare, lambire.

tonic agg. tonico, corroborante. ♦ **tonic** s. (med.) tonico, energetico.

tonight avv. e s. stanotte, stasera.

tonnage s. tonnellaggio, stazza.

tonsil s. tonsilla.

tonsillitis s. tonsillite.

tonsure s. tonsura.

to **tonsure** vt. tonsurare.

too avv. **1.** troppo **2.** anche, pure **3.** inoltre.

took V. to take.

tool s. **1.** arnese, attrezzo, utensile **2.** (fig.) strumento.

tooth s. (pl. teeth) **1.** dente, zanna **2.** dente (di pettine, forchetta ecc.) || — -paste, dentifricio; — -pick, stuzzicadenti.

toothache s. mal di denti.

toothbrush s. spazzolino da denti.

toothing s. dentatura, dentellatura.

toothless agg. sdentato.

toothy agg. dai denti sporgenti.

top[1] s. **1.** cima, sommità **2.** (fig.) apice **3.** parte superiore, "capote" di automobile.

top[2] s. trottola.

topaz s. topazio.

topic s. argomento, soggetto.

topical agg. d'attualità.

topographer s. topografo.

topographic(al) agg. topografico.

topography s. topografia.

topology s. topologia.

toponymy s. toponomastica.

topsail s. vela di gabbia.

topsyturvy agg. sottosopra, capovolto. ♦ **topsyturvy** s. capovolgimento, disordine, scompiglio. ♦ **topsyturvy** avv. sottosopra.

to **topsyturvy** vt. mettere sossopra.

toque s. berretto, tocco.

torch s. torcia, fiaccola || electric —, lampadina tascabile.

torchlight s. luce di fiaccole, torce || — procession, fiaccolata.

tore V. to tear.

torment s. tormento, tortura.

to **torment** vt. tormentare.

torn V. to tear.

tornado s. ciclone.

torpedo s. **1.** (zool.) torpedine **2.** (mar.) siluro || — -boat, torpediniera; — boat destroyer, cacciatorpediniere.

to **torpedo** vt. silurare.

torpid agg. torpido, apatico.

torpor s. torpore.

torrefaction s. torrefazione.

to **torrefy** vt. torrefare.

torrent s. torrente (anche fig.).

torrential agg. torrenziale.

torrid agg. torrido.

torsion s. torsione.

tortoise s. tartaruga.

torture s. tortura, tormento (anche fig.).

to **torture** vt. torturare, tormentare.

torturous agg. tormentoso.

toss s. **1.** lancio **2.** movimento del capo.

to **toss** vt. **1.** gettare, lanciare **2.** agitare, scuotere **3.** disarcionare. ♦ to **toss** vi. **1.** agitarsi, smaniare **2.** tirare a sorte **3.** (mar.) beccheggiare.

total agg. totale, completo. ♦ **total** s. totale.

totalitarian agg. totalitario.

totalitarianism s. totalitarismo.

totality s. totalità.

totalizator s. totalizzatore.

to **totalize** vt. e vi. totalizzare.

totalizer s. totalizzatore.

to **totter** vi. camminare barcollando.

tottering agg. vacillante, malsicuro.

touch s. **1.** tocco, colpetto **2.** tatto **3.** contatto, rapporto.

to **touch** vt. **1.** toccare **2.** sfiorare **3.** (fig.) colpire, commuovere. ♦ to **touch** vi. essere in contatto, confinare.

touchiness s. suscettibilità.

touching agg. toccante, commovente. ♦ **touching** prep. riguardo a.

touchstone s. pietra di paragone.

touchwood s. esca (per accendere il fuoco).

touchy agg. permaloso.

tough agg. **1.** duro **2.** forte, robusto **3.** (fig.) inflessibile **4.** difficile **5.** violento.

to **toughen** vt. indurire. ♦ to **toughen** vi. indurirsi.

toughness s. **1.** durezza **2.** inflessibilità.

tour s. giro, viaggio, escursione.

to **tour** vt. e vi. fare un viaggio.

tourism s. turismo.
tourist s. turista.
tourmalin(e) s. tormalina.
tournament s. torneo.
to **tousle** vt. scompigliare, arruffare.
tow s. rimorchio.
toward(s) prep. 1. verso, in direzione di 2. riguardo a 3. verso, circa (di tempo).
towel s. asciugamano || — -horse, porta-asciugamano.
tower s. torre.
to **tower** vi. torreggiare.
towing s. rimorchio.
town s. 1. città 2. cittadinanza || — -council, consiglio comunale; — -planning, piano regolatore; chief —, capoluogo.
townhall s. municipio.
townhouse s. residenza di città.
townscape s. veduta (di città).
townsfolk s. abitanti di una città.
township s. territorio, giurisdizione di una città.
townsman s. cittadino.
townspeople s. cittadinanza.
townward(s) avv. verso la città.
toxic(al) agg. tossico.
toxicity s. tossicità.
toxicologist s. tossicologo.
toxicology s. tossicologia.
toxin s. tossina.
toy s. 1. giocattolo 2. bazzecola, storiella.
to **toy** vi. giocherellare, trastullarsi.
toyish agg. 1. simile a giocattolo 2. insignificante.
toyshop s. negozio di giocattoli.
trabeation s. trabeazione.
trace s. traccia, orma.
to **trace** vt. 1. tracciare 2. seguire le tracce 3. rintracciare || to — back, risalire.
traceable agg. 1. rintracciabile 2. che si può tracciare.
trachea s. trachea.
tracheal agg. tracheale.
tracheitis s. tracheite.
trachyte s. trachite.
tracing s. 1. tracciato 2. calco, ricalco.
track s. 1. traccia, orma 2. sentiero, corso (anche fig.) 3. (sport) pista 4. (ferr.) binario || sound — (cine), colonna sonora.
to **track** vt. 1. inseguire, pedinare 2. tracciare un sentiero. ♦ to **track** vi. posare i binari.
tract[1] s. periodo, tratto, spazio.

tract[2] s. opuscolo.
tractability s. arrendevolezza.
tractable agg. arrendevole.
traction s. 1. trazione 2. contrazione.
tractor s. trattore.
trade s. 1. mestiere 2. commercio, traffico 3. commercianti (pl.) || — bank, banca commerciale; — dispute, vertenza sindacale; — -mark, marchio di fabbrica; — -show (cine), anteprima per la critica; free- —, libero scambio.
to **trade** vt. e vi. commerciare, negoziare.
trader s. 1. commerciante 2. nave mercantile.
trading s. commercio.
tradition s. tradizione.
traditional agg. tradizionale.
traditionalism s. tradizionalismo.
traditionalist s. tradizionalista.
to **traduce** vt. calunniare.
traffic s. 1. traffico, commercio 2. traffico, circolazione || — lights, semaforo; — jam, ingorgo stradale.
tragedian s. 1. tragediografo 2. attore tragico.
tragedy s. tragedia.
tragic(al) agg. tragico.
tragicomedy s. tragicommedia.
tragicomic(al) agg. tragicomico.
trail s. 1. traccia, striscia 2. pista, orma 3. cammino, sentiero.
to **trail** vt. 1. trascinare 2. seguire le tracce di. ♦ to **trail** vi. trascinarsi.
trailer s. 1. inseguitore, cacciatore 2. rimorchio 3. (cine) film di prossima programmazione.
train s. 1. treno: express — (o fast —), rapido; slow —, accelerato 2. seguito, corteo 3. serie, successione, fila.
to **train** vt. 1. allevare, educare 2. esercitare, allenare, addestrare. ♦ to **train** vi. 1. esercitarsi, allenarsi 2. viaggiare in ferrovia.
trainer s. istruttore, allenatore.
training s. educazione, ammaestramento, allenamento.
trait s. tratto, fattezza, caratteristica.
traitor s. traditore.
trajectory s. traiettoria.
tram s. 1. tram 2. carrello da miniera || — -conductor, tranviere.
trammel s. 1. tramaglio 2. intoppo.
tramp s. 1. calpestio 2. viaggio a piedi.

to **tramp** *vt.* **1.** camminare pesantemente **2.** viaggiare a piedi **3.** vagabondare.

trample *s.* calpestio.

to **trample** *vt.* **1.** calpestare **2.** (*fig.*) offendere. ♦ to **trample** *vi.* camminare pesantemente.

tramway *s.* tranvia.

to **tranquillize** *vt.* tranquillizzare.

tranquillizer *s.* (*med.*) tranquillante.

to **transact** *vt.* e *vi.* negoziare, trattare affari.

transaction *s.* **1.** affare, operazione **2.** (*giur.*) transazione **3.** atti (*di congresso ecc.*) (*pl.*).

transactor *s.* negoziatore.

transalpine *agg.* e *s.* transalpino.

transatlantic *agg.* transatlantico.

to **transcend** *vt.* trascendere, superare.

transcendence *s.* trascendenza.

transcendent *agg.* trascendente.

transcendental *agg.* trascendentale.

transcendentalism *s.* trascendentalismo.

transcontinental *agg.* transcontinentale.

to **transcribe** *vt.* trascrivere.

transcript *s.* riproduzione, copia.

transcription *s.* trascrizione.

transept *s.* transetto.

transfer *s.* **1.** trasferimento, cessione **2.** (*giur.*) trapasso **3.** decalcomania.

to **transfer** *vt.* trasferire, cedere.

transferable *agg.* trasferibile.

transfiguration *s.* trasfigurazione.

to **transfigure** *vt.* trasfigurare.

to **transfix** *vt.* trafiggere.

transfocator *s.* (*cine*) teleobiettivo.

to **transform** *vt.* trasformare.

transformable *agg.* trasformabile.

transformation *s.* trasformazione.

transformer *s.* trasformatore.

transformism *s.* trasformismo.

to **transfuse** *vt.* **1.** travasare **2.** fare una trasfusione (*di sangue*).

transfusion *s.* trasfusione.

to **transgress** *vt.* trasgredire. ♦ to **transgress** *vi.* commettere una violenza, peccare.

transgression *s.* trasgressione.

transgressor *s.* trasgressore.

transient *agg.* passeggero, transitorio.

transistor *s.* (*radio*) transistor.

transit *s.* **1.** transito, passaggio **2.** trasporto.

transition *s.* transizione.

transitive *agg.* transitivo.

transitory *agg.* transitorio.

translatable *agg.* traducibile.

to **translate** *vt.* tradurre.

translation *s.* **1.** traduzione **2.** trasferimento, assunzione (*al cielo*).

translator *s.* traduttore.

translucent *agg.* traslucido, diafano, trasparente.

to **transmigrate** *vi.* trasmigrare.

transmigration *s.* trasmigrazione.

transmissible *agg.* trasmissibile.

transmission *s.* trasmissione.

to **transmit** *vt.* trasmettere.

transmitter *s.* trasmettitore.

transoceanic *agg.* transoceanico.

transparence *s.* trasparenza.

transparent *agg.* **1.** trasparente, limpido **2.** chiaro, evidente.

to **transpire** *vt.* e *vi.* traspirare.

to **transplant** *vt.* trapiantare.

transplantation *s.* trapianto.

transport *s.* **1.** trasporto (*anche fig.*) **2.** mezzo di trasporto.

transportable *agg.* trasportabile.

transposal *s.* trasposizione.

transposition *s.* trasposizione (*di parole, cifre ecc.*).

transubstantiation *s.* transustanziazione.

transversal *agg.* e *s.* trasversale.

trap *s.* trappola ‖ — *-door*, botola.

to **trap** *vt.* prendere in trappola.

trapezium *s.* trapezio.

trapper *s.* chi tende trappole.

trash[1] *s.* rifiuto.

trash[2] *s.* guinzaglio.

to **trash** *vt.* sfrondare.

trashy *agg.* senza valore.

traumatic *agg.* traumatico.

travel *s.* **1.** viaggi (*pl.*): — *agency*, agenzia di viaggi **2.** (*mecc.*) corsa.

to **travel** *vi.* viaggiare.

traveller *s.* viaggiatore.

travelling *agg.* **1.** viaggiante **2.** di, da viaggio **3.** mobile. ♦ **travelling** *s.* il viaggiare.

traverse *agg.* trasversale. ♦ **traverse** *s.* **1.** trasversale **2.** traversata.

to **traverse** *vt.* **1.** traversare **2.** muovere lateralmente. ♦ to **traverse** *vi.* **1.** fare una traversata **2.** muoversi lateralmente **3.** girare su un perno.

travertin(e) *s.* travertino.

travesty *s.* parodia.

trawl *s.* (*mar.*) strascico.

trawler s. pescnereccio a strascico.

tray s. vassoio || *ash*- —, portace-nere.

treacherous *agg.* traditore, sleale.

treacherousness, treachery s. tra-dimento, slealtà.

tread s. 1. passo 2. suola 3. batti-strada.

to tread (trod, trodden) *vt.* e *vi.* camminare. ♦ to tread (trod, trodden) *vt.* 1. percorrere 2. cal-pestare.

treadle s. pedale.

treason s. tradimento.

treasure s. tesoro.

to treasure *vt.* 1. ammassare 2. cu-stodire gelosamente.

treasurer s. tesoriere.

treasury s. 1. tesoreria 2. Ministe-ro del Tesoro.

treat s. festa.

to treat *vt.* 1. trattare 2. offrire.

treatise s. trattato.

treatment s. 1. trattamento 2. (*med.*) cura.

treaty s. trattato.

treble *agg.* 1. triplo, triplice 2. (*mus.*) di soprano, parte di so-prano.

to treble *vt.* triplicare. ♦ to treble *vi.* triplicarsi.

tree s. 1. albero 2. trave || — *-frog*, raganella.

trefoil s. trifoglio.

trellis s. graticcio.

tremble s. tremito.

to tremble *vi.* tremare.

trembling *agg.* tremante, tremolan-te. ♦ trembling s. tremito.

tremendous *agg.* tremendo.

tremor s. tremore.

tremulous *agg.* tremulo.

trench s. 1. fosso 2. trincea.

to trench *vt.* e *vi.* scavare, solcare, scavare trincee.

trenchant *agg.* tagliente, incisivo, efficace.

trencher s. tagliere.

trend s. direzione, orientamento, tendenza.

to trend *vi.* tendere.

trepan s. trapano.

to trepan *vt.* trapanare.

trepidation s. 1. tremito 2. trepi-dazione.

trespass s. 1. trasgressione 2. vio-lazione.

to trespass *vi.* 1. commettere una violazione 2. peccare.

trespasser s. 1. trasgressore 2. pec-catore.

trestle s. 1. cavalletto 2. intelaia-tura.

trial s. 1. processo 2. prova, espe-rimento.

triangle s. triangolo.

triangular *agg.* triangolare.

triangulation s. triangolazione.

tribal *agg.* tribale.

tribe s. tribù.

tribune[1] s. tribuno.

tribune[2] s. tribuna.

tributary *agg.* e s. tributario.

tribute s. tributo.

trichromatic *agg.* tricromico.

trick s. 1. trucco 2. imbroglio 3. mania.

to trick *vt.* ingannare.

trickery s. inganno.

trickish *agg.* scaltro.

trickle s. gocciolio.

to trickle *vi.* gocciolare.

tricky *agg.* 1. scaltro 2. intricato.

tricolour *agg.* e s. tricolore.

tricycle s. triciclo.

trident s. tridente.

tridimensional *agg.* tridimensio-nale.

triennial *agg.* triennale.

trifle s. sciocchezza.

to trifle *vi.* scherzare.

trifler s. persona leggera.

trifling *agg.* 1. insignificante 2. fri-volo.

trigeminal *agg.* e s. trigemino.

trigeminus s. trigemino.

trigger s. grilletto.

trigonometry s. trigonometria.

trihedron s. triedro.

trill s. trillo.

to trill *vt.* e *vi.* trillare.

trillion s. 1. trilione 2. (*amer.*) bi-lione.

trilogy s. trilogia.

trim *agg.* ordinato. ♦ trim s. 1. ordine 2. assetto 3. (*cine*) taglio.

to trim *vt.* 1. ordinare 2. tagliare.

trimester s. trimestre.

trimmer s. decoratore.

trimming s. 1. guarnizione 2. ba-stonatura.

trinity s. trinità.

trinket s. ninnolo.

trinomial s. trinomio.

trip s. 1. gita, viaggio 2. passo agile 3. passo falso.

to trip *vi.* 1. saltellare 2. inciam-pare. ♦ to trip *vt.* 1. far inciampare 2. (*mecc.*) liberare.

tripartite *agg.* tripartito.

tripartition *s.* tripartizione.

tripe *s.* 1. trippa 2. (*gergo*) ciarpame, sciocchezze (*pl.*).

triple *agg.* triplo.

to **triple** *vt.* triplicare. ◆ to **triple** *vi.* triplicarsi.

triplicate *agg.* triplicato. ◆ **triplicate** *s.* triplice copia.

to **triplicate** *vt.* triplicare.

tripod *s.* 1. treppiede 2. tripode.

tripper *s.* gitante.

triptych *s.* trittico.

trisyllabic(al) *agg.* trisillabico.

trite *agg.* trito.

to **triturate** *vt.* triturare.

triumph *s.* trionfo.

to **triumph** *vi.* trionfare.

triumphant *agg.* trionfante.

triumvir *s.* triumviro.

triumvirate *s.* triumvirato.

trivalent *agg.* trivalente.

trivial *agg.* banale.

triviality *s.* banalità.

trod V. *to tread.*

trodden V. *to tread.*

troglodyte *s.* troglodita.

troglodytic(al) *agg.* trogloditico.

trolley *s.* carrello || — *bus*, filobus; — *line*, linea tranviaria.

troop *s.* 1. gruppo 2. truppe (*pl.*).

to **troop** *vi.* 1. radunarsi 2. sfilare.

trophy *s.* trofeo.

tropic *agg.* tropico.

tropical *agg.* tropicale.

tropism *s.* tropismo.

troposphere *s.* troposfera.

trot *s.* trotto.

to **trot** *vt.* far trottare. ◆ to **trot** *vi.* trottare.

trotter *s.* trottatore.

trouble *s.* guaio, disturbo.

to **trouble** *vt.* disturbare. ◆ to **trouble** *vi.* preoccuparsi.

troublesome *agg.* fastidioso.

trough *s.* 1. truogolo 2. condotto, solco 3. depressione (*atmosferica*).

trousers *s. pl.* calzoni

trout *s.* trota.

trowel *s.* cazzuola.

truce *s.* tregua.

truck[1] *s.* baratto, scambio.

truck[1] *s.* 1. carrello 2. (*amer.*) autocarro.

to **truck**[1] *vt.* barattare.

to **truck**[2] *vt.* trasportare (*su carrello*).

trucker *s.* camionista.

truculent *agg.* truculento.

to **trudge** *vi.* camminare faticosamente.

true *agg.* vero, esatto || *out of* —, sfasato.

truffle *s.* tartufo.

truly *avv.* 1. veramente 2. esattamente.

to **trump** *vt.* ingannare || *to* — *up a charge*, inventare un'accusa.

trumpery *agg.* illusorio. ◆ **trumpery** *s.* orpello.

trumpet *s.* tromba.

to **trumpet** *vi.* 1. suonare la tromba 2. barrire. ◆ to **trumpet** *vt.* strombazzare.

trumpeter *s.* trombettiere.

truncate *agg.* tronco, troncato.

truncheon *s.* manganello.

trunk *s.* 1. tronco 2. baule 3. proboscide || — *-call*, comunicazione interurbana. ◆ **trunks** *s. pl.* calzoni corti.

truss *s.* 1. fascio 2. (*arch.*) capriata.

trust *s.* 1. fede, fiducia 2. incarico di fiducia 3. (*econ.*) "trust", consorzio monopolistico.

to **trust** *vt.* e *vi.* confidare, fidarsi di, dar credito || *to* — *so. with sthg.*, affidare qc. a qu.

trustee *s.* 1. (*comm.*) fiduciario 2. (*giur.*) curatore.

truster *s.* chi si fida.

trustful *agg.* fiducioso.

trustworthy *agg.* degno di fiducia.

truth *s.* verità.

truthful *agg.* 1. vero 2. fedele.

try *s.* tentativo || — *-on*, prova (*di abiti*); — *-out* (*mecc.*), prova.

to **try** *vt.* provare, tentare || *to* — *for sthg.*, cercare di ottenere qc.; *to* — *on*, provare (*di abiti*); *to* — *out*, sottoporre a dura prova.

trying *agg.* 1. difficile 2. difficilmente sopportabile.

tub *s.* tinozza, vasca.

tube *s.* 1. tubo 2. camera d'aria 3. (*fam.*) ferrovia sotterranea.

tuber *s.* 1. tubero 2. tubercolo.

tubercular *agg.* 1. tubercolare 2. tubercoloso.

tuberculosis *s.* tubercolosi.

tuberculous *agg.* tubercoloso.

tubing *s.* tubatura.

tubular, tubulous *agg.* tubolare.

tuck *s.* piega (*di abito*).

to **tuck** *vt.* 1. (ri)piegare 2. pigiare || *to* — *up*, rimboccare.

Tuesday *s.* martedì.

tuff *s.* tufo vulcanico.

tuft *s*. **1.** ciuffo **2.** fiocco **3.** cespuglio.

tug *s*. strappo || — *-of-war*, tiro alla fune.

to **tug** *vt*. e *vi*. **1.** tirare **2.** dare strattoni.

tugboat *s*. (*mar.*) rimorchiatore.

tuition *s*. istruzione.

tulip *s*. tulipano.

tumble *s*. **1.** caduta **2.** confusione.

to **tumble** *vi*. **1.** cadere **2.** agitarsi **3.** precipitarsi **4.** fare acrobazie. ◆ to **tumble** *vt*. **1.** far cadere **2.** scompigliare.

tumble-down *agg*. in rovina.

tumbler *s*. **1.** acrobata **2.** bicchiere (*senza piede*).

tumefaction *s*. tumefazione.

to **tumefy** *vt*. tumefare. ◆ to **tumefy** *vi*. tumefarsi.

tumescence *s*. tumescenza.

tumescent *agg*. gonfio.

tumid *agg*. tumido.

tumidity *s*. gonfiore.

tumour *s*. tumore.

tumult *s*. tumulto.

tumultuous *agg*. tumultuoso.

tumulus *s*. (*pl.* -li) tumulo.

tun *s*. botte.

tuna *s*. tonno.

tune *s*. **1.** tono **2.** accordo **3.** motivo || *in* —, intonato; *out of* —, stonato.

to **tune** *vt*. (*mus.*) accordare || *to* — *up*, mettere a punto. ◆ to **tune** *vi*. essere in armonia.

tuneful *agg*. armonioso.

tuner *s*. **1.** (*mus.*) accordatore **2.** (*radio*) sintonizzatore.

tungsten *s*. tungsteno.

tunic *s*. tunica.

Tunisian *agg*. e *s*. tunisino.

to **tunnel** *vi*. costruire un tunnel. ◆ to **tunnel** *vt*. perforare.

tunny *s*. tonno.

turban *s*. turbante.

turbid *agg*. torbido.

turbidity *s*. torbidezza.

turbine *s*. turbina.

turbojet *s*. turbogetto || — *engine*, turboreattore.

turbulence *s*. turbolenza.

turbulent *agg*. turbolento.

tureen *s*. zuppiera.

turf *s*. **1.** zolla erbosa **2.** torba **3.** campo da corse || — *-accountant*, allibratore.

turgid *agg*. turgido.

turgidity *s*. turgidezza.

Turk *agg*. e *s*. turco.

turkey *s*. tacchino.

Turkish *agg*. turco.

turmoil *s*. agitazione.

turn *s*. **1.** giro **2.** curva **3.** turno **4.** servizio **5.** attitudine || — *-out*, assemblea, sciopero, produzione; — *-table*, piattaforma girevole, giradischi.

to **turn** *vi*. **1.** girarsi, volgersi **2.** diventare. ◆ to **turn** *vt*. **1.** girare, volgere **2.** mutare **3.** tornire || *to* — *off*, chiudere, spegnere; *to* — *on*, aprire, accendere; *to* — *down*, abbassare; *to* — *out*, scacciare, produrre, spegnere, risultare; *to* — *over*, rovesciare.

turnabout *s*. **1.** giostra **2.** inversione (*di rotta*).

turncoat *s*. voltagabbana.

turner *s*. tornitore.

turning *s*. **1.** giro, svolta **2.** tornitura.

turning-point *s*. svolta decisiva, momento critico.

turnip *s*. rapa.

turnkey *s*. secondino.

turnout *s*. **1.** folla **2.** equipaggio.

turnover *s*. **1.** rovesciamento **2.** (*comm.*) giro **3.** torta.

turnpike *s*. strada a pedaggio.

turnspit *s*. girarrosto.

turpentine *s*. trementina.

turpitude *s*. turpitudine.

turquoise *s*. turchese.

turret *s*. torretta.

turtle *s*. **1.** tartaruga **2.** — (-*dove*), tortora.

Tuscan *agg*. e *s*. toscano.

tusk *s*. zanna.

tussle *s*. zuffa.

to **tussle** *vi*. azzuffarsi.

tutelar(y) *agg*. tutelare.

tutor *s*. istitutore.

to **tutor** *vt*. **1.** istruire **2.** controllare.

tutorial *agg*. di istitutore.

tutorship *s*. mansione di istitutore.

twang *s*. **1.** suono acuto **2.** suono nasale.

to **twang** *vi*. **1.** avere un suono acuto **2.** parlare con voce nasale.

tweet *s*. cinguettio.

to **tweet** *vi*. cinguettare.

tweezers *s*. *pl*. pinzette.

twelfth *agg*. e *s*. dodicesimo.

twelve *agg*. e *s*. dodici.

twentieth *agg*. e *s*. ventesimo.

twenty *agg*. e *s*. venti.

twice *avv.* due volte.
twig *s.* ramoscello.
twilight *s.* **1.** crepuscolo **2.** luce fioca.
twin *agg.* e *s.* gemello.
to **twin** *vt.* accoppiare. ♦ to **twin** *vi.* accoppiarsi.
twine *s.* **1.** spago, corda **2.** groviglio.
twinge *s.* fitta, dolore.
twinkle *s.* **1.** scintillio **2.** ammicco || *in a* —, in un batter d'occhio.
to **twinkle** *vi.* **1.** scintillare **2.** ammiccare.
twinkling *s.* balenio.
twirl *s.* piroetta, rotazione.
to **twirl** *vt.* e *vi.* girare, roteare.
twist *s.* **1.** filo ritorto **2.** torsione **3.** curva.
to **twist** *vt.* **1.** torcere **2.** travisare. ♦ to **twist** *vi.* **1.** torcersi **2.** serpeggiare.
twister *s.* **1.** torcitore **2.** truffatore.
twisty *agg.* **1.** tortuoso **2.** disonesto.
to **twit** *vt.* biasimare.
twitch *s.* **1.** strattone **2.** tic nervoso.
twitter *s.* **1.** pigolio **2.** agitazione.
to **twitter** *vi.* **1.** pigolare **2.** essere ansioso.
two *agg.* e *s.* due.
twofold *agg.* doppio. ♦ **twofold** *avv.* doppiamente.
twopence *s.* due penny (*valore*).
tycoon *s.* (*amer.*) magnate.
type *s.* **1.** tipo **2.** simbolo **3.** (*tip.*) carattere tipografico || — *-setting* (*tip.*), composizione.
to **type** *vt.* **1.** rappresentare **2.** dattilografare.
    written) *vt.* e *vi.* dattilografare.
to **typewrite (typewrote, type-typewriter** *s.* dattilografo.
typewriting *s.* dattilografia.
typewritten V. *to typewrite.*
typewrote V. *to typewrite.*
typhoon *s.* tifone.
typhus *s.* tifo.
typic(al) *agg.* tipico.
to **typify** *vt.* **1.** incarnare **2.** esemplificare.
typist *s.* dattilografo.
typographer *s.* tipografo.
typographic(al) *agg.* tipografico.
typography *s.* tipografia.
tyrannic(al) *agg.* tirannico.
tyrannicide *s.* **1.** tirannicida **2.** tirannicidio.
to **tyrannize** *vt.* e *vi.* tiranneggiare.
tyrannous *agg.* tirannico.

tyranny *s.* tirannia.
tyrant *s.* tiranno.
tyre *s.* V. *tire.*
Tyrrhene, Tyrrhenian *agg.* e *s.* tirreno.
Tzigane *agg.* e *s.* tzigano.

U

ubication *s.* ubicazione.
ugliness *s.* bruttezza.
ugly *agg.* **1.** brutto **2.** vile, turpe.
ulcer *s.* ulcera, piaga (*anche fig.*).
to **ulcerate** *vt.* ulcerare. ♦ to **ulcerate** *vi.* ulcerarsi.
ulceration *s.* ulcerazione.
ulcerous *agg.* ulceroso.
ulna *s.* (*pl.* -ae) (*anat.*) ulna.
ultimate *agg.* ultimo, finale, definitivo.
ultra *agg.* ultra, estremo, eccessivo. ♦ **ultra** *s.* estremista.
ultramarine *agg.* oltremarino.
ultramontane *agg.* e *s.* oltremontano.
ultramundane *agg.* oltremondano.
ultra-red *agg.* infrarosso.
ultrasonic *agg.* ultrasonico.
ultraviolet *agg.* ultravioletto.
umbilical *agg.* ombelicale.
umbrella *s.* ombrello || — *-stand,* portaombrelli.
umpire *s.* (*giur.; sport*) arbitro.
unabashed *agg.* imperturbato.
unabated *agg.* non diminuito, non scemato.
unable *agg.* incapace, inabile.
unabridged *agg.* non abbreviato, completo || — *edition,* edizione integrale.
unacceptable *agg.* inaccettabile.
unaccomplished *agg.* incompleto, incompiuto.
unaccountability *s.* inesplicabilità.
unaccountable *agg.* inesplicabile.
unaccustomed *agg.* non abituale, insolito.
unachievable *agg.* ineseguibile.
unacquainted *agg.* **1.** ignaro di, non al corrente di **2.** sconosciuto, poco familiare.
unacquired *agg.* non acquisito, innato.
unactive *agg.* inattivo.
unadapted *agg.* inadatto.

unadorned *agg.* disadorno.
unadvisable *agg.* non consigliabile, inopportuno.
unaffected *agg.* 1. senza affettazione, semplice 2. insensibile.
unafraid *agg.* impavido.
unalienable *agg.* inalienabile.
unallied *agg.* senza relazione, senza connessione.
unalterable *agg.* inalterabile.
unamendable *agg.* incorreggibile.
to **unanchor** *vi.* toglier l'ancora.
♦ to **unanchor** *vt.* disancorare.
unanimated *agg.* inanimato.
unanimity *s.* unanimità.
unanimous *agg.* unanime.
unannounced *agg.* non annunciato, imprevisto.
unanswerable *agg.* 1. a cui non si può rispondere 2. irrefutabile.
unanswered *agg.* senza risposta.
unappealable *agg.* inappellabile.
unappeasable *agg.* implacabile.
unappeased *agg.* insoddisfatto.
unapplied *agg.* non impiegato, inapplicato.
unappreciated *agg.* non apprezzato, incompreso.
unapprehensive *agg.* 1. lento nell'apprendere 2. non apprensivo.
unapproachable *agg.* inaccessibile.
unapt *agg.* 1. inadatto 2. inetto.
unargued *agg.* indiscusso.
to **unarm** *vt.* disarmare.
unarmed *agg.* disarmato, inerme.
unartful *agg.* privo di artifici, ingenuo.
unascertainable *agg.* non verificabile.
unascertained *agg.* sconosciuto, non accertato.
unasked *agg.* non richiesto.
unaspiring *agg.* senza ambizione.
unassailable *agg.* inattaccabile.
unassailed *agg.* inattaccato.
unasserted *agg.* non asserito.
unassuming *agg.* modesto, senza pretese.
unattackable *agg.* inattaccabile.
unattainable *agg.* inaccessibile.
unattempted *agg.* intentato.
unauthorized *agg.* 1. non autorizzato 2. illecito.
unavailable *agg.* 1. inutile, vano 2. non disponibile.
unavenged *agg.* impunito.
unavoidable *agg.* inevitabile.
unaware *agg.* inconsapevole, inconscio.

unawareness *s.* inconsapevolezza.
unawares *avv.* inconsapevolmente, inconsciamente.
unbalance *s.* squilibrio.
to **unbalance** *vt.* sbilanciare.
to **unbandage** *vt.* sbendare.
unbearable *agg.* insopportabile.
unbeaten *agg.* 1. insuperato, non battuto 2. non frequentato.
unbecoming *agg.* disdicevole.
unbelief *s.* incredulità, scetticismo.
unbelievable *agg.* incredibile.
unbelieving *agg.* incredulo, scettico.
to **unbend** (**unbent, unbent**) *vt.* 1. raddrizzare 2. allentare, slegare.
♦ to **unbend** (**unbent, unbent**) *vi.* raddrizzarsi.
unbias(s)ed *agg.* imparziale, senza preconcetti.
to **unbind** (**unbound, unbound**) *vt.* sciogliere, slegare.
to **unbolt** *vt.* disserrare, aprire.
unborn *agg.* non nato, nascituro, che deve venire.
to **unbosom** *vt.* rivelare, confidare.
♦ to **unbosom** *vi.* sfogarsi: *to — oneself to* so., aprirsi con qu.
unbound V. *to unbind.*
unbreakable *agg.* infrangibile.
unbreathable *agg.* irrespirabile.
to **unbreech** *vt.* togliere i calzoni.
to **unbridle** *vt.* sbrigliare, dare libero corso a (*anche fig.*).
unbridled *agg.* incontrollato, senza briglia.
unbroken *agg.* 1. intatto, intero, inviolato 2. incessante.
unbruised *agg.* non ammaccato, illeso.
to **unbuckle** *vt.* sfibbiare, slacciare.
to **unburden** *vt.* 1. scaricare, alleggerire 2. (*fig.*) alleviare.
unburied *agg.* insepolto.
to **unbury** *vt.* disseppellire.
to **unbutton** *vt.* sbottonare. ♦ to **unbutton** *vi.* sbottonarsi.
uncalled *agg.* non chiamato, non invitato: — *for,* superfluo, gratuito.
uncanny *agg.* misterioso, irreale.
uncared-for *agg.* negletto, abbandonato.
unceasing *agg.* incessante.
uncensurable *agg.* incensurabile.
uncertain *agg.* 1. incerto, malsicuro 2. irresoluto.
uncertainty *s.* 1. incertezza 2. irresolutezza.
to **unchain** *vt.* sciogliere da catene.

unchanged agg. immutato.
uncharged agg. 1. non carico 2. non incriminato.
uncharitable agg. poco caritatevole.
to **uncharm** vt. liberare da un incantesimo.
unchaste agg. impuro.
unchecked agg. sfrenato.
uncivil agg. 1. scortese, maleducato 2. indecoroso.
uncivilized agg. non civilizzato.
to **unclasp** vt. slacciare. ♦ to **unclasp** vi. allentare la stretta.
uncle s. zio.
uncombed agg. spettinato.
uncomely agg. 1. sgraziato 2. sconveniente.
uncomfortable agg. 1. scomodo, a disagio 2. spiacevole.
uncommon agg. insolito, raro.
uncompared agg. incomparato.
uncompelled agg. non costretto, spontaneo.
unconcerned agg. indifferente, noncurante.
unconcerning agg. irrilevante, che non interessa.
unconditional agg. incondizionato.
uncongenial agg. 1. antipatico, spiacevole 2. non congeniale.
unconquerable agg. invincibile, indomabile.
unconquered agg. invitto, indomito.
unconscionable agg. 1. irragionevole 2. senza scrupoli.
unconscious agg. 1. inconscio, ignaro 2. privo di sensi. ♦ **unconscious** s. inconscio.
unconsciousness s. 1. inconsapevolezza 2. stato di incoscienza.
unconsolable agg. inconsolabile.
unconstitutional agg. incostituzionale.
unconstrained agg. 1. non costretto, libero 2. disinvolto.
unconstraint s. 1. assenza di costrizione, libertà 2. spontaneità.
uncontrollable agg. incontrollabile.
uncontrolled agg. senza controllo, sfrenato.
unconventional agg. non convenzionale, disinvolto.
unconvertible agg. inconvertibile.
unconvincing agg. non convincente.
to **uncork** vt. sturare, stappare.

uncountable agg. innumerevole.
to **uncouple** vt. 1. sguinzagliare 2. staccare.
uncouth agg. 1. ordinario, rozzo 2. desolato.
to **uncover** vt. 1. scoprire 2. spogliare. ♦ to **uncover** vi. togliersi il cappello.
uncovered agg. 1. scoperto, senza tetto 2. spogliato 3. senza cappello.
unction s. 1. unzione 2. unguento.
unctuous agg. grasso, untuoso (anche fig.).
uncultivable agg. non coltivabile.
uncultivated agg. incolto, non coltivato.
uncut agg. intonso, non tagliato.
undaunted agg. intrepido, impavido.
to **undeceive** vt. disingannare.
undecided agg. 1. indeciso, non risolto 2. indefinito 3. irresoluto.
undeclinable agg. indeclinabile.
undecomposable agg. indecomponibile.
undefended agg. 1. indifeso 2. (giur.) non assistito da difesa legale.
undeniable agg. innegabile.
under prep. 1. sotto, al di sotto di 2. in corso di 3. meno di. ♦ **under** avv. sotto, al di sotto ‖ —-age, minorenne.
underbrush s. sottobosco.
to **undercharge** vt. far pagare troppo poco.
underclothes s. pl. biancheria intima (sing.).
undercover agg. segreto.
undercurrent s. 1. corrente sottomarina 2. (fig.) attività, tendenza nascosta.
to **underdo** (**underdid, underdone**) vt. e vi. 1. agire in modo insufficiente 2. cuocere poco.
underdone V. to underdo. ♦ **underdone** agg. poco cotto.
to **underestimate** vt. sottovalutare.
underfed agg. denutrito.
to **underfeed** (**underfed, underfed**) vt. nutrire insufficientemente.
to **undergo** (**underwent, undergone**) vt. 1. subire, essere sottoposto a 2. sopportare.
undergraduate s. studente universitario.
underground agg. sotterraneo. ♦ **underground** s. 1. sottosuolo 2. metropolitana.

underground avv. **1.** sottoterra **2.** (pol.) clandestinamente.

underhand agg. **1.** clandestino, segreto **2.** furbo, astuto. ◆ **underhand** avv. segretamente, clandestinamente.

to **underline** vt. sottolineare.

underlining s. sottolineatura.

undermentioned agg. sottoindicato.

to **undermine** vt. **1.** minare, scalzare **2.** (fig.) indebolire, insidiare.

underneath avv. di sotto, al di sotto.

to **underpay** (**underpaid, underpaid**) vt. pagare inadeguatamente.

to **underrate** vt. sottovalutare.

underscriber s. sottoscrittore.

undersea agg. sottomarino.

to **undersell** (**undersold, undersold**) vt. svendere.

undershrub s. sottobosco.

undersignature s. firma in calce.

undersold V. to undersell.

to **understand** (**understood, understood**) vt. e vi. **1.** capire, comprendere **2.** dedurre, supporre **3.** sentir dire.

understandable agg. comprensibile.

understanding s. **1.** comprensione **2.** patto, intesa || on this —, a queste condizioni.

to **understate** vt. minimizzare.

understatement s. attenuazione del vero.

understood V. to understand.

to **undertake** (**undertook, undertaken**) vt. e vi. **1.** intraprendere **2.** incaricarsi di **3.** prendere in appalto.

undertaker s. **1.** impresario **2.** imprenditore di pompe funebri.

undertaking s. **1.** l'intraprendere **2.** (comm.) impresa **3.** (giur.) promessa, obbligazione.

undertook V. to undertake.

undervaluation s. **1.** scarsa stima **2.** svalutazione.

to **undervalue** vt. sottovalutare.

underwater agg. subacqueo || fishing —, pesca subacquea.

underwent V. to undergo.

underworld s. **1.** bassifondi (pl.) **2.** oltretomba.

to **underwrite** (**underwrote, underwritten**) vt. e vi. **1.** sottoscrivere, firmare **2.** (comm.) assicurare.

undeserved agg. immeritato.

undeserving agg. immeritevole.

undesirable agg. indesiderabile.

undestroyable agg. indistruttibile.

undetected agg. non scoperto.

undetermined agg. **1.** indeterminato **2.** indeciso.

undid V. to undo.

undies s. pl. biancheria intima (sing.).

undine s. ondina.

undisciplined agg. indisciplinato.

undiscriminating agg. che non distingue, che non fa distinzioni.

undiscussed agg. indiscusso.

indisputed agg. incontestato.

undissembled agg. non dissimulato.

undistinguished agg. indistinto.

undisturbed agg. indisturbato.

undividable agg. indivisibile.

to **undo** (**undid, undone**) vt. **1.** disfare, sciogliere **2.** annullare, rovinare.

undoing s. **1.** disfacimento **2.** rovina.

undone[1] V. to undo. ◆ **undone** agg. disfatto, rovinato.

undone[2] agg. incompiuto.

undoubtable agg. indubitabile.

undoubted agg. indubbio.

undreamed agg. non sognato, impensato.

to **undress** vt. svestire. ◆ to **undress** vi. svestirsi.

undue agg. **1.** non dovuto, indebito **2.** inadatto.

to **undulate** vi. **1.** ondeggiare **2.** essere ondulato.

undulation s. ondulazione.

undulatory agg. ondulatorio.

unduly avv. indebitamente.

to **unearth** vt. **1.** dissotterrare, portare alla luce **2.** far uscire dalla tana (un animale).

unearthly agg. ultraterreno || — hour, ora impossibile.

uneasily avv. **1.** a disagio, con difficoltà **2.** con ansia.

uneasiness s. **1.** disagio, pena **2.** ansia.

uneasy agg. **1.** a disagio **2.** ansioso, inquieto.

uneatable agg. immangiabile.

uneducated agg. rozzo, ignorante.

uneffected agg. non effettuato.

unembarrassed agg. a proprio agio, disinvolto.

unemployed agg. **1.** disoccupato **2.** non usato.

unemployment s. disoccupazione

|| — *benefit,* sussidio di disoccupazione.

unending *agg.* eterno, senza fine.

unequal *agg.* **1.** ineguale **2.** inadeguato, incapace.

unequalled *agg.* ineguagliato.

unerring *agg.* infallibile, sicuro.

uneven *agg.* **1.** ineguale, irregolare **2.** ruvido, non livellato.

unevenness *s.* **1.** disuguaglianza, irregolarità **2.** dislivello.

uneventful *agg.* pacifico, senza avvenimenti importanti.

unexceptionable *agg.* ineccepibile.

unexhausted *agg.* inesausto.

unexpected *agg.* inatteso.

unexpensive *agg.* poco costoso.

unexplored *agg.* inesplorato.

unextinguishable *agg.* inestinguibile.

unfadable *agg.* **1.** che non può appassire **2.** solido (*di colore*).

unfading *agg.* **1.** che non appassisce **2.** che non sbiadisce.

unfailing *agg.* **1.** infallibile, sicuro **2.** immancabile.

unfair *agg.* sleale: — *competition,* concorrenza sleale.

unfairness *s.* slealtà, ingiustizia.

unfaithful *agg.* **1.** infedele, sleale **2.** inesatto.

unfaithfulness *s.* **1.** infedeltà **2.** inesattezza.

unfaltering *agg.* fermo, non esitante.

unfamiliar *agg.* poco familiare.

unfashionable *agg.* fuori moda.

to **unfasten** *vt.* slacciare, slegare. ♦ to **unfasten** *vi.* slacciarsi, slegarsi.

unfathomable *agg.* insondabile.

unfavourable *agg.* sfavorevole.

unfeeling *agg.* insensibile, spietato.

unfinished *agg.* **1.** incompleto **2.** non rifinito.

unfit *agg.* **1.** inadatto, disadatto **2.** inabile.

unfitness *s.* **1.** inidoneità **2.** debole costituzione.

to **unfold** *vt.* **1.** aprire, schiudere **2.** svelare. ♦ to **unfold** *vi.* **1.** aprirsi, schiudersi **2.** svelarsi.

unforbearing *agg.* insofferente, impaziente.

unforeseeing *agg.* imprevidente.

unforeseen *agg.* imprevisto.

unforgettable *agg.* indimenticabile.

unforgiving *agg.* senza misericordia.

unforgotten *agg.* inobliato.

unfortunate *agg.* sfortunato.

unfortunately *avv.* sfortunatamente.

unfounded *agg.* infondato.

to **unfreeze (unfroze, unfrozen)** *vt.* disgelare, scongelare. ♦ to **unfreeze (unfroze, unfrozen)** *vi.* disgelarsi.

unfrequent *agg.* infrequente.

unfriendly *agg.* poco amichevole.

to **unfrock** *vt.* spretare.

unfroze V. to *unfreeze.*

unfrozen V. to *unfreeze.*

unfruitful *agg.* infruttuoso.

unfruitfulness *s.* infruttuosità.

to **unfurl** *vt.* e *vi.* spiegare, spiegarsi (*di bandiere ecc.*).

unfurnished *agg.* **1.** non ammobiliato **2.** sfornito.

ungainly *agg.* goffo, maldestro.

ungentlemanlike *agg.* indegno di un gentiluomo.

ungirt *agg.* senza cintura.

to **unglue** *vt.* scollare. ♦ to **unglue** *vi.* scollarsi.

ungodly *agg.* **1.** empio **2.** malvagio.

ungraceful *agg.* sgraziato.

ungrammatical *agg.* sgrammaticato.

ungrateful *agg.* ingrato.

ungrounded *agg.* **1.** infondato **2.** senza preparazione.

unguarded *agg.* sguarnito, senza difesa.

unguent *s.* unguento.

unhandy *agg.* **1.** maldestro **2.** poco maneggevole.

unhappiness *s.* infelicità.

unhappy *agg.* infelice, triste.

unharmed *agg.* intatto, illeso.

unharmful *agg.* innocuo.

unhealthily *avv.* in modo malsano, poco igienicamente.

unhealthy *agg.* **1.** malsano, insalubre **2.** (*fig.*) dannoso **3.** malaticcio.

unheard *agg.* **1.** non udito **2.** non ascoltato **3.** sconosciuto, strano || — *-of,* inaudito.

to **unhinge** *vt.* scardinare.

unholy *agg.* profano, empio.

to **unhook** *vt.* sganciare. ♦ to **unhook** *vi.* sganciarsi.

unhoped *agg.* insperato, inatteso.

to **unhorse** *vt.* **1.** disarcionare **2.** staccare i cavalli da.

unhuman *agg.* sovrumano.

unhurt *agg.* illeso, incolume.

unhurtful *agg.* innocuo.

unicellular agg. unicellulare.
unification s. unificazione.
uniform agg. uniforme, costante. ♦
  uniform s. uniforme, divisa.
to **uniform** vt. uniformare.
uniformity s. uniformità.
to **unify** vt. unificare.
unilateral agg. unilaterale.
unilaterally avv. unilateralmente.
unimaginable agg. inimmaginabile.
unimpaired agg. inalterato, intatto.
unimpassioned agg. spassionato,
  calmo.
unimpeachable agg. incensurabile.
unimportance s. scarsa importanza.
unimportant agg. privo d'importanza.
unimposing agg. poco imponente,
  che non fa soggezione.
uninhabitable agg. inabitabile.
uninhabited agg. disabitato.
uninominal agg. uninominale.
unintelligent agg. stupido.
unintelligible agg. inintelligibile.
unintended agg. 1. involontario 2.
  (giur.) non intenzionale.
uninteresting agg. non interessante.
uninviting agg. poco attraente.
union s. unione, associazione, lega
  || (trade) —, sindacato; the Union
  Jack, la bandiera del Regno Unito.
unionism s. tendenza ad unirsi.
unionist s. unionista.
uniparous agg. uniparo.
unique agg. 1. unico, solo 2. eccezionale.
uniqueness s. unicità.
unisexual agg. unisessuale.
unison s. 1. (mus.) unisono 2. (fig.)
  concordia.
unit s. 1. unità, unità di misura 2.
  complesso, insieme.
unitary agg. unitario.
to **unite** vt. unire. ♦ to **unite** vi.
  1. unirsi 2. mettersi d'accordo.
united agg. unito, collegato.
unity s. 1. unità 2. armonia.
universal agg. universale.
universality s. universalità.
to **universalize** vt. universalizzare.
universe s. universo.
university s. università.
univocal agg. univoco, non ambiguo.
to **unjoint** vt. disgiungere.
unjust agg. ingiusto.
unjustifiable agg. ingiustificabile.
unjustified agg. ingiustificato.
unkempt agg. trascurato, sciatto.

unkind agg. 1. sgarbato, scortese 2.
  crudele.
unkindness s. scortesia.
unknown agg. sconosciuto, ignoto.
unlawful agg. illegale.
to **unlearn (unlearnt, unlearnt)**
  (anche reg.) vt. disimparare.
unleavened agg. non lievitato || —
  bread, pane azzimo.
unless cong. a meno che, salvo che.
unlike agg. dissimile, diverso. ♦
  unlike avv. diversamente. ♦ un-
  like prep. diversamente da.
unlikelihood s. inverosimiglianza,
  improbabilità.
unlikely agg. inverosimile, improbabile.
unlimited agg. illimitato, sconfinato.
to **unline** vt. sfoderare.
unlined[1] agg. senza fodera.
unlined[2] agg. senza rughe.
unliterary agg. non letterario.
to **unload** vt. 1. scaricare 2. (fig.)
  alleggerire.
to **unlock** vt. aprire (con chiave).
unlooked-for agg. imprevisto.
to **unloose** vt. slegare.
unlosable agg. che non può essere
  perso.
unlovable agg. poco amabile, antipatico.
unlucky agg. 1. sfortunato 2. di
  cattivo augurio.
to **unman** vt. 1. evirare 2. abbrutire 3. togliere forza.
unmarred agg. non sciupato.
unmarried agg. non coniugato.
to **unmask** vt. togliere la maschera
  (anche fig.). ♦ to **unmask** vi. togliersi la maschera.
unmatched agg. senza rivali.
unmentionable agg. innominabile,
  irripetibile.
unmerciful agg. spietato.
unmethodical agg. non metodico.
unminded agg. negletto.
unmindful agg. 1. immemore 2. incurante.
unmistakable agg. indubbio, ine-
  quivocabile.
to **unmoor** vt. e vi. togliere gli ormeggi a.
to **unnail** vt. schiodare.
unnatural agg. innaturale, contro
  natura.
unnavigable agg. non navigabile.
unnecessary agg. non necessario.
unneeded agg. inutile, non neces-

sario.

to **unnerve** vt. snervare.

unnoticed agg. inosservato.

unobjectionable agg. ineccepibile.

unobliging agg. poco compiacente.

unobservant agg. 1. inosservante 2. distratto.

unobserved agg. inosservato.

unobtrusive agg. discreto, modesto.

unoffending agg. inoffensivo.

unofficial agg. ufficioso.

to **unpack** vt. e vi. 1. disfare (le valigie) 2. disimballare.

unpalatable agg. di gusto sgradevole.

unpardonable agg. imperdonabile.

unpaved agg. non lastricato.

unperceivable agg. impercettibile.

unperceived agg. inavvertito.

unperishable agg. duraturo, imperituro.

unpleasant agg. spiacevole, sgradevole.

unpliable agg. poco piacevole.

unpoetic(al) agg. poco poetico.

to **unpoison** vt. svelenire.

unpolluted agg. incontaminato.

unpopular agg. impopolare.

unpopularity s. impopolarità.

unprecise agg. impreciso.

unpredictable agg. imprevedibile.

unpredicted agg. imprevisto.

unpremeditated agg. non premeditato.

unprepared agg. impreparato.

unpreparedness s. impreparazione.

unprepossessed agg. senza prevenzioni.

unprepossessing agg. senza attrattive, antipatico.

unpresentable agg. impresentabile.

unpriestly agg. che non si addice a un prete.

unprincely agg. che non si addice a un principe.

unprintable agg. non adatto ad essere pubblicato.

unproductive agg. improduttivo.

unprofitable agg. poco vantaggioso.

unprofitableness s. infruttuosità.

unpronounceable agg. impronunciabile.

unprovable agg. indimostrabile.

unpublished agg. inedito.

unqualified agg. 1. incompetente 2. non abilitato 3. (giur.) senza restrizioni.

to **unqualify** vt. 1. inabilitare 2. squalificare.

unquenchable agg. inestinguibile, insaziabile (anche fig.).

unquestionable agg. incontestabile, indiscutibile.

unquestioned agg. indiscusso.

unquiet agg. inquieto.

unquoted agg. 1. non citato 2. (comm.) non quotato (di titoli).

to **unravel** vt. districare. ♦ to **unravel** vi. districarsi.

unreachable agg. irraggiungibile.

unready agg. 1. impreparato 2. tardo, lento.

unreal agg. irreale.

unreality s. irrealtà.

unrealizable agg. irrealizzabile.

unreasonable agg. irragionevole.

unrecognizable agg. irriconoscibile.

unredeemed agg. 1. irredento 2. non controbilanciato 3. (comm.) non estinto.

unrelated agg. senza rapporti, senza legami.

unreliable agg. 1. non fidato 2. inattendibile.

unrepealed agg. (giur.) non abrogato.

unrequired agg. non richiesto.

unrest s. inquietudine.

unrestrained agg. non represso.

unrestricted agg. senza limitazioni.

unrevenged agg. invendicato.

unripe agg. immaturo, acerbo (anche fig.).

unrivalled agg. impareggiabile.

to **unroll** vt. svolgere. ♦ to **unroll** vi. svolgersi.

unruly agg. sregolato, indisciplinato.

to **unsaddle** vt. dissellare, disarcionare.

unsafe agg. malsicuro.

unsatisfied agg. 1. insoddisfatto 2. non convinto.

unsavoury agg. insipido, scipito.

unscholarly agg. 1. indegno di un letterato 2. non erudito.

to **unscrew** vt. svitare.

unscriptural agg. non conforme alle Sacre Scritture.

to **unseal** vt. dissigillare.

unseasonable agg. 1. fuori stagione 2. (fig.) intempestivo.

unseemliness s. indecenza.

unseemly agg. sconveniente, indecente.

unseizable agg. inafferrabile.

unselfish agg. disinteressato.

unselfishness s. disinteresse.

unsettled *agg.* **1.** disordinato **2.** sconvolto, turbato **3.** mutevole, indeciso.

to **unsew** (**unsewed, unsewn**) *vt.* scucire.

unshaken *agg.* non scosso, fermo.

to **unsheathe** *vt.* sguainare.

to **unshoe** (**unshod, unshod**) *vt.* **1.** togliere le scarpe **2.** togliere i ferri a (*un cavallo*).

unshrinkable *agg.* irrestringibile.

unskilfulness *s.* incapacità, imperizia.

unskilled *agg.* inesperto, inabile.

unsocial *agg.* asociale.

unsold *agg.* invenduto.

to **unsolder** *vt.* dissaldare.

unsolved *agg.* insoluto.

unsound *agg.* **1.** malsano, malato **2.** guasto, avariato.

unspeakable *agg.* **1.** inesprimibile **2.** inqualificabile.

unstable *agg.* **1.** instabile **2.** (*fig.*) mutevole.

unsteadiness *agg.* incostanza, volubilità.

unsteady *agg.* instabile, incostante.

unsubstantial *agg.* **1.** inconsistente **2.** illusorio.

unsuccessful *agg.* mal riuscito, sfortunato.

unsuitable *agg.* inadatto, non appropriato.

unsure *agg.* **1.** malsicuro, precario **2.** incerto.

unsurpassed *agg.* insorpassato.

unsuspected *agg.* insospettato, non sospetto.

unsustainable *agg.* insostenibile.

untamable *agg.* indomabile.

untame *agg.* selvaggio, non addomesticato.

untaught *agg.* poco istruito, ignorante.

unteachable *agg.* **1.** difficile da insegnare **2.** non educabile.

unthinkable *agg.* inimmaginabile.

to **unthread** *vt.* sfilare, togliere il filo a.

untidily *avv.* disordinatamente.

untidy *agg.* disordinato, trasandato.

to **untie** *vt.* slegare. ♦ to **untie** *vi.* slegarsi.

until *prep.* fino a. ♦ **until** *cong.* finché.

untimeliness *s.* intempestività, inopportunità.

untimely *agg.* **1.** prematuro **2.** inopportuno. ♦ **untimely** *avv.* **1.** pre-

maturamente **2.** inopportunamente.

untiring *agg.* instancabile.

untitled *agg.* senza titolo.

to **untomb** *vt.* dissotterrare.

untouchable *agg.* **1.** intoccabile **2.** (*fig.*) irraggiungibile.

untouched *agg.* **1.** non toccato, intatto **2.** illeso, indenne.

untoward *agg.* **1.** restio, caparbio **2.** infausto.

untranslatable *agg.* intraducibile.

untravelled *agg.* che non ha viaggiato.

untrodden *agg.* non calpestato, non battuto.

untrue *agg.* **1.** falso, menzognero **2.** infedele.

untrustworthy *agg.* indegno di fiducia.

to **untune** *vt.* scordare (*uno strumento musicale*).

unusable *agg.* inutilizzabile.

unusual *agg.* insolito, inusitato.

unutterable *agg.* indescrivibile, impronunciabile.

unvarying *agg.* invariabile.

to **unveil** *vt.* **1.** togliere il velo a **2.** (*fig.*) rivelare.

unwary *agg.* incauto, sconsiderato.

unwatchful *agg.* non vigilante, disattento.

unweaned *agg.* non svezzato.

unweary *agg.* non stanco, indefesso.

unwell *agg.* indisposto, ammalato.

unwieldy *agg.* **1.** ingombrante **2.** impacciato.

unwilling *agg.* **1.** riluttante **2.** involontario.

unwillingly *avv.* malvolentieri.

unwillingness *s.* **1.** riluttanza **2.** malavoglia.

to **unwind** (**unwound, unwound**) *vt.* srotolare. ♦ to **unwind** (**unwound, unwound**) *vi.* srotolarsi.

unwise *agg.* malaccorto.

unwitting *agg.* inconsapevole.

unworldly *agg.* spirituale, non mondano.

unworthy *agg.* indegno, spregevole.

unwound *V.* to *unwind*.

to **unwrap** *vt.* disfare, svolgere.

unwritten *agg.* non scritto ‖ — *law*, legge tramandata oralmente.

unwrought *agg.* **1.** non lavorato **2.** grezzo.

up[1] *avv.* **1.** su, in su, in alto **2.** in piedi ‖ — *to*, fino a; *hurry —*, spicciati; *the game is* —, tutto è perduto. ♦ **up** *prep.* su, su per, in cima a || — *now*, fino ad ora.

up[2] *agg.* ascendente, che va verso l'alto || — *-train*, treno per Londra.

up-and-down *agg.* **1.** che va in su e in giù **2.** oscillante.

to **upbraid** *vt.* rimproverare.

upheaval *s.* **1.** sollevamento **2.** agitazione.

uphill *agg.* **1.** in salita **2.** (*fig.*) difficile. ♦ **uphill** *avv.* in salita. ♦ **uphill** *s.* salita.

to **uphold (upheld, upheld)** *vt.* **1.** sostenere, sorreggere **2.** (*fig.*) appoggiare, patrocinare.

to **upholster** *vt.* tappezzare, imbottire.

upholsterer *s.* tappezziere.

upholstery *s.* tappezzeria, imbottitura.

upkeep *s.* mantenimento, manutenzione.

upland *agg.* montuoso. ♦ **upland** *s.* zona montuosa.

upon *prep.* V. *on*.

upper *agg.* **1.** superiore, più alto **2.** più lontano (*dall'ingresso ecc.*) || *the Upper House*, la Camera dei Lords.

uppercut *s.* (*sport*) "uppercut", colpo dal basso in alto.

upright *agg.* **1.** ritto, diritto, eretto **2.** retto, integro. ♦ **upright** *avv.* in piedi, perpendicolarmente.

uprightness *s.* **1.** perpendicolarità **2.** rettitudine.

uproar *s.* tumulto, chiasso.

uproarious *agg.* tumultuoso, chiassoso.

to **uproot** *vt.* sradicare, svellere.

ups and downs *s. pl.* **1.** ondulazioni (*del terreno*) **2.** (*fig.*) vicissitudini, alti e bassi.

to **upset (upset, upset)** *vt.* **1.** rovesciare **2.** disturbare, sconvolgere. ♦ to **upset (upset, upset)** *vi.* rovesciarsi, capovolgersi.

upset *agg.* **1.** rovesciato, capovolto **2.** (*fig.*) sconvolto, turbato. ♦ **upset** *s.* **1.** rovesciamento **2.** disordine.

upshot *s.* esito, risultato.

upside-down *avv.* capovolto, sottosopra.

upstairs *agg. e avv.* al piano superiore, di sopra.

upstanding *agg.* **1.** eretto, diritto **2.** (*fig.*) franco, leale.

up-to-date *agg.* aggiornato, all'ultima moda.

upward(s) *agg.* ascendente, rivolto verso l'alto. ♦ **upward** *avv.* **1.** in su, in alto **2.** al di sopra.

uranium *s.* uranio.

urban *agg.* urbano, di città.

urbane *agg.* urbano, cortese.

urbanity *s.* urbanità, cortesia.

urbanization *s.* urbanizzazione.

to **urbanize** *vt.* urbanizzare.

urchin *s.* monello.

uretic *agg. e s.* diuretico.

urge *s.* **1.** impulso, stimolo **2.** spinta, sprone.

to **urge** *vt. e vi.* **1.** spingere, stimolare **2.** consigliare, raccomandare.

urgency *s.* **1.** urgenza, premura **2.** bisogno urgente, necessità.

urgent *agg.* urgente, pressante.

uric *agg.* urico.

to **urinate** *vi.* orinare.

urine *s.* orina.

urn *s.* **1.** urna **2.** bricco.

us *pron. pers. compl. pl.* ci, noi: *three of* —, tre di noi.

usable *agg.* usabile, servibile.

usage *s.* **1.** uso, trattamento, impiego **2.** usanza.

use *s.* **1.** uso, impiego **2.** utilità, vantaggio **3.** (*giur.*) usufrutto.

to **use** *vt.* **1.** usare, adoperare **2.** trattare || *to* — *up*, consumare.

used *agg.* **1.** usato, adoperato **2.** abituato || — *-up*, esaurito.

useful *agg.* utile, pratico.

usefulness *s.* utilità, vantaggio.

useless *agg.* inutile, vano.

uselessness *s.* inutilità.

user *s.* **1.** utente **2.** (*giur.*) usufruttuario.

usher *s.* usciere.

to **usher** *vt.* precedere (*in qualità di usciere*).

usual *agg.* usuale, abituale || *as* —, come al solito.

usually *avv.* di solito, abitualmente.

usufruct *s.* (*giur.*) usufrutto.

usufructuary *agg. e s.* usufruttuario.

usurer *s.* usuraio.

to **usurp** *vt.* usurpare.

usurpation *s.* usurpazione.

usurper *s.* usurpatore.

usury *s.* usura (*anche fig.*).

utensil *s.* utensile, arnese.

uterine *agg.* uterino.

uterus *s.* (*pl.* -ri) utero.

utilitarian *s.* utilitarista.

utilitarianism *s.* utilitarismo.
utility *s.* utilità, vantaggio.
utilizable *agg.* utilizzabile.
utilization *s.* utilizzazione.
to **utilize** *vt.* utilizzare.
utmost *agg.* e *s.* **1.** estremo, ultimo **2.** massimo, sommo ‖ *to do one's* —, fare del proprio meglio.
Utopian *s.* utopista.
utter *agg.* complèto, totale.
to **utter** *vt.* **1.** emettere **2.** esprimere, pronunciare.
utterable *agg.* esprimibile.
utterance *s.* espressione, sfogo.
uttering *s.* **1.** messa in circolazione **2.** spaccio (*di assegni ecc.*).
utterly *avv.* completamente, totalmente.
uttermost *agg.* e *s.* V. *utmost.*
uxoricide *s.* **1.** uxoricida **2.** uxoricidio.

V

vacancy *s.* **1.** vuoto, lacuna **2.** posto vacante ‖ *no* —, completo (*di alberghi ecc.*).
vacant *agg.* **1.** vuoto, vacante **2.** non occupato.
to **vacate** *vt.* lasciar vacante, sgomberare ‖ *to* — *a seat*, dare le dimissioni.
vacation *s.* **1.** il ritirarsi, il lasciar libero **2.** vacanze: *long* —, vacanze estive (*pl.*).
to **vaccinate** *vt.* e *vi.* vaccinare.
vaccination *s.* vaccinazione.
vaccine *s.* vaccino.
to **vacillate** *vi.* **1.** vacillare **2.** (*fig.*) esitare.
vacillating *agg.* **1.** vacillante **2.** incostante, irresoluto.
vacillation *s.* **1.** vacillamento **2.** esitazione.
vacillatory *agg.* V. *vacillating.*
vacuity *s.* vacuità (*anche fig.*).
vacuous *agg.* **1.** vacuo, vuoto **2.** sciocco, ozioso.
vacuum *s.* vuoto pneumatico ‖ — *cleaner*, aspirapolvere.
vagabond *s.* viandante, vagabondo.
vagary *s.* fantasticheria, capriccio.
vagrancy *s.* vagabondaggio, accattonaggio.
vagrant *agg.* e *s.* vagabondo.

vague *agg.* vago, impreciso.
vaguely *avv.* vagamente.
vagueness *s.* indeterminatezza.
vain *agg.* **1.** vano, inutile **2.** vanitoso.
vainglorious *agg.* vanaglorioso.
vainglory *s.* vanagloria.
vainly *avv.* **1.** inutilmente **2.** vanitosamente.
valance *s.* **1.** drappeggio **2.** cortina (*di un letto*).
valediction *s.* addio, commiato.
valedictory *agg.* d'addio, di saluto.
 ◆ **valedictory** *s.* discorso d'addio.
valence *s.* (*chim.*) valenza.
valerian *s.* valeriana.
valet *s.* valletto.
valiant *agg.* valoroso, prode.
valid *agg.* valido, legittimo.
to **validate** *vt.* render valido, convalidare.
validity *s.* validità.
validly *avv.* validamente.
valley *s.* valle, vallata.
valorization *s.* valorizzazione.
to **valorize** *vt.* valorizzare.
valour *s.* valore.
valuable *agg.* **1.** di valore, prezioso **2.** valutabile.
valuation *s.* **1.** valutazione, stima **2.** considerazione.
value *s.* **1.** valore, prezzo **2.** (*fig.*) pregio, importanza ‖ — *in exchange*, valore effettivo.
to **value** *vt.* **1.** valutare, stimare **2.** considerare, dar valore.
valueless *agg.* di nessun valore.
valuer *s.* estimatore.
valve *s.* **1.** valvola **2.** valva.
vamp[1] *s.* **1.** rappezzamento **2.** (*mus.*) accompagnamento.
vamp[2] *s.* (*gergo*) donna fatale.
vampire *s.* vampiro.
van *s.* **1.** furgone **2.** vagone ferroviario ‖ *luggage* —, bagagliaio; *prison* —, cellulare.
Vandal *agg.* e *s.* vandalo.
Vandalic *agg.* vandalico.
vandalism *s.* vandalismo.
vane *s.* **1.** banderuola **2.** pala (*di mulino a vento ecc.*).
vanguard *s.* avanguardia (*anche fig.*).
vanilla *s.* vaniglia.
to **vanish** *vi.* svanire, sparire.
vanishing *s.* il dileguarsi, lo sparire.
vanity *s.* vanità ‖ — *-case*, borsetta col necessario per il trucco.

to **vanquish** *vt.* vincere, conquistare. ,

vanquisher *s.* conquistatore

vantage *s.* vantaggio.

vapid *agg.* insulso.

vaporization *s.* evaporazione.

to **vaporize** *vt.* far evaporare. ♦ to **vaporize** *vi.* **1.** evaporare **2.** (*fig.*) volatilizzarsi.

vaporizer *s.* vaporizzatore.

vaporous *agg.* vaporoso.

vapour *s.* vapore, esalazione.

to **vapour** *vi.* **1.** evaporare **2.** (*fig.*) vantarsi.

vapouring *agg.* che evapora. ♦ **vapouring** *s.* vanteria.

vapourish *agg.* **1.** pieno di vapori **2.** depresso.

vapours *s. pl.* depressione (*sing.*), allucinazioni.

variability *s.* variabilità, mutevolezza.

variable *agg.* variabile, incostante.

variance *s.* **1.** variazione **2.** disaccordo.

variant *agg.* differente, contrastante. ♦ **variant** *s.* variante.

variation *s.* variazione, modificazione. ♦ **variations** *s. pl.* (*mat.*) variazioni.

varicoloured *agg.* variopinto.

varicose *agg.* varicoso.

varied *agg.* **1.** vario, variato **2.** variopinto.

to **variegate** *vt.* variegare, screziare.

variegated *agg.* variegato, screziato.

variegation *s.* screziatura.

variety *s.* varietà, diversità || — show (*teat.*), spettacolo di varietà.

various *agg.* alcuni, molti (*pl.*).

variously *avv.* variamente.

varnish *s.* **1.** vernice, lacca **2.** (*fig.*) apparenza, aspetto esteriore || nail —, smalto per unghie.

to **varnish** *vt.* **1.** verniciare, laccare **2.** (*fig.*) mascherare.

varnishing *s.* verniciatura, laccatura.

to **vary** *vt.* variare, cambiare. ♦ to **vary** *vi.* essere differente.

vase *s.* vaso.

vaseline *s.* vaselina.

vassal *s.* vassallo.

vassallage *s.* vassallaggio.

vast *agg.* ampio, immenso, vasto.

vastness *s.* vastità.

vat *s.* tino, tinozza.

vault[1] *s.* **1.** volta, soffitto a volta **2.** cantina **3.** sepolcro **4.** (*fig.*) volta celeste.

vault[2] *s.* volteggio.

to **vault** *vi.* volteggiare. ♦ to **vault** *vt.* saltare.

vaulting *s.* **1.** il costruire volte **2.** costruzione a volta.

to **vaunt** *vt.* vantare. ♦ to **vaunt** *vi.* vantarsi.

veal *s.* (*cuc.*) vitello.

vector *s.* vettore.

vectorial *agg.* vettoriale.

veer *s.* **1.** cambiamento di direzione **2.** (*mar.*) virata.

to **veer** *vi.* **1.** cambiare direzione **2.** (*mar.*) virare.

vegetable *agg.* vegetale. ♦ **vegetable** *s.* **1.** vegetale **2.** ortaggio. ♦ **vegetables** *s. pl.* verdura (*sing.*).

vegetal *agg.* vegetale.

vegetarian *agg.* e *s.* vegetariano.

to **vegetate** *vi.* vegetare (*anche fig.*).

vegetation *s.* **1.** vegetazione **2.** il vegetare.

vegetative *agg.* vegetativo.

vehemence *s.* veemenza.

vehement *agg.* veemente, impetuoso.

vehicle *s.* veicolo.

veil *s.* **1.** velo, cortina **2.** (*fig.*) apparenza, pretesto.

to **veil** *vt.* **1.** velare, coprire **2.** (*fig.*) dissimulare, nascondere.

veiling *s.* **1.** il velare **2.** velo, schermo.

vein *s.* **1.** (*anat.; geol.; fig.*) vena **2.** venatura, nervatura.

to **vein** *vt.* venare, coprire di venature.

veined *agg.* **1.** venato **2.** con venature, nervature.

velleity *s.* velleità.

velocipede *s.* velocipede.

velocity *s.* velocità.

velvet *agg.* di velluto, vellutato. ♦ **velvet** *s.* velluto.

velvety *agg.* vellutato, morbido.

venal *agg.* venale.

venality *s.* venalità.

to **vend** *vt.* vendere.

vendor *s.* venditore.

to **veneer** *vt.* **1.** impiallacciare **2.** (*fig.*) mascherare.

veneer, veneering *s.* **1.** impiallacciatura **2.** (*fig.*) maschera, vernice.

venerable *agg.* venerabile.

to **venerate** *vt.* venerare.

veneration *s.* venerazione.

venereal *agg.* venereo.

Venetian *agg.* e *s.* veneziano || —

blinds, shades, persiana alla veneziana.

vengeance s. vendetta || *to take — on so.,* vendicarsi di qu.

vengeful agg. vendicativo, vendicatore.

venial agg. veniale.

venom s. veleno (*di animali*).

venomous agg. velenoso.

venous agg. 1. venoso 2. con nervature.

vent[1] s. spacco, apertura (*di abito*).

vent[2] s. 1. sbocco, apertura, foro 2. (*fig.*) sfogo || *to give — to,* dar libero corso a.

to vent vt. 1. svuotare, esalare 2. (*fig.*) sfogare.

to ventilate vt. 1. ventilare 2. (*fig.*) discutere, rendere manifesto.

ventilation s. 1. ventilazione 2. discussione.

ventral agg. ventrale, addominale.

ventricle s. ventricolo.

ventriloquism s. ventriloquio.

ventriloquist s. ventriloquo.

venture s. 1. avventura, azzardo 2. (*comm.*) speculazione.

to venture vt. avventurare, arrischiare. ♦ **to venture** vi. avventurarsi, arrischiarsi.

venturer s. avventuriero.

venue s. sede giurisdizionale.

veracious agg. verace.

veracity s. veracità.

veranda(h) s. veranda.

verb s. verbo.

verbal agg. 1. verbale 2. orale, a parole.

verbally avv. verbalmente, oralmente.

verbiage s. verbosità.

verbose agg. verboso, prolisso

verdant agg. verdeggiante.

verdict s. verdetto.

verdigris s. verderame.

verge s. 1. orlo, limite || *on the — of,* sul punto di 2. bacchetta, verga.

to verge vi. 1. confinare, essere contiguo, adiacente 2. (*fig.*) rasentare: *to — on madness,* rasentare la pazzia.

verifiable agg. verificabile.

verification s. verifica.

verifier s. verificatore.

to verify vt. 1. verificare, controllare 2. (*giur.*) autenticare.

verily avv. in verità.

verisimilar agg. verosimile.

verisimilitude s. verosimiglianza.

verism s. verismo.

veritable agg. vero, genuino.

verity s. verità, realtà.

vermiform s. vermiforme.

vermin s. *coll.* insetti parassiti.

verminous agg. infestato da parassiti.

vernacular s. vernacolo, dialetto nativo. ♦ **vernacular** agg. vernacolo, nativo.

versatile agg. versatile, multiforme.

versatility s. versatilità.

verse s. 1. verso 2. strofa 3. componimento in versi.

versification s. versificazione.

to versify vt. e vi. 1. comporre in versi 2. narrare in versi.

version s. versione, traduzione.

vertebra s. (*pl.* -ae) vertebra.

vertebral agg. vertebrale.

vertebrate agg. e s. vertebrato.

vertex s. (*pl.* -tices) vertice, apice, sommità.

vertical agg. verticale. ♦ **vertical** s. piano verticale, verticale.

verticality s. posizione verticale, perpendicolarità.

very agg. 1. vero e proprio, autentico 2. (*uso enfatico*) esatto, stesso: *at that — moment,* in quello stesso istante. ♦ **very** avv. molto, assai.

vessel s. 1. vaso, recipiente 2. nave, vascello.

vest s. 1. panciotto 2. camiciola, davantino.

to vest vt. 1. conferire, investire 2. (*giur.*) assegnare 3. parare (*di altari ecc.*). ♦ **to vest** vi. passare per eredità.

vestal s. vestale.

vestibule s. vestibolo, entrata, portico di chiesa.

vestige s. vestigio, traccia.

vestment s. veste (*spec. liturgica*).

vestry s. 1. sagrestia 2. assemblea parrocchiale.

vesture s. rivestimento, veste.

veteran agg. e s. veterano.

veterinary agg. e s. veterinario.

to vex vt. 1. vessare, opprimere 2. irritare.

vexation s. 1. vessazione, oppressione 2. irritazione.

vexatious agg. 1. irritante, fastidioso 2. (*giur.*) vessatorio.

vexed agg. 1. vessato, oppresso 2. irritato.

via *prep.* per, via, attraverso: — *air mail*, per via aerea.
viability *s.* vitalità.
viable *agg.* vitale.
viaduct *s.* viadotto.
vial *s.* fiala.
viand *s.* vivanda, cibo.
vibrant *agg.* vibrante, tremante.
to vibrate *vi.* vibrare, risuonare. ◆ to **vibrate** *vt.* far vibrare.
vibration *s.* vibrazione, tremolio.
vibrator *s.* vibratore.
vibratory *agg.* **1.** vibratorio **2.** vibrante.
vicar *s.* **1.** curato (*nella Chiesa d'Inghilterra*) **2.** vicario (*Chiesa Cattolica*).
vicariate *s.* vicariato.
vice[1] *s.* **1.** immoralità, depravazione **2.** vizio.
vice[2] *s.* (*mecc.*) morsa.
vice[3] *s.* sostituto, vice.
vice[4] *prep.* in luogo di.
viceroy *s.* viceré.
vicinity *s.* **1.** vicinanza, prossimità **2.** affinità.
vicious *agg.* **1.** vizioso, immorale **2.** maligno **3.** bizzarro (*di animali*) **4.** difettoso, scorretto.
vicissitude *s.* vicissitudine.
victim *s.* vittima.
victor *s.* vincitore.
victorious *agg.* vittorioso.
victory *s.* vittoria.
to victual *vt.* vettovagliare, approvvigionare. ◆ to **victual** *vi.* approvvigionarsi.
victualling *s.* vettovagliamento, approvvigionamento.
victuals *s. pl.* vettovaglie, viveri.
to vie *vi.* gareggiare.
view *s.* **1.** vista, sguardo **2.** veduta, panorama **3.** opinione **4.** scopo, mira **5.** (*giur.*) sopralluogo || *point of —*, punto di vista; — *-finder* (*foto*), mirino.
to view *vt.* **1.** guardare attentamente **2.** esaminare.
viewer *s.* **1.** chi guarda **2.** telespettatore **3.** ispettore.
viewless *agg.* **1.** senza vista (*di casa ecc.*) **2.** invisibile.
viewpoint *s.* punto di vista.
vigil *s.* veglia.
vigilance *s.* vigilanza.
vigilant *agg.* vigilante, vigile.
vigorous *agg.* vigoroso, forte.
Viking *s.* vichingo.
vigour *s.* vigore, energia.

vigorously *avv.* vigorosamente.
vile *agg.* vile, spregevole.
vileness *s.* viltà, bassezza.
to vilify *vt.* diffamare.
villa *s.* villa.
village *s.* villaggio, paese.
villager *s.* abitante di villaggio.
villain *s.* furfante, scellerato.
villainous *agg.* scellerato, infame.
villainy *s.* scelleratezza.
to vindicate *vt.* **1.** rivendicare **2.** giustificare, difendere.
vindication *s.* **1.** rivendicazione **2.** giustificazione, difesa.
vindictive *agg.* vendicativo.
vine *s.* vite || — *-leaf*, pampino; — *-dresser*, vignaiuolo.
vinegar *s.* aceto.
vinery *s.* serra per viti.
vineyard *s.* vigneto, vigna.
vintage *s.* **1.** vendemmia **2.** annata.
vintager *s.* vendemmiatore.
vintner *s.* vinaio.
to violate *vt.* **1.** violare, trasgredire **2.** profanare.
violation *s.* **1.** violazione, trasgressione **2.** profanazione.
violator *s.* **1.** violatore, trasgressore **2.** profanatore.
violence *s.* violenza, veemenza.
violent *agg.* violento, impetuoso.
violet *agg.* violetto, viola. ◆ **violet** *s.* viola mammola.
violin *s.* violino.
violoncellist *s.* violoncellista.
viper *s.* vipera (*anche fig.*).
virgin *agg. e s.* vergine.
virginal *agg.* verginale.
virginity *s.* verginità.
virile *agg.* virile.
virility *s.* virilità.
virtual *agg.* virtuale, effettivo.
virtuality *s.* potenzialità, virtualità.
virtue *s.* **1.** virtù, moralità, forza d'animo **2.** qualità, merito.
virtuosity *s.* virtuosismo.
virtuous *agg.* virtuoso, morale.
virulence *s.* virulenza.
virulent *agg.* virulento.
virus *s.* virus.
visa *s.* visto consolare.
to visa *vt.* vistare (*un passaporto*).
visceral *agg.* viscerale.
viscid *agg.* viscido.
viscidity *s.* viscidità.
viscose *s.* viscosa.
viscosity *s.* viscosità.
viscount *s.* visconte.
viscous *agg.* viscoso.

visibility s. visibilità.

visible agg. visibile, evidente, manifesto.

vision s. **1.** visione, immaginazione **2.** vista, capacità visiva.

visional agg. irreale.

visionary s. visionario.

visit s. visita: *to pay a —*, fare una visita.

to visit vt. e vi. visitare, fare una visita.

visitation s. **1.** visita ufficiale **2.** castigo divino.

visitor s. visitatore, ospite.

visor s. visiera.

visual agg. visuale, visivo.

to visualize vt. **1.** rendere visibile **2.** prospettare. ♦ **to visualize** vi. diventare visibile.

vital agg. vitale, essenziale.

vitality s. vitalità.

to vitalize vt. vivificare.

vitals s. pl. organi vitali.

vitamin s. vitamina.

to vitiate vt. **1.** viziare **2.** (*giur.*) invalidare.

vitiation s. **1.** corruzione **2.** (*giur.*) l'invalidare.

viticulture s. viticoltura.

vitreous agg. vitreo.

vitrifiable agg. vetrificabile.

vitrification s. vetrificazione.

to vitrify vt. vetrificare. ♦ **to vitrify** vi. vetrificarsi.

vitriol s. vetriolo.

to vituperate vt. vituperare.

vituperation s. invettiva, biasimo.

vivacious agg. vivace, vispo.

vivacity s. vivacità, brio.

vivid agg. **1.** vivace, vigoroso **2.** vivido, colorito.

to vivify vt. vivificare, animare.

viviparous agg. viviparo.

vivisection s. vivisezione.

vixen s. **1.** volpe femmina **2.** megera.

vocabulary s. vocabolario.

vocal agg. vocale.

vocalization s. vocalizzazione.

to vocalize vt. e vi. vocalizzare.

vocation s. **1.** vocazione **2.** attitudine, inclinazione **3.** professione.

vocational agg. professionale.

vocative agg. e s. vocativo.

vociferous agg. clamoroso, vociferante.

vogue s. voga, moda.

voice s. voce || *with one —*, all'unanimità.

to voice vt. esprimere, dire.

voiced agg. **1.** dalla voce: *deep- —*, dalla voce profonda **2.** sonoro.

voiceless agg. senza voce, muto.

void agg. **1.** vuoto **2.** privo **3.** (*giur.*) nullo. ♦ **void** s. il vuoto.

to void vt. **1.** vuotare, liberare **2.** abrogare.

volatile agg. **1.** volatile, alato **2.** (*fig.*) incostante. ♦ **volatile** s. **1.** volatile **2.** (*chim.*) sostanza volatile.

to volatilize vt. volatilizzare. ♦ **to volatilize** vi. volatilizzarsi.

volcano s. vulcano.

volley s. **1.** scarica, raffica, salva || *— -ball*, palla a volo.

voltage s. (*elettr.*) voltaggio, tensione.

voltameter s. voltametro.

volubility s. speditezza (*di eloquio*), loquacità.

voluble agg. spedito (*di eloquio*), loquace.

volume s. **1.** volume **2.** tomo, libro **3.** massa.

volumetric(al) agg. volumetrico.

voluminous agg. **1.** in molti volumi **2.** (*fig.*) fecondo (*di scrittore*) **3.** voluminoso.

voluntarily avv. volontariamente.

voluntary agg. **1.** volontario, spontaneo **2.** voluto, fatto di proposito **3.** mantenuto da contributi non statali. ♦ **voluntary** s. azione volontaria.

volunteer s. volontario.

to volunteer vi. **1.** offrirsi volontariamente **2.** arruolarsi volontario.

voluptuary agg. **1.** voluttuario **2.** voluttuoso.

voluptuous agg. voluttuoso, sensuale.

voluptuousness s. voluttà, sensualità.

volute s. voluta, spirale.

vomit s. vomito.

to vomit vt. e vi. vomitare (*anche fig.*).

voracious agg. ingordo, vorace.

vortex s. vortice, gorgo.

vortical agg. vorticoso.

votary s. seguace, devoto.

vote s. voto, votazione.

to vote vt. e vi. votare.

voter s. elettore.

votive agg. votivo.

to vouch vt. e vi. **1.** attestare, garantire **2.** (*giur.*) citare come garante.

voucher *s.* **1.** testimone **2.** documento giustificativo.

to **vouchsafe** *vt.* concedere.

vow *s.* voto.

to **vow** *vi.* fare un voto.

vowel *s.* vocale.

voyage *s.* viaggio (*spec. per via d'acqua*) || *outward* —, viaggio di andata; *home* —, viaggio di ritorno.

to **voyage** *vi.* fare una traversata, navigare.

vulcanization *s.* vulcanizzazione.

vulgar *agg.* volgare, triviale.

vulgarism, vulgarity *s.* volgarità.

to **vulgarize** *vt.* **1.** rendere volgare **2.** divulgare.

vulnerability *s.* vulnerabilità.

vulnerable *agg.* vulnerabile.

vulture *s.* avvoltoio.

W

to **wabble** *vi.* vacillare, traballare.

wad *s.* **1.** tampone **2.** imbottitura **3.** rotolo (*di banconote*).

to **wad** *vt.* **1.** tamponare **2.** imbottire.

wadable *agg.* guadabile.

wadding *s.* ovatta.

waddle *s.* andatura ondeggiante.

to **waddle** *vi.* camminare ondeggiando.

wade *s.* guado.

to **wade** *vt.* guadare. ♦ to **wade** *vi.* procedere faticosamente.

wader *s.* **1.** chi passa a guado **2.** (*zool.*) trampoliere. ♦ **waders** *s. pl.* stivaloni impermeabili.

wading *s.* il guadare.

wafer *s.* **1.** cialda **2.** disco adesivo.

waft *s.* soffio.

to **waft** *vt.* sospingere. ♦ to **waft** *vi.* fluttuare.

wag *s.* **1.** cenno **2.** scodinzolio.

to **wag** *vt.* scuotere. ♦ to **wag** *vi.* scuotersi || *to have a wagging tongue*, avere la lingua troppo lunga.

to **wage** *vt.* intraprendere (*guerra*).

to **wager** *vt.* e *vi.* scommettere.

wages *s. pl.* salario (*sing.*) || —-earner, salariato.

to **waggle** V. *to wag.*

wag(g)on *s.* carro || *tea-* —, car-

rello da tè.

waif *s.* relitto (*anche fig.*).

wail *s.* gemito.

to **wail** *vt.* e *vi.* gemere.

wainscot *s.* rivestimento in legno.

to **wainscot** *vt.* rivestire in legno.

waist *s.* cintola.

waistband *s.* cintura.

waistbelt *s.* cinturone.

waistcoat *s.* panciotto.

wait *s.* **1.** attesa **2.** agguato.

to **wait** *vt.* e *vi.* (*for so., sthg.*) aspettare (*qu., qc.*) || *to* — *on*, servire.

waiter *s.* **1.** cameriere **2.** vassoio.

waiting *s.* attesa || — *-room*, sala d'aspetto; *to keep* —, fare aspettare.

waitress *s.* cameriera.

to **waive** *vt.* rinunciare a, mettere da parte.

wake¹ *s.* **1.** scia **2.** pista.

wake² *s.* **1.** risveglio **2.** veglia (*funebre*).

to **wake** (**waked** e **woke, waked, woke(n)**) *vt.* svegliare. ♦ to **wake** (**waked** e **woke, waked, woke(n)**) *vi.* svegliarsi.

wakeful *agg.* sveglio.

wakefulness *s.* veglia.

to **waken** V. *to wake.*

wakening *s.* risveglio.

waking *agg.* sveglio. ♦ **waking** *s.* **1.** risveglio **2.** veglia.

walk *s.* **1.** passeggiata **2.** andatura **3.** (*fig.*) rango || *to take a* —, fare una passeggiata.

to **walk** *vi.* passeggiare, andare a piedi || *to* — *off*, andarsene.

walker *s.* camminatore.

walkie-talkie *s.* (*radio*) trasmettitore-ricevitore portatile.

walking *s.* il camminare || — *tour*, escursione a piedi.

walkover *s.* facile vittoria.

wall *s.* muro || — *paper*, carta da parato; *main* —, muro maestro.

to **wall** *vt.* circondare di mura || *to* — *up*, murare.

wallet *s.* portafoglio.

wall-eye *s.* glaucoma.

Walloon *agg.* e *s.* vallone.

to **wallop** *vt.* **1.** bastonare **2.** percuotere, sculacciare.

wallow *s.* pantano.

to **wallow** *vi.* sguazzare.

walnut *s.* noce.

walrus *s.* tricheco.

waltz *s.* valzer.

to **waltz** vi. ballare il valzer.

wan agg. pallido.

to **wan** vi. impallidire.

wand s. bacchetta magica.

wander s. vagabondaggio.

to **wander** vi. 1. vagare 2. vaneggiare.

wanderer s. vagabondo.

wandering agg. 1. errante 2. delirante. ♦ **wandering** s. 1. vagabondaggio 2. delirio.

wane s. declino.

to **wane** vi. 1. declinare 2. decrescere 3. essere in fase calante.

to **wangle** vt. ottenere con intrighi.

want s. 1. mancanza 2. bisogno: to be in — of, aver bisogno di.

to **want** vt. 1. volere 2. aver bisogno di 3. mancare.

wanted agg. ricercato: to be — by the police, essere ricercato dalla polizia.

wanting prep. senza, in mancanza di.

wanton agg. 1. licenzioso 2. capriccioso 3. arbitrario 4. lascivo.

to **wanton** vi. 1. scherzare 2. comportarsi dissolutamente.

wantonness s. 1. dissolutezza 2. capriccio.

war s. guerra: — Office, Ministero della Guerra.

to **war** vi. guerreggiare.

warble s. trillo.

to **warble** vt. e vi. trillare.

warbling agg. melodioso. ♦ **warbling** s. gorgheggio.

ward s. 1. guardia 2. reparto 3. rione 4. tutela 5. pupillo.

to **ward** vt. parare: to — off a blow, parare un colpo.

warden s. 1. guardiano 2. direttore 3. governatore.

wardenship s. carica di direttore, governatore.

warder s. 1. guardiano 2. carceriere.

wardrobe s. guardaroba.

wardroom s. (mar.) quadrato ufficiali.

wardship s. tutela.

ware agg. conscio, circospetto.

to **ware** vt. fare attenzione a.

wares s. pl. 1. articoli 2. vasellame (sing.).

warehouse s. magazzino.

to **warehouse** vt. depositare in magazzino.

warehouseman s. 1. magazziniere 2. commerciante all'ingrosso.

warfare s. operazione bellica.

warfaring agg. bellicoso.

warily avv. cautamente.

wariness s. cautela.

warlike agg. guerriero.

warlikeness s. bellicosità.

warlock s. stregone.

warm agg. 1. caldo 2. animato.

to **warm** vt. 1. scaldare 2. animare. ♦ to **warm** vi. 1. scaldarsi 2. animarsi.

warmer s. riscaldatore.

warm-hearted agg. bonario, cordiale.

warming s. riscaldamento.

warmonger s. guerrafondaio.

warmth s. calore.

to **warn** vt. avvertire || to — off, invitare ad allontanarsi.

warning s. (pre)avviso || — light, spia luminosa.

warp s. 1. ordito 2. deformazione.

to **warp** vt. 1. curvare 2. (fig.) alterare. ♦ to **warp** vi. 1. curvarsi 2. (fig.) alterarsi.

warpath s. sentiero di guerra.

warping s. deformazione, pervertimento.

warrant s. 1. garanzia, garante 2. (giur.; comm.) ordine, autorizzazione.

to **warrant** vt. 1. garantire 2. giustificare.

warrantable agg. 1. giustificabile 2. legittimo.

warrantee s. chi riceve una garanzia.

warranter, -tor s. garante.

warranty s. 1. garanzia 2. autorizzazione.

warrior s. guerriero.

warship s. nave da guerra.

wart s. verruca.

wartime s. tempo di guerra.

wary agg. cauto.

was V. to be.

wash s. 1. lavata 2. bucato 3. sciacquio 4. brodaglia 5. mano (di colore).

to **wash** vt. 1. lavare 2. bagnare 3. gettare. ♦ to **wash** vi. 1. lavarsi 2. essere lavabile || to — up, rigovernare (le stoviglie); to — over, sommergere.

washable agg. lavabile.

washbasin s. catino.

washboard s. asse per lavare.

washer s. 1. lavandaio 2. (mecc.) lavatrice 3. (mecc.) rondella.

washerwoman s. lavandaia.
washhouse s. lavanderia.
washing s. **1.** lavaggio **2.** bucato **3.** risciacquatura || — -*machine*, lavatrice.
whashout s. erosione, dilatamento.
washroom s. **1.** lavanderia **2.** gabinetto.
washstand s. lavabo.
washy agg. **1.** annacquato **2.** scialbo.
wasp s. vespa.
waspish agg. pungente.
waspishness s. irascibilità.
wastage s. logorio.
waste agg. **1.** deserto **2.** di scarto.
♦ **waste** s. **1.** spreco **2.** scarto **3.** deserto || — -*basket*, cestino per rifiuti; — -*paper*, carta straccia.
to **waste** vt. **1.** consumare **2.** sprecare **3.** rovinare. ♦ to **waste** vi. **1.** consumarsi **2.** rovinarsi.
wasteful agg. **1.** rovinoso **2.** prodigo.
waster s. dissipatore.
wasting agg. **1.** logorante **2.** devastante. ♦ **wasting** s. **1.** sciupio **2.** deperimento **3.** devastazione.
watch s. **1.** orologio (*da polso*) **2.** guardia || — -*fire*, fuoco di bivacco; *to be on the* —, stare in guardia.
to **watch** vt. **1.** osservare **2.** stare a guardia di. ♦ to **watch** vi. **1.** vegliare **2.** aspettare.
watcher s. **1.** spettatore **2.** sorvegliante.
watchful agg. attento.
watchfulness s. **1.** vigilanza **2.** cautela.
watchmaker s. orologiaio.
watchman s. guardia (*notturna*).
watchword s. parola d'ordine.
water s. acqua || *to hold* —, non fare acqua, (*fig.*) essere logico; — -*bottle*, borraccia; — -*colour*, acquarello; — -*colourist*, acquarellista; — -*closet*, gabinetto; — -*gate*, chiusa; — -*line*, linea di galleggiamento; — -*meadow*, marcita; — -*polo*, pallanuoto; *drinking* —, acqua potabile.
to **water** vt. **1.** bagnare **2.** diluire **3.** abbeverare **4.** secernere || *to make one's mouth* —, far venire l'acquolina in bocca. ♦ to **water** vi. **1.** abbeverarsi **2.** riempirsi di acqua.
waterfall s. cascata.

watering s. **1.** annaffiamento **2.** diluizione **3.** abbeverarsi **4.** rifornimento d'acqua **5.** secrezione || — -*can*, — -*pot*, annaffiatoio.
waterman s. (*pl.* -men) barcaiolo.
watermark s. **1.** filigrana **2.** indicatore di livello **3.** livello d'acqua.
watermelon s. anguria.
waterproof agg. e s. impermeabile.
to **waterproof** vt. impermeabilizzare.
watershed s. **1.** spartiacque **2.** bacino idrico.
watertight agg. stagno.
waterway s. canale navigabile.
waterworks s. pl. impianto idrico (*sing.*).
watery agg. **1.** acquoso **2.** lacrimoso.
wattle s. **1.** fascina **2.** vimine.
wave s. **1.** onda, ondata **2.** cenno (*della mano*).
to **wave** vi. **1.** ondeggiare **2.** far cenno (*con la mano*). ♦ to **wave** vt. **1.** far ondeggiare **2.** ondulare **3.** chiamare (*con un cenno di mano*).
waved agg. ondulato.
wave-length s. lunghezza d'onda.
waveless agg. liscio.
wavelet s. piccola onda.
wavelike agg. ondeggiante.
to **waver** vi. vacillare.
wavering s. **1.** oscillazione **2.** esitazione.
wavily avv. a onde.
waviness s. ondulazione.
waving s. **1.** ondeggiamento, ondulazione **2.** sventolio **3.** cenno.
wavy agg. **1.** ondulato **2.** ondeggiante.
wax s. **1.** cera **2.** paraffina.
to **wax**[1] vt. incerare.
to **wax**[2] vi. **1.** crescere **2.** aumentare.
waxen agg. di, come cera.
way s. **1.** via **2.** maniera **3.** punto di vista **4.** stato || *to make* —, far posto; *this* —, per di qua; *in a* —, in un certo senso; *by the* —, tra parentesi; *one*- —, senso unico; *out of the* —, fuori mano.
waybill s. lista dei passeggeri.
wayfarer s. viandante.
to **waylay** vt. tendere un agguato a.
wayside s. margine della strada.
wayward agg. **1.** indocile **2.** capriccioso.
waywardness s. ostinazione.
we pron. sogg. noi.

weak *agg.* **1.** debole **2.** diluito.

to **weaken** *vi.* indebolirsi. ♦ to **weaken** *vt.* indebolire.

weakling *s.* persona debole.

weakly *agg.* debole.

weakness *s.* debolezza.

weal[1] *s.* benessere, prosperità.

weal[2] *s.* livido.

wealth *s.* ricchezza.

wealthy *agg.* ricco.

to **wean** *vt.* **1.** svezzare **2.** togliere il vizio a.

weaning *s.* svezzamento.

weapon *s.* arma.

wear *s.* **1.** uso, usura **2.** durata **3.** abbigliamento.

to **wear (wore, worn)** *vt.* **1.** indossare **2.** logorare **3.** stancare || *to — out*, logorare, stancare. ♦ to **wear (wore, worn)** *vi.* **1.** logorarsi **2.** stancarsi **3.** durare || *to — out*, logorarsi, stancarsi.

wearily *avv.* stancamente.

weariness *s.* **1.** stanchezza **2.** tedio.

wearing *agg.* **1.** logorante **2.** da indossare. ♦ **wearing** *s.* **1.** logorio **2.** l'indossare.

wearisome *agg.* **1.** faticoso **2.** tedioso.

weary *agg.* **1.** stanco **2.** annoiato.

to **weary** *vt.* **1.** affaticare **2.** annoiare. ♦ to **weary** *vi.* **1.** affaticarsi **2.** annoiarsi.

weasel *s.* donnola.

weather *s.* tempo (*atmosferico*) || *— -glass*, barometro; *— -report*, bollettino metereologico.

to **weather** *vt.* **1.** esporre all'aria **2.** superare || *to — a storm*, resistere a una burrasca. ♦ to **weather** *vi.* alterarsi.

weathercock *s.* banderuola.

weathering *s.* alterazione (*di tempo*).

weave *s.* tessuto.

to **weave (wove, woven)** *vt.* **1.** tessere, intrecciare **2.** (*fig.*) ideare.

weaver *s.* tessitore.

weaving *s.* **1.** tessitura **2.** orditura.

web *s.* **1.** tela **2.** (*fig.*) trama **3.** membrana || *cob- —*, ragnatela.

to **wed** *vt.* sposare. ♦ to **wed** *vi.* sposarsi.

wedding *s.* nozze (*pl.*) || *— -breakfast*, rinfresco di nozze; *— -ring*, fede nuziale.

wedge *s.* cuneo.

to **wedge** *vt.* **1.** incuneare **2.** fendere con cunei.

wedlock *s.* vincolo matrimoniale.

Wednesday *s.* mercoledì.

wee *agg.* minuscolo || *a — bit*, un tantino.

weed *s.* erbaccia. ♦ **weeds** *s. pl.* gramaglie.

to **weed** *vt.* **1.** sarchiare **2.** estirpare.

weeding *s.* sarchiatura.

week *s.* settimana || *today —*, oggi a otto; *— in — out*, una settimana dopo l'altra.

weekday *s.* giorno feriale.

week-end *s.* fine settimana.

weekly *agg.* e *s.* settimanale. ♦ **weekly** *avv.* settimanalmente.

weep *s.* pianto.

to **weep (wept, wept)** *vt.* e *vi.* **1.** piangere **2.** trasudare || *to — out*, piangere disperatamente.

weeper *s.* **1.** chi piange **2.** velo, nastro di lutto.

weeping *s.* **1.** pianto **2.** trasudamento.

weft *s.* trama (*di tessuto*).

to **weigh** *vt.* e *vi.* **1.** pesare **2.** (*fig.*) ponderare || *to — down*, piegare; *to — anchor* (*mar.*), levar l'ancora.

weigh-house *s.* pesa pubblica.

weighing *s.* pesatura || *— -machine*, pesa.

weight *s.* **1.** peso **2.** importanza || *to put on —*, ingrassare.

to **weight** *vi.* appensantire, caricare.

weightiness *s.* **1.** pesantezza **2.** (*fig.*) importanza.

weightless *agg.* senza peso.

weighty *agg.* **1.** pesante **2.** (*fig.*) importante.

weir *s.* chiusa, diga.

weird *agg.* **1.** fatale **2.** misterioso.

welcome *agg.* gradito. ♦ **welcome** *s.* benvenuto.

to **welcome** *vt.* dare il benvenuto a, gradire.

to **weld** *vt.* saldare. ♦ to **weld** *vi.* saldarsi.

welding *s.* saldatura.

welfare *s.* benessere || *— contributions*, oneri previdenziali; *— state*, stato assistenziale; *— work*, assistenza sociale.

well[1] *s.* **1.** fonte, pozzo **2.** tromba delle scale.

well[2] *avv.* e *s.* bene || *as —*, pure; *as — as*, oltre a, oltre che; *to be —*, star bene; *to get —*, guarire.

to **well** *vi.* sgorgare.

well-advised *agg.* saggio.

well-being *s.* benessere.

well-bred *agg.* educato.

well-doing *s.* buona condotta.

well-done *agg.* (*cuc.*) ben cotto.

well-meaning *agg.* ben intenzionato.

well-off *agg.* agiato.

well-read *agg.* colto, ben educato.

well-timed *agg.* opportuno.

well-to-do *agg.* agiato.

Welsh *agg.* gallese.

Welshman *s.* gallese.

went V. *to go.*

wept V. *to weep.*

were V. *to be* ‖ *as it* —, per così dire.

west *agg.* occidentale. ♦ **west** *avv.* a, verso ovest. ♦ **west** *s.* ovest.

westerly *agg.* 1. dall'ovest 2. verso ovest. ♦ **westerly** *avv.* verso ovest.

western *agg.* occidentale.

westerner *s.* occidentale.

to westernize *vt.* occidentalizzare. ♦ **to westernize** *vi.* occidentalizzarsi.

westward *agg.* e *avv.* verso ovest.

westwards *avv.* verso ovest.

wet *agg.* 1. umido 2. piovoso ‖ — *blanket*, guastafeste. ♦ **wet** *s.* 1. umidità 2. tempo piovoso.

to wet *vt.* bagnare. ♦ **to wet** *vi.* bagnarsi.

wet-nurse *s.* nutrice.

wetting *s.* bagnatura.

whale *s.* balena ‖ — -*boat*, baleniera.

to whale *vi.* andare a caccia di balene.

whalebone *s.* stecca di balena.

whaler *s.* 1. baleniere 2. baleniera.

wharf *s.* banchina.

to wharf *vt.* attraccare.

what *agg.* 1. (*int.*) quale? quali? che? 2. (*rel.*) (quello) ... che 3. (*escl.*) che! ♦ **what** *pron.* 1. (*int.*) che?, che cosa? 2. (*rel.*) ciò che 3. (*escl.*) quanto! ‖ — *for?*, perché mai?; — *is he?*, che cosa fa? ♦ **what** *inter.* come!

whatever *agg.* qualunque. ♦ **whatever** *pron.* qualunque cosa. ♦ **whatever** *avv.* affatto.

whatsoever V. *whatever.*

wheat *s.* grano.

to wheedle *vt.* lusingare.

wheel *s.* 1. ruota 2. volante ‖ *wheels within wheels*, retroscena.

to wheel *vt.* 1. far ruotare 2. spingere (*su un veicolo a ruote*). ♦

to wheel *vi.* ruotare.

wheelbarrow *s.* carriola.

wheeze *s.* respiro affannoso.

to wheeze *vi.* ansimare.

whelp *s.* cucciolo.

when *avv.* e *cong.* quando.

whence *avv.* da dove.

whenever *avv.* tutte le volte che.

where *avv.* dove.

whereabout(s) *avv.* e *cong.* dove. ♦ **whereabout(s)** *s.* luogo.

whereas *cong.* mentre.

whereby *avv.* 1. (*int.*) come? 2. (*rel.*) per cui.

wherefore *avv.* 1. (*int.*) perché 2. (*rel.*) perciò.

wherein *avv.* 1. (*int.*) come? dove? 2. (*rel.*) in cui.

whereof *avv.* 1. (*int.*) di che? 2. (*rel.*) di cui.

whereon *avv.* 1. (*int.*) su che? 2. (*rel.*) su cui.

whereto *avv.* 1. (*int.*) verso dove? a che scopo? 2. (*rel.*) a cui.

whereupon *avv.* 1. (*int.*) su che? 2. (*rel.*) dopo di che.

wherever *avv.* dovunque.

whet *s.* 1. affilatura 2. (*fig.*) stimolante.

to whet *vt.* 1. affilare 2. stimolare.

whether *cong.* se ‖ — ... *or*, o...o.

whey *s.* siero (*del latte*).

which *agg.* 1. (*int.*) quale?, quali? 2. (*rel.*) il, la quale, i, le quali. ♦ **which** *pron.* 1. (*int.*) quale?, quali?, chi? 2. (*rel.*) il, la quale, i, le quali; il che ‖ *I cannot tell* — *is* —, non so distinguerli l'uno dall'altro.

whichever *agg.* qualunque. ♦ **whichever** *pron.* qualunque cosa.

whiff *s.* 1. soffio 2. sbuffo.

to whiff *vt.* e *vi.* 1. soffiare 2. emettere sbuffi.

whig *agg.* e *s.* (*pol. inglese*) liberale.

while *cong.* 1. mentre 2. sebbene. ♦ **while** *s.* momento ‖ *once in a* —, una volta tanto; *the* —, frattanto.

to while *vt. to* — *away the time*, ammazzare il tempo.

whilst V. *while.*

whim *s.* capriccio.

whimper *s.* 1. piagnucolio 2. uggiolio.

to whimper *vi.* 1. piagnucolare 2. uggiolare.

whimsical *agg.* stravagante.

whimsicality s. stravaganza.

whimsy agg. capriccioso. ◆ whim-sy s. capriccio.

whine s. piagnisteo.

to whine v. to whimper.

whinny s. nitrito.

to whinny vi. nitrire.

whip s. frusta.

to whip vt. 1. frustare 2. frullare. ◆ to whip vi. precipitarsi || to — away, partire improvvisamente; to — out, pronunciare con violenza, tirar fuori.

whipper-snapper s. gradasso.

whirl s. 1. vortice 2. (fig.) confusione.

to whirl vt. 1. far roteare 2. trascinare. ◆ to whirl vi. 1. roteare 2. correr via 3. (fig.) esser confuso.

whirligig s. giostra.

whirlpool s. gorgo.

whirlwind s. turbine.

whir(r) s. 1. ronzio 2. frullio (d'ali) 3. rombo (di motore).

to whir(r) vi. 1. ronzare 2. frullare (d'ali) 3. rombare (di motore).

whisk s. 1. scopino 2. frullino 3. movimento rapido.

to whisk vt. 1. spazzare 2. (cuc.) frullare 3. agitare. ◆ to whisk vi. guizzare via.

whisker s. 1. basetta 2. baffo.

whisper s. 1. mormorio 2. diceria.

to whisper vt. e vi. mormorare, bisbigliare.

whistle s. fischio.

to whistle vt. e vi. 1. fischiare 2. chiamare con un fischio.

whistler s. 1. chi fischia 2. marmotta canadese.

whit s. 1. inezia 2. atomo.

Whit agg. di Pentecoste.

white agg. e s. bianco || — feather, viltà; — -livered, codardo.

to whiten vt. e vi. imbiancare.

whitener s. 1. imbianchino 2. candeggiante.

whiteness s. bianchezza.

whitening s. 1. imbiancamento 2. candeggiamento.

whitesmith s. lattoniere.

whitethorn s. biancospino.

whitewash s. 1. calce 2. (fig.) riabilitazione.

to whitewash vt. 1. imbiancare 2. (fig.) riabilitare.

whitewasher s. imbianchino.

whitewashing s. 1. imbiancatura 2. riabilitazione.

whiting s. calce.

whitish agg. biancastro.

whitlow s. patereccio.

Whitsunday s Pentecoste.

whiz s. sibilo.

who pron. 1. (int.) chi? 2. (rel.) il, la quale, i, le quali.

whoever pron. chiunque.

whole agg. tutto, intero. ◆ whole s. 1. il tutto, l'intero 2. il complesso || as a —, nell'insieme; on the —, nel complesso.

wholeness s. totalità.

wholesale agg. e avv. all'ingrosso. ◆ wholesale s. vendita all'ingrosso.

to wholesale vt. e vi. vendere all'ingrosso.

wholesaler s. venditore all'ingrosso.

wholesome agg. salutare.

wholly avv. totalmente.

whom pron. compl. di who.

whomever pron. compl. chiunque.

whomsoever V. whomever.

whoop s. ululato.

whooping-cough s. pertosse.

whorl s. spirale.

whose pron. 1. (int.) di chi? 2. (rel.) del, della quale, dei, delle quali.

whosever pron. di chiunque.

whosoever V. whoever.

why avv. 1. (int.) perché? 2. (rel.) per cui. ◆ why cong. perché. ◆ why inter. perbacco.

wick s. lucignolo.

wicked agg. malvagio.

wickedness s. malvagità.

wicker s. vimine.

wicket s. 1. sportello 2. cancelletto.

wide agg. 1. largo 2. alto (di tessuto) 3. spalancato: — open, spalancato. ◆ wide avv. largamente.

wide-awake agg. 1. completamente sveglio 2. (fig.) vigilante.

widely avv. largamente.

to widen vt. allargare. ◆ to widen vi. allargarsi.

widespread agg. esteso.

widow s. vedova.

widower s. vedovo.

widowhood s. vedovanza.

width s. 1. larghezza 2. altezza (di stoffa).

to wield vt. 1. brandire 2. esercitare (autorità ecc.).

wife s. (pl. wives) moglie.

wig s. (fam.) sgridata.

wild *agg.* **1.** selvaggio, selvatico **2.** agitato **3.** pazzo **4.** avventato **5.** disordinato. ♦ **wild** *s.* deserto. ♦ **wild** *avv.* **1.** selvaggiamente **2.** impulsivamente **3.** sfrenatamente.

wilderness *s.* deserto.

wild-goose chase *s.* impresa vana, impossibile.

wildness *s.* **1.** selvatichezza **2.** furore.

wile *s.* astuzia.

wilful *agg.* **1.** ostinato **2.** premeditato.

wilfulness *s.* **1.** ostinazione **2.** premeditazione.

will *s.* **1.** volontà **2.** testamento || *free* —, libero arbitrio.

will *v. ausiliare (usato per il futuro)* *he. — be*, egli sarà **2.** *v. dif.* volere: *I — go*, io voglio andare, io andrò *(futuro volitivo)*.

to will *vt. e vi.* **1.** disporre **2.** lasciare per testamento.

willed *agg. strong* —, di forte volontà.

willing *agg.* **1.** volonteroso **2.** disposto || — *or not*, volente o nolente.

willingly *avv.* volentieri.

willow *s.* — *(tree)*, salice: *weeping* —, salice piangente.

willy-nilly *agg. e avv.* volente o nolente.

wily *agg.* astuto.

wimple *s.* **1.** soggolo **2.** arricciatura.

to win (won, won) *vt. e vi.* vincere || *to — back*, riconquistare.

wince *s.* sussulto.

to wince *vi.* trasalire.

winch *s.* **1.** argano **2.** manovella.

wind[1] *s.* **1.** vento **2.** respiro || *to get — of*, aver sentore di; — *-breaker*, giacca a vento; — *-cone*, manica a vento.

wind[2] *s.* **1.** svolta, curva **2.** giro di carica.

to wind[1] *vt.* **1.** fiutare **2.** sfiatare.

to wind[2] (wound, wound) *vt.* **1.** avvolgere **2.** *(una molla)* caricare **3.** girare || *to — off*, svolgere. ♦ **to wind (wound, wound)** *vi.* **1.** serpeggiare **2.** avvolgersi || *to — off*, svolgersi.

windbag *s.* **1.** otre *(di cornamusa)* **2.** *(fig.)* parolaio.

winder *s.* **1.** manovella **2.** avvolgitore.

winding *agg.* tortuoso. ♦ **winding** *s.* **1.** tortuosità **2.** tornante **3.** spira

4. caricamento **5.** ritorcitura.

windlass *s.* argano.

windmill *s.* mulino a vento.

window *s.* finestra, finestrino || — *-dresser*, vetrinista; *French-* —, porta finestra.

windpipe *s.* trachea.

windscreen *s.* parabrezza || — *wiper*, tergicristallo.

windshield *s.* *(amer.)* parabrezza.

windward *agg.* contro vento. ♦ **windward** *s.* sopravvento.

windy *agg.* **1.** ventoso **2.** verboso.

wine *s.* vino.

wing *s.* **1.** ala **2.** battente *(di porta)* **3.** *(teat.)* quinta || *on the* —, in volo; *to take* —, spiccare il volo.

winged *agg.* alato.

wink *s.* **1.** battito di palpebre **2.** ammicco **3.** *(fig.)* istante.

to wink *vi.* **1.** battere le palpebre **2.** ammiccare **3.** scintillare.

winner *s.* vincitore.

winning *agg.* **1.** vincitore **2.** suadente. ♦ **winning** *s.* vittoria.

to winnow *vt. e vi.* vagliare.

winsome *agg.* incantevole.

winter *s.* inverno. ♦ **winter** *agg.* invernale.

to winter *vi.* svernare.

wintered *agg.* gelato.

winterly *V.* *wintry*.

wintriness *s.* rigore invernale.

wintry *agg.* invernale, freddo.

wipe *s.* **1.** asciugatura **2.** spolverata.

to wipe *vt.* **1.** asciugare **2.** strofinare || *to — off*, cancellare.

wiper *s.* **1.** chi pulisce **2.** strofinaccio.

wire *s.* **1.** filo metallico **2.** telegramma || — *netting*, rete metallica; *barbed* —, filo spinato.

to wire *vt. e vi.* **1.** legare con filo metallico **2.** prendere in trappola **3.** telegrafare.

wired *agg.* munito di filo metallico, di rete metallica.

wireless *agg.* senza fili. ♦ **wireless** *s.* radiotelegrafia.

to wireless *vt. e vi.* radiotelegrafare.

wire-puller *s.* intrigante, eminenza grigia.

wiry *agg.* **1.** di, simile a filo metallico **2.** *(fig.)* resistente.

wisdom *s.* saggezza.

wise *agg.* **1.** saggio **2.** edotto, informato.

wise *s.* modo, maniera.

wiseacre *s.* saccente.

wisely *avv.* saggiamente.

wish *s.* **1.** desiderio **2.** augurio: *best wishes,* i migliori auguri.

to **wish** *vt.* e *vi.* **1.** desiderare **2.** augurare || *I wish I were,* vorrei essere; *I wish I had,* vorrei avere; *I wish I could,* vorrei potere.

wisher *s.* **1.** chi desidera **2.** chi augura.

wishful *agg.* desideroso.

wishing *agg.* desideroso. ♦ **wishing** *s.* desiderio.

wistaria *s.* glicine.

wistful *agg.* **1.** desideroso **2.** pensoso.

wistfully *avv.* **1.** con desiderio **2.** pensosamente.

wistfulness *s.* **1.** bramosia **2.** raccoglimento.

wit *s.* **1.** ingegno **2.** spirito **3.** persona di spirito || *to live by one's wits,* vivere di espedienti; *to be at one's wits' end,* non saper più cosa fare.

witch *s.* strega.

to **witch** *vt.* stregare.

witchcraft *s.* **1.** stregoneria *2.* fascino.

witch-doctor *s.* stregone.

witchery *s.* V. *witchcraft.*

witching *agg.* magico.

with *prep.* **1.** con **2.** presso **3.** a causa di, per, da.

to **withdraw** (**withdrew, withdrawn**) *vt.* ritirare. ♦ to **withdraw** (**withdrew, withdrawn**) *vi.* ritirarsi.

withdrawal *s.* **1.** ritirata, ritiro **2** ritrattazione.

withdrawn V. *to withdraw.*

withdrew V. *to withdraw.*

withe *s.* vimine.

to **wither** *vt.* e *vi.* avvizzire.

withering *s.* avvizzimento.

to **withhold** (**withheld, withheld**) *vt.* **1.** trattenere **2.** rifiutare **3.** nascondere.

within *prep.* entro. ♦ **within** *avv.* dentro.

without *prep.* senza, senza di. ♦ **without** *cong.* senza (che). ♦ **without** *avv.* fuori.

to **withstand** (**withstood, withstood**) *vt.* resistere a, fronteggiare.

withstander *s.* oppositore.

withstood V. *to withstand.*

witness *s.* **1.** testimone: *eye- —,* testimone oculare **2.** testimonianza.

to **witness** *vt.* **1.** essere testimone a **2.** mostrare. ♦ to **witness** *vi.* testimoniare.

witticism *s.* arguzia.

wittily *avv.* spiritosamente.

wittiness *s.* spirito.

wittingly *avv.* consapevolmente.

witty *agg.* spiritoso.

wives V. *wife.*

wizard *s.* mago.

to **wobble** V. *to wabble.*

woe *s.* dolore.

woeful *agg.* doloroso.

woke V. *to wake.*

woken V. *to wake.*

wolf *s.* (*pl.* wolves) lupo || *she- —,* lupa.

to **wolf** *vt.* divorare.

wolfish *agg.* da lupo.

woman, *s.* (*pl.* women) donna.

womanhood *s.* **1.** femminilità **2.** maturità (*della donna*) **3.** condizione di donna.

womanish *agg.* **1.** effeminato **2.** femminile.

womankind *s.* le donne (*in genere*).

womanlike *agg.* femminile. ♦ **womanlike** *avv.* femminilmente.

womanliness *s.* femminilità.

womanly *agg.* femminile.

womb *s.* **1.** ventre **2.** grembo **3.** utero.

women V. *woman.*

won V. *to win.*

wonder *s.* **1.** prodigio **2.** meraviglia.

to **wonder** *vi.* **1.** domandarsi **2.** stupirsi.

wonderful *agg.* meraviglioso.

wonderingly *avv.* con meraviglia.

wonderland *s.* paese delle meraviglie.

wondrous *agg.* mirabile.

wont *agg.* abituato. ♦ **wont** *s.* abitudine.

wonted *agg.* abituato, abituale.

to **woo** *vt.* corteggiare.

wood *s.* **1.** bosco **2.** legno || *— -cutter,* boscaiolo.

woodcock *s.* beccaccia.

woodcut *s.* **1.** incisione su legno **2.** xilografia.

wooden *agg.* di legno.

woodiness *s.* **1.** boscosità **2.** legnosità.

woodland *s.* terreno boscoso.

woodman *s.* **1.** guardaboschi **2.** taglialegna.

woodpecker *s.* picchio.

woodwork s. lavoro in legno.
woody agg. 1. boscoso 2. legnoso.
wooer s. corteggiatore.
wool s. 1. lana 2. peluria di animale || *cotton* —, ovatta.
wool(l)en agg. di lana. ◆ **wool(l)en** s. stoffa di lana.
woolly agg. 1. di lana, lanoso 2. (fig.) confuso.
word s. parola || *by — of mouth*, oralmente.
to **word** vt. esprimere.
wordiness s. verbosità.
wording s. espressione.
wordy agg. verboso.
wore V. to wear.
work s. lavoro || *out of* —, disoccupato. ◆ **works** s. pl. 1. meccanismo (sing.) 2. fabbrica, officina (sing.).
to **work** vt. 1. lavorare 2. far funzionare 3. dirigere || *to — in*, introdurre; *to — off*, liberarsi di; *to — out*, calcolare; *to — up*, elaborare. ◆ to **work** vi. 1. lavorare 2. funzionare 3. agitarsi.
workable agg. 1. eseguibile 2. lavorabile.
workaday agg. lavorativo.
workday s. giorno feriale.
worker s. lavoratore || *skilled —*, operaio qualificato.
workhouse s. ospizio di mendicità.
working agg. 1. laborioso 2. funzionante. ◆ **working** s. 1. lavorio 2. funzionamento 3. lavorazione || *— clothes*, abiti da lavoro; *— expenses*, spese d'esercizio.
workless agg. senza lavoro.
workman s. operaio.
workmanship s. 1. abilità 2. fattura.
workroom s. laboratorio.
workshop s. officina.
workwoman s. operaia.
world s. mondo: *all over the —*, in tutto il mondo.
worldliness s. 1. condizione terrena 2. mondanità.
worldly agg. 1. terreno 2. mondano.
world-wide agg. diffuso, noto in tutto il mondo.
worm s. verme || *— screw*, vite senza fine.
to **worm** vt. carpire || *to — one's way*, insinuarsi.
wormwood s. assenzio.
worn V. to wear. ◆ **worn** agg. 1.

consumato 2. indebolito || *— out*, logoro, (fig.) esausto.
worried agg. 1. preoccupato 2. tormentato.
worrier s. seccatore.
worrisome agg. 1. irritante 2. preoccupato.
worry s. 1. ansia 2. guaio.
to **worry** vt. tormentare. ◆ to **worry** vi. preoccuparsi.
worrying agg. 1. preoccupante 2. tormentoso.
worse agg. (comp. di bad e ill) peggiore, peggio. ◆ **worse** avv. e s. peggio || *all the —*, tanto peggio; *so much the — for*, tanto peggio per; *none the —*, ugualmente; *— and —*, di male in peggio.
worship s. adorazione.
to **worship** vt. e vi. adorare, venerare.
worshipper s. 1. adoratore 2. fedele.
worst agg. (superl. di bad e ill) peggiore, pessimo. ◆ **worst** avv. e s. peggio || *at (the) —*, nella peggiore delle ipotesi.
worsted agg. di lana pettinata.
worth agg. degno. ◆ **worth** s. valore.
worthily avv. degnamente.
worthiness s. 1. valore 2. dignità.
worthless agg. 1. senza valore 2. indegno.
worthlessness s. 1. mancanza di valore 2. indegnità.
worthy agg. degno, meritevole. ◆ **worthy** s. persona illustre.
would v. dif. 1. (ausiliare del condiz.) *he — go*, egli andrebbe 2. (passato ind. imperfetto, congiuntivo, condiz.) volere 3. (imperfetto ind.) solere: *he — come every day*, soleva venire ogni giorno.
would-be agg. sedicente.
wound s. ferita.
to **wound** vt. ferire.
wound V. to wind.
wove V. to weave.
woven V. to weave.
wrack s. distruzione, rovina.
to **wrangle** vi. discutere.
wrangler s. attaccabrighe.
wrap s. sciarpa, coperta, mantello.
to **wrap** vt. avvolgere || *to — up*, impacchettare. ◆ to **wrap** vi. avvolgersi.
wrapper s. 1. imballatore 2. carta da imballo 3. copertina.

wrapping s. involucro || — *paper*, carta da imballaggio.
wrath s. ira.
wrathful agg. irato.
wrathfulness s. ira
wreath s. ghirlanda.
to **wreathe** vt. 1. intrecciare 2. inghirlandare 3. attorcigliare. ♦ to **wreathe** vi. innalzarsi in spire.
wreathy agg. 1. inghirlandato 2. a forma di ghirlanda.
wreck s. 1. naufragio (*anche fig.*) 2. relitto.
to **wreck** vt. rovinare. ♦ to **wreck** vi. naufragare.
wreckage V. *wreck*.
wren s. scricciolo.
wrench s. 1. strappo 2. (*mecc.*) chiave inglese.
to **wrench**, to **wrest** vt. 1. strappare 2. torcere.
wrestle s. lotta.
to **wrestle** vi. lottare.
wrestler s. lottatore.
wrestling s. (*sport.*) lotta
wretch s. disgraziato.
wretched agg. 1. disgraziato 2. scadente.
wretchedness s. 1. disgrazia 2. squallore.
wriggle s. contorsione.
to **wriggle** vt. contorcere. ♦ to **wriggle** vi. 1. contorcersi 2. (*fig.*) dar risposte evasive.
wring s. 1. torsione 2. dolore acuto.
to **wring** (**wrung, wrung**) vt. 1. torcere 2. estorcere 3. stringere || *to — out*, spremere, (*fig.*) strappare.
wringer s. 1. torcitore 2. torchio.
wringing agg. lancinante (*di dolore*). ♦ **wringing** s. torcitura.
wrinkle[1] s. 1. ruga 2. grinza.
wrinkle[2] s. stratagemma.
to **wrinkle** vt. 1. corrugare 2. spiegazzare. ♦ to **wrinkle** vi. corrugarsi.
wrinkled, wrinkly agg. 1. corrugato 2. rugoso.
wrinkledness s. rugosità.
wrist s. polso.
wristband s. polsino.
to **write** (**wrote, written**) vt. scrivere || *to — back*, rispondere; *to — down*, annotare, descrivere; *to — off*, cancellare; *to — out*, copiare, emettere un assegno.
writer s. scrittore.
writhe s. contorcimento.

to **writhe** vt. contorcere. ♦ to **writhe** vi. 1. contorcersi 2. (*fig.*) fremere.
writing s. 1. lo scrivere 2. scrittura 3. scritto || — *-desk*, scrivania; — *-paper*, carta da lettere.
written V. *to write*.
wrong agg. 1. sbagliato 2. ingiusto 3. illegale. ♦ **wrong** avv. 1. erroneamente 2. ingiustamente.
wrong s. 1. torto 2. male || — *-doer*, peccatore, offensore; — *-doing*, peccato, offesa.
to **wrong** vt. 1. far torto a 2. imbrogliare.
wrongful agg. V. *wrong*.
wrongfulness s. ingiustizia.
wrongly avv. V. *wrong*.
wrote V. *to write*.
wrought agg. lavorato || — *-iron*, ferro battuto.
wrung V. *to wring*.
wry agg. storto.
to **wry** vt. contorcere. ♦ to **wry** vi. contorcersi.
wryly avv. per traverso.

X

xenophobe s. xenofobo.
xenophobia s. xenofobia.
xerophilous agg. xerofilo.
Xmas s. Natale.
X-ray agg. attr. a, di raggi X.
to **X-ray** vt. sottoporre a raggi X.
X-rays s. pl. raggi X.
xylograph s. xilografia.
xylographer s. xilografo.
xylographic(al) agg. xilografico.
xylography s. xilografia.
xylophone s. xilofono.
xylophonist s. xilofonista.

Y

yacht s. panfilo.
to **yacht** vi. fare crociere su panfilo.
yachtsman s. (*pl.* -men) proprietario di panfilo.
to **yank** vt. e vi. strappare, dare uno

strattone.
yap s. guaito.
to **yap** vi. guaire.
yard s. **1.** iarda **2.** cortile **3.** cantiere: *ship- —*, cantiere navale.
yarn s. **1.** filo **2.** (fig.) storia.
yawl s. (naut.) iole, piccola imbarcazione.
yawn s. **1.** sbadiglio **2.** apertura.
to **yawn** vi. **1.** sbadigliare **2.** aprirsi.
yawning agg. **1.** sonnolento **2.** spalancato.
yea avv. sì.
year s. anno: *— by —*, di anno in anno; *all the — round*, per tutto l'anno; *New Year's Day*, Capodanno.
yearbook s. annuario.
yearling agg. di un anno d'età. ◆ **yearling** s. animale di un anno.
yearlong agg. che dura un anno.
yearly agg. annuale. ◆ **yearly** avv. annualmente.
to **yearn** vi. languire || *to — for, after sthg.*, bramare qc.
yearning s. brama. ◆ **yearning** agg. bramoso.
yeast s. **1.** lievito **2.** fermento.
to **yeast** vi. **1.** lievitare **2.** fermentare.
yell s. urlo.
to **yell** vt. e vi. urlare.
yeller s. urlatore.
yellow agg. e s. giallo.
to **yellow** vt. e vi. ingiallire.
yellowish agg. giallastro.
yelp s. guaito.
to **yelp** vi. guaire.
yeoman s. piccolo proprietario terriero.
yes avv. sì.
yesterday avv. e s. ieri: *the day before —*, l'altro ieri; *— week*, ieri a otto.
yet avv. **1.** ancora **2.** già || *as —*, finora. ◆ **yet** cong. tuttavia.
yew s. *— (-tree)* tasso.
yield s. **1.** produzione **2.** (comm.) rendita.
to **yield** vt. e vi. **1.** produrre, rendere **2.** cedere || *to — oneself up*, arrendersi.
yielding agg. **1.** pieghevole **2.** docile.
yoke s. **1.** giogo **2.** barra (del timone) **3.** coppia (di animali).
to **yoke** vt. aggiogare.
yolk s. tuorlo.

yonder agg. quello là, di laggiù. ◆ **yonder** avv. là.
you pron. pers. **1.** tu, te, ti **2.** voi, ve, vi **3.** (forma di cortesia) Lei, Loro.
young agg. giovane || *— people*, i giovani (in genere).
youngster s. giovanetto.
your agg. poss. **1.** tuo **2.** vostro **3.** (forma di cortesia) Suo.
yours pron. poss. **1.** tuo **2.** vostro **3.** (forma di cortesia) Suo, Loro || *— truly*, *— faithfully*, distinti saluti.
yourself pron. r. **1.** tu stesso, ti, te, te stesso **2.** (forma di cortesia) Lei stesso.
yourselves pron. r. **1.** voi stessi, vi **2.** (forma di cortesia) Loro stessi.
youth s. **1.** gioventù **2.** ragazzo.
youthful agg. **1.** giovane **2.** giovanile.
youthfulness s. aspetto giovanile.
Yugoslav agg. e s. iugoslavo.

Z

zeal s. zelo.
zealot s. fanatico.
zealous agg. zelante.
zed s. zeta.
zenith s. zenit.
zephyr s. zeffiro.
zero s. **1.** zero **2.** (fig.) nullità.
zest s. **1.** gusto **2.** aroma.
zigzag agg. e avv. a zigzag.
to **zigzag** vi. andare a zigzag.
zinc s. zinco.
to **zinc** vt. zincare.
zincking s. zincatura.
zincograph s. zincografia.
to **zincograph** vt. imprimere su lastre di zinco.
zincographer s. zincografo.
zincography s. zincografia.
Zionism s. sionismo.
Zionist s. e agg. sionista.
zip s. fischio || *— (-fastener)*, cerniera lampo.
to **zip** vi. sibilare.
zipper s. cerniera lampo.
zircon s. zircone.
zirconium s. zirconio.
zodiac s. zodiaco.
zodiacal agg. zodiacale.

zonal, zonary *agg.* zonale.
zonate(d) *agg.* a zone.
zonation *s.* zonatura.
zone *s.* zona.
zoo *s.* zoo.
zoological *agg.* zoologico.
zoologist *s.* zoologo.
zoology *s.* zoologia.
zoom *s.* **1.** rombo **2.** (*aer.*) salita a candela.
to zoom *vi.* **1.** rombare **2.** (*aer.*) salire a candela.

zoomorphic *agg.* zoomorfo.
zoomorphism *s.* zoomorfismo.
zoophilist *s.* zoofilo.
zoophilous *agg.* zoofilo.
zoophily *s.* zoofilia.
zoophobia *s.* zoofobia.
zootechnic *agg.* zootecnico.
zootechnics, zootechny *s.* zootecnica.
zootomic(al) *agg.* zootomico.
zouave *s.* zuavo.
zygoma *s.* (*pl.* zygomata) zigomo.

NOMI PROPRI, STORICI E GEOGRAFICI

Abel Abele.
Abraham Abramo.
Abyssinia Abissinia.
Achilles Achille.
Adam Adamo.
Adolph Adolfo.
Adonis Adone.
Adriatic Sea Mar Adriatico.
Aegean Sea Mar Egeo
Aeneas Enea.
Aeschylus Eschilo.
Aesop Esopo.
Afghanistan Afganistan.
Agamemnon Agamennone.
Agatha Agata.
Agnes Agnese.
Ajax Aiace.
Albert Alberto
Aldous Aldo.
Alec, Alex *dim. di* Alexander.
Alexander Alessandro.
Alexandra Alessandra.
Alexis Alessio.
Alfred Alfredo.
Algiers Algeri.
Alps *pl.* Alpi.
Alsace Alsazia.
Amazon Rio delle Amazzoni.
Ambrose Ambrogio.
Andes *pl.* Ande.
Andrew Andrea.
Andy *dim. di* Andrew.
Angel Angelo.
Ann(e) Anna.
Annie *dim. di* Ann(e).
Antarctica Antartide.
Anthony Antonio.
Antoninus Antonino.
Antony Antonio.
Apennines *pl.* Appennini.
Aphrodite Afrodite.
Apulia Puglia.
Aragon Aragona.
Archimedes Archimede.
Ariadne Arianna.
Aristophanes Aristofane.
Aristotle Aristotele.
Armand Armando.
Arnold Arnaldo.
Arthur Arturo.
Athens Atene.
Atlantic Atlantico.

Augustin Agostino.
Augustus Augusto.
Azores *pl.* Azzorre.

Babel Babele.
Babylon Babilonia.
Bacchus Bacco.
Balearic Islands Baleari.
Balkans *pl.* Balcani.
Balthazar Baldassarre.
Baltic Sea Mar Baltico.
Baltimore Baltimora.
Baptist Battista.
Barcelona Barcellona.
Barnabas, Barnaby Barnaba.
Bartholomew Bartolomeo.
Basel Basilea.
Basil Basilio.
Beatrix Beatrice.
Belgium Belgio.
Belgrade Belgrado.
Benedict Benedetto.
Bengal Bengala.
Ben *dim. di* Benjamin.
Benjamin Beniamino.
Benny *dim. di* Benjamin.
Berlin Berlino.
Bermudas *pl.* Bermude.
Bern Berna.
Bernard Bernardo.
Bertha Berta.
Bess *dim. di* Elizabeth.
Bethlehem Betlemme.
Betty *dim. di* Elizabeth.
Bill(y) *dim. di* William.
Blanche Bianca.
Bob(by) *dim. di* Robert.
Bohemia Boemia.
Boniface Bonifacio.
Bosporus Bosforo.
Brandenburg Brandeburgo.
Brazil Brasile.
Brittany Bretagna.
Brutus Bruto.
Burma Birmania.

Cadiz Cadice.
Caesar Cesare.
Cain Caino.
Caius Caio.

Calvin Calvino.
Cambodia Cambogia.
Canada Canadà.
Capitol Campidoglio.
Caribbean Sea Mar dei Caraibi.
Caroline Carolina.
Carpathian Mountains *pl*. Carpazi.
Carthage Cartagine.
Cashmere Cascemir.
Caspian Sea Mar Caspio.
Cassiopeia Cassiopea.
Cassius Cassio.
Catherine Caterina.
Cato Catone.
Caucasus Caucaso.
Cecil Cecilio.
Channel (The) La Manica.
Charlemagne Carlomagno.
Charles Carlo.
Charlie *dim. di* Charles.
Charlotte Carlotta.
Chile Cile.
China Cina.
Christ Cristo.
Christine Cristina.
Christopher Cristoforo.
Cicero Cicerone.
Cinderella Cenerentola.
Clara Clara, Chiara.
Claude, Claudius Claudio.
Clement Clemente.
Clementine Clementina.
Clytemnestra Clitennestra.
Cologne Colonia.
Connie *dim. di* Constance.
Conrad Corrado.
Constance Costanza.
Constantine Costantino.
Constantinople Costantinopoli.
Corinth Corinto.
Cornelius Cornelio.
Cornwall Cornovaglia.
Crete Creta.
Cynthia Cinzia.
Cyprus Cipro.
Cyril Cirillo.
Cyrus Ciro.
Czechoslovakia Cecoslovacchia.

Daisy *dim. di* Margaret.
Damascus Damasco.
Damocles Damocle.
Dan *dim. di* Daniel.
Daniel Daniele.
Danny *dim. di* Daniel.
Danube Danubio.
Danzig Danzica.

Daphne Dafne.
Dardanelles *pl*. Dardanelli.
Darius Dario.
Dave *dim. di* David.
Deb(by) *dim. di* Deborah.
Deborah Debora.
Delphi Delfo.
Democritus Democrito.
Demosthenes Demostene.
Denmark Danimarca.
Dick *dim. di* Richard.
Dido Didone.
Diocletian Diocleziano.
Diogenes Diogene.
Dionysius Dionigi, Dionisio.
Dominic Domenico.
Domitian Domiziano.
Dorothy Dorotea.
Dublin Dublino.

Ed(dy) *dim. di* Edmund, Edward.
Edgar Edgardo.
Edinburgh Edimburgo.
Edmund Edmondo.
Edward Edoardo.
Egypt Egitto.
Eire (Stato Libero di) Irlanda.
Eleanor Eleonora.
Electra Elettra.
Elias, Elijah Elia.
Eliza Elisa.
Elizabeth Elisabetta.
Emanuel Emanuele.
Emily Emilia.
England Inghilterra.
Epaminondas Epaminonda.
Epicurus Epicuro.
Erasmus Erasmo.
Ernest Ernesto.
Esther Ester.
Ethiopia Etiopia.
Euclid Euclide.
Eugene Eugenio.
Euphrates Eufrate.
Euripides Euripide.
Europe Europa.
Eve Eva.
Evelyn Evelina.
Ezekiel Ezechiele.

Faust(us) Fausto.
Felix Felice.
Ferdinand Ferdinando.
Finland Finlandia.
Florence Firenze.
France Francia.
Frances Francesca.

Francis Francesco.
Frank Franco.
Frankfurt Francoforte.
Fred(dy) *dim. di* Frederic.
Frederic Federico.

Gabriel Gabriele.
Galilee Galilea.
Gascony Guascogna.
Gaule Gallia.
Geneva Ginevra.
Genoa Genova.
Geoffrey Goffredo.
George Giorgio.
Gerard Gerardo.
Germany Germania.
Gibraltar Gibilterra.
Gilbert Gilberto.
Golgotha Golgota.
Goliath Golia.
Grace Grazia.
Great Britain Gran Bretagna.
Greece Grecia.
Greenland Groenlandia.
Gregory Gregorio.
Guiana Guaiana.
Gustavus Gustavo.
Guy Guido.

Hadrian Adriano.
Hague (The) L'Aia.
Hamburg Amburgo.
Hamlet Amleto.
Hannibal Annibale.
Harold Aroldo.
Harriet Enrichetta.
Harry *dim. di* Harold, Henry.
Hebrides *pl.* Ebridi.
Hector Ettore.
Helen Elena.
Hellas Ellade.
Henrietta Enrichetta.
Henry Arrigo, Enrico.
Heraclitus Eraclito.
Herbert Erberto.
Hercules Ercole.
Hermes Ermete.
Herod Erode.
Herodotus Erodoto.
Hesiod Esiodo.
Hilary Ilario.
Himalaya Imalaia.
Hindustan Indostan.
Hippolytus Ippolito.
Holland Olanda.
Homer Omero.
Horace, Horatio Orazio.

Hubert Uberto.
Hugh Ugo.
Humbert Umberto.
Hungary Ungheria.

Icarus Icaro.
Iceland Islanda.
Ignatius Ignazio.
Innocent Innocente.
Ionian Sea Mar Ionio.
Ireland Irlanda.
Iris Iride.
Isaac Isacco.
Isabel Isabella.
Isaiah Isaia.
Ishmael Ismaele.
Isis Iside.
Israel Israele.
Italy Italia.

Jack(ie) *dim. di* John.
Jacob Giacobbe.
Jamaica Giamaica.
James Giacomo.
Jane Giovanna.
Janet *dim. di* Jane.
Japan Giappone.
Jason Giasone.
Java Giava.
Jean Giovanna.
Jeffrey Goffredo.
Jehovah Geova.
Jenny *dim. di* Jean.
Jeremiah Geremia.
Jericho Gerico.
Jerome Gerolamo.
Jerry *dim. di* Gerard, Jerome.
Jerusalem Gerusalemme.
Jesus Gesù.
Jim(my) *dim. di* James.
Jo *dim. di* Josephine.
Joan Giovanna.
Job Giobbe.
Joe *dim. di* Joseph.
John Giovanni.
Johnny *dim. di* John.
Jonah, Jonas Giona.
Jonathan Gionata.
Jordan Giordano.
Joseph Giuseppe.
Josephine Giuseppina.
Joshua Giosuè.
Jove Giove.
Judas, Jude Giuda.
Judea Giudea.
Judith Giuditta.
Judy *dim. di* Judith.

Julia Giulia.
Julian Giuliano.
Juliana Giuliana.
Julie Giulia.
Juliet Giulietta.
Julius Giulio.
Juno Giunone.
Jupiter Giove.
Juvenal Giovenale.

Kashmir Cascemir.
Kate, Kitty dim. di Catherine.
Korea Corea.

Lambert Lamberto.
Laocoon Laocoonte.
Lapland Lapponia.
Larry dim. di Lawrence.
Latium Lazio.
Launcelot Lancillotto.
Lausanne Losanna.
Lawrence Lorenzo.
Lazarus Lazzaro.
Leander Leandro.
Lebanon Libano.
Leghorn Livorno.
Leo(n) Leone.
Leonard Leonardo.
Leonidas Leonida.
Leopold Leopoldo.
Lethe Lete.
Letitia Letizia.
Lewis Luigi.
Libya Libia.
Liège Liegi.
Lisbon Lisbona
Livy Livio.
Liza, Lizzie, Liz(zy) dim. di Elizabeth.
Lombardy Lombardia.
London Londra.
Lou dim. di Louise.
Louis Luigi.
Louise Luigia, Luisa.
Louvain Lovanio.
Lucerne Lucerna.
Lucian Luciano.
Lucifer Lucifero.
Lucius Lucio.
Lucretius Lucrezio.
Lucy Lucia.
Luke Luca.
Luther Lutero.
Luxemburg Lussemburgo.
Lycurgus Licurgo.
Lydia Lidia.
Lyons Lione.

Magdalene Maddalena.
Mag(gie) dim. di Margaret.
Majorca Maiorca.
Malaya Malesia.
Manchuria Manciuria.
Manfred Manfredi.
Mantua Mantova.
Marathon Maratona.
Marcellus Marcello.
Margaret Margherita.
Margie dim. di Margaret.
Marianne Marianna.
Marius Mario.
Mark Marco.
Mars Marte.
Martha Marta.
Martial Marziale.
Martin Martino.
Mary Maria.
Matilda Matilde.
Matt dim. di Matthew.
Matthew Matteo.
Matty dim. di Martha, Matilda.
Maurice Maurizio.
Max dim. di Maximilian.
Maximilian Massimiliano.
May dim. di Mary.
Mediterranean Mediterraneo.
Meg dim. di Margaret.
Menelaus Menelao.
Mephistopheles Mefistofele.
Mercury Mercurio.
Merlin Merlino.
Methuselah Matusalemme.
Meuse Mosa.
Mexico Messico.
Michael Michele.
Mick(ey) dim. di Michael.
Midas Mida.
Mike dim. di Michael.
Milan Milano.
Minos Minosse.
Minotaur Minotauro.
Mithridates Mitridate.
Mohammed Maometto.
Moll(y) dim. di Mary.
Moluccas pl. Molucche.
Monaco (Principato di) Monaco.
Morocco Marocco.
Moscow Mosca.
Moses Mosè.
Mozambique Mozambico.
Munich Monaco di Baviera.
Mycenae Micene.

Naples Napoli.
Napoleon Napoleone.
Narcissus Narciso.

Nell(y) *dim. di* Helen.
Neptune Nettuno.
Nero Nerone.
Netherlands *pl.* Paesi Bassi.
Newfoundland Terranova.
New Zealand Nuova Zelanda.
Nice Nizza.
Nicholas Nicola.
Nick *dim. di* Nicholas.
Nile Nilo.
Noah Noè.
Normandy Normandia.
Norway Norvegia.

Oedipus Edipo.
Oliver Oliviero.
Olympus Olimpo.
Ophelia Ofelia.
Orestes Oreste.
Orion Orione.
Orkneys *pl.* Orcadi.
Orpheus Orfeo.
Osiris Osiride.
Oswald Osvaldo.
Othello Otello.
Ovid Ovidio.

Pacific Pacifico.
Paddy *dim. di* Patrick.
Padua Padova.
Palestine Palestina.
Pancras Pancrazio.
Papua Papuasia.
Paris[1] Paride.
Paris[2] Parigi.
Parnassus Parnaso.
Parthenon Partenone.
Pat *dim. di* Patricia, Patrick.
Patricia Patrizia.
Patrick Patrizio.
Paul Paolo.
Paula Paola.
Pauline Paolina.
Peg(gy) *dim.* di Margaret.
Peking Pechino.
Peloponnesus Peloponneso.
Pennsylvania Pensilvania.
Pericles Pericle.
Perseus Perseo.
Peru Perù.
Pete *dim. di* Peter.
Peter Pietro.
Phaedra Fedra.
Pharsalus Farsalo.
Philadelphia Filadelfia.
Philip Filippo.
Philippi Filippi.

Philippines *pl.* Filippine.
Piedmont Piemonte.
Pigmalion Pigmalione.
Pindar Pindaro.
Piraeus Pireo.
Pius Pio.
Plato Platone.
Pliny Plinio.
Plutarch Plutarco.
Poland Polonia.
Poll(y) *dim. di* Mary.
Polynesia Polinesia.
Pompey Pompeo.
Portugal Portogallo.
Prague Praga.
Prometheus Prometeo.
Ptolemy Tolomeo.
Pyrenees *pl.* Pirenei.
Pythagoras Pitagora.

Quentin Quintino.

Rachel Rachele.
Ramses Ramsete.
Raphael Raffaele, Raffaello.
Raymond Raimondo.
Remus Remo.
Rhine Reno.
Rhodes Rodi.
Rhone Rodano.
Richard Riccardo.
Rob *dim. di* Robert.
Robert Roberto.
Roderick Rodrigo.
Roger Ruggero.
Roland Orlando, Rolando.
Rome Roma.
Romulus Romolo.
Rosalie Rosalia.
Rosalind Rosalinda.
Rose Rosa.
Roumania Romania.
Roxana Rossana.
Rudolph Rodolfo.
Rudy *dim. di* Rudolph.

Sadie, Sally *dim. di* Sarah.
Sam *dim. di* Samuel.
Samson Sansone.
Samuel Samuele.
Sappho Saffo.
Sarah Sara.
Sardinia Sardegna.
Satan Satana.
Saturn Saturno.
Savoy Savoia.

Saxony Sassonia.
Scipion Scipione.
Scotland Scozia.
Sean Giovanni.
Sebastian Sebastiano.
Sibyl Sibilla.
Sicily Sicilia.
Silvester Silvestro.
Simeon Simeone.
Simon Simone.
Simplon Sempione.
Smyrna Smirne.
Socrates Socrate.
Sodom Sodoma.
Solomon Salomone.
Somaliland Somalia.
Sophia Sofia.
Sophocles Sofocle.
Soudan Sudan.
Spain Spagna.
Stephen Stefano.
Steve *dim. di* Stephen.
Stockholm Stoccolma.
Strasbourg Strasburgo.
Sue *dim. di* Susan(nah).
Sulla Silla.
Susy *dim. di* Susan(nah).
Susan(nah) Susanna.
Sweden Svezia.
Switzerland Svizzera.
Sylvia Silvia.
Syracuse Siracusa.
Syria Siria.

Tacitus Tacito.
Tangier(s) Tangeri.
Ted(dy) *dim. di* Edward.
Telemachus Telemaco.
Terence Terenzio.
Tess *dim. di* Theresa.
Thailand Tailandia.
Thames Tamigi.
Thebes Tebe.
Themistocles Temistocle.
Theodoric Teodorico.
Theresa Teresa.
Thermopylae *pl.* Termopili.
Theseus Teseo.
Thomas Tommaso.
Tiber Tevere.
Tiberius Tiberio.
Tirol Tirolo.
Titian Tiziano.
Titus Tito.
Tobias Tobia.
Toby *dim. di* Tobias.

Tom(my) *dim. di* Thomas.
Tonkin, Tonking Tonchino.
Tony *dim. di* Ant(h)ony.
Trajan Traiano.
Tristan, Tristram Tristano.
Troy Troia.
Tully Tullio.
Tunis Tunisi.
Turin Torino.
Turkey Turchia.
Tuscany Toscana.
Tyrol Tirolo.
Tyrrhenian Sea Mar Tirreno.

Ukraine Ucraina.
Ulysses Ulisse.
United States of America Stati
    Uniti d'America.
Urban Urbano.
Ursula Orsola.
USA Stati Uniti d'America.
USSR URSS (Unione Repubbliche
    Socialiste Sovietiche).

Valentine Valentino.
Valerius Valerio.
Vatican Vaticano.
Venetia Veneto.
Venice Venezia.
Venus Venere.
Vesuvius Vesuvio.
Victor Vittorio.
Victoria Vittoria.
Vincent Vincenzo.
Virgil Virgilio.
Vivian Viviana, Viviano.
Vulcan Vulcano.

Wales Galles.
Walter Gualtiero.
Warsaw Varsavia.
Will *dim. di* William.
William Guglielmo.
Willy *dim. di* William.

Xerxes Serse.

Yugoslavia Iugoslavia.

Zachary Zaccaria.
Zurich Zurigo.

SIGLE E ABBREVIAZIONI USATE
NEI PAESI DI LINGUA INGLESE

a., 1. *about*: c., circa **2.** *acre*: acro **3.** *approved*: approvato, riconosciuto dallo Stato.

A.A., *Automobile Association*: A.C., Automobile Club.

A.A.R., *against all risks*: contro ogni rischio.

Abp., *Archbishop*: arcivescovo.

abr., 1. *abridged*: ridotto (*di edizione*) **2.** *abridgment*: compendio.

A.C., *alternating current*: c.a., corrente alternata.

a/c, ac., *account*: c., conto.

A.D., *Anno Domini* (= *dopo Cristo*): d.C., dopo Cristo.

adj., *adjourned*: aggiornato.

Adm., *Admiral*: ammiraglio.

adv., *advertisement*: inserzione.

A.E.C., *Atomic Energy Commission*: C.E.A., Commissione per l'energia atomica.

A.F., *Air Force*: A.M., Aeronautica Militare.

Ala., *Alabama*.

Alas., *Alaska*.

alt., 1. *alternate*: alternata **2.** *alternating*: alternata.

a.m., *ante meridiem, before noon*: antimeridiano.

Am(er)., 1. *America*: Am., Amer., America **2.** *American*: am., amer., americano.

anon., *anonymous*: anonimo.

A.P., *Associated Press*: Stampa Associata.

app., *appendix*: app., appendice.

approx., *approximately*: appross., approssimativamente.

Apr., *April*: apr., aprile.

apt., *apartment*: appartamento.

Ariz., *Arizona*.

Ark., *Arkansas*.

arr., 1. *arrival*: arr., arrivo **2.** *arrived*: arr., arrivato.

ass., *association*: ass., associazione.

at. no., *atomic number*: n.a., numero atomico.

att(y)., *attorney*: proc., procuratore.

at. wt., *atomic weight*: p. at., peso atomico.

Aug., *August*: ago., agosto.

avdp., *avoirdupois*: avoirdupois.

ave., *avenue*: v.le, viale.

b., 1. *book*: l., libro **2.** *born*: n., nato.

B.A., *Bachelor of Arts*: diplomato in lettere.

Bap(t)., *Baptist*: Battista.

B.B.C., *British Broadcasting Corporation*: Ente Radiofonico Britannico.

B.C., *Before Christ*: a.C., avanti Cristo.

B/E, b.e., *bill of exchange*: cambiale.

B.E.A., *British European Airways*: Linee Aeree Europee Britanniche.

Beds., *Bedfordshire*.

Berks., *Berkshire*.

bet., *between*: fra.

B/L, *bill of lading*: polizza di carico.

blvd., *boulevard*: boulevard.

B.M., *British Museum*: Museo Britannico.

B.M.A., *British Medical Association*: Associazione Medica Britannica.

B.O.A.C., *British Overseas Airways Corporation*: Società aerea d'oltremare britannica.

B. of A., *Bank of America*: Banca d'America.

B. of E., *Bank of England*: Banca d'Inghilterra.

Bp., *Bishop*: vesc., vescovo.

bros., *brothers*: F.lli, Fratelli.

b.s., 1. *balance sheet*: bilancio di esercizio **2.** *bill of sale*: atto di vendita.

bsh., *bushel*: staio.

Bucks., *Buckinghamshire*.

bul(l)., *bulletin*: boll., bollettino.

c., 1. *centigrade*: c., centigrado **2.** *cent*: cent., centesimo **3.** *chapter*: cap., capitolo.

C/A, *current account*: c/c, conto corrente.

ca., 1. *cathode*: catodo **2.** *about*: ca., circa.

Cal(if)., *California*.

Cam(b)., *Cambridge*.

Cambs., *Cambridgeshire*.

Can., 1. *Canada*: Canada **2.** *Canadian*: canadese.

Cantab., *of Cambridge*: cantabrigense.

cap., 1. *chapter*: cap., capitolo **2.** *capital*: capitale.

Capt., *Captain*: cap., capitano.

Card., *Cardinal*: card., cardinale.

cc., 1. *chapters*: capp., capitoli **2.** *cubic centimetres*: cmc., centimetri cubi.

C.D., *Corps Diplomatique*: C.D., Corpo Diplomatico.

C.E.D., *Community for European Defence*: C.E.D., Comitato per la Difesa Europea.

Celt., *Celtic*: celtico.

cent., 1. *centigrade*: c., centigrado **2.** *centimetre*: cm., centimetro **3.** *central*: centrale **4.** *century*: sec., secolo.

c.f., *cost and freight*: c.f., costo e nolo.

C.F.I., c.f.i., *cost, freight and insurance*: costo, nolo e assicurazione.

Ch., 1. *Church*: Chiesa **2.** *China*: Cina **3.** *Chinese*: cinese.

ch(ap)., *chapter*: cap., capitolo.

Ches(h)., *Cheshire*.

Chr., 1. *Christ*: Cristo **2.** *Christian*: cristiano.

C.I.A., *Central Intelligence Agency*: Organizzazione centrale d'informazioni (Servizio segreto americano).

c.i.f., *cost, insurance, freight*: c.i.f., costo, assicurazione e nolo.

cm., *centimetre*: cm., centimetro.

Co., 1. *Company*: s., società **2.** *County*: contea.

c/o, *care of*: c/o, presso.

C.O.D., c.o.d., *cash on delivery*: pagamento alla consegna.

Col., 1. *Colonel*: col., colonnello **2.** *Colorado*.

coll., 1. *colleague*: collega **2.** *college*: coll., collegio **3.** *colloquial*: fam., familiare.

Colo., *Colorado*.

Conn., *Connecticut*.

Consol., *consolidated*: consolidato.

cont(d)., *continued*: continuo, ininterrotto.

coop., *co-operative*: coop., cooperativa.

corp., *corporation*: **1.** corporazione **2.** (*amer.*) s.r.l., società a responsabilità limitata.

Corn(w), *Cornwall*.

c.o.s., *cash on shipment*: pagamento alla spedizione.

C.P., *Communist Party*: P.C., Partito Comunista.

cp., *compare*: cfr., confrontare.

Ct., *Connecticut*.

cu., *cubic*: c., cubico.

Cumb., *Cumberland*.

C.U.P., *Cambridge University Press*: Edizioni dell'Università di Cambridge.

d., 1. *date*: data **2.** *dead*: m., morto **3.** *penny, pence*: penny, pence.

d.c., *direct current*: c.c., corrente continua.

D.A.B., *Dictionary of American Biography*: Dizionario della Biografia Americana.

Dak., *Dakota*.

D.C., *District of Columbia*: Distretto della Columbia.

D.D., *Doctor of Divinity*: dottore in teologia.

dd., d/d, *delivered*: consegnato.

Dec., *December*: dic., dicembre.

Del., *Delaware*.

dep., 1. *department*: reparto, ufficio; (*am.*) ministero **2.** *deputy*: deputato.

Devon., *Devonshire*.

Dir., *director*: dirett., direttore.

disc., *discount*: sconto.

D. Lit., *Doctor of Literature*: dottore in letteratura.

D.N.B., *Dictionary of National Biography*: Dizionario della Biografia Nazionale.

dol., *dollar*: dollaro.

Dorset., *Dorsetshire*.

doz., *dozen*: dozz., dozzina.

D.P., *Displaced Person*: profugo.

Dr., 1. *Doctor*: dott., dottore **2.** *Debtor*: debitore.

dz., *dozen*: dozz., dozzina.

E., 1. *East*: E, Est **2.** *English*: inglese.

ea., *each*: cad., cadauno.

E.B., *Encyclopaedia Britannica*: Enciclopedia Britannica.

E.C.A., *Economic Co-operation Administration*: Amministrazione della cooperazione economica.

E.C.M., *European Common Market*: M.E.C., Mercato Comune Europeo.

ed., **1.** *edited*: ed., edito **2.** *edition*: ed., edizione.

E.D.C., *European Defence Community*: C.E.D., Comunità per la difesa europea.

edit., V. *ed.*

Edin., *Edinburgh*.

e.g., *for example*: p. es., per esempio.

Emp., *Emperor*: imperatore.

enc(l)., *enclosure*: all., allegato.

Eng., **1.** *England*: Inghilterra **2.** *English*: inglese.

esp(ec)., *especially*: spec., specialmente.

Esq., *Esquire* (*titolo di cortesia usato negli indirizzi*): Egr., egregio.

etc., *and so on*: ecc., eccetera.

Eur., **1.** *Europe*: Europa **2.** *European*: europeo.

ex., **1.** *examined*: esaminato **2.** *example*: es., esempio **3.** *excepted*: eccetto **4.** *executive*: esecutivo.

exc., *except(ed)*: eccettuato.

F., *Fahrenheit*: F., Fahrenheit.

f., *frequency*: f., frequenza.

F.A.O., *Food and Agricultural Organization*: Organizzazione per l'agricoltura e l'alimentazione.

F.B.I., *Federal Bureau of Investigation*: Ufficio federale d'investigazione.

Feb., *February*: feb., febbraio.

Fed., **1.** *Federal*: fed., federale **2.** *Federation*: federazione.

Fla., **Flor.**, *Florida*.

F.O., *Foreign Office*: M.AA.EE., Ministero degli affari esteri.

F.O.B., **f.o.b.**, *free on board*: f.o.b., franco bordo.

fol., *folio*: folio.

fol(l)., *following*: seg., seguente.

Fr., **1.** *Father*: P., padre **2.** *France*: Francia **3.** *French*: francese **4.** *Friday*: ven., venerdì.

Fri., *Friday*: ven., venerdì.

ft., *foot*, *feet*: piede, piedi.

g., **1.** *conductance*: conduttanza **2.** *gender*: genere **3.** *gram*: g., grammo **4.** *guinea*: ghinea.

Ga., *Georgia*.

gal(l)., *gallon*: gallone.

G.B., *Great Britain*: Gran Bretagna.

Gen., *General*: gen., generale.

gen., **1.** *gender*: genere **2.** *generally*: gen., generalmente.

gent., *gentleman*: gentiluomo, signore.

G.H.Q., *General Headquarters*: Q.G., quartier generale.

G.I., *Government Issue*: promulgazione ministeriale.

Gloster., *Gloucestershire*.

G-Man., *Government Man*: soldato governativo.

G.O.P., *Grand Old Party* (*U.S. Republican Party*): Partito Repubblicano Americano.

G.P.O., *General Post Office*: Posta centrale.

H, *hydrogen*: H., idrogeno.

h., **1.** *hour*: h., ora **2.** *high*: A., alto.

H.B.M., *His (Her) Britannic Majesty*: S.M.B., Sua Maestà Britannica.

H.C., *House of Commons*: Camera dei Comuni.

H.E., *His Excellency*: S.E., Sua Eccellenza.

Hereford., *Herefordshire*.

Herts., *Hertfordshire*.

hf., *half*: metà.

H.H., **1.** *His Holiness*: S.S., Sua Santità **2.** *His (Her) Highness*: S.A., Sua Altezza.

hhd., *hogshead*: hogshead (*misura di capacità l. 238,5*).

H.L., *House of Lords*: Camera Alta.

H.M., *His (Her) Majesty*: V.M., Vostra Maestà.

H.M.S., *His (Her) Majesty's Service*: servizio di Sua Maestà.

Hon., *Honourable*: on., onorèvole.

H.P., **1.** *high pressure*: alta pressione **2.** *horse power*: H.P., cavalli vapore.

hr., *hour*: h., ora.

H.S., *High School*: scuola media superiore.

Hunts., *Huntingdonshire*.

I(a)., *Iowa*.

ib(id)., *in the same place*: ibid., nello stesso luogo.

I.D., *Intelligence Department*: reparto informazioni.

id., *the same*: id., come sopra.

Id(a)., *Idaho*.

i.e., *that is*: cioè.

Ill., *Illinois*.

in., *inch*: pollice (*misura*).

inc., 1. *incorporated*: incorporato **2.** *including*: incluso.

inst., *instant (the present month)*: c.m., corrente mese.

I.O.U., *I owe you*: pagherò.

I.Q., *Intelligence Quotient*: Q.I., quoziente d'intelligenza.

Ire., *Ireland*.

Ja(n)., *January*: genn., gennaio.

J.P., *Justice of the Peace*: giudice di pace.

Jr., jun., *junior*: iun., junior.

Kan(s)., *Kansas*.

kg., *kilogram*: kg., chilogrammo.

kilo., 1. *kilogram*: chilogrammo **2.** *kilometre*: km., chilometro.

K.K.K., *Ku Klux Klan*: K.K.K., Ku Klux Klan.

km., *kilometre*: km., chilometro.

K.O., *knock out*: fuori combattimento.

kw., *kilowatt*: kw., chilowatt.

Ky., *Kentucky*.

L., *pound*: L.st., lira sterlina.

l., 1. *litre*: l., litro **2.** *long*: lungo.

La., *Louisiana*.

Lancs., *Lancashire*.

Lat., *Latin*: latino.

lat., *latitude*: latitudine.

lb., *pound*: libbra.

L.C.D., *lowest common denominator*: m.c.d., minimo comun denominatore.

L.C.M., *least common multiple*: m.c.m., minimo comune multiplo.

Leics., *Leicestershire*.

L.F., *low frequency*: b.f., bassa frequenza.

Lieut., *Lieutenant*: luogotenente.

Lincs., *Lincolnshire*.

LL.D., *Doctor of Laws*: dottore in legge.

Lon., *London*: Londra.

lon(g)., *longitude*: longitudine.

L.P., 1. *Labour Party*: Partito Laburista **2.** *Long Play*: microsolco.

L.R., *Lloyd's Register*: Registro dei Lloyd.

Ltd., *limited*: s.r.l., società a responsabilità limitata.

m., 1. *male*: m., maschio **2.** *metre*: m., metro **3.** *mile*: miglio **4.** *minute*: m., minuto **5.** *month*: m., mese.

M.A., *Master of Arts*: laureato in lettere.

Mad., Madm., *Madam*: sig.ra, signora.

Maj., *Major*: magg., maggiore.

Mar., *March*: mar., marzo.

Mass., *Massachusetts*.

max., *maximum*: mass., massimo.

M.C., *Member of Congress*: membro del Congresso.

Md., *Maryland*.

M.D., *Doctor of Medicine*: dottore in medicina.

Mdx., *Middlesex*.

Me., *Maine*.

M.F., *medium frequency*: m.f., media frequenza.

mg(m)., *milligram*: mg., milligrammo.

Mich., *Michigan*.

Minn., *Minnesota*.

Miss., *Mississippi*.

mm., *millimetre*: mm., millimetro.

Mo., 1. *Missouri* **2.** *Monday*: lun., lunedì.

M.O., *money order*: ordine di pagamento.

Mon., *Monday*: lun., lunedì.

Mont., *Montana*.

M.P., 1. *Military Police*: Polizia militare **2.** *Member of Parliament*: membro del Parlamento.

mph., *miles per hour*: miglia orarie.

Mr., *Mister*: sig., signor.

Mrs., *Mistress*: sig.ra, signora.

M/S, *motorship*: M/n, motonave.

MS., *manuscript*: ms., manoscritto.

MSS., *manuscripts*: mss., manoscritti.

Mt., *mount*: M., monte.

mus., 1. *museum*: mus., museo **2.** *music*: musica.

N., *North*: N, Nord.

n., 1. *born*: n., nato **2.** *number*: n., numero.

N.A.T.O., *North Atlantic Treaty Organization*: P.A., Patto atlantico.

N.B.C., *National Broadcasting Company*: Compagnia radiofonica nazionale.

N.C., *North Carolina*.

N.C.O., *non-commissioned officer*: s. uff., sottufficiale.

N. D(ak)., *North Dakota*.

Neb(r)., *Nebraska*.

Nev., *Nevada*.

New M., *New Mexico*.

N.H., *New Hampshire.*

N.J., *New Jersey.*

N. M(ex)., *New Mexico.*

no., *number*: n., numero.

Norf., *Norfolk.*

Northum(b)., *Northumberland*

nos., *numbers*: numeri.

Notts., *Nottinghamshire.*

Nov., *November*: nov., novembre.

N.Y., *New York*: Nuova York.

O., *Ohio.*

Oct., *October*: ott., ottobre.

O.E.D., *Oxford English Dictionary*: Dizionario Inglese Oxford.

Okla., *Oklahoma.*

op. cit., *in the work cited*: op. cit., opera citata.

Ore(g)., *Oregon.*

O.U.P., *Oxford University Press*: Edizioni dell'Università di Oxford.

Ox(f)., *Oxford.*

Oxon., 1. *Oxford* 2. *of Oxford*: ossoniese 3. *Oxfordshire ounce*: oncia.

P., *(car-)park*: P., parcheggio.

p., 1. *page*: p., pagina 2. *past*: pass., passato.

Pa., *Pennsylvania.*

P.A.A., *Pan American Airways*: Linee aeree panamericane.

par., *paragraph*: parag., paragrafo.

pat., 1. *patent*: brev., brevetto 2. *patented*: brevettato.

P.A.Y.E., *pay as you earn (trattenuta di ricchezza mobile)*: R.M., ricchezza mobile.

pd., *paid*: pagato.

Penn(a). v. *Pa.*

Ph. D., *Doctor of Philosophy*: dottore in filosofia.

P.M., *Prime Minister*: Primo Ministro.

p.m., *post meridiem (after noon)*: pomeridiano.

P.O., p.o., 1. *Post Office*: U.P., f-ficio postale 2. *postal order*: V., vaglia.

P.O.B., *post office box*: C.P., casella postale.

p.o.d., *pay on delivery*: pagamento alla consegna.

pp., *pages*: pagg., pagine.

prep., *preparation*: preparazione.

Pres., *President*: pres., presidente.

Prof., *Professor*: prof., professore.

prox., *next*: prossimo.

P.S., *postscript*: P.S., poscritto.

p.t.o., *please turn over*: voltare pagina.

Q.M.G., *Quartermaster General*: capo dipartimento amministrazione e alloggi.

qu., 1. *quart*: misura di capacità (l. 1.136) 2. *quarter*: quarto.

quot., *quotation*: citazione.

R., r., 1. *river*: f., fiume 2. *road*: strada.

R.A.C., *Royal Automobile Club*: Regio Automobile Club.

R.A.D.I.A.C., *Radioactivity Detection Identification and Computation*: Rivelazione, identificazione e calcolo della radioattività.

R.A.F., *Royal Air Force*: Regia Aviazione militare.

R.C., 1. *Red Cross*: C.R., Croce Rossa 2. *Roman Catholic*: Cattolico Romano.

R.C.A., *Radio Corporation of America*: Associazione Radiofonica Americana.

re., *reference* 1. ref., referenza 2. riferimento.

rec., 1. *receipt*: ricevuta 2. *record*: record.

reg., 1. *region*: regione 2. *register*: reg., registro 3. *regular*: regolare.

Rev., *Reverend*: rev., reverendo.

R.H., *Royal Highness*: A.R., Altezza Reale.

R.N., *Royal Navy*: Regia Marina.

Rt. Hon., *Right Honourable*: molto onorevole.

Rt. Rev., *Right Reverend*: molto reverendo.

Ry., *Railway*: ferrovia.

S., *South*: S, Sud.

s., 1. *second*: secondo 2. *shilling*: scellino.

Sat., *Saturday*: sab., sabato.

S.C., *South Carolina.*

sch., *school*: sc., scuola.

Scot., 1. *Scotland*: Scozia 2. *Scottish*: scozzese.

S. D(ak)., *South Dakota.*

sec., 1. *second*: secondo 2. *section*: sezione 3. *secretary*: segr., segretario

Sen., 1. *Senate*: senato 2. *senator*: senatore 3. *senior*: senior.

Sept., *September*: sett., settembre.

Sergt., *sergeant*: serg., sergente.

sh., *shilling*: scellino.

S.H.A.P.E., *Supreme Headquarters Allied Powers Europe*: quartier generale delle Forze alleate in Europa.

Shrops., *Shropshire*.

So., **1**. *South*: S, Sud **2**. *Southern*: sudista.

Soc., *society*: s., società.

Somerset., *Somersetshire*.

spec., **1**. *special*: spec., speciale **2**. *specification*: specificazione.

sp. gr., *specific gravity*: gravità specifica.

sq., *square*: p.za, piazza.

Sr., **1**. *senior*: senior **2**. *Sir*: Sir **3**. *sister*: sorella.

SS, S/S, *steamship*: piroscafo.

St., **1**. *Saint*: s., santo **2**. *street*: via.

st., *stone*: misura di peso (*Kg. 6,350*).

Staffs., *Staffordshire*.

ster., **stg.**, *sterling*: L.st., lira sterlina.

St. Ex., *Stock Exchange*: Borsa valori.

Sun(d)., *Sunday*: dom., domenica.

Sup. Ct., *Supreme Court*: C.S., Corte suprema.

supp(l)., *supplement*: supplemento.

Sur., *Surrey*.

Sus., *Sussex*.

S.W., **1**. *South Wales*: Galles del sud **2**. *South West*: S.O., sud ovest.

Swit., **Swtz.**, *Switzerland*: Svizzera.

syn., *synonym*: sinonimo

Sy., *Surrey*.

t., **1**. *ton*: t., tonnellata **2**. *volume*: v., volume.

T.B., *tuberculosis*: tbc, tubercolosi.

tel., **1**. *telegram*: telegramma **2**. *telegraph*: telegrafo **3**. *telephone*: tel., telefono.

Tenn., *Tennessee*.

Tex., *Texas*.

Thur(s)., *Thursday*: giov., giovedì.

T.O., *turn over*: voltare.

T.U., *Trade-Union*: Sindacato.

Tu(es)., *Tuesday*: mar., martedì.

TV., *television*: TV, televisione.

T.W.A., *Trans World Airlines*: linee aeree intercontinentali.

U., **1**. *Union*: U., unione **2**. *University*: Università.

U.K., *United Kingdom*: R.U., Regno Unito.

U.N., *United Nations*: N.U., Nazioni Unite.

U.N.E.S.C.O., *United Nations Educational Scientific and Cultural Organization*: Organizzazione culturale, scientifica e per l'educazione delle Nazioni Unite.

U.N.I.C.E.F., *United Nations International Children's Emergency Fund*: Fondo d'emergenza internazionale per l'infanzia delle Nazioni Unite.

U.N.O., *United Nations Organization*: O.N.U., Organizzazione delle Nazioni Unite.

U.P., *United Press*: Stampa associata.

U.S., *United States*: S.U., Stati Uniti.

U.S.A., **1**. *United States of America*: S.U.A., Stati Uniti d'America **2**. *United States Army*: Esercito degli Stati Uniti.

U.S.A.E.C., *United States Atomic Energy Commission*: commissione per l'energia atomica degli Stati Uniti.

U.S.A.F., *United States Air Force*: Aviazione militare degli Stati Uniti.

U.S.I.S., *United States Information Service*: Servizio informazioni degli Stati Uniti.

U.S.N., *United States Navy*: Marina degli Stati Uniti.

U.S.S.R., *Union of Soviet Socialist Republics*: U.R.S.S., Unione delle repubbliche socialiste sovietiche.

U.S.S., *United States Ship*: nave degli Stati Uniti.

Ut., *Utah*.

v., *verse*: v., verso.

Va., *Virginia*.

Vat., *Vatican*: Vaticano.

Ven., *Venerable*: Ven., venerabile.

V.H.F., *very high frequency*: altissima frequenza.

Vic(t)., *Victoria*.

V.I.P., *Very Important Person*: Persona molto importante.

viz., *namely*: cioè.

vol., *volume*: vol., volume.

V.P., *Vice-President*: vicepresidente.

vs., *against*: contro.

Vt., *Vermont*.

Vul(g)., *Vulgate*: Vulgata.

vv., *verses*: vv., versi.

w., *watt*: W., watt.

W., 1. *West*: O, Ovest **2.** *Washington.*

w., 1. *week*: settimana **2.** *wife*: moglie **5.** *with*: con.

Warwick., *Warwickshire.*

Wash., *Washington.*

W.D., *War Department*: Ministero della Guerra.

Wed., *Wednesday*: mer., mercoledì.

Westm., *Westminster.*

Westmore., *Westmoreland.*

whf., *wharf*: pontile.

Wis(c)., *Wisconsin.*

wk., 1. *week*: settimana **2.** *work*: lavoro.

w.l., *wave length*: lunghezza d'onda.

Worcs., *Worcestershire.*

W.R.A.C., *Women's Royal Army Corps*: Regio corpo d'armata femminile.

wt., *weight*: peso.

W.Va., *West Virginia*: Virginia dell'ovest.

Wy(o)., *Wyoming.*

Xmas., *Christmas*: Natale.

y., 1. *yard*: iarda **2.** *year*: anno.

yd., *yard*: iarda.

Y.H.A., *Youth Hostels Association*: Associazione Ostelli per la gioventù.

Y.M.C.A., *Young men's Christian Association*: Associazione Cristiana per i giovani.

yr., 1. *year*: anno **2.** *your*: vostro.

Yorks., *Yorkshire.*

yrs., 1. *years*: anni **2.** *yours*: vostri.

Y.W.C.A., *Young Women's Christian Association*: Associazione Cristiana per le giovani.

Z., *atomic number*: n.a., numero atomico.

&, *and*: e.

&c., *and so forth*: etc., ecc., eccetera.

PREFACE TO THE ITALIAN-ENGLISH SECTION OF THE
PICCOLO DIZIONARIO ITALIANO-INGLESE

1. The first part of the English-Italian section of the **Compact Dictionary** contains information in Italian designed to help in its use. It gives rules of pronunciation, a list of irregular verbs, tables of comparison of the English and American units and metric system, information on the English and American currency, a list of cardinal and ordinal numbers, and an explanatory list of the abbreviations used.

A similar introduction is included here to help in the use of the Italian-English section.

2. Since Italian presents particular problems with its verbs we have provided a list of irregular verbs in general use. We have not included their compounds, as they are conjugated in the same way.

Those verbs which take *essere* as an auxiliary are indicated by means of a single star. Those which take *essere* when used intransitively and *avere* when used transitively have a double star.

With the past definite tense we have shown the 1st person singular only, since the 3rd person singular and the 3rd person plural follow the same pattern, while the 2nd person singular and plural are regular in form e.g.: *prendere* – **presi**, *prendesti*, **prese**, *prendemmo, prendeste*, **presero**.

3. There are two points concerning the current use of verbs which the student of Italian may well find helpful:

a) there is a tendency in modern Italian towards a more frequent use of the perfect tense to represent completed past action (though such irrefutable statements of the past as, for example, *Dante died in 1321* would still always be translated as *Dante morì . . .*);

b) though the polite form in the singular, with *Lei* and the 3rd person of the verb, is regularly used e.g.: *Lei scrive in inglese?* (Are you writing in English?), the plural form addressed to more than one person is now more frequently the 2nd person plural with *Voi*, instead of the 3rd person plural with *Loro* e.g.: *Voi scrivete in inglese?* rather than *Loro scrivono in inglese?*

4. As some Italian nouns have irregular plurals or do not change their form in the plural we have included a list of the more commonly used ones.

5. In illustrating the possible alternative translations for the Italian words listed, the following symbols have been adopted:

a) a double line (‖) after the initial translation or translations indicates a grammatical change from, for example, an adjective to a noun or a pronoun to an adverb;

b) a lozenge (♦) indicates something more than just an alternative translation, showing, for example, a figurative or idiomatic use;

c) the numbers printed in large type (1., 2., 3., etc.) indicate the various alternative meanings;

d) the small numbers ([1], [2], [3], etc.) indicate words of identical form but different meaning.

The Alphabet

The Italian alphabet consists of 21 letters only. j *(i lunga)*, k *(cappa)*, w *(doppio vu)*, x *(ics)*, y *(ipsilon)* do not occur in the alphabet, though they are used for the spelling of foreign words e.g.: *judo, kimono, watt, xenofobia, yacht*. In some cases y is replaced by i, e.g. *raion* for rayon. ch replaces k, e.g. *chilogramma* for kilogram. ph is represented by f, e.g. *fobia* for phobia. x occurs in certain expressions such as *ex-presidente, extraterritoriale*, etc.

Letter	Name	Letter	Name
a	*a*	m	*emme*
b	*bi*	n	*enne*
c	*ci*	o	*o*
d	*di*	p	*pi*
e	*e*	q	*cu*
f	*effe*	r	*erre*
g	*gi*	s	*esse*
h	*acca*	t	*ti*
i	*i*	u	*u*
l	*elle*	v	*vu*
		z	*zeta*

Pronunciation

Since Italian is a phonetic language, once the rules of pronunciation are learnt, it is possible to pronounce most words correctly, though it is not always easy to tell on which syllable the tonic stress falls.

The Vowels

Italian vowels are pure sounds and should be pronounced well forward in the mouth:

A	like a in far	*gala*
close E	like a in fate	*seta*
open E	like e in ten	*pelle*
I	like i in machine	*vino*
close O	like o in store	*corte*
open O	like o in spot	*motto*
U	like oo in spoon	*uso*

The Consonants

In the case of double consonants each consonant is sounded, with the voice rising on them and falling on the following vowel.

The consonants **B, D, F, L, M, N, P, Q, T** and **V** are pronounced very much as in English. The rest are as follows:

C   1. before **a, o, u**, and consonants, including **h**: like **c** in cat, as in *casa, crema, chilo*;

     2. before **e** or **i**: like **ch** in chip, as in *cena, cibo*.

G   1. before **a, o, u** and consonants, including **h** but not including **l** and **n**: like **g** in gap, as in *gala, grido, ghiro*;

     2. before **e** or **i**: like **g** in gem, as in *gente, gita*.

gli like **lli** in billion, as in *figlia*; (a few exceptions have the **gli** pronounced as in English, e.g. *anglicano, negligente*).

gn like **ni** in onion, as in *signore*.

H   is always silent and occurs in very few words, except as shown above to harden the **c** and **g** sounds before **e** and **i**.

Q   is always followed by **u**, like **qu** in quick, as in *quinto*.

R   is rolled, rather as in **rr** Scottish pronunciation, as in *pera, serra*.

S   1. is voiced, like **s** in rose, as in *rosa, esatto,* or when followed by **b, d, g, l, m, n, r, v**, the voiceless consonants, as in *sdegno, svelto*;

     2. is unvoiced like **s** in sap, at the beginning of a word, or when it is doubled, as in *sega, rosso*.

sc 1. before **e** or **i** is like **sh** in shot, as in *scena*;

     2. before **a, o** and **u** is like **sk** in skate, as in *scarpa, scopo, scudo*;

     3. an **h** after it and before **e** or **i** makes it like **sk**, as in *schema, schiena*;

     4. an **i** after it and before **a, o** or **u** makes it like **sh**, as in *scialle, sciocco, sciupare*.

Z   1. voiced like **ds** in treads, as in *zio*;

     2. unvoiced like **ts** in wits, as in *forza*.

Accentuation

In printed and written Italian an accent is used to indicate when the toni stress falls on a final vowel such as in *città* or *caffè*. It is also used to distinguish between two words which are spelt and pronounced alike but have different meanings:

è = is	*e* = and
dà = he gives	*da* = from, by, of, etc.

It also occurs on some monosyllabic words as in *già* and *più*.

In print the acute accent is used to indicate a stress on a final **e** as in *perché* or *né*, though in handwriting the grave accent is more usual. In modern Italian the grave accent is normally used elsewhere and we have followed this practice.

As a general rule the tonic stress is on the penultimate syllable, but this is not by any means always so. The grave and acute accents have been used to show where the stress falls when it does not fall on the penultimate syllable. The open and close e are distinguished in the accepted way by means of è and é, e.g. *créscere, crédere, festival, férvido,* and the grave accent is used everywhere else, e.g. *càndido, moltitùdine.*

IRREGULAR ITALIAN VERBS†

Accendere – *p. def.* accesi, *p.p.* acceso

Accludere – see alludere

Addurre – *pres.* adduco, *p. def.* addussi, *fut.* addurrò, *p.p.* addotto

Affliggere – *p. def.* afflissi, *p.p.* afflitto

Alludere – *p. def.* allusi, *p.p.* alluso

Andare* – *pres.* vado, vai, va, andiamo, andate, vanno *fut.* andrò

Annettere – *p. def.* annettei (annessi), *p.p.* annesso

Apparire* – *pres.* apparisco, *p. def.* apparii (apparvi, apparsi), *p.p.* apparso

Appendere – *p. def.* appesi, *p.p.* appeso

Ardere – *p. def.* arsi, *p.p.* arso

Aspergere – *p. def.* aspersi, *p.p.* asperso

Assalire – *pres.* assalgo (assalisco), assalgono

Assolvere – *p. def.* assolsi (assolvei, assolvetti), *p.p.* assolto

Assumere – *p. def.* assunsi, *p.p.* assunto

Bere – *pres.* bevo, *p. def.* bevvi, *fut.* berrò

Cadere* – *p. def.* caddi, *fut.* cadrò

Cedere – *p. def.* cedei (cedetti)

Chiedere – *p. def.* chiesi, *p.p.* chiesto

Chiudere – *p. def.* chiusi, *p.p.* chiuso

Cingere – *p. def.* cinsi, *p.p.* cinto

Cogliere – *pres.* colgo, colgono, *p. def.* colsi, *p.p.* colto

Comprimere – *p. def.* compressi, *p.p.* compresso

Conoscere – *p. def.* conobbi, *p.p.* conosciuto

Consumare – *p. def.* consumai (consunsi), *p.p.* consumato (consunto)

Correre** – *p. def.* corsi, *p.p.* corso

Costruire – *p.p.* costruito (costrutto)

Crescere* – *p. def.* crebbi, *p.p.* cresciuto

Cucire – *pres.* cucio

Cuocere – *pres.* cuocio, cuoci, cuoce. cociamo, cocete, cuociono, *p. def.* cossi, *p.p.* cotto

Dare – *pres.* do, dai, dà, diamo, date, danno, *p. def.* diedi (detti), desti, *fut.* darò, *p.p.* dato

† Verbs which take *essere* are indicated by one star.

Those taking *avere* and *essere* have two stars.

Decidere – *p. def.* decisi, *p.p.* deciso
Difendere – *p. def.* difesi, *p.p.* difeso
Dipendere** – *p. def.* dipesi, *p.p.* dipeso
Dipingere – *p. def.* dipinsi, *p.p.* dipinto
Dire – *pres.* dico, dite, *p. def.* dissi, *fut.* dirò, *p.p.* detto
Dirigere – *p. def.* diressi, *p.p.* diretto
Discutere – *p. def.* discussi, *p.p.* discusso
Dissolvere – *p. def.* dissolsi (dissolvei), *p.p.* dissolto
Distinguere – *p. def.* distinsi, *p.p.* distinto
Dividere – *p. def.* divisi, *p.p.* diviso
Dolersi* – *pres.* mi dolgo, ti duoli, si duole, ci doliamo, vi dolete, si dolgono, *p. def.* mi dolsi, *fut.* mi dorrò
Dovere – *pres.* devo (debbo), devi, deve, dobbiamo, dovete, devono (debbono), *fut.* dovrò

Eccellere – *p. def.* eccelsi, *p.p.* eccelso
Emergere* – *p. def.* emersi, *p.p.* emerso
Ergere – *p. def.* ersi, *p.p.* erto
Erigere – *p. def.* eressi, *p.p.* eretto
Esigere – *p.p.* esatto
Espellere – *p. def.* espulsi, *p.p.* espulso
Esplodere** – *p. def.* esplosi, *p.p.* esploso
Evadere* – *p. def.* evasi, *p.p.* evaso

Fare – *pres.* faccio (fo), fai, fa, facciamo, fate, fanno, *imper.* facevo, *p. def.* feci, *fut.* farò, *p.p.* fatto
Fendere – *p. def.* fendei (fendetti), *p.p.* fesso (fenduto)
Figgere – *p. def.* fissi, *p.p.* fisso (fitto)
Fingere – *p. def.* finsi, *p.p.* finto
Fondere – *p. def.* fusi, *p.p.* fuso
Frangere – *p. def.* fransi, *p.p.* franto
Friggere – *p. def.* frissi, *p.p.* fritto

Giacere* – *pres.* giaccio, giacciono, *p. def.* giacqui, *p.p.* giaciuto
Giungere* – *p. def.* giunsi, *p.p.* giunto
Godere – *fut.* godrò

Incutere – *p. def.* incussi (incutei), *p.p.* incusso
Indulgere – *p. def.* indulsi, *p.p.* indulto
Intridere – *p. def.* intrisi, *p.p.* intriso
Invadere – *p. def.* invasi, *p.p.* invaso

Ledere – *p. def.* lesi, *p.p.* leso
Leggere – *p. def.* lessi, *p.p.* letto

Mettere – *p. def.* misi, *p.p.* messo

Mordere – *p. def.* morsi, *p.p.* morso

Morire* – *pres.* muoio, muori, muore, moriamo, morite, muoiono, *fut.* morrò, *p.p.* morto

Mungere – *p. def.* munsi, *p.p.* munto

Muovere – *pres.* moviamo, movete, *p. def.* mossi, *p.p.* mosso

Nascere* – *p. def.* nacqui, *p.p.* nato

Nascondere – *p. def.* nascosi, *p.p.* nascosto

Nuocere – *pres.* noccio, nociamo, nocete, nocciono, *p. def.* nocqui, *p.p.* nociuto

Offrire – *p. def.* offrii (offersi), *p.p.* offerto

Parere* – *pres.* paio, paiamo, paiono, *p. def.* parvi, *fut.* parrò, *p.p.* parso

Percuotere – *p.p.* percosso

Perdere – *p. def.* persi (perdei, perdetti), *p.p.* perduto (perso)

Persuadere – *p. def.* persuasi, *p.p.* persuaso

Piacere* – *pres.* piaccio, piaci, piace, piacciamo, piacete, piacciono, *p. def.* piacqui, *p.p.* piaciuto

Piangere – *p. def.* piansi, *p.p.* pianto

Piovere** – *p. def.* piovve, piovvero

Porgere – *p. def.* porsi, *p.p.* porto

Porre – *pres.* pongo, poni, pone, poniamo, ponete, pongono, *p. def.* posi, *fut.* porrò, *p.p.* posto

Potere – *pres.* posso, puoi, può, possiamo, potete, possono, *fut.* potrò

Prediligere – *p. def.* predilessi, *p.p.* prediletto

Prendere – *p. def.* presi, *p.p.* preso

Proteggere – *p. def.* protessi, *p.p.* protetto

Pungere – *p. def.* punsi, *p.p.* punto

Radere – *p. def.* rasi, *p.p.* raso

Redimere – *p. def.* redensi, *p.p.* redento

Reggere – *p. def.* ressi, *p.p.* retto

Rendere – *p. def.* resi, *p.p.* reso

Ridere – *p. def.* risi, *p.p.* riso

Rifulgere** – *p. def.* rifulsi, *p.p.* rifulso

Rispondere – *p. def.* risposi, *p.p.* risposto

Rodere – *p. def.* rosi, *p.p.* roso

Rompere – *p. def.* ruppi, *p.p.* rotto

Salire** – *pres.* salgo, salgono

Sapere – *pres.* so, sai, sa, sappiamo, sapete, sanno, *p. def.* seppi, *fut.* saprò

Scegliere – *pres.* scelgo, scelgono, *p. def.* scelsi, *p.p.* scelto

Scendere** – *p. def.* scesi, *p.p.* sceso

Scindere – *p. def.* scissi, *p.p.* scisso

Sciogliere – *pres.* sciolgo, sciolgono, *p. def.* sciolsi, *p.p.* sciolto

Scrivere – *p. def.* scrissi, *p.p.* scritto

Scuotere – *p. def.* scossi, *p.p.* scosso

Sedere* – *pres.* siedo (seggo), siedi, siede, sediamo, sedete, siedono (seggono)

Soddisfare – *pres.* soddisfo (soddisfaccio, soddisfò), soddisfi (soddisfai), soddisfa, soddisfiamo (soddisfacciamo), soddisfate, soddisfano (soddisfanno), *p. def.* soddisfeci, *p.p.* soddisfatto

Sorgere* – *p. def.* sorsi, *p.p.* sorto

Spargere – *p. def.* sparsi, *p.p.* sparso

Spegnere – *p. def.* spensi, *p.p.* spento

Spendere – *p. def.* spesi, *p.p.* speso

Spingere – *p. def.* spinsi, *p.p.* spinto

Stare* – *pres.* sto, stai, sta, stiamo, state, stanno, *imperf.* stavo, *p. def.* stetti, *p.p.* stato

Stringere – *p. def.* strinsi, *p.p.* stretto

Struggere – *p. def.* strussi, *p.p.* strutto

Svellere – *pres.* svello (svelgo), svellono (svelgono), *p. def.* svelsi, *p.p.* svelto

Svenire* – *p. def.* svenni

Tacere – *pres.* taccio, taci, tace, taciamo, tacete, tacciono, *p. def.* tacqui, *p.p.* taciuto

Tendere – *p. def.* tesi, *p.p.* teso

Tenere – *pres.* tengo, tieni, tiene, teniamo, tenete, tengono, *p. def.* tenni, *fut.* terrò

Tingere – *p. def.* tinsi, *p.p.* tinto

Togliere – *pres.* tolgo, tolgono, *p. def.* tolsi, *p.p.* tolto

Torcere – *p. def.* torsi, *p.p.* torto

Trarre – *pres.* traggo, trai, trae, traiamo, traete, traggono, *imperf.* traevo, *p. def.* trassi, *fut.* trarrò, *p.p.* tratto

Uccidere – *p. def.* uccisi, *p.p.* ucciso

Udire – *pres.* odo, odi, ode, udiamo, udite, odono, *fut.* udrò (udirò)

Ungere – *p. def.* unsi, *p.p.* unto

Uscire* – *pres.* esco, esci, esce, usciamo, uscite, escono

Valere** – *pres.* valgo, valgono, *p. def.* valsi, *fut.* varrò, *p.p.* valso

Vedere – *pres.* vedo (veggo), vedono (veggono), *p. def.* vidi, *fut.* vedrò, *p.p.* visto

Venire* – *pres.* vengo, vieni, viene, veniamo, venite, vengono, *p. def.* venni, *fut.* verrò

Vilipendere – *p. def.* vilipesi, *p.p.* vilipeso

Vincere – *p. def.* vinsi, *p.p.* vinto

Vivere** – *p. def.* vissi, *p.p.* vissuto

Volere – *pres.* voglio, vuoi, vuole, vogliamo, volete, vogliono, *p. def.*
  volli, *fut.* vorrò
Volgere – *p. def.* volsi, *p.p.* volto

IRREGULAR PLURALS OF NOUNS

l'autobus	gli autobus
il bar	i bar
il caffè	i caffè
la città	le città
la frutta	le frutta
il re	i re
il braccio	le braccia
il bue	i buoi
il centinaio	le centinaia
il dito	le dita
il ginocchio	le ginocchia
la guancia	le guance
il labbro	le labbra
il lenzuolo	le lenzuola
la mano	le mani
il migliaio	le migliaia
l'orecchio	le orecchie
il paio	le paia
l'uomo	gli uomini

ITALIAN MONEY

Italian bank notes are issued in the following denominations:

500 lire	10,000 lire
1000 lire	50,000 lire
2000 lire	100,000 lire.
5000 lire	

The one hundred thousand lire notes are not negotiable outside Italy.

Coins are issued in five, ten, twenty, fifty, one hundred and five hundred pieces.

NUMERALS

Cardinal		*Cardinal cont.*	
1	uno	3	tre
2	due	4	quattro

Cardinal		Cardinal cont.	
5	cinque	29	ventinove
6	sei	30	trenta
7	sette	31	trentuno
8	otto	32	trentadue
9	nove	38	trentotto
10	dieci	40	quaranta
11	undici	50	cinquanta
12	dodici	60	sessanta
13	tredici	70	settanta
14	quattordici	80	ottanta
15	quindici	90	novanta
16	sedici	100	cento
17	diciassette	101	centouno
18	diciotto	105	centocinque
19	diciannove	150	centocinquanta
20	venti	200	duecento
21	ventuno	300	trecento
22	ventidue	1000	mille
23	ventitré	1100	millecento
24	ventiquattro	1200	milleduecento
25	venticinque	2000	duemila
26	ventisei	100,000	centomila
27	ventisette	1,000,000	un milione
28	ventotto		

Ordinal

1st	primo
2nd	secondo
3rd	terzo
4th	quarto
5th	quinto
6th	sesto
7th	settimo
8th	ottavo
9th	nono
10th	decimo
11th	undicesimo or decimo primo
12th	dodicesimo or decimo secondo
20th	ventesimo
21st	ventunesimo or ventesimo primo
22nd	ventiduesimo or ventesimo secondo

30th	trentesimo·
40th	quarantesimo
50th	cinquantesimo
101st	centunesimo
200th	duecentesimo
1000th	millesimo
1205th	milleduecentocinquesimo
1,000,000th	milionesimo

ABBREVIATIONS USED IN THE DICTIONARY

abbr.	abbreviation	*(dial.)*	dialect
(aer.)	aviation	*dif.*	defective
agg.	adjective	*dim.*	diminutive
(agr.)	agriculture	*dimostr.*	demonstrative
(amer.)	American		
amm.	administrative	*ecc., etc.*	etcetera
(anat.)	anatomy	*(eccl.)*	ecclesiastical
(ant.)	archaic	*(econ.)*	economics
(arch.)	architecture	*(edil.)*	building industry
art.	article	*(elettr.)*	electricity
(arte)	art	*escl.*	exclamation
assol.	absolute		
(astr.)	astronomy	*f.*	feminine
attr.	attribute	*(fam.)*	familiar
aus.	auxiliary	*(farm.)*	pharmaceutical
(auto)	motoring	*(ferr.)*	railway
avv.	adverb	*(fig.)*	figurative
		(fil.)	philosophy
(bot.)	botany	*(fis.)*	physics
(biol.)	biology	*(foto)*	photography
		fut.	future
(chim.)	chemistry		
(chir.)	surgery	*gen.*	genitive
(cine)	cinematography	*general.*	generally
coll.	collective	*(geogr.)*	geography
(comm.)	commerce	*(geol.)*	geology
comp.	comparative	*(geom.)*	geometry
compl.	complement	*ger.*	gerund
condiz.	conditional	*(gergo)*	jargon, slang
cong.	conjunction	*(giorn.)*	journalism
(costr.)	building	*(giur.)*	legal
(cuc.)	cooking	*(gramm.)*	grammar

i.	intransitive	*pl.*	plural
id.	idem	*(poet.)*	poetical
imp.	impersonal	*(pol.)*	political
imperat.	imperative	*(pop.)*	popular
imperf.	imperfect	*poss.*	possessive
ind.	indicative	*p.p.*	past participle
indef.	indefinite	*prep.*	preposition
inf.	infinitive	*pred.*	predicate
int.	interrogative	*pres.*	present
inter.	interjection	*pron.*	pronoun
(iron.)	ironic	*prov.*	proverbial
irr.	irregular	*(psicol.)*	psychology
(itt.)	ichthyology		
		qc.	something
(lat.)	Latin, Latinism	*qu.*	someone
loc. avv.	adverbial phrase		
loc. cong.	conjunctive phrase	*r.*	reflexive
		(radio)	radio
loc. prep.	prepositional phrase	*rec.*	reciprocal
		reg.	regular
(lett.)	literature	*rel.*	relative
		(relig.)	religion
m.	masculine		
(mar.)	naval, maritime	*s.*	masculine and feminine noun
(mat.)	mathematics		
(mecc.)	mechanics	*semidif.*	partly defective
(med.)	medicine	*sf.*	feminine noun
(metal.)	metallurgy	*sm.*	masculine noun
(mil.)	military	*(scherz.)*	humourous
(min.)	mineralogy	*(scol.)*	scolastic
(mit.)	mythology	*(scult.)*	sculpture
(mus.)	music	*sing.*	singular
		so	someone
neg.	negative	*sogg.*	subject
(neol.)	neologism	*sost.*	noun
		spec.	especially
ogg.	object	*(spreg.)*	pejorative
(ott.)	optics	*sthg.*	something
		(stor.)	history
p.	participle	*superl.*	superlative
pass.	past		
p. def.	past definite	*t.*	transitive
pers.	personal	*(teat.)*	theatre
(pitt.)	painting	*(tec.)*	technical

(tel.)	telephony	v. dif.	defective verb
(teol.)	theology	vi.	instransitive verb
(tip.)	typography	(v. irr.)	irregular verb
(tv.)	television	(volg.)	vulgar
		vr.	reflexive verb
(us.)	usage	v. semidif.	partially defective verb
v.	verb	vt.	transitive verb
V.	cf.		
(vezz.)	diminutive	(zool.)	zoology

A

a, ad *prep.* **1.** (*termine*) to: *l'ho dato a te*, I gave it to you **2.** (*moto a luogo*) *vado alla stazione*, I am going to the station **3.** (*stato in luogo*) in, at: *vivo a Milano*, I live in Milan; *sono a casa*, I am at home **4.** (*tempo determinato*) at, on, in: *al mio arrivo*, on my arrival **5.** (*iterativo*): *due, tre volte al giorno*, twice, three times a day.
àbaco (*arch.*) *sm.* abacus.
abate *sm.* abbot.
abbacchiare *vt.* (*di frutta*) to beat (*v. irr.*) down. ♦ **abbacchiarsi** *vr.* to feel (*v. irr.*) down-hearted.
abbacchiato *agg.* down-hearted.
abbacinare *vt.* to dazzle.
àbbaco *sm.* elementary arithmetic book.
abbagliante *agg.* dazzling: *fari abbaglianti*, dazzling beams.
abbagliare *vt.* to dazzle, to blind (with).
abbaglio *sm.* **1.** dazzling **2.** (*errore*) blunder.
abbaiare *vi.* to bark.
abbaino *sm.* garret.
abbandonare *vt.* **1.** to leave (*v. irr.*), to forsake (*v. irr.*), to abandon **2.** (*rinunciare*) to give (*v. irr.*) up.
abbandonato *agg.* **1.** (*trascurato*) neglected **2.** (*di casa*) deserted **3.** (*di persona*) forsaken.
abbandono *sm.* **1.** (*di persona che viene abbandonata*) forsaking **2.** (*rinuncia*) giving up.
abbarbicare *vi.* to take (*v. irr.*) root. ♦ **abbarbicarsi** *vr.* to cling (*v. irr.*) (*anche fig.*).
abbaruffarsi *vr.* to quarrel.
abbassamento *sm.* lowering || — *di temperatura*, fall (in temperature).
abbassare *vt.* **1.** to lower, to pull down || — *la testa*, to bend (*v. irr.*) one's head **2.** (*ridurre*) to reduce. ♦ **abbassarsi** *vr.* to stoop (down).
abbasso *avv.* **1.** (*al di sotto*) below **2.** (*giù*) down **3.** (*al piano terreno, dopo aver sceso le scale*) downstairs. ♦ **abbasso!** *inter.* down with!
abbastanza *avv.* **1.** enough **2.** (*discretamente*) quite.

abbàttere *vt.* to pull down. ♦ **abbàttersi** *vr.* to be discouraged.
abbattimento *sm.* **1.** throwing down **2.** (*morale*) dejection.
abbattuto *agg.* disheartened.
abbazìa *sf.* abbey.
abbecedario *sm.* primer.
abbellimento *sm.* embellishment.
abbellire *vt.* to embellish.
abbeverare *vt.* to water. ♦ **abbeverarsi** *vr.* to water.
abbeveratoio *sm.* trough.
abbiccì *sm.* **1.** alphabet **2.** (*principi elementari*) primer.
abbiente *agg.* well-to-do, wealthy.
abbigliamento *sm.* clothes || *industria dell'—*, clothing industry.
abbigliare *vt.* to dress.
abbinare *vt.* to couple.
abbindolare *vt.* to cheat.
abbisognare *vi.* to need, to be necessary.
abboccamento *sm.* interview.
abboccare *vt. e vi.* **1.** to bite (*v. irr.*) **2.** (*fig.*) to be taken in. ♦ **abboccarsi** *vr.* to confer (with).
abbonacciarsi *vi.* **1.** (*di vento*) to drop **2.** (*di mare*) to smooth down.
abbonamento *sm.* **1.** subscription **2.** (*ferr.*) season-ticket.
abbonare *vt.* **1.** to make (*v. irr.*) (*so.*) a subscriber **2.** (*defalcare*) to make a discount. ♦ **abbonarsi** *vr.* to subscribe (to).
abbonato *sm.* **1.** subscriber **2.** (*ferr.*) season-ticket holder.
abbondante *agg.* plentiful.
abbondanza *sf.* plenty.
abbondare *vi.* to have plenty (of), to be plentiful.
abbonire *vt.* to calm.
abbordàbile *agg.* accessible.
abbordaggio *sm.* boarding.
abbordare *vt.* **1.** (*mar.*) to board **2.** (*una persona*) to open conversation (with).
abborracciare *vi.* to bungle.
abbottonare *vt.* to button (up). ♦ **abbottonarsi** *vr.* to button one's clothes (up).
abbottonatura *sf.* **1.** button-holes **2.** (*l'abbottonarsi*) buttoning.
abbozzare *vt.* to sketch || — *un sorriso*, to smile faintly.
abbozzo *sm.* sketch.
abbozzolarsi *vr.* to cocoon.
abbracciare *vt.* **1.** to embrace **2.** (*comprendere*) to include **3.** (*afferrare*) to grasp **4.** (*con lo sguardo*)

to take (v. irr.) in. ♦ **abbracciarsi** vr. to embrace.
abbraccio sm. embrace.
abbrancare vt. to grasp. ♦ **abbrancarsi** vr. to cling (v. irr.) (to).
abbreviare vt. to shorten, to abridge.
abbreviazione sf. abbreviation.
abbrivare vt. to get (v. irr.) under way.
abbrivo sm. freshway.
abbronzare vt. 1. to bronze 2. (al sole) to tan. ♦ **abbronzarsi** vr. to get (v. irr.) tanned.
abbronzatura sf. tanning.
abbruciacchiare vt. to scorch.
abbrustolire vt. to toast, to roast.
abbrutimento sm. brutalization.
abbrutire vt. to brutalize.
abbuffarsi vr. to stuff oneself.
abbuiarsi vr. to get (v. irr.) dark.
abbuono sm. allowance.
abburattare vt. to sift.
abdicare vi. to abdicate.
abdicazione sf. abdication.
aberrare vi. to stray.
aberrazione sf. aberration.
abetaia sf. fir-wood.
abete sm. fir-tree.
abietto agg. abject, base.
abiezione sf. abjection.
abigeato sm. cattle-stealing.
àbile agg. 1. able, skilful 2. (a fare qc.) clever at.
abilità sf. ability, skill.
abilitare vt. to qualify.
abilitazione sf. qualification || esame di —, qualifying examination.
abisso sm. abyss.
abitàbile agg. inhabitable.
abitàcolo sm. (aer.) cockpit.
abitante sm. inhabitant.
abitare vi. to inhabit, to live in.
abitato sm. inhabited place.
abitazione sf. habitation, house.
àbito sm. 1. (da uomo) suit 2. (da donna) dress.
abituale agg. usual, customary.
abituare vt. to accustom. ♦ **abituarsi** vr. to get (v. irr.) used (to).
abitudinario agg. methodical. ♦ **abitudinario** sm. routinist.
abitùdine sf. habit, custom.
abituro sm. slum dwelling.
abiura sf. abjuration.
abiurare vt. to abjure.
ablazione sf. ablation.

abluzione sf. ablution.
abnegazione sf. self-denial.
abnorme agg. abnormal.
abolire vt. to abolish.
abolizione sf. abolition, repeal.
abominare vt. to loathe.
abominévole agg. abominable.
aborìgeni sm. pl. the natives.
aborrimento sm. abhorrence.
aborrire vt. to hate, to loathe.
abortire vi. to miscarry.
aborto sm. miscarriage.
abrasione sf. abrasion.
abrogare vt. 1. to abrogate 2. (giur.) to repeal.
abrogazione sf. 1. abrogation 2. (giur.) repeal.
àbside sf. apse.
abulìa sf. (fig.) lack of will-power.
abùlico agg. (fig.) lacking in will-power.
abusare vi. to abuse.
abusivo agg. abusive.
abuso sm. abuse.
acacia sf. acacia.
acanto sm. acanthus.
acca sf. letter H.
accademia sf. academy.
accadèmico agg. academical. ♦ **accadèmico** sm. academician.
accademismo sm. academism.
accadere vi. to happen.
accaduto sm. event.
accagliarsi vr. 1. to curdle 2. (del sangue) to coagulate.
accalappiacani sm. dog-catcher.
accalappiare vt. 1. to catch (v. irr.) 2. (fig.) to ensnare.
accalcarsi vr. to crowd.
accaldarsi vi. 1. to get (v. irr.) heated 2. (fig.) to get excited.
accaldato agg. hot.
accalorarsi vr. to get (v. irr.) excited.
accampamento sm. camp.
accampare vt. to camp: — diritti, to lay (v. irr.) claims (to).
accanimento sm. 1. fury 2. (tenacia) tenacity.
accanirsi vr. 1. (infierire) to rage 2. (ostinarsi) to persist.
accanito agg. 1. (senza pietà) relentless 2. obstinate.
accanto avv. beside, near, by || accanto a, by, near, at the side of.
accantonare vt. to set (v. irr.) aside.
accaparrare vt. to buy (v. irr.) up.

accapigliarsi *vr.* to come (*v. irr.*) to blows, to quarrel.

accappatoio *sm.* bath-gown.

accapponarsi *vr.* to get (*v. irr.*) goose-flesh.

accarezzare *vt.* **1.** to caress, to stroke **2.** (*fig.*) to entertain.

accartocciare *vt.* **1.** to wrap up **2.** (*spiegazzare*) to crumple.

accasare *vt.* to marry, to give (*v. irr.*) in marriage. ♦ **accasarsi** *vr.* to get (*v. irr.*) married.

accasciarsi *vi.* **1.** to fall (*v. irr.*) to the ground **2.** (*fig.*) to lose (*v. irr.*) heart.

accatastare *vt.* to heap up.

accattivarsi *vi.* to win (*v. irr.*).

accattonaggio *sm.* begging.

accattone *sm.* beggar.

accavallare *vt.* to overlap: — le gambe, to cross one's legs.

accecamento *sm.* **1.** blinding **2.** (*fig.*) lack of perception.

accecare *vt.* to blind. ♦ **accecarsi** *vr.* to blind oneself.

accèdere *vi.* **1.** to approach **2.** (*entrare*) to enter **3.** (*comm.*) to comply (with).

accelerare *vt.* **1.** to quicken **2.** (*di velocità*) to accelerate.

accelerato *sm.* (*ferr.*) slow train.

acceleratore *sm.* accelerator.

accelerazione *sf.* acceleration.

accèndere *vt.* **1.** to light **2.** (*di fiammiferi*) to strike (*v. irr.*) **3.** (*di radio, luce ecc.*) to switch on **4.** (*fig.*) to inflame. ♦ **accèndersi** *vr.* **1.** to light up **2.** (*prender fuoco*) to catch (*v. irr.*) fire || — in volto, to blush.

accendino *sm.* **accendisìgaro** *sm.* (cigarette-)lighter.

accennare *vi.* **1.** to make (*v. irr.*) a sign **2.** (*menzionare*) to mention **3.** (*alludere*) to allude.

accenno *sm.* **1.** sign **2.** (*fig.*) hint.

accensione *sf.* **1.** lighting **2.** (*mecc.*) ignition || *chiavetta d'—*, ignition-key.

accentare *vt.* to accent, to stress.

accentazione *sf.* accentuation, stressing.

accento *sm.* **1.** accent **2.** (*tonico*) stress.

accentramento *sm.* centralization.

accentrare *vt.* to centralize.

accentuare *vt.* to accentuate, to stress. ♦ **accentuarsi** *vr.* to get (*v. irr.*) worse, to increase.

accerchiamento *sm.* surrounding.

accerchiare *vt.* to surround.

accertamento *sm.* **1.** assurance **2.** (*controllo*) verification.

accertare *vt.* **1.** to assure **2.** (*verificare*) to verify.

acceso *agg.* **1.** lit up **2.** (*in volto*) blushing **3.** (*d'ira*) in a temper.

accessìbile *agg.* **1.** open to **2.** (*di persona*) approachable.

accesso *sm.* **1.** admission **2.** (*di malattia, passione*) fit.

accessorio *agg.* accessory. ♦ **accessori** *sm. pl.* fittings.

accetta *sf.* hatchet.

accettare *vt.* **1.** to accept **2.** (*consentire*) to consent.

accetto *agg.* welcome.

accezione *sf.* meaning.

acchiappare *vt.* to catch (*v. irr.*).

acchito *sm.* di primo —, at first sight, at once.

acciacco *sm.* infirmity.

acciaierìa *sf.* steel-mill.

acciaio *sm.* steel.

acciarino *sm.* **1.** flint-lock **2.** (*di fucile*) gun-lock.

accidentale *agg.* accidental.

accidentato *agg.* uneven.

accidente *sm.* chance, accident.

accidenti *inter.* damn.

accidia *sf.* sloth.

accigliarsi *vr.* to frown.

accingersi *vr.* to set (*v. irr.*) about (doing).

acciottolare *vt.* to cobble.

acciottolato *sm.* cobbled paving.

acciottolio *sm.* clatter.

acciuffare *vt.* to catch (*v. irr.*), to seize.

acciuga *sf.* anchovy.

acclamare *vt.* **1.** to acclaim **2.** (*applaudire*) to applaud.

acclamazione *sf.* acclamation, applause.

acclimatazione *sf.* acclimatization.

acclùdere *vt.* to enclose.

accluso *agg.* enclosed.

accoccolarsi *vr.* to squat down.

accodarsi *vr.* to follow.

accogliente *agg.* comfortable, hospitable.

accoglienza *sf.* reception, welcome.

accògliere *vt.* **1.** to receive **2.** (*fare buona accoglienza*) to welcome **3.** (*una richiesta*) to grant.

accòlito *sm.* acolyte.

accollatura *sf.* neckline.

accoltellare *vt.* to stab.

accomiatare *vt.* **1.** to give (*v. irr.*) leave **2.** (*licenziare*) to dismiss. ♦ **accomiatarsi** *vr.* to take (*v. irr.*) leave (of).

accomodamento *sm.* **1.** adjustment **2.** (*conciliazione*) conciliation.

accomodante *agg.* yielding.

accomodare *vt.* **1.** (*riparare*) to repair **2.** (*sistemare*) to settle **3.** (*far comodo*) to suit.

accompagnamento *sm.* **1.** (*l'accompagnare*) accompanying **2.** (*seguito*) retinue **3.** (*mus.*) accompaniment.

accompagnare *vt.* **1.** to accompany **2.** (*— qu. alla stazione*) to see (*v. irr.*) so. off **3.** (*mus.*) to accompany.

accompagnatore *sm.* **1.** companion **2.** (*mus.*) accompanist.

accomunare *vt.* to join, to associate. ♦ **accomunarsi** *vr.* to join.

acconciare *vt.* **1.** to adjust, to adorn **2.** (*capelli*) to dress.

acconciatura *sf.* hair-style.

acconsentire *vi.* **1.** to consent **2.** (*annuire*) to assent.

accontentare *vt.* to satisfy. ♦ **accontentarsi** *vr.* to be content (with).

acconto *sm.* account.

accoppare *vt.* to kill.

accoppiamento *sm.* **1.** coupling **2.** (*di buoi al giogo*) yoking **3.** (*mecc.*) connection.

accoppiare *vt.* **1.** to couple **2.** (*fig.*) to match. ♦ **accoppiarsi** *vr.* to couple, to mate.

accoppiata *sf.* (*ippica*) fourecast.

accorato *agg.* sorrowful.

accorciare *vt.* to shorten.

accordare *vt.* **1.** to grant **2.** (*mus.*) to tune **3.** (*armonizzare*) to match. ♦ **accordarsi** *vr.* to agree (upon).

accordatore *sm.* tuner.

accordo *sm.* **1.** agreement ‖ *come d'—*, as agreed **2.** (*mus.*) chord **3.** (*fig.*) harmony.

accorgersi *vr.* **1.** (*percepire*) to perceive **2.** (*rendersi conto*) to realize.

accorgimento *sm.* **1.** sagacity **2.** (*stratagemma*) clever device.

accòrrere *vi.* to run (*v. irr.*), to hasten: *— in aiuto*, to rush to the help.

accortezza *sf.* sagacity.

accorto *agg.* shrewd.

accostare *vt.* **1.** to draw (*v. irr.*) near **2.** (*porte, finestre ecc.*) to set (*v. irr.*) ajar. ♦ **accostarsi** *vr.* to come (*v. irr.*) near.

accotonare *vt.* to raise.

accotonatura *sf.* raising.

accozzaglia *sf.* huddle: *un'— di gente*, a motley crowd.

accozzare *vt.* to huddle. ♦ **accozzarsi** *vr.* to huddle.

accreditamento *sm.* (*comm.*) crediting.

accreditare *vt.* to credit. ♦ **accreditarsi** *vr.* to gain credit.

accréscere *vt.* to increase.

accrescimento *sm.* increase.

accrescitivo *agg.* e *sm.* augmentative.

accucciarsi *vr.* to crouch.

accudire *vi.* to look after: *— alla casa*, to do (*v. irr.*) the housework.

accumulare *vt.* to heap up.

accumulatore *sm.* accumulator.

accuratezza *sf.* accuracy, care.

accurato *agg.* careful, precise.

accusa *sf.* charge.

accusare *vt.* **1.** to accuse, to charge (with) **2.** (*sentire*) to feel (*v. irr.*) **3.** (*comm.*) to acknowledge.

accusativo *agg.* e *sm.* accusative.

accusato *sm.* accused.

accusatore *sm.* prosecutor: *pubblico —*, public prosecutor.

acerbo *agg.* **1.** unripe **2.** (*acido*) sour.

àcero *sm.* maple.

acetilene *sm.* acetylene.

aceto *sm.* vinegar.

acetone *sm.* acetone.

acidità *sf.* **1.** acidity **2.** (*di stomaco*) hyperchlorhydria.

àcido *agg.* sour. ♦ **àcido** *sm.* acid.

acìdulo *agg.* acidulous.

àcino *sm.* (*di uva*) grape.

acme *sf.* **1.** acme **2.** (*di malattia*) crisis (*pl.* -ses).

acne *sf.* acne.

aconfessionale *agg.* nondenominational.

acqua *sf.* **1.** water: *— marina*, sea water; *— piovana*, rain water; *— potabile*, drinking water **2.** (*pioggia*) rain: *— a catinelle*, heavy rain.

acquaforte *sf.* etching.

acquaio *sm.* sink.

acquamarina *sf.* aquamarine.

acquaragia *sf.* turpentine.

acquario *sm.* aquarium.

acquasanta *sf.* holy water.

acquasantiera *sf.* stoup.

acquàtico *agg.* aquatic.

acquattarsi *vr.* 1. to crouch 2. (*nascondersi*) to hide (*v. irr.*).

acquavite *sf.* brandy.

acquazzone *sm.* downpour.

acquedotto *sm.* aqueduct.

acquerellista *sm.* water-colourist.

acquerello *sm.* water-colour.

acquerùgiola *sf.* drizzle.

acquiescente *agg.* acquiescent.

acquiescenza *sf.* acquiescence.

acquirente *sm.* buyer.

acquisire *vt.* to acquire.

acquistare *vt.* 1. (*comperare*) to buy (*v. irr.*) 2. (*ottenere*) to get (*v. irr.*) 3. (*fig.*) to gain || — *terreno*, to make (*v. irr.*) progress.

acquisto *sm.* purchase || *fare acquisti*, to go (*v. irr.*) shopping.

acquitrino *sm.* marsh.

acquolina *sf.* drizzle: *far venire l'— in bocca*, to make (*v. irr.*) so.'s mouth water.

acre *agg.* 1. sour 2. (*fig.*) sarcastic 3. (*pungente*) pungent.

acrèdine *sf.* 1. acridity 2. (*fig.*) acrimony.

acrimonia *sf.* acrimony.

acròbata *s.* acrobat.

acròbatico *agg.* acrobatic.

acrobazìa *sf.* acrobatics (*pl.*) || *fare delle acrobazie*, to perform stunts.

acròpoli *sf.* acropolis.

acuire *vt.* to sharpen: — *l'interesse*, to stimulate interest.

acùleo *sm.* 1. (*bot.*) prickle 2. (*zool.*) sting.

acume *sm.* insight.

acuminare *vt.* to sharpen.

acùstica *sf.* acoustics.

acutezza *sf.* 1. sharpness 2. (*di mente*) perspicacity.

acutizzare *vt.* to make (*v. irr.*) acute. ♦ **acutizzarsi** *vr.* to grow (*v. irr.*) acute.

acuto *agg.* 1. sharp 2. (*di angoli, accenti*) acute 3. (*intenso*) intense 4. (*di suono*) shrill. ♦ **acuto** *sm.* (*mus.*) high note.

adagiare *vt.* to lay (*v. irr.*) down with care. ♦ **adagiarsi** *vr.* to lie (*v. irr.*) down.

adagio[1] *avv.* 1. slowly 2. (*con cautela*) cautiously 3. (*con delicatezza*) gently.

adagio[2] *sm.* proverb, saying.

adamantino *agg.* adamantine.

adamìtico *agg.* adamic.

adattàbile *agg.* adaptable.

adattamento *sm.* 1. adaptation 2. (*assestamento*) adjustment.

adattare *vt.* to adapt, to fit. ♦ **adattarsi** *vr.* 1. to adapt oneself 2. (*attagliarsi*) to fit.

adatto *agg.* 1. fit, proper 2. (*che va bene*) suitable (for).

addebitare *vt.* to debit.

addébito *sm.* charge: *fare un — a qu. per qc.*, to charge so. with sthg.

addendo *sm.* addendum (*pl.* -da).

addensamento *sm.* 1. thickening 2. (*di persone*) crowding.

addensare *vt.* 1. to thicken. ♦ **addensarsi** *vr.* 1. to thicken 2. (*di folla*) to crowd.

addentare *vt.* to bite (*v. irr.*).

addentellato *sm.* 1. (*arch.*) toothing 2. (*fig.*) stepping-stone.

addentrarsi *vr.* to penetrate: — *in una questione*, to probe a question.

addentro *avv.* inside.

addestramento *sm.* 1. training 2. (*mil.*) drilling.

addestrare *vt.* 1. to train 2. (*mil.*) to drill.

addetto *agg.* employed (in). ♦ **addetto** *sm.* attaché.

addietro *avv.* 1. (*di spazio*) behind 2. (*di tempo*) before, ago || *era venuto due giorni —*, he had come two days before.

addìo *inter.* good-bye.

addirittura *avv.* 1. quite 2. (*in esclamazioni*) really!

addirsi *vr.* to become (*v. irr.*).

additare *vt.* to point at.

addizionale *agg.* additional.

addizionare *vt.* to sum up.

addizionatrice *sf.* adding-machine, adder.

addizione *sf.* addition.

addobbare *vt.* to adorn.

addobbo *sm.* 1. decoration 2. (*eccl.*) sacred ornaments (*pl.*).

addolcire *vt.* 1. to sweeten 2. (*fig.*) to soften. ♦ **addolcirsi** *vr.* to become (*v. irr.*) soft(er).

addolorare *vt.* to grieve. ♦ **addolorarsi** *vr.* to be grieved.

addolorato *agg.* grieved, sorry.

addome *sm.* abdomen.

addomesticare *vt.* to tame.

addominale *agg.* abdominal.

addormentare *vt.* 1. to send (*v. irr.*) to sleep 2. (*med.*) to anaesthetize. ✦ **addormentarsi** *vr.* **1.** to fall (*v. irr.*) asleep **2.** (*fig.*) to go (*v. irr.*) to sleep.

addossare *vt.* **1.** to lean **2.** (*attribuire*) to lay (*v. irr.*). ✦ **addossarsi** *vr.* **1.** (*affollarsi*) to crowd **2.** (*prendere su di sé*) to take (*v. irr.*) upon oneself.

addosso *avv. prep.* **1.** on, upon: *mettere qc. —*, to put (*v. irr.*) sthg. on; *togliere qc. d'—*, to take (*v. irr.*) sthg. off **2.** (*vicino a*) close to: *la casa è — alla montagna*, the house is close to the mountain || *dare —*, to assault, to contradict.

addottrinare *vt.* to instruct. ✦ **addottrinarsi** *vr.* to instruct oneself.

addurre *vt.* **1.** to put (*v. irr.*) forward: *— una scusa*, to plead **2.** (*citare*) to quote.

adeguamento *sm.* **1.** proportionment **2.** (*adattamento*) adaptation.

adeguare *vt.* **1.** to proportionate **2.** (*adattare*) to conform. ✦ **adeguarsi** *vr.* to conform oneself, to adapt oneself.

adeguato *agg.* **1.** proportionate **2.** (*adatto*) convenient, fit **3.** (*giusto*) fair.

adémpiere *vt.* **1.** (*compiere*) to fulfil **2.** (*eseguire*) to carry out. ✦ **adémpiersi** *vr.* (*avverarsi*) to come (*v. irr.*) true.

adempimento *sm.* **1.** fulfilment **2.** (*esecuzione*) carrying out.

adenòidi *sf. pl.* adenoids.

adepto *sm.* **1.** adept **2.** (*seguace*) follower.

aderente *agg.* **1.** adherent **2.** (*di abito*) close-fitting.

aderenza *sf.* **1.** adherence **2.** (*med.*) adhesion **3.** (*pl.*) connections.

aderire *vi.* **1.** (*stare vicino e fig.*) to adhere, to stick **2.** (*consentire*) to comply with **3.** (*parteggiare per*) to take sides (with).

adescamento *sm.* **1.** enticement **2.** (*seduzione*) seduction.

adescare *vt.* **1.** to entice **2.** (*sedurre*) to seduce.

adesione *sf.* adhesion: *dare la propria — ad un partito*, to join a party.

adesivo *agg.* adhesive.

adesso *avv.* now, at present, at the moment.

adiacente *agg.* adjacent.

adibire *vt.* to use as.

àdipe *sm.* fat.

adiposo *agg.* adipose.

adirarsi *vr.* to get (*v. irr.*) angry.

adirato *agg.* angry.

adire *vt.* (*giur.*) to apply to: *— le vie legali*, to take (*v. irr.*) legal steps.

àdito *sm.* entry: *dare —*, to give (*v. irr.*) rise.

adocchiare *vt.* **1.** to glance **2.** (*scorgere*) to catch (*v. irr.*) sight of.

adolescente *agg.* teen-aged, adolescent. ✦ **adolescente** *sm.* teen-ager.

adolescenza *sf.* adolescence.

adombrare *vt.* **1.** to shade **2.** (*nascondere*) to conceal **3.** (*simboleggiare*) to symbolize. ✦ **adombrarsi** *vr.* **1.** to resent **2.** (*di cavallo*) to shy.

adoperare *vt.* to use. ✦ **adoperarsi** *vr.* to endeavour.

adoràbile *agg.* charming.

adorare *vt.* to adore, to worship.

adorazione *sf.* adoration, worship.

adornare *vt.* to adorn.

adorno *agg.* adorned.

adottare *vt.* to adopt.

adottivo *agg.* adoptive.

adozione *sf.* adoption: *patria d'—*, adopted country.

adrenalina *sf.* adrenalin.

adulare *vt.* to flatter.

adulatore *agg.* flattering. ✦ **adulatore** *sm.* flatterer.

adulazione *sf.* flattery.

adùltera *sf.* adulteress.

adulterare *vt.* **1.** to adulterate **2.** (*fig.*) to falsify.

adulterino *agg.* adulterine.

adulterio *sm.* adultery.

adùltero *agg.* adulterous. ✦ **adùltero** *sm.* adulterer.

adulto *agg. e sm.* grown-up, adult.

adunanza *sf.* meeting.

adunco *agg.* hooked.

aerare *vt.* **1.** to air **2.** (*chim.*) to aerate.

aerazione *sf.* **1.** airing **2.** (*chim.*) aeration.

aèreo *agg.* aerial || *per via aerea*, by air. ✦ **aèreo** *sm.* **1.** plane **2.** (*radio*) aerial.

aerodinàmica *sf.* aerodynamics.

aeròdromo *sm.* aerodrome.

aerolito *sm.* aerolite.

aeromodello *sm.* model aircraft.

aeronàuta *sm.* aeronaut.

aeronàutica *sf.* aeronautics.

aeronave *sf.* airship.

aeronavigazione *sf.* air navigation

aeroplano *sm.* (aero)plane, aircraft || — *a razzo*, rocket plane; — *passeggeri*, passenger plane; — *da bombardamento*, bomber.

aeroporto *sm.* airport.

aerosòl *sm.* aerosol.

aerostàtica *sf.* aerostatics.

aeròstato *sm.* aerostat.

aerostazione *sf.* air-terminal.

aerotassì *sm.* airtaxi.

aerotrasportare *vt.* to air-bear.

afa *sf.* sultriness.

afasìa *sf.* aphasia.

affàbile *agg.* affable.

affabilità *sf.* affability, kindness.

affaccendarsi *vr.* to busy oneself.

affaccendato *agg.* busy.

affacciare *vt.* 1. to show (*v. irr.*) 2. (*un dubbio*) to raise. ♦ **affacciarsi** *vr.* 1. to show oneself 2. (*su un luogo*) to face.

affamare *vt.* to starve (out).

affamato *agg.* 1. hungry 2. (*fig.*) eager. ♦ **affamato** *sm.* starveling.

affamatore *sm.* starver.

affannare *vt.* to trouble, to worry. ♦ **affannarsi** *vr.* 1. to worry oneself 2. (*affaccendarsi*) to busy oneself.

affanno *sm.* 1. breathlessness 2. (*pena*) worry.

affannoso *agg.* 1. breathless || *respiro* —, difficult breathing 2. (*ansioso*) anxious.

affare *sm.* 1. affair, business: — *di cuore*, love affair; *questo è* — *nostro*, this is our business 2. (*comm.*) business: *fare affari*, to do (*v. irr.*) business || (*pol.*) *affari esteri*, foreign affairs; (*in Gran Bretagna*) *Ministero degli Affari Esteri*, Foreign Office.

affarista *sm.* speculator.

affascinante *agg.* charming.

affascinare *vt.* to charm.

affaticamento *sm.* weariness.

affaticare *vt.* to tire. ♦ **affaticarsi** *vr.* 1. to get (*v. irr.*) tired 2. (*lavorare molto*) to work hard.

affatto *avv.* 1. completely, quite 2. (*in frasi negative*) at all: *niente* —, not at all.

affatturare *vt.* to bewitch.

affermare *vt.* 1. to affirm 2. (*fig.*) to assert. ♦ **affermarsi** *vr.* to make (*v. irr.*) a name for oneself.

affermativo *agg.* affirmative.

affermazione *sf.* 1. statement 2. (*successo*) achievement.

afferrare *vt.* to grasp 2. (*fig.*) to seize. ♦ **afferrarsi** *vr.* to grasp at, to clutch at.

affettare[1] *vt.* (*tagliare a fette*) to slice.

affettare[2] *vt.* (*ostentare*) to affect.

affettato[1] *agg.* sliced.

affettato[2] *agg.* (*ostentato*) affected.

affettatrice *sf.* slicing machine.

affettazione *sf.* affectation, show.

affettivo *agg.* emotional.

affetto[1] *sm.* affection: *portare* — *a qu.*, to set (*v. irr.*) one's affection on so.

affetto[2] *agg.* affected (with).

affettuosità *sf.* tenderness.

affettuoso *agg.* tender, affectionate.

affezionarsi *vr.* to grow (*v. irr.*) fond of.

affezione *sf.* 1. affection 2. (*med.*) affection, disease.

affiancare *vt.* to flank. ♦ **affiancarsi** *vr.* to line up (with).

affiatamento *sm.* concord.

affiatare *vt.* 1. to bring (*v. irr.*) together 2. (*mus.*) to tune. ♦ **affiatarsi** *vr.* to become (*v. irr.*) familiar (with).

affibbiare *vt.* 1. to buckle 2. (*fig.*) to shift (upon).

affidamento *sm.* trust, confidence: *dare* —, to inspire confidence.

affidare *vt.* 1. to entrust 2. (*consegnare*) to commit. ♦ **affidarsi** *vr.* to rely upon.

affievolire *vt.* to weaken. ♦ **affievolirsi** *vr.* to grow (*v. irr.*) weak.

affiggere *vt.* to post up: — *lo sguardo*, to fix one's eyes (on).

affilare *vt.* to sharpen. ♦ **affilarsi** *vr.* (*dimagrire*) to thin.

affilato *agg.* 1. sharp 2. (*di naso, viso*) thin.

affiliare *vt.* to affiliate.

affiliato *sm.* member, associate.

affiliazione *sf.* affiliation.

affinamento *sm.* 1. refining 2. (*fig.*) sharpening.

affinare *vt.* 1. to refine 2. (*assottigliare*) to make (*v. irr.*) thin. ♦ **affinarsi** *vr.* 1. to refine, to improve 2. (*assottigliarsi*) to become (*v. irr.*) thin.

affinché *cong.* so that, in order that.

affine *agg.* like, similar.

affinità *sf.* affinity.

affiorare *vi.* to appear on the surface.

affissare *vt.* to affix.

affissione *sf.* bill-posting.

affisso *sm.* 1. (*avviso*) bill 2. (*cartello*) placard 3. (*manifesto*) poster.

affittacàmere *sm. e sf.* landlord, landlady.

affittare *vt.* 1. (*dare in affitto*) to let (*v. irr.*) 2. (*prendere in affitto*) to rent 3. (*noleggiare*) to hire.

affitto *sm.* rent.

afflato *sm.* afflatus.

affliggere *vt.* 1. to distress 2. (*di malattie*) to afflict. ♦ **affliggersi** *vr.* to worry.

afflitto *agg.* sad, sorrowful.

afflizione *sf.* 1. affliction 2. (*flagello*) calamity.

afflosciarsi *vr.* 1. to become (*v. irr.*) flabby 2. (*fig.*) to weaken.

affluente *sm.* affluent.

affluenza *sf.* 1. (*di acque*) flow 2. (*di persone*) crowd 3. (*abbondanza*) plenty.

affluire *vi.* 1. (*di acque*) to flow 2. (*di persone*) to crowd 3. (*di cose*) to pour in.

afflusso *sm.* afflux.

affogamento *sm.* drowning.

affogare *vt.* 1. to drown 2. (*fig.*) to smother. ♦ **affogarsi** *vr.* to drown oneself.

affogato *agg.* 1. drowned 2. (*fig.*) oppressed || *uova affogate*, poached eggs.

affollamento *sm.* overcrowding, throng.

affollare *vt.* 1. to crowd 2. (*fig.*) to overwhelm. ♦ **affollarsi** *vr.* to press up.

affollato *agg.* crowded.

affondare *vt.* 1. (*sommergere*) to sink (*v. irr.*) 2. (*immergere*) to plunge.

affossamento *sm.* ditching.

affossare *vt.* to ditch. ♦ **affossarsi** *vr.* to become (*v. irr.*) hollow.

affrancamento *sm.* release.

affrancare *vt.* 1. to release 2. (*con francobollo*) to stamp. ♦ **affrancarsi** *vr.* to free oneself.

affrancato *agg.* 1. free 2. (*con francobollo*) stamped.

affrancatura *sf.* postage.

affranto *agg.* broken-hearted || (*dalla fatica*) worn out.

affratellarsi *vr.* to fraternize.

affresco *sm.* fresco.

affrettare *vt.* 1. to hasten 2. (*anticipare*) to anticipate. ♦ **affrettarsi** *vr.* to make (*v. irr.*) haste.

affrettatamente *avv.* hastily.

affrettato *agg.* 1. hasty 2. (*trascurato*) careless.

affrontare *vt.* 1. to face 2. (*fig.*) to deal (*v. irr.*) with. ♦ **affrontarsi** *vr.* (*venire alle mani*) to come (*v. irr.*) to blows.

affronto *sm.* insult.

affumicare *vt.* 1. to fill with smoke 2. (*cuc.*) to smoke.

affumicato *agg.* 1. blackened by smoke 2. (*cuc.*) smoked || *lenti affumicate*, sun-glasses.

affusolare *vt.* to taper.

afonìa *sf.* aphonia.

àfono *agg.* voiceless.

aforisma *sm.* aphorism.

afoso *agg.* sultry.

africano *agg. e sm.* African.

afroasiàtico *agg.* Afro-Asiatic.

afta *sf.* aphtha.

àgata *sf.* agate.

àgave *sf.* agave.

agenda *sf.* note-book.

agente *sm.* agent.

agenzìa *sf.* agency.

agevolare *vt.* to make (*v. irr.*) easy.

agevolazione *sf.* facilitation.

agévole *agg.* 1. easy 2. (*di strada*) smooth.

agevolmente *avv.* easily.

agganciare *vt.* 1. to hook 2. (*ferr.*) to couple up.

aggeggio *sm.* device.

aggettare *vi.* to jut out.

aggettivo *agg.* adjective.

agghiacciare *vt.* to freeze (*v. irr.*). ♦ **agghiacciarsi** *vr.* to freeze.

agghindare *vt.* to array. ♦ **agghindarsi** *vr.* to dress (oneself) up.

aggiogare *vt.* to yoke.

aggiornamento *sm.* 1. (*rinvio*) adjournment 2. (*di un libro*) revision.

aggiornare *vt.* 1. (*rinviare*) to adjourn 2. (*mettere al corrente*) to bring (*v. irr.*) up to date. ♦ **aggiornarsi** *vr.* to brush up one's knowledge.

aggiornato *agg.* up-to-date.

aggirare *vt.* to go (*v. irr.*) round || — *l'ostacolo*, to avoid an obstacle. ♦ **aggirarsi** *vr.* to wander about, to go about.

aggiudicare *vt.* to award. ♦ **ag-**

giudicarsi *vr.* to win (*v. irr.*).

aggiudicazione *sf.* award.

aggiùngere *vt.* to add. ♦ aggiùngersi *vr.* to join.

aggiunta *sf.* 1. addition 2. (*aumento*) increase.

aggiunto *agg.* added, joined. ♦ aggiunto *sm.* assistant.

aggiustare *vt.* 1. (*riparare*) to mend 2. (*sistemare*) to arrange. ♦ aggiustarsi *vr.* (*accomodarsi*) to make (*v. irr.*) oneself comfortable.

agglomerato *sm.* agglomerate.

agglutinare *vt.* to agglutinate.

aggraffare *vt.* to seize.

aggranchire *vt.* to benumb.

aggrapparsi *vr.* to cling (*v. irr.*) (to), to get (*v. irr.*) hold (of).

aggravante *agg.* aggravating. ♦ aggravante *sf.* (*giur.*) aggravating circumstance.

aggravare *vt.* to aggravate, to overburden. ♦ aggravarsi *vr.* to grow (*v. irr.*) worse.

aggravato *agg.* 1. overburdened 2. (*med.*) worse.

aggraziare *vt.* to make (*v. irr.*) graceful.

aggredire *vt.* to assault.

aggregare *vt.* to associate. ♦ aggregarsi *vr.* to join.

aggressione *sf.* aggression, assault.

aggressività *sf.* aggressiveness.

aggressivo *agg.* aggressive.

aggressore *sm.* aggressor.

aggrottare *vt.* to frown.

aggrovigliare *vt.* to entangle.

aggrovigliarsi *vr.* to get (*v. irr.*) entangled.

aggruppare *vt.* to group.

agguantare *vt.* to catch (*v. irr.*).

agguato *sm.* ambush.

agguerrire *vt.* to inure (for war). ♦ agguerrirsi *vr.* to get (*v. irr.*) inured.

agiatamente *avv.* in ease and comfort.

agiato *agg.* well-to-do.

àgile *agg.* nimble.

agilità *sf.* nimbleness.

agio *sm.* comfort, ease, leisure.

agiografia *sf.* hagiography.

agire *vi.* to act.

agitare *vt.* 1. to agitate 2. (*scuotere*) to shake (*v. irr.*) 3. to stir (*anche fig.*). ♦ agitarsi *vr.* to be agitated.

agitatore *sm.* 1. agitator 2. (*mecc.*) stirrer.

agitazione *sf.* 1. agitation 2. (*eccitazione*) excitement 3. (*di folla*) tumult.

aglio *sm.* garlic.

agnello *sm.* lamb.

agnosticismo *sm.* agnosticism.

ago *sm.* 1. needle 2. (*mecc.*) tongue.

agognare *vt.* to long (for sthg.).

agonìa *sf.* agony, pangs (*pl.*) of death.

agonismo *sm.* athletic spirit.

agonizzante *agg.* dying.

agonizzare *vi.* to be in one's death agony.

agorafobia *sf.* agoraphobia.

agosto *sm.* August.

agraria *sf.* agriculture.

agrario *agg.* agrarian. ♦ agrario *sm.* 1. land-owner 2. (*esperto*) agriculturist.

agreste *agg.* agrestic, rustic.

agretto *agg.* sourish.

agricolo *agg.* agricultural.

agricoltore *sm.* farmer.

agricoltura *sf.* agriculture.

agrifoglio *sm.* holly.

agrimensore *sm.* land-surveyor.

agro *agg.* sour. ♦ agro *sm.* sourness.

agrodolce *agg.* bitter-sweet, sourish.

agronomìa *sf.* agronomy.

agronòmico *agg.* agronomical.

agrònomo *sm.* agronomist.

agrumi *sm. pl.* citrus fruit (*sing.*).

aguzzare *vt.* to sharpen.

aguzzino *sm.* 1. gaoler, jailer 2. (*fig.*) torturer.

aguzzo *agg.* sharp, pointed.

ahimè *inter.* alas.

aia *sf.* threshing-floor.

aio *sm.* tutor.

airone *sm.* heron.

aitante *agg.* vigorous, stout.

aiuola *sf.* flower-bed.

aiutante *sm.* 1. assistant 2. (*mil.*) adjutant: — *di campo*, aide-de-camp.

aiutare *vt.* to help. ♦ aiutarsi *vr.* (*ingegnarsi*) to make (*v. irr.*) shift. ♦ aiutarsi *vr. rec.* to help (one another).

aiuto *sm.* 1. help: *chiedere* —, to call for help 2. (*chi aiuta*) help, helper 3. (*pl.*) (*mil.*) reinforcements.

aizzare *vt.* to incite, to rouse.

ala *sf.* wing.

alabarda *sf.* halberd.

alabastro sm. alabaster.
àlacre agg. brisk, industrious.
alacrità sf. alacrity.
alamaro sm. frog.
alambicco sm. still.
alano sm. Great Dane.
alba sf. dawn.
albanese agg. e sm. Albanian.
àlbatro sm. albatross.
albeggiare vi. to dawn.
alberare vt. 1. to plant with trees
2. (mar.) to mast.
alberato agg. planted with trees.
alberatura sf. (mar.) masting.
albergatore sm. hotel-keeper.
alberghiero agg. hotel (attributivo): industria alberghiera. hotel
trade.
albergo sm. hotel.
àlbero sm. 1. tree 2. (mar.) mast
3. (mecc.) shaft.
albicocca sf. apricot.
albino agg. e sm. albino.
albo sm. 1. list, roll: — degli avvocati, Law List; — d'onore, roll
of honour 2. (per fotografie ecc.)
album 3. (tavola per affissione)
notice-board.
album sm. album.
albume sm. albumen.
albumina sf. albumin.
alca sf. auk.
alcalino agg. e sm. alkaline.
alce sm. elk.
alchimìa sf. alchemy.
alcòlico agg. alcoholic.
alcolismo sm. alcoholism.
alcolizzato agg. e sm. alcoholic.
alcool sm. alcohol.
alcova sf. alcove.
alcunché pron. anything, something.
alcuno agg. 1. (frasi affermative)
some, a few 2. (frasi negative) any.
♦ **alcuno** pron. 1. (frasi affermative) somebody, someone 2. (frasi negative) anybody, anyone.
aldilà sm. hereafter.
aleatorio agg. aleatory.
aleggiare vi. 1. to flutter 2. (fig.)
to hover (about).
alettone sm. aileron.
alfa sf. alpha.
alfabeto sm. alphabet.
alfiere sm. 1. ensign 2. (scacchi)
bishop.
alga sf. seaweed.
àlgebra sf. algebra.
algèbrico agg. algebraic, algebraical.

aliante sm. glider.
àlibi sm. alibi.
alienare vt. to alienate, to estrange.
♦ **alienarsi** vr. to alienate oneself, to become (v. irr.) estranged.
alienato agg. lunatic; mad; estranged, alienated. ♦ **alienato** sm.
1. lunatic, madman (pl. -men) 2.
alienated person, estranged person.
alienazione sf. alienation, estrangement.
alienista sm. alienist, psychiatrist.
alieno agg. averse, opposed.
alimentare[1] vt. to feed (v. irr.), to
nourish.
alimentare[2] agg. alimentary || ge-
neri alimentari, foodstuffs; negozio di generi alimentari, grocery
store.
alimentazione sf. nourishment,
feeding.
alimento sm. food.
alìnea sf. paragraph.
alìquota sf. aliquot, rate.
aliscafo sm. hydrofoil boat.
aliseo sm. trade-wind.
àlito sm. breath.
allacciare vt. 1. to lace, to connect
2. (fig.) to establish. ♦ **allacciarsi** vr. 1. (abbracciarsi) to embrace
2. (aggrovigliarsi) to get (v. irr.)
entangled, to be entangled.
allagare vt. to flood, to inundate.
allampanato agg. lean, lanky.
allargamento sm. widening, enlargement.
allargare vt. to widen, to enlarge,
to extend. ♦ **allargarsi** vr. to
widen, to extend, to spread (v.
irr.).
allarmante agg. alarming.
allarmare vt. to alarm. ♦ **allar-
marsi** vr. to get (v. irr.) frightened.
allarme sm. alarm, warning, alert.
allattamento sm. breast-feeding,
nursing.
allattare vt. to suckle, to nurse.
alleanza sf. alliance.
allearsi vr. to ally, to become (v.
irr.) allies.
alleato agg. allied. ♦ **alleato** sm.
ally.
allegare vt. 1. to allege 2. (accludere) to enclose.
allegato sm. enclosure.
alleggerimento sm. lightening, relief.
alleggerire vt. to lighten, to re-

lieve, to unburden. ◆ **alleggerirsi** *vr.* to relieve oneself.
allegorìa *sf.* allegory.
allegòrico *agg.* allegoric(al).
allegramente *agg.* cheerfully, merrily.
allegrìa *sf.* cheerfulness, mirth.
allegro *agg.* merry, cheerful, jolly.
allegrone *sm.* jolly fellow.
allenamento *sm.* training.
allenare *vt.* to train. ◆ **allenarsi** *vr.* to train (oneself).
allenatore *sm.* trainer; (*di squadre*) coach.
allentamento *sm.* **1.** loosening **2.** (*di velocità*) slackening.
allentare *vt.* to slacken, to loosen, to relax: — *il freno*, to release the brake. ◆ **allentarsi** *vr.* to slacken.
allergìa *sf.* allergy.
allèrgico *agg.* allergic.
allestimento *sm.* preparation, fitting out || — *scenico*, staging.
allestire *vt.* to prepare, to fit out.
allettamento *sm.* enticement, allurement.
allettante *agg.* alluring, enticing.
allettare *vt.* to allure, to entice.
allevamento *sm.* **1.** breeding, raising || (*di bambino*) bringing up **2.** (*luogo*) stock-farm || — *di cavalli*, stud-farm.
allevare *vt.* **1.** (*bambini*) to bring (*v. irr.*) up **2.** (*animali*) to breed (*v. irr.*), to rear.
allevatore *sm.* breeder.
alleviare *vt.* to relieve, to alleviate.
allibire *vi.* to be left speechless, to be struck dumb.
allibito *agg.* struck dumb, speechless.
allibratore *sm.* bookmaker.
allietare *vt.* to cheer. ◆ **allietarsi** *vr.* to cheer up.
allievo *sm.* **1.** pupil **2.** (*mil.*) cadet.
alligatore *sm.* alligator.
allineamento *sm.* **1.** alignment || (*tip.*) — *di caratteri*, ranging of characters **2.** (*mil.*) dressing.
allineare *vt.* **1.** to line up, to align: — *delle cifre*, to tabulate figures **2.** (*mil.*) to dress; (*in ordine di marcia*) to form up. ◆ **allinearsi** *vr.* **1.** to get (*v. irr.*) into line **2.** (*mil.*) to dress || *allineatevi*, draw up! **3.** (*pol.*) to be aligned with.
allocco *sm.* **1.** owl **2.** (*fig.*) fool.

allocuzione *sf.* allocution: *fare un'—*, to deliver a speech.
allòdola *sf.* skylark, lark.
allogare *vt.* to lodge.
allogazione *sf.* lease.
alloggiare *vt.* **1.** to lodge, to house, to put (*v. irr.*) up **2.** (*mil.*) to quarter; (*in casa privata*) to billet. ◆ **alloggiare** *vi.* **1.** to lodge, to live **2.** (*mil.*) to quarter; (*in casa privata*) to be billeted.
alloggio *sm.* **1.** lodging || *indennità di —*, living-out allowance **2.** (*mil.*) quarters (*pl.*).
allontanamento *sm.* **1.** removal **2.** (*licenziamento*) dismissal.
allontanare *vt.* **1.** to remove, to drive (*v. irr.*) away: — *un pericolo*, to evert a danger **2.** (*licenziare*) to dismiss, to turn out. ◆ **allontanarsi** *vr.* to go (*v. irr.*) away, to depart.
allora *avv.* **1.** then **2.** (*quindi*) so.
allorché *cong.* when.
alloro *sm.* laurel.
àlluce *sm.* big toe.
allucinare *vt.* **1.** to dazzle **2.** (*dare allucinazioni*) to hallucinate.
allucinato *agg.* hallucinated.
allucinazione *sf.* hallucination.
allùdere *vi.* to allude (to), to hint (at).
alluminio *sm.* aluminium.
allunaggio *sm.* mooning.
allunare *vi.* to moon.
allungàbile *agg.* extensible.
allungamento *sm.* lengthening, stretching.
allungare *vt.* **1.** to lengthen, to extend, to stretch || — *il passo*, to quicken one's steps || — *il collo*, to stretch one's neck || — *gli orecchi*, to strain one's ears || (*fig.*) — *le mani su qc.*, to lay (*v. irr.*) hands on sthg. ◆ **allungarsi** *vr.* to lengthen, to grow (*v. irr.*) longer, to draw (*v. irr.*) out.
allusione *sf.* allusion, hint.
allusivo *agg.* allusive.
alluvionato *agg.* flooded || *zone alluvionate*, flood-areas. ◆ **alluvionato** *sm.* flood-victim.
alluvione *sf.* flood.
almanaccare *vi.* to fantasticate.
almanacco *sm.* almanac.
almeno *avv.* at least.
alno *sm.* alder-tree.
aloè *sm.* aloe.

alone sm. halo.
alpaca sm. alpaca.
alpe sf. alp.
alpestre agg. alpine.
alpinismo sm. (mountain-)climbing, mountaineering.
alpinista s. (mountain-)climber.
alpino agg. Alpine.
alquanto avv. somewhat, rather.
altalena sf. swing.
altana sf. roof-terrace.
altare sm. altar.
alterare vt. to alter; (salute) to impair; (cibo) to adulterate. ♦ **alterarsi** vr. 1. to alter, to change 2. (andare a male) to go (v. irr.) bad 3. (turbarsi) to be upset || la sua voce si alterò, his voice faltered.
alterazione sf. 1. alteration 2. (deteriorazione) deterioration 3. (turbamento) emotion; (della voce) faltering.
alterco sm. altercation.
alterigia sf. haughtiness.
alternanza sf. alternation.
alternare vt. to alternate. ♦ **alternarsi** vr. to alternate.
alternativa sf. alternative.
alterno agg. alternate.
altero agg. lofty, proud.
altezza sf. 1. height 2. (di tessuto) width 3. (di suono) pitch 4. (fig.) essere all'— di qc., to be equal to sthg.; to be up to sthg. 5. (titolo) highness.
altezzoso agg. haughty.
alticcio agg. tight, tipsy.
altimetro sm. altimeter.
altitudine sf. altitude.
alto agg. 1. high, tall: un uomo —, a tall man || alta direzione, top management 2. (di suono) loud || ad alta voce, aloud, loudly 3. (profondo) deep: acqua alta, deep water 4. (geogr.) northern, upper 5. (stor.) early. ♦ **alto** sm. height || alti e bassi, ups and downs. ♦ **alto** avv. high, up || mani in —, hands up.
altoforno sm. blast-furnace.
altolocato agg. high-ranking, high-class.
altoparlante sm. loud-speaker.
altopiano sm. plateau.
altresì avv. likewise, also.
altrettanto agg. correlativo as much (...as); (pl.) as many (...as) || (neg.) as (o so) much (:..as); (pl.)

as (o so) many... (as): egli ha altrettante possibilità quanto me, he has as many chances as I. ♦ **altrettanto** 1. as much; (pl.) as many 2. (lo stesso) the same: — a voi!, the same to you!. ♦ **altrettanto** avv. 1. (con agg. e avv.) as (...as); (neg.) as (o so) ...as) 2. (coi verbi) as much (as).
altrimenti avv. otherwise. ♦ **altrimenti** cong. otherwise, else.
altro agg. indef. 1. other || un —, another 2. (differente) different 3. (con pronomi int.) else: chi altro?, who else? 4. (in più) more: leggerò altri due libri, I shall read two more books 5. (susseguente) next: verrò l'altra domenica, I shall come next Sunday 6. (antecedente) last: andai l'altro mese, I went last month.
altronde 1. (nella loc. avv.) d'—, on the other hand 2. (tuttavia) however.
altrove avv. elsewhere, somewhere else.
altrui agg. other people's, someone else's. ♦ **l'altrui** sm. the property of others.
altruismo sm. unselfishness.
altruistico agg. unselfish.
altura sf. height.
alunno sm. pupil.
alveare sm. beehive.
alveo sm. river-bed.
alzaia sf. towing-line || strada d'—, towing-path.
alzare vt. 1. to lift, to raise 2. (erigere) to build (v. irr.) 3. (mar.) to hoist. ♦ **alzarsi** vr. (dal letto) to get (v. irr.) up 2. (in piedi) to stand (v. irr.) up 3. (in altezza) to grow (v. irr.) tall.
alzata sf. 1. raising 2. (l'alzarsi) rising.
amabile agg. amiable.
amabilità sf. amiability.
amaca sf. hammock.
amalgama sm. amalgam.
amalgamare vt. to amalgamate.
amante s. 1. lover 2. (fig.) fond.
amanuense sm. copyist.
amaranto sm. amaranth.
amare vt. 1. to love, to be fond of 2. (richiedere) to require.
amareggiare vt. 1. to make (v. irr.) bitter 2. (fig.) to sadden. ♦ **amareggiarsi** vr. to worry.
amarena sf. sour black cherry.

amaretto *sm.* macaroon.
amarezza *sf.* **1.** bitterness **2.** (*fig.*) sorrow.
amaro *agg.* bitter. ♦ **amaro** *sm.* (*liquore*) bitters (*pl.*).
amatore *sm.* **1.** lover **2.** (*chi si occupa d'arte per diletto*) amateur.
amàzzone *sf.* **1.** Amazon **2.** (*fig.*) masculine woman.
ambage *sf.* ambages (*pl.*) || *senza ambagi*, plainly.
ambasciata *sf.* **1.** embassy **2.** (*messaggio*) message.
ambasciatore *sm.* ambassador.
ambedue *agg.* e *pron.* both.
ambientare *vt.* **1.** to acclimatize **2.** (*fatti, personaggi ecc.*) to place. ♦ **ambientarsi** *vr.* to get (*v. irr.*) accustomed.
ambiente *sm.* **1.** ambient **2.** (*fig.*) milieu **3.** (*stanza*) room.
ambiguità *sf.* ambiguity.
ambiguo *agg.* ambiguous.
ambio *sm.* amble.
ambire *vt.* to desire.
àmbito *sm.* ambit.
ambivalente *agg.* ambivalent.
ambivalenza *sf.* ambivalence.
ambizione *sf.* ambition.
ambizioso *agg.* ambitious.
ambo *sm.* ambo.
ambra *sf.* amber.
ambrosia *sf.* ambrosia.
ambulante *agg.* itinerant || *venditore* —, pedlar.
ambulanza *sf.* ambulance.
ambulatorio *sm.* surgery.
ameba *sf.* amoeba.
amebìasi *sf.* amoebiasis (*pl.* -ses).
amenità *sf.* **1.** amenity **2.** (*facezia*) joke.
ameno *agg.* **1.** pleasant **2.** (*divertente*) funny: *un tipo* —, a funny chap.
americanismo *sm.* Americanism.
americano *agg.* e *sm.* American.
ametista *sf.* amethyst.
amianto *sm.* amianthus.
amichévole *agg.* friendly.
amicizia *sf.* friendship || *fare* —, to make (*v. irr.*) friends with.
amico *sm.* friend.
amidatura *sf.* starching.
àmido *sm.* starch.
ammaccare *vt.* to bruise.
ammaccatura *sf.* bruise.
ammaestramento *sm.* **1.** (*addestramento*) training **2.** (*insegnamento*) teaching **3.** (*di animali*) taming.

ammaestrare *vt.* **1.** (*addestrare*) to train **2.** (*insegnare*) to teach (*v. irr.*) **3.** (*di animali*) to tame.
ammainare *vt.* to furl.
ammalarsi *vr.* to fall (*v. irr.*) ill.
ammalato *agg.* **1.** (*pred.*) ill **2.** (*attr.*) sick. ♦ **ammalato** *sm.* sick person, patient.
ammaliare *vt.* to bewitch.
ammaliatrice *sf.* bewitcher.
ammanco *sm.* shortage || — *di cassa*, deficit.
ammanettare *vt.* to handcuff.
ammannire *vt.* to prepare.
ammansire *vt.* **1.** to tame **2.** (*fig.*) to calm. ♦ **ammansirsi** *vr.* **1.** to become (*v. irr.*) tamed **2.** to calm down.
ammarare *vi.* **1.** to alight (on water) **2.** (*di capsule spaziali*) to splash down.
ammassare *vt.* to heap. ♦ **ammassarsi** *vr.* to gather.
ammasso *sm.* heap.
ammattire *vi.* to get (*v. irr.*) mad.
ammazzare *vt.* to kill.
ammazzatoio *sm.* slaughter-house.
ammenda *sf.* amends (*pl.*).
amméttere *vt.* **1.** (*lasciar entrare*) to admit, to receive **2.** (*concedere, supporre*) to acknowledge, to suppose.
ammezzato *sm.* mezzanine.
ammezzire *vi.* to become (*v. irr.*) over-ripe.
ammiccare *vi.* to wink (at).
ammina *sf.* amine.
amministrare *vt.* **1.** to manage **2.** (*giur.; eccl.*) to administer.
amministrativo *agg.* administrative.
amministratore *sm.* manager.
amministrazione *sf.* management.
ammiràbile *agg.* admirable.
ammiraglio *sm.* admiral.
ammirare *vt.* to admire.
ammiratore *sm.* **1.** admirer **2.** (*di attori ecc.*) fan.
ammirazione *sf.* admiration.
ammirévole *agg.* admirable.
ammissìbile *agg.* admissible.
ammobiliamento *sm.* furnishing.
ammobiliare *vt.* to furnish.
ammodernare *vt.* to modernize.
ammodo *agg.* nice, proper.
ammogliare *vt.* to marry. ♦ **ammogliarsi** *vr.* to get (*v. irr.*) mar-

ried.

ammollare *vt.* 1. to soak 2. (*ammorbidire*) to soften.

ammollire *vt.* to soften.

ammonìaca *sf.* ammonia.

ammonire *vt.* 1. to admonish 2. (*avvisare*) to warn.

ammonizione *sf.* 1. admonition 2. (*rimprovero*) reproof 3. (*avvertimento*) warning.

ammontare *vi.* to amount.

ammonticchiare *vt.* to heap (up).

ammorbare *vt.* to taint.

ammorbidire *vt.* to soften.

ammortamento *sm.* redemption || *quota d'—*, depreciation allowance.

ammortire *vt.* to numb.

ammortizzare *vt.* to redeem.

ammosciare *vt.* to become (*v. irr.*) flabby.

ammucchiare *vt.* to heap (up).

ammuffire *vi.* 1. to grow (*v. irr.*) musty 2. (*fig.*) to languish: *— in casa*, to languish at home.

ammutinamento *sm.* mutiny.

ammutinarsi *vr.* to mutiny.

ammutinato *agg.* mutinous. ♦ **ammutinato** *sm.* mutineer.

ammutolire *vi.* 1. to become (*v. irr.*) dumb 2. (*essere ammutolito da altri*) to be struck dumb.

amnesìa *sf.* loss of memory.

amnistìa *sf.* amnesty.

amnistiare *vt.* to amnesty.

amo *sm.* fish-hook.

amorale *agg.* amoral.

amoralità *sf.* amorality.

amore *sm.* 1. love || *— di sé*, selfishness 2. (*persona o cosa amata*) beloved || *per amore di*, for the sake of.

amoreggiare *vi.* to flirt.

amoretto *sm.* flirtation.

amorévole *agg.* loving.

amorevolezza *sf.* lovingness.

amorfo *agg.* amorphous.

amorino *sm.* Cupid.

amoroso *agg.* 1. loving 2. (*fig.*) amorous: *poesia —*, amorous verse.

amovìbile *agg.* movable.

amperòmetro *sm.* amperometer.

ampiezza *sf.* width, (*anche fig.*) breadth.

ampio *agg.* 1. wide 2. (*di abito*) comfortable.

amplesso *sm.* embrace.

ampliamento *sm.* amplification.

ampliare *vt.* 1. to amplify 2. (*aumentare*) to increase. ♦ **ampliar-**

si *vr.* to widen.

amplificare *vt.* 1. to enlarge 2. (*fig.; fis.*) to amplify.

amplificatore *sm.* amplifier.

amplificazione *sf.* amplification.

ampolla *sf.* 1. phial 2. (*per olio, aceto ecc.*) cruet.

ampollosità *sf.* pomposity.

ampolloso *agg.* pompous: *stile —*, bombastic style.

amputare *vt.* to amputate.

amputazione *sf.* amputation.

amuleto *sm.* amulet.

anabbaglianti *sm. pl.* lower beams

anabolismo *sm.* anabolism.

anacoreta *sm.* anchorite.

anacronismo *sm.* anachronism.

anacronistico *agg.* anachronistic.

anàgrafe *sf.* registry office.

anagramma *sm.* anagram.

analcòlico *agg.* soft.

anale *agg.* anal.

analfabeta *sm.* illiterate.

analfabetismo *sm.* illiteracy.

analgèsico *agg.* e *sm.* analgesic.

anàlisi *sf.* analysis (*pl.* -ses).

analìtico *agg.* analytical.

analizzare *vt.* to analyse.

analogamente *avv.* likewise.

analogìa *sf.* analogy.

anàlogo *agg.* similar.

ànanas *sm.* pine-apple.

anarchìa *sf.* anarchy.

anàrchico *agg.* anarchic. ♦ **anàrchico** *sm.* anarchist.

anatema *sm.* anathema.

anatomìa *sf.* anatomy.

anatòmico *agg.* anatomic.

anatomista *sm.* anatomist.

ànatra *sf.* duck.

anatròccolo *sm.* duckling.

anca *sf.* hip.

ancestrale *agg.* ancestral.

anche *avv.* 1. (*pure*) also, too 2. (*in frasi neg.*) either: *anch'io non verrò*, I will not come either 3. (*con comp.*) even, still: *ciò è anche peggio*, it is still worse 4. (*persino*) even. ♦ **anche** *cong.* (*anche se*) even if, even though

ancheggiare *vi.* to waddle.

anchilosato *agg.* ankylosed.

anchilosi *sf.* ankylosis.

àncora *sf.* 1. anchor: *levar l'—*, to weigh anchor 2. (*fig.*) hope: *— di salvezza*, last hope.

ancora *avv.* 1. (*tuttora*) still 2. (*in frasi neg.*) yet 3. (*di nuovo*) again 4. (*davanti a comp.*) still, even

5. (*con pron. e agg. quantitativi*) more: — *molte persone*, many more people **6.** («*di più*» *in frasi affermative*) some more: *voglio ancora caffè*, I want some more coffee **7.** («*di più*» *in frasi neg. e dubitative*) any more: *hai ancora caffè?*, have you any more coffee? **8.** (*più a lungo*) longer: *leggi ancora un po'*, read a little longer.

ancoraggio *sm.* anchorage.

ancorare *vt.* to anchor.

ancorché *cong.* even if, even though.

andamento *sm.* **1.** (*tendenza*) trend **2.** (*procedimento*) proceeding.

andante *agg.* **1.** (*scadente*) plain **2.** (*comm.*) current **3.** (*mus.*) andante.

andare *vi.* **1.** (*anche fig.*) to go (*v. irr.*): — *a cavallo*, to go on horseback; — *a far compere*, to go shopping; — *a piedi*, to go on foot; — *a zonzo*, to lounge about; — *e venire*, to come (*v. irr.*) and go; — *in bicicletta*, to ride (*v. irr.*) a bicycle; — *in treno*, to go by train; — *a male*, to go bad **2.** (*essere molto venduto*) to be in demand **3.** (— *bene*, *di indumento*) to fit || — *avanti* (*di orologi*), to be fast; — *indietro* (*di orologi*), to be slow. ♦ **andàrsene** *vr.* to go away.

andata *sf.* going: — *e ritorno*, going there and back || *biglie'to di sola* —, single ticket || *biglietto di* — *e ritorno*, return ticket.

andatura *sf.* **1.** gait **2.** (*velocità*) pace.

andazzo *sm.* habit, custom.

andicappare *vt.* to handicap.

andirivieni *sm.* coming and going.

àndito *sm.* passage.

andrògino *agg.* androgynous. ♦ **andrògino** *sm.* androgyne.

androne *sm.* lobby.

aneddòtico *agg.* anecdotic.

anèddoto *sm.* anecdote.

anelare *vi.* **1.** to gasp **2.** (*fig.*) to long for.

anèlito *sm.* **1.** gasp **2.** (*fig.*) longing for.

anello *sm.* ring: — *di fidanzamento*, engagement ring; — *di matrimonio*, wedding ring || — *di catena*, link of a chain.

anemìa *sf.* anaemia.

anèmico *agg.* anaemic.

anèmone *sm.* anemone.

anestesìa *sf.* anaesthesia.

anestesista *s.* anaesthetist.

anestètico *agg. e sm.* anaesthetic.

anestetizzare *vt.* to anaesthetize.

anfibio *agg.* amphibious. ♦ **anfibio** *sm.* (*zool.*; *mil.*) amphibian.

anfiteatro *sm.* amphitheatre.

anfitrione *sm.* amphitryon.

ànfora *sf.* amphora (*pl.* -ae).

anfrattuoso *agg.* anfractuous.

angèlico *agg.* angelic(al).

àngelo *sm.* angel.

angherìa *sf.* vexation.

angina *sf.* angina.

angioma *sm.* angioma.

anglicano *agg. e sm.* Anglican.

angolare *agg.* angular.

àngolo *sm.* **1.** corner **2.** (*fis.*; *geom.*) angle.

angoloso *agg.* angular.

angoscia *sf.* anguish.

angosciare *vt.* to anguish.

angoscioso *agg.* **1.** (*che dà angoscia*) distressing **2.** (*pieno di angoscia*) full of anguish.

anguilla *sf.* **1.** eel **2.** (*fig.*) elusive person.

anguria *sf.* water-melon.

angustia *sf.* **1.** narrowness **2.** (*tribolazione*) distress.

angustiare *vt.* to afflict. ♦ **angustiarsi** *vr.* to worry.

angusto *agg.* **1.** narrow **2.** (*fig.*) mean.

ànice *sm.* anise.

anidride *sf.* anhydride.

anilina *sf.* aniline.

ànima *sf.* **1.** soul || *esalare l'*—, to die || *vender l'*— *a caro prezzo*, to sell (*v. irr.*) one's life dearly. **2.** (*parte centrale*, *nerbo*) soul, heart **3.** (*cuore*, *sentimento*) feeling, heart **4.** (*persona*) person: *Torino ha oltre un milione di anime*, Turin has over one million persons.

animale *sm. e agg.* animal.

animalesco *agg.* beastly.

animare *vt.* to enliven, to give (*v. irr.*) life. ♦ **animarsi** *vr.* to become (*v. irr.*) lively.

animatamente *avv.* animatedly.

animato *agg.* **1.** living **2.** (*vivace*) lively.

animatore *sm.* animator.

animazione *sf.* briskness.

animismo *sm.* animism.

ànimo *sm.* **1.** mind: *ho in animo di fare ciò*, I have a mind to do that **2.** (*coraggio*) courage **3.** (*inclinazione*) disposition.

animosità sf. animosity.
animoso agg. 1. brave 2. (ostile) malevolent.
anisetta sf. anisette.
ànitra sf. duck.
annacquare vt. 1. to water 2. (fig.) to moderate.
annaffiare vt. to water.
annaffiatoio sm. watering-can.
annali sm. pl. annals.
annaspare vi. to grope.
annaspío sm. groping.
annata sf. 1. year 2. (raccolto) crop.
annebbiare vt. 1. to dim 2. (fig.) to dull. ♦ **annebbiarsi** vr. (della vista) to blur.
annegamento sm. drowning.
annegare vt. to drown. ♦ **annegarsi** vr. to drown oneself.
annegato agg. drowned.
annerimento sm. blackening.
annerire vt. to blacken.
annessione sf. annexation.
annesso agg. 1. connected 2. (accluso) enclosed.
annèttere vt. to annex.
annichilazione sf. annihilation.
annichilimento sm. annihilation.
annichilire vt. to annihilate.
annidarsi vr. 1. to nestle 2. (nascondersi) to hide (v. irr.).
annientamento sm. 1. destruction 2. (di desideri) frustration.
annientare vt. to destroy.
anniversario agg. e sm. anniversary.
anno sm. 1. year: — bisestile, leap-year || Capo d'—, New Year's Day || durante tutto l'—, all the year round 2. (periodo lungo e indeterminato) a long time 3. (nell'indicare l'età) to be ... years old: ho 10 anni, I am 10 years old.
annodare vt. to knot: — amicizie, to make friends.
annoiare vt. to bore, to tire. ♦ **annoiarsi** vr. to be bored.
annoiato agg. bored.
annoiatore sm. tiresome person.
annoso agg. old.
annotare vt. 1. (corredare di note) to annotate 2. (prendere nota) to take (v. irr.) a note (of).
annotazione sf. note.
annottare vi. to grow (v. irr.) dark.
annuale agg. yearly.
annuario sm. year-book.
annuire vi. to nod.
annullamento sm. cancellation.

annullare vt. 1. to annul 2. (comm.) to cancel.
annunciare vt. 1. to announce 2. (predire) to foretell (v. irr.).
annunciatore sm. announcer.
annuncio sm. 1. notice 2. (presagio) presage.
ànnuo agg. yearly.
annusare vt. 1. to smell 2. (tabacco) to take (v. irr.) snuff.
annuvolarsi vr. 1. to get (v. irr.) cloudy 2. (fig.) to become (v. irr.) gloomy.
ano sm. anus.
anòdino agg. anodyne.
ànodo sm. anode.
anomalìa sf. anomaly.
anòmalo agg. anomalous.
anònima sf. joint-stock company.
anònimo agg. anonymous. ♦ **anònimo** sm. anonym.
anormale agg. abnormal.
anormalità sf. abnormality.
ansa sf. 1. (insenatura) creek 2. (di fiume) bend 3. (manico) handle.
ansante agg. panting.
ansare vi. to pant.
ansia sf. anxiety.
ansietà sf. anxiety.
ansimare vi. to pant.
ansioso agg. 1. anxious 2. (desideroso) eager.
ànsito sm. panting.
anta sf. 1. shutter 2. (di armadio) door.
antagonismo sm. antagonism.
antagonista s. antagonist.
antàrtico agg. Antarctic.
antecedente agg. previous. ♦ **antecedente** sm. antecedent.
antecessore sm. predecessor.
antefatto sm. antecedent fact.
anteguerra sm. pre-war time.
antenato sm. ancestor.
antenna sf. 1. (zool.) antenna (pl. -nae) 2. (radio) aerial.
anteporre vt. to place before, to put (v. irr.) before.
anteprima sf. preview.
anteriore agg. 1. (nello spazio) fore 2. (nel tempo) previous, former.
antiabbaglianti sm. pl. anti-dazzle.
antiaèreo agg. anti-aircraft.
antibattèrico agg. e sm. antibacterial.
antibiòtico agg. e sm. antibiotic.
anticaglia sf. worthless antique.
anticamente avv. in ancient times.
anticàmera sf. ante-room || fare —,

to be kept waiting.

anticarro *agg.* anti-tank.

antichità *sf.* **1.** antiquity **2.** (*oggetti antichi*) antiques (*pl.*).

anticipare *vt.* **1.** to anticipate **2.** (*di danaro*) to pay in advance.

anticipatamente *avv.* in advance.

anticipato *agg.* **1.** advanced **2.** (*comm.*) in advance.

anticipazione *sf.* anticipation.

anticipo *sm.* advance: *essere in —*, to be before time **2.** (*caparra*) earnest money.

anticlericale *agg. e s.* anticlerical.

anticlericalismo *sm.* anticlericalism.

antico *agg.* **1.** ancient **2.** (*all'antica*) old-fashioned.

anticonformista *s.* nonconformist.

anticongelante *sm.* anti-freeze.

anticorpo *sm.* antibody.

anticostituzionale *agg.* anticonstitutional.

antidatare *vt.* to antedate.

antidiluviano *agg. e sm.* antediluvian.

antidoto *sm.* antidote.

antiestetico *agg.* antiaesthetic.

antifascismo *sm.* antifascism.

antifascista *s. e agg.* antifascist.

antifebbrile *sm.* febrifuge.

antifecondativo *sm.* anti-conceptive.

antifona *sf.* antiphon: *capire l'—* to take (*v. irr.*) a hint.

antifurto *sm.* antitheft device.

antigàs *agg.* anti-gas: *maschera —*, gas-mask.

antigienico *agg.* unhealthy.

antilope *sf.* antelope.

antimilitarismo *sm.* antimilitarism.

antincendio *agg.* antifire: *pompa —*, fire-pump.

antinebbia *agg.* *faro —*, fog-light.

antinevralgico *agg.* antineuralgic.

antinomìa *sf.* antinomy.

antiparticella *sf.* antiparticle.

antipasto *sm.* hors-d'oeuvre.

antipatìa *sf.* dislike.

antipàtico *agg.* disagreeable.

antipodi *sm. pl.* antipodes.

antiquariato *sm.* antique-dealing.

antiquario *sm.* antique-dealer.

antiquato *agg.* old-fashioned.

antireumàtico *agg.* antirheumatic.

antirùggine *agg.* anti-rust.

antisemitismo *sm.* anti-Semitism.

antisèttico *agg. e sm.* antiseptic.

antispàstico *agg.* antispasmodic.

antistante *agg.* before, in front of.

antìtesi *sf.* antithesis (*pl.* -ses).

antitetànico *agg.* antitetanic.

antitètico *agg.* antithetic(al).

antitòssico *agg.* antitoxic.

antivigilia *sf.* the day before the eve.

antologìa *sf.* anthology.

antològico *agg.* anthological.

antonomasia *sf.* antonomasia || *per —*, antonomastically.

antracite *sf.* anthracite.

antro *sm.* **1.** cave **2.** (*tana*) den.

antropocentrismo *sm.* anthropocentrism.

antropofagìa *sf.* anthropophagy.

antropòfago *agg.* anthropophagous. ♦ **antropòfago** *sm.* cannibal.

antropologìa *sf.* anthropology.

antropòlogo *sm.* anthropologist.

antropomorfo *agg.* anthropomorphous.

anulare *agg.* annular. ♦ **anulare** *sm.* ring-finger.

anzi *cong.* **1.** (*al contrario*) on the contrary **2.** (*in più*) moreover || *— che*, rather than; *— che no*, rather. ♦ **anzi** *avv.* before: *— tempo*, before time.

anzianità *sf.* seniority.

anziano *agg.* **1.** elderly **2.** (*in cariche, uffici ecc.*) senior.

anziché *cong.* **1.** rather than **2.** (*invece di*) instead of.

anzidetto *agg.* above-mentioned.

anzitempo *avv.* before time.

aorta *sf.* aorta.

apartìtico *agg.* non-sectarian.

apatìa *sf.* apathy, indifference.

apàtico *agg.* listless.

ape *sf.* bee.

aperitivo *sm.* aperitif.

apertamente *avv.* openly.

aperto *agg.* open.

apertura *sf.* **1.** opening **2.** (*di mente*) broad-mindedness **3.** (*ampiezza di un arco*) span: *— alare*, wing-span.

àpice *sm.* apex.

apicoltura *sf.* bee-keeping.

apnea *sf.* apnoea.

apocalisse *sf.* apocalypse.

apocalìttico *agg.* apocalyptic(al).

apòcrifo *agg.* apocryphal || *libri apocrifi*, Apocrypha.

apòfisi *sf.* apophysis.

apogeo *sm.* apogee.

apòlide *agg.* stateless. ♦ **apòlide** *sm.* stateless person.

apolìtico *agg.* non-political.
apologìa *sf.* apologia.
apologista *s.* apologist.
apòlogo *sm.* apologue.
apoplessìa *sf.* apoplexy.
apoplèttico *agg.* apoplectic: *colpo* —, apoplectic fit.
apostasìa *sf.* apostasy.
apòstata *sm.* apostate.
apòstolo *sm.* apostle.
apostrofare *vt.* to apostrophize.
apòstrofe *sf.* apostrophe.
apòstrofo *sm.* apostrophe.
apoteosi *sf.* apotheosis.
appagare *vt.* 1. to satisfy, to gratify 2. (*la sete*) to quench one's thirst.
appaiare *vt.* 1. to couple 2. (*armonizzare colori, vestiario ecc.*) to match.
appallottolare *vt.* to roll into a ball.
appaltare *vt.* to give (*v. irr.*) out by contract.
appaltatore *sm.* contractor.
appalto *sm.* contract, bid.
appannaggio *sm.* apanage.
appannamento *sm.* 1. (*di metalli*) tarnishing 2. (*di vetri ecc.*) clouding 3. (*di vista*) dimming.
appannare *vt.* 1. (*di metalli*) to tarnish 2. (*di vetri ecc.*) to cloud 3. (*di vista*) to dim.
apparato *sm.* 1. apparatus 2. (*mostra*) display.
apparecchiare *vt.* to prepare: — *la tavola*, to lay (*v. irr.*) the table.
apparecchio *sm.* 1. set 2. (*aereoplano*) aeroplane || — *fotografico*, camera; — *telefonico*, telephone; — *radio*, radio set.
apparentare *vt.* to relate.
apparente *agg.* 1. (*illusorio*) seeming 2. (*chiaro*) apparent, obvious.
apparentemente *avv.* seemingly.
apparenza *sf.* 1. appearance 2. (*aspetto*) look 3. (*pompa*) show.
apparire *vi.* 1. to appear 2. (*aver l'aspetto*) to look 3. (*risultare*) to result.
appariscente *agg.* 1. striking 2. (*vistoso*) showy.
apparizione *sf.* apparition.
appartamento *sm.* flat.
appartarsi *vr.* to retire.
appartenenza *sf.* belonging.
appartenere *vi.* 1. to belong (to) 2. (*essere membro*) to be a member (of).

appassionare *vt.* to impassion. ♦
appassionarsi *vr.* to become (*v. irr.*) fond of.
appassionato *agg.* 1. passionate 2. (*di musica, arte ecc.*) keen (on).
appassire *vi.* to wither.
appellare *vt.* to name, to call. ♦
appellarsi *vr.* to appeal.
appellativo *sm.* appellative.
appello *sm.* 1. (*giur.*) appeal 2. (*chiamata*) call 3. (*esortazione*) appeal.
appena *avv.* 1. (*a fatica*) hardly 2. (*molto poco*) very little 3. (*da poco*) just: *ero* — *arrivato*, I had just arrived || *non* —, as soon as.
appèndere *vt.* to hang (*v. irr.*).
appendice *sf.* appendix || *romanzo d'*—, serial.
appendicite *sf.* appendicitis.
appesantire *vt.* to make (*v. irr.*) heavy. ♦ appesantirsi *vr.* to grow (*v. irr.*) heavy.
appestare *vt.* 1. to infect 2. (*spargere odore*) to stink (*v. irr.*).
appestato *agg.* 1. plague-stricken 2. (*fig.*) tainted. ♦ appestato *sm.* plague-stricken person.
appetenza *sf.* 1. appetite 2. (*desiderio*) longing (for sthg.).
appetìbile *agg.* pleasing.
appetire *vt.* to desire.
appetito *sm.* appetite.
appezzamento *sm.* plot of land.
appianare *vt.* 1. to level 2. (*fig.*) to smooth.
appiattarsi *vr.* 1. to crouch 2. (*stare in agguato*) to lie (*v. irr.*) in wait 3. (*nascondersi*) to hide (*v. irr.*).
appiattire *vt.* to flatten.
appiccare *vt.* (*il fuoco*) to set (*v. irr.*) fire.
appiccicare *vt.* 1. to stick (*v. irr.*) 2. (*appioppare*) to palm off.
appiccicoso *agg.* sticky.
appiè *prep.* 1. (*al di sotto*) below 2. (*ai piedi*) at the foot: — *del letto*, at the foot of the bed.
appiedare *vt.* to dismount.
appiedato *agg.* dismounted.
appieno *avv.* fully.
appigliarsi *vr.* to get (*v. irr.*) hold of: — *ad un pretesto*, to take (*v. irr.*) a pretext.
appiglio *sm.* 1. support 2. (*fig.*) pretext.
appiombo *sm.* perpendicularity.
appioppare *vt.* 1. to give (*v. irr.*)

|| — *uno schiaffo*, to slap 2. (*affibbiare*) to palm off.

appisolarsi *vr.* to doze off.

applaudire *vt.* e *vi.* to applaud.

applauditore *sm.* applauder.

appláuso *sm.* 1. applause (*solo sing.*) 2. (*fig.*) praise.

applicare *vt.* 1. to apply 2. (*giur.*) to carry out 3. (*accostare*) to set (*v. irr.*). ♦ **applicarsi** *vr.* to apply oneself.

applicazione *sf.* 1. application 2. (*fig.*) care 3. (*guarnizione*) trimming.

appoggiare *vt.* 1. to lean (*v. irr.*) 2. (*posare*) to lay (*v. irr.*) 3. (*fig.*) to back. ♦ **appoggiarsi** *vr.* 1. to lean (*v. irr.*) 2. (*fig.*) to rely (on).

appoggio *sm.* 1. support 2. (*fig.*) assistance 3. (*colui che dà —*) supporter.

appollaiarsi *vr.* to perch.

apporre *vt.* to affix.

apportare *vt.* 1. to bring (*v. irr.*) 2. (*produrre*) to produce.

apporto *sm.* contribution.

appositamente *avv.* on purpose.

appòsito *agg.* 1. special 2. (*adatto*) fit.

apposizione *sf.* 1. (*gramm.*) apposition 2. (*l'apporre*) affixing.

apposta *avv.* expressly.

appostare *vt.* (*mil.*) to place. ♦ **appostarsi** *vr.* to lie (*v. irr.*) in ambush.

apprèndere *vt.* to learn (*v. irr.*).

apprendista *sm.* apprentice.

apprendistato *sm.* apprenticeship.

apprensione *sf.* 1. concern 2. (*l'apprendere*) learning.

appresso *avv.* near, close by. ♦ **appresso** *prep.* near, close to.

apprestamento *sm.* preparation.

apprestare *vt.* to prepare.

apprettare *vt.* to dress.

apprezzàbile *agg.* appreciable.

apprezzamento *sm.* 1. appreciation 2. (*giudizio*)·opinion.

apprezzare *vt.* 1. to appreciate 2. (*valutare*) to value.

approdare *vi.* 1. to land 2. (*fig.*) to be of use.

approfittare *vi.* to profit (by). ♦ **approfittarsi** *vr.* 1. to avail oneself 2. (*abusare*) to take (*v. irr.*) undue advantage.

approfondire *vt.* 1. to make (*v. irr.*) deeper 2. (*fig.*) to examine closely.

approntare *vt.* to make (*v. irr.*) ready.

appropriarsi *vr.* to take (*v. irr.*) possession of.

appropriato *agg.* fit, suitable.

appropriazione *sf.* appropriation: — *indebita*, embezzlement.

approssimarsi *vr.* 1. to come (*v. irr.*) near 2. (*di tempo*) to draw (*v. irr.*) near.

approssimativamente *avv.* approximately.

approssimativo *agg.* approximative.

approssimazione *sf.* approximation.

approvare *vt.* 1. to approve (of) 2. (*promuovere*) to pass.

approvazione *sf.* approval.

approvvigionamento *sm.* 1. (*l'approvvigionare*) supplying 2. (*provviste*) supplies.

approvvigionare *vt.* to supply provisions (to).

appuntamento *sm.* appointment.

appuntare *vt.* 1. to sharpen 2. (*prender nota*) to note 3. (*biasimare*) to blame.

appuntellare *vt.* 1. to prop 2. (*fig.*) to support.

appuntino *avv.* nicely.

appuntito *agg.* pointed.

appunto[1] *sm.* 1. note 2. (*critica*) blame.

appunto[2] *avv.* exactly, just.

appurare *vt.* to verify.

apribottiglie *sm.* bottle-opener.

aprile *sm.* April: *pesce d'—*, April fool.

aprire *vt.* to open: — *le braccia a qc.*, to welcome so.

apriscàtole *sm.* tin-opener.

àquila *sf.* eagle.

aquilino *agg.* aquiline.

aquilone *sm.* 1. (*vento del nord*) north wind 2. (*giocattolo*) kite.

aquilotto *sm.* eaglet.

arabescare *vt.* to decorate with arabesques.

arabesco *sm.* arabesque.

aràbico *agg.* Arabic.

aràbile *agg.* arable.

àrabo *agg.* e *sm.* Arab.

aràchide *sf.* peanut.

aragosta *sf.* lobster.

aràldico *agg.* heraldic

araldo *sm.* herald.

arancia *sf.* orange.

aranciata *sf.* orange squash.
aranciera *sf.* orangery.
arancio *agg.* (*colore*) orange. ♦ **arancio** *sm.* orange-tree.
arancione *agg.* orange-coloured.
arare *vt.* to plough.
aratore *sm.* ploughman (*pl.* -men).
aratro *sm.* plough.
aratura *sf.* ploughing.
arazzo *sm.* arras.
arbitraggio *sm.* 1. (*sport*) umpirage 2. (*comm.*) arbitrage.
arbitrare *vt.* 1. to arbitrate 2. (*calcio, boxe*) to referee.
arbitrario *agg.* arbitrary.
arbitrio *sm.* 1. will: *libero* —, free will 1. (*atto arbitrario*) arbitrary act.
àrbitro *sm.* 1. (*sport*) umpire 2. (*calcio, boxe*) referee 3. (*giur.*) arbitrator.
arboricoltore *sm.* arboriculturist.
arboricoltura *sf.* arboriculture.
arboscello *sm.* shrub.
arbusto *sm.* shrub.
arca *sf.* ark || — *di scienza*, eminent scholar.
arcàdico *agg.* e *sm.* Arcadian.
arcàico *agg.* 1. archaic 2. (*di parole, stile*) obsolete.
arcaismo *sm.* 1. archaism 2. (*parola arcaica*) obsolete word.
arcàngelo *sm.* archangel.
arcano *agg.* mysterious.
archeologìa *sf.* archaeology.
archeològico *agg.* archaeologic(al).
archeòlogo *sm.* archaeologist.
archètipo *sm.* archetype.
archetto *sm.* 1. small arch 2. (*mus.*) bow.
architettare *vt.* 1. to draw (*v. irr.*) the plans 2. (*fig.*) to devise.
architetto *sm.* architect.
architettònico *agg.* architectonic.
architettura *sf.* architecture.
architrave *sm.* architrave.
archiviare *vt.* 1. to place in the archives 2. (*comm.*) to file.
archivio *sm.* 1. archives (*pl.*) 2. (*comm.*) file.
archivista *sm.* archivist.
arciduca *sm.* archduke.
arciere *sm.* archer.
arcigno *agg.* gruff.
arcimiliardario *sm.* multimillionaire.
arcipèlago *sm.* archipelago (*pl.* -goes).
arcivescovado *sm.* archbishopric.

arcivéscovo *sm.* archbishop.
arco *sm.* 1. (*arma*) bow 2. (*geom.*) arc 3. (*arch.*) arch 4. (*mus.*) bow.
arcobaleno *sm.* rainbow.
arcolaio *sm.* wool-winder.
arcuare *vt.* 1. to arch 2. (*piegare*) to bend (*v. irr.*).
ardente *agg.* 1. burning 2. (*fig.*) passionate.
ardentemente *avv.* ardently.
àrdere *vt.* to burn (*v. irr.*).
ardesia *sf.* slate.
ardire *vi.* 1. to dare 2. (*avere l'impudenza*) to have the impudence.
ardito *agg.* 1. bold 2. (*rischioso*) risky.
ardore *sm.* 1. fierce heat 2. (*fig.*) passion.
àrduo *agg.* 1. hard 2. (*erto*) steep.
àrea *sf.* 1. area 2. (*sfera d'azione*) sphere.
arena *sf.* 1. (*sabbia*) sand 2. (*arch.*) arena.
arenarsi *vr.* to get (*v. irr.*) stranded (*anche fig.*).
arengario *sm.* tribune.
areòpago *sm.* Areopagus.
àrgano *sm.* 1. (*mar.*) capstan 2. (*mecc.*) windlass.
argentare *vt.* to silver.
argènteo *agg.* silvery.
argenterìa *sf.* silver ware.
argentino *agg.* silvery.
argento *sm.* silver.
argilla *sf.* clay.
argilloso *agg.* clayey.
arginare *vt.* 1. to dam 2. (*fig.*) to check.
àrgine *sm.* bank.
argomentare *vt.* to infer. ♦ **argomentare** *vi.* to argue.
argomentazione *sf.* reasoning.
argomento *sm.* 1. subject 2. (*prova a sostegno*) argument.
arguire *vt.* to deduce.
argutezza *sf.* shrewdness.
arguto *agg.* 1. sharp 2. (*faceto*) witty.
arguzia *sf.* wit.
aria *sf.* 1. air: — *condizionata*, air conditioning || *corrente d'*—, draught || *camera d'*—, inner tube || *andare all'*—, to fall (*v. irr.*) through 2. (*aspetto*) look 3. (*mus.*) tune.
ariano *agg.* e *sm.* Aryan.
ariditá *sf.* 1. aridity 2. (*di cuore*) lack of feeling.
àrido *agg.* 1. arid 2. (*di cuore*)

lacking feeling.
arieggiare *vt.* **1.** to air **2.** (*rassomigliare*) to look like **3.** (*imitare*) to imitate.
arieggiato *agg.* aired.
ariete *sm.* ram.
aringa *sf.* herring.
arioso *agg.* airy.
aristocràtico *agg.* aristocratic. ♦ **aristocràtico** *sm.* aristocrat.
aristocrazia *sf.* aristocracy.
aristotèlico *agg.* e *sm.* Aristotelian.
aritmètica *sf.* arithmetic.
aritmètico *agg.* arithmetic(al).
arlecchinata *sf.* harlequinade.
arlecchino *sm.* harlequin.
arma *sf.* weapon, arm: *armi bianche*, side-arms; *armi da fuoco*, fire-arms || *galleria d'armi*, armoury.
armadietto *sm.* **1.** (*per medicinali, strumenti ecc.*) cabinet **2.** (*per abiti*) locker.
armadio *sm.* **1.** (*per stoviglie*) cupboard **2.** (*per abiti*) wardrobe.
armaiolo *sm.* armourer.
armamentario *sm.* **1.** instruments (*pl.*) **2.** (*armeria*) armoury.
armamento *sm.* arming.
armare *vt.* to arm.
armata *sf.* army.
armatore *sm.* **1.** shipbuilder **2.** (*chi possiede una nave*) shipowner.
armatura *sf.* **1.** armour **2.** (*impalcatura*) scaffolding.
armeggiare *vi.* **1.** to handle arms **2.** (*darsi da fare*) to busy oneself **3.** (*tramare*) to manoeuvre.
armeggìo *sm.* **1.** handling of arms **2.** (*l'affaccendarsi*) bustling **3.** (*intrigo*) manoeuvre.
armento *sm.* herd.
armerìa *sf.* armoury.
armiere *sm.* gunsmith.
armistizio *sm.* armistice.
armonìa *sf.* harmony.
armònica *sf.* (*a bocca*) mouth-organ.
armònico *agg.* harmonic.
armonio *sm.* harmonium.
armonioso *agg.* harmonious.
armonista *s.* harmonist.
armonizzare *vt.* to harmonize. ♦ **armonizzare** *vi.* **1.** to harmonize **2.** (*di colori*) to match.
arnese *sm.* **1.** (*strumento*) tool **2.** (*aggeggio*) gadget.
arnia *sf.* beehive.
aroma *sm.* flavour.
aromàtico *agg.* aromatic.

aromatizzare *vt.* to flavour.
arpa *sf.* harp.
arpeggiare *vi.* to play the harp.
arpeggio *sm.* arpeggio.
arpista *s.* harpist.
arra *sf.* earnest.
arrabattarsi *vr.* to bestir oneself.
arrabbiare *vi.* **1.** to become (*v. irr.*) angry **2.** (*di cane*) to be affected with rabies. ♦ **arrabbiarsi** *vr.* to get (*v. irr.*) angry.
arrabbiato *agg.* **1.** angry **2.** (*di cane*) rabid.
arrabbiatura *sf.* rage.
arraffare *vt.* to grasp.
arrampicarsi *vr.* to climb.
arrampicata *sf.* climb.
arrampicatore *sm.* **1.** mountain climber **2.** (*fig.*) social climber.
arrancare *vi.* **1.** to plod along **2.** (*zoppicare*) to limp **3.** (*affaticarsi*) to get (*v. irr.*) tired.
arrangiamento *sm.* arrangement.
arrangiare *vt.* to arrange. ♦ **arrangiarsi** *vr.* to manage.
arrecare *vt.* **1.** to bring (*v. irr.*) **2.** (*causare*) to cause.
arredamento *sm.* furnishing.
arredare *vt.* to furnish.
arredatore *sm.* internal decorator.
arredo *sm.* piece of furniture.
arrèndersi *vr.* **1.** to surrender **2.** (*fig.*) to give (*v. irr.*) it up.
arrendévole *agg.* **1.** pliant **2.** (*fig.*) docile.
arrestare *vt.* **1.** to stop **2.** (*trarre in arresto*) to arrest. ♦ **arrestarsi** *vr.* to stop.
arresto *sm.* arrest.
arretrare *vt.* **1.** to pull back **2.** (*ritirare*) to withdraw (*v. irr.*).
arretrato *agg.* backward.
arricchimento *sm.* enrichment.
arricchire *vt.* to enrich. ♦ **arricchirsi** *vr.* to grow (*v. irr.*) rich.
arricciare *vt.* to curl: — *il naso*, to turn up one's nose.
arrìdere *vi.* to be favourable.
arringare *vt.* to harangue.
arringatore *sm.* haranguer.
arrischiare *vt.* to risk. ♦ **arrischiarsi** *vr.* to venture.
arrivare *vi.* **1.** to arrive (at), (in) **2.** (*fig.*) to attain.
arrivato *agg.* (*fig.*) successful.
arrivederci *inter.* goodbye.
arrivismo *sm.* social climbing.
arrivista *sm.* social climber.
arrivo *sm.* arrival.

arrogante *agg.* arrogant.
arroganza *sf.* arrogance.
arrogarsi *vr.* to arrogate to one-self.
arrossire *vi.* to blush.
arrostire *vt.* 1. to roast 2. (*di pane*) to toast.
arrosto *sm.* roast.
arrotare *vt.* to grind (*v. irr.*): — *i denti*, to grind one's teeth.
arrotino *sm.* knife-grinder.
arrotolare *vt.* to roll up.
arrotondare *vt.* 1. to round 2. (*di cifre*) to make (*v. irr.*) a round figure.
arrovellarsi *vr.* to worry.
arroventare *vt.* to make (*v. irr.*) red-hot.
arruffare *vt.* to ruffle.
arruffone *sm.* muddler
arrugginire *vi.* to rust.
arruolare *vt.* to enrol.
arsenale *sm.* 1. (*cantiere*) ship-yard 2. (*deposito di armi*) arsenal.
arsènico *sm.* arsenic.
arsura *sf.* 1. (*siccità*) drought 2. (*sete*) parching thirst.
arte *sf.* art || *belle arti*, fine arts.
artefatto *agg.* adulterated.
artéfice *sm.* maker.
arteria *sf.* 1. artery 2. (*di traffico*) thoroughfare.
arteriosclerosi *sf.* arteriosclerosis.
artesiano *agg.* artesian.
àrtico *agg.* arctic.
articolare *vt.* to articulate.
articolazione *sf.* articulation.
articolo *sm.* 1. (*gramm.; di giornale*) article || — *di fondo*, editorial 2. (*comm.*) item.
artificiale *agg.* artificial.
artificio *sm.* 1. device 2. (*astuzia*) cunning.
artigianato *sm.* handicraft.
artigiano *sm.* craftsman (*pl.* -men).
artigliere *sm.* gunner.
artiglieria *sf.* artillery.
artiglio *sm.* claw.
artista *sm.* artist.
artìstico *agg.* artistic(al).
arto *sm.* limb: — *artificiale*, artificial limb.
artrite *sf.* arthritis (*pl.* -ides).
artrosi *sf.* arthrosis.
arzigògolo *sm.* subtlety.
arzillo *agg.* lively, brisk.
ascella *sf.* armpit.
ascendente *sm.* 1. ascendancy 2. (*antenato*) ancestor.

ascendenza *sf.* ancestry.
ascéndere *vi.* (*anche fig.*) to rise (*v. irr.*).
ascensione *sf.* 1. ascension 2. (*scalata*) climb.
ascensore *sm.* lift.
ascesa *sf.* ascent.
ascesi *sf.* mystical practice.
ascesso *sm.* abscess.
asceta *sm.* ascetic.
ascètico *agg.* ascetical.
ascetismo *sm.* asceticism.
ascia *sf.* axe.
ascissa *sf.* abscissa (*pl.* -sae).
asciugacapelli *sm.* hair-drier.
asciugamano *sm.* towel.
asciugare *vt.* 1. to dry 2. (*con un panno*) to wipe. ♦ **asciugarsi** *vr.* to dry up.
asciugatoio *sm.* towel.
asciutto *agg.* 1. (*anche fig.*) dry 2. (*magro*) thin.
ascoltare *vt.* 1. to listen (to) 2. (*assistere*) to attend: — *le lezioni*, to attend classes.
ascolto *sm.* listening.
ascrìvere *vt.* 1. to count 2. (*attribuire*) to ascribe. ♦ **ascrìversi** *vr.* to claim.
asepsi *sf.* asepsis.
asessuale *agg.* asexual.
asèttico *agg.* aseptic.
asfaltare *vt.* to asphalt.
asfalto *sm.* asphalt.
asfissìa *sf.* 1. asphyxia 2. (*da gas*) gassing.
asfissiare *vt.* 1. to asphyxiate 2. (*con gas*) to gas.
asiàtico *agg. e sm.* Asiatic.
asilo *sm.* 1. shelter 2. (*scuola materna*) infant-school.
asimmetria *sf.* asymmetry.
asimmètrico *agg.* asymmetrical.
asineria *sf.* stupidity.
asinità *sf.* asininity.
àsino *sm.* 1. ass 2. (*fig.*) jackass.
asma *sf.* asthma.
asmàtico *agg.* asthmatical.
asociale *agg.* asocial.
àsola *sf.* buttonhole.
aspàrago *sm.* asparagus.
aspèrgere *vt.* to sprinkle.
asperità *sf.* 1. asperity 2. (*di superfici*) unevenness 3. (*di carattere*) harshness.
aspersorio *sm.* aspergillum.
aspettare *vt.* to wait (for). ♦ **aspettarsi** *vr.* to expect.
aspettativa *sf.* 1. expectation 2.

(esonero temporaneo) temporary retirement.

aspetto *sm.* look || *di bell'aspetto*, good-looking || *sala d'—*, waiting--room.

àspide *sm.* asp.

aspirante *agg.* aspirant. ♦ **aspirante** *sm.* candidate, applicant.

aspirapòlvere *sm.* vacuum cleaner, hoover.

aspirare *vt.* to inspire. ♦ **aspirare** *vi.* to aspire (to).

aspiratore *sm.* aspirator.

aspirazione *sf.* 1. aspiration 2. *(mecc.)* suction.

aspirina *sf.* aspirin.

asportare *vt.* 1. to remove 2. *(med.)* to extirpate.

asportazione *sf.* 1. removal 2. *(med.)* extirpation.

asprezza *sf.* 1. sourness 2. *(fig.)* harshness.

asprigno *agg.* sourish.

aspro *agg.* 1. sour 2. *(fig.)* harsh.

assaggiare *vt.* to taste.

assaggio *sm.* 1. tasting 2. *(campione)* sample.

assai *avv.* 1. *(con agg. e avv.)* very 2. *(con comp.)* much: *— meglio*, much better.

assalire *vt.* 1. to assail 2. *(di malattia)* to attack.

assalitore *sm.* assailer.

assaltare *vt.* to assault.

assalto *sm.* assault, attack.

assaporare *vt.* 1. to savour 2. *(fig.)* to enjoy.

assassinare *vt.* to murder.

assassinio *sm.* murder.

assassino *sm.* murderer.

asse *sf.* 1. *(tavola di legno)* board 2. *(geom.)* axis *(pl. axes)* 3. *(stor.)* Axis.

assecondare *vt.* to favour.

assediare *vt.* to bèsiege.

assedio *sm.* siege.

assegnamento *sm.* assignment || *fare — su qualcuno*, to rely on so.

assegnare *vt.* 1. to assign 2. *(un premio)* to award.

assegno *sm.* cheque: *— al portatore*, cheque to bearer; *— circolare*, banker's draft; *— sbarrato*, crossed cheque.

assemblea *sf.* 1. meeting 2. *(corpo deliberante)* assembly.

assembramento *sm.* concourse of people.

assembrarsi *vr.* to assemble.

assennatezza *sf.* common sense.

assennato *agg.* sensible.

assenso *sm.* assent.

assentarsi *vr.* to go *(v. irr.)* away.

assente *agg.* absent.

assenteismo *sm.* absenteeism.

assentire *vi.* 1. to assent (to) 2. *(col capo)* to nod (in assent).

assenza *sf.* absence.

assenzio *sm.* absinth.

asserire *vt.* to affirm.

asserragliarsi *vr.* to barricade oneself.

asserto *sm.* assertion.

assertore *sm.* 1. assertor 2. *(difensore)* defender, champion.

asservimento *sm.* enslavement.

asservire *vt.* to enslave, to subdue.

asserzione *sf.* statement.

assessorato *sm.* assessorship.

assessore *sm.* 1. *(alle imposte)* assessor 2. *(comunale)* councillor responsible for a municipal region.

assestamento *sm.* 1. adjustment 2. *(definitivo)* settlement 3. *(del terreno)* settling.

assestare *vt.* to arrange: *— un colpo*, to deal *(v. irr.)* a blow. ♦ **assestarsi** *vr.* to settle (down).

assetato *agg.* 1. thirsty 2. *(fig.)* eager (for).

assetto *sm.* order.

assicurare *vt.* 1. *(legare)* to fasten 2. *(promettere)* to assure 3. *(affermare)* to affirm 4. *(comm.)* to insure.

assicurata *sf.* registered letter.

assicurato *agg.* insured, assured. ♦ **assicurato** *sm.* insurant.

assicuratore *sm.* insurer.

assicurazione *sf.* 1. assurance 2. *(comm.)* insurance.

assideramento *sm.* frost-bite.

assiduità *sf.* assiduity.

assìduo *agg.* assiduous.

assieme *avv.* V. *insieme.*

assieparsi *vr.* to crowd (round).

assillante *agg.* urging.

assillare *vt.* to urge.

assillo *sm.* 1. urge 2. *(fig.)* worry.

assimilàbile *agg.* assimilable.

assimilare *vt.* to assimilate, to absorb.

assimilazione *sf.* assimilation.

assioma *sm.* axiom.

assiomàtico *agg.* axiomatic.

assise *sf. pl.* assizes.

assistente *sm.* assistant.

assistenza *sf.* assistance.

assistenziale agg. charitable.
assistere vt. 1. to assist 2. (curare) to nurse. ◆ **assistere** vi. to attend (sthg.).
assito sm. 1. wooden partition 2. (pavimento) plank floor.
asso sm. 1. (carte) ace 2. (sport) champion || piantare in —, to leave (v. irr.) in the lurch.
associare vt. to join. ◆ **associarsi** vr. to associate.
associato sm. member.
associazione sf. association.
assodare vt. 1. to consolidate 2. (accertare) to ascertain.
assoggettare vt. to subject. ◆ **assoggettarsi** vr. to submit oneself.
assolato agg. sunny.
assoldare vt. to recruit.
assolo sm. (mus.) solo.
assolutamente avv. absolutely.
assolutismo sm. absolutism.
assolutista agg. e sm. absolutist.
assoluto agg. e sm. absolute.
assoluzione sf. 1. (eccl.) absolution 2. (giur.) discharge.
assòlvere vt. 1. (teol.) to absolve 2. (giur.) to discharge 3. (eseguire) to accomplish.
assomigliante agg. like.
assomigliare vi. to look like.
assommare vt. e vi. to add, to amount (to).
assonanza sf. assonance.
assonnarsi vr. to fall (v. irr.) asleep.
assonnato agg. sleepy.
assopimento sm. dozing.
assopire vt. to make (v. irr.) dozy. ◆ **assopirsi** vr. to doze off.
assorbente agg. absorbing || carta —, blotting-paper.
assorbimento sm. absorption.
assorbire vt. to absorb.
assordante agg. deafening.
assordare vt. to deafen.
assortimento sm. assortment.
assortire vt. 1. to stock 2. (fig.) to match.
assorto agg. absorbed.
assottigliamento sm. 1. thinning 2. (riduzione) reduction.
assottigliare vt. 1. to thin 2. (diminuire) to reduce. ◆ **assottigliarsi** vr. to grow (v. irr.) thin.
assuefare vt. to accustom. ◆ **assuefarsi** vr. to accustom oneself.
assuefazione sf. custom.
assùmere vt. 1. to assume 2. (in

servizio) to employ 3. (informazioni) to make (v. irr.) inquiries.
assunzione sf. 1. (ascesa) accession 2. (impiego) engagement 3. (teol.) Assumption.
assurdamente avv. absurdly.
assurdità sf. absurdity.
assurdo agg. absurd. ◆ **assurdo** sm. absurdity.
assùrgere vi. to rise (v. irr.).
asta sf. 1. pole 2. (di bandiera) flagstaff 3. (di occhiali) bar 4. (di bilancia) arm (of balance) 5. (vendita all'asta) auction(-sale).
astante agg. present. ◆ **astante** sm. on-looker.
astemio agg. abstemious. ◆ **astemio** sm. teetotaller.
astenersi vr. to abstain.
astenìa sf. asthenia.
astensione sf. abstention.
astensionista sm. abstentionist.
asterisco sm. asterisk.
asteròide sm. asteroid.
asticciola sf. pothook.
astigmàtico agg. astigmatic.
astigmatismo sm. astigmatism.
astinenza sf. abstinence.
astio sm. resentment.
astiosamente avv. resentfully.
astioso agg. resentful.
astracàn sm. astrakhan.
astràgalo sm. 1. (bot.) astragalus (pl. -li) 2. (arch.) astragal.
astrale agg. astral.
astrarre vt. to abstract. ◆ **astrarsi** vr. to think (v. irr.) about sthg. else.
astrattismo sm. (arte) abstractionism.
astratto agg. abstract.
astrazione sf. abstraction.
astringente agg. e sm. astringent.
astro sm. star.
astrolabio sm. astrolabe.
astrologia sf. astrology.
astròlogo sm. astrologer.
astronàuta sm. astronaut.
astronave sf. space-ship.
astronomìa sf. astronomy.
astronòmico agg. astronomic(al).
astrònomo sm. astronomer.
astrusità sf. abstruseness.
astruso agg. abstruse.
astuccio sm. case, box: — per occhiali, spectacle-case.
astuto agg. cunning.
astuzia sf. 1. (qualità) cunning 2. (atto) trick.

atassìa sf. ataxy.
atàvico agg. atavic.
atavismo sm. atavism.
ateismo sm. atheism.
àteo agg. atheistic. ♦ **àteo** sm. atheist.
atleta sm. athlete.
atlètica sf. athletics.
atlètico agg. athletic.
atmosfera sf. atmosphere.
atollo sm. atoll.
atòmico agg. atomic.
atomismo sm. atomism.
atomìstica sf. atomic theory.
atomizzatore sm. atomizer.
àtomo sm. (anche fig.) atom.
atonìa sf. atony.
àtono agg. atonic.
atrio sm. (entrance-)hall.
atroce agg. dreadful.
atrocità sf. atrocity.
atrofìa sf. atrophy.
atrofizzare vt. to atrophy.
atrofizzato agg. atrophic.
atropina sf. atropine.
attaccabottoni sm. buttonholer.
attaccabrighe sm. quarrelsome fellow.
attaccamento sm. attachment: avere dell'—, to entertain an attachment (for).
attaccante sm. attacker.
attaccapanni sm. cloak-stand.
attaccare vt. 1. (unire) to attack 2. (appiccicare) to stick (v. irr.) 3. (cucire) to sew (v. irr.) 4. (assalire) to attack 5. (mus.) to open. ♦ **attaccarsi** vr. 1. (appigliarsi) to cling (v. irr.) 2. (affezionarsi) to become (v. irr.) fond of.
attaccatura sf. junction: — della manica, arm-hole.
attacchino sm. bill-poster.
attacco sm. 1. (mil.) attack 2. (med.) fit 3. (mecc.) connection || — elettrico, connecting plug.
attagliarsi vr. to suit.
attanagliare vt. to pinch.
attardarsi vr. to delay.
attecchire vi. 1. to take (v. irr.) root 2. (aver fortuna) to find (v. irr.) favour.
atteggiamento sm. attitude.
atteggiarsi vr. to assume an attitude: — a vittima, to pose as a victim.
attempato agg. elderly.
attendente sm. orderly.

attèndere vt. 1. (aspettare) to wait for 2. (aspettarsi) to expect 3. (accudire, frequentare) to attend.
attendìbile agg. reliable.
attenere vi. to concern. ♦ **attenersi** vr. 1. to cling (v. irr.) (on), (to) 2. (seguire) to conform.
attentamente avv. 1. attentively 2. (con cura) carefully.
attentare vi. to attempt. ♦ **attentarsi** vr. to dare.
attentato sm. attempt (upon).
attenti sm. attention: stare sull'—, to stand (v. irr.) at attention.
attento agg. attentive, careful.
attenuante agg. extenuating.
attenuare vt. 1. to attenuate 2. (giur.) to extenuate.
attenuazione sf. 1. attenuation 2. (di colpa) extenuation.
attenzione sf. 1. attention 2. care: fate —, take care 3. (riguardo) regard.
atterraggio sm. landing.
atterrare vt. to knock down. ♦ **atterrare** vi. (aer.) to land.
atterrire vt. to terrify. ♦ **atterrirsi** vr. to take (v. irr.) fright.
attesa sf. wait.
attestare vt. to attest.
attestato sm. 1. certificate 2. (prova) proof.
atticciato agg. sturdy.
àttico sm. attic.
attiguo agg. adjoining.
attillarsi vr. to spruce oneself up.
attillato agg. close-fitting.
àttimo sm. moment.
attinente agg. pertaining.
attinenza sf. relationship.
attìngere vt. to draw (v. irr.): — acqua da un pozzo, to draw water from a well; — denaro da qu., to draw on so. for money.
attirare vt. to attract, to draw (v. irr.) (anche fig.).
attitùdine sf. turn, disposition.
attivare vt. to make (v. irr.) active.
attivista s. activist.
attività sf. 1. activity 2. (comm.) profit: — e passività, assets and liabilities.
attivizzare vt. to make (v. irr.) active.
attivo agg. active.
attizzare vt. to stir up.
attizzatoio sm. poker.
atto¹ sm. 1. act 2. (azione) action 3. (fatto) deed: un — buono, a

good deed.

atto² *agg.* fit.

attònito *agg.* astonished.

attore *sm.* actor: — *cinematografico,* screen actor.

attorniare *vt.* to surround.

attorno *avv.* e *prep.* about, round, around: *non c'è nessuno —,* there is nobody about; — *alla tavola,* round the table; *le colline — al villaggio,* the hills around the village ‖ *darsi d'—,* to busy oneself.

attraccaggio *sm.* mooring.

attraccare *vi.* to moor.

attraente *agg.* charming, attractive.

attrarre *vt.* to attract, to draw (*v. irr.*) (*anche fig.*).

attrattiva *sf.* attraction, appeal.

attraversamento *sm.* crossing.

attraversare *vt.* **1.** to cross **2.** (*ostacolare*) to thwart.

attraverso *avv.* **1.** (*di luogo*) across, through: — *il fiume,* across the river **2.** (*di tempo*) through.

attrazione *sf.* attraction, appeal.

attrezzare *vt.* to equip.

attrezzatura *sf.* equipment.

attrezzista *sm.* (*teat.*) property-man.

attrezzo *sm.* tool.

attribuire *vt.* **1.** to attribute **2.** (*assegnare*) to assign **3.** (*addossare*) to put (on).

attributo *sm.* attribute.

attribuzione *sf.* attribution.

attrice *sf.* actress: — *cinematografica,* screen actress.

attrito *sm.* **1.** friction **2.** (*fig.*) dissension.

attruppamento *sm.* trooping

attrupparsi *vr.* to troop.

attuàbile *agg.* feasible.

attuale *agg.* present.

attualità *sf.* the moment: *cosa d'—,* topical question.

attualmente *avv.* at present.

attuare *vt.* to carry out.

attutire *vt.* to mitigate: — *un rumore,* to deaden a noise.

audace *agg.* bold.

audacia *sf.* boldness.

audiovisivo *agg.* audiovisual.

auditore *sm.* listener.

auditorio *sm.* **1.** auditorium **2.** (*pubblico*) audience.

audizione *sf.* **1.** (*fisiol.*) hearing **2.** (*teat.*) performance.

àuge *sm.* summit: *essere in —,* to enjoy great favour.

augurale *agg.* augural.

augurare *vt.* to wish.

augurio *sm.* wish ‖ *auguri di Natale e Capodanno,* season's greetings.

augusto *agg.* august.

àula *sf.* hall, room: — *di scuola,* school-room.

aumentare *vt.* to increase.

aumento *sm.* increase.

àureo *agg.* **1.** gold **2.** (*dorato*) golden.

auréola *sf.* halo.

auricola *sf.* auricle.

auricolare *agg.* auriculan.

aurifero *agg.* auriferous.

aurora *sf.* dawn (*anche fig.*).

auscultare *vt.* to auscultate.

auscultazione *sf.* auscultation.

ausiliare *agg.* auxiliary.

ausilio *sm.* **1.** help **2.** (*difesa*) defence.

auspicare *vt.* to augur.

auspicio *sm.* **1.** (*stor.*) auspice, omen: *di buon, cattivo —,* of good, ill omen **2.** (*augurio*) wish.

austerità *sf.* austerity.

austero *agg.* austere.

australe *agg.* austral.

australiano *agg.* e *sm.* Australian.

austrìaco *agg.* e *sm.* Austrian.

autarchìa *sf.* autarky.

autenticare *vt.* to certify.

autenticazione *sf.* authentication.

autenticità *sf.* authenticity.

autèntico *agg.* **1.** authentic **2.** (*genuino*) genuine.

autista *sm.* driver: — *di piazza,* taxi-driver.

àuto *sf.* car: — *da corsa,* racing car; — *aperta,* open car; — *di serie,* production-model car; — *fuori serie,* special-body car.

autoambulanza *sf.* ambulance.

auto-attrezzi *sf.* breakdown-lorry.

autobiografìa *sf.* autobiography.

autobiògrafo *sm.* autobiographer.

autoblinda *sf.* armoured car.

autobotte *sf.* tank truck.

àutobus *sm.* (motor-) bus.

autoclave *sf.* autoclave.

autocontrollo *sm.* self-control.

autòcrate *sm.* autocrat.

autocrazia *sf.* autocracy.

autocrìtica *sf.* self-criticism.

autòctono *agg.* autochthonous. ♦ **autòctono** *sm.* native.

autodafé *sm.* auto-da-fé (*pl.* autos--da-fé).

autodeterminazione *sf.* self-determination.

autodidatta *s.* self-taught person.

autòdromo *sm.* motor-racing track.

autoeducazione *sf.* self-education.

autofinanziamento *sm.* self-financing.

autògeno *agg.* autogenous.

autogoverno *sm.* self-government.

autografare *vt.* to autograph.

autògrafo *agg.* autographic(al). ♦ **autògrafo** *sm.* autograph.

autolesione *sf.* self-injury.

autolesionismo *sm.* self-injuring.

autolettiga *sf.* ambulance.

autolinea *sf.* bus line.

automa *sm.* automaton, robot.

automàtico *agg.* automatic: *pistola, fucile* —, automatic pistol, gun || *distributore* —, slot machine.

automatismo *sm.* automatism.

automazione *sf.* automation.

automòbile *sf.* V. *auto.*

automobilismo *sm.* motoring.

automobilista *sm.* motorist.

automotrice *sf.* rail-car.

autonoleggio *sm.* car rental.

autonomìa *sf.* autonomy: — *di volo,* flight range.

autonomismo *sm.* self-government.

autònomo *agg.* self-governing.

autoparco *sm.* car-park.

autopilota *sm.* automatic pilot.

autopompa *sf.* fire-engine.

autoposteggio *sm.* parking.

autopsìa *sf.* autopsy.

autoradio *sf.* car radio-set.

autore *sm.* author.

autorespiratore *sm.* aqualung.

autorévole *agg.* authoritative.

autorevolezza *sf.* authoritativeness.

autorimessa *sf.* garage.

autorità *sf.* authority.

autoritario *agg.* authoritative.

autoritratto *sm.* self-portrait.

autorizzare *vt.* 1. (*dare autorità*) to empower 2. (*permettere*) to permit.

autorizzazione *sf.* permission, consent.

autoscuola *sf.* driving school.

autostazione *sf.* filling station.

autostòp *sm.* hitch-hiking.

autostoppista *sm.* hitch-hiker.

autostrada *sf.* motor-way.

autosuggestione *sf.* auto-suggestion.

autotreno *sm.* motor-lorry.

autrice *sf.* authoress.

autunnale *agg.* autumnal.

autunno *sm.* autumn.

ava *sf.* 1. grandmother 2. (*antenata*) ancestress.

avallare *vt.* to guarantee.

avallo *sm.* guarantee.

avambraccio *sm.* forearm.

avamposto *sm.* outpost.

avanguardia *sf.* vanguard: *essere all'*—, to be in the van.

avannotto *sm.* fry.

avanscoperta *sf.* scouting party: *andare all'*—, to scout.

avanspettàcolo *sm.* introductory variety turn.

avanti *avv.* 1. (*di luogo*) forward: *andare* —, to move forward 2. (*a chi bussa*) « come in » 3. (*di tempo*) before || (*di orologio*) fast: *il mio orologio è avanti di 20 minuti,* my watch is twenty minutes fast. ♦ **avanti** *prep.* before. ♦ **avanti che** *cong.* before (*con ger.*).

avantieri *avv.* the day before yesterday.

avanzamento *sm.* 1. advancing 2. (*progresso*) advancement 3. (*promozione*) promotion.

avanzare *vt.* 1. to advance 2. (*fig.*) to put (*v. irr.*) forward 3. (*promuovere*) to promote. ♦ **avanzare** *vi.* to advance. ♦ **avanzarsi** *vr.* to advance.

avanzata *sf.* advance.

avanzato *agg.* 1. advanced 2. (*promosso*) promoted.

avanzo *sm.* remnant || — *di galera,* jail-bird || — *di stoffa,* scrap of cloth.

avarìa *sf.* damage.

avariato *agg.* damaged.

avarizia *sf.* avarice.

avaro *agg.* avaricious.

avena *sf.* oats (*p*)

avere *vt.* 1. (*general. e come v. ausiliare*) to have: *ho molti libri,* I have many books; *ho letto questo giornale,* I have read this newspaper 2. (*possedere*) to own, to have got: *ha una grande casa,* he owns, has got a big house 3. (*ottenere*) to get (*v. irr.*): *ebbi quell'impiego,* I got that job 4. (*indossare*) to wear (*v. irr.*): *aveva (indosso) un abito rosso,* she was wearing a red dress 5. (*dovere*) to have to: *ho molte cose da fare,*

I have many things to do 6. (di anni) to be ... years old: ho 10 anni, I am ten years old.

aviatore sm. airman (pl. -men), pilot.

aviazione sf. 1. aviation 2. (arma) Air Force.

avicoltura sf. bird-rearing.

avidità sf. 1. avidity 2. (ingordigia) greed 3. (brama) eagerness.

àvido agg. 1. avid 2. (ingordo) greedy 3. (desideroso) eager.

aviere sm. airman (pl. -men).

aviogetto sm. jet(-plane).

aviolìnea sf. airline.

aviotrasportare vt. to air-bear (v. irr.).

aviotrasporto sm. air-transport.

avitaminosi sf. avitaminosis.

avito agg. ancestral.

avo sm. 1. grandfather 2. (antenato) ancestor 3. (pl.) forefathers.

avorio sm. ivory.

avulso agg. uprooted.

avvalersi vr. to avail oneself.

avvaloramento sm. strengthening.

avvalorare vt. 1. to give (v. irr.) value to 2. (rafforzare) to strengthen.

avvampare vi. to flare up (anche fig.).

avvantaggiare vt. to advantage, to better. ♦ **avvantaggiarsi** vr. to profit (by).

avvedersi vr. to perceive.

avvedutamente avv. shrewdly.

avvedutezza sf. shrewdness.

avveduto agg. shrewd.

avvelenamento sm. poisoning.

avvelenare vt. to poison.

avvelenatore sm. poisoner.

avvenente agg. charming, pretty.

avvenenza sf. charm, loveliness.

avvenimento sm. event.

avvenire[1] vi. imp. to happen.

avvenire[2] sm. future.

avventarsi vr. to throw (v. irr.) oneself.

avventatamente avv. rashly.

avventatezza sf. rashness.

avventato agg. rash.

avventizio agg. 1. temporary 2. (giur.) adventitious.

avvento sm. 1. (eccl.) Advent 2. arrival 3. (assunzione al trono) accession.

avventore sm. customer.

avventura sf. adventure.

avventurarsi vr. to venture.

avventuriero sm. adventurer.

avventuroso agg. adventurous.

avverarsi vr. to come (v. irr.) true.

avverbiale agg. adverbial.

avverbio sm. adverb.

avversare vt. to oppose.

avversario agg. contrary. ♦ **avversario** sm. opponent.

avversione sf. aversion, dislike.

avversità sf. adversity, misfortune.

avverso agg. unfavourable.

avvertenza sf. 1. (avviso) warning 2. (attenzione, cura) attention, care.

avvertibile agg. perceptible.

avvertimento sm. warning.

avvertire vt. 1. (avvisare) to inform 2. (mettere in guardia) to warn 3. (osservare) to notice.

avvezzare vt. to accustom.

avvezzo agg. accustomed, used.

avviamento sm. starting.

avviare vt. to start.

avvicinamento sm. approach.

avvicinare vt. to approach. ♦ **avvicinarsi** vr. 1. to approach 2. (essere simile) to be similar.

avvicendare vt. to alternate. ♦ **avvicendarsi** vr. to alternate.

avvicendamento sm. alternation.

avvilente agg. 1. discouraging 2. (umiliante) humiliating.

avvilimento sm. 1. dejection 2. (umiliazione) humiliation.

avvilire vt. 1. (scoraggiare) to dishearten 2. (umiliare) to humiliate. ♦ **avvilirsi** vr. 1. to lose heart 2. (umiliarsi) to abase oneself.

avvilito agg. 1. downcast 2. (umiliato) humbled.

avviluppare vt. 1. to wrap up 2. (aggrovigliare) to entangle. ♦ **avvilupparsi** vr. 1. to wrap oneself up 2. (aggrovigliarsi) to get (v. irr.) entangled.

avvinazzarsi vr. to get (v. irr.) drunk.

avvinazzato agg. tipsy.

avvincente agg. engaging.

avvincere vt. to enthral.

avvinghiarsi vr. to cling (v. irr.).

avvìo sm. start: prendere l'—, to start off.

avvisaglia sf. (primo segno) foreshadowing.

avvisare vt. 1. to inform, to let (v. irr.) know 2. (mettere in guardia) to warn.

avviso sm. 1. notice 2. (consiglio) warning 3. (manifesto) poster 4.

(*opinione*) opinion.

avvistare *vt.* to sight.

avvitamento *sm.* spin.

avvitare *vt.* 1. (*mecc.*) to screw 2. (*aer.*) to spin.

avviticchiarsi *vr.* to twist round.

avvocato *sm.* 1. lawyer 2. (*civilista*) solicitor.

avvocatura *sf.* legal profession.

avvòlgere *vt.* 1. to wrap (*anche fig.*) 2. (*arrotolare*) to roll up.

avvolgimento *sm.* 1. winding 2. (*di pacchi*) wrapping up 3. (*elettr.*) winding.

avvoltoio *sm.* vulture (*anche fig.*).

azalea *sf.* azalea.

azienda *sf.* firm, concern: — *industriale*, manufacturing concern; — *agricola*, farm.

aziendale *agg.* firm, concern.

àzimut *sm.* azimuth.

azimutale *agg.* azimuthal.

azionamento *sm.* working.

azionare *vt.* to set (*v. irr.*) in action, to work.

azionario *agg.* share: *capitale* —, share capital.

azione *sf.* 1. action 2. (*comm.*) share.

azionista *s.* shareholder.

azotare *vt.* to azotize.

azoto *sm.* azote.

azteco *agg. e sm.* Aztec.

azzannare *vt.* to seize in the jaws.

azzardare *vt.* to risk, to venture.

azzardo *sm.* hazard || *gioco d'*—, game of chance.

azzeccare *vt.* to guess, to hit (*v. irr.*) the mark.

àzzimo *agg.* unleavened: *pane* —, unleavened bread.

azzoppare *vt.* to lame. ♦ **azzopparsi** *vr.* to become (*v. irr.*) lame.

azzuffarsi *vr.* to come (*v. irr.*) to blows.

azzurro *agg.* blue.

azzurrògnolo *agg.* bluish.

B

babbeo *sm.* blockhead.

babbo *sm.* father, daddy.

babbuccia *sf.* slipper.

babbuino *sm.* baboon.

babele *sf.* babel.

bacare *vi.* **bacarsi** *vr.* to rot.

bacato *agg.* rotten.

bacca *sf.* berry.

baccalà *sm.* stockfish.

baccanale *sm.* bacchanal.

baccano *sm.* uproar.

baccante *sf.* Bacchante.

baccarà *sm.* baccarat.

baccellierato *sm.* bachelorship.

baccelliere *sm.* bachelor.

baccello *sm.* pod.

bacchetta *sf.* 1. rod 2. (*di direttore d'orchestra*) baton 3. (*di tamburo*) drumstick.

bacchettata *sf.* rod stroke.

bacchettone *sm.* bigot.

bacchiare *vt.* to beat (*v. irr.*) down.

bàcchico *agg.* Bacchic.

bacheca *sf.* show-case.

bachelite *sf.* bakelite.

bacherozzo *sm.* 1. (*scarafaggio*) cockroach 2. (*bruco*) maggot.

bachicoltura *sf.* silkworm breeding.

baciamano *sm.* hand-kissing.

baciapile *sm.* bigot.

baciare *vt.* to kiss. ♦ **baciarsi** *vr.* rec. to kiss each other.

bacile *sm.* basin.

bacillo *sm.* bacillus (*pl.* -li).

bacinella *sf.* basin.

bacino *sm.* 1. basin 2. (*anat.*) pelvis 3. (*mar.*) dock: — *di carenaggio*, dry dock.

bacio *sm.* kiss.

baciucchiare *vt.* to kiss repeatedly.

baco *sm.* worm: — *da seta*, silkworm.

bada *sf.* (*nella loc.*) *tenere a* — *qu.*, to hold (*v. irr.*) so. at bay.

badare *vi.* to mind (*so., sthg.*): *senza* — *a spese*, regardless of expense.

badessa *sf.* abbess.

badìa *sf.* abbey.

badilante *sm.* navvy.

badile *sm.* shovel.

baffo *sm.* 1. moustache: *portare i baffi*, to wear (*v. irr.*) a moustache || *ridere sotto i baffi*, to laugh in one's sleeve 2. (*sgorbio*) smear.

bagagliaio *sm.* luggage van.

bagaglio *sm.* luggage (*solo sing.*) || *fare i bagagli*, to pack || *disfare i bagagli*, to unpack.

bagarinaggio *sm.* cornering.

bagattella *sf.* trifle.

baggianata *sf.* 1. (*azione*) foolish action 2. (*discorso*) nonsense.

bagliore *sm.* flash.

bagnante *sm.* bather.
bagnare *vt.* 1. to wet 2. (*immergere*) to dip 3. (*di mare, fiume*) to wash. ♦ **bagnarsi** *vr.* 1. to get (*v. irr.*) wet 2. (*fare bagni in mare ecc.*) to bathe.
bagnato *agg.* wet.
bagnino *sm.* bathing attendant.
bagno *sm.* 1. bath: *far un* —, to take (*v. irr.*) a bath; — *di sole*, sun-bath 2. (*in mare ecc.*) bathe || *fare il* —, to .bathe || *costume da* —, bathing-costume.
bagnomarìa *sm.* bain-marie.
bagordo *sm.* revelry.
baia[1] *sf.* (*scherzo*) joke || *dare la* — *a qu.*, to make (*v. irr.*) fun of so.
baia[2] *sf.* (*geogr.*) bay.
baionetta *sf.* bayonet.
bàita *sf.* Alpine hut.
balaustrata *sf.* balustrade.
balbettare *vt.* e *vi.* to stammer.
balbettìo *sm.* stammer.
balbuzie *sf.* stammer.
balbuziente *agg.* stammering. ♦ **balbuziente** *s.* stammerer.
balconata *sf.* balcony.
balcone *sm.* balcony.
baldacchino *sm.* canopy.
baldanza *sf.* boldness.
baldanzoso *agg.* bold.
baldo *agg.* bold.
baldoria *sf.* revel: *far* —, to make (*v. irr.*) merry.
balena *sf.* whale: *stecca di* —, whalebone.
balenare *vi.* 1. to lighten 2. (*di idea*) to flash.
baleno *sm.* lightning || *in un* —, in the twinkling of an eye.
balestra *sf.* 1. crossbow 2. (*mecc.*) leaf spring.
balia *sf.* wet nurse: — *asciutta*, dry-nurse.
balìa *sf.* mercy: *in* — *di*, at the mercy of.
balìstica *sf.* ballistics.
balla *sf.* 1. (*di cotone, di lana*) bale 2. (*volg.; fandonia*) tall story 3. (*fig.; mucchio*) heap.
ballare *vt.* e *vi.* to dance.
ballata *sf.* ballad.
ballatoio *sm.* gallery.
ballerina *sf.* 1. dancer 2. (*classica*) ballerina.
ballerino *sm.* 1. dancer 2. (*classico*) ballet-dancer.
balletto *sm.* ballet.

ballo *sm.* 1. dance 2. (*festa*) ball || *essere in* —; to be on the go; *tirare in* —, to call in question.
bellottaggio *sm.* second ballot.
balneare *agg.* bathing || *stazione* —, seaside resort.
balocco *sm.* toy.
balordàggine *sf.* 1. dullness 2. (*azione*) foolish action 3. (*discorso*) nonsense.
balordo *agg.* e *sm.* stupid.
balsàmico *agg.* balmy.
bàlsamo *sm.* balm.
baluardo *sm.* bulwark.
balza *sf.* 1. cliff 2. (*di vestito*) flounce.
balzano *agg.* 1. queer 2. (*di cavallo*) white-footed.
balzare *vi.* to jump.
balzo *sm.* jump: *cogliere la palla al* —, to seize an opportunity.
bambagia *sf.* cotton-wool.
bambina *sf.* 1. little girl, child (*pl.* children) 2. (*in fasce*) baby.
bambinaia *sf.* nurse.
bambino *sm.* 1. little boy, child (*pl.* children) 2. (*in fasce*) baby || *dare alla luce un* —, to bring (*v. irr.*) forth a child.
bamboccio *sm.* 1. (*bambola*) ragdoll 2. (*fig.*) simpleton.
bàmbola *sf.* doll.
bambù *sm.* bamboo.
banale *agg.* banal.
banalità *sf.* banality.
banana *sf.* banana.
banano *sm.* banana-tree.
banca *sf.* bank.
bancarella *sf.* stall.
bancario *agg.* bank: *libretto* —, passbook. ♦ **bancario** *sm.* bank clerk.
bancarotta *sf.* bankruptcy: *fare* —, to go (*v. irr.*) bankrupt.
banchetto *sm.* banquet.
banchiere *sm.* banker.
banchina *sf.* 1. (*molo*) wharf 2. (*terrapieno*) embankment.
banchisa *sf.* ice-pack.
banco *sm.* 1. bench 2. (*di chiesa*) pew 3. (*di negozio*) counter 4. (*di nebbia, di sabbia, di gioco*) bank.
banconota *sf.* banknote.
banda *sf.* 1. (*lato*) side 2. (*mus.; striscia di stoffa*) band 3. (*di delinquenti*) gang.
banderuola *sf.* weathercock.
bandiera *sf.* flag, colours (*pl.*).
bandire *vt.* 1. to proclaim 2. (*esi-*

liare, eliminare) to banish.
bandito *sm.* outlaw.
bando *sm.* **1.** ban **2.** (*esilio*) banishment || *essere al* —, to be banished **3.** (*annunzio*) announcement.
bar *sm.* bar.
bara *sf.* coffin.
baracca *sf.* hut.
baraccone *sm.* booth.
baraonda *sf.* chaos.
barare *vi.* to cheat.
bàratro *sm.* abyss.
barattare *vt.* to exchange.
baratto *sm.* barter.
baràttolo *sm.* **1.** jar **2.** (*di metallo*) tin.
barba *sf.* beard: *fare, farsi la* —, to shave. || (*fig.*) *in* — *a*, in spite of.
barbabiètola *sf.* beet-root.
barbarie *sf.* **1.** barbarousness **2.** (*crudeltà*) barbarity.
bàrbaro *agg. e sm.* barbarian.
barbiere *sm.* barber.
barbone *sm.* **1.** (*straccione*) tramp **2.** (*cane*) poodle.
barbuto *agg.* bearded.
barca *sf.* boat: *andare in* —, to go (*v. irr.*) boating.
barcaiolo *sm.* boatman (*pl.* -men).
barcamenarsi *vr.* to wangle.
barcollare *vi.* to stagger.
barcone *sm.* long boat.
bardare *vt.* to harness. ♦ **bardarsi** *vr.* to dress up.
barella *sf.* stretcher.
barile *sm.* barrel.
barista *sm.* barman (*pl.* -men). ♦ **barista** *sf.* barmaid.
baritonale *agg.* baritone.
barìtono *sm.* baritone.
barlume *sm.* glimmer.
baro *sm.* cheat.
barocco *agg. e sm.* baroque.
baromètrico *agg.* barometric(al).
baròmetro *sm.* barometer.
barone *sm.* baron.
baronessa *sf.* baroness.
barra *sf.* **1.** bar **2.** (*mar.*) helm.
barricare *vt.* to barricade.
barricata *sf.* barricade.
barriera *sf.* **1.** barrier **2.** (*fig.*) obstacle.
barrire *vi.* to trumpet.
barrito *sm.* trumpet.
barroccio *sm.* cart.
baruffa *sf.* quarrel.
barzelletta *sf.* joke.
basalto *sm.* basalt.

basamento *sm.* base.
basare *vt.* to base.
basco *agg. e sm.* Basque. ♦ **basco** *sm.* (*berretto*) beret.
base *sf.* base.
basette *sf. pl.* whiskers.
bàsico *agg.* basic.
basilare *agg.* basic.
basìlica *sf.* basilica.
basìlico *sm.* basil.
basilisco *sm.* basilisk.
bassezza *sf.* baseness.
basso *agg.* **1.** low **2.** (*di statura*) short **3.** (*abietto*) base. ♦ **basso** *avv.* low. ♦ **basso** *sm.* **1.** bottom **2.** (*mus.*) bass.
bassofondo *sm.* shallow || *i bassifondi della società*, the underworld.
bassopiano *sm.* lowland.
bassorilievo *sm.* bas-relief.
bassotto *agg.* thick-set. ♦ **bassotto** *sm.* (*cane*) dachshund.
bassoventre *sm.* belly.
basta *inter.* stop it!: — *con*, enough of.
bastardo *agg. e sm.* **1.** bastard **2.** (*di animali*) mongrel.
bastare *vi.* to be enough.
bastimento *sm.* ship.
bastione *sm.* **1.** rampart **2.** (*mil.*) bastion.
basto *sm.* pack-saddle.
bastonare *vt.* to cane.
bastonata *sf.* blow with a cane.
bastonatura *sf.* caning.
bastone *sm.* stick, staff.
batacchio *sm.* clapper.
batisfera *sf.* bathysphere.
batista *sf.* batiste.
batosta *sf.* blow.
batrace *sm.* batrachian.
battaglia *sf.* battle, fight || (*fig.*) *cavallo di* —, favourite subject, favourite piece.
battagliare *vi.* to battle, to fight (*v. irr.*), to struggle.
battagliero *agg.* **1.** warlike **2.** (*fig.*) fierce.
battaglione *sm.* battalion.
battelliere *sm.* boatman (*pl.* -men).
battello *sm.* boat.
battente *sm.* **1.** (*picchiotto*) knocker **2.** (*di porta*) wing.
bàttere *vt.* **1.** to beat (*v. irr.*), to strike (*v. irr.*) (*anche delle ore*) **2.** (*scrivere a macchina*) to type || — *le mani*, to clap hands; — *i piedi*, to stamp; *in un batter d'oc-*

chio, in the twinkling of an eye.
♦ **bàttere** *vi.* 1. to knock 2. (*pulsare*) to throb. ♦ **bàttersi** *vr.* to fight (*v. irr.*).

batterìa *sf.* 1. battery 2. (*da cucina*) kitchen utensils.

battèrio *sm.* bacterium (*pl.* -ia).

batteriologìa *sf.* bacteriology.

battésimo *sm.* baptism: *nome di* —, Christian name.

battezzare *vt.* to baptize.

battibaleno *sm.* (*nella loc. avv.*) *in un* —, in a twinkling.

battibecco *sm.* squabble.

batticuore *sm.* 1. throb 2. (*fig.*) fear.

battimano *sm.* clap.

battipanni *sm.* carpet-beater.

battistero *sm.* baptistery.

battistrada *sm.* 1. outrider 2. (*di pneumatico*) tread || *fare da* —, to lead (*v. irr.*) the way.

bàttito *sm.* 1. beat 2. (*mecc.*) knock.

battitore *sm.* 1. beater 2. (*cricket, baseball*) batsman (*pl.* -men).

battitura *sf.* thrashing.

battuta *sf.* 1. beating: — *di caccia*, beating 2. (*di spirito*) witty remark 3. (*mus.*) bar 4. (*teat.*) cue 5. (*tennis*) service.

batùffolo *sm.* flock.

baule *sm.* trunk.

bauxite *sf.* bauxite.

bava *sf.* 1. slaver 2. (*di lumaca*) slime.

bavaglino *sm.* bib.

bavaglio *sm.* gag: *mettere il* — *a qu.* (*fig.*), to gag so.

bàvero *sm.* collar.

bazàr *sm.* bazaar.

bazza *sf.* slipper-chin.

bazzècola *sf.* trifle.

bazzicare *vt. e vi.* to frequent.

bazzotto *agg.* soft-boiled.

be' *inter.* well.

beare *vt.* to make (*v. irr.*) so. happy.
♦ **bearsi** *vr.* to rejoice (at).

beatificazione *sf.* beatification.

beatitùdine *sf.* beatitude.

beato *agg.* 1. happy 2. (*relig.*) blessed.

beccaccia *sf.* woodcock.

beccaccino *sm.* snipe.

beccare *vt.* 1. to peck 2. (*fam. per acchiappare*) to catch (*v. irr.*). ♦ **beccarsi** *vr.* 1. (*procurarsi*) to get (*v. irr.*) 2. (*litigare*) to quarrel.

beccata *sf.* peck.

beccheggiare *vi.* to pitch.

beccheggio *sm.* pitching.

becchime *sm.* birdseed.

becchino *sm.* grave-digger.

becco *sm.* 1. beak 2. (*caprone*) billy-goat 3. (*fig.*) cuckold.

beccuccio *sm.* (*di teiera ecc.*) spout.

beduino *agg. e sm.* Bedouin.

befana *sf.* 1. "befana" 2. (*fig. fam.*) hag.

beffa *sf.* mockery: *farsi* — *di*, to laugh at; (*ingannare*) to make (*v. irr.*) a fool of.

beffardo *agg.* mocking. ♦ **beffardo** *sm.* mocker.

beffare *vt.* to mock. ♦ **beffarsi** *vr.* to laugh at.

beffeggiare *vt.* V. *beffare.*

bega *sf.* 1. quarrel 2. (*problema intricato*) entangled affair.

beghina *sf.* bigot.

begonia *sf.* (*bot.*) begonia.

belare *vi.* to bleat.

belato *sm.* bleat.

belga *agg. e sm.* Belgian.

bella *sf.* 1. beauty 2. (*innamorata*) sweetheart || *copiare in* —, to make (*v. irr.*) a fair copy.

belladonna *sf.* (*bot.; farm.*) belladonna.

belletto *sm.* rouge.

bellezza *sf.* beauty: *istituto di* —, beauty parlour.

bellicismo *sm.* warlikeness.

bèllico *agg.* 1. war (*attributivo*) 2. (*del tempo di guerra*) wartime.

bellicoso *agg.* warlike.

belligerante *agg. e sm.* belligerent.

belligeranza *sf.* belligerence.

bellimbusto *sm.* dandy.

bello *agg.* 1. fine, beautiful 2. (*di uomo*) handsome || *nel bel mezzo*, right in the middle. ♦ **bello** *sm.* 1. (*la bellezza*) beauty 2. (*innamorato*) sweetheart || *sul più* —, at the right moment; *ora viene il* —, now you'll hear the best of it.

belva *sf.* wild beast.

belvedere *sm.* 1. observation post 2. (*arch.*) belvedere.

bemolle *sm.* (*mus.*) flat.

benché *cong.* though.

benda *sf.* bandage.

bendaggio *sm.* bandage.

bendare *vt.* to bandage.

bene *sm.* good: *per il tuo* —, for your sake; *voler* —, to love. ♦

beni *sm. pl.* property || — *immobili*, real estate; — *di consumo*, consumer goods. ♦ **bene** *avv.* 1. well 2. (*molto*) very 3. (*nientemeno*) no less than || *star* —, to be well; *andar* —, to suit.

benedetto *agg.* blessed.

benedire *vt.* to bless.

benedizione *sf.* blessing.

benefattore *sm.* benefactor.

beneficare *vt.* to help.

beneficenza *sf.* charity.

beneficiario *agg. e sm.* beneficiary.

beneficiata *sf.* benefit.

beneficio *sm.* 1. benefit 2. (*eccl.; giur.*) benefice.

benèfico *agg.* 1. beneficent 2. (*vantaggioso*) beneficial.

benemerenza *sf.* merit.

benemèrito *agg.* well-deserving.

beneplàcito *sm.* consent: *a tuo* —, as you like.

benèssere *sm.* welfare.

benestante *agg.* well-off. ♦ **benestante** *s.* well-to-do person.

benestare *sm.* assent.

benevolenza *sf.* benevolence.

benèvolo *agg.* benevolent.

bengala *sm.* Bengal light.

beniamino *sm.* darling.

benignità *sf.* 1. benignity 2. (*di clima*) mildness.

benigno *agg.* 1. benign 2. (*di clima*) mild.

beninteso *avv.* of course.

benpensante *agg.* sensible || *i benpensanti*, the right thinking.

benservito *sm.* testimonial.

bensì *cong.* but.

benvenuto *agg. sm. inter.* welcome || *dare il — a qu.*, to welcome so.

benvolere *vt.* to like: *farsi* —, to make (*v. irr.*) oneself liked.

benzina *sf.* petrol.

benzinaio *sm.* filling station attendant.

benzolo *sm.* benzol.

beone *sm.* drunkard.

beota *agg. e sm.* Bœotian.

bèrbero *agg. e sm.* Berber.

berciare *vi.* to bawl.

bere *vt.* to drink (*v. irr.*) || *darla a* — (*fig.*), to tell (*v. irr.*) tall stories.

bergamotto *sm.* (*bot.; farm.*) bergamot.

berillo *sm.* beryllium.

berlina *sf.* 1. (*carrozza*) berline 2. (*automobile*) limousine 3. (*gogna*) pillory: *mettere alla* —, to pillory.

bernòccolo *sm.* bump.

berretta *sf.* cap.

berretto *sm.* cap.: — *con visiera*, peaked cap.

bersagliare *vt.* 1. to shoot (*v. irr.*) (at) 2. (*fig.*) to torment.

bersaglio *sm.* target: *tiro al* —, target-shooting || *colpire il* —, to hit (*v. irr.*) the mark.

besciamella *sf.* cream-sauce.

bestemmia *sf.* swear.

bestemmiare *vi.* to swear (*v. irr.*).

bestia *sf.* beast || *montare in* —, to lose (*v. irr.*) one's temper.

bestiale *agg.* beastly.

bestialità *sf.* 1. beastliness 2. (*fig.*) foolishness || *dire* —, to talk nonsense; *fare* —, to make (*v. irr.*) blunders.

bestiame *sm.* cattle.

béttola *sf.* tavern.

betulla *sf.* birch.

bevanda *sf.* drink.

beveraggio *sm.* beverage.

bevitore *sm.* drinker.

bevuta *sf.* 1. draught 2. (*il bere*) drinking.

biada *sf.* fodder.

biancastro *agg.* whitish.

biancheggiare *vi. e vt.* 1. (*essere bianco*) to be white 2. (*diventare, far diventare bianco*) to whiten.

biancheria *sf.* linen.

bianco *agg.* white || *in* —, blank; *di punto in* —, suddenly.

biancore *sm.* whiteness.

biancospino *sm.* hawthorn.

biascicare *vt.* to mumble.

biasimare *vt.* to blame.

biasimévole *agg.* blamable.

biàsimo *sm.* blame.

Bibbia *sf.* Bible.

bìbita *sf.* drink.

bìblico *agg.* biblical.

bibliografia *sf.* bibliography.

bibliogràfico *agg.* bibliographic(al).

biblioteca *sf.* 1. library 2. (*scaffale*) bookcase.

bibliotecario *sm.* librarian.

bica *sf.* stack.

bicamerale *agg.* (*pol.*) bicameral.

bicarbonato *sm.* bicarbonate.

bicchiere *sm.* glass.

bicèfalo *agg.* V. *bicipite*.

bicicletta *sf.* bicycle: *andare in* —, to cycle.

bicìpite *agg.* two-headed. ♦ **bicìpite** *sm.* biceps.

bicocca *sf.* hut.
bicolore *agg.* two-coloured.
bidè *sm.* bidet.
bidello *sm.* porter.
bidente *sm.* pitchfork.
bidone *sm.* **1.** can **2.** (*fam.*) swindle.
bieco *agg.* sinister.
biella *sf.* (*mecc.*) connecting rod.
biennale *agg.* biennial.
bietola *sf.* beet.
biennio *sm.* biennium (*pl.* -nia).
bifase *agg.* (*elettr.*) two-phase.
bifolco *sm.* boor.
biforcarsi *vr.* to fork.
biforcazione *sf.* fork.
biforcuto *agg.* forked.
bigamìa *sf.* bigamy.
bìgamo *agg.* bigamous. ♦ **bìgamo**
sm. bigamist.
bighellonare *vi.* to lounge.
bighellone *sm.* lounger.
bigio *agg.* grey.
bigiotterìa *sf.* trinkets (*pl.*).
biglia *sf.* (biliard-)ball.
bigliettaio *sm.* **1.** conductor **2.** (*di
stazione*) booking-clerk.
biglietterìa *sf.* **1.** booking-office **2.**
(*di teatro*) box-office.
biglietto *sm.* **1.** card: — *di visita*,
visiting card **2.** (*di tram ecc.*)
ticket: — *di andata e ritorno*,
return ticket; *mezzo* —, half-
fare ticket **3.** (*banconota*) banknote.
bigodino *sm.* (hair-)curler.
bigotto *agg.* bigoted. ♦ **bigotto**
sm. bigot.
bikini *sm.* bikini.
bilancia *sf.* balance, scales (*pl.*).
bilanciare *vt.* to balance.
bilanciere *sm.* **1.** balance-wheel **2.**
(*mar.*) outrigger.
bilancio *sm.* budget: *fare il* —, to
strike (*v. irr.*) the balance.
bilaterale *agg.* bilateral.
bile *sf.* **1.** bile **2.** (*ira*) anger.
biliardo *sm.* billiards (*pl.*).
bìlico *sm.* **1.** balance **2.** (*fig.*) uncer-
tainty || *mettere in* —, to balance;
stare in —, to be balanced.
bilingue *agg.* bilingual.
bilione *sm.* billion.
bilioso *agg.* bilious.
bimba *sf.* V. *bambina*.
bimbo *sm.* V. *bambino*.
bimensile *agg.* fortnightly.
bimestrale *agg.* bimestrial.
bimestre *sm.* (period of) two
months.

bimotore *agg.* two-engined: *aereo*
—, two-engined plane.
binario *sm.* track: — *morto*, dead-
-end track.
binòcolo *sm.* binoculars (*pl.*).
binomio *sm.* binomial.
biòccolo *sm.* flock: — *di neve*,
snow-flake.
biochìmica *sf.* biochemistry.
biofìsica *sf.* biophysics.
biografìa *sf.* biography.
biogràfico *agg.* biographic(al).
biògrafo *sm.* biographer.
biologìa *sf.* biology.
biològico *agg.* biologic(al).
biòlogo *sm.* biologist.
biondo *agg.* fair.
biosfera *sf.* biosphere.
biòssido *sm.* dioxide.
bipartizione *sf.* bipartition.
bipede *agg.* e *sm.* biped.
biplano *sm.* biplane.
bipolare *agg.* bipolar.
birba *sf.* scapegrace.
birbante *s.* rogue.
birbonata *sf.* knavery.
birbone *sm.* rogue.
bireattore *sm.* two-engined jet.
birichino *sm.* urchin. ♦ **birichino**
agg. naughty.
birillo *sm.* skittle.
biro *sf.* ball-point pen.
biroccio *sm.* cart.
birra *sf.* beer.
birrerìa *sf.* **1.** beer-house **2.** (*fabbrica*) brewery.
bisaccia *sf.* packsack.
bisbètico *agg.* cantankerous.
bisbigliare *vt.* to whisper.
bisbiglio *sm.* whisper.
bisboccia *sf.* spree: *far* —, to revel.
bisca *sf.* gambling-house.
biscia *sf.* snake.
biscotto *sm.* biscuit.
bisessuale *agg.* bisexual.
bisestile *agg. anno* —, leap year.
bisettimanale *agg.* bi-weekly.
bisettrice *sf.* bisector.
bisìllabo *agg.* disyllabic. ♦ **bisìllabo** *sm.* disyllable.
bislacco *agg.* odd.
bislungo *agg.* oblong.
bismuto *sm.* bismuth.
bisnipote *s.* great-grandchild (*pl.*
-children).
bisnonna *sf.* great-grandmother.
bisognare *vi. imp.* to be neces-
bisnonno *sm.* great-grandfather.
sary, must.

bisogno sm. **1.** need **2.** (povertà) necessity || aver —, to need.
bisognoso agg. needy.
bisonte sm. bison.
bissare vt. to give (v. irr.) an encore (of sthg.).
bistecca sf. beefsteak.
bisticciare vi. to squabble.
bisticcio sm. **1.** squabble **2.** (gioco di parole) pun
bistrattare vt. to ill-treat.
bistro sm. bistre.
bisturi sm. lancet.
bitòrzolo sm. bump.
bitume sm. bitumen.
bivacco sm. bivouac.
bivalente agg. bivalent.
bivio sm. **1.** fork **2.** (fig.) alternative.
bizantino agg. e sm. Byzantine.
bizza sf. freak || fare le bizze, to be peevish.
bizzarria sf. **1.** peculiarity **2.** (cosa) curiosity **3.** (atto, detto) extravagance.
bizzarro agg. strange.
bizzoso agg. **1.** freakish **2.** (irascibile) irascible
blandire vt. to soothe
blandizia sf. blandishment.
blando agg. bland.
blasone sm. **1.** blazon **2.** (nobiltà) nobility
blaterare vi. e vt. to prate.
bleso agg. lisping || pronuncia blesa, lisp. ♦ **bleso** sm. lisper.
blindare vt. (mil.) to armour.
bloccare vt. to block, to stop. ♦ **bloccarsi** vr. to jam.
blocco sm. **1.** block **2.** (mil.) blockade.
blu agg. e sm. blue.
bluff sm. bluff.
blusa sf. blouse.
boa[1] sf. (mar.) buoy.
boa[2] sm. (zool.) boa.
bobina sf. bobbin.
bocca sf. mouth: — da incendio, fire-plug; — dello stomaco, pit of the stomach; chiudere la — a qu., to silence so.
boccaccia sf. grimace.
boccale sm. jug.
boccaporto sm. hatchway.
boccata sf. mouthful.
boccheggiare vi. to gasp.
bocchino sm. mouthpiece.
boccia sf. **1.** water-bottle **2.** (sport) bowl.
bocciare vt. **1.** (respingere) to

reject **2.** (agli esami) to fail.
bocciatura sf. failure.
boccio sm. bud.
boccone sm. **1.** bit **2.** (boccata) mouthful **3.** (esca) bait.
bocconi avv. lying face downwards.
boia sm. executioner.
boicottare vt. to boycott.
bolgia sf. **1.** (fig.) bedlam **2.** (di inferno) pit.
bòlide sm. (astr.) bolide.
bolla sf. **1.** bubble **2.** (vescica) blister **3.** (eccl.) bull.
bollare vt. **1.** (timbrare) to stamp **2.** (a fuoco e fig.) to brand.
bollato agg. **1.** stamped: carta bollata, stamped paper **2.** (a fuoco e fig.) branded.
bollente agg. boiling.
bolletta sf. **1.** bill **2.** (ricevuta) receipt || essere in — (fig.), to be (v. irr.) penniless.
bollettario sm. counterfoil-book.
bollettino sm. **1.** bulletin **2.** (comm.) list, note.
bollire vi. e vt. to boil.
bollito sm. boiled meat.
bollitore sm. **1.** boiler **2.** (bricco) kettle.
bollitura sf. boiling.
bollo sm. stamp.
bollore sm. **1.** boil **2.** (fig.) excitement.
bolscevico agg. e sm. Bolshevist.
bolscevismo sm. Bolshevism.
boma sf. (mar.) boom.
bomba sf. bomb.
bombardamento sm. bombardment.
bombardare vt. to bombard; (generalmente da aereo) to bomb.
bombardiere sm. **1.** (soldato) bombardier **2.** (aereo) bomber.
bombetta sf. bowler.
bòmbola sf. bottle.
bomboniera sf. candy-box.
bonaccia sf. dead calm.
bonaccione agg. good-natured. ♦ **bonaccione** sm. good-natured man (pl. men).
bonarietà sf. good nature.
bonario agg. good-natured, friendly.
bonìfica sf. reclamation.
bonificare vt. **1.** to reclaim **2.** (comm.) to grant an allowance.
bonomìa sf. good nature.
bontà sf. goodness.
bonzo sm. bonze.
borbottare vi. e vt. **1.** to mumble

2. (*lamentarsi*) to grumble.
borbottìo *sm.* **1.** mumbling **2.** (*protesta*) grumbling.
bordare *vt.* to border.
bordeggiare *vi.* to tack.
bordello *sm.* bawdyhouse.
bordo *sm.* **1.** edge **2.** (*mar.*) board: *a —,* on board.
bordura *sf.* border.
bòrea *sf.* Boreas.
boreale *agg.* boreal: *aurora —,* aurora borealis.
borgata *sf.* village.
borghese *agg.* **1.** middle-class **2.** (*comune*) plain **3.** (*civile*) civilian: *in —,* in civilian dress. ♦ **borghese** *s.* middle-class person.
borghesìa *sf.* middle class(es): *l'alta —,* the upper middle class(es); *la piccola —,* the lower middle class(es).
borgo *sm.* village.
borgomastro *sm.* burgomaster.
boria *sf.* arrogance.
bòrico *agg.* boric.
borioso *agg.* arrogant.
borotalco *sm.* talcum powder.
borraccia *sf.* flask.
borsa[1] *sf.* bag || *— per documenti,* brief case; *— di studio,* scholarship.
borsa[2] *sf.* (*comm.*) Stock Exchange.
borsaiolo *sm.* pickpocket.
borseggiare *vt.* to pick pockets.
borsellino *sm.* purse.
borsetta *sf.* (hand-)bag.
boscaglia *sf.* brushwood.
boscaiolo *sm.* woodman (*pl.* -men).
boschetto *sm.* grove.
bosco *sm.* wood.
boscoso *agg.* woody.
bòssolo *sm.* cartridge-case.
botànica *sf.* botany.
bòtola *sf.* trap-door.
botta *sf.* **1.** blow **2.** (*battuta*) sarcastic remark || *dare un sacco di botte a qu.,* to whack so.
botte *sf.* barrel.
bottega *sf.* shop.
bottegaio *sm.* shop-keeper.
bottiglia *sf.* bottle.
bottiglieria *sf.* wine shop.
bottino *sm.* booty: *far —,* to plunder.
botto *sm.* blow || *di —,* suddenly.
bottone *sm.* button || *attaccare un — (fig.),* to buttonhole.
bovaro *sm.* cowherd.
bovini *sm. pl.* cattle (*sing.*).

bozza *sf.* **1.** (*gonfiore*) swelling **2.** (*tip.*) proof **3.** (*abbozzo*) draft || *correggere le bozze,* to proofread.
bozzetto *sm.* sketch.
bòzzolo *sm.* cocoon.
braccare *vt.* to hunt.
braccetto (*nella loc. avv.*) *a —,* arm-in-arm.
bracciale *sm.* **1.** (*fascia che si porta al braccio*) arm-band **2.** (*braccialetto*) bracelet.
braccialetto *sm.* bracelet.
bracciante *sm.* labourer.
bracciata *sf.* **1.** armful **2.** (*di nuoto*) stroke.
braccio *sm.* arm: *essere in — a qu.,* to be in so.'s arms || *— di mare,* sound.
bracco *sm.* hound.
bracconaggio *sm.* poaching.
bracconiere *sm.* poacher.
brace *sf.* embers (*pl.*).
brache *sf. pl.* **1.** trousers **2.** (*mutande*) drawers.
brachicèfalo *agg.* brachycephalous.
braciere *sm.* brazier.
braciola *sf.* chop.
bradicardìa *sf.* (*med.*) bradycardia.
brado *agg.* wild.
brama *sf.* longing.
bramare *vt.* to long for (sthg.).
bramosìa *sf.* covetousness.
bramoso *agg.* eager for (sthg.).
branca *sf.* **1.** claw **2.** (*settore*) branch.
branchia *sf.* gill.
branco *sm.* **1.** herd **2.** (*di pecore*) flock **3.** (*di pesci*) shoal **4.** (*di lupi e fig.*) pack.
brancolare *vi.* to grope.
branda *sf.* **1.** camp-bed **2.** (*mar.*) bunk.
brandello *sm.* **1.** rag **2.** (*pezzetto*) bit || *coi vestiti a brandelli,* in rags; *fare a brandelli,* to tear (*v. irr.*) up.
brandire *vt.* to brandish.
brano *sm.* piece.
brasato *sm.* braised beef.
brasiliano *agg. e sm.* Brazilian.
bravata *sf.* bravado.
bravo *agg.* clever, good || *—!,* well done!; *su, da —!,* be a good boy!
bravura *sf.* **1.** cleverness **2.** (*coraggio*) bravery || (*mus.*) *pezzo di —,* bravura.
breccia *sf.* breach: *essere sulla —,* to stand (*v. irr.*) in the breach.
brefotrofio *sm.* foundling hospital.

bretella *sf.* brace.
breve *agg.* short.
brevettare *vt.* to patent.
brevetto *sm.* patent.
breviario *sm.* breviary.
brevità *sf.* brevity.
brezza *sf.* breeze.
bricco *sm.* kettle, pot.
bricconata *sf.* roguish trick.
briccone *sm.* rogue.
briciola *sf.* crumb.
briciolo *sm.* bit.
briga *sf.* 1. trouble 2. (*lite*) quarrel: *attaccar* —, to pick a quarrel.
brigadiere *sm.* 1. « brigadiere » 2. (*ufficiale nell'Esercito Britannico assegnato al comando di brigata*) brigadier.
brigante *sm.* robber.
brigantino *sm.* (*mar.*) brig.
brigare *vi.* to intrigue.
brigata *sf.* 1. party 2. (*mil.*) brigade.
briglia *sf.* bridle || *a* — *sciolta*, at full gallop.
brillante *agg.* e *sm.* brilliant.
brillantina *sf.* brilliantine.
brillare *vi.* 1. to shine (*v. irr.*). ♦ **brillare** *vt.* 1. (*riso ecc.*) to hull 2. (*una mina*) to blast.
brillo *agg.* tipsy.
brina *sf.* hoarfrost.
brinare *vi. imp.*: *ha brinato*, there has been a frost.
brinata *sf.* hoarfrost.
brindare *vi.* to toast: — *a qu.*, to toast so.
brindello *sm.* rag.
brindisi *sm.* toast.
brio *sm.* liveliness.
brioso *agg.* lively.
britànnico *agg.* British.
brìvido *sm.* 1. shiver 2. (*di paura, orrore*) shudder.
brizzolato *agg.* grizzled.
brocca *sf.* jug.
broccato *sm.* brocade.
bròccolo *sm.* broccoli.
brodaglia *sf.* slops (*pl.*).
brodo *sm.* broth.
broglio *sm.* intrigue: — *elettorale*, gerry-mander.
bromo *sm.* bromine.
bromuro *sm.* bromide.
bronchiale *agg.* bronchial.
bronchite *sf.* bronchitis.
broncio *sm.* pout || *fare il* —, to pout.
bronco *sm.* bronchus (*pl.* -chi).

broncopolmonite *sf.* bronchopneumonia.
brontolare *vi.* e *vt.* to grumble.
brontolìo *sm.* grumbling.
brontolone *sm.* grumbler.
brontosàuro *sm.* brontosaurus.
brònzeo *agg.* 1. bronze (*attributivo*) 2. (*simile a bronzo*) bronzy.
bronzo *sm.* bronze || *faccia di* —, brazen-faced person.
brossura *sf.* paper-back binding || *in* —, paper-bound.
brucare *vt.* to browse (on).
bruciacchiare *vt.* to scorch.
bruciacchiatura *sf.* scorching.
bruciapelo (*nella loc. avv.*) *a* —, point-blank.
bruciare *vt.* e *vi.* to burn (*v. irr.*).
bruciatore *sm.* burner.
bruciatura *sf.* burn.
bruciore *sm.* burning, smart (*anche fig.*).
bruco *sm.* caterpillar.
brùffolo *sm.* pimple.
brughiera *sf.* heath.
brulicare *vi.* to swarm (with).
brulichìo *sm.* swarm.
brullo *agg.* bare.
bruma *sf.* mist.
brumoso *agg.* misty.
brunire *vt.* to burnish.
brunitura *sf.* burnishing.
bruno *agg.* brown.
bruscamente *avv.* roughly.
brusco *agg.* 1. rough 2. (*di sapore*) sour.
brusìo *sm.* buzz.
brutale *agg.* brutal.
brutalità *sf.* brutality.
bruto *agg.* e *sm.* brute.
bruttezza *sf.* ugliness.
brutto *agg.* 1. ugly 2. (*cattivo*) bad.
bruttura *sf.* 1. ugly thing 2. (*azione*) base action.
bùbbola *sf.* lie.
bubbone *sm.* bubo.
bubbònico *agg.* bubonic.
buca *sf.* hole: — *delle lettere*, letter-box.
bucaneve *sm.* snowdrop.
bucaniere *sm.* buccaneer.
bucare *vt.* 1. to pierce 2. (*una gomma*) to puncture 3. (*biglietti*) to punch.
bucato *sm.* 1. washing 2. (*i panni*) laundry.
buccia *sf.* peel.
bucherellare *vt.* to riddle.

buco *sm.* hole.

bucòlico *agg.* bucolic.

buddismo *sm.* Buddhism.

buddista *s.* Buddhist.

budello *sm.* **1.** bowel **2.** (*strada stretta*) alley **3.** (*tubo*) narrow tube.

budino *sm.* pudding.

bue *sm.* ox (*pl.* oxen): *carne di* —, beef.

bùfalo *sm.* buffalo.

bufera *sf.* **1.** storm **2.** (*di vento*) gale.

buffetto *sm.* fillip: *dare un* —, to fillip.

buffo *agg.* funny || *opera buffa*, comic opera.

buffonata *sf.* buffoonery.

buffone *sm.* **1.** clown, fool **2.** (*di corte*) court jester **3.** (*fig.*) unreliable person.

bugìa *sf.* **1.** lie **2.** (*portacandela*) flat candlestick.

bugiardo *agg.* false. ◆ **bugiardo** *sm.* liar.

bugigàttolo *sm.* lumber-room.

buio *agg. e sm.* dark: — *pesto*, pitch dark.

bulbo *sm.* **1.** bulb **2.** (*di occhio*) eyeball.

bùlgaro *agg. e sm.* Bulgarian.

bulinare *vt.* to engrave.

bulino *sm.* burin.

bullonare *vt.* (*mecc.*) to bolt.

bullone *sm.* bolt.

buonanotte *sf.* good night.

buonasera *sf.* good evening.

buoncostume *sm.*: *squadra del* —, vice squad.

buongiorno *sm.* **1.** (*di mattina*) good morning **2.** (*di pomeriggio*) good afternoon **3.** (*a ogni ora incontrandosi, fam.*) hullo **4.** (*a ogni ora lasciandosi*) goodbye.

buongustaio *sm.* gourmet.

buongusto *sm.* good taste.

buono *agg.* **1.** good **2.** (*di tempo*) fine || *alla buona*, informal; *a buon diritto*, by right; *di buon grado*, willingly. ◆ **buono** *sm.* **1.** good **2.** (*persona*) good person **3.** (*comm.*) bond **4.** (*tagliando*) coupon.

buonsenso *sm.* (common) sense.

buontempone *sm.* merry fellow.

buonumore *sm.* V. *umore*.

buonuomo *sm.* **1.** good-natured man (*pl.* men) **2.** simple man (*pl.* men).

burattinaio *sm.* puppet showman (*pl.* -men).

burattino *sm.* puppet.

burbanzoso *agg.* haughty.

bùrbero *agg.* gruff.

burla *sf.* trick || *per* —, in fun.

burlare *vt.* to play a trick on (so.). ◆ **burlarsi** *vr.* to make (*v. irr.*) fun of.

burlesco *agg.* farcical.

burlone *sm.* joker.

buròcrate *sm.* bureaucrat.

burocràtico *agg.* bureaucratic.

burocrazìa *sf.* bureaucracy; (*in Inghilterra*) Civil Service.

burrasca *sf.* storm.

burrascoso *agg.* stormy.

burrificio *sm.* dairy.

burro *sm.* butter.

burrone *sm.* ravine.

burroso *agg.* buttery.

buscarsi *vr.* to get (*v. irr.*) || *buscarle*, to get a thrashing.

bussare *vi.* to knock: — *alla porta*, to knock at the door.

busse *sf. pl.* blows: *prendere le* —, to get (*v. irr.*) a thrashing.

bùssola *sf.* compass: *perdere la* — (*fig.*), to lose (*v. irr.*) one's head.

bussolotto *sm.* dice-box || *fare il giuoco dei bussolotti* (*anche fig.*), to juggle.

busta *sf.* **1.** envelope **2.** (*astuccio*) case.

bustarella *sf.* bribe.

bustina *sf.* (*mil.*) service cap.

busto *sm.* **1.** bust **2.** (*indumento per donna*) corset.

butano *sm.* (*chim.*) butane.

buttare *vt.* **1.** to throw (*v. irr.*) **2.** (*sprecare*) to waste || — *all'aria*, to upset (*v. irr.*); — *a terra*, to knock down.

butterato *agg.* pitted.

buzzo *sm.* belly || *di* — *buono*, very eagerly.

C

càbala *sf.* cab(b)ala.

cabalìstico *agg.* cab(b)alistic(al).

cabina *sf.* **1.** box, hut: — *balneare*, bathing hut; — *telefonica*, telephone box **2.** (*aer.; mar.*) cabin.

cablogramma *sm.* cable.

cabotaggio *sm.* cabotage: *nave di piccolo —,* coasting vessel.

cacao *sm.* **1.** (*bot.*) cacao **2.** (*polvere, bevanda*) cocoa.

cacare *vi.* to evacuate one's bowels.

cacarella *sf.* diarrhoea.

cacatoa, cacatùa *sm.* cockatoo.

cacca *sf.* excrement.

caccia *sf.* hunt, hunting || *— grossa,* big game || *cane da —,* sporting dog; *stagione di —,* shooting season; *andare a —,* to go (*v. irr.*) hunting; *andare a — di uccelli,* to go shooting. ♦ **caccia** *sm.* (*aer.*) fighter.

cacciagione *sf.* game.

cacciare *vt.* **1.** to hunt **2.** (*mil.; mar.*) to chase **3.** (*scacciare*) to expel **4.** (*mettere*) to put (*v. irr.*).

cacciatore *sm.* hunter (*anche fig.*).

cacciatorpediniere *sf.* (torpedo-boat) destroyer.

cacciavite *sm.* screwdriver.

cachi *sm.* persimmon.

cacio *sm.* cheese || *essere alto come un soldo di —,* to be very short.

cacofonìa *sf.* cacophony.

cactus *sm.* cactus (*pl.* cacti).

cadauno *agg. e pron. indef.* each.

cadàvere *sm.* corpse.

cadavèrico *agg.* **1.** corpse-like **2.** (*pallido*) deadly pale.

cadente *agg.* **1.** falling **2.** (*di astri*) setting || *stella —,* shooting star || *età —,* decrepit old age.

cadenza *sf.* **1.** cadence **2.** (*ritmo*) rhythm **3.** (*accento*) accent.

cadere *vi.* **1.** to fall (*v. irr.*) (*anche fig.*): *— bocconi,* to fall flat on one's face; *— in mare,* to fall overboard; *— addormentato,* to fall asleep; *— a proposito,* to fall in the nick of time; *— dal sonno,* to be overcome by sleep; *— nell'errore,* to fall into error || *far —,* to knock down; (*fig.*) to bring (*v. irr.*) about the fall of **2.** (*tramontare, di astri*) to set (*v. irr.*) **3.** (*calare*) to drop **4.** (*far fiasco*) to fail.

cadetto *agg. e sm.* cadet.

caducità *sf.* caducity.

caduco *agg.* perishable, decaying.

caduta *sf.* **1.** fall, falling **2.** (*fig.*) downfall, ruin **3.** (*fis.*) drop.

caffè *sm.* **1.** coffee: *— macinato,* ground coffee; *— nero,* black coffee **2.** (*locale*) coffee-house.

caffeina *sf.* caffeine.

caffettiera *sf.* coffee-pot.

cafone *sm.* boor.

cagionévole *agg.* sickly, weak.

cagliarsi *vr.* to curdle.

cagna *sf.* bitch.

cagnara *sf.* **1.** furious barking **2.** (*fig.*) uproar.

cagnesco *agg. in —,* surlily || *guardare in —,* to scowl at.

cagnolino *sm.* **1.** (*cucciolo*) puppy **2.** (*cane piccolo*) small dog.

caimano *sm.* cayman.

cala *sf.* **1.** creek **2.** (*mar.*) hold.

calabrone *sm.* hornet.

calamaio *sm.* ink-stand.

calamaro *sm.* calamary.

calamita *sf.* magnet (*anche fig.*).

calamità *sf.* calamity, misfortune.

calamitare *vt.* to magnetize (*anche fig.*).

calamitoso *agg.* calamitous.

calandra *sf.* **1.** (*zool.*) wood-lark **2.** (*mecc.*) calender.

calare *vt.* to lower, to drop || *cala la tela,* the curtain drops. ♦ **calare** *vi.* **1.** to descend **2.** (*di astri*) to set (*v. irr.*) **3.** (*di febbre*) to abate **4.** (*comm.*) to fall (*v. irr.*). ♦ **calarsi** *vr.* to let (*v. irr.*) oneself down.

calata *sf.* descent.

calca *sf.* crowd.

calcagno *sm.* heel || *stare alle calcagna di qu.,* to follow so. closely.

calcare¹ *vt.* **1.** to tread (*v. irr.*) **2.** (*premere*) to press down || *— la mano* (*fig.*), to exaggerate.

calcare² *sm.* limestone.

calcàreo *agg.* calcareous.

calce *sf.* lime || *in —* (*loc. avv.*), at the foot.

calcestruzzo *sm.* concrete.

calciare *vi.* to kick.

calciatore *sm.* footballer.

calcificare *vt.* to calcify.

calcificazione *sf.* calcification.

calcina *sf.* lime.

calcinaccio *sm.* debris (*solo sing.*).

calcinare *vt.* to calcine.

calcio¹ *sm.* **1.** kick **2.** (*giuoco*) football || *— d'inizio,* kick-off; *— di rigore,* penalty **3.** (*di arma*) butt.

calcio² *sm.* (*chim.*) calcium.

calco *sm.* **1.** (*scult.*) cast **2.** (*di disegno*) drawing.

calcolàbile *agg.* computable.

calcolare *vt.* **1.** to calculate, to compute **2.** (*prevedere*) to estimate.

calcolatore *sm.* (electronic) computer || *regolo —,* slide-rule.

calcolatrice *sf.* calculating machine.

càlcolo *sm.* 1. calculation 2. (*med.*) stone.

calcomanìa *sf.* . transfer.

caldaia *sf.* 1. kier 2. (*per produzione di vapore*) boiler.

caldamente *avv.* warmly.

caldeggiare *vt.* to favour.

caldeggiatore *sm.* supporter.

calderaio *sm.* tinker.

calderone *sm.* 1. cauldron 2. (*fig.*) medley.

caldo *agg.* 1. warm; (*molto caldo*) hot 2. (*fig.*) ardent. ♦ **caldo** *sm.* heat || *far* (*a*), to be warm, to be hot.

caleidoscopio *sm.* kaleidoscope.

calendario *sm.* calendar.

calende *sf. pl.* kalends || *rimandare alle — greche*, to put off till doomsday.

calesse *sm.* gig, calash.

calessino *sm.* gig.

calibrare *vt.* to calibrate.

calibratura *sf.* calibration.

càlibro *sm.* 1. calibre 2. (*di persona*) caliber, importance.

càlice *sm.* 1. (*eccl.*) chalice 2. (*bicchiere*) goblet, drinking-cup.

calìgine *sf.* thick fog, smog.

callifugo *sm.* corn-plaster.

calligrafìa *sf.* handwriting.

calligràfico *agg.* calligraphic.

callìgrafo *sm.* calligrapher: *perito —*, handwriting expert.

callista *sm.* chiropodist.

callo *sm.* corn.

callosità *sf.* callosity.

calloso *agg.* callous.

calma *sf.* calm.

calmante *agg.* calming, soothing. ♦ **calmante** *sm.* (*farm.*) sedative.

calmare *vt.* 1. to calm 2. (*metter pace*) to appease.

calmo *agg.* calm, quiet.

calo *sm.* 1. shrinkage 2. (*comm.*) drop.

calore *sm.* 1. (*forte*) heat; (*moderato*) warmth 2. (*fig.*) warmth, eagerness.

calorìa *sf.* calory.

calorìfero *sm.* heating apparatus, radiator.

caloroso *agg.* 1. warm, hearty 2. (*che non sente freddo*) not feeling the cold.

calotta *sf.* 1. cap: — *cranica*, skull-cap 2. (*geom.*) bowl.

calpestare *vt.* to tread (*v. irr.*):

vietato — l'erba, keep off the grass.

calpestìo *sm.* trampling (of feet).

calunnia *sf.* slander.

calunniare *vt.* to slander.

calunniatore *sm.* slanderer.

calvizie *sf.* baldness.

calvo *agg.* bald.

calza *sf.* 1. (*corta*) sock; (*da donna*) stocking 2. (*lavoro a maglia*) knitting || *fare la —*, to knit.

calzamaglia *sf.* tights (*pl.*).

calzare *vt.* to put (*v. irr.*) on. ♦ **calzare** *vi.* to fit.

calzatura *sf.* shoe || *negozio di calzature*, shoe-shop.

calzaturificio *sm.* boot factory.

calzettone *sm.* heavy sock.

calzino *sm.* sock.

calzolaio *sm.* shoemaker.

calzolerìa *sf.* shoemaker's shop.

calzoni *sm. pl.* trousers.

camaleonte *sm.* chameleon (*anche fig.*).

cambiale *sf.* bill (of exchange): — *a vista*, bill at sight; *emettere una —*, to issue a bill; *girare una —*, to endorse a bill; *protestare una —*, to note a bill || — *pagherò*, promissory note.

cambiamento *sm.* change.

cambiare *vt.* to change (*anche fig.*). ♦ **cambiarsi** *vr.* to change.

cambio *sm.* 1. change 2. (*econ.*) exchange 3. (*mecc.*) change-gear 4. (*auto*) gear || *in —*, in exchange for, instead of.

camelia *sf.* (*bot.*) camellia.

càmera *sf.* 1. room: — *da letto*, bedroom; — *dei bambini*, nursery; — *degli ospiti*, guest-room || *musica da —*, chamber music 2. (*pol.*) Chamber House: *camera dei deputati*, Chamber of Deputies 3. (*tec.*) chamber || — *oscura*, dark room; — *d'aria*, inner tube.

camerata¹ *sm.* comrade, mate.

camerata² *sf.* dormitory.

cameratismo *sm.* comradeship.

cameriera *sf.* 1. maid 2. (*di albergo*) chambermaid 3. (*di ristorante*) waitress.

cameriere *sm.* 1. man-servant (*pl.* men-) 2. (*di ristorante*) waiter.

càmice *sm.* 1. overall 2. (*eccl.*) surplice.

camicetta *sf.* blouse.

camicia *sf.* 1. (*da uomo*) shirt || — *da notte* (*da uomo*), night-shirt

2. (*da donna*) chemise || — *da notte* (*da donna*), night-dress **3.** (*tec.*) jacket || *è nato con la* —, he was born with a silver spoon in his mouth.

caminetto *sm.* fireplace.

camino *sm.* **1.** (*focolare*) fireplace **2.** (*comignolo*) chimney.

camion *sm.* lorry.

camioncino *sm.* van.

camionista *sm.* lorry-driver.

cammello *sm.* camel.

cammeo *sm.* cameo.

camminare *vi.* **1.** to walk || — *a grandi passi*, to stride (*v. irr.*) along; — *in punta di piedi*, to walk on tiptoe **2.** (*di meccanismi*) to go (*v. irr.*), to work **3.** (*discorsi, affari ecc.*) to proceed.

camminata *sf.* **1.** walk **2.** (*andatura*) gait.

camminatore *sm.* walker.

cammino *sm.* way.

camomilla *sf.* (*bot.*) camomile: *una tazza di* —, a cup of camomile-tea.

camoscio *sm.* chamois: *pelle di* —, chamois leather.

campagna *sf.* **1.** country: *casa di* —, country-house; *andare in* —, to go (*v. irr.*) into the country; *essere in* —, to be in the country **2.** (*tenuta*) estate **3.** (*mil.*) campaign **4.** (*villeggiatura*) holidays.

campana *sf.* bell.

campanaro *sm.* bell-ringer.

campanello *sm.* door-bell: — *d'allarme*, alarm-bell.

campanile *sm.* bell-tower.

campanilismo *sm.* parochialism.

campare *vi.* to live.

campeggiatore *sm.* camper.

campeggio *sm.* camping.

campestre *agg.* rural, rustic || *corsa* —, cross-country race.

campionario *sm.* set of samples, sample case || *fiera campionaria*, trade fair.

campionato *sm.* championship.

campione *sm.* **1.** champion **2.** (*comm.*) sample.

campo *sm.* **1.** (*mil.*) field **2.** (*sport*) sport ground || — *da tennis*, tennis court **3.** (*terreno*) field || — *di battaglia*, battle-field.

camuffare *vt.* to disguise.

canadese *agg. e sm.* Canadian.

canaglia *sf.* **1.** rabble **2.** (*di persona malvagia*) rascal.

canale *sm.* **1.** canal **2.** (*braccio di mare*) channel **3.** (*condotto*) pipe **4.** (*tv.*) channel.

cànapa *sf.* hemp.

canarino *sm.* canary.

cancellare *vt.* **1.** (*a penna*) to cross out; (*con una gomma*) to rub out; (*con un panno*) to wipe out **2.** (*fig.*) efface.

cancellatura *sf.* **1.** erasure **2.** (*fig.*) effacement.

cancellerìa *sf.* **1.** (*pol.*) chancellery **2.** (*materiale di* —) stationery articles **3.** (*giur.*) record-office.

cancelliere *sm.* **1.** (*pol.*) chancellor **2.** (*giur.*) recorder.

cancello *sm.* gate.

cancrena *sf.* gangrene.

cancro *sm.* cancer.

candeggina *sf.* chloride.

candela *sf.* **1.** candle: — *di sego*, tallow candle; *al lume di* —, by candle-light **2.** (*auto*) sparking plug.

candelabro *sm.* branched candlestick.

candeliere *sm.* candlestick.

candelotto *sm.* short thick candle: — *fumogeno*, smoke candle.

candidato *sm.* candidate.

candidatura *sf.* candidature.

càndido *agg.* **1.** snow-white **2.** (*innocente*) innocent.

candito *agg.* candied. ♦ **candito** *sm.* sugar candy.

candore *sm.* **1.** whiteness **2.** (*innocenza*) innocence.

cane *sm.* **1.** dog: — *da caccia*, sporting dog; — *pastore*, sheep dog; — *da guardia*, watch-dog **2.** (*persona spietata*) brute **3.** (*di fucile*) cock.

cànfora *sf.* camphor.

canguro *sm.* kangaroo.

canìcola *sf.* the height of summer.

canile *sm.* kennel.

canino *agg.* canine: *dente* —, canine tooth.

canna *sf.* **1.** reed **2.** (*coltivata*) cane || — *da zucchero*, sugar cane **3.** (*tubo*) pipe **4.** (*di arma*) barrel **5.** (*da pesca*) (fishing-)rod.

cannella *sf.* **1.** (*bot.*) cinnamon **2.** (*di botte*) spout.

cannello *sm.* **1.** torch **2.** (*chim.*) pipe.

canneto *sm.* canebrake.

cannìbale *sm.* cannibal.

cannocchiale *sm.* binoculars (*pl.*) || — *da campagna*, field glasses; — *da teatro*, opera glasses.

cannone sm. 1. gun: — antiaereo, anti-aircraft gun; — anticarro, anti-tank gun 2. (fig.) ace.

cannuccia sf. 1. thin cane: — per sorbire bibite, straw.

cànone sm. canon: — d'affitto, rent; — della radio, radio-licence fee.

canònica sf. rectory.

canònico agg. canonical || diritti canonici, canon law. ♦ **canònico** sm. canon.

canonizzare vt. to canonize.

canoro agg. singing.

canottaggio sm. 1. rowing, boating 2. (come attività) boating.

canottiera sf. vest.

canotto sm. small boat.

canovaccio sm. 1. (per asciugare stoviglie) dish-cloth; 2. (per ricamo) canvas 3. (trama di un'opera) plot.

cantante sm. singer.

cantare vt. 1. to sing (v. irr.) 2. (del gallo) to crow 3. (fare la spia) to squeal.

cantata sf. song.

canterellare vt. e vi. to sing (v. irr.) softly, to hum.

càntico sm. hymn.

cantiere sm. yard.

cantilena sf. sing-song.

cantina sf. cellar.

cantiniere sm. cellarman (pl. -men).

cantino sm. chanterelle.

canto[1] sm. singing.

canto[2] sm. (angolo) corner || dal — mio, for my part; da un — on one hand.

cantonata sf. corner: prendere una —, to make (v. irr.) a blunder.

cantone sm. 1. corner 2. (geogr.) canton.

cantoniera sf. 1. (mobile) corner cupboard 2. (casa) roadman's house 3. (ferr.) signalman's house.

cantoniere sm. signalman (pl. -men).

canuto agg. hoary.

canzonare vt. to make (v. irr.) fun of.

canzone sf. song.

canzonetta sf. 1. short song 2. (poet.) canzonet.

canzonettista s. 1. music-hall singer 2. (autore di canzoni) songwriter.

caolino sm. kaolin.

caos sm. chaos.

capace agg. 1. able 2. (idoneo) fit 3. (abile) clever.

capacità sf. 1. ability, cleverness 2. (capienza) capacity.

capanna sf. hut.

capanno sm. 1. (da caccia) shooting-box 2. (per bagnanti) bathing-box.

caparbierìa sf. stubbornness.

caparbio agg. stubborn.

caparra sf. caution-money.

capeggiare vt. to lead (v. irr.).

capello sm. hair (solo sing.) || acconciatura dei capelli, hairdress; farsi tagliare i capelli, to have one's hair cut; avere un diavolo per —, to be furious.

capezzale sm. bolster.

capézzolo sm. nipple.

capienza sf. capacity.

capigliatura sf. hair.

capillare agg. capillary.

capillarità sf. capillarity.

capinera sf. blackcap.

capire vt. to understand (v. irr.).

capitale sm. capital. ♦ **capitale** agg. 1. (che riguarda la vita) capital 2. (principale) main.

capitalismo sm. capitalism.

capitalista s. capitalist.

capitalizzare vt. to capitalize. ♦ **capitalizzare** vi. (accumulare denaro) to save.

capitano sm. captain, leader.

capitare vi. 1. (giungere) to arrive 2. (accadere) to happen, to befall (v. irr.).

capitello sm. (arch.) capital.

capitolare vi. to capitulate.

capitolare sm. capitulary. ♦ **capitolare** agg. capitular.

capitolo sm. chapter.

capitòmbolo sm. tumble.

capo sm. 1. head || avere mal di —, to have a headache; senza — né coda, without rhyme or reason 2. (estremità) end || da un — all'altro, from end to end; andare a —, new line; in — a un anno, within a year; Capo d'Anno, New Year's day 3. (geogr.) cape 4. (chi comanda) leader.

capobanda sm. 1. (mus.) bandmaster 2. (di una banda di criminali) ringleader.

capocuoco sm. head cook.

capocordata sm. first man on the rope.

capodanno sm. New Year's day.

capofamiglia s. head of a family.

capofila *sm.* file-leader.
capofitto. (*nella loc. avv.*) *a —*, headlong || *cadere, tuffarsi a —*, to fall (*v. irr.*), to dive head first.
capogiro *sm.* dizziness.
capolavoro *sm.* masterpiece.
capolìnea *sm.* terminus (*pl.* -ni).
capolino *sm.* small head || *far —*, to peep in.
capoluogo *sm.* main town.
caporale *sm.* corporal.
caporedattore *sm.* editor in chief.
caposaldo *sm.* **1.** datum point **2.** (*mil.*) stronghold **3.** (*fondamento*) main point.
caposcuola *sm.* leader of a movement.
capostazione *sm.* station-master.
capotare *vi.* **1.** (*di aerei*) to somersault **2.** (*di auto*) to turn over.
capoufficio *sm.* head-clerk.
capoverso *sm.* **1.** (*in poesia*) beginning of a line **2.** (*in prosa*) beginning of a paragraph.
capovòlgere *vt.* to turn upside down. ♦ **capovòlgersi** *vr.* to capsize.
cappa *sf.* **1.** (*mantello*) cloak **2.** (*di prete*) cape **3.** (*fig.*) vault || *— del camino*, chimney.
cappella *sf.* chapel.
cappellano *sm.* chaplain.
cappello *sm.* **1.** hat: *— a cilindro*, top-hat; *— di paglia*, straw hat; **2.** (*introduzione*) preamble.
càppero *sm.* caper.
cappone *sm.* capon.
cappotto *sm.* **1.** coat **2.** (*di gioco*) capot.
cappuccino *sm.* **1.** (*eccl.*) capuchin **2.** (*bevanda*) white coffee.
cappuccio *sm.* hood.
capra *sf.* goat.
capretto *sm.* kid.
capriccio *sm.* whim: *fare i capricci*, to be naughty.
caprino *agg.* goatish.
capriola[1] *sf.* caper: *far capriole*, to cut (*v. irr.*) capers.
capriola[2] *sf.* (*femmina del capriolo*) doe.
capriolo *sm.* roe-deer.
càpsula *sf.* **1.** capsule **2.** (*di dente*) crown.
captare *vt.* (*radio*) to pick up.
capzioso *agg.* captious.
carabina *sf.* carabine.
carabiniere *sm.* carabineer.
caracollare *vi.* to caracole.

caraffa *sf.* **1.** (*per acqua*) carafe **2.** (*per vino*) decanter.
caràmbola *sf.* cannon: *far —*, to cannon.
carambolare *vi.* to cannon.
caramella *sf.* sugar-drop, toffee.
caramellare *vt.* to coat with burnt sugar.
caramello *sm.* caramel.
carato *sm.* carat.
caràttere *sm.* **1.** character, temper **2.** (*caratteristica*) character **3.** (*tip.*) type.
caratterista *s.* character actor (actress).
caratterìstico *agg.* characteristic. ♦ **caratterìstica** *sf.* characteristic.
caravella *sf.* caravel.
carbonaio *sm.* coal merchant.
carbone *sm.* coal || *— di legna*, charcoal; *— fossile*, pit coal; *miniera di —*, coal-mine.
carbonerìa *sf.* Carbonarist movement.
carbonìfero *agg.* carboniferous.
carbonio *sm.* carbon.
carbonizzare *vt.* **1.** to carbonize **2.** (*di legno*) to char.
carburante *sm.* fuel.
carburatore *sm.* carburettor.
carburazione *sf.* carburation.
carcassa *sf.* carcass.
carcerazione *sf.* imprisonment.
càrcere *sm.* prison, jail.
carceriere *sm.* jailer.
carciofo *sm.* artichoke.
cardano *sm.* (*mecc.*) cardan joint.
cardare *vt.* to card.
cardìaco *agg.* cardiac || *disturbi cardiaci*, heart-disease.
cardinale *agg. e sm.* cardinal.
càrdine *sm.* **1.** hinge, pivot **2.** (*fig.*) foundation.
cardiòlogo *sm.* cardiologist.
cardiopatìa *sf.* cardiopathy.
cardo *sm.* **1.** (*bot.*) thistle **2.** (*cuc.*) cardoon **3.** (*mecc.*) carding machine.
carena *sf.* **1.** (*mar.*) keel **2.** (*aer.*) hull **3.** (*zool.*) càrina (*pl.* -nae).
carenza *sf.* want, lack.
carestìa *sf.* famine.
carezza *sf.* caress.
carezzévole *agg.* caressing.
cariàtide *sf.* caryatid.
cariato *agg.* decayed.
càrica *sf.* **1.** (*pubblico ufficio*) office: *entrare in —*, to take (*v.*

irr.) office **2.** (*mil.*) charge **3.** (*di arma da fuoco; elettr.*) charge **4.** (*di orologio*) winding up.

caricare *vt.* **1.** to load **2.** (*mil.; elettr.*) to charge **3.** (*di orologio*) to wind (*v. irr.*) up.

caricatore *sm.* **1.** loader **2.** (*di arma*) magazine.

caricatura *sf.* caricature.

càrico¹ *agg.* **1.** loaded, laden (*anche fig.*) **2.** (*di caffè*) strong **3.** (*elettr.*) charged.

càrico² *sm.* **1.** (*di nave*) freight; (*di veicolo*) load; (*di animale da soma*) burden **2.** (*fig.*) load, weight **3.** (*accusa*) charge || (*comm.*) essere a — di qu., to be charged to so.

carie *sf.* decay.

carino *agg.* pretty, nice.

carità *sf.* **1.** (*amore; teol.*) charity **2.** (*elemosina*) alms.

carlinga *sf.* cockpit.

carlona (*nella loc. avv.*) alla —, carelessly.

carminio *agg.* carmine.

carnagione *sf.* complexion.

carnale *agg.* carnal.

carne *sf.* **1.** flesh **2.** (*come alimento*) meat || — di manzo, beef; — di vitello, veal; — in scatola, tinned meat; — congelata, frozen meat.

carnéfice *sm.* executioner.

carneficina *sf.* slaughter.

carnevale *sm.* carnival.

carnìvoro *agg.* carnivorous.

caro *agg.* **1.** dear **2.** (*costoso*) dear, expensive.

carogna *sf.* carrion.

carosello *sm.* carousel.

carota *sf.* carrot.

caròtide *sf.* carotid.

carovana *sf.* caravan.

carovita *sm.* high cost of living.

carpa *sf.* carp.

carpentiere *sm.* carpenter.

carpire *vt.* **1.** to snatch **2.** (*con astuzia*) to swindle.

carponi *avv.* on all fours.

carràbile *agg.* cart: passo —, driveway.

carreggiata **1.** (*solco*) track **2.** (*strada*) cartway.

carrellata *sf.* dolly shot.

carrello *sm.* **1.** (*ferr.*) wag(g)on **2.** (*aer.*) landing gear **3.** (*cine; tv.*) dolly **4.** (*di macchina per scrivere*)

carriage.

carriera *sf.* career || di gran —, at full speed.

carriola *sf.* wheelbarrow.

carrista *sm.* (*mil.*) tankman (*pl. -men*).

carro *sm.* **1.** (*a due ruote*) cart **2.** (*a quattro ruote*) wag(g)on || — armato, tank.

carrozza *sf.* carriage: — diretta, through coach; — viaggiatori, passenger car.

carrozzàbile *agg.* practicable.

carrozzella *sf.* **1.** cab **2.** (*per bambini*) perambulator; (*fam.*) pram.

carrozzerìa *sf.* body.

carrozziere *sm.* body-maker.

carrozzone *sm.* **1.** lumbering coach **2.** (*di zingari*) caravan.

carruba *sf.*, **carrubo** *sm.* carob.

carrùcola *sf.* pulley.

carta *sf.* paper: — da lettere, writing-paper; — carbone, carbon paper; — d'identità, identity card; — stradale, road-map.

cartaio *sm.* paper-maker.

cartamodello *sm.* dressmaker's pattern.

cartamoneta *sf.* paper-money.

cartapesta *sf.* paper-pulp.

cartavetrata *sf.* sand-paper.

carteggio *sm.* **1.** correspondence **2.** (*collezione di lettere*) collection of letters.

cartella *sf.* **1.** (*da scuola*) satchel **2.** (*di cuoio*) brief-case.

cartello *sm.* **1.** bill **2.** (*pubblicitario*) poster **3.** (*stradale*) traffic sign **4.** (*econ.*) cartel.

cartellone *sm.* **1.** (*pubblicitario*) poster **2.** (*teat.*) bill.

cartellonista *sm.* commercial artist.

cartiera *sf.* paper-mill.

cartilàgine *sf.* cartilage.

cartoccio *sm.* paper-bag.

cartografìa *sf.* cartography.

cartolerìa *sf.* stationer's shop.

cartolina *sf.* postcard: — illustrata, picture postcard.

cartoncino *sm.* thin card.

cartone *sm.* cardboard || cartoni animati, cartoons.

cartuccia *sf.* cartridge || mezza — (*fig.*), shrimp.

casa *sf.* **1.** (*abitazione*) house **2.** (*ambiente familiare*) home || amico di —, family friend; donna di —, housewife; nostalgia di —, home-sickness; *andare a —*, to go (*v. irr.*) home; *restare a —*, to stay at home; *essere in —*, to be in **3.** (*stirpe*) house, dynasty, family.

casacca *sf.* coat.

casaccio (*nella loc. avv.*) *a —*, at random.

casalinga *sf.* housewife.

casalingo *agg.* homely: *cucina casalinga*, plain cooking.

casato *sm.* **1.** (*cognome*) surname **2.** (*origine, nascita*) birth.

cascame *sm.* waste.

cascamorto *sm.* spoon: *fare il —*, to run (*v. irr.*) after.

cascante *agg.* **1.** (*debole*) weak **2.** (*floscio*) flabby (*anche fig.*).

cascare *vi.* **1.** to fall (*v. irr.*) **2.** (*con rumore*) to crash || *— dalle nuvole*, to be struck with amazement; *— dal sonno*, to be overcome with sleep.

cascata *sf.* **1.** (*caduta*) fall **2.** (*d'acqua*) waterfall **3.** (*fig.*) cascade.

cascina *sf.* **1.** dairy farm **2.** (*cascinale*) farmstead.

casco *sm.* **1.** helmet **2.** (*per asciugare i capelli*) dryer.

casella *sf.*: *— postale*, post-box.

casellante *sm.* **1.** (*ferr.*) signalman (*pl.* -men) **2.** (*di passaggio a livello*) crossing keeper.

casellario *sm.* **1.** set of pigeon-holes **2.** (*giur.*) *— penale*, records-office.

casereccio *agg.* homely: *pane —*, home-made bread.

caserma *sf.* barracks (*pl.*).

caso *sm.* **1.** chance **2.** (*fatto*) case **3.** (*possibilità*) way, possibility || *a —*, at random; *per —*, by chance.

càspita *inter.* good gracious!

cassa *sf.* **1.** case, box **2.** (*comm.*) cash || *libro di —*, cash-book; *pagamento per —*, cash-payment; *sportello di —*, cashier's window **3.** (*mus.*) case || *gran —*, bass-drum.

cassaforte *sf.* safe.

cassapanca *sf.* chest.

cassazione *sf.* (*giur.*) cassation.

casseruola *sf.* saucepan.

cassetto *sm.* drawer.

cassettone *sm.* chest of drawers.

cassiere *sm.* cashier.

casta *sf.* caste.

castagna *sf.* chestnut.

castagnaccio *sm.* chestnut-tart.

castagno *sm.* chestnut-tree.

castano *agg.* nut-brown.

castellano *sm.* lord of a castle.

castello *sm.* castle.

castigare *vt.* to punish.

castigatezza *sf.* moderation.

castigato *agg.* **1.** (*casto*) chaste **2.** (*emendato*) castigated.

castigo *sm.* punishment.

castità *sf.* chastity.

casto *agg.* chaste.

castoro *sm.* beaver.

castrare *vt.* to castrate.

castrato *sm.* (*cuc.*) mutton.

castroneria *sf.* stupidity.

casuale *agg.* casual.

casualità *sf.* casualness.

cataclisma *sm.* cataclysm (*anche fig.*).

catacomba *sf.* catacomb.

catafalco *sm.* catafalque.

catafascio (*nella loc. avv.*) *andare a —*, to go (*v. irr.*) to rack and ruin; *a —*, topsyturvy.

catalessi *sf.* catalepsy.

catalizzatore *sm.* catalyst.

catalogare *vt.* to catalogue.

catàlogo *sm.* catalogue.

catapecchia *sf.* hovel.

catapulta *sf.* catapult.

catarifrangente *sm.* reflector.

catarro *sm.* catarrh.

catarsi *sf.* catharsis.

catasta *sf.* pile, heap.

catasto *sm.* cadastre.

catàstrofe *sf.* catastrophe.

catastròfico *agg.* catastrophic(al).

catechismo *sm.* catechism.

catechizzare *vt.* **1.** to catechize **2.** (*fig.*) to persuade.

catecùmeno *sm.* catechumen.

categorìa *sf.* category, class.

categòrico *agg.* categorical, absolute.

catena *sf.* **1.** chain **2.** (*fig.*) bond.

catenaccio *sm.* bolt.

cateratta *sf.* cataract.

catèrva *sf.* **1.** (*di persone*) crowd **2.** (*di cose*) great quantity.

catino *sm.* basin.

catione *sm.* (*fis.*) cation.

càtodo *sm.* cathode.

catramare *vt.* to tar.

catrame *sm.* tar.

càttedra *sf.* **1.** desk **2.** (*l'ufficio dell'insegnare*) teaching post **3.** (*di università*) chair.

cattedrale *sf.* cathedral.

cattiveria *sf.* wickedness.

cattività *sf.* captivity.

cattivo *agg.* e *sm.* bad || — *scritto-re*, poor writer.
cattolicésimo *sm.* catholicism.
cattòlico *agg.* catholic.
cattura *sf.* **1.** capture **2.** (*arresto*) arrest: *mandato di* —, warrant of arrest.
catturare *vt.* **1.** to capture **2.** (*arrestare*) to arrest.
cauccíù *sm.* india-rubber.
càusa *sf* **1.** cause **2.** (*giur.*) law suit || *far* — *a qu.*, to sue so. (for).
causare *vt.* to cause.
càustico *agg.* caustic (*anche fig.*)
cautela *sf.* caution.
cautelare *vt.* to protect. ♦ **caute-larsi** *vr.* to take (*v. irr.*) precautions.
cauterizzare *vt.* to cauterize.
càuto *agg.* cautious, prudent.
cauzione *sf.* **1.** guarantee **2.** (*per essere rilasciato dalla polizia*) bail.
cava *sf.* quarry.
cavalcare *vt.* to ride (*v. irr.*). ♦ **cavalcare** *vi.* to ride on horseback.
cavalcavìa *sm.* fly-over bridge.
cavalcioni (a) *loc. avv.* astride.
cavaliere *sm.* **1.** rider **2.** (*di ordine cavalleresco*) knight.
cavalla *sf.* mare.
cavalleresco *agg.* knightly.
cavallerìa *sf.* **1.** (*mil.*) cavalry **2.** (*stor.*) chivalry.
cavalletta *sf.* grasshopper.
cavalletto *sm.* **1.** trestle **2.** (*foto*) tripod **3.** (*per pittori*) easel.
cavallo *sm.* **1.** horse: — *da corsa*, racehorse; — *a dondolo*, rocking-horse; — *da soma*, pack-horse; *ferro di* —, horse-shoe **2.** (*ginnastica*) vaulting-horse **3.** (*cavallo vapore*) horse-power (*abbr.* H.P.).
cavallone *sm.* (*maroso*) billow.
cavare *vt.* to take (*v. irr.*) off || — *un dente*, to pull out a tooth || *cavarsela*, to get (*v. irr.*) off.
cavatappi, cavaturàccioli *sm.* cork-screw.
caverna *sf.* cave.
cavernoso *agg.* cavernous || *voce cavernosa*, very deep voice.
cavezza *sf.* halter.
cavia *sf.* cavy.
caviale *sm.* caviar.
caviglia *sf.* ankle.
cavillare *vi.* to cavil (at).
cavillo *sm.* cavil.
cavità *sf.* cavity.

cavo *agg.* hollow, empty. ♦ **cavo** *sm.* cable, rope.
cavolfiore *sm.* cauliflower.
càvolo *sm.* cabbage.
cazzotto *sm.* punch || *fare a cazzot-ti*, to come (*v. irr.*) to blows.
cazzuola *sf.* trowel.
cece *sm.* chick-pea.
cecità *sf.* blindness (*anche fig.*).
cecoslovacco *agg.* e *sm.* Czechoslovak.
cèdere *vt.* e *vi.* **1.** (*dare*) to give (*v. irr.*) **2.** (*trasferire*) to hand over **3.** (*vendere*) to dispose of. ♦ **cè-dere** *vi.* **1.** to surrender **2.** (*venir meno*) to subside **3.** (*essere inferiore*) to be second to.
cedimento *sm.* **1.** yielding **2.** (*fig.*) giving up.
cèdola *sf.* coupon.
cedrata *sf.* citron syrup.
cedrina *sf.* lemon-scented verbena.
cedro *sm.* **1.** citron-tree **2.** (*frutto*) citron.
cedrone *agg.* e *sm.* (*gallo*) capercaillie.
cefalea *sf.* cephalea.
cefalgìa *sf.* cephalalgy.
ceffone *sm.* slap in the face.
celare *vt.* to conceal, to hide (*v. irr.*).
celebrare *vt.* to celebrate || — *un anniversario*, to keep (*v. irr.*) an anniversary.
celebrazione *sf.* celebration.
cèlebre *agg.* celebrated.
celebrità *sf.* celebrity.
cèlere *agg.* quick, swift.
celerità *sf.* quickness.
celeste *agg.* **1.** light-blue **2.** (*del cielo*) heavenly.
celia *sf.* jest.
celiare *vi.* to jest.
celibato *sm.* bachelorhood.
cèlibe *agg.* e *sm.* single. ♦ **cèlibe** *sm.* bachelor.
cella *sf.* cell.
cèllula *sf.* cell.
cellulare *agg.* cellular || *segregazione* —, close confinement.
cellulite *sf.* cellulitis.
cellulòide *sf.* celluloid.
cellulosa *sf.* cellulose.
celta *sm.* Celt.
cèltico *agg.* Celtic.
cémbalo *sm.* **1.** (*tamburello*) tambourine **2.** (*spinetta*) spinet.
cementare *vt.* to cement (*anche fig.*).

cementazione *sf.* cementation.

cementificio *sm.* cement-factory.

cemento *sm.* cement: — *armato,* reinforced concrete.

cena *sf.* **1.** (*pasto serale leggero*) supper **2.** (*pranzo*) dinner || *far* —, to have supper.

cenàcolo *sm.* **1.** supper-room **2.** (*di artisti*) artistic coterie || *il — di Leonardo da Vinci,* Leonardo's Last Supper.

cenare *vi.* to have (*v. irr.*) supper.

cenciaio *sm.* ragman (*pl.* -men).

cencio *sm.* **1.** rag **2.** (*vestito logoro*) tatters (*pl.*).

cencioso *agg.* ragged, tattered.

cénere *sf.* ash (*general. al pl.*).

cenno *sm.* **1.** (*segno*) sign **2.** (*allusione*) hint **3.** (*breve notizia*) notice || *fare un — col capo,* to nod || *a un vostro — (comm.),* on hearing from you.

cenobio *sm.* coenobium (*pl.* -ia).

cenone *sm.* **1.** (*di Natale*) Christmas eve dinner **2.** (*di Capodanno*) New Year's eve dinner.

censimento *sm.* census.

censire *vt.* **1.** to take (*v. irr.*) a census of **2.** (*di proprietà*) to assess.

censo *sm.* **1.** (*stor.*) census **2.** (*ricchezza*) wealth.

censore *sm.* **1.** censor **2.** (*fig.*) critic.

censorio *agg.* censorial.

censura *sf.* **1.** (*ufficio di censore*) censorship **2.** (*azione di censura*) censure.

censurare *vt.* **1.** to censor **2.** (*fig.*) to censure.

centàuro *sm.* **1.** centaur **2.** (*fig., motociclista*) motorcyclist.

centellinare *vt.* to sip.

centenario *agg. e sm.* **1.** centennial **2.** (*di persona*) centenarian. ♦ **centenario** *sm.* (*commemorazione*) centenary.

centesimale *agg.* centesimal.

centèsimo *agg.* (the) hundredth. ♦ **centèsimo** *sm.* (one) hundredth (of *sthg.*) **2.** (*di dollaro*) cent **3.** (*di franco*) centime || *non avere un —,* to be penniless.

centigrado *agg.* centigrade.

centigrammo *sm.* centigramme.

centìlitro *sm.* centilitre.

centìmetro *sm.* centimetre.

centinaio *sm.* hundred.

cento *agg. e num. card.* hundred || *— di questi giorni,* many happy

returns of the day.

centrale *agg.* central. ♦ **centrale** *sf.* **1.** — *elettrica,* power station **2.** — *telefonica,* exchange.

centralinista *s.* operator.

centralino *sm.* telephone exchange.

centralismo *sm.* centralism.

centrare *vt.* to hit (*v. irr.*) the centre.

centrìfuga *sf.* centrifuge.

centrìfugo *agg.* centrifugal.

centrino *sm.* doily.

centrìpeto *agg.* centripetal.

centrismo *sm.* centrism.

centro *sm.* **1.** centre **2.** (*istituto*) institute.

centuplicare *vt.* **1.** to centuplicate **2.** (*fig.*) to increase.

cèntuplo *agg. e sm.* centuple.

centuria *sf.* (*stor.*) century.

centurione *sm.* (*stor.*) centurion.

ceppo *sm.* **1.** stump **2.** (*fig.*) stock.

cera *sf.* **1.** wax **2.** (*aspetto*) look || *avere bella —,* to look well.

ceralacca *sf.* sealing-wax.

ceràmica *sf.* **1.** (*arte*) ceramics **2.** (*pezzo*) piece of pottery.

ceramista *sm.* ceramist.

cerato *agg.* waxed || *tela cerata,* wax-cloth.

cerbiatto *sm.* fawn.

cerbottana *sf.* **1.** blowgun **2.** (*giocattolo*) pea-shooter.

cercare *vt.* **1.** to look for **2.** (*per consultazione*) to look up **3.** (*a tentoni*) to fumble for **4.** (*chiedere*) to ask (for). ♦ **cercare** *vi.* to try.

cercatore *sm.* seeker: — *d'oro,* gold-digger; (*amer.*) prospector.

cerchia *sf.* circle.

cerchiare *vt.* to hoop.

cerchiatura *sf.* hooping.

cerchietto *sm.* **1.** small ring **2.** (*gioco*) quoit.

cerchio *sm.* **1.** circle **2.** (*gioco*) hoop.

cerchione *sm.* rim.

cereale *sm.* cereals (*pl.*).

cerebrale *agg.* cerebral.

cèreo *agg.* waxen.

ceretta *sf.* **1.** boot polish **2.** (*per depilare*) wax.

cerimonia *sf.* **1.** ceremony **2.** (*pompa*) pomp.

cerimoniale *sm.* ceremonial.

cerimoniere *sm.* Master of Ceremonies.

cerimonioso *agg.* ceremonious

cerino *sm.* match.

cerniera *sf.* **1.** (*di occhiali, porte, finestre*) hinge **2.** (*di borsetta*) clasp **3.** (*lampo*) zipper.

cèrnita *sf.* choice, selection.

cero *sm.* large candle.

cerone *sm.* make-up.

cerotto *sm.* plaster.

certamente *avv.* certainly, undoubtedly.

certezza *sf.* certainty.

certificare *vt.* to certify, to attest.

certificato *sm.* certificate.

certo¹ *agg. indef.* **1.** certain: *un — Mr. Smith,* a (certain) Mr. Smith **2.** (*qualche*) some: *certe persone lo riconobbero,* some people recognized him; *dopo un — tempo,* after some time **3.** (*tale, di tal genere*) such. ◆ **certi** *pron. indef. pl.* some people.

certo² *agg.* certain. ◆ **certo** *avv.* certainly.

certuni *pron. indef.* some.

cerùleo *agg.* sky-blue.

cerva *sf.* (*zool.*) hind.

cervella *sf.* brain.

cervelletto *sm.* cerebellum.

cervello *sm.* **1.** brain **2.** (*intelligenza, mente*) understanding, mind.

cervellòtico *agg.* far-fetched.

cervicale *agg.* cervical.

cervice *sf.* nape.

cèrvidi *sm. pl.* cervidae.

cervo *sm.* deer (*inv. al pl.*).

cesàreo *agg.* Caesarean ‖ *taglio —,* Caesarean operation.

cesarismo *sm.* Caesarism.

cesellare *vt.* to chisel (*anche fig.*).

cesellatura *sf.* chisel work.

cesello *sm.* chisel.

cesoia *sf.* shears (*pl.*).

cespuglio *sm.* bush, thicket.

cespuglioso *agg.* bushy.

cessare *vt. e vi.* to cease, to stop.

cessazione *sf.* cessation.

cessione *sf.* transfer.

cesso *sm.* lavatory.

cesta *sf.* basket.

cestaio *sm.* **1.** basket-maker **2.** (*chi vende*) basket-vendor.

cestinare *vt.* (*fig.*) to refuse.

cestino *sm.* small basket: *— da lavoro,* work-basket; *— da viaggio,* luncheon-basket; *— per la carta straccia,* waste-paper basket.

cesto *sm.* (*sport*) basket.

cesura *sf.* caesura.

cetàceo *agg. e sm.* cetacean.

ceto *sm.* ciass, rank.

cetra *sf.* cithern, lyre.

cetriolino *sm.* gherkin.

cetriolo *sm.* cucumber.

che¹ *pron. rel.* **1.** (*sogg., riferito a persone*) who, that: *l'uomo — mi parlò,* the man who (that) spoke to me **2.** (*sogg., riferito a cose e animali*) which, that: *ecco il cane — mi fu regalato,* here is the dog which (that) was given to me **3.** (*ogg., riferito a persone*) whom: *è la ragazza più graziosa — abbia mai incontrato,* she is the prettiest girl whom I ever met **4.** (*ogg., riferito a cose e animali*) which: *questo è il libro — le darò,* this is the book which I shall give her **5.** *il —,* which **6.** (*riferito a tempo*) when.

che² *agg. int.* **1.** what: *— musica preferisci?,* what music do you prefer? **2.** which: *— libro scegli?,* which book do you choose? ◆ **che** *pron. int.* what: *— è questo?,* what is this? ◆ **che** *agg. escl.* what, what a. ◆ **che** *pron. ind.* something.

che³ *cong.* **1.** that **2.** (*comparativo*) than: *è più bella che intelligente,* she is more beautiful than intelligent **3.** (*correlativo*) whether: *— tu venga o no,* whether you come or not. ◆ **che** *inter.* what!

checché *pron. indef.* whatever.

checchessia *pron. indef.* anything.

chepì *sm.* (*mil.*) kepi.

cherosene *sm.* kerosene.

cherubino *sm.* cherub.

chetamente *avv.* quietly, secretly.

chetare *vt.* to quiet. ◆ **chetarsi** *vr.* to quiet down.

chetichella (*nella loc. avv.*) *alla —,* on the sly, secretly.

cheto *agg.* quiet.

chi *pron. rel.* **1.** (*colui che*) he (*ogg.* him) who (*ogg.* whom) **2.** (*colei che*) she (*ogg.* her) who (*ogg.* whom) **3.** (*coloro che*) they (*ogg.* them) who (*ogg.* whom) **4.** (*gen.*) those, the person who(m). ◆ **chi** *pron. indef.* **1.** whoever, anyone **2.** (*qualcuno che*) someone who. ◆ **chi** *pron. int.* **1.** (*sogg.*) who **2.** (*ogg.*) whom **3.** which: *— di voi?,* which of you? **4.** (*specificazione poss.*) whose: *di — è questa casa?,* whose house is this?

chiàcchiera *sf.* chatter.

chiacchierare *vi.* to chat.

chiacchierata *sf.* chat.

chiacchierone *sm.* chatterbox.

chiamare *vt.* to call || *mandare a —,* to send (*v. irr.*) for; *— al telefono,* to call up. ♦ **chiamarsi** *vr.* to be called || *come ti chiami?,* what's your name?

chiamata *sf.* call, appeal.

chiara *sf. — d'uovo,* white (of an egg).

chiaretto *sm.* (*vino*) claret.

chiarezza *sf.* **1.** clearness **2.** (*fig.*) evidence.

chiarificare *vt.* to clarify.

chiarificazione *sf.* **1.** clarification **2.** (*fig.*) frank explanation.

chiarimento *sm.* explanation.

chiarire *vt.* **1.** to clarify, to clear up **2.** (*spiegare*) to explain.

chiaro *agg.* **1.** clear, evident **2.** (*di luce*) light.

chiarore *sm.* **1.** light **2.** (*luce tenue*) faint light.

chiaroscuro *sm.* light and shade.

chiaroveggente *agg.* **1.** clear-sighted **2.** (*che ha facoltà divinatorie*) clairvoyant.

chiassata *sf.* row.

chiasso *sm.* noise, uproar.

chiassone *sm.* noisy person.

chiassoso *agg.* **1.** noisy **2.** (*fig.*) showy.

chiatta *sf.* barge.

chiavarda *sf.* bolt.

chiave *sf.* **1.** key **2.** (*mus.*) clef.

chiavistello *sm.* latch, bolt.

chiazza *sf.* spot, stain.

chicchessia *pron. indef.* anyone.

chicco *sm.* **1.** grain **2.** (*di grandine*) hailstone **3.** (*di caffè*) coffee-bean **4.** (*di uva*) grape.

chiedere *vt.* **1.** to ask: *— qc. a qu.,* (*per sapere*) to ask so. sthg., (*per avere*) to ask so. for sthg. **2.** (*riferito a un prezzo*) to charge.

chierichetto *sm.* altar boy.

chiesa *sf.* church.

chiglia *sf.* (*mar.*) keel.

chilo[1] *sm.* (*med.*) chyle || *fare il —,* to take (*v. irr.*) a nap.

chilo[2] *sm.* kilo.

chilogrammo *sm.* kilogram.

chilometraggio *sm.* distance in kilometres.

chilòmetro *sm.* kilometre.

chìlowatt *sm.* kilowatt.

chimera *sf.* chimera.

chìmica *sf.* chemistry.

chìmico *agg.* chemical. ♦ **chìmico**
sm. chemist.

china *sf.* slope.

chinare *vt.* to bend (*v. irr.*), to bow. ♦ **chinarsi** *vr.* to bend (*v. irr.*) down.

chincaglierìa *sf.* **1.** small fancy articles (*pl.*) **2.** (*negozio*) fancy goods shop.

chinino *sm.* quinine.

chioccia *sf.* brooding-hen.

chiòcciola *sf.* snail || *scala a —,* spiral staircase.

chiodato *agg.* nailed.

chiodo *sm.* **1.** nail **2.** (*fig.*) fixed idea.

chioma *sf.* hair.

chiosco *sm.* **1.** kiosk **2.** (*per giornali, frutta e verdura*) stand.

chiostro *sm.* cloister.

chiromante *s.* chiromancer.

chiromanzìa *sf.* chiromancy.

chirurgìa *sf.* surgery.

chirurgo *sm.* surgeon.

chissà *inter.* goodness knows.

chitarra *sf.* guitar.

chiùdere *vt.* **1.** to shut (*v. irr.*) || *— a chiave,* to lock **2.** (*terminare*) to close **3.** (*rinchiudere*) to shut (*v. irr.*) up.

chiunque *pron.* **1.** (*sogg.*) anyone who, whoever **2.** (*ogg.*) whomever, anyone **3.** (*specificazione possessiva*) *di —,* whosoever.

chiuso *agg.* closed, shut || *— a chiave,* locked.

chiusura *sf.* closing.

ci *pron.* **1.** (*ogg.*) us: *essi — amano,* they love us **2.** (*riflessivo*) ourselves: *noi — laviamo,* we wash ourselves **3.** (*rec. fra due persone*) each other: *mia madre ed io — guardammo,* my mother and I looked at each other **4.** (*rec. fra più persone*) one another **5.** (*dimostrativo*) this, that, it: *non badarci,* pay no attention to it. ♦ **ci** *avv. di luogo* there (*là*), here (*qui*).

ciabatta *sf.* slipper.

ciambella *sf.* ring-shaped cake.

ciambellano *sm.* chamberlain.

ciancia *sf.* idle talk || *ciance!,* nonsense!

cianciare *vi.* to chatter.

cianografìa *sf.* blueprint.

cianuro *sm.* cyanide.

ciao *inter.* **1.** (*incontrandosi*) hullo **2.** (*congedandosi*) bye-bye.

ciarla *sf.* **1.** loquacity **2.** (*notizia*

falsa) false report.

ciarlare *vi.* to talk idly.

ciarlatano *sm.* charlatan.

ciascuno *agg.* every. ♦ **ciascuno** *pron.* **1.** (*con valore distributivo*) each **2.** (*tutti*) everybody, everyone.

cibernètica *sf.* cybernetics.

cibo *sm.* food.

ciborio *sm.* ciborium (*pl.* -ia).

cicala *sf.* cicada.

cicatrice *sf.* scar.

cicatrizzare *vt.* to cicatrize, to heal. ♦ **cicatrizzarsi** *vr.* to cicatrize, to heal.

cicerone *sm.* guide.

ciclamino *sm.* cyclamen.

cìclico *agg.* cyclic.

ciclismo *sm.* cycling.

ciclista *s.* cyclist.

ciclo *sm.* **1.** cycle **2.** (*di malattia*) course.

ciclone *sm.* hurricane.

ciclòpico *agg.* Cyclopean.

ciclostilare *vt.* to mimeograph.

ciclostile *sm.* cyclostyle.

ciclotrone *sm.* cyclotron.

cicogna *sf.* stork.

cicuta *sf.* hemlock.

cieco *agg.* blind (*anche fig.*). ♦ **cieco** *sm.* blind man.

cielo *sm.* **1.** sky **2.** (*aria*) air **3.** (*paradiso*) Heaven.

cifra *sf.* **1.** figure, number **2.** (*segno di cifrario*) cipher.

cifrare *vt.* **1.** to cipher **2.** (*ricamare in cifra*) to mark.

ciglio *sm.* **1.** eyelash **2.** (*bordo*) edge.

cigno *sm.* swan.

cilecca *sf.* failure || *far* —, to miss fire, (*fig.*) to fail.

cileno *agg.* Chilean.

cilicio *sm.* **1.** hairshirt **2.** (*relig.*) cilice.

ciliegia *sf.* cherry.

ciliegio *sm.* cherry-tree.

cilindrata *sf.* (*auto*) displacement.

cilindro *sm.* **1.** (*geom.; auto*) cylinder **2.** (*cappello*) top-hat.

cima *sf.* **1.** top, summit: *in* —, at the top **2.** (*fig.*) genius.

cìmbali *sm. pl. essere in* —, to be tipsy.

cimentare *vt.* to put (*v. irr.*) to the test. ♦ **cimentarsi** *vr.* to venture upon.

cimitero *sm.* cemetery, graveyard.

cinabro *sm.* cinnabar.

cincillà *sf.* chinchilla.

cineasta *sm.* cinematographer.

cinecàmera *sf.* cine-camera.

cinedilettante *sm.* film-amateur.

cinegiornale *sm.* news-reel.

cìnema *sm.* **1.** cinema, pictures (*pl.*) **2.** (*locale*) cinema **3.** (*amer.*) movies (*pl.*).

cinemàtica *sf.* kinematics.

cinematografìa *sf.* cinematography.

cinematògrafo *sm.* cinema.

cinèreo *agg.* cinereous, ashen-grey.

cinese *agg. e sm.* Chinese.

cineteca *sf.* film library.

cinètica *sf.* kinetics.

cìngere *vt.* **1.** to engird **2.** (*circondare*) to surround.

cinghia *sf.* **1.** strap **2.** (*mecc.*) belt.

cinghiale *sm.* (*zool.*) wild boar.

cìnico *agg.* cynical. ♦ **cìnico** *sm.* cynic.

cinismo *sm.* cynicism.

cinocèfalo *sm.* cynocephalus (*pl.* -ali).

cinòdromo *sm.* greyhound racing-track.

cinofilìa *sf.* dog-love.

cinquanta *agg.* fifty.

cinquantenario *sm.* fiftieth anniversary.

cinque *agg.* five.

cinquecento *agg.* five hundred.

cinta *sf.* town-walls (*pl.*): *muro di* —, boundary walls.

cinto *sm.* belt. ♦ **cinto** *agg.* surrounded.

cintola *sf.* waist: *dalla* — *in giù*, below the waist; *dalla* — *in su*, above the waist.

cintura *sf.* belt.

cinturone *sm.* belt.

ciò *pron.* that, this, it.

ciocca *sf.* (*di capelli*) lock.

cioccolata *sf.* chocolate.

cioccolatino *sm.* chocolate.

cioccolato *sm.* chocolate.

cioè *cong.* that is.

ciondolare *vi.* **1.** to dangle **2.** (*fig.*) to lounge.

ciòndolo *sm.* pendant.

ciondoloni *avv.* dangling.

ciòtola *sf.* cup, bowl.

ciòttolo *sm.* pebble.

cipolla *sf.* onion.

cipresso *sm.* cypress.

cipria *sf.* powder: *piumino per* —, powder puff.

circa *prep. e avv.* about, nearly || — *a*, as to.

circo *sm.* circus.

circolante *agg.* circulating: *moneta* —, currency.

circolare¹ *agg.* circular. ♦ **circolare** *sf.* circular letter.

circolare² *vi.* to circulate.

circolatorio *agg.* circulatory.

circolazione *sf.* **1.** circulation **2.** (*traffico*) traffic **3.** (*comm.*) currency.

circolo *sm.* **1.** circle **2.** (*associazione*) club.

circoncìdere *vt.* to circumcise.

circoncisione *sf.* circumcision.

circondare *vt.* to surround (*anche fig.*).

circonferenza *sf.* circumference.

circonflesso *agg.* circumflex.

circonlocuzione *sf.* circumlocution.

circonvallazione *sf.* ring-road.

circonvenire *vt.* to circumvent.

circonvoluzione *sf.* circumvolution.

circoscrivere *vt.* to circumscribe.

circoscrizione *sf.* **1.** circumscription **2.** (*territorio*) area.

circospetto *agg.* circumspect.

circospezione *sf.* circumspection.

circostante *agg.* **1.** surrounding **2.** (*attr.*) neighbouring.

circostanza *sf.* circumstance, occasion: *in queste circostanze*, under these circumstances; *in quella* —, on that occasion.

circostanziale *agg.* circumstantial.

circostanziare *vt.* to detail.

circuire *vt.* **1.** to surround **2.** (*fig.*) to circumvent.

circùito *sm.* circuit.

cirillico *agg.* cyrillic.

cirrosi *sf.* cirrhosis.

cisalpino *agg.* cisalpine.

cisposo *agg.* blear.

ciste *sf.* cyst.

cisterna *sf.* **1.** cistern **2.** (*serbatoio*) tank.

cistifèllea *sf.* gall-bladder.

cistite *sf.* cystitis.

citare *vt.* **1.** (*menzionare*) to mention **2.** (*da un libro o da un discorso ecc.*) to quote **3.** (*giur.*) to summon.

citazione *sf.* **1.** (*da un discorso, un libro ecc.*) quotation **2.** (*giur.*) summons (*pl.*).

citòfono *sm.* interphone.

citologìa *sf.* (*biol.*) cytology.

citrato *sm.* citrate.

cìtrico *agg.* citric.

città *sf.* **1.** town: — *di provincia*, country town; — *natale*, home town; *gente di* —, townspeople; *vita di* —, town life **2.** (*metropoli*) city.

cittadella *sf.* **1.** citadel **2.** (*baluardo*) stronghold.

cittadina *sf.* **1.** small town **2.** (*donna che abita in città*) woman citizen.

cittadinanza *sf.* **1.** (*abitanti*) people of the city **2.** (*nazionalità*) citizenship: *diritto di* —, right of citizenship.

cittadino *sm.* **1.** (*che abita in città*) town-dweller **2.** (*che appartiene a uno stato*) citizen. ♦ **cittadino** *agg.* town.

ciuffo *sm.* **1.** forelock **2.** (*di penne, peli, erba*) tuft.

ciurma *sf.* crew.

civetta *sf.* **1.** owl **2.** (*fig.*) coquette.

civetterìa *sf.* coquetry.

cìvico *agg.* civic.

civile *agg.* **1.** civil **2.** (*che riguarda la civiltà*) civilized **3.** (*gentile*) polite **4.** (*non ecclesiastico o non militare*) civilian.

civilizzare *vt.* to civilize.

civilizzazione *sf.* civilization.

civiltà *sf.* **1.** civilization **2.** (*cortesia*) politeness.

civismo *sm.* civic virtues (*pl.*).

clamore *sm.* uproar.

clamoroso *agg.* noisy.

clandestino *agg.* clandestine, secret.

clarinetto, clarino *sm.* clarinet.

classe *sf.* class || *di* — (*qualità*), first-rate.

classicismo *sm.* classicism.

clàssico *agg.* classical. ♦ **clàssico** *sm.* classic.

classìfica *sf.* **1.** classification **2.** (*sport*) position.

classificare *vt.* to classify.

classificazione *sf.* classification.

claudicare *vi.* to limp.

clàusola *sf.* **1.** clause **2.** (*riserva*) reserve.

claustrofobìa *sf.* claustrophobia.

clava *sf.* club.

clavicémbalo *sm.* harpsichord.

clavìcola *sf.* collar-bone.

clemente *agg.* clement, mild.

clemenza *sf.* clemency, mildness.

cleptòmane *agg. e sm.* kleptomaniac.

cleptomanìa *sf.* kleptomania.

clericale *agg.* clerical.

clero *sm.* clergy.

cliente sm. 1. customer 2. (di medico, avvocato) client.

clientela sf. 1. customers (pl.) 2. (di medico, avvocato) practice 3. (comm.) connection.

clima sm. climate.

clinica sf. nursing-home.

clinico agg. clinical. ♦ **clinico** sm. clinician.

clistere sm. enema.

cloaca sf. cloaca.

cloro sm. chlorine.

clorofilla sf. chlorophyll.

cloroformio sm. chloroform.

cloruro sm. chloride.

coabitare vi. to cohabit.

coabitazione sf. cohabitation.

coadiuvante agg. coadjuvant.

coadiuvare vt. to help.

coagulare vt. 1. to coagulate 2. (del latte) to curdle.

coagulazione sf. coagulation.

coàgulo sm. 1. curd 2. (di sangue) blood-clot.

coalizione sf. alliance, coalition.

coalizzare vt. to unite. ♦ **coalizzarsi** vr. to form a coalition.

coartare vt. to force.

coatto agg. forced: domicilio —, forced residence.

cobalto sm. cobalt.

cobelligerante agg. e sm. co-belligerent.

cobra sm. cobra.

cocaina sf. cocaine.

cocainòmane s. cocainist.

coccarda sf. cockade.

cocchiere sm. coachman (pl. -men).

cocchio sm. coach.

còccige sm. coccyx (pl. -yges).

coccinella sf. ladybird.

cocciniglia sf. cochineal.

coccio sm. 1. (terracotta) crock, pot 2. (pezzo rotto) fragment of pottery.

cocciutàggine sf. stubbornness.

cocciuto agg. stubborn.

cocco sm. 1. (frutto) coconut 2. (albero) coconut-tree 3. (fam. vezz.) darling.

coccodrillo sm. crocodile.

coccolare vt. to pet, to fondle.

cocente agg. 1. hot, scalding 2. (fig.) deep, bitter.

cocòmero sm. water-melon.

cocùzzolo sm. 1. crown 2. (vetta) top.

coda sf. 1. tail 2. (fila) queue: fare la —, to queue up.

codardo agg. cowardly. ♦ **codardo** sm. coward.

codesto agg. 1. that (pl. those) 2. (come « tale ») such. ♦ **codesto** pron. that one (pl. those ones).

còdice sm. 1. code: — civile, Civil Law 2. (manoscritto antico) codex.

codificare vt. to codify.

coefficiente sm. coefficient.

coercitivo agg. coercive.

coercizione sf. compulsion.

coerente agg. coherent.

coerenza sf. coherence.

coesione sf. cohesion.

coesistenza sf. coexistence.

coesìstere vi. to coexist.

coetàneo agg. e sm. contemporary || Carlo ed io siamo coetanei, Charles and I are the same age.

cofanetto sm. casket: — di gioielli, jewel box.

còfano sm. 1. coffer 2. (auto) bonnet.

cògliere vt. 1. to pick up, to pluck 2. (sorprendere) to catch (v. irr.) 3. (colpire) to hit (v. irr.) 4. (afferrare) to seize: — la palla al balzo, to seize the opportunity.

cognata sf. sister-in-law.

cognato sm. brother-in-law.

cognizione sf. 1. knowledge 2. (giur.) cognizance.

cognome sm. surname.

coincidenza sf. 1. coincidence 2. (ferr.) connection.

coincìdere vi. to coincide, to clash.

coinvòlgere vt. to involve.

còito sm. coition.

colabrodo sm. strainer.

colaggio sm. 1. (di liquidi) leakage 2. (metal.) casting.

colare vt. 1. to strain 2. (fondere) to cast (v. irr.). ♦ **colare** vi. to drip.

colata sf. 1. (metal.) casting 2. (quantità di metallo fuso) cast 3. (di lava) flow.

colato agg. strained, filtered.

colazione sf. 1. (del mattino) breakfast 2. (di mezzogiorno) lunch.

colbacco sm. busby.

colei pron. dimostr. 1. (sogg.) she; (ogg.) her 2. — che, she who, she whom (sogg.); her who, her whom (ogg.): — che viene qui è mia sorella, she who is coming here is my sister; — che vedi è Maria, she whom you see is Mary; vedi — che viene?, can you see her who is coming?; sono stata aiutata da —

che odiavo, I have been helped by her whom I hated.

coleòttero *sm.* coleopter.

colera *sm.* cholera.

colesterolo *sm.* cholesterol.

còlica *sf.* colic.

colino *sm.* strainer.

colite *sf.* colitis.

colla *sf.* glue || — *di farina,* paste.

collaborare *vi.* to collaborate.

collaboratore *sm.* collaborator.

collaborazione *sf.* collaboration.

collaborazionismo *sm.* collaborationism.

collaborazionista *sm.* collaborationist.

collana *sf.* **1.** necklace **2.** (*raccolta*) collection **3.** (*di libri*) series.

collare *sm.* collar.

collasso *sm.* breakdown: — *cardiaco,* heart failure.

collaterale *agg.* collateral.

collaudare *vt.* to test.

collaudatore *sm.* **1.** tester **2.** (*aer.*) test pilot **3.** (*auto*) test-driver.

collàudo *sm.* test: *fare un — di qc.,* to put (*v. irr.*) sthg. to the test.

collazionare *vt.* to collate.

colle *sm.* hill.

collega *sm.* colleague.

collegamento *sm.* **1.** connection **2.** (*mecc.*) linkwork || *essere in —,* to be in touch.

collegare *vt.* to connect, to link.

collegiale *agg.* collegial. ♦ **collegiale** *sm.* boarder.

collegio *sm.* **1.** college **2.** (*scuola con convitto*) boarding-school.

còllera *sf.* anger || *essere in —,* to be angry.

collèrico *agg.* hot-tempered.

colletta *sf.* collection.

collettivismo *sm.* collectivism.

collettività *sf.* collectivity.

collettivizzare *vt.* to collectivize.

collettivizzazione *sf.* collectivization.

collettivo *agg.* collective.

colletto *sm.* collar.

collettore *agg.* collecting. ♦ **collettore** *sm.* **1.** (*esattore; raccoglitore*) collector **2.** (*mecc.*) manifold **3.** (*elettr.*) commutator.

collezionare *vt.* to collect.

collezione *sf.* collection.

collezionista *sm.* collector.

collimare *vi.* **1.** (*essere d'accordo*) to agree (with) **2.** (*coincidere*) to coincide.

collina *sf.* hill.

collinoso *agg.* hilly.

collirio *sm.* eye-wash.

collisione *sf.* collision (*anche fig.*), impact.

collo *sm.* **1.** neck: *allungare il —,* to crane one's neck || *a rotta di —,* at breakneck speed; *tra capo e —,* unexpectedly **2.** (*pacco*) parcel, package.

collocamento *sm.* **1.** placing **2.** (*impiego*) employment || *agenzia di —,* employment bureau **3.** (*comm.*) disposal.

collocare *vt.* **1.** to place **2.** (*impiegare*) to employ **3.** (*comm.*) to sell (*v. irr.*), to dispose (of sthg.). ♦ **collocarsi** *vr.* **1.** to place oneself **2.** (*impiegarsi*) to get a situation.

collocazione *sf.* **1.** placing **2.** (*comm.*) sale **3.** (*di libri in biblioteche*) press-mark.

colloidale *agg.* colloidal.

colloquio *sm.* **1.** conversation, talk **2.** (*intervista*) interview.

collusione *sf.* collusion.

colluttazione *sf.* scuffle: *venire a —,* to come (*v. irr.*) to grips.

colmare *vt.* **1.** to fill up **2.** (*fig.*) to fill, to overwhelm.

colmo *agg.* full, brimful. ♦ **colmo** *sm.* top, summit, climax || *per — di sfortuna,* as a crowning misfortune; *è il —!,* that beats everything.

colomba *sf.* dove.

colombaia *sf.* dove-cot.

colombo *sm.* pigeon: — *viaggiatore,* carrier-pigeon.

colonia *sf.* colony.

coloniale *agg.* colonial.

colonialismo *sm.* colonialism.

colonialista *sm.* colonialist.

colonizzare *vt.* to colonize.

colonizzatore *sm.* colonizer.

colonizzazione *sf.* colonization.

colonna *sf.* column (*anche fig.*), pillar || — *d'acqua,* fall of water.

colonnato *sm.* colonnade.

colonnello *sm.* colonel.

colono *sm.* **1.** farmer **2.** (*abitante di una colonia*) settler.

colorante *agg.* colouring. ♦ **colorante** *sm.* dye.

colorare *vt.* to colour. ♦ **colorarsi** *vr.* **1.** to colour **2.** (*di persona*) to blush, to flush.

colorazione *sf.* colouring.

colore *sm.* **1.** colour ‖ *biancheria di —*, coloured linen; *gente di —*, coloured people; *colori a olio*, oil-paints **2.** (*aspetto*) look.

colorire *vt.* to colour.

colorito *sm.* complexion.

coloritura *sf.* colouring.

coloro *pron. dimostr.* **1.** they (*sogg.*); them (*compl.*) **2.** *— che*, they who, they whom (*sogg.*); them who, them whom (*compl.*): *— studiano saranno premiati*, they who study will be given a prize; *— tu vedi sono i miei amici*, they whom you see are my friends; *amerò sempre — mi amano*, I shall always love them who love me; *ti presenterò a — hai visto ieri*, I shall introduce you to them whom you saw yesterday.

colossale *agg.* colossal.

colosso *sm.* colossus (*pl.* -si).

colpa *sf.* **1.** fault **2.** (*colpevolezza*) guilt.

colpévole *agg.* guilty.

colpevolezza *sf.* guilt, guiltiness.

colpire *vt.* **1.** to hit (*v. irr.*), to strike (*v. irr.; anche fig.*) **2.** (*di arma da fuoco*) to shoot (*v. irr.*).

colpo *sm.* **1.** blow, stroke (*anche fig.*): *— di fortuna*, stroke of luck; *— apoplettico*, stroke of apoplexy ‖ *— d'aria*, draught; *a — d'occhio*, at a glance; *a — sicuro*, without any risk; *senza — ferire*, without resistance **2.** (*di arma da fuoco*) shot.

colposo *agg.* unpremeditated: *omicidio —*, manslaughter.

coltellata *sf.* stab.

coltello *sm.* knife: *— a serramanico*, jack-knife; *affilare un —*, to sharpen a knife.

coltivàbile *agg.* cultivable.

coltivare *vt.* to cultivate (*anche fig.*), to till, to farm.

coltivatore *sm.* **1.** tiller, farmer **2.** (*di patate, tabacco ecc.*) grower.

coltivazione *sf.* **1.** tilling, farming **2.** (*di patate, tabacco ecc.*) growing.

colto *agg.* (*istruito*) learned.

coltre *sf.* blanket, coverlet.

colui *pron. dimostr.* **1.** he (*sogg.*) him (*compl.*) **2.** *— che*, he who, he whom (*sogg.*); him who, him whom (*compl.*): *— che ti ha salutato è mio fratello*, he who has greeted you is my brother; *— che vedesti ieri è un mio vecchio ami-*

co, he whom you saw yesterday is an old friend of mine; *daranno il premio a — che studierà*, they will give the prize to him who studies; *fui aiutata da — che avevo aiutato*, I was helped by him whom I had helped.

coma *sm.* coma.

comandamento *sm.* **1.** command, precept **2.** (*relig.*) commandment.

comandante *sm.* commander.

comandare *vt.* **1.** to order, to command **2.** (*essere al comando*) to command, to be in command of.

comando *sm.* **1.** (*ordine*) order **2.** (*autorità*) command **3.** (*sede del comandante*) headquarters (*pl.*).

comatoso *agg.* comatose.

combaciare *vi.* to fit together.

combattente *sm.* **1.** fighting man **2.** (*soldato*) soldier, service man.

combattentìstico *agg.* soldier (like) (*attr.*).

combàttere *vt. e vi.* to fight (*v. irr.*) (*anche fig.*).

combattimento *sm.* **1.** combat, fight, battle **2.** (*boxe*) match.

combattività *sf.* pugnacity.

combattivo *agg.* pugnacious.

combinare *vt.* **1.** to combine **2.** (*di colori*) to match **3.** (*concludere*) to conclude **4.** (*progettare*) to plan.

combinazione *sf.* **1.** combination **2.** (*sistemazione*) arrangement **3.** (*caso, coincidenza*) chance, coincidence.

combrìccola *sf.* **1.** band **2.** (*comitiva*) party.

combustìbile *agg.* combustible. ♦ **combustìbile** *sm.* fuel.

combustione *sf.* combustion.

combutta *sf.* **1.** gang: *essere in —*, to be hand in glove **2.** (*congiura*) plot.

come *avv.* **1.** (*simile a*) like: *è proprio — suo padre*, he is just like his father **2.** (*in qualità di, modale*) as: *ti parlo — amico*, I am speaking to you as a friend **3.** (*in comp.*) as ... as; so ... as: *Carlo è studioso — me*, Charles is as studious as I; *Carlo non è studioso — me*, Charles is not so studious as I **4.** (*int.*) how: *— va?*, How are you? **5.** (*escl.*) how: *— è interessante questo libro!*, How interesting this book is! ♦ **come** *prep.* **1.** (*tempo-*

rale) as, as soon as: — *sentii la sua voce lo riconobbi*, as soon as I heard his voice I recognized him 2. (*come se*) as if: *mi guarda — se mi conoscesse*, he is looking at me as if he knew me || — *Dio volle*, in God's good time; — *segue*, as follows; — *d'accordo*, as agreed.

cometa *sf.* comet.

comicità *sf.* comicality.

còmico *agg.* comical, funny. ♦ **còmico** *sm.* comedian.

comìgnolo *sm.* chimney-pot.

cominciare *vt.* to begin (*v. irr.*), to start.

comitato *sm.* committee.

comitiva *sf.* party, company.

comizio *sm.* meeting.

comma *sm.* paragraph.

commedia *sf.* 1. comedy, play 2. (*fig.*) pretence || *recitare la —*, to play a part.

commediante *sm.* 1. player 2. (*fig.*) shammer.

commediògrafo *sm.* playwright.

commemorare *vt.* to commemorate.

commemorativo *agg.* memorial.

commemorazione *sf.* commemoration.

commendàbile *agg.* commendable.

commendatizia *sf.* letter of recommendation.

commensale *sm.* table-companion.

commentare *vt.* to comment (on).

commentario *sm.* (*lett.*) commentary.

commentatore *sm.* commentator.

commento *sm.* commentary.

commerciàbile *agg.* negotiable.

commerciale *agg.* commercial.

commercializzare *vt.* to commercialize.

commerciante *sm.* 1. trader 2. (*uomo d'affari*) business-man (*pl.* -men) || — *all'ingrosso*, wholesale dealer; — *al minuto*, retailer.

commerciare *vi.* to trade, to deal (*v. irr.*) (in).

commercio *sm.* 1. commerce, trade 2. (*affari*) business || — *all'ingrosso*, wholesale trade; — *al minuto*, retail trade; — *d'importazione, esportazione*, import, export trade; *essere in —*, to be on sale; *essere fuori —*, to be out of sale; *essere in — (di un commerciante)*, to be in business.

commessa *sf.* shop assistant, shop-girl.

commesso *sm.* clerk, shopman (*pl.* -men), shop assistant || — *viaggiatore*, commercial traveller.

commestìbile *agg.* eatable. ♦ **commestìbili** *sm. pl.* foodstuffs.

comméttere *vt.* 1. to commit, to do (*v. irr.*), to make (*v. irr.*) 2. (*ordinare*) to order.

commiato *sm.* 1. (*preso*) leave 2. (*dato*) dismissal.

commilitone *sm.* fellow-soldier.

comminatoria *sf.* commination.

comminatorio *agg.* comminatory.

commiserare *vt.* to pity.

commiserazione *sf.* pity.

commissariato *sm.* 1. (*carica di commissario*) commissaryship 2. (*ufficio*) commissary's office.

commissario *sm.* commissary.

commissionare *vt.* (*comm.*) to order.

commissionario *sm.* (*comm.*) commission agent.

commissione *sf.* 1. errand: *fare una —*, to go (*v. irr.*) on an errand 2. (*comm.*) commission, order 3. (*comitato*) commission, committee.

commisurare *vt.* to compare.

committente *sm.* purchaser, buyer.

commosso *agg.* moved, affected.

commovente *agg.* moving, touching, affecting.

commozione *sf.* 1. emotion 2. (*med.*) concussion: — *cerebrale*, concussion of the brain.

commuòvere *vt.* to move, to touch. ♦ **commuòversi** *vr.* to be moved.

commutàbile *agg.* commutable.

commutare *vt.* to commute.

commutativo *agg.* commutative.

commutatore *sm.* commutator.

comò *sm.* chest of drawers.

comodino *sm.* night-table.

comodità *sf.* convenience, comfort.

còmodo *agg.* 1. useful 2. (*conveniente*) convenient 3. (*confortevole*) comfortable 4. (*maneggevole*) handy.

compagnìa *sf.* 1. company: *tener —*, to keep (*v. irr.*) company 2. (*gruppo di persone*) party 3. (*società*) company.

compagno *sm.* companion, mate, comrade || — *di giuochi*, playmate; — *di stanza*, room-mate; — *di studi*, fellow-student.

compagnone sm. jolly good fellow.

comparàbile agg. comparable.

comparare vt. to compare.

comparativo agg. (gramm.) comparative.

comparato agg. comparative.

compare sm. 1. (compagno) comrade, partner 2. (padrino) godfather 3. (testimone di matrimonio) witness 4. (complice) accomplice.

comparire vi. 1. to appear 2. (sembrare) to show (v. irr.) oneself 3. (far bella mostra) to show (v. irr.) off.

comparizione sf. appearance: (giur.) mandato di —, summons.

comparsa sf. 1. appearance 2. (teat.; cine) supernumerary 3. (giur.) appearance.

compartecipare vi. to share in.

compartimento sm. 1. compartment 2. (circoscrizione) department.

compartizione sf. distribution.

compassato agg. 1. stiff, formal 2. (di discorso) restrained.

compassione sf. pity, commiseration.

compasso sm. compasses (pl.).

compatìbile agg. consistent.

compatibilità sf. consistency.

compatimento sm. pity, compassion.

compatire vt. to pity.

compatriota sm. fellow-countryman (pl. -men). ♦ **compatriota** sf. fellow-countrywoman (pl. -women).

compattezza sf. 1. compactness 2. (di associazione, partito) unity.

compatto agg. compact, solid.

compendiare vt. to abridge, to sum up.

compendio sm. 1. abridgement, summary.

compenetrare vt. to penetrate.

compensàbile agg. remunerable.

compensare vt. 1. to compensate 2. (ricompensare) to reward.

compensato sm. ply-wood.

compensazione sf. 1. compensation, indemnity 2. (comm.) clearing.

compenso sm. 1. compensation 2. (rimunerazione) reward, retribution.

còmpera sf. purchase.

competente agg. competent.

competenza sf. 1. competence 2. (onorario) fee.

compètere vi. 1. (gareggiare) to vie 2. (spettare) to be due, to belong.

competitivo agg. competitive.

competitore sm. competitor, rival.

competizione sf. competition.

compiacente agg. obliging.

compiacenza sf. 1. kindness 2. (soddisfazione) satisfaction.

compiacere vt. to please, to gratify. ♦ **compiacersi** vr. 1. to be pleased (with), to congratulate 2. (degnarsi) to condescend.

compiacimento sm. 1. satisfaction 2. (congratulazione) congratulation.

compiàngere vt. 1. to pity, to sympathize (with) 2. (disprezzare) to despise.

compianto agg. regretted. ♦ **compianto** sm. regret.

còmpiere vt. 1. (finire) to finish 2. (eseguire) to accomplish 3. (adempiere) to do (v. irr.): — il proprio dovere, to do one's duty 4. (di età) ho compiuto 30 anni, I am now 30 years old.

compilare vt. to compile: — un documento, to draw (v. irr.) up a document; — una lista, to make (v. irr.) a list.

compilazione sf. 1. compilation 2. (comm.) drawing up.

compimento sm. 1. (il compire) completion 2. (conclusione) achievement.

compitare vt. to spell (v. irr.).

compitezza sf. politeness, refinement.

compito agg. polite.

còmpito sm. 1. task, duty 2. (scolastico, a casa) homework; (a scuola) class-work.

compiutamente avv. completely.

compiutezza sf. completeness.

compiuto agg. complete.

compleanno sm. birthday: buon —!, happy birthday!.

complementare agg. complementary.

complemento sm. 1. complement 2. (gramm.) — indiretto, indirect object 3. (mil.) truppe di —, reserve.

complessato agg. neurotic.

complessione sf. constitution.

complessità sf. complexity.

complessivamente avv. on the whole.

complessivo agg. total, inclusive.

complesso agg. complex, complicated. ♦ **complesso** *sm.* **1.** whole **2.** (*industriale*) plant, set **3.** (*mus.*) band.

completamente *avv.* completely.

completare *vt.* to complete, to finish.

completezza *sf.* completeness.

completo *agg.* **1.** complete, whole **2.** (*pieno*) full. ♦ **completo** *sm.* (*vestito*) suit.

complicare *vt.* to complicate.

complicato *agg.* complicated.

complicazione *sf.* complication: *salvo complicazioni*, if no complications set in.

còmplice *s.* accomplice.

complicità *sf.* accomplicity.

complimentare *vt.* to compliment. ♦ **complimentarsi** *vr.* to congratulate (so.).

complimento *sm.* **1.** compliment **2.** (*congratulazione*) congratulation.

complottare *vi.* to plot.

complotto *sm.* plot, conspiracy.

compluvio *sm.* (*arch.*) compluvium (*pl.* -ia).

componente *agg.* component. ♦ **componente** *sm.* **1.** member **2.** (*chim.*) component.

componimento *sm.* **1.** (*lett.; mus.; scol.*) composition **2.** (*giur.*) settlement.

comporre *vt.* **1.** to compose: — *una poesia*, to write (*v. irr.*) a poem; — *un numero telefonico*, to dial a number **2.** (*chim.*) to compound **3.** (*assestare*) to arrange.

comportamento *sm.* behaviour.

comportare *vt.* to involve, to require. ♦ **comportarsi** *vr.* to behave (oneself).

compòsito *agg.* composite.

compositore *sm.* **1.** (*mus.*) composer **2.** (*tip.*) compositor.

composizione *sf.* **1.** composition **2.** (*conciliazione*) composition, agreement **3.** (*tip.*) composing.

composta *sf.* compote.

compostezza *sf.* **1.** composure **2.** (*dignità*) self-respect.

composto *agg.* **1.** compound **2.** (*ordinato*) tidy **3.** (*calmo*) calm ‖ *stare* —, to sit (*v. irr.*) still. ♦ **composto** *sm.* compound.

comprare *vt.* **1.** to buy (*v. irr.*): — *a credito*, to buy on credit; — *per contanti*, to buy for cash; — — *all'ingrosso*, to buy wholesale **2.** (*corrompere*) to bribe.

compratore *sm.* buyer, purchaser.

compravéndita *sf.* marketing.

comprèndere *vt.* **1.** (*includere*) to include, to take (*v. irr.*) in **2.** (*capire*) to understand (*v. irr.*) **3.** (*rendersi conto*) to realize.

comprensìbile *agg.* intelligible.

comprensibilità *sf.* intelligibility.

comprensione *sf.* **1.** comprehension, understanding **2.** (*compassione*) sympathy.

comprensivo *agg.* **1.** comprehensive **2.** (*che capisce*) comprehending **3.** (*che prova simpatia*) sympathetic.

compressa *sf.* **1.** tablet **2.** (*di garza*) compress.

compressibilità *sf.* compressibility.

compressione *sf.* compression.

comprìmere *vt.* **1.** to compress **2.** (*fig.*) to restrain, to repress.

compromesso *sm.* compromise.

compromettente *agg.* compromising.

comprométtere *vt.* to compromise, to involve.

comproprietà *sf.* joint ownership.

comproprietario *sm.* joint owner.

comprovare *vt.* to prove.

compunto *agg.* filled with compunction, contrite.

computare *vt.* to compute.

computisterìa *sf.* book-keeping.

còmputo *sm.* reckoning.

comunale *agg.* communal, municipal.

comunardo *sm.* (*stor.*) Communard.

comune[1] *agg.* **1.** common **2.** (*abituale*) frequent, usual.

comune[2] *sm.* **1.** commune **2.** (*edificio*) Town Hall.

comunella *sf.* cabal: *far — con qu.*, to consort.

comunemente *avv.* commonly, usually.

comunicàbile *agg.* communicable.

comunicabilità *sf.* communicability.

comunicante *agg.* communicating.

comunicare *vt.* **1.** to communicate, to transmit **2.** (*relig.*) to communicate. ♦ **comunicarsi** *vr.* to receive Holy Communion.

comunicativa *sf.* communicativeness.

comunicativo *agg.* communicative.

comunicato *sm.* bulletin.

comunicazione *sf.* communication: —

comunione *sf.* **1.** communion: —

di idee, similarity of ideas 2. (*re-lig.*) Holy Communion.

comunismo *sm.* communism.

comunista *s.* communist.

comunità *sf.* community.

comunque *avv.* however, anyhow.

con *prep.* 1. (*compagnia, unione, strumento*) with: *venne — me*, he came with me; *scrivo — questa penna*, I write with this pen 2. (*stato, condizione*) in: — *il freddo sto meglio*, in cold weather I feel better 3. (*mezzo di trasporto*) by: *arriverò col treno delle 3*, I shall arrive by the three o'clock train 4. (*per mezzo di*) by means of.

conato *sm.* effort ‖ *avere conati di vomito*, to feel (*v. irr.*) sick.

conca *sf.* 1. basin, pot 2. (*valle*) valley.

concatenamento *sm.* concatenation.

concatenare *vt.* to concatenate.

concatenazione *sf.* concatenation.

còncavo *agg.* concave, hollow.

concèdere *vt.* 1. to grant, to bestow 2. (*permettere*) to allow.

concentramento *sm.* concentration: *campo di —*, concentration camp.

concentrare *vt.* to concentrate. ♦ **concentrarsi** *vr.* to concentrate.

concentrato *agg.* concentrated. ♦ **concentrato** *sm.* concentrated food.

concentrazione *sf.* concentration.

concèntrico *agg.* concentric.

concepìbile *agg.* conceivable.

concepimento *sm.* conception.

concepire *vt.* 1. to conceive 2. (*nutrire speranze, timori*) to entertain 3. (*formulare*) to express.

concerìa *sf.* tannery.

concèrnere *vt.* to concern, to relate to.

concertare *vt.* 1. (*mus.*) to harmonize 2. (*stabilire*) to plan, to arrange.

concertato *agg.* concerted (*anche mus.*), arranged.

concertista *s.* concert artist.

concertìstico *agg.* concert.

concerto *sm.* concert.

concessionario *sm.* concessionary agent.

concessione *sf.* 1. concession 2. (*permesso*) permission.

concetto *sm.* concept.

concettuale *agg.* conceptual.

concezionale *agg.* conceptional.

concezione *sf.* conception.

conchiglia *sf.* shell.

concia *sf.* 1. (*di pelli*) tanning 2. (*di tabacco*) curing.

conciare *vt.* 1. (*pelli*) to tan 2. (*tabacco*) to cure 3. (*fig.*) to ill-treat 4. (*insudiciare*) to soil. ♦ **conciarsi** *vr.* to get (*v. irr.*) dirty.

conciatore *sm.* tanner.

conciatura *sf.* tanning.

conciliàbile *agg.* compatible, consistent.

conciliabilità *sf.* compatibility.

conciliàbolo *sm.* conventicle, secret talk.

conciliante *agg.* conciliatory.

conciliare *vt.* 1. to reconcile 2. (*procacciare*) to win (*v. irr.*), to gain. ♦ **conciliarsi** *vr.* to win (*v. irr.*).

conciliare *agg.* conciliar.

conciliatore *agg.* conciliatory. ♦ **conciliatore** *sm.* peacemaker ‖ *giudice —*, Justice of the Peace.

conciliazione *sf.* conciliation.

concilio *sm.* Council.

concimaia *sf.* dung-hill, dung-pit.

concimare *vt.* to dung.

concimazione *sf.* dunging.

concime *sm.* 1. (*organico*) dung 2. (*chimico*) fertilizer.

concio *sm.* dung.

concionare *vi.* to harangue.

concione *sf.* harangue.

concisione *sf.* concision.

conciso *agg.* concise, brief.

concistoro *sm.* (*eccl.*) concistory.

concitare *vt.* to excite, to stir (up).

concitazione *sf.* excitement, agitation.

concittadino *sm.* fellow-citizen.

conclamare *vt.* to acclaim.

conclave *sm.* (*eccl.*) conclave.

concludente *agg.* 1. conclusive 2. (*di persona*) energetic.

conclùdere *vt.* 1. to conclude, to finish 2. (*dedurre*) to infer 3. (*fare*) to do (*v. irr.*).

conclusionale *sf.* (*giur.*) pleadings (*pl.*).

conclusione *sf.* 1. conclusion 2. (*risultato*) issue, result.

conclusivo *agg.* conclusive.

concomitante *agg.* concomitant.

concomitanza *sf.* concomitance.

concordanza *sf.* agreement.

concordare *vi.* to agree. ♦ **concordare** *vt.* 1. to agree upon 2.

(*mettere d'accordo*) to reconcile **3.** (*gramm.*) to put (*v. irr.*) in concord.

concordatario *agg.* **1.** (*eccl.*) of concordat **2.** (*giur.; comm.*) composition.

concordato *sm.* **1.** convention **2.** (*eccl.*) concordat **3.** (*giur.; comm.*) agreement, composition.

concorde *agg.* concordant, agreeing: *volontà —*, unanimous will.

concordemente *avv.* concordantly.

concordia *sf.* concord, agreement.

concorrente *agg.* **1.** concurrent **2.** (*rivale*) competing. ♦ **concorrente** *sm.* **1.** candidate **2.** (*rivale*) competitor.

concorrenza *sf.* **1.** (*affluenza*) concourse **2.** (*comm.*) competition || *fare —*, to compete with; *— sleale*, unfair competition.

concorrenziale *agg.* competitive.

concòrrere *vi.* **1.** to come (*v. irr.*) together **2.** (*contribuire*) to concur, to contribute **3.** (*partecipare*) to share in **4.** (*mettersi in gara*) to compete.

concorso *sm.* **1.** (*affluenza*) rush, crowd, concourse **2.** (*gara*) competition **3.** (*sport*) contest.

concretàre *vt.* **1.** to make (*v. irr.*) concrete **2.** (*concludere*) to realize.

concretezza *sf.* concreteness.

concreto *agg.* **1.** concrete, real **2.** (*solido*) solid.

concrezione *sf.* concretion.

concubina *sf.* concubine.

concubinaggio, concubinato *sm.* concubinage.

conculcare *vt.* to trample on.

concupire *vt.* to covet, to lust after.

concupiscenza *sf.* concupiscence, lust.

concussione *sf.* (*giur.*) concussion.

condanna *sf.* **1.** condemnation **2.** (*sentenza*) sentence: *— a morte*, death sentence **3.** (*pena*) penalty.

condannàbile *agg.* condemnable.

condannare *vt.* **1.** to sentence **2.** (*fig.*) to condemn **3.** (*riprovare*) to blame.

condannato *agg.* sentenced. ♦ **condannato** *sm.* condemned man.

condensàbile *agg.* condensable.

condensabilità *vt.* condensability.

condensazione *sf.* condensation.

condensare *vt.* to condense.

condensatore *sm.* condenser.

condimento *sm.* seasoning, dressing.

condire *vt.* to season; (*anche fig.*) to flavour.

condirettore *sm.* joint manager.

condiscendente *agg.* complying.

condiscendenza *sf.* **1.** compliance **2.** (*degnazione*) condescension.

condiscèndere *vi.* **1.** to comply with **2.** (*degnarsi*) to condescend.

condiscépolo *sm.* schoolfellow.

condivìdere *vt.* to share (*anche fig.*).

condizionale *agg. e sm.* conditional. ♦ **condizionale** *sf.* (*giur.*) conditional sentence.

condizionamento *sm.* conditioning.

condizionare *vt.* to condition.

condizione *sf.* **1.** condition: *a — che*: on condition that **2.** (*ceto*) rank, station.

condoglianza *sf.* condolence.

condominio *sm.* joint ownership.

condòmino *sm.* joint-owner.

condonare *vt.* to remit.

condono *sm.* remission.

condotta *sf.* **1.** conduct, behaviour.

condotto *agg. medico —*, doctor employed by the local authority. ♦ **condotto** *sm.* **1.** conduit, pipeline **2.** (*anat.*) duct.

conducente *sm.* driver.

conducibilità *sf.* (*fis.*) conductibility.

condurre *vt.* **1.** (*guidare*) to lead (*v. irr.*) **2.** (*accompagnare*) to take (*v. irr.*) **3.** (*governare, trattare*) to manage: *— i propri affari*, to manage one's business **4.** (*vivere*) to lead (*v. irr.*): *— una vita triste*, to lead a sad life. ♦ **condurre** *vi.* to lead (*v. irr.*): *questa strada conduce a Milano*, this route leads to Milan. ♦ **condursi** *vr.* to behave.

conduttività *sf.* conductivity.

conduttivo *agg.* conducting.

conduttore *agg.* conducting. ♦ **conduttore** *sm.* **1.** leader, guide **2.** (*di veicoli*) driver **3.** (*fis.*) conductor.

conduttura *sf.* **1.** duct, conduit **2.** (*di tubazioni*) piping.

conduzione *sf.* **1.** management **2.** (*fis.*) conduction.

confabulare *vi.* to confabulate.

confacente *agg.* suitable, proper.

confarsi *vr.* to suit, to become (*v. irr.*).

confederale *agg.* confederal.

confederare *vt.* to confederate.

confederazione *sf.* **1.** Confederation **2.** (*alleanza*) confederacy.

conferenza *sf.* **1.** lecture **2.** (*assemblea*) conference.

conferenziere *sm.* lecturer.

conferimento *sm.* bestowal.

conferire *vt.* to confer, to bestow. ♦ **conferire** *vi.* **1.** to have an interview **2.** (*giovare*) to be useful.

conferma *sf.* confirmation.

confermare *vt.* to confirm. ♦ **confermarsi** *vr.* to prove oneself.

confermazione *sf.* confirmation.

confessare *vt.* **1.** to confess **2.** (*riconoscere, ammettere*) to admit. ♦ **confessarsi** *vr.* (*eccl.*) to go (*v. irr.*) to confession.

confessionale *agg.* confessional. ♦ **confessionale** *sm.* confessional.

confessione *sf.* **1.** confession **2.** (*ammissione*) admission **3.** (*memorie*) memoirs (*pl.*).

confessore *sm.* confessor.

confetteria *sf.* confectionery.

confettiere *sm.* confectioner.

confetto *sm.* comfit.

confettura *sf.* **1.** (*confetti*) sweetmeats (*pl.*) **2.** (*marmellata*) jam || — *d'arance*, marmalade.

confezionare *vt.* **1.** to make (*v. irr.*) up **2.** (*di piatti*) to prepare **3.** (*di pacchi*) to pack up.

confezione *sf.* **1.** manufacture **2.** (*preparazione*) preparation **3.** (*pl.*) (*abiti*) ready-to-wear clothes **4.** (*imballaggio*) packing.

conficcare *vt.* to hammer, to drive (*v. irr.*). ♦ **conficcarsi** *vr.* to run (*v. irr.*) into.

confidare *vt.* to confide. ♦ **confidare** *vi.* **1.** to confide, to trust **2.** (*fare assegnamento*) to rely (on).

confidente *agg.* trustful. ♦ **confidente** *sm.* **1.** confidant **2.** (*di polizia*) police spy.

confidenza *sf.* **1.** (*fiducia*) confidence **2.** (*cosa confidata*) secret **3.** (*familiarità*) familiarity || *essere in — con qu.*, to be on familiar terms with so.

confidenziale *agg.* confidential: *strettamente —*, strictly confidential.

confidenzialmente *avv.* confidentially.

configgere *vt.* to drive (*v. irr.*) in.

configurare *vt.* to configure, to shape.

configurazione *sf.* configuration, shape.

confinante *agg.* **1.** neighbouring **2.** (*fig.*) bordering.

confinare *vi.* to border on. ♦ **confinare** *vt.* **1.** to banish **2.** (*fig.*) to confine.

confinario *agg.* border.

confinato *agg.* interned.

confine *sm.* **1.** border, frontier **2.** (*fig.*) limit, boundary.

confino *sm.* internment, political confinement.

confisca *sf.* confiscation.

confiscàbile *agg.* confiscable.

confiscare *vt.* to confiscate.

confitto *agg.* **1.** nailed, driven in **2.** (*fig.*) fixed.

conflagrare *vi.* to break (*v. irr.*) out.

conflagrazione *sf.* **1.** conflagration **2.** (*fig.*) sudden out-break (of war).

conflitto *sm.* **1.** conflict **2.** (*fig.*) clash.

confluente *sm.* confluent.

confluenza *sf.* confluence.

confluire *vi.* to flow together.

confòndere *vt.* **1.** to confuse **2.** (*scambiare una persona per un'altra*) to mistake (*v. irr.*) **3.** (*turbare*) to confound. ♦ **confòndersi** *vr.* **1.** to get (*v. irr.*) mixed up **2.** (*mescolarsi*) to mingle **3.** (*turbarsi*) to be disconcerted.

confondìbile *agg.* liable to be confused.

conformare *vt.* to conform. ♦ **conformarsi** *vr.* to conform.

conformato *agg.* shaped.

conformazione *sf.* conformation.

conforme *agg.* **1.** conforming **2.** (*simile*) similar **3.** (*fedele*) true || — *a*, in conformity with. ♦ **conforme a·** *loc. avv.* in conformity with.

conformismo *sm.* time-serving.

conformista *s.* **1.** time-server **2.** (*relig.*) conformist.

conformìstico *agg.* conformist.

conformità *sf.* conformity.

confortàbile *agg.* consolable.

confortante *agg.* consoling.

confortare *vt.* **1.** to comfort **2.** (*incoraggiare*) to encourage.

confortatore *agg.* comforting. ♦ **confortatore** *sm.* comforter.

confortatorio *agg.* comforting.

confortévole *agg.* **1.** comforting **2.** (*comodo*) comfortable.

confortevolmente *avv.* comfortably.

conforto *sm.* 1. comfort, solace 2. (*incoraggiamento*) encouragement.

confratello *sm.* brother (*pl.* brethren).

confratèrnita *sf.* brotherhood.

confrontàbile *agg.* comparable.

confrontare *vt.* 1. to compare 2. (*giur.*) to confront.

confronto *sm.* 1. comparison 2. (*giur.*) confrontation || *nei confronti di*, to, towards; *in — a*, in comparison with.

confucianésimo *sm.* confucianism.

confusamente *avv.* confusedly.

confusionario *agg.* blundering, unmethodical. ♦ **confusionario** *sm.* bungler, muddler.

confusione *sf.* confusion, medley.

confusionismo *sm.* general confusion.

confuso *agg.* 1. confused, mixed, vague 2. (*indistinto*) indistinct 3. (*imbarazzato*) embarrassed.

confutàbile *agg.* confutable.

confutare *vt.* to confute.

confutazione *sf.* confutation.

congedare *vt.* 1. to dismiss 2. (*mil.*) to discharge. ♦ **congedarsi** *vr.* to take (*v. irr.*) one's leave.

congedato *agg.* dischargee.

congedo *sm.* 1. (*commiato*) leave 2. (*mil.*) leave, discharge || *essere in —*, to be on leave.

congegnare *vt.* 1. (*mecc.*) to assemble 2. (*fig.*) to devise.

congegno *sm.* 1. device, gear 2. (*fig.*) device, scheme.

congelamento *sm.* 1. freezing 2. (*med.*) congelation.

congelare *vt.* to freeze (*v. irr.*), to congeal.

congelato *agg.* congealed, frozen (*anche comm.*).

congelatore *sm.* freezer.

congènere *agg.* 1. akin (*attr.*) 2. similar (*pred.*).

congeniale *agg.* congenial.

congènito *agg.* congenital, innate.

congestionare *vt.* to congest.

congestionato *agg.* congested: *viso —*, flushed face.

congestione *sf.* congestion.

congettura *sf.* conjecture, supposition.

congetturare *vt.* to conjecture.

congiùngere *vt.* 1. to join 2. (*collegare*) to connect.

congiuntiva *sf.* conjunctiva.

congiuntivite *sf.* conjunctivitis.

congiuntivo *agg.* conjunctive. ♦ **congiuntivo** *sm.* (*gramm.*) subjunctive.

congiunto *agg.* 1. joined, united 2. (*collegato*) connected. ♦ **congiunto** *sm.* relative.

congiuntura *sf.* 1. point of junction 2. (*circostanza, situazione*) circumstance, situation 3. (*econ.*) trend, trade cycle.

congiunzione *sf.* 1. connection 2. (*gramm.; astr.*) conjunction.

congiura *sf.* conspiracy, plot.

congiurare *vi.* to conspire, to plot.

congiurato *sm.* conspirator, plotter.

conglobamento *sm.* conglobation.

conglobare *vt.* 1. to conglobate 2. (*di tasse, debiti ecc.*) to combine.

conglobazione *sf.* conglobation.

conglomerato *sm.* 1. (*geol.*) conglomerate 2. (*etnico; pol.*) grouping.

congratularsi *vr.* to congratulate.

congratulazione *sf.* congratulation.

congregazione *sf.* assembly, congregation (*anche eccl.*).

congressista *s.* member of a congress.

congresso *sm.* congress.

congruo *agg.* 1. (*coerente*) congruous 2. (*adeguato*) adequate.

conguagliare *vt.* 1. to equalize 2. (*comm.*) to balance.

coniare *vt.* to coin (*anche fig.*).

cònico *agg.* conic(al).

conìfera *sf.* conifer.

coniglio *sm.* 1. rabbit 2. (*fig.*) faint-hearted.

conio *sm.* 1. (*attrezzo per coniare*) minting die 2. (*impronta*) coin, brand 3. (*invenzione di nuove parole*) coinage.

coniugale *agg.* conjugal: *vita —*, married life.

coniugare *vt.* 1. to conjugate 2. (*unire in matrimonio*) to marry.

coniugato *agg.* married.

coniugazione *sf.* conjugation.

còniuge *sm.* husband. ♦ **còniuge** *sf.* wife.

connaturale *agg.* connatural, innate.

connaturato *agg.* deeply rooted.

connazionale *sm.* fellow-countryman (*pl.* -men). ♦ **connazionale** *sf.* fellow-countrywoman (*pl.* -women).

connessione *sf.* connection.

connesso *agg.* connected.

connèttere *vt.* 1. (*unire*) to connect, to join 2. (*fig.*) to associate, to link || *non connettere*, to talk at random.

connettivo *agg.* connective.

connivente *agg.* conniving (at).

connotato *sm.* description, feature || *i connotati*, description.

connubio *sm.* 1. marriage 2. (*fig.*) union.

cono *sm.* cone: — *gelato*, ice-cream cone.

conoscente *sm.* acquaintance.

conoscenza *sf.* 1. knowledge || *venire a — di qc.*, to become (*v. irr.*) acquainted with sthg. 2. (*persona*) acquaintance 3. (*sensi*) consciousness.

conòscere *vt.* 1. to know (*v. irr.*): — *di vista*, to know by sight; — *di fama*, to know by reputation; — *dalla voce*, to recognize by one's voice 2. (*fare la conoscenza*) to meet (*v. irr.*).

conoscìbile *agg.* 1. knowable 2. (*riconoscibile*) recognizable.

conoscitivo *agg.* cognitive.

conoscitore *sm.* expert, good judge.

conosciuto *agg.* well-known, renowned.

conquista *sf.* conquest.

conquistare *vt.* 1. to conquer 2. (*fig.*) to win (*v. irr.*).

conquistatore *sm.* 1. conqueror 2. (*rubacuori*) lady-killer.

consacrare *vt.* 1. (*eccl.*) to consecrate 2. (*dedicare*) to devote.

consacrazione *sf.* consecration.

consanguineità *sf.* consanguinity.

consanguineo *agg.* consanguine, akin. ♦ **consanguineo** *sm.* kinsman (*pl.* -men).

consapévole *agg.* aware, conscious.

consapevolezza *sf.* 1. consciousness 2. (*conoscenza*) knowledge.

conscio *agg.* conscious.

consecutivo *agg.* 1. following 2. (*di seguito*) running: *per due giorni consecutivi*, for two days running 3. (*gramm.*) consecutive.

consegna *sf.* 1. (*comm.*) delivery: — *contro assegno*, cash on delivery; — *mancata*, nondelivery; *ordine di —*, delivery-note; *effettuare la —*, to effect delivery 2. (*deposito*) consignment 3. (*mil.*) orders (*pl.*) || — *in caserma*, confi-

nement to barracks.

consegnare *vt.* 1. to deliver 2. (*mil.*) to confine to barracks.

conseguente *agg.* consequent.

conseguenza *sf.* consequence.

conseguìbile *agg.* attainable.

conseguimento *sm.* attainment.

conseguire *vt.* to attain, to achieve, to get (*v. irr.*).

consenso *sm.* 1. consent 2. (*matrimoniale*) licence.

consensuale *agg.* by mutual consent.

consentire *vi.* to consent, to agree. ♦ **consentire** *vt.* to allow.

consenziente *agg.* consenting.

conserto *agg.* interwoven, folded: *a braccia conserte*, with folded arms.

conserva *sf.* preserve || — *di frutta*, jam; — *di pomodoro*, tomato sauce.

conservare *vt.* to preserve ♦ **conservarsi** *vr.* to keep (*v. irr.*).

conservativo *agg.* conservative.

conservatore *agg.* 1. preserving 2. (*pol.*) conservative. ♦ **conservatore** *sm.* 1. preserver 2. (*pol.*) conservative.

conservatorio *sm.* academy of music.

conservazione *sf.* preservation || *istinto di —*, instinct of self-preservation.

considerare *vt.* 1. to consider, to think (*v. irr.*) of 2. (*reputare*) to deem, to judge. ♦ **considerarsi** *vr.* to consider oneself.

considerato *agg.* considerate || — *che*, considering that.

considerazione *sf.* 1. consideration 2. (*stima*) esteem, regard || *avere — per qu.*, to have regard for so.

considerévole *agg.* considerable.

consigliare *vt.* to advise. ♦ **consigliarsi** *vr.* to ask so.'s advice, to consult (with).

consigliere *sm.* 1. counsellor 2. (*membro di un consiglio*) councillor.

consiglio *sm.* 1. advice (*solo sing.*) 2. (*corpo di persone*) council.

consiliare *agg.* of a council.

consìmile *agg.* similar.

consistente *agg.* firm, substantial.

consistenza *sf.* 1. consistence 2. (*comm.*) on hand: — *di cassa*, cash on hand.

consìstere *vi.* to consist.

consociare vt. to associate.
consociato agg. associated.
consociazione sf. association.
consocio sm. co-partner.
consolante agg. cheering.
consolare[1] vt. to console, to comfort. ◆ **consolarsi** vr. to be comforted.
consolare[2] agg. consular.
consolato sm. consulate.
consolatore agg. consoling. ◆ **consolatore** sm. consoler.
consolazione sf. consolation, solace.
cònsole sm. consul.
consolidamento sm. consolidation.
consolidare vt. to consolidate, to strengthen.
consolidato agg. consolidated.
consonante sf. consonant.
consonanza sf. consonance (anche fig.).
cònsono agg. in accordance (with).
consorella sf. (eccl.) sister.
consorte sm. consort, husband. ◆ **consorte** sf. consort, wife.
consorteria sf. faction.
consorzio sm. society: — agrario, agricultural union.
constare vi. 1. (essere composto) to consist 2. (risultare) to be within one's knowledge || da quanto mi consta, as far as I know.
constatare vt. V. costatare.
constatazione sf. V. costatazione.
consueto agg. usual, customary.
consuetudinario agg. customary, consuetudinary.
consuetùdine sf. 1. custom, habit 2. (comm.) rule.
consulente sm. adviser.
consulenza sf. advice.
consulta sf. 1. consultation 2. (corpo consultivo) council.
consultare vt. 1. to consult 2. (esaminare) to examine.
consultazione sf. consultation: libro di —, reference book.
consultivo agg. consultative.
consulto sm. consultation.
consumare vt. 1. to consume 2. (di abiti) to wear (v. irr.) 3. (dissipare) to waste 4. (compiere) to commit.
consumato agg. 1. (perfetto) accomplished 2. (logoro) worn out 3. (divorato) consumed.
consumatore sm. consumer.
consumazione sf. 1. consumption 2. (giur.) consummation 3. (bibita) drink.

consumo sm. consumption || per proprio uso e —, for one's private use.
consuntivo agg. final: bilancio —, final balance.
consunzione sf. consumption.
contàbile agg. bookkeeping. ◆ **contàbile** sm. bookkeeper.
contabilità sf. bookkeeping.
contachilòmetri sm. speedometer.
contadino sm. countryman (pl. -men), peasant. ◆ **contadino** agg. rustic.
contado sm. countryside.
contagiare vt. to infect.
contagio sm. contagion (anche fig.), infection.
contagioso agg. contagious, infectious (anche fig.).
contagiri sm. revolution counter.
contagocce sm. dropper.
contaminare vt. 1. to pollute, to infect 2. (un testo letterario) to corrupt.
contaminazione sf. contamination (anche fig.), pollution.
contante agg. ready. ◆ **contante** sm. ready money || pagare in contanti, to pay cash.
contare vt. 1. to count, to number 2. (considerare) to consider 3. (proporsi) to think (v. irr.) of || conto di andare a Milano domani, I think of going to Milan tomorrow 4. (aspettarsi) to expect. ◆ **contare** vi. 1. (avere importanza) to count, to be important 2. (fare assegnamento) to rely on.
contatore sm. meter: — del gas, gas-meter; — dell'acqua, water-meter; — della luce, electric power-meter.
contatto sm. 1. contact, touch: essere in —, to be in touch 2. (elettr.) contact.
conte sm. 1. Count 2. (in Gran Bretagna) Earl.
contea sf. 1. earldom 2. (divisione territoriale) county.
conteggiare vt. to count.
conteggio sm. computation.
contegno sm. 1. behaviour 2. (atteggiamento) attitude.
contegnoso agg. 1. dignified 2. (altero) stiff.
contemperamento sm. adaptation.
contemperare vt. to adapt.
contemplare vt. 1. to behold (v.

irr.), to admire **2.** (*giur.*) to consider.

contemplativo *agg.* contemplative.

contemplatore *sm.* contemplator.

contemplazione *sf.* contemplation.

contempo (*nella loc. avv.*) **nel —,** in the meantime.

contemporaneamente *avv.* at the same time.

contemporaneità *sf.* contemporaneousness.

contemporàneo *agg. e sm.* contemporary.

contendente *agg.* contending, opposing. ♦ **contendente** *sm.* opponent, rival.

contèndere *vt.* to contend, to refuse. ♦ **contèndersi** *vr. rec.* to contend.

contenere *vt.* **1.** to contain, to hold (*v. irr.*) **2.** (*trattenere*) to repress. ♦ **contenersi** *vr.* **1.** (*comportarsi*) to behave **2.** (*dominarsi*) to contain oneself.

contenitore *sm.* container.

contentare *vt.* to content. ♦ **contentarsi** *vr.* to be content (with).

contentezza *sf.* pleasure, joy.

contento *agg.* content, pleased.

contenuto *sm.* contents (*pl.*).

contenzioso *agg.* contentious.

conterìe *sf. pl.* glass beads.

conterràneo *sm.* fellow-countryman (*pl.* -men) ‖ (*femm.*) fellow-countrywoman (*pl.* -women).

contesa *sf.* **1.** contest **2.** (*litigio*) quarrel.

contessa *sf.* countess.

contestàbile *agg.* questionable.

contestare *vt.* **1.** to contest, to challenge, to deny **2.** (*notificare*) to declare.

contestazione *sf.* dispute, objection: *sollevare contestazioni,* to raise objections.

contesto *sm.* context.

contiguità *sf.* contiguity.

contiguo *agg.* neighbouring.

continentale *agg.* continental.

continente *agg.* moderate. ♦ **continente** *sm.* continent.

continenza *sf.* continence.

contingentamento *sm.* allotment.

contingentare *vt.* to allot.

contingenza *sf.* **1.** emergency **2.** (*circostanza*) circumstance **3.** (*fil.*) contingency.

continuamente *avv.* continuously.

continuare *vt. e vi.* **1.** to go (*v.*

irr.) on (with) **2.** (*riprendere*) to resume.

continuativo *agg.* continuative.

continuato *agg.* **1.** (*ininterrotto*) continuous **2.** (*che si ripete*) continual.

continuatore *sm.* continuator.

continuazione *sf.* continuation.

continuità *sf.* continuity.

continuo *agg.* **1.** (*ininterrotto*) continuous **2.** (*che si ripete*) continual.

conto *sm.* **1.** (*anche comm.*) account: *fare i conti,* to make (*v. irr.*) up accounts **2.** (*di albergo ecc.*) bill **3.** (*assegnamento*) reliance: *far — su,* to rely on **4.** (*stima*) regard ‖ *persona di poco —,* person of little account; *rendere — di,* to answer for; *rendersi —,* to realize; *mettersi per proprio —,* to set (*v. irr.*) for oneself.

contòrcere *vt.* to twist. ♦ **contòrcersi** *vr.* to twist.

contorcimento *sm.* twisting.

contornare *vt.* **1.** to surround **2.** (*con guarnizioni*) to trim.

contorno *sm.* **1.** outline **2.** (*orlo*) border **3.** (*cuc.*) vegetables (*pl.*).

contorsione *sf.* contortion.

contorsionismo *sm.* writhing.

contorsionista *s.* contorsionist.

contorto *agg.* twisted.

contrabbandare *vt.* to smuggle.

contrabbandiere *sm.* smuggler.

contrabbando *sm.* smuggling.

contrabbassista *sm.* double-bass player.

contrabbasso *sm.* double-bass.

contraccambiare *vt.* to return.

contraccambio *sm.* return ‖ *rendere il —,* to retaliate (upon).

contraccolpo *sm.* **1.** counterblow **2.** (*fig.*) reaction.

contraccusa *sf.* countercharge.

contrada *sf.* **1.** quarter **2.** (*paese*) country.

contraddanza *sf.* country-dance.

contraddire *vt.* to contradict. ♦ **contraddirsi** *vr.* to contradict oneself. ♦ **contraddirsi** *v. rec.* to contradict one another, each other.

contraddistìnguere *vt.* to mark.

contraddittore *sm.* opposer.

contraddittorio *agg.* contradictory. ♦ **contraddittorio** *sm.* debate.

contraddizione *sf.* contradiction, discrepancy.

contraente *agg.* contracting. ♦

contraente *sm.* contractor.
contraèrea *sf.* anti-aircraft artillery.
contraèreo *agg.* anti-aircraft.
contraffare *vt.* to counterfeit.
contraffatto *agg.* counterfeit.
contraffattore *sm.* **1.** (*falsificatore*) counterfeiter **2.** (*imitatore*) imitator.
contrafforte *sm.* buttress.
contraggenio *sm.* dislike || *a* (*di*) —, unwillingly.
contràlbero *sm.* (*mecc.*) countershaft.
contralto *sm.* contralto.
contrammiraglio *sm.* rear-admiral.
contrappasso *sm.* retaliation.
contrappello *sm.* second roll-call.
contrappesare *vt.* to counterbalance.
contrappeso *sm.* counterbalance.
contrapporre *vt.* to oppose, to contrast || — *qc. a qu.*, to set (*v. irr.*) sthg. against so.
contrapposizione *sf.* contraposition.
contrapposto *agg.* opposite || *per* —, on the contrary. ♦ **contrapposto** *sm.* opposite.
contrappunto *sm.* counterpoint.
contrariamente *avv.* on the contrary || — *ad ogni aspettativa*, contrary to all expectation.
contrariare *vt.* **1.** to oppose **2.** (*irritare*) to annoy.
contrarietà *sf.* **1.** opposition **2.** (*avversità*) misfortune.
contrario *agg.* **1.** contrary, opposed **2.** (*nocivo*) harmful **3.** (*riluttante*) unwilling || *al* —, on the contrary. ♦ **contrario** *sm.* contrary.
contrarre *vt.* to contract.
contrassegnare *vt.* to mark.
contrassegno *sm.* **1.** countersign **2.** (*segno*) mark **3.** (*distintivo*) badge.
contrastare *vi.* to be in contrast. ♦ **contrastare** *vt.* to oppose.
contrastato *agg.* opposed.
contrasto *sm.* **1.** contrast **2.** (*dissidio*) conflict.
contrattaccare *vt.* to counterattack.
contrattacco *sm.* counterattack.
contrattare *vt.* to negotiate: — *il prezzo*, to haggle about the price.
contrattazione *sf.* dealing, negotiation.
contrattempo *sm.* **1.** (*incidente*) mishap **2.** (*inconveniente*) inconvenience.

contràttile *agg.* contractile.
contratto *sm.* contract.
contratto *agg.* contracted.
contrattuale *agg.* contractual.
contravveleno *sm.* antidote.
contravvenire *vi.* to infringe.
contravventore *sm.* transgressor.
contravvenzione *sf.* **1.** violation **2.** (*multa*) fine.
contrazione *sf.* contraction.
contribuente *sm.* taxpayer.
contribuire *vi.* to contribute.
contributo *sm.* contribution.
contribuzione *sf.* contribution.
contristarsi *vr.* to grieve.
contrito *agg.* contrite.
contrizione *sf.* contrition.
contro *prep.* **1.** against **2.** (*in opposizione a*) contrary to || — *assegno*, cash on delivery.
controbàttere *vt.* (*confutare*) to disprove, to confute.
controbilanciare *vt.* to counterbalance.
controcampo *sm.* (*cine*) reverse shot.
controcorrente *sf.* counter-current. ♦ **controcorrente** *loc. avv.* against the stream.
controffensiva *sf.* counter-offensive.
controfigura *sf.* double.
controfirmare *vt.* to countersign.
controindicare *vt.* (*med.*) to contra-indicate.
controindicazione *sf.* (*med.*) contra-indication.
controllare *vt.* **1.** to control **2.** (*verificare*) to verify, to check **3.** (*ispezionare*) to inspect **4.** (*comm.*) to audit.
controllo *sm.* **1.** control **2.** (*verifica*) check, verification **3.** (*ispezione*) inspection **4.** (*comm.*) audit.
controllore *sm.* **1.** controller **2.** (*ferr.*) ticket-inspector.
controluce *avv.* against the light. ♦ **controluce** *sf.* counterlight.
contromarca *sf.* pass-out check (ticket).
controparte *sf.* counter-party.
contropartita *sf.* **1.** (*comm.*) counter-item **2.** (*compenso*) compensation.
contropelo *sm.* wrong way of the hair || *fare il* —, to shave against the lie of the hair.
controproducente *agg.* having opposite effect.

controproposta *sf.* counter-proposal.

controprova *sf.* 1. countercheck 2. (*giur.*) counter-evidence.

contrórdine *sm.* counter-order: *dare un —*, to countermand an order.

controriforma *sf.* counter-reformation.

controrivoluzione *sf.* counter-revolution.

controsenso *sm.* self-contradiction, absurdity.

controspionaggio *sm.* counter-espionage.

controstòmaco *avv.* reluctantly.

controvelaccio *sm.* (*mar.*) main royal.

controvento *avv.* against the wind.

controversia *sf.* controversy.

controverso *agg.* controversial.

controvertibile *agg.* controvertible.

controvoglia *avv.* unwillingly.

contumace *agg.* guilty of default.

contumacia *sf.* default.

contumaciale *agg.* (*giur.*) judgement by default.

contumelia *sf.* insult, abuse.

contundente *agg.* blunt: *corpo —*, blunt instrument.

conturbare *vt.* 1. to perturb 2. (*eccitare*) to thrill.

contusione *sf.* bruise.

contuso *agg.* bruised.

convalescente *agg. e sm.* convalescent.

convalescenza *sf.* convalescence.

convalidare *vt.* to ratify, to confirm.

convegno *sm.* meeting.

convenévole *agg.* convenient, proper. ♦ **convenévoli** *sm. pl.* compliments.

conveniente *agg.* 1. convenient (for) 2. (*economicamente vantaggioso*) profitable.

convenienza *sf.* 1. convenience 2. (*vantaggio economico*) profit 3. (*buona creanza*) propriety.

convenire *vi.* 1. to convene 2. (*essere d'accordo*) to agree 3. (*essere utile*) to be convenient.

convento *sm.* 1. convent 2. (*di suore*) nunnery.

conventuale *agg.* conventual.

convenuto *agg.* agreed upon. ♦ **convenuto** *sm.* 1. agreement 2. *i convenuti*, the persons present.

convenzionale *agg.* conventional.

convenzionare *vt.* to make (*v. irr.*) an agreement.

convenzione *sf.* convention.

convergente *agg.* convergent.

convergenza *sf.* convergence.

convèrgere *vi.* to converge.

conversare *vi.* to talk.

conversatore *sm.* talker.

conversazione *sf.* conversation, talk.

conversione *sf.* 1. (*anche fig.*) conversion 2. (*mil.*) wheel.

convertibile *agg.* convertible.

convertire *vt.* 1. (*pol.; relig.*) to convert 2. (*mutare*) to turn, to change. ♦ **convertirsi** *vr.* to be converted.

convessità *sf.* convexity.

convesso *agg.* convex.

convìncere *vt.* to convince, to persuade.

convinto *agg.* convinced, persuaded.

convinzione *sf.* persuasion, firm belief.

convitato *sm.* guest.

convito *sm.* banquet.

convitto *sm.* boarding-school.

convivente *agg.* cohabiting.

convivenza *sf.* cohabitation, life in common.

convìvere *vi.* to live together.

convocare *vt.* to convene, to summon.

convocazione *sf.* convocation, summoning.

convogliare *vt.* 1. (*scortare*) to escort 2. (*trasportare*) to carry away 3. (*indirizzare*) to address.

convoglio *sm.* 1. (*treno*) train 2. (*mil.; mar.*) convoy.

convolare *vi.* to fly (*v. irr.*) together: *— a giuste nozze*, to get (*v. irr.*) married.

convulsione *sf.* convulsion.

convulso *agg.* convulsive.

cooperare *vi.* to co-operate, to collaborate.

cooperativa *sf.* 1. co-operative society 2. (*di consumo*) co-operative store.

cooperativo *agg.* co-operative.

cooperatore *sm.* co-operator.

cooperazione *sf.* co-operation, collaboration.

coordinamento *sm.* co-ordination.

coordinare *vt.* to co-ordinate.

coordinata *sf.* co-ordinate.

coordinativo *agg.* co-ordinative.

coordinato *agg.* co-ordinate.

coordinatore *agg.* co-ordinative. ♦
   coordinatore *sm.* co-ordinator.
coordinazione *sf.* co-ordination.
coorte *sf.* **1.** (*mil.*) cohort **2.** (*folla*)
   crowd.
copale *sf.* **1.** copal **2.** (*pelle*) patent
   leather.
copeco *sm.* copeck.
coperchio *sm.* lid, cover (*anche
   mecc.*).
coperta *sf.* **1.** blanket: — *da viaggio*, rug; — *scozzese*, plaid **2.**
   (*mar.*) deck.
copertina *sf.* cover: — *di libro*,
   book-cover.
coperto *agg.* **1.** (*riparato*) covered,
   sheltered ‖ — *di ferro*, iron-clad;
   mettere al —, to shelter from **2.**
   (*di cielo*) overcast **3.** (*nascosto*)
   hidden. ♦ **coperto** *sm.* cover.
copertone *sm.* tyre.
copertura *sf.* **1.** covering **2.** (*di mobili*) cover.
copia *sf.* **1.** copy **2.** (*foto*) print.
copiare *vt.* to copy.
copiativo *agg.* *matita copiativa*,
   copying pencil.
copiatura *sf.* copying.
copione *sm.* script.
copiosamente *avv.* plentifully.
copioso *agg.* plentiful.
copista *sm.* copyist.
coppa *sf.* **1.** cup **2.** (*auto*) pan.
coppella *sf.* (*metal.*) cupel.
coppellare *vt.* (*metal.*) to cupel.
coppia *sf.* **1.** (*di persone e cose*)
   couple **2.** (*di animali*) pair ‖ *una
   — di buoi*, a yoke.
copricapo *sm.* hat.
coprifuoco *sm.* curfew.
copriletto *sm.* coverlet.
coprire *vt.* **1.** to cover **2.** (*nascondere*) to conceal **3.** (*coprire un suono*) to drown.
copto *agg.* coptic. ♦ **copto** *sm.*
   copt.
copulativo *agg.* (*gramm.*) copulative.
copulazione *sf.* copulation.
coraggio *sm.* **1.** courage, bravery,
   heart **2.** (*sfrontatezza*) impudence.
coraggiosamente *avv.* bravely.
coraggioso *agg.* brave, bold.
corale *agg.* choral.
corallifero *agg.* coralliferous.
corallo *sm.* coral.
corazza *sf.* **1.** cuirass **2.** (*bot.; zool.*)
   armour, carapace.
corazzare *vt.* **1.** to armour **2.** (*fig.*)

to strengthen. ♦ **corazzarsi** *vr.*
   to harden oneself.
corazzata *sf.* (*mar.*) battleship.
corazziere *sm.* cuirassier.
corbellerìa *sf.* **1.** foolish action **2.**
   (*sciocchezza*) nonsense.
corda *sf.* **1.** rope **2.** (*mus.*) string.
cordaio *sm.* **1.** (*chi fabbrica corde*)
   rope-maker **2.** (*chi vende corde*)
   rope-seller.
cordame *sm.* cordage.
cordata *sf.* rope: *in* —, on the rope.
cordiale *agg.* cordial, hearty. ♦
   cordiale *sm.* (*liquore*) cordial.
cordialità *sf.* cordiality.
cordialmente *avv.* cordially.
cordicella *sf.* string.
cordigliera *sf.* cordillera.
cordite *sf.* cordite.
cordoglio *sm.* deep sorrow.
cordone *sm.* **1.** cord **2.** (*mil.*) cordon.
coreano *agg.* e *sm.* Korean.
coreografìa *sf.* choreography.
coreogràfico *agg.* **1.** choreographic
   2. (*fig.*) spectacular.
coreògrafo *sm.* choreographer.
coriàceo *agg.* coriaceous, tough.
coriàndolo *sm.* confetti (*pl.*).
coricare *vt.* to lay (*v. irr.*) down.
   ♦ **coricarsi** *vr.* to lie (*v. irr.*)
   down.
corifeo *sm.* coryphaeus (*pl.* -aei).
corinzio *agg.* e *sm.* Corinthian.
corista *sm.* chorus-singer.
cormorano *sm.* (*zool.*) cormorant.
cornacchia *sf.* rook, crow.
cornamusa *sf.* bagpipe.
cornata *sf.* butt.
còrnea *sf.* cornea.
cornetta *sf.* cornet.
cornice *sf.* frame.
cornicione *sm.* **1.** (*arch.*) cornice
   2. (*di finestre, porte*) label **3.** (*di
   gronda*) eaves (*pl.*).
cornificare *vt.* **1.** (*di moglie*) to
   cuckold **2.** (*di marito*) to be unfaithful to.
corno *sm.* horn ‖ (*inter.*) *un* —, not
   at all.
cornuto *agg.* horned. ♦ **cornuto**
   sm. (*fig.*) cuckold.
coro *sm.* **1.** chorus **2.** (*eccl.*) choir.
corolla *sf.* corolla.
corollario *sm.* corollary.
corona *sf.* **1.** crown: — *del rosario*,
   rosary crown; — *del dente*, crown
   2. (*mecc.*) rim **3.** (*relig.*) (*tonsura*)
   tonsure.

coronamento *sm.* **1.** crowning **2.** (*completamento*) fulfilment.

coronare *vt.* to crown (*anche fig.*).

coronario *agg.* coronary.

corpo *sm.* **1.** body || *a — morto*, desperately; *combattere a — a —*, to fight (*v. irr.*) hand to hand; *passare sul — di qu.*, to pass over so. **2.** (*cadavere*) corpse **3.** (*collettività*) corps || *— insegnante*, teaching staff.

corporale *agg.* corporal.

corporativismo *sm.* (*econ.*) corporative system.

corporativo *agg.* (*econ.*) corporative.

corporatura *sf.* build, size.

corporazione *sf.* corporation.

corpòreo *agg.* corporeal.

corpulento *agg.* corpulent, stout.

corpulenza *sf.* stoutness.

corpuscolare *agg.* corpuscular.

corpùscolo *sm.* corpuscle.

corredare *vt.* **1.** to equip **2.** (*accompagnare*) to accompany.

corredino *sm.* baby's outfit.

corredo *sm.* **1.** outfit **2.** (*di sposa*) trousseau **3.** (*bagaglio*) wealth, store: *— di cultura*, store of knowledge.

corrèggere *vt.* **1.** to correct **2.** (*di bevande*) to lace. ♦ **corrèggersi** *vr.* to amend, to correct oneself.

correggia *sf.* leather strap.

correlativo *agg.* correlative.

correlazione *sf.* correlation.

corrente[1] *agg.* **1.** (*che scorre*) running **2.** (*circolante*) current **3.** (*comm.*) inst. (*abbrev. di instant*) || *conto —*, current account **4.** (*andante*) common.

corrente[2] *sf.* **1.** current (*anche fig.*), stream **2.** (*di aria*) draught.

correntemente *avv.* fluently.

còrrere *vi.* **1.** to run (*v. irr.*): *— dietro a qu.*, to run after; *— a gambe levate*, to run as hard as one can || *lasciar —*, to take (*v. irr.*) no notice of sthg. **2.** (*di tempo*) to pass **3.** (*di voci*) to be abroad.

corresponsàbile *agg.* jointly responsible.

corresponsione *sf.* payment.

correttezza *sf.* **1.** correctness **2.** (*onestà*) honesty **3.** (*decoro, educazione*) propriety, politeness.

correttivo *agg. e sm.* corrective.

corretto *agg.* **1.** correct, exact **2.** (*irreprensibile*) faultless **3.** (*di bevanda*) laced.

correttore *sm.* corrector || *— di bozze*, proof-reader.

correzionale *agg.* correctional.

correzione *sf.* correction || *— di bozze*, proof-reading; *casa di —*, house of correction.

corridoio *sm.* **1.** passage **2.** (*di treno*) corridor.

corridore *sm.* **1.** runner **2.** (*sport*) racer.

corriera *sf.* coach.

corriere *sm.* **1.** messenger **2.** (*chi trasporta merci*) carrier **3.** (*posta*) mail.

corrimano *sm.* handrail.

corrispettivo *agg.* correlative. ♦ **corrispettivo** *sm.* **1.** equivalent **2.** (*compenso*) compensation.

corrispondente *agg. e sm.* correspondent.

corrispondenza *sf.* correspondence.

corrispòndere *vi.* **1.** to correspond (with) **2.** (*ricambiare sentimenti ecc.*) to return. ♦ **corrispòndere** *vt.* to pay.

corrisposto *agg.* **1.** (*contraccambiato*) returned **2.** (*pagato*) paid.

corroborante *agg. e sm.* corroborant.

corroborare *vt.* to strengthen.

corròdere *vt.* to corrode.

corròmpere *vt.* **1.** to corrupt (*anche fig.*), to pollute **2.** (*con denaro*) to bribe.

corrosione *sf.* corrosion.

corrosivo *agg. e sm.* corrosive.

corrucciarsi *vr.* to get (*v. irr.*) angry.

corrucciato *agg.* angry, worried.

corruccio *sm.* anger, worry.

corrugamento *sm.* corrugation: *— della fronte*, wrinkling of the forehead.

corrugare *vt.* to wrinkle.

corruttìbile *agg.* corruptible.

corruttore *agg.* corrupting. ♦ **corruttore** *sm.* **1.** corrupter **2.** (*con denaro*) briber.

corruzione *sf.* **1.** corruption **2.** (*con denaro*) bribery.

corsa *sf.* **1.** run **2.** (*sport*) race **3.** (*su veicolo pubblico*) trip || *prezzo della —*, fare; (*ferr.*) *perdere la —*, to miss the train.

corsaro *sm.* corsair.

corsetto *sm.* corset.

corsìa *sf.* **1.** passage **2.** (*di ospedale*) ward **3.** (*di strada*) lane.

corsiero *sm.* steed.
corsivo *agg.* cursive. ♦ **corsivo** *sm.* (*tip.*) italics (*pl.*).
corso *sm.* 1. course (*anche fig.*) 2. (*di acque*) water-course.
corte *sf.* 1. court 2. (*cortile*) court-yard 3. (*corteggiamento*) courtship.
corteccia *sf.* 1. bark 2. (*anat.*) cortex.
corteggiare *vt.* 1. to woo 2. (*adulare*) to flatter.
corteggiatore *sm.* suitor, lover.
corteo *sm.* train, procession: — *funebre*, funeral train.
cortese *agg.* kind.
cortesia *sf.* 1. kindness, politeness 2. (*favore*) favour || *per* —, please.
cortigiano *sm.* 1. courtier 2. (*adulatore*) flatterer.
cortile *sm.* courtyard || *animali da* —, poultry.
cortina *sf.* curtain: — *di ferro* (*pol.*), iron curtain.
cortisone *sm.* cortisone.
corto *agg.* short: *a* — *di*, short of.
cortocircuito *sm.* short circuit.
cortometraggio *sm.* short (film).
corvetta *sf.* (*mar.*) corvette.
corvino *agg.* 1. corvine 2. (*nero*) raven(-black).
corvo *sm.* raven.
cosa *sf.* 1. thing 2. (*faccenda*) matter || *nessuna* —, nothing; *ogni* —, everything; *che* —?, what?.
cosacco *agg. e sm.* Cossack.
coscia *sf.* 1. thigh 2. (*cuc.*) leg.
cosciente *agg.* 1. conscious 2. (*conscio*) aware.
coscienza *sf.* 1. conscience 2. (*consapevolezza*) consciousness.
coscienziosamente *avv.* conscientiously.
coscienzioso *agg.* conscientious.
cosciotto *sm.* leg: — *di manzo*, leg of beef.
coscritto *sm.* recruit.
coscrizione *sf.* conscription.
cosecante *sf.* cosecant.
coseno *sm.* (*mat.*) cosine.
così *avv.* so: *e* — *via*, and so on; — *come*, — *pure*, as well as; — ... *come*, — ... *quanto*, as ... as; — *da*, so ... as: *non è* — *sciocco da farlo*, he is not so foolish as to do that.
cosicché *cong.* so that.
cosiddetto *agg.* so-called.
cosiffatto *agg.* such, similar.

cosmesi *sf.* beauty culture.
cosmetico *agg. e sm.* cosmetic.
còsmico *agg.* cosmic.
cosmo *sm.* cosmos.
cosmogonìa *sf.* cosmogony.
cosmografìa *sf.* cosmography.
cosmògrafo *sm.* cosmographer.
cosmologìa *sf.* cosmology.
cosmonàuta *s.* astronaut.
cosmonàutica *sf.* astronautics.
cosmopolita *agg. e sm.* cosmopolitan.
cosmopolitismo *sm.* cosmopolitanism.
coso *sm.* (*fam.*) 1. (*cosa*) thing 2. (*individuo*) fellow.
cospàrgere *vt.* 1. to strew (*v. irr.*) 2. (*sale, zucchero ecc.*) to sprinkle.
cospetto *sm.* presence: *al* — *di*, in the presence of.
cospicuità *sf.* conspicuousness.
cospicuo *agg.* 1. (*visibile*) conspicuous 2. (*notevole*) remarkable.
cospirare *vi.* to plot.
cospiratore *sm.* plotter.
cospirazione *sf.* plot.
costa *sf.* 1. coast, shore 2. (*venatura*) rib 3. (*di monte*) side 4. (*di libro*) back.
costà *avv.* there.
costaggiù *avv.* down there.
costale *agg.* costal.
costante *agg.* steady. ♦ **costante** *sf.* constant.
costanza *sf.* 1. firmness 2. (*perseveranza*) perseverance || *con* —, steadily.
costare *vi.* to cost (*v. irr.*).
costassù *avv.* up there.
costata *sf.* chop.
costatare *vt.* 1. (*accertare*) to ascertain 2. (*notare*) to notice.
costatazione *sf.* 1. ascertainment 2. (*osservazione*) remark.
costato *sm.* chest.
costeggiare *vt.* 1. to follow the coast of 2. (*per terra*) to skirt. ♦ **costeggiare** *vi.* to coast along.
costei *pron.* 1. (*sogg.*) she 2. (*compl.*) her 3. this woman, that woman.
costellare *vt.* to scatter.
costellazione *sf.* constellation.
costernare *vt.* to dismay. ♦ **costernarsi** *vr.* to be dismayed (at).
costernazione *sf.* dismay.
costì *avv.* there.
costiera *sf.* stretch of coast.
costiero *agg.* coastal || *nave costiera*, coaster.

costipare *vt.* **1.** (*un terreno*) to tamp **2.** (*ammassare*) to amass. ♦ **costiparsi** *vr.* **1.** (*raffreddarsi*) to catch (*v. irr.*) a cold **2.** (*di intestino*) to become (*v. irr.*) constipated.

costipato *agg.* essere —, to have a cold.

costipazione *sf.* **1.** (*raffreddore*) cold **2.** (*intestinale*) constipation **3.** (*di terreno*) tamping.

costituente *agg.* constituent.

costituire *vt.* **1.** to constitute, to form **2.** (*nominare*) to appoint. ♦ **costituirsi** *vr.* (*consegnarsi*) to give (*v. irr.*) oneself up.

costituito *agg.* constituted.

costitutivo *agg.* constitutive.

costituto *sm.* (*giur.*) interrogation of the accused.

costituzionale *agg.* constitutional.

costituzionalismo *sm.* constitutionalism.

costituzionalità *sf.* constitutionality.

costituzione *sf.* **1.** establishment **2.** (*pol.; med.*) constitution.

costo *sm.* cost: ad ogni —, at all cost; a nessun —, in no case.

còstola *sf.* rib ∥ stare alle costole, to watch over.

costoletta *sf.* cutlet.

costone *sm.* side.

costoro *pron.* **1.** (*sogg.*) they **2.** (*compl.*) them **3.** these people, those people.

costoso *agg.* expensive, dear.

costrìngere *vt.* **1.** (*stringere*) to press **2.** (*obbligare*) to compel.

costrizione *sf.* **1.** (*restringimento*) constriction **2.** (*obbligo*) compulsion.

costruire *vt.* to build (*v. irr.*).

costruttivo *agg.* constructive.

costruttore *agg.* building. ♦ **costruttore** *sm.* builder.

costruzione *sf.* construction, building.

costui *pron.* **1.** (*sogg.*) he **2.** (*compl.*) him **3.** this man, that man.

costumato *agg.* **1.** (*virtuoso*) virtuous **2.** (*educato*) polite.

costume *sm.* **1.** (*usanza*) custom **2.** (*personale*) habit **3.** (*condotta*) morals (*pl.*) **4.** (*vestito*) costume.

costumista *sm.* costume-designer.

cotangente *sf.* (*mat.*) cotangent.

cotenna *sf.* **1.** pigskin **2.** (*del cranio*) scalp **3.** (*del lardo*) rind.

còtica *sf.* V. cotenna.

cotogna *sf.* quince.

cotognata *sf.* quince jam.

cotoletta *sf.* cutlet.

cotone *sm.* cotton.

cotoniere *sm.* cotton-spinner.

cotoniero *agg.* cotton.

cotonificio *sm.* cotton-mill.

cotonina *sf.* calico.

cotta[1] *sf.* (*eccl.*) surplice.

cotta[2] *sf.* **1.** (*cottura*) cooking **2.** (*infornata*) batch **3.** (*fam.*) prendere una — per, to have a crush on.

cottimista *sm.* pieceworker.

còttimo *sm.* piecework: lavorare a —, to work by the job; lavoro a —, job-work; contratto a —, job contract.

cotto *sm.* brickwork.

cottura *sf.* **1.** cooking **2.** (*in forno*) baking.

coturno *sm.* cothurnus (*pl.* -ni).

cova *sf.* **1.** (*il covare*) brooding **2.** (*nido*) nest.

covare *vt.* **1.** to brood **2.** (*fig.*) to brood over **3.** (*di fuoco; passioni*) to smoulder **4.** (*di malattia*) to be latent.

covata *sf.* brood.

covo *sm.* den.

covone *sm.* sheaf (*pl.* sheaves).

cozza *sf.* mussel.

cozzare *vi.* **1.** to strike (*v. irr.*) **2.** (*venire in collisione*) to collide.

cozzo *sm.* **1.** clash, collision **2.** (*conflitto*) conflict.

crampo *sm.* cramp.

cranio *sm.* skull.

crasso *agg.* crass, gross: ignoranza crassa, gross ignorance.

cratere *sm.* crater.

cràuti *sm. pl.* sauerkraut (*sing.*)

cravatta *sf.* neck-tie.

creanza *sf.* politeness.

creare *vt.* **1.** .to create **2.** (*causare*) to cause **3.** (*nominare*) to appoint **4.** (*costituire*) to form.

creativo *agg.* creative.

creato *sm.* creation.

creatore *agg.* creating. ♦ **creatore** *sm.* creator.

creatura *sf.* creature.

creazione *sf.* creation.

credente *sm.* believer.

credenza[1] *sf.* belief.

credenza[2] *sf.* (*buffet*) sideboard.

credenziale *agg.* credential: lettera —, credential.

crédere vt. e vi. 1. (pensare) to think (v. irr.) 2. (prestar fede) to believe. ♦ **crédersi** vr. to think (v. irr.). oneself.

credìbile agg. 1. credible 2. (di persona) trustworthy.

credibilità sf. credibility.

creditizio agg. credit.

crédito sm. 1. (comm.) credit: a —, on credit 2. (stima) esteem.

creditore sm. creditor.

credo sm. creed.

credulità sf. credulity.

credulone agg. credulous.

crema sf. cream.

cremagliera sf. rack: ferrovia a —, rack-railway.

cremare vt. to cremate.

crematorio agg. crematory: forno —, crematory.

cremazione sf. cremation.

cremerìa sf. creamery.

crèmisi agg. e sm. crimson.

crèolo agg. e sm. creole.

crepa sf. crack.

crepaccio sm. crevasse.

crepacuore sm. heart-break: morire di —, to die of a broken heart.

crepapelle (nella loc. avv.) ridere a —, to roar with laughter; mangiare a —, to eat to excess.

crepare vi. to crack.

crepella sf. crepoline.

crepitare vi. to crackle.

crepitìo sm. crackle.

crepuscolare agg. crepuscular.

crepùscolo sm. twilight.

crescente agg. growing.

crescenza sf. growth.

créscere vi. 1. to grow (v. irr.) 2. (aumentare) to increase.

crescione sm. (bot.) water-cress.

créscita sf. 1. growth 2. (aumento) increase.

crèsima sf. confirmation.

cresimare vt. to confirm.

creso sm. Croesus.

crespo agg. crisp.

cresta sf. 1. crest 2. (di gallo) comb.

crestina sf. maid-servant's cap.

creta sf. clay.

cretinerìa sf. 1. idiocy 2. (azione) foolish action 3. (detto) nonsense.

cretinismo sm. idiocy.

cretino agg. e sm. idiot.

cricca sf. gang.

cricco sm. jack.

criminale agg. e sm. criminal.

criminalista s. 1. (avvocato) criminal lawyer 2. (studioso) criminologist.

criminalità sf. criminality.

crimine sm. crime.

criminologìa sf. criminology.

criminosità sf. criminality.

criminoso agg. criminal.

crine sm. horse-hair.

criniera sf. mane.

crinolina sf. crinoline.

criolite sf. cryolite.

cripta sf. crypt.

crisàlide sf. chrysalid.

crisantemo sm. chrysanthemum.

crisi sf. 1. crisis (pl. -ses) 2. (med.) fit.

crisma sm. 1. (eccl.) chrism 2. (fig.) approval || con tutti i crismi, approved, praised.

cristallerìa sf. 1. crystal-ware 2. (fabbrica) crystal manufactory.

cristalliera sf. glass case.

cristallino agg. e sm. crystalline.

cristallizzare vt. e vi., **cristallizzarsi** vr. to crystallize.

cristallizzazione sf. crystallization.

cristallo sm. 1. crystal 2. (lastra di vetro) plate glass.

cristallografìa sf. crystallography.

cristianésimo sm. Christianity.

cristiania sm. (sport) Christiania.

cristianità sf. 1. (i cristiani) Christendom 2. (cristianesimo) Christianity.

cristiano agg. e sm. Christian.

criterio sm. 1. principle 2. opinion 3. (buon senso) sense.

crìtica sf. 1. criticism 2. (saggio) critical essay 3. (i critici) the critics (pl.).

criticamente avv. critically.

criticare vt. 1. to criticize 2. (biasimare) to blame.

criticismo sm. 1. criticism 2. (stor.) critical philosophy.

crìtico agg. critical. ♦ **crìtico** sm. critic.

criticone sm. fault-finder.

crittògama sf. (bot.) cryptogam.

crittografìa sf. cryptography.

crittogramma sm. cryptogram.

crivellare vt. to riddle.

crivellatura sf. riddling.

crivello sm. riddle.

croato agg. e sm. Croatian.

croccante agg. crisp. ♦ **croccante** sm. almond sweetmeat.

crocchetta *sf.* croquette.
crocchia *sf.* bun.
crocchio *sm.* group.
croce *sf.* cross.
crocerossina *sf.* Red Cross nurse.
crociata *sf.* crusade.
crociato *sm.* crusader.
crocicchio *sm.* cross-road.
crociera *sf.* **1.** cruise **2.** (*arch.*) cross-vault.
crocifiggere *vt.* to crucify.
crocifissione *sf.* crucifixion.
crocifisso *sm.* crucifix.
croco *sm.* (*bot.*) crocus.
crogiuolo *sm.* crucible.
crollare *vi.* to fall (*v. irr.*) down.
crollo *sm.* **1.** breakdown **2.** (*caduta*) falling down.
croma *sf.* (*mus.*) quaver.
cromare *vt.* to chromium-plate.
cromàtico *agg.* chromatic.
cromatismo *sm.* chromatism.
cromatografìa *sf.* chromatography.
cromatura *sf.* chromium plating.
cromo *sm.* chromium.
cromolitografìa *sf.* chromolithography.
cromosoma *sm.* chromosome.
crònaca *sf.* **1.** chronicle **2.** (*di giornale*) news.
crònico *agg.* chronic. ♦ **crònico** *sm.* chronic invalid.
cronista *.m.* reporter.
cronistoria *sf.* chronicle.
cronologìa *sf.* chronology.
cronològico *agg.* chronological.
cronometraggio *sm.* time-study.
cronometrare *vt.* to time.
cronometrìa *sf.* timing.
cronòmetro *sm.* stop watch.
crosta *sf.* **1.** crust **2.** (*tec.*) coating.
crostàcei *sm. pl.* Crustacea.
crostata *sf.* (*cuc.*) tart.
cròtalo *sm.* rattlesnake.
crucciare *vt.*, **crucciarsi** *vr.* to worry.
cruciale *agg.* crucial.
cruciverba *sm.* cross-word puzzle.
crudele *agg.* cruel.
crudeltà *sf.* cruelty.
crudezza *sf.* **1.** (*di stagione*) harshness **2.** (*di parole*) coarseness **3.** (*di cibo*) rawness.
crudo *agg.* **1.** raw **2.** (*poco cotto*) underdone **3.** (*aspro, rigido*) harsh **4.** (*rozzo*) coarse.
cruento *agg.* bloody.
crumiro *sm.* blackleg.
cruna *sf.* needle's eye.

crusca *sf.* bran.
cruscotto *sm.* dashboard.
cubaggio *sm.* cubage.
cubano *agg. e sm.* Cuban.
cubatura *sf.* cubature.
cubetto *sm.* — *di ghiaccio*, ice cube.
cùbico *agg.* cubic.
cubismo *sm.* cubism.
cubitale *agg. a caratteri cubitali*, in very large letters.
cùbito *sm.* **1.** (*misura*) cubit **2.** (*avambraccio*) forearm.
cubo *sm.* cube.
cuccagna *sf.* abundance ‖ *albero della* —, greasy pole.
cuccetta *sf.* berth.
cucchiaiata *sf.* spoonful.
cucchiaino *sm.* **1.** tea-spoon, coffee-spoon **2.** (*il contenuto*) tea-spoon-ful.
cucchiaio *sm.* spoon.
cuccia *sf.* dog-house.
cùcciolo *sm.* puppy.
cùccuma *sf.* kettle.
cucina *sf.* **1.** kitchen **2.** (*modo di cucinare*) cooking **3.** (*culinaria*) cookery **4.** (*stufa*) stove.
cucinare *vt.* to cook.
cuciniere *sm.* man-cook.
cucire *vt.* **1.** to sew (*v. irr.*) **2.** (*med.*) to stitch.
cucito *sm.* needlework.
cucitrice *sf.* **1.** seamstress **2.** (*macchinetta*) stapler.
cucitura *sf.* **1.** seam **2.** (*di fogli*) stapling.
cucù *sm.* (*zool.*) cuckoo.
cucùrbita *sf.* gourd.
cuffia *sf.* **1.** cap. **2.** (*radio*) head-phone.
cugina *sf.* cousin.
cugino *sm.* cousin.
cui *pron. rel.* **1.** (*di possesso*) whose; (*di possesso, solo per animali e cose*) of which: *l'uomo la — casa*, the man whose house; *il libro le — pagine*, the book the pages of which **2.** (*altri casi, per persone*) whom; (*altri casi, per animali e cose*) which: *l'uomo con — parlai*, the man to whom I spoke; *il libro di — parlai*, the book about which I spoke ‖ *in — (dove)*, where; *in — (quando)* when.
culaccio *sm.* rump.
culatta *sf.* breech.
culinaria *sf.* cookery.
culinario *agg.* culinary.

culla *sf.* cradle.
cullare *vt.* to rock, to lull (*anche fig.*).
culminante *agg.* culminant: *momento* —, climax.
culminare *vi.* to culminate.
cùlmine *sm.* 1. summit 2. (*fig.*) apex.
culo *sm.* bottom; (*volg.*) ass.
culto *sm.* 1. cult 2. (*religione*) religion 3. (*adorazione*) worship.
cultore *sm.* lover.
cultura *sf.* culture.
culturale *agg.* cultural.
cumulare *vt.* to heap up.
cumulativo *agg.* cumulative.
cumulatore *sm.* hoarder.
cumulazione *sf.* hoarding.
cùmulo *sm.* 1. heap 2. (*nube*) cumulus (*pl.* -li).
cuna *sf.* cradle.
cuneiforme *agg.* cuneiform, wedge-shaped.
cùneo *sm.* wedge.
cunetta *sf.* 1. (*stradale*) road bump 2. (*scolo*) gutter.
cunìcolo *sm.* underground passage, shaft.
cuòcere *vt.* 1. to cook 2. (*in forno, fornace*) to bake.
cuoco *sm.* cook.
cuoiame *sm.* leather and hides.
cuoio *sm.* leather || — *capelluto*, scalp.
cuore *sm.* heart.
cupezza *sf.* 1. darkness 2. (*tristezza*) gloom.
cupidìgia *sf.* cupidity, greed.
cùpido *agg.* greedy.
cupo *agg.* 1. dark 2. (*triste*) gloomy 3. (*profondo*) deep.
cùpola *sf.* dome.
cùpreo *agg.* cupreous.
cùprico *agg.* cupric.
cura *sf.* 1. care 2. (*med.*) treatment || *casa di* —, nursing-home.
curàbile *agg.* curable.
curante *agg. medico* —, attending physician.
curare *vt.* 1. (*aver cura di*) to take (*v. irr.*) care of 2. (*med.*) to treat 3. (*una pubblicazione*) to edit. ♦ **curarsi** *vr.* (*seguire una cura*) to follow a treatment.
curaro *sm.* curare.
curato *sm.* vicar.
curatore *sm.* trustee.
curdo *agg.* Kurdish. ♦ **curdo** *sm.* Kurd.

curia *sf.* 1. (*eccl.*) see 2. (*giur.*) court of justice.
curie *sm.* curie.
curiosare *vi.* to pry.
curiosità *sf.* 1. curiosity 2. (*stranezza*) oddity.
curioso *agg.* curious.
currìculum *sm.* curriculum (*pl.* -la).
cursore *sm.* 1. messenger 2. (*mecc.*) slider.
curva *sf.* bend.
curvare *vt.* to bend (*v. irr.*). ♦ **curvarsi** *vr.* 1. to bend (*v. irr.*) 2. (*inclinarsi*) to bow.
curvatura *sf.* 1. bending 2. (*arch.*) sweep.
curvilìneo *agg.* curvilinear.
curvo *agg.* bent.
cuscinetto *sm.* small cushion || — *a sfera*, ball bearing.
cuscino *sm.* 1. cushion 2. (*guanciale*) pillow 3. (*mecc.*) pillow.
custode *sm.* keeper.
custodia *sf.* 1. care 2. (*tutela*) guardianship 3. (*astuccio*) case.
custodire *vt.* 1. to keep (*v. irr.*) 2. (*aver cura di*) to look after.
cutàneo *agg.* skin: *malattia cutanea*, skin disease.
cute *sf.* skin.

D

da *prep.* 1. (*provenienza*) from: *vengo* — *Milano*, I come from Milan 2. (*moto a luogo*) to: *andremo* — *loro*, we shall go to their house 3. (*stato in luogo*) at: *vivo* — *mia zia*, I live at my aunt's 4. (*moto per luogo*) through: *passai* — *Roma*, I passed through Rome 5. (*tempo, durata*) for: *siamo qui* — *due mesi*, we have been here for two months; (*a partire da*) since: *lo conosco dal 1955*, I have known him since 1955 6. (*agente*) by: *fu aiutato* — *sua sorella*, he was helped by his sister 7. (*come*) like: *si comportano* — *bambini*, they are behaving like children || *fare* —, to act as.
dabbasso *avv.* 1. below, down below 2. (*al piano inferiore*) downstairs.

dabbenàggine *sf.* ingenuousness.
dabbene *agg.* honest.
daccapo *avv.* over again, from the beginning.
dacché *cong.* since.
dadaismo *sm.* dadaism.
dado *sm.* **1.** die (*pl.* dice) **2.** (*cuc.*) cube **3.** (*mecc.*) nut.
daffare *sm.* work ‖ *darsi* —, to be on the go.
dagherrotipìa *sf.* daguerreotypy.
dagherròtipo *sm.* daguerreotype.
dàgli, dài *inter.* go on.
dàino *sm.* fallow-deer (*invariato al pl.*).
dalìa *sf.* dahlia.
daltònico *agg.* colour-blind.
daltonismo *sm.* colour-blindness.
d'altronde *avv.* on the other hand.
dama *sf.* **1.** lady of rank **2.** (*al ballo*) partner **3.** (*giuoco*) draughts (*pl.*).
damasco *sm.* damask.
damerino *sm.* dandy.
damiere *sm.* draughtboard.
damigella *sf.* maid of honour.
damigiana *sf.* demijohn.
danaroso *agg.* wealthy.
danese *agg.* Danish. ♦ **danese** *sm.* Dane.
dannare *vt.* to damn ‖ *far* —, to drive (*v. irr.*) so. mad. ♦ **dannarsi 1.** to be damned **2.** (*fig.*) to strive (*v. irr.*) hard.
dannato *agg.* damned. ♦ **dannato** *sm.* damned soul.
dannazione *sf.* damnation: —!, damn!
danneggiamento *sm.* damage.
danneggiare *vt.* **1.** to damage **2.** (*di persone*) to injure.
danno *sm.* **1.** damage **2.** (*a persona*) injury ‖ *recare* — *a qu.*, to do (*v. irr.*) so. harm.
dannoso *agg.* harmful.
dantesco *agg.* Dantesque.
danza *sf.* dance.
danzante *agg.* dancing: *trattenimento* —, dance.
danzare *vt. e vi.* to dance.
danzatore *sm.* dancer.
dappertutto *avv.* everywhere.
dappocàggine *sf.* ineptitude.
dappoco *agg.* inept.
dappresso *avv.* near-by.
dapprima *avv.* at first.
dardeggiare *vt. e vi.* to dart.
dardo *sm.* dart.
dare *sm.* debit. ♦ **dare** *vt.* to give

(*v. irr.*): — *origine, luogo a qc.*, to give rise; — *a bere a qu. che*, to give so. to believe that; — *ad intendere*, to give to understand; — *a pensare*, to give food for thought ‖ — *atto di qc.*, to acknowledge; *può darsi, maybe*; — *alla testa*, to go (*v. irr.*) to one's head; — *nell'occhio*, to stand (*v. irr.*) out. ♦ **darsi** *vr.* to devote oneself ‖ — *al bere*, to take (*v. irr.*) to drink; — *ammalato*, to pretend to be ill; — *da fare*, to busy oneself; *darsela a gambe*, to take (*v. irr.*) to one's heels.
dàrsena *sf.* wet dock.
darvinismo *sm.* Darwinism.
data *sf.* date: *in* — *d'oggi*, under to-day's date.
datare *vt.* to date.
dativo *sm.* dative.
dato *agg.* **1.** given **2.** (*stabilito*) stated **3.** (*dedito*) addicted ‖ — *e non concesso*, supposing that. ♦ **dato** *sm.* datum (*pl.* -ta). ♦ **dato che** *cong.* since, as.
datore *sm.* giver ‖ — *di lavoro*, employer.
dàttero *sm.* **1.** date **2.** (*albero*) date-palm.
dattilografare *vt.* to typewrite.
dattilografia *sf.* typewriting.
dattilògrafo *sm.* typist.
dattiloscritto *agg.* typewritten. ♦ **dattiloscritto** *sm.* typescript.
dattorno *avv.* round, about.
davanti *avv.* before, in front. ♦ **davanti** *sm.* front. ♦ **davanti** *agg.* front. ♦ **davanti a** (*loc. prep.*) before.
davantino *sm.* ruffle.
davanzale *sm.* window-sill.
davvero *avv.* really, indeed.
daziario *agg.* toll.
daziere *sm.* exciseman (*pl.* -men).
dazio *sm.* **1.** toll, duty **2.** (*ufficio daziario*) toll-house **3.** (*di consumo*) excise.
dea *sf.* goddess.
deambulare *vi.* to walk about.
deambulatorio *agg. e sm.* deambulatory.
deambulazione *sf.* deambulation.
debellare *vt.* **1.** to defeat **2.** (*fig.*) to overcome (*v. irr.*).
debilitante *agg.* weakening.
debilitare *vt.* to weaken.
debilitazione debilitation.

debitamente *avv.* duly.
débito *agg.* due, proper. ♦ **débito**
sm. debt: *fare un* —, to run (*v. irr.*) into debt.
debitore *sm.* debtor.
débole *agg.* weak.
debolezza *sf.* weakness.
debosciato *agg.* debauched.
debuttante *sm.* **1.** novice **2.** (*di ragazza in società*) debutante.
debuttare *vi.* **1.** to make (*v. irr.*) one's debut **2.** (*di ragazza in società*) to come (*v. irr.*) out.
debutto *sm.* **1.** debut **2.** (*di ragazza in società*) coming out.
dècade *sf.* **1.** (*di giorni*) ten days **2.** (*di anni*) ten years.
decadente *agg.* **1.** decaying **2.** (*lett.*) decadent.
decadenza *sf.* decay, decline.
decadere *vi.* to decline || — *da un diritto*, to lose (*v. irr.*) a right.
decaduto *agg.* impoverished.
decaedro *sm.* decahedron.
decagrammo *sm.* decagram.
decalcare *vt.* to transfer.
decalcificare *vt.* to decalcify.
decàlitre *sm.* decalitre.
decàlogo *sm.* decalogue.
decàmetro *sm.* decametre.
decampare *vi.* **1.** to decamp **2.** (*fig.*) to recede.
decano *sm.* **1.** senior **2.** (*eccl.*) dean.
decantare *vt.* **1.** to extol **2.** (*chim.*) to decant.
decantazione *sf.* (*chim.*) decantation.
decapitare *vt.* to behead.
decappottàbile *agg.* (*auto*) convertible.
decasìllabo *agg.* decasyllabic. ♦ **decasìllabo** *sm.* decasyllable.
decatissaggio *sm.* decatizing.
decèdere *vi.* to die.
decelerare *vt.* to decelerate.
decennale *agg.* decennial.
decenne *agg.* **1.** ten years old (*predicativo*) **2.** ten-year-old (*attributivo*).
decennio *sm.* ten-year period.
decente *agg.* decent, proper.
decentramento *sm.* decentralization.
decentrare *vt.* to decentralize.
decenza *sf.* decency.
decesso *sm.* death.
decìdere *vt.* to decide. ♦ **decìdersi** *vr.* to make (*v. irr.*) up one's
mind.
decifrare *vt.* **1.** to decipher **2.** (*fam.*) to make (*v. irr.*) out.
decifrazione *sf.* deciphering.
decigrammo *sm.* decigram.
decìlitro *sm.* decilitre.
decimale *agg. e sm.* decimal.
decimare *vt.* to decimate.
decimazione *sf.* decimation.
decìmetro *sm.* decimetre.
dècimo *agg.* tenth.
decina *sf.* ten, half-a-score.
decisione *sf.* decision.
decisivo *agg.* decisive.
deciso *agg.* **1.** resolute, firm **2.** (*definito*) decided.
declamare *vt. e vi.* to declaim.
declamatorio *agg.* declamatory.
declamazione *sf.* declamation.
declassare *vt.* to degrade.
declinàbile *agg.* declinable.
declinante *agg.* declining.
declinare *vt.* **1.** to decline || — *le proprie generalità*, to say (*v. irr.*) one's name and surname. ♦ **declinare** *vi.* **1.** (*del sole*) to set (*v. irr.*) **2.** (*degradare*) to slope **3.** (*venir meno*) to decline.
declinazione *sf.* (*gramm.*) declension.
declino *sm.* decline.
declivio *sm.* declivity.
decollaggio *sm.* (*aer.*) take-off.
decollare *vi.* to take (*v. irr.*) off.
decollo *sm.* take-off.
decolorante *agg.* decolorating. ♦ **decolorante** *sm.* decolorant.
decolorare *vt.* to decolorate.
decolorazione *sf.* decoloration || — *dei capelli*, hair bleaching.
decomponìbile *agg.* decomposable.
decomporre *vt.* to decompose.
decomposizione *sf.* **1.** decomposition **2.** (*putrefazione*) putrefaction.
decongelare *vt.* to defrost.
decongestionare *vt.* to decongest.
decorare *vt.* to decorate: — *al valore*, to decorate for bravery.
decorativo *agg.* decorative.
decoratore *sm.* decorator.
decorazione *sf.* decoration.
decoro *sm.* dignity.
decoroso *agg.* decorous, proper.
decorrenza *sf.* expiration: *con — da*, beginning from.
decòrrere *vi.* **1.** to pass || *a — da*, to begin (*v. irr.*) from **2.** (*comm.*) to run (*v. irr.*), to have effect.
decorso *sm.* **1.** period **2.** (*il passa-*

re) passing.

decrepitezza *sf.* decrepitude.

decrèpito *agg.* decrepit.

decréscere *vi.* to decrease.

decretare *vt.* **1.** to decree **2.** (*concedere*) to confer.

decreto *sm.* decree: — *legge*, Order in Council.

decuplicare *vt.* to decuple.

dècuplo *sm.* decuple, ten times as much.

decurtare *vt.* to reduce.

dèdalo *sm.* maze.

dèdica *sf.* dedication.

dedicare *vt.* to dedicate. ♦ **dedicarsi** *vr.* to devote oneself.

dedicatorio *agg.* dedicatory.

dèdito *agg.* **1.** given up **2.** (*a vizio*) addicted.

dedizione *sf.* devotion.

dedurre *vt.* **1.** to infer, to deduce **2.** (*defalcare*) to deduct.

deduttivo *agg.* deductive.

deduzione *sf.* deduction.

defalcare *vt.* to deduct.

defalco *sm.* deduction.

defecare *vi.* to defecate.

defenestrare *vt.* **1.** to throw (*v. irr.*) out of the window **2.** (*fig.*) to dismiss.

defenestrazione *sf.* defenestration.

deferente *agg.* deferential.

deferenza *sf.* compliance, deference.

deferire *vt.* **1.** to submit **2.** (*giur.*) to remit.

defezionare *vi.* to desert.

defezione *sf.* **1.** defection **2.** (*mil.*) desertion.

deficiente *agg.* **1.** insufficient **2.** (*idiota*) mentally deficient. ♦ **deficiente** *sm.* idiot.

deficienza *sf.* **1.** deficiency, lack **2.** (*idiozia*) mental deficiency.

dèficit *sm.* deficit.

definìbile *agg.* definable.

definire *vt.* **1.** to define **2.** (*determinare, risolvere*) to determine.

definitivo *agg.* final.

definito *agg.* definite.

definizione *sf.* **1.** definition **2.** (*risoluzione*) settlement.

deflagrante *agg.* deflagrating.

deflagrare *vi.* to deflagrate.

deflagrazione *sf.* deflagration.

deflazione *sf.* deflation.

deflèttere *vi.* to deflect.

deflettore *sm.* baffle.

deflorare *vt.* to deflower.

deflorazione *sf.* defloration.

defluire *vi.* to flow down.

deflusso *sm.* **1.** downflow **2.** (*di marea*) ebb-tide.

deformante *agg.* deforming.

deformare *vt.* **1.** to deform, to disfigure **2.** (*alterare*) to alter. ♦ **deformarsi** *vr.* **1.** (*mecc.*) to warp **2.** to get (*v. irr.*) deformed.

deformazione *sf.* **1.** deformation **2.** (*mecc.*) buckling.

deforme *agg.* deformed.

deformità *sf.* deformity.

defraudare *vt.* to defraud.

defunto *agg.* e *sm.* dead.

degenerare *vi.* to degenerate.

degenerazione *sf.* degeneration.

degènere *agg.* degenerate.

degente *sm.* patient.

degenza *sf.* stay in hospital.

deglutizione *sf.* swallowing.

degnarsi *vr.* to condescend.

degnazione *sf.* condescension.

degno *agg.* worthy, deserving.

degradante *agg.* degrading.

degradare *vt.* to degrade.

degradazione *sf.* degradation.

degustare *vt.* to taste.

deiezione *sf.* dejection.

deificare *vt.* to deify.

deismo *sm.* deism.

deità *sf.* deity.

delatore *sm.* delator.

delazione *sf.* delation, informing.

delèbile *agg.* erasable.

dèlega *sf.* **1.** delegation **2.** (*procura*) proxy.

delegare *vt.* to delegate.

delegato *sm.* delegate.

delegazione *sf.* **1.** delegation **2.** (*commissione*) committee.

deleterio *agg.* harmful.

delfino *sm.* **1.** (*zool.*) dolphin **2.** (*fig.*) probable successor **3.** (*stor.*) dauphin.

deliberare *vt.* to decide.

deliberazione *sf.* deliberation.

delicatezza *sf.* delicacy.

delicato *agg.* **1.** delicate **2.** (*scrupoloso*) scrupulous **3.** (*discreto*) discreet, tactful.

delimitare *vt.* to delimit.

delimitazione *sf.* delimitation.

delineare *vt.* to outline.

delineazione *sf.* delineation.

delinquente *sm.* delinquent.

delinquenza *sf.* criminality.

delìnquere *vi.* to commit an offence.

deliquio *sm.* swoon.

delirare *vi.* to rave.
delirio *sm.* delirium, frenzy (*anche fig.*).
delitto *sm.* crime.
delittuoso *agg.* criminal.
delizia *sf.* delight.
deliziare *vt.* to delight.
delizioso *agg.* 1. delightful 2. (*di sapore, profumo*) delicious.
delta *sm.* delta.
deltòide *agg.* e *sm.* deltoid.
delucidare *vt.* to explain.
delucidazione *sf.* explanation.
delùdere *vt.* to disappoint.
delusione *sf.* disappointment.
demagogìa *sf.* demagogy.
demagògico *agg.* demagogic.
demagogo *sm.* demagogue.
demandare *vt.* to commit.
demaniale *agg.* (owned by the) State.
demanio *sm.* State property.
demarcare *vt.* to mark the boundaries of.
demarcazione *sf.* demarcation.
demente *agg.* insane. ♦ **demente** *sm.* madman (*pl.* -men).
demenza *sf.* insanity.
demeritare *vt.* to forfeit. ♦ **demeritare** *vi.* to deserve censure.
demèrito *sm.* demerit.
demiurgo *sm.* demiurge.
democràtico *agg.* democratic. ♦ **democràtico** *sm.* democrat.
democratizzare *vt.* to democratize.
democrazìa *sf.* democracy.
democristiano *sm.* christian-democrat.
demografìa *sf.* demography.
demogràfico *agg.* demographic(al).
demolire *vt.* to demolish.
demolitore *sm.* 1. demolisher 2. (*fig.*) iconoclast.
demolizione *sf.* 1. demolition 2. (*fig.*) destruction.
dèmone *sm.* 1. demon 2. (*diavolo*) devil.
demonìaco *agg.* demoniac(al).
demonio *sm.* 1. devil 2. (*fig.*) demon.
demonologìa *sf.* demonology.
demoralizzare *vt.* to demoralize. ♦ **demoralizzarsi** *vr.* to lose (*v. irr.*) heart.
demoralizzazione *sf.* demoralization.
denaro *sm.* 1. money 2. (*moneta antica*) denarius (*pl.* -rii).
denaturare *vt.* to denature.

dendrologìa *sf.* dendrology.
denegare *vt.* to deny.
denicotinizzare *vt.* to denicotinize.
denigrare *vt.* to denigrate.
denigratore *sm.* denigrator.
denigrazione *sf.* denigration.
denominare *vt.* to name.
denominativo *agg.* denominative.
denominatore *sm.* denominator.
denominazione *sf.* denomination.
denotare *vt.* to signify.
densità *sf.* density.
denso *agg.* thick.
dentale *agg.* dental.
dentario *agg.* dental, tooth (*attr.*).
dentato *agg.* toothed.
dentatura *sf.* 1. set of teeth 2. (*di ingranaggio*) toothing.
dente *sm.* tooth (*pl.* teeth).
dentellare *vt.* to indent.
dentellatura *sf.* indentation.
dentello *sm.* 1. (*mecc.*) tooth 2. (*arch.*) dentil 3. (*tacca*) notch.
dentiera *sf.* dental plate.
dentifricio *agg.* tooth (*attr.*) ♦ **dentifricio** *sm.* tooth-paste.
dentina *sf.* dentine.
dentista *sm.* dentist.
dentìstico *agg.* dental: *gabinetto* —, dentist's surgery.
dentizione *sf.* teething.
dentro *avv.* in, inside. ♦ **dentro** *prep.* 1. in, inside 2. (*di tempo*) (with)in.
denudare *vt.* 1. to strip 2. (*scoprire*) to lay (*v. irr.*) bare. ♦ **denudarsi** *vr.* to strip.
denudazione *sf.* denudation.
denuncia *sf.* 1. denunciation 2. (*dichiarazione*) statement: — *dei redditi*, statement of one's income.
denunciare *vt.* 1. to denounce 2. (*dichiarare*) to report 3. (*giur.*) — *qu.*, to inform against so.
denutrito *agg.* underfed.
denutrizione *sf.* underfeeding.
deodorante *agg.* deodorizing. ♦ **deodorante** *sm.* deodorant.
deodorare *vt.* to deodorize.
deontologìa *sf.* deontology.
depauperamento *sm.* impoverishment.
depauperare *vt.* to impoverish.
depennare *vt.* to cross out.
deperìbile *agg.* perishable.
deperimento *sm.* 1. (*di salute*) wasting away 2. (*per un dolore*) pining away 3. (*di cose*) deterioration.

deperire vi. 1. (di salute) to waste away 2. (per un dolore) to pine. away 3. (di cose) to deteriorate.

depilare vt. to remove hair (from).

depilatore sm. hair-remover.

depilatorio agg. hair-removing.

depilazione sf. hair-removal.

deploràbile agg. deplorable.

deplorare vt. 1. (essere spiacenti) to deplore 2. (lagnarsi di) to complain of.

deplorazione sf. 1. (biasimo) blame 2. (rimpianto) regret.

deplorévole agg. 1. deplorable 2. (biasimevole) blamable.

deporre vt. 1. to lay (v. irr.) 2. (da una carica) to remove from (an) office 3. (depositare) to deposit 4. (giur.) to witness. ♦ **deporre** vi. (giur.) to give (v. irr.) evidence.

deportare vt. to deport.

deportato agg. deported. ♦ **deportato** sm. convict.

deportazione sf. deportation.

depositante sm. depositor.

depositare vt. to deposit: — merci, to store goods.

depositario sm. trustee.

depòsito sm. 1. deposit 2. (luogo in cui depositare) warehouse 3. (per bagagli) left-luggage room.

deposizione sf. deposition.

depravare vt. to corrupt.

depravazione sf. corruption.

deprecàbile agg. deprecable.

deprecare vt. to deprecate.

deprecativo agg. deprecatory.

deprecazione sf. deprecation.

depredamento sm. plunder.

depredare vt. to plunder, to ravage.

depressione sf. depression.

depressivo agg. depressing.

depresso agg. depressed.

depressore sm. depressor.

deprezzamento sm. depreciation.

deprezzare vt. to depreciate.

deprimente agg. depressing.

deprìmere vt. to depress.

depurare vt. to depurate.

depurativo agg. depurative.

depuratore sm. 1. depurator 2. (mecc.) cleaner.

depurazione sf. purification, depuration.

deputare vt. to depute.

deputato sm. deputy.

deputazione sf. deputation.

deragliamento sm. derailment.

deragliare vi. to go (v. irr.) off the rails.

derattizzare vt. to clear by deratization.

derattizzazione sf. deratization.

derelitto agg. forlorn.

deretano sm. posterior.

derìdere vt. to laugh at, to make (v. irr.) fun of.

derisìbile agg. laughable.

derisione sf. mockery.

derisorio agg. derisory.

deriva sf. drift.

derivare vi. 1. to derive 2. (originarsi) to rise (v. irr.). ♦ **derivare** vt. to derive.

derivativo agg. derivative.

derivato agg. derived. ♦ **derivato** sm. 1. derivative 2. (sottoprodotto) by-product.

derivazione sf. 1. derivation 2. (elettr.) shunt.

derma sm. derm.

dermatologìa sf. dermatology.

dermatològico agg. dermatological.

dermatòlogo sm. dermatologist.

dèroga sf. derogation.

derogare vi. to derogate.

derrata sf. 1. victual 2. (alimentare) food-stuff.

derubare vt. to rob (so. of).

desco sm. dinner table.

descrittivo agg. descriptive.

descrìvere vt. to describe.

descrivìbile agg. describable.

descrizione sf. description.

desèrtico agg. desert.

deserto agg. e sm. desert.

desideràbile agg. desirable.

desiderare vt. 1. to wish 2. (desiderare di avere) to wish for.

desiderio sm. wish.

desideroso agg. desirous, eager (for).

designare vt. to appoint.

designazione sf. designation.

desinare vi. to dine, to have dinner. ♦ **desinare** sm. dinner.

desinenza sf. ending.

desìstere vi. to cease, to leave (v. irr.) off.

desolare vt. 1. to desolate 2. (addolorare) to distress.

desolato agg. (spiacente) sorry.

desolazione sf. 1. desolation 2. (dolore) grief, sorrow.

dèspota sm. despot.

destare vt. 1. to wake (v. irr.) 2.

(*suscitare*) to rouse. ♦ **destarsi** *vr.* to wake (*v. irr.*) up.

destinare *vt.* 1. to destine 2. (*devolvere*) to assign.

destinatario *sm.* addressee.

destinazione *sf.* destination.

destino *sm.* 1. destiny 2. (*sorte*) lot.

destituire *vt.* to dismiss.

destituzione *sf.* dismissal.

desto *agg.* awake.

destra *sf.* 1. right hand 2. (*parte destra*) right, right side: *alla tua* —, on your right; *tenere la* —, to keep (*v. irr.*) right.

destramente *avv.* skilfully.

destreggiarsi *vr.* to manage.

destrezza *sf.* dexterity.

destriero *sm.* steed.

destrina *sf.* dextrine.

destro *agg.* 1. right 2. (*abile*) clever. ♦ **destro** *sm.* opportunity.

desueto *agg.* unusual, obsolete.

desuetùdine *sf.* disuse.

desùmere *vt.* 1. to infer 2. (*trarre*) to draw (*v. irr.*).

detenere *vt.* 1. to hold (*v. irr.*) 2. (*tener prigioniero*) to keep (*v. irr.*) in prison.

detentore *sm.* holder.

detenuto *agg.* imprisoned. ♦ **detenuto** *sm.* prisoner.

detenzione *sf.* 1. possession 2. (*il detenere*) holding 3. (*galera*) detention.

detergente *agg. e sm.* detergent.

detèrgere *vt.* to cleanse.

deterioramento *sm.* deterioration.

deteriorare *vt.* 1. to deteriorate 2. (*danneggiare*) to damage.

deteriore *agg.* worse.

determinàbile *agg.* determinable.

determinante *agg.* determinant.

determinare *vt.* 1. to determine 2. (*causare*) to cause.

determinativo *agg.* determinative || *articolo* —, definite article.

determinato *agg.* 1. determinate 2. (*particolare*) special 3. (*deciso*) resolute.

determinazione *sf.* determination.

determinismo *sm.* determinism.

deterrente *sm.* deterrent.

detersivo *agg. e sm.* detersive.

detestàbile *agg.* detestable.

detestare *vt.* to loathe.

detettore *sm.* detector.

detonante *agg.* explosive.

detonare *vi.* to detonate.

detonatore *sm.* detonator.

detonazione *sf.* explosion.

detrarre *vt.* to deduct.

detrattore *sm.* detractor.

detrazione *sf.* 1. deduction 2. (*fig.*) detraction.

detrimento *sm.* detriment.

detrìtico *agg.* detrital.

detrito *sm.* rubble, debris.

detronizzare *vt.* to depose.

detronizzazione *sf.* dethronement.

detta (*nella loc. avv.*) *a* — *di qu.*, according to what so. says.

dettagliante *sm.* retailer.

dettagliare *vt.* to detail.

dettagliatamente *avv.* in detail.

dettaglio *sm.* 1. detail 2. (*comm.*) retail.

dettame *sm.* dictate.

dettare *vt.* 1. to dictate 2. (*suggerire*) to suggest || — *la legge*, to lay (*v. irr.*) down the law.

dettato *sm.* dictation.

detto *agg.* 1. called 2. (*sopraddetto*) said, above-mentioned. ♦ **detto** *sm.* saying.

deturpare *vt.* to disfigure.

deturpazione *sf.* disfigurement.

devalutazione *sf.* depreciation.

devastare *vt.* to ravage, to ruin.

devastatore *agg.* ravaging. ♦ **devastatore** *sm.* ravager.

devastazione *sf.* devastation.

deviare *vi.* to deviate || *non* —! (*non cambiare discorso*), stick to the point! ♦ **deviare** *vt.* to divert.

deviazione *sf.* 1. deviation 2. (*stradale*) detour || — *ferroviaria*, shunting.

deviazionismo *sm.* deviationism.

devoluzione *sf.* devolution.

devòlvere *vt.* 1. (*giur.*) to devolve, to assign 2. (*adoperare*) to employ.

devoto *agg.* 1. devout, affectionate 2. (*relig.*) pious, religious.

devozione *sf.* devotion, piety.

di *prep.* 1. of 2. (*partitivo*) some, any: *dammi del pane*, give me some bread; *hai dello zucchero?*, have you any sugar? 3. (*tempo*) in, during: — *mattina*, in the morning 4. (*argomento*) of, about 5. (*paragone coi comparativi*) than: *è più graziosa* — *sua sorella*, she is prettier than her sister 6. (*nei superl.*) of, in 7. (*modo*) with, in.

dì *sm.* day.

diabete *sm.* diabetes.

diabètico *agg. e sm.* diabetic.

diabòlico *agg.* diabolic(al).

diàcono *sm.* deacon.

diadema *sm.* diadem.

diàfano *agg.* diaphanous.

diaframma *sm.* diaphragm.

diàgnosi *sf.* diagnosis (*pl.* -ses).

diagnosticare *vt.* to diagnose.

diagnòstico *agg.* diagnostic.

diagonale *agg.* diagonal. ♦ **diagonale** *sf.* diagonal.

diagonalmente *avv.* diagonally.

diagramma *sm.* diagram.

dialettale *agg.* dialectal.

dialèttica *sf.* dialectics.

dialèttico *agg.* dialectic. ♦ **dialèttico** *sm.* dialectic.

dialetto *sm.* dialect.

diàlisi *sf.* dialysis (*pl.* -ses).

dialogare *vi.* to hold (*v. irr.*) a dialogue.

diàlogo *sm.* dialogue.

diamante *sm.* diamond.

diametralmente *avv.* diametrically.

diàmetro *sm.* diameter.

diàmine *inter.* good heavens!

dianzi *avv.* just, just now.

diapositiva *sf.* slide.

diarchìa *sf.* diarchy.

diario *sm.* diary.

diarrea *sf.* diarrhoea.

diaspro *sm.* jasper.

diatonìa *sf.* diatony.

diatriba *sf.* diatribe.

diavolerìa *sf.* 1. devilry 2. (*fam.*) trick.

diavoletto *sm.* imp.

diàvolo *sm.* devil.

dibàttere *vt.* to debate. ♦ **dibàttersi** *vr.* to struggle.

dibàttito *sm.* debate, discussion.

dibattuto *agg.* controversial.

diboscamento *sm.* deforestation.

diboscare *vt.* to deforest.

dicastero *sm.* office.

dicembre *sm.* December.

dicerìa *sf.* gossip, rumour.

dichiarare *vt.* to declare.

dichiarato *agg.* declared.

dichiarazione *sf.* declaration.

diciannove *agg.* nineteen.

diciannovenne *agg.* 1. nineteen years old (*pred.*) 2. nineteen-year-old (*attr.*).

diciannovèsimo *agg.* nineteenth.

diciassette *agg.* seventeen.

diciassettenne *agg.* 1. seventeen years old (*pred.*) 2. seventeen-year-old (*attr.*).

diciassettèsimo *agg.* seventeenth.

diciottenne *agg.* 1. eighteen years old (*pred.*) 2. eighteen-year-old (*attr.*).

diciottèsimo *agg.* eighteenth.

diciotto *agg.* eighteen.

dicitore *sm.* speaker.

dicitura *sf.* wording.

didascalìa *sf.* 1. explanation 2. (*cine*) subtitles (*pl.*).

didascàlico *agg.* didactic.

didàttica *sf.* didactics.

didàttico *agg.* didactic(al).

didentro *sm.* inside.

didietro *sm.* back.

dieci *agg.* ten.

diecina *sf.* ten, half a score.

diedro *sm.* dihedral.

dielèttrico *agg.* dielectric.

diesis *sm.* sharp.

dieta *sf.* diet.

dietètico *agg.* dietetic.

dietòlogo *sm.* dietician.

dietro *avv.* behind. ♦ **dietro** *prep.* behind, after. ♦ **dietro** *sm.* back, rear.

dietrofrònt *sm.* about turn!

difatti *avv.* as a matter of fact.

difèndere *vt.* to defend.

difendìbile *agg.* defensible.

difensiva *sf.* defensive.

difensivo *agg.* defensive.

difensore *agg.* defending. ♦ **difensore** *sm.* 1. defender 2. (*giur.*) defending counsel 3. (*di un'idea ecc.*) supporter.

difesa *sf.* defence.

difettare *vi.* to be wanting.

difettivo *agg.* defective.

difetto *sm.* defect.

difettoso *agg.* defective.

diffamare *vt.* to defame.

diffamatore *sm.* defamer.

diffamatorio *agg.* defamatory.

diffamazione *sf.* defamation.

differente *agg.* unlike, different.

differentemente *avv.* differently.

differenza *sf.* difference.

differenziale *agg. e sm.* differential.

differenziare *vt.* to differentiate.

differenziato *agg.* differentiated.

differenziazione *sf.* differentiation.

differìbile *agg.* that can be deferred.

differimento *sm.* deferment.

differire *vi.* (*essere diverso*) to differ (from). ♦ **differire** *vt.* to delay.

difficile *agg.* difficult.

difficilmente *avv.* with difficulty.

difficoltà *sf.* difficulty.

difficoltoso *agg.* difficult.

diffida *sf.* warning, intimation.

diffidare *vi.* to distrust. ♦ **diffidare** *vt.* to give (*v. irr.*) warning.

diffidente *agg.* suspicious.

diffidenza *sf.* **1.** distrust **2.** (*sospetto*) suspicion.

diffòndere *vt.* to diffuse, to spread (*v. irr.*). ♦ **diffòndersi** *vr.* to spread (*v. irr.*).

difforme *agg.* **1.** different **2.** shapeless.

difformità *sf.* difference, deformity.

diffrazione *sf.* diffraction.

diffusamente *avv.* diffusely.

diffusione *sf.* **1.** diffusion, spreading **2.** (*di giornale*) circulation.

diffuso *agg.* diffuse.

diffusore *sm.* diffusor.

difilato *avv.* straight.

diftèrico *agg.* diphtheric.

difterite *sf.* diphtheria.

diga *sf.* dam.

digerente *agg.* digestive.

digeribile *agg.* digestible.

digeribilità *sf.* digestibility.

digerire *vt.* to digest.

digestione *sf.* digestion.

digestivo *agg. e sm.* digestive.

digesto *sm.* digest.

digitale *agg.* digital || *impronte digitali,* finger-prints. ♦ **digitale** *sf.* digitalis, (*fam.*) foxglove.

digiunare *vi.* to fast.

digiunatore *sm.* faster.

digiuno¹ *agg.* **1.** fasting **2.** (*fig.*) lacking (in).

digiuno² *sm.* fast.

dignità *sf.* dignity.

dignitario *sm.* dignitary.

dignitosamente *avv.* with dignity.

dignitoso *agg.* dignified.

digradante *agg.* **1.** sloping **2.** (*pitt.*) shading.

digradare *vi.* **1.** to slope down **2.** (*pitt.*) to shade off.

digressione *sf.* digression.

digressivo *agg.* digressive.

digrignare *vt.* to gnash.

digrossamento *sm.* **1.** reducing **2.** (*sbozzo*) rough-hewing.

digrossare *vt.* **1.** to reduce **2.** (*sbozzare*) to rough-hew.

dilacerare *vt.* to tear (*v. irr.*).

dilagare *vi.* to spread (*v. irr.*).

dilaniare *vt.* to tear (*v. irr.*) to pieces.

dilapidare *vt.* to squander.

dilapidatore *sm.* squanderer.

dilapidazione *sf.* squandering.

dilatàbile *agg.* dilatable.

dilatabilità *sf.* dilatability.

dilatare *vt.,* **dilatarsi** *vr.* **1.** to dilate **2.** (*fis.*) to expand.

dilatazione *sf.* dilatation.

dilatorio *agg.* dilatory.

dilavamento *sm.* washing away.

dilavare *vt.* to wash away.

dilazionare *vt.* to defer.

dilazione *sf.* delay, respite.

dileggiare *vt.* to mock.

dileggio *sm.* mockery.

dileguare *vt.* to disperse. ♦ **dileguarsi** *vr.* to disappear.

dilemma *sm.* dilemma.

dilettante *sm.* amateur.

dilettantismo *sm.* amateurism.

dilettare *vt.* to delight. ♦ **dilettarsi** *vr.* to take (*v. irr.*) delight (in).

dilettévole *agg.* delightful.

diletto *agg.* beloved. ♦ **diletto** *sm.* delight.

diligente *agg.* diligent.

diligenza *sf.* **1.** diligence **2.** (*carrozza*) stage-coach.

dilucidare *vt.* V. *delucidare.*

dilucidazione *sf.* V. *delucidazione.*

diluente *sm.* diluent.

diluire *vt.* **1.** to dilute **2.** (*fig.*) to water down.

diluizione *sf.* dilution.

dilungarsi *vr.* to speak (*v. irr.*) diffusely.

diluviale *agg.* **1.** torrential **2.** (*geol.*) diluvial.

diluviano *agg.* diluvial.

diluviare *vi.* **1.** to pour **2.** (*fig.*) to shower.

diluvio *sm.* deluge, flood.

dimagramento *sm.* thinning.

dimagrante *agg.* slimming.

dimagrare *vi.* to thin.

dimagrire *vi.* V. *dimagrare.*

dimenare *vt.* **1.** (*la coda*) to wag **2.** to wave. ♦ **dimenarsi** *vr.* to move about restlessly.

dimensione *sf.* dimension, size.

dimenticanza *sf.* **1.** (*svista*) oversight **2.** (*oblio*) oblivion.

dimenticare *vt.,* **dimenticarsi** *vr.* to forget (*v. irr.*).

dimèntico *agg.* forgetful.

dimesso *agg.* **1.** modest **2.** (*trasandato*) shabby.

dimestichezza sf. familiarity.
dìmetro sm. dimeter.
diméttere vt. to dismiss || — dall'ospedale, to discharge. ♦ **diméttersi** vr. to resign.
dimezzamento sm. halving.
dimezzare vt. to halve.
diminuendo sm. 1. (mat.) minuend 2. (mus.) diminuendo.
diminuìbile agg. diminishable.
diminuire vt. e vi. to lessen, to diminish.
diminutivo agg. e sm. diminutive.
diminuzione sf. lessening, reduction.
dimissionare vt. to oblige (so.) to resign.
dimissionario agg. resigning.
dimissione sf. resignation || dare le dimissioni, to resign.
dimissoria sf. dimissory letter.
dimodoché cong. so that.
dimora sf. residence, lodgings (pl.).
dimorare vi. to stay, to live.
dimorfismo sm. dimorphism.
dimorfo agg. dimorphic.
dimostràbile agg. demonstrable.
dimostrabilità sf. demonstrability.
dimostrante sm. demonstrant.
dimostrare vt. 1. to show (v. irr.) 2. (provare) to demonstrate. ♦ **dimostrarsi** vr. to show oneself.
dimostrativo agg. e sm. demonstrative.
dimostratore sm. demonstrator.
dimostrazione sf. demonstration.
dina sf. dyne.
dinàmica sf. dynamics.
dinamicamente avv. dynamically.
dinamicità sf. dynamism, energy.
dinàmico agg. 1. dynamic 2. (fig.) energetic.
dinamismo sm. 1. dynamism 2. (fig.) energy.
dinamitardo sm. dynamiter.
dinamite sf. dynamite.
dìnamo sf. dynamo.
dinamòmetro sm. dynamometer.
dinanzi prep. before, in front of. ♦ **dinanzi** avv. before, in front, forward.
dìnaro sm. dinar.
dinasta sm. dynast.
dinastìa sf. dynasty.
dinàstico agg. dynastic(al).
dìndo sm. turkey.
diniego sm. denial.
dinoccolato agg. slouching.
dinosàuro sm. dinosaur.

dintorni sm. pl. surroundings.
dintorno avv. e prep. 1. round, round about 2. (circa) about.
dio sm. god: Marte, il — della guerra, Mars, the god of war. ♦ **Dio** sm. God: — ci.assista!, — non voglia!, God help us, God forbid.
diocesano agg. diocesan.
diòcesi sf. diocese.
diòdo sm. diode.
dionea sf. dionaea.
dionisìaco agg. Dionysiac.
diorama sm. diorama.
diorite sf. diorite.
diottrìa sf. diopter.
diòttrica sf. dioptrics.
diòttrico agg. dioptric.
dipanamento sm. winding into a ball.
dipanare vt. 1. to wind (v. irr.) into a ball 2. (fig.) to disentangle.
dipanatoio sm. skein-winder.
dipartimentale agg. departmental.
dipartimento sm. department.
dipartire vi. to depart. ♦ **dipartirsi** vr. 1. to go (v. irr.) away 2. (morire) to pass away.
dipartita sf. 1. departure 2. (morte) death.
dipendente agg. dependent (on). ♦ **dipendente** sm. employee.
dipendenza sf. dependence (on).
dipèndere vi. 1. (derivare) to be due 2. (essere subordinato, vivere a carico) to depend (on).
dipìngere vt. to paint.
dipinto agg. painted. ♦ **dipinto** sm. painting.
diplegìa sf. diplegia.
diplococco sm. diplococcus (pl. -ci).
diploma sm. diploma.
diplomare vt. to confer a diploma (upon so.). ♦ **diplomarsi** vr. to get (v. irr.) a diploma.
diplomàtica sf. diplomatics.
diplomaticamente avv. diplomatically.
diplomàtico agg. diplomatic. ♦ **diplomàtico** sm. diplomat.
diplomato agg. holding a diploma. ♦ **diplomato** sm. graduate.
diplomazìa sf. diplomacy.
diplopìa sf. diplopia.
dipnoi sm. pl. Dipnoi.
dipodìa sf. dipody.
dipoi avv. then.
diporto sm. recreation, diversion ||

viaggiare per —, to travel on pleasure.

dipresso (*nella loc. avv.*) *a un* —, approximately.

dìptero *agg.* dipteral.

diradamento *sm.* 1. thinning 2. (*di nebbia, gas*) rarefaction.

diradare *vt.* 1. to thin out 2. (*rendere meno frequente*) to do (*v. irr.*) less frequent. ♦ **diradarsi** *vr.* 1. to clear away 2. (*divenire meno frequente*) to become (*v. irr.*) less frequent.

diramare *vt.* to issue, to spread (*v. irr.*).

diramazione *sf.* 1. branching 2. (*diffusione*) diffusion 3. (*per radio*) broadcasting.

dire *vt.* 1. (*nel senso di enunciare e quando introduce il discorso diretto*) to say (*v. irr.*): *dice che ha sonno*, he says he is sleepy: « *venite* », *ci disse*, « come », he said to us 2. (*nel senso di raccontare e quando è enunciata la persona cui si parla*) to tell (*v. irr.*): *gli dissi di venire*, I told him to come || *si dice*, they say; *mi si dice*, I am told; *inutile* — *che*, it goes without saying that; *vale a* —, that is to say; *sentir* —, to hear (*v. irr.*); *voler* —, to mean (*v. irr.*).

dire *sm.* words (*pl.*), speech.

direttamente *avv.* directly.

direttìssima *sf. per* —, summarily.

direttìssimo *sm.* (*ferr.*) fast train.

direttiva *sf.* directions (*pl.*).

direttivo *agg.* 1. leading 2. (*comm.*) managing.

diretto *agg.* direct, straight.

direttore *sm.* 1. (*comm.; amm.*) manager 2. (*di scuola*) headmaster.

direttoriale *agg.* directorial.

direttorio *sm.* executive board.

direttrice *sf.* 1. (*comm.; amm.*) manageress 2. (*di scuola*) headmistress.

direzionale *agg.* directional || *centro* —, office district.

direzione *sf.* 1. direction, course 2. (*di società*) management 3. (*di giornale*) editorship 4. (*di scuola*) headmastership 5. (*sede*) administrative office.

dirigente *agg.* directing, leading. ♦ **dirigente** *sm.* director, manager, leader.

dirìgere *vt.* 1. (*indirizzare*) to direct 2. (*guidare*) to lead (*v. irr.*) 3. (*sovraintendere*) to supervise. ♦ **dirigersi** *vr.* to turn one's steps towards.

dirigìbile *sm.* airship.

dirigismo *sm.* state planning.

dirigista *sm.* supporter of state planning.

dirimente *agg.* diriment.

dirìmere *vt.* to settle.

dirimpettaio *sm.* person living just opposite.

dirimpetto *avv.* face to face, opposite.

diritta *sf.* right, right-hand: *a* —, on the right.

dirittamente *avv.* straight.

diritto *agg.* straight, upright || *rigare* —, to behave properly. ♦ **diritto** *sm.* 1. right 2. (*tassa, tributo*) due 3. (*legge*) law.

dirittura *sf.* 1. straight line 2. (*rettitudine*) uprightness 3. (*sport*) — *d'arrivo*, home stretch.

dirizzare *vt.* 1. to direct 2. (*erigere*) to raise 3. (*raddrizzare; fig.*) to put (*v. irr.*) right, to straighten.

dirizzone *sm.* inconsiderate action.

diroccamento *sm.* demolition.

diroccare *vt.* to demolish.

diroccato *agg.* 1. (*demolito*) dismantled 2. (*in rovina*) crumbled.

dirompente *agg.* disruptive.

diròmpere *vt.* 1. (*di lino, canapa ecc.*) to scutch 2. (*rompere*) to break (*v. irr.*).

dirottare *vt.* to divert. ♦ **dirottare** *vi.* to change course.

dirotto *agg.* excessive: *pianto* —, desperate crying; *piove a* —, it is pouring.

dirozzamento *sm.* 1. (*lo sbozzare*) rough-hewing 2. (*fig.*) refinement.

dirozzare *vt.* 1. (*sbozzare*) to rough-hew 2. (*fig.*) to refine.

dirugginire *vt.* to remove the rust from.

dirupamento *sm.* 1. falling down 2. (*di luogo*) abruptness.

dirupato *agg.* 1. abrupt 2. (*roccioso*) rocky.

dirupo *sm.* precipice.

disabbellire *vt.* to spoil the beauty of. ♦ **disabbellirsi** *vr.* to lose (*v. irr.*) one's beauty.

disabitato *agg.* 1. uninhabited 2. (*abbandonato*) deserted.

disabituare *vt.* to disaccustom. ♦ **disabituarsi** *vr.* to give (*v. irr.*)

up the habit of.
disaccordo *sm.* disagreement.
disacerbare *vt.* to appease.
disadatto *agg.* **1.** unfit **2.** (*che non si addice*) unbecoming.
disadornare *vt.* to disadorn.
disadorno *agg.* **1.** unadorned **2.** (*spoglio*) bare.
disaffezionarsi *vr.* to lose (*v. irr.*) one's affection (for).
disaffezionato *agg.* estranged.
disaffezione *sf.* estrangement.
disagévole *agg.* uncomfortable.
disagiatamente *avv.* uncomfortably.
disagiato *agg.* **1.** uncomfortable **2.** (*povero*) needy.
disagio *sm.* **1.** uneasiness ‖ *essere a —,* to be uneasy **2.** (*disturbo*) inconvenience **3.** (*pl.; privazioni*) privations.
disamare *vt.* to cease to love.
disàmina *sf.* examination.
disaminare *vt.* to examine carefully.
disancorarsi *vr.* **1.** to weigh anchor **2.** (*fig.*) to break (*v. irr.*) all connections (with).
disanimarsi *vr.* to lose (*v. irr.*) heart.
disappetenza *sf.* lack of appetite.
disapprèndere *vt.* to forget (*v. irr.*).
disapprovare *vt.* to disapprove (of).
disapprovazione *sf.* disapproval.
disappunto *sm.* disappointment.
disarcionare *vt.* to unsaddle.
disarmare *vt.* to disarm.
disarmato *agg.* disarmed.
disarmo *sm.* disarmament.
disarmonìa *sf.* discord.
disarmonicamente *avv.* discordantly.
disarmònico *agg.* discordant.
disarmonizzare *vt.* to disharmonize.
disarticolare *vt.* to disjoint.
disarticolazione *sf.* disjointing.
disastro *sm.* disaster.
disastroso *agg.* disastrous.
disattento *agg.* inattentive.
disattenzione *sf.* inattention: *errore di —,* a slip of the pen.
disavanzo *sm.* deficit.
disavveduto *agg.* heedless.
disavventura *sf.* **1.** mishap **2.** (*sfortuna*) misfortune.
disavvertenza *sf.* inadvertence.

disavvezzo *agg.* unaccustomed.
disazotare *vt.* to remove nitrogen from.
disborso *sm.* disbursement.
disbrigo *sm.* dispatch.
disbrogliare *vt.* to disentangle.
discacciare *vt.* to turn out.
discapitare *vi.* to suffer damage.
discàpito *sm.* disadvantage.
discàrico *sm.* **1.** discharge **2.** (*scusa*) defence.
discendente *agg.* descending. ♦
discendente *sm.* descendant.
discendenza *sf.* **1.** descent **2.** (*discendenti*) offspring.
discéndere *vt.* **1.** to descend, to go (*v. irr.*) down **2.** (*di astri*) to sink (*v. irr.*) **3.** (*di prezzi*) to fall (*v. irr.*).
discépolo *sm.* disciple.
discèrnere *vt.* **1.** to discern **2.** (*distinguere*) to distinguish.
discernibile *agg.* discernible.
discernimento *sm.* discernment.
discesa *sf.* **1.** descent **2.** (*declivio*) slope **3.** (*caduta*) fall **4.** (*invasione*) invasion.
dischiùdere *vt.* to disclose.
dischiuso *agg.* disclosed.
discinto *agg.* ungirt.
disciplina *sf.* **1.** (*materia di studio*) doctrine **2.** (*regola*) discipline.
disciplinàbile *agg.* disciplinable.
disciplinare[1] *vt.* to discipline.
disciplinare[2] *agg.* disciplinary.
disciplinarmente *avv.* with discipline.
disciplinatamente *avv.* with discipline.
disciplinato *agg.* disciplined.
disco *sm.* **1.** disk **2.** (*mus.*) record **3.** (*sport*) discus **4.** (*ferr.*) disk signal.
discòbolo *sm.* discus-thrower.
discòide *agg.* discoid.
discolo *sm.* wild boy, little scamp.
discolpa *sf.* excuse.
discolpare *vt.* to clear.
disconoscente *aff.* ungrateful.
disconoscenza *sf.* ungratitude.
disconòscere *vt.* to refuse to recognize.
disconoscimento *sm.* **1.** refusal to recognize **2.** (*ingratitudine*) ingratitude.
discontinuità *sf.* discontinuity.
discontinuo *agg.* discontinuous.
discordante *agg.* **1.** discordant **2.** (*diverso*) different **3.** (*di colori*)

clashing.

discordanza *sf.* discordance.

discordare *vi.* 1. to disagree 2. (*di colori*) to clash 3. (*di suoni*) to jar.

discorde *agg.* discordant (with).

discordemente *avv.* discordantly.

discordia *sf.* discord.

discòrrere *vi.* to talk.

discorsivo *agg.* talkative.

discorso *sm.* speech.

discostare *vt.* to shift.

discosto *agg.* far, distant. ♦ **discosto** *avv.* at some distance.

discoteca *sf.* record library.

discreditare *vt.* to discredit.

discrédito *sm.* discredit.

discrepante *agg.* differing.

discrepanza *sf.* discrepancy.

discretamente *avv.* 1. (*con discrezione*) discreetly 2. (*sufficientemente*) fairly 3. (*piuttosto*) rather.

discreto *agg.* 1. (*che ha discrezione*) discreet 2. (*moderato*) moderate 3. (*abbastanza buono*) fairly good.

discrezionale *agg.* discretionary.

discrezione *sf.* discretion.

discriminante *agg.* discriminating.

discriminare *vt.* to discriminate.

discriminazione *sf.* discrimination.

discussione *sf.* discussion.

discusso *agg.* discussed.

discùtere *vt.* to discuss.

discutìbile *agg.* questionable.

disdegnare *vt.* to disdain.

disdegno *sm.* disdain.

disdegnosamente *avv.* disdainfully.

disdegnoso *agg.* disdainful.

disdetta *sf.* 1. (*giur.*) notice of leave 2. (*sfortuna*) bad luck.

disdettare *vt.* to give (*v. irr.*) notice.

disdicévole *agg.* unbecoming.

disdire *vt.* 1. (*ritrattare*) to take (*v. irr.*) back, to retract 2. (*annullare*) to cancel.

disegnare *vt.* 1. to draw (*v. irr.*) 2. (*progettare*) to plan.

disegnatore *sm.* designer.

disegno *sm.* 1. drawing 2. (*di tessuto*) pattern 3. (*di edificio*) plan 4. (*schizzo*) sketch 5. (*fig.*) design, plan.

diseredare *vt.* to disinherit.

diseredato *agg.* 1. poor, destitute 2. (*privato di eredità*) disinherited.

disertare *vt.* 1. to desert 2. (*abbandonare*) to leave (*v. irr.*).

disertore *sm.* deserter.

diserzione *sf.* desertion.

disfacimento *sm.* 1. (*il disfare*) undoing 2. (*decadimento*) decay.

disfare *vt.* 1. to undo (*v. irr.*) 2. (*slegare*) to untie.

disfasia *sf.* dysphasia.

disfatta *sf.* defeat.

disfattismo *sm.* defeatism.

disfattista *agg. e s.* defeatist.

disfatto *agg.* 1. (*distrutto*) ruined 2. (*slegato*) undone 3. (*molto stanco*) worn out.

disfavore *sm.* disfavour.

disfida *sf.* challenge.

disfunzione *sf.* disorder.

disgelare *vt. e vi.* to thaw.

disgelo *sm.* thaw.

disgiùngere *vt.* to disjoin.

disgiungimento *sm.* disjoining.

disgiuntamente *avv.* separately.

disgiuntivamente *avv.* disjunctively.

disgiuntivo *agg.* disjunctive.

disgiunto *agg.* disjoined.

disgiunzione *sf.* disjunction.

disgrazia *sf.* 1. misfortune 2. (*sfavore*) disfavour || cadere in —, to lose (*v. irr.*) so.'s favour 3. (*fatto involontario*) accident.

disgraziatamente *avv.* unfortunately.

disgraziato *agg.* 1. unlucky, wretched 2. (*deforme*) misshapen.

disgregamento *sm.* disintegration.

disgregare *vt.* to disgregate, to break (*v. irr.*) up.

disgregazione *sf.* disgregation.

disguido *sm.* miscarriage.

disgustare *vt.* to disgust, to sicken. ♦ **disgustarsi** *vr.* to become (*v. irr.*) disgusted (with).

disgusto *sm.*, 1. disgust 2. (*avversione*) dislike.

disgustoso *agg.* disgusting.

disidratare *vt.* to dehydrate.

disidratazione *sf.* dehydration.

disillùdere *vt.* to undeceive.

disillusione *sf.* disillusion.

disilluso *agg.* undeceived, disappointed.

disimballaggio *sm.* unpacking.

disimballare *vt.* to unpack.

disimpacciare *vt.* to disembarrass.

disimparare *vt.* to forget (*v. irr.*).

disimpegnare *vt.* 1. to redeem 2. (*liberare da un impegno*) to release. ♦ **disimpegnarsi** *vr.* **1.** to disengage oneself **2.** (*cavarsela*) to manage.

disimpegno *sm.* **1.** redemption **2.** (*il liberarsi da un impegno*) disengagement.

disincagliare *vt.* to get (*v. irr.*) afloat.

disincantare *vt.* to disenchant.

disincantato *agg.* disenchanted.

disincanto *sm.* disenchantment.

disinfestare *vt.* to disinfest.

disinfettante *sm.* disinfectant.

disinfettare *vt.* to disinfect.

disinfezione *sf.* disinfection.

disingannare *vt.* to undeceive.

disinganno *sm.* **1.** undeceiving **2.** (*delusione*) disappointment.

disinnescare *vt.* to defuse.

disinnestare *vt.* to disengage.

disinnesto *sm.* disengagement, release.

disinserire *vt.* to disconnect.

disintegrare *vt.* to disintegrate.

disintegratore *sm.* disintegrator.

disintegrazione *sf.* disintegration.

disinteressare *vt.* **1.** to disinterest **2.** (*comm.*) to buy (*v. irr.*) out. ♦ **disinteressarsi** *vr.* to take (*v. irr.*) no interest (in).

disinteressato *agg.* **1.** disinterested **2.** (*altruistico*) unselfish.

disinteresse *sm.* **1.** indifference **2.** (*altruismo*) unselfishness.

disintossicare *vt.* to unpoison.

disintossicazione *sf.* unpoisoning.

disinvolto *agg.* unconstrained, free-and-easy.

disinvoltura *sf.* unconstraint, free-and-easy way.

disistima *sf.* disesteem.

disistimare *vt.* to disesteem.

dislivello *sm.* **1.** difference of level **2.** (*di acque*) rise **3.** (*di strade*) gradient **4.** (*ineguaglianza*) inequality.

dislocamento *sm.* **1.** displacement **2.** (*mil.*) dislocation.

dislocare *vt.* **1.** to displace **2.** (*mil.*) to dislocate.

dislocazione *sf.* removal, dislocation.

dismisura *sf.* excess || *a* —, excessively.

disobbedire *vi.* V. *disubbidire*.

disobbligare *vt.* to release from duty. ♦ **disobbligarsi** *vr.* to free oneself from duty.

disoccupato *agg.* unemployed. ♦

disoccupato *sm.* unemployed person.

disoccupazione *sf.* unemployment.

disonestà *sf.* **1.** dishonesty **2.** (*atto disonesto*) fraud.

disonesto *agg.* dishonest, fraudulent.

disonorante *agg.* shameful.

disonorare *vt.* to dishonour.

disonore *sm.* dishonour, shame.

disonorévole *agg.* dishonourable.

disopra *avv.* **1.** above, over **2.** (*in cima*) on top **3.** (*ai piani superiori*) upstairs. ♦ **disopra** *sm.* top, upper part. ♦ **al disopra di**, **disopra a** *prep.* above.

disordinare *vt.* to disorder.

disordinatamente *avv.* untidily.

disordinato *agg.* untidy, disorderly.

disòrdine *sm.* **1.** disorder, untidiness **2.** (*sregolatezza*) disorderliness **3.** (*tumulto*) disorder, tumult.

disorgànico *agg.* inorganic.

disorganizzare *vt.* to disorganize.

disorganizzato *agg.* disorganized.

disorganizzazione *sf.* disorganization.

disorientamento *sm.* disorientation, confusion.

disorientare *vt.* **1.** to disorientate **2.** (*sconcertare*) to bewilder.

disorientato *agg.* bewildered, puzzled.

disormeggiare *vt.* to unmoor.

disossare *vt.* to bone.

disossidante *sm.* deoxidizer.

disossidare *vt.* to deoxidize.

disossidazione *sf.* deoxidation.

disotto *avv.* **1.** below, underneath **2.** (*al piano inferiore*) downstairs. ♦ **disotto** *sm.* underside, lower part. ♦ **al disotto di**, **disotto a** *prep.* under, beneath, below.

dispaccio *sm.* dispatch.

disparato *agg.* disparate.

disparere *sm.* difference of opinion.

dìspari *agg.* odd.

disparità *sf.* disparity.

disparte *avv.* aside, apart: *starsene in* —, to stand (*v. irr.*) aside; (*fig.*) to stand aloof; *mettere in* —, to put (*v. irr.*) aside; (*per uno scopo*) to put by.

dispendio *sm.* **1.** heavy expense **2.** (*di forza, tempo*) waste.

dispendioso *agg.* expensive.

dispensa *sf.* **1.** pantry **2.** (*mobile*) sideboard **3.** (*pubblicazione perio-*

dica) number **4.** (*esenzione; eccl.*) dispensation.

dispensare *vt.* **1.** (*distribuire*) to deal (*v. irr.*) out **2.** (*esentare*) to exempt, to dispense.

dispensario *sm.* dispensary.

dispensato *agg.* exempted.

dispensatore *sm.* distributor, dispenser.

dispepsìa *sf.* dyspepsia.

dispèptico *agg.* dyspeptic.

disperare *vi.* to despair, to lose (*v. irr.*) all hope. ♦ **disperarsi** *vr.* to give (*v. irr.*) oneself up to despair.

disperatamente *avv.* desperately.

disperato *agg.* **1.** despairing **2.** (*senza speranza*) hopeless || *essere* — (*di malato*), to be far gone. ♦ **disperato** *sm.* **1.** (*miserabile*) destitute **2.** (*forsennato*) madman (*pl.* -men).

disperazione *sf.* despair.

disperdere *vt.* to disperse **2.** (*consumare*) to waste.

dispersione *sf.* **1.** dispersion **2.** (*elettr.*) leak.

dispersivo *agg.* dispersive.

disperso *agg.* missing, lost.

dispetto *sm.* **1.** spite: *a — di*, in spite of **2.** (*stizza*) vexation.

dispettoso *agg.* spiteful.

displacere [1] *vi.* **1.** to dislike || *mi dispiace*, I am sorry; (*in espressioni di cortesia*) *se non vi dispiace*, if you please **2.** (*essere sgradevole*) to be disagreeable.

displacere [2] *sm.* **1.** regret **2.** (*disapprovazione*) displeasure **3.** (*fastidio*) tròuble.

dispiegare *vt.* **1.** (*allargare*) to spread (*v. irr.*) out **2.** (*le vele*) to unfurl.

displuvio *sm.* **1.** watershed || *linea di —*, ridge **2.** (*arch.*) hip.

disponìbile *agg.* available.

disponibilità *sf.* availability.

disporre *vt.* **1.** to arrange **2.** (*preparare*) to dispose **3.** (*deliberare*) to order.

dispositivo *sm.* (*mecc.*) device.

disposizione *sf.* **1.** disposition, arrangement **2.** (*ordine*) order, direction || *a —*, at one's disposal **3.** (*inclinazione*) bent.

disposto *agg.* **1.** ready, willing **2.** (*ben disposto fisicamente*) strong.

dispòtico *agg.* despotic.

dispotismo *sm.* despotism.

dispregiativamente *avv.* disparagingly.

dispregiativo *agg.* depreciative. ♦ **dispregiativo** *sm.* (*gramm.*) pejorative.

dispregiatore *sm.* contemner.

dispregio *sm.* contempt.

disprezzàbile *agg.* despicable.

disprezzare *vt.* **1.** to despise **2.** (*considerare di poco conto*) to look down on.

disprezzo *sm.* contempt.

disputa *sf.* discussion.

disputàbile *agg.* disputable.

disputare *vi.* e *vt.* to discuss.

disquisizione *sf.* disquisition.

dissaldare *vt.* to unsolder.

dissanguamento *sm.* **1.** bleeding **2.** (*fig.*) impoverishment.

dissanguare *vt.* **1.** to bleed **2.** (*fig.*) to impoverish. ♦ **dissanguarsi** *vr.* (*fig.*) to become (*v. irr.*) impoverished.

dissanguato *agg.* **1.** bloodless **2.** (*fig.*) impoverished.

dissanguatore *sm.* (*fig.*) blood-sucker.

dissapore *sm.* disagreement.

dissecare *vt.* to dissect.

disseccamento *sm.* drying up.

disseccante *agg.* drying up. ♦ **disseccante** *sm.* desiccative.

disseccare *vt.* **1.** to dry up **2.** (*cibo*) to desiccate.

disselciare *vt.* to unpave.

disseminare *vt.* to disseminate.

disseminato *agg.* strewn.

disseminatore *agg.* disseminating. ♦ **disseminatore** *sm.* disseminator.

disseminazione *sf.* dissemination.

dissennatamente *avv.* madly.

dissennatezza *sf.* **1.** madness **2.** (*avventatezza*) rashness.

dissennato *agg.* **1.** mad **2.** (*avventato*) rash.

dissensione *sf.* dissension.

dissenso *sm.* dissent.

dissenterìa *sf.* dysentery.

dissentèrico *agg.* dysenteric.

dissentire *vi.* to dissent.

dissenziente *agg.* dissenting. ♦ **dissenziente** *sm.* dissenter.

disseppellimento *sm.* disinterment.

disseppellire *vt.* **1.** to disinter **2.** (*fig.*) to revive.

disserrare *vt.* to unfasten.

dissertare *vi.* to dissertate (on).

dissertatore *sm.* dissertator.

dissertazione *sf.* dissertation.
dissestare *vt.* 1. (*finanziariamente*) to ruin 2. (*mettere fuori posto*) to derange.
dissestato *agg.* (*di persona*) ruined.
dissesto *sm.* 1. trouble 2. (*fallimento*) bankruptcy.
dissetante *agg.* refreshing: *bibita* —, refreshing drink.
dissetare *vt.* to quench the thirst of. ♦ **dissetarsi** *vr.* 1. to quench one's thirst 2. (*bere*) to drink (*v. irr.*); (*di animali*) to water.
dissezione *sf.* dissection.
dissidente *agg.* e *sm.* dissident.
dissidenza *sf.* dissidence.
dissidio *sm.* 1. dissension, disagreement 2. (*litigio*) quarrel.
dissigillare *vt.* to unseal.
dissìmile *agg.* unlike.
dissimmetrìa *sf.* dissymetry.
dissimulare *vt.* to dissemble.
dissimulatamente *avv.* dissemblingly.
dissimulatore *sm.* dissimulator.
dissimulazione *sf.* dissimulation.
dissipare *vt.* to dissipate. ♦ **dissiparsi** *vr.* to dissipate, to vanish.
dissipatezza *sf.* dissipation.
dissipatore *sm.* waster.
dissipazione *sf.* dissipation.
dissociàbile *agg.* dissociable.
dissociare *vt.* to dissociate.
dissociazione *sf.* dissociation.
dissodamento *sm.* tillage.
dissodare *vt.* to till.
dissolùbile *agg.* dissoluble.
dissolubilità *sf.* dissolubility.
dissolutezza *sf.* dissoluteness.
dissoluto *agg.* dissolute.
dissoluzione *sf.* dissolution.
dissolvente *agg.* e *sm.* dissolvent.
dissòlvere *vt.* 1. to dissolve 2. (*disperdere*) to dispel. ♦ **dissòlversi** *vr.* to dissolve.
dissolvimento *sm.* dissolution.
dissomigliante *agg.* dissimilar (to).
dissomiglianza *sf.* dissimilarity.
dissomigliare *vi.* to be unlike. ♦ **dissomigliarsi** *vr.* to differ from.
dissonante *agg.* dissonant.
dissonanza *sf.* 1. dissonance 2. (*fig.*) discordance.
dissonare *vi.* 1. to be out of tune 2. (*fig.*) to discord (with).
dissotterramento *sm.* disinterment.
dissotterrare *vt.* to disinter.

dissuadere *vt.* to dissuade.
dissuasione *sf.* dissuasion.
distaccamento *sm.* 1. detaching 2. (*mil.*) detachment.
distaccare *vt.* to detach. ♦ **distaccarsi** *vr.* to come (*v. irr.*) off.
distacco *sm.* 1. detaching 2. (*partenza*) leaving 3. (*indifferenza*) unconcern.
distante *agg.* distant. ♦ **distante** *avv.* far, far off, far away.
distanza *sf.* distance.
distanziare *vt.* 1. to space 2. (*lasciare indietro*) to distance.
distanziato *agg.* 1. spaced 2. (*sport*) outdistanced.
distare *vi.* to be far: *quanto dista?*, how far is it?
distèndere *vt.* 1. (*allungare*) to stretch 2. (*spalmare*) to spread (*v. irr.*) 3. (*porre, stendere*) to lay (*v. irr.*). ♦ **distèndersi** *vr.* 1. to spread (*v. irr.*) 2. (*sdraiarsi*) to lie (*v. irr.*) down 3. (*rilassarsi*) to relax.
distensione *sf.* 1. (*di nervi, tensione*) relaxation 2. (*pol.*) distension.
distensivo *agg.* relaxing.
distesa *sf.* expanse || *a* —, continuously.
distesamente *avv.* diffusely.
disteso *agg.* 1. (*teso*) extended 2. (*giacente*) lying 3. (*esteso*) extensive || *per* —, diffusely.
distico *sm.* couplet.
distillare *vt.* to distil.
distillato *agg.* distilled. ♦ **distillato** *sm.* distillate.
distillatoio *sm.* still.
distillatore *sm.* distiller.
distillazione *sf.* distillation.
distillerìa *sf.* distillery.
distinguere *vt.* 1. to distinguish 2. (*contrassegnare*) to mark.
distinta *sf.* list.
distintivo *agg.* distinctive. ♦ **distintivo** *sm.* badge.
distinto *agg.* 1. distinct 2. (*garbato*) distinguished.
distinzione *sf.* 1. distinction 2. (*riguardo*) regard 3. (*raffinatezza*) refinement.
distogliere *vt.* 1. (*dissuadere*) to dissuade 2. (*distrarre*) to divert. ♦ **distògliersi** *vr.* to be distracted.
distorsione *sf.* distortion.
distrarre *vt.* 1. (*distogliere*) to divert 2. (*divertire*) to entertain.

distrattamente *avv.* **1.** absent-mindedly **2.** (*inavvertitamente*) inadvertently.

distratto *agg.* **1.** absent-minded **2.** (*disattento*) inattentive.

distrazione *sf.* **1.** absent-mindedness **2.** (*disattenzione*) inattention **3.** (*divertimento*) recreation.

distretta *sf.* urgent need.

distretto *sm.* district || — *militare*, recruiting centre.

distrettuale *agg.* district.

distribuibile *agg.* distributable.

distribuire *vt.* to distribute.

distributivo *agg.* e *sm.* distributive.

distributore *agg.* distributing. ♦ **distributore** *sm.* distributor || — *di benzina*, petrol pump.

distribuzione *sf.* distribution.

districare *vt.* to disentangle.

distruggere *vt.* **1.** to destroy **2.** (*struggere*) to consume. ♦ **distruggersi** *vr.* (*consumarsi*) to pine (away).

distruggibile *agg.* destroyable.

distruttivo *agg.* destroying.

distrutto *agg.* destroyed.

distruttore *agg.* destroying. ♦ **distruttore** *sm.* destroyer.

distruzione *sf.* destruction.

disturbare *vt.* to disturb.

disturbato *agg.* **1.** disturbed **2.** (*indisposto*) unwell.

disturbatore *sm.* disturber.

disturbo *sm.* **1.** trouble, inconvenience **2.** (*malattia*) trouble, illness **3.** (*radio*) disturbance.

disubbidiente *agg.* disobedient.

disubbidienza *sf.* disobedience.

disubbidire *vi.* to disobey.

disuguaglianza *sf.* **1.** inequality **2.** (*di terreno*) unevenness.

disuguale *agg.* **1.** unequal **2.** (*irregolare*) irregular **3.** (*differente*) different.

disumanamente *avv.* inhumanly.

disumanare *vt.* to divest of humanity.

disumanità *sf.* inhumanity.

disumano *agg.* inhuman.

disumidire *vt.* to dry.

disunione *sf.* disunion.

disunire *vt.* to disunite. ♦ **disunirsi** *vr.* to become (*v. irr.*) disunited.

disunito *agg.* disunited.

disusare *vt.* to disuse.

disusato *agg.* disused.

disuso *sm.* disuse.

ditale *sm.* thimble.

ditata *sf.* finger-mark.

ditirambico *agg.* dithyrambic.

ditirambo *sm.* dithyramb.

dito *sm.* **1.** finger **2.** (*del piede* toe.

ditta *sf.* firm.

dittafono *sm.* dictaphone.

dittatore *sm.* dictator.

dittatoriale *agg.* dictatorial.

dittatorio *agg.* dictatorial.

dittatura *sf.* dictatorship.

dittico *sm.* diptych.

dittongo *sm.* diphthong.

diuresi *sf.* diuresis.

diuretico *agg.* diuretic.

diurno *agg.* diurnal, daytime.

diuturnamente *avv.* for a long time.

diuturno *agg.* diuturnal.

diva *sf.* **1.** goddess **2.** (*cine*) star.

divagare *vi.* to wander **2.** (*divertire*) to amuse. ♦ **divagarsi** *vr.* **1.** to be distracted **2.** (*divertirsi*) to amuse oneself.

divagazione *sf.* digression.

divampare *vi.* to blaze.

divano *sm.* divan, sofa.

divaricamento *sm.* straddle.

divaricare *vt.* to open wide || — *le gambc*, to part one's legs wide.

divario *sm.* difference.

divedere *vt.* **1.** (*nella loc. avv.*) *dare a* —, to show (*v. irr.*) clearly **2.** (*dar a credere*) to make (*v. irr.*) believe.

divellere *vt.* to uproot.

divenire[1] *vi.* **1.** to become (*v. irr.*) **2.** (*mutarsi lentamente*) to grow (*v. irr.*).

divenire[2] *sm.* becoming: *l'essere e il* —, being and becoming.

diverbio *sm.* quarrel.

divergente *agg.* divergent.

divergenza *sf.* divergence.

divergere *vi.* **1.** to diverge **2.** (*scostarsi*) to wander.

diversamente *avv.* **1.** differently **2.** (*altrimenti*) otherwise.

diversificare *vt.* to diversify. ♦ **diversificarsi** *vr.* to differ.

diversione *sf.* diversion.

diversità *sf.* diversity.

diversivo *agg.* **1.** deviating **2.** (*che distrae*) diverting. ♦ **diversivo** *sm.* diversion, distraction.

diverso *agg.* different.

divertente *agg.* amusing.

divertimento sm. amusement.

divertire vt. to amuse, to entertain ♦ **divertirsi** vr. to enjoy oneself, to have a good time.

divezzamento sm. weaning.

divezzare vt. to wean.

dividendo sm. dividend.

divìdere vt. 1. to divide 2. (condividere) to share.

divieto sm. prohibition.

divinamente avv. divinely.

divinare vt. to divine.

divinatore sm. diviner.

divinatorio agg. divinatory.

divinazione sf. divination.

divincolarsi vr. to wriggle.

divinità sf. divinity.

divinizzare vt. to deify.

divino agg. divine.

divisa sf. 1. uniform 2. (valuta) currency.

divisare vt. to plan.

divisìbile agg. divisible.

divisibilità sf. divisibility.

divisionale agg. divisional.

divisione sf. 1. division 2. (amm.) department.

divisionismo sm. pointillism.

divisionista s. pointillist.

divismo sm. stardom, star worship.

diviso agg. 1. divided 2. (separato) separated 3. (condiviso) shared.

divisore sm. divisor.

divisorio agg. dividing.

divo sm. 1. deity 2. (cine) star.

divorare vt. to devour.

divoratore agg. devouring.

divorziare vi. to divorce, to be divorced.

divorziato agg. divorced. ♦ **divorziato** sm. divorcee.

divorzio sm. divorce (anche fig.).

divulgàbile agg. that may be divulged.

divulgare vt. to spread (v. irr.).

divulgativo agg. divulging.

divulgatore sm. divulger.

divulgazione sf. divulgation, spreading.

dizionario sm. dictionary.

dizionarista s. lexicographer.

dizione sf. 1. diction 2. (pronuncia) pronunciation.

do sm. (mus.) C.

doccia sf. shower.

docente agg. teaching. ♦ **docente** sm. teacher ‖ libero —, fully established university lecturer.

docenza sf. teaching.

dòcile agg. docile.

docilità sf. docility.

documentare vt. to document.

documentario sm. documentary.

documentarista s. documentary film-maker.

documentato agg. documented.

documentazione sf. 1. documentation 2. pl. (documenti) papers.

documento sm. document.

dodecaedro sm. dodecahedron.

dodecafonìa sf. dodecaphony.

dodecafònico agg. dodecaphonic.

dodecàgono sm. dodecagon.

dodecasillabo sm. dodecasyllable.

dodicèsimo agg. twelfth.

dòdici agg. twelve.

doga sf. stave.

dogana sf. customs (pl.).

doganale agg. customs (attr.): dichiarazione —, customs entry.

doganiere sm. customs officer.

doge sm. doge.

doglia sf. 1. sharp pains 2. (pl., med.) throes.

dogma sm. dogma.

dogmàtico agg. dogmatic(al).

dogmatismo sm. dogmatism.

dolce agg. 1. sweet 2. (mite) mild 3. (tec.) soft. ♦ **dolce** sm. 1. sweet 2. (torta) cake.

dolcezza sf. 1. sweetness 2. (di clima) mildness.

dolciario agg. confectionary.

dolciastro agg. sweetish.

dolcificare vt. 1. to sweeten 2. (fig.) to mitigate.

dolcificazione sf. sweetening.

dolciumi sm. pl. sweets.

dolente agg. 1. afflicted, grieved 2. (spiacente) sorry.

dolere vi. 1. to ache 2. (rincrescere) to regret. ♦ **dolersi** vr. to regret.

dolicocèfalo agg. dolichocephalic.

dòllaro sm. dollar.

dolmen sm. dolmen.

dolo sm. fraud.

dolomite sf. dolomite.

dolomìtico agg. dolomitic.

dolorante agg. aching.

dolore sm. 1. pain, ache 2. (fig.) sorrow, grief.

dolorosamente avv. 1. painfully 2. (morale) sadly.

doloroso agg. 1. painful 2. (che causa dolore) grievous.

doloso agg. fraudulent.

domàbile agg. tamable.

domànda sf. 1. question, request

2. (*richiesta scritta*) application.

domandare *vt.* to ask (so. for sthg.). ♦ **domandarsi** *vr.* to wonder.

domani *avv.* tomorrow.

domare *vt.* **1.** to tame **2.** (*sottomettere*) to subdue.

domatore *sm.* tamer.

domattina *avv.* tomorrow morning.

doménica *sf.* Sunday.

domenicale *agg.* Sunday (*attr.*).

domenicano *agg.* dominican.

domèstica *sf.* maid.

domèstico *agg. e sm.* domestic || *lavori domestici*, household duties.

domiciliare *agg.* domiciliary.

domiciliarsi *vr.* to settle (in).

domiciliato *agg.* resident, living.

domicilio *sm.* **1.** house, dwelling **2.** (*giur.*) domicile.

dominante *agg.* dominant.

dominare *vt.* to dominate.

dominatore *sm.* ruler.

dominazione *sf.* domination.

dominio *sm.* **1.** domination **2.** (*territorio*) dominion **3.** (*giur.*) domain || *di — pubblico*, known to everybody.

dòmino *sm.* domino.

donare *vt.* to give (*v. irr.*) ♦ **donare** *vi.* (*addirsi*) to suit.

donatore *sm.* donor.

donazione *sf.* **1.** donation **2.** (*somma elargita per uno scopo*) grant.

donchisciottesco *agg.* quixotic.

donde *avv.* whence, from where || *ne ha ben —*, he has good reason for it.

dondolamento *sm.* swinging.

dondolare *vt. e vi.* to swing (*v. irr.*) ♦ **dondolarsi** *vr.* to swing, to rock.

dondolìo *sm.* swinging.

dòndolo *sm.* **1.** (*altalena*) swing || *a —*, rocking.

donna *sf.* woman (*pl.* women).

donnaiolo *sm.* ladies' man (*pl.* men).

donnesco *agg.* womanlike.

dònnola *sf.* weasel.

dono *sm.* gift.

donzella *sf.* damsel.

dopo *avv.* **1.** (*di luogo*) after, next **2.** (*dietro*) behind **3.** (*di tempo*) after, then **4.** (*più tardi*) later. ♦ **dopo** *prep.* (*di luogo e tempo*) after.

dopodomani *avv.* the day after tomorrow.

dopoguerra *sm.* post-war period.

dopopranzo *sm.* afternoon.

dopotutto *avv.* after all.

doppiaggio *sm.* (*cine*) dubbing.

doppiamente *avv.* **1.** doubly **2.** (*con inganno*) deceitfully.

doppiare *vt.* **1.** to double **2.** (*cine*) to dub.

doppiato *agg.* **1.** doubled **2.** (*cine*) dubbed.

doppiatura *sf.* doubling.

doppietta *sf.* double-barrelled gun.

doppiezza *sf.* **1.** doubleness **2.** (*ambiguità*) double-dealing.

doppio *agg.* **1.** double **2.** (*ambiguo*) double-faced. ♦ **doppio** *sm.* twice as much, twice as many.

doppiofondo *sm.* double bottom.

doppione *sm.* **1.** double **2.** (*di parola*) doublet.

doppiopetto *sm.* double-breasted.

dorare *vt.* to gild.

dorato *agg.* **1.** gilded **2.** (*color oro*) golden.

doratore *sm.* gilder.

doratura *sf.* gilding.

dòrico *agg.* doric.

dorìfora *sf.* potato-beetle.

dormicchiare *vi.* to doze.

dormiente *agg.* sleeping. ♦ **dormiente** *sm.* sleeper.

dormiglione *sm.* sleepy-head.

dormire *vi.* **1.** to sleep (*v. irr.*) || *— tra due guanciali*, to set (*v. irr.*) one's mind at rest **2.** (*fig.*) to remain inactive.

dormita *sf.* sleep.

dormitorio *sm.* dormitory.

dormiveglia *sm.* drowsiness.

dorsale *agg.* dorsal: *spina —*, backbone.

dorso *sm.* **1.** back **2.** (*di monte*) ridge.

dosàbile *agg.* measurable.

dosaggio *sm.* dosage.

dosare *vt.* to proportion: *— le parole*, to weigh one's words.

dosatura *sf.* dosage.

dose *sf.* dose: *una buona — di*, a good deal of.

dossale *sm.* dossal.

dosso *sm.* back: *togliersi di —*, to take (*v. irr.*) off.

dotare *vt.* **1.** to give (*v. irr.*) a dowry **2.** (*fornire di una rendita*) to endow **3.** (*fornire*) to provide (with).

dotato *agg.* **1.** gifted (with) **2.** (*e-*

quipaggiato) provided (with).
dotazione *sf.* endowment.
dote *sf.* 1. dowry 2. (*qualità*) endowment.
dotto[1] *agg.* learned. ♦ **dotto** *sm.* scholar.
dotto[2] *sm.* (*anat.*) duct.
dottorale *agg.* doctoral.
dottorato *sm.* doctorate.
dottore *sm.* 1. doctor 2. (*laureato*) graduate.
dottoressa *sf.* 1. (*laureata*) graduate 2. (*in medicina*) lady doctor.
dottrina *sf.* doctrine.
dottrinale *agg.* doctrinal.
dottrinario *sm.* doctrinaire.
dottrinarismo *sm.* doctrinairism.
dove *avv.* where.
dovere[1] *vi.* 1. (*obbligo*) must (*v. dif.*): *devi lavorare*, you must work 2. to have to 3. (*possibilità, predestinazione*) to be to: *doveva diventare un grande scrittore*, he was to become a great writer 4. (*devo?, dobbiamo?, nel senso di: vuoi che?*) shall (*v. dif.*): *devo aprire la finestra?*, shall I open the window? 5. (*al condizionale*) ought to, should (*v. dif.*): *dovresti essere gentile*, you ought to be kind; *dovremmo partire*, we should leave 6. (*al congiuntivo*) should, were to: *se dovesse venire*, if he should come, if he were to come 7. (*essere obbligati*) to be obliged, to be forced 8. (*essere da attribuire, dover arrivare*) to be due: *lo si deve al mio ritardo*, this is due to my being late; *il treno deve arrivare alle 4*, the train is due at 4 a.m. ♦ **dovere** *vt.* (*essere debitore in tutti i sensi*) to owe: *ti devo 1000 lire*, I owe you one thousand lire; *ti devo la vita*, I owe you my life.
dovere[2] *sm.* duty: *fare il proprio* —, to do (*v. irr.*) one's duty.
doverosamente *avv.* dutifully.
doveroso *agg.* dutiful.
dovizia *sf.* plenty.
dovizioso *agg.* abundant.
dovunque *avv.* 1. everywhere 2. (*seguito da verbo*) wherever.
dovuto *agg.* 1. due 2. (*equo*) fair. ♦ **dovuto** *sm.* due.
dozzina *sf.* dozen.
dozzinale *agg.* cheap, common.
draconiano *agg.* draconian.
draga *sf.* dredger.

dragaggio *sm.* dredging.
dragamine *sm.* mine-sweeper.
dragare *vt.* to dredge.
draglia *sf.* stay.
drago *sm.* dragon.
dragona *sf.* sword-knot.
dragone *sm.* dragon.
dramma *sm.* drama.
drammàtica *sf.* dramatics.
drammaticamente *avv.* dramatically.
drammaticità *sf.* tragicalness.
drammàtico *agg.* dramatic.
drammatizzare *vt.* to dramatise.
drammaturgìa *sf.* dramaturgy.
drammaturgo *sm.* dramatist.
drappeggiare *vt.* to drape.
drappeggio *sm.* draping.
drappello *sm.* squad.
drapperìa *sf.* drapery.
drappo *sm.* cloth.
dràstico *agg.* drastic.
drenaggio *sm.* drainage.
drenare *vt.* to drain.
drìade *sf.* 1. (*mit.*) dryad 2. (*bot.*) dryas (*pl.* -ades).
dribblare *vt.* to dribble.
drìtta *sf.* 1. right hand, right 2. (*mar.*) starboard.
dritto *agg.* 1. (*non storto*) straight 2. (*eretto, onesto*) upright. ♦ **dritto** *sm.* right side.
drizza *sf.* halyard.
drizzare *vt.* to straighten.
droga *sf.* 1. drug 2. (*spezia*) spices (*pl.*).
drogare *vt.* 1. to drug 2. (*condire*) to spice.
drogherìa *sf.* grocery.
droghiere *sm.* grocer.
dromedario *sm.* dromedary.
drùido *sm.* druid.
drupa *sf.* drupe.
dualismo *sm.* dualism.
dualità *sf.* duality.
dubbiezza *sf.* dubiousness.
dubbio *sm.* doubt: *mettere in* —, to question. ♦ **dubbio** *agg.* dubious.
dubbioso *agg.* doubtful.
dubitare *vi.* to doubt.
dubitativo *agg.* dubitative.
duca *sm.* duke.
ducale *agg.* ducal.
ducato *sm.* 1. dukedom 2. (*moneta*) ducat.
duchessa *sf.* duchess.
due *agg.* two.
duecentèsimo *agg.* two hundredth.

duecentesco *agg.* thirteenth century (*attr.*).

duecento *sm.* two hundred || *il* —, the thirteenth century.

duellare *vi.* to duel.

duello *sm.* duel: — *all'ultimo sangue*, duel to the death.

duetto *sm.* duet.

duna *sf.* dune.

dunque *cong.* **1.** (*perciò*) therefore **2.** (*rafforzativo*) well, then. ◆ **dunque** *sm. venire al* —, to come (*v. irr.*) to the point.

duodenale *agg.* duodenal.

duodeno *sm.* duodenum.

duomo *sm.* cathedral.

duplicare *vt.* to duplicate.

duplicato *sm.* duplicate.

dùplice *agg.* twofold.

duplicità *sf.* double-dealing.

durabilità *sf.* durability.

duralluminio *sm.* duralumin.

durante *prep.* during.

durare *vi.* **1.** to last **2.** (*perseverare*) to persist **3.** (*resistere*) to hold (*v. irr.*) out. ◆ **durare** *vt.* to endure || *chi la dura la vince*, slow and steady wins the race.

durata *sf.* **1.** duration, length **2.** (*periodo*) term **3.** (*di un oggetto*) endurance.

duraturo *agg.* lasting.

durévole *agg.* durable.

durezza *sf.* **1.** hardness **2.** (*rigidità*) stiffness.

duro *agg.* **1.** hard **2.** (*di voce*) harsh || *avere il sonno* —, to sleep (*v. irr.*) like a log; *avere la testa dura*, to be a block-head, to be stubborn.

durone *sm.* hard skin.

dùttile *agg.* ductile.

duttilità *sf.* ductility.

E

e *cong.* and: *e... e*, both... and.

ebanista *sm.* cabinet-maker.

ebanisteria *sf.* **1.** (*bottega*) cabinet-maker's shop **2.** (*arte*) cabinet-making.

ebanite *sf.* ebonite.

èbano *sm.* ebony.

ebbene *cong.* well: —*?*, what about it?

ebbrezza *sf.* **1.** drunkenness **2.** (*fig.*) elation.

ebbro *agg.* **1.** drunken **2.** (*fig.*) mad.

ebdomadario *agg.* weekly. ◆ **ebdomadario** *sm.* weekly paper.

èbete *agg.* idiotic. ◆ **èbete** *sm.* idiot.

ebollizione *sf.* boiling.

ebràico *agg.* Hebrew.

ebreo *agg.* Hebrew, Jewish. ◆ **ebreo** *sm.* Hebrew, Jew.

ecatombe *sf.* massacre.

eccedente *agg.* excessive, in excess (*pred.*). ◆ **eccedente** *sm.* (*comm.*) exceeding.

eccedenza *sf.* excess, surplus: — *di peso*, overweight.

eccèdere *vt.* to exceed. ◆ **eccèdere** *vi.* to go (*v. irr.*) too far.

eccellente *agg.* excellent.

eccellenza *sf.* **1.** excellence **2.** (*titolo*) excellency.

eccèllere *vi.* to excel.

eccelso *agg.* sublime.

eccentricità *sf.* eccentricity.

eccèntrico *agg.* eccentric.

eccepire *vi.* to object.

eccessivo *agg.* excessive.

eccesso *sm.* excess.

eccètera *sm.* et cetera (*abbr.* etc.), and so on.

eccetto *prep.* except, but, save. ◆ **eccetto che** *cong.* **1.** except that **2.** (*purché*) provided that.

eccettuare *vt.* to except.

eccettuato *agg.* excluded.

eccezionale *agg.* exceptional.

eccezione *sf.* exception.

ecchìmosi *sf.* bruise.

eccidio *sm.* bloodshed.

eccitàbile *agg.* excitable.

eccitabilità *sf.* excitability.

eccitamento *sm.* excitement.

eccitante *agg.* e *sm.* excitant.

eccitare *vt.* to excite. ◆ **eccitarsi** *vr.* to get (*v. irr.*) excited.

eccitatore *agg.* excitative. ◆ **eccitatore** *sm.* exciter.

eccitazione *sf.* excitement.

ecclesiàstico *agg.* ecclesiastical.

ecco *avv.* here, there (*in unione con le voci del verbo* to be *al pres. ind.*): — *il mio cappello!*, here is my hat! || — *tutto*, that's all; *quand'* —, when suddenly.

eccome *inter.* and how!

echeggiare *vi.* to echo (with sthg.).

echinoderma *sm.* echinoderm.

eclèttico *agg.* e *sm.* eclectic.

eclettismo *sm.* eclecticism.
eclissare *vt.* 1. to eclipse 2. (*fig.*) to overshadow.
eclisse, eclissi *sf.* eclipse.
eclìttica *sf.* ecliptic.
eclìttico *agg.* ecliptic.
eco *sf.* echo.
economato *sm.* 1. steward's office 2. (*in università*) bursar's office.
economìa *sf.* 1. economy 2. (*scienza*) economics.
econòmico *agg.* 1. economic 2. (*a buon prezzo*) cheap.
economista *s.* economist.
economizzare *vt.* to economize.
ecònomo *agg.* economical. ♦ **ecònomo** *sm.* 1. steward 2. (*di università*) bursar.
ecumènico *agg.* ecumenical.
eczema *sm.* eczema.
edema *sm.* oedema.
eden *sm.* Eden.
èdera *sf.* ivy.
edìcola *sf.* newspaper kiosk.
edicolista *sm.* news-agent.
edificante *agg.* edifying.
edificare *vt.* 1. to build (*v. irr.*) (up) 2. (*fig.*) to edify.
edificatore *sm.* 1. builder 2. (*fig.*) edifier.
edificazione *sf.* 1. building 2. (*fig.*) edification.
edificio *sm.* building.
edile *agg.* building: *perito* —, master-builder. ♦ **edile** *sm.* (*stor. romana*) aedile.
edilizia *sf.* building industry.
edilizio *agg.* building (*attr.*).
èdito *agg.* published.
editore *sm.* publisher.
editorìa *sf.* book industry.
editoriale *agg. e sm.* editorial.
editrice *agg.*: *casa* —, publishing house.
editto *sm.* edict.
edizione *sf.* edition, issue.
edonismo *sm.* hedonism.
edonista *s.* hedonist.
edotto *agg.* aware: *rendere* —, to inform.
educanda *sf.* boarding-school girl.
educandato *sm.* girls' boarding--school.
educare *vt.* 1. to educate 2. (*allevare*) to bring (*v. irr.*) up.
educativo *agg.* educational.
educato *agg.* well-bred, polite.
educatore *sm.* educator.
educazione *sf.* 1. education 2.

(*buone maniere*) good manners (*pl.*).
edulcorare *vt.* to edulcorate.
efebo *sm.* ephebe.
efèlide *sf.* freckle.
effemèride *sf.* ephemeris (*pl.* -ides).
effeminare *vt.* to effeminate. ♦ **effeminarsi** *vr.* to become (*v. irr.*) effeminate.
effeminatezza *sf.* effeminacy.
efferatezza *sf.* brutality.
efferato *agg.* brutal.
effervescente *agg.* sparkling.
effervescenza *sf.* effervescence.
effettivamente *avv.* actually, indeed.
effettivo *agg.* actual.
effetto *sm.* 1. effect, result ‖ *in effetti*, as a matter of fact 2. (*comm.*) bill.
effettuàbile *agg.* feasible.
effettuare *vt.* to carry out: — *un piano*, to carry out a plan. ♦ **effettuarsi** *vr.* (*aver luogo*) to take (*v. irr.*) place.
effettuazione *sf.* accomplishment.
efficace *agg.* effective, efficacious.
efficacia *sf.* efficacy.
efficiente *agg.* efficient.
efficienza *sf.* efficiency.
effigiare *vt.* to portray.
effigie *sf.* image.
effìmera *sf.* (*fam.*) mayfly.
effìmero *agg.* ephemeral.
effluvio *sm.* exhalation.
effòndere *vt.* to pour forth. ♦ **effòndersi** *vr.* to spread (*v. irr.*) (about).
effrazione *sf.* (*giur.*) house-breaking, burglary.
effusione *sf.* 1. shedding 2. (*cordialità*) cordiality 3. (*pl., manifestazioni*) effusions.
effusivo *agg.* effusive.
egemonìa *sf.* hegemony.
egemònico *agg.* hegemonic.
ègida *sf.* 1. aegis 2. (*fig.*) protection.
egiziano *agg. e sm.* Egyptian.
egli *pron.* he: — *stesso*, he himself.
ègloga *sf.* eclogue.
egocèntrico *agg.* egocentric. ♦ **egocèntrico** *sm.* egocentric man.
egocentrismo *sm.* egocentrism.
egoismo *sm.* selfishness.
egoista *agg. e sm.* egoist.
egotismo *sm.* self-conceit.
egregiamente *avv.* eminently.
egregio *agg.* eminent ‖ (*nelle lettere*) — *Signore*, Dear Sir.

eguaglianza, eguagliare, eguale ecc. V. *uguaglianza, uguagliare, uguale* ecc.

egualità *sf.* equality.

eiaculare *vi.* to ejaculate.

eiaculazione *sf.* ejaculation.

eiezione *sf.* ejection.

elaborare *vt.* to elaborate.

elaborato *agg.* elaborate.

elaborazione *sf.* **1.** elaboration **2.** (*di piano*) formulation.

elargire *vt.* to lavish.

elargizione *sf.* donation.

elasticità *sf.* **1.** elasticity **2.** (*agilità*) nimbleness.

elasticizzare *vt.* to make (*v. irr.*) elastic.

elàstico *agg.* **1.** elastic **2.** (*agile*) nimble. ♦ **elàstico** *sm.* rubber band.

elce *sm.* ilex.

elefante *sm.* elephant.

elefantesco *agg.* elephantine.

elefantìasi *sf.* elephantiasis.

elegante *agg.* elegant, smart.

eleganza *sf.* smartness.

elèggere *vt.* **1.** to elect **2.** (*nominare*) to appoint.

eleggìbile *agg.* eligible.

eleggibilità *sf.* eligibility.

elegìa *sf.* elegy.

elegìaco *agg.* elegiac.

elementare *agg.* elementary: *scuola* —, primary school.

elemento *sm.* **1.** element **2.** (*componente*) component **3.** (*pl., rudimenti*) rudiments **4.** (*persona*) person.

elemòsina *sf.* alms: *chiedere l'*—, to beg.

elemosinare *vt. e vi.* to beg (for).

elencare *vt.* to list.

elenco *sm.* list: — *telefonico*, telephone directory.

elettivo *agg.* elective.

eletto *agg.* elect, chosen.

elettorale *agg.* electoral.

elettorato *sm.* electorate.

elettore *sm.* voter.

elettràuto *sm.* **1.** (*officina*) car electrical repairs (*pl.*) **2.** (*meccanico*) car electrician.

elettricista *sm.* electrician.

elettricità *sf.* electricity.

elèttrico *agg.* electric.

elettrificare *vt.* to electrify.

elettrificazione *sf.* electrification.

elettrizzare *vt.* to electrify.

elettrocalamita *sf.* electro-magnet.

elettrocardiogramma *sm.* electrocardiogram.

elettrodinàmica *sf.* electrodynamics.

elèttrodo *sm.* electrode.

elettrodomèstici *sm. pl.* electrical household appliances.

elettrògeno *agg.* generating electricity.

elettròlisi *sf.* electrolysis.

elettromagnètico *agg.* electro-magnetic.

elettromotore *sm.* dynamo.

elettromotrice *sf.* electric rail car.

elettrone *sm.* electron.

elettrònica *sf.* electronics.

elettrònico *agg.* electronic.

elettrotècnica *sf.* electrical technology.

elettrotreno *sm.* electric train.

elevamento *sm.* elevation.

elevare *vt.* **1.** to elevate **2.** (*erigere*) to erect **3.** (*mat.*) to raise. ♦ **elevarsi** *vr.* to rise (*v. irr.*).

elevatezza *sf.* loftiness.

elevato *agg.* elevated, high.

elevatore *sm.* elevator.

elevazione *sf.* **1.** elevation **2.** (*l'elevare*) rising **3.** (*mat.*) raising.

elezione *sf.* election.

èlica *sf.* **1.** (*aer.*) propeller **2.** (*mar.*) screw.

elicoidale *agg.* helicoidal.

elicòttero *sm.* helicopter.

elìdere *vt.* to annul. ♦ **elidersi** *vr. rec.* to annul each other.

eliminare *vt.* to eliminate. ♦ **eliminarsi** *vr.* to be eliminated.

eliminatoria *sf.* preliminary heat.

eliminazione *sf.* elimination, expulsion.

elio *sm.* helium.

eliocèntrico *agg.* heliocentric.

eliografìa *sf.* heliography.

elioterapìa *sf.* heliotherapy.

eliotipìa *sf.* heliotypy.

eliporto *sm.* heliport.

elisione *sf.* elision.

elisìr *sm.* elixir.

èlitra *sf.* elytrum (*pl.* -ra).

ella *pron. she:* — *stessa*, she herself.

ellènico *agg.* Hellenic.

ellenismo *sm.* Hellenism.

ellenista *s.* Hellenist.

ellisse *sf.* ellipse.

ellissi *sf.* ellipsis (*pl.* -ses).

ellìttico *sm.* elliptic(al).

elmetto *sm.* helmet.

elmo *sm.* helmet.

elocuzione *sf.* elocution.

elogiàbile *agg.* praiseworthy.

elogiare *vt.* to eulogize, to praise.

elogiatore *sm.* eulogist.

elogio *sm.* eulogy, praise.

eloquente *agg.* eloquent.

eloquenza *sf.* eloquence.

elucubrare *vt.* to lucubrate: — *su, intorno a qc.*, to lucubrate on, about sthg.

elucubrazione *sf.* lucubration.

elùdere *vt.* to elude.

elusivo *agg.* elusive.

elvètico *agg.* Helvetic.

elzeviro *sm.* 1. elzevir 2. *(giorn.)* leading literary article.

emaciare *vt.* to emaciate. ♦ **emaciarsi** *vr.* to become (*v. irr.*) emaciated.

emaciato *agg.* emaciated.

emanare *vt.* 1. to issue 2. *(vapori, profumi)* to exhale.

emanazione *sf.* emanation.

emancipare *vt.* to emancipate.

emancipato *agg.* emancipated.

emancipazione *sf.* emancipation.

emàtico *agg.* haematic.

ematoma *sm.* haematoma (*pl. -ata*).

ematosi *sf.* haematosis.

embargo *sm.* embargo.

emblema *sm.* 1. emblem 2. *(simbolo)* symbol.

emblemàtico *agg.* emblematic.

embolìa *sf.* embolism.

èmbolo *sm.* embolus (*pl. -li*).

embrionale *agg.* embryonic.

embrione *sm.* embryo.

emendamento *sm.* 1. amendment 2. *(correzione)* emendation.

emendare *vt.* 1. to amend 2. *(correggere)* to emend.

emergenza *sf.* emergency.

emèrgere *vi.* 1. to emerge 2. *(fig.)* to emerge, to appear.

emèrito *agg.* emeritus.

emeroteca *sf.* newspaper library.

emersione *sf.* emersion.

eméttere *vt.* 1. to emit 2. *(di suono)* to utter 3. *(emanare)* to deliver 4. *(banconote)* to issue.

emiciclo *sm.* hemicycle.

emicrania *sf.* headache.

emigrante *agg. e sm.* emigrant.

emigrare *vi.* to emigrate.

emigrato *sm.* emigrant.

emigrazione *sf.* emigration.

eminente *agg.* outstanding, eminent.

eminenza *sf.* eminence.

emiro *sm.* emir.

emisfèrico *agg.* hemispheric(al).

emisfero *sm.* hemisphere.

emissario *sm.* emissary.

emissione *sf.* 1. emission 2. *(econ.)* issue.

emistichìo *sm.* hemistich.

emittente *agg.* issuing || *stazione* — *(radio)*, broadcasting station.

emofilìa *sf.* haemophilia.

emoglobina *sf.* haemoglobin.

emolliente *agg.* emollient.

emolumento *sm.* emolument.

emorragìa *sf.* haemorrhage.

emorròidi *sf. pl.* haemorrhoids.

emòstasi *sf.* haemostasis.

emostàtico *agg.* haemostatic.

emoteca *sf.* blood bank.

emotività *sf.* emotionality.

emotivo *agg.* emotional.

emottisi *sf.* haemoptysis.

emozionante *agg.* touching, exciting, thrilling.

emozionare *vt.* to move. ♦ **emozionarsi** *vr.* to get (*v. irr.*) excited.

emozione *sf.* emotion, thrill.

empiastro *sm.* plaster.

empietà *sf.* impiety.

empio *agg.* impious.

empire *vt.* to fill.

empìrico *agg. e sm.* empiric.

empirismo *sm.* empiricism.

emporio *sm.* department store.

emulare *vt.* to emulate.

emulazione *sf.* emulation.

èmulo *sm.* rival.

emulsionare *vt.* to emulsify.

emulsione *sf.* emulsion.

encefalite *sf.* encephalitis.

encèfalo *sm.* encephalon (*pl. -ala*).

encìclica *sf.* encyclic.

enciclopedìa *sf.* encyclopaedia.

enciclopèdico *agg.* encyclopaedic.

enclìtico *agg.* enclitic.

encomiàbile *agg.* praiseworthy.

encomiare *vt.* to commend.

encomio *sm.* panegyric.

endecasìllabo *agg.* hendecasyllabic. ♦ **endecasìllabo** *sm.* hendecasyllable.

endèmico *agg.* endemic.

endocardio *sm.* endocardium.

endocardite *sf.* endocarditis.

endòcrino *agg.* endocrine.

endocrinologìa *sf.* endocrinology.

endovenoso *agg.* intravenous. ♦ **endovenosa** *sf.* intravenous injection.

energètico *agg.* e *sm.* tonic.
energìa *sf.* energy.
energicamente *avv.* energetically.
enèrgico *agg.* energetic(al).
energùmeno *sm.* energumen.
ènfasi *sf.* emphasis.
enfàtico *agg.* emphatic.
enfiagione *sf.* swelling.
enfisema *sm.* emphysema.
enfitèusi *sf.* emphyteusis.
enigma *sm.* enigma, puzzle.
enigmàtico *agg.* puzzling.
enigmista *sm.* enigmatographer.
enigmìstica *sf.* enigmatography.
enigmìstico *agg.* puzzle (*attr.*).
ennèsimo *agg.* nth: *ennesima potenza,* nth power.
enologìa *sf.* oenology.
enòlogo *sm.* oenologist.
enorme *agg.* huge.
enormità *sf.* **1.** hugeness **2.** (*fig.*) absurdity.
ente *sm.* **1.** being **2.** (*comm.*) body, corporation.
enterite *sf.* enteritis.
enteroclisma *sm.* enema.
enterocolite *sf.* enterocolitis.
entità *sf.* entity.
entomologìa *sf.* entomology.
entomòlogo *sm.* entomologist.
entrambi *pron.* e *agg.* both.
entrante *agg.* (*con espressioni di tempo*) next, coming.
entrare *vi.* to enter, to come (*v. irr.*) in, to go (*v. irr.*) in || *non c'entra,* this has got nothing to do with it; — *correndo,* to run (*v. irr.*) in; — *in carica,* to come (*v. irr.*) into office; — *in società,* to go into partnership (with); — *precipitosamente,* to rush in; — *in giuoco,* to come into play; — *in vigore,* to come into force.
entrata *sf.* **1.** entrance, entry **2.** (*rendita*) income.
entratura *sf.* entrance.
entro *prep.* **1.** (*luogo*) inside **2.** (*tempo*) in, within, by: — *due giorni,* within two days; — *lunedì,* by Monday.
entrobordo *sm.* inboard.
entroterra *sm.* inland.
entusiasmante *agg.* exciting.
entusiasmare *vt.* to raise enthusiasm in. ♦ **entusiasmarsi** *vr.* to become (*v. irr.*) enthusiastic.
entusiasmo *sm.* enthusiasm
entusiasta *agg.* enthusiast: *essere — di qc.,* to be crazy about sthg.

entusiàstico *agg.* enthusiastic(al).
enucleare *vt.* to enucleate.
enucleazione *sf.* enucleation.
enumerare *vt.* to enumerate.
enumerazione *sf.* enumeration.
enunciare *vt.* to state: — *un teorema,* to enunciate a theorem.
enunciato *sm.* proposition, terms (*pl.*).
enunciazione *sf.* enunciation.
enuresi *sf.* enuresis.
enzima *sm.* enzyme.
eòlico *agg.* Aeolian.
epàtico *agg.* hepatic.
epatite *sf.* hepatitis.
èpica *sf.* epic.
epicentro *sm.* epicentre.
èpico *agg.* epic.
epicureismo *sm.* **1.** epicurism **2.** (*fil.*) epicureanism.
epicureo *agg.* e *sm.* Epicurean.
epidemìa *sf.* epidemic.
epidèmico *agg.* epidemical.
epidèrmico *agg.* epidermic.
epidèrmide *sf.* epidermis, skin.
Epifanìa *sf.* Epiphany, Twelfth Night.
epìgono *sm.* imitator, follower.
epìgrafe *sf.* epigraph.
epigrafia *sf.* epigraphy.
epigramma *sm.* epigram.
epigrammista *s.* epigrammatist.
epilessìa *sf.* epilepsy.
epilèttico *agg.* e *sm.* epileptic.
epìlogo *sm.* epilogue.
episcopale *agg.* episcopal.
episcopato *sm.* episcopacy.
episòdico *agg.* episodic(al).
episodio *sm.* episode.
epìstola *sf.* epistle.
epistolare *agg.* epistolary.
epistolario *sm.* letters (*pl.*).
epitaffio *sm.* epitaph.
epitalamio *sm.* epithalamium (*pl.* -ia).
epitelio *sm.* epithelium.
epìteto *sm.* epithet.
epìtome *sf.* epitome.
època *sf.* **1.** epoch **2.** (*età*) age **3.** (*data*) date || *far —,* to mark an epoch.
epopea *sf.* **1.** epopee **2.** (*serie di fatti eroici*) epos.
eppure *cong.* yet.
epulone *sm.* glutton.
epurare *vt.* to purge.
epurazione *sf.* purge.
equamente *avv.* fairly.
equànime *agg.* equanimous.

equanimità *sf.* equanimity, impartiality.
equatore *sm.* equator.
equatoriale *agg.* equatorial.
equazione *sf.* equation.
equestre *agg.* equestrian.
equidistante *agg.* equidistant.
equidistanza *sf.* equidistance.
equilàtero *agg.* equilateral.
equilibrare *vt.* to balance.
equilibrato *agg.* 1. balanced 2. (*fig.*) well-balanced.
equilibrio *sm.* balance, equilibrium.
equilibrismo *sm.* acrobatics (*pl.*).
equilibrista *s.* acrobat.
equino *agg.* equine.
equinozio *sm.* equinox.
equipaggiamento *sm.* equipment, outfit.
equipaggiare *vt.* to equip, to fit out.
equipaggio *sm.* (*mar.; aer.*) crew.
equiparàbile *agg.* comparable.
equiparare *vt.* to equalize.
equiparazione *sf.* equalization.
equipollente *agg.* equipollent.
equipollenza *sf.* equipollence.
equità *sf.* equity, fairness.
equitazione *sf.* riding.
equivalente *agg.* equivalent.
equivalenza *sf.* equivalence.
equivalere *vi.* to be equivalent. ♦ **equivalersi** *vr.* to be equivalent.
equivocàbile *agg.* mistakable.
equivocare *vi.* to misunderstand (*v. irr.*).
equìvoco *agg.* equivocal, ambiguous. ♦ **equìvoco** *sm.* equivocation.
equo *agg.* fair.
era *sf.* era, epoch.
erariale *agg.* fiscal.
erario *sm.* Treasury.
erba *sf.* grass || *in —*, green; (*fig.*) budding: *un poeta in —*, a budding poet.
erbaccia *sf.* weed.
erbàceo *agg.* herbaceous.
erbaggio *sm.* vegetable.
erbario *sm.* herbarium.
erbetta *sf.* new grass.
erbivéndolo *sm.* greengrocer.
erbìvoro *agg.* herbivorous.
erborista *s.* herborist.
erboso *agg.* grassy.
èrcole *sm.* Hercules.
ercùleo *agg.* Herculean.
erede *sm.* heir. ♦ **erede** *sf.* heiress.
eredità *sf.* inheritance.

ereditare *vt.* to inherit.
ereditarietà *sf.* hereditariness.
ereditario *agg.* hereditary.
ereditiera *sf.* heiress.
eremita *sm.* hermit.
eremitaggio *sm.* hermitage.
èremo *sm.* hermitage.
eresia *sf.* heresy.
erètico *agg.* heretical.
erèttile *agg.* erectile.
eretto *agg.* 1. upright 2. (*costruito*) built.
erezione *sf.* 1. erection 2. (*costruzione*) building.
ergastolano *sm.* convict (serving a life sentence).
ergàstolo *sm.* life imprisonment.
èrgere *vt.* to raise. ♦ **èrgersi** *vr.* to rise (*v. irr.*).
èrica *sf.* heather.
erìgere *vt.* to erect, to build (*v. irr.*). ♦ **erìgersi** *vr.* to set up (for).
erma *sf.* herma (*pl.* -ae).
ermafrodito *agg.* hermaphrodite.
ermellino *sm.* ermine.
ermenèuta *sm.* hermeneut.
ermenèutica *sf* hermeneutics.
ermètico *agg.* 1. (*tec.*) airtight 2. (*oscuro*) obscure.
ermetismo *sm.* obscurity.
ernia *sf.* hernia.
erniario *agg.* hernial.
erodere *vt.* to wear (*v. irr.*) away.
eroe *sm.* hero.
erogare *vt.* 1. to distribute 2. (*elett.; idraulica*) to deliver.
erogazione *sf.* 1. distribution 2. (*elettr.; idraulica*) delivery.
eròico *agg.* heroic.
eroina *sf.* 1. heroine 2. (*farm.*) heroin.
eroismo *sm.* heroism.
eròmpere *vi.* to burst (*v. irr.*) forth.
erosione *sf.* erosion.
erosivo *agg.* erosive.
eròtico *agg.* erotic.
erotismo *sm.* eroticism.
erotòmane *s.* erotomaniac.
èrpete *sm.* herpes.
érpice *sm.* harrow.
errabondo *agg.* wandering.
errante *agg.* errant.
errare *vi.* 1. (*vagare*) to wander 2. (*sbagliare*) to err.
erràtico *agg.* erratic.
errato *agg.* wrong.
erròneo *agg.* erroneous.

errore sm. error, mistake.
erta sf. steep ‖ stare all'—, to be on the look-out.
erto agg. steep.
erudire vt. to teach (v. irr.). ♦ **erudirsi** vr. to get (v. irr.) educated.
erudito agg. learned. ♦ **erudito** sm. scholar.
erudizione sf. erudition, learning.
eruttare vt. to erupt.
eruttivo agg. eruptive.
eruzione sf. eruption.
esacerbare vt. to embitter.
esacerbazione sf. embitterment.
esaedro sm. hexahedron.
esagerare vt. to exaggerate. ♦ **esagerare** vi. to go (v. irr.) too far, to exceed.
esagerato agg. 1. exaggerated 2. (di prezzo) exorbitant.
esagerazione sf. exaggeration.
esagitare vt. to stir violently.
esagonale agg. hexagonal.
esagono sm. hexagon.
esalare vt. to exhale. ♦ **esalare** vi. to exhale, to rise (v. irr.).
esalazione sf. exhalation.
esaltare vt. to exalt. ♦ **esaltarsi** vr. 1. (vantarsi) to boast 2. (infervorarsi) to become (v. irr.) excited.
esaltato agg. excited. ♦ **esaltato** sm. hot-head.
esaltazione sf. 1. exaltation 2. (eccitazione) excitement.
esame sm. examination: dare un —, to take (v. irr.) an examination; essere respinto ad un —, to fail in an examination.
esametro sm. hexameter.
esaminando sm. candidate.
esaminare vt. to examine.
esaminatore sm. examiner.
esangue agg. bloodless.
esanime agg. lifeless.
esasperare vt. to exasperate. ♦ **esasperarsi** vr. to become (v. irr.) irritated.
esasperato agg. exasperated.
esasperazione sf. exasperation.
esattamente avv. exactly, just.
esattezza sf. exactitude.
esatto agg. exact, right.
esattore sm. collector.
esattoria sf. collector's office.
esaudimento sm. satisfaction.
esaudire vt. to grant.
esauriente agg. exhaustive.

esaurimento sm. exhaustion.
esaurire vt. to exhaust. ♦ **esaurirsi** vr. to get (v. irr.) exhausted.
esaurito agg. 1. exhausted 2. (di persona) worn out 3. (che ha l'esaurimento nervoso) suffering from a nervous breakdown 4. (di libro) out of print.
esàusto agg. exhausted.
esautorare vt. to deprive of authority.
esazione sf. collection.
esborso sm. outlay.
esca sf. 1. bait 2. (materiale infiammabile) tinder 3. (di esplosivo) fuse.
escandescenza sf. outburst of rage ‖ dare in escandescenze, to lose (v. irr.) one's temper.
escatologìa sf. eschatology.
escavatore sm. digger.
escavatrice sf. digger.
escavazione sf. digging out.
eschimese agg. e sm. Eskimo.
esclamare vi. to exclaim.
esclamativo agg. exclamatory: punto —, exclamation mark.
esclamazione sf. exclamation.
esclùdere vt. to exclude, to leave (v. irr.) out.
esclusione sf. exclusion ‖ ad — di, except.
esclusiva sf. 1. patent 2. (diritto esclusivo) sole right.
esclusività sf. exclusiveness.
esclusivo agg. exclusive, sole.
escluso agg. 1. excluded 2. (eccettuato) excepted.
escogitare vt. to contrive.
escoriare vt. to graze.
escoriazione sf. abrasion.
escremento sm. excrement.
escrescenza sf. excrescence.
escursione sf. excursion, trip.
escursionista s. excursionist.
escussione sf. examination.
esecràbile agg. execrable.
esecrare vt. to execrate.
esecrazione sf. execration.
esecutivo agg. executive.
esecutore sm. 1. executor 2. (di musica) performer 3. (carnefice) executioner.
esecuzione sf. 1. execution 2. (mus.) performance.
esedra sf. exedra (pl. -ae).
esegesi sf. exegesis (pl. -ses).
esegeta s. exegete.
eseguìbile agg. feasible.

eseguire vt. 1. to execute, to carry out 2. (mus.) to perform.

esempio sm. 1. example, instance 2. (modello perfetto) pattern.

esemplare agg. exemplary. ♦ **esemplare** sm. 1. pattern, specimen 2. (di libro) copy.

esemplificare vt. to exemplify.

esemplificazione sf. exemplification.

esentare vt. to exempt.

esente agg. exempt, free.

esenzione sf. exemption.

esequie sf. pl. exequies.

esercente sm. shop-keeper.

esercire vt. to manage (a business) || — un negozio, to keep (v. irr.) a shop.

esercitare vt. 1. to exercise 2. (una professione) to practice 3. (addestrare) to train. ♦ **esercitarsi** vr. to practice.

esercitazione sf. 1. exercise 2. (allenamento) training 3. (mil.) drill.

esercito sm. army.

esercizio sm. 1. exercise 2. (negozio) shop 3. (comm.) — finanziario, financial year.

esibire vt. to exhibit, to show (v irr.).

esibizione sf. exhibition, show.

esibizionismo sm. exhibitionism, showing-off.

esibizionista s. exhibitionist.

esigente agg. exacting.

esigenza sf. 1. demand, exigence 2. (pretesa) pretension.

esigere vt. 1. (comm.) to collect 2. (richiedere con autorità) to insist on 3. (pretendere) to exact.

esigibile agg. 1. exigible 2. (riscuotibile) collectable.

esiguità sf. exiguity.

esiguo agg. exiguous, scanty.

esilarante agg. exhilarating.

esilarare vt. to exhilarate.

esile agg. slender.

esiliare vt. to exile. ♦ **esiliarsi** vr. to go (v. irr.) into exile.

esiliato agg. banished. ♦ **esiliato** sm. exile.

esilio sm. exile.

esimere vt. to free, to excuse. ♦ **esimersi** vr. to evade (sthg.).

esimio agg. excellent.

esistente agg. 1. existing 2. (di cose) extant.

esistenza sf. existence.

esistenziale agg. existential.

esistenzialismo sm. existentialism.

esistenzialista agg. e s. existentialist.

esistere vi. to exist.

esitante agg. hesitating: voce —, faltering voice.

esitare vi. 1. to hesitate 2. (di voce) to falter.

esitazione sf. hesitation: senza —, unhesitatingly.

esito sm. result, outcome.

esiziale agg. ruinous.

esodo sm. exodus.

esofago sm. oesophagus.

esogeno agg. exogenous.

esonerare vt. to exonerate.

esonero sm. exoneration.

esorbitante agg. exorbitant.

esorbitanza sf. exorbitance.

esorbitare vi. to exceed.

esorcismo sm. exorcism.

esorcista sm. exorcist.

esorcizzare vt. to exorcize.

esorcizzatore sm. exorcizer.

esordiente agg. beginning. ♦ **esordiente** sm. beginner.

esordio sm. preamble, beginning.

esordire vi. 1. to begin (v. irr.) 2. (in arte) to make (v. irr.) one's debut.

esortare vt. to exhort.

esortativo agg. exhortative.

esortazione sf. exhortation.

esosità sf. greediness.

esoso agg. greedy.

esoterico agg. esoteric.

esotermico agg. exothermic.

esotico agg. exotic.

esotismo sm. exoticism.

espandere vt. to spread (v. irr.) (out). ♦ **espandersi** vr. to spread.

espansione sf. expansion.

espansionismo sm. expansionism.

espansività sf. effusiveness.

espansivo agg. effusive.

espatriare vi. to emigrate.

espatrio sm. expatriation.

espediente sm. expedient.

espellere vt. to expel.

esperanto sm. Esperanto.

esperienza sf. experience.

esperimento sm. 1. experiment 2. (esame) test 3. (tentativo) trial.

esperire vt. to try.

esperto agg. e sm. expert.

espettorante agg. e sm. expectorant.

espettorare vt. to expectorate.

espettorazione *sf.* expectoration.

espiare *vt.* to expiate.

espiatorio *agg.* expiatory: *capro —*, scapegoat.

espiazione *sf.* expiation.

espirare *vt. e vi.* to expire.

espirazione *sf.* expiration.

espletare *vt.* to dispatch.

espletazione *sf.* dispatching.

esplicare *vt.* to explicate: *— un'attività*, to have an activity.

esplicativo *agg.* explanatory.

esplicazione *sf.* explication.

esplicito *agg.* explicit.

esplòdere *vi.* to explode, to burst (*v. irr.*).

esplorare *vt.* 1. to explore 2. (*mil.*) to scout.

esploratore *sm.* 1. explorer 2. (*mil.*) scout.

esplorazione *sf.* 1. exploration 2. (*mil.*) scouting expedition.

esplosione *sf.* 1. explosion, blast 2. (*fig.*) outbreak.

esplosivo *agg. e sm.* explosive.

esponente *sm.* exponent.

esporre *vt.* 1. to show (*v. irr.*) 2. (*a rischio*) to venture 3. (*spiegare*) to expound 4. (*mettere in vista*) to display. ♦ **esporsi** *vr.* to expose oneself.

esportare *vt.* to export.

esportatore *agg.* exporting. ♦ **esportatore** *sm.* exporter.

esportazione *sf.* export, exportation.

esposimetro *sm.* exposure-meter.

espositore *sm.* exhibitor.

esposizione *sf.* 1. exposure 2. (*mostra*) exhibition 3. (*eloquio*) exposition.

esposto *sm.* petition.

espressamente *avv.* 1. expressly 2. (*appositamente*) on purpose.

espressione *sf.* expression.

espressionismo *sm.* expressionism.

espressionista *s.* expressionist.

espressivo *agg.* expressive.

espresso *agg.* express.

esprìmere *vt.* to express.

esprimìbile *agg.* expressible.

espropriare *vt.* to dispossess.

espropriazione *sf.* expropriation.

espugnare *vt.* to conquer.

espugnatore *sm.* conqueror.

espugnazione *sf.* conquest.

espulsione *sf.* expulsion.

espulsivo *agg. e sm.* expulsive.

espulsore *sm.* ejector.

espùngere *vt.* to expunge.

espurgare *vt.* 1. to expurgate 2. (*un libro*) to bowdlerize.

espurgazione *sf.* 1. expurgation 2. (*un libro*) to bowdlerize.

essa *pron.* 1. (*sogg.*) she, (*compl.*) her 2. (*riferito a cose o animali*) it.

esse *sf.* letter S.: *a —*, S-shaped.

essenza *sf.* essence.

essenziale *agg.* essential.

essenzialità *sf.* essentiality.

èssere *vi.* to be ‖ *c'è, ci sono*, there is, there are.

èssere *sm.* 1. being 2. (*esistenza*) existence.

essi *pron.* (*sogg.*) they, (*compl.*) them.

essiccare *vt.* to dry.

essiccatoio *sm.* drier.

essiccazione *sf.* drying process.

esso *pron.* 1. (*sogg.*) he, (*compl.*) him 2. (*per cose o animali*) it.

essudato *sm.* exudate.

essudazione *sf.* exudation.

est *sm.* east.

èstasi *sf.* ecstasy: *andare in —*, to go (*v. irr.*) into ecstasies; *mandare in —*, to throw (*v. irr.*) into ecstasies.

estasiare *vt.* to enrapture. ♦ **estasiarsi** *vr.* to be enraptured.

estate *sf.* summer.

estàtico *agg.* ecstatic.

estemporàneo *agg.* extempore.

estèndere *vt.* to extend.

estendìbile *agg.* extensible.

estensione *sf.* 1. extension 2. (*distesa*) expanse, extent 3. (*mus.*) range.

estensivo *agg.* extensive.

estensore *sm.* 1. compiler 2. (*giur.*) drafts-man (*pl.* -men) 3. (*sport*) chest-expander.

estenuante *agg.* exhausting.

estenuare *vt.* to tire out.

estenuazione *sf.* exhaustion.

esteriore *agg.* outward. ♦ **esteriore** *sm.* exterior, outside.

esteriorità *sf.* outward appearance.

esternamente *avv.* externally, outside.

esternare *vt.* to express, to utter.

esterno *agg.* outer, external.

èstero *agg.* foreign. ♦ **èstero** *sm.* foreign countries (*pl.*) ‖ *all'—*, abroad.

esterofilia *sf.* xenomania.

esterrefatto *agg.* aghast, amazed.

esteso *agg.* large, wide || *per —*, in detail.

esteta *s.* aesthete.

estètica *sf.* aesthetics.

estètico *agg.* aesthetic.

estetismo *sm.* aestheticism.

èstimo *sm.* estimate.

estìnguere *vt.* **1.** to put (*v. irr.*) out **2.** (*saldare*) to extinguish || *— la propria sete*, to slake one's thirst. ♦ **estìnguersi** *vr.* (*finire*) to die.

estinguìbile *agg.* extinguishable.

estinto *agg.* **1.** extinct **2.** (*morto*) dead. ♦ **estinto** *sm.* deceased man.

estintore *sm.* extinguisher.

estinzione *sf.* **1.** extinction **2.** (*di sete*) quenching **3.** (*di debito*) paying off.

estirpare *vt.* **1.** to extirpate **2.** (*di denti*) to pull out.

estirpazione *sf.* **1.** extirpation **2.** (*di denti*) extraction.

estivo *agg.* summer (*attr.*).

estòrcere *vt.* to extort.

estorsione *sf.* extortion.

estradare *vt.* to extradite.

estradizione *sf.* extradition.

estràneo *agg.* extraneous, alien. ♦ **estràneo** *sm.* stranger.

estraniare *vt.* to estrange. ♦ **estraniarsi** *vr.* to get (*v. irr.*) estranged.

estrarre *vt.* to draw (*v. irr.*) out: *— a sorte*, to draw by lot.

estrattivo *agg.* extractive.

estratto *sm.* **1.** extract **2.** (*riassunto*) excerpt **3.** (*comm.*) *— conto*, statement of account.

estrattore *sm.* extractor.

estrazione *sf.* **1.** extraction **2.** (*di lotteria*) drawing.

estremamente *avv.* extremely.

estremismo *sm.* extremism.

estremista *s.* extremist: *— di destra*, extreme rightist; *— di sinistra*, extreme leftist.

estremità *sf.* extremity, end.

estremo *agg.* **1.** utmost **2.** (*eccessivo*) intense **3.** (*drastico*) drastic. ♦ **estremo** *sm.* extreme.

estrinsecare *vt.* to express. ♦ **estrinsecarsi** *vr.* to be expressed.

estrinsecazione *sf.* expression.

estrìnseco *agg.* extrinsic(al).

estro *sm.* **1.** inspiration **2.** (*capriccio*) whim.

estrométtere *vt.* to turn out.

estromissione *sf.* expulsion.

estroso *agg.* **1.** (*ispirato*) inspired **2.** freakish.

estroverso *agg.* extroverted.

estuario *sm.* estuary.

esuberante *agg.* exuberant.

esuberanza *sf.* exuberance.

esulare *vi.* **1.** to go (*v. irr.*) into exile **2.** (*fig.*) to be beyond.

esulcerare *vt.* to exulcerate.

esulcerazione *sf.* exulceration.

èsule *sm.* **1.** exile **2.** (*profugo*) refugee.

esultante *agg.* rejoicing.

esultanza *sf.* exultation.

esultare *vi.* to rejoice.

esumare *vt.* to exhume.

esumazione *sf.* exhumation.

età *sf.* age || *che — hai?*, how old are you?; *avere la stessa —*, to be the same age; *una persona di mezza —*, a middle-aged person.

ètere *sm.* ether.

etèreo *agg.* ethereal.

eternare *vt.* to make (*v. irr.*) eternal.

eternità *sf.* eternity.

eterno *agg.* eternal, everlasting.

eteròclito *agg.* **1.** heteroclite **2.** (*fig.*) irregular.

eterodossìa *sf.* heterodoxy.

eterodosso *agg.* heterodox.

eterogeneità *sf.* heterogeneity.

eterogèneo *agg.* heterogeneous.

ètica *sf.* ethics.

etichetta *sf.* **1.** label **2.** (*galateo*) etiquette.

etichettare *vt.* to stick (*v. irr.*) a label (on).

ètico *agg.* ethical.

etilene *sm.* ethylene.

etìlico *agg.* ethylic.

etilismo *sm.* alcoholism.

etimologìa *sf.* etymology.

etimològico *agg.* etymologic(al).

ètnico *agg.* ethnic(al).

etnografìa *sf.* ethnography.

etnologìa *sf.* ethnology.

etnòlogo *sm.* ethnologist.

etrusco *agg. e sm.* Etruscan.

ettàgono *sm.* heptagon.

èttaro *sm.* hectare.

etto *sm.* hectogram.

ettòlitro *sm.* hectolitre.

ettòmetro *sm.* hectometre.

eucalipto *sm.* eucalyptus.

eucaristìa *sf.* Eucharist, Holy Communion.

eucaristico *agg.* Eucharistic.
eufemismo *sm.* euphemism.
eufonia *sf.* euphony.
eufònico *agg.* euphonic(al).
euforbia *sf.* Euphorbia.
euforìa *sf.* euphoria.
eufòrico *agg.* euphoric.
eunuco *sm.* eunuch.
euritmia *sf.* eurhythmy.
europeismo *sm.* Europeanism.
europeo *agg. e sm.* European.
eurovisione *sf.* Eurovision.
eutanasìa *sf.* euthanasia.
evacuare *vt.* to evacuate.
evacuazione *sf.* evacuation.
evàdere *vi.* to escape. ♦ **evàdere**
vt. (*burocratico*) **1.** to dispatch **2.**
(*eludere*) to evade.
evanescente *agg.* vanishing.
evangèlico *agg.* evangelic(al).
evangelista *sm.* evangelist.
evangelizzare *vt.* to evangelize.
evaporare *vi.* to evaporate.
evaporazione *sf.* evaporation.
evasione *sf.* **1.** escape **2.** (*comm.*)
dare — a una pratica, to dispatch
a business.
evasivo *agg.* evasive.
evaso *sm.* runaway.
evasore *sm.* evader: *— fiscale*, tax
evader.
evenienza *sf.* event, occurrence:
per ogni —, for any occasion.
evento *sm.* event.
eventuale *agg.* possible.
eventualità *sf.* eventuality.
eventualmente *avv.* in case.
evidente *agg.* evident, obvious,
clear.
evidenza *sf.* evidence.
evìncere *vt.* (*giur.*) to evict.
evirare *vt.* to evirate.
evitàbile *agg.* avoidable.
evitare *vt.* **1.** to avoid **2.** (*sfuggire*)
to escape.
evo *sm.* age: *il Medio Evo*, the
Middle Ages.
evocare *vt.* to evoke, to recall.
evocativo *agg.* evocative.
evocazione *sf.* evocation.
evolutivo *agg.* evolutive.
evoluto *agg.* well-developed, modern.
evoluzione *sf.* evolution.
evoluzionismo *sm.* evolutionism.
evòlvere *vt.* to evolve.
evviva *inter.* hurray.
ex libris *sm.* ex libris.
extra *agg.* extra.

extraterritoriale *agg.* extraterritorial.
eziologìa *sf.* aetiology.

F

fa¹ *sm.* (*mus.*) F.
fa² *avv.* ago: *un anno —*, a year ago.
fabbisogno *sm.* needs (*pl.*).
fàbbrica *sf.* **1.** factory || *— di au-
tomobili*, motor works; *— di
mattoni*, brickyard; *— di carta*,
paper-mill; *capo —*, fore-man (*pl.*
-men); *marchio di —*, trade-mark
2. (*fabbricazione*) manufacture.
fabbricàbile *agg.* manufacturable ||
area —, housing area.
fabbricante *sm.* manufacturer.
fabbricare *vt.* **1.** (*produrre*) to
manufacture **2.** (*costruire*) to build
(*v. irr.*) **3.** (*fare*) to make (*v. irr.*).
fabbricato *sm.* building || *imposta
sui fabbricati*, house tax.
fabbricazione *sf.* **1.** manufacture,
make **2.** (*costruzione*) building.
fabbro *sm.* blacksmith.
fabbroferraio *sm.* blacksmith.
faccenda *sf.* matter; business (*solo
sing.*) || *— di stato*, state affair
2. (*lavori domestici*) housework
(*solo sing.*).
faccendiere *sm.* busybody.
faccetta *sf.* little face **2.** (*geom.*)
facet.
facchinàggio *sm.* porterage.
facchino *sm.* porter.
faccia *sf.* **1.** face: *che — tosta!*,
what a face!; *a — a —*, face to face
2. (*aspetto*) look, expression **3.** (*lato, superficie*) face, side.
facciale *agg.* facial.
facciata *sf.* **1.** front, façade **2.** (*pagina*) page.
face *sf.* torch.
faceto *agg.* facetious, witty.
facezia *sf.* witty remark, joke: *dire delle facezie*, to crack jokes.
fachiro *sm.* fakir.
fàcile *agg.* **1.** easy **2.** (*trattabile*)
docile **3.** (*pronto*) ready **4.** (*incline*) inclined **3.** (*probabile*) likely.
facilità *sf.* **1.** facility **2.** (*attitudine*) aptitude.
facilitare *vt.* to make (*v. irr.*)
easier

facilitazione *sf.* **1.** facilitation **2.** (*agevolazione*) facility.

facilone *sm.* slipshod fellow.

facinoroso *agg.* lawless. ♦ **facinoroso** *sm.* lawless man.

facoltà *sf.* faculty.

facoltativo *agg.* facultative: *fermata facoltativa*, request stop.

facoltoso *agg.* wealthy.

facondia *sf.* eloquence.

facondo *agg.* eloquent.

facsìmile *sm.* facsimile.

factotum *sm.* factotum

faggeto *sm.* beech-wood.

faggio *sm.* beech.

fagiano *sm.* pheasant.

fagiolino *sm.* French bean.

fagiolo *sm.* bean.

fagocita, fagocito *sm.* phagocyte.

fagocitare *vt.* **1.** to phagocyte **2.** (*fig.*) to absorb.

fagocitosi *sf.* phagocytosis.

fagotto[1] *sm.* bundle.

fagotto[2] *sm.* (*mus.*) bassoon.

faina *sf.* beech-marten.

falange *sf.* phalanx (*pl.* -nges).

falcata *sf.* **1.** curvet **2.** (*di persona*) stride.

falce *sf.* **1.** sickle **2.** (*da fieno*) scythe **3.** (*di luna*) crescent.

falciare *vt.* **1.** to mow (*v. irr.*) **2.** (*fig.*) to mow down.

falciatore *sm.* mower.

falciatrice *sf.* mowing-machine.

falciatura *sf.* mowing.

falcidiare *vt.* to reduce.

falco *sm.* hawk: *avere occhi di —*, to be hawk-eyed.

falconerìa *sf.* falconry.

falconiere *sm.* hawker.

falda *sf.* **1.** (*strato*) stratum (*pl.* -ta) **2.** (*di neve*) flake **3.** (*di cappello*) brim **4.** (*di monte*) slope.

falegname *sm.* joiner.

falegnamerìa *sf.* **1.** joinery **2.** (*bottega*) joiner's shop.

falena *sf.* moth.

falla *sf.* leak.

fallace *agg.* false, disappointing.

fallacia *sf.* fallacy.

fallibile *agg.* liable to make mistakes.

fàllico *agg.* phallic.

fallimentare *agg.* bankruptcy.

fallimento *sm.* **1.** bankruptcy **2.** (*fig.*) failure.

fallire *vi.* **1.** to fail **2.** (*comm.*) to go (*v. irr.*) bankrupt **3.** (*fam.*) to go under.

fallito *agg.* **1.** (*comm.*) bankrupt **2.** (*fig.*) unsuccessful. ♦ **fallito** *sm.* **1.** (*comm.*) bankrupt **2.** (*fig.*) failure.

fallo *sm.* **1.** fault: *senza —*, without fail **2.** (*anat.*) phallus (*pl.* -li).

falò *sm.* bonfire.

falpalà *sm.* furbelow.

falsare *vt.* **1.** to misrepresent **2.** (*falsificare*) to falsify.

falsariga *sf.* **1.** ruling paper **2.** (*fig.*) pattern, model.

falsario *sm.* **1.** forger **2.** (*di monete*) coiner.

falsetto *sm.* falsetto.

falsificàbile *agg.* falsifiable.

falsificare *vt.* to falsify, to counterfeit.

falsificatore *sm.* **1.** falsifier **2.** (*di monete*) coiner.

falsificazione *sf.* falsification, forgery.

falsità *sf.* **1.** falseness **2.** (*menzogna*) falsehood **3.** (*ipocrisia*) insincerity.

falso *agg.* **1.** false **2.** (*falsificato*) forged.

fama *sf.* fame, renown, reputation: *acquistarsi —*, to win (*v. irr.*) fame; *avere cattiva —*, to have a bad reputation.

fame *sf.* **1.** hunger: *avere —*, to be hungry: *far morire di —*, to starve **2.** (*carestia*) famine.

famèlico *agg.* ravenous.

famigerato *agg.* ill-famed.

famiglia *sf.* family.

familiare *agg.* **1.** domestic, homely **2.** (*intimo, anche fig.*) familiar **3.** (*senza cerimonie*) informal. ♦ **familiare** *sm.* relative.

familiarità *sf.* familiarity: *avere — con qu.*, to be familiar with so.

famoso *agg.* famous, celebrated.

fanale *sm.* **1.** lamp **2.** (*auto*) light: *— anteriore*, head-light; *— di coda*, (*aer.*) tail light, (*auto*) rear lamp; *— di posizione*, parking lights (*pl.*).

fanàtico *agg.* fanatical. ♦ **fanàtico** *sm.* **1.** fanatic **2.** (*fam.*) fan.

fanatismo *sm.* fanaticism.

fanatizzare *vt.* to fanaticize.

fanciulla *sf.* young girl.

fanciullàggine *sf.* **1.** childishness **2.** (*azione infantile*) childish action.

fanciullesco *agg.* childish.

fanciullezza *sf.* childhood.

fanciullo sm. young boy, child (pl. children).

fandonia sf. lie.

fanello sm. linnet.

fanfara sf. 1. brass band 2. (suono di trombe) fanfare.

fanfaronata sf. boasting.

fanfarone sm. boaster.

fangaia sf. muddy road.

fanghiglia sf. slush.

fango sm. 1. mud: gettare del — addosso a qu., to throw (v. irr.) mud at so.; cadere nel —, to fall (v. irr.) very low 2. (med.) mud-baths (pl.).

fangoso agg. muddy.

fannullone sm. idler.

fanone sm. whalebone.

fantaccino sm. foot-soldier.

fantascienza sf. science fiction.

fantasia sf. 1. imagination, fancy 2. (inventiva) inventiveness 3. (articoli fantasia) fancy goods.

fantasioso agg. fanciful.

fantasma sm. ghost.

fantasmagorìa sf. phantasmagoria.

fantasmagòrico agg. phantasmagoric.

fantasticare vt. to daydream.

fantasticherìa sf. daydream.

fantàstico agg. 1. fanciful 2. (bizzarro) queer 3. (fam.) extraordinary.

fante sm. 1. infantryman (pl. -men) 2. (delle carte) knave, jack.

fanterìa sf. infantry.

fantesca sf. maid-servant.

fantino sm. jockey.

fantoccio sm. puppet (anche fig.).

fantomàtico agg. mysterious.

farabutto sm. blackguard.

faraona sf. guinea-hen.

faraone sm. Pharaoh.

farcire vt. to stuff.

farcito agg. stuffed.

fardello sm. 1. bundle 2. (fig.) burden.

fare vt. 1. (in senso generale) to do (v. irr.): cosa fai?, what are you doing?; ecco fatto!, that's done!; — del proprio meglio, to do one's best; 2. (fabbricare, produrre) to make (v. irr.): — amicizia, to make friends; — un errore, to make a mistake; — in fretta, to make haste 3. (essere, esercitare una professione) to be: faccio l'insegnante, I am a teacher 4. (reputare) to think (v. irr.): la facevo

più intelligente, I thought she was more intelligent 5. (segnare le ore): che ora fa il tuo orologio?, what time is it by your watch? 6. (praticare) to go (v. irr.) in for || — le carte, to shuffle; — fagotto, to pack up; — una passeggiata, to go for a walk; — colazione, to have breakfast; — bella, brutta figura, to cut (v. irr.) a fine, a poor figure; — compassione, to rouse compassion; — aspettare qu., to keep (v. irr.) so. waiting; — avere, sapere, vedere a qu., to let (v. irr.) so. have, know, see. ◆ **fare** vi. 1. (di condizioni atmosferiche): che tempo fa?, what is the weather like? 2. (far caldo, freddo) to be hot, cold 3. (essere adatto) to suit. ◆ **farsi** vr. to become (v. irr.), to grow (v. irr.) || — animo, to take (v. irr.) courage.

fare sm. manners (pl).

faretra sf. quiver.

farfalla sf. butterfly.

farfugliare vt. to mumble.

farina sf. meal, flour.

farìnaceo agg. farinaceous.

faringe sf. pharynx (pl. -nges).

faringite sf. pharyngitis.

farinoso agg. mealy, floury.

fariseo agg. e sm. Pharisee.

farmacèutico agg. pharmaceutic.

farmacìa sf. 1. pharmacy 2. (negozio) chemist's shop.

farmacista sm. chemist.

fàrmaco sm. medicine, remedy (anche fig.).

farmacologìa sf. pharmacology.

farmacopea sf. pharmacopoeia.

farneticare vi. to rave.

faro sm. 1. lighthouse 2. (auto) headlight.

farràgine sf. medley, mixture.

farraginoso agg. confused.

farsa sf. farce.

farsesco agg. farcical.

fascetta sf. 1. small band 2. (med.) bandage 3. (edit.) wrapper.

fascia sf. 1. band 2. (med.) bandage 3. (dei bambini) swaddling-band.

fasciame sm. planking.

fasciare vt. 1. to bind (v. irr.) (up) 2. (dei neonati) to swaddle.

fasciatura sf. 1. dressing 2. (di neonato) swaddling.

fascìcolo sm. booklet.

fascina sf. faggot.

fàscino *sm.* charm, fascination.

fàscio *sm.* **1.** bundle **2.** (*geom.*) sheaf **3.** (*di luce*) beam.

fascismo *sm.* Fascism.

fascista *agg.* e *s.* Fascist.

fase *sf.* **1.** stage **2.** (*elettr.*) phase **3.** (*auto*) stroke.

fastello *sm.* faggot.

fastidio *sm.* **1.** trouble: *dare — a qu.*, to give (*v. irr.*) so. trouble **2.** (*contrarietà*) annoyance.

fastidioso *agg.* tiresome.

fastigio *sm.* **1.** pediment **2.** (*fig.*) height.

fasto *sm.* pomp.

fastosità *sf.* pomp, splendour.

fastoso *agg.* magnificent.

fasullo *agg.* false.

fata *sf.* fairy.

fatale *agg.* fatal, inevitable.

fatalismo *sm.* fatalism.

fatalista *agg.* e *s.* fatalist.

fatalità *sf.* fatality.

fatica *sf.* weariness, fatigue.

faticare *vi.* to toil, to work hard.

faticata *sf.* drudgery.

faticoso *agg.* hard, tiring.

fatìdico *agg.* fatidical.

fato *sm.* **1.** fate, destiny **2.** (*sorte*) lot.

fatta *sf.* kind, sort.

fattìbile *agg.* practicable.

fattispecie *sf.* case in point: *nella —*, in this case.

fattivo *agg.* **1.** effective **2.** (*attivo*) busy.

fatto *sm.* **1.** fact **2.** (*azione*) deed **3.** (*avvenimento*) event || *sapere il — proprio*, to know (*v. irr.*) one's business; *venire al —*, to go (*v. irr.*) to the point; *in — di*, as regards.

fattore *sm.* **1.** factor **2.** (*agr.*) farmer.

fattorìa *sf.* farm.

fattorino *sm.* errand-boy.

fattucchiere *sm.* wizard.

fattura *sf.* **1.** making **2.** (*lavorazione*) work **3.** (*comm.*) invoice **4.** (*stregoneria*) sorcery.

fatturare *vt.* **1.** to adulterate **2.** (*comm.*) to invoice.

fatturazione *sf.* (*comm.*) invoicing.

fatuità *sf.* fatuity.

fatuo *agg.* **1.** fatuous **2.** (*vanitoso*) vain || *fuoco —*, will-o'-the-visp.

fàuci *sf. pl.* **1.** jaws **2.** (*di persona*) throat (*sing.*).

fàuna *sf.* fauna.

fàuno *sm.* faun.

fàusto *agg.* propitious.

fautore *sm.* supporter.

fava *sf.* broad bean || *pigliare due piccioni con una —*, to kill two birds with one stone.

favella *sf.* speech.

favellare *vi.* to speak (*v. irr.*).

favilla *sf.* spark (*anche fig.*).

favo *sm.* **1.** honeycomb **2.** (*med.*) favus.

fàvola *sf.* **1.** fable **2.** (*frottola*) idle story **3.** (*oggetto di pettegolezzo*) byword.

favoloso *agg.* fabulous.

favore *sm.* favour.

favoreggiamento *sm.* favouring.

favoreggiare *vt.* to favour.

favoreggiatore *sm.* abettor.

favorévole *agg.* favourable.

favorire *vt.* **1.** to favour **2.** (*aiutare*) to help **3.** (*promuovere*) to foster.

favoritismo *sm.* favouritism.

favorito *agg.* e *sm.* favourite.

fazione *sf.* faction.

fazioso *agg.* factious.

fazzoletto *sm.* **1.** handkerchief **2.** (*da collo*) neckerchief.

febbraio *sm.* February.

febbre *sf.* fever.

febbricitante *agg.* feverish.

febbrìfugo *agg.* febrifugal. ♦ **febbrìfugo** *sm.* febrifuge.

febbrile *agg.* feverish.

fecale *agg.* fecal.

feccia *sf.* dregs (*pl.*) (*anche fig.*).

feci *sf. pl.* excrement (*sing.*).

fècola *sf.* starch.

fecondare *vt.* to fecundate.

fecondazione *sf.* fecundation.

fecondità *sf.* fecundity.

fecondo *agg.* fecund.

fede *sf.* **1.** faith, belief **2.** (*fiducia*) trust.

fedele *agg.* faithful.

fedeltà *sf.* fidelity.

fèdera *sf.* pillow-case.

federale *agg.* federal.

federalismo *sm.* federalism.

federativo *agg.* federative.

federato *agg.* federate.

federazione *sf.* federation.

fedìfrago *sm.* traitor.

fedina *sf.* criminal record.

fégato *sm.* **1.** liver **2.** (*fig.*) courage.

fegatoso *agg.* **1.** bilious **2.** (*fig.*) irritable.

felce *sf.* fern.

feldspato *sm.* felspar.

felice *agg.* **1.** happy **2.** (*fortunato*) lucky **3.** (*piacevole*) pleasant.

felicità *sf.* happiness.

felicitarsi *vr.* to congratulate (so. on sthg.).

felicitazioni *sf. pl.* congratulation (*sing.*).

felino *agg.* e *sm.* feline.

fellone *sm.* villain, traitor.

fellonia *sf.* felony, treason.

felpato *agg.* **1.** plushy **2.** (*fig.*) soft || *a passi felpati*, stealthily.

feltro *sm.* felt.

feluca *sf.* **1.** (*mar.*) felucca **2.** (*cappello*) cocked hat.

fémmina *sf.* female || *mala* —, bad woman.

femminile *agg.* **1.** female **2.** (*da donna*) feminine.

femminilità *sf.* womanliness.

femminismo *sm.* feminism.

femminuccia *sf.* **1.** simple woman **2.** (*uomo senza coraggio*) coward.

fèmore *sm.* thigh-bone.

fendente *sm.* cutting blow.

fèndere *vt.* to rend (*v. irr.*).

fenditura *sf.* cleft, fissure.

fenice *sf.* phoenix.

fènico *agg.* phenic.

fenolo *sm.* phenol.

fenomenale *agg.* phenomenal.

fenomenismo *sm.* phenomenalism.

fenòmeno *sm* phenomenon (*pl.* -na).

fenomenologìa *sf.* phenomenology.

ferace *agg.* fruitful, rich (*anche fig.*).

ferale *agg.* feral, deadly.

fèretro *sm.* coffin.

ferie *sf. pl.* holidays.

feriale *agg.* working: *giorno* —, working-day.

ferimento *sm.* wounding.

ferino *agg.* ferine, wild.

ferire *vt.* to wound, to hurt (*v. irr.*).

ferita *sf.* wound (*anche fig.*).

ferito *agg.* wounded, injured.

feritoia *sf.* loophole.

ferma *sf.* **1.** (*mil.*) service **2.** (*caccia*) pointing.

fermacarte *sm.* paper-weight.

fermaglio *sm.* **1.** clasp **2.** (*per gioielli*) brooch **3.** (*per carte*) clip.

fermare *vt.* **1.** to stop, to arrest **2.** (*fissare*) to fix (*anche fig.*) **3.** (*giur.*) to hold (*v. irr.*). ♦ **fermarsi** *vr.* **1.** to stop **2.** (*soggiornare*) to stay **3.** (*fare una pausa*) to pause.

fermata *sf.* **1.** stop **2.** (*pausa*) pause.

fermentare *vi.* to ferment (*anche fig.*).

fermentazione *sf.* fermentation.

fermento *sm.* **1.** ferment **2.** (*fig.*) turmoil, ferment.

fermezza *sf.* firmness, strength.

fermo *agg.* **1.** still **2.** (*irremovibile*) steady, firm || *mano ferma*, firm hand; *volontà ferma*, unfaltering will. ♦ **fermo** *sm.* **1.** (*mecc.*) lock, catch, stop **2.** (*giur.*) provisional arrest.

fermoposta *sm.* poste-restante.

feroce *agg.* fierce, cruel.

ferocia *sf.* fierceness.

ferraglia *sf.* scrap-iron.

ferragosto *sm.* **1.** August holiday **2.** (*in Inghilterra*) August Bank holiday.

ferraio *sm.* blacksmith.

ferramenta *sf. pl.* hardware (*sing.*).

ferramento *sm.* iron tool.

ferrare *vt.* **1.** to fit with iron **2.** (*di cavalli*) to shoe.

ferrato *agg.* **1.** ironshod **2.** (*di scarpe*) hobnailed **3.** (*strada ferrata*) railway **4.** (*fig.*) well read.

ferratura *sf.* shoeing.

fèrreo *agg.* iron (*attr.*).

ferriera *sf.* iron-foundry.

ferro *sm.* iron: — *battuto*, wrought iron; — *da stiro*, flat-iron; — *da calza*, knitting needle || *i ferri del mestiere*, the tools of the trade; *tocca* —!, touch wood!

ferroso *agg.* ferrous.

ferrovìa *sf.* railway.

ferroviario *agg.* railway (*attr.*).

ferroviere *sm.* railwayman (*pl.* -men).

ferruginoso *agg.* ferruginous.

fèrtile *agg.* fertile (*anche fig.*).

fertilità *sf.* fertility.

fertilizzante *agg.* fertilizing. ♦ **fertilizzante** *sm.* fertilizer.

fertilizzare *vt.* to fertilize.

fèrula *sf.* rod.

fervente *agg.* burning, ardent (*anche fig.*).

fèrvido *agg.* fervid, ardent || *fervidi auguri*, best wishes.

fervore *sm.* fervour, heat.

fessura *sf.* **1.** crack **2.** (*per liquidi*) leak.

festa *sf.* **1.** (*giorno di riposo*) holiday **2.** (*religiosa*) feast **3.** (*anniversario*) birthday **4.** (*onomasti-*

co) Saint's day **5.** (*banchetto, ballo*) feast, ball || *giorno di* —, festal day.

festaiolo *sm.* reveller.

festante *agg.* rejoicing.

festeggiamento *sm.* celebration.

festeggiare *vt.* **1.** to celebrate **2.** (*accogliere festosamente*) to give (*v. irr.*) a hearty welcome.

festévole *agg.* festive.

festino *sm.* feast.

fèstival *sm.* festival.

festività *sf.* festivity.

festivo *agg.* **1.** festive **2.** (*domenicale*) Sunday (*attr.*).

festone *sm.* festoon.

festoso *agg.* joyous.

festuca *sf.* straw.

feticcio *sm.* fetish.

feticismo *sm.* fetishism.

feticista *s.* fetishist.

fètido *agg.* foetid, foul.

feto *sm.* foetus.

fefore *sm.* stink.

fetta *sf.* **1.** slice **2.** (*piccolo pezzo*) piece.

fettuccia *sf.* tape.

feudale *agg.* feudal.

feudalésimo *sm.* feudalism.

feudatario *sm.* feudatory.

fèudo *sm.* feud.

fiaba *sf.* **1.** fable **2.** (*falsità*) falsehood.

fiabesco *agg.* fairy-like.

fiacca *sf.* weariness || *battere la* — (*fam.*), to be sluggish.

fiaccare *vt.* to exhaust. ♦ **fiaccarsi** *vr.* to break (*v. irr.*) down.

fiacchezza *sf.* weakness, weariness.

fiacco *agg.* weak, exhausted.

fiàccola *sf.* torch.

fiaccolata *sf.* torchlight procession.

fiala *sf.* phial.

fiamma *sf.* **1.** flame **2.** (*molto viva*) blaze.

fiammante *agg.* **1.** flaming **2.** (*fig.*) bright || *nuovo* —, brand-new.

fiammata *sf.* blaze.

fiammeggiante *agg.* blazing, burning.

fiammeggiare *vi.* to blaze, to flame, to burn.

fiammifero *sm.* match: *accendere un* —, to strike (*v. irr.*) a match.

fiammingo *agg.* Flemish. ♦ **fiammingo** *sm.* Fleming.

fiancata *sf.* **1.** side **2.** (*mar.*) broadside.

fiancheggiare *vt.* **1.** to flank **2.** (*fig.*) to support.

fiancheggiatore *sm.* flanker, supporter.

fianco *sm.* **1.** hip, side (*anche fig.*) **2.** (*di animali; mil.*) flank.

fiasca *sf.* flask.

fiasco *sm.* flask || *fare* —, to fail utterly.

fiatare *vi.* to breathe: *senza* —, without speaking.

fiato *sm.* breath.

fibbia *sf.* buckle.

fibra *sf.* **1.** fibre **2.** (*costituzione*) constitution.

fibroma *sm.* fibroma (*pl.* -ata).

fibroso *agg.* fibrous.

fibula *sf.* **1.** fibula **2.** (*med.*) splint-bone.

ficcanaso *sm.* meddler.

ficcare *vt.* to thrust (*v. irr.*); to drive (*v. irr.*) (in). ♦ **ficcarsi** *vr.* to interfere || — *in testa qc.*, to get (*v. irr.*) sthg. into one's head.

fico *sm.* fig.

fidanzamento *sm.* engagement.

fidanzare *vt.* to engage. ♦ **fidanzarsi** *vr.* to become (*v. irr.*) engaged (to so.).

fidanzata *sf.* fiancée.

fidanzato *sm.* fiancé.

fidare *vi.* to trust. ♦ **fidarsi** *vr.* trust (upon so., sthg.).

fidato *agg.* reliable.

fideiussione *sf.* suretyship.

fidente *agg.* confiding.

fido *agg.* faithful. ♦ **fido** *sm.* **1.** devoted follower **2.** (*comm.*) credit.

fiducia *sf.* trust, confidence: — *in se stessi*, self-confidence.

fiduciario *agg.* fiduciary. ♦ **fiduciario** *sm.* fiduciary, trustee.

fiducioso *agg.* trusting, hopeful.

fiele *sm.* **1.** gall **2.** (*fig.*) hatred.

fienagione *sf.* haymaking.

fienile *sm.* hay-loft.

fieno *sm.* hay: *asma da* —, hay-asthma.

fiera *sf.* **1.** fair **2.** (*esposizione*) exhibition || — *campionaria*, samples fair.

fierezza *sf.* fierceness.

fiero *agg.* proud.

fièvole *agg.* **1.** feeble **2.** (*di luce, suono*) dim.

figgere *vt.* to fix.

figlia *sf.* daughter.

figliare *vt.* to bring (*v. irr.*) forth.

figliastra *sf.* step-daughter.
figliastro *sm.* step-son.
figlio *sm.* son.
figlioccia *sf.* goddaughter.
figlioccio *sm.* godson.
figliolanza *sf.* children (*pl.*), family.
figliolo *sm.* son.
figura *sf.* **1.** figure **2.** (*illustrazione*) illustration, picture **3.** (*personaggio di romanzi, opere teatrali ecc.*) character || *fare una bella, brutta* —, to cut (*v. irr.*) a fine, poor figure.
figurare *vt.* **1.** to represent **2.** (*far figura*) to look smart **3.** (*apparire*) to appear.
figurativo *agg.* figurative.
figurato *agg.* **1.** (*illustrato*) illustrated **2.** (*di linguaggio, senso*) figurative.
figurazione *sf.* figuration.
figurinista *s.* dress-designer.
figurino *sm.* fashion-plate.
figuro *sm.* scoundrel.
fila *sf.* **1.** row, file **2.** (*coda*) queue: *fare la* —, to queue (up).
filaccia *sf.* lint.
filamento *sm.* filament.
filamentoso *agg.* filamentous.
filanda *sf.* spinning-mill.
filandaia *sf.* spinner.
filante *agg.:* *stella* — **1.** (*astr.*) falling-star **2.** (*di carta*) (paper) streamer.
filantropìa *sf.* philanthropy.
filàntropo *sm.* philanthrope.
filare[1] *vt.* **1.** to spin (*v. irr.*) **2.** (*correre*) to run (*v. irr.*) **3.** (*amoreggiare*) to flirt.
filare[2] *sm.* row, line.
filarmònico *agg. e sm.* philharmonic.
filastrocca *sf.* nursery rhyme.
filatelìa *sf.* stamp-collecting.
filatèlico *agg.* philatelic. ♦ **filatèlico** *sm.* philatelist.
filato *agg.* **1.** spun **2.** (*di seguito*) running.
filatura *sf.* spinning.
filettare *vt.* (*mecc.*) to thread.
filettatura *sf.* (*mecc.*) threading.
filetto *sm.* **1.** (*filo sottile*) thin thread **2.** (*mecc.*) thread || — *della lingua*, fraenum.
filiale *agg.* filial. ♦ **filiale** *sf.* branch house.
filiazione *sf.* filiation.
filibustiere *sm.* **1.** filibuster **2.** (*fig.*) adventurer, rascal.

filiera *sf.* **1.** (*mecc.*) screw cutting die **2.** (*ind. tess.*) spinneret.
filiforme *agg.* threadlike.
filigrana *sf.* **1.** filigree **2.** (*di carta*) watermark.
filìppica *sf.* philippic.
fillòssera *sf.* phylloxera.
film *sm.* picture || *girare un* —, to shoot (*v. irr.*) a picture.
filmare *vt.* to film.
filo *sm.* **1.** thread **2.** (*ind. tessile*) yarn **3.** (*tec.*) wire || *un* — *d'acqua*, a fine stream of water; *un* — *d'aria*, a breath of air.
fìlobus *sm.* trolley-bus.
filologìa *sf.* philology.
filòlogo *sm.* philologist.
filone *sm.* **1.** (*di pane*) long loaf **2.** (*min.*) vein.
filosofare *vi.* to philosophize.
filosofìa *sf.* philosophy.
filòsofo *sm.* philosopher.
filovìa *sf.* trolley-bus line.
filtrare *vt.* to filter, to strain.
filtro *sm.* **1.** filter **2.** (*colino*) strainer.
filza *sf.* **1.** string **2.** (*fig.*) series (*pl.*) **3.** (*cucito*) running stitch.
finale *agg.* last, final.
finalità *sf.* aim, end.
finalmente *avv.* **1.** at last **2.** (*in conclusione*) finally.
finanche *avv.* even.
finanza *sf.* finance.
finanziamento *sm.* financing.
finanziare *vt.* to finance.
finanziario *agg.* financial.
finanziatore *sm.* financing capitalist.
finanziere *sm.* financier.
finché *cong.* **1.** till, until **2.** (*per tutto il tempo che*) as long as.
fine[1] *sf.* end || *alla fin* —, after all. ♦ **fine** *sm.* (*scopo*) purpose.
fine[2] *agg.* fine, thin.
finestra *sf.* window.
finestrino *sm.* window.
finezza *sf.* **1.** thinness **2.** (*acume*) subtlety **3.** (*raffinatezza*) refinement **4.** (*gentilezza*) kindness.
fingere *vi.* to pretend. ♦ **fingersi** *vr.* to feign oneself.
finimenti *sm. pl.* harness (*sing.*).
finimondo *sm.* **1.** end of the world **2.** (*fig.*) catastrophe.
finire *vi.* to finish, to end **2.** (*interrompersi*) to stop || — *con*, to end by: *finii con l'andare*, I ended by going.
finitezza *sf.* perfection.

finìtimo *agg.* bordering.

finito *agg.* 1. finished, ended 2. (*rovinato*) done for.

finitura *sf.* finishing.

fino *prep.* 1. (*di tempo*) till, until, up to: — *a dicembre*, till December 2. (*di spazio*) as far as: *andammo fino a Roma*, we went as far as Rome 3. (*fino da*) from 4. (*a partire da*) since.

finocchio *sm.* fennel.

finora *avv.* till now, so far.

finta *sf.* 1. sham 2. (*scherma*) feint.

fintantoché *avv.* V. *finché.*

finto *agg.* false.

finzione *sf.* pretence, duplicity.

fio *sm.* penalty: *pagare il —,* to pay (*v. irr.*) the penalty (of).

fioccare *vi.* 1. to snow 2. (*fig.*) to shower.

fiocco *sm.* 1. ribbon 2. (*di lana*) staple 3. (*falda*) flake 4. (*di neve*) snowflake.

fiocina *sf.* harpoon.

fioco *agg.* 1. (*rauco*) hoarse 2. (*debole*) weak 3. (*di luce*) dim 4. (*di voce*) faint.

fionda *sf.* sling.

fioraio *sm.* florist.

fiorame *sm.* floral design.

fiordaliso *sm.* bluebottle.

fiordo *sm.* fjord.

fiore *sm.* 1. flower 2. (*fioritura*) bloom: *essere in —* (*anche fig.*), to 'be in bloom 3. (*parte scelta*) the best part 4. (*nelle carte*) clubs (*pl.*).

fiorente *agg.* 1. blooming 2. (*fig.*) flourishing.

fioretto *sm.* 1. little flower 2. (*relig.*) act of mortification 3. (*scherma*) foil.

fioricultore *sm.* floriculturist.

fiorino *sm.* florin.

fiorire *vi.* 1. to flower, to bloom, to blossom 2. (*fig.*) to flourish.

fiorista *s.* florist.

fiorito *agg.* 1. flowery 2. (*in fiore*) in bloom.

fioritura *sf.* 1. flowering 2. (*fig.*) flourishing.

fiotto *sm.* wave, stream: *a fiotti,* in streams.

firma *sf.* signature.

firmamento *sm.* firmament.

firmare *vt.* to sign.

firmatario *sm.* 1. signatory 2. (*comm.*) signer.

fisarmònica *sf.* accordion.

fisarmonicista *s.* accordionist.

fiscale *agg.* 1. fiscal 2. (*inquisitorio*) strict.

fiscalismo *sm.* rigorism.

fischiare *vi.* 1. to whistle 2. (*di segnale acustico*) to hoot 3. (*di serpente; per disapprovare*) to hiss 4. (*nelle orecchie*) to buzz 5. (*di proiettili*) to whiz.

fischiata *sf.* 1. whistling 2. (*di disapprovazione*) hissing.

fischiettare *vt.* to whistle softly.

fischietto *sm.* whistle.

fischio *sm.* 1. whistle 2. (*di serpente; di disapprovazione*) hiss 3. (*segnali acustici*) hoot 4. (*nelle orecchie*) buzzing.

fisco *sm.* public treasury.

fisica *sf.* physics.

fisico *agg.* physical, bodily. ♦ **fisico** *sm.* 1. (*scienziato*) physicist 2. (*costituzione*) physique.

fisima *sf.* caprice, whim.

fisiologìa *sf.* physiology.

fisiològico *agg.* physiologic(al).

fisiòlogo *sm.* physiologist.

fisionomìa *sf.* 1. features (*pl.*) 2. (*carattere*) character.

fisionomista *sm.* physiognomist.

fisioterapìa *sf.* physiotherapy.

fissaggio *sm.* fixing.

fissare *vt.* 1. to fix 2. (*guardare fisso*) to gaze 3. (*prenotare*) to book. ♦ **fissarsi** *vr.* 1. to be fixed 2. (*stabilirsi*) to settle down.

fissato *agg.* 1. fixed 2. (*fam.*) obsessed.

fissatore *sm.* 1. fixer 2. (*foto*) fixing bath.

fissazione *sf.* fixed idea.

fissione *sf.* fission.

fissità *sf.* fixity.

fisso *agg.* fixed.

fistola *sf.* 1. Pan-pipe 2. (*patol.*) fistula.

fitologìa *sf.* phytology.

fitta *sf.* stitch.

fittàvolo *sm.* tenant farmer.

fittizio *agg.* fictitious.

fitto[1] *agg.* 1. (*conficcato*) driven in 2. (*denso*) thick.

fitto[2] *sm.* rent.

fiumana *sf.* 1. broad stream 2. (*fig.*) crowd, stream.

fiume *sm.* 1. river 2. (*fig.*) flood.

fiutare *vt.* 1. to smell (*v. irr.*) 2. (*fig.*) to guess.

fiuto *sm.* 1. scent, smell 2. (*fig.*) intuition.

flàccido *agg.* flabby.
flacone *sm.* vial.
flagellare *vt.* 1. to flagellate 2. (*fig.*) to scourge.
flagellazione *sf.* flagellation.
flagello *sm.* 1. scourge, whip 2. (*fig.*) scourge, plague.
flagrante *agg.* flagrant || *cogliere qu. in —*, to catch (*v. irr.*) so. in the open act.
flagranza *sf.* flagrancy.
flanella *sf.* flannel.
flato *sm.* flatus.
flatulenza *sf.* flatulence.
flautato *agg.* fluted.
flautista *sm.* flute-player.
flàuto *sm.* flute.
flèbile *agg.* plaintive, feeble.
flebite *sf.* phlebitis.
fleboclisi *sf.* phleboclysis.
flebòtomo *sm.* phlebotomist.
flemma *sf.* coolness, phlegm.
flemmàtico *agg.* phlegmatic.
flèmmone *sm.* phlegmon.
flessibile *agg.* flexible, pliant (*anche fig.*).
flessibilità *sf.* flexibility.
flessione *sf.* flexion, bending.
flessuosità *sf.* 1. flexuosity 2. (*di corpo*) suppleness.
flessuoso *agg.* 1. flexuous 2. (*di corpo*) supple.
flèttere *vt.* to bend (*v. irr.*).
flirtare *vi.* to flirt.
flogìstico *agg.* (*med.*) phlogistic.
flora *sf.* flora.
floreale *agg.* floral.
floricoltore *sm.* floriculturist.
floricoltura *sf.* floriculture.
floridezza *sf.* prosperity.
flòrido *agg.* 1. prosperous 2. (*fig.*) buxom 3. (*di colorito*) ruddy.
florilegio *sm.* florilegium (*pl.* -ia).
floscio *agg.* flabby.
flotta *sf.* fleet: *— metropolitana* (*in Gran Bretagna*), the Home Fleet.
flottante *agg.* floating.
flottiglia *sf.* flotilla.
fluente *agg.* fluent (*anche fig.*).
fluidità *sf.* fluency.
flùido *agg. e sm.* fluid.
fluire *vi.* to flow.
fluorescente *agg.* fluorescent.
fluorescenza *sf.* 1. (*fig.*) fluorescence 2. (*elettr.*) glow.
fluorìdrico *agg.* hydrofluoric.
fluorite *sf.* fluorite.
fluoro *sm.* fluorine.
fluoruro *sm.* fluoride.

flussione *sf.* fluxion.
flusso *sm.* 1. (*di marea*) flood(-tide) 2. (*fig.*) flux.
flutto *sm.* wave.
fluttuante *agg.* 1. fluctuating, floating 2. (*incerto*) irresolute.
fluttuare *vi.* to fluctuate, to waver.
fluttuazione *sf.* fluctuation.
fluviale *agg.* river (*attr.*).
fobìa *sf.* phobia, aversion.
foca *sf.* seal.
focaccia *sf.* cake || *rendere pan per —*, to give (*v. irr.*) tit for tat.
focaia *sf. pietra —*, flint.
focale *agg.* focal.
foce *sf.* mouth.
focolaio *sm.* centre of infection.
focolare *sm.* 1. hearth 2. (*caminetto*) fireplace 3. (*fig.*) home.
focoso *agg.* hot, fiery.
fòdera *sf.* lining.
foderare *vt.* to line.
fòdero *sm.* scabbard, sheath.
foga *sf.* impetuosity.
foggia *sf.* 1. (*moda*) fashion 2. (*maniera*) way 3. (*forma*) shape.
foggiare *vt.* to shape.
foglia *sf.* leaf (*pl.* leaves) || *mangiare la —*, to take (*v. irr.*) the hint.
fogliame *sm.* foliage, leafage.
foglio *sm.* sheet.
fogna *sf.* sewer.
fognatura *sf.* sewage.
foia *sf.* lust.
fola *sf.* 1. fable 2. (*fandonia*) fib.
folata *sf.* (*di vento*) gust.
folclore *sm.* folklore.
folclorìstico *agg.* folkloristic.
folgorante *agg.* flashing, dazzling.
folgorare *vt.* to strike (*v. irr.*) with lightning.
folgorazione *sf.* 1. (*elettr.*) electrocution 2. (*fig.*) fulmination.
fòlgore *sf.* thunderbolt.
folla *sf.* crowd.
folle *agg.* 1. mad 2. (*mecc.*) idle 3. (*auto*) neutral.
folleggiare *vi.* 1. to behave foolishly 2. (*divertirsi*) to make (*v. irr.*) merry.
folletto *sm.* 1. imp 2. (*ragazzo*) restless child.
follìa *sf.* madness || *amare qu. alla —*, to be madly in love with so.
folto *agg.* thick. ♦ **folto** *sm.* thick.
fomentare *vt.* to foster.
fomentatore *sm.* fomenter.
fomento *sm.* fomentation.

fonda *sf.* anchorage || *nave alla —,* ship at anchor.

fòndaco *sm.* draper's shop.

fondale *sm.* 1. (*teat.*) background 2. (*mar.*) depth.

fondamentale *agg.* fundamental.

fondamento *sm.* 1. foundation: *gettare le fondamenta,* to lay (*v. irr.*) the foundation 2. (*fig.*) basis, ground.

fondare *vt.* to found. ♦ **fondarsi** *vr.* to base oneself on.

fondatezza *sf.* foundation, ground.

fondato *agg.* well-grounded.

fondatore *sm.* founder.

fondazione *sf.* 1. foundation 2. (*istituzione*) institution.

fòndere *vt.* 1. to melt 2. (*fondere in forma*) to cast (*v. irr.*) 3. (*unire*) to blend.

fonderìa *sf.* foundry.

fondiario *agg.* land (*attr.*).

fondista *sm.* long-distance runner.

fonditore *sm.* melter, caster.

fonditura *sf.* 1. melting 2. (*colata*) casting.

fondo *agg.* deep. ♦ **fondo** *sm.* 1. (*parte inferiore*) bottom 2. (*estremità*) end 3. (*indole*) nature 4. (*possedimento*) estate 5. (*capitale*) fund || *articolo di —,* leading article.

fonema *sm.* phoneme.

fonètica *sf.* phonetics.

fonogramma *sm.* phonogram.

fonologìa *sf.* phonology.

fontana *sf.* fountain.

fontanella *sf.* (*anat.*) fontanel.

fonte *sf.* spring, source (*anche fig.*).

foraggio *sm.* forage.

foràneo *agg.* 1. rural 2. (*mar.*) outer.

forare *vt.* 1. to pierce 2. (*di pneumatico*) to puncture 3. (*di biglietti*) to punch.

foratura *sf.* 1. piercing 2. (*di pneumatico*) puncture.

fòrbici *sf. pl.* scissors.

forbire *vt.* 1. to clean 2. (*di stile*) to polish.

forbito *agg.* 1. elegant 2. (*di stile*) polished.

forca *sf.* 1. fork 2. (*patibolo*) gallows.

forcella *sf.* 1. forked stick 2. (*mecc.*) fork 3. (*per capelli*) hairpin.

forchetta *sf.* fork.

forcina *sf.* hairpin.

fòrcipe *sm.* forceps (*pl.*).

forcuto *agg.* forked.

forense *agg.* forensic.

foresta *sf.* forest, (*anche fig.*), wood.

forestale *agg.* forestal: *guardia —,* forester.

foresterìa *sf.* guest-rooms (*pl.*).

forestiero *agg.* foreign. ♦ **forestiero** *sm.* foreigner.

fòrfora *sf.* dandruff, scurf.

forgiare *vt.* 1. to forge 2. (*modellare*) to shape.

forma *sf.* 1. form, shape 2. (*tec.*) mould.

formaggio *sm.* cheese.

formale *agg.* 1. formal 2. (*solenne*) solemn.

formalismo *sm.* formalism.

formalista *agg. e s.* formalist.

formalità *sf.* formality.

formalizzarsi *vr.* to be shocked (at, by).

formare *vt.* 1. to form 2. (*fare*) to make (*v. irr.*), to create 3. (*modellare*) to shape 4. (*addestrare*) to train. ♦ **formarsi** *vr.* 1. to form 2. (*crescere, affinarsi*) to grow (*v. irr.*), to develop.

formativo *agg.* formative.

formato *sm.* 1. form 2. (*misura*) size 3. (*di libro*) format.

formazione *sf.* formation.

formica *sf.* ant.

formichiere *sm.* ant-eater.

formicolare *vi.* 1. to swarm 2. (*sentire un formicolio*) to tingle.

formicolìo *sm.* 1. swarming 2. (*intorpidimento*) tingling.

formidàbile *agg.* formidable.

fòrmula *sf.* formula (*pl. -ae*).

formulare *vt.* to formulate.

fornace *sf.* furnace.

fornaio *sm.* 1. baker 2. (*negozio*) baker's shop.

fornello *sm.* stove.

fornire *vt.* 1. to supply (with), to provide (with) 2. (*equipaggiare*) to equip (with).

fornito *agg.* 1. furnished (with), supplied (with) 2. (*equipaggiato*) equipped (with).

fornitore *sm.* furnisher, supplier.

fornitura *sf.* 1. (*il fornire*) supplying 2. (*attrezzatura*) furniture, fitting.

forno *sm.* 1. (*da cucina*) oven 2. (*metal.*) furnace.

foro[1] *sm.* hole.

foro[2] *sm.* 1. court of justice 2. (*gli avvocati*) the Bár 3. (*stor.*) forum.

forse *avv.* 1. perhaps, maybe 2. (*circa*) about.

forsennato *agg.* mad, frantic.

forte *agg.* 1. strong (*anche fig.*) 2. (*di mali*) severe 3. (*violento*) heavy 4. (*di suono*) loud. ♦ **forte** *sm.* 1. strong man 2. (*punto di forza*) strong point 3. (*fortezza*) fortress. ♦ **forte** *avv.* strongly.

fortezza *sf.* stronghold, fortress.

fortificare *vt.* to strengthen, to fortify (*anche fig.*).

fortificazione *sf.* fortification.

fortino *sm.* block-house.

fortúito *agg.* fortuitous, accidental.

fortuna *sf.* 1. luck 2. (*ricchezza*) fortune, wealth 3. (*riuscita*) success 4. (*emergenza*) emergency.

fortunale *sm.* storm.

fortunato *agg.* lucky.

fortunoso *agg.* 1. stormy 2. (*fig.*) eventful.

forùncolo *sm.* boil.

foruncolosi *sf.* furunculosis.

forviare *vt.* to lead (*v. irr.*) astray.

forza *sf.* 1. strength 2. (*fig.*) power || — *di volontà*, will-power; *a* — *di*, by dint of 3. (*mil.*) force.

forzare *vt.* 1. to force, to compel 2. (*scassinare*) to pick the lock of.

forzato *agg.* forced. ♦ **forzato** *sm.* convict.

forziere *sm.* coffer.

forzoso *agg.* forced.

foschìa *sf.* haze, mist.

fosco *agg.* 1. dark, hazy 2. (*di aspetto*) gloomy.

fosfato *sm.* phosphate.

fosforescente *agg.* phosphorescent.

fosforescenza *sf.* phosphorescence.

fòsforo *sm.* 1. phosphorus 2. (*fig.*) intelligence.

fossa *sf.* 1. ditch 2. (*cavità*) hollow 3. (*tomba*) grave.

fossato *sm.* ditch.

fòssile *agg. e sm.* fossil || *carbon* —, pit-coal.

fosso *sm.* ditch.

foto *sf.* photo.

fotocèllula *sf.* photoelectric cell.

fotocopia *sf.* photocopy.

fotogènico *agg.* photogenic.

fotografare *vt.* to photograph.

fotografia *sf.* 1. (*arte fotogràfica*) photography 2. (*immagine fotogràfica*) photograph || — *istantanea*, snapshot; *fare una* —, to take (*v. irr.*) a photograph.

fotògrafo *sm.* photographer.

fotomontaggio *sm.* photomontage.

fra *prep.* V. *tra.*

fra' *sm.* (*relig.*) Brother.

frac *sm.* tail-coat.

fracassare *vt.* to smash, to shatter.

fracasso *sm.* 1. noise, hubbub 2. (*di cose rotte*) crash.

fracco *sm.* 1. a great deal 2. (*di botte*) a good thrashing.

fràdicio *agg.* 1. rotten 2. (*bagnato*) wet through.

fràgile *agg.* 1. fragile 2. (*fig.*) frail.

fragilità *sf.* fragility (*anche fig.*).

fràgola *sf.* strawberry.

fragore *sm.* loud noise.

fragoroso *agg.* noisy.

fragrante *agg.* fragrant.

fragranza *sf.* fragrance.

fraintèndere *vt.* to misunderstand (*v. irr.*).

frammassone *sm.* freemason.

frammassonerìa *sf.* freemasonry.

frammentario *agg.* fragmentary.

frammento *sm.* fragment.

frammétere *vt.* to interpose. ♦ **framméttersi** *vr.* to interpose, to intrude.

frammezzare *vt.* to intersperse.

frammezzo *prep.* V. *tra.*

frammischiare *vt.* to intermingle. ♦ **frammischiarsi** *vr.* to intermingle.

frana *sf.* landslide.

franare *vi.* 1. (*di terreno*) to slide (*v. irr.*) down 2. (*di casa*) to fall (*v. irr.*) in.

francescano *agg. e sm.* Franciscan.

francese *agg.* French. ♦ **francese** *sm.* Frenchman (*pl.* -men).

francesismo *sm.* Gallicism.

franchezza *sf.* frankness, outspokenness.

franchigia *sf.* 1. immunity 2. (*postale*) post-free 3. (*mar.*) furlough.

franco¹ *agg.* 1. frank, outspoken 2. (*libero; comm.*) free: *un porto* —, a free port; — *a bordo*, free on board; — *di spese*, free of charge.

franco² *sm.* franc.

francobollo *sm.* stamp.

francotiratore *sm.* sharp-shooter.

frangente *sm.* 1. (*mar.*) breaker 2. (*situazione difficile*) emergency.

fràngere *vt.* 1. to break (*v. irr.*) 2. (*schiacciare*) to crush.

frangetta *sf.* fringe.

frangia *sf.* 1. fringe 2. (*fig.*) embellishment.

frangiare *vt.* to fringe.
frangìbile *agg.* frangible.
frangibilità *sf.* frangibility.
frangiflutti *agg.* e *sm.* breakwater.
frangizolle *sm.* (*agr.*) clod-smasher.
franoso *agg.* crumbling.
frantoio *sm.* oil-mill.
frantumare *vt.* to shatter.
frantume *sm.* fragment || *andare in frantumi*, to break (*v. irr.*) into fragments.
frappé *sm.* shake.
frapporre *vt.* to interpose. ♦ **frapporsi** *vr.* to interpose.
frasario *sm.* jargon.
frasca *sf.* 1. leafy branch 2. (*donna leggera*) coquette.
frascheggiare *vi.* 1. to rustle 2. (*civettare*) to flirt.
fraschetta *sf.* 1. twig 2. (*fig.*) frivolous girl.
frase *sf.* sentence.
fraseggiare *vi.* to phrase.
fraseologìa *sf.* phraseology.
fràssino *sm.* ash-tree.
frastagliare *vt.* to indent.
frastagliato *agg.* indented.
frastaglio *sm.* indentation.
frastornare *vt.* to disturb.
frastuono *sm.* noise, uproar, hubbub.
frate *sm.* 1. friar 2. (*come appellativo*) Brother.
fratellanza *sf.* brotherhood, fraternity.
fratellastro *sm.* half-brother.
fratello *sm.* brother || *fratelli siamesi*, Siamese twins.
fraternità *sf.* brotherhood, fraternity.
fraternizzare *vi.* to fraternize.
fraternizzazione *sf.* fraternization.
fraterno *agg.* brotherly.
fratricida *agg.* fratricidal. ♦ **fratricida** *s.* fratricide.
fratricidio *sm.* fratricide.
fratta *sf.* thicket.
frattaglie *sf. pl.* chitterlings.
frattanto *avv.* meantime, meanwhile.
frattempo (*nella loc. avv.*) *nel —*, in the meanwhile.
fratto *agg.* broken, crushed.
frattura *sf.* fracture.
fratturare *vt.* to fracture, to break (*v. irr.*). ♦ **fratturarsi** *vr.* to fracture, to break.
fraudolento *agg.* fraudulent.
fraudolenza *sf.* fraudulence.

frazionamento *sm.* division.
frazionare *vt.* to divide.
frazionario *agg.* fractional.
frazione *sf.* fraction.
freccia *sf.* arrow.
frecciata *sf.* (*fig.*) gibe.
freddare *vt.* 1. to cool 2. (*ammazzare*) to kill.
freddezza *sf.* coldness, coldheartedness.
freddo *agg.* cold. ♦ **freddo** *sm.* cold: *avere —*, to be cold; *tremare di —*, to shiver with cold.
freddoloso *agg.* sensitive to cold.
freddura *sf.* pun.
fregagione *sf.* massage.
fregare *vt.* 1. to rub 2. (*imbrogliare; volg.*) to swindle.
fregata[1] *sf.* rubbing.
fregata[2] *sf.* (*nave*) frigate.
fregatura *sf.* swindle.
fregiare *vt.* to decorate, to adorn.
fregio *sm.* 1. ornament 2. (*arch.*) frieze.
frego *sm.* stroke: *tirare un — su qc.*, to cross sthg. out.
frégola *sf.* heat.
fremente *agg.* quivering: *— d'ira*, fuming.
frèmere *vi.* to quiver, to tremble.
frèmito *sm.* quiver, thrill.
frenare *vt.* 1. to brake 2. (*trattenere*) to restrain.
frenata *sf.* braking.
frenesìa *sf.* 1. frenzy 2. (*desiderio sfrenato*) immoderate desire.
frenètico *agg.* 1. frantic 2. (*entusiastico*) enthusiastic.
freno *sm.* 1. brake || *bloccare i freni*, to jam the brakes; *togliere il —*, to release the brake 2. (*ritegno*) check restraint || *mordere il —*, to fret under restraint; *stringere i freni*, to shorten the reins 3. (*di cavallo*) bit.
frenologìa *sf.* phrenology.
frequentare *vt.* 1. to frequent 2. (*di scuola*) to attend 3. (*di lvogo pubblico*) to patronize.
frequentato *agg.* 1. frequented 2. (*di scuola*) attended 3. (*di luogo pubblico*) patronized.
frequentatore *sm.* 1. frequenter 2. (*cliente assiduo*) regular customer.
frequente *agg.* frequent.
frequenza *sf.* 1. frequency 2. (*affluenza*) concourse 3. (*assiduità*) attendance.

fresa *sf*. milling machine.
fresatrice *sf*. milling machine.
freschezza *sf*. freshness (*anche fig.*), coolness.
fresco *agg*. 1. fresh 2. (*di temperatura*) cool.
frescura *sf*. coolness.
fretta *sf*. haste, hurry: *avere* —. to be in a hurry.
frettoloso *agg*. hurried.
freudiano *agg*. Freudian.
friàbile *agg*. crumbly.
friabilità *sf*. friability.
fricassea *sf*. fricassee.
friggere *vt*. to fry || *andare a farsi* —, to go (*v. irr.*) to the devil.
friggitorìa *sf*. fried food shop.
frigidezza, **frigidità** *sf*. frigidity.
frìgido *agg*. frigid (*anche fig.*).
frignare *vi*. to whimper.
frigorìfero *agg*. refrigerant. ♦ **frigorìfero** *sm*. 1. refrigerator 2. (*fam.*) fridge.
fringuello *sm*. finch.
frittata *sf*. omelette.
frittella *sf*. pancake.
fritto *agg*. fried.
frittura *sf*. fry.
frivolezza *sf*. 1. frivolity 2. (*cosa frivola*) trifle.
frìvolo *agg*. frivolous.
frizionare *vt*. to rub, to massage.
frizione *sf*. 1. rub, rubbing, massage 2. (*auto*) clutch.
frizzante *agg*. 1. biting 2. (*di bevanda*) sparkling.
frizzare *vi*. 1. to tingle 2. (*di bevanda*) to sparkle.
frizzo *sm*. 1. witticism 2. (*scherno*) gibe.
frodare *vt*. to defraud.
frodatore *sm*. defrauder.
frode *sf*. fraud, swindle.
frodo *sm*. smuggling || *cacciare di* —, to poach; *cacciatore di* —, poacher.
frollare *vt*. to hang. ♦ **frollare** *vi*. to become (*v. irr.*) tender.
frollatura *sf*. hanging.
frollo *agg*. tender, high || *pasta frolla*, pastry.
fronda[1] *sf*. leafy branch.
fronda[2] *sf*. (*rivolta*) rebellion: *vento di* —, trouble brewing.
frondoso *agg*. leafy.
frontale *agg*. frontal.
fronte *sf*. 1. forehead: — *ampia, sfuggente*, broad, receding forehead 2. (*arch.*) front || *di* — *a*, in front

of; *far* — *a*, to face. ♦ **fronte** *sm*. 1. (*mil.*) front 2. (*pol.*) union.
fronteggiare *vt*. to face.
frontespizio *sm*. 1. (*arch.*) frontispiece 2. (*di libro*) title page.
frontiera *sf*. frontier, border.
frontone *sm*. 1. pediment 2. (*di porta, finestra*) gable.
frònzolo *sm*. frill || *senza fronzoli*, plain.
frotta *sf*. 1. crowd 2. (*di animali*) flock.
fròttola *sf*. fib.
frugacchiare *vi*. to rummage.
frugale *agg*. frugal.
frugalità *sf*. frugality.
frugare *vi*. to search, to rummage.
frùgolo *sm*. lively child.
fruire *vi*. to enjoy, to avail oneself of.
fruizione *sf*. fruition.
frullare *vi*. 1. to whip, to beat (*v. irr.*) up 2. (*di ali*) to whir.
frullato *sm*. — *di frutta*, fruit-shake.
frullatore *sm*. mill.
frullino *sm*. whisk.
frullìo *sm*. whirring.
frullo *sm*. whir.
frumento *sm*. wheat.
frusciare *vi*. to rustle.
fruscìo *sm*. rustle.
frusta *sf*. 1. whip 2. (*cuc.*) whisk.
frustare *vt*. to whip, to lash.
frustata *sf*. lash.
frustino *sm*. riding-whip.
frusto *agg*. worn-out, thread-bare.
frustrare *vt*. to frustrate.
frutta *sf*. fruit: — *candita*, candied fruit; — *sciroppata*, fruit in syrup; — *cotta*, compote.
fruttare *vi*. 1. to bear (*v. irr.*) fruit, to pay (*v. irr.*) 2. (*comm.*) to yield.
frutteto *sm*. orchard.
frutticultura *sf*. fruit-growing.
fruttiera *sf*. fruit-dish.
fruttìfero *agg*. 1. fruitful 2. (*econ.*) interest-bearing: *buono* —, interest-bearing security.
fruttificare *vi*. to bear (*v. irr.*) fruit.
fruttivéndolo *sm*. greengrocer.
frutto *sm*. fruit || *frutti di mare*, edible mussels.
fruttuoso *agg*. fruitful, profitable.
fu *agg*. late.
fucilare *vt*. to shoot (*v. irr.*).
fucilata *sf*. shot.
fucilazione *sf*. shooting.

fucile *sm.* rifle, gun: — *ad aria compressa*, air-gun; — *da caccia*, shotgun; *calcio del* —, butt; *canna del* —, gun-barrel; *caricare un* —, to load a gun.

fucilerìa *sf.* 1. rifle fire 2. (*insieme di fucili*) musketry.

fuciliere *sm.* rifleman (*pl.* -men).

fucina *sf.* forge.

fucinare *vt.* to forge.

fuco *sm.* 1. drone 2. (*bot.*) fucus.

fucsia *sf.* fuchsia.

fuga *sf.* 1. flight, escape 2. (*di innamorati*) elopement 3. (*falla, apertura*) escape, leak 4. (*mus.*) fugue.

fugace *agg.* short-lived, transient.

fugacità *sf.* fugacity.

fugare *vt.* 1. to put (*v. irr.*) to flight, to disperse 2. (*scacciare*) to dispel.

fuggévole *agg.* flying, ephemeral.

fuggiasco *agg. e sm.* runaway.

fuggire *vi.* 1. to run (*v. irr.*) away, to flee (*v. irr.*) 2. (*di innamorati*) to elope. ♦ **fuggire** *vt.* to shun.

fuggitivo *agg. e sm.* fugitive.

fulcro *sm.* fulcrum (*pl.* -ra).

fùlgido *agg.* shining.

fulgore *sm.* brightness.

fulìggine *sf.* soot.

fulìginoso *agg.* sooty.

fulminante *agg.* fulminant. ♦ **fulminante** *sm.* 1. (*chim.*) fulminate 2. (*di arma*) primer.

fulminare *vt.* 1. to strike (*v. irr.*) by lightning 2. (*colpire*) to strike.

fulminato *agg.* 1. struck by lightning 2. (*fig.*) thunder-struck.

fùlmine *sm.* lightning.

fulmìneo *agg.* flashing.

fulvo *agg.* tawny.

fumaiolo *sm.* smoke-stack.

fumante *agg.* smoking, steaming.

fumare *vt. e vi.* to smoke.

fumarola *sf.* fumarole.

fumata *sf.* 1. smoke 2. (*segnale*) smoke signal.

fumatore *sm.* smoker.

fumetto *sm.* strip cartoon || *giornali a fumetti*, comics.

fumista *s.* stove-repairer.

fumo *sm.* 1. smoke || *venditore di* —, windbag; *andare in* —, to end in smoke 2. (*vapore*) fume (*anche fig.*) 3. (*di pentole*) steam.

fumògeno *agg.* smoke-producing.

fumoso *agg.* smoky.

funàmbolo *sm.* rope-dancer.

fune *sf.* 1. rope 2. (*cavo*) cable.

fùnebre *agg.* 1. funeral: *canto* —, dirge; *carro* —, hearse 2. (*cupo*) gloomy.

funerale *sm.* funeral || *i funerali*, the obsequies.

funerario *agg.* funerary.

funèreo *agg.* funereal.

funestare *vt.* to afflict.

funesto *agg.* baneful, woeful.

fungaia *sf.* mushroom-bed.

fùngere *vi.* to act (as).

fungo *sm.* mushroom.

funicolare *sf.* funicular.

funivìa *sf.* telpherage.

funzionale *agg.* functional.

funzionamento *sm.* working.

funzionare *vi.* 1. to act (as) 2. (*andar bene*) to work.

funzionario *sm.* official.

funzione *sf.* 1. function 2. (*carica*) office 3. (*relig.*) service.

fuochista *sm.* stoker.

fuoco *sm.* 1. fire 2. (*cine; foto; mat.*) focus: *mettere a* —, to focus.

fuorché *cong.* except, but.

fuori *avv.* 1. out, outdoors 2. (*all'estero*) abroad. ♦ **fuori (di)** *prep.* out of, outside.

fuoribordo *sm.* outboard motor.

fuoriclasse *sm.* first-rater.

fuorigioco *sm., agg. e avv.* off-side.

fuorilegge *sm.* outlaw.

fuoriserie *agg. e sm.* special body car.

fuoruscito *sm.* exile, refugee.

fuorviare *vt.* to lead (*v. irr.*) astray.

furberìa *sf.* cunning.

furbo *agg.* cunning, shrewd.

furente *agg.* furious, mad.

furerìa *sf.* orderly room.

furetto *sm.* ferret.

furfante *sm.* rascal, scamp.

furgoncino *sm.* small van.

furgone *sm.* van.

furia *sf.* fury: *montare su tutte le furie*, to fly (*v. irr.*) into a fury.

furibondo *agg.* furious.

furioso *agg.* 1. furious 2. (*violento*) violent.

furore *sm.* fury: *far* —, to be a hit.

furoreggiare *vi.* to be all the rage.

furtivo *agg.* stealthy.

furto *sm.* theft.

fuscello *sm.* 1. twig, straw 2. (*fig.*) thin person.

fusìbile *sm.* fuse.

fusione *sf.* 1. fusion 2. (*di società comm.*) merging.

fuso sm. spindle || — orario, time zone.

fusoliera sf. fuselage.

fustigare vt. to flog.

fusto sm. 1. (bot.) stalk 2. (tronco umano) trunk 3. (per benzina) drum 4. (di legno per liquori) barrel 5. (giovane prestante) muscle--man (pl. -men) 6. (di colonna) shaft.

fùtile agg. trifling.

futilità sf. trifle.

futurismo sm. futurism.

futurista agg. e sm. futurist.

futuro agg. e sm. future.

G

gabbamondo sm. swindler.

gabbare vt. to swindle.

gabbia sf. 1. cage 2. (per imballaggio) crate.

gabbiano sm. sea-gull.

gabellare vt. (far credere) to pass off as.

gabinetto sm. 1. (studio) study 2. (pol.) cabinet 3. (latrina) water-closet, toilet.

gagà sm. dandy.

gagliardamente avv. vigorously.

gagliardetto sm. pennon.

gagliardo agg. vigorous.

gaglioffo sm. rascal.

gaiezza sf. 1. cheerfulness 2. (di colore) brightness.

gaio agg. 1. cheerful 2. (di colore) bright.

gala sf. 1. (trina) frill 2. (festa) gala: abito di —, gala dress.

galante agg. e sm. gallant || lettera —, love letter; fare il —, to flirt.

galanteria sf. 1. gallantry 2. (complimento) compliment.

galantina sf. galantine.

galantuomo sm. honest man.

galassia sf. galaxy.

galateo sm. 1. good manners (pl.) 2. (libro) book of manners.

galena sf. galena.

galeone sm. galleon.

galeotto sm. 1. convict 2. (mezzano) pander 3. (mar.) galley-slave.

galera sf. 1. jail 2. (mar.) galley.

galileo agg. e sm. Galilean.

galla[1] (nella loc. avv.) a —, afloat || stare a —, to float; venire a —, to come (v. irr.) to the surface; (fig.) to come to light.

galla[2] sf. (bot.) gall.

galleggiamento sm. floating: linea di —, water-line.

galleggiante agg. floating, afloat (pred.). ♦ **galleggiante** sm. 1. float 2. (boa) buoy.

galleggiare vi. to float.

galleria sf. 1. tunnel 2. (d'arte, in teatro) gallery.

gallese agg. Welsh. ♦ **gallese** sm. Welshman (pl. -men).

galletta sf. biscuit.

gallina sf. 1. hen 2. (cibo) chicken.

gallinàceo agg. e sm. gallinacean.

gallio sm. gallium.

gallismo sm. cocksure behaviour (towards women).

gallo sm. 1. cock 2. (stor.) Gaul.

gallonato agg. gallooned.

gallone sm. 1. braid, galloon 2. (mil.) chevron stripes (pl.) 3. (misura) gallon.

galoppante agg. galloping.

galoppare vi. to gallop.

galoppata sf. gallop.

galoppatoio sm. riding-track.

galoppino sm. 1. errand-boy 2. (tirapiedi) drudge.

galoppo sm. gallop: al —, at a gallop, (fig.) at full speed; andare al gran —, to ride (v. irr.) full gallop.

galoscia sf. galosh.

galvànico agg. galvanic.

galvanizzare vt. 1. to galvanize 2. (rivestire di metallo) to electroplate.

galvanizzazione sf. 1. galvanization 2. (rivestitura di metallo) electroplating.

galvanoplàstica sf. galvanoplastics.

gamba sf. leg || avere le gambe lunghe, to be long-legged; male in —, down at heel; in — (fig.), smart.

gambale sm. 1. legging 2. (di armatura) jamb.

gamberetto sm. shrimp.

gàmbero sm. 1. (di mare) lobster 2. (d'acqua dolce) crayfish || andare come un —, to go (v. irr.) backwards.

gambo sm. stem.

gamma sf. range: — di lunghezza d'onda, waveband.

ganascia *sf.* jaw || *mangiare a quattro ganasce*, to eat (*v. irr.*) voraciously.

gancio *sm.* hook.

ganga *sf.* gang.

gànghero *sm.* hinge || *andare fuori dai gangheri*, to lose (*v. irr.*) one's temper.

ganglio *sm.* ganglion (*pl.* -ia).

gangsterismo *sm.* gangsterism.

ganimede *sm.* dandy.

gara *sf.* competition.

garagista *sm.* garage keeper.

garante *sm.* **1.** warranter **2.** (*per un imputato*) bail || *essere —*, to answer for.

garantire *vt.* **1.** to warrant **2.** (*farsi garante per*) to answer for **3.** (*un imputato*) to go (*v. irr.*) bail for.

garanzìa *sf.* **1.** warranty, guarantee **2.** (*somma di —*) security **3.** (*cauzione*) bail || *dare, non dare —*, to be reliable, unreliable; *a — di*, as a guarantee for.

garbare *vi.* to like.

garbatamente *avv.* politely.

garbatezza *sf.* politeness.

garbato *agg.* polite.

garbo *sm.* politeness || *con bel —*, with a good grace.

garbuglio *sm.* entanglement.

gardenia *sf.* gardenia.

gareggiare *vi.* to compete.

garganella (*nella loc. avv.*) *bere a —*, to gulp down.

gargarismo *sm.* gargle.

gargarizzare *vi.* to gargle.

garibaldino *agg. e sm.* Garibaldian.

garitta *sf.* **1.** sentry-box **2.** (*torretta*) look-out turret **3.** (*di guardiano*) cabin.

garòfano *sm.* carnation || *chiodo di —*, clove.

garrese *sm.* withers (*pl.*).

garretto *sm.* **1.** back of heel **2.** (*di animale*) hock.

garrire *vi.* **1.** (*di bandiere*) to flutter, to flap **2.** (*di uccelli*) to chirp.

gàrrulo *agg.* talkative.

garza *sf.* gauze.

garzone *sm.* shop-boy, apprentice.

gas *sm.* gas.

gasolio *sm.* gas oil.

gasometro *sm.* gasholder.

gassare *vt.* to gas.

gassato *agg.* aerated || *acqua gassata*, soda-water.

gassista *sm.* gas-fitter.

gassògeno *sm.* gas producer.

gassoso *agg.* **1.** gaseous **2.** (*gassato*) aerated.

gàstrico *agg.* gastric.

gastrite *sf.* gastritis.

gastroenterite *sf.* gastroenteritis.

gastronomìa *sf.* gastronomy.

gastronòmico *agg.* gastronomic(al).

gatta *sf.* she-cat.

gattabuia *sf.* jail.

gatto *sm.* cat.

gattopardo *sm.* leopard.

gaudente *agg.* **1.** jolly **2.** (*dissipato*) fast. ♦ **gaudente** *sm.* fast person.

gàudio *sm.* joy.

gavetta *sf.* mess-tin.

gavitello *sm.* buoy.

gazza *sf.* magpie.

gazzarra *sf.* din.

gazzella *sf.* gazelle.

gazzetta *sf.* gazette.

gelare *vt.* e *vi.* to freeze (*v. irr.*).

gelata *sf.* frost.

gelataio *sm.* ice-cream vendor.

gelaterìa *sf.* ice-cream shop.

gelatina *sf.* **1.** (*cuc.*) jelly **2.** (*chim.*) gelatine.

gelatinoso *agg.* gelatinous.

gelato *agg.* frozen, icy. ♦ **gelato** *sm.* ice-cream.

gèlido *agg.* icy (*anche fig.*).

gelo *sm.* **1.** intense cold **2.** (*fig.*) chill **3.** (*ghiaccio*) ice **4.** (*brina*) frost.

gelone *sm.* chilblain.

gelosìa *sf.* **1.** jealousy **2.** (*cura*) care **3.** (*persiana*) shutter.

geloso *agg.* jealous.

gelso *sm.* mulberry(-tree).

gelsomino *sm.* jasmine.

gemebondo *agg.* groaning.

gemelli *sm. pl.* (*di polsino*) cuff-links.

gemello *agg. e sm.* twin.

gèmere *vi.* to groan.

gèmito *sm.* groan.

gemma *sf.* **1.** gem **2.** (*bot.*) bud.

gemmare *vi.* (*bot.*) to bud.

gendarme *sm.* policeman (*pl.* -men).

gendarmerìa *sf.* **1.** police-force **2.** (*caserma*) police-station.

genealogìa *sf.* genealogy.

genealògico *agg.* genealogical.

generàbile *agg.* generable.

generale[1] *agg.* general || *quartier —*, headquarters (*pl.*).

generale² *sm.* general.

generalità *sf.* generàlity || *dare le proprie* —, to give (*v. irr.*) one's particulars.

generalizzare *vt.* to generalize.

generalizzazione *sf.* generalization.

generare *vt.* 1. to beget (*v. irr.*) 2. (*produrre, anche tec.*) to produce. ♦ **generarsi** *vr.* to be born.

generatore *agg.* generative. ♦ **generatore** *sm.* generator.

generazione *sf.* generation.

gènere *sm.* 1. kind 2. (*gramm.*) gender 3. (*letterario*) genre 4. (*prodotto*) product || *generi alimentari,* foodstuffs; *generi di prima necessità,* commodities.

genèrico *agg.* generic, vague.

gènero *sm.* son-in-law.

generosità *sf.* generosity.

generoso *agg.* generous.

gènesi *sf.* genesis (*pl.* -ses).

genètica *sf.* genetics.

genètico *agg.* genetic.

genetlìaco *sm.* birthday.

gengiva *sf.* gum.

genìa *sf.* 1. race 2. (*spreg.*) tribe.

geniale *agg.* clever.

genialità *sf.* 1. cleverness 2. (*genio*) genius.

gènio *sm.* genius || *andare a* —, to please.

genitale *agg.* e *sm.* genital.

genitivo *sm.* genitive.

genitore *sm.* 1. parent 2. (*padre*) father.

genitrice *sf.* mother.

gennaio *sm.* January.

genocidio *sm.* genocide.

gentaglia *sf.* rabble.

gente *sf.* people: *c'è molta* —, there are a lot of people; *le genti dell'Asia,* the peoples of Asia.

gentildonna *sf.* lady.

gentile *agg.* 1. kind 2. (*cortese*) polite || *è — da parte sua,* it is kind of him.

gentilezza *sf.* 1. kindness 2. (*cortesia*) politeness 3. (*favore*) favour.

gentilizio *agg.* noble: *stemma* —, coat of arms.

gentiluomo *sm.* gentleman (*pl.* -men).

genuflessione *sf.* genuflection.

genuflèttersi *vr.* to kneel down.

genuinità *sf.* genuineness.

genuino *agg.* genuine.

genziana *sf.* gentian.

geodesìa *sf.* geodesy.

geofìsica *sf.* geophysics.

geografìa *sf.* geography.

geogràfico *agg.* geographic(al) || *carta geografica,* map.

geògrafo *sm.* geographer.

geologìa *sf.* geology.

geològico *agg.* geologic(al).

geòlogo *sm.* geologist.

geòmetra *sm.* 1. geometer 2. (*agrimensore*) land-surveyor.

geometrìa *sf.* geometry.

geomètrico *agg.* geometric(al).

geopolìtica *sf.* geopolitics.

geòrgico *agg.* georgic.

geranio *sm.* geranium.

gerarca *sm.* leader.

gerarchìa *sf.* hierarchy.

gerente *sm.* manager.

gerenza *sf.* management.

gergo *sm.* 1. slang 2. (*di una classe professionale*) jargon.

germànico *agg.* Germanic.

germanio *sm.* germanium.

germanismo *sm.* Germanism.

germanista *s.* Germanist.

germanìstica *sf.* Germanic studies.

germano¹ *agg.* e *sm.* German.

germano² *agg.* german: *fratello* —, brother-german.

germe *sm.* germ.

germicida *agg.* germicidal. ♦ **germicida** *sm.* germicide.

germinare *vi.* V. germogliare.

germinazione *sf.* germination.

germogliare *vi.* 1. to sprout 2. (*fig.*) to spring (*v. irr.*) (up).

germoglio *sm.* germ.

geroglifico *sm.* hieroglyphic.

gerontologìa *sf.* gerontology.

gerundio *sm.* gerund.

gessetto *sm.* chalk.

gesso *sm.* 1. chalk 2. (*med.; scult.; edil.*) plaster.

gesta *sf. pl.* deeds.

gestante *sf.* pregnant woman.

gestazione *sf.* gestation.

gesticolare *vi.* to gesticulate.

gestione *sf.* management.

gestire¹ *vt.* to manage.

gestire² *vi.* to gesture.

gesto *sm.* gesture || *un bel* —, a noble deed.

gestore *sm.* manager.

gesuita *sm.* Jesuit.

gesuìtico *agg.* Jesuitic(al).

gettare *vt.* 1. to throw (*v. irr.*), (*anche metal.; edil.*) to cast (*v. irr.*) 2. (*bot.*) to sprout 3. (*fruttare*) to yield || *— le fondamenta,* to lay (*v. irr.*) the foundations; — *un grido*, to utter a cry. ♦ **gettarsi** *vr.* (*di fiume*) to flow.

gettata *sf.* 1. throw 2. (*edil.; metal.*) cast 3. (*di arma*) range 4. (*molo*) jetty.

gèttito *sm.* (*delle imposte*) yield.

getto *sm.* 1. throw 2. (*mecc.; di liquidi*) jet 3. (*bot.*) sprout 4. (*metal.; edil.*) casting ‖ *di* —, effortlessly; *a* — *continuo*, continuously.

gettone *sm.* 1. counter: — *telefonico*, telephone counter 2. (*contromarca*) check ‖ *macchina a* —, slot-machine.

geyser *sm.* geyser.

gheriglio *sm.* kernel.

gherminella *sf.* trick: *fare una* —, to play a trick (on).

ghermire *vt.* to clutch.

ghette *sf. pl.* spats.

ghetto *sm.* 1. ghetto 2. (*insieme degli ebrei*) Jewry.

ghiacciaia *sf.* 1. ice-box 2. (*stanza*) ice-house.

ghiacciaio *sm.* glacier.

ghiacciare *vi.* e *vt.* to freeze (*v. irr.*).

ghiacciato *agg.* 1. frozen 2. (*molto freddo*) icy.

ghiaccio *sm.* ice.

ghiacciolo *sm.* icicle.

ghiaia *sf.* gravel.

ghiaioso *agg.* gravelly.

ghianda *sf.* acorn.

ghiàndola *sf.* gland.

ghibellino *agg.* e *sm.* Ghibelline.

ghigliottina *sf.* guillotine.

ghigliottinare *vt.* to guillotine.

ghignare *vi.* to grin.

ghigno *sm.* grin.

ghìngheri (*nella loc. avv.*) *mettersi in* —, to dress up.

ghiotto *agg.* 1. greedy 2. (*appetitoso*) dainty.

ghiottone *sm.* glutton.

ghiottonerìa *sf.* 1. gluttony 2. (*cibo prelibato*) dainty.

ghiribizzo *sm.* whim.

ghirigoro *sm.* doodle.

ghirlanda *sf.* wreath.

ghiro *sm.* dormouse (*pl.* dormice) ‖ *dormire come un* —, to sleep (*v. irr.*) like a log.

ghisa *sf.* cast iron.

già *avv.* 1. already 2. (*un tempo*) once 3. (*certamente*) of course.

giacca *sf.* coat, jacket.

giacché *cong.* as, since.

giacente *agg.* 1. lying 2. (*di capitale*) uninvested 3. (*di posta*) unclaimed.

giacenza *sf.* lying ‖ *capitale in* —, uninvested capital; *lettera in* —, unclaimed letter; *merci in* —, goods in stock.

giacere *vi.* to lie (*v. irr.*).

giaciglio *sm.* couch.

giacimento *sm.* (*min.*) deposit: — *di petrolio*, oil-field.

giacinto *sm.* hyacinth.

giacobino *sm.* e *agg.* Jacobin.

giada *sf.* jade.

giaggiolo *sm.* iris.

giaguaro *sm.* jaguar.

giallastro *agg.* yellowish.

giallo *agg.* yellow ‖ *romanzo, film, dramma* —, thriller.

giammai *avv.* never.

giansenismo *sm.* Jansenism.

giansenista *s.* Jansenist.

giapponese *agg.* e *sm.* Japanese (*invariato al pl.*).

giara *sf.* jar.

giardinaggio *sm.* gardening.

giardinetta *sf.* station wagon.

giardiniere *sm.* gardener.

giardino *sm.* garden ‖ — *d'infanzia*, nursery-school.

giarrettiera *sf.* garter.

giavellotto *sm.* javelin: *lancio del* —, javelin throwing.

gibbosità *sf.* hump.

giberna *sf.* cartridge-pouch.

gigante *sm.* giant ‖ *fare passi da* —, to make (*v. irr.*) rapid progress.

giganteggiare *vi.* to tower.

gigantesco *agg.* gigantic.

gigantismo *sm.* giantism.

gigione *sm.* ham.

giglio *sm.* lily.

gilè *sm.* waistcoat.

gincana *sf.* gymkhana.

gineceo *sm.* gynaeceum (*pl.* -ea).

ginecologìa *sf.* gynaecology.

ginecològico *agg.* gynaecological.

ginecòlogo *sm.* gynaecologist.

ginepraio *sm.* 1. juniper thicket 2. (*fig.*) fix: *ficcarsi in un* —, to get (*v. irr.*) into a scrape.

ginepro *sm.* juniper.

ginestra *sf.* broom.

gingillarsi *vr.* to dawdle.

gingillo *sm.* 1. knick-knack 2. (*balocco*) plaything.

ginnasio *sm.* 1. grammar school 2.

(*in Italia e stor.*) gymnasium (*pl.* -ia).

ginnasta *sm.* athlete.

ginnàstica *sf.* gymnastics.

gìnnico *agg.* gymnastic, athletic.

ginocchiata *sf.* blow with the knee.

ginocchiera *sf.* 1. knee-guard 2. (*mecc.*) toggle.

ginocchio *sm.* 1. knee: *in* —, on one's knees 2. (*mecc.*) bend.

ginocchioni *avv.* on one's knees.

giocare *vi.* 1. to play 2. (*d'azzardo*) to gamble 3. (*scommettere*) to bet (*v. irr.*) 4. (*in borsa*) to speculate. ♦ **giocare** *vt.* 1. to play 2. (*ingannare*) to deceive. ♦ **giocarsi** *vr.* (*beffarsi*) to trifle (with).

giocata *sf.* 1. game 2. (*puntata*) stake.

giocatore *sm.* 1. player 2. (*d'azzardo*) gambler 3. (*in borsa*) stock-jobber.

giocàttolo *sm.* toy.

giocherellare *vi.* to toy.

gioco *sm.* 1. play 2. (*regolato da norme*) game 3. (*d'azzardo*) gambling 4. (*scherzo*) joke || *per* —, for fun; — *di pazienza*, puzzle; — *di parole*, pun; *essere in* —, to be involved.

giocoforza *sm.* necessary: *è* —, it is absolutely necessary.

giocoliere *sm.* juggler.

giocondità *sf.* gaiety.

giocondo *agg.* gay.

giocosità *sf.* playfulness.

giocoso *agg.* playful.

giogaia *sf.* mountain range.

giogo *sm.* 1. yoke 2. (*di monte*) summit.

gioia *sf.* 1. joy 2. (*gioiello*) jewel.

gioielleria *sf.* 1. jewelry 2. (*negozio*) jeweller's shop.

gioielliere *sm.* jeweller

gioiello *sm.* jewel

gioioso *agg.* joyful.

gioire *vi.* to rejoice (at).

giornalaio *sm.* newsman (*pl.* -men).

giornale *sm.* 1. newspaper 2. (*comm.*) journal || — *radio*, news bulletin; *cine* —, news-reel.

giornaliero *agg.* daily.

giornalismo *sm.* 1. journalism 2. (*la stampa*) press.

giornalista *s.* journalist, reporter.

giornalìstico *agg.* journalistic || *ambiente* —, press.

giornalmente *avv.* daily.

giornata *sf.* day: *lavorare a* —, to work by the day || *donna a* —, charwoman (*pl.* -women).

giorno *sm.* day: *di* —, by day; *a giorni*, in a few days' time; *due volte al* —, twice a day; *un* — (*avv.*), one day || — *festivo*, holiday.

giovamento *sm.* benefit || *trarre* — *da*, to benefit by.

giòvane *agg.* young. ♦ **giòvane** *sm.* young man (*pl.* -men). ♦ **giòvane** *sf.* young woman (*pl.* women).

giovanetta *sf.* girl.

giovanetto *sm.* boy.

giovanile *agg.* 1. juvenile 2. (*da giovane*) youthful.

giovanotto *sm.* young man (*pl.* men).

giovare *vi.* to be of use. ♦ **giovare** *vt.* to be good (for). ♦ **giovarsi** *vr.* to benefit (by).

giovedì *sm.* Thursday.

giovenca *sf.* heifer.

gioventù *sf.* youth.

gioviale *agg.* jolly.

giovialità *sf.* jollity.

giovinastro *sm.* hooligan.

giovincello *sm.* lad.

giovinezza *sf.* youth.

giràbile *agg.* endorsable.

giradischi *sm.* record player.

giradito *sm.* whitlow.

giraffa *sf.* giraffe.

giramento *sm.* turning: — *di capo*, giddiness; *avere un* —, to feel (*v. irr.*) giddy.

giramondo *sm.* 1. wanderer 2. (*turista*) globe-trotter.

giràndola *sf.* 1. (*fuoco d'artificio*) Catherine-wheel 2. (*fig.*) fickle person.

girandolare *vi.* to saunter.

girandolone *sm.* saunterer.

girante *sm.* 1. (*comm.*) endorser 2. (*mecc.*) impeller (*di pompa*), wheel (*di turbina*).

girare *vi. e vt.* 1. to turn 2. (*evitare*) to avoid 3. (*viaggiare*) to tour 4. (*vagare*) to stroll 5. (*comm.*) to endorse 6. (*riprendere un film*) to shoot (*v. irr.*). ♦ **girarsi** *vr.* to turn.

girarrosto *sm.* spit.

girasole *sm.* sunflower.

girata *sf.* 1. turn 2. (*comm.*) endorsement.

giratario *sm.* (*comm.*) endorsee.

giravolta *sf.* **1.** turning **2.** (*fig.*) shift || *fare una* —, to turn round.

girello *sm.* **1.** (*per bambini*) go-cart **2.** (*parte di bue*) rump.

giretto *sm.* stroll: *fare un* —, to take (*v. irr.*) a short walk.

girévole *agg.* revolving.

girino *sm.* tadpole.

giro *sm.* **1.** turn **2.** (*viaggio*) tour **3.** (*passeggiata*) stroll **4.** (*percorso*) round || *a* — *di posta*, by return of post; — *d'affari*, turnover; *nel* — *di pochi giorni*, in a few days' time; *fare un* — *in auto*, to go (*v. irr.*) for a drive in a car; *fare un* — *in bicicletta*, to take (*v. irr.*) a ride on a bicycle.

girondino *agg. e sm.* Girondist.

gironzolare *vi.* to stroll.

giroscopio *sm.* gyroscope.

girotondo *sm.* round dance.

girovagare *vi.* to wander.

giròvago *agg.* wandering. ♦ **giròvago** *sm.* tramp || *venditore* —, pedlar.

gita *sf.* trip: *fare una* —, to take (*v. irr.*) a trip.

gitano *sm.* Spanish gipsy.

gitante *s.* tripper.

giù *avv.* **1.** down **2.** (*dabbasso*) downstairs || — *per*, down; *su per*, approximately.

giubba *sf.* coat.

giubbetto *sm.* **1.** jacket **2.** (*da donna*) bodice.

giubbotto *sm.* (heavy) coat.

giubilare *vi.* to exult.

giubileo *sm.* jubilee.

giùbilo *sm.* rejoicing.

giudàico *agg.* Judaic.

giudaismo *sm.* Judaism.

giudeo *agg.* Jewish. ♦ **giudeo** *sm.* Jew. ♦ **giudea** *sf.* Jewess.

giudicare *vt.* **1.** to judge **2.** (*pensare*) to think (*v. irr.*).

giùdice *sm.* judge || *i giudici*, the Bench.

giudiziario *agg.* judicial.

giudizio *sm.* **1.** judgement **2.** (*causa*) trial **3.** (*sentenza*) sentence **4.** (*buon senso*) common sense || *far* —, to behave oneself; *rinviare a* —, to commit for trial.

giudizioso *agg.* sensible.

giùggiola *sf.* jujube || *andare in brodo di giuggiole*, to be extremely pleased.

giuggiolone *sm.* simpleton.

giugno *sm.* June.

giugulare *agg.* jugular.

giuliano *agg.* Julian.

giulivo *agg.* cheerful.

giullare *sm.* jester.

giumenta *sf.* (*cavalla*) mare.

giunca *sf.* junk.

giunco *sm.* reed.

giùngere *vi.* **1.** to arrive (at), to reach (sthg.) **2.** (*riuscire*) to succeed (in). ♦ **giùngere** *vt.* (*congiungere*) to join.

giungla *sf.* jungle.

giunta[1] *sf.* **1.** addition: *per* —, in addition **2.** (*di peso*) make-weight.

giunta[2] *sf.* — *comunale*, town council.

giunto *sm.* (*mecc.*) joint.

giuntura *sf.* juncture.

giunzione *sf.* **1.** connection **2.** (*giunto*) joint || *fare una* —, to joint.

giuramento *sm.* oath: *sotto* —, on oath.

giurare *vt.* to swear (*v. irr.*).

giurato *sm.* juryman (*pl.* -men) || *i giurati*, the jury (*sing.*).

giurìa *sf.* jury.

giurìdico *agg.* juridical: *stato* —, legal status.

giurisdizione *sf.* jurisdiction.

giurisprudenza *sf.* law.

giurista *sm.* jurist.

giustezza *sf.* **1.** exactness **2.** (*tip.*) measure.

giustificàbile *agg.* justifiable.

giustificare *vt.* to justify.

giustificazione *sf.* justification.

giustizia *sf.* justice.

giustiziare *vt.* to execute.

giustiziato *sm.* executed man.

giustiziere *sm.* **1.** executioner **2.** (*vendicatore*) avenger.

giusto *agg.* **1.** just **2.** (*esatto*) right **3.** (*legittimo*) legitimate.

glabro *agg.* hairless.

glaciale *agg.* icy: *regione* —, ice region.

glaciazione *sf.* glaciation.

gladiatore *sm.* gladiator.

gladìolo *sm.* gladiolus.

glande *sm.* glans (*pl.* -ndes).

glàndola *sf.* V. *ghiandola*.

glandolare *agg.* glandular.

glassare *vt.* **1.** (*con zucchero*) to ice **2.** (*con gelatina*) to glaze.

glàuco *agg.* glaucous.

glaucoma *sm.* glaucoma.

gleba *sf.* clod || *servo della* —, serf.

gli¹ *art.* **1.** the **2.** (*in senso generico non si traduce*): — *stranieri amano l'Italia*, foreigners love Italy **3.** (*si traduce col possessivo coi capi di vestiario ecc.*): *si tolse* — *occhiali*, he took off his glasses.

gli² *pron.* **1.** (*per persona*) him, to him **2.** (*per cosa*) it, to it ‖ — *mandai un libro*, I sent him a book, I sent a book to him.

glicerina *sf.* glycerine.

glicine *sm.* wistaria.

glicògeno *sm.* glycogen.

glielo *pron.* it (to) him; it (to) her; him to him; him to her; it to it.

globale *agg.* total.

globo *sm.* globe.

globulare *agg.* globular.

glòbulo *sm.* (*biol.*) corpuscle.

gloria *sf.* glory.

gloriarsi *vr.* to glory (in).

glorificare *vt.* to glorify.

glorificazione *sf.* glorification.

glorioso *agg.* glorious.

glossa *sf.* gloss.

glossario *sm.* glossary.

glòttide *sf.* glottis.

glottologìa *sf.* glottology.

glottològico *agg.* glottological.

glottòlogo *sm.* glottologist.

glucosio *sm.* glucose.

glùteo *sm.* gluteus (*pl.* -ei).

glutinato *agg.* gluten (*attr.*).

glùtine *sm.* gluten.

gnomo *sm.* gnome.

gnosticismo *sm.* gnosticism.

gnòstico *agg.* e *sm.* gnostic.

gobba *sf.* **1.** hump (*anche fig.*) **2.** (*donna* —) humpbacked woman.

gobbo *agg.* **1.** humpbacked **2.** (*curvo*) bent. ♦ **gobbo** *sm.* humpback.

goccia *sf.* **goccio** *sm.* drop.

gocciolare *vi.* e *vt.* to drip.

gocciolìo *sm.* dripping.

godere *vi.* e *vt.* to enjoy ‖ *godersela*, to have a good time.

godereccio *agg.* **1.** (*amante dei godimenti*) pleasure-loving **2.** (*che dà godimento*) pleasant.

godimento *sm.* enjoyment.

goffàggine *sf.* **1.** clumsiness **2.** (*atto goffo*) clumsy action.

goffo *agg.* clumsy.

gogna *sf.* pillory: *mettere alla* —, to pillory.

gola *sf.* **1.** throat: *aver mal di* —, to have a sorethroat **2.** (*golosità*) gluttony: *far* —, to tempt **3.** (*geogr.*) gorge.

goletta *sf.* (*mar.*) schooner.

golf *sm.* **1.** jersey **2.** (*gioco*) golf.

golfo *sm.* gulf.

goliàrdico *agg.* of students.

goliardo *sm.* university student.

golosità *sf.* **1.** greediness **2.** (*cibo prelibato*) dainty.

goloso *agg.* greedy. ♦ **goloso** *sm.* glutton.

gòmena *sf.* rope.

gomitata *sf.* nudge ‖ *farsi avanti a gomitate*, to elbow one's way.

gòmito *sm.* **1.** elbow **2.** (*di strada*) sharp bend ‖ — *a* —, side by side.

gomìtolo *sm.* clew.

gomma *sf.* **1.** rubber **2.** (*sostanza resinosa*) gum **3.** (*pneumatico*) tyre.

gommapiuma *sf.* foam rubber.

gòndola *sf.* gondola.

gonfalone *sm.* standard.

gonfiare *vt.* **1.** to swell (*v. irr.*) **2.** (*esagerare*) to exaggerate. ♦ **gonfiarsi** *vr.* to swell (*anche fig.*).

gonfiatura *sf.* **1.** swelling **2.** (*esagerazione*) exaggeration.

gonfio *agg.* **1.** swollen **2.** (*di stile*) bombastic.

gonfiore *sm.* swelling.

gong *sm.* gong.

gongolante *agg.* rejoicing (at).

gongolare *vi.* to rejoice (at).

goniòmetro *sm.* goniometer.

gonna *sf.* **1.** skirt **2.** (*di costume storico anche maschile*) gown.

gonnellino *sm.* — *scozzese*, kilt.

gonzo *sm.* blockhead.

gorgheggiare *vi.* to trill.

gorgheggio *sm.* trill.

gorgo *sm.* whirlpool.

gorgogliare *vi.* to gurgle.

gorgoglio *sm.* gurgling.

gorilla *sm.* gorilla.

gota *sf.* cheek.

gòtico *agg.* Gothic.

gotta *sf.* gout.

governàbile *agg.* governable.

governante *sm.* **1.** ruler **2.** (*statista*) statesman (*pl.* -men). ♦ **governante** *sf.* **1.** housekeeper **2.** (*bambinaia*) nurse.

governare *vt.* **1.** to govern, to rule **2.** (*badare a*) to look after **3.** (*mar.*) to steer.

governativo *agg.* government (*attributivo*).

governatore *sm.* governor.

governo *sm.* **1.** government **2.** (*dominio*) rule **3.** (*comm.*) management **4.** (*mar.*) steerage ‖ — *della* *casa*, housekeeping.

gozzo *sm.* **1.** goitre **2.** (*di uccello*) crop.

gozzoviglia *sf.* revelry.

gozzovigliare *vi.* to revel.

gozzuto *agg.* goitrous.

gracchiare *vi.* to croak.

gracidare *vi.* to croak.

gracidìo *sm.* croaking.

gràcile *agg.* frail.

gracilità *sf.* frailty.

gradassata *sf.* boastfulness, brag.

gradasso *sm.* boaster, braggart.

gradatamente *avv.* gradually.

gradazione *sf.* **1.** gradation **2.** (*sfumatura*) shade.

gradévole *agg.* agreeable.

gradimento *sm.* **1.** pleasure **2.** satisfaction **3.** (*approvazione*) approval.

gradinata *sf.* **1.** flight of steps **2.** (*negli stadi*) tiers of seats.

gradino *sm.* **1.** step **2.** (*di stadio*) stage.

gradire *vt.* **1.** to like **2.** (*accettare*) to accept.

gradito *agg.* **1.** (*piacevole*) pleasant **2.** (*ben accetto*) welcome.

grado *sm.* **1.** degree **2.** (*mil.*) rank || *essere in* —, to be able; *di buon* —, willingly.

graduale *agg.* gradual.

gradualità *sf.* graduality.

graduare *vt.* to graduate.

graduato *agg.* **1.** graded **2.** (*di strumento*) graduated. ♦ **graduato** *sm.* non-commissioned officer.

graduatoria *sf.* **1.** classification **2.** (*sport*) position.

graduazione *sf.* graduation.

graffa *sf.* clip.

graffiare *vt.* to scratch.

graffiatura *sf.* scratch.

graffio *sm.* scratch.

graffito *sm.* graffito (*pl.* -ti).

grafìa *sf.* **1.** writing **2.** (*ortografia*) spelling.

gràfico *agg.* graphic. ♦ **gràfico** *sm.* graph.

grafite *sf.* graphite.

grafologìa *sf.* graphology.

grafòlogo *sm.* graphologist.

grafòmane *s.* graphomaniac.

grafomanìa *sf.* graphomania.

gragnuola *sf.* **1.** hail **2.** (*fig.*) shower.

gramaglie *sf. pl.* mourning (*sing.*): *mettersi in* —, to go (*v. irr.*) into mourning.

gramigna *sf.* couch-grass.

graminàcee *sf. pl.* Gramineae.

grammàtica *sf.* grammar.

grammaticale *agg.* grammatical.

grammàtico *sm.* grammarian.

grammo *sm.* gram.

grammòfono *sm.* gramophone.

gramo *agg.* **1.** miserable **2.** (*scarso*) scanty.

grana *sf.* **1.** grain **2.** (*noia*) trouble **3.** (*denaro*) dough.

granaglie *sf. pl.* corn (*sing.*).

granaio *sm.* barn.

granata[1] *sf.* (*scopa*) broom.

granata[2] *sf.* (*mil.*) grenade.

granatiere *sm.* grenadier.

granatina *sf.* grenadine.

granato *agg.* **1.** garnet red **2.** (*fatto a grani*) grainy.

grancassa *sf.* big drum.

granchio *sm.* crab || *prendere un* —, to make (*v. irr.*) a blunder.

grande *agg.* **1.** great **2.** (*esteso*) large **3.** (*grosso*) big **4.** (*alto*) high; (*di statura*) tall **5.** (*adulto*) grownup.

grandeggiare *vi.* **1.** to tower **2.** (*ostentare*) to show (*v. irr.*) off.

grandezza *sf.* **1.** greatness **2.** (*dimensione*) size **3.** (*estensione*) largeness **4.** (*grandiosità*) grandeur **5.** (*liberalità*) liberality **6.** (*mat.*) quantity.

grandiloquenza *sf.* magniloquence.

grandinare *vi.* to hail (*anche fig.*).

grandinata *sf.* hail-storm.

gràndine *sf.* hail.

grandiosità *sf.* grandeur.

grandioso *agg.* grand.

granduca *sm.* Grand Duke.

granducato *sm.* Grand Duchy.

granduchessa *sf.* Grand Duchess.

granello *sm.* grain.

granita *sf.* grated-ice drink.

granìtico *agg.* granitic.

granito *sm.* granite.

granìvoro *agg.* granivorous.

grano *sm.* **1.** grain **2.** (*frumento*) wheat **3.** (*ogni cereale*) corn.

granturco *sm.* maize.

granulare *agg.* granular.

granuloma *sm.* granuloma.

granuloso *agg.* granulose.

grappa[1] *sf.* (*per unire blocchi di legno ecc.*) cramp.

grappa[2] *sf.* (*liquore*) "grappa".

gràppolo *sm.* cluster.

grassaggio *sm.* greasing.

grassatore *sm.* robber.

grassazione sf. robbery.
grassetto sm. (tip.) heavytype.
grassezza sf. fatness.
grasso agg. fat. ♦ **grasso** sm. **1.** fat **2.** (lubrificante) grease.
grassoccio agg. plump.
grata sf. grating.
graticciata sf. trellis-work.
graticola sf. **1.** grill **2.** (di forno) grate.
graticolato sm. **1.** trellis **2.** (inferriata) grating.
gratifica sf. bonus.
gratificare vt. to gratify.
gratificazione sf. gratuity.
gratis avv. free.
gratitùdine sf. gratitude.
grato agg. **1.** grateful **2.** (gradito) welcome **3.** (piacevole) pleasant.
grattacapo sm. trouble.
grattacielo sm. skyscraper.
grattare vt. **1.** to scratch **2.** (grattugiare) to grate.
grattugia sf. grater.
grattugiare vt. to grate.
gratùito agg. **1.** free **2.** (ingiustificato) gratuitous.
gravame sm. **1.** burden **2.** (ipoteca) mortgage.
gravare vi. to weigh. ♦ **gravare** vt. to burden.
grave agg. **1.** grave **2.** (pesante) heavy **3.** (importante, pericoloso) serious.
gravezza sf. **1.** (pesantezza) heaviness **2.** (serietà) gravity **3.** (stanchezza) weariness.
gravidanza sf. pregnancy.
gràvido agg. **1.** (di femmina) pregnant **2.** (fig.) fraught (with).
gravità sf. **1.** gravity **2.** (severità) severity.
gravitare vi. to gravitate.
gravitazionale agg. gravitational.
gravitazione sf. gravitation.
gravosità sf. heaviness.
gravoso agg. heavy.
grazia sf. **1.** grace **2.** (favore) favour **3.** (clemenza) mercy **4.** (teol.) grace **5.** Sua, Vostra Grazia, His, Her, Your Grace ‖ in — di, owing to.
graziare vt. to pardon.
grazie inter. thank you!, thanks! — tante, many thanks!
grazioso agg. pretty, graceful.
greca sf. **1.** (disegno) Greek fret **2.** (mil.) zig-zag braid.
grecale sm. north-east wind.

grecìsmo sm. Hellenism.
grecista s. Hellenist.
greco agg. e sm. Greek.
greco-romano agg. Graeco-Roman.
gregario sm. **1.** follower **2.** (aiutante) helper.
gregge sm. flock.
greggio agg. **1.** raw **2.** (di tessuto) unbleached **3.** (di metallo e fig.) unrefined.
gregoriano agg. Gregorian.
grembiale, grembiule sm. apron.
grembo sm. **1.** lap **2.** (ventre materno) womb **3.** (fig.) bosom.
gremire vt. to fill.
gremito agg. filled (with).
greppia sf. crib.
gres sm. stoneware.
greto sm. **1.** (di fiume) gravel bank **2.** (di mare) shingly shore.
grettezza sf. meanness.
gretto agg. mean, narrow-minded.
greve agg. heavy.
grezzo agg. V. greggio.
gridare vt. e vi. **1.** to cry **2.** (gridare forte, protestare) to cry out: gridò per il dolore, he cried out with pain.
grido sm. cry ‖ di —, famous.
grifagno agg. **1.** rapacious **2.** (fig.) fierce.
grifo sm. snout.
grifone sm. griffin.
grigiastro agg. greyish.
grigio agg. grey: — perla, pearl grey.
grigiore sm. greyness.
griglia sf. **1.** (di finestra) shutter **2.** (di forno) grate **3.** (grata, graticola) grill ‖ cuocere alla —, to grill.
grilletto sm. trigger.
grillo sm. **1.** cricket **2.** (fig.) fancy.
grillotalpa sm. mole-cricket.
grimaldello sm. picklock.
grinfia sf. clutch.
grinta sf. grim face.
grinza sf. **1.** (di pelle) wrinkle **2.** (di stoffa) crease ‖ (fig.) non fa una —, it is quite correct.
grinzoso agg. **1.** (di pelle) wrinkly **2.** (di stoffa) creasy.
grisù sm. fire-damp.
gronda sf. eaves (pl.).
grondaia sf. **1.** gutter **2.** (tubo di discesa) gutter pipe.
grondante agg. dripping.
grondare vi. to drip ‖ — sangue, to bleed (v. irr.).
groppa sf. back.

groppo *sm.* knot: *avere un — in gola,* to have a lump in one's throat.

groppone *sm.* back: *piegare il —,* to submit.

grossa *sf. dormire della —,* to sleep *(v. irr.)* soundly.

grossezza *sf.* **1.** bigness **2.** *(dimensione)* size **3.** *(spessore)* thickness.

grossista *s.* wholesaler.

grosso *agg.* **1.** *(anche fig.)* big **2.** *(denso)* thick.

grossolanità *sf.* coarseness.

grossolano *agg.* coarse: *errore —,* blunder.

grotta *sf.* cave.

grottesco *agg.* grotesque.

groviera *sf.* gruyère.

groviglio *sm.* tangle.

gru *sf.* *(zool.; mecc.)* crane.

gruccia *sf.* **1.** crutch **2.** *(per abiti)* dress-hanger **3.** *(per uccelli)* perch.

grufolare *vi.* to root.

grugnire *vi.* to grunt.

grugnito *sm.* grunt.

grugno *sm.* snout.

grumo *sm.* clot.

grumoso *agg.* clotted.

gruppo *sm.* group.

grùzzolo *sm.* hoard; *(risparmi)* savings *(pl.).*

guadàbile *agg.* fordable.

guadagnare *vt.* **1.** to gain **2.** *(col lavoro)* to earn.

guadagno *sm.* **1.** earnings *(pl.)* **2.** *(comm.)* profits *(pl.)* **3.** *(fig.)* gain.

guadare *vt.* to ford.

guado *sm.* ford.

guai *inter.* woe!

guaina *sf.* **1.** *(bot.; fodero per armi)* sheath **2.** *(custodia, astuccio)* case **3.** *(anat.)* theca *(pl.* -ae*).*

guaio *sm.* trouble.

guaire *vi.* to yelp.

guaito *sm.* yelp.

gualcire *vt.* to rumple.

gualdrappa *sf.* saddle-cloth.

guancia *sf.* cheek.

guanciale *sm.* pillow ‖ *dormire fra due guanciali,* to have no worries.

guantaio *sm.* glover.

guantiera *sf.* **1.** *(scatola per guanti)* glove-box **2.** *(vassoio)* tray.

guantificio *sm.* glove-factory.

guanto *sm.* glove.

guantone *sm.* boxing-glove.

guardabarriere *sm.* gate-keeper.

guardaboschi *sm.* forester.

guardacaccia *sm.* gamekeeper.

guardacoste *sm.* coastguard.

guardalìnee *sm.* *(sport)* linesman *(pl.* -men*).*

guardamano *sm.* *(di scala)* hand-rail.

guardapesca *sm.* fishing warden.

guardaportone *sm.* doorkeeper.

guardare *vt.* **1.** to look (at) **2.** *(proteggere)* to protect. ♦ **guardare** *vi.* **1.** *(tentare)* to try **2.** *(essere orientato)* to face. ♦ **guardarsi** *vr.* *(da),* to beware (of).

guardaroba *sm.* **1.** wardrobe **2.** *(in teatro ecc.)* cloak-room.

guardarobiera *sf.* **1.** *(nei locali pubblici)* cloak-room attendant **2.** *(in alberghi e case private)* linen maid.

guardarobiere *sm.* *(nei locali pubblici)* cloak-room attendant.

guardasala *sm.* ticket-collector.

guardasigilli *sm.* keeper of the seals.

guardavìa *sm.* guard-rail.

guardia *sf.* guard ‖ *— medica,* first-aid station; *fare la — a,* to guard; *mettere in —,* to warn.

guardiamarina *sm.* midshipman *(pl.* -men*).*

guardiano *sm.* **1.** keeper **2.** *(di armenti)* herdsman *(pl.* -men*)* ‖ *— notturno,* night watchman *(pl.* -men*).*

guardina *sf.* guard-room.

guardingo *agg.* wary.

guardiola *sf.* guard-room.

guarìbile *agg.* **1.** curable **2.** *(di ferita)* healable.

guarigione *sf.* recovery.

guarire *vt.* **1.** to cure **2.** *(una ferita)* to heal. ♦ **guarire** *vi.* **1.** to recover **2.** *(di ferita)* to heal.

guaritore *sm.* healer.

guarnigione *sf.* garrison.

guarnire *vt.* **1.** to trim **2.** *(cuc.)* to garnish **3.** *(fornire)* to furnish **4.** *(mecc.)* to pack.

guarnitura, guarnizione *sf.* **1.** trimming **2.** *(cuc.)* garniture **3.** *(mecc.)* packing.

guasconata *sf.* gasconade.

guascone *agg. e sm.* *(anche fig.)* Gascon.

guastafeste *s.* kill-joy.

guastamestieri *sm.* bungler.

guastare *vt.* **1.** to spoil *(v. irr.)* **2.** *(danneggiare)* to damage.

guastatore *sm.* **1.** destroyer **2.** *(mil.)* sapper.

guasto *agg.* **1.** damaged **2.** (*marcio*) rotten **3.** (*corrotto*) tainted **4.** (*mecc.*) out of order.

guasto *sm.* **1.** damage **2.** (*mecc.*) breakdown || *ci deve essere un —*, there must be something wrong.

guatare *vt.* to gaze (at).

guazzabuglio *sm.* mess.

guazzare *vi.* **1.** to paddle **2.** (*rotolarsi*) to wallow **3.** (*di liquidi in recipienti*) to splash about.

guazzo *sm.* (*pitt.*) gouache. .

guelfo *agg.* e *sm.* Guelph.

guercio *agg.* squinting. ♦ **guercio** *sm.* squinter.

guerra *sf.* war.

guerrafondaio *sm.* warmonger.

guerreggiante *agg.* e *sm.* belligerent.

guerreggiare *vi.* to fight (*v. irr.*), to war.

guerresco *agg.* **1.** war (*attr.*) **2.** (*bellicoso*) warlike.

guerriero *agg.* warlike. ♦ **guerriero** *sm.* warrior.

guerriglia *sf.* guerrilla.

guerrigliero *sm.* **1.** guerrilla **2.** partisan.

gufo *sm.* owl.

guglia *sf.* spire.

gugliata *sf.* needleful.

guida *sf.* **1.** guide **2.** (*auto*) drive || *patente di —*, driving licence; *— telefonica*, telephone book.

guidare *vt.* **1.** to guide **2.** (*auto*) to drive (*v. irr.*).

guidatore *sm.* driver.

guidoslitta *sf.* bobsleigh.

guinzaglio *sm.* leash: *mettere al —*, to leash.

guisa *sf.* manner || *a — di*, like.

guitto *sm.* strolling player.

guizzante *agg.* **1.** darting **2.** (*di luce*) flashing **3.** (*di pesci*) wriggling.

guizzare *vi.* **1.** to dart **2.** (*di luce*) to flash **3.** (*di pesci*) to wriggle.

guizzo *sm.* **1.** dart **2.** (*di luce*) flash **3.** (*di pesci*) wriggle.

guscio *sm.* shell.

gustare *vt.* **1.** to enjoy **2.** (*assaggiare*) to taste.

gustativo *agg.* gustative.

gustatore *sm.* taster.

gusto *sm.* **1.** taste **2.** (*gradimento*) liking || *di, con —*, with relish.

gustoso *agg.* **1.** (*saporito*) tasty **2.** (*piacevole*) pleasant.

guttaperca *sf.* gutta-percha.

gutturale *agg.* guttural.

H

harem *sm.* harem.

hascisc *sm.* hashish.

hawaiano *agg.* e *sm.* Hawaiian.

hurrà *inter.* hurrah.

i *art.* the.

iarda *sf.* yard.

iato *sm.* hiatus.

iattanza *sf.* boastfulness.

iattura *sf.* misfortune.

ibèrico *agg.* e *sm.* Iberian.

ibernazione *sf.* hibernation.

ibisco *sm.* hibiscus.

ibridazione *sf.* hybridization.

ibridismo *sm.* hybridism.

ìbrido *agg.* e *sm.* hybrid.

icona *sf.* icon.

iconoclasta *sm.* iconoclast.

idea *sf.* idea.

ideàbile *agg.* imaginable.

ideale *agg.* e *sm.* ideal.

idealismo *sm.* idealism.

idealista *s.* idealist.

idealìstico *agg.* idealistic.

idealizzare *vt.* to idealize.

idealizzazione *sf.* idealization.

ideare *vt.* to conceive, to devise.

ideatore *sm.* inventor, deviser.

ideazione *sf.* ideation.

idèntico *agg.* identic.

identificàbile *agg.* identifiable.

identificare *vt.* to identify.

identificazione *sf.* identification.

identità *sf.* identity.

ideografia *sf.* ideography.

ideogramma *sm.* ideogram.

ideologìa *sf.* ideology.

ideològico *agg.* ideologic(al).

ideologismo *sm.* ideology.

ideòlogo *sm.* ideologist.

idilliaco *agg.* idyllic.

idillio *sm.* idyl.

idioma *sm.* language.

idiomàtico *agg.* idiomatic.

idiosincrasìa *sf.* idiosyncrasy.

idiota *sm.* idiot. ♦ **idiota** *agg.* idiotic.

idiotismo *sm.* idiom.

idiozìa *sf.* idiocy.

idolatra *sm.* idolater.

idolatrare vt. to worship.
idolatrìa sf. idolatry.
ìdolo sm. idol.
idoneità sf. fitness.
idòneo agg. fit.
idrante sm. hydrant.
idratare vt. to hydrate.
idrato sm. hydrate.
idràulica sf. hydraulics.
idràulico agg. hydraulic. ♦ **idràulico** sm. plumber.
ìdrico agg. water.
idrocarburo sm. hydrocarbon.
idrocefalìa sf. hydrocephalus.
idrocèfalo sm. hydrocephalus.
idroelèttrico agg. hydroelectric.
idròfilo agg. absorbent: cotone —, cotton wool.
idrofobìa sf. rabies.
idròfobo agg. 1. rabid 2. (fig.) furious.
idrògeno sm. hydrogen.
idrografìa sf. hydrography.
idròlisi sf. hydrolysis (pl. -ses).
idrologìa sf. hydrology.
idròpico agg. dropsical.
idropisìa sf. dropsy.
idroscalo sm. seaplane station.
idrostàtica sf. hydrostatics.
idrovolante sm. seaplane.
idròvora sf. water-scooping machine.
iella sf. bad luck.
iena sf. 1. hyaena 2. (fig.) vixen.
ieràtico agg. hieratic(al).
ieri avv. yesterday.
iettatore sm. evil-eyed man.
iettatura sf. evil-eye.
igiene sf. 1. hygiene 2. (sistema sanitario) sanitation.
igiènico agg. sanitary.
igienista s. hygienist.
ignaro agg. ignorant.
ignavia sf. laziness.
ignavo agg. lazy.
ìgneo agg. igneous.
ignòbile agg. mean.
ignominia sf. ignominy.
ignominioso agg. ignominious.
ignorante agg. e sm. ignorant.
ignoranza sf. ignorance.
ignorare vt. to ignore.
ignoto agg. unknown.
ignudo agg. naked.
igrometrìa sf. hygrometry.
iguana sf. iguana.
il art. the.
ilare agg. cheerful.
ilarità sf. hilarity.

ilìaco agg. iliac.
illanguidire vt. to weaken.
illazione sf. illation.
illécito agg. illicit.
illegale agg. illegal.
illegalità sf. illegality.
illeggìbile agg. illegible.
illegittimità sf. illegitimacy.
illegìttimo agg. illegitimate.
illeso agg. unhurt.
illibatezza sf. purity.
illibato agg. pure.
illiberale agg. illiberal.
illimitato agg. unlimited.
illividire vt. to make (v. irr.) livid. ♦ **illividire** vi. to turn livid.
illogicità sf. illogicality.
illogico agg. illogical.
illùdere vt. to delude. ♦ **illùdersi** vr. to delude oneself.
illuminante agg. illuminating.
illuminare vt. to light up.
illuminazione sf. lighting.
illuminismo sm. Illuminism.
illusione sf. illusion.
illusionismo sm. illusionism.
illusionista s. conjurer.
illuso agg. deluded. ♦ **illuso** sm. day-dreamer.
illusorio agg. illusory.
illustrare vt. to illustrate.
illustrativo agg. illustrative.
illustrato agg. illustrated || cartolina illustrata, picture post-card.
illustrazione sf. illustration.
illustre agg. renowned.
imbacuccare vt. to muffle up.
imbaldanzire vt. to embolden. ♦ **imbaldanzirsi** vr. to grow (v. irr.) bold.
mballaggio sm. packing.
imballare vt. to pack (up). ♦ **imballarsi** vr. (di motori) to race.
imbalsamare vt. 1. to embalm 2. (di animali) to stuff.
imbalsamatore sm. 1. embalmer 2. (di animali) stuffer.
imbalsamazione sf. 1. embalming 2. (di animali) stuffing.
imbambolato agg. dull.
imbandierare vt. to deck with flags.
imbandire vt. 1. (la tavola) to lay (v. irr.) 2. to prepare.
imbarazzante agg. embarrassing.
imbarazzare vt. to embarrass. ♦ **imbarazzarsi** vr. to meddle.
imbarazzato agg. embarrassed.
imbarazzo sm. embarrassment.

imbarcadero sm. landing-stage.
imbarcare vt. to take (v. irr.) on board. ♦ **imbarcarsi** vr. to embark.
imbarcazione sf. boat.
imbarco sm. embarkation.
imbastardire vt. to debase.
imbastardito agg. debased.
imbastire vt. 1. to tack 2. (fig.) to put (v. irr.) together.
imbastitura sf. tacking.
imbàttersi vr. to meet (v. irr.) (with).
imbattìbile agg. invincible.
imbattibilità sf. invincibility.
imbavagliare vt. to gag.
imbeccare vt. 1. to feed (v. irr.) 2. (fig.) to prompt.
imbeccata sf. 1. beakful 2. (fig.) prompting.
imbecille agg. e sm. imbecile.
imbecillità sf. imbecility.
imbelle agg. weak.
imbellettare vt. to make (v. irr.) up.
imbellire vt. to embellish.
imberbe agg. beardless.
imbestialire vi. to get (v. irr.) furious. ♦ **imbestialirsi** vr. to get furious.
imbévere vt. to imbue with.
imbiancamento sm. whitening.
imbiancare vt. 1. to whiten 2. (i muri) to whitewash.
imbiancatura sf. 1. (di muri) whitewashing 2. (di tessuti) bleaching.
imbianchino sm. house painter.
imbiondire vt. to make (v. irr.) fair. ♦ **imbiondire** vi. to become (v. irr.) fair.
imbizzarrirsi vr. 1. to become (v. irr.) restive 2. (adirarsi) to fire up.
imboccare vt. 1. to feed (v. irr.) 2. (di strada) to enter.
imboccatura sf. 1. mouth 2. (di strumento) mouthpiece.
imbonimento sm. sales talk.
imbonire vt. to allure.
imbonitore sm. charlatan.
imborghesimento sm. getting into middle-class habits.
imborghesire vt. to give (v. irr.) middle-class habits. ♦ **imborghesirsi** vr. to acquire middle-class habits.
imboscare vt. 1. to put (v. irr.) into safe keeping 2. (mil.) to help to evade military service. ♦ **im-**

boscarsi vr. 1. to lie (v. irr.) in ambush 2. (mil.) to evade military service.
imboscata sf. ambush.
imboscato sm. shirker.
imboschimento sm. afforestation.
imboschire vt. to afforest.
imbottigliamento sm. bottling || — stradale, traffic jam.
imbottigliare vt. 1. to bottle 2. (fig.) to block.
imbottire vt. 1. to stuff 2. (di vestiti) to wad 3. (fig.) — la testa, to cram. ♦ **imbottirsi** vr. 1. to fill oneself (with), to stuff oneself (with) 2. (coprirsi) to wrap oneself (into).
imbottita sf. quilt.
imbottito agg. stuffed, filled || panino —, sandwich.
imbottitura sf. 1. stuffing 2. (di vestiti) wadding.
imbracciare vt. 1. to put (v. irr.) sthg. on one's hands 2. (di fucile) to bring (v. irr.) to firing position.
imbrancare vt. to herd.
imbrattacarte sm. scribbler.
imbrattamento sm. soiling.
imbrattare vt. to soil.
imbrattatele sm. dauber.
imbrigliamento sm. bridling.
imbrigliare vt. to bridle.
imbrigliatura sf. bridling.
imbroccare vt. 1. to hit (v. irr.) 2. (fig.) to guess.
imbrogliare vt. 1. to cheat 2. (confondere) to confuse.
imbroglio sm. cheat, swindle.
imbroglione sm. cheat, swindler.
imbronciarsi vr. to pout.
imbronciato agg. sulky.
imbrunire vi. 1. to brown 2. (farsi sera) to get (v. irr.) dark.
imbrunire sm. nightfall.
imbruttire vt. to make (v. irr.) ugly. ♦ **imbruttirsi** vr. to become (v. irr.) ugly.
imbucare vt. to post.
imburrare vt. to butter.
imbuto sm. funnel.
imene sm. hymen.
imeneo sm. wedding.
imenòttero sm. hymenopteron (pl. -ra).
imitare vt. to imitate.
imitativo agg. imitative.
imitatore sm. imitator.
imitazione sf. imitation.

immacolato *agg.* spotless.

immagazzinare *vt.* to store (up).

immaginàbile *agg.* imaginable.

immaginare *vt.* to imagine.

immaginario *agg.* imaginary.

immaginativa *sf.* imagination.

immaginativo *agg.* imaginative.

immaginazione *sf.* imagination.

immàgine *sf.* image.

immalinconire *vt.* to make (*v. irr.*) melancholy. ♦ **immalinconire** *vi.* to grow (*v. irr.*) sad.

immancàbile *agg.* unfailing.

immane *agg.* 1. huge 2. (*fig.*) frightful.

immanente *agg.* immanent.

immanenza *sf.* immanence.

immangiàbile *agg.* uneatable.

immarcescìbile *agg.* incorruptible.

immateriale *agg.* immaterial.

immaterialità *sf.* immateriality.

immatricolare *vt.* to matriculate. ♦ **immatricolarsi** *vr.* to matriculate.

immatricolazione *sf.* matriculation.

immaturità *sf.* immaturity.

immaturo *agg.* 1. (*di frutto*) unripe 2. (*di persona*) immature.

immedesimare *vt.* 1. to unify. ♦ **immedesimarsi** *vr.* to identify oneself (with).

immedesimazione *sf.* unifying.

immediatamente *avv.* at once.

immediatezza *sf.* immediateness.

immediato *agg.* immediate.

immemoràbile *agg.* immemorial.

immèmore *agg.* forgetful.

immensità *sf.* immensity.

immenso *agg.* immense.

immèrgere *vt.* to immerse. ♦ **immèrgersi** *vr.* to immerse oneself.

immeritato *agg.* undeserved.

immeritévole *agg.* undeserving.

immersione *sf.* immersion.

imméttere *vt.* to let (*v. irr.*) in. ♦ **imméttersi** *vr.* to penetrate.

immigrante *agg. e sm.* immigrant.

immigrare *vi.* to immigrate.

immigrato *agg.* immigrated. ♦ **immigrato** *sm.* immigrant.

immigrazione *sf.* immigration.

imminente *agg.* impending.

imminenza *sf.* imminence.

immischiare *vt.* to involve. ♦ **immischiarsi** *vr.* to meddle (with).

immiserimento *sm.* impoverishing.

immiserire *vt.* to impoverish. ♦

immiserirsi *vr.* 1. to become (*v. irr.*) poor 2. (*fig.*) to weaken.

immissario *sm.* affluent.

immissione *sf.* letting in.

immòbile *agg.* immobile || *beni immobili,* immovables.

immobiliare *agg.* immovable.

immobilismo *sm.* ultra-conservatism.

immobilità *sf.* immobility.

immobilizzare *vt.* 1. to immobilize 2. (*comm.*) to lock up.

immobilizzazione *sf.* 1. immobilization 2. (*comm.*) locking up.

immoderato *agg.* immoderate.

immodestia *sf.* immodesty.

immodesto *agg.* immodest.

immolare *vt.* to immolate.

immondezza *sf.* dirtiness.

immondezzaio *sm.* garbage heap.

immondizia *sf.* 1. filth 2. (*spazzatura*) garbage.

immondo *agg.* dirty.

immorale *agg.* immoral.

immoralità *sf.* immorality.

immortalare *vt.* to immortalize.

immortale *agg.* immortal.

immortalità *sf.* immortality.

immoto *agg* motionless.

immune *agg.* immune.

immunità *sf.* immunity.

immunizzare *vt.* to immunize.

immunizzazione *sf.* immunization.

immusonirsi *vr.* to sulk.

immusonito *agg.* sulky.

immutàbile *agg.* immutable.

immutabilità *sf.* immutability.

impacchettare *vt.* to package.

impacciare *vt.* to hamper.

impacciato *agg.* 1. embarrassed 2. (*goffo*) awkward.

impaccio *sm.* hindrance.

impacco *sm.* compress.

impadronirsi *vr.* to take (*v. irr.*) possession (of).

impagàbile *agg.* priceless.

impaginare *vt.* to make-up.

impaginatore *sm.* maker-up.

impaginazione *sf.* making-up.

impagliare *vt.* 1. to cover with straw 2. (*di animali*) to stuff with straw.

impagliatore *sm.* 1. chair-mender 2. (*di animali*) stuffer.

impagliatura *sf.* 1. chair-mending 2. (*di animali*) stuffing.

impalare *vt.* to impale.

impalato *agg.* stiff.

impalcatura *sf.* 1. scaffolding 2.

(*di corna di cervo*) antlers (*pl.*).
impallidire *vi.* to turn pale.
impallinare *vt.* to shot.
impalmare *vt.* to marry.
impalpàbile *agg.* impalpable.
impalpabilità *sf.* impalpability.
impanare *vt.* **1.** (*cuc.*) to bread **2.** (*mecc.*) to thread.
impantanare *vt.* to swamp. ♦ **impantanarsi** *vr.* to swamp (*anche fig.*).
impaperarsi *vr.* to slip up.
impappinarsi *vr.* to stammer.
imparagonàbile *agg.* incomparable.
imparare *vt.* to learn (*v. irr.*).
impareggiàbile *agg.* unparalleled.
imparentare *vt.* to relate. ♦ **imparentarsi** *vr.* to become (*v. irr.*) related (to).
impari *agg.* unequal.
imparisìllabo *agg. e sm.* imparisyllabic.
imparruccato *agg.* bewigged.
impartire *vt.* to impart.
imparziale *agg.* impartial.
imparzialità *sf.* impartiality.
impassìbile *agg.* impassive, unmoved.
impassibilità *sf.* impassibility.
impastare *vt.* to knead ‖ — *i colori*, to impaste.
impastato *agg.* **1.** kneaded **2.** (*fig.*) full.
impastatore *sm.* kneader.
impastatrice *sf.* kneading-machine.
impasto *sm.* **1.** dough **2.** (*miscuglio*) mixture.
impastoiare *vt.* (*fig.*) to impede.
impatto *sm.* impact.
impaurire *vt.* to frighten. ♦ **impaurirsi** *vr.* to get (*v. irr.*) scared.
impaurito *agg.* afraid: *sguardo* —, fearful look.
impàvido *agg.* fearless.
impaziente *agg.* impatient.
impazientirsi *vr.* to lose (*v. irr.*) one's patience.
impazienza *sf.* impatience.
impazzare *vi.* to be at one's height.
impazzata (*nella loc. avv.*) *all'*—, madly.
impazzire *vi.* to go (*v. irr.*) mad.
impeccàbile *agg.* faultless.
impeciare *vt.* to pitch.
impedimento *sm.* obstacle.
impedire *vt.* to prevent (from).
impegnare *vt.* **1.** (*dare in pegno*) to pawn **2.** (*prenotare*) to reserve,

to book. ♦ **impegnarsi** *vr.* to engage (oneself).
impegnativo *agg.* binding ‖ *lavoro* —, exacting job.
impegno *sm.* engagement.
impegolarsi *vr.* (*fig.*) to get (*v. irr.*) involved.
impelagarsi *vr.* to get (*v. irr.*) in trouble.
impellente *agg.* urgent.
impellicciare *vt.* to fur.
impellicciatura *sf.* veneering.
impenetràbile *agg.* impenetrable.
impenetrabilità *sf.* impenetrableness.
impenitente *agg.* impenitent.
impennacchiare *vt.* to plume.
impennarsi *vr.* **1.** (*di cavallo*) to rear **2.** (*fig.*) to rear up.
impennata *sf.* (*di cavallo*) rearing **2.** (*fig.*) bristling.
impensàbile *agg.* unthinkable.
impensato *agg.* unexpected.
impensierire *vt.* to worry.
imperante *agg.* ruling.
imperare *vi.* to rule (over).
imperativo *agg.* imperative.
imperatore *sm.* emperor.
imperatrice *sf.* empress.
impercettìbile *agg.* imperceptible.
impercettibilità *sf.* imperceptibility.
imperdonàbile *agg.* unpardonable.
imperfetto *agg.* **1.** (*gramm.*) imperfect **2.** (*fig.*) faulty.
imperfezione *sf.* imperfection.
imperiale[1] *agg.* imperial.
imperiale[2] *sm.* imperial.
imperialismo *sm.* imperialism.
imperialista *s.* imperialist.
imperialìstico *agg.* imperialistic
imperio *sm.* command, authority.
imperioso *agg.* imperious.
imperito *agg.* unskilful.
imperituro *agg.* everlasting.
imperizia *sf.* unskilfulness.
imperlare *vt.* to bead. ♦ **imperlarsi** *vr.* to bead.
impermalirsi *vr.* to resent (sthg.).
impermeàbile *agg.* impermeable. ♦ **impermeàbile** *sm.* raincoat.
impermeabilità *sf.* impermeability.
impermeabilizzare *vt.* to waterproof.
impermeabilizzazione *sf.* waterproofing.
imperniare *vt.* to pivot (upon).
impero *sm.* empire.
imperscrutàbile *agg.* inscrutable.

imperscrutabilità *sf.* inscrutableness.

impersonale *agg.* impersonal.

impersonalità *sf.* impersonality.

impersonare *vt.* to impersonate. ♦ **impersonarsi** *vr.* to materialize.

impertèrrito *agg.* undaunted.

impertinente *agg.* impertinent.

impertinenza *sf.* impertinence.

imperturbàbile *agg.* impassive.

imperturbabilità *sf.* imperturbability.

imperturbato *agg.* imperturbed.

imperversare *vi.* to rage.

impervio *agg.* inaccessible.

ìmpeto *sm.* 1. rush, impetus 2. (*impulso*) impulse.

impetrare *vt.* to impetrate.

impettito *agg.* stiff.

impetuosità *sf.* impetuosity.

impetuoso *agg.* impetuous.

impiantare *vt.* to found.

impiantito *sm.* 1. (*di legno*) parquet floor 2. (*di piastrelle*) tiled floor.

impianto *sm.* plant, installation.

impiastricciare *vt.* to daub.

impiastro *sm.* 1. plaster 2. (*fig.*) bore.

impiccagione *sf.* hanging.

impiccare *vt.* to hang.

impiccato *agg.* hanged. ♦ **impiccato** *sm.* hanged man.

impicciare *vt.* to hinder. ♦ **impicciarsi** *vr.* to meddle (in).

impiccio *sm.* hindrance.

impiccolire *vt.* to make (*v. irr.*) smaller.

impiegare *vt.* 1. to employ 2. (*spendere*) to spend (*v. irr.*) 3. (*comm.*) to invest.

impiegatizio *agg.* white-collar (*attributivo*).

impiegato *agg.* employed. ♦ **impiegato** *sm.* employee, clerk.

impiego *sm.* 1. employment 2. (*uso*) use.

impietosire *vt.* to move tò pity. ♦ **impietosirsi** *vr.* to feel (*v. irr.*) sorry (for).

impietrire *vt.* to petrify.

impigliare *vt.* to entangle.

impigrire *vt.* to make (*v. irr.*) lazy.

impinguare *vt.* 1. to fatten 2. (*fig.*) to enrich.

impiombare *vt.* 1. to plumb 2. (*otturare*) to fill 3. (*coprire di piombo*) to lead.

impiombatura *sf.* 1. plumbing 2. (*otturazione*) filling 3. (*copertura di piombo*) leading.

implacàbile *agg.* implacable.

implacabilità *sf.* implacability.

implicare *vt.* to involve.

implìcito *agg.* implicit.

implorare *vt.* to implore.

implorazione *sf.* entreaty.

implume *agg.* featherless.

impolìtico *agg.* impolitic.

impollinare *vt.* to pollinate.

impollinazione *sf.* pollination.

impoltronire *vt.* to make (*v. irr.*) lazy. ♦ **impoltronirsi** *vr.* to grow (*v. irr.*) lazy.

impolverare *vt.* to cover with dust.

impolverato *agg.* dusty.

impomatare *vt.* to pomade. ♦ **impomatarsi** *vr.* to pomade oneself.

imponderàbile *agg.* imponderable.

imponderabilità *sf.* imponderability.

imponente *agg.* imposing.

imponenza *sf.* grandeur, majesty.

imponìbile *agg.* taxable.

imponibilità *sf.* taxability.

impopolare *agg.* unpopular.

impopolarità *sf.* unpopularity.

imporporarsi *vr.* to purple.

imporre *vt.* to impose: — *un nome*, to give (*v. irr.*) a name. ♦ **imporsi** *vr.* 1. to impose oneself 2. (*avere successo*) to become (*v. irr.*) popular.

importante *agg.* important.

importanza *sf.* importance.

importare *vi. imp.* to matter, to care. ♦ **importare** *vt.* (*comm.*) to import.

importatore *sm.* importer.

importazione *sf.* import.

importo *sm.* amount.

importunare *vt.* to importune, to bother.

importunità *sf.* importunity.

importuno *agg.* boring. ♦ **importuno** *sm.* bore.

imposizione *sf.* imposition.

impossessarsi *vr.* to take (*v. irr.*) possession (of).

impossìbile *agg.* impossible.

impossibilità *sf.* impossibility.

impossibilitato *agg.* unable.

imposta *sf.* 1. tax 2. (*edil.*) shutter.

impostare *vt.* 1. to start 2. (*di lettera*) to post.

impostazione *sf.* general lines (*pl.*).

impostore *sm.* impostor.

impostura *sf*. 1. imposture 2. (*frode*) fraud.

impotente *agg*. powerless. ♦ impotente *agg. e sm.* (*med.*) impotent.

impotenza *sf*. impotence.

impoverimento *sm*. impoverishment.

impoverire *vt*. to impoverish. ♦ **impoverirsi** *vr*. to become (*v. irr.*) poor.

impraticàbile *agg*. impracticable: *strada* —, impassable road.

impraticabilità *sf*. impracticability.

impratichire *vt*. to train. ♦ **impratichirsi** *vr*. to get (*v. irr.*) trained.

imprecare *vi*. to curse.

imprecazione *sf*. curse.

imprecisàbile *agg*. indeterminable.

imprecisato *agg*. undetermined.

imprecisione *sf*. 1. vagueness 2. (*inesattezza*) inaccuracy.

impreciso *agg*. inaccurate.

impregnare *vt*. to impregnate (with). ♦ **impregnarsi** *vr*. to become (*v. irr.*) imbued (with).

imprèndere *vt*. to undertake (*v. irr.*).

imprendìbile *agg*. elusive, invincible.

imprenditore *sm*. 1. entrepreneur 2. (*edil.*) contractor.

impreparato *agg*. unprepared.

impreparazione *sf*. unpreparedness.

impresa *sf*. 1. (*iniziativa*) undertaking 2. (*gesta*) deed 3. (*azienda*) firm, company.

impresario *sm*. 1. contractor 2. (*teat.*) manager.

imprescindìbile *agg*. unavoidable.

imprescrittìbile *agg*. indefeasible.

impressionàbile *agg*. impressionable.

impressionabilità *sf*. impressionability.

impressionante *agg*. frightening.

impressionare *vt*. 1. to impress 2. (*foto*) to expose.

impressione *sf*. impression.

impressionismo *sm*. impressionism.

impressionista *s*. impressionist.

impresso *agg*. printed.

imprestare *vt*. to lend (*v. irr.*).

imprevedìbile *agg*. unforeseeable.

impreveduto *agg*. unforeseen.

imprevidente *agg*. improvident.

imprevidenza *sf*. improvidence.

imprevisto *agg*. unexpected. ♦ **imprevisto** *sm*. unforeseen event.

impreziosire *vt*. to make (*v. irr.*) precious. ♦ **impreziosirsi** *vr*. to become (*v. irr.*) precious.

imprigionamento *sm*. imprisonment.

imprigionare *vt*. to imprison.

imprìmere *vt*. to impress.

improbàbile *agg*. improbable.

improbabilità *sf*. improbability.

ìmprobo *agg*. 1. dishonest 2. (*faticoso*) hard.

improduttività *sf*. unproductiveness.

improduttivo *agg*. unproductive.

impronta *sf*. 1. impression: — *del piede, digitale,* footprint, fingerprint 2. (*fig.*) mark.

improntare *vt*. 1. to prepare 2. (*fig.*) to mark.

improntitùdine *sf*. impudence.

impronunciàbile *agg*. unpronounceable.

improperio *sm*. insult.

improprietà *sf*. impropriety.

improprio *agg*. improper.

improrogàbile *agg*. undelayable.

impròvvido *agg*. improvident.

improvvisamente *avv*. suddenly.

improvvisare *vt. e vi*. to improvise. ♦ **improvvisarsi** *vr*. to act.

improvvisata *sf*. surprise.

improvvisatore *sm*. improviser.

improvvisazione *sf*. improvisation.

improvviso *agg*. sudden.

imprudente *agg*. imprudent.

imprudenza *sf*. imprudence.

impudente *agg*. impudent.

impudenza *sf*. impudence.

impudicizia *sf*. immodesty.

impudico *agg*. shameless, immodest.

impugnàbile *agg*. (*giur.*) impugnable.

impugnabilità *sf*. (*giur.*) impugnment.

impugnare *vt*. 1. to grasp, to hold 2. (*giur.*) to impugn.

impugnatura *sf*. hilt.

impulsività *sf*. impulsiveness.

impulsivo *agg*. impulsive.

impulso *sm*. impulse.

impunemente *avv*. safely.

impunità *sf*. impunity.

impunito *agg*. unpunished.

impuntare *vi*. to stumble (over).

♦ **impuntarsi** *vr.* 1. to jib 2. (*ostinarsi*) to stick (*v. irr.*) (to).

impuntura *sf.* stitching.

impurità *sf.* impurity.

impuro *agg.* impure.

imputàbile *agg.* 1. imputable 2. (*giur.*) chargeable (with).

imputare *vt.* 1. to impute 2. (*giur.*) to charge (with).

imputato *sm.* defendant.

imputazione *sf.* imputation.

imputridimento *sm.* putrefaction.

imputridire *vi.* to rot.

in *prep.* (*stato in luogo*) in, at: *essere — campagna, — città*, to be in the country, in town; *essere — casa, — chiesa*, to be at home, at church 2. (*moto a luogo*) to: *andò — America*, he went to America 3. (*moto dentro luogo*) into: *va' nello studio*, go into the study 4. (*coi mezzi di trasporto*) by: *sono venuto — treno*, I came by train.

inàbile *agg.* 1. unable 2. (*non idoneo*) unfit.

inabilità *sf.* 1. inability 2. (*inidoneità*) unfitness.

inabilitare *vt.* to disable.

inabilitazione *sf.* disability.

inabissamento *sm.* sinking.

inabissarsi *vr.* to sink (*v. irr.*).

inabitàbile *agg.* uninhabitable.

inabitabilità *sf.* uninhabitableness.

inabitato *agg.* 1. uninhabited 2. (*deserto*) deserted.

inaccessìbile *agg.* inaccessible.

inaccessibilità *sf.* inaccessibility.

inaccettàbile *agg.* unacceptable.

inaccettabilità *sf.* unacceptableness.

inacerbire *vt.* to exacerbate. ♦ **inacerbirsi** *vr.* to grow (*v. irr.*) bitter.

inacidire *vt.* to sour. ♦ **inacidirsi** *vr.* to turn sour.

inacidito *agg.* sour.

inadattàbile *agg.* unadaptable.

inadattabilità *sf.* inadaptability.

inadatto *agg.* 1. unfit (for) 2. (*sconveniente*) unbecoming.

inadeguato *agg.* inadequate.

inadempìbile *agg.* unfulfillable.

inadempiente *agg.* defaulting.

inadempienza *sf.* non-execution.

inafferràbile *agg.* unseizable.

inalare *vt.* to inhale.

inalatore *sm.* inhaler.

inalazione *sf.* inhalation.

inalberare *vt.* to hoist. ♦ **inalberarsi** *vr.* 1. to rear up 2. (*fig.*) to lose (*v. irr.*) one's temper.

inalienàbile *agg.* inalienable.

inalienabilità *sf.* inalienability.

inalteràbile *agg.* inalterable.

inalterabilità *sf.* inalterability.

inalterato *agg.* unaltered.

inalveare *vt.* to canalize.

inamidare *vt.* to starch.

inammissìbile *agg.* inadmissible.

inammissibilità *sf.* inadmissibility.

inamovìbile *agg.* irremovable.

inamovibilità *sf.* irremovability.

inane *agg.* inane.

inanellare *vt.* to curl.

inanimato *agg.* lifeless.

inanità *sf.* inanity.

inappagàbile *agg.* unsatisfiable.

inappagato *agg.* unsatisfied.

inappellàbile *agg.* inappellable.

inappetenza *sf.* inappetence.

inapplicàbile *agg.* inapplicable.

inapprezzàbile *agg.* priceless.

inappuntàbile *agg.* 1. irreproachable 2. (*nel vestire*) faultlessly dressed.

inarcamento *sm.* bending, arching.

inarcare *vt.* to bend (*v. irr.*) || — *le sopracciglia*, to raise one's brows. ♦ **inarcarsi** *vr.* to arch.

inargentare *vt.* to silver.

inaridire *vt.* to dry. ♦ **inaridirsi** *vr.* to dry up.

inarticolato *agg.* inarticulate.

inascoltato *agg.* unheard.

inaspettato *agg.* unexpected.

inasprimento *sm.* embitterment.

inasprire *vt.* to embitter. ♦ **inasprirsi** *vr.* to become (*v. irr.*) embittered.

inattaccàbile *agg.* unassailable.

inattendìbile *agg.* unreliable.

inatteso *agg.* unexpected.

inattività *sf.* inactivity.

inattivo *agg.* inactive.

inattuàbile *agg.* impracticable.

inattuale *agg.* outdated.

inaudito *agg.* unheard of.

inaugurale *agg.* inaugural.

inaugurare *vt.* to inaugurate.

inaugurazione *sf.* inauguration.

inavvedutezza *sf.* carelessness.

inavveduto *agg.* careless.

inavvertenza *sf.* inadvertence.

inavvertito *agg.* unperceived.

inazione *sf.* inaction.

incagliare *vt.* to hinder. ♦ **incagliarsi** *vr.* to strand.

incaglio *sm* 1. stranding 2. (*fig.*) obstacle.

incalcolàbile *agg.* incalculable.

incallire *vi.* to harden. ♦ **incallirsi** *vr.* to harden.

incallito *agg.* hardened.

incalzante *agg.* 1. pursuing 2. (*fig.*) pressing.

incalzare *vt.* 1. to pursue 2. (*fig.*) to urge.

incameramento *sm.* confiscation.

incamerare *vt.* to confiscate.

incamminare *vt.* to set (*v. irr.*) going. ♦ **incamminarsi** *vr.* to set out (for).

incanalamento *sm.* canalization.

incanalare *vt.* to canalize.

incancellàbile *agg.* indelible.

incancrenire *vi.* to become (*v. irr.*) gangrenous.

incandescente *agg.* white-hot.

incandescenza *sf.* incandescence.

incantamento *sm.* charm.

incantare *vt.* to charm. ♦ **incantarsi** *vr.* to be charmed.

incantato *agg.* enchanted.

incantatore *agg.* enchanting. ♦ **incantatore** *sm.* enchanter.

incantésimo *sm.* spell.

incantévole *agg.* charming.

incanto[1] *sm.* enchantment.

incanto[2] *sm.* (*comm.*) auction: *vendere all'—*, to sell (*v. irr.*) by auction.

incanutire *vi.* to grow (*v. irr.*) hoary.

incapace *agg.* unable.

incapacità *sf.* incapacity.

incaparbirsi *vr.* to become (*v. irr.*) obstinate.

incappare *vi.* to get (*v. irr.*) into, to stumble.

incappucciare *vt.* to hood. ♦ **incappucciarsi** *vr.* to put (*v. irr.*) on one's hood.

incapricciarsi *vr.* to take (*v. irr.*) a fancy (to).

incapsulare *vt.* to capsule.

incarcerare *vt.* to imprison.

incarcerazione *sf.* imprisonment.

incaricare *vt.* to charge (so. with). ♦ **incaricarsi** *vr.* to charge oneself (with).

incaricato *agg.* charged (with). ♦ **incaricato** *sm.* appointee.

incàrico *sm.* task, duty.

incarnare *vt.* to embody. ♦ **incarnarsi** *vr.* to take (*v. irr.*) body.

incarnato *sm.* complexion.

incarnazione *sf.* incarnation.

incarnire *vi.* to grow (*v. irr.*) into flesh.

incartamento *sm.* dossier.

incartapecorire *vi.* to wrinkle.

incartapecorito *agg.* wrinkled with age.

incartare *vt.* to wrap in paper.

incarto *sm.* set of papers.

incartocciare *vt.* to wrap up in a cornet.

incasellare *vt.* to put (*v. irr.*) in squares.

incassamento *sm.* 1. boxing 2. (*mecc.; arch.*) embedding.

incassare *vt.* 1. to box 2. (*riscuotere*) to cash.

incassatura *sf.* hollow.

incasso *sm.* 1. collection 2. (*di spettacoli*) receipts (*pl.*).

incastellamento *sm.* 1. fortifications (*pl.*) 2. (*arch.*) scaffolding.

incastellare *vt.* to fortify with battlements.

incastellatura *sf.* 1. frame 2. (*arch.*) scaffolding.

incastonare *vt.* to set (*v. irr.*).

incastonatura *sf.* setting.

incastrare *vt.* 1. to embed 2. (*adattare*) to fit in. ♦ **incastrarsi** *vr.* 1. to fit 2. (*impigliarsi*) to get (*v. irr.*) stuck.

incastro *sm.* joint.

incatenamento *sm.* chaining.

incatenare *vt.* to chain. ♦ **incatenarsi** *vr.* to be linked (with).

incatramare *vt.* to tar.

incattivire *vt.* to exasperate. ♦ **incattivirsi** *vr.* to get (*v. irr.*) crossed.

incàuto *agg.* rash.

incavare *vt.* to hollow out.

incavatura *sf.* hollowness.

incavo *sm.* hollow.

incèdere *vi.* to advance.

incendiare *vt.* to set (*v. irr.*) on fire.

incendiario *agg. e sm.* incendiary.

incendio *sm.* fire.

incenerire *vt.* to reduce to ashes.

incensamento *sm.* 1. incensation 2. (*fig.*) flattery.

incensare *vt.* 1. to incense 2. (*fig.*) to flatter.

incenso *sm.* incense.

incensuràbile *agg.* irreproachable.

incensurato *agg.* blameless: *essere —*, to be a first-offender.

incentivo *sm.* incentive.

inceppamento sm. 1. obstacle 2. (mecc.) jam.

inceppare vt. 1. to clog 2. (ostacolare) to encumber. ♦ **incepparsi** vr. to jam.

incerare vt. to wax.

incertezza sf. uncertainty, doubt.

incerto agg. uncertain. ♦ **incerto** sm. uncertainty.

incespicare vi. to stumble.

incessante agg. unceasing.

incesto sm. incest.

incestuoso agg. incestuous.

incetta sf. cornering: fare — di, to make (v. irr.) a corner in.

incettare vt. to corner.

incettatore sm. cornerer.

inchiesta sf. inquiry, investigation.

inchinare vt. to bow. ♦ **inchinarsi** vr. to bow (down).

inchino sm. bow.

inchiodare vt. to nail.

inchiodatura sf. nailing.

inchiostro sm. ink.

inciampare vi. to stumble.

inciampo sm. obstacle.

incidentale agg. 1. incidental 2. (gramm.) parenthetic.

incidente agg. incident. ♦ **incidente** sm. accident.

incidenza sf. incidence.

incìdere[1] vt. 1. to cut (v. irr.) 2. (intagliare) to engrave 3. (su disco, nastro ecc.) to record.

incìdere[2] vi. to weigh heavily: — sul bilancio, to weigh heavily on one's budget.

incinta agg. f. pregnant.

incipiente agg. incipient.

incipriare vt. to powder. ♦ **incipriarsi** vr. to powder (oneself).

incirca (nella loc. avv.) all'—, about.

incisione sf. 1. cut 2. (arte) engraving 3. (su disco, nastro ecc.) recording.

incisività sf. sharpness.

incisivo agg. incisive. ♦ **incisivo** sm. (anat.) incisor.

inciso sm. parenthetic clause: per —, incidentally.

incisore sm. engraver.

incitamento sm. urge.

incitare vt. to urge, to stimulate.

incitrullire vi. to become (v. irr.) silly.

incivile agg. 1. uncivilized 2. (scortese) rude.

incivilimento sm. civilization.

incivilire vt. to civilize. ♦ **incivilirsi** vr. to become (v. irr.) civilized.

inciviltà sf. 1. barbarism 2. (fig.) rudeness.

inclassificàbile agg. unclassifiable.

inclemente agg. 1. inclement: tempo —, inclement weather 2. (spietato) merciless.

inclemenza sf. 1. (di tempo) inclemency 2. (crudeltà) mercilessness.

inclinare vt. to incline, to bend (v. irr.).

inclinato agg. inclined (anche fig.).

inclinazione sf. 1. inclination 2. (attitudine) bent.

incline agg. disposed.

inclito agg. famous.

inclùdere vt. to include.

inclusione sf. inclusion.

inclusivo agg. inclusive.

incluso agg. 1. included 2. (accluso) enclosed.

incoccare vt. to nock.

incoercìbile agg. irrepressible.

incoercibilità sf. irrepressibleness.

incoerente agg. incoherent.

incoerenza sf. incoherence.

incògnita sf. 1. (mat.) unknown quantity 2. (fig.) uncertainty.

incògnito agg. unknown. ♦ **incògnito** sm. incognito (pl. -tos).

incollamento sm. pasting.

incollare vt. to stick (v. irr.). ♦ **incollarsi** vr. to stick.

incollatrice sf. sizing-machine.

incollatura[1] sf. sticking.

incollatura[2] sf. (ippica) neck.

incollerire vi. to get (v. irr.) angry. ♦ **incollerirsi** vr. to get angry.

incollerito agg. angry.

incolonnamento sm. column formation.

incolonnare vt. to form into columns. ♦ **incolonnarsi** vr. to rank.

incolore agg. colourless.

incolpàbile agg. accusable.

incolpare vt. to charge (with), to accuse (of). ♦ **incolparsi** vr. to accuse oneself.

incolpévole agg. blameless.

incolto agg. uncultivated.

incòlume agg. unhurt.

incolumità sf. safety.

incombente agg. impending.

incombenza sf. errand, task.

incòmbere vi. 1. (spettare) to be

one's job **2.** (*sovrastare*) to impend (over).

incombustìbile *agg.* incombustible.

incominciare *vt. e vi.* V. *cominciare.*

incommensuràbile *agg.* incommensurable.

incommensurabilità *sf.* incommensurability.

incommerciàbile *agg.* not negotiable.

incommutàbile *agg.* incommutable.

incomodare *vt.* to annoy. ♦ **incomodarsi** *vr.* to trouble.

incomodità *sf.* uncomfortableness.

incòmodo *agg.* uncomfortable || *essere d'* —, to be in the way.

incomparàbile *agg.* incomparable.

incompatìbile *agg.* incompatible.

incompatibilità *sf.* incompatibility.

incompetente *agg.* incompetent.

incompetenza *sf.* incompetence.

incompiuto *agg.* unfinished.

incompletezza *sf.* incompleteness.

incompleto *agg.* incomplete.

incompostezza *sf.* disorder.

incomposto *agg.* disorderly.

incomprensìbile *agg.* incomprehensibile.

incomprensibilità *sf.* incomprehensibility.

incomprensione *sf.* incomprehension.

incompreso *agg.* **1.** not understood **2.** (*non apprezzato*) unappreciated.

incomputàbile *agg.* incalculable.

incomunicàbile *agg.* incommunicable.

incomunicabilità *sf.* incommunicability.

inconcepìbile *agg.* inconceivable.

inconciliàbile *agg.* irreconcilable.

inconciliabilità *sf.* irreconcilability.

inconcludente *agg.* **1.** inconclusive **2.** (*di persona*) good-for-nothing.

inconcusso *agg.* unshaken.

incondizionato *agg.* unconditional.

inconfessàbile *agg.* unavowable.

inconfessato *agg.* unconfessed.

inconfondìbile *agg.* unmistakable.

inconfutàbile *agg.* irrefutable.

incongruente *agg.* incongruous.

incongruenza *sf.* incongruity.

incòngruo *agg.* incongruous.

inconsapévole *agg.* unconscious, unaware.

inconsapevolezza *sf.* unconsciousness, unawareness.

inconscio *agg. e sm.* unconscious.

inconseguente *agg.* inconsequent.

inconseguenza *sf.* inconsequence.

inconsideratezza *sf.* rashness.

inconsiderato *agg.* rash.

inconsistente *agg.* insubstantial.

inconsistenza *sf.* insubstantiality.

inconsolàbile *agg.* inconsolable.

inconsueto *agg.* unusual.

inconsulto *agg.* unadvised, rash.

incontaminato *agg.* unpolluted.

incontentàbile *agg.* insatiable.

incontentabilità *sf.* insatiability.

incontestàbile *agg.* incontestable.

incontinente *agg.* incontinent.

incontinenza *sf.* incontinence.

incontrare *vt.* to meet (*v. irr.*). ♦ **incontrarsi** *vr.* to meet || *i nostri gusti non si incontrano*, our tastes do not agree.

incontrastàbile *agg.* incontestable.

incontrastato *agg.* uncontested.

incontro[1] *sm.* **1.** meeting **2.** (*sport*) match.

incontro[2] *prep.* — *a*, towards, to.

incontrollàbile *agg.* uncontrollable.

incontrollato *agg.* uncontrolled.

incontrovertìbile *agg.* indisputable.

inconveniente *sm.* inconvenience, drawback.

inconvertìbile *agg.* inconvertible.

inconvertibilità *sf.* inconvertibility.

incoraggiamento *sm.* encouragement.

incoraggiante *agg.* encouraging.

incoraggiare *vt.* to encourage.

incorniciare *vt.* to frame.

incorniciatura *sf.* framing.

incoronamento *sm.* V. *coronamento.*

incoronare *vt.* V. *coronare.*

incoronazione *sf.* coronation.

incorporare *vt.* to incorporate.

incorporazione *sf.* incorporation.

incorpòreo *agg.* incorporeal.

incorreggìbile *agg.* incorrigible.

incòrrere *vi.* to incur, to suffer (sthg.).

incorretto *agg.* incorrect.

incorrotto *agg.* incorrupt.

incorruttìbile *agg.* incorruptible.

incorruttibilità *sf.* incorruptibility.

incosciente *agg.* **1.** unconscious **2.** (*irresponsabile*) reckless. ♦ **incosciente** *sm.* irresponsible.

incoscienza *sf.* **1.** unconsciousness **2.** (*spericolatezza*) rashness.

incostante *agg.* inconstant: *tempo* —, changeable weather.

incostituzionale *agg.* unconstitutional.

incostituzionalità *sf.* unconstitutionality.

incredìbile *agg.* incredible.

incredibilità *sf.* incredibility.

incredulità *sf.* incredulity.

incrèdulo *agg.* incredulous.

incrementare *vt.* to increase.

incremento *sm.* increase.

increscioso *agg.* unpleasant.

increspamento *sm.* 1. (*di acque*) rippling 2. (*di capelli*) ruffling.

increspare *vt.*, **incresparsi** *vr.* 1. (*di acque*) to ripple 2. (*di capelli*) to ruffle.

incretinire *vt.* to make (*v. irr.*) stupid. ♦ **incretinirsi** *vr.* to dull.

incriminàbile *agg.* impeachable.

incriminare *vt.* to impeach.

incriminazione *sf.* 1. (*l'accusare*) crimination 2. (*atto d'accusa*) indictment.

incrinare *vt.* to crack. ♦ **incrinarsi** *vr.* to crack.

incrinatura *sf.* crack.

incriticàbile *agg.* uncensurable.

incrociare *vt.* to cross. ♦ **incrociarsi** *vr.* to cross.

incrociatore *sm.* cruiser.

incrocio *sm.* 1. crossing || — *stradale*, cross-road 2. (*di razze*) crossbreed.

incrollàbile *agg.* unshakable.

incrostare *vt.* to incrust. ♦ **incrostarsi** *vr.* to become (*v. irr.*) incrusted.

incrostazione *sf.* incrustation.

incrudelimento *sm.* toughening.

incrudelire *vi.* to become (*v. irr.*) cruel || — *contro* qu., to be pitiless towards so.

incrudire *vi.* to grow (*v. irr.*) worse.

incruento *agg.* bloodless.

incubatrice *sf.* incubator.

incubazione *sf.* incubation.

ìncubo *sm.* nightmare.

incùdine *sf.* anvil.

inculcare *vt.* to inculcate.

incunàbolo *sm.* incunabulum.

incuneare *vt.* to wedge. ♦ **incunearsi** *vr.* to wedge oneself.

incupire *vt.* e *vi.* to darken. ♦ **incupirsi** *vr.* to become (*v. irr.*) gloomy.

incuràbile *agg.* e *sm.* incurable.

incurabilità *sf.* incurability.

incurante *agg.* careless, heedless.

incuria *sf.* heedlessness.

incuriosire *vt.* to make (*v. irr.*) curious. ♦ **incuriosirsi** *vr.* to become (*v. irr.*) curious.

incuriosito *agg.* made curious.

incursione *sf.* raid.

incurvare *vt.* e **incurvarsi** *vr.* bend (*v. irr.*), to curve.

incurvatura *sf.* bend.

incustodito *agg.* unguarded.

incùtere *vt.* to rouse.

ìndaco *sm.* indigo.

indaffarato *agg.* busy.

indagare *vt.* to investigate.

indagatore *agg.* investigating.

indàgine *sf.* 1. research, investigation 2. (*giur.*) inquiry.

indebitare *vt.* to involve in debt. ♦ **indebitarsi** *vr.* to run (*v. irr.*) into debt.

indébito *agg.* undue.

indebolimento *sm.* weakening.

indebolire *vt.* to weaken. ♦ **indebolirsi** *vr.* to weaken.

indecente *agg.* indecent.

indecenza *sf.* indecency.

indecifràbile *agg.* 1. indecipherable 2. (*di calligrafia*) illegible.

indecisione *sf.* indecision.

indeciso *agg.* 1. irresolute 2. (*di cose*) undecided.

indeclinàbile *agg.* 1. indeclinable 2. (*che non si può eludere*) unavoidable.

indecoroso *agg.* unseemly.

indefesso *agg.* indefatigable.

indefinìbile *agg.* indefinable.

indefinito *agg.* indefinite.

indeformàbile *agg.* indeformable.

indegno *agg.* 1. unworthy 2. (*spregevole*) disgraceful.

indelèbile *agg.* indelible.

indelicatezza *sf.* indelicacy.

indelicato *agg.* tactless.

indemoniato *agg.* 1. possessed 2. (*fig.*) frantic. ♦ **indemoniato** *sm.* demoniac.

indenne *agg.* undamaged.

indennità *sf.* allowance.

indennizzare *vt.* to indemnify.

indennizzo *sm.* indemnity.

inderogàbile *agg.* intransgressible.

indescrivìbile *agg.* indescribable.

indesideràbile *agg.* undesirable.

indeterminàbile *agg.* indeterminable.

indeterminatezza *sf.* vagueness.

indeterminativo *agg.* (*gramm.*) indefinite.

indeterminato *agg.* indeterminate.

indeterminazione *sf.* indetermination.

indi *avv.* **1.** (*di tempo*) then **2.** (*di luogo*) (from) thence.

indiano *agg.* Indian: — *d'America*, Red Indian; *in fila indiana*, in Indian file.

indiavolato *agg.* frenzied, furious.

indicare *vt.* **1.** to show (*v. irr.*) **2.** (*col dito*) to point at.

indicativo *agg.* indicative.

indicato *agg.* **1.** (*adatto*) suitable **2.** (*consigliabile*) advisable.

indicatore *agg.* indicatory. ♦ **indicatore** *sm.* indicator.

indicazione *sf.* indication.

indice *sm.* **1.** (*dito della mano*) forefinger **2.** (*di libro, statistica ecc.*) index.

indicibile *agg.* inexpressible.

indietreggiare *vi.* to withdraw (*v. irr.*).

indietro *avv.* (*di spazio, tempo*) back, behind.

indifendibile *agg.* indefensible.

indifeso *agg.* undefended.

indifferente *agg.* indifferent.

indifferenza *sf.* indifference.

indifferibile *agg.* undelayable.

indigeno *agg. e sm.* native.

indigente *agg.* indigent, poor.

indigenza *sf.* indigence.

indigestione *sf.* indigestion.

indigesto *agg.* **1.** indigestible **2.** (*fig.*) heavy.

indignare *vt.* to make (*v. irr.*) indignant. ♦ **indignarsi** *vr.* to get (*v. irr.*) angry.

indignazione *sf.* indignation.

indimenticabile *agg.* unforgettable.

indimostrabile *agg.* indemonstrable.

indipendente *agg.* independent (of). ♦ **indipendente** *sm.* (*pol.*) independent.

indipendenza *sf.* independence.

indire *vt.* to call, to announce.

indiretto *agg.* indirect.

indirizzare *vt.* to address. ♦ **indirizzarsi** *vr.* **1.** (*dirigersi*) to set (*v. irr.*) out (for) **2.** (*rivolgersi*) to address oneself (to).

indirizzo *sm.* **1.** address **2.** (*linea di condotta*) trend.

indisciplina *sf.* indiscipline.

indisciplinato *agg.* undisciplined.

indiscretezza *sf.* indiscretion.

indiscreto *agg.* indiscreet.

indiscrezione *sf.* indiscretion.

indiscriminato *agg.* indiscriminate.

indiscusso *agg.* undiscussed.

indiscutibile *agg.* unquestionable.

indispensabile *agg.* indispensable.

indispettire *vt.* to vex. ♦ **indispettirsi** *vr.* to become (*v. irr.*) vexed.

indispettito *agg.* vexed.

indisponente *agg.* irritating.

indisporre *vt.* to irritate.

indisposizione *sf.* indisposition.

indisposto *agg.* unwell (*pred.*).

indissolubile *agg.* indissoluble.

indissolubilità *sf.* indissolubility.

indistinto *agg.* indistinct.

indistruttibile *agg.* indestructible.

indisturbato *agg.* undisturbed.

individuale *agg.* individual.

individualismo *sm.* individualism.

individualista *s.* individualist.

individualistico *agg.* individualistic.

individuare *vt.* to single out.

individuo *sm.* individual.

indivisibile *agg.* indivisible.

indivisibilità *sf.* indivisibility.

indiviso *agg.* undivided.

indiziare *vt.* to make (*v. irr.*) suspect.

indiziario *agg.* presumptive.

indiziato *agg. e sm.* suspect.

indizio *sm.* **1.** indication **2.** (*giur.*) circumstantial proof.

indocile *agg.* indocile.

indocilità *sf.* indocility.

indoeuropeo *agg. e sm.* Indo-European.

indole *sf.* nature, disposition || *un ragazzo di buona* —, a good-natured boy.

indolente *agg.* indolent.

indolenza *sf.* indolence.

idolenzimento *sm.* numbness.

indolenzire *vt.* to numb. ♦ **indolenzirsi** *vr.* to become (*v. irr.*) numb.

indolenzito *agg.* numb.

indolore *agg.* painless.

indomabile *agg.* untamable.

indomani *sm.* next day || *all'* —, on the day after.

indomito *agg.* indomitable.

indorare *vt.* V. dorare.

indossare *vt.* **1.** (*avere indosso*) to wear (*v. irr.*) **2.** (*mettere indosso*) to put (*v. irr.*) on.

indossatrice *sf.* mannequin.
indosso *avv.* on.
indotto *agg.* (*spinto*) driven.
indovinare *vt.* to guess.
indovinello *sm.* riddle.
indovino *sm.* soothsayer.
indubbio *agg.* undoubted.
indubitàbile *agg.* indubitable.
indugiare *vi.* to delay, to hesitate.
indugio *sm.* delay.
indulgente *agg.* indulgent.
indulgenza *sf.* indulgence.
indùlgere *vi.* to indulge (in).
indulto *sm.* **1.** (*eccl.*) indult **2.** (*giur.*) free pardon.
indumento *sm.* garment.
indurimento *sm.* hardening.
indurire *vt.* e *vi.* to harden. ♦ **indurirsi** *vr.* to harden.
indurre *vt.* to induce, to get (*v. irr.*) || — *in errore*, to mislead (*v. irr.*). ♦ **indursi** *vr.* to bring (*v. irr.*) oneself (to).
industria *sf.* industry.
industriale *agg.* industrial. ♦ **industriale** *sm.* industrialist, manufacturer.
industrialismo *sm.* industrialism.
industrializzare *vt.* to industrialize.
industrializzazione *sf.* industrialization.
industriarsi *vr.* to do (*v. irr.*) one's best.
industrioso *agg.* industrious.
induttivo *agg.* inductive.
induttore *agg.* inductor.
induzione *sf.* induction.
inebetire *vt.* e *vi.* to dull.
inebetito *agg.* dull.
inebriante *agg.* inebriating.
inebriare *vt.* **1.** to make (*v. irr.*) drunk **2.** (*fig.*) to inebriate. ♦ **inebriarsi** *vr.* **1.** to get (*v. irr.*) drunk **2.** (*fig.*) to go (*v. irr.*) into raptures.
ineccepìbile *agg.* unexceptionable.
inedia *sf.* starvation.
inèdito *agg.* unpublished.
ineducato *agg.* ill-bred.
ineffàbile *agg.* ineffable.
inefficace *agg.* ineffective.
inefficacia *sf.* inefficacy.
inefficiente *agg.* inefficient.
inefficienza *sf.* ineffectiveness.
ineguaglianza *sf.* inequality.
ineguale *agg.* **1.** unlike **2.** (*irregolare*) irregular **3.** (*di superficie*) uneven.

ineleggìbile *agg.* ineligible.
ineleggibilità *sf.* ineligibility.
ineluttàbile *agg.* ineluctable.
ineluttabilità *sf.* inevitableness.
inenarràbile *agg.* unutterable.
inequivocàbile *agg.* unmistakable
'nerente *agg.* concerning.
inerme *agg.* unarmed.
inerpicarsi *vr.* to climb (up).
inerte *agg.* inert.
inerzia *sf.* inertness.
inesattezza *sf.* inaccuracy.
inesatto *agg.* incorrect.
inesaudito *agg.* ungranted.
inesauribile *agg.* inexhaustible.
inesàusto *agg.* unexhausted.
ineseguibile *agg.* inexecutable.
inesigìbile *agg.* **1.** uncollectable **2.** (*di assegno*) worthless.
inesistente *agg.* inexistent.
in:sistenza *sf.* inexistence.
in:soràbile *agg.* inexorable.
inesorabilità *sf.* inexorability.
inesperienza *sf.* inexperience.
inesperto *agg.* unskilled.
inespiàbile *agg.* inexpiable.
inesplicàbile *agg.* inexplicable.
inesploràbile *agg.* inexplorable.
inesplorato *agg.* unexplored.
inespressivo *agg.* inexpressive.
inespresso *agg.* implied.
inesprimìbile *agg.* inexpressible.
inespugnàbile *agg.* inexpugnable.
inespugnabilità *sf.* inexpugnability.
inestimàbile *agg.* inestimable.
inestinguìbile *agg.* unquenchable.
inestirpàbile *agg.* ineradicable.
inestricàbile *agg.* inextricable.
inettitùdine *sf.* unfitness.
inetto *agg.* **1.** unapt **2.** (*dappoco*) good-for-nothing.
inevaso *agg.* outstanding, unanswered.
inevitàbile *agg.* inevitable.
inezia *sf.* trifle.
infagottare *vt.* to muffle up. ♦ **infagottarsi** *vr.* to muffle oneself up.
infallìbile *agg.* infallible.
infallibilità *sf.* infallibility.
infamante *agg.* shameful.
infamare *vt.* to defame, to disgrace.
infame *agg.* wicked.
infamia *sf.* infamy.
infangare *vt.* to muddy. ♦ **infangarsi** *vr.* to become (*v. irr.*) muddy.
infanticida *s.* child-murderer.

infanticidio sm. child-murder.

infantile agg. childlike, childish.

infantilismo sm. infantilism.

infanzia sf. **1.** infancy **2.** (coll.) children (pl.).

infarcire vt. V. farcire.

infarinare vt. to flour. ◆ **infarinarsi** vr. to get (v. irr.) covered with flour.

infarinatura sf. **1.** flouring **2.** (fig.) smattering.

infarto sm. infarct.

infastidire vt. to annoy. ◆ **infastidirsi** vr. to get (v. irr.) bored.

infaticàbile agg. tireless.

infatti cong. in fact.

infatuare vt. to infatuate. ◆ **infatuarsi** vr. to get (v. irr.) crazy (about).

infatuato agg. crazy (about).

infatuazione sf. infatuation.

infàusto agg. unlucky.

infecondità sf. sterility.

infecondo agg. steril.

infedele agg. unfaithful. ◆ **infedele** sm. infidel.

infedeltà sf. unfaithfulness.

infelice agg. **1.** unhappy **2.** (non appropriato) ill-timed. ◆ **infelice** s. wretch.

infelicità sf. unhappiness.

inferiore agg. **1.** inferior **2.** (più basso) lower **3.** (al di sotto) below. ◆ **inferiore** sm. inferior.

inferiorità sf. inferiority.

inferire vt. **1.** (dedurre) to inœer **2.** (dare) to inflict.

infermerìa sf. infirmary.

infermiera sf. nurse.

infermiere sm. hospital attendant.

infermità sf. infirmity.

infermo agg. e sm. invalid.

infernale agg. **1.** infernal **2.** (fig.) awful.

inferno sm. hell.

inferocire vt. to enrage. ◆ **inferocire** vi. to get (v. irr.) fierce.

inferriata sf. grating.

infervorare vt. to excite. ◆ **infervorarsi** vr. to get (v. irr.) excited.

infervorato agg. fervent.

infestare vt. to infest.

infestazione sf. infestation.

infettare vt. to infect. ◆ **infettarsi** vr. to become (v. irr.) infected.

infettivo agg. contagious.

infetto agg. infected.

infezione sf. infection.

infiacchimento sm. weakening.

infiacchire vt. e vi. to weaken. ◆ **infiacchirsi** vr. to become (v. irr.) weak.

infiammàbile agg. inflammable.

infiammabilità sf. inflammability.

infiammare vt. **1.** to set (v. irr.) on fire **2.** (fig.) to inflame. ◆ **infiammarsi** vr. **1.** to take (v. irr.) fire **2.** (fig.) to get (v. irr.) excited.

infiammato agg. inflamed (with).

infiammatorio agg. inflammatory.

infiammazione sf. inflammation.

infiascare vt. to put (v. irr.) into flasks.

inficiare vt. **1.** to invalidate **2.** (giur.) to impugn.

infido agg. false.

infierire vi. to be pitiless.

infìggere vt. **1.** to infix **2.** (conficcare) to drive (v. irr.) (into).

infilare vt. **1.** to thread **2.** (introdurre) to insert **3.** (passare per) to enter. ◆ **infilarsi** vr. to slip into.

infilata sf. row.

infiltrarsi vr. to penetrate.

infiltrazione sf. infiltration.

infilzare vt. **1.** to transfix **2.** (conficcare) to stick (v. irr.). ◆ **infilzarsi** vr. **1.** to run (v. irr.) oneself through **2.** (conficcarsi) to get (v. irr.) stuck.

infilzata sf. string.

ìnfimo agg. lowest.

infine avv. at last.

infingardàggine sf. laziness.

infingardo agg. lazy.

infinità sf. infinity.

infinitamente avv. infinitely.

infinitesimale agg. infinitesimal.

infinito agg. boundless. ◆ **infinito** sm. **1.** infinite **2.** (gramm.) infinitive.

infioccare vt. to tassel.

infiorare vt. to flower.

infirmare vt. to invalidate.

infischiarsi vr. not to care (about).

infittire vi. to thicken. ◆ **infittirsi** vr. to thicken.

inflazione sf. inflation.

inflazionìstico agg. inflationary.

inflessìbile agg. inflexible.

inflessibilità sf. inflexibility.

inflessione sf. inflexion.

inflìggere vt. to inflict.

influente agg. influential.

influenza sf. **1.** influence **2.** (med.) (fam.) 'flu.

influenzare vt. to influence.

influire vi. to exert influence (on, upon, over).

influsso sm. influence.

infocare vt. 1. to heat up 2. to inflame.

infocato agg. 1. red hot 2. (fig.) inflamed.

infoltire vi. to thicken.

infondatezza sf. groundlessness.

infondato agg. groundless.

infóndere vt. to infuse.

inforcare vt. 1. to pitchfork 2. (montare a cavalcioni) to get (v. irr.) on || — gli occhiali, to put (v. irr.) on one's glasses.

informale agg. informal.

informare vt. 1. to inform 2. (dare forma) to shape. ♦ **informarsi** vr. to inquire (about).

informativo agg. informative.

informato agg. informed.

informatore sm. informer.

informazione sf. information (solo sing.), news (pl.).

informe agg. shapeless.

infornare vt. to put (v. irr.) into an oven.

infornata sf. batch.

infortunarsi vr. to get (v. irr.) injured.

infortunato agg. injured.

infortunio sm. accident.

infortunìstica sf. industrial accident research.

infossamento sm. hollow.

infossare vt. to hollow. ♦ **infossarsi** vr. to become (v. irr.) hollow.

infradiciare vt. 1. to drench 2. (marcire) to rot (v. irr.).

inframmettenza sf. interference.

inframméttere vt. to interpose. ♦ **inframméttersi** vr. to meddle (with).

infràngere vt. 1. to shatter 2. (trasgredire) to infringe. ♦ **infràngersi** vr. to break (v. irr.) (up).

infrangibile agg. unbreakable: vetro —, shatter-proof glass.

infranto agg. 1. shattered, broken 2. (di legge) infringed.

infrarosso agg. infrared.

infrasettimanale agg. midweek.

infrastruttura sf. infrastructure.

infrazione sf. infraction.

infreddolirsi vr. to feel (v. irr.) cold.

infreddolito agg. chilly.

infrequente agg. infrequent.

infrollirsi vr. 1. to become (v. irr.) tender 2. (di selvaggina) to become (v. irr.) high.

infruttìfero agg. unfruitful.

infruttuoso agg. 1. unfruitful 2. (fig.) useless.

infuori (loc. prep.) all'—, except.

infuriare vi. to enrage. ♦ **infuriarsi** vr. to flare up.

infusione sf. infusion.

infuso agg. infused. ♦ **infuso** sm. infusion.

infusorio sm. infusorial.

ingabbiare vt. 1. to cage 2. (fig.) to lock up.

ingaggiare vt. to engage.

ingaggio sm. engagement.

ingagliardire vt. to strengthen. ♦ **ingagliardirsi** vr. to strengthen.

ingannare vt. to deceive || — il tempo, to while away the time. ♦ **ingannarsi** vr. to be mistaken.

ingannatore agg. deceiving. ♦ **ingannatore** sm. deceiver.

ingannévole agg. deceitful.

inganno sm. deception, fraud.

ingarbugliare vt. to entangle. ♦ **ingarbugliarsi** vr. to get (v. irr.) mixed up.

ingegnarsi vr. to contrive (to).

ingegnere sm. engineer.

ingegnerìa sf. engineering.

ingegno sm. talent.

ingegnosità sf. ingeniousness.

ingegnoso agg. ingenious.

ingelosire vt. to make (v. irr.) jealous. ♦ **ingelosirsi** vr. to become (v. irr.) jealous.

ingenerare vt. to engender.

ingeneroso agg. selfish.

ingente agg. huge.

ingentilire vt. to refine.

ingenuità sf. naïveness.

ingenuo agg. naïve.

ingerenza sf. interference.

ingerimento sm. swallowing.

ingerire vt. to swallow.

ingessare vt. to plaster.

ingessatura sf. 1. plastering 2. (med.) plaster cast.

inghiaiare vt. to gravel.

inghiottire vt. 1. to swallow 2. (di acque ecc.) to engulf 3. (sopportare) to lump.

inghirlandare vt. to wreathe.

ingiallire vt. e vi. to yellow.

ingigantire vt. to magnify. ♦ **ingigantire** vi. to become (v. irr.) gigantic.

inginocchiarsi *vr.* to kneel (*v. irr.*) (down).

inginocchiatoio *sm.* kneeler.

ingioiellare *vt.* to bejewel.

ingiú *avv.* down, downwards.

ingiùngere *vt.* to order.

ingiuntivo *agg.* injunctive.

ingiunzione *sf.* injunction.

ingiuria *sf.* insult.

ingiuriare *vt.* to insult.

ingiurioso *agg.* insulting.

ingiustamente *avv.* unjustly.

ingiustificàbile *agg.* unjustifiable.

ingiustificato *agg.* unjustified.

ingiustizia *sf.* unjustice.

ingiusto *agg.* unjust.

inglese *agg.* English. ♦ **inglese** *sm.* Englishman (*pl.* -men) ‖ *gli Inglesi,* the English (people).

inglobare *vt.* to inglobe.

inglorioso *agg.* inglorious.

ingobbire *vi.* to become (*v. irr.*) humpbacked. ♦ **ingobbirsi** *vr.* to become humpbacked.

ingoiare *vt.* to swallow.

ingolfarsi *vr.* (*fig.*) to throw (*v. irr.*) oneself (into).

ingollare *vt.* to gulp down.

ingolosire *vt.* to make (*v. irr.*) greedy.

ingombrante *agg.* cumbersome.

ingombrare *vt.* to encumber.

ingombro *agg.* encumbered (with). ♦ **ingombro** *sm.* encumbrance.

ingommare *vt.* 1. to gum 2. (*incollare*) to stick (*v. irr.*).

ingordigia *sf.* greed.

ingordo *agg.* greedy.

ingorgare *vt.* to choke. ♦ **ingorgarsi** *vr.* to become (*v. irr.*) choked.

ingorgo *sm.* 1. obstruction 2. (*del traffico*) traffic jam.

ingozzare *vt.* to gulp.

ingranaggio *sm.* 1. gear 2. (*fig.*) mechanism.

ingranare *vt.* 1. to put (*v. irr.*) into gear 2. (*auto*) — *una marcia,* to engage a gear. ♦ **ingranare** *vi.* (*fam.*) to get (*v. irr.*) along (with).

ingrandimento *sm.* 1. enlargement 2. (*ott.*) magnification.

ingrandire *vt.* 1. to enlarge 2. (*ott.*) to magnify. ♦ **ingrandirsi** *vr.* to become (*v. irr.*) larger.

ingrassare *vt.* 1. to fatten 2. (*lubrificare*) to grease. ♦ **ingrassare** *vi.* to grow (*v. irr.*) fat.

ingrasso *sm.* fattening.

ingratitùdine *sf.* ingratitude.

ingrato *agg.* ungrateful. ♦ **ingrato** *sm.* ingrate.

ingravidare *vt.* to make (*v. irr.*) pregnant. ♦ **ingravidare** *vi.* to become (*v. irr.*) pregnant.

ingraziarsi *vr.* to get (*v. irr.*) into so.'s good graces.

ingrediente *sm.* ingredient.

ingresso *sm.* 1. entry 2. (*entrata*) entrance 3. (*accesso*) admittance.

ingrossamento *sm.* enlargement.

ingrossare *vt.* e *vi.* to enlarge. ♦ **ingrossarsi** *vr.* to become (*v. irr.*) bigger.

ingrosso (*nella loc. avv.*) all'—, wholesale.

ingualcìbile *agg.* crease-resistant.

inguarìbile *agg.* incurable.

inguinale *agg.* inguinal.

inguine *sm.* inguen.

ingurgitare *vt.* to swallow.

inibire *vt.* to inhibit.

inibito *agg.* inhibited.

inibizione *sf.* inhibition.

iniettare *vt.* to inject.

iniezione *sf.* injection.

inimicare *vt.* to alienate. ♦ **inimicarsi** *vr.* to estrange from oneself.

inimicizia *sf.* enmity.

inimitàbile *agg.* incomparable, inimitable.

inimmaginàbile *agg.* unimaginable.

inintelligìbile *agg.* unintelligible.

ininterrotto *agg.* continuous, unceasing.

iniquità *sf.* iniquity.

iniquo *agg.* 1. unfair 2. (*malvagio*) wicked.

iniziale *agg.* initial, starting. ♦ **iniziale** *sf.* initial.

iniziare *vt.* 1. to begin (*v. irr.*), to start 2. (*introdurre*) to initiate.

iniziativa *sf.* initiative.

iniziato *agg.* e *sm.* initiate.

iniziazione *sf.* initiation.

inizio *sm.* beginning.

innaffiare *vt.* to water.

innaffiatoio *sm.* watering-pot.

innalzamento *sm.* elevation.

innalzare *vt.* 1. to raise 2. (*rendere più alto*) to heighten. ♦ **innalzarsi** *vr.* to rise (*v. irr.*).

innamoramento *sm.* falling in love.

innamorare *vt.* to charm. ♦ **innamorarsi** *vr.* to fall (*v. irr.*) in love (with)

innamorato *agg.* in love (with). ♦ **innamorato** *sm.* lover.

innanzi *avv.* 1. forward, on 2. (*di fronte*) in front of 3. (*più avanti*) further || *d'ora* —, from now on. ♦ **innanzi** *prep.* before.

innato *agg.* inborn.

innaturale *agg.* unnatural.

innegàbile *agg.* undeniable.

inneggiare *vi.* 1. to exalt 2. (*acclamare*) to cheer.

innervare *vt.* to innervate.

innervosire *vt.* to get (*v. irr.*) on so.'s nerves. ♦ **innervosirsi** *vr.* to get nervous.

innescamento *sm.* priming.

innescare *vt.* to prime.

innesco *sm.* primer.

innestare *vt.* 1. (*agr.; med.*) to graft 2. (*mecc.*) to engage.

innesto *sm.* 1. (*agr.; med.*) graft 2. (*mecc.*) clutch.

inno *sm.* hymn || — *nazionale*, national anthem.

innocente *agg.* e *sm.* innocent.

innocenza *sf.* innocence.

innocuità *sf.* innocuousness.

innocuo *agg.* harmless.

innominàbile *agg.* unmentionable.

innovare *vt.* to innovate.

innovatore *agg.* innovating. ♦ **innovatore** *sm.* innovator.

innovazione *sf.* innovation.

innumerévole *agg.* numberless.

inoculare *vt.* to inoculate.

inoculazione *sf.* inoculation.

inodoro *agg.* odourless.

inoffensivo *agg.* harmless.

inoltrare *vt.* to forward. ♦ **inoltrarsi** *vr.* to advance.

inoltrato *agg.* advanced, late.

inoltre *avv.* moreover, besides.

inoltro *sm.* 1. (*di merci*) forwarding 2. (*di documenti*) sending on.

inondare *vt.* to flood.

inondazione *sf.* flood.

inoperosità *sf.* inactivity.

inoperoso *agg.* inactive.

inopinàbile *agg.* inconceivable.

inopinato *agg.* unexpected.

inopportunità *sf.* inopportunity.

inopportuno *agg.* inopportune.

inoppugnàbile *agg.* incontestable.

inoppugnabilità *sf.* incontestability.

inorgànico *agg.* inorganic.

inorgoglire *vt.* to make (*v. irr.*) proud. ♦ **inorgoglirsi** *vr.* to become (*v. irr.*) proud.

inorridire *vt.* to horrify. ♦ **inorridire** *vi.* to be horrified.

inospitale *agg.* inhospitable.

inosservanza *sf.* inobservance.

inosservato *agg.* unobserved.

inossidàbile *agg.* rust-proof || *acciaio* —, stainless steel.

inquadramento *sm.* framing.

inquadrare *vt.* 1. to frame 2. (*fig.*) to set (*v. irr.*) 3. (*mil.*) to rank 4. (*foto, cine*) to frame.

inquadratura *sf.* (*cine*) shot.

inqualificàbile *agg.* despicable.

inquietante *agg.* worrying.

inquietare *vt.* to worry. ♦ **inquietarsi** *vr.* to get (*v. irr.*) angry.

inquieto *agg.* 1. restless 2. (*preoccupato*) worried 3. (*arrabbiato*) angry.

inquietùdine *sf.* 1. restlessness 2. (*preoccupazione*) anxiety.

inquilino *sm.* tenant.

inquinamento *sm.* defilement.

inquinare *vt.* to defile.

inquirente *agg.* investigating.

inquisire *vt.* to investigate. ♦ **inquisire** *vi.* to inquire.

inquisitore *agg.* inquiring. ♦ **inquisitore** *sm.* inquisitor.

inquisizione *sf.* inquisition.

insabbiamento *sm.* (*fig.*) hindering.

insabbiare *vt.* 1. to sand 2. (*fig.*) to hinder.

insaccare *vt.* to sack.

insalata *sf.* salad.

insalatiera *sf.* salad-bowl.

insalubre *agg.* unhealthy.

insalubrità *sf.* insalubrity.

insanàbile *agg.* incurable.

insanguinare *vt.* to cover (with blood). ♦ **insanguinarsi** *vr.* to become (*v. irr.*) bloodstained.

insano *agg.* insane.

insaponare *vt.* to soap.

insaponatura *sf.* soaping.

insaporire *vt.* to flavour.

insaporo *agg.* flavourless.

insaputa *sf.* (*nella loc. avv.*) *all'*— *di*, unknown (to).

insaziàbile *agg.* insatiable.

insaziabilità *sf.* insatiability.

insaziato *agg.* unappeased.

inscatolare *vt.* to tin.

inscenare *vt.* to stage.

inscindìbile *agg.* inseparable.

inscrìvere *vt.* 1. (*a una scuola, esame ecc.*) to enrol 2. (*scrivere, scolpire; geom.*) to inscribe.

insediamento *sm.* installation.
insediare *vt.* to install. ♦ **insediarsi** *vr.* to install oneself.
insegna *sf.* 1. insignia (*pl.*) 2. (*bandiera*) flag 3. (*di negozio*) sign-board.
insegnamento *sm.* 1. teaching 2. (*precetto, lezione*) precept, lesson.
insegnante *agg.* teaching. ♦ **insegnante** *s.* teacher.
insegnare *vt.* to teach (*v. irr.*).
inseguimento *sm.* pursuit.
inseguire *vt.* to pursue.
inseguitore *sm.* pursuer.
insellare *vt.* to saddle.
inselvatichire *vi.* to grow (*v. irr.*) wild.
insenatura *sf.* inlet, creek.
insensatezza *sf.* 1. craziness 2. (*atto insensato*) foolish action.
insensato *agg.* foolish, crazy.
insensibile *agg.* 1. insensible 2. (*indifferente*) indifferent 3. (*frigido*) unfeeling.
insensibilità *sf.* 1. insensibility 2. (*indifferenza*) indifference.
insensibilmente *avv.* 1. (*impercettibilmente*) imperceptibly, slightly 2. (*senza sentimento*) insensibly.
inseparàbile *agg.* inseparable.
insepolto *agg.* unburied.
inserimento *sm.* insertion.
inserire *vt.* 1. to insert 2. (*elcttr.*) to connect.
inserto *sm.* 1. file, dossier 2. (*cine, stampa*) insert.
inservìbile *agg.* useless.
inserviente *sm.* attendant.
inserzione *sf.* 1. insertion 2. (*pubblicitaria*) advertisement.
inserzionista *sm.* advertiser.
insetticida *agg.* e *sm.* insecticide.
insettìvoro *agg.* insectivorous. ♦ **insettìvoro** *sm.* insectivore.
insetto *sm.* insect.
insicurezza *sf.* insecurity.
insidia *sf.* 1. snare 2. (*pericolo*) danger.
insidiare *vt.* to endanger || — *la vita di una persona*, to attempt a person's life.
insidioso *agg.* insidious.
insieme *avv.* 1. together 2. (*allo stesso tempo*) at the same time. ♦ **insieme** *prep.* together (with). ♦ **insieme** *sm.* whole: *nell'—*, as a whole || *sguardo d'—*, comprehensive view.
insigne *agg.* famous.

insignificante *agg.* insignificant.
insignire *vt.* to confer (sthg. upon).
insincerità *sf.* insincerity.
insincero *agg.* insincere.
insindacàbile *agg.* undisputable.
insinuante *agg.* insinuating.
insinuare *vt.* to hint. ♦ **insinuarsi** *vr.* to insinuate oneself.
insinuazione *sf.* hint, insinuation.
insipidezza *sf.* insipidness.
insipido *agg.* 1. tasteless 2. (*fig.*) insipid.
insistente *agg.* 1. insistent, steady 2. (*molesto*) irritating.
insistenza *sf.* insistence.
insistere *vi.* to insist (on).
ìnsito *agg.* inborn, inherent.
insoddisfatto *agg.* dissatisfied (with).
insoddisfazione *sf.* dissatisfaction (with).
insofferente *agg.* intolerant.
insofferenza *sf.* intolerance.
insoffrìbile *agg.* unbearable.
insolazione *sf.* sunstroke.
insolente *agg.* e *sm.* insolent.
insolentire *vt.* to insult.
insolenza *sf.* insolence.
insòlito *agg.* unusual.
insolùbile *agg.* insoluble.
insolubilità *sf.* insolubility.
insoluto *agg.* 1. unsolved 2. (*non pagato*) unpaid.
insolvente *agg.* insolvent.
insolvenza *sf.* insolvency.
insolvìbile *agg.* 1. (*di debito*) unpayable 2. (*di persona*) insolvent.
insolvibilità *sf.* insolvency.
insomma *avv.* finally, in short.
insondàbile *agg.* unfathomable.
insonne *agg.* sleepless.
insonnia *sf.* insomnia.
insonnolito *agg.* drowsy, sleepy.
insopportàbile *agg.* unbearable.
insopprimìbile *agg.* insuppressible.
insòrgere *vi.* 1. to rise (*v. irr.*) 2. (*protestare*) to protest, to rebel 3. (*manifestarsi*) to arise (*v. irr.*).
insormontàbile *agg.* insurmountable.
insorto *sm.* rebel.
insospettàbile *agg.* beyond suspicion.
insospettato *agg.* unsuspected.
insospettire *vt.* to make (*v. irr.*) suspicious. ♦ **insospettirsi** *vr.* to grow (*v. irr.*) suspicious.
insostenìbile *agg.* unsustainable.
insostituìbile *agg.* irreplaceable.

insozzare *vt.* 1. to soil 2. (*fig.*) to disgrace.
insperàbile *agg.* beyond hope.
insperato *agg.* unhoped for.
inspiegàbile *agg.* inexplicable.
inspirare *vt.* to breathe in.
inspirazione *sf.* breathing in, inhalation.
instàbile *agg.* unstable || *tempo* —, unsettled weather.
instabilità *sf.* 1. instability 2. (*fig.*) fickleness.
installare *vt.* to install. ♦ **installarsi** *vr.* to settle.
installazione *sf.* installation.
instancàbile *agg.* untiring.
instaurare *vt.* to set (*v. irr.*) up.
instaurazione *sf.* establishment.
instradare *vt.* to direct, to coach.
insú *avv.* up, upwards.
insubordinatezza *sf.* insubordination.
insubordinato *agg.* insubordinate.
insubordinazione *sf.* insubordination.
insuccesso *sm.* failure.
insudiciare *vt.* to soil.
insufficiente *agg.* insufficient.
insufficienza *sf.* 1. insufficiency 2. (*scol.*) low mark.
insulare *agg.* insular.
insulina *sf.* insulin.
insulsàggine *sf.* 1. silliness 2. (*cosa insulsa*) nonsense.
insulso *agg.* silly.
insultare *vt.* to insult.
insulto *sm.* insult.
insuperàbile *agg.* insuperable.
insuperato *agg.* unsurpassed.
insuperbire *vt.* to elate. ♦ **insuperbirsi** *vr.* to pride oneself (on).
insurrezionale *agg.* insurrectional.
insurrezione *sf.* insurrection.
insussistente *agg.* unfounded.
intaccare *vt.* 1. to notch 2. (*chim.*) to etch 3. (*fig.*) to injure.
intacco *sm.* notch.
intagliare *vt.* 1. to carve 2. (*incidere*) to engrave.
intaglio *sm.* 1. carving 2. (*incisione*) engraving.
intangìbile *agg.* intangible.
intanto *avv.* meanwhile.
intarsiare *vt.* to inlay.
intarsio *sm.* inlay.
intasamento *sm.* obstruction.
intasare *vt.* to obstruct.
intascare *vt.* to pocket.

intatto *agg.* intact.
intavolare *vt.* 1. to plank 2. (*iniziare*) to begin (*v. irr.*), to start.
integèrrimo *agg.* strictly honest.
integràbile *agg.* integrable.
integrale *agg.* integral: (*mat.*) *calcolo* —, integral calculus.
integrante *agg.* integrant.
integrare *vt.* to integrate.
integrazione *sf.* integration.
integrità *sf.* integrity.
integro *agg.* 1. integral 2. (*onesto*) honest.
intelaiatura *sf.* 1. framework 2. (*di finestre*) sash.
intellettivo *agg.* intellective.
intelletto *sm.* intellect.
intellettuale *agg. e sm.* intellectual.
intellettualismo *sm.* intellectualism.
intelligente *agg.* intelligent.
intelligenza *sf.* intelligence.
intelligìbile *agg.* intelligible.
intelligibilità *sf.* intelligibility.
intemerata *sf.* reprimand.
intemerato *agg.* faultless.
intemperante *agg.* intemperate.
intemperanza *sf.* intemperance.
intemperie *sf. pl.* inclemency of the weather (*sing.*).
intempestività *sf.* untimeliness.
intempestivo *agg.* untimely.
intendente *agg.* expert. ♦ **intendente** *sm.* superintendent.
intendenza *sf.* superintendence.
intèndere *vt.* 1. (*capire*) to understand (*v. irr.*) 2. (*significare*) to mean (*v. irr.*) 3. (*avere intenzione di*) to intend to. ♦ **intèndersi** *vr.* 1. (*avere cognizione*) to be a good judge 2. (*mettersi d'accordo*) to come (*v. irr.*) to an agreement.
intendimento *sm.* 1. understanding 2. (*intenzione*) intention.
intenditore *sm.* 1. good judge 2. (*d'arte*) connoisseur.
intenerimento *sm.* 1. softening 2. (*fig.*) tenderness.
intenerire *vt.* 1. to soften 2. (*fig.*) to move to pity. ♦ **intenerirsi** *vr.* to be moved to pity.
intensificare *vt.* to intensify.
intensificazione *sf.* intensification.
intensità *sf.* intensity.
intensivo *agg.* intensive.
intenso *agg.* intense.
intentàbile *agg.* 1. unattemptable 2. (*giur.*) suable.

intentare *vt.* to bring (*v. irr.*).

intento *agg.* intent. ♦ **intento** *sm.* aim, purpose.

intenzionale *agg.* deliberate.

intenzionato *agg.* disposed.

intenzione *sf.* intention.

intepidire *vt.* to warm, to make (*v. irr.*) tepid. ♦ **intepidirsi** *vr.* to get (*v. irr.*) tepid.

interamente *avv.* wholly, entirely.

intercalare *agg.* intercalary. ♦ **intercalare** *sm.* pet phrase.

intercalare *vt.* to intercalate.

intercambiàbile *agg.* interchangeable.

intercèdere *vi.* to intercede, to plead.

intercessione *sf.* intercession.

intercessore *sm.* intercessor.

intercettare *vt.* to intercept.

intercettatore *sm.* interceptor.

intercettazione *sf.* interception.

intercomunale *sf.* (*tel.*) long-distance call.

intercontinentale *agg.* intercontinental.

intercòrrere *vi.* 1. to pass 2. (*accadere*) to happen.

intercostale *agg.* intercostal.

interdetto *agg.* 1. prohibited 2. (*giur.*) interdicted. ♦ **interdetto** *sm.* interdict.

interdipendente *agg.* interdependent.

interdipendenza *sf.* interdependence.

interdire *vt.* to interdict.

interdizione *sf.* interdiction.

interessamento *sm.* concern.

interessante *agg.* interesting.

interessare *vt.* 1. to interest 2. (*riguardare*) to concern. ♦ **interessarsi** *vr.* 1. to be interested (in) 2. (*provvedere*) to take (*v. irr.*) care (of).

interessato *agg.* interested.

interesse *sm.* interest.

interessenza *sf.* share, profit.

interezza *sf.* wholeness.

interferenza *sf.* interference.

interferire *vi.* to interfere.

interiezione *sf.* interjection.

interinale *agg.* temporary.

interiora *sf. pl.* entrails.

interiore *agg.* inner. ♦ **interiore** *sm.* interior, inside.

interiorità *sf.* inwardness.

interiormente *avv.* 1. (*intimamente*) innerly 2. (*nell'interno*) inside.

interlìnea *sf.* 1. interline 2. (*tip.*) lead.

interlineare *vt.* 1. to interline 2. (*tip.*) to lead (*v. irr.*).

interlineare *vt.* to interline.

interlocutore *sm.* interlocutor.

interlocutorio *agg.* interlocutory.

interloquire *vi.* to join in the conversation.

interludio *sm.* interlude.

intermediario *agg.* intermediary. ♦ **intermèdiario** *sm.* 1. go-between 2. (*comm.*) middleman (*pl.* -men).

intermedio *agg.* intermediate, middle.

intermezzo *sm.* 1. intermission 2. (*mus.*) intermezzo.

interminàbile *agg.* endless.

intermittente *agg.* intermittent.

intermittenza *sf.* intermittence.

internamento *sm.* internment.

internare *vt.* to intern.

internato *agg.* interned. ♦ **internato** *sm.* (*scol.*) boarding-school.

internazionale *agg.* international.

internazionalismo *sm.* internationalism.

internazionalizzare *vt.* to internationalize.

interno *agg.* 1. internal, interior 2. (*interiore*) inner. ♦ **interno** *sm.* interior.

intero *agg.* 1. whole 2. (*intatto*) intact.

interpellanza *sf.* interrogation.

interpellare *vt.* 1. (*pol.*) to interpellate 2. (*giur.*) to summon 3. (*chiedere*) to ask.

interplanetario *agg.* interplanetary.

interpolare *vt.* to interpolate.

interpolazione *sf.* interpolation.

interporre *vt.* to interpose.

interpretare *vt.* 1. to interpret, to render 2. (*teat.*) to play.

interpretativo *agg.* interpretative.

interpretazione *sf.* 1. interpretation 2. (*cine*) starring 3. (*mus.*) performance 4. (*teat.*) acting.

intèrprete *s.* 1. interpreter 2. (*teat.; cine*) actor, player.

interpunzione *sf.* punctuation.

interramento *sm.* burial.

interrare *vt.* 1. to bury 2. (*riempire di terra*) to fill up with earth.

interrogare *vt.* to question.

interrogativo *agg.* interrogative || punto —, question mark. ♦ **interrogativo** *sm.* interrogative.

interrogatore *agg.* interrogating. ♦
interrogatore *sm.* examiner.
interrogatorio *sm.* examination.
interrogazione *sf.* **1.** interrogation
2. (*scol.*) oral test.
interròmpere *vt.* to interrupt. ♦
interròmpersi *vr.* to stop.
interrotto *agg.* interrupted || *strada interrotta*, blocked road.
interruttore *sm.* (*elettr.*) switch.
interruzione *sf.* interruption.
intersecare *vt.* to intersect.
intersezione *sf.* intersection.
interstizio *sm.* interstice.
intervallare *vt.* to space.
intervallo *sm.* **1.** interval **2.** (*spazio*) space.
intervenire *vi.* **1.** to intervene **2.** (*essere presenti*) to be present.
interventismo *sm.* interventionism.
interventista *s.* interventionist.
intervento *sm.* **1.** intervention **2.** (*presenza*) presence **3.** (*chir.*) operation.
intervenuto *agg.* present. ♦ **intervenuto** *sm.* person present.
intervista *sf.* interview.
intervistare *vt.* to interview.
intesa *sf.* agreement.
inteso *agg.* **1.** agreed (upon) **2.** (*mirante*) aiming (at).
intèssere *vt.* to interweave (*v. irr.*).
intestare *vt.* to head, to register. ♦
intestarsi *vr.* to be determinated.
intestatario *sm.* holder.
intestato *agg.* **1.** headed **2.** (*giur.*) registered **3.** (*senza testamento*) intestate **4.** (*ostinato*) stubborn.
intestazione *sf.* **1.** title **2.** (*di lettera ecc.*) heading.
intestinale *agg.* intestinal.
intestino *sm.* intestine.
intimare *vt.* **1.** (*ordinare*) to order **2.** (*ingiungere*) to summon.
intimazione *sf.* **1.** order **2.** (*ingiunzione*) summons.
intimidatorio *agg.* intimidatory.
intimidazione *sf.* intimidation.
intimidire *vt.* **1.** to make (*v. irr.*) shy **2.** (*impaurire*) to intimidate.
intimità *sf.* **1.** privacy **2.** (*familiarità*) familiarity.
intimo *agg.* **1.** intimate **2.** (*profondo*) deep. ♦ **intimo** *sm.* **1.** (*amico*) intimate **2.** (*animo*) soul || *nell'—*, at heart.
intimorire *vt.* to frighten. ♦ **intimorirsi** *vr.* to get (*v. irr.*)

frightened.
intìngere *vt.* to dip.
intìngolo *sm.* **1.** gravy **2.** (*salsa*) sauce.
intirizzire *vt.* to benumb.
intitolare *vt.* **1.** to entitle **2.** (*dedicare*) to dedicate.
intoccàbile *agg. e sm.* untouchable.
intolleràbile *agg.* intolerable.
intollerante *agg.* intolerant.
intolleranza *sf.* intolerance.
intonacare *vt.* to plaster.
intonacatura *sf.* plastering.
intònaco *sm.* plaster.
intonare *vt.* **1.** to tune **2.** (*cantilenare*) to intone. ♦ **intonarsi** *vr.* **1.** to harmonize (with) **2.** (*di colori*) to match.
intonato *agg.* **1.** in tune **2.** (*di colori*) matching.
intonazione *sf.* **1.** intonation **2.** (*di strumenti*) tuning **3.** (*di colori, voce*) tone.
intonso *agg.* (*di libri*) uncut.
intontimento *sm.* stunning.
intontire *vt.* to stun.
intoppare *vt.* to stumble (on).
intoppo *sm.* **1.** obstacle **2.** (*fig.*) hitch.
intorbidare *vt.* to make (*v. irr.*) muddy. ♦ **intorbidarsi** *vr.* to become (*v. irr.*) muddy.
intorno *avv.* round, around. ♦ **intorno a** *prep.* **1.** round, around **2.** (*circa, su di*) about.
intorpidimento *sm.* numbness.
intorpidire *vt.* to benumb. ♦ **intorpidirsi** *vr.* to grow (*v. irr.*) numb.
intossicare *vt.* to poison.
intossicazione *sf.* poisoning.
intraducìbile *agg.* untranslatable.
intralciare *vt.* to hinder, to interfere.
intralcio *sm.* hindrance.
intrallazzo *sm.* **1.** plotting **2.** (*imbroglio*) swindle.
intramezzare *vt.* to interpose, to alternate.
intramontàbile *agg.* everlasting.
intramuscolare *agg.* intermuscular.
intransigente *agg.* strict, intransigent.
intransigenza *sf.* intransigence.
intransitivo *agg. e sm.* intransitive.
intrappolare *vt.* to entrap.
intraprendente *agg.* enterprising.
intraprendenza *sf.* enterprise.

intraprèndere *vt.* **1.** to undertake (*v. irr.*), to start **2.** (*una professione*) to go (*v. irr.*) in for.

intrattàbile *agg.* intractable.

intrattenere *vt.* to entertain. ◆ intrattenersi *vr.* **1.** to linger **2.** (*dilungarsi*) to dwell (*v. irr.*).

intravedere *vt.* **1.** (*vedere di sfuggita*) to catch (*v. irr.*) a glimpse of **2.** (*vedere indistintamente*) to see (*v. irr.*) indistinctly.

intrecciare *vt.* **1.** to interlace || — danze, to dance **2.** (*capelli, nastri*) to plait.

intreccio *sm.* **1.** interlacement **2.** (*di romanzi*) plot.

intrèpido *agg.* brave, fearless.

intricare *vt.* to tangle. ◆ intricarsi *vr.* to get (*v. irr.*) entangled.

intrico *sm.* tangle.

intrìdere *vt.* to soak.

intrigante *agg.* crafty. ◆ intrigante *sm.* intriguer.

intrigare *vi.* to intrigue. ◆ intrigarsi *vr.* to meddle (with).

intrigo *sm.* intrigue, plot.

intrìnseco *agg.* intrinsic.

intristire *vi.* **1.** to pine away **2.** (*incattivire*) to grow (*v. irr.*) wicked.

introdotto *agg.* **1.** (*importato*) imported **2.** (*conosciuto*) well-known.

intriso *agg.* soaked (with), imbrued.

introdurre *vt.* **1.** to introduce **2.** (*far entrare*) to show (*v. irr.*) in. ◆ introdursi *vr.* to get (*v. irr.*) into, to slip into.

introduttivo *agg.* introductory.

introduzione *sf.* introduction.

introitare *vt.* to cash.

intròito *sm.* profit.

intromèttere *vt.* to introduce. ◆ intromettersi *vr.* to interfere.

intromissione *sf.* intrusion.

intronare *vt.* to stun.

introspettivo *agg.* introspective.

introspezione *sf.* introspection.

introvàbile *agg.* not to be found.

introversione *sf.* introversion.

introverso *agg.* introverted. ◆ introverso *sm.* introvert.

intrufolarsi *vr.* to intrude (in).

intruglio *sm.* bad mixture.

intruppamento *sm.* trooping.

intrupparsi *vr.* to troop.

intrusione *sf.* intrusion.

intruso *sm.* intruder.

intuìbile *agg.* guessable.

intuire *vt.* to guess, to perceive.

intuitivo *agg.* intuitive.

intùito *sm.* intuition, insight.

intuizione *sf.* intuition.

inturgidimento *sm.* swelling.

inturgidire *vi.* to swell (up). inturgidirsi *vr.* to swell (up).

inuguale *agg.* unlike.

inumanità *sf.* inhumanity.

inumano *agg.* inhuman.

inumare *vt.* to inter.

inumazione *sf.* interment.

inumidire *vt.* to moisten. ◆ inumidirsi *vr.* to moisten.

inurbanità *sf.* incivility.

inurbano *agg.* uncivil.

inurbarsi *vr.* to inurbate.

inusitato *agg.* unusual.

inùtile *agg.* useless.

inutilità *sf.* uselessness.

inutilizzàbile *agg.* unusable.

invadente *agg.* intrusive.

invadenza *sf.* intrusiveness.

invàdere *vt.* to invade.

invaghimento *sm.* fancy (for).

invaghirsi *vr.* to take (*v. irr.*) a fancy (for), to fall (*v. irr.*) in love (with).

invaghito *agg.* fond (of), infatuated.

invalere *vi.* to prevail.

invalicàbile *agg.* impassable.

invalidare *vt.* to invalidate.

invalidazione *sf.* invalidation.

invalidità *sf.* invalidity.

invàlido *agg. e sm.* invalid.

invalso *agg.* prevailed.

invano *avv.* in vain.

invariàbile *agg.* **1.** invariable **2.** (*di tempo*) unchangeable.

invariabilità *sf.* invariability.

invariato *agg.* unchanged.

invasamento *sm.* obsession.

invasare *vt.* to possess.

invasato *agg.* possessed. ◆ invasato *sm.* possessed person.

invasione *sf.* invasion.

invasore *sm.* invader.

invecchiamento *sm.* ageing.

invecchiare *vt.* to make (*v. irr.*) old. ◆ invecchiare *vi.* to grow (*v. irr.*) old.

invece *avv.* on the contrary || — di, instead of.

inveire *vi.* to rail (at).

invelenire *vt.* to embitter.

invendìbile *agg.* unsaleable.

invendicato *agg.* unavenged.

invenduto *agg.* unsold.

inventare vt. to invent.
inventariare vt. to inventory.
inventario sm. inventory || con beneficio d'—, with reservation.
inventiva sf. inventiveness.
inventivo agg. inventive.
inventore sm. inventor.
invenzione sf. invention.
inverdire vi. to turn green.
inverecondia sf. immodesty.
inverecondo agg. immodest.
inverificàbile agg. unverifiable.
invernale agg. **1.** winter (attr.) **2.** (da inverno) wintry.
invernata sf. wintertime.
inverno sm. winter.
invero avv. indeed.
inverosimiglianza sf. unlikelihood.
inverosìmile agg. unlikely.
inversione sf. inversion.
inverso agg. **1.** (mat.) inverse **2.** opposite, contrary. ♦ **inverso** sm. oppòsite, contrary.
invertebrato agg. e sm. invertebrate.
invertìbile agg. invertible.
invertire vt. to invert || — la marcia, to reverse.
invertito sm. invert.
invertitore sm. reverse gear.
investigare vt. to inquire.
investigativo agg. investigative.
investigatore sm. detective.
investigazione sf. investigation.
investimento sm. **1.** investment **2.** collision **3.** (stradale) running down.
investire vt. **1.** to invest (with) **2.** (comm.) to invest **3.** (assalire) to assail **4.** (auto) to run (v. irr.) down.
investitore sm. (comm.) investor.
investitura sf. investiture.
inveterato agg. inveterate.
invetriata sf. glass window.
invettiva sf. invective.
inviare vt. to send (v. irr.).
inviato sm. **1.** messenger **2.** (in diplomazia) envoy **3.** (in giornalismo) correspondent.
invidia sf. envy: per —, out of envy.
invidiàbile agg. enviable.
invidiare vt. to envy.
invidioso agg. envious.
invigorire vt. to strengthen. ♦ **invigorirsi** vr. to strengthen.
inviluppare vt. to envelop, to wrap up.
invincìbile agg. invincible.

invincibilità sf. invincibility.
invìo sm. **1.** (per posta) mailing **2.** (di merci) forwarding **3.** (per nave) shipment **4.** (di danaro) remittance.
inviolàbile agg. inviolable.
inviolabilità sf. inviolability.
inviperirsi vr. to become (v. irr.) furious.
inviperito agg. furious.
invischiare vt. **1.** to lime **2.** (fig.) to entangle. ♦ **invischiarsi** vr. to get (v. irr.) entangled.
invisìbile agg. invisible.
invisibilità sf. invisibility.
inviso agg. disliked.
invitante agg. inviting.
invitare vt. **1.** to invite **2.** (domandare) to request.
invitato agg. invited. ♦ **invitato** sm. guest.
invito sm. invitation.
invitto agg. unconquered.
invocare vt. to invoke.
invocazione sf. invocation.
invogliare vt. to tempt.
involare vt. to abduct. ♦ **involarsi** vr. to flee, to run (v. irr.) away.
involontario agg. unintentional.
involto sm. bundle, parcel.
invòlucro sm. **1.** envelope **2.** (bot.) involucre.
involutivo agg. involutionary.
involuto agg. involved.
involuzione sf. **1.** involution **2.** (decadenza) decline.
invulneràbile agg. invulnerable.
invulnerabilità sf. invulnerability.
inzaccherare vt. to muddy. ♦ **inzaccherarsi** vr. to get (v. irr.) muddy.
inzuppare vt. **1.** to soak **2.** (intingere) to dip.
io pron. I: — stesso, I myself.
iodato agg. iodized. ♦ **iodato** sm. iodate.
iodio sm. iodine.
iole sf. gig.
ione sm. ion.
iònico agg. Ionic.
ionizzazione sf. ionization.
ionosfera sf. ionosphere.
iosa (nella loc. avv.) a —, in plenty.
iperalimentazione sf. hypernutrition.
ipèrbole sf. hyperbole.
iperbòlico agg. hyperbolic(al).
iperbòreo agg. hyperborean.

ipercrìtico *agg.* hypercritical.
ipermetropìa *sf.* hypermetropia.
ipermètrope *agg.* hypermetropic.
ipernutrizione *sf.* hypernutrition.
ipersensìbile *agg.* hypersensitive.
ipersensibilità *sf.* hypersensitivity.
ipertensione *sf.* hypertension.
iperteso *agg.* e *sm.* hypertensive.
ipertrofìa *sf.* hypertrophy.
ipnosi *sf.* hypnosis.
ipnòtico *agg.* hypnotic.
ipnotismo *sm.* hypnotism.
ipnotizzare *vt.* to hypnotize.
ipnotizzatore *sm.* hypnotizer.
ipocondrìa *sf.* hypochondria.
ipocondrìaco *agg.* e *sm.* hypochondriac.
ipocrisìa *sf.* hypocrisy.
ipòcrita *agg.* hypocritical. ♦ **ipòcrita** *sm.* hypocrite.
ipodèrmico *agg.* hypodermic.
ipodermoclisi *sf.* hypodermoclysis.
ipòfisi *sf.* hypophysis.
ipoteca *sf.* mortgage.
ipotecare *vt.* to mortgage.
ipotenusa *sf.* hypotenuse.
ipòtesi *sf.* 1. hypothesis (*pl.* -ses) 2. (*supposizione*) supposition.
ipotètico *agg.* hypothetical.
ìppica *sf.* horse-racing.
ìppico *agg.* horse (*attr.*).
ippocampo *sm.* hippocampus (*pl.* -pi).
ippocastano *sm.* horse-chestnut.
ippòdromo *sm.* race-course.
ippopòtamo *smi.* hippopotamus.
ira *sf.* anger, rage.
iracondo *agg.* irascible.
irascìbile *agg.* irritable.
irascibilità *sf.* irritability.
irato *agg.* angry.
iridato *agg.* iridescent.
ìride *sf.* iris.
iridescente *agg.* iridescent.
iridescenza *sf.* iridescence.
irlandese *agg.* Irish.
ironìa *sf.* irony.
irònico *agg.* ironic(al).
ironizzare *vi.* to make (*v. irr.*) ironical remarks.
iroso *agg.* wrathful.
irradiamento *sm.* irradiation.
irradiare *vt.* to irradiate.
irradiazione *sf.* V. *irradiamento.*
irraggiare *vt.* V. *irradiare.*
irraggiungìbile *agg.* unreachable.
irragionévole *agg.* unreasonable.
irrancidire *vi.* to grow (*v. irr.*) rank.

irrazionale *agg.* irrational.
irrazionalità *sf.* irrationality.
irreale *agg.* unreal.
irrealizzàbile *agg.* unrealizable.
irrealtà *sf.* unreality.
irreconciliàbile *agg.* irreconcilable.
irrecuperàbile *agg.* irrecoverable.
irrefrenàbile *agg.* unrestrainable.
irrefutàbile *agg.* irrefutable.
irregolare *agg.* irregular.
irregolarità *sf.* irregularity.
irremovìbile *agg.* 1. immovable 2. (*inflessibile*) inflexible.
irreparàbile *agg.* irreparable.
irreperìbile *agg.* elusive: *rendersi —*, to hide (*v. irr.*) oneself.
irreprensìbile *agg.* irreproachable.
irrequietezza *sf.* restlessness.
irrequieto *agg.* restless.
irresistìbile *agg.* irresistible.
irresolutezza *sf.* irresolution.
irresoluto *agg.* hesitating.
irrespiràbile *agg.* unbreathable.
irresponsàbile *agg.* irresponsible.
irresponsabilità *sf.* irresponsibility.
irrestringìbile *agg.* unshrinkable.
irretire *vt.* to snare.
irreversìbile *agg.* irreversible.
irreversibilità *sf.* irreversibility.
irrevocàbile *agg.* irrevocable.
irriconoscìbile *agg.* unrecognizable.
irrìdere *vt.* to laugh at.
irriducìbile *agg.* irreducible.
irriflessione *sf.* thoughtlessness.
irriflessivo *agg.* thoughtless.
irrigàbile *agg.* irrigable.
irrigare *vt.* to irrigate.
irrigazione *sf.* irrigation.
irrigidimento *sm.* stiffening.
irrigidire *vt.* to stiffen. ♦ **irrigidirsi** *vr.* to stiffen.
irriguo *agg.* well-watered.
irrilevante *agg.* insignificant.
irrimediàbile *agg.* irremediable.
irrisione *sf.* mockery.
irrisorio *agg.* derisory, paltry.
irrispettoso *agg.* disrespectful.
irritàbile *agg.* 1. (*di persona*) irritable 2. (*di pelle*) sensitive.
irritabilità *sf.* 1. (*di persona*) irritability 2. (*di pelle*) sensitiveness.
irritante *agg.* irritating.
irritare *vt.* to irritate. ♦ **irritarsi** *vr.* 1. to grow (*v. irr.*) angry 2. (*di pelle*) to become (*v. irr.*) irritated.
irritazione *sf.* 1. irritation 2. (*di pelle*) inflammation.

irriverente *agg.* disrespectful.
irriverenza *sf.* irreverence.
irrobustire *vt.* to strengthen. ♦
irrobustirsi *vr.* to strengthen.
irròmpere *vi.* **1.** to break (*v. irr.*)
into **2.** (*di acque*) to overflow.
irrorare *vt.* to sprinkle.
irroratrice *sf.* sprayer.
irruente *agg.* impetuous.
irruenza *sf.* impetuosity.
irruvidire *vt.* to roughen.
irruzione *sf.* irruption: *fare* —,
to rush into.
irsuto *agg.* shaggy.
irto *agg.* bristling (with).
iscritto *sm.* member.
iscrìvere *vt.* **1.** (*a scuola, esami
ecc.*) to enrol **2.** (*registrare*) to record **3.** (*scolpire*) to engrave. ♦
iscrìversi *vr.* to enter, to join.
iscrizione *sf.* **1.** inscription **2.** (*a
scuola, esami ecc.*) entry || *do-
manda d'*—, application.
islàmico *agg.* Islamic.
islamismo *sm.* Islamism.
isocronismo *sm.* isochronism.
isola *sf.* island.
isolamento *sm.* **1.** isolation **2.**
(*elettr.*) insulation || — *acustico*,
sound-proofing.
isolano *agg.* insular. ♦ **isolano** *sm.*
islander.
isolante *agg.* insulating. ♦ **isolante** *sm.* insulator.
isolare *vt.* **1.** to isolate **2.** (*elettr.*)
to insulate || — *acusticamente*, to
soundproof. ♦ **isolarsi** *vr.* to
seclude oneself.
isolato *agg.* **1.** isolated **2.** (*elettr.*)
insulated. ♦ **isolato** *sm.* (*edil.*)
block.
isolatore *sm.* insulator.
isolazionismo *sm.* isolationism.
isolazionista *s.* isolationist.
isolotto *sm.* islet.
isomorfismo *sm.* isomorphism.
isomorfo *agg.* isomorphous.
isòscele *agg.* isosceles.
isotèrmico *agg.* isothermal.
isòtopo *sm.* isotope.
isòtropo *sm.* isotrope.
ispànico *agg.* Hispanic.
ispanismo *sm.* Hispanicism.
ispanista *s.* Hispanist.
ispettorato *sm.* inspectorate.
ispettore *sm.* inspector.
ispezionare *vt.* to inspect.
ispezione *sf.* inspection.
ispido *agg.* hispid.

ispirare *vt.* to inspire (with). ♦
ispirarsi *vr.* to draw (*v. irr.*) one's
inspiration (from).
ispirato *agg.* **1.** inspired **2.** (*basato*)
imbued (with).
ispiratore *agg.* inspiring. ♦ **ispiratore** *sm.* inspirer.
ispirazione *sf.* inspiration.
israeliano *agg. e sm.* Israeli.
israelita *agg. e s.* Israelite.
issare *vt.* to hoist.
istantànea *sf.* snapshot: *fare un'*—,
to snapshot.
istantaneità *sf.* instantaneousness.
istantàneo *agg.* instantaneous.
istante *sm.* instant || *all'*—, *sull'*—,
instantly.
istanza *sf.* **1.** request, instance **2.**
(*supplica*) entreaty **3.** (*domanda
scritta*) application.
istèrico *agg.* hysteric(al). ♦ **istèrico** *sm.* hysterical man (*pl.* -men).
isterilire *vt.* to sterilize. ♦ **isteri-
lirsi** *vr.* to become (*v. irr.*) barren.
isterismo *sm.* hysteria.
istigare *vt.* to instigate.
istigatore *sm.* instigator.
istigazione *sf.* instigation.
istintivo *agg.* instinctive.
istinto *sm.* instinct.
istituire *vt.* **1.** to institute **2.** (*fondare*) to found **3.** (*giur.*) to appoint.
istituto *sm.* **1.** institute **2.** (*istituzione*) institution **3.** (*scuola*)
school.
istitutore *sm.* tutor.
istitutrice *sf.* governess.
istituzionale *agg.* institutional.
istituzione *sf.* institution.
istmo *sm.* isthmus (*pl.* -mi).
istologìa *sf.* histology.
ìstrice *sm.* hedgehog.
istrione *sm.* **1.** (*teat.*) histrion **2.**
(*ciarlatano*) quack.
istriònico *agg.* histrionic.
istruire *vt.* **1.** to teach (*v. irr.*) **2.**
(*dare istruzioni*) to instruct, to di-
rect **3.** (*giur.*) to institute. ♦
istruirsi *vr.* to educate oneself.
istruito *agg.* learned.
istruttivo *agg.* instructive.
istruttore *sm.* instructor: *giudice*
—, examining magistrate.
istruttoria *sf.* examination || *apri-
re ·l'*—, to open proceedings.
istruzione *sf.* **1.** education **2.** (*cultura*) learning **3.** (*insegnamento*)
teaching **4.** (*ordine*) instruction.

istupidire vt. to make (v. irr.) stupid. ♦ **istupidirsi** v.r. to become (v. irr.) stupid.
italiano agg. e sm. Italian.
itinerario sm. itinerary.
itterizia sf. jaundice.
ittiologìa sf. ichthyology.
ittiòlogo sm. ichthyologist.
iugoslavo agg. e sm. Yugoslav.
iugulare agg. jugular.
iuta sf. jute.
ivi avv. there.

L

la[1] art. the. ♦ **la** pron. 1. (per donna) her 2. (per animale e cosa) it 3. (forma di cortesia) you.
la[2] sm. (mus.) A.
là avv. there || l'al di —, the hereafter; — per —, on the spot; al di — di, beyond; più in —, (spazio) further on, (tempo) later on.
labbro sm. lip.
labiale agg. labial.
làbile agg. fleeting: memoria —, weak memory.
labirinto sm. labyrinth.
laboratorio sm. 1. laboratory 2. (artigianale) workshop.
laboriosità sf. laboriousness.
laborioso agg. laborious.
laburismo sm. labourism.
laburista agg. labour || partito —, Labour Party. ♦ **laburista** s. Labourite.
lacca sf. lacquer.
laccare vt. to lacquer.
laccatura sf. lacquering.
laccio sm. 1. string || lacci da scarpe, shoe-laces 2. (trappola) snare || prendere al — (fig.), to ensnare.
laceramento sm. tearing.
lacerante agg. rending.
lacerare vt. to tear (v. irr.) (up), to rend (v. irr.) (anche fig.). ♦ **lacerarsi** vr. to tear.
lacerazione sf. laceration.
làcero agg. 1. torn 2. (med.) lacerated.
laconicità sf. laconicism.
lacònico agg. laconic(al).
làcrima sf. tear.
lacrimale agg. lachrymal.

lacrimare vi. to weep (v. irr.).
lacrimazione sf. lachrymation.
lacrimévole agg. tearful.
lacrimògeno agg. lachrymatory: gas —, tear-gas.
lacrimoso agg. tearful.
lacuna sf. gap.
lacunoso agg. lacunous.
lacustre agg. lacustrine.
laddove cong. whereas. ♦ **laddove** avv. (there) where.
ladra sf. woman thief.
ladro agg. thieving. ♦ **ladro** sm. thief: al —!, stop thief!
ladrocinio sm. theft.
ladrone sm. robber.
ladronerìa sf. robbery.
laggiù avv. down there.
lagna sf. lament.
lagnanza sf. complaint.
lagnarsi vr. to complain (of).
lago sm. lake.
laguna sf. lagoon.
lagunare agg. lagoon (attr.).
laicato sm. laity.
laicismo sm. laicism.
laicizzare vt. to laicize.
làico agg. laic. ♦ **làico** sm. layman (pl. -men).
laidezza sf. ugliness, foulness.
làido agg. 1. dirty 2. (brutto) ugly.
lama[1] sf. blade.
lama[2] sm. (zool.) llama.
lama[3] sm. (monaco buddista) lama.
lambiccare vt. to distil || lambiccarsi il cervello, to rack one's brains.
lambiccato agg. 1. distilled 2. (ricercato) over-elaborate.
lambicco sm. alembic.
lambire vt. to lick.
lamella sf. lamella (pl. -lae).
lamentare vt. to lament. ♦ **lamentarsi** vr. to moan.
lamentazione sf. lamentation.
lamentela sf. complaint.
lamentévole agg. mournful.
lamento sm. moan.
lamentoso agg. mournful.
lametta sf. razor-blade.
lamiera sf. sheet.
làmina sf. lamina (pl. -nae).
laminare vt. to laminate.
laminato sm. 1. (tessuto) lamé 2. (metallo) rolled section.
laminatoio sm. rolling-mill.
làmpada sf. lamp.
lampadario sm. chandelier, lamp holder.

lampadina *sf.* bulb.

lampante *agg.* glaring, evident.

lampeggiamento *sm.* 1. flashing, lightning 2. (*di fari, semafori ecc.*) winking 3. (*di auto*) to blink.

lampeggiare *vi.* 1. to flash, to lighten 2. (*di fari, semafori ecc.*) to wink.

lampeggiatore *sm.* 1. winking light 2. (*di auto*) blinker.

lampione *sm.* street-lamp.

lampo *sm.* 1. lightning 2. (*luce istantanea, anche fig.*) flash || *chiusura* —, zip-fastener.

lampone *sm.* raspberry.

lampreda *sf.* lamprey.

lana *sf.* wool.

lancetta *sf.* 1. (*di quadrante*) hand 2. (*di chirurgo*) lancet.

lancia[1] *sf.* lance.

lancia[2] *sf.* (*mar.*) launch || — *di salvataggio*, lifeboat.

lanciafiamme *sm.* flame-thrower.

lanciare *vt.* 1. to throw (*v. irr.*) 2. (*fig.*) to launch || — *un'occhiata*, to cast (*v. irr.*) a glance. ♦ **lanciarsi** *vr.* to dash.

lanciatore *sm.* thrower.

lanciere *sm.* lancer.

lancinante *agg.* piercing.

lancio *sm.* 1. throwing 2. (*pubblicitario*) launching.

landa *sf.* moor.

languido *agg.* languid.

languire *vi.* to languish.

languore *sm.* languor.

laniero *agg.* woollen.

lanificio *sm.* wool factory.

lanolina *sf.* lanolin.

lanoso *agg.* woolly.

lanterna *sf.* lantern.

lanugine *sf.* down.

laparotomìa *sf.* laparotomy.

lapidare *vt.* to stone.

lapidario *agg.* lapidary.

lapidazione *sf.* lapidation.

làpide *sf.* 1. tablet 2. (*sepolcrale*) tombstone.

lapis *sm.* pencil.

lardellare *vt.* to lard.

lardo *sm.* lard, bacon.

larga (*nella loc. avv.*) *alla* —, **away** (from).

largheggiare *vi.* to abound (with).

larghezza *sf.* 1. breadth 2. (*liberalità*) liberality 3. (*abbondanza*) plenty.

largire *vt.* to bestow (upon).

largitore *sm.* bestower.

largizione *sf.* bestowal.

largo *agg.* broad, wide. ♦ **largo** *sm.* 1. (*mar.*) open sea 2. (*piazza*) square || *prendere il* —, to set (*v. irr.*) sail; (*fig.*) to run (*v. irr.*) away; *andare al* —, to take (*v. irr.*) to the open sea; *fare* —, to make (*v. irr.*) room.

làrice *sm.* larch.

laringe *sf.* larynx.

laringite *sf.* laryngitis.

larva *sf.* larva (*pl.* -ae).

lasciapassare *sm.* pass.

lasciare *vt.* 1. to leave (*v. irr.*) 2. (*permettere*) to let (*v. irr.*), to allow. ♦ **lasciarsi** *vr. rec.* (*separarsi*) to part.

làscito *sm.* legacy.

lascivia *sf.* lust.

lascivo *agg.* lustful.

lassativo *agg.* e *sm.* laxative.

lasso *sm.* lapse: *dopo un certo* — *di tempo*, after a lapse of time.

lassù *avv.* up there.

lastra *sf.* 1. (*vetro*) glass' sheet 2. (*di pietra*) slab 3. (*di metallo, foto*) plate.

lastricare *vt.* to pave.

lastricatura *sf.* paving.

làstrico *sm.* pavement || *essere sul* — (*fig.*), to be destitute.

latente *agg.* latent.

laterale *agg.* side: *via* —, by-street.

lateralmente *avv.* sideways.

laterizi *sm. pl.* bricks.

làtice *sm.* latex.

latifondista *sm.* landowner.

latifondo *sm.* large landed estate.

latinismo *sm.* Latinism.

latinista *s.* Latinist.

latinità *sf.* Latinity.

latino *agg.* e *sm.* Latin.

latitante *agg.* absconding: *essere* —, to be in hiding. ♦ **latitante** *s.* absconder.

latitanza *sf.* hiding: *darsi alla* —, to evade arrest.

latitùdine *sf.* latitude.

lato[1] *sm.* 1. side 2. (*fig.*) point of view || *d'altro* —, on the other hand; *da un* —, on the one hand.

lato[2] *agg.* wide || *in senso* —, in a broad sense.

latore *sm.* bearer.

latrare *vi.* to bark.

latrato *sm.* barking.

latrina *sf.* lavatory.

latta *sf.* tin.

lattaio sm. milkman (pl. -men).
lattante agg. unweaned. ♦ **lattante** s. suckling (baby).
latte sm. milk.
làtteo agg. milky.
latterìa sf. dairy.
latticini sm. pl. dairy products.
lattiera sf. milk-jug.
lattiginoso agg. 1. milky 2. (bot.) lactescent.
lattoniere sm. tinker.
lattosio sm. lactose.
lattuga sf. lettuce.
laudativo agg. laudatory.
làurea sf. degree.
laureare vt. to confer a degree (on). ♦ **laurearsi** vr. to graduate.
laureato agg. graduated. ♦ **laureato** sm. graduate || — in lettere, Doctor of Literature Degree.
làuro sm. laurel.
làuto agg. sumptuous || lauti guadagni, large profits.
lavà sf. lava.
lavàbile agg. washable.
lavabo sm. washbowl.
lavaggio sm. washing: — a secco, dry cleaning.
lavagna sf. 1. blackboard 2. (ardesia) slate.
lavanda[1] sf. 1. washing 2. (med.) lavage.
lavanda[2] sf. (bot.) lavender.
lavandaia sf. laundress.
lavanderìa sf. laundry.
lavandino sm. sink.
lavapiatti s. dish-washer.
lavare vt. to wash: — a secco, to dry-clean. ♦ **lavarsi** vr. to wash (oneself).
lavata sf. wash || dare una — di capo (fig.), to scold.
lavativo sm. 1. (med.) enema 2. (fig.) lazy-bones.
lavatoio sm. 1. wash-house 2. (asse per lavare) wash-board.
lavatrice sf. 1. washer 2. (lavabiancheria) washing machine.
lavatura sf. washing.
lavina sf. landslip.
lavorante sm. worker.
lavorare vi. e vt. to work.
lavorativo agg. working || ora lavorativa, man-hour.
lavoratore agg. working. ♦ **lavoratore** sm. worker || — a giornata, day-labourer.
lavorazione sf. 1. processing 2. (fattura) work 3. (agr.) tilling || —

a mano, handwork.
lavorìo sm. intense activity.
lavoro sm. 1. work 2. (occupazione) job || — a ore, work by the hour; lavori di casa, housework; — su ordinazione, work to order; eccesso di —, overwork; — in proprio, self-employment.
lazzaretto sm. lazaretto.
lazzarone sm. slacker.
lazzo sm. joke.
le art. the. ♦ **le** pron. 1. (sing.) her, to her 2. (pl.) them 3. (forma di cortesia) you, to you.
leale agg. 1. loyal 2. (corretto) fair.
lealtà sf. 1. loyalty 2. (correttezza) fairness.
lebbra sf. leprosy.
lebbrosario sm. leper hospital.
lebbroso agg. leprous. ♦ **lebbroso** sm. leper.
leccapiedi sm. bootlicker.
leccare vt. to lick. ♦ **leccarsi** vr. to lick (oneself).
leccata sf. licking.
leccornìa sf. dainty.
lécito agg. 1. lawful 2. (giusto) right 3. (permesso) allowed. ♦ **lécito** sm. right.
lèdere vt. 1. to injure 2. (danneggiare) to damage.
lega sf. 1. league 2. (di metalli) alloy || di buona —, genuine; di cattiva —, low.
legaccio sm. string.
legale agg. legal, lawful || procedere per vie legali, to have recourse to the law. ♦ **legale** sm. lawyer.
legalità sf. legality.
legalizzare vt. 1. to legalize 2. (autenticare) to authenticate.
legalizzazione sf. 1. legalization 2. (autenticazione) authentication.
legame sm. 1. string 2. (vincolo) tie 3. (connessione) link.
legamento sm. 1. string 2. (anat.) ligament.
legare[1] vt. 1. to tie 2. (di metalli) to alloy (with) 3. (aver connessione) to be connected. ♦ **legarsi** vr. to bind (v. irr.) oneself.
legare[2] vt. (giur.) to bequeath.
legatario sm. legatee.
legato[1] sm. 1. ambassador 2. (eccl.) legate.
legato[2] sm. (giur.) legacy.
legatore sm. binder.
legatorìa sf. bookbinder's establishment.

legatura *sf.* **1.** binding **2.** (*mus.; med.*) ligature.
legazione *sf.* legation.
legge *sf.* **1.** law **2.** (*singola*) act **3.** (*regola*) rule || *progetto di* —, bill; *a norma di* —, according to the law; *a termini di* —, as by law enacted.
leggenda *sf.* legend.
leggendario *agg.* legendary.
lèggere *vt.* to read (*v. irr.*).
leggerezza *sf.* lightness.
leggero *agg.* light.
leggiadrìa *sf.* loveliness.
leggiadro *agg.* lovely.
leggìbile *agg.* readable.
leggìo *sm.* **1.** reading-desk **2.** (*mus.*) music-stand.
legiferare *vi.* to legislate.
legionario *agg. e sm.* legionary.
legione *sf.* legion.
legislativo *agg.* legislative.
legislatore *sm.* legislator.
legislatura *sf.* legislature.
legislazione *sf.* legislation.
legittimare *vt.* to legitimate.
legittimazione *sf.* legitimation.
legittimità *sf.* legitimacy.
legìttimo *agg.* legitimate.
legna *sf.* wood || — *da ardere*, firewood.
legnaia *sf.* wood-store.
legname *sm.* **1.** wood **2.** (*da costruzione*) timber.
legnata *sf.* blow with a cudgel.
legno *sm.* wood || *di* —, wooden.
legnosità *sf.* woodiness.
legnoso *agg.* **1.** woody **2.** (*duro*) tough.
legume *sm.* legume.
leguminoso *agg.* leguminous.
lei *pron.* **1.** (*sogg.*) she, (*compl.*) her **2.** (*forma di cortesia*) you.
lembo *sm.* **1.** edge **2.** (*pezzo*) strip.
lemma *sm.* lemma.
lèmure *sm.* lemur. ◆ **lèmuri** *sm. pl.* (*mit.*) lemures.
lena *sf.* **1.** energy **2.** (*respiro*) breath.
lenire *vt.* to soothe.
lenone *sm.* pander.
lente *sf.* lens: — *d'ingrandimento*, magnifying lens || *lenti*, glasses.
lentezza *sf.* slowness.
lenticchia *sf.* lentil.
lentìggine *sf.* freckle.
lentigginoso *agg.* freckly.
lento *agg.* **1.** slow **2.** (*non teso*) loose.

lenza *sf.* fishing-line.
lenzuolo *sm.* sheet.
leone *sm.* lion.
leonessa *sf.* lioness.
leonino *agg.* leonine.
leopardo *sm.* leopard.
lèpido *agg.* witty.
lepidòttero *sm.* lepidopteron (*pl. -era*).
leporino *agg.* leporine || *labbro* —, hare-lip.
lepre *sf.* hare.
lercio *agg.* filthy.
lèsbica *agg. e sf.* Lesbian.
lésina *sf.* awl.
lesinare *vi.* to be stingy. ◆ **lesinare** *vt.* to grudge.
lesionare *vt.* to damage, to injure.
lesione *sf.* **1.** lesion, injury **2.** (*danno*) damage.
lesivo *agg.* harmful.
leso *agg.* **1.** injured **2.** (*danneggiato*) damaged.
lessare *vt.* to boil.
lessicale *agg.* lexical.
lèssico *sm.* lexicon.
lessicografìa *sf.* lexicography.
lessicologìa *sf.* lexicology.
lesso *agg.* boiled. ◆ **lesso** *sm.* boiled meat.
lestezza *sf.* quickness.
lesto *agg.* quick.
lestofante *sm.* swindler.
letale *agg.* lethal.
letamaio *sm.* dunghill.
letame *sm.* dung.
letàrgico *agg.* **1.** lethargic **2.** (*di animali, in inverno*) hibernating; (*id., in estate*) estivating.
letargo *sm.* **1.** lethargy **2.** (*di animali, in inverno*) hibernation; (*id., in estate*) estivation.
letizia *sf.* joy.
lèttera *sf.* letter || *alla* —, literally.
letterale *agg.* literal.
letterario *agg.* literary.
letterato *agg.* lettered. ◆ **letterato** *sm.* literary man.
letteratura *sf.* literature.
lettiga *sf.* stretcher.
letto *sm.* bed || *camera da* —, bedroom; *vagone* —, sleeping-car.
lettore *sm.* reader.
lettura *sf.* reading.
leucemìa *sf.* leukaemia.
leucociti *sm. pl.* leucocytes.
leucoma *sm.* leucoma.
leva[1] *sf.* **1.** lever **2.** (*fig.*) stimulus || *far* — *sui sentimenti di qu.*, to

play on so.'s feelings.

leva² sf. (mil.) draft: essere di —, to be due for draft.

levante sm. 1. east 2. (vento) levanter.

levare vt. 1. (sollevare) to raise 2. (togliere) to take (v. irr.) off. ♦ **levarsi** vr. 1. to rise (v. irr.) 2. (togliersi) to take off.

levata sf. 1. (di sole) rising 2. (di posta) collection || — di scudi rebellion.

levataccia sf. early rising.

levatoio agg. ponte —, drawbridge.

levatrice sf. midwife (pl. -wives).

levatura sf. intelligence.

levigare vt. to smooth.

levigatezza sf. smoothness.

levigato agg. smooth.

levitazione sf. levitation.

levriere sm. greyhound.

lezione sf. 1. lesson 2. (universitaria) lecture 3. (lett.) reading.

leziosàggine sf. affectation.

lezioso agg. affected.

lezzo sm. stench.

li pron. them.

lì avv. there: — vicino, near there; — dentro, in there || — per —, at first; di — a poco, soon after; giù di — (press'a poco), thereabouts; essere — per, to be on the point of.

liana sf. liana.

libagione sf. libation.

libbra sf. pound.

libeccio sm. Southwest wind.

libello sm. libel.

libèllula sf. dragonfly.

liberale agg. e sm. liberal.

liberalismo sm. liberalism.

liberalità sf. generosity.

liberalizzare vt. to liberalize.

liberare vt. 1. to free 2. (da pericoli) to rescue 3. (sbarazzare) to rid (v. irr.) (of). ♦ **liberarsi** vr. (sbarazzarsi) to get (v. irr.) rid (of).

liberatore agg. liberating. ♦ **liberatore** sm. deliverer.

liberazione sf. liberation.

libero agg. free.

liberoscambista agg. e sm. free-trader.

libertà sf. liberty, freedom.

libertario agg. e sm. libertarian.

liberticida agg. e sm. liberticide.

libertinaggio sm. libertinage.

libertino agg. e sm. libertine.

libìdine sf. lust.

libidinoso agg. lustful.

libido sf. lustfulness.

libraio sm. bookseller.

librarsi vr. to hover.

librerìa sf. 1. bookshop 2. (mobile) bookcase.

libresco agg. bookish.

libretto sm. 1. booklet 2. (d'opera) libretto || — di assegni, cheque-book; — di risparmio, savings-book; — personale, record-book.

libro sm. book.

licenza sf. 1. (abuso) licence 2. (permesso) permission, leave 3. (documento) licence.

licenziamento sm. dismissal.

licenziare vt. to dismiss. ♦ **licenziarsi** vr. to give (v. irr.) up one's job.

licenziosità sf. licentiousness.

licenzioso agg. licentious.

lichene sm. lichen.

licitazione sf. sale by auction.

lido sm. shore.

lieto agg. glad.

lieve agg. slight.

lievitare vi. to rise (v. irr.). ♦ **lievitare** vt. to leaven.

lievitazione sf. leavening.

lièvito sm. 1. yeast 2. (fermento) ferment.

ligio agg. faithful, observant (of).

lignaggio sm. lineage.

ligneo agg. wooden.

lignite sf. lignite.

lillà sm. lilac.

lilliputiano agg. e sm. Lilliputian.

lima sf. file.

limaccioso agg. slimy.

limare vt. 1. to file 2. (fig.) to polish.

limatrice sf. (mecc.) shaping-machine.

limatura sf. filing.

limbo sm. limbo.

limitare vt. to limit. ♦ **limitarsi** vr. (controllarsi) to check oneself.

limitatezza sf. limitation.

limitativo agg. limitative.

limitato agg. limited.

limitazione sf. limitation: — delle nascite, birth-control.

lìmite sm. limit: — di velocità, speed-limit || — di rottura, breaking-point.

lìmitrofo agg. neighbouring.

limo sm. slime.

limonata sf. lemonade.

limone *sm.* lemon.
limpidezza *sf.* clearness.
limpido *agg.* limpid, clear.
lince *sf.* lynx.
linciaggio *sm.* lynching
linciare *vt.* to lynch.
lindo *agg.* neat.
linea *sf.* line || *aereo di* —, air-liner; *mantenere la* —, to keep (*v. irr.*) one's figure.
lineamenti *sm. pl.* 1. features 2. (*linee essenziali*) outlines.
lineare *agg.* 1. linear 2. (*fig.*) unswerving.
lineetta *sf.* 1. dash 2. (*trattino d'unione*) hyphen.
linfa *sf.* (*biol.*) lymph.
linfàtico *agg.* lymphatic.
linfatismo *sm.* lymphatism.
lingotto *sm.* ingot.
lingua *sf.* 1. tongue 2. (*linguaggio*) language.
linguacciuto *agg.* talkative.
linguaggio *sm.* language.
linguetta *sf.* 1. flap 2. (*mecc.; di scarpe*) tongue.
linguista *s.* linguist.
linguìstica *sf.* linguistics.
linguìstico *agg.* linguistic.
linimento *sm.* liniment.
lino *sm.* flax.
linòleum *sm.* linoleum.
linone *sm.* lawn.
linotipìa *sf.* linotyping.
linotipista *s.* linotypist.
liquefare *vt.* to liquefy. ♦ **liquefarsi** *vr.* to liquefy.
liquefazione *sf.* liquefaction.
liquidare *vt.* 1. to liquidate 2. (*comm.*) to sell (*v. irr.*) off, to settle || — *una questione*, to settle a question.
liquidatore *sm.* liquidator.
liquidazione *sf.* liquidation, sale.
lìquido *agg. e sm.* liquid || *denaro* —, cash.
liquirìzia *sf.* liquorice.
liquore *sm.* liqueur || *i liquori*, spirits.
liquoroso *agg.* liqueur-like.
lira *sf.* 1. (*moneta*) lira 2. (*mus.*) lyre.
lìrica *sf.* 1. lyric poetry 2. (*teatro lirico*) opera.
lìrico *agg.* lyric(al). ♦ **lìrico** *sm.* lyrist.
lirismo *sm.* lyrism.
lisciare *vt.* 1. to smooth 2. (*adulare*) to flatter. ♦ **lisciarsi** *vr.* to

sleek oneself.
liscio *agg.* 1. smooth 2. (*di bevanda*) undiluted 3. (*semplice*) plain 4. (*di capelli*) sleek.
lisciva *sf.* lye.
liso *agg.* threadbare.
lista *sf.* 1. (*elenco*) list, note 2. (*striscia*) stripe.
listare *vt.* 1. to stripe 2. (*bordare*) to border.
listino *sm.* list.
litanìa *sf.* litany.
lite *sf.* 1. quarrel, wrangle 2. (*giur.*) lawsuit.
litigante *sm.* 1. wrangler 2. (*giur.*) litigant.
litigare *vi.* 1. to quarrel 2. (*giur.*) to litigate.
litigio *sm.* quarrel.
litigioso *agg.* quarrelsome.
litografìa *sf.* 1. lithography 2. (*pezzo singolo*) lithograph.
litogràfico *agg.* lithographic.
litorale *agg.* littoral. ♦ **litorale** *sm.* coast.
litro *sm.* litre.
liturgìa *sf.* liturgy.
litùrgico *agg.* liturgic(al).
liuto *sm.* lute.
livellamento *sm.* levelling.
livellare *vt.* to level.
livellatrice *sf.* bulldozer.
livello *sm.* level: *a* — *del mare*, at sea-level; *passaggio a* —, level-crossing; *essere allo stesso* — *di*, to be on a level with.
lìvido *agg.* livid. ♦ **lìvido** *sm.* bruise.
livore *sm.* 1. (*invidia*) envy 2. (*odio*) hatred.
livrea *sf.* livery.
lizza *sf.* competition, lists (*pl.*) || *essere in* — (*fig.*), to be competing.
lo *art.* the. ♦ **lo** *pron.* 1. (*per uomo*) him 2. (*per animale, cosa*) it || — *credo*, I think so.
lobo *sm.* lobe.
locale *agg.* local. ♦ **locale** *sm.* 1. room 2. (*ritrovo*) place.
località *sf.* locality, spot.
localizzare *vt.* to localize.
localizzazione *sf.* localization.
locanda *sf.* inn.
locandiere *sm.* innkeeper.
locandina *sf.* play-bill.
locare *vt.* to rent.
locatario *sm.* tenant.
locativo *agg.* locative || *valore* —, rental value.

locatore *sm.* lessor.
locazione *sf.* lease.
locomotiva *sf.* locomotive.
locomotore *agg. e sm.* locomotive.
locomozione *sf.* locomotion.
locusta *sf.* locust.
locuzione *sf.* locution.
lodàbile *agg.* laudable.
lodare *vt.* to praise
lodatore *sm.* praiser.
lode *sf.* praise.
lodévole *agg.* praiseworthy.
logaritmo *sm.* logarithm.
loggia *sf.* **1.** (*arch.*) loggia **2.** (*massonica*) lodge.
loggione *sm.* gallery.
lògica *sf.* logic.
logicità *sf.* logicality.
lògico *agg.* logical. ◆ **lògico** *sm.* logician.
logìstica *sf.* logistics.
logìstico *agg.* logistic(al).
loglio *sm.* darnel.
logomachìa *sf.* logomachy.
logoramento *sm.* **1.** wear **2.** (*fig.*) wasting away.
logorante *agg.* wearing.
logorare *vt.* to wear (*v. irr.*) (out, down). ◆ **logorarsi** *vr.* to wear (out, down).
logorio *sm.* wear and tear.
lògoro *agg.* worn (out, down).
lombàggine *sf.* lumbago.
lombardo *agg. e sm.* Lombard.
lombare *agg.* lumbar.
lombi *sm. pl.* loins.
lombrico *sm.* earth-worm.
longànime *agg.* forbearing.
longanimità *sf.* forbearance.
longevità *sf.* longevity.
longevo *agg.* longevous.
longitudinale *agg.* longitudinal.
longitùdine *sf.* longitude.
lontananza *sf.* distance: *in* —, in the distance.
lontano *agg.* **1.** far **2.** (*nel tempo*) far off, distant **3.** (*vago*) vague. ◆ **lontano** *avv.* far || *da* —, from afar.
lontra *sf.* otter.
loquace *agg.* talkative.
loquacità *sf.* talkativeness.
loquela *sf.* glibness.
lordare *vt.* to soil. ◆ **lordarsi** *vr.* to get (*v. irr.*) dirty.
lordo *agg.* **1.** (*sporco*) filthy **2.** (*di peso*) gross.
loro *agg. poss.* their. ◆ **loro** *pron. poss.* theirs. ◆ **loro** *pron. pers.*

1. (*sogg.*) they, (*compl.*) them **2.** (*forma di cortesia*) you.
losanga *sf.* lozenge.
losco *agg.* **1.** (*bieco*) sinister **2.** (*sospetto*) suspicious.
loto *sm.* **1.** (*fango*) mud **2.** (*bot.*) lotus.
lotta *sf.* **1.** struggle **2.** (*sport*) wrestling.
lottare *vi.* **1.** to struggle **2.** (*sport*) to wrestle.
lottatore *sm.* **1.** struggler **2.** (*sport*) wrestler.
lotterìa *sf.* lottery.
lottizzare *vt.* to lot.
lottizzazione *sf.* division into lots.
lotto *sm.* **1.** lot **2.** (*gioco*) state lottery.
lozione *sf.* lotion.
lubricità *sf.* lubricity.
lùbrico *agg.* **1.** lubricous **2.** (*fig.*) lascivious.
lubrificante *agg.* lubricating. ◆ **lubrificante** *sm.* lubricant.
lubrificare *vt.* to lubricate.
lubrificazione *sf.* lubrication.
lucchetto *sm.* padlock.
luccicante *agg.* glittering.
luccicare *vi.* to glitter.
luccichìo *sm.* glitter.
lùcciola *sf.* **1.** firefly **2.** (*senz'ali*) glow-worm.
luce *sf.* light || *alla* — *del sole* (*fig.*), openly; *dare alla* — *un bambino*, to give (*v. irr.*) birth to a child; *mettere in* —, to show (*v. irr.*); *venire alla* — (*nascere*), to be born.
lucente *agg.* bright.
lucentezza *sf.* brightness.
lucerna *sf.* oil-lamp.
lucernario *sm.* skylight.
lucèrtola *sf.* lizard.
lucidare *vt.* to polish.
lucidatrice *sf.* **1.** floor-polisher **2.** (*mecc.*) polishing machine.
lucidatura *sf.* polishing.
lucidezza *sf.* **1.** brightness **2.** (*di mente*) lucidness.
lucidità *sf.* lucidity.
lùcido *agg.* **1.** lucid **2.** (*lucidato*) glossy. ◆ **lùcido** *sm.* **1.** (*per scarpe*) shoe-polish **2.** (*lucidezza*) shine.
lucìgnolo *sm.* wick.
lucrare *vt.* to profit.
lucrativo *agg.* profitable.
lucro *sm.* profit: *a scopo di* —, for the sake of gain.
ludibrio *sm.* mockery

luglio *sm.* July.
lùgubre *agg.* lugubrious.
lui *pron.* 1. (*sogg.*) he 2. (*compl.*) him.
lumaca *sf.* snail.
lume *sm.* light || *al — di candela*, by candle-light; *perdere il — della ragione*, to be blinded by anger.
lumeggiare *vt.* (*fig.*) to put (*v. irr.*) in evidence.
luminare *sm.* luminary.
luminescenza *sf.* luminescence.
luminosità *sf.* brightness.
luminoso *agg.* bright.
luna *sf.* moon: —, *calante*, waning moon; — *crescente*, waxing moon || *chiaro di —*, moonlight; — *di miele*, honeymoon; *avere la —* (*fig.*), to be in the sulks.
lunare *agg.* lunar.
lunario *sm.* almanac || *sbarcare il —*, to make (*v. irr.*) both ends meet.
lunàtico *agg.* moody.
lunazione *sf.* lunation.
lunedì *sm.* Monday.
lunetta *sf.* lunette.
lungàggine *sf.* slowness, delay.
lunghezza *sf.* length.
lungimirante *agg.* far-sighted.
lungo *agg.* 1. long: *a —*, long; *a — andare*, in the long run 2. (*lento*) slow || *in — e in largo*, far and wide; *di gran lunga*, by far. ♦ **lungo** *prep.* 1. along 2. (*durante*) during.
lungofiume *sm.* embankment.
lungolago *sm.* lake-front.
lungomare *sm.* sea-front.
lungometraggio *sm.* feature film.
luogo *sm.* place: — *di nascita*, birthplace; *sul —*, on the spot; *aver —*, to take (*v. irr.*) place; *dar —*, to cause.
luogotenente *sm.* lieutenant.
lupa *sf.* she-wolf.
lupanare *sm.* brothel.
lupara *sf.* shotgun.
lupino *sm.* (*bot.*) lupine.
lupo *sm.* wolf || — *di mare*, sea-dog; *in bocca al —!*, good luck!
lùppolo *sm.* hop.
lùrido *agg.* dirty.
luridume *sm.* dirt.
lusinga *sf.* allurement, flattery.
lusingare *vt.* to allure, to flatter.
lusinghiero *agg.* alluring, flattering.
lussare *vt.* to dislocate.
lussazione *sf.* dislocation.

lusso *sm.* luxury.
lussuoso *agg.* luxurious, rich.
lussureggiante *agg.* luxuriant.
lussureggiare *vi.* to thrive (*v. irr.*).
lussuria *sf.* lust.
lussurioso *agg.* lustful.
lustrale *agg.* lustral.
lustrare *vt.* to polish.
lustrascarpe *sm.* shoeblack.
lustratura *sf.* polish.
lustrino *sm.* spangle.
lustro *agg.* shining, shiny. ♦ **lustro** *sm.* lustre.
luteranésimo *sm.* Lutheranism.
luterano *agg. e sm.* Lutheran.
lutto *sm.* mourning: *mettere il —*, to go (*v. irr.*) into mourning.
luttuoso *agg.* mournful.

M

ma *cong.* 1. but 2. (*tuttavia*) however, still.
màcabro *agg.* macabre.
macaco *sm.* 1. macaque 2. (*fig.*) runt.
macché *inter.* you don't say it!
maccheroni *sm. pl.* macaroni (*sing.*).
macchia[1] *sf.* spot, stain.
macchia[2] *sf.* (*boscaglia*) bush: *darsi alla —*, to take (*v. irr.*) to the bush.
macchiare *vt.* to stain. ♦ **macchiarsi** *vr.* 1. to get (*v. irr.*) stained 2. (*fig.*) to soil oneself.
macchiato *agg.* spotted.
macchietta *sf.* 1. caricature 2. (*di persona*) character.
màcchina *sf.* 1. engine, machine: — *calcolatrice*, calculating machine; — *per cucire*, sewing-machine; — *da presa*, cine-camera; — *per scrivere*, typewriter; — *fotografica*, camera; *fatto a —*, machine-made; *andare in —* (*di giornali*), to go (*v. irr.*) to press 2. (*automobile*) car.
macchinale *agg.* mechanical.
macchinare *vt.* to plot.
macchinario *sm.* machinery.
macchinazione *sf.* machination.
macchinista *sm.* 1. (*ferr.*) engine-driver 2. (*teat.*) scene-shifter.
macchinoso *agg.* complicated.

macedonia sf. (cuc.) fruit-salad.
macellaio sm. butcher.
macellare vt. to slaughter.
macellerìa sf. butcher's shop.
macello sm. 1. (luogo dove si macella) slaughter-house 2. (massacro) slaughter.
macerare vt. 1. to soak 2. (di lino, canapa) to ret. ♦ **macerarsi** vr. (fig.) to waste (away).
maceratoio sm. rettery.
macerazione sf. 1. soaking 2. (industria tessile) retting.
macerie sf. pl. rubble (sing.), ruins.
màcero sm. (per canapa e lino) retting-ground: carta da —, waste-paper.
machiavèllico agg. Machiavellian.
machiavellismo sm. Machiavellism.
macigno sm. boulder.
macilento agg. emaciated.
macilenza sf. emaciation.
màcina sf. grindstone.
macinacaffè sm. coffee-mill.
macinapepe sm. pepper-mill.
macinare vt. 1. to grind (v. irr.), to mince.
macinino sm. grinder.
maciullare vt. to crush.
macrocèfalo agg. macrocephalous.
macrocosmo sm. macrocosm.
macromolècola sf. macromolecule.
macroscòpico agg. macroscopic.
maculato agg. spotted.
madia sf. 1. kitchen cupboard 2. (per pane) kneading trough.
màdido agg. wet: — di sudore, bathed in sweat.
madonna sf. 1. (titolo) Lady, My Lady 2. (relig.) The Virgin Mary, Our Lady 3. (pitt.) Madonna.
madornale agg. huge.
madre sf. mother.
madrepatria sf. mother-country.
madreperla sf. mother-of-pearl.
madreperlàceo agg. pearly.
madrèpora sf. madrepore.
madrepòrico agg. madreporic.
madrevite sf. 1. nut screw 2. (utensile) die.
madrigale sm. madrigal.
madrina sf. godmother.
maestà sf. majesty.
maestosità sf. majesty.
maestoso agg. majestic.
maestra sf. (scol.) teacher.
maestrale sm. mistral.
maestranza sf. skilled workers (pl.).

maestrìa sf. skill, ability.
maestro sm. 1. (scol.) teacher 2. (uomo dotto) master 3. (mus.) conductor, "maestro" || albero —, mainmast.
mafia sf. "Mafia".
maga sf. sorceress.
magagna sf. flaw, imperfection.
magari inter. if only! ♦ **magari** avv. (forse) perhaps, maybe. ♦ **magari** cong. even if.
magazzinaggio sm. storage.
magazziniere sm. store-keeper.
magazzino sm. warehouse || fondi di —, unsold stock.
maggese sm. fallow land.
maggio sm. May.
maggiolino sm. May-bug.
maggiorana sf. marjoram.
maggioranza sf. majority, most (of).
maggiorare vt. to increase.
maggiorazione sf. increase, charge.
maggiordomo sm. butler.
maggiore agg. 1. (più grande, ampio) greater, larger 2. (più vecchio) older: il —, the oldest 3. (di fratelli) elder (fra due), eldest (fra molti). ♦ **maggiore** sm. 1. (mil.) major 2. (superiore) superior.
maggiorenne agg. of age: diventare —, to come (v. irr.) of age. ♦ **maggiorenne** sm. major.
maggiorente sm. notable.
maggioritario agg. majority (attr.).
maggiormente avv. more, much more.
magìa sf. magic.
màgiaro agg. e sm. Magyar.
magicamente avv. magically.
màgico agg. magical.
magistrale agg. 1. magisteral || scuola —, teachers' institute 2. (eccellente) masterly.
magistralmente avv. skilfully.
magistrato sm. Magistrate.
magistratura sf. magistracy.
maglia sf. 1. (di lavoro a maglia) stitch || lavorare a —, to knit (v. irr.) 2. (indumento) vest 3. (di catena) link.
magliaia sf. knitter.
maglierìa sf. hosiery.
maglificio sm. hosiery.
maglio sm. 1. mallet 2. (mecc.) hammer.
maglione sm. sweater.
magma sm. magma.
magnanimità sf. magnanimity.

magnànimo agg. magnanimous.
magnate sm. magnate.
magnesia sf. magnesia.
magnesio sm. magnesium. lampo al —, flash.
magnete sm. magnet.
magnètico agg. magnetic.
magnetismo sm. magnetism.
magnetite sf. magnetite.
magnetizzare vt. to magnetize.
magnetizzatore sm. magnetizer.
magnetizzazione sf. magnetization.
magnetòfono sm. tape-recorder.
magnetòmetro sm. magnetometer.
magnificamente avv. magnificently.
magnificare vt. to extol, to glorify.
magnificenza sf. magnificence.
magnìfico agg. magnificent.
magniloquente agg. magniloquent.
magniloquenza sf. magniloquence.
magnolia sf. magnolia.
mago sm. wizard.
magra sf. (di fiumi) low water.
magrezza sf. thinness.
magro agg. 1. thin 2. (di carni) lean.
mah inter. who knows!
mai avv. 1. ever 2. (non mai) never: — e poi —, never never; — più, never more; caso —, if; non si sa —, you never can tell; meglio tardi che —, better late than never.
maiale sm. 1. pig 2. (carne) pork.
maièutica sf. maieutics.
maiòlica sf. majolica.
maionese sf. mayonnaise
mais sm. maize.
maiùscola sf. capital letter.
maiuscoletto sm. small capitals.
maiùscolo agg. capital.
malaccorto agg. ill-advised
malachìte sf. malachite.
malacreanza sf. rudeness.
malafede sf. bad faith.
malaffare sm. 1. donna di —, whore 2. gente di —, crooks (pl.).
malagévole agg. difficult, hard.
malagrazia sf. bad grace.
malalingua sf. backbiter.
malamente avv. badly.
malandato agg. in bad condition.
malandrino sm. 1. brigand 2. (fam.) rogue.
malànimo sm. malevolence.
malanno sm. 1. calamity 2. (malattia) illness.

malapena (nella loc. avv.) a —, hardly.
malaria sf. malaria.
malaticcio agg. sickly.
malato agg. sick, ill. ♦ **malato** sm. patient.
malattìa sf. sickness, disease.
malauguratamente avv. unluckily.
malaugurato agg. ill-fated.
malaugurio sm. ill-omen.
malavita sf. underworld.
malavoglia sf., unwillingness ‖ di —, reluctantly.
malcapitato agg. unlucky. ♦ **malcapitato** sm. victim.
malconcio agg. 1. battered 2. (contuso) bruised.
malcontento agg. dissatisfied (with). ♦ **malcontento** sm. discontent.
malcostume sm. immorality, corruption.
maldestro agg. awkward.
maldicente agg. disparaging. ♦ **maldicente** sm. slanderer.
maldicenza sf. backbiting.
maldisposto agg. ill-disposed, hostile.
male sm. 1. evil 2. (malattia) illness, disease 3. (dolore fisico) pain ‖ — di testa, headache. ♦ **male** avv. badly, ill.
maledettamente avv. awfully.
maledetto agg. cursed.
malèdico agg. slanderous.
maledire vt. to curse.
maledizione sf. curse, malediction ‖ —! (inter.), damn!
maleducato agg. rude, impolite.
maleducazione sf. rudeness.
malefatta sf. mischief.
maleficio sm. sorcery.
malèfico agg. harmful.
malerba sf. weed.
malese agg. e sm. Malay.
malèssere sm. 1. malaise 2. (disagio) uneasiness.
malestro sm. mischief.
malevolenza sf. malevolence.
malèvolo agg. malevolent.
malfamato agg. ill-famed.
malfatto agg. 1. ill-shaped 2. (di abito) ill-fitting.
malfattore sm. evil-doer.
malfermo agg. shaky ‖ salute malferma, poor health.
malfido agg. unreliable.
malfondato agg. ill-grounded.

malformato *agg.* malformed.
malformazione *sf.* malformation.
malgarbo *sm.* bad grace.
malgoverno *sm.* misgovernment, misrule.
malgrado *prep. e avv.* in spite of.
♦ **malgrado (che)** *cong.* though, although.
malìa *sf.* (*fascino*) fascination.
maliarda *sf.* 1. (*donna affascinante*) fascinating woman 2. (*maga*) witch.
malignamente *avv.* maliciously.
malignare *vi.* to speak (*v. irr.*) ill (of).
malignità *sf.* malice.
maligno *agg.* malicious: *tumore* —, malignant tumor.
malinconìa *sf.* melancholy.
malinconicamente *avv.* sadly.
malincònico *agg.* melancholy.
malincuore (*nella loc. avv.*) *a* —, unwillingly.
malintenzionato *agg.* ill-disposed.
malinteso *agg.* misplaced. ♦ **malinteso** *sm.* misunderstanding.
malizia *sf.* 1. malice 2. (*astuzia*) cunning.
maliziosamente *avv.* artfully.
malizioso *agg.* malicious, mischievous.
malleàbile *agg.* malleable.
malleabilità *sf.* malleability.
malleverìa *sf.* bail.
malloppo *sm.* swag.
malmenare *vt.* to manhandle.
malmesso *ag.* poorly dressed.
malnato *agg.* ill-bred.
malocchio *sm.* evil eye.
malora *sf.* ruin || *va alla* —!, go to the devil!
malore *sm.* illness.
malpensante *agg.* wrong-thinking.
malsano *agg.* unhealthy.
malsicuro *agg.* unsafe.
malta *sf.* mortar.
maltempo *sm.* bad weather.
maltenuto *agg.* untidy.
maltese *agg. e sm.* Maltese.
malto *sm.* malt.
maltolto *agg.* ill-gotten. ♦ **maltolto** *sm.* ill-gotten property.
maltosio *sm.* maltose.
maltrattamento *sm.* maltreatment.
maltrattare *vt.* to maltreat.
maltusianismo *sm.* Malthusianism.
maltusiano *agg. e sm.* Malthusian.
malumore *sm.* ill-humour.
malva *sf.* mallow.

malvagio *agg.* wicked.
malvagità *sf.* wickedness.
malversatore *sm.* embezzler.
malversazione *sf.* embezzlement.
malvisto *agg.* unpopular (with).
malvivente *sm.* gangster.
malvivenza *sf.* delinquency.
malvolentieri *avv.* unwillingly.
malvolere *sm.* ill-will.
malvolere *vi.* to dislike.
mamma *sf.* mama, mummy.
mammalucco *sm.* (*fam.*) simpleton.
mammella *sf.* 1. mamma (*pl.* -ae) 2. (*di animali da latte*) udder.
mammìfero *agg.* mammiferous. ♦ **mammìfero** *sm.* mammal.
màmmola *sf.* sweet-smelling violet.
mammùt *sm.* mammoth.
manata *sf.* slap.
manca *sf.* 1. left hand 2. (*parte sinistra*) left || *a dritta e a* —, on all sides.
mancante *agg.* incomplete.
mancanza *sf.* 1. lack, shortage 2. (*fallo*) fault || *sentire la* — *di qu.*, to miss so.
mancare *vi.* 1. to be lacking (in) 2. (*non esserci*) to be missing 3. (*venir meno*) to fail 4. (*agire scorrettamente*) to wrong (so.).
mancato *agg.* unsuccessful.
manchévole *agg.* defective.
manchevolezza *sf.* defect, fault.
mancia *sf.* tip || *dare la* — *a qu.*, to tip so.
manciata *sf.* handful.
mancina *sf.* left-hand.
mancino *agg.* left-handed. ♦ **mancino** *sm.* left-hander.
manco *avv.* not even.
mandamento *sm.* district.
mandante *sm.* 1. instigator 2. (*giur.*) principal.
mandare *vt.* 1. to send (*v. irr.*) 2. (*spedire*) to forward 3. (*emettere*) to give (*v. irr.*) out.
mandarino *sm.* mandarin.
mandata *sf.* batch || — *di chiave*, turn.
mandatario *sm.* mandatary.
mandato *sm.* 1. mandate 2. (*comm.* agency 3. (*giur.*) warrant.
mandìbola *sf.* mandible.
mandola *sf.* mandola.
mandolinista *s.* mandolinist.
mandolino *sm.* mandolin.
màndorla *sf.* almond.
màndorlo *sm.* almond-tree.

mandràgora *sf.* mandrake.
mandria *sf.* herd.
mandriano *sm.* herdsman (*pl.* -men).
maneggévole *agg.* handy.
maneggiare *vt.* to handle.
maneggio *sm.* 1. (*equitazione*) riding-ground 2. (*uso*) use 3. (*intrigo*) plot.
manesco *agg.* rough, aggressive.
manette *sf. pl.* handcuff (*sing.*).
manforte *sf.* help.
manganellare *vt.* to cudgel.
manganello *sm.* cudgel.
manganese *sm.* manganese.
mangereccio *agg.* eatable.
mangiàbile *agg.* eatable.
mangiare *vt.* to eat (*v. irr.*).
mangiata *sf.* square meal.
mangiatoia *sf.* manger.
mangime *sm.* fodder.
mangiucchiare *vt.* to nibble (at).
manìa *sf.* mania.
maniaco *agg.* 1. maniac 2. (*fig.*) crazy. ♦ **maniaco** *sm.* maniac.
mànica *sf.* sleeve || *essere di — larga, stretta*, to be indulgent, strict.
manicheismo *sm.* Manicheism.
manicheo *agg. e sm.* Manichean.
manichino *sm.* manikin.
mànico *sm.* handle.
manicomio *sm.* mental hospital.
manicotto *sm.* 1. muff 2. (*mecc.*) sleeve.
maniera *sf.* manner, way.
manierato *agg.* affected.
manierismo *sm.* mannerism.
maniero *sm.* castle.
manifattura *sf.* manufacture.
manifatturiero *agg.* manufacturing.
manifestante *s.* demonstrator.
manifestare *vt.* 1. to manifest, to show (*v. irr.*) 2. (*pol.*) to demonstrate.
manifestazione *sf.* 1. manifestation 2. (*pol.*) demonstration.
manifesto *agg.* manifest, clear, obvious. ♦ **manifesto** *sm.* 1. (*affisso*) poster 2. (*volantino*) leaflet 3. (*dichiarazione*) manifesto.
maniglia *sf.* handle.
manigoldo *sm.* scoundrel.
manioca *sf.* manioc.
manipolare *vt.* to manipulate.
manipolatore *sm.* manipulator.
manipolazione *sf.* manipulation.
manìpolo *sm.* (*eccl.; stor.*) maniple.
maniscalco *sm.* blacksmith.

manna *sf.* 1. manna 2. (*fig.*) blessing.
mannaia *sf.* 1. axe 2. (*della ghigliottina*) knife.
mannaro *agg. lupo —*, werewolf.
mano *sf.* hand: *fatto a —*, hand-made; *stringere la —*, to shake (*v. irr.*) hands with || *a — armata*, by force of arms; *sotto —*, underhand.
manodòpera *sf.* labour.
manòmetro *sm.* manometer.
manométtere *vt.* to tamper with.
manomissione *sf.* tampering.
manòpola *sf.* 1. knob 2. (*impugnatura*) handle.
manoscritto *agg.* handwritten. ♦ **manoscritto** *sm.* manuscript.
manovale *sm.* hodman (*pl.* -men).
manovella *sf.* crank.
manovra *sf.* manoeuvre, operation.
manovràbile *agg.* manoeuvrable.
manovrare *vt.* 1. to manoeuvre 2. (*mecc.*) to operate.
manovratore *sm.* operator, driver.
manrovescio *sm.* back-handed slap.
mansarda *sf.* mansard.
mansione *sf.* function.
mansuefare *vt.* to tame.
mansueto *agg.* meek, mild.
mansuetùdine *sf.* meekness.
mantella *sf.* cape.
mantello *sm.* cloak.
mantenere *vt.* to keep (*v. irr.*), to maintain: *— la parola*, to keep one's word.
mantenimento *sm.* maintenance.
màntice *sm.* bellows (*pl.*).
manto *sm.* cloak.
manuale *agg.* manual. ♦ **manuale** *sm.* handbook.
manubrio *sm.* 1. handle 2. (*di bicicletta ecc.*) handle-bar.
manufatto *agg.* hand-made. ♦ **manufatto** *sm.* hand-manufactured article.
manutèngolo *sm.* abettor.
manutenzione *sf.* maintenance, servicing.
manzo *sm.* 1. (*zool.*) steer 2. (*carne*) beef.
maomettano *agg. e sm.* Mohammedan.
mappa *sf.* map.
mappamondo *sm.* globe.
marachella *sf.* trick.
marasma *sm.* 1. (*med.*) marasmus 2. (*fig.*) decadence.
maratona *sf.* marathon race.

marca *sf*. brand: — *di fabbrica*, trade mark.

marcare *vt*. 1. to mark 2. (*sport*) to score.

marcato *agg*. marked, branded.

marcatore *sm*. 1. marker 2. (*sport*) scorer.

marcatura *sf*. 1. marking 2. (*sport*) scoring.

marchesa *sf*. 1. marchioness 2. (*se non è inglese*) marquise.

marchesato *sm*. marquisate.

marchese *sm*. marquis.

marchiano *agg*. enormous, glaring.

marchiare *vt*. to brand.

marchiatura *sf*. branding.

marchio *sm*. 1. stamp 2. (*a fuoco*) brand 3. (*fig.; comm.*) mark.

marcia *sf*. 1. (*auto*) gear 2. (*mil.; mus.*) march.

marciapiede *sm*. 1. pavement 2. (*ferr.*) platform.

marciare *vi*. to march.

marciatore *sm*. (*sport*) road-walker.

marcio *agg*. 1. rotten 2. (*fig.*) corrupted. ♦ marcio *sm*. (*fig.*) corruption.

marcire *vi*. 1. (*guastarsi*) to go (*v. irr.*) bad 2. (*decomporsi*) to rot (*v. irr.*).

marciume *sm*. rottenness.

marco *sm*. mark.

marconigrafia *sf*. marconigraphy.

mare *sm*. sea.

marea *sf*. tide.

mareggiata *sf*. sea-storm.

maremma *sf*. maremma (*pl.* -me).

maremoto *sm*. seaquake.

mareògrafo *sm*. tide-gauge.

maresciallo *sm*. marshal.

margarina *sf*. margarine.

margherita *sf*. daisy.

marginale *agg*. marginal.

marginare *vt*. 1. to border 2. (*tip.*) to margin.

marginatura *sf*. 1. edging 2. (*tip.*) furniture.

màrgine *sm*. 1. border, edge 2. (*fig.*) margin.

marina *sf*. 1. navy 2. (*costa*) sea-shore 3. (*pitt.*) sea-scape.

marinaio *sm*. sailor.

marinara *sf*. 1. (*cappotto*) duffle coat 2. (*cappello*) sailor hat.

marinare *vt*. (*cuc.*) to pickle || — *la scuola*, to play truant.

marinaresco *agg*. sailor-like.

marinaro *agg*. 1. maritime 2. sail-

or-like. ♦ marinaro *sm*. sailor.

marineria *sf*. 1. seamanship 2. (*marina*) navy.

marino *agg*. sea (*attr.*).

mariolo *sm*. rogue.

marionetta *sf*. puppet.

maritale *agg*. marital.

maritare *vt*. to marry. ♦ maritarsi *vr*. to get (*v. irr.*) married.

marito *sm*. husband.

marìttimo *agg*. maritime || *città marittima*, sea-town; *commercio* —, shipping business. ♦ marìttimo *sm*. seafarer || *i marittimi*, seafolk (*sing.*).

marmaglia *sf*. rabble.

marmellata *sf*. 1. jam 2. (*d'arance*) marmalade.

marmista *sm*. marble-cutter.

marmitta *sf*. 1. (*cuc.*) stock-pot 2. (*auto*) silencer's muffler.

marmo *sm*. marble.

marmocchio *sm*. kid.

marmòreo *agg*. marble.

marmotta *sf*. 1. marmot 2. (*di persona*) lazy-bones.

marna *sf*. marl.

marocchino *agg*. Moroccan. ♦ marocchino *sm*. 1. (*persona*) Moroccan 2. (*cuoio*) Morocco leather.

maroso *sm*. billow.

marra *sf*. 1. (*agr.*) hoe 2. (*mar.*) fluke.

marrone *agg*. brown. ♦ marrone *sm*. chestnut.

martedì *sm*. Tuesday.

martellamento *sm*. hammering.

martellare *vt*. 1. to hammer 2. (*mil.*) to pound 3. (*pulsare*) to throb.

martellata *sf*. hammer-blow.

martello *sm*. hammer.

martinetto *sm*. jack.

martingala *sf*. half-belt.

màrtire *sm*. martyr.

martirio *sm*. martyrdom.

martirizzare *vt*. to martyrize.

martirologio *sm*. martyrology.

màrtora *sf*. marten.

martoriare *vt*. to torture.

marxismo *sm*. Marxism.

marxista *agg. e s*. Marxist.

marzapane *sm*. marzipan.

marziale *agg*. martial.

marziano *sm*. Martian.

marzo *sm*. March.

mascalzonata *sf*. knavery.

mascalzone *sm*. rascal.

mascella *sf*. jaw.

mascellare agg. jaw (attr.).
màschera sf. 1. mask 2. (figura mascherata) masker 3. (cosmesi) face-pack 4. (inserviente di cinema, teatro) usher.
mascheramento sm. masking.
mascherare vt. to mask.
mascherata sf. masquerade.
maschietto sm. male.
maschile agg. male.
maschio[1] agg. 1. male 2. (virile) manly. ♦ **maschio** sm. 1. (di animale) (uccelli) cock, (mammiferi) bull (attributivi) 2. (di uomo) male 3. (bambino) boy.
maschio[2] sm. (torre) donjon.
mascolinità sf. masculinity.
masnada sf. gang.
masnadiere sm. highwayman (pl. -men).
masochismo sm. masochism.
masonite sf. masonite.
massa sf. mass, heap.
massacrante agg. exhausting.
massacrare vt. to massacre.
massacratore sm. slaughterer.
massacro sm. massacre.
massaggiare vt. to massage.
massaggiatore sm. masseur.
massaggiatrice sf. masseuse.
massaggio sm. massage.
massaia sf. housewife (pl. -wives).
massello sm. ingot.
masserìa sf. farm.
masserizie sf. pl. household goods.
massicciata sf. road-bed.
massiccio agg. solid. ♦ **massiccio** sm. massif.
màssima sf. maxim, rule || in linea di —, on the whole; accordo di —, general agreement.
massimalismo sm. Maximalism.
massimalista s. Maximalist.
màssimo agg. 1. greatest, highest 2. (l'estremo) utmost 3. (il più lungo) longest. ♦ **màssimo** sm. 1. most 2. (il meglio) best 3. (mat.; fis.) maximum.
masso sm. boulder.
massone sm. freemason.
massonerìa sf. freemasonry.
mastello sm. tub.
masticare vt. to chew.
masticazione sf. mastication.
màstice sm. rubber.
mastino sm. mastiff.
mastite sf. mastitis.
mastodonte sm. 1. (zool.) mastodon 2. (fig.) giant.

mastodòntico agg. colossal.
mastòide sf. mastoid.
mastoidite sf. mastoiditis.
mastro sm. 1. (libro) ledger 2. (appellativo) Master.
masturbazione sf. masturbation.
matassa sf. 1. hank 2. (fig.) tangle.
matemàtica sf. mathematics.
matemàtico agg. mathematical. ♦ **matemàtico** sm. mathematician.
materasso sm. mattress.
materia sf. matter, subject.
materiale agg. 1. material 2. (rozzo) rough. ♦ **materiale** sm. material.
materialismo sm. materialism.
materialista s. materialist.
materialìstico agg. materialistic.
materializzare vt. to materialize.
maternità sf. maternity.
materno agg. motherly, maternal || scuola materna, nursery-school.
matita sf. pencil.
matriarcato sm. matriarchy.
matrice sf. 1. matrix (pl. matrices) 2. (comm.) counterfoil.
matricida s. matricide.
matricidio sm. matricide.
matrìcola sf. 1. matricula, register || numero di —, matriculation number 2. (scol.) freshman (pl. -men).
matricolato agg. matriculated || briccone —, arrant knave.
matrigna sf. stepmother.
matrimoniale agg. matrimonial.
matrimonio sm. 1. marriage 2. (cerimonia nuziale) wedding.
matrona sf. matron.
matta sf. 1. mad woman (pl. women) 2. (al gioco) jolly joker.
mattacchione sm. joker.
mattatoio sm. slaughter-house.
matterello sm. rolling-pin.
mattina sf. morning.
mattinata sf. 1. morning 2. (teat.) matinée.
mattiniero agg. early-rising.
mattino sm. morning.
matto[1] agg. mad, crazy. ♦ **matto** sm. madman (pl. -men).
matto[2] agg. 1. (non lucido) mat 2. (di gioielli) false.
mattone sm. 1. brick 2. (fig.) bore.
mattonella sf. tile.
mattutino agg. morning (attr.). ♦ **mattutino** sm. (eccl.) matins (pl.).
maturare vi. e vt. to ripen, to mature (anche fig.).

maturazione *sf.* maturation, ripening (*anche fig.*).

maturità *sf.* ripening, maturity (*anche fig.*).

maturo *agg.* ripe, mature (*anche fig.*).

mausoleo *sm.* mausoleum.

mazurca *sf.* mazurka.

mazza *sf.* **1.** (*clava*) club **2.** (*martello di legno*) mallet.

mazzata *sf.* heavy blow (*anche fig.*).

mazziere *sm.* **1.** mace-bearer **2.** (*di carte*) dealer.

mazzo *sm.* **1.** bunch **2.** (*di carte*) pack || *fare il —*, to shuffle **3.** (*di fiori*) bouquet.

mazzolino *sm.* (*di fiori*) posy.

mazzuolo *sm.* mallet.

me *pron.* **1.** me **2.** (*me stesso*) myself.

meandro *sm.* **1.** meander **2.** (*labirinto*) maze.

meato *sm.* meatus.

meccànica *sf.* mechanics.

meccànico *agg.* mechanical. ♦ **meccànico** *sm.* mechanic.

meccanismo *sm.* **1.** gear **2.** (*movimento*) motion.

meccanizzare *vt.* to mechanize.

meccanizzazione *sf.* mechanization.

meccanografia *sf.* mechanography.

meccanogràfico *agg.* mechanographic.

mecenate *sm.* Maecenas.

mecenatismo *sm.* patronage.

medaglia *sf.* medal.

medaglione *sm.* **1.** locket **2.** (*arch.*) medallion.

medaglista *sm.* **1.** (*incisore*) medallist **2.** (*collezionista*) collector of medals.

medésimo *agg. e pron.* V. **stesso**.

media *sf.* **1.** average: *alla — di*, at an average of **2.** (*mat.*) mean.

mediana *sf.* median line.

mediànico *agg.* mediumistic.

mediano *agg.* **1.** medial, middle (*attr.*) **2.** (*geom.; anat.; bot.*) median. ♦ **mediano** *sm.* (*sport*) half-back.

mediante *prep.* by, by means of, through.

mediato *agg.* indirect.

mediatore *sm.* **1.** mediator **2.** (*comm.*) broker.

mediazione *sf.* **1.** mediation **2.** (*comm.*) brokerage.

medicamento *sm.* medicament.

medicare *vt.* to dress.

medicastro *sm.* quack (doctor).

medicazione *sf.* **1.** medication **2.** (*di ferita*) dressing.

medicina *sf.* medicine.

medicinale *sm.* medicinal.

mèdico *agg.* medical. ♦ **mèdico** *sm.* physician, doctor.

medievale *agg.* medieval.

medio *sm.* **1.** (*dito*) middle finger **2.** (*mat.*) mean. ♦ **medio** *agg.* **1.** middle **2.** (*normale, che risulta da una media*) average.

mediocre *agg.* second-rate.

mediocrità *sf.* mediocrity.

medioevo *sm.* Middle Ages (*pl.*).

meditabondo *agg.* thoughtful.

meditare *vt.* **1.** to ponder **2.** (*avere un'intenzione*) to meditate.

meditativo *agg.* meditative.

meditazione *sf.* meditation.

mediterràneo *agg.* **1.** inland **2.** Mediterranean.

medium *sm.* medium.

medusa *sf.* medusa (*pl.* -ae).

mefistofèlico *agg.* satanic.

mefitico *agg.* poisonous.

megaciclo *sm.* megacycle.

megàfono *sm.* megaphone.

megalòmane *sm.* megalomaniac.

megalomanìa *sf.* megalomania.

megatone *sm.* megaton.

meglio *avv.* **1.** (*comp.*) better **2.** (*superl. rel.*) best. ♦ **meglio** *agg.* **1.** (*comp.*) better: *questo vestito è — di quello*, this dress is better than that **2.** (*superl. rel.*) best. ♦ **meglio** *sm.* best, best thing || *in mancanza di —*, for lack of anything better. ♦ **meglio** *sf.* *avere la —*, to have the better || *alla —*, as well as possible.

mela *sf.* apple.

melacotogna *sf.* quince.

melagrana *sf.* pomegranate.

melanismo *sm.* melanism.

melanzana *sf.* aubergine.

melassa *sf.* molasses (*pl.*).

melato *agg.* **1.** sweetened with honey **2.** (*fig.*) honeyed.

melenso *agg.* dull, silly.

mellifluo *agg.* honeyed.

melma *sf.* slime.

melmoso *agg.* slimy.

melo *sm.* apple-tree.

melodìa *sf.* melody.

melòdico *agg.* melodic.

melodioso *agg.* melodious.

melodramma *sm.* **1.** opera **2.** (*fig.*) melodrama.

melodrammàtico agg. **1.** operatic **2.** (fig.) melodramatic.

melograno sm. pomegranate-tree.

melòmane s. melomaniac.

melomanìa sf. melomania.

melone sm. melon.

membra sf. pl. limbs.

membrana sf. membrane.

membratura sf structure.

membro sm. **1.** member **2.** (anat.) limb.

memoràbile agg. memorable.

memorandum sm. memorandum (pl. -da).

mèmore agg. mindful.

memoria sf. **1.** memory: — di ferro, cast-iron memory || a —, by heart **2.** (ricordo) memory, recollection.

memoriale sm. **1.** (petizione) memorial **2.** (libro di memorie) memoirs (pl.).

memorialista s. memorialist.

menabò sm. dummy.

menadito (nella loc. avv.) a —, perfectly || sapere qc. a —, to have sthg. at one's finger-tips.

menagramo sm. bearer of ill-luck.

menare vt. (condurre) to lead (v. irr.) || — vanto, to boast; — il can per l'aia, to beat (v. irr.) about the bush; — buono, gramo, to bring (v. irr.) good, bad luck.

mendace agg. mendacious, false.

mendacia sf. mendacity.

mendicante sm. beggar.

mendicare vi. to beg.

mendicità sf. mendicity.

mendico agg. e sm. mendicant.

menestrello sm. minstrel.

meninge sf. meninx (pl. meninges).

menisco sm. meniscus.

meno avv. **1.** (comp.) less **2.** (superl. rel.) least || fare a —, to do (v. irr.) without; non poter fare a —, cannot help: non posso fare a — di andare, I cannot help going **3.** (mat.) minus. ◆ **meno** prep. but for || a — che (non), unless. ◆ **meno** agg. **1.** (comp. sing.) less: è — bella di sua sorella, she is less beautiful than her sister **2.** (comp. con s. pl.) fewer: ho — libri di te, I have fewer books than you **3.** (superl. rel. sing.) the least: è il — intelligente dei miei amici, he is the least intelligent of my friends **4.** (superl. rel. con s. pl.) the fewest (raro).

◆ **meno** sm. **1.** (comp.) less **2.** (superl. rel.) the least.

menomare vt. to lessen.

menomato agg. **1.** lessened **2.** (di vista, udito) impaired.

menomazione sf. **1.** lessening **2.** (di arti, sensi) impairment **3.** (di persona) disablement.

menopàusa sf. menopause.

mensa sf. table.

mensile agg. monthly. ◆ **mensile** sm. **1.** (salario) month's salary **2.** (pubblicazione mensile) monthly.

mensilità sf. monthly instalment || tredicesima —, Christmas bonus.

mensilmente avv. monthly, once a month.

mènsola sf. **1.** bracket **2.** (scaffale) shelf (pl. -lves).

menta sf. mint.

mentale agg. mental.

mentalità sf. mentality.

mente sf. mind: persona dalla — ristretta, narrow-minded person; aguzzare la —, to sharpen one's wits.

mentecatto agg. insane. ◆ **mentecatto** sm. madman (pl. -men).

mentina sf. peppermint-drop.

mentire vi. to lie.

mentito agg. false: sotto mentite spoglie, under false pretences.

mentitore sm. liar.

mento sm. chin.

mentolo sm. menthol.

mèntore sm. mentor.

mentre cong. **1.** (temporale) while, as, when **2.** (avversativo) whereas, while **3.** (finché) as long as, while. ◆ **mentre** sm. moment: in quel —, at that moment.

menzionare vt. to mention.

menzione sf. mention.

menzogna sf. falsehood.

menzognero agg. **1.** (di persona) mendacious **2.** (di cosa) false.

meraviglia sf. wonder: sopraffatto dalla —, wonder-struck; non fa — che, nessuna — che, no wonder.

meravigliare vt. to astonish. ◆ **meravigliarsi** vr. to be astonished (at).

meravigliato agg. astonished.

meraviglioso agg. wonderful.

mercante sm. merchant.

mercanteggiare vi. (tirare sul prezzo) to bargain, to haggle.

mercantile agg. mercantile. ◆ **mercantile** sm. cargo boat.

mercantilismo *sm.* mercantilism.
mercanzìa *sf.* merchandise.
mercato *sm.* market || *a buon —*, cheap.
merce *sf.* goods (*pl.*).
mercé *sf.* mercy.
mercede *sf.* pay, reward.
mercenario *agg. e sm.* mercenary.
merceologìa *sf.* technology of marketable goods.
mercerìa *sf.* **1.** haberdashery **2.** (*negozio*) haberdasher's shop.
mercerizzato *agg.* mercerized.
merciaio *sm.* haberdasher.
mercoledì *sm.* Wednesday: *— delle Ceneri*, Ash Wednesday.
mercurio *sm.* mercury, quicksilver.
merenda *sf.* afternoon snack.
meretrice *sf.* prostitute.
meretricio *sm.* prostitution.
meridiana *sf.* sun-dial.
meridiano *agg. e sm.* meridian.
meridionale *agg.* Southern. ♦ **meridionale** *sm.* Southerner.
meridione *sm.* south.
meringa *sf.* meringue.
merino *sm.* merino.
meritare *vt.* to deserve.
meritévole *agg.* deserving.
mèrito *sm.* merit || *in — a*, as to.
meritorio *agg.* meritorious, deserving.
merletto *sm.* lace.
merlo *sm.* **1.** blackbird **2.** (*sciocco*) simpleton.
merluzzo *sm.* codfish.
mero *agg.* **1.** pure **2.** (*fig.*) mere.
mesata *sf.* **1.** month **2.** (*paga di un mese*) month's pay.
méscere *vt.* to pour (out).
meschinità *sf.* meanness.
meschino *agg.* mean. ♦ **meschino** *sm.* wretch.
méscita *sf.* pouring (out).
mescolanza *sf.* **1.** mixing **2.** (*miscuglio*) mixture.
mescolare *vt.* **1.** to mix **2.** (*tè, caffè, liquori, tabacco*) to blend. ♦ **mescolarsi** *vr.* to mingle.
mescolatrice *sf.* mixer.
mese *sm.* month.
messa *sf.* **1.** (*eccl.*) Mass **2.** (*azione del mettere*) putting, setting: *— a punto*, setting up || *— a fuoco*, focusing.
messaggero *sm.* messenger.
messaggio *sm.* **1.** message **2.** (*allocuzione*) address.
messale *sm.* missal.

messe *sf.* crop, harvest.
messìa *sm.* Messiah.
messiànico *agg.* Messianic.
messianismo *sm.* Messianism.
messicano *agg. e sm.* Mexican.
messinscena *sf.* staging.
mestare *vt.* to stir.
mestiere *sm.* **1.** trade **2.** (*perizia*) skill **3.** (*lavoro*) work.
mestizia *sf.* sadness.
méstola *sf.* ladle.
méstolo *sm.* ladle.
mestruazione *sf.* menstruation.
meta *sf.* **1.** destination **2.** (*scopo*) aim, purpose: *senza —*, aimless.
metà *sf.* **1.** half (*pl.* halves) **2.** (*parte mediana*) middle **3.** (*coniuge*) *la mia —*, my better half.
metabolismo *sm.* metabolism.
metafìsica *sf.* metaphysics.
metàfora *sf.* metaphor.
metafòrico *agg.* metaphoric(al).
metàllico *agg.* metallic.
metallo *sm.* metal.
metallurgìa *sf.* metallurgy.
metallùrgico *agg.* metallurgic(al). ♦ **metallùrgico** *sm.* metallurgist.
metalmeccànico *sm.* metallurgist and mechanic.
metamòrfico *agg.* metamorphic.
metamorfismo *sm.* metamorphism.
metamòrfosi *sf.* metamorphosis (*pl.* -ses).
metano *sm.* methane.
metapsìchica *sf.* metapsychics.
metapsìchico *agg.* metapsychic(al).
metàstasi *sf.* metastasis (*pl.* -ses).
metempsicosi *sf.* metempsychosis (*pl.* -ses).
metèora *sf.* meteor.
meteòrico *agg.* meteoric.
meteorite *sm.* meteorite.
meteorologìa *sf.* meteorology.
meteorològico *agg.* meteorological || *previsioni meteorologiche*, weather-forecast (*sing.*).
meteoròlogo *sm.* meteorologist.
meticcio *agg. e sm.* mestizo (*pl.* -za).
meticoloso *agg.* meticulous.
metodicità *sf.* methodicalness.
metòdico *agg.* methodical.
metodista *agg. e s.* Methodist.
mètodo *sm.* method.
metodologìa *sf.* methodology.
metodològico *agg.* methodological.
mètopa *sf.* metope.
metraggio *sm.* **1.** length (in metres) **2.** (*cine*) *corto, lungo —*, short, full-length film.

mètrica *sf.* prosody.

mètrico *agg.* metric.

metrite *sf.* metritis.

metro *sm.* 1. metre 2. (*strumento per misurare*) rule.

metrònomo *sm.* metronome.

metronotte *sm.* night-watch.

metròpoli *sf.* metropolis (*pl.* -ses).

metropolitana *sf.* underground.

metropolitano *agg.* metropolitan.

méttere *vt.* 1. to put (*v. irr.*) || — *in chiaro qc.*, to make (*v. irr.*) sthg. clear; — *in dubbio qc.*, to doubt sthg.; — *in serbo*, to lay (*v. irr.*) aside; — *in moto*, to start; — *in luce*, to emphasize; — *in guardia qu.*, to put so. on his guard; — *le mani su qc.*, to take (*v. irr.*) possession of; — *le mani sul fuoco per qu.*, to speak (*v. irr.*) for so. 2. (*impiegare, di tempo*) to take 3. (*indossare*) to put on 4. (*paragonare*) to compare. ♦ mettersi *vr.* 1. to put oneself || — *in contatto con qu.*, to get (*v. irr.*) in touch with so.; — *in testa di fare qc.*, to take into one's head to do sthg.; — *sotto*, to get down to it 2. (*incominciare*) to begin (*v. irr.*) 3. (*indossare*) to put (*v. irr.*) on.

mettifoglio *sm.* (*tip.*) feeder.

mezzadrìa *sf.* métayage.

mezzadro *sm.* métayer.

mezzaluna *sf.* 1. half-moon 2. (*emblema islamico*) crescent 3. (*cuc.*) mincing-knife.

mezzana[1] *sf.* (*mar.*) mizzen sail.

mezzana[2] *sf.* procuress.

mezzano *agg.* middle. ♦ mezzano *sm.* go-between.

mezzanotte *sf.* midnight.

mezzatinta *sf.* half-tone.

mezzo[1] *agg.* 1. half 2. (*medio*) middle. ♦ mezzo *avv.* half. ♦ in mezzo a *prep.* 1. in the middle of 2. (*fra molti*) among 3. (*fra due*) between.

mezzo[2] *sm.* 1. means 2. (*fis.*) medium.

mezzo[3] *agg.* (*marcio*) rotten.

mezzobusto *sm.* bust.

mezzocerchio *sm.* semicircle.

mezzodì *sm.* midday, noon.

mezzofondo *sm.* middle-distance race.

mezzogiorno *sm.* 1. midday 2. (*Sud*) South.

mezzosoprano *sm.* mezzo-soprano.

mi[1] *pron.* 1. me 2. (*me stesso*) myself 3. (*a me*) to me.

mi[2] *sm.* (*mus.*) E, mi.

miagolare *vi.* to mew.

miagolìo *sm.* mewing.

miasma *sm.* miasma.

mica *sf.* mica.

miccia *sf.* fuse.

michetta *sf.* roll.

micidiale *agg.* lethal, deadly.

micino *sm.* kitten, pussy.

micosi *sf.* mycosis (*pl.* -ses).

microbio *sm.* microbe.

microbiologìa *sf.* microbiology.

microcosmo *sm.* microcosm.

microfilm *sm.* microfilm.

micròfono *sm.* microphone.

microfotografìa *sf.* microphotography.

micrometrìa *sf.* micrometry.

micròmetro *sm.* micrometer.

micron *sm.* micron.

microrganismo *sm.* microorganism.

microscopìa *sf.* microscopy.

microscòpico *agg.* microscopic(al).

microscopio *sm.* microscope.

microsolco *sm.* long-playing record.

microtelèfono *sm.* microtelephone.

midolla *sf.* crumb.

midollare *agg.* medullar.

midollo *sm.* marrow: — *spinale*, spinal cord.

miele *sm.* honey.

mietere *vt.* to reap.

mietitrice *sf.* reaper.

mietitura *sf.* reaping.

migliaio *sm.* thousand.

miglio[1] *sm.* (*bot.*) millet.

miglio[2] *sm.* (*misura di lunghezza*) mile.

miglioramento *sm.* improvement.

migliorare *vt.* to better, to improve.

migliore *agg.* 1. (*comp.*) better: *questo libro è — di quello*, this book is better than that 2. (*superl.*) the best: *è il — alunno della classe*, he is the best pupil in his class.

miglioria *sf.* improvement.

mignatta *sf.* leech.

mignolo *sm.* little finger.

migrare *vi.* to migrate.

migratore *agg.* migratory. ♦ migratore *sm.* migrant.

migratorio *agg.* migratory.

migrazione *sf.* migration.

miliardario *sm.* multi-millionaire.

miliardo sm. a thousand millions.
miliare agg. pietra —, milestone.
milionario sm. millionaire.
milione sm. million.
milionèsimo agg. millionth.
militante agg. militant.
militare[1] agg. military. ♦ **militare** sm. soldier.
militare[2] vi. 1. to be a soldier 2. (lavorare a favore di) to support.
militaresco agg. soldierlike.
militarismo sm. militarism.
militarista sm. militarist.
militarizzare vt. to militarize.
militarizzazione sf. militarization.
militarmente avv. militarily.
milite sm. militiaman (pl. -men).
milizia sf. Army.
miliziano sm. militiaman (pl. -men).
millantare vt. to boast of. ♦ **millantarsi** vr. to boast.
millantatore sm. boaster.
millanterìa sf. boasting.
mille agg. one thousand.
millenario agg. e sm. millenary.
millennio sm. millennium.
millepiedi sm. millepede.
millèsimo agg. thousandth.
milligrammo sm. milligram.
millimetro sm. millimetre.
milza sf. spleen.
mimare vt. e vi. to mime.
mimètico agg. mimetic.
mimetismo sm. 1. (di animali) mimicry 2. (mil.) camouflage.
mimetizzare vt. to camouflage.
mimetizzazione sf. camouflage.
mìmica sf. 1. (teat.) mimic art 2. (di gesti) gesticulation.
mìmico agg. miming, mimic.
mimo sm. mime.
mimosa sf. mimosa.
mina sf. mine.
minaccia sf. threat.
minacciare vt. to threaten.
minaccioso agg. threatening.
minare vt. 1. to mine 2. (fig.) undermine.
minareto sm. minaret.
minatore sm. miner.
minatorio agg. threatening.
minchione sm. simpleton.
minerale agg. mineral. ♦ **minerale** sm. mineral.
mineralizzare vt. to mineralize.
mineralogìa sf. mineralogy.
minerario agg. mining (attr.).
minestra sf. soup.
mingherlino agg. slim.

miniare vt. 1. to paint in miniature 2. (di manoscritti) to illuminate.
miniato agg. illuminated.
miniatura sf. miniature.
miniaturista sm. miniaturist.
miniera sf. mine.
minigonna sf. miniskirt.
minimamente avv. not in the least.
minimizzare vt. to minimize.
mìnimo agg. least, slightest, smallest. ♦ **mìnimo** sm. minimum..
minio sm. red lead.
ministeriale agg. ministerial.
ministero sm. ministry: — dell'Istruzione, ministry of Education || — degli Esteri, dell'Interno, Foreign, Home Office; — del Tesoro, Treasury.
ministro sm. minister.
minoranza sf. minority.
minorare vt. to diminish.
minorato agg. disabled.
minorazione sf. 1. (diminuzione) reduction 2. (invalidità) disablement.
minore agg. 1. (comp.) (più piccolo) smaller, less; (più basso) lower; (più corto) shorter; (più giovane) younger 2. (superl.) the smallest, least, lowest, shortest, youngest.
minorile agg. juvenile.
minorenne agg. under age. ♦ **minorenne** s. minor.
minorile agg. juvenile.
minorità sf. minority.
minoritario agg. minority (attr.).
minuetto sm. minuet.
minugia sf. gut.
minùscolo agg. small letter.
minuta sf. rough copy.
minutaglia sf. bits and pieces (pl.).
minuto[1] agg. 1. minute 2. (dettagliato) detailed.
minuto[2] sm. minute.
minuto[3] sm. (comm.) retail.
minuzia sf. trifle.
minuziosamente avv. minutely.
minuziosità sf. minuteness.
minuzioso agg. minute, detailed.
minùzzolo sm. crumb.
mio agg. my. ♦ **mio** pron. mine
miocardìa sf. myocardia.
miocardio sm. myocardium.
miocardite sf. myocarditis.
miocene sm. miocene.
mìope agg. short-sighted.
miopìa sf. myopia.

mira *sf.* **1.** aim: *prendere la —,* to take (*v. irr.*) aim **2.** (*fig.*) aim, design.

miràbile *agg.* admirable.

mirabilia *sf. pl.* wonders.

mirabolante *agg.* astonishing.

miràcolo *sm.* miracle: *fare miràcoli,* to do (*v. irr.*) miracles, (*fig.*) to work wonders.

miracoloso *agg.* miraculous.

miraggio *sm.* mirage.

mirare *vt.* to look at. ♦ **mirare** *vi.* to aim (at).

miriade *sf.* myriad.

miriagrammo *sm.* myriagram.

miriàmetro *sm.* myriametre.

miriàpodi *sm. pl.* Myriapoda.

mirifico *agg.* wondrous.

mirino *sm.* **1.** sight **2.** (*foto*) view-finder.

mirra *sf.* myrrh.

mirtillo *sm.* bilberry.

mirto *sm.* myrtle.

misantropìa *sf.* misanthropy.

misàntropo *sm.* misanthrope.

miscela *sf.* **1.** mixture **2.** (*di caffè, tè, liquori, tabacco*) blend.

miscelare *vt.* **1.** to mix **2.** (*di caffè, tabacco, liquori ecc.*) to blend.

miscellànea *sf.* miscellany.

mischia *sf.* fray.

mischiare *vt.* to mix, to mingle.

mischiatura *sf.* **1.** (*il mischiare*) mixing **2.** (*miscuglio*) mixture.

misconòscere *vt.* not to acknowledge.

miscredente *agg.* misbelieving. ♦ **miscredente** *sm.* misbeliever.

miscredenza *sf.* misbelief.

miscuglio *sm.* **1.** mixture **2.** (*amalgama*) blend.

miseràbile *agg.* **1.** miserable **2.** (*scarso*) poor **3.** (*vile*) despicable, mean. ♦ **miseràbile** *sm.* wretch.

miserando *agg.* miserable.

miserévole *agg.* miserable, pitiable.

miseria *sf.* **1.** misery, poverty **2.** (*scarsità*) lack **3.** (*inezia*) trifle.

misericordia *sf.* mercy.

misericordioso *agg.* merciful.

mìsero *agg.* **1.** poor, scanty **2.** (*meschino*) wretched.

misfatto *sm.* misdeed.

misoginìa *sf.* misogyny.

misògino *agg.* misogynous. ♦ **misògino** *sm.* misogynist.

misoneismo *sm.* misoneism.

missaggio *sm.* mixing.

missile *sm.* missile.

missionario *sm.* missionary.

missione *sf.* mission.

missiva *sf.* letter.

misteriosamente *avv.* mysteriously.

misterioso *agg.* mysterious.

mistero *sm.* mystery.

mìstica *sf.* mysticism.

misticismo *sm.* mysticism.

mìstico *agg.* mystic.

mistificare *vt.* to mystify.

mistificatore *sm.* mystifier.

mistificazione *sf.* mystification.

misto *agg.* mixed.

mistura *sf.* mixture.

misura *sf.* **1.** (*misurazione, precauzione*) measure **2.** (*taglia*) size **3.** (*limite*) limit.

misuràbile *agg.* measurable.

misurare *vt.* **1.** to measure **2.** (*tec.*) to gauge **3.** (*limitare*) to limit. ♦ **misurarsi** *vr.* to compete.

misurato *agg.* measured.

misuratore *sm.* **1.** (*persona che misura*) measurer **2.** (*strumento*) gauge.

misurazione *sf.* measurement.

misurino *sm.* small measure.

mite *agg.* gentle, meek.

mitezza *sf.* gentleness, meekness.

mìtico *agg.* mythical.

mitigare *vt.* **1.** to mitigate **2.** (*passioni*) to appease **3.** (*dolori*) to relieve. ♦ **mitigarsi** *vr.* to be appeased.

mitigazione *sf.* **1.** mitigation **2.** (*di passioni*) appeasement **3.** (*di dolore*) relief.

mìtilo *sm.* mussel.

mito *sm.* myth.

mitologìa *sf.* mythology.

mitològico *agg.* mythological.

mitòmane *s.* mythomaniac.

mitomanìa *sf.* mythomania.

mitra[1] *sf.* (*eccl.*) mitre.

mitra[2] *sm.* (*mil.*) tommy-gun.

mitraglia *sf.* grape-shot.

mitragliare *vt.* to machine-gun.

mitragliatore *sm.* machine-gunner.

mitragliatrice *sf.* machine-gun.

mitragliere *sm.* machine-gunner.

mitrale *agg.* mitral.

mitrato *agg.* mitred.

mitridàtico *agg.* mithridatic.

mitridatismo *sm.* mithridatism.

mittente *sm.* sender.

mnemònica *sf.* mnemonics.

mnemònico *agg.* mnemonic.

mo' (*nella loc. prep.*) *a — di,* like.

mòbile *agg.* **1.** movable || *scala —*, escalator; *beni mobili*, personal property **2.** (*mutevole*) inconstant. ♦ **mòbile** *sm.* piece of furniture.

mobilia *sf.* furniture.

mobiliare[1] *agg.* movable, personal.

mobiliare[2] *vt.* to furnish.

mobilità *sf.* **1.** mobility **2.** (*fig.*) inconstancy.

mobilitare *vt.* to mobilize.

mobilitazione *sf.* mobilization.

mocassino *sm.* moccasin.

moccioso *agg.* snivelling. ♦ **moccioso** *sm.* young scoundrel, brat.

mòccolo *sm.* **1.** candle-end **2.** (*bestemmia*) curse.

moda *sf.* **1.** fashion: *di —*, in fashion; *fuori —*, out of fashion || *alla —*, fashionable **2.** (*abitudine, modo*) manner, way: *alla — di*, after the manner of.

modale *agg.* modal.

modalità *sf.* modality.

modanatura *sf.* moulding.

mòdano *sm.* model.

modella *sf.* model.

modellare *vt.* to model, to shape.

modellatore *sm.* modeller.

modellazione *sf.* modelling.

modello *sm.* **1.** model, pattern **2.** (*stampo*) mould.

moderare *vt.* to moderate, to check.

moderato *agg.* moderate.

moderatore *agg.* moderating. ♦ **moderatore** *sm.* moderator.

moderazione *sf.* moderation.

modernismo *sm.* modernism.

modernità *sf.* modernity.

modernizzare *vt.* to modernize.

moderno *agg.* modern, up-to-date (*attr.*).

modestia *sf.* modesty: *— a parte*, modesty apart.

modesto *agg.* modest.

modicità *sf.* **1.** moderateness **2.** (*di prezzi*) cheapness.

mòdico *agg.* moderate: *a prezzo —*, cheap.

modìfica *sf.* alteration, change.

modificare *vt.* to modify.

modificazione *sf.* V. *modifica.*

modista *sf.* milliner.

modisterìa *sf.* milliner's shop.

modo *sm.* **1.** way, manner **2.** (*gramm.*) mood **3.** (*mezzo*) means: *in nessun —*, by no means || *di — che*, so (that); *in — da*, so as to; *in che —*, how; *in qualche —*, anyhow; *oltre —*, beyond measure.

modulare *vt.* to modulate.

modulato *agg.* modulated.

modulazione *sf.* modulation

mòdulo *sm.* form.

moffetta *sf.* skunk.

mògano *sm.* mahogany.

moggio *sm.* bushel.

mogio *agg.* depressed.

moglie *sf.* wife (*pl.* wives).

moina *sf.* simpering.

mola[1] *sf.* **1.** (*di mulino*) millstone **2.** (*per arrotare*) grindstone.

mola[2] *sf.* (*itt.*) sun-fish.

molare[1] *vt.* to grind (*v. irr.*).

molare[2] *agg.* molar. ♦ **molare** *sm.* (*dente*) molar (tooth).

molatura *sf.* grinding.

molazza *sf.* muller.

mole *sf.* **1.** mass, bulk **2.** (*dimensione*) size.

molècola *sf.* molecule.

molecolare *agg.* molecular.

molestare *vt.* to molest, to tease.

molestatore *agg.* molesting. ♦ **molestatore** *sm.* molester.

molestia *sf.* nuisance, trouble.

molesto *agg.* troublesome.

molibdeno *sm.* molybdenum.

molitorio *agg.* molinary.

molla *sf.* **1.** spring **2.** (*incentivo*) spur.

mollare *vt.* **1.** (*allentare*) to slacken **2.** (*mar.*) to let (*v. irr.*) go. ♦ **mollare** *vi.* to give (*v. irr.*) in.

molle *agg.* **1.** soft **2.** (*floscio*) flabby **3.** (*debole*) weak **4.** (*inzuppato*) soaking wet. ♦ **molle** *sf. pl.* tongs.

molleggiamento *sm.* **1.** (*elasticità*) springiness **2.** (*di veicoli*) springing system.

molleggiare *vi.* to be springy.

molleggiato *agg.* sprung.

molleggio *sm.* (*di veicoli*) suspension.

molletta *sf.* **1.** (*per il bucato*) clothes-peg **2.** (*per i capelli*) hair-pin.

mollettiere *sf. pl.* puttees.

mollettone *sm.* thick flannel.

mollezza *sf.* **1.** (*morbidezza*) softness **2.** (*debolezza*) weakness.

mollica *sf.* crumb.

mollo *agg.* damp: *mettere a —*, to steep.

mollusco *sm.* mollusc.

molo *sm.* pier, wharf.

moltéplice *agg.* manifold.

molteplicità *sf.* multiplicity.

moltìplica sf. (mecc.) chain gearing.
moltiplicando sm. multiplicand.
moltiplicare vt. to multiply.
moltiplicatore sm. multiplier.
moltiplicazione sf. multiplication.
moltìssimo agg. indef. **1.** very much (pl. very many) **2.** (di tempo) very long. ♦ **moltìssimo** avv. a great deal, very much.
moltitùdine sf. multitude.
molto agg. indef. **1.** (sing.) much, a great deal of, a lot of, plenty of **2.** (pl.) many, a good many, a lot of, plenty of **3.** (di tempo) long. ♦ **molto** avv. **1.** very **2.** (con comp.) much, far **3.** (di tempo) long, a long time.
momentaneamente avv. at the moment.
momentàneo agg. momentary.
momento sm. **1.** moment || dal — che, since **2.** (tempo, circostanza) time **3.** (opportunità) chance.
mònaca sf. nun.
monacale agg. monastic.
mònaco sm. monk.
mònade sf. monad.
monarca sm. monarch.
monarchìa sf. monarchy.
monàrchico agg. monarchic.
monastero sm. monastery.
monàstico agg. monastic.
moncherino sm. stump.
monco agg. **1.** maimed **2.** (fig.) incomplete.
moncone sm. stump.
mondanità sf. **1.** society life **2.** worldliness.
mondano agg. worldly.
mondare vt. **1.** to clean || — il grano, to winnow the corn **2.** (fig.) to cleanse.
mondiale agg. world-wide, world (attr.).
mondina sf. rice-weeder.
mondo[1] sm. world: fare il giro del —, to go (v. irr.) round the world; da che — è —, since the world began.
mondo[2] agg. clean.
monellerìa sf. prank.
monello sm. little rascal, urchin.
moneta sf. **1.** money (solo sing.) **2.** (ogni singolo pezzo) coin **3.** (spiccioli) change.
monetario agg. monetary.
monetizzare vt. to monetize.
mongolfiera sf. montgolfier.
mongolismo sm. mongolism.

mòngolo agg. Mongolian. ♦ **mòngolo** sm. Mongol.
mongolòide agg. e sm. mongoloid.
monile sm. jewel.
monismo sm. monism.
mònito sm. warning.
monoblocco sm. monobloc.
monòcolo sm. monocle.
monocromàtico agg. monochromatic.
monòcromo agg. monochrome.
monodìa sf. monody.
monogamìa sf. monogamy.
monògamo agg. monogamous. ♦ **monògamo** sm. monogamist.
monografìa sf. monograph.
monogràfico agg. monographic.
monogramma sm. monogram.
monolìtico agg. monolithic.
monòlogo sm. monologue, soliloquy.
monometallismo sm. monometallism.
monomio sm. monomial.
monopàttino sm. scooter.
monoplano sm. monoplane.
monopolio sm. monopoly.
monopolista sm. monopolist.
monopolizzare vt. to monopolize.
monoposto agg. e sm. single-seater.
monorotaia sf. monorail.
monosillàbico agg. monosyllabic.
monosìllabo sm. monosyllable.
monoteismo sm. monotheism.
monoteista s. monotheist.
monoteìstico agg. monotheistic.
monotipo sm. monotype.
monotonìa sf. monotony.
monòtono agg. monotonous.
monovalente agg. monovalent.
monsignore sm. monsignor (pl. -ri).
monsone sm. monsoon.
montacàrichi sm. goods-lift.
montaggio sm. **1.** assembly: linea di —, assembly line **2.** (cine) editing **3.** (foto) montage.
montagna sf. mountain.
montagnoso agg. mountainous.
montanaro agg. mountain (attr.). ♦ **montanaro** sm. mountaineer.
montante sm. **1.** (boxe) uppercut **2.** (mecc.; edil.) vertical rod.
montare vt. **1.** (mettere insieme) to assemble **2.** (cavalcare) to ride (v. irr.) **3.** (di panna) to whip. ♦ **montare** vi. **1.** to climb **2.** (alzarsi, aumentare) to rise (v. irr.). ♦ **montarsi** vr. to get (v. irr.) excited.

montatore *sm.* assembler.
montatura *sf.* **1.** fitting **2.** (*fig.*) hot hair.
montavivande *sm.* dumb-waiter.
monte *sm.* **1.** mount (*seguito dal nome*) **2.** mountain || *andare a —*, to come (*v. irr.*) to nothing; *mandare a —*, to cause to fail.
montone *sm.* **1.** ram **2.** (*carne*) mutton.
montuosità *sf.* hilliness.
montuoso *agg.* hilly.
monumentale *agg.* monumental.
monumento *sm.* monument.
mora[1] *sf.* (*bot.*) mulberry.
mora[2] *sf.* (*giur.*) delay.
morale *agg.* moral. ♦ **morale** *sm.* morale. ♦ **morale** *sf.* **1.** morals (*pl.*) **2.** (*fil.*) ethics **3.** (*conclusione*) moral.
moralismo *sm.* moralism.
moralista *s.* moralist.
moralìstico *agg.* moralistic.
moralità *sf.* morality.
moralizzare *vt.* to moralize.
moralizzazione *sf.* moralization.
moratorio *agg.* moratory.
morbidezza *sf.* softness.
mòrbido *agg.* soft.
morbillo *sm.* measles (*pl.*).
morbo *sm.* disease, plague.
morbosità *sf.* morbidity.
morboso *agg.* morbid.
mordace *agg.* biting, pungent.
mordacità *sf.* mordacity.
mordente *sm.* **1.** (*mus.*) mordent **2.** (*spirito aggressivo*) bite.
mòrdere *vt.* **1.** to bite (*v. irr.*) **2.** (*tormentare*) to torment || *— il freno*, to strain at the leash; *— la polvere*, to bite the dust.
morena *sf.* moraine.
morènico *agg.* morainic.
morente *agg.* dying. ♦ **morente** *sm.* dying man.
moresco *agg.* Moorish.
morfina *sf.* morphine.
morfinòmane *s.* morphinomaniac.
morfologìa *sf.* morphology.
morfològico *agg.* morphologic(al).
morganàtico *agg.* morganatic.
moribondo *agg.* dying. ♦ **moribondo** *sm.* dying man.
morigeratezza *sf.* moderation.
morigerato *agg.* moderate, sober.
morire *vi.* **1.** to die **2.** (*di luci e colori*) to fade **3.** (*di suoni*) to die out **4.** (*tramontare*) to set (*v. irr.*) ♦ **morire** *sm.* death.

mormone *agg.* e *sm.* Mormon.
mormorare *vt.* to murmur. ♦ **mormorare** *vi.* (*parlar male*) to gossip.
mormorìo *sm.* **1.** murmur **2.** (*lamento*) complaining **3.** (*malignità*) evil gossip.
moro *agg.* dark. ♦ **moro** *sm.* **1.** moor **2.** (*bot.*) mulberry-tree.
morra *sf.* "morra".
morsa *sf.* vice.
morsetto *sm.* (*mecc.*) clamp.
morsicare *vt.* to bite (*v. irr.*).
morsicatura *sf.* bite.
morsicchiare *vt.* to nibble.
morso *sm.* **1.** bite **2.** (*puntura, stimolo*) sting, pang **3.** (*del cavallo*) bit **4.** (*boccone*) morsel, bit.
mortaio *sm.* mortar.
mortale *agg.* mortal, deadly.
mortalità *sf.* mortality.
mortalmente *avv.* mortally.
mortaretto *sm.* cracker.
morte *sf.* death || *pena di —*, capital punishment; *dar la — a qu.*, to kill so.; *odiare a — qu.*, to hate so. like poison.
mortella *sf.* myrtle.
mortìfero *agg.* lethal.
mortificare *vt.* **1.** to humiliate **2.** (*reprimere*) to mortify.
mortificato *agg.* humiliated.
mortificazione *sf.* mortification.
morto *agg.* **1.** dead || *natura morta* (*pitt.*), still life; *stanco —*, dead tired **2.** (*senza vivacità*) dull. ♦ **morto** *sm.* dead man.
mortorio *sm.* funeral.
mortuario *agg.* mortuary.
mosaicista *s.* mosaicist.
mosàico *sm.* mosaic.
mosca *sf.* fly.
moscatello *sm.* muscatel.
moscato *sm.* (*vino*) muscatel. ♦ **moscato** *agg.* *noce moscata*, nutmeg.
moscerino *sm.* gnat.
moschea *sf.* mosque.
moschettiere *sm.* musketeer.
moschetto *sm.* musket.
moscio *agg.* flabby.
moscone *sm.* blue-bottle.
mossa *sf.* **1.** movement **2.** (*spostamento al gioco; fig.*) move **3.** (*sport*) starting post.
mossiere *sm.* (*sport*) starter.
mosso *agg.* **1.** (*di mare*) rough **2.** (*di capelli*) wavy.
mosto *sm.* must.

mostra *sf.* **1.** (*esposizione*) show, exhibition **2.** (*vetrina*) shop-window **3.** (*ostentazione*) display.

mostrare *vt.* **1.** to show (*v. irr.*) **2.** (*ostentare*) to show (*v. irr.*) off **3.** (*dimostrare*) to prove **4.** (*fingere*) to pretend.

mostrina *sf.* collar badge.

mostro *sm.* monster.

mostruosamente *avv.* monstrously.

mostruosità *sf.* monstrosity.

mostruoso *agg.* monstrous. for **2.** (*giur.*) to allege.

mota *sf.* mud, mire.

motivare *vt.* **1.** to state the reason

motivazione *sf.* **1.** motivation **2.** (*giur.*) opinion.

motivo *sm.* **1.** reason || *a — di*, owing to; *senza —*, groundless **2.** (*mus.*) theme.

moto *sm.* **1.** motion, movement **2.** (*esercizio fisico*) exercise **3.** (*impulso*) impulse. ♦ **moto** *sf.* motor-cycle.

motobarca *sf.* motor-boat.

motocarrozzetta *sf.* side-car.

motocicletta *sf.* motor-cycle.

motociclismo *sm.* motor-cycling.

motociclista *s.* motor-cyclist.

motofurgone *sm.* van.

motore *agg.* motor, driving. ♦ **motore** *sm.* engine, motor.

motorista *sm.* engineer.

motorizzare *vt.* to motorize. ♦ **motorizzarsi** *vr.* to buy (*v. irr.*) a car, a motor-cycle.

motorizzazione *sf.* motorization.

motoscafo *sm.* motor-boat.

motoveicolo *sm.* motor vehicle.

motrice *sf.* **1.** tractor **2.** (*ferr.*) engine.

motteggiare *vt.* to make (*v. irr.*) fun of. ♦ **motteggiare** *vi.* to joke.

motteggiatore *agg.* joking. ♦ **motteggiatore** *sm.* joker.

motteggio *sm.* **1.** (*il motteggiare*) raillery **2.** (*detto arguto*) joke.

mottetto *sm.* motet.

motto *sm.* **1.** word **2.** (*proverbio*) saying **3.** (*facezia*) witticism.

movente *sm.* motive, cause.

movenza *sf.* movements (*pl.*).

movìbile *agg.* movable.

movimentare *vt.* to enliven.

movimentato *agg.* **1.** lively **2.** (*pieno di movimento*) eventful.

movimento *sm.* **1.** movement **2.**

(*traffico, trambusto*) traffic, bustle.

moviola *sf.* film-editing machine.

mozione *sf.* motion.

mozzare *vt.* to cut (*v. irr.*) off.

mozzicone *sm.* **1.** stump **2.** (*di sigaretta*) butt.

mozzo[1] *agg.* cut (off).

mozzo[2] *sm.* **1.** (*di ruota*) hub **2.** (*mar.*) ship-boy.

mucca *sf.* cow.

mucchio *sm.* heap, mass.

mùcido *agg.* mouldy. ♦ **mùcido** *sm.* mould.

muco *sm.* mucus.

mucosa *sf.* mucous membrane.

mucoso *agg.* mucous.

muffa *sf.* mould.

muffire *vi.* to mildew.

muflone *sm.* moufflon.

mugghiare *vi.* **1.** to bellow **2.** (*fig.*) to roar **3.** (*del vento*) to howl.

mugghio *sm.* **1.** bellow **2.** (*fig.*) roar **3.** (*del vento*) howl.

muggire *vi.* V. *mugghiare.*

muggito *sm.* V. *mugghio.*

mughetto *sm.* lily of the valley.

mugnaio *sm.* miller.

mugolare *vi.* **1.** to howl **2.** (*piagnucolare*) to whimper.

mugolìo *sm.* **1.** howling **2.** (*piagnucolio*) whimpering.

mugugnare *vi.* to mumble.

mulattiera *sf.* mule-track.

mulattiere *sm.* mule-driver.

mulatto *sm.* mulatto.

muliebre *agg.* feminine, womanly.

mulinare *vt.* **1.** to whirl **2.** (*fig.*) to brood (over).

mulinello *sm.* **1.** (*d'acqua*) whirlpool **2.** (*d'aria*) whirlwind **3.** (*rapido movimento*) twirl.

mulino *sm.* mill.

mulo *sm.* mule.

multa *sf.* fine.

multare *vt.* to fine.

multicolore *agg.* many-coloured.

multiforme *agg.* multiform.

mùltiplo *agg.* e *sm.* multiple.

mummia *sf.* mummy.

mummificare *vt.* to mummify.

mummificazione *sf.* mummification.

mùngere *vt.* to milk.

mungitore *sm.* milker.

mungitura *sf.* milking.

municipale *agg.* municipal.

municipalità *sf.* municipality.

municipalizzare *vt.* to municipalize.

municipalizzazione *sf.* municipalization.

municipio *sm.* 1. municipality 2. (*palazzo*) townhall 3. (*stor.*) municipium (*pl.* -ia).

munificenza *sf.* munificence.

munifico *agg.* munificent.

munire *vt.* 1. (*fortificare*) to fortify 2. (*provvedere*) to supply (with).

munizione *sf.* munition.

muovere *vt.* to move. ♦ **muoversi** *vr.* to move, to stir || *muoviti!* hurry up!

mura¹ *sf.* (*mar.*) tack.

mura² *sf. pl.* walls.

muraglia *sf.* wall.

muraglione *sm.* massive wall.

murale *agg.* mural.

murare *vt.* 1. to wall up 2. (*cingere di mura*) to wall.

murario *agg.* building (*attr.*).

murata *sf.* ship's side.

muratore *sm.* bricklayer.

muratura *sf.* masonry || *lavoro in* —, brickwork.

murena *sf.* moray.

muriatico *agg.* muriatic.

muricciolo *sm.* low wall.

murice *sm.* murex.

muro *sm.* wall || *armadio a* —, built-in cupboard; — *del suono*, sound barrier.

musa *sf.* muse.

muschiato *agg.* musky.

muschio¹ *sm.* (*sostanza odorosa*) musk.

muschio² *sm.* (*bot.*) moss.

muscolare *agg.* muscular.

muscolatura *sf.* musculature.

muscolo *sm.* muscle.

muscoloso *agg.* muscular.

muscoso *agg.* mossy.

museo *sm.* museum.

museruola *sf.* muzzle.

musica *sf.* music.

musicale *agg.* musical.

musicalità *sf.* musicality.

musicante *sm.* musician.

musicare *vt.* to set (*v. irr.*) to music.

musicista *sm.* musician.

musico *sm.* musician.

musicologia *sf.* musicology.

musicologo *sm.* musicologist.

musivo *agg.* mosaic (*attr.*).

muso *sm.* 1. muzzle 2. (*broncio*) long face: *fare il* —, to pull a long face.

musone *sm.* 1. large muzzle 2. (*per-*

sona che tiene il broncio) sulky person.

musoneria *sf.* sulkiness.

mussare *vi.* to froth.

mussolina *sf.* muslin.

mustelidi *sm. pl.* mustelidae.

musulmano *agg. e sm.* Muslim.

muta *sf.* 1. (*di cani*) pack of hounds 2. (*della guardia*) change 3. (*biol.*) moult.

mutabile *agg.* changeable.

mutabilità *sf.* 1. (*di cosa*) changeability 2. (*di persona*) fickleness.

mutamento *sm.* change.

mutande *sf. pl.* drawers.

mutandine *sf. pl.* trunks.

mutare *vt.* 1. to change 2. (*di animali*) to shed (*v. irr.*), to moult. ♦ **mutarsi** *vr.* to change.

mutazione *sf.* change.

mutevole *agg.* changeable.

mutilare *vt.* 1. to maim 2. (*fig.*) to mutilate.

mutilato *agg.* 1. maimed 2. (*fig.*) mutilated. ♦ **mutilato** *sm.* cripple.

mutilazione *sf.* 1. maiming 2. (*fig.*) mutilation.

mutilo *agg.* mutilated.

mutismo *sm.* dumbness.

muto *agg.* 1. dumb || *carta geografica muta*, blank map 2. (*fonetica*) mute.

mutria *sf.* stand-offishness.

mutua *sf.* national insurance || *medico della* —, panel doctor.

mutualistico *agg.* insurance (*attr.*).

mutualità *sf.* mutual help.

mutuare *vt.* 1. (*dare in mutuo*) to lend (*v. irr.*) 2. (*prendere a mutuo*) to borrow.

mutuatario *sm.* borrower.

mutuato *agg.* insured.

mutuo *agg.* mutual. ♦ **mutuo** *sm.* loan.

N

nababbo *sm.* nabob.

nacchera *sf.* castanet.

nafta *sf.* 1. oil 2. (*chim.*) naphtha.

naftalina *sf.* moth-balls (*pl.*).

naia¹ *sf.* (*zool.*) cobra.

naia² *sf.* (*mil.*) *fare la* —, to do (*v. irr.*) one's bit.

nàiade *sf.* naiad.

nàilon *sm.* nylon.

nandù *sm.* nandu.

nanismo *sm.* nanism.

nano *sm.* dwarf.

nappa *sf.* tassel.

narcisismo *sm.* narcissism.

narcisista *sm.* narcissist.

narciso *sm.* narcissus.

narcosi *sf.* narcosis (*pl.* -ses).

narcòtico *agg.* e *sm.* narcotic.

narcotizzare *vt.* to narcotize.

narice *sf.* nostril.

narrare *vt.* to tell (*v. irr.*).

narrativa *sf.* fiction.

narrativo *agg.* narrative.

narratore *sm.* **1.** story-teller **2.** (*scrittore*) writer.

narrazione *sf.* narration.

narvalo *sm.* narwhal.

nasale *agg.* nasal.

nascente *agg.* rising.

nàscere *vi.* **1.** to be born **2.** (*di piante*) to spring (*v. irr.*) up **3.** (*di fiume; sorgere*) to rise (*v. irr.*) **4.** (*avere origine*) to originate ‖ *far —*, to give (*v. irr.*) rise to.

nàscita *sf.* **1.** birth **2.** (*origine*) origin.

nascituro *sm.* unborn child.

nascòndere *vt.* to hide (*v. irr.*). ♦ **nascòndersi** *vr.* to hide (oneself).

nascondiglio *sm.* hiding-place.

nascosto *agg.* hidden ‖ *di —*, secretly.

nasello *sm.* (*itt.*) whiting.

naso *sm.* nose ‖ *a lume di —*, by guesswork; *ficcare il — in qc.*, to poke one's nose into sthg.; *avere buon —*, to be shrewd.

nassa *sf.* bow-net.

nastro *sm.* **1.** ribbon **2.** (*tec.*) tape.

natale *agg.* native. ♦ **Natale** *sm.* Christmas.

natalità *sf.* birth-rate.

natalizio *agg.* Christmas (*attr.*).

natante *agg.* floating. ♦ **natante** *sm.* watercraft.

natatoia *sf.* fin.

natatorio *agg.* swimming (*attr.*).

nàtica *sf.* buttock.

natività *sf.* nativity.

nativo *agg.* **1.** native **2.** (*innato*) inborn.

nato *agg.* born.

natura *sf.* nature.

naturale *agg.* natural.

naturalezza *sf.* naturalness, simplicity.

naturalismo *sm.* naturalism.

naturalista *s.* naturalist.

naturalizzare *vt.* to naturalize.

naturalizzazione *sf.* naturalization.

naturalmente *avv.* naturally, of course.

naturismo *sm.* naturism.

naturista *s.* naturist.

naufragare *vi.* **1.** to be shipwrecked **2.** (*fig.*) to be wrecked.

naufragio *sm.* **1.** shipwreck **2.** (*fig.*) wreck.

nàufrago *sm.* shipwrecked person.

nàusea *sf.* disgust, nausea ‖ *avere la —*, to feel (*v. irr.*) sick.

nauseabondo *agg.* nauseating.

nauseare *vt.* to make (*v. irr.*) sick.

nàutica *sf.* navigation.

nàutico *agg.* nautical.

navale *agg.* naval.

navata *sf.* **1.** (*centrale*) nave **2.** (*laterale*) aisle.

nave *sf.* ship.

navetta *sf.* shuttle.

navicella *sf.* (*aer.*) nacelle.

navigàbile *agg.* navigable.

navigabilità *sf.* navigability.

navigare *vi.* to sail.

navigato *agg.* (*fig.*) cunning.

navigatore *sm.* navigator.

navigazione *sf.* navigation.

naviglio *sm.* **1.** fleet **2.** (*nave*) craft.

nazionale *agg.* national.

nazionalismo *sm.* nationalism.

nazionalista *s.* nationalist.

nazionalità *sf.* nationality.

nazionalizzare *vt.* to nationalize.

nazionalizzazione *sf.* nationalization.

nazionalsocialismo *sm.* National Socialism.

nazione *sf.* nation.

nazismo *sm.* Nazism.

nazista *agg.* e *sm.* Nazi.

nazzareno *agg.* e *sm.* Nazarene.

ne *pron.* **1.** of him, about him; of her, about her; of it, about it; of them, about them; of this, about this; of that, about that **2.** (*partitivo*) some: *— ho*, I have some; any: *non — ho*, I haven't any. ♦ **ne** (*particella avv. di moto da luogo*) from there.

né *cong.* **1.** neither, nor **2.** (*né... né...*) neither... nor; (*in presenza di altra negazione*) either... or.

neanche *avv.* not even. ♦ **neanche** *cong.* neither, nor: *essi non anda-*

rono e — io, they did not go and neither did I.

nebbia *sf.* fog.

nebbioso *agg.* foggy.

nebulizzare *vt.* to nebulize.

nebulizzatore *sm.* nebulizer.

nebulosa *sf.* nebula (*pl.* -ae).

nebulosità *sf.* **1.** nebulosity **2.** (*fig.*) haziness.

nebuloso *agg.* **1.** nebulous **2.** (*fig.*) vague.

necessario *agg.* necessary. ♦ **necessario** *sm.* **1.** necessary **2.** (*l'indispensabile*) necessities (*pl.*).

necessità *sf.* **1.** necessity **2.** (*bisogno*) need.

necessitare *vi.* to need.

necrologìa *sf.* obituary-notice.

necrologio *sm.* **1.** necrology **2.** (*annuncio*) obituary.

necròpoli *sf.* necropolis.

necrosi *sf.* necrosis (*pl.* -ses).

necrotizzare *vt.* to necrotize.

nefandezza *sf.* wickedness.

nefando *agg.* wicked.

nefasto *agg.* ill-omened.

nefrite *sf.* nephritis.

nefrìtico *agg.* nephritic. ♦ **nefrìtico** *sm.* nephritic subject.

negare *vt.* **1.** to deny **2.** (*rifiutare*) to refuse.

negativa *sf.* (*anche foto*) negative.

negativo *agg.* negative.

negato *agg.* **1.** refused, denied **2.** (*inadatto*) unfit (for).

negatore *agg.* negatory. ♦ **negatore** *sm.* denier.

negazione *sf.* **1.** denial **2.** (*gramm.*) negative **3.** (*cosa diametralmente opposta all'altra*) negation.

neghittoso *agg.* slothful.

negletto *agg.* **1.** neglected **2.** (*di aspetto*) slovenly.

negligente *agg.* negligent, careless.

negligenza *sf.* negligence, carelessness.

negoziàbile *agg.* negotiable.

negoziante *sm.* **1.** merchant, trader **2.** (*chi ha negozio*) shopkeeper.

negoziare *vt.* to negotiate.

negoziato *agg.* negotiated. ♦ **negoziato** *sm.* negotiation.

negozio *sm.* **1.** shop **2.** (*commercio*) trade **3.** (*faccenda*) affair.

negriero *agg.* slave (*attr.*). ♦ **negriero** *sm.* slave-trader.

negro *agg. e sm.* **1.** negro **2.** (*spreg.*) nigger.

negròide *agg. e s.* negroid.

negromante *sm.* necromancer.

negromanzìa *sf.* necromancy.

nembo *sm.* **1.** raincloud **2.** (*fig.*) multitude.

nèmesi *sf.* nemesis (*pl.* -ses).

nemico *agg.* **1.** adverse **2.** (*del nemico*) enemy (*attr.*). ♦ **nemico** *sm.* enemy.

neo[1] *sm.* **1.** mole **2.** (*fig.*) flaw.

neo[2] *agg.* neo.

neocapitalismo *sm.* neo-capitalism.

neocapitalista *agg. e sm.* neo-capitalist.

neocapitalìstico *agg.* neo-capitalistic.

neoclassicismo *sm.* neo-classicism.

neoclàssico *agg.* neo-classic.

neofascismo *sm.* neofascism.

neofascista *agg. e s.* neofascist.

neòfita *sm.* **1.** neophyte **2.** (*fig.*) beginner.

neolìtico *agg.* Neolithic.

neologismo *sm.* neologism.

neon *sm.* neon: *insegna al —*, neon sign.

neonato *agg.* new-born. ♦ **neonato** *sm.* (new-born) baby.

neorealismo *sm.* Neorealism.

neorealista *agg. e sm.* neorealist.

neozelandese *agg.* New Zealand (*attr.*). ♦ **neozelandese** *s.* New Zealander.

nepotismo *sm.* nepotism.

nerastro *agg.* blackish.

nerbo *sm.* **1.** sinew **2.** (*fig.*) strength, vigour.

nerboruto *agg.* brawny.

neretto *sm.* (*tip.*) boldface.

nerezza *sf.* blackness.

nero *agg.* black.

nerofumo *sm.* lamp-black.

nerògnolo *agg.* blackish.

nerume *sm.* mass of black.

nervatura *sf.* ribbing.

nervo *sm.* nerve.

nervosamente *agg.* nervously.

nervosismo *sm.* nervousness.

nervoso *agg.* nervous, irritable.

nèspola *sf.* medlar.

nèspolo *sm.* medlar(-tree).

nesso *sm.* connection.

nessuno *agg.* **1.** no **2.** (*in presenza di altra neg.*) any. ♦ **nessuno** *pron.* **1.** (*per persone*) nobody, no one; (*per cose*) none **2.** (*in presenza di altra neg.*) anybody (*solo per persone*), anyone, any || *— di*, none of, (*in presenza di altra neg.*) any of.

nèttare *sm.* nectar.

nettare *vt.* to clean.

nettezza *sf.* cleanness: — *urbana*, municipal street cleansing.

netto *agg.* 1. clean, spotless (*anche fig.*) 2. (*comm.*) net.

nettunio *sm.* neptunium.

neurite *sf.* neuritis.

neurochirurgìa *sf.* neurosurgery.

neurologìa *sf.* neurology.

neuròlogo *sm.* neurologist.

neuropàtico *agg.* neuropathic. ♦ neuropàtico *sm.* neuropath.

neuropatologìa *sf.* neuropathology.

neurosi *sf.* neurosis (*pl.* -ses).

neurovegetativo *agg.* vegetative nervous.

neutrale *agg.* neutral.

neutralismo *sm.* neutralism.

neutralista *s.* neutralist.

neutralità *sf.* neutrality.

neutralizzare *vt.* to neutralize.

neutralizzazione *sf.* neutralization.

nèutro *agg.* 1. neutral 2. (*gramm.; bot.; zool.*) neuter.

neutrone *sm.* neutron.

neve *sf.* snow.

nevicare *vi.* to snow: *nevica*, it is snowing.

nevicata *sf.* snowfall.

nevischio *sm.* sleet.

nevoso *agg.* snowy.

nevralgìa *sf.* neuralgia.

nevràlgico *agg.* neuralgic.

nevrastenìa *sf.* neurasthenia.

nevrastènico *agg.* neurasthenic.

nevròtico *agg.* e *sm.* neurotic.

nibbio *sm.* kite.

nicchia *sf.* niche.

nicchiare *vi.* to shilly-shally.

nichel *sm.* nickel.

nichelare *vt.* to nickel.

nichelatura *sf.* nickel-plating.

nichelino *sm.* nickel coin.

nichilismo *sm.* nihilism.

nichilista *s.* nihilist.

nicotina *sf.* nicotine.

nidiata *sf.* 1. nest 2. (*covata*) brood || *una — di bambini*, a swarm of children.

nidificare *vi.* to nest.

nido *sm.* nest.

niente *pron.* 1. nothing 2. (*in presenza di altre negazioni*) anything.

nimbo *sm.* halo.

ninfa *sf.* nymph.

ninfea *sf.* water-lily.

ninfòmane *sf.* nymphomaniac.

ninnananna *sf.* lullaby.

ninnolo *sm.* 1. knick-knack 2. (*balocco*) plaything.

nipote *sm.* 1. (*di nonno*) grand-son 2. (*di zio*) nephew. ♦ nipote *sf.* 1. (*di nonno*) grand-daughter 2. (*di zio*) niece.

nippònico *agg.* e *sm.* Japanese.

nirvana *sm.* nirvana.

nitidezza *sf.* neatness.

nìtido *agg.* neat, clear.

nitrato *sm.* nitrate.

nìtrico *agg.* nitric.

nitrire *vi.* to whinny.

nitrito[1] *sm.* (*di cavallo*) whinny.

nitrito[2] *sm.* (*chim.*) nitrite.

nitroglicerina *sf.* nitroglycerin.

nìveo *agg.* snowy.

no *avv.* no.

nòbile *agg.* e *sm.* noble.

nobiliare *agg.* nobiliary.

nobilitare *vt.* to ennoble.

nobilitazione *sf.* ennobling.

nobilmente *avv.* nobly.

nobiltà *sf.* nobility.

nocca *sf.* knuckle.

nocchiere *sm.* helmsman (*pl.* -men).

nocciola *sf.* hazel-nut.

nòcciolo *sm.* 1. stone 2. (*ciò che è essenziale*) heart.

nocciolo *sm.* (*bot.*) hazel-tree.

noce *sm.* walnut-tree. ♦ noce *sf.* walnut || *guscio di —* (*barchetta*), cockle-shell; — *moscata*, nutmeg.

nocivo *agg.* noxious, harmful.

nodo *sm.* knot.

nodoso *agg.* knotty.

noi *pron.* 1. (*sogg.*) we 2. (*compl.*) us.

noia *sf.* 1. boredom 2. (*fastidio*) worry, nuisance.

noioso *agg.* 1. boring 2. (*molesto*) annoying.

noleggiante *sm.* (*mar.*) charterer.

noleggiare *vt.* 1. to hire 2. (*di navi*) to charter.

noleggiatore *sm.* hirer.

noleggio *sm.* 1. hire 2. (*mar.*) freight.

nolente *agg.* unwilling || *volente o —*, willy-nilly.

nolo *sm.* 1. hire 2. (*mar.*) freight.

nòmade *agg.* e *s.* nomad.

nomadismo *sm.* nomadism.

nome *sm.* 1. name 2. (*di battesimo*) Christian name || *senza —*, nameless; *a — di*, on behalf of; *per —*, by name 3. (*gramm.*) noun.

nomea *sf.* notoriety.

nomenclatura *sf.* nomenclature.

nomìgnolo *sm.* nickname.

nòmina *sf.* appointment.

nominale *agg.* nominal.

nominalismo *sm.* nominalism.

nominalista *s.* nominalist.

nominalmente *avv.* nominally.

nominare *vt.* 1. to name 2. (*eleggere*) to appoint.

nominativo *agg.* 1. nominative 2. (*comm.*) registered. ◆ **nominativo** *sm.* name.

non *avv.* not.

nona *sf.* 1. (*eccl.*) Nones (*pl.*) 2. (*mus.*) ninth.

nonagenario *agg.* ninety years old (*pred.*); ninety-year-old (*attr.*). ◆ **nonagenario** *sm.* nonagenarian.

nonconformista *s.* non-conformist.

noncurante *agg.* careless.

noncuranza *sf.* carelessness.

nondimeno *avv.* nevertheless.

nonna *sf.* grandmother.

nonno *sm.* grandfather: *i miei nonni*, my grandparents.

nonnulla *sm.* trifle.

nono *agg.* ninth.

nonostante *prep.* notwithstanding || — *che*, though, although.

nonsenso *sm.* nonsense.

non-ti-scordar-di-me *sm.* forget-me-not.

nord *sm.* north.

nordamericano *agg. e sm.* North American.

nòrdico *agg.* 1. northern 2. (*dell'Europa settentrionale*) Nordic. ◆ **nòrdico** *sm.* 1. Northerner 2. (*dell'Europa settentrionale*) Nordic.

nordista *sm.* (*stor. amer.*) Federal.

norma *sf.* 1. rule, norm 2. (*istruzioni*) instruction, direction || *a — di legge*, according to law.

normale *agg. e sm.* 1. normal 2. (*che dà una norma*) standard.

normalità *sf.* normality.

normalizzare *vt.* to normalize.

normalizzazione *sf.* normalization.

normalmente *avv.* usually.

normanno *agg. e sm.* Norman: *anglo-—*, (*stor.*) Anglo-Norman.

normativo *agg.* normative.

normògrafo *sm.* stencil.

norvegese *agg. e sm.* Norwegian.

nosocòmio *sm.* hospital.

nostalgìa *sf.* home-sickness.

nostàlgico *agg.* homesick.

nostrano *agg.* home (*attr.*), national.

nostro *agg.* our: *i nostri amici*, our friends. ◆ **nostro** *pron.* ours: *questa casa è nostra*, this house is ours. ◆ **nostro** *sm.* 1. *viviamo del* —, we live on our own income 2. *il Nostro* (*di autore*), the Author 3. *i nostri*, our family.

nostromo *sm.* boatswain.

nota *sf.* 1. note 2. (*lista*) list.

notàbile *agg.* notable.

notaio *sm.* notary.

notare *vt.* to note.

notariato *sm.* profession of notary.

notarile *agg.* notarial.

notazione *sf.* notation.

notévole *agg.* remarkable, notable.

notevolmente *avv.* remarkably.

notìfica *sf.* 1. notification 2. (*giur.*) service.

notificare *vt.* 1. to notify 2. (*informare*) to inform 3. (*giur.*) to serve.

notizia *sf.* 1. news (*pl. con costruzione sing.*), piece of news (*solo sing.*) 2. (*informazione*) information (*solo sing.*) 3. (*dato*) note: *notizie biografiche*, biographical notes.

notiziario *sm.* news (*pl., con costruzione sing.*).

noto *agg.* well-known. ◆ **noto** *sm.* the known.

notoriamente *avv.* notoriously.

notorietà *sf.* notoriety.

notorio *agg.* 1. (*in senso sfavorevole*) notorious 2. well-known.

nottàmbulo *agg.* noctambulous. ◆ **nottàmbulo** *sm.* night-bird.

nottata *sf.* night.

notte *sf.* night.

nottetempo *avv.* by night.

notturno *agg.* night (*attr.*). ◆ **notturno** *sm.* (*mus.*) nocturne.

novanta *agg.* ninety.

novantenne *agg.* 1. ninety years old (*pred.*) 2. ninety-year-old (*attr.*).

novantèsimo *agg.* ninetieth.

novatore *sm.* innovator.

nove *agg.* nine.

novecento *agg.* nine hundred.

novella *sf.* short story, tale.

novellino *agg.* inexperienced. ◆ **novellino** *sm.* beginner.

novellista *s.* short-story writer.

novellìstica *sf.* story-telling.

novello *agg.* 1. new, spring (*attr.*) 2. (*nuovo*) second: *un — Raffaello*, a second Raffaello.

novembre *sm.* November.
novena *sf.* novena (*pl.* -ae).
nòvero *sm.* number **2.** (*categoria*) class.
novilunio *sm.* new moon.
novità *sf.* **1.** novelty **2.** (*notizia*) news (*pl. con costruzione sing.*), piece of news (*solo sing.*).
noviziato *sm.* novitiate.
novizio *sm.* novice.
nozione *sf.* notion.
nozze *sf. pl.* wedding (*sing.*).
nube *sf.* cloud.
nubifragio *sm.* downpour.
nùbile *agg.* unmarried, single. ◆ **nùbile** *sf.* single woman.
nuca *sf.* nape.
nucleare *agg.* nuclear.
nucleina *sf.* nuclein.
nùcleo *sm.* nucleus (*pl.* -ei).
nudismo *sm.* nudism.
nudista *s.* nudist.
nudità *sf.* nakedness.
nudo *agg.* naked, bare.
nùgolo *sm.* cloud.
nulla *pron.* V. *niente.*
nullaosta *sm.* permit.
nullatenente *agg.* without property. ◆ **nullatenente** *s.* person without property.
nullità *sf.* **1.** (*di cose*) nullity **2.** (*di persone*) nonentity.
nullo *agg.* (*giur.*) null, void.
nume *sm.* numen, deity.
numeràbile *agg.* numerable.
numerabilità *sf.* numerability.
numerale *agg.* numeral.
numerare *vt.* **1.** to count **2.** (*segnare con numero*) to number.
numerato *agg.* **1.** counted **2.** (*segnato con un numero*) numbered.
numerario *agg.* numerary. ◆ **numerario** *sm.* (*comm.*) ready cash.
numeratore *sm.* (*mat.*) numerator.
numerazione *sf.* **1.** numbering **2.** (*mat.*) numeration.
numericamente *avv.* numerically.
numèrico *agg.* numerical.
nùmero *sm.* number.
numeroso *agg.* numerous.
numismàtica *sf.* numismatics.
numismàtico *agg.* numismatic. ◆ **numismàtico** *sm.* numismatist.
nunziatura *sf.* (*eccl.*) nunciature.
nunzio *sm.* nuncio.
nuòcere *vi.* to damage, to harm.
nuora *sf.* daughter-in-law.
nuotare *vi.* to swim (*v. irr.*).
nuotata *sf.* swim.

nuotatore *sm.* swimmer.
nuoto *sm.* swimming: *gara di* —, swimming-race.
nuova *sf.* news (*pl. con costruzione sing.*), piece of news (*solo sing.*).
nuovamente *avv.* again.
nuovo *agg.* new: — *di zecca, fiammante*, brand-new.
nutazione *sf.* nutation.
nutrice *sf.* wet-nurse.
nutriente *agg.* nourishing.
nutrimento *sm.* **1.** feeding **2.** (*fig.*) nourishment.
nutrire *vt.* **1.** to feed (*v. irr.*) **2.** (*mantenere*) to maintain **3.** (*di sentimenti, passioni*) to foster. ◆ **nutrirsi** *vr.* to feed (on).
nutritivo *agg.* nourishing.
nutrito *agg.* fed, nourished.
nutrizione *sf.* **1.** feeding **2.** (*fig.*) nourishment.
nùvola *sf.* cloud.
nuvoloso *agg.* overcast, cloudy.
nuziale *agg.* wedding (*attr.*).

O

o *cong.* or ‖ *o ... o*, either ... or: — *tu* — *tua madre dovete venire*, either you or your mother must come; — *l'uno* — *l'altro*, either: *prendi* — *l'uno* — *l'altro*, take either.
òasi *sf.* oasis (*pl.* -ses).
obbligare *vt.* to compel. ◆ **obbligarsi** *vr.* to bind (*v. irr.*) oneself.
obbligatorietà *sf.* compulsoriness.
obbligatorio *agg.* compulsory.
obbligazione *sf.* **1.** obligation **2.** (*comm.*) bond.
obbligazionista *sm.* bond-holder.
òbbligo *sm.* obligation: *assumersi l'*—, to undertake (*v. irr.*).
obbrobrio *sm.* disgrace.
obbrobrioso *agg.* disgraceful.
obelisco *sm.* obelisk.
oberare *vt.* to burden.
obesità *sf.* obesity.
obeso *agg.* obese.
òbice *sm.* howitzer.
obiettare *vt.* to object.
obiettivamente *avv.* objectively.
obiettivismo *sm.* objectivism.
obiettività *sf.* objectivity.

obiettivo *agg.* objective. ♦ **obiettivo** *sm.* **1.** (*mil.*) objective **2.** (*scopo*) aim **3.** (*foto*) lens.

obiettore *sm.* objector: — *di coscienza*, conscientous objector.

obiezione *sf.* objection.

obitorio *sm.* morgue.

oblatore *sm.* donor.

oblazione *sf.* donation.

obliare *vt.* to forget (*v. irr.*).

oblìo *sm.* oblivion.

obliquamente *avv.* obliquely.

obliquità *sf.* obliquity.

obliquo *agg.* oblique.

obliterare *vt.* to obliterate.

obliterazione *sf.* obliteration.

oblò *sm.* porthole.

oblungo *agg.* oblong.

òboe *sm.* oboe.

òbolo *sm.* offering.

obsoleto *agg.* obsolete.

oca *sf.* goose (*pl.* geese): *pelle d'—*, goose flesh; *penna d'—*, goose-quill.

occasionale *agg.* occasional.

occasionalismo *sm.* occasionalism.

occasionalmente *avv.* occasionally.

occasione *sf.* occasion.

occhiaia *sf.* eye-socket ‖ *avere le occhiaie*, to have rings under one's eyes.

occhiali *sm. pl.* spectacles, glasses.

occhialuto *agg.* spectacled, wearing spectacles (*pred.*).

occhiata *sf.* look, glance.

occhiataccia *sf.* glare.

occhieggiare *vt.* to cast (*v. irr.*) glances (at). ♦ **occhieggiare** *vi.* to peep (at).

occhiello *sm.* **1.** button-hole **2.** (*mecc.*) eye.

occhietto *sm. fare l'— a qu.*, to wink at so.

occhio *sm.* eye ‖ *costare un —*, to be terribly expensive; *chiudere un — su*, to turn a blind eye to; *dare nell'—*, to strike (*v. irr.*) the eye; *tenere d'—*, to keep (*v. irr.*) an eye on; *in un batter d'—*, in the twinkling of an eye.

occidentale *agg.* west, western. ♦ **occidentale** *s.* westerner.

occidentalizzare *vt.* to occidentalize.

occidente *sm.* west.

occipitale *agg.* occipital.

occìpite *sm.* occiput (*pl.* occipita).

occlusione *sf.* occlusion.

occlusivo *agg.* occlusive.

occorrente *agg.* necessary. ♦ **occorrente** *sm.* the necessary.

occorrenza *sf. all'—*, in case of need.

occòrrere *vi.* **1.** (*imp.*) to be necessary **2.** (*abbisognare*) to need.

occultamento *sm.* concealment.

occultare *vt.* to hide (*v. irr.*), to conceal. ♦ **occultarsi** *vr.* to hide.

occultatore *sm.* hider.

occultismo *sm.* occultism.

occulto *agg.* **1.** occult **2.** (*nascosto*) hidden.

occupante *agg.* occupying. ♦ **occupante** *s.* occupant.

occupare *vt.* **1.** to occupy **2.** (*ingaggiare*) to employ. ♦ **occuparsi** *vr.* **1.** (*impiegarsi*) to find (*v. irr.*) a job **2.** (*badare*) to attend (to).

occupato *agg.* engaged ‖ *essere —* (*fare un lavoro*), to work.

occupazione *sf.* **1.** occupation **2.** (*lavoro*) job.

oceànico *agg.* oceanic.

ocèano *sm.* ocean.

oceanografìa *sf.* oceanography.

ocello *sm.* ocellus (*pl.* -li).

ocra *sf.* ochre.

oculare *agg.* ocular, eye (*attr.*). ♦ **oculare** *sm.* (*fis.*) eyepiece.

oculatezza *sf.* shrewdness.

oculato *agg.* prudent.

oculista *sm.* oculist.

oculìstica *sf.* ophthalmology.

odalisca *sf.* odalisque.

ode *sf.* ode.

odiare *vt.* to hate.

odierno *agg.* of today, today's.

odio *sm.* hatred.

odioso *agg.* hateful.

odontàlgico *agg.* odontalgic.

odontoiatra *s.* odontologist, dentist.

odontoiatrìa *sf.* odontology.

odontoiàtrico *agg.* odontological.

odorare *vt. e vi.* to smell (*v. irr.*).

odorato *sm.* smell.

odore *sm.* smell.

odorìfero *agg.* odoriferous.

odoroso *agg.* fragrant.

offèndere *vt.* to offend. ♦ **offendersi** *vr.* to be offended (at, by); to feel (*v. irr.*) hurt (by).

offensiva *sf.* offensive.

offensivo *agg.* offensive.

offensore *sm.* offender.

offerente *s.* **1.** offerer **2.** (*a un'asta*) bidder.

offerta *sf.* offer, donation.
offesa *sf.* offence.
offeso *agg.* offended, injured.
officiare *vi.* to officiate.
officina *sf.* workshop.
officinale *agg.* officinal.
offrire *vt.* to offer. ♦ **offrirsi** *vr.* to offer (oneself).
offuscamento *sm.* **1.** dimming **2.** (*oscurità*) dimness.
offuscare *vt.* to dim. ♦ **offuscarsi** *vr.* to grow (*v. irr.*) dim.
oftalmìa *sf.* ophthalmia.
oftàlmico *agg.* ophthalmic.
oftalmologìa *sf.* ophthalmology.
oftalmoscopìa *sf.* ophthalmoscopy.
oftalmoscopio *sm.* ophthalmoscope.
oggettivamente *avv.* objectively.
oggettivare *vt.* to objectify.
oggettivazione *sf.* objectification.
oggettivismo *sm.* objectivism.
oggettività *sf.* objectivity.
oggettivo *agg.* objective.
oggetto *sm.* object.
oggi *avv.* today.
ogiva *sf.* ogive.
ogivale *agg.* ogival.
ogni *agg.* every, each || *in — modo*, anyhow; *in — luogo*, everywhere.
ogniqualvolta *cong.* whenever.
ognuno *pron.* everybody, everyone || *— di*, each of.
oleandro *sm.* oleander.
oleario *agg.* oil (*attr.*).
oleato *agg.* oiled || *carta oleata*, grease-proof paper.
oleificio *sm.* oil mill.
oleodotto *sm.* oil pipeline.
oleografìa *sf.* **1.** oleography **2.** (*pezzo singolo*) oleograph.
oleoso *agg.* oily.
olezzare *vi.* to smell (*v. irr.*) sweetly.
olezzo *sm.* fragrance.
olfattivo *agg.* olfactory.
olfatto *sm.* smell.
oliare *vt.* to oil.
oliatore *sm.* oil-can.
oliera *sf.* cruet.
oligarca *sm.* oligarch.
oligarchìa *sf.* oligarchy.
oligàrchico *agg.* oligarchic(al).
oligocene *sm.* Oligocene.
olimpìaco *agg.* V. *olimpico.*
olimpìade *sf.* Olympiad || *le Olimpiadi*, Olympic games.
olìmpico *agg.* Olympic.
olimpiònico *agg.* Olympic games (*attr.*). ♦ **olimpiònico** *sm.*

Olympic champion.
olio *sm.* oil.
oliva *sf.* olive.
olivastro *agg.* olive.
oliveto *sm.* olive-grove.
olivo *sm.* olive.
olmo *sm.* elm.
olocàusto *sm.* holocaust.
ològrafo *agg.* holograph.
oltraggiare *vt.* to outrage.
oltraggio *sm.* outrage.
oltraggioso *agg.* outrageous.
oltramontano *agg.* e *sm.* ultramontane.
oltranza *sf.* (*nella loc. avv.*) *a —*, to the bitter end.
oltranzista *sm.* extremist.
oltre *avv.* **1.** (*di luogo*) further, farther **2.** (*di tempo*) longer. ♦ **oltre** *prep.* **1.** (*di luogo*) beyond **2.** (*più di*) over **3.** (*in aggiunta*) in addition to. ♦ **oltre a, che** *cong.* besides.
oltrecortina *avv.* beyond the Iron Curtain.
oltremare *avv.* overseas: *d'—*, overseas (*attr.*).
oltremodo *avv.* extremely.
oltrepassare *vt.* to go (*v. irr.*) beyond || *— i limiti* (*fig.*), to go (*v. irr.*) too far.
oltretomba *sm.* hereafter.
omaccione *sm.* burly man (*pl.* men).
omaggio *sm.* **1.** homage **2.** (*offerta*) gift.
ombelicale *agg.* umbilical.
ombelico *sm.* navel.
ombra *sf.* **1.** shade (*anche spettro*) **2.** (*immagine proiettata, parvenza*) shadow || *dar — a qu.*, to overshadow so.
ombreggiare *vt.* to shade.
ombreggiatura *sf.* shading.
ombrella *sf.* (*bot.*) umbel.
ombrellìfero *agg.* umbelliferous.
ombrellino *sm.* parasol.
ombrello *sm.* umbrella.
ombrellone *sm.* sunshade.
ombretto *sm.* eye shadow.
ombrina *sf.* umbrina.
ombrosità *sf.* **1.** shadiness **2.** (*di persona*) touchiness **3.** (*di cavallo*) skittishness.
ombroso *agg.* **1.** shady **2.** (*di persona*) touchy **3.** (*di cavallo*) skittish.
omega *sm.* omega.
omelìa *sf.* homily.
omeopatia *sf.* homeopathy.

omeopàtico agg. homeopathic. ♦
omeopàtico sm. homeopath
omèrico agg. Homeric.
òmero sm. humerus (pl. -ri).
omertà sf. silence.
omesso agg. omitted.
ométtere vt. to omit, to leave out.
omicida agg. homicidal. ♦ **omicida** s. homicide.
omicidio sm. homicide.
omissione sf. omission.
òmnibus sm. bus.
omogeneità sf. homogeneity.
omogeneizzare vt. to homogenize.
omogèneo agg. homogeneous.
omologare vt. 1. to homologate 2. (sport) to ratify.
omologazione sf. 1. homologation 2. (sport) ratification.
omòlogo agg. homologous.
omonimìa sf. homonymy.
omònimo agg. homonymous. ♦
omònimo sm. homonym.
omosessuale agg. e s. homosexual.
omosessualità sf. homosexuality.
oncia sf. ounce.
onda sf. wave || mettere in — (radio), to broadcast (v. irr.).
ondata sf. wave: a ondate, in waves.
onde avv. 1. whence 2. (affinché) so that 3. (cosicché) therefore 4. (da, con cui) from, by, with which.
ondeggiamento sm. 1. waving 2. (di barca) rolling 3. (esitazione) wavering.
ondeggiante agg. 1. waving 2. (di barca) rolling 3. (esitante) wavering.
ondeggiare vi. 1. to wave 2. (di barca) tò roll 3. (esitare) to waver.
ondina sf. undine.
ondoso agg. undulatory.
ondulare vt. to wave.
ondulato agg. 1. wavy 2. (tec.) corrugated.
ondulatorio agg. undulatory.
ondulazione sf. 1. undulation 2. (di capelli) wave.
onerare vt. to burden.
ònere sm. burden || — fiscale, tax.
oneroso agg. burdensome.
onestà sf. 1. honesty 2. (castità) chastity.
onesto agg. 1. honest 2. (casto) chaste.
ònice sf. onyx.
onìrico agg. oneiric.

onnipotente agg. cmnipotent. ♦
Onnipotente (l') sm. the Almighty.
onnipotenza sf. omnipotence.
onnipresente agg. omnipresent.
onnisciente agg. omniscient.
onniscienza sf. omniscience.
onniveggente agg. omnipercipient.
onnìvoro agg. omnivorous. ♦ **onnìvoro** sm. omnivore.
onomàstico agg. onomastic. ♦
onomàstico sm. name-day.
onomatopea sf. onomatopoeia.
onomatopèico agg. onomatopoeic.
onoràbile agg. honourable.
onorabilità sf. honourableness.
onoranza sf. honour.
onorare vt. to honour. ♦ **onorarsi** vr. to be proud (of).
onorario agg. honorary. ♦ **onorario** sm. fee.
onorato agg. 1. honoured 2. (onesto) honourable.
onore sm. honour || farsi —, to excel; a onor del vero, to tell (v. irr.) the truth; serata d'—, gala night.
onorévole agg. honourable.
onorificenza sf. 1. honour 2. (decorazione) decoration.
onorìfico agg. honorific(al).
onta sf. 1. shame 2. (offesa) insult || ad — di, in spite of.
ontano sm. alder.
ontologìa sf. ontology.
ontològico agg. ontological.
opacità sf. opacity.
opàco agg. 1. opaque 2. (di suoni, colori) dull.
opale sm. opal.
opalescente agg. opalescent.
opalino agg. opaline.
òpera sf. 1. work 2. (melodramma) opera 3. (istituto) institution.
operàbile agg. 1. workable. 2. (chir.) operable.
operaio agg. working. ♦ **operaio** sm. worker: — specializzato, skilled worker.
operante agg. operating.
operare vi. to work, to operate (anche med.).
operativo agg. operative.
operato agg. (di tessuto) diapered. ♦ **operato** sm. 1. (condotta) behaviour 2. (chi ha subito un'operazione) operated patient.
operatore sm. 1. operator 2. (cine) cameraman (pl. -men).

operatorio *agg.* operating.
operazione *sf.* operation: *fare un'— a qu.*, to perform an operation on so.; *subire un'—*, to undergo (*v. irr.*) an operation.
operetta *sf.* operetta.
operistico *agg.* opera (*attr.*).
operosità *sf.* industry.
operoso *agg.* industrious.
opificio *sm.* factory.
opimo *agg.* fertile.
opinàbile *agg.* thinkable.
opinare *vi.* to think (*v. irr.*).
opinione *sf.* opinion: *secondo l'— di qu.*, in so.'s opinion.
opossum *sm.* opossum.
oppiare *vt.* to opiate.
oppiato *agg. e sm.* opiate.
oppio *sm.* opium.
oppiòmane *s.* opium-addict.
opponente *agg. e sm.* opponent.
opponìbile *agg.* opposable.
opporre *vt.* 1. to oppose 2. (*obiettare*) to object. ♦ **opporsi** *vr.* to object (to), to be opposed.
opportunismo *sm.* opportunism.
opportunista *s.* opportunist.
opportunìstico *agg.* opportunistic.
opportunità *sf.* 1. (*occasione*) opportunity 2. (*l'essere opportuno*) timeliness.
opportuno *agg.* 1. opportune 2. (*giusto*) right.
oppositore *sm.* opponent.
opposizione *sf.* opposition || *fare — (a qu., qc.)*, to oppose (so., sthg.).
opposto *agg. e sm.* opposite.
oppressione *sf.* oppression.
oppressivo *agg.* oppressive.
oppresso *agg.* oppressed.
oppressore *sm.* oppressor.
opprimente *agg.* oppressive.
opprìmere *vt.* to oppress.
oppugnare *vt.* to assail.
oppure *cong.* 1. or 2. (*altrimenti*) or else.
optare *vi.* to opt.
opulento *agg.* opulent.
opulenza *sf.* opulence.
opùscolo *sm.* pamphlet.
opzione *sf.* option.
ora¹ *sf.* 1. hour 2. (*tempo*) time: *che — è?*, what time is it?; *— di punta*, rush hour; *all'—*, by the hour; *di — in —*, hourly; *di buon'—*, early; *— legale*, summer time; *non veder l'— di*, to look forward to.

ora² *avv.* now || *— come —*, at the moment; *d'— in poi*, from now on; *fino ad —*, so far; *sin d'—*, now; *prima d'—*, before; *or —*, just. ♦ **ora che** *cong.* now (that).
oràcolo *sm.* oracle.
òrafo *sm.* goldsmith.
orale *agg. e sm.* oral.
oralmente *avv.* orally.
oramai *avv.* V. *ormai*.
orango *sm.* orang-outang.
orario *agg.* 1. time (*attr.*) 2. (*all'ora*) per hour. ♦ **orario** *sm.* 1. hours (*pl.*) 2. (*tabella*) time-table || *in —*, on time.
orata *sf.* dory.
oratore *sm.* orator.
oratoria *sf.* oratory.
oratorio *sm.* oratory.
orazione *sf.* 1. oration 2. (*preghiera*) prayer.
orbare *vt.* to bereave (*v. irr.*).
orbene *avv.* well.
òrbita *sf.* orbit.
orbitale *agg.* orbital.
orbo *agg.* (*di un occhio*) one-eyed.
orchestra *sf.* orchestra.
orchestrale *agg.* orchestral. ♦ **orchestrale** *s.* member of an orchestra.
orchestrare *vt.* to orchestrate.
orchestrazione *sf.* orchestration.
orchestrina *sf.* band.
orchidea *sf.* orchid.
orcio *sm.* pitcher.
orco *sm.* ogre.
orda *sf.* horde.
ordigno *sm.* device.
ordinale *agg. e sm.* ordinal.
ordinamento *sm.* 1. arrangement 2. (*regolamento*) code, system.
ordinanza *sf.* 1. order 2. (*attendente mil.*) batman (*pl.* -men).
ordinare *vt.* 1. to order 2. (*mettere in ordine*) to put (*v. irr.*) in order 3. (*eccl.*) to ordain 4. (*med.*) to prescribe. ♦ **ordinarsi** *vr.* 1. to straighten up 2. (*mil.*) to draw (*v. irr.*) up.
ordinario *agg. e sm.* ordinary.
ordinata *sf.* 1. (*mat.*) ordinate 2. (*aer.; mar.*) frame.
ordinatamente *avv.* tidily.
ordinato *agg.* tidy, orderly.
ordinazione *sf.* 1. order 2. (*med.*) prescription 3. (*eccl.*) ordination.
òrdine *sm.* order || *— d'idee*, scheme of things; *all'— del giorno*,

on the agenda; *per — di*, by order of; *parola d'—*, password; *di prim'—*, firstclass (*attr.*).
ordire *vt.* 1. to warp 2. (*fig.*) to plot.
ordito *sm.* warp.
orecchiàbile *agg.* catchy.
orecchino *sm.* earring.
orecchio *sm.* ear.
orecchioni *sm. pl.* mumps.
oréfice *sm.* jeweller.
oreficerìa *sf.* 1. jeweller's art 2. (*negozio*) jeweller's shop.
òrfano *agg. e sm.* orphan.
orfanotrofio *sm.* orphanage.
organetto *sm.* barrel-organ || *suonatore di —*, organ-grinder.
organicità *sf.* organic unity.
organico[1] *agg.* organic.
organico[2] *sm.* staff.
organismo *sm.* 1. organism 2. (*ente*) body.
organista *s.* organist.
organizzàbile *agg.* organizable.
organizzare *vt.* to organize.
organizzatore *sm.* organizer.
organizzazione *sf.* organization.
òrgano *sm.* organ.
organza *sf.* organza.
organzino *sm.* organzine.
orgasmo *sm.* orgasm.
orgia *sf.* orgy.
orgiàstico *agg.* orgiastic.
orgoglio *sm.* pride.
orgoglioso *agg.* proud.
orientale *agg.* eastern.
orientalista *s.* orientalist.
orientamento *sm.* orientation || *perdere l'—*, to lose (*v. irr.*) one's bearings.
orientare *vt.* to orient. ♦ **orientarsi** *vr.* 1. to find (*v. irr.*) one's bearings 2. (*tendere*) to tend.
oriente *sm.* east.
orifiamma *sf.* oriflamme.
orifizio *sm.* orifice.
orìgano *sm.* origan.
originale *agg.* 1. original 2. (*strano*) odd. ♦ **originale** *sm.* 1. original 2. (*persona eccentrica*) eccentric.
originalità *sf.* 1. originality 2. (*stranezza*) oddity.
originare *vt. e vi.* to originate.
originariamente *avv.* originally.
originario *agg.* original.
orìgine *sf.* origin || *avere —*, to originate; *dare —*, to cause.
origliare *vi.* to eavesdrop.

orina *sf.* urine.
orinale *sm.* chamber pot.
orinare *vi.* to urinate.
orinatoio *sm.* public lavatory.
orizzontale *agg.* horizontal.
orizzontalmente *avv.* horizontally.
orizzontare *vt.*, **orizzontarsi** *vr.* V. *orientare*, *orientarsi*.
orizzonte *sm.* horizon.
orlare *vt.* 1. (*bordare*) to edge 2. (*fare l'orlo*) to hem.
orlatura *sf.* hemming.
orlo *sm.* 1. (*di abito ecc.*) hem 2. (*bordatura*) border 3. (*estremità*) edge 4. (*di oggetto rotondo*) rim || *— a giorno*, hem-stitch; *sull'— della rovina*, on the verge of ruin.
orma *sf.* 1. mark 2. (*traccia*) trace 3. (*di piede*) footprint || *seguire le orme di qu.*, to follow in so.'s footsteps; *tornare sulle proprie orme*, to go (*v. irr.*) back on one's tracks.
ormai *avv.* 1. (by) now 2. (*al passato*) (by) then.
ormeggiare *vt.* to moor. ♦ **ormeggiarsi** *vr.* to moor.
ormeggio *sm.* mooring.
ormone *sm.* hormone.
ormònico *agg.* hormonic.
ornamentale *agg.* ornamental.
ornamentazione *sf.* ornamentation.
ornamento *sm.* ornament.
ornare *vt.* to adorn.
ornato *agg.* 1. adorned (with) 2. (*di stile*) ornate.
ornitologìa *sf.* ornithology.
ornitològico *agg.* ornithological.
ornitòlogo *sm.* ornithologist.
oro *sm.* gold || *d'—*, golden.
orografìa *sf.* orography.
orogràfico *agg.* orographic(al).
orologerìa *sf.* 1. (*arte*) horology 2. (*negozio*) watchmaker's shop || *movimento d'—*, clock movement.
orologiaio *sm.* watchmaker.
orologio *sm.* 1. watch 2. (*a muro, da tavolo*) clock.
oròscopo *sm.* horoscope.
orpello *sm.* tinsel.
orrendamente *avv.* dreadfully.
orrendo *agg.* dreadful.
orrìbile *agg.* horrible.
orribilmente *avv.* horribly.
òrrido *agg.* frightful.
orripilante *agg.* terrifying.
orrore *sm.* horror.
orsa *sf.* she-bear: *— Maggiore*,

Great Bear; — *Minore*, Little Bear.

orsacchiotto *sm.* 1. young bear 2. (*giocattolo*) Teddy bear.

orso *sm.* bear.

ortaggio *sm.* vegetable.

ortensia *sf.* hydrangea.

ortica *sf.* nettle.

orticaria *sf.* nettle-rash.

orticultore *sm.* horticulturist.

orticultura *sf.* horticulture.

orto *sm.* 1. kitchen garden 2. (*di orticoltore*) market garden.

ortodossìa *sf.* orthodoxy.

ortodosso *agg.* orthodox.

ortofruttìcolo *agg.* horticultural.

ortogonale *agg.* orthogonal.

ortografìa *sf.* orthography, spelling.

ortogràfico *agg.* orthographic(al).

ortolano *sm.* 1. market-gardener 2. (*negoziante*) greengrocer.

ortopedìa *sf.* orthopedics.

ortopèdico *agg.* orthopedic. ♦ **ortopèdico** *sm.* orthopedist.

orzaiolo *sm.* sty.

orzata *sf.* (*bibita*) orgeat.

orzo *sm.* barley.

osanna *sf.* hosanna.

osare *vi.* to dare (*v. semidif.*). ♦ **osare** *vt.* (*tentare*) to attempt.

oscenità *sf.* obscenity.

osceno *agg.* obscene.

oscillare *vi.* 1. to swing (*v. irr.*) 2. (*di fiamma; opinioni*) to waver 3. (*elettr.*) to oscillate 4. (*di prezzi*) to fluctuate.

oscillatore *sm.* oscillator.

oscillatorio *agg.* oscillatory.

oscillazione *sf.* 1. swing 2. (*di fiamma; opinioni*) wavering 3. (*elettr.*) oscillation 4. (*di prezzi*) fluctuation.

oscillògrafo *sm.* oscillograph.

oscurantismo *sm.* obscurantism.

oscurantista *agg. e s.* obscurantist.

oscurare *vt.* 1. to darken 2. (*fig.*) to overshadow. ♦ **oscurarsi** *vr.* to darken.

oscurità *sf.* 1. darkness 2. (*fig.*) obscurity.

oscuro *agg.* 1. dark 2. (*sconosciuto, umile*) obscure 3. (*difficile*) hard, difficult 4. (*sconosciuto*) unknown.

osmosi *sf.* osmosis (*pl.* -ses).

ospedale *sm.* hospital.

ospedaliero *agg.* hospital (*attr.*).

ospitale *agg.* hospitable.

ospitalità *sf.* hospitality.

ospitare *vt.* to entertain.

òspite *s.* 1. (*chi ospita, uomo*) host; (*id., donna*) hostess 2. (*chi è ospitato*) guest.

ospizio *sm.* 1. (*per poveri*) alms-house 2. (*per trovatelli*) foundling hospital 3. (*per vecchi ecc.*) home (for the old etc.).

ossario *sm.* charnel-house, ossuary.

ossatura *sf.* 1. skeleton 2. (*di edificio, discorso*) framework.

òsseo *agg.* bony.

ossequente *agg.* respectful.

ossequio *sm.* 1. homage 2. (*obbedienza*) obedience 3. (*saluti*) regards (*pl.*).

ossequiosità *sf.* deference.

ossequioso *agg.* deferential.

osservàbile *agg.* observable.

osservante *agg.* observant.

osservanza *sf.* 1. observance 2. (*ossequio*) regards (*pl.*).

osservare *vt.* 1. to observe 2. (*esaminare*) to examine.

osservatore *agg.* observing. ♦ **osservatore** *sm.* observer.

osservatorio *sm.* observatory.

osservazione *sf.* 1. observation: *in —*, under observation 2. (*rimprovero*) reproach.

ossessionante *agg.* haunting.

ossessionare *vt.* to haunt.

ossessione *sf.* obsession.

ossessivo *agg.* haunting.

ossesso *sm.* person possessed.

ossìa *cong.* (*cioè*) that is.

ossidàbile *agg.* oxidizable.

ossidare *vt.* to oxidize. ♦ **ossidarsi** *vr.* to oxidize.

ossidazione *sf.* oxidation.

òssido *sm.* oxide.

ossìdrico *agg.* oxyhydrogen.

ossificare *vt.* to ossify. ♦ **ossificarsi** *vr.* to ossify.

ossificazione *sf.* ossification.

ossigenare *vt.* 1. to oxygenate 2. (*di capelli*) to peroxide.

ossigenato *agg.* 1. oxygenated 2. (*di capelli*) peroxided || *acqua ossigenata*, hydrogen peroxide.

ossìgeno *sm.* oxygen.

osso *sm.* bone || *in carne e ossa*, in flesh and blood; *avere le ossa rotte*, to be aching all over.

ossuto *agg.* bony.

ostacolare *vt.* to hamper.

ostàcolo *sm.* 1. obstacle 2. (*sport*) hurdle || *corsa ippica ad ostacoli*, steeple-chase.

ostaggio *sm.* hostage.

oste *sm.* innkeeper.
osteggiare *vt.* to oppose.
ostello *sm.* — *della gioventù,* (youth) hostel.
ostensorio *sm.* monstrance.
ostentare *vt.* 1. to show (*v. irr.*) off 2. (*fingere*) to feign.
ostentatamente *avv.* ostentatiously.
ostentazione *sf.* ostentation.
osteologìa *sf.* osteology.
osterìa *sf.* pub.
ostètrica *sf.* midwife (*pl.* -wives).
ostetricia *sf.* obstetrics.
ostètrico *sm.* obstetrician.
ostia *sf.* 1. wafer 2. (*eccl.*) host.
òstico *agg.* 1. irksome 2. (*di sapore*) unpalatable 3. (*fig.*) difficult.
ostile *agg.* hostile.
ostilità *sf.* hostility.
ostinarsi *vr.* to persist (in).
ostinato *agg.* stubborn.
ostinazione *sf.* obstinacy.
ostracismo *sm.* ostracism.
òstrica *sf.* oyster.
ostricaio *sm.* oyster-seller.
ostricultura *sf.* oyster-breeding.
ostruire *vt.* to obstruct.
ostruzione *sf.* obstruction.
ostruzionismo *sm.* obstructionism.
ostruzionista *s.* obstructionist.
otaria *sf.* otary.
otite *sf.* otitis.
otorinolaringoiatra *s.* otorhinolaryngologist.
otorinolaringoiatrìa *sf.* otorhinolaryngology.
ottaedro *sm.* octahedron.
ottagonale *agg.* octagonal.
ottàgono *sm.* octagon.
ottanta *agg.* eighty.
ottantenne *agg.* eighty years old, eighty-year-old (*attr.*).
ottantèsimo *agg.* eightieth.
ottava *sf.* octave.
ottavo *agg.* e *sm.* eighth.
ottemperanza *sf.* compliance.
ottemperare *vi.* to comply (with).
ottenebrare *vt.* to cloud.
ottenere *vt.* to obtain, to get (*v. irr.*).
ottetto *sm.* octet.
òttica *sf.* optics.
òttico *agg.* optic(al). ♦ **òttico** *sm.* optician.
ottimismo *sm.* optimism.
ottimista *s.* optimist.
ottimìstico *agg.* optimistic.
òttimo *agg.* best, very good. ♦ **òttimo** *sm.* optimum (*pl.* -ma).

otto *agg.* eight.
ottobre *sm.* October.
ottocento *agg.* eight hundred. ♦ **ottocento** *sm.* l'—, the nineteenth century.
ottomana *sf.* ottoman.
ottomano *agg.* e *sm.* Ottoman.
ottone *sm.* brass.
ottuagenario *agg.* e *sm.* octogenarian.
otturare *vt.* to stop. ♦ **otturarsi** *vr.* to stop.
otturatore *sm.* (*foto*) shutter.
otturazione *sf.* stopping.
ottusità *sf.* obtuseness.
ottuso *agg.* obtuse.
ovaia *sf.* ovary.
ovale *agg.* e *sm.* oval.
ovatta *sf.* 1. wadding 2. (*cotone idrofilo*) cotton-wool.
ovattare *vt.* to stuff with wadding.
ovazione *sf.* ovation.
ove *avv.* where.
ovest *sm.* west.
ovile *sm.* fold.
ovino *agg.* ovine. ♦ **ovino** *sm.* sheep (*invariato al pl.*).
ovìparo *agg.* oviparous.
ovòide *agg.* egg-shaped.
òvolo *sm.* (*fungo*) agaric.
ovulazione *sf.* ovulation.
òvulo *sm.* ovule.
ovunque *avv.* 1. everywhere 2. (*in qualsiasi posto*) anywhere. ♦ **ovunque** *cong.* wherever.
ovvero *cong.* or.
ovviare *vi.* to obviate (sthg.).
ovvio *agg.* obvious.
oziare *vi.* to loaf, to idle.
ozio *sm.* idleness.
oziosamente *avv.* idly.
ozono *sm.* ozone.

P

pacare *vt.* to calm.
pacatezza *sf.* calmness.
pacato *agg.* calm.
pacca *sf.* slap.
pacchetto *sm.* packet.
pacchia *sf.* godsend.
pacchianata *sf.* coarse action.
pacchiano *agg.* coarse.
pacco *sm.* 1. (*postale*) parcel 2. (*collo*) package.

paccottiglia *sf.* cheap stuff.
pace *sf.* peace || *darsi* —, to set (*v. irr.*) one's mind at rest.
pachiderma *sm.* pachyderm.
pachistano *agg. e sm.* Pakistani.
pacificare *vt.* 1. to pacify 2. (*riconciliare*) to reconcile. ♦ **pacificarsi** *vr.* to become (*v. irr.*) reconciled.
pacificazione *sf.* 1. pacification 2. (*riconciliazione*) reconciliation.
pacifico *agg.* 1. pacific 2. (*evidente*) self-evident.
pacifismo *sm.* pacifism.
pacifista *s.* pacifist.
pacioccone *sm.* easy-going person.
padella *sf.* frying-pan.
padiglione *sm.* pavilion.
padre *sm.* father.
padrino *sm.* godfather.
padronale *agg.* (*privato*) private || *casa* —, manor-house.
padronanza *sf.* mastery: — *di sé*, self-control.
padrone *sm.* 1. master 2. (*proprietario*) owner 3. (*di casa, albergo*) landlord || *essere* — *di sé*, to have self-control; *padronissimo!*, do as you like!
paesaggio *sm.* landscape.
paesano *agg.* rural. ♦ **paesano** *sm.* peasant.
paese *sm.* 1. (*nazione, territorio*) country 2. (*villaggio*) village.
paesista *s.* landscape painter.
paffuto *agg.* chubby.
paga *sf.* pay, wages (*pl.*): *libro* —, wages book; *giorno di* —, pay day.
pagàbile *agg.* payable.
pagaia *sf.* paddle.
pagamento *sm.* payment.
paganésimo *sm.* paganism.
pagano *agg. e sm.* pagan.
pagare *vt.* to pay (*v. irr.*).
pagella *sf.* schoolreport.
paggio *sm.* page.
pagherò *sm.* promissory note.
pàgina *sf.* page.
paglia *sf.* straw.
pagliacciata *sf.* buffoonery.
pagliaccio *sm.* clown.
pagliaio *sm.* strawstack.
pagliericcio *sm.* paillasse.
paglierino *agg.* straw-coloured.
paglietta *sf.* 1. (*cappello*) straw-hat 2. (*paglia di ferro*) steel-wool 3. (*trucioli per imballaggio*) wood-shavings (*pl.*) 4. (*trucioli, di carta*) paper-wool.

pagnotta *sf.* round loaf (*pl.* -aves).
pagoda *sf.* pagoda.
paio *sm.* 1. (*di cose necessariamente unite*) pair 2. (*due*) couple.
pala *sf.* 1. shovel 2. (*di remo, elica*) blade 3. (*di ruota*) paddle || — *d'altare*, altar-piece.
paladino *sm.* 1. paladin 2. (*fig.*) champion.
palafitta *sf.* 1. pile 2. (*abitazione*) pile-dwelling.
palafreniere *sm.* groom.
palafreno *sm.* palfrey.
palanchino *sm.* palanquin.
palata *sf.* 1. shovelful 2. (*colpo*) blow with a shovel || *a palate* (*fig.*), in plenty.
palatale *agg.* palatal.
palatino *agg.* palatine.
palato *sm.* palate.
palazzo *sm.* palace.
palco *sm.* 1. (*di teatro*) box 2. (*pedana*) stand.
palcoscènico *sm.* stage.
paleocristiano *agg.* paleo-christian.
paleografia *sf.* paleography.
paleògrafo *sm.* paleographer.
paleontologia *sf.* paleontology.
paleontològico *agg.* paleontologic(al).
paleontòlogo *sm.* paleontologist.
palesare *vt.* to reveal.
palese *agg.* evident.
palestra *sf.* gymnasium.
paletta *sf.* (*di capostazione*) signal stick.
palinodìa *sf.* palinode.
palissandro *sm.* rosewood.
palizzata *sf.* palisade.
palla *sf.* 1. ball 2. (*pallottola*) bullet.
pallacanestro *sf.* basket-ball.
pallanuoto *sf.* water-polo.
pallavolo *sf.* volley-ball.
palleggiare *vi.* (*calcio*) to dribble. ♦ **palleggiare** *vt.* to toss. ♦ **palleggiarsi** *vr. rec.* to shift on one another.
palleggio *sm.* 1. (*calcio*) dribbling 2. (*tennis*) tossing.
palliativo *agg. e sm.* palliative.
pallidezza *sf.* paleness.
pàllido *agg.* pale.
pallino *sm.* 1. (*di fucile*) shot 2. (*mania*) craze.
palloncino *sm.* 1. balloon 2. (*lampioncino*) Chinese lantern.
pallone *sm.* ball || *gioco del* —, football.

pallore *sm.* pallor.
pallòttola *sf.* 1. pellet 2. (*mil.*) bullet.
pallottoliere *sm.* abacus (*pl.* -ci).
palma[1] *sf.* (*della mano*) palm.
palma[2] *sf.* (*albero*) palm(-tree).
palmare *agg.* 1. (*anat.*) palmar 2. (*evidente*) clear.
palmato *agg.* 1. (*bot.*) palmate 2. (*zool.*) webbed.
palmeto *sm.* palm-grove.
palmìpede *agg. e sm.* palmiped.
palmo *sm.* palm.
palo *sm.* 1. pole 2. (*per fondamenta, ormeggio*) pile || — *indicatore*, signpost; *fare il* —, to be on the lookout.
palombaro *sm.* diver.
palpàbile *agg.* tangible.
palpare *vt.* 1. to finger 2. (*med.*) to palpate.
pàlpebra *sf.* eyelid || *battere le palpebre*, to blink.
palpitante *agg.* 1. throbbing 2. (*fig.*) fascinating.
palpitare *vi.* to throb (with sthg.).
palpitazione *sf.* 1. throbbing 2. (*med.*) palpitation.
pàlpito *sm.* throb.
paltò *sm.* overcoat.
palude *sf.* marsh.
paludoso *agg.* marshy.
pàmpino *sm.* vine-leaf (*pl.* -leaves).
panacea *sf.* panacea.
panare *vt.* to bread.
panca *sf.* bench.
pancetta *sf.* 1. (*cu persona*) pot-belly.
panchina *sf.* bench.
pancia *sf.* belly.
panciera *sf.* body-belt.
panciotto *sm.* waistcoat.
panciuto *agg.* pot-bellied.
pancotto *sm.* panada.
pàncreas *sm.* pancreas.
pancreàtico *agg.* pancreatic.
pandemonio *sm.* pandemonium.
pane *sm.* bread.
panegìrico *sm.* panegyric.
panetterìa *sf.* bakery.
panettiere *sm.* baker.
pànfilo *sm.* yacht.
pangermanismo *sm.* Pan-Germanism.
pànico *agg. e sm.* panic.
panico *sm.* (*bot.*) millet.
paniere *sm.* basket.
panificare *vi.* to make (*v. irr.*) bread.

panificazione *sf.* bread-making.
panificio *sm.* bakery.
panino *sm.* roll: — *imbottito*, sandwich.
panna[1] *sf.* cream: — *montata*, whipped cream.
panna[2] *sf. restare in* —, to have a breakdown.
pannello *sm.* 1. (*edil.*) panel 2. (*di stoffa*) light cloth.
panno *sm.* 1. cloth (*pl.* cloths) 2. *pl.* (*vestiti*) clothes.
pannocchia *sf.* cob.
pannolino *sm.* 1. (*per bambini*) napkin 2. (*assorbente igienico*) sanitary towel.
panorama *sm.* view.
panslavismo *sm.* Pan-slavism.
pantagruèlico *agg.* Pantagruelian.
pantaloni *sm. pl.* trousers || — *corti*, shorts.
pantano *sm.* 1. mire 2. (*luogo pantanoso; fig.*) quagmire.
panteismo *sm.* pantheism.
panteista *s.* pantheist.
panteìstico *agg.* pantheistic(al).
pantera *sf.* panther.
pantòfola *sf.* slipper.
pantògrafo *sm.* pantograph.
pantomima *sf.* pantomime.
panzana *sf.* fib.
paonazzo *agg.* purple.
papa *sm.* pope.
papà *sm.* daddy.
papale *agg.* papal.
papalina *sf.* skull-cap.
papato *sm.* papacy.
papàvero *sm.* poppy || *alto* —, (*fig.*) bigwig.
pàpera *sf.* 1. (*zool.*) duckling 2. (*errore*) slip 3. (*teat.*) fluff.
papilla *sf.* papilla (*pl.* -ae).
papillare *agg.* papillary.
papiro *sm.* papyrus (*pl.* -ri).
papirologìa *sf.* papyrology.
papismo *sm.* popery.
papista *s.* papist.
pappa *sf.* pap.
pappagallo *sm.* parrot || *ripetere a* —, to parrot.
pappagorgia *sf.* double chin.
pappare *vt.* to gorge. ♦ **papparsi** *vr.* to eat up.
pàprica *sf.* paprika.
paràbola *sf.* 1. parable 2. (*geom.; mil.*) parabola.
parabòlico *agg.* parabolic.
parabrezza *sm.* windscreen.
paracadutare *vt.* to parachute. ♦

paracadutarsi *vr.* to bail out.
paracadute *sm.* parachute.
paracadutismo *sm.* parachutism.
paracadutista *sm.* **1.** parachutist **2.** (*mil.*) paratrooper.
paracarro *sm.* wayside post.
paradigma *sm.* paradigm.
paradisìaco *agg.* paradisiac(al).
paradiso *sm.* paradise.
paradossale *agg.* paradoxical.
paradosso *sm.* paradox.
parafango *sm.* mudguard.
paraffina *sf.* paraffin.
parafrasare *vt.* to paraphrase.
paràfrasi *sf.* paraphrase.
parafùlmine *sm.* lightning-rod.
paragonàbile *agg.* comparable.
paragonare *vt.* to compare.
paragone *sm.* comparison: *a — di*, in comparison with.
paràgrafo *sm.* paragraph.
paràlisi *sf.* palsy.
paralìtico *agg. e sm.* paralytic.
paralizzare *vt.* to paralyze.
parallela *sf.* parallel: *le parallele* (*sport*), parallel bars.
parallelepìpedo *sm.* parallelepiped (*pl.* -da).
parallelismo *sm.* parallelism.
parallelo *agg. e sm.* parallel.
parallelogrammo *sm.* parallelogram.
paralume *sm.* lamp-shade.
paramento *sm.* **1.** hanging **2.** (*eccl.*) vestment.
paràmetro *sm.* parameter.
paraninfo *sm.* paranymph.
paranoia *sf.* paranoia.
paranòico *agg. e sm.* paranoiac.
paraocchi *sm. pl.* blinkers.
parapetto *sm.* **1.** parapet **2.** (*davanzale*) sill.
parapiglia *sm.* turmoil.
parapioggia *sm.* umbrella.
parare *vt.* **1.** (*riparare*) to shield **2.** (*evitare*) to parry **3.** (*ornare*) to decorate || *andare a —*, to drive (*v. irr.*) at. ♦ **pararsi** *vr.* **1.** (*comparire*) to appear **2.** (*adornarsi*) to deck oneself.
parasole *sm.* parasol.
parassita *agg.* parasitic. ♦ **parassita** *s.* parasite.
parassitismo *sm.* parasitism.
parastatale *agg.* State controlled || *ente —*, semi-governmental body.
parata *sf.* **1.** parade **2.** (*sport*) parry || *fare una —* (*sport*), to parry.
paratìa *sf.* bulkhead.

paratifo *sm.* paratyphoid.
parato *sm.* hanging || *carta da parati*, wallpaper.
paratoia *sf.* cataract.
paraurti *sm.* bumper.
paravento *sm.* screen.
parcella *sf.* fee.
parcheggiare *vt.* to park.
parcheggio *sm.* **1.** parking **2.** (*luogo*) car park.
parco[1] *sm.* park: *— di divertimenti*, fun-fair.
parco[2] *agg.* sparing.
parecchio *agg.* quite a lot of. ♦ **parecchio** *avv.* quite a lot, quite (+ *agg.*). ♦ **parecchio** *pron.* a good deal of it, several (*pl.*).
pareggiare *vt.* **1.** (*livellare*) to level **2.** (*comm.*) to balance **3.** (*parificare una scuola*) to recognize officially. ♦ **pareggiare** *vi.* (*sport*) to draw (*v. irr.*).
pareggio *sm.* **1.** (*comm.*) balance **2.** (*sport*) draw, tie.
parentado *sm.* V. *parentela*.
parente *sm.* relative.
parentela *sf.* **1.** relationship **2.** (*i parenti*) relatives.
parèntesi *sf.* **1.** parenthesis (*pl.* -ses) **2.** (*segno grafico*) bracket.
parere[1] *vi.* **1.** to seem **2.** (*essere simile a*) to look like **3.** (*pensare*) to think (*v. irr.*) (of).
parere[2] *sm.* opinion.
paresi *sf.* paresis.
parete *sf.* wall: *— divisoria*, partition.
pàrgolo *sm.* little child (*pl.* children).
pari *agg.* **1.** equal, same **2.** (*simile*) like **3.** (*divisibile per due*) even. ♦ **pari** *sm.* equal, peer.
paria *sm.* pariah.
parietale *agg.* parietal.
parificazione *sf.* **1.** (*comm.*) balance **2.** (*scuola*) official recognition **3.** (*livellamento*) levelling.
parigino *agg. e sm.* Parisian.
pariglia *sf.* pair.
parimenti *avv.* likewise.
parità *sf.* equality.
paritario *agg.* equalitarian.
parlamentare[1] *agg.* parliamentary. ♦ **parlamentare** *sm.* Member of Parliament.
parlamentare[2] *vi.* to parley.
parlamentarismo *sm.* parliamentarism.

parlamento *sm.* parliament.

parlantina *sf.* talkativeness ‖ *aver buona —*, to be a glib talker.

parlare *vi.* to speak (*v. irr.*), to talk.

parlare *sm.* 1. (*discorso*) speech 2. (*chiacchiere*) talk 3. (*idioma*) language.

parlato *agg. cinema —*, talkies (*pl.*).

parlatore *sm.* speaker.

parlatorio *sm.* parlour.

parlottare *vi.* to mutter.

parodìa *sf.* parody.

parodiare *vt.* to parody.

parodista *s.* parodist.

parola *sf.* 1. word 2. (*facoltà di parlare, discorso*) speech ‖ *parole incrociate*, crosswords; *gioco di parole*, pun; *far —*, to mention; *restare senza —*, to be left speechless; *venire a parole con*, to have words with; *rivolgere la — a qu.*, to address so.; *avere la — facile*, to be a glib talker.

parolaccia *sf.* nasty word: *dire parolacce*, to swear (*v. irr.*).

parolaio *sm.* 1. chatterbox 2. (*di scrittore*) word-monger.

paroliere *sm.* « lyrics » writer.

parossismo *sm.* paroxysm.

paròtide *sf.* parotid.

parricida *s.* parricide.

parricidio *sm.* parricide.

parrocchia *sf.* parish.

parrocchiale *agg.* parish (*attr.*).

parrocchiano *sm.* parishioner.

pàrroco *sm.* 1. (*cattolico*) parish priest 2. (*protestante*) parson.

parrucca *sf.* wig.

parrucchiere *sm.* hairdresser.

parsimonia *sf.* thriftiness.

parsimonioso *agg.* thrifty.

parte *sf.* 1. part 2. (*lato*) side 3. (*porzione*) share 4. (*pol.; comm.; giur.*) party ‖ *da —*, aside: *da di*, from; *da — a —*, right through; *da una — ... dall'altra*, on one hand ... on the other; *la maggior — di*, most (of); *a — ciò*, apart from that; *farsi da —*, to get (*v. irr.*) out of the way; *fare la — di*, to play.

partecipante *s.* 1. sharer 2. (*chi annuncia*) spokesman (*pl.* -men) 3. (*chi presenzia*) the bystander.

partecipare *vi.* 1. to share (in) 2. (*esser presente*) to be present. ♦ **partecipare** *vt.* to announce.

partecipazione *sf.* 1. sharing 2. (*esser presente*) presence 3. (*annuncio*) announcement 4. (*biglietto*) card.

partécipe *agg.* 1. sharing 2. (*informato*) acquainted ‖ *rendere — qu. di qc.*, to acquaint so. with sthg.

parteggiare *vi.* to take (*v. irr.*) sides (with).

partenogènesi *sf.* parthenogenesis.

partenza *sf.* 1. departure, leaving 2. (*sport*) start ‖ *punto di —*, starting-point; *essere in —*, to be leaving.

particella *sf.* particle.

participiale *agg.* participial.

participio *sm.* participle.

particolare *agg.* particular. ♦ **particolare** *sm.* detail.

particolareggiato *agg.* detailed.

particolarismo *sm.* particularism.

particolarità *sf.* 1. particularity 2. (*dettaglio*) detail.

partigiano *agg. e sm.* partisan.

partire[1] *vi.* 1. to leave (*v. irr.*) 2. (*muoversi, iniziare, anche fig.*) to start ‖ *a — da*, (beginning) from.

partire[2] *vt.* to separate.

partita *sf.* 1. (*giocata*) game, match 2. (*di merce*) lot 3. (*in contabilità*) entry ‖ *dar — vinta* (*fig.*), to give (*v. irr.*) in.

partitivo *agg. e sm.* partitive.

partito *sm.* party.

partitura *sf.* (*mus.*) score.

partizione *sf.* division.

parto *sm.* 1. delivery 2. (*fig.*) product.

partoriente *agg.* parturient. ♦ **partoriente** *sf.* lying-in woman.

partorire *vt.* to bring (*v. irr.*) forth, to beget (*v. irr.*) (*anche fig.*).

parvenza *sf.* 1. appearance 2. (*ombra*) shadow.

parziale *agg.* partial.

parzialità *sf.* partiality.

parzialmente *avv.* partially.

pàscere *vt. e vi.* 1. to feed (*v. irr.*) 2. (*al pascolo*) to graze. ♦ **pàscersi** *vr.* to feed (on).

pascià *sm.* pasha.

pasciuto *agg.* fed.

pascolare *vt. e vi.* to pasture.

pàscolo *sm.* pasture ‖ *essere al —*, to be grazing.

Pasqua *sf.* Easter.

pasquale *agg.* Easter (*attr.*).

passàbile *agg.* passabl-

passabilmente *avv.* passably.

passaggio *sm.* 1. passage 2. (*traversata*) crossing || *dare un — in macchina*, to give (*v. irr.*) a lift; *vietato il —*, no thoroughfare; *di —*, of transition; (*incidentalmente*) incidentally.

passamanerìa *sf.* passementerie.

passamano *sm.* (*fettuccia*) braid.

passamontagna *sm.* snow-cap.

passante *sm.* 1. (*di cinghia ecc.*) loop 2. (*persona*) passer-by.

passaporto *sm.* passport.

passare *vi.* 1. to pass 2. (*andare*) to call (on so., at sthg.). ◆ **passare** *vt.* 1. to pass 2. (*di tempo*) to spend (*v. irr.*) 3. (*sopportare, trafiggere*) to pass through.

passatempo *sm.* pastime.

passatista *s.* traditionalist.

passato *agg.* 1. past 2. (*scorso*) last. ◆ **passato** *sm.* 1. past 2. (*cuc.*) mash.

passaverdura *sm.* vegetable masher.

passeggero *agg.* passing. ◆ **passeggero** *sm.* passenger.

passeggiare *vi.* to walk, to take (*v. irr.*) a walk.

passeggiata *sf.* 1. walk 2. (*in auto*) drive 3. (*in bicicletta, a cavallo*) ride 4. (*lungomare*) promenade.

passeggino *sm.* perambulator.

passeggio *sm.* 1. walk 2. (*gente che passeggia*) promenaders (*pl.*) || *andare a —*, to go (*v. irr.*) for a walk.

passeràceo *sm. e agg.* passerine.

passerella *sf.* 1. (*ponte pedonale*) footbridge 2. (*provvisoria*) trestle-bridge 3. (*mar.; edil.*) gangway 4. (*teat.*) parade.

pàssero *sm.* sparrow.

passìbile *agg.* liable (to).

passiflora *sf.* passion-flower.

passino *sm.* strainer.

passionale *agg.* 1. passional 2. (*appassionato*) passionate.

passione *sf.* passion.

passivamente *avv.* passively.

passività *sf.* 1. passivity 2. (*comm.*) liabilities (*pl.*).

passivo *agg.* passive. ◆ **passivo** *sm.* 1. passive 2. (*comm.*) liabilities (*pl.*).

passo *sm.* 1. step 2. (*andatura*) pace 3. (*di montagna*) pass 4. (*brano, passaggio*) passage 5. (*cine*)

gauge 6. (*tec.*) pitch || *passo passo*, very slowly; *segnare il —*, to mark time; *camminare a grandi passi*, to stride (*v. irr.*).

pasta *sf.* 1. paste 2. (*pasticcino*) cake 3. (*per minestre*) "pasta".

pasteggiare *vi.* to feed (*v. irr.*) (on).

pastella *sf.* (*cuc.*) batter.

pastello *sm.* pastel: *matita, disegno a —*, pastel.

pasticca *sf.* tablet.

pasticcerìa *sf.* confectionery.

pasticciare *vt. e vi.* to make (*v. irr.*) a mess (of).

pasticciere *sm.* confectioner.

pasticcino *sm.* cake.

pasticcio *sm.* 1. (*cuc.*) pie 2. (*fig.*) mess || *essere nei pasticci*, to be in trouble.

pasticcione *sm.* bungler.

pastificio *sm.* « pasta » factory.

pastiglia *sf.* tablet.

pasto *sm.* meal.

pastoia *sf.* hobble.

pastone *sm.* mash.

pastorale *agg.* pastoral.

pastore *sm.* 1. shepherd 2. (*relig.*) parson.

pastorizia *sf.* stock-raising.

pastorizzare *vt.* to pasteurize.

pastorizzazione *sf.* pasteurization.

pastosità *sf.* 1. mellowness 2. (*morbidezza*) doughiness.

pastoso *agg.* 1. mellow 2. (*morbido*) doughy.

pastrano *sm.* overcoat.

pastura *sf.* pasture.

patacca *sf.* 1. (*macchia*) spot 2. (*cosa senza valore*) worthless object.

patata *sf.* potato: *— americana*, sweet potato || *— fritta*, chip; (*id., croccante*) crisp.

patema *sm.* worry.

patentato *agg.* licenced.

patente *agg.* patent. ◆ **patente** *sf.* licence.

patereccio *sm.* whitlow.

paternale *sf.* scolding || *fare una — a qu.*, to lecture so.

paternalismo *sm.* paternalism.

paternalìstico *agg.* paternalistic.

paternità *sf.* paternity.

paterno *agg.* paternal.

pateticamente *avv.* pathetically.

patètico *agg. e sm.* pathetic.

patibolare *agg.* sinister.

patìbolo *sm.* scaffold.

patimento *sm.* pain.

pàtina *sf.* 1. patina 2. (*di vernice*)

coat of varnish **3.** (*sulla lingua*)
coat **4.** (*su carta, terracotta*) glaze.

patinare *vt.* **1.** to varnish **2.** (*carta, terracotta*) to glaze.

patire *vt. e vi.* to suffer: — *il freddo*, to suffer from the cold || — *la fame*, to starve.

patito *agg.* sickly. ◆ **patito** *sm.* (*fig.*) fan.

patògeno *agg.* pathogenic.

patologìa *sf.* pathology.

patològico *agg.* pathologic(al).

patòlogo *sm.* pathologist.

patria *sf.* **1.** country, fatherland **2.** (*luogo natale*) birthplace.

patriarca *sm.* patriarch.

patriarcale *agg.* patriarchal.

patriarcato *sm.* patriarchate.

patricida *s.* V. *parricida*.

patrigno *sm.* stepfather.

patrimoniale *agg.* patrimonial.

patrimonio *sm.* patrimony.

patrio *agg.* **1.** native **2.** (*páterno*) paternal.

patriota *s.* patriot.

patriottardo *sm. e agg.* jingoist.

patriòttico *agg.* patriotic.

patriottismo *sm.* patriotism.

patriziato *sm.* patriciate.

patrizio *sm. e agg.* patrician.

patrocinante *sm.* pleader.

patrocinare *vt.* **1.** (*sostenere*) to support **2.** (*giur.*) to plead.

patrocinio *sm.* **1.** support **2.** (*giur.*) pleading.

patronato *sm.* **1.** patronage **2.** (*istituto benefico*) charitable institution.

patronessa *sf.* patroness.

patrono *sm.* **1.** patron **2.** (*giur.*) counsel for the defence.

patteggiare *vi.* to come (*v. irr.*) to terms.

pattinaggio *sm.* skating.

pattinare *vi.* to skate.

pattinatore *sm.* skater.

pàttino *sm.* **1.** (*a rotelle*) roller-skate **2.** (*da ghiaccio*) ice-skate **3.** (*di slitta*) shoe **4.** (*aer.*) skid **5.** (*mecc.*) sliding-block.

patto *sm.* **1.** agreement, pact **2.** (*condizione*) term || *a — che*, provided that; *a nessun —*, by no means.

pattuglia *sf.* patrol.

pattugliare *vi.* to patrol.

pattuire *vi.* to reach an agreement (upon). ◆ **pattuire** *vt.* to agree (on).

pattume *sm.* rubbish.

pattumiera *sf.* dust-bin.

pauperismo *sm.* pauperism.

paura *sf.* **1.** fear, dread **2.** (*spavento*) fright, scare.

pauroso *agg.* fearful.

pàusa *sf.* pause.

pavesare *vt.* to dress (with flags).

pavese *sm.* (*mar.*) hoist.

pavimentare *vt.* **1.** to pave **2.** (*una stanza*) to floor.

pavimento *sm.* floor.

pavone *sm.* peacock.

pavoneggiarsi *vr.* to show (*v. irr.*) off.

pazientare *vi.* to have patience.

paziente *agg. e sm.* patient.

pazienza *sf.* patience || —!, never mind!

pazzesco *agg.* foolish.

pazzìa *sf.* **1.** madness **2.** (*azione, idea pazza*) folly || *fare pazzie*, to act like a fool.

pazzo *agg.* mad. ◆ **pazzo** *sm.* madman (*pl.* -men).

pecca *sf.* fault || *senza —*, faultless.

peccaminoso *agg.* sinful.

peccare *vi.* **1.** to sin **2.** (*errare*) to err **3.** (*esser manchevole*) to lack (sthg.).

peccato *sm.* sin || *che —!*, what a pity!; *è un — che*, it is a pity that.

peccatore *sm.* sinner.

pece *sf.* pitch.

pècora *sf.* **1.** sheep (*pl. invariato*) **2.** (*femmina*) ewe.

pecoraio *sm.* shepherd.

peculato *sm.* peculation.

peculiare *agg.* peculiar.

peculiarità *sf.* peculiarity.

peculio *sm.* money.

pecuniario *agg.* pecuniary.

pedaggio *sm.* toll.

pedagogìa *sf.* pedagogy.

pedagògico *agg.* pedagogic(al).

pedagogista *s.* pedagogist.

pedagogo *sm.* pedagogue.

pedalare *vi.* to pedal.

pedale *sm.* pedal.

pedaliera *sf.* **1.** (*aer.*) rudder-bar **2.** (*mus.*) pedal keyboard.

pedana *sf.* **1.** (*sport*) spring-board **2.** (*piedistallo*) stand.

pedante *agg.* pedantic. ◆ **pedante** *s.* pedant.

pedanterìa *sf.* pedantry.

pedantesco *agg.* pedantic.

pedata *sf.* **1.** kick **2.** (*impronta*) footprint.

pedemontano *agg.* piedmont.
pederasta *sm.* homosexual.
pederastìa *sf.* homosexuality.
pedestre *agg.* pedestrian.
pediatra *s.* pediatrist.
pediatrìa *sf.* pediatrics.
pedicure *s.* chiropodist.
pedilùvio *sm.* foot-bath.
pedina *sf.* 1. (*alla dama*) piece 2. (*agli scacchi*) pawn || *muovere una — (anche fig.)*, to make (*v. irr.*) a move.
pedinare *vt.* to shadow.
pedonale *agg.* pedestrian (*attr.*): *passaggio —*, pedestrian crossing.
pedone *sm.* pedestrian || *strada riservata ai pedoni*, footpath.
pedùncolo *sm.* stalk.
peggio *agg.* (*comp.*) worse. ♦ **peggio** *sm.* the worst. ♦ **peggio** *avv.* 1. (*comp.*) worse 2. (*superl. rel.*) the worst || *— per lui*, so much the worse for him; *alla —*, at worst; *avere la —*, to get (*v. irr.*) the worst of it.
peggioramento *sm.* aggravation.
peggiorare *vt.* to make (*v. irr.*) worse. ♦ **peggiorare** *vi.* to get (*v. irr.*) worse.
peggiorativo *agg. e sm.* pejorative.
peggiore *agg.* 1. (*comp.*) worse: *questo libro è — di quello*, this book is worse than that 2. (*superl. rel.*) the worst: *era il suo — nemico*, he was his worst enemy.
pegno *sm.* pledge || *dare qc. in —*, to pledge sthg.; *polizza di —*, pawn-ticket; *agenzia di pegni*, pawnshop.
pelàgico *agg.* pelagic.
pelame *sm.* hair.
pelapatate *sm.* potato peeler.
pelare *vt.* 1. to unhair 2. (*sbucciare*) to peel 3. (*spellare*) to skin 4. (*far pagare caro*) to fleece. ♦ **pelarsi** *vr.* to lose (*v. irr.*) one's hair.
pelato *agg.* bald.
pelatura *sf.* 1. unhairing 2. (*sbucciatura*) peeling.
pellaio *sm.* furrier.
pellame *sm.* hides (*pl.*).
pelle *sf.* skin; (*di animale grosso*) hide || *articoli in —*, leather articles; *amici per la —*, bosom friends.
pellegrina *sf.* (*mantella*) tippet.
pellegrinaggio *sm.* pilgrimage: *in —*, on a pilgrimage.

pellegrinare *vi.* to wander, to roam.
pellegrino *sm.* pilgrim.
pellerossa *agg. e sm.* redskin.
pelletterìa *sf.* 1. leather goods 2. (*negozio*) leather goods shop.
pellicano *sm.* pelican.
pelliccerìa *sf.* 1. furriery 2. (*negozio*) furrier's shop.
pelliccia *sf.* fur.
pellicciaio *sm.* furrier.
pellìcola *sf.* film: *— a passo ridotto*, substandard film.
pelo *sm.* hair: *per un —*, by a hair's breadth; *cercare il — nell'uovo*, to split (*v. irr.*) hairs || *non avere peli sulla lingua*, to be outspoken.
peloso *agg.* hairy.
pelota *sf.* pelota.
peltro *sm.* pewter.
peluria *sf.* down || *coperto di —*, downy.
pelvi *sf.* pelvis.
pèlvico *agg.* pelvic.
pena *sf.* 1. (*punizione*) punishment 2. (*dolore*) pain 3. (*disturbo*) trouble || *essere in —*, to worry; *aver — di*, to pity; *a mala —*, hardly; *non ne vale la —*, it is not worth while.
penale *agg.* 1. criminal 2. (*relativo alla pena*) penal.
penalista *sm.* criminal lawyer.
penalità *sf.* penalty.
penalizzare *vt.* to penalize.
penare *vi.* 1. to suffer 2. (*far fatica*) to be hardly able.
pendaglio *sm.* pendant.
pendente *agg.* 1. pendent 2. (*inclinato*) leaning. ♦ **pendente** *sm.* pendant.
pendenza *sf.* 1. slope 2. (*grado d'inclinazione*) gradient 3. (*giur.*) pending suit 4. (*comm.*) outstanding account.
pèndere *vi.* 1. to hang (*v. irr.*) 2. (*inclinare*) to lean (*v. irr.*) 3. (*essere in declino*) to slope 4. (*incombere*) to overhang (*v. irr.*) 5. (*essere incerto*) to waver.
pendìo *sm.* slope.
pèndola *sf.* pendulum-clock.
pendolare *agg.* pendular.
pèndolo *sm.* pendulum.
pèndulo *agg.* pendulous.
pene *sm.* penis.
penetràbile *agg.* penetrable.
penetrabilità *sf.* penetrability.

penetrante *agg.* piercing.

penetrare *vi.* e *vt.* **1.** to penetrate **2.** (*con fatica; di freddo, suono*) to pierce **3.** (*furtivamente*) to steal (*v. irr.*) (into).

penetrazione *sf.* penetration.

penicillina *sf.* penicillin.

peninsulare *agg.* peninsular.

penisola *sf.* peninsula.

penitente *agg.* e *s.* penitent.

penitenza *sf.* **1.** (*teol.*) penance **2.** (*pentimento*) repentance **3.** (*nei giochi*) forfeit.

penitenziale *agg.* penitential.

penitenziario *agg.* penitentiary. ◆ **penitenziario** *sm.* jail.

penna *sf.* **1.** pen **2.** (*di uccello*) feather.

pennacchio *sm.* **1.** plume **2.** (*mil.*) panache.

pennecchio *sm.* wool on the distaff.

pennellare *vi.* **1.** to brush **2.** (*med.*) to paint.

pennellata *sf.* touch (of the brush).

pennellessa *sf.* flat brush.

pennello *sm.* brush.

pennino *sm.* nib.

pennone *sm.* (*mar.*) yard.

pennuto *agg.* feathered. ◆ **pennuto** *sm.* bird.

penombra *sf.* half-light

penoso *agg.* painful.

pensare *vi.* e *vt.* **1.** to think (*v. irr.*) (of) **2.** (*badare*) to look after || *pensa ai fatti tuoi*, mind your own business.

pensata *sf.* thought, idea.

pensatore *sm.* thinker.

pensiero *sm.* **1.** thought **2.** (*opinione*) mind, opinion **3.** (*ansia*) worry.

pensieroso *agg.* thoughtful.

pensile *agg.* hanging || *giardino* —, roof garden.

pensilina *sf.* **1.** penthouse **2.** (*di attesa*) shelter.

pensionàbile *agg.* pensionable.

pensionante *s.* boarder.

pensionato[1] *agg.* retired. ◆ **pensionato** *sm.* pensioner, retired person.

pensionato[2] *sm.* (*istituto*) hostel.

pensione *sf.* **1.** (*assegno vitalizio*) pension || *essere in* —, to be retired; *mettere in* —, to pension off **2.** (*albergo*) boarding-house || *essere a* —, to be boarding (at); — *completa*, full board.

pensoso *agg.* pensive.

pentaedro *sm.* pentahedron.

pentàgono *sm.* pentagon.

pentagramma *sm.* (*mus.*) pentagram.

pentàmetro *sm.* pentameter.

pentano *sm.* pentane.

Pentecoste *sf.* Pentecost, Whitsunday.

pentimento *sm.* repentance.

pentirsi *vr.* **1.** to repent **2.** (*rimpiangere*) to regret.

pèntodo *sm.* pentode.

péntola *sf.* pot.

penùltimo *agg.* e *sm.* last but one.

penuria *sf.* shortage, penury.

penzolare *vi.* to dangle.

penzoloni *agg.* **1.** (*dondolante*) dangling **2.** (*pèndente*) hanging.

peocio *sm.* mussel.

peonia *sf.* peony.

pepaiola *sf.* pepper-box.

pepare *vt.* to pepper.

pepato *agg.* peppery (*anche fig.*).

pepe *sm.* pepper.

peperone *sm.* pepper: *peperoni sott'aceto*, pickled peppers.

pepita *sf.* nugget.

peplo *sm.* peplum.

pepsina *sf.* pepsin.

peptone *sm.* peptone.

per *prep.* **1.** for: *fallo — me*, do it for me **2.** (*moto per luogo*) through: *passai per Roma*, I passed through Rome **3.** (*entro, per mezzo di*) by: *devo farlo — la fine dell'anno*, I have to do it by the end of the year; — *telegramma*, by telegram **4.** (*causa*) owing to, because of: *non potemmo andare — la nebbia*, we couldn't go owing to (because of) fog || — *l'addietro*, in the past; — *caso*, by chance; — *nulla*, not at all; — *sempre*, for ever; — *tempo*, early. ◆ **per** *cong.* **1.** (*finale*) to, in order to **2.** (*causale*) for.

pera *sf.* pear.

peràcido *sm.* peracid.

perbacco *inter.* by Jove.

perbene *agg.* respectable.

percalle *sm.* percale.

percentuale *agg.* per cent. ◆ **percentuale** *sf.* percentage.

percepìbile *agg.* **1.** perceptible **2.** (*di somme*) receivable.

percepire *vt.* **1.** to perceive **2.** (*di stipendio*) to receive.

percettìbile *agg.* perceptible.
percettivo *agg.* perceptive.
percezione *sf.* perception.
perché *cong.* 1. (*int.*) why 2. (*nelle risposte*) because 3. (*affinché*) so that. ◆ **perché** *sm.* reason, why: *chiedersi il* —, to wonder why.
perciò *cong.* therefore, so.
perclorato *sm.* perchlorate.
percòrrere *vt.* 1. to cover 2. (*attraversare*) to run (*v. irr.*) through.
percorso *sm.* 1. (*distanza*) distance 2. (*tragitto*) way 3. (*tracciato*) course.
percossa *sf.* blow.
percuòtere *vt.* to strike (*v. irr.*).
percussione *sf.* percussion.
percussore *sm.* percussion-pin.
perdente *agg.* losing. ◆ **perdente** *s.* loser.
pèrdere *vt.* 1. to lose (*v. irr.*) 2. (*di treno, occasione*) to miss 3. (*far acqua*) to leak. ◆ **pèrdersi** *vr.* 1. to get (*v. irr.*) lost 2. (*svanire*) to fade 3. (*rovinarsi*) to be ruined || — *d'animo*, to lose heart.
perdifiato (*nella loc. avv.*) *a* —, with all one's strength.
perdigiorno *sm.* idler.
pèrdita *sf.* 1. loss 2. (*falla, fuga*) leak.
perditempo *sm.* waste of time.
perdizione *sf.* perdition.
perdonàbile *agg.* pardonable.
perdonare *vt.* 1. to forgive (*v. irr.*) 2. (*risparmiare*) to spare. ◆ **perdonarsi** *vr.* to forgive oneself. ◆ **perdonarsi** *v. rec.* to forgive each other (one another).
perdono *sm.* forgiveness || *chiedere* —, to beg one's pardon.
perdurare *vi.* to continue.
perdutamente *avv.* desperately.
perduto *agg.* lost.
peregrinare *vi.* to wander, to roam.
peregrinazione *sf.* wandering, roaming.
peregrino *agg.* rare.
perenne *agg.* 1. perennial 2. (*eterno*) everlasting.
perennemente *avv.* 1. perennially 2. (*per sempre*) for ever.
perentorio *agg.* peremptory.
perequazione *sf.* equalization.
perfettamente *avv.* perfectly.
perfettìbile *agg.* perfectible.
perfettibilità *sf.* perfectibility.
perfetto *agg.* perfect. ◆ **perfetto**

sm. (*gramm.*) perfect.
perfezionamento *sm.* perfecting.
perfezionare *vt.* 1. to perfect 2. (*migliorare*) to improve. ◆ **perfezionarsi** *vr.* to improve.
perfezione *sf.* perfection: *alla* —, to perfection.
perfidamente *avv.* wickedly.
perfidia *sf.* wickedness.
pèrfido *agg.* wicked.
perfino *avv.* even.
perforare *vt.* 1. to pierce 2. (*d biglietti, schede*) to punch 3 (*mecc.*) to drill, to bore.
perforatore *agg.* perforating. ◆ **perforatore** *sm.* perforator.
perforatrice *sf.* (*macchina*) drill; punch.
perforazione *sf.* 1. perforation 2. (*mecc.*) drilling 3. (*di biglietti, schede*) punching.
pergamena *sf.* parchment.
pèrgola *sf.* bower.
pergolato *sm.* arbour.
pericardio *sm.* pericardium (*pl.* -ia).
pericolante *agg.* tottering.
perìcolo *sm.* danger || *mettere in* —, to endanger; *correre un* —, to be in danger.
pericolosamente *avv.* dangerously.
pericoloso *agg.* dangerous.
periferìa *sf.* 1. periphery 2. (*di città*) suburbs (*pl.*).
perifèrico *agg.* 1. peripheral 2. (*suburbano*) suburban.
perìfrasi *sf.* periphrasis (*pl.* -ses).
perifràstico *agg.* periphrastic.
perigèo *sm.* perigee.
perìmetro *sm.* perimeter.
periodicità *sf.* periodicity.
periòdico *agg. e sm.* periodical.
perìodo *sm.* period.
peripezìa *sf.* vicissitude.
pèriplo *sm.* circumnavigation.
perire *vi.* to perish.
periscopio *sm.* periscope.
peristilio *sm.* peristyle.
perito *sm.* 1. expert 2. (*comm.*) estimator.
peritonite *sf.* peritonitis.
perituro *agg.* perishable.
perizia *sf.* 1. (*abilità*) skill 2. (*valutazione*) survey.
perla *sf.* pearl.
perlàceo *agg.* pearly.
perlìfero *agg.* pearl (*attr.*).
perlomeno *avv.* at least.
perlustrare *vt.* 1. to reconnoitre 2. (*di polizia*) to patrol.

perlustratore *sm.* scout.

perlustrazione *sf.* 1. reconnaissance 2. (*di polizia*) patrol || *essere in* —, to be on a reconnaissance.

permalosità *sf.* touchiness.

permaloso *agg.* touchy.

permanente *agg.* permanent. ♦ permanente *sf.* permanent wave.

permanentemente *avv.* permanently.

permanenza *sf.* 1. permanence 2. (*soggiorno*) stay.

permanere *vi.* 1. to remain 2. (*durare*) to last.

permanganato *sm.* permanganate.

permeàbile *agg.* permeable.

permeabilità *sf.* permeability.

permeare *vt.* to permeate.

permesso *agg.* allowed. ♦ permesso *sm.* 1. leave: *in* —, on leave 2. (*autorizzazione*) licence || *documento di* —, permit.

perméttere *vt.* to allow || *permettete?*, may I? ♦ perméttersi *vr.* (*prendersi la libertà*) to take (*v. irr.*) the liberty (of) || — *il lusso*, to afford.

pèrmuta *sf.* exchange.

permutàbile *agg.* exchangeable.

permutare *vt.* to exchange.

permutazione *sf.* permutation.

pernice *sf.* partridge.

pernicioso *agg.* pernicious.

perno *sm.* pivot.

pernottamento *sm.* overnight stay.

pernottare *vi.* to stay overnight.

pero *sm.* pear-tree.

però *cong.* but.

peronòspora *sf.* mildew.

perorare *vt.* to plead.

perorazione *sf.* pleading.

peròssido *sm.* peroxide.

perpendicolare *agg. e sf.* perpendicular.

perpetrare *vt.* to perpetrate.

perpetuamente *avv.* perpetually.

perpetuare *vt.* to perpetuate. ♦ perpetuarsi *vr.* to last.

perpetuità *sf.* perpetuity.

perpetuo *agg.* perpetual: *in* —, perpetually.

perplessità *sf.* perplexity.

perplesso *agg.* perplexed: *rendere* —, to perplex.

perquisire *vt.* to search.

perquisizione *sf.* search.

persecutore *sm.* persecutor.

persecuzione *sf.* persecution.

perseguìbile *agg.* (*giur.*) prosecu-table.

perseguire *vt.* 1. to pursue 2. (*giur.*) to prosecute.

perseguitare *vt.* to persecute.

perseguitato *sm.* persecuted person.

perseverante *agg.* persevering.

perseveranza *sf.* perseverance.

perseverare *vi.* to persevere.

persiana *sf.* shutter.

persiano *agg. e sm.* Persian.

persistente *agg.* persistent.

persistenza *sf.* persistence.

persìstere *vi.* to persist.

persona *sf.* person: *di* —, personally; — *giuridica*, artificial person.

personaggio *sm.* 1. personage 2. (*di romanzo ecc.*) character.

personale *agg.* personal. ♦ personale *sm.* 1. staff 2. (*corporatura*) figure.

personalità *sf.* personality: — *giuridica*, legal status.

personalmente *avv.* personally.

personificare *vt.* 1. to personify 2. (*teat.*) to play.

personificazione *sf.* personification.

perspicace *agg.* shrewd.

perspicacia *sf.* shrewdness

perspicuo *agg.* perspicuous.

persuadere *vt.* to persuade. ♦ persuadersi *vr.* to convince oneself.

persuasione *sf.* persuasion.

persuasivo *agg.* persuasive.

pertanto *cong.* therefore.

pèrtica *sf.* perch.

pertinace *agg.* pertinacious.

pertinacia *sf.* pertinacity.

pertinente *agg.* pertinent.

pertinenza *sf.* pertinence.

pertosse *sf.* whooping cough.

pertugio *sm.* hole.

perturbare *vt.* to disturb.

perturbatore *agg.* disturbing. ♦ perturbatore *sm.* disturber.

perturbazione *sf.* disturbance.

pervàdere *vt.* to pervade.

pervenire *vi.* to arrive (at).

perversione *sf.* perversion.

perversità *sf.* perversity.

perverso *agg.* perverse.

pervertire *vt.* to pervert. ♦ pervertirsi *vr.* to go (*v. irr.*) astray.

pervicace *agg.* obstinate.

pervicacia *sf.* obstinacy.

pervinca *sf.* periwinkle.

pesa *sf.* 1. (*luogo*) weigh-house 2. (*apparecchio*) weighing-machine.

pesante *agg.* heavy.

pesantezza *sf.* heaviness.
pesare *vt.* to weigh. ◆ **pesare** *vi.*
1. to weigh 2. (*fig.*) to lie (*v. irr.*)
heavy.
pesata *sf.* weighing.
pesca[1] *sf.* (*bot.*) peach.
pesca[2] *sf.* 1. (*il pescare*) fishing 2.
(*industria*) fishery 3. (*il pescato*)
catch.
pescaggio *sm.* (*mar.*) draught.
pescare *vt.* 1. to fish 2. (*fig.*) to
fish out 3. (*cogliere sul fatto*) to
catch (*v. irr.*) red-handed 4. (*carte*)
to draw (*v. irr.*). ◆ **pescare** *vi.*
to draw.
pescatore *sm.* 1. fisher 2. (*con lenza*) angler.
pesce *sm.* fish: — *rosso*, goldfish;
— *persico*, perch.
pescecane *sm.* shark.
peschereccio *agg.* fishing. ◆ **peschereccio** *sm.* fishing-boat.
pescheria *sf.* 1. fish-shop 2. (*mercato*) fish-market.
peschiera *sf.* fish-pond.
pesciaiola *sf.* (*cuc.*) fish-kettle.
pesco *sm.* peach-tree.
pescoso *agg.* fishy.
pesista *sm.* weight thrower.
peso *sm.* weight: *a* —, by weight.
pessimismo *sm.* pessimism.
pessimista *agg.* pessimistic. ◆ **pessimista** *s.* pessimist.
pessimìstico *agg.* pessimistic.
pèssimo *agg.* worst, very bad.
pesta *sf.* 1. track 2. (*difficoltà*) difficulty.
pestaggio *sm.* scuffle.
pestare *vt.* 1. to pound 2. (*picchiare*) to beat (*v. irr.*) 3. (*calpestare*) to tread (*v. irr.*) on.
pestata *sf.* 1. (*lo schiacciare*) pounding 2. (*il calpestare*) treading.
peste *sf.* plague.
pestello *sm.* pestle.
pestifero *agg.* pestiferous.
pestilenza *sf.* plague.
pestilenziale *agg.* pestilential.
pesto *agg.* pounded: *buio* —, pitch
dark; *avere gli occhi pesti*, to have
rings under one's eyes.
pètalo *sm.* petal.
petardo *sm.* petard.
petizione *sf.* petition.
petraia *sf.* 1. (*cava*) quarry 2. (*mucchio di pietre*) heap of stones.
petrografia *sf.* petrography.
petroliera *sf.* tanker.
petrolifero *agg.* oil (*attr.*).

petrolio *sm.* oil.
pettégola *sf.* gossiper.
pettegolare *vi.* to gossip.
pettegolezzo *sm.* gossip.
pettégolo *agg.* gossipy. ◆ **pettégolo** *sm.* gossiper.
pettinare *vt.* to comb. ◆ **pettinar-
si** *vr.* to comb one's hair.
pettinato *sm.* worsted.
pettinatrice *sf.* 1. hairdresser 2.
(*industria tessile*) comber.
pettinatura *sf.* 1. hairdo 2. (*industria tessile*) combing.
pèttine *sm.* comb.
pettirosso *sm.* robin.
petto *sm.* 1. breast 2. (*torace*) chest
|| — *a* —, face to face; *prendere
di* —, to face.
pettorale *agg. e sm.* pectoral.
pettorina *sf.* stomacher.
pettoruto *agg.* 1. full-breasted 2.
(*fig.*) haughty.
petulante *agg.* pert.
petulanza *sf.* pertness.
petunia *sf.* petunia.
pezza *sf.* 1. patch 2. (*macchia*) spot
|| — *di stoffa*, roll.
pezzato *agg.* spotted.
pezzente *agg.* beggarly. ◆ **pezzente** *s.* ragamuffin.
pezzo *sm.* piece: *fare a pezzi*, to
tear (*v. irr.*) to pieces; *a pezzi e
bocconi*, piecemeal; — *grosso* (*fig.*),
bigwig; — *di ricambio*, spare part.
pezzuola *sf.* handkerchief.
piacente *agg.* pleasant.
piacere[1] *sm.* 1. pleasure 2. (*favore*)
favour || *per* —, please; —! (*nelle
presentazioni*), how do you do!
piacere[2] *vi.* to like: *gli piace leggere*, he likes reading, he likes to
read; *come pare e piace*, as one
pleases.
piacévole *agg.* pleasant.
piacimento *sm.* pleasure, liking: *a*
—, as much as one likes.
piaga *sf.* 1. sore 2. (*calamità*)
plague 3. (*fig.*) nuisance.
piagnisteo *sm.* moaning.
piagnucolare *vi.* to whimper.
piagnucolio *sm.* whimper.
piagnucoloso *agg.* whimpering.
pialla *sf.* plane.
piallare *vt.* to plane.
piallatrice *sf.* planer.
piallatura *sf.* 1. planing 2. (*trucioli*) shavings (*pl.*).
piana *sf.* plane.
pianeggiante *agg.* level.

pianella *sf.* **1.** (*pantofola*) slipper **2.** (*mattonella*) flat tile.

pianeròttolo *sm.* landing.

pianeta *sm.* planet.

piangente *agg.* weeping, crying.

piàngere *vi.* to cry, to weep (*v. irr.*). ♦ **piàngere** *vt.* to weep **2.** (*un lutto*) to mourn || *— a calde lacrime*, to weep one's heart out.

pianificare *vt.* to plan.

pianificazione *sf.* planning.

pianista *s.* pianist.

piano[1] *agg.* **1.** flat **2.** (*chiaro*) clear **3.** (*semplice*) simple.

piano[2] *sm.* **1.** plain **2.** (*di casa*) floor, storey **3.** (*strato*) layer **4.** (*superficie piana, livello*) plane **5.** (*progetto*) plan **6.** (*cine*) primo —, close up || *— stradale*, roadway; *in primo* —, in the foreground.

piano[3] *avv.* **1.** (*lentamente*) slowly **2.** (*sommessamente*) softly **3.** (*con cautela*) gently.

pianoforte *sm.* piano.

pianola *sf.* barrel-organ.

pianta *sf.* **1.** plant **2.** (*carta topografica*) map **3.** (*del piede*) sole || *di sana — (completamente)*, completely; (*di nuovo*) anew.

piantagione *sf.* plantation.

piantare *vt.* **1.** to plant **2.** (*conficcare*) to drive (*v. irr.*) **3.** (*lasciare*) to leave (*v. irr.*) || *piantarla*, to stop.

piantatore *sm.* planter.

pianterreno *sm.* ground-floor.

pianto *sm.* **1.** tears (*pl.*): *scoppiare in* —, to burst (*v. irr.*) into tears **2.** (*dolore*) grief.

piantonamento *sm.* guarding.

piantonare *vt.* to guard.

piantone[1] *sm.* soldier on guard.

piantone[2] *sm.* (*agr.*) shoot.

pianura *sf.* plain.

piastra *sf.* **1.** plate **2.** (*di marmo*) slab **3.** (*moneta*) piastre.

piastrella *sf.* tile.

piastrellare *vt.* to tile.

piastrellatura *sf.* tiling.

piastrina *sf.* plaque.

piattaforma *sf.* platform.

piattello *sm.* pan || *tiro al* —, trap-shooting.

piattino *sm.* saucer.

piatto[1] *agg.* flat.

piatto[2] *sm.* **1.** dish **2.** (*portata*) course **3.** (*di lama*) flat **4.** (*di grammofono*) turn-table.

piazza *sf.* **1.** square **2.** (*comm.*) market || *mettere qc. in* —, to make (*v. irr.*) sthg. public.

piazzaforte *sf.* stronghold.

piazzale *sm.* large square.

piazzamento *sm.* place.

piazzare *vt.* to place. ♦ **piazzarsi** *vr.* (*sport*) to be placed.

piazzista *sm.* salesman (*pl.* -men).

picaresco *agg.* picaresque.

picca *sf.* pike || *picche (alle carte)*, spades (*pl.*).

piccante *agg.* **1.** piquant **2.** (*salace*) spicy.

piccarsi *vr.* to plume oneself (on).

piccato *agg.* resentful.

picchettare *vt.* **1.** to peg out **2.** (*mil.*) to picket.

picchetto *sm.* **1.** peg **2.** (*mil.*) picket: *essere di* —, to be on picket.

picchiare *vt.* e *vi.* **1.** (*percuotere*) to beat (*v. irr.*) **2.** (*battere*) to strike (*v. irr.*) **3.** (*bussare*) to knock **4.** (*aer.*) to pitch || *— in testa (di motore)*, to ping. ♦ **picchiarsi** *vr. rec.* to fight (*v. irr.*).

picchiata *sf.* **1.** beating **2.** (*aer.*) dive || *scendere in* —, to dive.

picchiatello *agg.* slightly crazy.

picchiettare *vt.* **1.** (*battere*) to tap **2.** (*chiazzare*) to spot.

picchiettato *agg.* spotted.

picchiettìo *sm.* tapping.

picchio[1] *sm.* **1.** (*colpo*) blow **2.** (*alla porta*) knock.

picchio[2] *sm.* (*zool.*) woodpecker.

picchiotto *sm.* door-knocker.

piccinerìa *sf.* meanness.

piccino *agg.* **1.** little **2.** (*fig.*) mean.

piccionaia *sf.* **1.** pigeon-house **2.** (*teat.*) gallery.

piccione *sm.* pigeon.

picco *sm.* peak || *a* —, vertically; *colare a* —, *mandare a* —, to sink (*v. irr.*).

piccolezza *sf.* **1.** smallness **2.** (*meschinità*) meanness **3.** (*inezia*) trifle.

piccolo *agg.* **1.** small, little **2.** (*di statura, breve*) short **3.** (*giovane*) young **4.** (*meschino*) mean **5.** (*leggero*) light.

piccone *sm.* pick(axe).

piccozza *sf.* axe.

pidocchieria *sf.* meanness.

pidocchio *sm.* **1.** louse (*pl.* lice) **2.** (*fig.*) miser.

pidocchioso *agg.* **1.** lousy **2.** (*fig.*) stingy.

piede *sm.* foot (*pl.* feet): *a piedi*, on foot || *a — libero*, on bail; *prender —*, to get (*v. irr.*) a footing.

piedistallo *sm.* pedestal.

piega *sf.* 1. fold 2. (*fatta ad arte*) pleat 3. (*segno*) crease || *messa in — (di capelli)*, set.

piegàbile *agg.* folding.

piegamento *sm.* 1. folding 2. (*flessione*) flexing.

piegare *vt.* 1. to fold 2. (*flettere, anche fig.*) to bend (*v. irr.*). ◆ **piegare** *vi.* 1. (*voltare*) to turn 2. (*curvarsi*) to bend. ◆ **piegarsi** *vr.* to bend.

piegatrice *sf.* (*mecc.*) bending-machine.

pieghettare *vt.* to pleat.

pieghévole *agg.* 1. pliable 2. (*atto a essere piegato*) folding. ◆ **pieghévole** *sm.* folder.

pieghevolezza *sf.* pliability.

piena *sf.* 1. flood, spate 2. (*folla*) crowd.

pienamente *avv.* fully.

pienezza *sf.* 1. fullness 2. (*massimo grado*) height.

pieno *agg.* full: *— zeppo*, full up; *in — (completamente)*, fully, (*esattamente*) exactly, (*nel mezzo*) in the middle; *in — giorno*, in broad daylight. ◆ **pieno** *sm.* (*il colmo*) middle || *fare il — (auto)*, to fill up.

pietà *sf.* 1. pity 2. (*relig.*) piety || *aver — di*, to have mercy on; *far —*, to arouse pity; *per —!*, for pity's sake!

pietanza *sf.* 1. main course 2. (*piatto*) dish.

pietismo *sm.* pietism.

pietosamente *avv.* pitifully.

pietoso *agg.* pitiful.

pietra *sf.* stone: *posare la prima —*, to lay the foundation stone.

pietraia *sf.* V. petraia.

pietrificare *vt.* to petrify. ◆ **pietrificarsi** *vr.* to petrify.

pietrina *sf.* flint.

pietrisco *sm.* rubble.

pietroso *agg.* stony.

piffero *sm.* pipe.

pigiama *sm.* pyjamas (*pl.*).

pigia pigia *sm.* awful crush.

pigiare *vt.* to press. ◆ **pigiarsi** *vr.* to crowd.

pigione *sf.* rent: *stare a — presso*, to lodge with.

pigmentato *agg.* pigmented.

pigmentazione *sf.* pigmentation.

pigmento *sm.* pigment.

pigmeo *sm.* pigmy.

pigna *sf.* pinecone.

pignatta *sf.* pot.

pignolerìa *sf.* faultfinding.

pignolo *sm.* 1. (*bot.*) pine-seed 2. (*fig.*) faultfinder.

pignoramento *sm.* attachment.

pignorare *vt.* to distrain.

pigolare *vi.* to peep.

pigolìo *sm.* peep.

pigramente *avv.* 1. lazily 2. (*lentamente*) sluggishly.

pigrizia *sf.* 1. laziness 2. (*lentezza*) sluggishness.

pigro *agg.* 1. lazy 2. (*lento*) sluggish.

pila *sf.* pile: *— a secco*, dry battery.

pilastro *sm.* pillar.

pìllola *sf.* pill: *— anticoncezionale*, contraceptive (pill), the "pill".

pilone *sm.* 1. pylon 2. (*di ponte*) pier || *— d'ormeggio*, mooring-mast.

piloro *sm.* pylorus (*pl.* -ri).

pilota *sm.* 1. pilot 2. (*di auto*) driver.

pilotaggio *sm.* pilotage: *scuola di —*, flying-school.

pilotare *vt.* 1. to pilot 2. (*un'auto*) to drive (*v. irr.*).

piluccare *vt.* to nibble.

piluccone *sm.* nibbler.

pinacoteca *sf.* picture-gallery.

pinastro *sm.* pinaster.

pindàrico *agg.* Pindaric.

pineta *sf.* pinewood.

pingue *agg.* 1. fat 2. (*ricco*) rich.

pinguèdine *sf.* fatness.

pinguino *sm.* penguin.

pinna *sf.* 1. fin 2. (*sport*) flipper.

pinnàcolo[1] *sm.* pinnacle.

pinnàcolo[2] *sm.* (*gioco*) pinochle.

pino *sm.* pine (-tree).

pinolo *sm.* pine-seed.

pinta *sf.* pint.

pinza *sf.* pliers (*pl.*), pincers (*pl.*).

pinzetta *sf.* tweezers (*pl.*).

pio *agg.* pious || *opera pia*, charitable organization.

pioggia *sf.* rain: *sotto la —*, in the rain.

piolo *sm.* V. piuolo.

piombare *vt.* 1. to plumb 2. (*tip.*) to lead || *— un dente*, to stop a tooth. ◆ **piombare** *vi.* 1. (*cade-*

re) to fall (*v. irr.*) heavily **2.** (*assalire*) to assail **3.** (*precipitarsi*) to rush.

piombatura *sf.* sealing, leading.

piombino *sm.* **1.** plummet **2.** (*sigillo*) leaden seal.

♦ **piombo** *sm.* **1** lead **2.** (*sigillo*) leaden seal **3.** (*pallottola*) bullet ‖ *filo a* —, plumb line; *a* —, perpendicularly; *di* —, leaden; *andare coi piedi di* —, to proceed very cautiously.

pioniere *sm.* pioneer.

pioppeto *sm.* poplargrove.

pioppo *sm.* poplar.

piorrea *sf.* pyorrhoea.

piovano *agg.* rain (*attr.*).

piovasco *sm.* shower.

piòvere *vi.* to rain, to pour (*anche fig.*).

piovigginare *vi.* to drizzle.

piovigginoso *agg.* drizzly, rainy.

piovoso *agg.* rainy.

piovra *sf.* octopus.

pipa *sf.* pipe.

pipetta *sf.* (*chim.*) pipette.

pipistrello *sm.* bat.

pipita *sf.* agnail.

pira *sf.* pyre.

piramidale *ag.* pyramidal.

piràmide *sf.* pyramid.

pirata *sm.* pirate ‖ — *della strada*, hit-and-run driver.

piraterìa *sf.* piracy.

pìrico *agg.* *polvere pirica*, gunpowder.

pirite *sf.* pyrite(s).

piroetta *sf.* pirouette.

piroettare *vi.* to pirouette.

piroga *sf.* pirogue.

pirografìa *sf.* pyrography.

piròscafo *sm.* steamer.

pirotècnica *sf.* pyrotechnics.

pirotècnico *agg.* pyrotechnic(al): *spettacolo* —, fireworks. ♦ **pirotècnico** *sm.* pyrotechnist.

piscia *sf.* piss.

pisciare *vi.* to piss.

pisciata *sf.* piss.

pisciatoio *sm.* urinal.

piscicoltura *sf.* pisciculture.

piscina *sf.* swimming-pool.

pisello *sm.* pea.

pisolino *sm.* nap.

pista *sf.* **1.** (*traccia*) track **2.** (*di animale*) trail **3.** (*aer.*) strip.

pistacchio *sm.* pistachio.

pistillo *sm.* pistil.

pistola *sf.* pistol.

pistone *sm.* piston.

pitagòrico *agg. e sm.* Pythagorean: *tavola pitagorica*, multiplication table.

pitale *sm.* chamber pot.

pitocco *agg.* **1.** mean **2.** (*fig.*) stingy. ♦ **pitocco** *sm.* **1.** beggar **2.** (*fig.*) mean person.

pitone *sm.* python.

pitonessa *sf.* pythoness.

pittore *sm.* painter.

pittoresco *agg.* picturesque.

pittòrico *agg.* pictorial.

pittrice *sf.* paintress.

pittura *sf.* **1.** painting **2.** (*dipinto, descrizione*) picture **3.** (*vernice*) paint.

pitturare *vt.* to paint.

più *avv.* **1.** (*comp. di maggioranza con agg. polisillabi, con s., v. e avv.*) more: *questo libro è* — *costoso di quello*, this book is more expensive than that; *ho* — *libri di te*, I have more books than you; *lavoro* — *di te*, I work more than you **2.** (*comp. di maggioranza con agg. e avv. monosillabi e bisillabi terminanti in y, er, ow*) ...er: *è* — *gentile di lui*, he is kinder than he is **3.** (*superl. rel., corrispondente a* "*more*") the most, the more (*fra due*): *è il libro* — *costoso di tutti*, it is the most expensive book of all; *la* — *bella delle due sorelle*, the more beautiful of the two sisters **4.** (*superl. rel., corrispondente a* "*...er*") the ...est, the ...er (*fra due*): *è la persona* — *felice che conosca*, she is the happiest person I know; *è la* — *graziosa delle due sorelle*, she is the prettier of the sisters **4.** (*di tempo*) no longer, no more, not again ‖ *mai* —, never again. ♦ **più** *agg.* **1.** more **2.** (*diversi*) several. ♦ **più** *sm.* most: *il* — *è fatto*, most of it is done ‖ *i* —, most people (*al sing.*).

pluma *sf.* **1.** feather, down **2.** (*ornamento*) plume.

piumaggio *sm.* plumage.

piumino *sm.* **1.** down **2.** (*copriletto*) eiderdown **3.** (*per la cipria*) powder-puff **4.** (*per spolverare*) duster.

piuttosto *avv.* rather. ♦ **piuttosto che, di** *cong.* rather than.

piuolo *sm.* **1.** peg: *scala a piuoli*, ladder **2.** (*paletto*) post.

piva *sf.* bagpipe.
pivello *sm.* greenhorn.
piviere *sm.* plover.
pizzicàgnolo *sm.* delicatessen seller.
pizzicare *vt.* **1.** to pinch, to nip **2.** (*di insetti*) to bite (*v. irr.*) **3.** (*di sostanza acre*) to burn (*v. irr.*) **4.** (*con parole*) to tease **5.** (*sorprendere*) to catch (*v. irr.*). ♦ **pizzicare** *vi.* (*prudere*) to itch, to tingle.
pizzicherìa *sf.* **1.** delicatessen shop **2.** (*merci*) delicatessen.
pìzzico *sm.* **1.** pinch **2.** (*pizzicore*) itch **3.** (*fig.*) bit.
pizzicore *sm.* itch.
pizzicotto *sm.* pinch.
pizzo *sm.* **1.** lace (*solo sing.*) **2.** (*di montagna*) peak **3.** (*barba*) pointed beard.
placare *vt.* to appease: — *la fame di qu.*, to satisfy so.'s hunger; — *la sete di qu.*, to quench so.'s thirst. ♦ **placarsi** *vr.* to calm down.
placca *sf.* plaque.
placcare *vt.* to plate (sthg. with).
placcatura *sf.* plating.
placenta *sf.* placenta.
placidità *sf.* placidity.
plàcido *agg.* placid.
plaga *sf.* region.
plagiare *vt. e vi.* to plagiarize.
plagiario *agg.* plagiaristic. ♦ **plagiario** *sm.* plagiarist.
plagio *sm.* plagiarism.
planare *vi.* to glide down.
planata *sf.* glide.
plancia *sf.* (*mar.*) deck.
plancton *sm.* plankton.
planetario *agg.* planetary. ♦ **planetario** *sm.* planetarium (*pl.* -ia).
planimetrìa *sf.* planimetry, plan.
planimètrico *agg.* planimetric(al).
planisfero *sm.* planisphere.
plantìgrado *agg. e sm.* plantigrade.
plasma *sm.* plasma.
plasmare *vt.* to mould.
plàstica *sf.* **1.** (*operazione*) plastic operation **2.** (*materiale*) plastic.
plasticare *vt.* to plasticize.
plasticità *sf.* plasticity.
plàstico *agg.* plastic. ♦ **plàstico** *sm.* **1.** plastic model **2.** (*carta topografica*) relief map.
plastilina *sf.* plasticine.
plàtano *sm.* plane (-tree).
platea *sf.* pit: *poltrona di* —, stall.
plateale *agg.* coarse.

platinare *vt.* **1.** to platinize **2.** (*di capelli*) to bleach.
plàtino *sm.* platinum.
platònico *agg.* Platonic.
plaudente *agg.* applauding.
plausibile *agg.* plausible.
plàuso *sm.* **1.** applause **2.** (*lode*) praise.
plebaglia *sf.* mob.
plebe *sf.* populace.
plebeo *agg. e sm.* plebeian.
plebiscitario *agg.* plebiscitary.
plebiscito *sm.* plebiscite.
plenario *agg.* plenary.
plenilunio *sm.* plenilune.
plenipotenziario *agg. e sm.* plenipotentiary.
pleonasmo *sm.* pleonasm.
pleonàstico *agg.* pleonastic.
plesso *sm.* plexus.
plètora *sf.* plethora.
pletòrico *agg.* plethoric.
plettro *sm.* plectrum (*pl.* -ra).
plèura *sf.* pleura (*pl.* -rae).
pleurite *sf.* pleurisy.
plico *sm.* **1.** packet **2.** (*busta*) cover: *in* — *separato*, under separate cover.
plotone *sm.* platoon.
plùmbeo *agg.* leaden.
plurale *agg. e sm.* plural.
pluralismo *sm.* pluralism.
pluralità *sf.* plurality.
pluricellulare *agg.* multicellular.
plusvalore *sm.* plus value.
plutòcrate *sm.* plutocrat.
plutocrazìa *sf.* plutocracy.
pneumàtico *agg.* pneumatic, inflatable. ♦ **pneumàtico** *sm.* (*di auto*) tyre.
pneumatorace *sm.* pneumothorax.
pochezza *sf.* (*scarsità, ristrettezza*) scantiness, insufficiency.
pochìssimo *agg. e avv.* **1.** very little **2.** (*rarissimamente*) very seldom. ♦ **pochìssimi** *sm. pl.* very few.
poco *avv.* **1.** not very (*con agg. e avv.*), little (*con comp., p. passati, verbi*): *a* — *a* —, little by little; — *per volta*, a little at a time **2.** (*di tempo*) a short time ‖ *fra* —, soon. ♦ **poco** *agg.* **1.** little (*pl.* few) **2.** (*di tempo*) short. ♦ **poco** *pron. e sm.* little (*pl.* few): *un* — *di*, a little.
podere *sm.* farm.
poderoso *agg.* powerful.
podio *sm.* platform.

podismo sm. **1.** walking **2.** (sport) foot-racing.

podista sm. (sport) foot-racer.

podìstico agg. foot (attr.).

poema sm. poem.

poesìa sf. **1.** poetry **2.** (composizione poetica) poem.

poeta sm. poet.

poetare vi. to write (v. irr.) poetry.

poètico agg. poetic(al).

poggiapiedi sm. footstool.

poggiare vi. e vt. to rest. ♦ **poggiarsi** vr. to lean (v. irr.) against.

poggio sm. hillock.

poi avv. **1.** then **2.** (più tardi) later || d'ora in —, from now on.

poiché cong. since, as.

polacca sf. (mus.) polonaise.

polacco agg. Polish. ♦ **polacco** sm. Pole.

polare agg. polar || stella —, pole-star.

polarità sf. polarity.

polarizzare vt. to polarize.

polarizzato agg. polarizing. ♦ **polarizzatore** sm. polarizer.

polarizzazione sf. polarization.

polca sf. polka.

polèmica sf. polemic.

polèmico agg. e sm. polemic.

polemista s. polemist.

polemizzare vi. to polemize.

poliandrìa sf. polyandry.

policlìnico sm. polyclinic.

policromìa sf. polychromy.

policromo agg. polychrome.

polièdrico agg. **1.** polyhedral **2.** (fig.) versatile.

poliedro sm. polyhedron.

polifonìa sf. polyphony.

polifònico agg. polyphonic.

poligamìa sf. polygamy.

polìgamo agg. polygamous. ♦ **polìgamo** sm. polygamist.

poliglotta s. polyglot.

polìgono sm. polygon || — di tiro, shooting-range.

polimerizzazione sf. polymerization.

polìmero agg. polymeric. ♦ **polìmero** sm. polymer.

polimorfismo sm. polymorphism.

poliomielite sf. poliomyelitis.

poliomielìtico agg. polio (attr.). ♦ **poliomielìtico** sm. person who has had polio.

pòlipo sm. polyp.

polisìllabo agg. polysyllabic(al). ♦ **polisìllabo** sm. polysyllable.

politècnico agg. e sm. polytechnic.

politeismo sm. polytheism.

politeista agg. polytheistic. ♦ **politeista** s. polytheist.

polìtica sf. **1.** politics **2.** (linea di condotta) policy.

politicante sm. petty politician.

polìtico agg. **1.** political **2.** (sagace) politic || uomo —, politician.

polivalente agg. polyvalent.

polizìa sf. police (us. al pl.).

poliziesco agg. **1.** police (attr.) **2.** (di film ecc.) detective (attr.).

poliziotto sm. policeman (pl. -men).

pòlizza sf. **1.** policy **2.** (ricevuta) bill.

polla sf. spring.

pollaio sm. hen-house.

pollame sm. poultry.

pollastra sf. pullet.

pollastro sm. cockerel.

pòllice sm. **1.** thumb **2.** (del piede) big toe **3.** (misura) inch.

pollicoltore sm. poultryman (pl. -men).

pollicoltura sf. poultry-farming.

pòlline sm. pollen.

pollivéndolo sm. poulterer.

pollo sm. **1.** chicken **2.** (fig.) dupe.

polmonare agg. pulmonary.

polmone sm. lung: — d'acciaio, iron lung.

polmonite sf. pneumonia.

polo¹ sm. pole.

polo² sm. (sport) polo.

polpa sf. **1.** (di frutta) pulp **2.** (carne) lean meat.

polpaccio sm. calf (pl. calves).

polpastrello sm. finger-tip.

polpetta sf. meat-ball, croquette.

polposo agg. pulpy.

polsino sm. cuff.

polso sm. **1.** wrist **2.** (fig.) energy **3.** (pulsazione) pulse **4.** (polsino) cuff || tastare il — a qu., to feel (v. irr.) so.'s pulse; uomo di —, energetic man.

poltiglia sf. **1.** pulp **2.** (fanghiglia) mud.

poltrire vi. to idle.

poltrona sf. **1.** armchair **2.** (teat.) stall.

poltrone agg. idle. ♦ **poltrone** sm. idler.

poltronerìa sf. idleness.

pòlvere sf. **1.** dust **2.** (sostanza polverizzata) powder || togliere la —, to dust.

polveriera sf. powder-magazine.

polverizzare *vt.* to pulverize. ♦
  polverizzarsi *vr.* to pulverize.
polverone *sm.* cloud of dust.
polveroso *agg.* dusty.
pomata *sf.* salve.
pomello *sm.* **1.** (*di porta ecc.*) knob
  2. (*di guancia*) cheek-bone.
pomeridiano *agg.* **1.** afternoon
  (*attr.*) **2.** (*con le ore*) p. m. (post
  meridiem): *alle 5 pomeridiane*,
  at five o'clock.
pomeriggio *sm.* afternoon.
pòmice *sf.* pumice.
pomo *sm.* **1.** (*mela*) apple **2.** (*di
  porta ecc.*) knob.
pomodoro *sm.* tomato.
pompa *sf.* **1.** pump **2.** (*fasto*) pomp
  3. (*ostentazione*) display || *impresa
  di pompe funebri*, undertaker's
  business; *far — di sé*, to show (*v.
  irr.*) off.
pompare *vt.* **1.** to pump **2.** (*fig.*)
  to puff up.
pompelmo *sm.* grapefruit.
pompiere *sm.* fireman (*pl.* -men).
pomposità *sf.* pomposity.
pomposo *agg.* pompous.
ponderàbile *agg.* ponderable.
ponderabilità *sf.* ponderability.
ponderare *vt.* to ponder.
ponderatamente *avv.* after reflection.
ponderatezza *sf.* circumspection.
ponderato *agg.* pondered.
ponderazione *sf.* consideration.
ponderoso *agg.* ponderous.
ponente *sm.* west.
ponte *sm.* **1.** bridge: *— girevole*,
  swing bridge **2.** (*mar.*) deck **3.**
  (*impalcatura*) scaffold || *rompere i
  ponti con* (*fig.*), to break (*v. irr.*)
  with.
pontéfice *sm.* pope.
pontificale *agg.* pontifical.
pontificare *vi.* to pontificate.
pontificato *sm.* pontificate.
pontificio *agg.* papal.
pontile *sm.* landing-stage.
pontone *sm.* pontoon.
ponzare *vi.* to rack one's brains.
popolamento *sm.* peopling.
popolano *agg.* common. ♦ **popola-
  no** *sm.* man of the people || *i
  popolani*, the common people.
popolare[1] *vt.* to people. ♦ **popo-
  larsi** *vr.* to become (*v. irr.*) pop-
  ulated.
popolare[2] *agg.* **1.** popular **2.** (*tradizionale*) folk (*attr.*).

popolaresco *agg.* popular-like.
popolarità *sf.* popularity.
popolarizzare *vt.* to popularize.
popolazione *sf.* population.
pòpolo *sm.* **1.** (*gente*) people (*pl.*)
  2. (*nazione*) people.
popoloso *agg.* populous.
popone *sm.* melon.
poppa[1] *sf.* **1.** (*mar.*) stern || *avere il
  vento in —*, to sail before the
  wind; *a —*, astern.
poppa[2] *sf.* breast.
poppante *s.* suckling.
poppare *vt.* to suck.
poppata *sf.* suck: *ora della —*,
  feeding-time.
poppatoio *sm.* feeding-bottle.
populismo *sm.* populism.
populista *agg.* populistic. ♦ **populista** *s.* populist.
porcaro *sm.* swineherd.
porcellana *sf.* china (*solo sing.*).
porcherìa *sf.* **1.** dirt **2.** (*azione di-
  sonesta*) dirty trick **3.** (*detto indecente*) obscene word **4.** (*atto indecente*) obscene act **5.** (*cibo cattivo*) revolting stuff **6.** (*cose senza
  valore*) rubbish.
porcile *sm.* pigsty.
porcino *agg.* pig (*attr.*). ♦ **porcino** *sm.* (*fungo*) boletus.
porco *sm.* **1.** pig **2.** (*cuc.*) pork.
porcospino *sm.* porcupine.
pòrfido *sm.* porphyry.
pòrgere *vt.* **1.** to hand **2.** (*offrire*)
  to offer.
pornografìa *sf.* pornography.
pornogràfico *agg.* pornographic
poro *sm.* pore.
porosità *sf.* porosity.
poroso *agg.* porous.
pòrpora *sf.* purple.
porporato *sm.* Cardinal.
porre *vt.* **1.** to put (*v. irr.*) **2.** (*sup-
  porre*) to suppose || *— le fonda-
  menta*, to lay (*v. irr.*) the founda-
  tions; *— mano*, to begin (*v. irr.*).
porro *sm.* **1.** leek **2.** (*med.*) wart.
porta *sf.* **1.** door **2.** (*di mura ecc.*)
  gate **3.** (*sport*) goal.
portabagagli *sm.* **1.** luggage-rack
  2. (*facchino*) porter.
portabandiera *sm.* ensign.
portacarte *sm.* portfolio.
portacénere *sm.* ash-tray.
portachiavi *sm.* key-holder.
portacipria *sm.* compact.
portaèrei *sf.* aircraft carrier.
portaferiti *sm.* stretcher-bearer.

portafiori *sm:* flower-holder.
portafoglio *sm.* **1.** wallet **2.** (*pol.*) portfolio.
portafortuna *sm.* mascot.
portagioielli *sm.* jewel-case.
portalèttere *sm.* ·pòstman (*pl.* -men).
portamento *sm.* **1.** gait **2.** (*condotta*) behaviour.
portamonete *sm.* purse.
portantina *sf.* sedan-chair.
portaombrelli *sm.* umbrella-stand.
portaòrdini *sm.* messenger.
portapacchi *sm.* carrier.
portapenne *sm.* penholder.
portare *vt.* **1.** (*verso chi parla o ascolta*) to bring (*v. irr.*) **2.** (*lontano da chi parla, accompagnare*) to take (*v. irr.*) **3.** (*trasportare*) to carry **4.** (*condurre*) to lead (*v. irr.*) **5.** (*indossare*) to wear (*v. irr.*) **6.** (*avere*) to have.
portasapone *sm.* soap-dish.
portasigarette *sm.* cigarette-case.
portaspilli *sm.* pincushion.
portata *sf.* **1.** (*di pranzo*) course **2.** (*di arma, strumento ottico*) range **3.** (*di fiume*) flow **4.** (*di ponte, auto ecc.*) capacity **5.** (*stazza*) tonnage **6.** (*fig.*) importance.
portàtile *agg.* portable.
portatore *sm.* bearer.
portauovo *sm.* egg-cup.
portavoce *sm.* spokesman (*pl.* -men).
portello *sm.* hatch.
portento *sm.* prodigy.
portentosamente *avv.* prodigiously.
portentoso *agg.* prodigious.
porticato *sm.* arcade.
pòrtico *sm.* **1.** (*loggia*) porch **2.** (*porticato*) arcade.
portiera¹ *sf.* (*porta*) door.
portiera² *sf.* doorkeeper.
portiere *sm.* **1.** (*sport*) goal-keeper **2.** porter.
portinaio *sm.* door keeper.
portinerìa *sf.* porter's lodge.
porto¹ *sm.* **1.** port (*anche fig.*) **2.** (*bacino*) harbour (*anche fig.*).
porto² *sm.* (*trasporto*) carriage: *franco di* —, carriage paid || — *d'armi*, shooting licence; *condurre in* — (*fig.*), to carry out.
portoghese *agg. e sm.* Portuguese.
portone *sm.* main door.
portuale *agg.* harbour (*attr.*): *città* —, port. ♦ **portuale** *sm.* docker.

porzione *sf.* portion.
posa *sf.* **1.** (*il porre*) laying **2.** (*posizione*) posture **3.** (*affettazione*) pose **4.** (*pausa*) pause **5.** (*foto*) exposure || *mettersi in* —, to pose; *senza* —, incessantly.
posare *vt.* to lay (*v. irr.*). ♦ **posare** *vi.* **1.** (*aver fondamento*) to rest **2.** (*assumere un atteggiamento non spontaneo*) to pose **3.** (*di liquido*) to stand (*v. irr.*). ♦ **posarsi** *vr.* **1.** to settle **2.** (*aer.; di uccello*) to alight.
posata *sf.* **1.** (*coltello*) knife (*pl.* knives) **2.** (*forchetta*) fork **3.** (*cucchiaio*) spoon.
posato *agg.* staid.
poscritto *sm.* postscript.
positiva *sf.* (*foto*) positive.
positivamente *avv.* positively.
positivismo *sm.* positivism.
positivista *s.* positivist.
positivo *agg.* positive.
posizione *sf.* position.
posologìa *sf.* posology.
posporre *vt.* **1.** to place after **2.** (*posticipare*) to postpone.
possedere *vt.* to possess.
possedimento *sm.* V. *possesso*.
possente *agg.* powerful.
possessivo *agg.* possessive.
possesso *sm.* **1.** possession **2.** (*proprietà*) property.
possessore *sm.* possessor, owner.
possìbile *agg.* possible: *il più presto* —, as soon as possible; *fare il* —, to do (*v. irr.*) one's best.
possibilità *sf.* **1.** possibility **2.** (*potere*) power || — *finanziarie*, means.
possidente *sm.* **1.** man (*pl.* -men) of property **2.** (*terriero*) landowner.
posta *sf.* **1.** post, mail **2.** (*ufficio postale*) post-office || *fermo* —, poste restante; *a giro di* —, by return of post; *per* —, by mail **3.** (*al gioco*) stake.
postale *agg.* postal, post (*attr.*), mail (*attr.*): *per pacco* —, by parcel post; *spese postali*, postage.
postazione *sf.* stationing.
postbèllico *agg.* post-war (*attr.*).
postdatare *vt.* to postdate.
posteggiare *vt.* to park.
posteggiatore *sm.* **1.** car-park attendant **2.** (*venditore*) stall-keeper.
posteggio *sm.* car-park || — *di taxi*, taxi rank.
postelegrafònico *agg.* postal telegraph and telephone (*attr.*). ♦

postelegrafònico *sm.* post-office clerk.

postema *sf.* aposteme.

pòsteri *sm. pl.* descendants.

posteriore *agg.* **1.** (*nel tempo*) following **2.** (*nello spazio*) back, rear.

posterità *sf.* posterity.

posticcio *agg.* false. ◆ **posticcio** *sm.* toupee.

posticipare *vt.* to póstpone.

posticipazione *sf.* deferment.

postiglione *sm.* postilion.

postilla *sf.* (marginal) note.

postillare *vt.* to annotate.

postino *sm.* postman (*pl. -*men).

posto *sm.* **1.** place **2.** (*spazio*) room **3.** (*lavoro*) job **4.** (*posto a sedere*) seat **5.** (*stazione*) station || *al — di,* instead of.

postoperatorio *agg.* postoperative.

postribolo *sm.* brothel.

postulante *sm.* **1.** petitioner **2.** (*eccl.*) postulant.

postulare *vt.* to petition (for sthg.).

postulato *sm.* postulate.

pòstumo *agg.* posthumous.

potàbile *agg.* drinkable.

potare *vt.* to prune.

potassa *sf.* potash.

potàssico *agg.* potassic.

potassio *sm.* potassium.

potatore *sm.* pruner.

potatura *sf.* pruning.

potente *agg.* powerful.

potenza *sf.* power || *in — (avv.),* potentially, (*agg.*) potential.

potenziale *agg. e sm.* potential.

potenzialità *sf.* potentiality.

potenziamento *sm.* **1.** (*rafforzamento*) strengthening **2.** (*sviluppo*) development.

potenziare *vt.* **1.** (*rafforzare*) to strengthen **2.** (*sviluppare*) to develop.

potere[1] *vi.* **1.** can (*pres.*), could (*pass., condiz.*), to be able: *non può venire,* he cannot come **2.** (*eventualità, augurio, permesso*) may (*pres.*), might (*pass., condiz.*), to be allowed to: *può darsi,* maybe; *può darsi che venga,* he may come.

potere[2] *sm.* power.

potestà *sf.* power, authority.

poveraccio *sm.* poor devil.

pòvero *agg.* poor.

povertà *sf.* poverty.

pozione *sf.* potion.

pozza *sf.* pool.

pozzànghera *sf.* puddle.

pozzetto *sm.* **1.** (*di motore*) sump **2.** (*di fognatura*) drain well.

pozzo *sm.* well: *— nero,* cesspool; *— carbonifero,* coal-pit.

pragmatismo *sm.* pragmatism.

pragmatista *s.* pragmatist.

pragmatìstico *agg.* pragmatist.

prammàtica *sf.* custom: *di —,* customary.

prammàtico *agg.* pragmatic.

pranzare *vi.* to dine.

pranzo *sm.* **1.** dinner **2.** (*di mezzogiorno*) lunch.

prassi *sf.* praxis.

prataiolo *agg.* field (*attr.*).

praterìa *sf.* prairie.

pràtica *sf.* **1.** practice **2.** (*affare*) matter **3.** (*esperienza*) experience **4.** (*incartamento*) file **5.** (*trattativa*) dealing **6.** (*passo presso un'autorità*) step || *far —,* to practise; *aver — di,* to be familiar with.

praticàbile *agg.* practicable.

praticabilità *sf.* practicability.

praticaccia *sf.* practical knowledge.

praticante *agg.* practising.

praticare *vt.* **1.** to practise **2.** (*frequentare*) to frequent **3.** (*fare*) to make (*v. irr.*).

praticità *sf.* practicality.

pràtico *agg.* **1.** practical **2.** (*esperto*) skilled || *esser — di,* to be familiar with.

prativo *agg.* grass (*attr.*).

prato *sm.* **1.** meadow **2.** (*artificiale*) lawn.

pratolina *sf.* daisy.

pravo *agg.* perverse.

preallarme *sm.* prewarning.

preàmbolo *sm.* preface.

preannunziare *vt.* to portend.

preavvertire *vt.* to forewarn.

preavvisare *vt.* to forewarn.

preavviso *sm.* **1.** forewarning **2.** (*disdetta*) notice.

prebèllico *agg.* pre-war (*attr.*).

prebenda *sf.* **1.** (*eccl.*) prebend **2.** (*salario*) salary.

precarietà *sf.* precariousness.

precario *agg.* precarious.

precauzionale *agg.* precautionary.

precauzione *sf.* **1.** precaution **2.** (*cautela*) caution.

precedente *agg.* previous. ◆ **precedente** *sm.* precedent || *i precedenti* (*condotta*), record.

precedenza *sf.* precedence || *in —,* previously.

precèdere *vt.* to precede. ♦ **precèdere** *vi.* to come (*v. irr.*) first.

precessione *sf.* precession.

precettare *vt.* **1.** (*giur.*) to summon **2.** (*mil.*) to call to arms.

precetto *sm.* **1.** precept **2.** (*mil.*) call-up notice.

precettore *sm.* tutor.

precipitare *vt.* to precipitate. ♦ **precipitare** *vi.* **1.** to fall (*v. irr.*) **2.** (*chim.*) to precipitate. ♦ **precipitarsi** *vr.* to dash.

precipitato *agg. e sm.* precipitate.

precipitazione *sf.* **1.** (*atmosferica*) precipitation **2.** (*furia*) haste.

precipitoso *agg.* **1.** (*impetuoso*) headlong **2.** (*frettoloso*) hasty **3.** (*scosceso*) precipitous.

precipizio *sm.* precipice: *a —* (*precipitosamente*), headlong; (*a picco*) perpendicularly.

precipuo *agg.* principal.

precisare *vt.* to specify.

precisazione *sf.* specification.

precisione *sf.* **1.** precision **2.** (*chiarezza*) clarity.

preciso *agg.* **1.** precise **2.** (*accurato*) careful **3.** (*definito*) definite **4.** (*identico*) identical **5.** (*di ore*) sharp.

preclaro *agg.* prominent.

preclùdere *vt.* to preclude.

precoce *agg.* **1.** precocious **2.** (*di frutto, stagione*) early **3.** (*prematuro*) premature.

precocità *sf.* precociousness.

preconcetto *agg.* preconceived. ♦ **preconcetto** *sm.* prejudice.

preconizzare *vt.* to foretell (*v. irr.*).

precordi *sm. pl.* praecordia.

precòrrere *vt.* to anticipate.

precursore *agg.* precursory. ♦ **precursore** *sm.* forerunner.

preda *sf.* **1.** prey **2.** (*bottino*) booty || *cadere in —* a, to fall (*v. irr.*) a prey to; *far — di*, to plunder.

predace *agg.* predacious.

predare *vt.* to plunder.

predatore *agg.* predatory. ♦ **predatore** *sm.* plunderer.

predatorio *agg.* predatory.

predecessore *sm.* forerunner.

predella *sf.* **1.** platform **2.** (*sgabello*) stool.

predellino *sm.* **1.** (*di vettura*) footboard **2.** (*poggiapiedi*) footstool.

predestinare *vt.* to predestine.

predestinazione *sf.* **1.** predestina-

tion **2.** (*destino*) destiny.

predeterminare *vt.* to predetermine.

predeterminazione *sf.* predetermination.

predetto *agg.* **1.** (*suddetto*) above mentioned **2.** (*presagito*) foretold (*pred.*).

prediale *agg.* praedial.

prèdica *sf.* sermon: *fare la — a qu.*, to lecture so.

predicàbile *agg.* predicable.

predicare *vt. e vi.* to preach.

predicativo *agg.* predicate.

predicato *sm.* predicate: *essere in — per*, to be considered for.

predicatore *sm.* preacher.

predicatorio *agg.* preachifying.

predicazione *sf.* preaching.

predicozzo *sm.* lecture.

predigestione *sf.* preliminary digestion.

prediletto *agg.* favourite. ♦ **prediletto** *sm.* pet.

predilezione *sf.* predilection.

predilìgere *vt.* to prefer.

predire *vt.* to foretell (*v. irr.*).

predisporre *vi.* **1.** to predispose **2.** (*provvedere*) to arrange. ♦ **predisporsi** *vr.* to prepare oneself.

predisposizione *sf.* **1.** (*med.*) predisposition **2.** (*inclinazione*) bent.

predizione *sf.* prediction.

predominante *agg.* prevailing.

predominanza *sf.* prevalence.

predominare *vi.* to prevail.

predominio *sm.* predominance.

predone *sm.* plunderer.

preesistente *agg.* pre-existing.

preesistenza *sf.* pre-existence.

preesìstere *vi.* to pre-exist.

prefabbricare *vt.* to prefabricate.

prefazio *sm.* preface.

prefazione *sf.* preface.

preferenza *sf.* preference: *di —*, generally.

preferenziale *agg.* preferential.

preferìbile *agg.* preferable.

preferire *vt.* to prefer.

preferito *agg. e sm.* V. **prediletto**.

prefettizio *agg.* prefectorial.

prefetto *sm.* prefect.

prefettura *sf.* prefecture.

prefìggere *vt.* to (pre-)establish. ♦ **prefìggersi** *vr.* to be resolved: *— uno scopo*, to propose an aim to oneself.

prefigurare *vt.* to prefigure.

prefigurazione *sf.* prefiguration.

prefisso *sm.* prefix.

preformare *vt.* to preform.

pregare *vt.* **1.** to pray **2.** (*chiedere*) to beg.

pregévole *agg.* valuable.

preghiera *sf.* **1.** prayer **2.** (*domanda*) request.

pregiare *vt.* to esteem. ♦ **pregiarsi** *vr.* to beg (to).

pregiato *agg.* valuable: *vino —*, vintage wine.

pregio *sm.* **1.** (*valore*) value **2.** (*merito*) merit || *di —*, valuable.

pregiudicare *vt.* to prejudice.

pregiudicato *sm.* previous offender.

pregiudiziale *agg.* prejudicial

pregiudizio *sm.* prejudice.

pregnante *agg.* pregnant.

pregno *agg.* **1.** pregnant (with) **2.** (*pieno*) full (of).

pregustare *vt.* to foretaste.

preistoria *sf.* prehistory.

preistòrico *agg.* prehistoric.

prelatizio *agg.* prelatic.

prelato *sm.* prelate.

prelazione *sf.* pre-emption.

prelevamento *sm.* drawing: *fare un —* (*comm.*), to draw (*v. irr.*).

prelevare *vt.* to draw (*v. irr.*).

prelibare *vt.* to foretaste.

prelibato *agg.* excellent.

prelievo *sm.* V. *prelevamento.*

preliminare *agg.* preliminary.

prelùdere *vi.* to prelude (sthg.), to foreshadow (sthg.).

preludiare *vi.* to prelude.

preludio *sm.* prelude.

prematuro *agg.* premature.

premeditare *vt.* to premeditate.

premeditato *agg.* premeditated.

premeditazione *sf.* premeditation.

prèmere *vi.* **1.** to press **2.** (*importare*) to interest **3.** (*essere urgente*) to be urgent. ♦ **prèmere** *vt.* to press.

premessa *sf.* introduction.

premesso *agg.* previous.

preméttere *vt.* **1.** to premise **2.** (*mettere prima*) to put (*v. irr.*) before.

premiare *vt.* **1.** to give (*v. irr.*) a prize **2.** (*ricompensare*) to reward.

premiazione *sf.* awarding of prizes.

preminente *agg.* pre-eminent.

preminenza *sf.* pre-eminence.

premio *sm.* **1.** prize **2.** (*ricompensa*) reward **3.** (*comm.*) premium.

prèmito *sm.* tenesmus.

premolare *agg.* e *sm.* premolar.

premonitore *agg.* premonitory.

premorire *vi.* to predecease.

premunire *vt.* to forearm. ♦ **premunirsi** *vr.* to secure.

premura *sf.* **1.** (*cura*) care **2.** (*fretta*) hurry **3.** (*gentilezza*) kindness || *aver —*, to be in a hurry.

premuroso *agg.* **1.** (*servizievole*) helpful **2.** (*gentile*) obliging.

prèndere *vt.* **1.** to take (*v. irr.*) **2.** (*sorprendere, afferrare*) to catch (*v. irr.*) **3.** (*comprare, ottenere*) to get (*v. irr.*). ♦ **prèndersi** *vr.* to take || *che ti prende?*, what's the matter with you?

prendisole *sm.* sun-suit.

prenome *sm.* praenomen (*pl.* -mina).

prenotare *vt.* to book. ♦ **prenotarsi** *vr.* to engage oneself.

prenotazione *sf.* booking.

prènsile *agg.* prehensile.

prensione *sf.* prehension.

preoccupante *agg.* worrying.

preoccupare *vt.* to worry. ♦ **preoccuparsi** *vr.* to be worried (about).

preoccupazione *sf.* worry.

preordinare *vt.* to prearrange.

preparare *vt.* to prepare. ♦ **prepararsi** *vr.* to get (*v. irr.*) ready.

preparativo *sm.* preparation.

preparato *agg.* ready. ♦ **preparato** *sm.* (*med.*) preparation.

preparatore *sm.* preparer.

preparatorio *agg.* preparatory.

preparazione *sf.* preparation.

preponderante *agg.* preponderant.

preponderanza *sf.* preponderance.

preporre *vt.* **1.** to put (*v. irr.*) before **2.** (*preferire*) to prefer **3.** (*mettere a capo*) to put at the head.

prepositivo *agg.* prepositional.

preposizione *sf.* preposition.

preposto *sm.* **1.** provost **2.** (*relig., prevosto*) parish priest.

prepotente *agg.* overbearing.

prepotentemente *avv.* overbearingly.

prepotenza *sf.* **1.** arrogance **2.** (*azione*) overbearing action.

preraffaellismo *sm.* Pre-Raphaelitism.

preraffaellita *agg.* e *s.* Pre-Raphaelite.

prerogativa *sf.* **1.** prerogative **2.** (*di persona*) faculty **3.** (*di cosa*) property.

presa *sf.* **1.** taking **2.** (*stretta*) grip

3. _(cattura)_ capture **4.** _(elettr.)_ plug **5.** _(pizzico)_ pinch ‖ _macchina da_ —, camera; _far_ — _(di cemento)_, to set _(v. irr.)_.

presagio _sm._ presage, omen.

presagire _vt._ **1.** to foresee _(v. irr.)_ **2.** _(essere presagio di)_ to forebode.

presago _agg._ _essere_ — _di (prevedere)_, to have a presentiment of.

presbiopìa _sf._ long-sightedness.

prèsbite _agg._ long-sighted.

presbiterianismo _sm._ Presbyterianism.

presbiteriano _agg._ e _sm._ Presbyterian.

presbiterio _sm._ presbytery.

prescégliere _vt._ to choose _(v. irr.)_.

prescelto _agg._ chosen.

prescienza _sf._ prescience.

prescìndere _vi._ to leave _(v. irr.)_ out of consideration: _a — da_, apart from.

prescritto _sm._ prescript.

prescrìvere _vt._ to prescribe.

prescrizione _sf._ **1.** regulation **2.** _(med.; giur.)_ prescription: _caduto in_ —, invalidated by prescription.

presentàbile _agg._ presentable.

presentare _vt._ **1.** to present **2.** _(mostrare)_ to show _(v. irr.)_ **3.** _(far conoscere)_ to introduce. ♦ **presentarsi** _vr._ **1.** to present oneself **2.** _(capitare)_ to occur.

presentatore _sm._ **1.** announcer **2.** _(teat.)_ showman _(pl._ -men).

presentazione _sf._ **1.** presentation **2.** _(di una persona)_ introduction.

presente _agg._ e _s._ present ‖ _i presenti_, the people present; _la_ — _(lettera)_, this letter.

presentemente _avv._ now.

presentimento _sm._ presentiment.

presentire _vt._ to foresee _(v. irr.)_.

presenza _sf._ **1.** presence **2.** _(frequenza)_ attendance.

prèsenziare _vt._ e _vi._ to be present (at).

presepio _sm._ crib.

preservare _vt._ to preserve.

preservativo _agg._ e _sm._ preservative.

preservazione _sf._ preservation.

prèside _sm._ headmaster. ♦ **prèside** _sf._ headmistress.

presidente _sm._ **1.** president **2.** _(di assemblea)_ chairman _(pl._ -men).

presidenza _sf._ **1.** presidency **2.** _(di assemblea)_ chairmanship **3.** _(di società)_ management **4.** _(insieme di direttori)_ board of directors **5.** _(di scuola)_ headmastership.

presidenziale _agg._ presidential.

presidiare _vt._ to garrison.

presidio _sm._ garrison.

presièdere _vt._ e _vi._ to preside (over, at).

pressa _sf._ press.

pressacarte _sm._ paper-weight.

pressante _agg._ pressing.

pressantemente _avv._ pressingly.

pressappoco _avv._ approximately.

pressare _vt._ to press.

pressi _sm. pl._ **1.** neighbourhood _(sing.)_ **2.** _(sobborghi)_ outskirts.

pressione _sf._ pressure: _fare_ — _su qu._ _(fig.)_, to put _(v. irr.)_ pressure on so.

presso _avv._ nearly: _a un di_ —, _press'a poco_, approximately; _da_ —, closely. ♦ **presso** _prep._ **1.** near **2.** _(a casa di)_ at **3.** _(nell'ufficio di)_ with **4.** _(fra)_ among **5.** _(negli indirizzi)_ c/o _(care of)_.

pressoché _avv._ almost.

pressurizzare _vt._ to pressurize.

pressurizzazione _sf._ pressurization.

prestabilire _vt._ to pre-arrange.

prestamente _avv._ quickly.

prestanome _sm._ man of straw.

prestante _agg._ good-looking.

prestanza _sf._ fine appearance.

prestare _vt._ V. _imprestare._ ♦ **prestarsi** _vr._ to volunteer.

prestatore _sm._ lender: — _d'opera_, workman _(pl._ -men).

prestazione _sf._ **1.** _(prestito)_ loan **2.** _(servizio)_ service **3.** _(sport)_ performance.

prestezza _sf._ quickness.

prestidigitatore _sm._ conjurer.

prestigio _sm._ prestige ‖ _gioco di_ —, conjuring trick.

prestigioso _agg._ **1.** _(affascinante)_ glamorous **2.** _(favoloso)_ fabulous.

prèstito _sm._ loan: _prendere in_ —, to borrow; _dare in_ —, to lend _(v. irr.)_.

presto[1] _agg._ — _di mano_, dexterous.

presto[2] _avv._ **1.** soon **2.** _(di buon'ora)_ early **3.** _(in fretta)_ quickly ‖ — _o tardi_, sooner or later; _al più_ —, as soon as possible. ♦ **presto!** _inter._ quick!

presùmere _vt._ to presume.

presumìbile _agg._ presumable.

presumibilmente _avv._ presumably.

presuntivo _agg._ presumptive.

presunto _agg._ supposed.

presuntuosamente *avv.* presumptuously.

presuntuosità *sf.* conceit.

presuntuoso *agg.* presumptuous.

presunzione *sf.* presumption.

presupporre *vt.* **1.** to presuppose **2.** (*supporre*) to suppose.

presupposizione *sf.* **1.** presupposition **2.** (*supposizione*) supposition.

presupposto *sm.* V. *presupposizione.*

prete *sm.* priest. .

pretendente *sm.* **1.** pretender. **2.** (*corteggiatore*) suitor.

pretèndere *vt.* **1.** to pretend **2.** (*esigere*) to want. ♦ **pretèndere** *vi.* to claim.

pretensione *sf.* pretension.

pretenzioso *agg.* **1.** pretentious **2.** (*presuntuoso*) conceited.

preterintenzionale *agg.* unintentional.

pretèrito *agg. e sm.* past.

pretesa *sf.* **1.** pretence **2.** (*richiesta*) claim || *avere molte pretese*, to be hard to please; *avanzare pretese su*, to claim rights over.

pretesto *sm.* **1.** pretext **2.** (*occasione*) occasion.

pretore *sm.* magistrate.

prettamente *avv.* purely.

pretto *agg.* pure.

pretura *sf.* magistrate's court.

prevalente *agg.* prevailing.

prevalenza *sf.* prevalence.

prevalere *vi.* to prevail.

prevaricare *vi.* **1.** to prevaricate **2.** (*abusare del potere*) to abuse one's office.

prevaricatore *sm.* prevaricator.

prevaricazione *sf.* **1.** prevarication **2.** (*abuso di potere*) abuse of office.

prevedere *vt.* **1.** to foresee (*v. irr.*) **2.** (*di legge, contratto*) to provide (for).

prevedìbile *agg.* foreseeable.

preveggente *agg.* foreseeing.

preveggenza *sf.* foresight.

prevenire *vt.* **1.** (*precedere*) to forestall **2.** (*evitare*) to prevent **3.** (*avvertire*) to warn.

preventivamente *avv.* **1.** beforehand **2.** (*in modo preventivo*) preventively.

preventivare *vt.* to estimate.

preventivo *agg.* **1.** preventive **2.** (*comm.*) estimated || *bilancio* —, budget. ♦ **preventivo** *sm.* estimate

preventorio *sm.* preventive sanatorium.

prevenuto *agg. essere* — *contro*, to have a prejudice against.

prevenzione *sf.* **1.** prejudice **2.** (*il prevenire*) prevention.

previdente *agg.* provident.

previdenza *sf.* providence: — *sociale*, social security.

previdenziale *agg.* social security (*attr.*).

previo *agg.* **1.** previous **2.** (*soggetto a*) subject to.

previsione *sf.* **1.** forecast **2.** (*comm.*) estimate.

previsto *agg.* **1.** foreseen **2.** (*comm.*) estimated **3.** (*giur.*) provided.

prevosto *sm.* V. *preposto.*

preziosismo *sm.* preciosity.

preziosità *sf.* preciousness.

prezioso *agg.* precious. ♦ **prezioso** *sm.* jewel.

prezzémolo *sm.* parsley.

prezzo *sm.* **1.** price, cost **2.** (*valore*) value || *a* — *di*, at the cost of.

prezzolare *vt.* to hire.

prezzolato *agg.* (*mercenario*) mercenary.

prigione *sf.* **1.** prison **2.** (*pena*) imprisonment.

prigionìa *sf.* imprisonment.

prigioniero *agg.* imprisoned. ♦ **prigioniero** *sm.* prisoner.

prillare *vi.* to twirl.

prima[1] *avv.* **1.** before **2.** (*in anticipo*) in advance **3.** (*un tempo*) once **4.** (*più presto*) earlier, sooner **5.** (*per prima cosa*) first || — *o poi*, sooner or later; *quanto* —, soon. ♦ **prima** *prep.* before. ♦ **prima che, di** *cong.* before.

prima[2] *sf.* **1.** (*ferr.; scuola*) first class **2.** (*teat.*) première.

primario *agg.* primary. ♦ **primario** *sm.* head physician.

primate *sm.* (*eccl.*) primate.

primati *sm. pl.* (*zool.*) Primates.

primaticcio *agg.* early.

primatista *s.* record-holder.

primato *sm.* **1.** supremacy **2.** (*sport*) record.

primavera *sf.* spring.

primaverile *agg.* spring (*attributivo*), springlike.

primeggiare *vi.* to excel.

primigenio *agg.* primigenial.

primìpara *sf.* primipara (*pl.* -ae).

primitivo *agg. e sm.* primitive.

primizia *sf.* **1.** (*frutta*) early fruit

2. (*verdura*) early vegetable **3.** (*novità*) novelty.
primo *agg.* **1.** first **2.** (*principale*) chief **3.** (*iniziale*) early **4.** (*prossimo*) next || *in un — tempo*, at first.
primogènito *agg.* e *sm.* first-born.
primogenitura *sf.* primogeniture.
primordiale *agg.* primeval.
primordi *sm. pl.* beginnings.
primula *sf.* primrose.
principale *agg.* principal. ♦ **principale** *sm.* master, boss.
principato *sm.* principality.
prìncipe *sm.* prince.
principesco *agg.* princely.
principessa *sf.* princess.
principiante *sm.* beginner.
principiare *vt.* e *vi.* to begin (*v. irr.*).
princìpio *sm.* **1.** (*inizio*) beginning **2.** (*norma*) principle: *per —*, on principle.
priora *sf.* prioress.
priorato *sm.* priorate.
priore *sm.* prior.
priorità *sf.* priority.
prisma *sm.* prism.
prismàtico *agg.* prismatic(al).
prìstino *agg.* former.
privare *vt.* to deprive.
privatista *s.* external student.
privativa *sf.* **1.** (*esclusiva*) sole right **2.** (*monopolio*) monopoly **3.** (*tabaccheria*) tobacconist's shop.
privativo *agg.* privative.
privato *agg.* **1.** private **2.** (*privo*) deprived. ♦ **privato** *sm.* private citizen.
privazione *sf.* **1.** (*disagio*) privation **2.** (*perdita*) loss.
privilegiare *vt.* to privilege.
privilegiato *agg.* **1.** privileged **2.** (*comm.*) preferred.
privilegio *sm.* privilege.
privo *agg.* devoid: *— di padre*, fatherless; *— di madre*, motherless.
pro¹ *prep.* for.
pro² *sm. a che —?*, what is the use of?
proavo *sm.* great grandfather.
probàbile *agg.* probable.
probabilismo *sm.* probabilism.
probabilità *sf.* probability.
pròbante *agg.* probatory.
probativo *agg.* probative.
probità *sf.* uprightness.
probiviri *sm. pl.* arbiters.

problema *sm.* problem.
problematicità *sf.* problematic nature.
problemàtico *agg.* problematic(al).
probo *agg.* upright.
proboscidati *sm. pl.* Proboscidea.
probòscide *sf.* trunk.
procaccia *sm.* postman (*pl. -men*).
procacciare *vt.* to get (*v. irr.*). ♦ **procacciarsi** *vr.* to get.
procacciatore *sm.* procurer.
procace *agg.* **1.** (*provocante*) provoking **2.** (*inverecondo*) immodest.
procacità *sf.* **1.** provocativeness **2.** (*inverecondia*) immodesty.
pro capite *loc. avv.* each.
procèdere *vi.* **1.** to proceed, to go (*v. irr.*) on **2.** (*agire*) to act.
procedimento *sm.* **1.** (*progressione*) course **2.** (*condotta*) behaviour **3.** (*giur.*) proceedings (*pl.*) **4.** (*tec.*) process.
procedura *sf.* **1.** procedure **2.** (*giur.*) practice.
procedurale *agg.* procedural.
procella *sf.* storm.
procellaria *sf.* stormy-petrel.
procelloso *agg.* stormy.
processare *vt.* to try: *far —*, to prosecute.
processionaria *sf.* processioner.
processione *sf.* procession.
processo *sm.* **1.** (*giur.*) trial **2.** (*med.; chim.; tec.*) process || *andare sotto —*, to be tried; *intentare un —*, to bring (*v. irr.*) an action.
processuale *agg.* trial (*attr.*).
procinto (*nella loc. avv.*) *in — di*, on the point of.
proclama *sm.* proclamation.
proclamare *vt.* to proclaim.
proclamatore *sm.* proclaimer.
proclamazione *sf.* proclamation.
proclive *agg.* inclined.
proclività *sf.* inclination.
procònsole *sm.* proconsul.
procrastinare *vt.* to postpone. ♦ **procrastinare** *vi.* to procrastinate.
procrastinazione *sf.* procrastination.
procreare *vt.* to procreate.
procreatore *sm.* procreator.
procreazione *sf.* procreation.
procura *sf.* **1.** proxy: *per —*, *by* proxy **2.** (*documento*) letter of attorney.
procurare *vt.* **1.** to get (*v. irr.*) **2.** (*causare*) to cause **3.** (*cercare*) to

try. ♦ **procurarsi** vr. to get (v. irr.).

procuratore sm. attorney.

prode agg. brave.

prodezza sf. 1. bravery 2. (azione) brave deed.

prodiere sm. bowman (pl. -men).

prodiero agg. forward.

prodigalità sf. lavishness.

prodigare vt. to lavish. ♦ **prodigarsi** vr. to do (v. irr.) all one can.

prodigio sm. prodigy.

prodigiosità sf. prodigiousness.

prodigioso agg. prodigious.

pròdigo agg. lavish.

proditoriamente avv. treacherously.

proditorio agg. treacherous.

prodotto sm. 1. product 2. (risultato) result 3. (agr.) produce.

pròdromo sm. 1. warning sign 2. (med.) symptom.

produrre vt. to produce. ♦ **prodursi** vr. 1. (causarsi) to cause oneself 2. (accadere) to happen 3. (esibirsi) to perform (before).

produttività sf. productivity.

produttivo agg. productive.

produttore agg. productive. ♦ **produttore** sm. producer.

produzione sf. production.

proemio sm. proem.

profanamente avv. profanely.

profanare vt. to profane.

profanatore agg. profaning. ♦ **profanatore** sm. profaner.

profanazione sf. profanation.

profanità sf. profanity.

profano agg. profane. ♦ **profano** sm. (persona inesperta) layman (pl. -men) || i profani, the laity.

proferire vt. 1. to pronounce 2. (dire) to utter.

professare vt. to profess.

professionale agg. professional: scuola —, vocational school.

professione sf. profession.

professionismo sm. professionalism.

professionista sm. 1. professional man 2. (sport) professional.

professorale agg. professorial.

professore sm. 1. teacher 2. (ordinario di università) professor.

profeta sm. prophet.

profetare vt. to prophesy.

profètico agg. prophetic(al).

profetizzare vt. V. profétare.

profezìa sf. prophecy.

profferire vt. 1. (offrire) to offer 2. (pronunciare) to utter.

profferta sf. offer.

proficuo agg. profitable.

profilare vt. 1. to profile 2. (orlare) to edge. ♦ **profilarsi** vr. 1. to be outlined 2. (apparire) to loom.

profilassi sf. prophylaxis.

profilato agg. 1. (delineato) outlined 2. (affilato) sharp 3. (orlato) edged. ♦ **profilato** sm. section.

profilàttico agg. e sm. prophylactic.

profilo sm. 1. (contorno) outline 2. (di viso) profile 3. (studio letterario) monograph.

profittare vi. 1. (trar profitto) to avail oneself (of) 2. (progredire) to make (v. irr.) progress 3. (guadagnare) to make profits.

profittatore sm. profiteer.

profittévole agg. profitable.

profitto sm. profit: trar —, to profit (by); mettere qc. a —, to make (v. irr.) good use of sthg.

profluvio sm. flood.

profondamente avv. deeply: dormire —, to sleep (v. irr.) soundly.

profòndere vt. to lavish. ♦ **profòndersi** vr. to be profuse (in, of).

profondità sf. depth.

profondo agg. deep. ♦ **profondo** sm. depth.

pròfugo sm. refugee.

profumare vt. to scent. ♦ **profumarsi** vr. to spray oneself with scent.

profumatamente avv. (fig.) dearly.

profumerìa sf. perfumery.

profumiere sm. perfumer.

profumo sm. perfume, scent.

profusamente avv. 1. profusely 2. (lungamente) at length.

profusione sf. profusion.

progenerare vt. to procreate.

progenie sf. progeny.

progenitore sm. ancestor.

progettare vt. to plan.

progettazione sf. planning.

progettista s. planner.

progetto sm. plan.

prognatismo sm. prognathism.

prognato agg. prognathous.

prògnosi sf. prognosis (pl. -ses).

programma sm. program(me).

programmare vt. to program(me).

programmatore sm. programmist.

programmazione sf. programming.

programmista *sm.* programmer.
progredire *vi.* 1. to advance 2. (*fig.*) to get (*v. irr.*) on 3. (*far progressi*) to make (*v. irr.*) progress.
progressione *sf.* progression.
progressista *agg. e s.* progressive.
progressivamente *avv.* progressively.
progressivo *agg.* progressive.
progresso *sm.* progress.
proibire *vt.* 1. to forbid (*v. irr.*) 2. (*impedire*) to prevent.
proibitivo *agg.* prohibitive.
proibizione *sf.* prohibition.
proibizionismo *sm.* prohibitionism.
proibizionista *agg. e s.* prohibitionist.
proiettare *vt.* 1. to project 2. (*cine*) to show (*v. irr.*) ♦ **proiettare** *vi.* to project. ♦ **proiettarsi** *vr.* to be projected.
proiettile *sm.* shell.
proiettore *sm.* 1. (*riflettore*) searchlight 2. (*cine*) projector.
proiezione *sf.* 1. projection 2. (*cine*) movie show || *macchina da* —, projector; *sala di* —, projection room.
prole *sf.* issue.
proletariato *sm.* proletariat.
proletario *agg. e sm.* proletarian.
proliferare *vi.* to proliferate.
proliferazione *sf.* proliferation.
prolifico *agg.* prolific.
prolissità *sf.* prolixity.
prolisso *agg.* prolix.
prologo *sm.* prologue.
prolungàbile *agg.* extendable.
prolungamento *sm.* extension.
prolungare *vt.* 1. to extend 2. (*differire*) to postpone. ♦ **prolungarsi** *vr.* 1. to extend 2. (*dilungarsi*) to dwell (*v. irr.*) (on).
prolusione *sf.* opening lecture.
promemoria *sm.* memorandum (*pl.* -da).
promessa *sf.* promise.
promettente *agg.* promising.
prométtere *vt.* to promise: — *bene*, to be full of promise.
prominente *agg.* prominent.
prominenza *sf.* prominence.
promiscuità *sf.* promiscuity.
promiscuo *agg.* mixed, promiscuous.
promontorio *sm.* promontory.
promosso *agg.* 1. (*a scuola*) successful 2. (*sostenuto*) promoted.

promotore *sm.* promoter.
promozione *sf.* promotion.
promulgare *vt.* to promulgate.
promulgatore *sm.* promulgator.
promulgazione *sf.* promulgation.
promuòvere *vt.* 1. to promote 2. (*a scuola*) to pass.
prònao *sm.* pronaos (*pl.* -aoi).
pronipote *sm.* 1. (*di bisnonno*) great-grandson, great-grandchild (*pl.* -children) 2. (*di prozio*) grandnephew || *i pronipoti* (*discendenti*), descendants. ♦ **pronipote** *sf.* 1. (*di bisnonno*) great-granddaughter, great-grandchild 2. (*di prozio*) grandniece.
prono *agg.* prone.
pronome *sm.* pronoun.
pronominale *agg.* pronominal.
pronosticare *vt.* 1. to forecast (*v. irr.*) 2. (*predire*) to foretell (*v. irr.*) 3. (*far prevedere*) to portend.
pronòstico *sm.* forecast.
prontezza *sf.* readiness.
pronto *agg.* 1. (*preparato*) ready 2. (*veloce*) prompt 3. (*al telefono*) hallo || — *soccorso*, first aid.
prontuario *sm.* handbook.
pronuncia *sf.* pronunciation.
pronunciamento *sm.* pronouncement.
pronunciare *vt.* 1. to pronounce 2. (*proferire*) to utter || — *un discorso*, to deliver a speech. ♦ **pronunciarsi** *vr.* to give (*v. irr.*) one's opinion.
pronunciato *agg.* pronounced.
propaganda *sf.* 1. propaganda 2. (*comm.*) advertising: *far* — (*comm.*), to advertise 3. (*pol.*) canvass.
propagandare *vt.* 1. to propagandize 2. (*comm.*) to advertise.
propagandista *s.* 1. propagandist 2. (*comm.*) advertiser.
propagandìstico *agg.* 1. propagandist 2. (*comm.*) advertising.
propagare *vt.* to propagate. ♦ **propagarsi** *vr.* to propagate.
propagatore *sm.* propagator.
propagazione *sf.* propagation.
propagginare *vt.* (*agr.*) to layer.
propàggine *sf.* 1. (*agr.*) layer 2. (*geogr.*) ramification 3. (*discendenza*) offspring.
propalare *vt.* to spread (*v. irr.*).
propano *sm.* propane.
propedèutica *sf.* propaedeutics.
propedèutico *agg.* propaedeutic(al).

propellente *agg.* propellent. ♦
propellente *sm.* propellant.
propèndere *vi.* to be inclined. ,
propensione *sf.* propensity.
propenso *agg.* inclined.
propilene *sm.* propylene.
propileo *sm.* propylaeum (*pl.* -laea).
propina *sf.* examiner's fee.
propinare *vt.* to give (*v. irr.*).
propiziare *vt.* to propitiate. ♦
propiziarsi *vr.* to gain so.'s favour.
propiziatore *sm.* propitiator.
propiziatorio *agg.* propitiatory.
propiziazione *sf.* propitiation.
propizio *agg.* favourable.
proponimento *sm.* resolution: *far —*, to resolve.
proporre *vt.* 1. to propose 2. (*suggerire*) to suggest. ♦ **proporsi** *vr.* to intend, to mean (*v. irr.*).
proporzionale *agg.* proportional.
proporzionalità *sf.* proportionality.
proporzionare *vt.* to proportion.
proporzionato *agg.* (*adeguato*) proportionate: *ben —*, well-proportioned.
proporzione *sf.* 1. proportion 2. (*rapporto*) ratio.
propòsito *sm.* 1. purpose 2. (*intenzione*) intention || *di —*, on purpose; *a — di*, with regard to; *a — (inter.)*, by the way; *a — (al momento giusto)*, at the right moment.
proposizione *sf.* sentence.
proposta *sf.* proposal.
proprietà *sf.* 1. property 2. (*l'essere proprietario*) ownership 3. (*correttezza*) propriety || *— letteraria*, copyright.
proprietario *agg.* proprietary. ♦
proprietario *sm.* 1. owner 2. (*di locanda*) landlord 3. (*possidente*) man of property || *— terriero*, landowner.
proprio *agg.* 1. (*rafforzativo del poss.*) own 2. (*adatto*) suitable 3. (*mat.; gramm.*) proper || *vero e —*, real. ♦ **proprio** *avv.* 1. (*esattamente*) exactly 2. (*veramente*) really || *— ora*, just now; *— così*, just like that.
propugnare *vt.* to support.
propugnatore *sm.* supporter.
propulsione *sf.* propulsion.
propulsivo *agg.* propulsive.
propulsore *sm.* propeller.
prora *sf.* bow.

proravìa (*nella loc. avv.*) *a —*, at the bow.
pròroga *sf.* 1. (*giur.*) adjournment 2. (*dilazione*) extension.
prorogàbile *agg.* 1. (*giur.*) adjournable 2. extensible.
prorogare *vt.* 1. to delay, to extend 2. (*giur.*) to postpone.
prorompente *agg.* bursting (out).
proròmpere *vi.* 1. to burst (*v. irr.*) (out) 2. (*di liquidi*) to gush out.
prosa *sf.* prose || *teatro di —*, drama; *compagnia di —*, dramatic company.
prosaicità *sf.* prosaism.
prosàico *agg.* prosaic.
prosapia *sf.* race.
prosàstico *agg.* prose (*attr.*).
prosatore *sm.* prose-writer.
proscenio *sm.* proscenium.
proscimmie *sf. pl.* lemurs.
prosciògliere *vt.* 1. (*da un obbligo*) to release 2. (*giur.*) to acquit.
proscioglimento *sm.* 1. release 2. (*giur.*) acquittal.
prosciugamento *sm.* 1. drying up 2. (*artificiale*) draining.
prosciugare *vt.* 1. to dry up 2. (*artificialmente*) to drain. ♦ **prosciugarsi** *vr.* to dry up.
prosciutto *sm.* ham.
proscritto *sm.* exile.
proscrìvere *vt.* to banish.
proscrizione *sf.* banishment.
prosecuzione *sf.* prosecution.
proseguimento *sm.* continuation.
proseguire *vt.* to continue. ♦ **proseguire** *vi.* to go (*v. irr.*) on.
proselitismo *sm.* proselytism.
prosèlito *sm.* proselyte.
prosieguo *sm.* course.
prosodìa *sf.* prosody.
prosopopea *sf.* (*fig.*) haughtiness.
prosperare *vi.* to prosper.
prosperità *sf.* prosperity.
pròspero *agg.* prosperous.
prosperoso *agg.* 1. prosperous 2. (*in salute*) healthy.
prospettare *vt.* 1. (*indicare*) to point out 2. (*guardare*) to look on to.
prospèttico *agg.* perspective (*attr.*).
prospettiva *sf.* 1. perspective 2. (*possibilità*) prospect.
prospetto *sm.* 1. view 2. (*fronte*) front 3. (*specchietto, programma*) prospectus.
prospezione *sf.* prospecting.
prospiciente *agg.* facing.

prossimità *sf.* closeness: *in — di,* near.

pròssimo *agg.* **1.** (*vicino*) near **2.** (*seguente*) next. ♦ **pròssimo** *sm.* fellow creatures (*pl.*), neighbour.

pròstata *sf.* prostate.

prosternare *vt.* to prostrate.

prostituire *vt.* to prostitute.

prostituta *sf.* prostitute.

prostituzione *sf.* prostitution.

prostrare *vt.* to prostrate. ♦ **prostrarsi** *vr.* to bow down.

prostrazione *sf.* prostration.

protagonista *s.* protagonist.

proteggere *vt.* to protect.

protèico *agg.* protein (*attr.*).

proteina *sf.* protein.

protèndere *vt.* to stretch (out): *— lo sguardo,* to gaze. ♦ **protèndersi** *vr.* to stretch oneself.

protervia *sf.* insolence.

protervo *agg.* insolent.

pròtesi *sf.* prosthesis.

protesta *sf.* protest.

protestante *agg. e s.* protestant.

protestantésimo *sm.* Protestantism.

protestare *vt. e vi.* to protest.

protesto *sm.* protest: *in —,* under protest; *lasciar andare una cambiale in —,* to dishonour a bill.

protettivo *agg.* protective.

protetto *agg.* protected. ♦ **protetto** *sm.* favourite.

protettorato *sm.* protectorate.

protettore *sm.* **1.** protector **2.** (*patrono*) patron.

protezione *sf.* **1.** protection **2.** (*patronato*) patronage.

protezionismo *sm.* protectionism.

protezionista *s.* protectionist.

proto *sm.* overseer.

protocollare *agg.* protocol (*attr.*).

protocollo *sm.* **1.** protocol **2.** (*registro*) record || *mettere a —,* to record; *carta —,* foolscap.

protone *sm.* proton.

protoplasma *sm.* protoplasm.

protòtipo *sm.* prototype.

protozòi *sm. pl.* Protozoa.

protrarre *vt.* **1.** to protract **2.** (*differire*) to defer. ♦ **protrarsi** *vr.* to go (*v. irr.*) on.

protrazione *sf.* **1.** protraction **2.** (*differimento*) deferment.

protuberanza *sf.* bulge.

prova *sf.* **1.** proof **2.** (*giur.*) evidence (*solo sing.*) **3.** (*esperimento, esame*) test **4.** (*tentativo*) try **5.**

(*sventura*) trial **6.** (*teat.*) rehearsal **7.** (*di abito*) fitting || *in —,* on trial; *dar — di essere,* to prove to be; *superare una —,* to pass a test.

provare *vt.* **1.** to prove **2.** (*tentare, mettere alla prova*) to try **3.** (*sentire*) to feel (*v. irr.*) **4.** (*di abiti*) to try on **5.** (*teat.*) to rehearse **6.** (*collaudare*) to test. ♦ **provarsi** *vr.* **1.** (*tentare*) to try **2.** (*cimentarsi*) to engage (in).

provenienza *sf.* origin.

provenire *vi.* to come (*v. irr.*).

provento *sm.* **1.** proceeds (*pl.*) **2.** (*reddito*) income.

proverbiale *agg.* proverbial

proverbio *sm.* proverb.

provetta *sf.* test-tube.

provetto *agg.* skilled.

provincia *sf.* province.

provinciale *agg. e s.* provincial: *strada —,* main road.

provincialismo *sm.* provincialism.

provino *sm.* **1.** (*teat.*) tryout **2.** (*cine*) test film.

provocante *agg.* **1.** provocative **2.** (*procace*) immodest.

provocare *vt.* **1.** to provoke **2.** (*causare*) to cause.

provocatore *sm.* provoker.

provocazione *sf.* provocation.

provvedere *vi.* **1.** to provide (for) **2.** (*badare a*) to see (*v. irr.*) (to) **3.** (*aver cura di*) to take (*v. irr.*) care of. ♦ **provvedere** *vt.* **1.** to provide **2.** (*preparare*) to prepare.

provvedimento *sm.* measure.

provveduto *agg.* **1.** provided (with) **2.** (*accorto*) wary.

provvidenza *sf.* providence: *essere una —,* to be providential.

provvidenziale *agg.* providential.

pròvvido *agg.* provident.

provvigione *sf.* **1.** (*comm.*) commission **2.** (*provvista*) supply.

provvisorietà *sf.* temporariness.

provvisorio *agg.* temporary: *in via provvisoria,* temporarily.

provvista *sf.* supply, provision (*specialmente di cibo*).

provvisto *agg.* **1.** supplied (with) **2.** (*fig.*) well-off.

prua *sf.* bow.

prudente *agg.* **1.** prudent **2.** (*cauto*) careful.

prudenza *sf.* **1.** prudence **2.** (*cautela*) care **3.** (*precauzione*) precaution.

prùdere *vi.* to itch.
prugna *sf.* plum.
prugno *sm.* plum-tree.
pruno *sm.* **1.** thorn-bush **2.** (*spina*) thorn.
pruriginoso *agg.* itching
prurito *sm.* itch.
prùssico *agg.* prussic.
pseudònimo *sm.* pseudonym.
psicanàlisi *sf.* psychoanalysis.
psicanalista *s.* psychoanalyst.
psicanalìtico *agg.* psychoanalytic(al).
psicanalizzare *vt.* to psychoanalyze.
psiche *sf.* psyche.
psichiatra *s.* psychiatrist.
psichiatrìa *sf.* psychiatry.
psichiàtrico *agg.* psychiatric(al).
psìchico *agg.* psychic(al).
psicologìa *sf.* psychology.
psicològico *agg.* psychologic(al).
psicòlogo *sm.* psychologist.
psicometrìa *sf.* psychometry.
psicopatìa *sf.* psychopathy.
psicopàtico *agg.* e *sm.* psychopathic.
psicopatologìa *sf.* psychopathology.
psicosi *sf.* psychosis (*pl.* -ses).
psicoterapìa *sf.* psychotherapy.
psittacosi *sf.* psittacosis.
pubblicàbile *agg.* publishable.
pubblicano *sm.* publican.
pubblicare *vt.* **1.** to publish **2.** (*di leggi ecc.*) to issue.
pubblicazione *sf.* publication: *fare le pubblicazioni di matrimonio*, to put up the banns.
pubblicista *s.* journalist.
pubblicità *sf.* **1.** publicity **2.** (*propaganda*) advertising || *fare —*, to advertise.
pubblicitario *agg.* advertising.
pùbblico *agg.* public. ♦ **pùbblico** *sm.* **1.** public **2.** (*in teatro ecc.*) audience **3.** (*cine*) moviegoers (*pl.*).
pube *sm.* pubis (*pl.* -bes).
pubertà *sf.* puberty.
pudibondo *agg.* demure.
pudicizia *sf.* demureness.
pudico *agg.* demure.
pudore *sm.* decency.
puericoltura *sf.* puericulture.
puerile *agg.* childish.
puerilità *sf.* childishness.
puèrpera *sf.* childwife (*pl.* -wives)
pugilato *sm.* boxing: *fare del —*, to box.

pùgile *sm.* boxer.
pugnalare *vt.* to stab.
pugnalata *sf.* **1.** stab **2.** (*fig.*) blow.
pugnale *sm.* dagger.
pugno *sm.* **1.** fist **2.** (*colpo*) punch **3.** (*manciata*) handful || *colpire col —*, to punch; *in —*, in one's hand; *di proprio —*, in one's own handwriting; *fare a pugni*, to fight (*v. irr.*), (*fig.*) to clash.
pula *sf.* chaff.
pulce *sf.* flea: *— in un orecchio*, suspicion.
pulcino *sm.* chick.
puledro *sm.* colt.
puleggia *sf.* pulley.
pulire *vt.* to clean: *pulirsi la bocca*, to wipe one's mouth.
pulito *agg.* clean.
pulitore *sm.* cleaner.
pulizìa *sf.* **1.** (*il pulire*) cleaning **2.** (*l'essere pulito*) cleanliness.
pullulare *vi.* to swarm (with).
pùlpito *sm.* pulpit.
pulsante *sm.* push button.
pulsare *vi.* to beat (*v. irr.*)
pulsazione *sf.* beat.
pulverulento *agg.* dusty.
pulvìscolo *sm.* dust: *— atmosferico*, motes (*pl.*).
puma *sm.* puma.
pungente *agg.* **1.** prickly **2.** (*fig.*) biting.
pùngere *vt.* **1.** to sting (*v. irr.*) **2.** (*di ago*) to prick **3.** (*fig.*) to tease. ♦ **pùngersi** *vr.* to prick oneself.
pungiglione *sm.* sting.
pungitopo *sm.* (*bot.*) butcher's broom.
pungolare *vt.* to goad.
pùngolo *sm.* goad.
punìbile *agg.* punishable.
punire *vt.* to punish: *— una offesa*, to revenge an insult.
punitivo *agg.* punitive.
punitore *agg.* punitory. ♦ **punitore** *sm.* punisher.
punizione *sf.* punishment.
punta *sf.* **1.** point **2.** (*estremità*) tip **3.** (*cima*) top **4.** (*un po'*) bit **5.** (*dolore, fitta*) twinge || *sulla — dei piedi*, on tiptoe; *avere qc. sulla — delle dita*, to have sthg. at one's finger-tips.
puntale *sm.* (*di bastone ecc.*) ferrule.
puntamento *sm.* aim.
puntare *vt.* **1.** to point (at) **2.** (*mirare*) to aim (at) **3.** (*spingere*) to

push **4.** (*scommettere*) to bet (*v. irr.*) || — *i piedi* (*fig.*), to put (*v. irr.*) one's foot down. ♦ **puntare** *vi.* to head.

puntata *sf.* **1.** (*al gioco*) stake **2.** (*di romanzo*) instalment.

puntatore *sm.* **1.** (*mil.*) marksman (*pl.* -men) **2.** (*al gioco*) better.

punteggiare *vt.* **1.** to punctuate **2.** (*nel disegno*) to dot.

punteggiatura *sf.* **1.** punctuation **2.** (*nel disegno*) dotting.

punteggio *sm.* (*sport*) score.

puntellare *vt.* to prop.

puntellatura *sf.* propping.

puntello *sm.* prop.

punteruolo *sm.* punch.

puntiglio *sm.* **1.** punctilio **2.** (*ostinazione*) obstinacy || *per* —, out of pique.

puntigliosamente *avv.* **1.** punctiliously **2.** (*ostinatamente*) obstinately.

puntiglioso *agg.* **1.** punctilious **2.** (*ostinato*) obstinate.

puntina *sf.* **1.** (*da fonografo*) needle **2.** (*da disegno*) drawing-pin.

puntino *sm.* dot: *puntini di sospensione*, dots || *a* —, properly.

punto[1] *sm.* **1.** point **2.** (*di cucito*) stitch **3.** (*voto*) mark **4.** (*gramm.*) full stop **5.** (*macchiolina*) dot || *due punti*, colon; — *e virgola*, semicolon; *mettere a* —, to set (*v. irr.*) up.

punto[2] *avv.* not at all.

punto[3] *agg. e pron.* not ... any.

puntone *sm.* (*edil.*) strut.

puntuale *agg.* punctual.

puntualità *sf.* punctuality.

puntualizzare *vt.* to stress.

puntualmente *avv.* punctually.

puntura *sf.* **1.** (*di insetto*) sting **2.** (*di ago*) prick **3.** (*iniezione*) injection **4.** (*dolore, fitta*) pain.

puntuto *agg.* pointed.

punzecchiamento *sm.* **1.** (*d'insetto*) stinging **2.** (*d'ago*) pricking **3.** (*fig.*) teasing.

punzecchiare *vt.* **1.** (*di insetti*) to sting (*v. irr.*) **2.** (*fig.*) to tease.

punzonare *vt.* to punch.

punzonatrice *sf.* (*mecc.*) punch.

punzonatura *sf.* punching.

punzone *sm.* punch.

pupàttola *sf.* doll.

pupazzetto *sm.* (*disegno*) sketch.

pupazzo *sm.* puppet.

pupilla *sf.* pupil.

pupillo *sm.* pupil.

pupo *sm.* baby.

purché *cong.* provided (that).

pure *avv.* **1.** (*anche*) also, too **2.** (*eppure*) yet **3.** (*di concessione*) as you like, of course. ♦ **pure** *cong.* **1.** (*con frasi concessive*) even though **2.** (*tuttavia*) but, yet. ♦ **pure di** *cong.* if only.

purè *sm.* purée: — *di patate*, mashed potatoes; *fare un* — *di verdura*, to mash vegetables.

purezza *sf.* purity.

purga *sf.* purgative, purge.

purgante *sm.* purgative, purge.

purgare *vt.* **1.** to purge **2.** (*di scritti*) to expurgate.

purgativo *agg.* purgative.

purgatorio *sm.* purgatory.

purificare *vt.* to purify.

purificatore *agg.* purificatory.

purificazione *sf.* purification.

purismo *sm.* purism.

purista *s.* purist.

puritanésimo *sm.* Puritanism.

puritano *agg. e sm.* Puritan.

puro *agg.* **1.** pure **2.** (*mero*) mere.

purosangue *sm.* thoroughbred.

purpùreo *agg.* purple.

purpurina *sf.* purpurin.

purtroppo *avv.* unfortunately.

purulento *agg.* purulent.

pus *sm.* pus.

pusillànime *agg.* pusillanimous. ♦ **pusillànime** *s.* coward.

pusillanimità *sf.* pusillanimity.

pùstola *sf.* pustule.

putacaso *loc. avv.* supposing.

putativo *agg.* putative.

putiferio *sm.* uproar: *sollevare un* —, to make (*v. irr.*) an uproar.

putrèdine *sf.* **1.** putridness **2.** (*cosa putrefatta*) rot.

putrefare *vi.* to rot. ♦ **putrefarsi** *vr.* to rot.

putrefatto *agg.* rotten.

putrefazione *sf.* putrefaction.

putrella *sf.* iron beam.

putrescenza *sf.* putrescence.

putrescìbile *agg.* putrescible.

putridità *sf.* rottenness.

pùtrido *agg.* rotten.

putridume *sm.* rot.

putto *sm.* putto (*pl.* -ti).

puzza *sf.* V. *puzzo*.

puzzare *vi.* to stink (*v. irr.*).

puzzo *sm.* stench.

pùzzola *sf.* polecat.

puzzolente *agg.* stinking.

Q

qua *avv.* here: *di — di*, on this side of; *per di —*, this way; *da quando in —?*, since when?

quàcchero *agg. e sm.* Quaker.

quaderno *sm.* exercise-book.

quadrangolare *agg.* quadrangular.

quadràngolo *sm.* quadrangle.

quadrante *sm.* 1. quadrant 2. (*di orologio*) dial.

quadrare *vt.* 1. (*geom.*) to square 2. (*formare*) to shape. ♦ **quadrare** *vi.* (*corrispondere*) to suit.

quadrato *agg.* 1. square 2. (*fig.*) strong. ♦ **quadrato** *sm.* 1. square 2. (*sport*) ring.

quadratura *sf.* 1. squaring 2. (*mat.*) quadrature.

quadrettato *agg.* 1. squared 2. (*di tessuto*) chequered.

quadriennale *agg.* quadrennial.

quadriennio *sm.* quadrennium (*pl.* -ia).

quadrifoglio *sm.* four-leaved clover.

quadriglia *sf.* quadrille.

quadrilàtero *sm.* quadrilateral.

quadrimotore *sm.* four-engined aircraft.

quadrivio *sm.* cross-roads.

quadro *agg.* V. *quadrato*. ♦ **quadro** *sm.* 1. picture 2. (*tabella*) table 3. (*teat.*) scene 4. (*elettr.*) board 5. (*mil.*) cadre || *galleria di quadri*, picture-gallery; *— riassuntivo*, summary; *— degli interruttori*, switch board.

quadrùmane *agg.* quadrumanous. ♦ **quadrùmane** *sm.* quadrumane.

quadrùpede *agg. e sm.* quadruped.

quadruplicare *vt.* to quadruple. ♦ **quadruplicarsi** *vr.* to quadruple.

quàdruplo *agg. e sm.* 1. quadruple 2. (*quattro volte tanto*) four times as much.

quaggiù *avv.* down here.

quaglia *sf.* quail.

qualche *agg.* (*in frasi affermative e interrogative che aspettano risposta affermativa*) some; (*in frasi interrogative, dubitative, condizionali*) any || *— volta*, sometimes; *in — luogo*, somewhere; *in — modo*, somehow.

qualcosa *pron.* something, anything (*per l'uso* V. *qualche*).

qualcuno *pron.* 1. somebody, someone 2. (*alcuni*) some, any: *— di*, some, any of (*per l'uso* V. *qualche*).

quale *pron. rel.* 1. (*per persone*) who (*sogg.*), whom (*altri casi*) 2. (*per animali, cose*) which 3. (*per tutti, solo sogg. e ogg.*) that || *del — (poss.)*, whose: *l'uomo la casa del —*, the man whose house. ♦ **quale** *agg. e pron. int.* 1. (*di che tipo*) what 2. (*scelta tra numero limitato*) which. ♦ **quale** *agg. escl.* what. ♦ **quale** *pron.* (*correlativo di "tale"*) as || *è tale e — suo fratello*, he is just like his brother.

qualìfica *sf.* 1. qualification 2. (*titolo*) title.

qualificare *vt.* to qualify.

qualificativo *agg.* qualifying.

qualificato *agg.* qualified: *operaio —*, skilled worker.

qualificazione *sf.* qualification.

qualità *sf.* 1. quality 2. (*specie*) kind 3. (*ufficio*) capacity.

qualitativo *agg.* qualitative.

qualora *cong.* in case.

qualsìasi *agg.* V. *qualunque*.

qualunque *agg.* 1. any 2. (*quale che sia*) whatever; (*riferito a numero limitato*) whichever 3. (*comune*) ordinary || *uno —*, anybody; *— cosa*, anything; *in — posto*, anywhere; *in — modo*, anyhow.

quando *avv. e cong.* when || *da —*, since; *da —?*, since when?; *quand'anche*, even though; *di — in —*, now and then.

quantità *sf.* quantity: *una gran — di*, a great deal of.

quantitativo *agg.* quantitative. ♦ **quantitativo** *sm.* V. *quantità*.

quanto *agg.* how much (*pl.* how many) || *tanto... —*, as much... as; *tanti... quanti*, as many... as; *— tempo?* how long? ♦ **quanto** *avv.* how, how much || *tanto —*, as much as; *tanto... —*, as... as; *tanto... — (sia... sia)*, both ...and; *— più... tanto più*, the more... the more; *— più... tanto meno*, the more... the less; *— a*, as for; *— prima*, soon; *per —*, however; *— fa?*, how much is it?

quantunque *cong.* though, although.

quaranta *agg.* forty.

quarantena *sf.* quarantine.

quarantenne *agg.* forty years old, forty-year-old (*attr.*).

quarantèsimo *agg.* fortieth.

quarantina *sf.* about forty: *aver*

passato la —, to be over forty.
quarésima *sf.* Lent.
quartetto *sm.* quartet.
quartiere *sm.* **1.** (*di una città*) quarter **2.** (*rione amministrativo*) district || — *generale*, headquarters (*pl.*).
quartina *sf.* quatrain.
quarto *agg.* fourth. ♦ **quarto** *sm.* quarter.
quarzo *sm.* quartz.
quasi *avv.* almost: — *mai*, hardly ever.
quassù *avv.* up here.
quaterna *sf.* set of four numbers.
quaternario *agg.* quaternary. ♦ **quaternario** *sm.* (*verso di una poesia*) line of four syllables.
quatto *agg.* **1.** squatting **2.** (*silenzioso*) silent || — —, very quietly.
quattordicèsimo *agg.* fourteenth.
quattòrdici *agg.* fourteen.
quattrini *sm. pl.* money (*us. al sing.*): *star male a* —, to be hard up.
quattro *agg.* four || *in* — *e* — *otto*, in no time; *fare il diavolo a* —, to make (*v. irr.*) a hullabaloo; *farsi in* —, to do (*v. irr.*) one's utmost.
quattrocchi (*nella loc. avv.*) *a* —, privately.
quattrocento *agg.* four hundred. ♦ **quattrocento** *sm. il* —, the fifteenth century.
quattromila *agg.* four thousand.
quegli *agg.* V. *quelli.* ♦ **quegli** *pron.* V. *egli.*
quei *agg. e pron.* V. *quelli.*
quella *agg. e pron.* V. *quello.*
quelle *agg. e pron.* V. *quelli.*
quelli *agg.* those. ♦ **quelli** *pron.* those, the ones.
quello *agg.* that. ♦ **quello** *pron.* that, the one || — *che* (*ciò che*), what; *tutto* — *che*, all that.
quercia *sf.* oak.
querela *sf.* **1.** complaint **2.** (*giur.*) action; *sporger* —, to bring (*v. irr.*) an action.
querelante *s.* plaintiff.
querelare *vt.* to proceed (against).
querelato *sm.* defendant.
quèrulo *agg.* querulous.
quesito *sm.* question.
questa *agg. e pron.* V. *questo.*
queste *agg. e pron.* V. *questo.*
questi *agg.* these. ♦ **questi** *pron.* **1.** these **2.** (*sing.*) this (man).

questionare *vi.* to quarrel.
questionario *sm.* questionnaire.
questione *sf.* **1.** question **2.** (*lite*) quarrel.
questo *agg.* this. ♦ **questo** *pron.* this, that || — *...quello* (*il primo... il secondo*) the former... the latter.
questore *sm.* questor.
questua *sf.* **1.** begging **2.** (*in chiesa*) collection.
questuante *agg.* begging. ♦ **questuante** *s.* beggar.
questuare *vi.* to beg.
questura *sf.* police-headquarters (*pl.*).
questurino *sm.* cop.
qui *avv.* here: *per di* —, this way; — *vicino*, close by; *da* — *innanzi*, from now on; *di* — *a un anno*, a year from now; *di* — *a otto giorni*, a week today; *fin* — (*di tempo*), so far.
quiescenza *sf.* quiescence.
quietanza *sf.* receipt.
quietare *vt.* to quiet. ♦ **quietarsi** *vr.* to quiet down.
quiete *sf.* quiet.
quietismo *sm.* quietism.
quieto *agg.* quiet || *star* — (*zitto*), to keep (*v. irr.*) quiet; *star* — (*fermo*), to keep (*v. irr.*) still; — —, very quietly.
quindi *avv.* **1.** therefore **2.** (*poi*) then.
quindicenne *agg.* fifteen years old, fifteen-year-old (*attr.*).
quindicèsimo *agg.* fifteenth.
quìndici *agg.* fifteen.
quindicina *sf.* **1.** about fifteen **2.** (*salario*) a fortnight's wages || *una* — *di giorni*, about a fortnight.
quindicinale *agg.* fortnightly.
quinquennale *agg.* quinquennial.
quinta *sf.* (*teat.*) wing || *dietro le quinte*, behind the scenes.
quintale *sm.* quintal.
quinterno *sm.* five sheets (*pl.*).
quintessenza *sf.* quintessence.
quintetto *sm.* quintet(te).
quinto *agg.* fifth.
quintuplicare *vt.* to quintuple.
quìntuplo *agg. e sm.* quintuple.
quisquilia *sf.* trifle.
quivi *avv.* here.
quota *sf.* **1.** share **2.** (*aer.*) altitude **3.** (*mar.*) depth || *perdere* —, to lose (*v. irr.*) height; *prender* —, to climb.

quotare *vt.* to quote. ♦ **quotarsi** *vr.* to subscribe.
quotato *agg.* 1. quoted 2. (*fig.*) esteemed.
quotazione *sf.* quotation.
quotidianamente *avv.* daily.
quotidiano *agg. e sm.* daily: *vita quotidiana,* everyday life.
quoziente *sm.* quotient.

R

rabàrbaro *sm.* rhubarb.
rabberciamento *sm.* patching (up).
rabberciare *vt.* to patch (up).
rabbia *sf.* 1. rage 2. (*idrofobia*) rabies ‖ *far — a qu.,* to make (*v. irr.*) so. angry.
rabbino *sm.* rabbi.
rabbioso *agg.* 1. (*med.*) rabid 2. (*fig.*) angry.
rabbonire *vt.* to calm down.
rabbrividire *vi.* 1. (*di freddo*) to shiver 2. (*di paura ecc.*) to shudder.
rabbuffare *vt.* 1. to ruffle 2. (*rimproverare*) to reprimand.
rabbuffo *sm.* rebuke.
rabbuiarsi *vr.* to darken.
rabdomante *s.* dowser.
rabdomanzìa *sf.* dowsing.
rabesco *sm.* V. *arabesco.*
raccapezzare *vt.* 1. (*raccogliere*) to gather 2. (*capire*) to understand (*v. irr.*). ♦ **raccapezzarsi** *vr.* to see (*v. irr.*) one's way.
raccapricciante *agg.* horrifying.
raccapricciare *vt.* to horrify. ♦ **raccapricciarsi** *vr.* to be horrified.
raccapriccio *sm.* horror.
raccattare *vt.* to pick up.
racchétta *sf.* racket.
racchio *agg.* ugly.
racchiùdere *vt.* to contain.
raccògliere *vt.* 1. to pick (up) 2. (*radunare*) to gather 3. (*far collezione*) to collect 4. (*accogliere*) to shelter 5. (*agr.*) to reap. ♦ **raccògliersi** *vr.* 1. to gather 2. (*concentrarsi*) to collect one's thoughts.
raccoglimento *sm.* 1. concentration 2. (*meditazione*) meditation.
raccogliticcio *agg.* picked up at random.

raccoglitore *sm.* 1. picker 2. (*collezionista*) collector 3. (*cartella*) folder.
raccolta *sf.* 1. (*agr.*) harvest; (*di frutta, cotone*) picking 2. (*collezione*) collection 3. (*adunanza*) gathering ‖ *fare la —,* to harvest; *chiamare a —,* to collect.
raccoltamente *avv.* intently.
raccolto *sm.* harvest.
raccomandàbile *agg.* recommendable.
raccomandare *vt.* 1. to recommend 2. (*esortare*) to urge 3. (*di lettere, pacchi*) to register. ♦ **raccomandarsi** *vr.* to beg (so.).
raccomandata *sf.* registered letter: *fare una —,* to register a letter.
raccomandazione *sf.* 1. recommendation 2. (*consiglio*) advice 3. (*di lettere, pacchi*) registration.
raccomodare *vt.* to mend.
raccontare *vt.* to tell (*v. irr.*) ‖ *si racconta,* it is said.
racconto *sm.* 1. tale 2. (*resoconto*) relation.
raccorciare *vt.* to shorten. ♦ **raccorciarsi** *vr.* to grow (*v. irr.*) shorter.
raccordare *vt.* to connect.
raccordo *sm.* 1. connection 2. (*mecc.*) union 3. (*ferr.*) siding.
ràchide *sf.* rachis (*pl.* -ides).
rachìtico *agg.* rickety.
rachitismo *sm.* rickets.
racimolare *vt.* to glean.
rada *sf.* roadstead.
radar *sm.* radar.
raddobbare *vt.* 1. (*mar.*) to repair 2. (*riparare*) to refit.
raddobbo *sm.* (*mar.*) repair.
raddolcimento *sm.* 1. sweetening 2. (*fig.*) softening.
raddolcire *vt.* 1. to sweeten 2. (*fig.*) to soften 3. (*alleviare*) to soothe. ♦ **raddolcirsi** *vr.* 1. to soften 2. (*alleviarsi*) to be soothed 3. (*mitigarsi*) to grow (*v. irr.*) milder.
raddoppiamento *sm.* doubling.
raddoppiare *vt.* to double. ♦ **raddoppiarsi** *vr.* to double.
raddoppio *sm.* doubling.
raddrizzamento *sm.* 1. straightening 2. (*correzione*) redressing.
raddrizzare *vt.* 1. to straighten 2. (*correggere*) to redress.
radente *agg.* 1. shaving 2. (*rasente*) grazing.

ràdere *vt.* **1.** to shave **2.** (*sfiorare*) to graze **3.** (*distruggere*) to raze.

radezza *sf.* **1.** thinness **2.** (*rarità*) infrequency.

radiale *agg.* radial.

radiante *agg.* radiant.

radiare *vt.* **1.** to radiate **2.** (*espellere*) to expel **3.** (*un nome*) to strike (*v. irr.*) off.

radiatore *sm.* radiator.

radiazione *sf.* **1.** radiation **2.** (*espulsione*) expulsion.

radicale *agg.* radical,

radicalismo *sm.* radicalism.

radicare *vi.* to root. ♦ **radicarsi** *vr.* to root.

radicato *agg.* deep-rooted.

radice *sf.* root.

radio[1] *sm.* (*anat.*) radius (*pl.* -dii).

radio[2] *sm.* (*chim.*) radium.

radio[3] *sf.* radio, wireless: *ponte* —, radiolink; *alla* —, on the radio; — *portatile ricevente e trasmittente*, walkie-talkie.

radioattività *sf.* radioactivity.

radioattivo *agg.* radioactive.

radioaudizione *sf.* **1.** broadcasting **2.** (*ascolto*) listening.

radiocomunicazione *sf.* wireless communication.

radiocrònaca *sf.* running commentary, radio account.

radiocronista *s.* radio commentator, wireless commentator.

radiodiffusione *sf.* broadcast.

radioestesìa *sf.* sensitivity to radiation.

radiofaro *sm.* radio beacon.

radiogonlòmetro *sm.* radio compass.

radiografare *vt.* to radiograph.

radiografìa *sf.* **1.** radiograph **2.** (*scienza*) radiography.

radiogramma *sm.* radiogram.

radiogrammòfono *sm.* radio--gramophone.

radiologìa *sf.* radiology.

radiòlogo *sm.* radiologist.

radioscopìa *sf.* radioscopy.

radioscòpico *agg.* radioscopic.

radiosità *sf.* radiance.

radioso *agg.* bright.

radiotècnica *sf.* radioengineering.

radiotècnico *sm.* radioengineer.

radiotelefonìa *sf.* radiotelephony.

radiotelèfono *sm.* radiotelephone.

radiotelegrafìa *sf.* radiotelegraphy.

radiotelegràfico *agg.* radiotelegraphic, wireless (*attr.*).

radiotelegrafista *s.* telegraphist.

radiotelevisione *sf.* radio and television.

radioterapìa *sf.* radiotherapy.

radiotrasméttere *vt.* to broadcast (*v. irr.*).

rado *agg.* **1.** thin **2.** (*non frequente*) infrequent ‖ *di* —, seldom.

radunare *vt.* to gather. ♦ **radunarsi** *vr.* to gather.

raduno *sm.* gathering.

radura *sf.* glade.

raffazzonare *vt.* to patch up.

raffermo *agg.* stale.

ràffica *sf.* **1.** gust **2.** (*di arma*) burst **3.** (*fig.*) hail.

raffigurare *vt.* to represent. ♦ **raffigurarsi** *vr.* (*immaginare*) to imagine.

raffinamento *sm.* **1.** refining **2.** (*fig.*) refinement.

raffinare *vt.* to refine. ♦ **raffinarsi** *vr.* to become (*v. irr.*) refined, to refine.

raffinatamente *avv.* refinedly.

raffinatezza *sf.* refinement.

raffinato *agg.* refined (*anche fig.*).

raffinazione *sf.* refining.

raffinerìa *sf.* refinery.

raffio *sm.* grapnel.

rafforzamento *sm.* strengthening.

rafforzare *vt.* to strengthen. ♦ **rafforzarsi** *vr.* to grow (*v. irr.*) stronger.

raffreddamento *sm.* **1.** cooling **2.** (*fig.*) coolness.

raffreddare *vt.* **1.** to cool **2.** (*fig.*) to lessen. ♦ **raffreddarsi** *vr.* **1.** to cool **2.** (*fig.*) to wane **3.** (*prendere un raffreddore*) to catch (*v. irr.*) a cold.

raffreddato *agg.* essere —, to have a cold.

raffreddatore *sm.* cooler.

raffreddore *sm.* cold.

raffrenare *vt.* to restrain.

raffrontare *vt.* to compare.

raffronto *sm.* comparison.

rafia *sf.* raffia.

ràgadi *sf. pl.* rhagades.

raganella *sf.* **1.** tree-frog **2.** (*strumento*) rattle.

ragazza *sf.* girl.

ragazzaglia *sf.* crowd of youngsters.

ragazzata *sf.* escapade.

ragazzo *sm.* boy: *da* —, as a boy.

raggelare *vt.* to freeze (*v. irr.*). ♦ **raggelarsi** *vr.* to freeze.

raggiante *agg.* radiant (with).

raggiare *vi.* 1. to shine (*v. irr.*) (with sthg.) 2. (*fig.*) to beam (with sthg.). ♦ **raggiare** *vt.* to radiate.

raggiera *sf.* halo of rays: *a* —, radially.

raggio *sm.* 1. ray 2. (*geom.*) radius 3. (*d'azione*) range 4. (*di ruota*) spoke || — *di sole*, sunbeam.

raggirare *vt.* to cheat.

raggiro *sm.* cheat.

raggiùngere *vt.* to reach.

raggiungimento *sm.* reaching.

raggiustare *vt.* 1. to repair 2. (*riordinare*) to rearrange.

raggomitolare *vt.* to roll up. ♦ **raggomitolarsi** *vr.* to roll oneself up.

raggranellare *vt.* to scrape together.

raggrinzire *vt.* to wrinkle. ♦ **raggrinzirsi** *vr.* to wrinkle, to become (*v. irr.*) wrinkled.

raggrumare *vt.* to clot. ♦ **raggrumarsi** *vr.* to clot.

raggruppamento *sm.* 1. grouping 2. (*gruppo*) group.

raggruppare *vt.* to group. ♦ **raggrupparsi** *vr.* to gather.

ragguagliare *vt.* 1. (*livellare*) to level 2. (*informare*) to inform 3. (*paragonare*) to compare 4. (*comm.*) to balance.

ragguaglio *sm.* 1. (*informazione*) information (*solo sing.*) 2. (*paragone*) comparison 3. (*comm.*) balance.

ragguardévole *agg.* considerable.

ragia *sf.* resin: *acqua* —, turpentine.

ragionamento *sm.* reasoning.

ragionare *vi.* 1. to reason (about) 2. (*discutere*) to discuss (sthg.).

ragionatore *sm.* reasoner.

ragione *sf.* 1. reason 2. (*diritto*) right 2. (*rapporto*) rate || *la* — *per cui*, the reason why; *a* — *veduta*, after due consideration; *aver* —, to be right; *a maggior* —, all the more reason; *aver* — *di qu.*, to get (*v. irr.*) the better of so.; — *sociale* (*comm.*), style.

ragioneria *sf.* bookkeeping.

ragionévole *agg.* 1. reasonable 2. (*di buon senso*) sensible.

ragionevolezza *sf.* reasonableness.

ragioniere *sm.* bookkeeper.

ragliare *vi.* to bray.

raglio *sm.* bray.

ragnatela *sf.* cobweb.

ragno *sm.* spider.

ragù *sm.* ragout.

raion *sm.* rayon.

rallegramenti *sm. pl.* congratulations.

rallegrare *vt.* to cheer (up). ♦ **rallegrarsi** *vr.* 1. to rejoice (at) 2. (*congratularsi*) to congratulate (so. on sthg.).

rallentamento *sm.* slowing down.

rallentare *vt.* to slacken. ♦ **rallentare** *vi.* 1. to slacken 2. (*di velocità*) to slow down. ♦ **rallentarsi** *vr.* to get (*v. irr.*) slack.

rallentatore *sm.* (*cine*) slow motion.

ramaiolo *sm.* ladle.

ramanzina *sf.* scolding.

ramare *vt.* to copper.

ramarro *sm.* green lizard.

ramazza *sf.* broom.

rame *sm.* copper.

ramìfero *agg.* copper-bearing (*attr.*).

ramificare *vi.* to ramify. ♦ **ramificarsi** *vr.* to ramify.

ramificazione *sf.* ramification.

ramingo *agg.* roving.

rammagliare *vt.* to mend a run.

rammaricare *vt.* to afflict. ♦ **rammaricarsi** *vr.* 1. to be sorry 2. (*lamentarsi*) to complain (of).

rammàrico *sm.* sorrow.

rammendare *vt.* to darn.

rammendatrice *sf.* darner.

rammendo *sm.* 1. darning 2. (*parte rammendata*) darn.

rammentare *vt.* to remember: — *qc. a qu.*, to remind so. of sthg. ♦ **rammentarsi** *vr.* to remember.

rammollimento *sm.* softening.

rammollire *vt.* to soften. ♦ **rammollirsi** *vr.* to soften, to go (*v. irr.*) soft.

rammollito *agg.* soft: *un vecchio* —, a dotard. ♦ **rammollito** *sm.* imbecile.

ramo *sm.* branch.

ramoscello *sm.* twig.

ramoso *agg.* branched.

rampa *sf.* 1. ramp 2. (*di scale*) flight.

rampante *agg.* rampant.

rampicante *agg.* climbing: *pianta* —, creeper.

rampino *sm.* hook.

rampogna *sf.* reproach.

rampollare *vi.* to spring (*v. irr.*).

rampollo *sm.* 1. (*d'acqua*) spring 2. (*di albero*) shoot 3. (*discendente*) offspring.

rampone *sm.* **1.** (*mar.*) harpoon **2.** (*da montagna*) crampon.

rana *sf.* frog: *uomo* —, frogman (*pl.* -men); *nuotare a* —, to swim (*v. irr.*) the breast stroke.

ràncido *agg.* **1.** rancid **2.** (*fig.*) trite || *sapere di* —, to have a rancid taste.

rancio *sm.* (*mil.*) mess.

rancore *sm.* grudge.

randagio *agg.* stray.

randellare *vt.* to cudgel.

randellata *sf.* blow with a cudgel.

randello *sm.* cudgel.

ranetta *sf.* rennet.

rango *sm.* rank.

rannicchiarsi *vr.* to crouch.

rannuvolamento *sm.* clouding over.

rannuvolare *vi.* to become (*v. irr.*) cloudy, to cloud over. ♦ **rannuvolarsi** *vr.* to get (*v. irr.*) cloudy.

ranocchio *sm.* frog.

rantolare *vi.* **1.** to wheeze **2.** (*in punto di morte*) to have the death-rattle.

ràntolo *sm.* **1.** wheeze **2.** (*di morte*) death-rattle.

ranùncolo *sm.* buttercup.

rapa *sf.* turnip.

rapace *agg.* greedy. ♦ **rapace** *sm.* bird of prey.

rapacità *sf.* greed.

rapare *vt.* to crop (so.'s hair).

rapato *agg.* shorn.

ràpida *sf.* rapid.

rapidità *sf.* swiftness.

ràpido *agg.* swift. ♦ **ràpido** *sm.* express (train).

rapimento *sm.* **1.** kidnapping **2.** (*di donna*) abduction **3.** (*fig.*) rapture.

rapina *sf.* robbery.

rapinare *vt.* to rob.

rapinatore *sm.* robber.

rapire *vt.* **1.** to kidnap **2.** (*una donna*) to abduct **3.** (*fig.*) to ravish.

rapitore *sm.* **1.** kidnapper **2.** (*di donna*) abductor.

rappacificare *vt.* to reconcile. ♦ **rappacificarsi** *vr.* to become (*v. irr.*) reconciled.

rappacificazione *sf.* reconciliation.

rappezzare *vt.* to patch.

rappezzatura *sf.* **1.** patching **2.** (*parte rappezzata*) patch.

rapporto *sm.* **1.** relation **2.** (*relazione*) report **3.** (*mat.*) ratio || *chiamare a* —, to summon; *andare a*

— *da*, to report to; *essere in buoni rapporti*, to be on good terms; *sotto tutti i rapporti*, in every respect.

rapprèndere *vi.* to coagulate. ♦ **rapprèndersi** *vr.* to coagulate.

rappresaglia *sf.* retaliation: *far* —, to retaliate.

rappresentàbile *agg.* performable.

rappresentante *s.* **1.** representative **2.** (*comm.*) agent.

rappresentanza *sf.* **1.** representation **2.** (*comm.*) agency || *in* — *di*, on behalf of.

rappresentare *vt.* **1.** to represent **2.** (*comm.*) to be agent (for) **3.** (*una parte*) to play **4.** (*un'opera teatrale*) to stage. ♦ **rappresentarsi** *vr.* to imagine.

rappresentativo *agg.* representative.

rappresentazione *sf.* **1.** representation **2.** (*teat.*) performance **3.** (*cine*) exhibition.

rapsodia *sf.* rhapsody.

rarefare *vt.* to rarefy. ♦ **rarefarsi** *vr.* to rarefy.

rarefatto *agg.* rarefied.

rarefazione *sf.* rarefaction.

rarità *sf.* rarity.

raro *agg.* rare: *rare volte*, seldom; *una bestia rara* (*fig.*), a queer fish.

rasare *vt.* **1.** to shave **2.** (*un prato*) to mow (*v. irr.*) **3.** (*lisciare*) to smooth. ♦ **rasarsi** *vr.* to shave.

rasato *agg.* **1.** shaven **2.** (*liscio*) smooth **3.** (*simile a raso*) satin (*attributivo*).

rasatura *sf.* **1.** shave **2.** (*di prato*) mowing.

raschiamento *sm.* **1.** scraping **2.** (*med.*) curettage.

raschiare *vt.* **1.** to scrape **2.** (*med.*) to curette || *raschiarsi la gola*, to clear one's throat.

raschiata *sf.* scraping.

raschiatoio *sm.* **1.** scraper **2.** (*med.*) curette.

raschiatura *sf.* scraping.

raschietto *sm.* **1.** scraper **2.** (*per cancellare*) eraser.

rasciugare *vt.* to dry.

rasentare *vt.* **1.** to graze **2.** (*confinare*) to border (on).

rasente *prep.* close to: *passare* —, to skim.

raso *agg.* V. *rasato*. ♦ **raso** *sm.* satin.

rasoio *sm.* razor.

raspa *sf.* rasp.

raspamento *sm.* rasping.

raspare *vt.* 1. to rasp 2. (*con le unghie*) to scratch 3. (*frugare*) to rummage.

rassegna *sf.* 1. (*rivista, recensione*) review 2. (*esame*) survey || *passare in* —, to inspect.

rassegnare *vt.* to hand in: — *le dimissioni*, to resign. ♦ **rassegnarsi** *vr.* to resign oneself.

rassegnato *agg.* resigned.

rassegnazione *sf.* resignation.

rasserenare *vt.* 1. to clear 2. (*fig.*) to cheer up. ♦ **rasserenarsi** *vr.* to clear up.

rassettare *vt.* 1. to tidy 2. (*riparare*) to mend.

rassicurante *agg.* reassuring.

rassicurare *vt.* to reassure. ♦ **rassicurarsi** *vr.* to be reassured.

rassicurazione *sf.* reassurance.

rassodamento *sm.* consolidation.

rassodare *vt.* 1. to consolidate 2. (*indurire*) to harden. ♦ **rassodarsi** *vr.* to harden.

rassomigliante *agg.* like, alike (*pred.*).

rassomiglianza *sf.* likeness.

rassomigliare *vi.* to be like. ♦ **rassomigliarsi** *vr. rec.* to be alike.

rassottigliare *vt.* V. *assottigliare.*

rastrellamento *sm.* 1. raking 2. (*mil.*) mopping up 3. (*di polizia*) combing 4. (*dragaggio*) dragging.

rastrellare *vt.* 1. to rake 2. (*mil.*) to mop up 3. (*di polizia*) to comb 4. (*dragare*) to drag.

rastrelliera *sf.* rack.

rastrello *sm.* rake.

rastremare *vt.* to taper. ♦ **rastremarsi** *vr.* to taper.

rata *sf.* instalment: *a rate*, by instalments.

rateale *agg.* by instalments.

rateare *vt.* to divide into instalments.

ratifica *sf.* ratification.

ratificare *vt.* to ratify.

ratificatore *sm.* ratifier.

ratificazione *sf.* V. *ratifica.*

ratto[1] *sm.* 1. kidnapping 2. (*di donna*) rape.

ratto[2] *sm.* (*topo*) rat.

rattoppare *vt.* to patch (up).

rattoppo *sm.* 1. patching up 2. (*toppa*) patch.

rattrappimento *sm.* 1. (*intorpidimento*) benumbing 2. (*contrazione*) contraction.

rattrappire *vt.* 1. (*contrarre*) to contract 2. (*intorpidire*) to benumb.

rattristare *vt.* to grieve. ♦ **rattristarsi** *vr.* 1. (*divenir triste*) to become (*v. irr.*) sad 2. (*essere triste*) to be sad.

raucèdine *sf.* hoarseness: *avere la* —, to have a hoarse voice.

ràuco *agg.* hoarse.

ravanello *sm.* radish.

ravvedersi *vr.* to mend one's way.

ravvedimento *sm.* reformation.

ravviamento *sm.* tidying (up).

ravviare *vt.* to tidy (up).

ravvicinamento *sm.* 1. approach 2. (*conciliazione*) reconciliation.

ravvicinare *vt.* 1. to bring (*v. irr.*) closer 2. (*riconciliare*) to reconcile 3. (*confrontare*) to compare. ♦ **ravvicinarsi** *vr.* 1. to draw (*v. irr.*) closer 2. (*riconciliarsi*) to become (*v. irr.*) reconciled.

ravvisàbile *agg.* recognizable.

ravvisare *vt.* to recognize.

ravvivamento *sm.* revival.

ravvivare *vt.* 1. to revive 2. (*rallegrare*) to brighten up || — *il fuoco*, to poke the fire. ♦ **ravvivarsi** *vr.* 1. to revive 2. (*rallegrarsi*) to brighten up.

raziocinante *agg.* reasoning.

raziocinio *sm.* 1. reason 2. (*buon senso*) common sense.

razionale *agg.* rational.

razionalismo *sm.* rationalism.

razionalista *s.* rationalist.

razionalità *sf.* rationality.

razionamento *sm.* rationing.

razionare *vt.* to ration.

razione *sf.* ration.

razza[1] *sf.* 1. race 2. (*di animali*) breed 3. (*genere*) kind.

razza[2] *sf.* (*itt.*) ray.

razzìa *sf.* 1. raid 2. (*insetticida*) insecticide || *far* —, to plunder.

razziale *agg.* racial.

razziare *vt.* to plunder.

razziatore *sm.* plunderer.

razzismo *sm.* racialism.

razzista *s.* racialist.

razzo *sm.* rocket.

razzolare *vi.* to scratch about.

re[1] *sm.* king.

re[2] *sm.* (*mus.*) D, re.

reagente *sm.* reagent.

reagire *vi.* to react.

reale¹ *agg.* real.
reale² *agg.* (*del re*) royal.
realismo *sm.* realism.
realista¹ *agg. e s.* realist.
realista² *agg. e s.* (*del re*) royalist.
realìstico *agg.* realistic.
realizzàbile *agg.* realizable. ♦ **realizzarsi** *vr.* 1. to be realized 2. (*avverarsi*) to come (*v. irr.*) true.
realizzatore *sm.* realizer.
realizzazione *sf.* 1. realization 2. (*teat.*) staging 3. (*cine*) production.
realtà *sf.* reality.
reame *sm.* kingdom.
reato *sm.* 1. offence 2. (*crimine*) crime.
reattivo *agg.* reactive. ♦ **reattivo** *sm.* reagent.
reattore *sm.* 1. reactor 2. (*aereo*) jet.
reazionario *agg. e sm.* reactionary.
reazione *sf.* reaction: *motore a —,* jet engine; *aereo a —,* jet.
reboante *agg.* 1. thundering 2. (*fig.*) bombastic.
rebus *sm.* rebus.
recalcitrare *vi.* V. *ricalcitrare.*
recapitare *vt.* to deliver.
recàpito *sm.* 1. (*consegna*) delivery 2. (*indirizzo*) address.
recare *vt.* 1. to bring (*v. irr.*) 2. (*fig.*) to bear (*v. irr.*) 3. (*causare*) to cause. ♦ **recarsi** *vr.* to go (*v. irr.*).
recèdere *vi.* to withdraw (*v. irr.*).
recensione *sf.* review.
recensire *vt.* to review.
recensore *sm.* reviewer.
recente *agg.* recent.
recentemente *avv.* recently.
recentissime *sf. pl.* latest news.
recessione *sf.* recession.
recessivo *agg.* receding.
recesso *sm.* 1. recess 2. (*recessione*) recession 3. (*giur.*) withdrawal.
recettivo *agg.* V. *ricettivo.*
recezione *sf.* reception.
recìdere *vt.* to cut (*v. irr.*) off.
recidiva *sf.* relapse.
recidività *sf.* 1. (*giur.*) recidivism 2. (*med.*) relapse.
recidivo *agg.* 1. (*giur.*) recidivous 2. (*med.*) relapsing. ♦ **recidivo** *sm.* 1. (*giur.*) recidivist 2. (*med.*) relapser.
recintare *vt.* to fence.
recinto *sm.* enclosure.
recipiente *sm.* vessel.

reciprocamente *avv.* reciprocally.
reciprocità *sf.* reciprocity.
recìproco *agg.* reciprocal.
recisamente *avv.* resolutely.
recisione *sf.* excision.
reciso *agg.* 1. cut 2. (*fig.*) resolute.
rècita *sf.* performance.
recitare *vt.* 1. to recite 2. (*teat.*) to act ‖ *— una parte,* to play a part.
recitativo *sm.* recitative.
recitazione *sf.* 1. recitation 2. (*teat.*) acting.
reclamante *sm.* claimant.
reclamare *vt.* to claim. ♦ **reclamare** *vi.* to complain.
reclamìstico *agg.* advertising.
reclamizzare *vt.* to advertise.
reclamo *sm.* complaint.
reclinare *vt.* to bow.
reclusione *sf.* 1. seclusion 2. (*prigionia*) imprisonment.
recluso *agg.* 1. secluded 2. (*imprigionato*) imprisoned. ♦ **recluso** *sm.* prisoner.
rècluta *sf.* 1. recruit 2. (*fig.*) novice.
reclutamento *sm.* enlistment.
reclutare *vt.* to enlist, to recruit.
recòndito *agg.* hidden.
recriminare *vi.* 1. to recriminate 2. (*lamentarsi*) to complain.
recriminazione *sf.* 1. recrimination 2. (*lamentela*) complaint.
recrudescente *agg.* recrudescent.
recrudescenza *sf.* recrudescence.
redarguire *vt.* to reproach.
redattore *sm.* 1. drawer 2. (*di giornale*) member of the editorial staff ‖ *— capo,* editor.
redazionale *agg.* editorial.
redazione *sf.* 1. drawing up 2. (*di giornale*) editing 2. (*i redattori*) editorial staff 3. (*ufficio*) editorial office.
redditività *sf.* profitableness.
redditizio *agg.* profitable.
rèddito *sm.* 1. income 2. (*dello Stato*) revenue.
redento *agg.* redeemed.
redentore *sm.* redeemer.
redenzione *sf.* redemption.
redìgere *vt.* to draw (*v. irr.*) up.
redìmere *vt.* to redeem.
redimìbile *agg.* redeemable.
rèdini *sf. pl.* reins.
redivivo *agg.* 1. restored to life 2. (*nuovo*) new.
rèduce *agg.* back from. ♦ **rèduce** *sm.* veteran.

referendum *sm.* referendum.
referenza *sf.* reference.
referenziare *vt.* to give (*v. irr.*) references.
referto *sm.* report.
refettorio *sm.* refectory.
refezione *sf.* meal.
refrattario *agg.* refractory: *terra refrattaria*, fireclay.
refrigerante *agg. e sm.* refrigerant.
refrigerare *vt.* to refrigerate.
refrigeratore *sm.* refrigerator.
refrigerazione *sf.* refrigeration.
refrigerio *sm.* **1.** cool **2.** (*sollievo*) relief.
refurtiva *sf.* stolen goods (*pl.*).
refuso *sm.* misprint, wrong fount.
regalare *vt.* **1.** to present (so. with sthg.) **2.** (*vendere a poco prezzo*) to sell (*v. irr.*) cheap.
regalato *agg.* (*venduto a buon prezzo*) cheap.
regale *agg.* regal.
regalia *sf.* (*mancia*) gratuity.
regalo *sm.* present: *in —,* as a present.
regata *sf.* regatta.
reggente *agg. e sm.* regent.
reggenza *sf.* regency.
règgere *vt.* **1.** (*sorreggere*) to hold (*v. irr.*) **2.** (*dirigere*) to run (*v. irr.*) **3.** (*gramm.*) to govern || *— una prova,* to stand (*v. irr.*) a test. ♦ **règgere** *vi.* **1.** (*resistere*) to hold (out) **2.** (*stare in piedi, anche fig.*) to stand. ♦ **règgersi** *vr.* **1.** (*sostenersi*) to stand **2.** (*appoggiarsi a*) to hold (on, to).
reggia *sf.* royal palace.
reggicalze *sm.* girdle.
reggimento *sm.* (*mil.*) regiment.
reggipetto *sm.* bra.
reggiseno *sm.* V. *reggipetto.*
reggitore *sm.* ruler.
regìa *sf.* **1.** (*teat.*) production **2.** (*cine*) direction || *— di,* produced, directed by.
regicida *sm.* regicide.
regicidio *sm.* regicide.
regime *sm.* **1.** regime **2.** (*mecc.*) speed **3.** (*dieta*) diet || *essere a —,* to be on a diet.
regina *sf.* queen.
regio *agg.* royal.
regionale *agg.* regional.
regionalismo *sm.* regionalism.
regionalista *s.* regionalist.
regione *sf.* **1.** region **2.** (*divisione amministrativa; fig.*) province.

regista *sm.* **1.** (*teat.*) producer **2.** (*cine*) director.
registràbile *agg.* registrable, recordable.
registrare *vt.* **1.** to register **2.** (*comm.*) to book **3.** (*segnare; cine*) to record **4.** (*su nastro*) to tape-record **5.** (*mecc.*) to adjust.
registratore *sm.* **1.** (*persona*) registrar **2.** (*strumento*) register: *— di cassa,* cash-register **3.** (*magnetofono*) taperecorder.
registrazione *sf.* **1.** registration **2.** (*comm.*) entry **3.** (*di suoni*) recording.
registro *sm.* **1.** register **2.** (*comm.*) book **3.** (*ufficio governativo*) registry.
regnante *agg.* reigning. ♦ **regnante** *s.* sovereign.
regnare *vi.* to reign.
regno *sm.* **1.** reign **2.** (*territorio; fig.*) kingdom.
règola *sf.* **1.** rule **2.** (*esempio*) example **3.** (*misura*) moderation || *in —,* in order; *è di —,* it is the custom.
regolamentare *agg.* prescribed: *non essere —,* to be against the rules.
regolamentarmente *avv.* according to the rules.
regolamentazione *sf.* regulations (*pl.*).
regolamento *sm.* regulation: *— dei conti,* settlement.
regolare[1] *vt.* **1.** to regulate **2.** (*sistemare*) to settle **3.** (*sintonizzare*) to tune (in). ♦ **regolarsi** *vr.* **1.** to act **2.** (*controllarsi*) to control oneself.
regolare[2] *agg.* regular.
regolarità *sf.* regularity.
regolarizzare *vt.* to regularize.
regolarizzazione *sf.* regularization.
regolatamente *avv.* **1.** regularly **2.** (*con moderazione*) moderately.
regolatezza *sf.* sobriety.
regolato *agg.* regular.
regolatore *agg.* regulating: *piano —,* townplan. ♦ **regolatore** *sm.* regulator.
regolazione *sf.* regulation.
règolo *sm.* rule: *— calcolatore,* slide rule.
regredire *vi.* to regress.
regressione *sf.* regression.
regressivo *agg.* regressive.
regresso *sm.* regress.

reietto *agg.* rejected. ♦ **reietto** *sm.* outcast.

reiezione *sf.* rejection.

reincarnare *vt.* to reincarnate. ♦ **reincarnarsi** *vr.* to be reincarnated.

reincarnazione *sf.* reincarnation.

reintegrare *vt.* 1. to restore 2. (*risarcire*) to indemnify.

reintegrazione *sf.* 1. restoration 2. (*risarcimento*) indemnification.

reità *sf.* 1. (*colpevolezza*) guiltiness 2. (*malvagità*) wickedness.

reiterare *vt.* to reiterate.

reiterazione *sf.* reiteration.

relativamente *avv.* comparatively: — *a*, as regards.

relativismo *sm.* relativism.

relativìstico *agg.* relativistic.

relatività *sf.* relativity.

relativo *agg.* 1. relative 2. (*rispettivo*) respective 3. (*attinente*) pertinent.

relatore *sm.* 1. relator 2. (*di leggi*) proposer.

relazionare *vt.* to relate.

relazione *sf.* 1. report 2. (*legame*) relation 3. (*contatto*) touch 4. (*conoscenza*) acquaintance || *aver* — *con*, to be connected with; *essere in buone relazioni*, to be on good terms; *mettersi in* — *con*, to get (*v. irr.*) into touch with; — *amorosa*, love affair.

relegare *vt.* to relegate.

relegazione *sf.* relegation.

religione *sf.* 1. religion 2. (*culto*) worship.

religiosità *sf.* piety.

religioso *agg. e sm.* religious.

reliquia *sf.* relic.

reliquario *sm.* reliquary.

relitto *sm.* 1. wreckage 2. (*di persona*) outcast.

remare *vi.* 1. to row 2. (*con pagaia*) to paddle.

remata *sf.* 1. row 2. (*colpo di remo*) stroke.

rematore *sm.* oarsman (*pl.* -men).

remiganti *sf. pl.* remiges.

remigare *vi.* 1. to row 2. (*di ali*) to flap.

reminiscenza *sf.* reminiscence.

remissione *sf.* (*giur.*) remission.

remissività *sf.* submissiveness.

remissivo *agg.* submissive.

remo *sm.* oar.

rèmora *sf.* 1. (*ostacolo*) obstacle 2. (*indugio*) delay 3. (*zool.*) remora.

remoto *agg.* remote: *passato* — (*gramm.*) past simple tense.

remunerare *vt.* to remunerate.

remunerativo *agg.* remunerative.

remunerazione *sf.* remuneration.

rena *sf.* sand.

renale *agg.* renal.

rèndere *vt.* 1. to render 2. (*fruttare*) to yield || — *conto di*, to account for; — *giustizia a qu.*, to do (*v. irr.*) so. justice. ♦ **rèndersi** *vr.* to become (*v. irr.*) || — *conto di*, to realize.

rendiconto *sm.* 1. statement 2. (*resoconto*) report.

rendimento *sm.* 1. rendering 2. (*resa*). output 3. (*efficienza*) efficiency.

rèndita *sf.* 1. revenue 2. (*privata*) income.

rene *sm.* kidney.

renella *sf.* gravel.

reni *sf. pl.* back (*sing.*).

renitente *agg.* reluctant || *essere* — *alla leva*, to fail to appear at the draft.

renitenza *sf.* reluctance || — *alla leva*, failure to register for national service.

renna *sf.* reindeer (*pl. invariato*).

renoso *agg.* sandy.

reo *agg.* guilty. ♦ **reo** *sm.* culprit.

reòmetro *sm.* rheometer.

reòstato *sm.* rheostat.

reparto *sm.* 1. department 2. (*mil.*) detachment.

repellente *agg.* repulsive.

repentaglio *sm.* danger: *a* —, in danger.

repentino *agg.* sudden.

reperìbile *agg.* to be found (*pred.*).

reperire *vt.* to find (*v. irr.*).

reperto *sm.* 1. (*giur.*) evidence 2. (*med.*) report.

repertorio *sm.* (*teat.*) repertoire.

rèplica *sf.* 1. reply 2. (*obiezione*) objection 3. (*copia*) copy 4. (*teat.*) performance || *avere molte repliche* (*teat.*), to have a long run.

replicare *vt.* 1. to reply 2. (*obiettare*) to object 3. (*ripetere*) to repeat.

reprensìbile *agg.* reprehensible.

reprensione *sf.* reprehension.

repressione *sf.* repression.

repressivo *agg.* repressive.

represso *agg.* repressed.

reprimenda *sf.* reprimand.

reprìmere *vt.* to repress.

rèprobo *agg. e sm.* reprobate.

repùbblica *sf.* republic.

repubblicano *agg. e sm.* republican.

reputare *vt.* **1.** to consider **2.** (*pensare*) to think (*v. irr.*).

reputazione *sf.* reputation.

requie *sf.* rest.

requisire *vt.* to requisition.

requisito *sm.* qualification.

requisitoria *sf.* **1.** indictment **2.** (*giur.*) summing up.

requisizione *sf.* requisition.

resa *sf.* (*rendimento*) yield **2.** (*capitolazione*) surrender || — *dei conti*, rendering of accounts.

rescìndere *vt.* to rescind.

rescindìbile *agg.* rescindable.

rescissione *sf.* rescission.

reseda *sf.* reseda.

resezione *sf.* resection.

residente *agg. e sm.* resident.

residenza *sf.* residence.

residenziale *agg.* residential.

residuare *vi.* to be left.

residuato *agg.* residual. ◆ residuato *sm.* — *di guerra*, war surplus.

residuo *agg.* remaining. ◆ residuo *sm.* residue: *residui radioattivi*, radioactive waste.

rèsina *sf.* resin.

resinoso *agg.* resinous.

resipiscenza *sf.* resipiscence.

resistente *agg.* **1.** resistant **2.** (*forte*) strong.

resistenza *sf.* resistance.

resìstere *vi.* **1.** to resist **2.** (*sopportare*) to endure.

resoconto *sm.* report.

respingente *sm.* buffer.

respìngere *vt.* **1.** to repel **2.** (*rimandare*) to return **3.** (*rifiutare*) to reject **4.** (*scol.*) to pluck.

respinta *sf.* V. *parata*.

respiràbile *agg.* breathable.

respirare *vt. e vi.* to breathe.

respiratore *sm.* respirator.

respiratorio *agg.* respiratory.

respirazione *sf.* respiration, breathing.

respiro *sm.* **1.** breath **2.** (*riposo*) respite.

responsàbile *agg.* responsible (for).

responsabilità *sf.* responsibility.

responso *sm.* **1.** response **2.** (*opinione*) opinion.

responsorio *sm.* responsory.

ressa *sf.* crowd: *far — intorno a*

qu., to crowd round so.

resta *sf.* **1.** (*di cipolla, aglio ecc.*) string **2.** (*di lancia*) rest.

restante *agg. e sm.* V. *rimanente*.

restare *vi.* V. *rimanere*.

restaurare *vt.* to restore.

restauratore *sm.* restorer.

restaurazione *sf.* restoration.

restàuro *sm.* restoration: *in —*, under repair.

restìo *agg.* loath, reluctant.

restituire *vt.* **1.** to return **2.** (*reintegrare*) to restore.

restituzione *sf.* **1.** return **2.** (*reintegrazione*) restoration.

resto *sm.* **1.** rest **2.** (*mat.*) remainder **3.** (*di denaro*) change || *resti*, remains; *del —*, on the other hand.

restringente *sm.* astringent.

restrìngere *vt.* **1.** (*contrarre*) to contract **2.** (*limitare*) to limit **3.** (*un vestito*) to tighten. ◆ restrìngersi *vr.* **1.** to get (*v. irr.*) narrower **2.** (*contrarsi*) to contract **3.** (*affollarsi*) to close up **4.** (*di tessuti*) to shrink (*v. irr.*).

restringimento *sm.* **1.** narrowing **2.** (*contrazione*) contraction **3.** (*limitazione*) limitation **4.** (*di tessuto*) shrinking **5.** (*di vestito*) tightening.

restrittivo *agg.* restrictive.

restrizione *sf.* restriction.

retaggio *sm.* heritage.

retata *sf.* **1.** haul **2.** (*di polizia*) roundup.

rete *sf.* **1.** net **2.** (*di letto*) wire netting **3.** (*intreccio*) network.

reticella *sf.* **1.** (*per capelli*) hair-net **2.** (*per bagagli*) luggage-rack.

reticente *agg.* reticent.

reticenza *sf.* reticence.

reticolato *sm.* **1.** (*mil.*) barbed-wire entanglement **2.** (*tracciato di linee*) network.

retìcolo *sm.* **1.** (*anat.*) reticulum (*pl.* -la) **2.** (*ott.*) reticle.

rètina *sf.* retina.

retina *sf.* V. *reticella*.

rètore *sm.* rhetorician.

retòrica *sf.* rhetoric.

retòrico *agg.* rhetorical.

retrarre *vt.* to retract.

retràttile *agg.* retractile.

retrattilità *sf.* retractility.

retribuire *vt.* to pay (*v. irr.*).

retribuzione *sf.* payment.

retrivo *agg.* reactionary.

retro *sm.* back.

retroattività *sf.* retroactivity.
retroattivo *agg.* retroactive.
retrobottega *sm.* back of the shop.
retrocèdere *vi.* to withdraw (*v. irt.*). ◆ **retrocèdere** *vt.* 1. (*mil.*) to degrade 2. to retrocede.
retrocessione *sf.* 1. retrocession 2. (*mil.*) degradation.
retrodatare *vt.* to date back.
retrògrado *agg.* 1. out-of-date 2. (*reazionario*) reactionary.
retroguardia *sf.* rear-guard.
retromarcia *sf.* reverse-gear.
retroscena *sf.* 1. back of the stage 2. (*fig.*) intrigue.
retrospettivo *agg.* retrospective.
retrostante *agg.* at the back.
retroterra *sm.* hinterland.
retroversione *sf.* 1. retroversion 2. (*di traduzione*) back version.
retrovie *sf. pl.* zone behind the front (*sing*).
retrovisore *sm.* specchietto —, driving mirror.
retta[1] *sf.* (*geom.*) straight line.
retta[2] *sf.* (*di pensione*) terms (*pl.*).
retta[3] *sf.* dar — a qu., to listen to so.
rettale *agg.* rectal.
rettamente *avv.* 1. (*giustamente*) rightly 2. (*onestamente*) honestly.
rettangolare *agg.* rectangular.
rettàngolo *sm.* rectangle.
rettìfica *sf.* 1. rectification 2. (*mecc.*) grinding.
rettificare *vt.* 1. to rectify 2. (*mecc.*) to grind (*v. irr.*).
rettificatrice *sf.* grinder.
rettificazione *sf.* V. *rettìfica*.
rettifilo *sm.* straight, stretch.
rèttile *sm.* reptile.
rettilìneo *agg.* rectilinear. ◆ **rettilìneo** *sm.* straight, stretch.
rettitùdine *sf.* righteousness, honesty.
retto *agg.* 1. straight 2. (*geom.; giusto*) right. ◆ **retto** *sm.*, (*anat.*) rectum (*pl.* -ta).
rettorato *sm.* rectorship.
rettore *sm.* 1. rector 2. (*di università*) chancellor.
rèuma *sm.* rheumàtism.
reumàtico *agg. e sm.* rheumatic.
reumatismo *sm.* V. *reuma*.
reverendo *agg.* reverend. ◆ **reverendo** *sm.* clergyman (*pl.* -men).
reversìbile *agg.* reversible.
reversibilità *sf.* reversibility.
reversione *sf.* reversion.

revisionare *vt.* 1. (*mecc.*) to overhaul 2. (*comm.*) to audit.
revisione *sf.* 1. revision 2. (*mecc.*) overhaul 3. (*comm.*) audit.
revisionismo *sm.* revisionism.
revisore *sm.* 1. reviser 2. (*comm.*) auditor.
reviviscenza *sf.* `reviviscence.
rèvoca *sf.* revocation.
revocàbile *agg.* revocable.
revocare *vt.* 1. (*richiamare*) to recall 2. (*giur.*) to revoke.
revocazione *sf.* revocation.
revolverata *sf.* revolver shot.
revulsione *sf.* revulsion.
revulsivo *agg.* revulsive.
riabbottonare *vt.* to button again.
riabilitare *vt.* to rehabilitate.
riabilitazione *sf.* rehabilitation.
riaccèndere *vt.* 1. to relight 2. (*radio, luce ecc.*) to turn on again. ◆ **riaccèndersi** *vr.* 1. to brighten again 2. (*riprender fuoco*) to catch (*v. irr.*) fire again.
riaccompagnare *vt.* to take (*v. irr.*) home.
riacquistare *vt.* 1. to buy (*v. irr.*) again 2. (*riprendere*) to recover.
riadattare *vt.* to adapt again. ◆ **riadattarsi** *vr.* (*rassegnarsi*) to resign oneself again.
riaddormentare *vt.* to send (*v. irr.*) to sleep again. ◆ **riaddormentarsi** *vr.* to fall (*v. irr.*) asleep again.
riaffacciare *vt.* to present again. ◆ **riaffacciarsi** *vr.* to reappear, to appear again.
riaffermare *vt.* to affirm again. ◆ **riaffermarsi** *vr.* to reaffirm oneself.
riafferrare *vt.* to grasp again. ◆ **riafferrarsi** *vr.* to catch (*v. irr.*) hold of (so., sthg.) again.
riallacciare *vt.* 1. to fasten again 2. (*riprendere*) to resume.
riallargare *vt.* to widen again. ◆ **riallargarsi** *vr.* to widen again.
rialto *sm.* rise, height.
rialzamento *sm.* 1. raising 2. (*rialzo*) rise, height.
rialzare *vt.* 1. to raise 2. (*rendere più alto*) to make (*v. irr.*) higher. ◆ **rialzarsi** *vr.* to rise (*v. irr.*) again.
rialzato *agg.* piano —, ground floor.
rialzo *sm.* 1. rise 2. (*di sostegno*) support.
riamare *vt.* to love again.

riammèttere *vt.* to readmit.
rianimare *vt.* to revive. ♦ **rianimarsi** *vr.* 1. (*riprendere allegria*) to cheer up 2. (*riprendere coraggio*) to take (*v. irr.*) courage again.
riapertura *sf.* reopening.
riapparire *vi.* to reappear.
riaprire *vt.* to open again. ♦ **riaprirsi** *vr.* to open again.
riarmare *vt.* to rearm. ♦ **riarmarsi** *vr.* to rearm.
riarmo *sm.* rearmament.
riarso *agg.* parched.
riassestare *vt.* to readjust. ♦ **riassestarsi** *vr.* to readjust.
riassettare *vt.* to put (*v. irr.*) in order again.
riassetto *sm.* rearrangement.
riassorbire *vt.* to reabsorb.
riassùmere *vt.* 1. (*assumere di nuovo*) to take (*v. irr.*) on again 2. (*riepilogare*) to sum up 3. (*riprendere*) to resume.
riassuntivo *agg.* summarizing.
riassunto *sm.* summary.
riattaccare *vt.* 1. (*con colla*) to stick (*v. irr.*) again 2. (*ricucire*) to sew (*v. irr.*) 3. (*riprendere*) to begin (*v. irr.*) again 4. (*mil.*) to attack again 5. (*tel.*) to hang (*v. irr.*) up. ♦ **riattaccarsi** *vr.* to stick again.
riattamento *sm.* repair.
riattare *vt.* to repair.
riattivare *vt.* to restore.
riavere *vt.* 1. to have again 2. (*ricuperare*) to get (*v. irr.*) back. ♦ **riaversi** *vr.* to recover.
riavvicinare *vt.* 1. to approach again 2. (*riconciliare*) to reconcile. ♦ **riavvicinarsi** *vr.* to approach again 2. (*riconciliarsi*) to be reconciled.
ribadire *vt.* to rivet.
ribaldèrìa *sf.* rascality.
ribaldo *sm.* rascal.
ribalta *sf.* 1. (*teat.*) footlights (*pl.*) 2. (*fig.*) limelight.
ribaltàbile *agg.* overturnable.
ribaltare *vt.* to overturn. ♦ **ribaltarsi** *vr.* to capsize.
ribassare *vt.* to reduce. ♦ **ribassare** *vi.* to fall (*v. irr.*).
ribasso *sm.* 1. fall 2. (*sconto*) discount.
ribàttere *vt.* 1. to beat (*v. irr.*) again 2. (*ribadire*) to rivet 3. (*confutare*) to confute. ♦ **ribàttere** *vi.* to insist.

ribattezzare *vt.* to rename.
ribellarsi *vr.* to rebel.
ribelle *agg.* rebellious. ♦ **ribelle** *s.* rebel.
ribellione *sf.* rebellion.
ribes *sm.* gooseberry.
riboccante *agg.* overflowing (with).
riboccare *vi.* to overflow (with).
ribollimento *sm.* ebullition.
ribollire *vi.* to boil.
ribollitura *sf.* reboiling.
ribrezzo *sm.* disgust: *fare* —, to disgust.
ributtante *agg.* disgusting.
ributtare *vt.* 1. to throw (*v. irr.*) again 2. (*respingere*) to repel 3. (*disgustare*) to disgust.
ricacciare *vt.* 1. (*respingere*) to push (out, back) 2. (*ficcare di nuovo*) to thrust (*v. irr.*) again. ♦ **ricacciarsi** *vr.* to plunge again.
ricadere *vi.* 1. to fall (*v. irr.*) again 2. (*avere una ricaduta*) to relapse 3. (*pendere*) to hang (*v. irr.*).
ricaduta *sf.* relapse.
ricalcare *vt.* 1. to pull down 2. (*un disegno*) to transfer || — le orme di qu., to tread (*v. irr.*) in so.'s steps.
ricalcitrante *agg.* recalcitrant.
ricalcitrare *vi.* to recalcitrate.
ricamare *vt.* e *vi.* to embroider.
ricamatore *sm.* embroiderer.
ricamatrice *sf.* embroideress.
ricambiare *vt.* 1. to change again 2. (*contraccambiare*) to return.
ricambio *sm.* 1. replacement 2. (*med.*) metabolism || *di* —, spare (*agg. attr.*).
ricamo *sm.* embroidery: *un* —, a piece of embroidery.
ricapitolare *vt.* to summarize || *ricapitolando*, in short.
ricapitolazione *sf.* summary.
ricaricare *vt.* 1. to reload 2. (*di batteria*) to recharge 3. (*di orologio*) to wind (*v. irr.*) up again.
ricascare *vi.* V. *ricadere.*
ricattare *vt.* to blackmail.
ricattatore *sm.* blackmailer.
ricattatorio *agg.* blackmailing.
ricatto *sm.* blackmail.
ricavare *vt.* 1. to draw (*v. irr.*) 2. (*ottenere*) to get (*v. irr.*).
ricavato *sm.* proceeds (*pl.*).
ricavo *sm.* V. *ricavato.*
riccamente *avv.* richly.
ricchezza *sf.* wealth (*solo sing.*).
riccio¹ *agg.* curly.

riccio² *sm.* **1.** curl **2.** (*bot.*) chestnut husk **3.** (*zool.*) hedgehog **4.** (*di mare*) sea-urchin.

ricciuto *agg.* curly.

ricco *agg.* rich: — *di*, rich in.

ricerca *sf.* **1.** search **2.** (*scientifica*) research **3.** (*indagine*) investigation.

ricercare *vt.* **1.** (*cercare*) to seek (*v. irr.*) for **2.** (*investigare*) to investigate **3.** (*cercare di nuovo*) to look for (so., sthg.) again.

ricercatezza *sf.* refinement.

ricercato *agg.* **1.** (*richiesto*) sought--after **2.** (*raffinato*) refined **3.** (*insolito*) far-fetched **4.** (*dalla polizia*) wanted.

ricercatore *sm.* **1.** searcher **2.** (*scientifico*) researcher.

ricetta *sf.* **1.** (*med.*) prescription **2.** (*cuc.*) recipe.

ricettàcolo *sm.* receptacle.

ricettare *vt.* (*custodire cose rubate*) to receive.

ricettario *sm.* **1.** (*med.*) book of prescriptions **2.** (*cuc.*) book of recipes.

ricettatore *sm.* receiver.

ricettazione *sf.* receiving of stolen goods.

ricettività *sf.* receptivity.

ricettivo *agg.* receptive.

ricevente *agg.* receiving. ♦ **ricevente** *s.* receiver.

ricévere *vt.* to receive.

ricevimento *sm.* **1.** receipt **2.** (*festa*) party.

ricevitore *sm.* receiver.

ricevitorìa *sf.* receiving-office.

ricevuta *sf.* receipt: *accusare* —, to acknowledge receipt.

ricezione *vt.* reception.

richiamare *vt.* **1.** to call again **2.** (*far tornare*) to recall **3.** (*attirare*) to attract **4.** (*rimproverare*) to rebuke ‖ — *all'ordine*, to call to order. ♦ **richiamarsi** *vr.* (*riferirsi*) to refer.

richiamata *sf.* recall.

richiamato *sm.* (*mil.*) re-drafted soldier.

richiamo *sm.* **1.** recall **2.** (*allettamento*) call.

richiedente *s.* applicant.

richièdere *vt.* **1.** to ask (for sthg., so.) again **2.** (*chiedere*) to ask for **3.** (*in restituzione*) to ask (for sthg.) back **4.** (*necessitare di*) to require.

richiesta *sf.* **1.** request: *dietro* —, at request **2.** (*comm.*) demand.

richiùdere *vt.* to close again. ♦ **richiùdersi** *vr.* to close again.

rìcino *sm.* castor-oil plant: *olio di* —, castor-oil.

ricognitore *sm.* (*mil.*) scout.

ricognizione *sf.* reconnaissance.

ricollegare *vt.* to connect. ♦ **ricollegarsi** *vr.* to be connected.

ricollocamento *sm.* replacement.

ricolmare *vt.* **1.** to fill up **2.** (*fig.*) to load.

ricolmo *agg.* **1.** full **2.** (*fig.*) loaded (with).

ricominciare *vt.* to begin (*v. irr.*) again.

ricomparire *vi.* to reappear.

ricompensa *sf.* reward: *in* —, as a reward.

ricompensare *vt.* to reward.

ricomperare *vt.* to buy (*v. irr.*) again.

ricomporre *vt.* to recompose.

ricomposizione *sf.* recomposition.

riconciliare *vt.* to reconcile. ♦ **riconciliarsi** *vr.* to be reconciled.

riconciliatore *sm.* reconciler.

riconciliazione *sf.* reconciliation.

ricondurre *vt.* to take (*v. irr.*) back, to bring (*v. irr.*) back.

riconferma *sf.* reconfirmation.

riconfermare *vt.* to reconfirm.

riconfortare *vt.* to cheer up. ♦ **riconfortarsi** *vr.* to cheer up.

ricongiùngere *vt.* to join again. ♦ **ricongiùngersi** *vr.* to join again.

ricongiungimento *sm.* reunion.

riconnèttere *vt.* to connect again.

riconoscente *agg.* grateful.

riconoscenza *sf.* gratitude.

riconòscere *vt.* to recognize.

riconoscìbile *agg.* recognizable.

riconoscimento *sm.* **1.** recognition **2.** (*ammissione*) admission.

riconquista *sf.* recapture.

riconquistare *vt.* to conquer again.

riconsegna *sf.* return.

riconsegnare *vt.* to redeliver.

riconsiderare *vt.* to reconsider.

riconversione *sf.* reconversion.

riconvocare *vt.* to resummon.

riconvocazione *sf.* resummons.

ricopiare *vt.* to copy.

ricopiatura *sf.* (re)copying.

ricoprire *vt.* **1.** to cover **2.** (*coprire di nuovo*) to cover again **3.** (*fig.*) to load.

ricordare *vt.* 1. to remember 2. (*chiamare alla memoria altrui*) to remind (so. of sthg.) 3. (*nominare*) to mention. ♦ **ricordarsi** *vr.* to remember.

ricordo *sm.* 1. memory 2. (*oggetto ricordo*) souvenir 3. (*memorie*) (*lett.*) memoirs (*pl.*).

ricorrente *agg.* recurrent.

ricorrenza *sf.* 1. recurrence 2. (*anniversario*) anniversary 3. (*occasione*) occasion.

ricòrrere *vi.* 1. (*ripetersi*) to recur 2. (*rivòlgersi*) to apply 3. (*fare appello*) to appeal 4. (*valersi*) to resort.

ricorso *sm.* 1. (*ritorno*) return 2. (*appello*) appeal || *su — di*, on a petition by.

ricostituente *agg. e sm.* tonic.

ricostituire *vt.* to form again. ♦ **ricostituirsi** *vr.* to form again.

ricostituzione *sf.* reconstitution.

ricostruire *vt.* to reconstruct.

ricostruttore *agg.* reconstructive. ♦ **ricostruttore** *sm.* reconstructor.

ricostruzione *sf.* reconstruction.

ricoverare *vt.* to shelter: *— in ospedale*, to hospitalize. ♦ **ricoverarsi** *vr.* to take (*v. irr.*) shelter.

ricòvero *sm.* 1. sheltering 2. (*in ospedale*) hospitalization 3. (*ospizio*) home.

ricreare[1] *vt.* to re-create.

ricreare[2] *vt.* (*divertire*) to recreate. ♦ **ricrearsi** *vr.* to recreate.

ricreativo *agg.* recreative.

ricreazione *sf.* recreation: *ora della —*, playtime.

ricrédersi *vr.* to change one's mind.

ricréscere *vi.* to grow (*v. irr.*) again.

ricréscita *sf.* fresh growth.

ricucire *vt.* 1. to sew (*v. irr.*) up 2. (*cucire di nuovo*) to sew (*v. irr.*) again.

ricucitura *sf.* sewing up.

ricuòcere *vt. e vi.* 1. to cook again 2. (*al forno*) to bake again.

ricuperàbile *agg.* recoverable.

ricuperare *vt.* 1. to recover 2. (*di tempo*) to make (*v. irr.*) up for.

ricùpero *sm.* recovery.

ricurvare *vt.* 1. to bend (*v. irr.*) 2. (*curvare di nuovo*) to bend again.

ricurvo *agg.* bent.

ricusàbile *agg.* refusable.

ricusare *vt.* to refuse.

ridacchiare *vi.* to giggle.

ridanciano *agg.* jolly.

ridare *vt.* 1. to give (*v. irr.*) again 2. (*restituire*) to return.

ridda *sf.* turmoil.

ridente *agg.* 1. smiling 2. (*di luogo*) charming.

ridere *vi.* to laugh (at): *per —*, for fun. ♦ **ridersi** *vr.* to make (*v. irr.*) fun (of).

ridestare *vt.* 1. to wake (*v. irr.*) (up) again 2. (*destare*) to awaken. ♦ **ridestarsi** *vr.* 1. to wake (up) again 2. (*destarsi*) to awake.

ridicolàggine *sf.* nonsense (*solo sing.*).

ridìcolo *agg.* ridiculous. ♦ **ridìcolo** *sm.* ridicule.

ridimensionare *vt.* to reorganize.

ridire *vt.* 1. to say (*v. irr.*) again, to tell (*v. irr.*) again 2. (*riferire*) to repeat 3. (*obiettare*) to object.

ridiscéndere *vi.* to come (*v. irr.*) down again, to go (*v. irr.*) down again.

ridiscòrrere *vi.* to talk again.

ridiventare *vi.* to become (*v. irr.*) again.

ridomandare *vt.* to ask again.

ridonare *vt.* 1. to give (*v. irr.*) again 2. (*restituire*) to give back.

ridondante *agg.* redundant.

ridondanza *sf.* redundancy.

ridondare *vi.* 1. to be redundant 2. (*risultare*) to redound.

ridosso (*nella loc. avv.*) *a — di*, close to.

ridotta *sf.* redoubt.

ridotto *agg.* 1. reduced 2. (*di libro*) abridged || *mal —*, in a sorry plight. ♦ **ridotto** *sm.* (*teat.*) foyer.

riducente *agg.* reducing. ♦ **riducente** *sm.* reducer.

riducìbile *agg.* reducible.

ridurre *vt.* 1. to reduce 2. (*adattare*) to. adapt 3. (*un libro*) to abridge. ♦ **ridursi** *vr.* 1. to be reduced 2. (*restringersi*) to shrink (*v. irr.*).

riduttore *agg. e sm.* V. *riducente*.

riduzione *sf.* 1. reduction 2. (*sconto*) discount 3. (*cine; tv*) adaptation 4. (*di libro*) abridgement.

riecheggiare *vt. e vi.* to re-echo.

riedificare *vt.* to rebuild (*v. irr.*).

riedificazione *sf.* rebuilding.

rieducare *vt.* to re-educate.

rieducazione *sf.* re-education.

rielaborare *vt.* to re-elaborate.

rielèggere *vt.* to re-elect.

rieleggìbile *agg.* re-elegible.

rielezione *sf.* re-election.

riemèrgere *vi.* to re-emerge.

riemersione *sf.* re-emergence.

riempìre *vt.* to fill. ♦ **riempìrsi** *vr.* to fill.

riempitivo *sm.* filling.

rientrante *agg.* receding.

rientranza *sf.* recess.

rientrare *vi.* 1. to re-enter 2. (*tornare*) to return 3. (*far parte*) to be part (of) 4. (*piegare in dentro*) to recede.

rientro *sm.* 1. recess 2. (*astronautica*) retro-firing 3. (*ritorno*) return.

riepilogare *vt.* to recapitulate.

riepìlogo *sm.* recapitulation.

riesame *sm.* re-examination.

riesaminare *vt.* to re-examine.

rièssere *vi.* to be again.

riesumare *vt.* 1. to exhume 2. (*fig.*) to bring (*v. irr.*) to light.

rievocare *vt.* to recall.

rievocazione *sf.* recalling.

rifacimento *sm.* 1. reconstruction 2. (*adattamento*) adaptation.

rifare *vt.* 1. to do (*v. irr.*) again, to make (*v. irr.*) again 2. (*ripercorrere*) to retrace 3. (*riparare*) to repair 4. (*imitare*) to imitate 5. (*indennizzare*) to indemnify. ♦ **rifarsi** *vr.* 1. to make up 2. (*vendicarsi*) to revenge oneself 3. (*risalire*) to go (*v. irr.*) back.

rifasciare *vt.* 1. to bandage again 2. (*un bambino*) to swaddle again.

riferìbile *agg.* 1. referable 2. (*raccontabile*) fit to be told.

riferimento *sm.* reference: *linea, punto di —*, datum-line, datum-point.

riferire *vt.* 1. to report 2. (*attribuire*) to ascribe. ♦ **riferìrsi** *vr.* to refer.

rificcare *vt.* to thrust (*v. irr.*) again.

rifilare *vt.* 1. to spin again 2. (*tagliare a filo*) to trim 3. (*appioppare*) to palm off.

rifilatura *sf.* 1. trimming 2. (*bordo*) border.

rifinimento *sm.* finishing touch.

rifinire *vt.* to finish.

rifinitura *sf.* V. *rifinimento*.

rifiorire *vi.* 1. to blossom again 2. (*fig.*) to flourish again.

rifioritura *sf.* reflorescence.

rifiutàbile *agg.* refusable.

rifiutare *vt.* to refuse.

rifiuto *sm.* refusal || *rifiuti*, waste (*solo sing.*); *i rifiuti della società*, the dregs of society.

riflessione *sf.* reflection.

riflessivo *agg.* 1. reflective 2. (*gramm.*) reflexive.

riflèsso *agg.* reflected, reflex (*anche fig.*). ♦ **riflèsso** *sm.* 1. reflection 2. (*di colore*) tint 3. (*med.*) reflex || *di —*, as a consequence; *per —*, indirectly.

riflèttere *vt. e vi.* to reflect. ♦ **riflèttersi** *vr.* to be reflected.

riflettore *sm.* 1. reflector 2. (*lampada*) searchlight.

rifluire *vi.* 1. to flow again 2. (*fluire indietro*) to flow back.

riflusso *sm.* ebb.

rifocillare *vt.* to give (*v. irr.*) refreshment. ♦ **rifocillàrsi** *vr.* to take (*v. irr.*) refreshment.

rifòndere *vt.* 1. to melt again 2. (*rimborsare*) to refund.

riforma *sf.* reformation.

riformare *vt.* 1. to reform 2. (*mil.*) to declare unfit for military service.

riformatore *sm.* reformer.

riformatorio *sm.* reformatory.

riformismo *sm.* reformism.

riformista *s.* reformist.

rifornimento *sm.* 1. supplying 2. (*aer.; auto*) refuelling 3. (*scorta*) supply || *stazione di —*, filling-station; *far — di benzina*, to fill up the tank.

rifornire *vt.* to supply (so. with).

rifornitore *sm.* supplier.

rifràngere *vt.* to refract. ♦ **rifràngersi** *vr.* to be refracted.

rifrangibilità *sf.* refrangibility.

rifrattore *sm.* refractor.

rifrazione *sf.* refraction.

rifritto *agg.* 1. fried again 2. (*fig.*) stale.

rifuggire *vi.* 1. to escape again 2. (*essere alieno*) to shrink (*v. irr.*).

rifugiarsi *vr.* to take (*v. irr.*) shelter.

rifugiato *agg. e sm.* refugee.

rifugio *sm.* 1. shelter 2. (*di montagna*) mountain hut.

rifùlgere *vi.* to shine (*v. irr.*) brightly (with sthg.).

rifusione *sf.* 1. re-melting 2. (*rimborso*) repayment.

riga *sf.* 1. line 2. (*fila*) row 3. (*regolo*) rule 4. (*striscia*) stripe 5. (*scriminatura*) parting 6. (*mus.*

stave || *mettersi in* —, to line up.

rigaglie *sf. pl.* giblets.

rigàgnolo *sm.* 1. rivulet 2. (*scolo*) gutter.

rigare *vt.* 1. to rule 2. (*solcare*) to furrow || — *diritto*, to behave well.

rigato *agg.* 1. ruled 2. (*a strisce*) striped 3. (*solcato*) furrowed.

rigattiere *sm.* second-hand dealer.

rigatura *sf.* 1. ruling 2. (*di arma*) rifling.

rigenerare *vt.* 1. to regenerate 2. (*mecc.*) to repair.

rigeneratore *agg.* regenerative. ♦ **rigeneratore** *sm.* regenerator.

rigenerazione *sf.* regeneration.

rigettare *vt.* 1. to throw (*v. irr.*) again 2. (*gettare indietro*) to throw back 3. (*vomitare*) to vomit 4. (*respingere*) to reject.

rigetto *sm.* rejection.

righello *sm.* ruler.

rigidezza *sf.* 1. stiffness 2. (*di clima*) rigour.

rigidità *sf.* V. rigidezza.

rìgido *agg.* 1. stiff 2. (*di clima*) rigorous.

rigirare *vt.* 1. to turn again 2. (*cambiare*) to change. ♦ **rigirare** *vi.* to walk about. ♦ **rigirarsi** *vr.* to turn about.

rigiro *sm.* 1. turning round 2. (*di parole*) involved expression.

rigo *sm.* V. riga.

rigoglio *sm.* bloom.

rigogliosità *sf.* luxuriancy.

rigoglioso *agg.* flourishing.

rigonfiamento *sm.* swelling.

rigonfiare *vt.* to swell (*v. irr.*). ♦ **rigonfiarsi** *vr.* to swell.

rigonfio *agg.* swollen (with). ♦ **rigonfio** *sm.* swelling.

rigore *sm.* 1. rigour 2. (*esattezza*) exactness || *di* —, compulsory; *a* —, according to the rules; *a* — *di termini*, in the strict sense, *area di* — (*sport*), penalty-area.

rigorismo *sm.* rigorism.

rigorista *s.* rigorist.

rigorosità *sf.* 1. rigour 2. (*esattezza*) preciseness.

rigoroso *agg.* 1. rigorous 2. (*esatto*) exact.

rigovernare *vt.* 1. to govern again 2. (*di piatti*) to wash up.

rigovernatura *sf.* washing-up.

riguadagnare *vt.* 1. to earn again

2. (*ricuperare, raggiungere*) to regain.

riguardare *vt.* 1. to look at (so., sthg.) again 2. (*esaminare*) to examine 3. (*considerare*) to regard. ♦ **riguardarsi** *vr.* to take (*v. irr.*) care of oneself.

riguardata *sf.* look.

riguardévole *agg.* 1. considerable 2. (*importante*) important.

riguardo *sm.* 1. regard 2. (*cura*) care || *persona di* —, person of consequence; — *a*, as regards; *a questo* —, in this connection.

riguardoso *agg.* respectful.

rigurgitare *vi.* 1. to overflow 2. (*di stomaco*) to regurgitate 3. (*brulicare*) to swarm (with).

rigùrgito *sm.* 1. overflow 2. (*di stomaco*) regurgitation 3. (*travaso*) extravasation 4. (*gorgo*) eddy.

rilanciare *vt.* 1. to throw (*v. irr.*) again 2. (*lanciare indietro*) to throw back 3. (*un'offerta*) to raise.

rilancio *sm.* 1. new throw 2. (*di offerta*) raising.

rilasciare *vt.* 1. to release 2. (*concedere*) to grant 3. (*emettere*) to issue. ♦ **rilasciarsi** *vr.* 1. to slacken 2. (*med.*) to prolapse 3. (*rilassarsi*) to relax.

rilascio *sm.* 1. release 2. (*concessione*) granting 3. (*emissione*) issue.

rilassamento *sm.* 1. slackening 2. (*med.*) prolapse 3. (*riposo*) relaxation.

rilassare *vt.* 1. to slacken 2. (*distendere*) to relax. ♦ **rilassarsi** *vr.* 1. to slacken 2. (*distendersi*) to relax.

rilassatezza *sf.* laxity.

rilegare *vt.* 1. to tie again 2. (*libri*) to bind (*v. irr.*).

rilegatura *sf.* binding.

rilèggere *vt.* to reread (*v. irr.*), to read (*v. irr.*) again.

rilento (*nella loc. avv.*) *a* —, slowly.

rilevamento *sm.* 1. (*topografico*) survey 2. (*mar.*) bearing 3. (*cambio*) relieving.

rilevante *agg.* prominent.

rilevare *vt.* 1. to take (*v. irr.*) off again 2. (*notare*) to notice 3. (*far notare*) to point out 4. (*prendere*) to take 5. (*topografia*) to survey 6. (*sostituire*) to relieve 7. (*comm.*) to take over.

rilevazione *sf.* V. *rilievo.*

rilievo *sm.* 1. relief 2. (*importanza*) importance 3. (*osservazione*) remark 4. (*topografico*) survey 5. (*comm.*) taking over || *mettere in* —, to stress.

rilucente *agg.* glittering.

rilùcere *vi.* to glitter.

riluttante *agg.* reluctant.

riluttanza *sf.* reluctance.

riluttare *vi.* to reluct (at).

rima *sf.* rhyme || *rispondere per le rime,* to give (*v. irr.*) tit for tat.

rimandare *vt.* 1. to send (*v. irr.*) again 2. (*restituire*) to send back 3. (*posporre*) to postpone 4. (*far riferimento*) to refer 5. (*agli esami*) to make (*v. irr.*) (so.) repeat (an exam).

rimando *sm.* 1. returning 2. (*differimento*) postponement 3. (*segno di richiamo*) reference-mark.

rimaneggiamento *sm.* 1. rearrangement 2. (*di opera letteraria*) adaptation 3. (*pol.*) shuffle.

rimaneggiare *vt.* 1. to rearrange 2. (*modificare*) to change 3. (*pol.*) to shuffle.

rimanente *agg.* remaining. ♦ **rimanente** *sm.* rest.

rimanenza *sf.* remainder.

rimanere *vi.* 1. to remain 2. (*avanzare*) to be left 3. (*essere sorpreso*) to be astonished.

rimangiare *vt.* to eat (*v. irr.*) again. ♦ **rimangiarsi** *vr.* to take (*v. irr.*) back.

rimarchévole *agg.* remarkable.

rimare *vt. e vi.* to rhyme.

rimarginare *vt.* to heal. ♦ **rimarginarsi** *vr.* to heal.

rimaritare *vt.* to marry again. ♦ **rimaritarsi** *vr.* to marry again.

rimasticare *vt.* 1. to chew again 2. (*fig.*) to muse.

rimasuglio *sm.* remains (*pl.*).

rimatore *sm.* rhymer.

rimbalzare *vi.* to rebound.

rimbalzello *sm.* ducks and drakes.

rimbalzo *sm.* rebound: *di* —, on the rebound.

rimbambimento *sm.* dotage.

rimbambire *vi.* to reach one's dotage.

rimbambito *agg.* in one's dotage (*pred.*): *un vecchio* —, a dotard.

rimbeccare *vt.* to retort.

rimbecco *sm.* retort.

rimbecillire *vi.* 1. to grow (*v. irr.*) stupid 2. (*per età*) to reach one's dotage.

rimbecillito *agg.* doting.

rimboccare *vt.* to tuck up. ♦ **rimboccarsi** *vr.* to tuck up.

rimbombante *agg.* thundering.

rimbombare *vi.* 1. to thunder 2. (*risuonare*) to resound.

rimbombo *sm.* roar.

rimborsàbile *agg.* repayable.

rimborsare *vt.* to reimburse.

rimborso *sm.* reimbursement.

rimboscare *vt.* V. *rimboschire.*

rimboschimento *sm.* reafforestation.
irr.) wooded again.

rimboschire *vt.* to reafforest. ♦ **rimboschirsi** *vr.* to become (*v. irr.*).

rimbrottare *vt.* to reproach.

rimbrotto *sm.* reproach.

rimediàbile *agg.* remediable.

rimediare *vi.* to find (*v. irr.*) a remedy (for).

rimedio *sm.* remedy.

rimembranza *sf.* memory.

rimembrare *vt.* to remember.

rimeritare *vt.* to reward.

rimescolamento *sm.* 1. stir 2. (*turbamento*) shock.

rimescolare *vt.* 1. to stir again 2. (*mescolare*) to stir. ♦ **rimescolarsi** *vr.* to be upset || *gli si rimescolò il sangue* (*per rabbia*), his blood boiled, (*per paura*), his blood ran cold.

rimescolìo *sm.* confusion.

rimessa *sf.* 1. replacing 2. (*per auto*) garage 3. (*di denaro*) remittance 4. (*di merci*) consignment || — *in gioco,* throw-in.

rimesso *agg.* 1. (*falso*) false 2. (*ristabilito*) well again 3. (*perdonato*) forgiven.

rimestare *vt.* V. *rimescolare.*

riméttere *vt.* 1. to put (*v. irr.*) again, to put back 2. (*consegnare*) to hand 3. (*mandare, perdonare*) to remit 4. (*affidare*) to leave (*v. irr.*) 5. (*vomitare*) to vomit || — *in gioco,* to throw (*v. irr.*) in; *rimetterci,* to lose (*v. irr.*). ♦ **riméttersi** *vr.* 1. (*affidarsi*) to rely on 2. (*ristabilirsi*) to recover 3. (*rasserenarsi*) to clear up.

rimirare *vt.* to gaze (at). ♦ **rimirarsi** *vr.* to admire oneself.

rimisurare *vt.* to measure again.

rimodellare *vt.* to remodel.

rimodernamento *sm.* modernization.

rimodernare *vt.* to modernize. ♦ **rimodernarsi** *vr.* to become up-to-date.

rimondare *vt.* to clean again.

rimonta *sf.* 1. (*mil.*) remount 2. (*sport*) catching up.

rimontare *vt.* 1. to go (*v. irr.*) up 2. (*ricomporre*) to reassemble. ♦ **rimontare** *vi.* 1. to remount 2. (*fig.*) to go back 3. (*sport*) to catch (*v. irr.*) up ‖ — *in auto*, to get (*v. irr.*) into a car again.

rimorchiare *vt.* to tow.

rimorchiatore *sm.* tug.

rimorchio *sm.* 1. tow 2. (*veicolo*) trailer.

rimòrdere *vt.* 1. to bite (*v. irr.*) again 2. (*fig.*) to prick.

rimorso *sm.* remorse.

rimosso *agg.* removed.

rimostranza *sf.* remonstrance: *fare le proprie rimostranze*, to remonstrate.

rimostrare *vi.* to remonstrate.

rimovìbile *agg.* removable.

rimozione *sf.* removal.

rimpacchettare *vt.* to package again.

rimpadronirsi *vr.* to seize again.

rimpagliare *vt.* 1. to re-cover with straw 2. (*imbottire*) to re-stuff with straw.

rimpallo *sm.* counterblow.

rimpannucciarsi *vr.* (*fig.*) to improve one's financial position.

rimpastare *vt.* 1. to knead again 2. (*fig.*) to rearrange.

rimpasto *sm.* 1. kneading again 2. (*fig.*) rearrangement 3. (*pol.*) reshuffle.

rimpatriare *vt.* to repatriate. ♦ **rimpatriare** *vi.* to return to one's country.

rimpatrio *sm.* repatriation.

rimpetto *avv.* opposite.

rimpiàngere *vt.* 1. to regret 2. (*una perdita*) to mourn.

rimpianto *sm.* regret.

rimpiattarsi *vr.* to hide (*v. irr.*) oneself.

rimpiattino *sm.* hide-and-seek.

rimpiazzare *vt.* to replace.

rimpiazzo *sm.* replacement.

rimpicciolire *vt.* to lessen. ♦ **rimpicciolirsi** *vr.* to lessen.

rimpiegare *vt.* to re-employ.

rimpiego *sm.* re-employment.

rimpinguare *vt.* 1. to fatten 2. (*arricchire*) to enrich. ♦ **rimpinguarsi** *vr.* 1. to fatten 2. (*arricchirsi*) to grow (*v. irr.*) rich.

rimpinzare *vt.* to stuff (with).

rimpolpare *vt.* V. *rimpinguare*.

rimproverare *vt.* to reproach.

rimpròvero *sm.* reproach: *muovere un —*, to reproach.

rimuginare *vt.* to brood over.

rimunerare *vt.* to remunerate.

rimuòvere *vt.* 1. to remove 2. (*dissuadere*) to dissuade 3. (*da una carica*) to dismiss.

rimutare *vt.* to change again.

rinascenza *sf.* Renaissance.

rinàscere *vi.* to revive.

rinascimentale *agg.* Renaissance (*attr.*).

rinascimento *sm.* Renaissance.

rinàscita *sf.* 1. rebirth 2. (*fig.*) revival.

rincagnarsi *vr.* to frown.

rincagnato *agg.* pug (*attr.*).

rincalzare *vt.* 1. (*rimboccare*) to tuck in 2. (*sostenere*) to prop up.

rincalzo *sm.* support: *a — di*, in support of.

rincantucciare *vt.* to put (*v. irr.*) in a corner. ♦ **rincantucciarsi** *vr.* to hide (*v. irr.*) in a corner.

rincarare *vt.* 1. to raise the price of 2. (*esagerare*) to exaggerate. ♦ **rincarare** *vi.* to become (*v. irr.*) more expensive.

rincaro *sm.* rise in prices.

rincasare *vi.* to return home.

rinchiùdere *vt.* to shut (*v. irr.*) up.

rincitrullire *vt.* to make (*v. irr.*) silly. ♦ **rincitrullirsi** *vr.* to grow (*v. irr.*) silly.

rincivilire *vt.* to civilize. ♦ **rincivilirsi** *vr.* 1. to become (*v. irr.*) civilized 2. (*raffinarsi*) to become refined.

rincollare *vt.* to paste again.

rincominciare *vt.* to begin (*v. irr.*) again.

rincontrare *vt.* to meet (*v. irr.*) again. ♦ **rincontrarsi** *vr.* to meet again.

rincontro *sm.* meeting.

rincoramento *sm.* encouragement.

rincorare *vt.* to encourage. ♦ **rincorarsi** *vr.* to pluck up courage.

rincòrrere *vt.* to run (*v. irr.*) after.

rincorsa *sf.* run-up.

rincréscere *vi.* 1. to be sorry: *mi*

rincresce, I am sorry 2. (*dar noia*) to mind: *ti rincresce aprire la finestra?*, do you mind opening the window?

rincrescimento *sm.* regret: *con mio —*, to my regret.

rincrudimento *sm.* aggravation.

rincrudire *vi.* 1. to aggravate 2. (*esacerbare*) to embitter 3. (*del tempo*) to get (*v. irr.*) worse.

rinculare *vi.* to recoil.

rinculo *sm.* recoil.

rinfacciare *vt.* to throw (*v. irr.*) (sthg.) in so.'s face.

rinfiancare *vt.* to support.

rinfilare *vt.* 1. to thread again 2. (*rinserire*) to insert again. ♦ **rinfilarsi** *vr.* 1. (*introdursi*) to slip again 2. (*rindossare*) to slip on again.

rinfiorare *vt.* to adorn with flowers again.

rinfittire *vt.* 1. to thicken 2. (*rendere più frequenti*) to make (*v. irr.*) more frequent. ♦ **rinfittirsi** *vr.* (*di lana*) to shrink (*v. irr.*).

rinfocolare *vt.* 1. to poke 2. (*fig.*) to stir up (again).

rinfoderare *vt.* to sheathe (again).

rinforzamento *sm.* strengthening.

rinforzare *vt.* 1. to strengthen 2. (*mecc.*) to stiffen. ♦ **rinforzarsi** *vr.* to become (*v. irr.*) stronger.

rinforzo *sm.* 1. strengthening 2. (*mil.*) reinforcements (*pl.*) 3. (*fig.*) support 4. (*mecc.*) stiffener.

rinfrancare *vt.* to encourage. ♦ **rinfrancarsi** *vr.* 1. (*migliorare*) to improve 2. (*riprendere coraggio*) to pluck up courage.

rinfrescamento *sm.* cooling.

rinfrescante *agg.* refreshing.

rinfrescare *vt.* 1. to cool 2. (*ristorare*) to refresh 3. (*rinnovare*) to renovate. ♦ **rinfrescare** *vi.* to cool.

rinfresco *sm.* 1. refreshments (*pl.*) 2. (*ricevimento*) cocktail party.

rinfusa (*nella loc. avv.*) *alla —*, in confusion.

ringalluzzire *vt.* to make (*v. irr.*) cocky. ♦ **ringalluzzirsi** *vr.* to become (*v. irr.*) cocky.

ringentilire *vt.* to refine.

ringhiare *vi.* to snarl.

ringhiera *sf.* 1. railing 2. (*di scale*) banisters (*pl.*).

ringhio *sm.* snarl.

ringhioso *agg.* snarling

ringiovanimento *sm.* rejuvenation.

ringiovanire *vt.* 1. to make (*v. irr.*) young again 2. (*far sembrare più giovane*) to make (so.) look younger. ♦ **ringiovanire** *vi.* 1. to grow (*v. irr.*) young again 2. (*sembrare più giovane*) to look younger.

ringiovanito *agg.* young again.

ringoiare *vt.* to swallow up again.

ringranare *vt.* to re-engage.

ringraziamento *sm.* thanks (*pl.*).

ringraziare *vt.* to thank.

ringuainare *vt.* V. *rinfoderare*.

rinite *sf.* rhinitis.

rinnegàbile *agg.* deniable.

rinnegamento *sm.* disowning.

rinnegare *vt.* to disown.

rinnegato *agg.* e *sm.* renegade.

rinnegatore *sm.* disowner.

rinnestare *vt.* 1. (*agr.*) to graft again 2. (*mecc.*) to re-engage.

rinnesto *sm.* 1. (*agr.*) new grafting 2. (*mecc.*) re-engagement.

rinnovàbile *agg.* renewable.

rinnovamento *sm.* renewal.

rinnovare *vt.* to renew. ♦ **rinnovarsi** *vr.* (*riaccadere*) to happen again.

rinnovatore *sm.* renewer.

rinnovazione *sf.* renewal.

rinnovellare *vt.* to renew. ♦ **rinnovellarsi** *vr.* to be renewed.

rinnovo *sm.* renewal.

rinoceronte *sm.* rhinoceros.

rinolaringite *sf.* rhinolaryngitis.

rinologìa *sf.* rhinology.

rinomanza *sf.* renown.

rinomato *agg.* renowned.

rinominare *vt.* 1. to name again 2. (*designare di nuovo*) to reappoint.

rinoplàstica *sf.* rhinoplasty.

rinoscopìa *sf.* rhinoscopy.

rinoscopio *sm.* rhinoscope.

rinsaccare *vt.* to pack again. ♦ **rinsaccarsi** *vr.* to shrug one's shoulders.

rinsaldamento *sm.* consolidation.

rinsaldare *vt.* to consolidate.

rinsanguare *vt.* 1. to supply with new blood 2. (*fig.*) to reinvigorate. ♦ **rinsanguarsi** *vr.* 1. to recover 2. (*finanziariamente*) to re-establish one's financial condition.

rinsanire *vi.* 1. to recover 2. (*rinsavire*) to return to reason.

rinsavimento *sm.* return to reason.

rinsavire *vi.* to recover one's wits.

rinsecchire *vi.* 1. to dry up 2. (*di persone*) to get (*v. irr.*) thin 3.

(*avvizzire*) to wither.

rinserrare *vt.* to shut (*v. irr.*) up (again).

rintanarsi *vr.* to shut (*v. irr.*) oneself up.

rintascare *vt.* to pocket again.

rintavolare *vt.* to start again.

rintoccare *vi.* **1.** (*di orologio*) to strike (*v. irr.*) **2.** (*di campana*) to toll.

rintocco *sm.* **1.** (*di orologio*) stroke **2.** (*di campana*) toll.

rintontire *vt.* to stun. ♦ **rintontirsi** *vr.* to be stunned.

rintracciare *vt.* **1.** to trace **2.** (*trovare*) to find (*v. irr.*) out.

rintronamento *sm.* booming.

rintronare *vt.* **1.** to deafen **2.** (*stordire*) to stun. ♦ **rintronare** *vi.* to boom.

rintuzzare *vt.* **1.** to blunt **2.** (*ribattere*) to retort.

rinuncia *sf.* renouncement.

rinunciare *vi.* to renounce (sthg.).

rinunciatario *agg.* releasee.

rinvenimento *sm.* recovery.

rinvenire *vt.* to find (*v. irr.*). ♦ **rinvenire** *vi.* **1.** to recover one's senses **2.** (*riprendere freschezza*) to revive **3.** (*riprendere morbidezza*) to soften.

rinverdire *vt.* (*ravvivare*) to reawaken. ♦ **rinverdire** *vi.* **1.** to turn green again **2.** (*ravvivarsi*) to revive.

rinvestimento *sm.* reinvestment.

rinvestire *vt.* **1.** to restore to the possession of **2.** (*comm.*) to reinvest.

rinviare *vt.* **1.** to put (*v. irr.*) off **2.** (*mandare indietro*) to return.

rinvigorimento *sm.* reinvigoration.

rinvigorire *vt.* to reinvigorate. ♦ **rinvigorirsi** *vr.* to regain strength.

rinvilire *vt.* to lower. ♦ **rinvilire** *vi.* to become (*v. irr.*) cheaper.

rinvìo *sm.* **1.** postponement **2.** (*il rimandare indietro*) returning.

rinvoltare *vt.* to wrap up again.

rinzaffare *vt.* **1.** to bung again **2.** (*arch.*) to rough in.

rinzaffatura *sf.* (*arch.*) roughing-in coat.

rio[1] *sm.* rivulet.

rio[2] *agg.* evil.

rioccupare *vt.* to reoccupy.

rioccupazione *sf.* reoccupation.

rionale *agg.* local, ward (*attr.*).

rione *sm.* ward, district.

riordinare *vt.* **1.** to tidy up **2.** (*riorganizzare*) to reorganize **3.** (*comandare di nuovo*) to order again.

riordinatore *sm.* **1.** rearranger **2.** (*riorganizzatore*) reorganizer.

riordinazione *sf.* **1.** rearrangement **2.** (*riorganizzazione*) reorganization **3.** (*nuova ordinazione*) new order.

riòrdino *sm.* V. riordinazione.

riorganizzare *vt.* to reorganize.

riorganizzatore *sm.* reorganizer.

riorganizzazione *sf.* reorganization.

riottosità *sf.* **1.** turbulence **2.** (*indocilità*) indocility.

riottoso *agg.* **1.** turbulent **2.** (*indocile*) indocile.

ripa *sf.* **1.** bank **2.** (*scarpata*) scarp.

ripagare *vt.* **1.** to repay (*v. irr.*) **2.** (*pagare di nuovo*) to pay (*v. irr.*) again.

riparare *vt.* **1.** (*proteggere*) to shelter **2.** (*aggiustare*) to repair **3.** (*risarcire*) to redress || — *un esame*, to repeat an exam. ♦ **riparare** *vi.* **1.** (*porre rimedio*) to remedy **2.** (*rifugiarsi*) to take (*v. irr.*) shelter. ♦ **ripararsi** *vr.* to take shelter.

riparatore *agg.* repairing. ♦ **riparatore** *sm.* repairer.

riparazione *sf.* **1.** repair: *in* —, under repair **2.** (*fig.*) reparation.

riparlare *vi.* to speak (*v. irr.*) again.

riparo *sm.* **1.** shelter **2.** (*rimedio*) remedy **3.** (*mecc.*) guard.

ripartire[1] *vi.* to start again.

ripartire[2] *vt.* to divide.

ripartizione *sf.* division.

ripassare *vi.* **1.** to pass again **2.** (*far visita*) to call again. ♦ **ripassare** *vt.* **1.** (*riattraversare*) to cross again **2.** (*dare di nuovo*) to pass again **3.** (*rileggere, rivedere*) to go (*v. irr.*) through **4.** (*mecc.*) to overhaul.

ripassata *sf.* **1.** (*revisione*) revision **2.** (*mecc.*) overhauling **3.** (*pulita*) cleaning **4.** (*mano di vernice*) new coat.

ripasso *sf.* **1.** (*ritorno*) return **2.** (*revisione*) revision **3.** (*di lezioni*) review.

ripensamento *sm.* reflection: *avere un* —, to change one's mind.

ripensare *vi.* **1.** to think (*v. irr.*) (of sthg., so.) again **2.** (*riconside-*

rare) to think over 3. (*cambiar parere*) to change one's mind: *ci ho ripensato*, I have changed my mind.

ripercòrrere *vt.* to travel over (sthg.) again.

ripercuòtere *vt.* to strike (*v. irr.*) again. ♦ **ripercuòtersi** *vr.* 1. to reverberate 2. (*fig.*) to influence (so., sthg.).

ripercussione *sf.* repercussion.

ripescare *vt.* 1. to catch (*v. irr.*) again 2. (*ritrovare*) to find (*v. irr.*) again.

ripetente *s.* repeater.

ripètere *vt.* to repeat.

ripetitore *sm.* 1. repeater 2. (*scol.*) private tutor.

ripetizione *sf.* 1. (*rifacimento*) repetition 2. (*ripasso*) revision 3. (*lezione privata*) private lesson || *arma a —*, repeater.

ripetuto *agg.* repeated.

ripiano *sm.* 1. (*terreno*) terrace 2. (*pianerottolo*) landing 3. (*scaffale*) shelf (*pl.* -lves).

ripicco *sm.* spite: *per —*, out of spite.

ripidezza *sf.* steepness.

ripido *agg.* steep.

ripiegamento *sm.* 1. folding 2. (*il curvare*) bending 3. (*mil.*) withdrawal.

ripiegare *vt.* 1. to bend (*v. irr.*) again 2. (*piegare*) to fold. ♦ **ripiegare** *vi.* 1. to bend 2. (*ritirarsi*) to withdraw (*v. irr.*). ♦ **ripiegarsi** *vr.* to bend.

ripiegatura *sf.* 1. folding 2. (*piega*) fold 2. (*curva*) bend.

ripiego *sm.* 1. expedient 2. (*rimedio*) remedy.

ripienezza *sf.* fullness.

ripieno *agg.* 1. full 2. (*cuc.*) stuffed (with). ♦ **ripieno** *sm.* 1. filling 2. (*cuc.*) stuffing.

ripigliare *vt.* V. *riprendere*.

ripiombare *vt.* to plunge back. ♦ **ripiombare** *vi.* to fall (*v. irr.*) again.

ripopolamento *sm.* 1. repeopling 2. (*di animali*) restocking.

ripopolare *vt.* 1. to repeople 2. (*di animali*) to restock.

riporre *vt.* 1. to replace 2. (*metter via*) to put (*v. irr.*) away 3. (*porre*) to place. ♦ **riporsi** *vr.* (*riprendere*) to resume.

riportare *vt.* 1. to bring (*v. irr.*)

again, to take (*v. irr.*) again 2. (*portare indietro*) to bring back, to take back 3. (*riferire*) to report 4. (*citare*) to quote 5. (*ricevere*) to get (*v. irr.*) 6. (*mat.*) to carry. ♦ **riportarsi** *vr.* (*tornare*) to go (*v. irr.*) back.

riporto *sm.* 1. (*mat.*) carry over 2. (*in borsa*) contango 3. (*ornamento*) appliqué.

riposante *agg.* restful.

riposare *vt.* 1. to rest 2. (*posare di nuovo*) to place back. ♦ **riposare** *vi.* to rest. ♦ **riposarsi** *vr.* to rest.

riposato *agg.* 1. (*fresco*) fresh 2. (*tranquillo*) quiet.

riposo *sm.* rest: *andare a —*, to retire.

ripostiglio *sm.* cupboard.

riprèndere *vt.* 1. to take (*v. irr.*) again 2. (*riavere*) to take back 3. (*riassumere, ricominciare*) to resume 4. (*ricuperare*) to recover 5. (*rimproverare*) to reprove 6. (*teat.*) to revive 7. (*cine*) to shoot (*v. irr.*). ♦ **riprèndersi** *vr.* 1. to recover 2. (*da turbamento*) to collect oneself 3. (*correggersi*) to correct oneself.

riprensione *sf.* reprehension.

riprensivo *agg.* reprehensive.

ripresa *sf.* 1. renewal 2. (*teat.; rinascita*) revival 3. (*riconquista*) recapture 4. (*da malattia*) recovery 5. (*cine*) shot 6. (*auto*) acceleration 7. (*registrazione*) recording 8. (*di pugilato*) round 9. (*sport*) second half.

ripresentare *vt.* to present again.

ripristinare *vt.* 1. to restore 2. (*rimettere in vigore*) to re-establish.

ripristino *sm.* 1. restoration 2. (*il rimettere in vigore*) re-establishment.

riproducìbile *agg.* reproducible.

riprodurre *vt.* to reproduce. ♦ **riprodursi** *vr.* to reproduce.

riproduttivo *agg.* reproductive.

riproduttore *agg.* reproducing. ♦ **riproduttore** *sm.* reproducer.

riproduzione *sf.* reproduction.

ripromèttere *vt.* to promise again. ♦ **ripromèttersi** *vr.* 1. to intend 2. (*aspettarsi*) to expect.

riproporre *vt.* to re-propose. ♦ **riproporsi** *vr.* to re-propose.

riprova *sf.* (new) proof.

riprovare *vt.* 1. to try again 2. (*sentire di nuovo*) to feel (*v. irr.*)

again 3. (*disapprovare*) to criticize 4. (*scol.*) to fail.

riprovazione *sf.* reprobation.

riprovévole *agg.* **1.** blamable **2.** (*spregevole*) despicable.

ripubblicare *vt.* to republish.

ripudiare *vt.* to repudiate.

ripudio *sm.* repudiation.

ripugnante *agg.* repugnant.

ripugnanza *sf.* repugnance.

ripugnare *vi.* **1.** (*disgustare*) to disgust **2.** (*essere contrario*) to be repugnant.

ripulire *vt.* **1.** to clean again **2.** (*pulire*) to clean **3.** (*fig.*) to polish **4.** (*saccheggiare*) to ransack.

ripulita *sf.* clean: *darsi una —*, to tidy oneself up.

ripulsa *sf.* repulse.

ripulsione *sf.* repulsion.

ripulsivo *agg.* repulsive.

riquadrare *vt.* **1.** to square **2.** (*una stanza*) to decorate.

riquadratura *sf.* **1.** square **2.** (*decorazione*) decoration.

riquadro *sm.* **1.** square **2.** (*su parete*) panel.

risacca *sf.* surf.

risaia *sf.* rice-field.

risalire *vt.* **1.** to go (*v. irr.*) up again **2.** (*contro corrente*) to go up: *— la corrente*, to go upstream. ♦ **risalire** *vi.* **1.** to go up again **2.** (*nel tempo*) to go back.

risaltare[1] *vi.* **1.** to show (*v. irr.*) up **2.** (*di persona*) to stand (*v. irr.*) out.

risaltare[2] *vt.* to jump again.

risalto *sm.* **1.** prominence **2.** (*rilievo*) relief.

risanàbile *agg.* **1.** curable **2.** (*bonificabile*) reclaimable.

risanamento *sm.* **1.** curing **2.** (*guarigione*) recovery **3.** (*bonifica*) reclamation **4.** (*fig.*) reformation || *— di quartiere*, slum-clearance.

risanare *vt.* **1.** to cure **2.** (*bonificare*) to reclaim **3.** (*un quartiere*) to clear (a slum). ♦ **risanare** *vi.* to recover.

risanatore *agg.* healing. ♦ **risanatore** *sm.* healer.

risapere *vt.* to come (*v. irr.*) to know.

risaputo *agg.* well-known.

risarcìbile *agg.* that can be indemnified.

risarcimento *sm.* indemnity.

risarcire *vt.* to indemnify.

risata *sf.* laugh: *scoppiare in una —*, to burst (*v. irr.*) out laughing.

riscaldamento *sm.* heating.

riscaldare *vt.* **1.** to warm (up) **2.** (*di casa*) to heat **3.** (*fig.*) to excite. ♦ **riscaldarsi** *vr.* to warm up.

riscaldo *sm.* inflammation.

riscattàbile *agg.* redeemable.

riscattare *vt.* to redeem.

riscatto *sm.* **1.** ransom **2.** (*redenzione*) redemption.

rischiaramento *sm.* brightening.

rischiarare *vt.* to light (*v. irr.*) (up). ♦ **rischiararsi** *vr.* **1.** to light up **2.** (*diventare più chiaro*) to get (*v. irr.*) clearer **3.** (*di cielo*) to clear up.

rischiare *vt.* to risk. ♦ **rischiare** *vi.* to run (*v. irr.*) the risk (of).

rischio *sm.* risk.

rischioso *agg.* risky.

risciacquare *vt.* to rinse. ♦ **risciacquarsi** *vr.* to rinse.

risciacquata *sf.* rinse.

risciacquatura *sf.* **1.** rinsing **2.** (*acqua*) dish-water.

riscontare *vt.* to rediscount.

risconto *sm.* rediscount.

riscontrare *vt.* **1.** (*controllare*) to check **2.** (*trovare*) to find (*v. irr.*) **3.** (*confrontare*) to compare.

riscontro *sm.* **1.** (*controllo*) checking **2.** (*confronto*) comparison **3.** (*risposta*) reply **4.** (*corrispondenza simmetrica*) pendant.

riscoprire *vt.* to discover again.

riscossa *sf.* **1.** (*rivolta*) revolt **2.** (*riscatto*) redemption || *andare alla —*, to counterattack.

riscossione *sf.* collection.

riscotìbile *agg.* collectable.

riscotimento *sm.* collection.

riscrìvere *vt.* **1.** to rewrite (*v. irr.*) **2.** (*in risposta*) to write (*v. irr.*) back.

riscuòtere *vt.* **1.** (*denaro*) to collect **2.** (*conseguire*) to win (*v. irr.*) **3.** (*scuotere*) to shake (*v. irr.*). ♦ **riscuòtersi** *vr.* (*trasalire*) to start.

riseccare *vt.* to dry up. ♦ **riseccarsi** *vr.* to dry up.

risedersi *vr.* to sit (*v. irr.*) down again.

risega *sf.* **1.** (*arch.*) offset **2.** (*della pelle*) fold.

riseminare *vt.* to sow (*v. irr.*) again.

risentimento *sm.* resentment: *con —*, resentfully.

risentire *vt.* **1.** (*sentire di nuovo*) to feel (*v. irr.*) again **2.** (*riudire*) to hear (*v. irr.*) again **3.** (*sentire*) to feel ‖ — *di qc.*, to show (*v. irr.*) traces of sthg.; (*di persona*) to feel the effect of sthg. ♦ **risentirsi** *vr.* to take (*v. irr.*) offence (at).

risentito *agg.* (*sdegnato*) resentful.

riserbare *vt.* V. *riservare*.

riserbo *sm.* **1.** reserve **2.** (*discrezione*) discretion.

riserva *sf.* **1.** reserve **2.** (*di caccia, pesca*) preserve.

riservare *vt.* to reserve. ♦ **riservarsi** *vr.* (*ripromettersi*) to intend: — *la diagnosi*, to refuse to formulate a definite diagnosis.

riservatezza *sf.* reservedness.

riservato *agg.* **1.** reserved **2.** (*segreto*) private.

risìbile *agg.* laughable.

risicoltore *sm.* rice-grower.

risicoltura *sf.* rice-growing.

risièdere *vi.* to reside.

risma *sf.* **1.** ream **2.** (*fig.*) kind.

riso[1] *sm.* (*bot.*) rice.

riso[2] *sm.* laugh.

risolare *vt.* to resole.

risolatura *sf.* resoling.

risollevare *vt.* **1.** to raise again **2.** (*confortare*) to cheer up. ♦ **risollevarsi** *vr.* **1.** to rise again **2.** (*confortarsi*) to cheer up.

risolutezza *sf.* resolution.

risolutivo *agg.* resolutive.

risoluto *agg.* resolute.

risoluzione *sf.* **1.** resolution **2.** (*giur.*) cancellation.

risòlvere *vt.* **1.** to resolve **2.** (*rescindere*) to rescind. ♦ **risòlversi** *vr.* **1.** (*decidersi*) to make (*v. irr.*) up one's mind **2.** (*mutarsi*) to turn (into) **3.** (*di malattia*) to clear up.

risolvìbile *agg.* **1.** resolvable **2.** (*rescindibile*) rescindable.

risonante *agg.* resonant.

risonanza *sf.* resonance.

risonare *vt.* **1.** to play again **2.** (*un campanello*) to ring (*v. irr.*) again. ♦ **risonare** *vi.* to resound.

risòrgere *vi.* **1.** to rise (*v. irr.*) again **2.** (*rifiorire*) to revive ‖ *far* —, to revive.

risorgimento *sm.* revival.

risorsa *sf.* resource.

risparmiare *vt.* **1.** to save **2.** (*evitare, salvare*) to spare.

risparmiatore *agg.* thrifty. ♦ **risparmiatore** *sm.* saver.

risparmio *sm.* saving: *senza* —, lavishly.

rispecchiare *vt.* to reflect. ♦ **rispecchiarsi** *vr.* to be reflected.

rispedire *vt.* **1.** to send (*v. irr.*) again **2.** (*spedire indietro*) to send back.

rispettàbile *agg.* respectable.

rispettabilità *sf.* respectability.

rispettare *vt.* **1.** to respect **2.** (*onorare*) to honour.

rispettivo *agg.* respective.

rispetto *sm.* respect: — *a*, as regards; *a* — *di*, in comparison to; *mancare di* — *a*, to be disrespectful to.

rispettoso *agg.* respectful.

risplendente *agg.* shining.

risplèndere *vi.* to shine (*v. irr.*).

rispolverare *vt.* **1.** to dust again **2.** (*fig.*) to brush up.

rispondente *agg.* answering (to).

rispondenza *sf.* correspondence.

rispòndere *vt. e vi.* **1.** to answer (so., sthg.) **2.** (*obbedire*) to respond ‖ — *di qu., qc.*, to answer for so., sthg.

risposare *vt.* V. *rimaritare*.

risposta *sf.* answer, reply.

rispuntare *vi.* **1.** to reappear **2.** (*risorgere*) to rise (*v. irr.*) again **3.** (*di germogli*) to sprout again.

rissa *sf.* brawl.

rissare *vi.* to brawl.

rissoso *agg.* quarrelsome.

ristabilimento *sm.* **1.** restoration **2.** (*di salute*) recovery.

ristabilire *vt.* to restore. ♦ **ristabilirsi** *vr.* **1.** to settle again **2.** (*rimettersi*) to recover.

ristagnamento *sm.* **1.** stagnation **2.** (*di sangue*) staunching.

ristagnare *vi.* to stagnate. ♦ **ristagnare** *vt.* to staunch.

ristagno *sm.* (*econ.*) slackness.

ristampa *sf.* reprint: *essere in* —, to be reprinting.

ristampare *vt.* to reprint.

ristare *vi.* **1.** (*cessare*) to stop **2.** (*rimanere*) to remain.

ristoràbile *agg.* restorable.

ristorante *sm.* restaurant.

ristorare *vt.* to refresh, to restore (*anche fig.*).

ristoratore *agg.* refreshing. ♦ **ristoratore** *sm.* restorer.

ristoro *sm.* **1.** relief **2.** (*cibo, be-*

vanda) refreshment || *luogo di —*, refreshment-room.

ristrettezza *sf.* 1. narrowness 2. (*insufficienza*) lack || *— di idee*, narrow-mindedness.

ristretto *agg.* 1. narrow 2. (*condensato*) condensed.

ristringere *vt.* 1. to tighten again 2. (*premere di nuovo*) to press again || *— la mano a qu.*, to shake (*v. irr.*) hands with so. again.

ristuccare *vt.* 1. (*edil.*) to replaster 2. (*nauseare*) to surfeit.

ristuccatura *sf.* (*edil.*) replastering.

ristudiare *vt.* to study again.

risucchiare *vt.* to suck (again).

risucchio *sm.* whirlpool.

risultante *agg. e sf.* resultant.

risultanza *sf.* result.

risultare *vi.* 1. to result 2. (*venire a sapere*) to turn out || *mi risulta*, I know.

risultato *sm.* result.

risurrezione *sf.* resurrection.

risuscitamento *sm.* resuscitation.

risuscitare *vt. e vi.* to resuscitate.

risvegliare *vt.* to wake (*v. irr.*) (up). ♦ **risvegliarsi** *vr.* to wake up.

risveglio *sm.* 1. awakening 2. (*fig.*) revival.

risvoltare *vt.* to turn up.

risvolto *sm.* 1. (*di giacca*) lapel 2. (*di calzoni*) turn-up.

ritagliare *vt.* 1. to cut (*v. irr.*) out 2. (*tagliare di nuovo*) to cut again.

ritaglio *sm.* 1. (*di stoffa*) remnant 2. (*di giornale*) clipping || *ritagli di tempo*, odd moments.

ritardare *vt.* to delay. ♦ **ritardare** *vi.* 1. to be late 2. (*di orologio*) to be slow.

ritardatario *sm.* late-comer.

ritardo *sm.* delay: *in —*, late.

ritegno *sm.* 1. reserve 2. (*freno*) restraint 3. (*riluttanza*) reluctance.

ritemprare *vt.* 1. to strengthen 2. (*metalli*) to harden again. ♦ **ritemprarsi** *vr.* to get (*v. irr.*) stronger.

ritenere *vt.* 1. to hold (*v. irr.*) 2. (*giudicare*) to consider 3. (*pensare*) to think (*v. irr.*).

ritentare *vt.* 1. to tempt again 2. (*riprovare*) to try again.

ritenuta *sf.* deduction.

ritenzione *sf.* retention.

ritingere *vt.* to dye again.

ritirare *vt.* 1. to withdraw (*v. irr.*)

2. (*farsi consegnare*) to collect. ♦ **ritirarsi** *vr.* 1. to retire 2. (*di stoffa*) to shrink (*v. irr.*).

ritirata *sf.* 1. retreat 2. (*latrina*) lavatory.

ritiro *sm.* 1. withdrawal 2. (*il ritirarsi*) retirement 3. (*luogo appartato*) retreat 4. (*il farsi consegnare*) collection.

ritmare *vt.* to mark.

ritmica *sf.* rhythmic(s).

ritmico *agg.* rhythmic(al).

ritmo *sm.* rhythm.

rito *sm.* rite: *essere di —*, to be customary.

ritoccare *vt.* to retouch.

ritoccatore *sm.* retoucher.

ritocco *sm.* retouch.

ritògliere *vt.* 1. to take (*v. irr.*) off again 2. (*riappropriarsi*) to take back. ♦ **ritògliersi** *vr.* to take off again.

ritòrcere *vt.* 1. to twist again 2. (*torcere*) to twist 3. (*rivolgere*) to retort. ♦ **ritòrcersi** *vr.* 1. to get (*v. irr.*) twisted 2. (*fig.*) to recoil (on, upon).

ritorcitura *sf.* twisting.

ritornare *vi.* to return.

ritornello *sm.* refrain.

ritorno *sm.* return: *— di fiamma*, backfire; *essere di —*, to be back.

ritorsione *sf.* retortion.

ritorto *agg.* twisted.

ritrarre *vt.* 1. to withdraw (*v. irr.*) 2. (*distogliere*) to turn away 3. (*rappresentare*) to represent 4. (*dedurre*) to understand (*v. irr.*). ♦ **ritrarsi** *vr.* to withdraw.

ritrattare *vt.* 1. to retract 2. (*trattare di nuovo*) to treat again.

ritrattazione *sf.* 1. retraction 2. (*nuova trattazione*) new treatment.

ritrattista *s.* portraitist.

ritrattìstica *sf.* portraiture.

ritratto *sm.* portrait.

ritrazione *sf.* retraction.

ritrito *agg.* stale.

ritrosìa *sf.* 1. (*riluttanza*) reluctance 2. (*timidezza*) shyness.

ritroso *agg.* 1. (*riluttante*) reluctant 2. (*timido*) shy || *a —*, backwards.

ritrovamento *sm.* finding.

ritrovare *vt.* 1. to find (*v. irr.*) again 2. (*ricuperare*) to recover 3. (*scoprire*) to discover. ♦ **ritrovarsi** *vr.* 1. to find oneself 2. (*rincontrarsi*) to meet (*v. irr.*) again.

ritrovato *sm.* **1.** invention **2.** (*scoperta*) discovery.

ritrovo *sm.* meeting-place, haunt.

ritto *agg.* upright.

rituale *agg.* e *sm.* ritual.

rituffare *vt.* to plunge again. ♦ **rituffarsi** *vr.* to plunge again.

riudire *vt.* to hear (*v. irr.*) again.

riunione *sf.* meeting.

riunire *vt.* **1.** to re-unite **2.** (*raccogliere*) to gather **3.** (*unire*) to join. ♦ **riunirsi** *vr.* **1.** to come (*v. irr.*) together again **2.** (*unirsi*) to unite **3.** (*incontrarsi*) to meet (*v. irr.*).

riuscire *vi.* **1.** to succeed (in), to be good (at) **2.** (*risultare*) to be **3.** (*uscire di nuovo*) to go (*v. irr.*) out again.

riuscita *sf.* **1.** issue **2.** (*successo*) success.

riutilizzare *vt.* to utilize again.

riva *sf.* **1.** (*di mare, lago*) shore **2.** (*di fiume*) bank.

rivale *agg.* e *sm.* rival.

rivaleggiare *vi.* to rival (so., sthg.).

rivalersi *vr.* **1.** to make (*v. irr.*) up for one's losses **2.** (*valersi di nuovo*) to make use again.

rivalicare *vt.* to recross.

rivalità *sf.* rivalry.

rivalsa *sf.* **1.** (*rivincita*) revenge **2.** (*risarcimento*) compensation **3.** (*comm.*) recourse.

rivalutare *vt.* **1.** to revalue **2.** (*elevare*) to raise.

rivalutazione *sf.* **1.** revaluation **2.** (*aumento*) rise.

rivangare *vt.* e *vi.* to dig (*v. irr.*) up again.

rivedere *vt.* **1.** to see (*v. irr.*) again **2.** (*revisionare*) to revise.

riveduta *sf.* look, revision.

rivelare *vt.* **1.** to reveal. ♦ **rivelarsi** *vr.* **1.** to reveal oneself **2.** (*dimostrarsi*) to prove.

rivelatore *agg.* revealing. ♦ **rivelatore** *sm.* **1.** revealer **2.** (*radio*) detector.

rivelazione *sf.* **1.** revelation **2.** (*fis.; radio*) detection.

rivéndere *vt.* **1.** to resell (*v. irr.*) **2.** (*al dettaglio*) to retail.

rivendicare *vt.* **1.** to claim **2.** (*vendicare*) to revenge.

rivendicatore *agg.* **1.** claiming **2.** (*vendicatore*) revenging. ♦ **rivendicatore** *sm.* **1.** claimant **2.** (*vendicatore*) revenger.

rivendicazione *sf.* claim.

rivéndita *sf.* **1.** resale **2.** (*spaccio*) shop.

rivenditore *sm.* retailer.

rivendùgliolo *sm.* V. *rigattiere*.

riverberare *vt.* to reverberate. ♦ **riverberarsi** *vr.* to reverberate.

rivèrbero *sm.* reverberation: *di* —, indirectly.

riverente *agg.* reverent.

riverenza *sf.* **1.** reverence **2.** (*inchino*) bow.

riverenziale *agg.* reverential.

riverire *vt.* **1.** to revere **2.** (*salutare*) to pay (*v. irr.*) one's respects (to).

riversare *vt.* **1.** to pour again **2.** (*versare*) to pour **3.** (*di fiume*) to flow. ♦ **riversarsi** *vr.* to flow.

riverso *avv.* on one's back.

rivestimento *sm.* **1.** covering **2.** (*interno*) lining.

rivestire *vt.* **1.** to dress again **2.** (*foderare*) to line (with sthg.) **3.** (*coprire*) to cover (with sthg.) **4.** (*fig.*) to hold (*v. irr.*).

riviera *sf.* coast || *la Riviera*, the Riviera.

rivierasco *agg.* coast (*attr.*).

rivincere *vt.* **1.** to win (*v. irr.*) again **2.** (*recuperare*) to win back.

rivincita *sf.* **1.** (*vendetta*) revenge **2.** (*sport*) return match **3.** (*al gioco*) return game.

rivista *sf.* **1.** review **2.** (*teat.*) revue **3.** (*mil.*) parade || *passare in* —, to review.

rivivere *vi.* e *vt.* to live again.

rivo *sm.* stream.

rivolere *vt.* **1.** to want again **2.** (*volere indietro*) to want back.

rivòlgere *vt.* **1.** to turn **2.** (*indirizzare*) to address. ♦ **rivòlgersi** *vr.* **1.** to turn **2.** (*parlando*) to address (so.) **3.** (*ricorrere, riferirsi*) to apply (to).

rivolgimento *sm.* **1.** upheaval **2.** (*cambio*) change.

rivolo *sm.* streamlet.

rivolta *sf.* revolt.

rivoltante *agg.* revolting.

rivoltare *vt.* **1.** to turn (over) again **2.** (*rovesciare*) to turn **3.** (*capovolgere*) to turn upside-down **4.** (*con l'interno all'esterno*) to turn inside out **5.** (*fig.*) to upset (*v. irr.*). ♦ **rivoltarsi** *vr.* **1.** to turn round **2.** (*rigirarsi*) to turn over **3.** (*ribellarsi*) to revolt **4.** (*fig.*) to turn.

rivoltella *sf.* revolver.

rivoltoso agg. e sm. rebel.

rivoluzionare vt. to revolutionize.

rivoluzionario agg. e sm. revolutionary.

rivoluzione sf. revolution.

rizoma sm. rhizome.

rizzare vt. to raise: — le orecchie, to prick one's ears. ♦ **rizzarsi** vr. 1. to stand (v. irr.) up 2. (di capelli) to stand on end.

roba sf. stuff, things (pl.).

robaccia sf. rubbish.

robinia sf. locust-tree.

robustezza sf. robustness.

robusto agg. robust.

rocambolesco agg. daring.

rocca[1] sf. 1. stronghold 2. (roccia) rock.

rocca[2] sf. (conocchia) distaff.

roccaforte sf. stronghold.

rocchetto sm. 1. spool 2. (elettr.) coil.

rocchio sm. 1. (di tronco) log 2. (di colonna) drum.

roccia sf. rock.

rocciatore sm. rock-climber.

roccioso agg. rocky.

roco agg. hoarse.

rodaggio sm. (auto) running in.

rodare vt. to run (v. irr.) in.

ròdere vt. 1. to gnaw 2. (corrodere) to corrode. ♦ **ròdersi** vr. 1. to worry 2. (di rabbia ecc.) to be consumed (with).

rodimento sm. 1. gnawing 2. (fig.) anxiety.

roditore agg. e sm. rodent.

rododendro sm. rhododendron.

rogare vt. to draw (v. irr.) up.

rogatoria sf. request.

rogazioni sf. pl. rogations.

roggia sf. irrigation ditch.

rògito sm. deed.

rogna sf. 1. scabies 2. (fig.) trouble.

rognone sm. kidney.

rognoso agg. scabby.

rogo sm. 1. fire 2. (pira) pyre 3. (supplizio) stake.

rollare vi. to roll.

rollìo sm. roll.

romancio agg. Romansh.

romànico agg. 1. (arch.) Romanesque 2. Romanic.

romano agg. e sm. Roman.

romanticheria sf. 1. (atteggiamento) romantic attitude 2. (azione) romantic deed.

romanticismo sm. Romanticism.

romàntico agg. e sm. romantic.

romanza sf. romance.

romanzare vt. to romanticize.

romanzesco agg. romantic.

romanziere sm. novelist.

romanzo[1] agg. Romance.

romanzo[2] sm. 1. novel 2. (storia incredibile) romance || — a puntate, serial; — a fumetti, comics.

romba sf. roar.

rombare vi. to rumble.

ròmbico agg. rhombic(al).

rombo[1] sm. (rumore) rumble.

rombo[2] sm. (geom.) rhomb.

rombo[3] sm. (itt.) brill.

romboèdrico agg. rhombohedral.

romboedro sm. rhombohedron (pl. -ra).

romboidale agg. rhomboid(al).

rombòide agg. e sm. rhomboid.

romeno agg. e sm. Rumanian.

romeo sm. pilgrim.

romitaggio sm. hermitage.

ròmito agg. solitary. ♦ **romito** sm. hermit.

romitorio sm. hermitage.

ròmpere vt. to break (v. irr.): — i ponti con qu., to break with so. ♦ **ròmpersi** vr. to break (up).

rompicapo sm. puzzle.

rompicollo sm. madcap: a —, headlong.

rompighiaccio sm. ice-breaker.

rompiscàtole s. nuisance.

rompitore sm. breaker.

ronca sf. pruning-knife (pl. -ives).

ronciglio sm. hook.

ròncola sf. pruning-hook.

ronda sf. 1. rounds (pl.) 2. (pattuglia) patrol.

rondella sf. washer.

ròndine sf. swallow: a coda di —, swallow-tailed.

rondinotto sm. young swallow.

rondò sm. 1. (mus.) rondo 2. (poet.) rondel 3. (piazza circolare) circus.

rondone sm. swift.

ronfare vi. to snore.

ronzare vi. 1. to buzz 2. (fig.) to hang (v. irr.) around.

ronzino sm. jade.

ronzìo sm. buzz.

ròrido agg. 1. (bagnato) wet 2. (rugiadoso) dewy.

rosa sf. rose || all'acqua di rose (fig.), moderate. ♦ **rosa** agg. e sm. pink.

rosàceo agg. rosy.

rosaio sm. rose-bush.

rosario sm. rosary.

rosato agg. rosy.

ròseo agg. rosy.

roseòla sf. roseola.

roseto sm. rose-garden.

rosetta sf. 1. rosette 2. (diamante) rose 3. (mecc.) washer.

rosicchiare vt. to gnaw.

rosmarino sm. rosemary.

rosolare vt. to brown. ♦ **rosolarsi** vr. 1. to get (v. irr.) brown 2. (prendere il sole) to bask.

rosolìa sf. German measles (pl.).

rosolio sm. rosolio.

rosone sm. rose-window.

rospo sm. toad.

rossastro agg. reddish.

rosseggiare vi. to be reddish.

rossetto sm. 1. (per labbra) lipstick 2. (per guance) rouge.

rossiccio agg. ruddy.

rosso agg. e sm. red: — d'uovo, yolk; diventar —, to flush.

rossore sm. flush.

rosticcerìa sf. rotisserie.

rosticciere sm. owner of a rotisserie.

rostro sm. 1. rostrum (pl. -ra) 2. (becco) beak.

rotàbile agg. carriage (attr.).

rotaia sf. 1. rail 2. (solco) rut.

rotare vi. e vt. to rotate, to revolve.

rotativa sf. rotary press.

rotativo agg. rotary.

rotatorio agg. rotating.

rotazione sf. rotation.

roteare vt. 1. to swing (v. irr.) 2. (gli occhi) to roll. ♦ **roteare** vi. to wheel.

rotella sf. small wheel.

rotocalco sm. 1. rotogravure 2. (rivista) illustrated magazine.

rotolamento sm. rolling.

rotolare vt. e vi. to roll. ♦ **rotolarsi** vr. to roll.

ròtolo sm. roll || andare a rotoli, to go (v. irr.) to rack and ruin; mandare a rotoli, to ruin.

rotolone sm. V. ruzzolone.

rotonda sf. rotunda.

rotondità sf. roundness.

rotondo agg. 1. round 2. (grassoccio) plump.

rotore sm. rotor.

rotta sf. 1. course 2. (rottura) breach 3. (sconfitta) rout || a — di collo, headlong; essere in — con, to be on bad terms with; mettere in —, to rout.

rottame sm. 1. wreck 2. (di scarto) scraps (pl.).

rotto agg. 1. broken 2. (stracciato) torn 3. (avvezzo) accustomed.

rottura sf. break(ing).

ròtula sf. knee-cap.

rovente agg. red-hot.

ròvere sm. oak.

rovesciamento sm. 1. overthrowing 2. (cambiamento) reversal.

rovesciare vt. 1. to overturn 2. (capovolgere) to turn upside down 3. (gettare) to throw (v. irr.) 4. (rivoltare) to turn inside out 5. (versare intenzionalmente) to pour 6. (versare accidentalmente) to spill 7. (abbattere) to overthrow (v. irr.). ♦ **rovesciarsi** vr. 1. to overturn 2. (riversarsi) to pour.

rovescio sm. 1. reverse 2. (opposto) opposite 3. (di pioggia) heavy shower 4. (di critiche ecc.) hail || a — (capovolto), upside down.

roveto sm. bramble-bush.

rovina sf. ruin.

rovinare vt. 1. to ruin 2. (sciupare) to spoil (v. irr.). ♦ **rovinare** vi. to crash.

rovinìo sm. 1. downfall 2. (rumore) crash.

rovinoso agg. ruinous.

rovistare vt. e vi. to rummage.

rovo sm. blackberry bush.

rozza sf. jade.

rozzezza sf. roughness.

rozzo agg. rough.

ruba sf. andare a —, to sell (v. irr.) like wildfire.

rubacchiare vt. to pilfer.

rubacuori agg. bewitching. ♦ **rubacuori** sm. lady-killer.

rubare vt. to steal (v. irr.).

ruberìa sf. theft.

rubicondo agg. ruddy.

rubinetterìa sf. plumbing fixtures (pl.).

rubinetto sm. tap.

rubino sm. ruby.

rubizzo agg. hale.

rublo sm. rouble.

rubrica sf. 1. (di giornale) column 2. (per indirizzi) addressbook.

rude agg. rough.

rùdere sm. ruin.

rudezza sf. roughness.

rudimentale agg. rudimentary.

rudimento sm. rudiment.

ruffiano sm. pander.

ruga sf. wrinkle.

ruggente agg. roaring.

rùggine *sf.* **1.** rust **2.** (*fig.*) grudge.
rugginoso *agg.* rusty.
ruggire *vi.* to roar.
ruggito *sm.* roar.
rugiada *sf.* dew: *goccia di —*, dew-drop.
rugiadoso *agg.* dewy.
rugosità *sf.* **1.** wrinkledness **2.** (*scabrosità*) ruggedness.
rugoso *agg.* **1.** wrinkled **2.** (*scabro*) rugged.
rullaggio *sm. pista di —*, taxi-track.
rullare *vi.* **1.** to roll **2.** (*di aereo*) to taxi.
rullino *sm.* roll.
rullìo *sm.* roll.
rullo *sm.* **1.** roll **2.** (*mecc.*) roller.
rum *sm.* rum.
ruminante *agg.* e *sm.* ruminant.
ruminare *vt.* to ruminate.
ruminazione *sf.* rumination.
rùmine *sm.* rumen.
rumore *sm.* **1.** noise **2.** (*diceria*) rumour || *far — (fig.)*, to arouse great interest.
rumoreggiare *vi.* **1.** to rumble **2.** (*fig.*) to rumour.
rumorìo *sm.* noise.
rumorista *sm.* noise-maker.
rumoroso *agg.* noisy.
ruolino *sm.* (*di marcia*) time schedule.
ruolo *sm.* **1.** roll, list **2.** (*teat.*) role **3.** (*amm.*) roster.
ruota *sf.* wheel.
rupe *sf.* cliff.
rupestre *agg.* rocky.
rurale *agg.* rural || *i rurali*, country people.
ruscello *sm.* brook.
ruspa *sf.* scraper.
ruspare *vi.* (*razzolare*) to scratch about.
russare *vi.* to snore.
russo *agg.* e *sm.* Russian.
rusticità *sf.* rusticity.
rùstico *agg.* **1.** rustic **2.** (*ritroso*) unsociable.
ruta *sf.* rue.
rutilante *agg.* glowing.
ruttare *vi.* to belch.
rutto *sm.* belch.
rùvido *agg.* rough.
ruzzare *vi.* to romp.
ruzzolare *vt.* to roll. ♦ ruzzolare *vi.* **1.** to roll **2.** (*cadere*) to tumble down.
ruzzolone *sm.* tumble: *fare un —*, to tumble down.

S

sàbato *sm.* Saturday.
sabba *sm.* witches' Sabbath.
sabbia *sf.* sand.
sabbiare *vt.* to sand.
sabbiatura *sf.* sand-bath.
sabbioso *agg.* sandy.
sabotaggio *sm.* sabotage.
sabotare *vt.* to sabotage.
sabotatore *sm.* saboteur.
sacca *sf.* bag.
saccarina *sf.* saccharine.
saccarosio *sm.* saccharose.
saccente *agg.* pedantic. ♦ saccente *s.* pedant.
saccheggiare *vt.* to sack.
saccheggio *sm.* sack.
sacchetto *sm.* small bag.
sacco *sm.* **1.** sack, bag || *colazione al —*, picnic; *mettere qu. nel —*, to take (*v. irr.*) so. in **2.** (*grande quantità*) a lot of.
saccoccia *sf.* pocket.
saccone *sm.* palliasse.
sacerdotale *agg.* sacerdotal.
sacerdote *sm.* priest.
sacerdozio *sm.* priesthood.
sacrale *agg.* sacral.
sacramentale *agg.* sacramental.
sacramentare *vi.* (*fig.*) to swear (*v. irr.*).
sacramento *sm.* sacrament.
sacrario *sm.* shrine.
sacrificare *vt.* to sacrifice.
sacrificio *sm.* sacrifice.
sacrilegio *sm.* sacrilege.
sacrìlego *agg.* sacrilegious.
sacrista *sm.* sacristan.
sacro *agg.* sacred, holy.
sacrosanto *agg.* **1.** sacrosanct **2.** (*indiscutibile*) absolute.
sàdico *agg.* sadistic. ♦ sàdico *sm.* sadist.
sadismo *sm.* sadism.
saetta *sf.* **1.** arrow **2.** (*fulmine*) thunderbolt.
saettare *vt.* **1.** to shoot (*v. irr.*) arrows at **2.** (*fig.*) to dart. ♦ saettare *vi.* to dart.
sàffico *agg.* Sapphic.
sagace *agg.* sagacious.
sagacia *sf.* sagacity.
saggezza *sf.* wisdom.
saggiare *vt.* to assay, to test.
saggiatore *sm.* **1.** assayer **2.** (*bilancia*) assay balance.
saggina *sf.* sorghum.

saggio[1] *agg.* wise. ◆ **saggio** *sm.* wise man (*pl.* men).

saggio[2] *sm.* 1. essay 2. (*campione*) sample 3. (*saggio ginnico*) display.

saggista *s.* essayist.

sagittario *sm.* 1. archer 2. (*astr.*) Sagittarius.

sàgoma *sf.* shape || è una —! (*fam.*), he is a character!

sagomare *vt.* to shape.

sagra *sf.* festival.

sagrato *sm.* church-square.

sagrestano *sm.* sacristan.

sagrestìa *sf.* sacristy.

saia *sf.* serge.

saio *sm.* habit.

sala *sf.* hall, room: — da pranzo, dining-room.

salace *agg.* salacious.

salacità *sf.* salacity.

salamandra *sf.* salamander.

salame *sm.* salami (*pl.*).

salamelecco *sm.* salaam.

salamoia *sf.* pickle.

salare *vt.* to salt.

salariale *agg.* salary (*attr.*).

salariato *agg.* wage-earning. ◆ **salariato** *sm.* wage-earner.

salario *sm.* wages (*pl.*).

salassare *vt.* to bleed (*v. irr.*).

salasso *sm.* 1. bleeding 2. (*fig.*) extortion.

salato *agg.* 1. salty 2. (*costoso*) dear 3. (*salace*) keen.

salatura *sf.* salting.

salda *sf.* starch-water.

saldamente *avv.* firmly.

saldare *vt.* 1. to solder, to weld 2. (*un conto*) to settle.

saldatore *sm.* solderer, welder.

saldatrice *sf.* welding machine.

saldatura *sf.* soldering, welding.

saldezza *sf.* firmness.

saldo[1] *agg.* firm.

saldo[2] *sm.* balance: — attivo, passivo, credit, debit balance.

sale *sm.* salt.

salesiano *agg. e sm.* Salesian.

salgemma *sm.* rock-salt.

sàlice *sm.* willow.

salicilato *sm.* salicylate.

saliente *agg.* important.

saliera *sf.* salt-cellar.

salina *sf.* salt-pit.

salino *agg.* saline, salt (*attr.*).

salire *vi.* 1. to rise (*v. irr.*), to go (*v. irr.*) up 2. (*di prezzi*) to increase.

saliscendi *sm.* 1. latch 2. (*alter-

narsi di salite e discese*) ups and downs (*pl.*).

salita *sf.* 1. slope, ascent 2. (*aumento*) rise.

saliva *sf.* saliva, spittle.

salivare *agg.* salivary.

salivare *vi.* to salivate.

salivazione *sf.* salivation.

salma *sf.* corpse.

salmastro *agg.* saltish.

salmo *sm.* psalm.

salmodìa *sf.* psalmody.

salmodiare *vi.* to sing (*v. irr.*) psalms.

salmone *sm.* salmon.

salnitro *sm.* saltpetre.

salone *sm.* large hall, reception-room.

salottiero *agg.* drawing-room (*attr.*).

salotto *sm.* sitting-room.

salpare *vi.* to set (*v. irr.*) sails.

salsa *sf.* sauce.

salsèdine *sf.* saltness.

salsiccia *sf.* sausage.

salsiera *sf.* sauce-boat.

salso *agg.* salt (*attr.*).

saltare *vt. e vi.* to jump, to leap (*v. irr.*): — di palo in frasca, to jump from one subject to another; far — una serratura, to break (*v. irr.*) a lock.

saltatore *agg.* jumping. ◆ **saltatore** *sm.* jumper.

saltellare *vi.* to hop.

saltimbanco *sm.* tumbler.

salto *sm.* jump, leap.

saltuario *agg.* desultory.

salubre *agg.* healthy.

salubrità *sf.* healthiness.

salume *sm.* salted meat.

salumiere *sm.* delicatessen seller.

salumerìa *sf.* delicatessen.

salutare[1] *agg.* healthy.

salutare[2] *vt.* to greet, to hail.

salute *sf.* health.

saluto *sm.* greeting, salute.

salva *sf.* volley (*anche fig.*): colpo a —, blank shot.

salvacondotto *sm.* safe-conduct.

salvadanaio *sm.* money-box.

salvagente *sm.* 1. life-belt 2. (*marciapiede*) traffic island.

salvaguardare *vt.* to safeguard.

salvaguardia *sf.* safeguard.

salvare *vt.* 1. to save (*anche fig.*) 2. (*trarre in salvo*) to rescue. ◆ **salvarsi** *vr.* to save oneself.

salvataggio *sm.* rescue.

salvatore *sm.* saviour, saver.

salve *inter.* hail.
salvezza *sf.* salvation.
salvia *sf.* sage.
salvietta *sf.* towel.
salvo *agg.* safe. ♦ **salvo** *prep.* except, save. ♦ **salvo che** *cong.* except that, unless.
sanàbile *agg.* curable, remediable.
sanare *vt.* to heal.
sanatorio *sm.* sanatorium (*pl.* -ia).
sancire *vt.* to sanction.
sanculotto *sm.* sansculotte.
sàndalo[1] *sm.* (*calzatura*) sandal.
sàndalo[2] *sm.* (*mar.*) punt.
sandolino *sm.* small canoe.
sangue *sm.* blood: *spargimento di* —, bloodshed; *perdita di* —, bleeding; — *freddo*, coolness; *a* — *freddo*, in cold blood; *farsi cattivo* —, to worry over; *buon* — *non mente*, blood will tell.
sanguigno *agg.* sanguineous, blood (*attr.*).
sanguinaccio *sm.* blood-sausage.
sanguinante *agg.* bleeding.
sanguinare *vi.* to bleed (*v. irr.*).
sanguinario *agg. e sm.* sanguinary: *uomo* —, bloodthirsty man.
sanguinoso *agg.* bloody.
sanguisuga *sf.* leech.
sanità *sf.* soundness, sanity.
sanitario *agg.* sanitary.
sano *agg.* 1. healthy 2. (*fig.*) sound 3. (*intero, intatto*) intact.
sansa *sf.* husk.
sànscrito *sm.* Sanskrit.
santarellina *sf.* goody-goody.
santificante *agg.* sanctifying.
santificare *vt.* to canonize: — *le feste*, to observe holy days.
santificazione *sf.* sanctification.
santino *sm.* small holy picture.
santìssimo *agg.* most holy: *il* — *Sacramento*, the Blessed Sacrament.
santità *sf.* holiness.
santo *agg.* 1. holy 2. (*seguito da nome proprio*) saint. ♦ **santo** *sm.* saint.
santone *sm.* santon.
santuario *sm.* sanctuary.
sanzionare *vt.* to ratify.
sanzione *sf.* sanction.
sapere[1] *vt.* 1. to know (*v. irr.*): *non* — *che fare*, to be at a loss what to do; *chi sa!*, who knows!; *non si sa mai*, you never know; *venire a* —, to hear (*v. irr.*) 2. (*essere capace*) can, to be able: *sai parlare inglese?*, can you speak English?; *non so farlo*, I am not able to do it. ♦ **sapere** *vi.* (*aver sapore*) to taste.
sapere[2] *sm.* 1. knowledge 2. (*cultura*) learning.
sàpido *agg.* sapid.
sapiente *agg.* wise. ♦ **sapiente** *sm.* sage.
sapienza *sf.* wisdom.
saponaria *sf.* soapwort.
saponata *sf.* lather (*solo sing.*).
sapone *sm.* soap: — *da barba*, shaving-soap; — *da bagno*, bath soap.
saponetta *sf.* cake of soap.
saponificare *vt.* to saponify.
saponificazione *sf.* saponification.
saponificio *sm.* soap-works (*pl. con costruzione sing.*).
sapore *sm.* taste, flavour (*anche fig.*).
saporire *vt.* to flavour.
saporitamente *avv.* savourily ∥ *dormire* —, to sleep (*v. irr.*) soundly.
saporito *agg.* savoury, tasty.
saputello *sm.* wiseacre.
saputo *agg.* 1. learned 2. (*noto*) well-known.
sarabanda *sf.* saraband.
saraceno *sm.* saracen.
saracinesca *sf.* rolling-shutter.
sarcasmo *sm.* sarcasm.
sarcàstico *agg.* sarcastic.
sarchiare *vt.* to weed.
sarchiatore *agg.* weeding. ♦ **sarchiatore** *sm.* weeder.
sarchiatura *sf.* weeding.
sarchio *sm.* hoe.
sarcòfago *sm.* sarcophagus (*pl.* -gi).
sardina *sf.* sardine.
sardònico *agg.* sardonic.
sarmento *sm.* runner.
sarta *sf.* dressmaker.
sartie *sf. pl.* shrouds.
sartina *sf.* grisette.
sarto *sm.* tailor.
sartorìa *sf.* 1. (*da uomo*) tailor's 2. (*da donna*) dressmaker's.
sassaia *sf.* stony place.
sassaiuola *sf.* 1. shower of stones 2. (*battaglia di sassi*) stone-fight.
sassata *sf.* blow with a stone.
sasso *sm.* stone: *a un tiro di* — *da*, within a stone's throw of.
sassofonista *sm.* saxophonist.
sassòfono *sm.* saxophone.
sassolino *sm.* pebble.
sàssone *agg. e sm.* Saxon.

sassoso *agg.* stony.

satànico *agg.* Satanic.

satèllite *sm.* satellite.

sàtira *sf.* satire.

satìrico *agg.* satirical.

sàtiro *sm.* satyr.

satollare *vt.* to satiate.

satollo *agg.* satiated.

sàtrapo *sm.* satrap.

saturare *vt.* to saturate.

saturazione *sf.* saturation.

saturnali *sm. pl.* saturnalia.

sàturo *agg.* saturated.

sàuro *agg.* sorrel.

savana *sf.* savannah.

savio *agg.* wise. ♦ savio *sm.* sage.

saziàbile *agg.* satiable.

saziare *vt.* to satisfy, to glut. ♦ saziarsi *vr.* to get (*v. irr.*) full.

sazietà *sf.* satiety: *mangiare, bere a —,* to eat (*v. irr.*), to drink (*v. irr.*) one's fill.

sazio *agg.* replete, full.

sbaciucchiare *vt.* to smother with kisses.

sbadatàggine *sf.* carelessness.

sbadato *agg.* careless.

sbadigliare *vi.* to yawn.

sbadiglio *sm.* yawn.

sbafare *vi.* to scrounge.

sbafatore *sm.* scrounger.

sbafo (*nella loc. avv.*) *prendere qc. a —,* to scrounge sthg.

sbagliare *vi.* to mistake (*v. irr.*). ♦ sbagliarsi *vr.* to make (*v. irr.*) a mistake.

sbagliato *agg.* wrong.

sbaglio *sm.* mistake.

sbalestrare *vt.* 1. to send (*v. irr.*) 2. (*fig.*) to flounder.

sballare *vt.* to unpack.

sballato *agg.* (*fig.*) foolhardy.

sballottamento *sm.* jolting.

sballottare *vt.* to jolt (about), to toss (about).

sbalordimento *sm.* amazement.

sbalordire *vt.* to amaze.

sbalorditivo *agg.* amazing.

sbalordito *agg.* amazed.

sbalzamento *sm.* 1. overthrow 2. (*fig.*) dismissal.

sbalzare¹ *vt.* to throw (*v. irr.*), to toss.

sbalzare² *vt.* (*arte*) to emboss.

sbalzato *agg.* (*arte*) embossed.

sbalzo *sm.* 1. bound, jump 2. (*cambio*) change.

sbancare *vt.* to leave (*v. irr.*) broke.

sbandamento *sm.* 1. dispersal 2. (*auto*) skid 3. (*mar.*) list.

sbandare *vt.* 1. to disperse 2. (*auto*) to cause a skid.

sbandata *sf.* V. *sbandamento.*

sbandato *sm.* straggler.

sbandierare *vt.* (*fig.*) to display.

sbaragliare *vt.* to rout.

sbaraglio *sm.* jeopardy: *mettere allo —,* to jeopardize.

sbarazzare *vt.* to clear up. ♦ sbarazzarsi *vr.* to get (*v. irr.*) rid (of).

sbarazzino *agg.* free and easy. ♦ sbarazzino *sm.* little scamp.

sbarbare *vt.* to shave.

sbarbatello *sm.* young colt.

sbarcare *vt. e vi.* to land, to disembark.

sbarco *sm.* 1. (*di passeggeri*) landing 2. (*di merci*) unloading.

sbarra *sf.* 1. bar 2. (*del timone*) tiller.

sbarramento *sm.* 1. barricade 2. (*di acque*) dam 3. (*mil.*) barrage.

sbarrare *vt.* 1. to bar: *— un assegno,* to cross a cheque 2. (*spalancare*) to open wide.

sbarrato *agg.* blocked || *occhi sbarrati,* wide open eyes.

sbatacchiamento *sm.* banging, slamming.

sbatacchiare *vt.* to bang, to slam.

sbàttere *vt.* 1. (*urtare contro*) to knock 2. (*scaraventare*) to throw (*v. irr.*) 3. (*chiudere violentemente*) to slam 4. (*di panna, uova*) to whip, to beat (*v. irr.*).

sbattezzare *vt.* to force to abjure Christianity.

sbattimento *sm.* banging.

sbattiuova *sm.* egg-whisk.

sbattuto *agg.* 1. depressed: *viso —,* tired face 2. (*di uova*) beaten.

sbavare *vi.* 1. to dribble 2. (*tip.*) to smudge.

sbavatura *sf.* 1. dribble 2. (*tip.*) smudge.

sbellicarsi *vr. — dalle risa,* to split (*v. irr.*) one's sides with laughter.

sbendare *vt.* to unbandage.

sberla *sf.* slap.

sberleffo *sm.* grimace.

sbertucciare *vt.* 1. to mock 2. (*sgualcire*) to crumple.

sbiadire *vi.* to fade.

sbiancare *vt.* to bleach. ♦ sbiancare *vi.* to turn white. ♦ sbiancarsi *vr.* to turn white.

sbieco agg. slanting: guardare qu. di —, to look askance at so.; tagliare una stoffa di —, to cut (v. irr.) a cloth on the bias.

sbigottimento sm. dismay.

sbigottire vt. to dismay. ♦ **sbigottirsi** vr. to be dismayed.

sbigottito agg. dismayed.

sbilanciare vt. to unbalance. ♦ **sbilanciarsi** vr. 1. to lose (v. irr.) one's balance 2. (fig.) to commit oneself.

sbilancio sm. lack of balance; disproportion.

sbilenco agg. crooked.

sbirciare vt. to cast (v. irr.) a sidelong glance.

sbirraglia sf. police (us. al pl.).

sbirro sm. policeman (pl. -men).

sbizzarrirsi vr. to satisfy one's whims.

sbloccare vt. to raise the blockade: — gli affitti, to decontrol rents.

sblocco sm. 1. raising the blockade 2. (mecc.) releasing the brake 3. (econ.) decontrol.

sboccare vi. 1. (di corso d'acqua) to flow 2. (di strada) to lead (v. irr.).

sboccato agg. (fig.) coarse.

sbocciare vi. to open, to blossom.

sboccio sm. blooming.

sbocco sm. outlet, exit.

sbocconcellare vt. to nibble.

sbollire vi. (fig.) to cool down.

sbolognare vt. to palm off.

sbornia sf. drunkenness: prendere la —, to get (v. irr.) drunk.

sborsamento sm. paying out.

sborsare vt. to pay (v. irr.) out.

sborso sm. 1. payment 2. (denaro sborsato) outlay.

sbottare vi. to burst (v. irr.) out.

sbotto sm. outburst.

sbottonare vt. to unbutton. ♦ **sbottonarsi** vr. 1. to undo (v. irr.) one's buttons 2. (fig.) to disclose one's feelings.

sbozzare vt. to sketch out.

sbracare vt. to unbreech.

sbracato agg. (fig.) unseemly.

sbracciare vi. to gesticulate. ♦ **sbracciarsi** vr. 1. to roll up one's sleeves 2. (agitarsi) to strive (v. irr.).

sbracciato agg. (di persona) with bare arms.

sbraitare vi. to shout.

sbranamento sm. tearing to pieces.

sbranare vt. to tear (v. irr.) to pieces.

sbrancare vt. to separate. ♦ **sbrancarsi** vr. to scatter.

sbrattare vt. to clean.

sbriciolamento sm. crumbling.

sbriciolare vt. to crumble.

sbrigare vt. to finish off, to get (v. irr.) through. ♦ **sbrigarsi** vr. to hurry up.

sbrigativo agg. quick, hasty.

sbrigliare vt. to unbridle.

sbrinamento sm. defrosting.

sbrinare vt. to defrost.

sbrindellare vt. to tear (v. irr.) to ribbons.

sbrodolare vt. to spill (v. irr.).

sbrodolone sm. 1. slovenly eater 2. (chi parla a lungo) babbler.

sbrogliare vt. to disentangle. ♦ **sbrogliarsi** vr. to extricate oneself.

sbronza sf. V. sbornia.

sbronzarsi vr. to get (v. irr.) drunk.

sbronzo agg. drunk.

sbruffare vt. to besprinkle. ♦ **sbruffare** vi. (fig.) to brag.

sbruffo sm. sprinkle.

sbruffone sm. braggart.

sbucare vi. 1. to come (v. irr.) out 2. (fig.) to spring (v. irr.).

sbucciare vt. 1. to peel 2. (sgranare) to shell.

sbucciatura sf. 1. peeling 2. (scalfittura) scratch.

sbudellamento sm. stabbing.

sbudellare vt. to stab.

sbuffare vi. 1. to pant, to puff 2. (per noia, ira) to snort.

sbuffo sm. 1. puff 2. (per noia, ira) snort.

sbugiardare vt. to give (v. irr.) the lie to.

sbullonare vt. to unbolt.

scabbia sf. scabies.

scabbioso agg. scabby.

scabro agg. rough.

scabrosità sf. 1. roughness 2. (fig.) difficulty.

scabroso agg. 1. rough 2. (fig.) scabrous.

scacchiera sf. chess-board.

scacchiere sm. (stor.) Exchequer.

scacchista sm. chess-player.

scacciacani sf. dummy pistol.

scacciare vt. 1. to drive (v. irr.) away 2. (da scuola) to expel.

scacciata sf. expulsion.

scaccino *sm.* church cleaner.

scacco *sm.* **1.** (*quadratino*) square **2.** (*disegno su tessuti*) check **3.** (*giuoco*) chess || — *matto*, checkmate.

scadente *agg.* **1.** poor **2.** (*comm.*) falling due.

scadenza *sf.* (*comm.*) maturity: *a breve, lunga scadenza* (*comm.*), at short, long maturity || *a breve* —, in a short time.

scadenzario *sm.* discount bill-book.

scadere *vi.* **1.** to expire **2.** (*di pagamenti ecc.*) to become (*v. irr.*) due **3.** (*peggiorare*) to fall (*v. irr.*) off.

scadimento *sm.* decay.

scafandro *sm.* diving-suit.

scaffalare *vt.* to shelve.

scaffalatura *sf.* shelving.

scaffale *sm.* shelf (*pl.* shelves).

scafo *sm.* hull, body.

scagionare *vt.* to acquit. ♦ **scagionarsi** *vr.* to exculpate oneself.

scaglia *sf.* **1.** scale **2.** (*di legno, pietra*) chip.

scagliare *vt.* to fling (*v. irr.*), to throw (*v. irr.*).

scaglionare *vt.* to divide into groups.

scaglione *sm.* **1.** group **2.** (*mil.*) echelon.

scaglioso *agg.* scaly.

scala *sf.* **1.** stairs (*pl.*) **2.** (*trasportabile*) ladder **3.** (*scala graduata*) scale || *salire, scendere le scale*, to go (*v. irr.*) upstairs, downstairs.

scalare[1] *agg.* gradual.

scalare[2] *vt.* **1.** to climb (up) **2.** (*diminuire*) to scale down.

scalata *sf.* climbing.

scalatore *sm.* climber.

scalcagnato *agg.* down-at-heel, shabby.

scalciare *vi.* to kick.

scalcinato *agg.* **1.** unplastered **2.** (*sciatto*) shabby.

scaldabagno *sm.* water-heater.

scaldaletto *sm.* bed-warmer.

scaldapiedi *sm.* foot-warmer.

scaldare *vt.* to heat, to warm. ♦ **scaldarsi** *vr.* to warm oneself, to get (*v. irr.*) warm.

scaldavivande *sm.* dish-warmer.

scaldino *sm.* hand-warmer.

scalea *sf.* flight of stairs.

scaleno *agg.* scalene.

scalfire *vt.* to scratch.

scalfittura *sf.* scratch.

scalinata *sf.* flight of steps.

scalino *sm.* step.

scalmanarsi *vr.* (*fig.*) to get (*v. irr.*) excited.

scalmanato *agg.* out of breath, excited.

scalmo *sm.* rowlock.

scalo *sm.* **1.** (*mar.; aer.*) port of call: *volo senza* —, non-stop flight **2.** (*ferr.*) goods station || *fare* — *a*, to touch at.

scalogna *sf.* bad luck.

scalognato *agg.* unlucky.

scalone *sm.* great staircase.

scaloppina *sf.* veal cutlet.

scalpellare *vt.* to chisel.

scalpellino *sm.* stone-cutter.

scalpello *sm.* chisel.

scalpicciare *vi.* to shuffle.

scalpiccìo *sm.* shuffling.

scalpitare *vi.* **1.** to paw **2.** (*di persona*) to stamp.

scalpitìo *sm.* **1.** pawing **2.** (*di persona*) stamping.

scalpore *sm.* fuss, noise.

scaltrezza *sf.* shrewdness.

scaltrire *vt.* to sharpen so.'s wits. ♦ **scaltrirsi** *vr.* to become (*v. irr.*) sharp.

scaltro *agg.* shrewd.

scalzacane *sm.* **1.** (*incompetente*) botcher **2.** (*malridotto*) down-and-out.

scalzare *vt.* **1.** to take (*v. irr.*) so.'s shoes and socks off **2.** (*fig.*) to undermine.

scalzo *agg.* barefoot.

scambiare *vt.* **1.** to exchange **2.** (*sbagliarsi*) to mistake (*v. irr.*).

scambiévole *agg.* reciprocal.

scambio *sm.* **1.** exchange **2.** (*ferr.*) points (*pl.*).

scambista *sm.* (*ferr.*) pointsman (*pl.* -men).

scamiciato *agg.* shirt-sleeved (*attr.*).

scamosciare *vt.* to chamois.

scamosciato *agg.* shammy.

scampagnata *sf.* trip into the country.

scampanare *vt.* to chime.

scampanellare *vi.* to ring (*v. irr.*) long and loudly.

scampanellata *sf.* loud long ring.

scampare *vi.* to escape || *l'hai scampata bella!*, you have had a narrow escape.

scampato *sm.* survivor.

scampo[1] *sm.* escape: *via di* —, escape.

scampo² sm. (itt.) shrimp.
scàmpolo sm. remnant.
scanalare vt. to channel.
scanalatura sf. groove.
scandagliare vt. to sound.
scandaglio sm. sounding-lead.
scandalizzare vt. to shock.
scandalizzato agg. shocked.
scàndalo sm. scandal: fare uno —, to stir up a scandal.
scandaloso agg. scandalous, shocking.
scandire vt. 1. to scan 2. (parole) to syllabize 3. (mus.) to stress.
scannare vt. 1. to cut (v. irr.) so.'s throat 2. (uccidere crudelmente) to slaughter.
scannatoio sm. slaughter-house.
scanno sm. seat.
scansafatiche sm. lazy-bones.
scansare vt. to avoid, to shun. ♦ **scansarsi** vr. to step aside.
scansìa sf. shelves (pl.).
scantinato sm. basement.
scantonamento sm. (l'evitare) avoiding.
scantonare vt. (evitare) to avoid. ♦ **scantonare** vi. to turn the corner.
scanzonato agg. unconventional.
scapaccione sm. slap.
scapatàggine sf. recklessness.
scapestrato agg. e sm. madcap.
scapigliare vt. to dishevel.
scapigliato agg. 1. dishevelled 2. (fig.) unruly.
scàpito sm. damage, detriment: a — di, to the detriment of.
scàpola sf. shoulder-blade.
scapolare agg. e sm. scapular.
scàpolo agg. single. ♦ **scàpolo** sm. bachelor.
scappamento sm. 1. escape 2. (di motori) exhaust.
scappare vi. to escape, to run (v. irr.) away || lasciarsi —, to miss.
scappata sf. 1. escape 2. (breve visita) call.
scappatella sf. prank.
scappatoia sf. loop-hole.
scappellarsi vr. to take (v. irr.) off one's hat.
scappellata sf. raising one's hat.
scappellotto sm. slap.
scarabeo sm. scarab.
scarabocchiare vt. e vi. to scribble.
scarabocchio sm. scribble.
scarafaggio sm. black-beetle.
scaramanzìa sf. per —, for luck.

scaramuccia sf. skirmish.
scaraventare vt. to hurl.
scarcerare vt. to release (from prison).
scarcerazione sf. release (from prison).
scardinare vt. to unhinge.
scàrica sf. 1. (di armi da fuoco; elettr.) discharge 2. (di proiettili, frecce; fig.) shower.
scaricabarili sm. fare a —, to lay (v. irr.) the blame on so. else.
scaricamento sm. unloading.
scaricare vt. to discharge.
scaricatoio sm. 1. wharf 2. (tubo) waste-pipe.
scaricatore sm. unloader: — di porto, docker.
scàrico sm. 1. (scolo) drain 2. (di merci) discharge. ♦ **scàrico** agg. 1. (di arma) unloaded 2. discharged.
scarlattina sf. scarlet fever.
scarlatto agg. scarlet.
scarmigliare vt. to dishevel.
scarnire vt. to take (v. irr.) flesh off.
scarno agg. thin, lean.
scarpa sf. shoe: — col tacco alto, high-heeled shoe; lucido per scarpe, shoe polish.
scarpata sf. scarp.
scarpone sm. boot.
scarroccio sm. (mar.) leeway.
scarrozzare vt. e vi. to drive (v. irr.) about.
scarsamente avv. scarcely.
scarseggiare vi. to be lacking (in).
scarsità vt. shortage, lack.
scarso agg. scanty, lacking in.
scartabellare vt. to look through.
scartafaccio sm. note-book.
scartamento sm. (ferr.) gauge: — ridotto, narrow gauge.
scartare¹ vt. (mettere da parte) to reject.
scartare² vi. to unwrap.
scartare³ vt. (sport) to swerve.
scarto¹ sm. 1. (cosa scartata) discard 2. (lo scartare) discarding.
scarto² sm. (deviazione) swerve.
scartocciare vt. to unwrap.
scartoffie sf. pl. heap of papers.
scassare vt. (rompere) to force open.
scassinare vt. to break (v. irr.) open.
scassinatore sm. 1. house-breaker 2. (di notte) burglar.

scasso *sm.* lock-picking, house-breaking: *furto con — (di giorno),* house-breaking; *(di notte)* burglary.

scatenamento *sm.* (*fig.*) outburst.

scatenare *vt.* **1.** (*aizzare*) to stir up **2.** (*suscitare*) to rouse. ♦ **scatenarsi** *vr.* **1.** to break (*v. irr.*) loose **2.** (*fig.*) to break out.

scàtola *sf.* **1.** box **2.** (*di latta*) tin.

scatolame *sm.* **1.** tins (*pl.*) **2.** (*cibo in scatola*) tinned food.

scattare *vi.* **1.** (*adirarsi*) to lose (*v. irr.*) one's temper **2.** to go (*v. irr.*) off; to spring (*v. irr.*). ♦ **scattare** *vt.* (*foto*) to shoot (*v. irr.*).

scatto *sm.* **1.** (*d'ira*) outburst || *di —,* suddenly; *a scatti,* in jerks **2.** (*rumore*) click **3.** (*di stipendio*) increase.

scaturire *vi.* **1.** to spring (*v. irr.*) **2.** (*derivare*) to originate.

scavalcare *vt.* **1.** (*gettare da cavallo*) to unhorse **2.** (*fig.*) to supplant **3.** (*passare sopra*) to step, to jump over.

scavare *vt.* **1.** to dig (*v. irr.*) **2.** (*archeologia*) to excavate.

scavatrice *sf.* excavator.

scavezzacollo *sm.* reckless fellow.

scavo *sm.* **1.** digging **2.** (*archeologia*) excavation.

scégliere *vt.* to choose (*v. irr.*), to pick out.

sceicco *sm.* sheik.

scelleratezza *sf.* **1.** wickedness **2.** (*atto scellerato*) misdeed.

scellerato *agg.* wicked. ♦ **scellerato** *sm.* wicked person.

scellino *sm.* shilling: *mezzo —,* sixpence.

scelta *sf.* choice.

scelto *agg.* choice, selected.

scemare *vi.* to diminish.

scemenza *sf.* stupidity.

scemo *agg.* e *sm.* stupid.

scempiare *vt.* to halve.

scempio[1] *agg.* stupid, foolish.

scempio[2] *sm.* havoc.

scena *sf.* **1.** scene **2.** (*palcoscenico*) stage: *colpo di —,* stage effect.

scenario *sm.* scenery.

scenata *sf.* row.

scéndere *vi.* **1.** to go (*v. irr.*) down, to come (*v. irr.*) down **2.** (*da un veicolo*) to get (*v. irr.*) off; (*da cavallo*), to dismount (from a horse) **3.** (*declinare*) to slope down **4.** (*di astri*) to sink (*v. irr.*) **5.** (*avere origini*) to descend.

scendiletto *sm.* bedside-carpet.

sceneggiare *vt.* to arrange into scenes.

sceneggiatore *sm.* scenarist.

sceneggiatura *sf.* screenplay.

scenicamente *avv.* scenically.

scenografia *sf.* scenography.

scèrnere *vt.* to choose (*v. irr.*).

scervellarsi *vr.* to rack one's brains.

scervellato *agg.* brainless. ♦ **scervellato** *sm.* brainless person.

scetticismo *sm.* scepticism.

scèttico *agg.* sceptical. ♦ **scèttico** *sm.* sceptic.

scettro *sm.* sceptre.

sceverare *vt.* to discern.

scevro *agg.* exempt.

scheda *sf.* card: *— elettorale,* voting-paper.

schedario *sm.* card-index.

scheggia *sf.* splinter, chip.

scheggiare *vt.* to chip, to splinter.

schelètrico *agg.* skeletal.

schèletro *sm.* skeleton.

schema *sm.* **1.** scheme **2.** (*tec.*) diagram.

schemàtico *agg.* schematic.

schematismo *sm.* schematism.

scherma *sf.* fencing.

schermaglia *sf.* skirmish.

schermare *vt.* **1.** to screen **2.** (*elettr.*) to shield.

schermirsi *vr.* to act coy.

schermitore *sm.* fencer.

schermo *sm.* **1.** protection **2.** (*cine*) screen **3.** (*fis.*) shield **4.** (*foto*) filter.

schernire *vt.* to laugh at.

scherno *sm.* mockery, derision.

scherzare *vi.* **1.** to joke **2.** (*considerare con leggerezza*) to trifle with.

scherzo *sm.* **1.** joke: *per —,* for fun **2.** (*effetto*) effects (*pl.*).

scherzosamente *avv.* playfully.

scherzoso *agg.* playful.

schettinare *vi.* to roller-skate.

schettini *sm. pl.* roller-skates.

schiaccianoci *sm.* nut-cracker.

schiacciante *agg.* (*decisivo*) overwhelming.

schiacciare *vt.* to crush, to squash.

schiacciasassi *sm.* steam-roller.

schiaffare *vt.* to hurl.

schiaffeggiare *vt.* to slap.

schiaffo *sm.* **1.** slap **2.** (*affronto*) slap in the face.

schiamazzare *vi.* to make (*v. irr.*) a din.

schiamazzo *sm.* din, uproar.

schiantare *vt.* to break (*v. irr.*). ♦
  schiantarsi *vr.* to break, to crash.
schiarimento *sm.* (*spiegazione*) explanation.
schiarire *vt.* to clear, to make (*v.
  irr.*) clear: — *i capelli*, to bleach
  one's hair. ♦ **schiarirsi** *vr.* (*fig.*)
  to brighten.
schiarita *sf.* **1.** clearing **2.** (*miglioramento*) improvement.
schiattare *vi.* to burst: — *di rabbia*, to burst with rage.
schiavista *sm.* **1.** anti-abolitionist
  2. (*mercante di schiavi*) slave-
  -trader.
schiavitù *sf.* slavery.
schiavo *agg. e sm.* slave.
schidionata *sf.* spitful.
schidione *sm.* spit.
schiena *sf.* **1.** back **2.** (*di monte*)
  ridge.
schienale *sm.* back.
schiera *sf.* **1.** formation **2.** (*gruppo
  di persone*) group.
schieramento *sm.* array.
schierare *vt.* to array. ♦ **schierarsi** *vr.* **1.** to draw (*v. irr.*) up **2.**
  (*parteggiare*) to side with.
schiettezza *sf.* openness, purity.
schietto *agg.* pure, open.
schifare *vt.* to loathe. ♦ **schifarsi**
  vr. to feel (*v. irr.*) disgusted
  (at).
schifezza *sf.* disgusting thing.
schifiltoso *agg.* squeamish.
schifo[1] *sm.* disgust.
schifo[2] *sm.* (*mar.*) skiff.
schifoso *agg.* disgusting.
schioccare *vi.* **1.** to crack **2.** (*le
  dita*) to snap **3.** (*le labbra*) to
  smack.
schiocco *sm.* **1.** crack **2.** (*di labbra*)
  smack.
schiodare *vt.* to unnail.
schiodatura *sf.* unnailing.
schioppettata *sf.* shot.
schioppo *sm.* gun.
schiùdere *vt.* to open. ♦ **schiùder-
  si** *vr.* to open.
schiuma *sf.* **1.** foam **2.** (*di vino,
  birra*) froth **3.** (*di sapone*) lather.
schiumare *vt.* to skim. ♦ **schiumare** *vi.* **1.** to foam **2.** (*di bevande*) to froth.
schiumarola *sf.* skimmer.
schiumoso *agg.* **1.** (*di mare*) foamy
  2. (*di bevande*) frothy **3.** (*di sapone*) lathery.
schiuso *agg.* open.

schivare *vt.* to avoid.
schivata *sf.* dodge.
schivo *agg.* shy, bashful.
schizofrenia *sf.* schizophrenia.
schizofrènico *agg.* schizophrenic. ♦
  schizofrènico *sm.* schizophrene.
schizzare *vt.* **1.** to splash, to spatter **2.** (*abbozzare*) to sketch. ♦
  schizzare *vi.* to spurt.
schizzata *sf.* splashing.
schizzatoio *sm.* spray.
schizzetto *sm.* spray.
schizzinoso *agg.* squeamish, fussy.
schizzo *sm.* **1.** splash, squirt **2.**
  (*pitt.*) sketch.
sci *sm.* ski.
scia *sf.* **1.** (*mar.*) wake **2.** (*traccia*)
  trail.
scià *sm.* shah.
sciàbica *sf.* trawl.
sciàbola *sf.* sabre.
sciabolata *sf.* sabre-cut.
sciabolatore *sm.* sabreur.
sciabordare *vi.* to wash.
sciabordìo *sm.* washing, lapping.
sciacallo *sm.* **1.** jackal **2.** (*fig.*) profiteer.
sciacquare *vt.* to rinse (out).
sciacquatura *sf.* **1.** rinsing **2.**
  (*acqua*) rinsing-water.
sciacquìo *sm.* rinsing.
sciacquone *sm.* flush.
sciagura *sf.* misfortune.
sciagurato *agg.* **1.** unlucky **2.** (*malvagio*) wicked. ♦ **sciagurato** *sm.*
  wretch.
scialacquare *vt.* to squander.
scialacquatore *sm.* squanderer.
scialacquìo *sm.* squandering.
scialare *vt.* to squander money.
scialbare *vt.* to plaster.
scialbo *agg.* pale, wan.
scialle *sm.* shawl.
scialo *sm.* waste.
scialuppa *sf.* boat.
sciamannato *agg.* slovenly.
sciamano *sm.* shaman.
sciamare *vi.* to swarm.
sciame *sm.* swarm.
sciancarsi *vr.* to become (*v. irr.*)
  lame.
sciancato *agg.* lame.
sciarada *sf.* charade.
sciare[1] *vi.* to ski.
sciare[2] *vi.* (*mar.*) to back water.
sciarpa *sf.* scarf.
sciàtica *sf.* sciatica.
sciàtico *agg.* sciatic.
sciatore *sm.* skier.

sciatterìa *sf.* slovenliness.
sciatto *agg.* **1.** slovenly, untidy **2.** (*di ·stile ecc.*) careless.
scìbile *sm.* knowledge.
sciccherìa *sf.* smartness.
scientífico *agg.* scientific.
scienza *sf.* science.
scienziato *sm.* scientist.
scilinguàgnolo *sm.* glib tongue.
scimitarra *sf.* scimitar.
scimmia *sf.* monkey, ape (*anche fig.*).
scimmiesco *agg.* monkeyish.
scimmiottare *vt.* to ape.
scimmiotto *sm.* young monkey.
scimpanzé *sm.* chimpanzee.
scimunito *agg.* silly. ♦ **scimunito** *sm.* blockhead.
scìndere *vt.* to divide: — *le questioni*, to deal (*v. irr.*) with each matter separately.
scintilla *sf.* spark.
scintillamento *sf.* sparkling.
scintillante *agg.* sparkling.
scintillare *vi.* to sparkle.
scintillìo *sm.* sparkling.
scintoismo *sm.* Shintoism.
scintoista *sm.* Shintoist.
scioccamente *avv.* foolishly.
sciocchezza *sf.* **1.** foolishness **2.** foolish thing **3.** trifle.
sciocco *agg.* silly.
sciògliere *vt.* **1.** to melt **2.** (*slegare, disfare*) to untie **3.** (*liberare*) to release **4.** (*risolvere*) to solve. ♦ **sciògliersi** *vr.* to dissolve, to get (*v. irr.*) loose.
scioglilingua *sm.* tongue-twister.
scioglimento *sm.* **1.** dissolution, breaking up **2.** (*epilogo*) unravelling.
sciolina *sf.* ski wax.
scioltezza *sf.* **1.** agility **2.** (*spigliatezza*) ease **3.** (*nel parlare*) fluency.
sciolto *agg.* **1.** melted **2.** (*slegato*) untied **3.** (*agile*) agile **4.** (*disinvolto*) easy ‖ *capelli sciolti,* loose hair; *avere la lingua sciolta,* to have a ready tongue; — *da obblighi,* free from obligations.
scioperante *sm.* striker.
scioperare *vi.* to strike (*v. irr.*).
scioperatàggine *sf.* laziness.
scioperato *agg.* lazy. ♦ **scioperato** *sm.* lazy fellow.
sciòpero *sm.* strike.
sciorinare *vt.* to air, to display (*anche fig.*).
sciovìa *sf.* ski-lift.

sciovinismo *sm.* chauvinism.
sciovinista *sm.* chauvinist.
scipitàggine *sf.* insipidity (*anche fig.*).
scipito *agg.* insipid.
scirocco *sm.* sirocco.
sciroppare *vt.* to syrup.
sciroppato *agg.* in syrup.
sciropposo *agg.* syrupy.
scisma *sm.* schism.
scismàtico *agg.* e *sm.* schismatic.
scissione *sf.* **1.** scission, split (*anche fig.*) **2.** (*fis.; biol.*) fission.
scisso *agg.* divided.
scissura *sf.* **1.** cleft, split **2.** (*fig.*) dissension.
sciupare *vt.* **1.** to spoil (*v. irr.*), to damage **2.** (*sprecare*) to waste.
sciupato *agg.* **1.** spoilt **2.** (*sprecato*) wasted.
sciupìo *sm.* waste.
sciupone *agg.* wasteful. ♦ **sciupone** *sm.* waster.
scivolamento *sm.* sliding.
scivolare *vi.* **1.** to slide (*v. irr.*) **2.** (*involontariamente*) to slip.
scivolata *sf.* **1.** slide **2.** (*involontaria*) slip.
scìvolo *sm.* **1.** (*aer.; mar.*) slipway **2.** skid.
scivolone *sm.* slip.
scivoloso *agg.* slippery.
sclerosi *sf.* sclerosis.
scleròtica *sf.* sclerotic.
scleròtico *agg.* sclerotic.
scoccare *vt.* e *vi.* **1.** to shoot (*v. irr.*) **2.** (*l'ora*) to strike (*v. irr.*).
scocciare *vt.* to bother.
scocciatore *sm.* bore.
scocciatura *sf.* bother.
scodella *sf.* bowl.
scodellare *vt.* to dish up.
scodinzolare *vi.* to wag the tail.
scodinzolìo *sm.* tail-wagging.
scogliera *sf.* cliff.
scoglio *sm.* **1.** rock **2.** (*fig.*) difficulty.
scoiare *vt.* V. *scuoiare.*
scoiàttolo *sm.* squirrel.
scolapasta *sm.* colander.
scolara *sf.* pupil, schoolgirl.
scolare *vt.* **1.** to drain **2.** (*in un colabrodo*) to strain.
scolaresca *sf.* student-body.
scolaro *sm.* pupil, schoolboy.
scolàstica *sf.* scholasticism.
scolàstico *agg.* **1.** school (*attr.*) **2.** (*dispregiativo*) bookish.
scolatoio *sm.* drain.

scolatura *sf.* draining.
scoliosi *sf.* scoliosis.
scollacciato *agg.* 1. (*di abito*) low--necked 2. (*fig.*) coarse.
scollare[1] *vt.* to cut (*v. irr.*) away the neck of.
scollare[2] *vt.* (*staccare*) to unglue.
scollato[1] *agg.* (*di abito*) low-necked.
scollato[2] *agg.* unglued.
scollatura *sf.* neckline.
scollo *sm.* neck-opening.
scolo *sm.* draining.
scolorare *vt.* to discolour. ◆ **scolorarsi** *vr.* to grow (*v. irr.*) pale.
scolorimento *sm.* discolouration.
scolorire *vt.* to bleach.
scolorito *agg.* faded, pale.
scolpare *vt.* to exculpate.
scolpire *vt.* to sculpture.
scombinare *vt.* to upset (*v. irr.*).
scombinato *agg.* screwy.
scombussolamento *sm.* upsetting.
scombussolare *vt.* to upset (*v. irr.*).
scommessa *sf.* bet.
scomméttere *vt.* to bet (*v. irr.*).
scommettitore *sm.* bettor.
scomodamente *avv.* uncomfortably.
scomodare *vt.* to trouble, to bother.
scomodità *sf.* lack of comfort.
scòmodo *agg.* uncomfortable.
scompaginamento *sm.* upsetting, upset.
scompaginare *vt.* to upset (*v. irr.*).
scompagnare *vt.* to break (*v. irr.*) up (a pair).
scompagnato *agg.* odd.
scomparire *vi.* 1. to disappear 2. (*non spiccare*) not to stand (*v. irr.*) out.
scomparsa *sf.* 1. disappearance 2. (*morte*) death.
scomparso *agg.* 1. disappeared 2. (*morto*) dead.
scompartimento *sm.* 1. partition 2. (*ferr.*) compartment.
scompartire *vt.* to divide, to share out.
scomparto *sm.* V. *scompartimento.*
scompenso *sm.* lack of balance: — *cardiaco*, cardiac decompensation.
scompiacenza *sf.* unkindness.
scompigliare *vt.* 1. to upset (*v. irr.*) 2. (*arruffare*) to ruffle.
scompigliatamente *avv.* confusedly.

scompiglio *sm.* confusion, disorder.
scomponìbile *agg.* decomposable.
scomponimento *sm.* decomposition.
scomporre *vt.* 1. to decompose 2. (*i lineamenti*) to distort.
scompostamente *avv.* in an unseemly manner.
scompostezza *sf.* unseemliness.
scomposto *agg.* 1. (*sguaiato*) unseemly 2. decomposed.
scomùnica *sf.* excommunication.
scomunicare *vt.* to excommunicate.
scomunicato *agg. e sm.* excommunicate.
sconcertante *agg.* disconcerting.
sconcertare *vt.* to disconcert, to baffle.
sconcertato *agg.* disconcerted.
sconcerto *sm.* perturbation.
sconcezza *sf.* indecency.
sconciamente *avv.* indecently.
sconcio *agg.* indecent.
sconclusionatamente *avv.* inconclusively.
sconclusionato *agg.* inconclusive.
scondito *agg.* 1. unseasoned 2. (*di insalata*) undressed.
sconfessare *vt.* to disown.
sconfessione *sf.* disowning.
sconfìggere *vt.* to defeat.
sconfinamento *sm.* 1. (*in paese straniero*) crossing the frontier 2. (*in proprietà privata*) trespass.
sconfinare *vi.* 1. (*in paese straniero*) to cross the frontier 2. (*in proprietà privata*) to trespass.
sconfinato *agg.* boundless.
sconfitta *sf.* defeat.
sconfitto *agg.* defeated.
sconfortante *agg.* discouraging.
sconfortare *vt.* to discourage.
sconfortato *agg.* discouraged.
sconforto *sm.* 1. discouragement 2. (*dolore*) sorrow.
scongiurare *vt.* 1. to beseech (*v. irr.*) 2. (*evitare*) to avoid.
scongiuro *sm.* exorcism.
sconnessione *sf.* disconnectedness.
sconnesso *agg.* 1. disconnected 2. (*fig.*) rambling.
sconnèttere *vt.* to disconnect. ◆ **sconnèttere** *vi.* to wander.
sconoscente *agg.* ungrateful.
sconoscenza *sf.* ingratitude.
sconòscere *vt.* to disown.
sconosciuto *agg.* unknown. ◆ **sconosciuto** *sm.* stranger.

sconquassare *vt.* to shatter.

sconquassato *agg.* ramshackle.

sconquasso *sm.* mess, disorder.

sconsacrare *vt.* to deconsecrate.

sconsideratezza *sf.* rashness.

sconsiderato *agg.* thoughtless.

sconsigliare *vt.* to advise against.

sconsigliato *agg.* rash.

sconsolante *agg.* discouraging.

sconsolare *vt.* to dishearten.

sconsolato *agg.* disconsolate.

scontàbile *agg.* discountable.

scontare *vt.* **1.** (*comm.*) to discount **2.** (*detrarre*) to deduct **3.** (*espiare*) to expiate.

scontato *agg.* (*previsto*) expected.

scontentare *vt.* to displease.

scontentezza *sf.* discontent.

scontento *agg.* displeased.

sconto *sm.* discount.

scontrarsi *vr.* to clash.

scontrino *sm.* ticket, check.

scontro *sm.* **1.** encounter **2.** (*di veicoli*) crash **3.** (*fig.*) clash.

scontrosamente *avv.* peevishly.

scontrosità *sf.* bad temper.

scontroso *agg.* bad-tempered.

sconveniente *agg.* **1.** unprofitable **2.** (*indecente*) unseemly.

sconvenientemente *avv.* unbecomingly.

sconvenienza *sf.* **1.** unprofitableness **2.** (*mancanza di correttezza*) unseemliness.

sconvolgente *agg.* upsetting.

sconvòlgere *vt.* to upset (*v. irr.*).

sconvolgimento *sm.* upsetting, confusion.

sconvolto *agg.* upset.

scopa *sf.* broom.

scopare *vt.* to sweep (*v. irr.*).

scoperchiare *vt.* to take (*v. irr.*) off the lid.

scoperta *sf.* discovery.

scopertamente *avv.* openly.

scoperto *agg.* uncovered || *automobile scoperta*, open car; *a capo —*, bare-headed; *giocare a carte scoperte*, to act openly.

scopino *sm.* street-sweeper.

scopo *sm.* aim, purpose: *senza —*, aimless.

scopolamina *sf.* scopolamine.

scoppiare *vi.* **1.** to burst (*v. irr.*) **2.** (*di guerre, epidemie ecc.*) to break (*v. irr.*) out.

scoppiettante *agg.* crackling.

scoppiettare *vi.* to crackle.

scoppiettìo *sm.* crackling.

scoppio *sm.* **1.** burst, explosion: *motore a —*, piston-engine **2.** (*di guerre, rivoluzioni ecc.*) outbreak.

scoprimento *sm.* **1.** discovering **2.** (*di monumento*) unveiling.

scoprire *vt.* **1.** to discover **2.** (*avvistare*) to sight **3.** (*togliere ciò che copre*) to uncover **4.** (*palesare*) to show (*v. irr.*). ♦ scoprirsi *vr.* (*rivelarsi*) to reveal oneself.

scopritore *sm.* discoverer.

scoraggiamento *sm.* discouragement.

scoraggiante *agg.* discouraging.

scoraggiare *vt.* to discourage. ♦ scoraggiarsi *vr.* to get (*v. irr.*) discouraged.

scoraggiato *agg.* discouraged.

scoramento *sm.* discouragement.

scorato *agg.* disheartened.

scorbùtico *agg.* **1.** (*med.*) scorbutic **2.** (*fig.*) ill-tempered.

scorbuto *sm.* scurvy.

scorciare *vt.* to shorten.

scorciatoia *sf.* short cut.

scorcio *sm.* **1.** foreshortening **2.** (*spazio di tempo*) end, close.

scordare[1] *vt.* to forget (*v. irr.*).

scordare[2] *vt.* (*mus.*) to untune.

scordato[1] *agg.* forgotten.

scordato[2] *agg.* (*mus.*) untuned.

scòrfano *sm.* **1.** sea-scorpion **2.** (*di persona*) fright: *che —!*, what a fright!

scòrgere *vt.* to perceive, to discern.

scoria *sf.* **1.** (*metal.*) dross **2.** (*fig.*) scum.

scornare *vt.* **1.** to horn **2.** (*fig.*) to humiliate.

scornato *agg.* humiliated.

scorno *sm.* shame.

scorpacciata *sf.* blow out: *fare una — di*, to stuff oneself with.

scorpione *sm.* scorpion.

scorporare *vt.* to disembody.

scòrporo *sm.* breaking up.

scorrazzare *vi.* to run (*v. irr.*) about.

scòrrere *vi.* **1.** to run (*v. irr.*) **2.** (*scivolare*) to glide **3.** (*fluire*) to flow **4.** (*di tempo*) to fly (*v. irr.*).

scorreria *sf.* raid.

scorrettezza *sf.* incorrectness.

scorretto *agg.* **1.** incorrect **2.** (*di costumi*) dissolute **3.** (*maleducato*) rude.

scorrévole *agg.* **1.** sliding **2.** (*fig.*) fluent.

scorrevolezza sf. fluency.

scorribanda sf. incursion, raid.

scorrimento sm. sliding.

scorsa sf. glance.

scorso agg. last, past.

scorsoio agg. running.

scorta sf. 1. escort 2. (provvista) supply || ruota di —, spare wheel.

scortare vt. to escort.

scortecciare vt. 1. to peel 2. (un albero) to bark.

scortese agg. rude, impolite.

scortesìa sf. rudeness.

scorticare vt. to skin.

scorticatura sf. scratch.

scortichino sm. flaying-knife.

scorza sf. 1. (corteccia) bark 2. (buccia) skin, rind.

scoscéndere vt. to split (v. irr.).

scoscendimento sm. 1. collapse 2. (di terreno) break.

scosceso agg steep, sloping.

scossa sf. shock, shake.

scosso agg. 1. shaken 2. (fig.) upset.

scossone sm. 1. shake 2. (strattone) jerk.

scostare vt. to shift, to move away. ♦ **scostarsi** vr. 1. to move away 2. (staccarsi) to turn off.

scostumatezza sf. dissoluteness.

scostumato agg. dissolute. ♦ **scostumato** sm. dissolute person.

scotennare vt. to scalp.

scottante agg. burning.

scottare vt. 1. to burn (v. irr.) 2. (cuc.) to half-cook 3. (fig.) to hurt (v. irr.).

scottatura sf. burn.

scotto[1] sm. score: pagare lo —, to pay (v. irr.) one's piper.

scotto[2] agg. overdone.

scovare vt. 1. to put (v. irr.) up 2. (scoprire) to discover.

scozzare vt. to shuffle.

scozzese agg. Scotch, Scottish. ♦ **scozzese** sm. Scotchman (pl. -men).

scozzonare vt. 1. to break (v. irr.) in 2. (fig.) to teach (v. irr.) the first elements.

screanzatamente avv. rudely.

screanzato agg. rude, impolite. ♦ **screanzato** sm. rude person.

screditare vt. to discredit.

screditato agg. discredited.

scrédito sm. discredit.

scremare vt. to skim.

scremato agg. skimmed: latte —, skim-milk.

scrematura sf. skimming.

screpolare vi. 1. to crack 2. (della pelle) to get (v. irr.) chapped.

screpolatura sf. 1. crack 2. (della pelle) chap.

screziare vt. to variegate.

screziato agg. variegated.

screziatura sf. variegation.

screzio sm. disagreement.

scribacchiare vt. e vi. to scribble.

scribacchino sm. scribbler.

scricchiolare vi. 1. to creak 2. (di denti) to grind (v. irr.).

scricchiolìo sm. 1. creaking 2. (di denti) grinding.

scrigno sm. casket: — di gioielli, jewel-case.

scriminatura sf. (hair-)parting.

scriteriato agg. senseless.

scritta sf. 1. inscription 2. (cartello) notice 3. (dicitura) caption.

scritto sm. writing.

scrittoio sm. writing-desk.

scrittore sm. writer.

scrittrice sf. woman writer.

scrittura sf. 1. writing: — a macchina, typewriting; — a mano, handwriting 2. (teat.) engagement 3. (giur.) deed.

scritturare vt. to engage.

scrivanìa sf. writing-desk.

scrivano sm. clerk, copyist.

scrivere vt. to write (v. irr.): — a mano, to write by hand; — a penna, a matita, to write in pen, in pencil; — sotto dettatura, to write from dictation; — a macchina, to typewrite (v. irr.) 2. (registrare) to enter, to record.

scroccare vt. to scrounge.

scrocco sm. vivere a —, to sponge one's living.

scroccone sm. sponger.

scrofa sf. sow.

scrofoloso agg. scrofulous.

scrollamento sm. 1. shaking 2. (di spalle) shrugging.

scrollare vt. 1. to shake (v. irr.) 2. (le spalle) to shrug.

scrollata sf. 1. (di testa) shake 2. (di spalle) shrug.

scrosciante agg. (di risa ecc.) roaring: pioggia —, pelting rain.

scrosciare vi. 1. (di pioggia) to pelt down 2. (fig.) to roar.

scroscio sm. 1. (di cascata, torrente ecc.) roar 2. (fig.) roar, burst || — di pioggia, shower.

scrostamento sm. peeling.

scrostare vt. 1. to take (v. irr.) the crust off, to peel off 2. (dei muri) to remove the plaster from a wall. ♦ **scrostarsi** vr. to fall (v. irr.) off, to peel off.

scrùpolo sm. scruple.

scrupolosamente avv. scrupulously.

scrupolosità sf. scrupulosity.

scrupoloso agg. scrupulous.

scrutare vt. to search, to scan.

scrutatore agg. searching, inquisitive. ♦ **scrutatore** sm. 1. searcher 2. (di elezioni) scrutineer.

scrutinare vt. to scrutinize.

scrutinio sm. 1. (di elezioni) poll 2. (scolastico) assignment of a term's marks 3. (attento esame) scrutiny.

scucire vt. to unsew (v. irr.), to unstitch. ♦ **scucirsi** vr. to rip.

scucito agg. 1. unsewn 2. (fig.) incoherent.

scucitura sf. unsewing.

scuderìa sf. stable.

scudetto sm. 1. small shield 2. (sport) (championship) shield.

scudiero sm. squire.

scudisciare vt. to lash.

scudisciata sf. lash.

scudiscio sm. switch, lash.

scudo sm. shield.

scuffia sf. (sbornia) drunkenness.

sculacciare vt. to spank.

sculacciata sf. spank.

sculettare vi. to waddle.

scultore sm. sculptor.

scultòreo agg. sculptural.

scultura sf. sculpture.

scuoiare vt. to skin.

scuola sf. school: — diurna, day-classes; — elementare, primary school; — media inferiore, superiore, secondary school; — pubblica, State school; maestro di —, schoolmaster.

scuòtere vt. 1. to shake (v. irr.) (anche fig.) 2. (agitare) to stir.

scuotimento sm. shaking.

scure sf. axe.

scurire vt. 1. to darken 2. (pitt.) to tone down. ♦ **scurirsi** vr. to grow (v. irr.) dark.

scuro agg. dark || faccia scura, grim face.

scurrile agg. scurrilous.

scurrilità sf. scurrility.

scusa sf. 1. excuse, apology 2. (pretesto) pretext.

scusàbile agg. excusable.

scusare vt. to excuse, to forgive (v. irr.) || scusi!, scusate!, sorry!, excuse me! ♦ **scusarsi** vr. to apologize.

sdebitarsi vr. 1. to pay (v. irr.) off one's debts 2. (disobbligarsi) to return a kindness.

sdegnare vt. 1. to disdain 2. (provocare lo sdegno) to enrage.

sdegnato agg. indignant.

sdegno sm. disdain, indignation.

sdegnosamente avv. disdainfully.

sdegnoso agg. 1. (di atti e parole) disdainful 2. (di persona) haughty.

sdentare vt. to break (v. irr.) the teeth.

sdentato agg. toothless.

sdilinquimento sm. mawkishness.

sdilinquirsi vr. to melt away.

sdoganamento sm. clearing (through the customs).

sdolcinato agg. sugary, affected.

sdolcinatura sf. mawkishness.

sdoppiamento sm. splitting.

sdoppiare vt. to split.

sdraia sf. deck-chair.

sdraiarsi vr. to lie (v. irr.) down.

sdrucciolare vi. to slip, to slide.

sdrucciolévole agg. slippery.

sdrucciolone sm. slip.

sdrucire vt. to tear (v. irr.).

sdrucito agg. torn.

se cong. 1. if 2. (dubitativo) whether || — mai, in case; — non altro, at least; — non che, except that; anche —, even if.

sé pron. pers. 1. one, him, her, it, them 2. (riflessivi) oneself, himself, herself, itself, themselves || una donna piena di —, a conceited woman; essere fuori di —, to be beside oneself; tornare in —, to recover consciousness; amore di —, selfishness; padronanza di —, self-control; un uomo sicuro di —, a self-confident man; un uomo che si è fatto da —, a self-made man; rispetto di —, self-respect.

sebàceo agg. sebaceous.

sebbene cong. though, although.

sebo sm. sebum.

secante sf. secant.

secca sf. 1. shoal 2. (siccità) drought.

seccamente avv. coldly.

seccante agg. (fig.) annoying, irritating || una cosa, persona —, a nuisance.

seccare vt. **1.** to dry up **2.** (annoiare) to annoy, to irritate. ◆ **seccarsi** vr. (infastidirsi) to be annoyed (with).

seccatore sm. bother.

seccatura sf. **1.** (essicamento) drying **2.** (noia) bother, nuisance.

secchia sf. pail, bucket.

secchiello sm. bucket.

secchio sm. V. **secchia.**

secco agg. **1.** dry **2.** (appassito) withered **3.** (magro) thin **4.** (brusco) sharp **5.** (freddo) cold.

secentesco agg. of the seventeenth century.

secèrnere vt. to secrete.

secessione sf. secession

secessionista agg. e sm. secessionist.

seco pron. with him, with her, with them.

secolare agg. **1.** secular **2.** (in opposizione a ecclesiastico) lay.

secolarizzare vt. to secularize.

secolarizzazione sf. secularization.

sècolo sm. **1.** century **2.** (epoca) epoch, age || Padre Carlo, al — John Smith, Father Charles, in the world John Smith.

seconda sf. (auto) second gear || a — di (loc. prep.), according to.

secondare vt. to favour.

secondario agg. secondary.

secondino sm. warder.

secondo[1] agg. **1.** second **2.** (favorevole) favourable. ◆ **secondo** sm. **1.** (minuto) second **2.** (ufficiale in seconda) executive officer.

secondo[2] prep. according to. ◆ **secondo** avv. second.

secrezione sf. secretion.

sèdano sm. celery.

sedare vt. to soothe.

sedativo agg. e sm. sedative.

sede sf. **1.** seat, centre **2.** (residenza) residence **3.** (eccl.) see **4.** (edificio per pubblici uffici) office.

sedentario agg. sedentary.

sedere[1] vi. **1.** (stare seduto) to sit (v. irr.), to be sitting **2.** (mettersi a sedere) to sit (down).

sedere[2] sm. bottom.

sedia sf. chair: — a dondolo, rocking-chair.

sedicenne agg. **1.** (attr.) sixteen--year-old **2.** (pred.) sixteen years old.

sedicente agg. would-be.

sedicèsimo agg. sixteenth.

sédici agg. sixteen.

sedile sm. seat, chair.

sedimentario agg. sedimentary.

sedimentazione sf. sedimentation.

sedimento sm. sediment.

sedizione sf. sedition.

sedizioso agg. seditious.

seducente agg. **1.** alluring **2.** (affascinante) charming.

sedurre vt. to seduce, to tempt.

seduta sf. sitting, session.

seduttore agg. seducing. ◆ **seduttore** sm. seducer.

seduzione sf. **1.** seduction **2.** (attrazione) attraction.

sega sf. saw.

ségala sf. rye.

segaligno agg. **1.** rye (attr.) **2.** (di persona) wiry.

segare vt. to saw (v. irr.).

segatura sf. sawdust.

seggio sm. chair, seat: — elettorale, poll.

sèggiola sf. chair.

seggiovìa sf. chair-lift.

segherìa sf. saw-mill.

seghettare vt. to jag.

segmentazione sf. segmentation.

segmento sm. segment.

segnalare vt. **1.** to signal **2.** (far notare) to point out. ◆ **segnalarsi** vr. to distinguish oneself.

segnalatore sm. **1.** signaller **2.** (segnalatore di direzione) direction indicator.

segnalazione sf. signal: — stradale, traffic signal.

segnale sm. signal: — di pericolo, allarme, danger, alarm signal; — di linea libera, occupata (tel.), ringing, engaged tone; — di passaggio a livello, level-crossing signal.

segnalètica sf. signals (pl.).

segnalètico agg. descriptive.

segnalibro sm. book-mark.

segnare vt. **1.** to mark **2.** (indicare) to show (v. irr.) **3.** (sport) to score. ◆ **segnarsi** vr. to cross oneself.

segnatura sf. **1.** marking **2.** (sport) scoring.

segno sm. **1.** sign, mark: passare il —, to overstep the mark **2.** (limite) limit **3.** (simbolo) symbol.

sego sm. tallow.

segregare vt. to segregate.

segregazione sf. segregation.

segreta sf. dungeon.

segretamente *avv.* in secret.

segretariato *sm.* secretariate.

segretario *sm.* secretary.

segreteria *sf.* **1.** secretariat **2.** (*di ministero*) secretariat of State.

segretezza *sf.* secrecy.

segreto *agg.* secret. ♦ **segreto** *sm.* **1.** secret: *nel — del cuore*, in the depths of one's heart **2.** (*parte interna, intimità*) secrecy.

seguace *sm.* follower, supporter.

seguente *agg.* following, next.

segugio *sm.* bloodhound.

seguire *vt. e vi.* **1.** to follow **2.** (*sorvegliare*) to supervise **3.** (*frequentare regolarmente*) to attend.

séguito *sm.* **1.** (*corteo*) retinue **2.** (*successione, sequela*) series **3.** (*continuazione*) continuation ‖ *il — alla prossima puntata*, to be continued **4.** (*comm.*): *a — di*, following up.

sei *agg.* six.

seicento *agg.* six hundred. ♦ **seicento** *sm.* the seventeenth century.

selce *sf.* flint.

selciare *vt.* to pave.

selciato *sm.* pavement.

selenio *sm.* selenium.

selenite *agg.* lunar. ♦ **selenite** *sf.* selenite.

selettività *sf.* selectivity.

selettivo *agg.* selective.

selettore *sm.* selector.

selezionare *vt.* to select.

selezione *sf.* selection.

sella *sf.* saddle.

sellaio *sm.* saddler.

sellare *vt.* to saddle.

sellino *sm.* saddle.

selva *sf.* **1.** wood **2.** (*fig.*) mass.

selvaggina *sf.* game.

selvaggio *agg.* wild, primitive. ♦ **selvaggio** *sm.* savage.

selvàtico *agg.* **1.** wild **2.** (*non socievole*) unsociable.

selvoso *agg.* woody.

semàforo *sm.* traffic-lights (*pl.*).

semàntica *sf.* semantics.

semàntico *agg.* semantic.

sembianza *sf.* features (*pl.*).

sembrare *vi.* **1.** to seem **2.** (*somigliare*) to look like.

seme *sm.* **1.** seed **2.** (*carte da giuoco*) suit.

sementa *sf.* **1.** seeds (*pl.*) **2.** (*epoca della semina*) seed-time.

semente *sf.* seeds (*pl.*).

semenza *sf.* seeds (*pl.*).

semenzaio *sm.* seed-bed.

semestrale *agg.* six-monthly (*attr.*).

semestralmente *avv.* twice a year.

semestre *sm.* half-year.

semiaperto *agg.* half-open.

semicerchio *sm.* semicircle.

semichiuso *agg.* half-closed.

semicircolare *agg.* semicircular.

semiconduttore *sm.* semiconductor.

semidiàmetro *sm.* semi-diameter.

semidio *sm.* demigod.

semifinale *sf.* semifinal.

semilavorato *agg. e sm.* semi-manufactured.

sémina *sf.* sowing.

seminàbile *agg.* fit to be sown.

seminagione *sf.* sowing.

seminare *vt.* to sow (*v. irr.*).

seminario *sm.* seminary.

seminarista *sm.* seminarist.

seminato *agg.* **1.** sown **2.** (*fig.*) strewn.

seminatore *sm.* sower.

seminfermità *sf.* partial infirmity: *— mentale*, partial insanity.

seminudo *agg.* half-naked.

semiserio *agg.* half-serious.

semisfera *sf.* hemisphere.

semita *s.* Semite.

semìtico *agg.* Semitic.

semitono *sm.* semitone.

semivivo *agg.* half-alive.

sémola *sf.* bran.

semolino *sm.* semolina.

semovente *agg.* self-moving.

sempiterno *agg.* everlasting.

sémplice *agg.* simple.

semplicione *sm.* simpleton.

semplicismo *sm.* superficiality.

semplicìstico *agg.* superficial.

semplicità *sf.* simplicity.

semplificare *vt.* to simplify.

semplificazione *sf.* simplification

sempre *avv.* **1.** always: *— avanti! always onward!*; *— meglio, peggio*, better and better, worse and worse; *per —*, for ever; *una volta per —*, once for all **2.** (*tuttora*) still: *vivi — qui?*, do you still live here?

sempreverde *sm.* evergreen.

sènape *sf.* mustard.

senato *sm.* senate.

senatore *sm.* senator.

senatoriale *agg.* senatorial.

senescenza *sf.* senescence.

senile *agg.* senile.

senilità *sf.* senility.

senno *sm.* sense, wisdom.

seno *sm.* **1.** breast, bosom **2.** (*grembo*) womb.

sensale *sm.* broker.

sensatezza *sf.* good sense.

sensato *agg.* sensible.

sensazionale *agg.* sensational.

sensazione *sf.* sensation, feeling.

sensibile *agg.* sensitive.

sensibilità *sf.* sensitiveness.

sensibilizzare *vt.* to sensitize.

sensibilmente *avv.* **1.** sensitively **2.** (*notevolmente*) sensibly.

sensitività *sf.* sensitivity.

sensitivo *agg.* **1.** sensory **2.** (*sensibile*) sensitive.

senso *sm.* **1.** sense **2.** (*sensazione*) sensation **3.** (*direzione*) direction, way **4.** (*modo*) way, manner.

sensorio *agg.* sensorial.

sensuale *agg.* sensual.

sensualità *sf.* sensuality.

sensualmente *avv.* sensually.

sentenza *sf.* **1.** sentence **2.** (*massima*) saying.

sentenziare *vi.* to judge, to hold (*v. irr.*).

sentenziosamente *avv.* sententiously.

sentenzioso *agg.* sententious.

sentiero *sm.* path.

sentimentale *agg.* sentimental.

sentimentalismo *sm.* sentimentalism.

sentimentalità *sf.* sentimentality.

sentimento *sm.* **1.** sentiment **2.** (*disposizione spirituale*) feeling.

sentinella *sf.* sentry.

sentire *vt.* **1.** to feel (*v. irr.*) **2.** (*udire*) to hear (*v. irr.*) **3.** (*gustare*) to taste **4.** (*odorare*) to smell (*v. irr.*) **5.** (*ascoltare*) to listen to. ◆ **sentirsi** *vr.* to feel.

sentitamente *avv.* heartily.

sentito *agg.* **1.** heart-felt **2.** (*udito*) heard || *per — dire*, by hearsay.

sentore *sm.* inkling: *aver — di*, to suspect.

senza *prep.* without: *— scarpe*, barefoot; *— fine*, endless; *— confronto*, unrivalled; *— numero*, countless; *— testa*, thoughtless.

senzatetto *s.* homeless person.

separare *vt.* to separate. ◆ **separarsi** *vr.* to separate.

separatamente *avv.* separately.

separatismo *sm.* separatism.

separatista *s.* separatist.

separativo *agg.* separative.

separato *agg.* separated.

separazione *sf.* separation.

sepolcrale *agg.* sepulchral.

sepolcro *sm.* sepulchre, tomb.

sepolto *agg.* buried.

sepoltura *sf.* burial.

seppellimento *sm.* burial.

seppellire *vt.* to bury.

seppia *sf.* cuttle-fish.

seppure *cong.* even if.

sequela *sf.* series (*invariato al pl.*).

sequenza *sf.* **1.** series **2.** (*cine*) sequence.

sequestrabile *agg.* seizable.

sequestrare *vt.* to seize.

sequestro *sm.* **1.** seizure **2.** (*per debiti*) distress.

sequoia *sf.* sequoia.

sera *sf.* evening.

seràfico *agg.* seraphic.

serafino *sm.* seraph.

serale *agg.* evening (*attr.*).

serata *sf.* **1.** evening **2.** (*ricevimento serale*) party.

serbare *vt.* **1.** (*mettere in serbo*) to put (*v. irr.*) aside **2.** (*conservare*) to keep (*v. irr.*) || *— odio, rancore*, to nourish hatred, rancour. ◆ **serbarsi** *vr.* to keep, to remain.

serbatoio *sm.* reservoir, tank.

serbo (*nella loc.*) *tenere in —*, to keep (*v. irr.*) aside.

serenamente *avv.* serenely.

serenata *sf.* serenade.

serenìssimo *agg.* Serene Highness.

serenità *sf.* serenity.

sereno *agg.* serene, clear || *giudizio —*, objective judgement.

sergente *sm.* sergeant.

sèrico *agg.* silk (*attr.*), silky.

sericoltore *sm.* silkgrower.

sericoltura *sf.* sericulture.

serie *sf.* **1.** series (*invariato al pl.*): *in —*, mass-produced **2.** (*assieme*) set **3.** (*fila*) row.

serietà *sf.* seriousness.

serio *agg.* serious, earnest.

sermone *sm.* **1.** sermon **2.** (*rimprovero*) lecture.

seròtino *agg.* evening (*attr.*).

serpe *sf.* snake.

serpeggiante *agg.* winding.

serpeggiare *vi.* to wind (*v. irr.*).

serpente *sm.* snake, serpent.

serpentina *sf.* **1.** coil **2.** (*di strada*) winding road.

serpentino *agg.* snakelike. ◆ **serpentino** *sm.* serpentine.

serra *sf.* greenhouse.

serraglio *sm.* **1.** menagerie **2.** (*del sultano*) seraglio.

serramànico (*nella loc. avv.*) *coltello a* —, flick-knife.

serramento *sm.* lock.

serrare *vt.* **1.** to shut (*v. irr.*), to close **2.** (*a chiave*) to lock **3.** (*stringere*) to tighten **4.** (*concludere*) to conclude.

serrata *sf.* (*econ.*) lockout.

serratura *sf.* lock: *buco della* —, keyhole.

serva *sf.* maid-servant.

servibile *agg.* usable.

servigio *sm.* service, favour.

servile *agg.* servile.

servilismo *sm.* servility.

servire *vt.* **1.** to serve **2.** (*di persona di servizio*) to wait on **3.** (*le carte*) to deal (*v. irr.*). ♦ **servire** *vi.* (*occorrere*) to need: *vi serve qualcosa?*, can I help you? ♦ **servirsi** *vr.* **1.** to use **2.** (*a tavola*) to help oneself (to).

servitore *sm.* servant.

servitù *sf.* **1.** servitude, slavery **2.** (*personale di servizio*) servants (*pl.*).

serviziévole *agg.* obliging.

servizio *sm.* **1.** service **2.** (*lavoro*) work: *fuori* —, off duty **3.** (*favore*) favour.

servo *sm.* **1.** servant **2.** (*schiavo*) slave.

servofreno *sm.* brake booster.

sèsamo *sm.* sesame.

sessanta *agg.* sixty.

sessantenne *agg.* **1.** (*attr.*) sixty-year-old **2.** (*pred.*) sixty years old. ♦ **sessantenne** *s.* sixty-year-old person.

sessantèsimo *agg.* sixtieth.

sessantina *sf.* about sixty: *un uomo sulla* —, a man in his sixties.

sessione *sf.* session.

sesso *sm.* sex.

sessuale *agg.* sexual.

sessualità *sf.* sexuality.

sestante *sm.* sextant.

sesterzio *sm.* sesterce.

sestetto *sm.* sextet.

sesto[1] *agg.* sixth.

sesto[2] *sm.* **1.** order **2.** (*arch.*) curve.

sèstuplo *agg. e sm.* sextuple.

seta *sf.* silk.

setacciare *vt.* to sieve.

setaccio *sm.* sieve.

sete *sf.* thirst: *avere* —, to be thirsty.

seterìa *sf.* **1.** silk factory **2.** (*negozio di seta*) silk shop.

setificio *sm.* silk factory.

sétola *sf.* **1.** bristle **2.** (*crine*) hair.

setta *sf.* sect.

settanta *agg.* seventy.

settantenne *agg.* **1.** (*attr.*) seventy-year-old **2.** (*pred.*) seventy years old. ♦ **settantenne** *s.* seventy-year-old person.

settantèsimo *agg.* seventieth.

settario *agg.* sectarian.

settarismo *sm.* sectarianism.

sette *agg.* seven.

settecentesco *agg.* of eighteenth century.

settecento *agg.* seven hundred. ♦ **settecento** *sm.* the eighteenth century.

settembre *sm.* September.

settentrionale *agg.* northern.

settentrione *sm.* north.

setticemìa *sf.* septicaemia.

sèttico *agg.* septic.

settimana *sf.* week.

settimanale *agg.* weekly. ♦ **settimanale** *sm.* weekly magazine.

settimino *sm.* seven months' child.

setto *sm.* septum (*pl.* -ta).

settore *sm.* **1.** (*geom.*) sector **2.** (*campo*) field.

settoriale *agg.* sectorial.

severità *sf.* severity.

severo *agg.* severe, strict.

sevizia *sf.* torture.

seviziare *vt.* to torture.

sezionamento *sm.* dissection.

sezionare *vt.* (*anat.*) to dissect.

sezione *sf.* **1.** section **2.** (*reparto*) department **3.** (*di scuola*) side.

sfaccendato *agg.* idle. ♦ **sfaccendato** *sm.* idler.

sfaccettare *vt.* to facet.

sfacchinare *vi.* to drudge.

sfacciatàggine *sf.* impudence.

sfacciato *agg.* **1.** impudent, cheeky **2.** (*di colori*) gaudy.

sfacelo *sm.* break-up.

sfaldamento *sm.* flaking.

sfaldarsi *vr.* to flake away.

sfamare *vt.* to appease so.'s hunger.

sfarfallare *vi.* to flutter about.

sfarzo *sm.* pomp.

sfarzoso *agg.* sumptuous.

sfasamento *sm.* **1.** (*mecc.; elettr.*) phase-displacement, phase-difference **2.** (*fig.*) inconsequence.

sfasato *agg.* **1.** out of phase **2.** (*fig.*) inconsequent.

sfasciare[1] *vt.* (*togliere le fasce*) to unbandage.

sfasciare[2] *vt.* to smash. ♦ **sfasciarsi** *vr.* to collapse.

sfasciato *agg.* (*rotto*) in pieces.

sfatare *vt.* to discredit.

sfaticato *agg.* lazy. ♦ **sfaticato** *sm.* lazy-bones.

sfatto *agg.* undone.

sfavillante *agg.* shining.

sfavillare *vi.* to shine (*v. irr.*), to sparkle.

sfavore *sm.* disfavour, discredit.

sfavorévole *agg.* unfavourable.

sfebbrato *agg.* without a temperature.

sfegatarsi *vr.* to wear (*v. irr.*) oneself out.

sfegatato *agg.* fanatic.

sfenòide *sm.* sphenoid.

sfera *sf.* 1. sphere 2. (*lancetta*) hand 3. (*mecc.*) ball.

sfericità *sf.* sphericity.

sfèrico *agg.* spherical.

sferragliare *vi.* to clang.

sferrare *vt.* 1. (*un attacco*) to launch 2. (*un colpo*) to land a blow. ♦ **sferrarsi** *vr.* to hurl oneself (at).

sferruzzare *vi.* to knit (*v. irr.*).

sferza *sf.* whip, lash (*anche fig.*).

sferzare *vt.* 1. to whip, to lash 2. (*fig.*) to reprimand.

sferzata *sf.* 1. lash 2. (*fig.*) sharp rebuke.

sfiancare *vt.* to wear (*v. irr.*) out.

sfiatare *vi.* to leak. ♦ **sfiatarsi** *vr.* to talk oneself hoarse.

sfiatato *agg.* out of breath.

sfiatatoio *sm.* vent.

sfibbiare *vt.* to unbuckle.

sfibramento *sm.* enfeeblement.

sfibrante *agg.* exhausting.

sfibrare *vt.* to weaken, to wear (*v. irr.*) out.

sfibratura *sf.* breaking.

sfida *sf.* challenge: *in tono di —,* defiantly.

sfidante *sm.* challenger.

sfidare *vt.* 1. to challenge 2. (*affrontare*) to face, to dare: *— la morte,* to face death.

sfiducia *sf.* mistrust: *avere —,* to mistrust.

sfiduciare *vt.* to discourage. ♦ **sfiduciarsi** *vr.* to become (*v. irr.*) discouraged.

sfiduciato *agg.* discouraged.

sfigurare *vt.* to spoil (*v. irr.*). ♦

sfigurare *vi.* to cut (*v. irr.*) a poor figure.

sfigurato *agg.* disfigured.

sfilacciare *vt.* to fray.

sfilacciato *agg.* frayed.

sfilare[1] *vt.* to unthread, to unstring (*v. irr.*).

sfilare[2] *vi.* to parade.

sfilata *sf.* 1. march, parade 2. (*fila*) line, string.

sfinge *sf.* sphinx.

sfinimento *sm.* exhaustion.

sfinire *vt.* to exhaust.

sfinitezza *sf.* extreme weakness.

sfinito *agg.* worn out.

sfintere *sm.* sphincter.

sfiorare *vt.* to graze, to touch on.

sfiorire *vi.* to wither, to fade.

sfiorito *agg.* faded, withered (*anche fig.*).

sfittare *vt.* to vacate.

sfitto *agg.* vacant.

sfocato *agg.* out of focus.

sfociare *vi.* to flow.

sfoderare *vt.* 1. to unline 2. (*sguainare*) to unsheathe 3. (*ostentare*) to display.

sfoderato *agg.* 1. unlined 2. (*sguainato*) unsheathed.

sfogare *vt.* to give (*v. irr.*) vent to. ♦ **sfogarsi** *vr.* to relieve one's feelings.

sfoggiare *vi.* to show (*v. irr.*) off.

sfoggio *sm.* show, ostentation.

sfoglia *sf.* 1. (*lamina*) foil 2. (*cuc.*) pastry.

sfogliare[1] *vt.* to pluck the petals off.

sfogliare[2] *vt.* 1. (*voltare le pagine*) to turn over the pages 2. (*dare un'occhiata*) to glance through.

sfogliata *sf.* 1. (*cuc.*) puff-pastry 2. (*di libro*) thumbing.

sfogo *sm.* vent, outlet.

sfolgoramento *sm.* blazing.

sfolgorante *agg.* flaming.

sfolgorare *vi.* to blaze.

sfolgorìo *sm.* blaze.

sfollagente *sm.* truncheon.

sfollamento *sm.* 1. dispersal 2. (*mil.*) evacuation.

sfollare *vt.* e *vi.* to disperse 2. (*mil.*) to evacuate.

sfollato *agg.* 1. evacuated. ♦ **sfollato** *sm.* evacuee.

sfoltire *vt.* to thin.

sfondamento *sm.* breaking.

sfondare *vt.* 1. (*rompere il fondo*) to break (*v. irr.*) the bottom 2.

(*mil.*) to break through. ♦ **sfon-dare** *vi.* to have success.

sfondato *agg.* **1.** without a bottom ‖ *scarpe sfondate*, worn-out shoes **2.** (*insaziabile*) voracious.

sfondo *sm.* background.

sforbiciare *vt.* to cut (*v. irr.*) with scissors.

sformare *vt.* **1.** to pull out of shape **2.** (*togliere dalla forma*) to remove from the mould. ♦ **sformarsi** *vr.* to get (*v. irr.*) out of shape.

sformato *agg.* shapeless.

sfornare *vt.* **1.** to take (*v. irr.*) out of the oven **2.** (*produrre*) to bring (*v. irr.*) out.

sfornito *agg.* destitute, lacking (in).

sfortuna *sf.* bad luck.

sfortunato *agg.* unlucky.

sforzare *vt.* to strain, to force. ♦ **sforzarsi** *vr.* to try hard.

sforzatamente *avv.* **1.** with much effort **2.** (*in modo forzato*) forcedly.

sforzato *agg.* **1.** forced **2.** (*fig.*) false.

sforzatura *sf.* (*cosa sforzata*) far--fetched thing.

sforzo *sm.* **1.** effort **2.** (*mecc.*) stress.

sfòttere *vt.* to pull so.'s legs.

sfracellare *vt.* to smash. ♦ **sfracellarsi** *vr.* to smash.

sfrangiare *vt.* to undo (*v. irr.*), to form a fringe. ♦ **sfrangiarsi** *vr.* to fray.

sfrangiatura *sf.* fraying.

sfrattare *vt.* to evict.

sfratto *sm.* eviction.

sfrecciare *vi.* to dart.

sfregamento *sm.* rubbing.

sfregare *vt.* to rub.

sfregiare *vt.* to disfigure.

sfregiato *agg.* disfigured.

sfregio *sm.* slash, scar.

sfrenare *vt.* to unbridle.

sfrenatezza *sf.* unrestraint.

sfrenato *agg.* wild, unbridled.

sfrigolare *vi.* to sizzle.

sfrigolio *sm.* sizzle.

sfringuellare *vi.* to twitter.

sfrondare *vt.* **1.** to strip off leaves **2.** (*fig.*) to curtail.

sfrontatezza *sf.* effrontery.

sfrontato *agg.* brazen, impudent. ♦ **sfrontato** *sm.* impudent fellow.

sfrusciare *vi.* to rustle.

sfruscìo *sm.* rustling.

sfruttamento *sm.* exploitation.

sfruttare *vt.* to exploit.

sfruttatore *sm.* profiteer.

sfuggente *agg.* receding: *sguardo* —, elusive look.

sfuggévole *agg.* transitory.

sfuggire *vi.* to escape, to slip. ♦ **sfuggire** *vt.* to avoid.

sfuggita *sf. di* —, quickly: *vedere qu. di* —, to have a glimpse of so.

sfumare *vt.* to shade. ♦ **sfumare** *vi.* **1.** to evaporate **2.** (*fig.*) to come (*v. irr.*) to nothing.

sfumatamente *avv.* softly.

sfumato *agg.* **1.** vanished **2.** (*di colori*) soft.

sfumatura *sf.* **1.** (*lo sfumare*) shading **2.** (*gradazione*) shade.

sfuriata *sf.* outburst.

sgabello *sm.* stool.

sgabuzzino *sm.* closet.

sgambettare *vi.* to kick (one's legs) about.

sgambetto *sm.* trip: *fare lo* —, to trip (so.); (*fig.*) to supplant.

sganasciamento *sm.* dislocation (of so.'s jaw).

sganasciarsi *vr.* — *dalle risa*, to laugh oneself silly.

sganascione *sm.* slap.

sganciare *vt.* **1.** to unhook **2.** (*ferr.*) to uncouple **3.** (*di bombe*) to release. ♦ **sganciarsi** *vr.* (*liberarsi di qu.*) to get (*v. irr.*) away (so.).

sgangherare *vt.* to unhinge.

sgangherato *agg.* **1.** unhinged **2.** (*sguaiato*) wild.

sgarbatamente *avv.* impolitely.

sgarbato *agg.* rude, impolite.

sgarberìa *sf.* rudeness.

sgarbo *sm.* offence.

sgargiante *agg.* gaudy.

sgarrare *vi.* **1.** to be wrong **2.** (*di orologio*) (*se è avanti*) to gain; (*se è indietro*) to lose (*v. irr.*).

sgattaiolare *vi.* to slip away.

sgelare *vi.* to thaw. ♦ **sgelarsi** *vr.* to thaw.

sgelo *sm.* thawing.

sghembo *agg.* oblique: *di* —, obliquely.

sgherro *sm.* hired assassin.

sghignazzare *vi.* to guffaw.

sghignazzata *sf.* guffaw.

sghimbescio (*nella loc. avv.*) *di* —, awry.

sghiribizzo *sm.* whim.

sgobbare *vi.* to work hard.

sgobbone *sm.* **1.** hard worker **2.** (*studentesco*) swot.

sgocciolare vi. to drip.

sgocciolìo sm. dripping.

sgolarsi vr. to shout oneself hoarse.

sgombrare vt. to clear.

sgombro agg. 1. clear (of) 2. (fig.) free (from).

sgomentare vt. to dismay.

sgomento agg. dismayed. ◆ **sgomento** sm. dismay.

sgominare vt. to rout.

sgonfiamento sm. deflation.

sgonfiare vt. to deflate.

sgonfio agg. deflated.

sgorbia sf. gouge.

sgorbiare vt. to scrawl.

sgorbio sm. 1. scrawl 2. (pittura mal fatta) daub 3. (fig.) deformed man (pl. men).

sgorgare vi. to gush, to flow.

sgozzare vt. to cut (v. irr.) so.'s throat.

sgradévole agg. unpleasant.

sgradito agg. 1. disagreeable 2. (mal accetto) unwelcome.

sgrammaticato agg. ungrammatical.

sgranare vt. 1. to shell: — gli occhi, to open one's eyes wide 2. (mangiare) to devour.

sgranatrice sf. husker.

sgranchire vt. to stretch.

sgranocchiare vt. to munch.

sgrassare vt. to take (v. irr.) the grease off: — il brodo, to skim the grease from the broth.

sgravare vt. 1. to lighten 2. (fig.) to relieve.

sgravio sm. 1. lightening 2. (fig.) relief.

sgraziato agg. awkward.

sgretolamento sm. pounding.

sgretolare vt. to pound. ◆ **sgretolarsi** vr. to crumble.

sgridare vt. to scold.

sgroppare¹ vt. (sciogliere) to untie.

sgroppare² vi. (di cavallo) to buck.

sgroppata sf. bucking.

sgrossamento sm. rough-shaping.

sgrossare vt. 1. to rough 2. (dirozzare) to refine.

sgrovigliare vt. to unravel.

sguaiato agg. 1. unbecoming 2. (volgare) coarse.

sguainare vt. to unsheathe.

sgualcire vt. to crease.

sgualdrina sf. harlot, whore.

sguardo sm. look, glance: dare uno —, to have a look.

sguarnire vt. 1. to untrim 2. (mil.) to dismantle.

sguàttero sm. scullery-boy.

sguazzare vi. to wallow.

sguinzagliare vt. to unleash.

sgusciare vt. to shell. ◆ **sgusciare** vi. to slip away.

si¹ pron. 1. (riflessivo) oneself, himself, herself, itself, themselves 2. (rec.) (fra due) each other; (fra molti) one another 3. (pron. indef.) one, people, we, they: — dice, people say.

si² sm. (mus.) si, B.

sì avv. yes: penso di —, I think so; — certo, certainly; e — che, yet; uno —, uno no, every other one; forse che —, forse che no, maybe yes, maybe no.

sia cong. 1. (o l'uno o l'altro) whether... or, either... or 2. (entrambi) both... and.

siamese agg. e s. Siamese.

sibarita s. sybarite.

siberiano agg. Siberian.

sibilante agg. 1. hissing 2. (fonetica) sibilant.

sibilare vi. to whistle, to hiss.

sibilla sf. sibyl.

sibillino agg. sibylline.

sibilo sm. hiss, whistle.

sicario sm. cut-throat.

sicché cong. 1. so... that 2. (dunque) therefore.

siccità sf. drought.

siccome cong. as, since.

siciliano agg. e sm. Sicilian.

sicomoro sm. sycamore.

sicumera sf. presumption.

sicura sf. safety belt.

sicurezza sf. 1. (certezza) certainty 2. (immunità da pericoli) safety || dispositivo di —, safety device; misura di —, precautionary measure; uscita di —, emergency door; rasoio, spilla di —, safety-razor, pin.

sicuro agg. 1. (certo) sure: — di sé, self-confident 2. (immune da pericoli) safe 3. (che non sbaglia) unfailing 4. (calmo, saldo) calm, steady 5. (esperto) skilful.

siderale agg. sidereal.

siderurgìa sf. metallurgy of iron.

siderùrgico agg. iron (attr.): stabilimento —, iron-works (pl.). ◆ **siderùrgico** sm. iron worker.

sidro sm. cider.

siepe sf. hedge.

siero *sm.* serum.

sieroso *agg.* serous.

sieroterapia *sf.* serotherapy.

siesta *sf.* nap.

siffatto *agg.* such.

sifilide *sf.* syphilis.

sifone *sm.* siphon.

sigaraia *sf.* cigar-seller.

sigaretta *sf.* cigarette.

sigaro *sm.* cigar.

sigillare *vt.* to seal.

sigillatura *sf.* sealing.

sigillo *sf.* seal.

sigla *sf.* monogram.

siglare *vt.* to initial.

significare *vt.* 1. to mean (*v. irr.*) 2. (*comunicare*) to signify 3. (*simboleggiare*) to represent.

significativo *agg.* meaningful.

significato *sm.* 1. meaning 2. (*valore*) import.

signora *sf.* 1. lady, woman (*pl.* women) 2. (*seguito da cognome*) Mrs: *la — Smith*, Mrs. Smith 3. (*vocativo*) Madam: *buon giorno —*, good morning Madam 4. (*padrona*) mistress 5. (*donna ricca*) rich lady 6. (*moglie*) wife (*pl.* wives).

signore *sm.* 1. gentleman, man (*pl.* -men) 2. (*seguito da cognome*) Mr.: *il — Smith*, Mr. Smith 3. (*padrone*) master 4. (*vocativo*) Sir: *sì —! yes*, Sir! 5. (*uomo ricco*) lord 6. (*Dio*) God, Lord.

signoreggiare *vt.* to rule.

signoria *sf.* 1. (*di uomo*) Lordship; (*di donna*) Ladyship 2. (*dominio*) dominion.

signorile *agg.* 1. (*riferito a uomo*) gentlemanlike; (*riferito a donna*) ladylike 2. (*elegante*) luxury.

signorilità *sf.* distinction, high class.

signorina *sf.* 1. young lady 2. (*seguito da cognome*) Miss: *la — Smith*, Miss Smith 3. (*vocativo*) Madam: *Buon giorno —*, good morning Madam 4. (*padroncina*) young mistress 5. (*donna non sposata*) unmarried woman.

signorotto *sm.* squire.

silenziatore *sm.* silencer.

silenzio *sm.* silence.

silenzioso *agg.* silent || *una strada silenziosa*, a noiseless street.

silfide *sf.* sylph.

silfo *sm.* sylph.

silice *sf.* silica.

silicio *sm.* silicon.

silicone *sm.* silicone.

silicosi *sf.* silicosis.

sillaba *sf.* syllable.

sillabare *vt.* to syllabize.

sillabo *sm.* summary.

sillogismo *sm.* syllogism.

sillogistico *agg.* syllogistic.

silo *sm.* silo (*pl.* silos).

siluramento *sm.* 1. torpedoing 2. (*fig.*) firing.

silurante *sf.* torpedo-boat.

silurare *vt.* 1. to torpedo 2. (*fig.*) to dismiss.

siluriano *agg. e sm.* Silurian.

siluro *sm.* (*mil.; zool.*) torpedo.

silvestre *agg.* sylvan.

silvicoltore *sm.* forester.

silvicoltura *sf.* forestry.

simbiosi *sf.* symbiosis.

simboleggiare *vt.* to symbolize.

simbolico *agg.* 1. symbolic 2. (*nominale*) nominal.

simbolismo *sm.* symbolism.

simbolista *agg. e sm.* symbolist.

simbolo *sm.* symbol.

similare *agg.* similar.

simile *agg.* 1. like, similar 2. (*pred.*) alike 3. (*tale*) such. ♦ **simile** *sm.* fellow-creature.

similitudine *sf.* 1. likeness 2. (*lett.*) simile.

simmetria *sf.* symmetry.

simmetrico *agg.* symmetric(al).

simonia *sf.* simony.

simoniaco *agg. e sm.* simoniac.

simpatia *sf.* liking.

simpatico *agg.* nice, pleasant.

simpatizzante *agg.* sympathizing. ♦ **simpatizzante** *s.* sympathizer.

simpatizzare *vi.* 1. to sympathize 2. (*rec.*) to take (*v. irr.*) a liking to each other.

simposio *sm.* symposium (*pl.* -ia).

simulacro *sm.* 1. simulacre 2. (*finzione*) sham.

simulare *vt.* to feign.

simulato *agg.* simulated.

simulatore *sm.* simulator.

simulazione *sf.* simulation.

simultaneità *sf.* simultaneity.

simultaneo *agg.* simultaneous (with).

sinagoga *sf.* synagogue.

sincerarsi *vr.* to make (*v. irr.*) sure.

sincerità *sf.* sincerity.

sincero *agg.* sincere, true.

sincopare *vt.* to syncopate.

sincopato agg. syncopated.
sìncope sf. 1. (med.) syncope 2. (mus.; gramm.) syncopation.
sincronismo sm. synchronism.
sincronizzare vt. to synchronize.
sincronizzazione sf. synchronization.
sindacale agg. trade-union (attr.).
sindacalismo sm. trade-unionism.
sindacalista s. trade-unionist.
sindacare vt. 1. to control 2. (criticare) to criticize.
sindacato sm. trade-union.
sìndaco sm. 1. mayor 2. (di società) auditor.
sìndrome sf. syndrome.
sinecura sf. sinecure.
sinfonìa sf. symphony.
sinfònico agg. symphonic.
singhiozzare vi. to sob.
singhiozzo sm. 1. hiccup 2. (di pianto) sob.
singolare agg. 1. singular 2. (singolo) single.
singolarità sf. singularity.
singolarmente avv. 1. (ad uno ad uno) singly 2. (segnatamente) particularly.
sìngolo agg. single, individual.
singulto sm. 1. hiccup 2. (di pianto) sob.
sinistra sf. 1. left: alla mia —, on my left 2. (mano) left hand 3. (parte) left-hand side || uomo di — (pol.), left-winger.
sinistramente avv. sinisterly.
sinistrato agg. 1. (di edificio) bomb-damaged 2. (di persona) injured. ♦ **sinistrato** sm. (damage) sufferer.
sinistro agg. 1. left 2. (truce) sinister, grim. ♦ **sinistro** sm. 1. accident, mishap 2. (boxe) left.
sinòlogo sm. Sinologist.
sinonimìa sf. synonymy.
sinònimo agg. synonymous. ♦ **sinònimo** sm. synonym.
sinora avv. till now, so far.
sinovite sf. synovitis.
sintassi sf. syntax.
sintàttico agg. syntactic(al).
sìntesi sf. synthesis (pl. -ses).
sintètico agg. synthetic.
sintetizzare vt. to synthetize.
sintomàtico agg. symptomatic.
sìntomo sm. symptom.
sintonìa sf. syntony.
sintonizzare vt. to tune in.
sinuosità sf. winding.

sinuoso agg. winding.
sinusite sf. sinusitis.
sionismo sm. Zionism.
sionista s. Zionist.
sipario sm. curtain.
sirena sf. 1. (mit.) siren, mermaid 2. (acustica) hooter.
siringa sf. syringe.
siringare vt. to syringe.
sìsmico agg. seismic.
sismògrafo sm. seismograph.
sismologìa sf. seismology.
sismòlogo sm. seismologist.
sistema sm. system: — di vita, way of life.
sistemare vt. 1. (mettere in ordine) to arrange 2. (definire) to settle.
sistemàtico agg. systematic(al).
sistemazione sf. 1. (ordine) arrangement 2. (collocazione di macchinari) layout 3. (il sistemarsi) settling 4. (lavoro) job.
sito sm. place.
situare vt. to place.
situazione sf. situation.
slabbrare vt. to chip the rim of.
slabbratura sf. chipping.
slacciare vt. 1. to untie 2. (sbottonare) to unbutton.
slanciarsi vr. to rush.
slanciato agg. slim.
slancio sm. 1. rush 2. (energia) energy.
slargare vt. to widen.
slattamento sm. weaning.
slattare vt. to wean.
slavato agg. pale.
slavina sf. landslide; (di neve) snowslide.
slavo agg. e sm. Slav.
sleale agg. unfair.
slealtà sf. disloyalty.
slegare vt. to untie.
slegato agg. 1. untied 2. (di discorso ecc.) disconnected.
slitta sf. sleigh.
slittamento sm. skidding.
slittare vi. 1. to slide (v. irr.) 2. (di ruote) to skid.
slogamento sm. dislocation.
slogare vt. to dislocate.
slogatura sf. dislocation.
sloggiare vi. to clear out. ♦ **sloggiare** vt. to drive (v. irr.) out.
smaccato agg. sickly-sweet.
smacchiare vt. to clean.
smacchiatore sm. stain-remover.
smacchiatura sf. cleaning.
smacco sm. mortification.

smagliante *agg.* dazzling.
smagliare *vt.* to unravel. ♦ **smagliarsi** *vr.* (*di calze*) to ladder.
smagliato *agg.* unravelled.
smagliatura *sf.* 1. (*di calze*) ladder.
smagnetizzare *vt.* to demagnetize.
smagnetizzazione *sf.* demagnetization.
smagrire *vt.* e *vi.* to thin.
smagrito *agg.* thin, grown thin.
smaliziare *vt.* to smarten up. ♦ **smaliziarsi** *vr.* to wisen.
smaliziato *agg.* cunning.
smaltare *vt.* to enamel: — *le unghie*, to paint one's nails.
smaltato *agg.* 1. enamelled 2. (*di unghie*) painted.
smaltire *vt.* to digest: — *la sbornia*, to get (*v. irr.*) over one's drunkenness.
smalto *sm.* enamel: — *per unghie*, nail-polish.
smancerìa *sf.* mawkishness.
smangiare *vt.* to corrode.
smania *sf.* 1. great desire 2. (*agitazione*) frenzy.
smaniare *vi.* 1. to yearn (for) 2. (*essere agitati*) to be restless.
smanioso *agg.* 1. eager 2. (*agitato*) restless.
smantellamento *sm.* dismantling.
smantellare *vt.* to dismantle.
smarcare *vt.* to unmark.
smargiassata *sf.* swagger.
smargiasserìa *sf.* bragging.
smargiasso *sm.* braggart.
smarginare *vt.* to trim the edge.
smarrimento *sm.* 1. loss 2. (*turbamento*) bewilderment.
smarrire *vt.* to lose (*v. irr.*). ♦ **smarrirsi** *vr.* 1. to lose one's way 2. (*di lettera, pacco*) to miscarry 3. (*turbarsi*) to be bewildered.
smascellarsi *vr.* to dislocate one's jaws.
smascherare *vt.* to unmask.
smembramento *sm.* dismemberment.
smembrare *vt.* to dismember.
smemorataggine *sf.* 1. lack of memory 2. (*dimenticanza*) lapse of memory.
smemorato *agg.* absent-minded.
smentire *vt.* to deny. ♦ **smentirsi** *vr.* 1. to contradict oneself 2. (*venir meno*) to be untrue to oneself.
smentita *sf.* denial.
smeraldo *sm.* emerald.

smerciare *vt.* to sell (*v. irr.*) off.
smercio *sm.* sale.
smerigliare *vt.* 1. to polish with emery 2. (*di vetri*) to frost glass.
smerigliato *agg.* emery: *carta smerigliata*, emery paper; *vetro* —, frosted glass.
smeriglio *sm.* emery.
smerlo *sm.* scallop.
smesso *agg.* cast off.
sméttere *vt.* to stop, to leave (*v. irr.*) off: — *un vestito*, to cast (*v. irr.*) off a dress.
smezzare *vt.* to halve.
smidollato *agg.* (*di persona*) spineless.
smilitarizzare *vt.* to demilitarize.
smilitarizzazione *sf.* demilitarization.
smilzo *agg.* thin.
sminuire *vt.* to diminish. ♦ **sminuirsi** *vr.* to belittle oneself.
sminuzzare *vt.* 1. (*tritare*) to mince 2. (*tagliuzzare*) to chop up 3. (*sbriciolare*) to crumble.
smistamento *sm.* 1. clearing 2. (*ferr.*) shunting 3. (*di corrispondenza*) sorting.
smistare *vt.* 1. (*di corrispondenza*) to sort out 2. (*ferr.*) to shunt.
smisuratamente *avv.* beyond measure.
smisurato *agg.* enormous, huge.
smobilitare *vt.* to demobilize.
smobilitazione *sf.* demobilization.
smoccolare *vt.* to snuff.
smoccolatoio *sm.* snuffers (*pl.*).
smoccolatura *sf.* snuffing.
smodato *agg.* immoderate.
smoderatezza *sf.* immoderateness.
smoderato *agg.* immoderate.
smontàbile *agg.* demountable.
smontaggio *sm.* disassembling.
smontare *vt.* 1. (*far scendere*) (*da cavallo*) to unhorse; (*da un'automobile*) to drop 2. (*scomporre in parti*) to take (*v. irr.*) to pieces 3. (*mecc.*) to disassemble 4. (*fig.*) to dishearten, to cool. ♦ **smontare** *vi.* 1. (*da un treno, tram ecc.*) to get (*v. irr.*) off 2. (*da un'automobile*) to get (*v. irr.*) out 3. (*da cavallo*) to dismount 4. (*dal lavoro*) to go (*v. irr.*) off duty 5. (*sbiadire*) to fade.
smorfia *sf.* grimace.
smorfioso *agg.* affected.
smorto *agg.* pale.
smorzamento *sm.* 1. (*di luci*) shad-

ing **2.** (*di colori*) toning down
3. (*di suoni*) lowering **4.** (*di sete;*
fig.) quenching.

smorzare *vt.* **1.** (*di luci*) to shade
2. (*di colori*) to tone down **3.** (*di
suoni*) to lower **4.** (*di sete; fig.*) to
quench **5.** (*spegnere*) to put (*v.
irr.*) down.

smottamento *sm.* landslip.

smottare *vi.* to slip.

smozzicare *vt.* **1.** to hack to pieces
2. (*di parole*) to clip.

smunto *agg.* pale.

smuòvere *vt.* **1.** to shift **2.** (*fig.*)
to move.

smussare *vt.* **1.** to round off **2.**
(*fig.*) to soften.

smussato *agg.* **1.** blunted **2.** (*fig.*)
softened.

snaturare *vt.* to pervert.

snaturato *agg.* unnatural.

snazionalizzare *vt.* to denationalize.

snebbiare *vt.* **1.** to dispel the fog
2. (*fig.*) to clear.

snellezza *sf.* slenderness.

snellire *vt.* **1.** to make (*v. irr.*)
slender **2.** (*fig.*) to simplify. ◆
snellirsi *vr.* to grow (*v. irr.*)
slender.

snello *agg.* slender.

snervante *agg.* enervating.

snervare *vt.* to enervate.

snidare *vt.* **1.** to flush **2.** (*fig.*) to
dislodge.

snobbare *vt.* to snob.

snobismo *sm.* snobbery.

snocciolare *vt.* **1.** to stone **2.** (*fig.*)
to tell (*v. irr.*).

snodare *vt.* **1.** to untie **2.** (*rendere
agile*) to make (*v. irr.*) supple. ◆
snodarsi *vr.* (*di strade*) to wind
(*v. irr.*).

snodato *agg.* **1.** supple **2.** (*di cosa*)
jointed.

snodo *sm.* joint.

soave *agg.* sweet.

soavità *sf.* sweetness.

sobbalzare *vi.* **1.** to jerk **2.** (*trasalire*) to start.

sobbalzo *sm.* **1.** jerk **2.** (*sussulto*)
start.

sobbarcarsi *vr.* to take (*v. irr.*)
upon oneself.

sobborgo *sm.* suburb.

sobillare *vt.* to stir up.

sobillatore *sm.* instigator.

sobrietà *sf.* sobriety.

sobrio *agg.* sober.

socchiùdere *vt.* **1.** to half-close **2.**
(*aprire un po'*) to half-open.

socchiuso *agg.* half-closed, half-
open.

sòccida *sf.* agistment.

soccòmbere *vi.* to succumb.

soccòrrere *vt.* to help, to assist.

soccorritore *agg.* helpful. ◆ **soccorritore** *sm.* helper.

soccorso *sm.* help || *pronto* —, first
aid.

socialdemocràtico *agg.* socialdem-
ocratic.

socialdemocrazìa *sf.* socialdem-
ocracy.

sociale *agg.* social.

socialismo *sm.* Socialism.

socialista *agg.* e *sm.* Socialist.

socialità *sf.* sociality.

socializzare *vt.* to socialize.

socializzazione *sf.* socialization.

società *sf.* **1.** society **2.** (*comm.*)
company: — *anonima*, joint-stock
company; — *a responsabilità limi-
tata*, limited company || *entrare in*
—, to enter into partnership.

sociévole *agg.* sociable.

socievolezza *sf.* sociability.

socio *sm.* **1.** member **2.** (*comm.*)
partner.

sociologìa *sf.* sociology.

sociològico *agg.* sociological.

sociòlogo *sm.* sociologist.

socràtico *agg.* Socratic.

soda *sf.* soda.

sodalizio *sm.* **1.** society **2.** (*confraternita*) brotherhood.

sodare *vt.* to consolidate.

sodatura *sf.* (*tessile*) fulling.

soddisfacente *agg.* satisfactory.

soddisfare *vt.* **1.** to satisfy **2.** (*a-
dempiere*) to fulfil **3.** (*far fronte
a*) to discharge **4.** (*riparare*) to
make (*v. irr.*) amends.

soddisfazione *sf.* satisfaction.

sodio *sm.* sodium.

sodo *agg.* solid, firm: *uovo* —,
hard-boiled egg; *darle sode a qu.*,
to strike (*v. irr.*) so. hard.

sofferente *agg.* **1.** suffering **2.** (*malaticcio*) poorly.

sofferenza *sf.* pain.

soffermare *vt.* to stop. ◆ **soffer-
marsi** *vr.* to stop.

soffiare *vt.* e *vi.* to blow (*v. irr.*):
soffiarsi il naso, to blow one's
nose.

soffiata *sf.* puff.

soffiato *agg.* puffed.

soffiatore *sm.* blower.
soffiatura *sf.* blowing.
sòffice *agg.* soft.
soffietto *sm.* **1.** bellows (*pl.*) **2.** (*edit.*) blurb.
soffio *sm.* puff, whiff.
soffione *sm.* **1.** blow-pipe **2.** (*geol.*) fumarole.
soffitta *sf.* garret.
soffitto *sm.* ceiling.
soffocamento *sm.* choking.
soffocante *agg.* choking: *caldo —,* sultry heat.
soffocare *vt.* **1.** to choke **2.** (*reprimere*) to repress.
soffocato *agg.* choked.
sòffoco *sm.* sultriness.
soffòndere *vt.* to suffuse.
soffrìggere *vt.* to fry slightly.
soffrire *vt.* **1.** to suffer **2.** (*sopportare*) to stand (*v. irr.*).
soffuso *agg.* suffused.
sofisma *sm.* sophism.
sofista *sm.* sophist.
sofìstica *sf.* sophistry.
sofisticare *vi.* to quibble. ♦ **sofisticare** *vt.* to adulterate.
sofisticato *agg.* **1.** sophisticated **2.** (*adulterato*) adulterated.
sofisticazione *sf.* adulteration.
sofisticherìa *sf.* quibbling.
sofìstico *agg.* sophistical.
soggettista *sm.* scenario writer.
soggettivismo *sm.* subjectivism.
soggettività *sf.* subjectivity.
soggettivo *agg.* subjective.
soggetto *agg. e sm.* subject.
soggezione *sf.* **1.** subjection **2.** (*timidezza*) shyness.
sogghignare *vi.* to sneer.
sogghigno *sm.* sneer.
soggiacere *vi.* to be subjected.
soggiogare *vt.* to subdue.
soggiornare *vi.* to stay.
soggiorno *sm.* stay: *stanza di —,* living-room.
soggiùngere *vt.* to add.
soglia *sf.* threshold.
sògliola *sf.* sole.
sognante *agg.* dreaming: *occhi sognanti,* dreamy eyes.
sognare *vt.* to dream (*v. irr.*): — *ad occhi aperti,* to have day-dreams.
sognatore *agg.* dreaming. ♦ **sognatore** *sm.* dreamer.
sogno *sm.* dream.
soia *sf.* soya.
solaio *sm.* attic.

solamente *avv.* only.
solare *agg.* **1.** solar **2.** (*radioso*) radiant.
solatìo *agg.* sunny.
solcare *vt.* **1.** to plough **2.** (*fig.*) to furrow.
solcato *agg.* **1.** ploughed **2.** (*fig.*) furrowed.
solcatura *sf.* ploughing, furrowing.
solco *sm.* **1.** (*agr.*) furrow **2.** (*ruga*) wrinkle **3.** (*mar.*) wake **4.** (*di ruota sul terreno*) track.
solcòmetro *sm.* log.
soldataglia *sf.* soldiery.
soldatesco *agg.* soldierly.
soldato *sm.* soldier.
soldo *sm.* **1.** penny **2.** (*denaro*) money **3.** (*salario*) pay: *essere al — di qu.,* to be in so.'s pay.
sole *sm.* sun: *bagno di —,* sun-bathing; *colpo di —,* sunstroke; *un giorno di —, senza —,* a sunny day, a sunless day; *tramonto del —,* sunset.
soleggiare *vt.* to sun-dry.
soleggiato *agg.* sunny.
solenne *agg.* solemn.
solennità *sf.* **1.** solemnity **2.** (*cerimonia*) ceremony.
solennizzare *vt.* to solemnize.
solenòide *sm.* solenoid.
solere *vi.* to use (*usato solo al passato*).
solerte *agg.* diligent.
solerzia *sf.* diligence.
soletta *sf.* sole.
solfa *sf.* **1.** scale **2.** (*fig.*) old story.
solfara *sf.* sulphur mine.
solfare *vt.* to sulphur.
solfatara *sf.* solfatara.
solfato *sm.* sulphate.
solfeggiare *vt.* to sol-fa.
solfeggio *sm.* solfeggio.
solfito *sm.* sulphite.
solfuro *sm.* sulphide.
solidale *agg.* solid (for).
solidamente *avv.* solidly.
solidarietà *sf.* solidarity.
solidarizzare *vi.* to be solid (for).
solidificare *vt.* to solidify.
solidificazione *sf.* solidification.
solidità *sf.* **1.** solidity **2.** (*di colori*) fastness.
sòlido *agg.* **1.** solid **2.** (*di colori*) fast **3.** (*fig.*) sound. ♦ **sòlido** *sm.* solid.
soliloquio *sm.* soliloquy.
solipsismo *sm.* solipsism.
solista *s.* soloist.

solitamente *avv.* usually.
solitario¹ *agg.* solitary. ♦ **solitario** *sm.* 1. hermit 2. .(*brillante*) solitaire.
solitario² *sm.* (*a carte*) solitaire.
sòlito *agg.* usual, customary: *essere* —, to be used to (doing); *di* —, usually.
solitùdine *sf.* loneliness.
sollazzare *vt.* to amuse.
sollazzo *sm.* amusement.
sollecitante *agg.* urging.
sollecitare *vt.* 1. (*far premura*) to urge 2. (*brigare*) to solicit 3. (*affrettare*) to hurry up.
sollecitazione *sf.* 1. solicitation 2. (*preghiera*) entreaty.
sollécito *agg.* 1. (*rapido*) prompt 2. (*preoccupato*) solicitous 3. (*premuroso*) obliging.
sollecitùdine *sf.* 1. (*rapidità*) promptness 2. (*interessamento*) concern 3. (*gentilezza*) kindness.
solleone *sm.* dog-days (*pl.*).
solleticante *agg.* alluring.
solleticare *vt.* to tickle.
sollético *sm.* 1. tickle: *soffrire il* —, to be ticklish 2. (*fig.*) itch.
sollevamento *sm.* lifting.
sollevare *vt.* 1. to lift 2. (*issare*) to hoist 3. (*fig.*) to raise 4. (*dar sollievo*) to relieve. ♦ **sollevarsi** *vr.* 1. to rise (*v. irr.*) 2. (*riaversi*) to recover 3. (*insorgere*) to rebel.
sollevato *agg.* (*rasserenato*) cheered up.
sollevazione *sf.* (*rivolta*) rising.
sollievo *sm.* relief.
sollùchero *sm.* andare in —, to go (*v. irr.*) into raptures.
solo *agg.* 1. alone (*pred.*): *da* —, by oneself. 2. (*unico*) only. ♦ **solo** *avv.* only.
solstizio *sm.* solstice.
soltanto *avv.* only.
solùbile *agg.* soluble.
solubilità *sf.* solubility.
soluzione *sf.* solution.
solvente *agg. e sm.* solvent.
solvenza *sf.* (*comm.*) solvency.
solvìbile *agg.* solvent.
solvibilità *sf.* solvency.
soma *sf.* load, burden.
somaràggine *sf.* stupidity.
somaro *sm.* ass.
somàtico *agg.* somatic.
somigliante *agg.* alike, similar.
somiglianza *sf.* likeness.
somigliare *vi.* to look like.

somma *sf.* 1. (*mat.*) addition 2. (*di denaro*) sum.
sommamente *avv.* extremely.
sommare *vt.* to add.
sommariamente *avv.* summarily.
sommario *agg. e sm.* summary.
sommèrgere *vt.* to submerge.
sommergìbile *agg.* submersible. ♦ **sommergìbile** *sm.* submarine.
sommergibilista *sm.* submariner.
sommersione *sf.* submersion.
sommerso *agg.* submerged.
sommessamente *avv.* 1. submissively 2. (*a bassa voce*) in a low voice.
sommesso *agg.* 1. submissive 2. (*di voce*) low.
somministrare *vt.* to administer.
somministratore *sm.* giver.
somministrazione *sf.* giving.
sommissione *sf.* V. *sottomissione*.
sommità *sf.* summit, top.
sommo¹ *agg.* 1. highest 2. (*fig.*) supreme.
sommo² *sm.* summit, top.
sommossa *sf.* rising.
sommovimento *sm.* movement, agitation.
sommozzatore *sm.* frogman (*pl.* -men).
sommuòvere *vt.* to stir up.
sonagliera *sf.* collar with bells.
sonaglio *sm.* 1. harness-bell 2. (*giocattolo*) rattle || *serpente a sonagli*, rattlesnake.
sonante *agg.* resounding || *denaro* —, ready money.
sonare *vt.* 1. to sound 2. (*musica*) to play 3. (*di orologio*) to strike (*v. irr.*). ♦ **sonare** *vi.* (*di campanello*) to ring (*v. irr.*).
sonata *sf.* (*mus.*) sonata.
sonatore *sm.* player.
sonda *sf.* 1. (*mar.*) sounding line 2. (*med.*) probe 3. (*min.*) drill.
sondaggio *sm.* 1. sounding 2. (*med.*) probing 3. (*min.*) drilling.
sondare *vt.* 1. to sound 2. (*fig.*) to throw (*v. irr.*) out.
sonerìa *sf.* 1. (*di orologio*) striking--mechanism 2. alarm.
sonetto *sm.* sonnet.
sonnacchiosamente *avv.* drowsily.
sonnacchioso *agg.* 1. sleepy 2. (*fig.*) torpid.
sonnambulismo *sm.* sleep-walking.
sonnàmbulo *sm.* sleep-walker.
sonnecchiare *vi.* to doze.
sonnellino *sm.* nap.

sonnìfero *sm.* sleeping pills (*pl.*).

sonno *sm.* sleep: — *profondo*, sound sleep.

sonnolento *agg.* drowsy.

sonnolenza *sf.* drowsiness.

sonoramente *avv.* sonorously.

sonorità *sf.* sonority.

sonorizzare *vt.* to post-score.

sonorizzazione *sf.* post-scoring.

sonoro *agg.* **1.** sonorous **2.** (*rumoroso*) loud **3.** (*cine*) sound.

sontuosamente *avv.* sumptuously.

sontuosità *sf.* sumptuousness.

sontuoso *agg.* sumptuous.

soperchierìa *sf.* V. *soverchierìa*.

sopire *vt.* **1.** to make (*v. irr.*) drowsy **2.** (*calmare*) to soothe.

sopore *sm.* doze.

soporìfero *agg.* soporific.

sopperire *vi.* **1.** to provide (for) **2.** (*supplire*) to make (*v. irr.*) up (for).

soppesare *vt.* **1.** to weigh in one's hand **2.** (*considerare*) to weigh.

soppiantare *vt.* to supplant.

soppiatto (*nella loc. avv.*) *di* —, stealthily.

sopportàbile *agg.* bearable.

sopportabilità *sf.* bearableness.

sopportabilmente *avv.* bearably.

sopportare *vt.* to bear (*v. irr.*).

sopportazione *sf.* endurance.

soppressare *vt.* to press.

soppressione *sf.* **1.** suppression **2.** (*abolizione*) abolition.

soppresso *agg.* **1.** suppressed **2.** (*abolito*) abolished.

sopprìmere *vt.* **1.** to suppress **2.** (*abolire*) to abolish.

sopra *prep.* **1.** (*con contatto*) on, upon **2.** (*senza contatto*) over **3.** (*al di sopra*) above. ♦ **sopra** *avv.* **1.** above **2.** (*al piano superiore*) upstairs.

soprabbondanza *sf.* V. *sovrabbondanza*.

soprabbondare *vi.* V. *sovrabbondare*.

sopràbito *sm.* overcoat.

sopraccaricare *vt.* V. *sovraccaricare*.

sopraccàrico *sm.* V. *sovraccàricó*.

sopraccennato *agg.* above-mentioned.

sopracciglio *sm.* eyebrow.

sopraccitato *agg.* V. *sopraddetto*.

sopraccoperta *sf.* **1.** (*di libro*) jacket **2.** (*di letto*) counterpane. ♦ **sopraccoperta** *avv.* (*mar.*) on deck.

sopraddetto *agg.* above-mentioned.

sopraelevare *vt.* **1.** (*edil.*) to increase the height of **2.** (*di strade, rotaie ecc.*) to bank.

sopraelevazione *sf.* **1.** (*edil.*) heightening **2.** (*di strade, rotaie ecc.*). superelevation.

sopraffare *vt.* to overwhelm.

sopraffazione *sf.* **1.** overwhelming **2.** (*abuso*) abuse.

sopraffino *agg.* first-rate.

sopraggiùngere *vi.* **1.** to arrive **2.** (*accadere*) to happen.

sopraggiunta *sf.* addition.

sopraindicato *agg.* V. *sopraddetto*.

sopralluogo *sm.* investigation on the spot.

soprammercato (*nella loc. avv.*) *per* —, moreover.

soprammèttere *vt.* to place on.

soprammòbile *sm.* knick-knack.

soprannaturale *agg.* supernatural.

soprannome *sm.* nickname.

soprannominare *vt.* to nickname.

soprannùmero *sm.* excess.

soprano *sm.* soprano.

soprappassaggio *sm.* overbridge.

soprappensiero *avv.* lost in thought.

soprappiù *sm.* extra, addition.

soprapprezzo *sm.* extra charge.

soprascarpa *sf.* galosh.

soprascritta *sf.* inscription.

soprascritto *agg.* above-written.

soprasensìbile *agg.* supersensible.

soprassalto *sm.* jerk: *di* —, all of a sudden.

soprassedere *vi.* **1.** to wait **2.** (*rimandare*) to postpone.

soprassoldo *sm.* extra pay.

soprastruttura *sf.* superstructure.

soprattassa *sf.* extra tax.

soprattutto *avv.* above all.

sopravanzare *vt.* **1.** (*superare*) to surpass **2.** (*avanzare*) to be left over.

sopravanzo *sm.* surplus.

sopravvalutare *vt.* to overrate.

sopravvenire *vi.* **1.** (*di persone*) to turn up **2.** (*di cose*) to come (*v. irr.*) about.

sopravvento *sm.* **1.** (*mar.*) windward **2.** (*fig.*) upper hand: *prendere il* —, to get (*v. irr.*) the upper hand.

sopravvissuto *agg. e sm.* surviving. ♦ **sopravvissuto** *sm.* survivor.

sopravvivenza *sf.* survival.

sopravvìvere *vi.* to survive.
sopruso *sm.* abuse of power.
soqquadro *sm.* confusion: *a* —, topsy-turvy.
sorbettare *vt.* to freeze (*v. irr.*).
sorbetto *sm.* sherbet.
sorbire *vt.* to sip. ♦ **sorbirsi** *vr.* to put (*v. irr.*) up with.
sorcio *sm.* mouse (*pl.* mice).
sordamente *avv.* dully.
sordidamente *avv.* filthily.
sordidezza *sf.* filthiness.
sòrdido *agg.* filthy.
sordina *sf.* (*mus.*) mute: *in* — (*fig.*), on the sly.
sordità *sf.* deafness.
sordo *agg.* deaf.
sordomuto *sm.* deaf-mute.
sorella *sf.* sister.
sorellastra *sf.* half-sister.
sorgente *sf.* spring, source.
sòrgere *vi.* to rise (*v. irr.*).
sorgiva *sf.* spring-water.
sorgivo *agg.* spring (*attr.*).
soriano *agg.* syrian: *gatto* —, tabby cat.
sormontare *vt.* 1. to surmount 2. (*superare*) to overcome (*v. irr.*).
sornione *agg.* sly. ♦ **sornione** *sm.* sly person.
sorpassare *vt.* 1. to overtake (*v. irr.*) 2. (*sport*) to outrun (*v. irr.*).
sorpassato *agg.* old-fashioned.
sorpasso *sm.* overtaking.
sorprendente *agg.* surprising.
sorprèndere *vt.* 1. (*cogliere inaspettatamente*) to catch (*v. irr.*) 2. (*meravigliare*) to surprise.
sorpresa *sf.* surprise: *di* —, by surprise.
sorrèggere *vt.* to support.
sorridente *agg.* smiling.
sorrìdere *vi.* 1. to smile 2. (*attrarre*) to appeal.
sorriso *sm.* smile.
sorsata *sf.* sip.
sorseggiare *vt.* to sip.
sorso *sm.* gulp, sip.
sorta *sf.* kind, sort.
sorte *sf.* 1. destiny, lot 2. (*avvenire*) future.
sorteggiare *vt.* to draw (*v. irr.*) lots (for).
sorteggio *sm.* draw.
sortilegio *sm.* witchcraft.
sortire[1] *vt.* to get (*v. irr.*).
sortire[2] *vi.* to come (*v. irr.*) out.
sortita *sf.* sally.
sorvegliante *sm.* overseer.

sorveglianza *sf.* overseeing.
sorvegliare *vt.* to oversee (*v. irr.*).
sorvolare *vt.* 1. to fly (*v. irr.*) over 2. (*passar sopra*) to pass over.
sorvolo *sm.* flying over.
sosia *sm.* double.
sospèndere *vt.* 1. (*attaccare*) to suspend 2. (*interrompere*) to defer.
sospensione *sf.* 1. (*incertezza; chim.*) suspension 2. (*interruzione*) interruption.
sospensiva *sf.* suspension.
sospensivo *agg.* suspensive.
sospeso *agg.* 1. hanging 2. (*interrotto*) suspended.
sospettàbile *agg.* liable to suspicion.
sospettare *vt.* to suspect.
sospetto *sm.* suspicion.
sospettosamente *avv.* suspiciously.
sospettoso *agg.* suspicious.
sospìngere *vt.* to drive (*v. irr.*) || *ad ogni piè sospinto*, at every moment.
sospirare *vi.* 1. to sigh 2. (*fig.*) to pine. ♦ **sospirare** *vt.* to long (for).
sospirato *agg.* (*desiderato*) longed for.
sospiro *sm.* sigh.
sosta *sf.* 1. (*fermata*) stop 2. (*pausa*) pause.
sostantivamente *avv.* substantively.
sostantivare *vt.* to substantivize.
sostantivo *sm.* substantive, noun.
sostanza *sf.* substance || *in* — (*in breve*), in short.
sostanziale *agg.* substantial.
sostanzialmente *avv.* substantially.
sostanzioso *agg.* substantial.
sostare *vi.* to stop.
sostegno *sm.* support.
sostenere *vt.* 1. to support 2. (*affermare*) to maintain 3. (*tener alto*) to keep (*v. irr.*) up.
sostenìbile *agg.* 1. supportable 2. (*di opinioni*) maintainable.
sostenimento *sm.* 1. support 2. (*sostentamento*) sustenance.
sostenitore *sm.* supporter.
sostentamento *sm.* sustenance.
sostenuto *agg.* 1. stiff, distant 2. (*comm.*) steady.
sostituìbile *agg.* replaceable.
sostituire *vt.* to replace.
sostituto *sm.* substitute.
sostituzione *sf.* replacement.
sostrato *sm.* substratum (*pl.* -ta).

sottacere vt. to keep (v. irr.) (sthg.) from.

sottaceti sm. pl. pickles.

sottana sf. 1. skirt 2. (di prete) cassock.

sottecchi (nella loc. avv.) di —, stealthily.

sotterfugio sm. subterfuge.

sotterramento sm. burial.

sotterrànea sf. underground.

sotterràneo agg. underground. ♦ **sotterràneo** sm. 1. (di basilica) vault 2. (di castello) dungeon.

sotterrare vt. to bury.

sottigliezza sf. 1. thinness 2. (acutezza) subtlety.

sottile agg. 1. thin 2. (fig.) subtle.

sottilizzare vi. to split (v. irr.) hairs.

sottilmente avv. 1. finely 2. (con acutezza) subtly.

sottintèndere vt. to imply.

sottinteso agg. implied. ♦ **sottinteso** sm. allusion.

sotto prep. 1. under 2. (al di sotto, più in basso) below, beneath 3. (in espressioni di tempo) — Natale, at Christmas; essere — gli esami, to be close to the exams. ♦ **sotto** avv. 1. underneath, below 2. (al piano di sotto) downstairs.

sottobanco loc. avv. underthecounter.

sottobosco sm. underbrush.

sottocchio avv. in front of: tenere qc. —, to keep (v. irr.) an eye on sthg.

sottochiave avv. under lock and key.

sottocoperta sf. (mar.) below deck.

sottocoppa sf. saucer.

sottocutàneo agg. subcutaneous.

sottofondo sm. 1. (edil.) foundation 2. (sfondo) background.

sottogamba (nella loc. avv.) prendere qc. —, to make (v. irr.) light of sthg.

sottolineare vt. 1. to underline 2. (fig.) to lay (v. irr.) stress (on).

sottolineatura sf. underlining.

sottomano avv. 1. (di nascosto) underhand 2. (a portata di mano) at hand.

sottomarino agg. e sm. submarine.

sottomesso agg. 1. subdued 2. (obbediente) submissive.

sottométtere vt. to subject. ♦ **sottométtersi** vr. to submit (oneself).

sottomissione sf. 1. subdual 2. (obbedienza) submission.

sottopassaggio sm. subway.

sottoporre vt. 1. (al giudizio di qu.) to submit 2. (subire, far subire) to subject 3. (esporre) to expose.

sottoposto sm. subordinate.

sottoprodotto sm. by-product.

sottoscritto agg. subscribed. ♦ **sottoscritto** sm. undersigned.

sottoscrìvere vt. 1. to sign 2. (comm.) to underwrite. ♦ **sottoscrìvere** vi. to subscribe.

sottoscrizione sf. subscription.

sottosegretario sm. under-secretary.

sottosopra avv. 1. upside down 2. (in disordine) topsy-turvy.

sottospecie sf. subspecies (invariato al pl.). ·

sottostante agg. below.

sottostare vi. 1. (essere sotto) to be below 2. (essere soggetto) to be subjected 3. (sottomettersi) to submit.

sottosuolo sm. subsoil.

sottotenente sm. second lieutenant.

sottotìtolo sm. subtitle.

sottovalutare vt. to undervalue.

sottovento avv. (mar.) leeward.

sottoveste sf. petticoat.

sottovoce avv. in a low voice.

sottrarre vt. 1. (mat.) to subtract 2. (portar via) to take (v. irr.) away 3. (rubare) to steal (v. irr.) 4. (salvare da) to deliver. ♦ **sottrarsi** vr. to avoid (sthg.).

sottrazione sf. subtraction.

sottufficiale sm. non-commissioned officer.

sovente avv. often, frequently.

soverchiare vi. to overcome (v. irr.).

soverchierìa sf. oppression.

soviètico agg. e sm. Soviet.

sovrabbondante agg. superabundant.

sovrabbondanza sf. superabundance.

sovrabbondare vi. to superabound.

sovraccaricare vt. to overload.

sovraccàrico sm. overload.

sovraccoperta sf. e avv. V. sopraccoperta.

sovranità sf. 1. sovereignty 2. (supremazia) supremacy.

sovrannaturale agg. V. soprannaturale.

sovrano *agg.* sovereign.
sovrappopolare *vt.* to overpopulate.
sovrappopolato *agg.* overpopulated.
sovrappopolazione *sf.* overpopulation.
sovrapporre *vt.* to superimpose.
sovrapposizione *sf.* superimposition.
sovrastampa *sf.* overprint.
sovrastante *agg.* impending, overhanging.
sovrastare *vi.* **1.** to overhang (*v. irr.*) over **2.** (*fig.*) to impend **3.** (*essere superiore*) to be superior.
sovreccedente *agg.* superabundant.
sovreccedenza *sf.* surplus.
sovreccitabile *agg.* overexcitable.
sovreccitabilità *sf.* overexcitability.
sovreccitare *vt.* to overexcite.
sovreccitazione *sf.* overexcitement.
sovrimposta *sf.* additional tax.
sovrimpressione *sf.* (*foto; cine*) superimposure.
sovrintendente *sm.* superintendent.
sovrintendenza *sf.* superintendence.
sovrumano *agg.* superhuman.
sovvenzionare *vt.* to subsidize.
sovvenzione *sf.* subsidy.
sovversione *sf.* overthrow.
sovversivo *agg.* subversive. ♦ **sovversivo** *sm.* subverter.
sovvertimento *sm.* subversion.
sovvertire *vt.* to overthrow (*v. irr.*).
sozzo *agg.* filthy.
sozzume *sm.* filth.
spaccalegna *sm.* wood-cutter.
spaccamontagne *sm.* braggart.
spaccapietre *sm.* stone-breaker.
spaccare *vt.* **1.** to split (*v. irr.*) **2.** (*rompere*) to break (*v. irr.*) || *il mio orologio spacca il minuto*, my watch is dead right; *il sole spacca le pietre*, the sun is blazing down.
spaccatura *sf.* split, cleft.
spacchettare *vt.* to unpack.
spacciare *vt.* **1.** (*vendere*) to sell (*v. irr.*) **2.** (*mettere in circolazione*) to circulate **3.** (*far credere*) to make (*v. irr.*) (so.) believe **4.** (*uccidere*) to kill. ♦ **spacciarsi** *vr.* to pretend to be || *lo danno per spacciato* (*di malato*), they give him up.
spacciato *agg.* done for.

spacciatore *sm.* **1.** seller **2.** (*di monete false*) forger.
spaccio *sm.* **1.** shop **2.** (*vendita*) sale.
spacco *sm.* **1.** split **2.** (*di abiti*) vent.
spacconata *sf.* bluff.
spaccone *sm.* boaster.
spada *sf.* sword.
spadaccino *sm.* fencer.
spadino *sm.* court-sword.
spadroneggiare *vi.* to lord it.
spaesato *agg.* (*fig.*) lost.
spaghetto *sm.* **1.** (*piccolo spago*) string **2.** (*fam.*) (*paura*) fright.
spagliare *vt.* to take (*v. irr.*) the straw off.
spagnoletta *sf.* **1.** (*di filo*) spool **2.** (*arachide*) peanut.
spagnolismo *sm.* Hispanicism.
spagnolo *agg.* Spanish. ♦ **spagnolo** *sm.* Spaniard.
spago *sm.* string.
spaiare *vt.* to uncouple.
spaiato *agg.* odd.
spalancare *vt.* to open wide.
spalancato *agg.* wide open.
spalare *vt.* to shovel away.
spalatore *sm.* shoveller.
spalatura *sf.* shovelling.
spalla *sf.* **1.** shoulder **2.** (*pl.*) back (*sing.*) **3.** (*teat.*) stooge man || *alle spalle*, behind; *vivere alle spalle di qu.*, to live on so.
spallata *sf.* **1.** push with the shoulders **2.** (*alzata di spalle*) shrug.
spalleggiare *vt.* to back.
spalletta *sf.* parapet.
spalliera *sf.* **1.** back **2.** (*di piante*) espalier.
spallina *sf.* **1.** shoulder-strap **2.** (*mil.*) epaulette.
spalluccia *sf.* *far spallucce*, to shrug one's shoulders.
spalmare *vt.* to smear.
spalto *sm.* glacis.
spampanare *vt.* to strip a vine of its leaves.
spàndere *vt.* **1.** to spread (*v. irr.*) **2.** (*versare*) to shed (*v. irr.*) **3.** (*scialacquare*) to squander.
spanna *sf.* span.
spannare *vt.* to skim.
spannocchiare *vt.* to husk.
spappolare *vt.* to pulp. ♦ **spappolarsi** *vr.* to become (*v. irr.*) mushy.
sparare[1] *vt.* to shoot (*v. irr.*), to fire.

sparare[2] *vt.* (*squartare*) to split (*v. irr.*).

sparata *sf.* 1. discharge 2. (*spacconata*) brag.

sparato *sm.* (*di camicia*) shirt--front.

sparatore *sm.* shooter.

sparatoria *sf.* shooting.

sparecchiare *vt.* to clear.

spareggio *sm.* 1. disparity 2. (*sport*) deciding game.

spàrgere *vt.* 1. to scatter 2. (*divulgare*) to spread (*v. irr.*) 3. (*versare; di luce*) to shed (*v. irr.*).

spargimento *sm.* 1. spreading 2. (*versamento*) shedding || — *di sangue*, bloodshed.

sparigliare *vt.* to unmatch.

sparire *vi.* to disappear.

sparizione *sf.* disappearance.

sparlare *vi.* to speak (*v. irr.*) badly.

sparo *sm.* shot.

sparpagliare *vt.* to scatter. ♦ **sparpagliarsi** *vr.* to scatter.

sparso *agg.* 1. (*versato*) shed 2. (*sciolto*) loose.

spartano *agg.* Spartan.

spartiacque *sm.* watershed.

spartineve *sm.* snow-plough.

spartire *vt.* to share out.

spartito *sm.* score.

spartizione *sf.* sharing.

sparuto *agg.* lean, spare.

sparviero *sm.* sparrow-hawk.

spasimante *sm.* wooer.

spasimare *vi.* 1. to suffer agonies 2. (*fig.*) to yearn.

spàsimo *sm.* pang.

spasmo *sm.* spasm.

spasmodicamente *avv.* spasmodically.

spasmòdico *agg.* spasmodic.

spassare *vt.* to amuse || *spassarsela*, to have a very good time.

spassionato *agg.* impartial.

spasso *sm.* 1. amusement: *che* —!, what fun! 2. (*passeggiata*) *andare a* —, to go (*v. irr.*) for a walk; *essere a* —, to be out of work.

spassoso *agg.* funny, amusing.

spàstico *agg.* spastic.

spato *sm.* spar.

spàtola *sf.* broad knife.

spatriare *vt.* V. *espatriare*.

spauracchio *sm.* 1. scarecrow 2. (*fig.*) bugbear.

spaurire *vt.* to frighten. ♦ **spaurirsi** *vr.* to get (*v irr.*) frightened.

spaurito *agg.* frightened.

spavalderìa *sf.* boldness.

spavaldo *agg.* bold, arrogant.

spaventapàsseri *sm.* scarecrow.

spaventare *vt.* to frighten, to scare. ♦ **spaventarsi** *vr.* to be frightened.

spaventato *agg.* frightened, scared.

spavento *sm.* fright.

spaventoso *agg.* dreadful, frightful.

spaziale *agg.* space (*attr.*).

spaziare *vt.* to space. ♦ **spaziare** *vi.* to range.

spaziatura *sf.* spacing.

spazieggiare *vt.* to space.

spazientirsi *vr.* to lose (*v. irr.*) one's patience.

spazio *sm.* 1. space 2. (*posto*) room.

spazioso *agg.* wide.

spazzacamino *sm.* chimney-sweep.

spazzamine *sm.* mine-sweeper.

spazzaneve *sm.* snow-plough.

spazzare *vt.* to sweep (*v. irr.*).

spazzata *sf.* sweep.

spazzatura *sf.* (*rifiuti*) sweepings (*pl.*): *bidone della* —, dust-bin; *carro della* —, dust-cart.

spazzino *sm.* 1. road-sweeper 2. (*spazzaturaio*) dustman (*pl.* -men).

spàzzola *sf.* brush || *capelli a* —, crew-cut.

spazzolare *vt.* to brush.

spazzolata *sf.* brush.

spazzolino *sm.* (small) brush: — *da denti*, tooth-brush.

spazzolone *sm.* scrubbing-brush.

specchiarsi *vr.* 1. to look at oneself in a mirror 2. (*riflettersi*) to be mirrored.

specchiera *sf.* looking-glass.

specchietto *sm.* 1. hand-mirror 2. (*tabella*) table || — *retrovisore*, driving-mirror.

specchio *sm.* 1. mirror 2. (*prospetto*) register 3. (*modello*) model || — *d'acqua*, sheet of water.

speciale *agg.* special.

specialista *s.* specialist.

specialità *sf.* speciality.

specializzare *vt.* to specialize. ♦ **specializzarsi** *vr.* to specialize.

specializzazione *sf.* specialization.

specie *sf.* 1. kind 2. (*scientifico; teol.*) species (*pl. invariato*) || *far* —, to surprise.

specificamente *avv.* specifically.

specificare *vt.* to specify.

specificazione *sf.* specification.

specìfico *agg.* e *sm.* specific.

specioso *agg.* specious.

speculare[1] *vi.* to speculate (on): — *al rialzo, al ribasso,* to speculate for the advance, for the fall.

speculare[2] *agg.* mirror-like.

speculativo *agg.* speculative.

speculatore *agg.* speculative. ◆ **speculatore** *sm.* speculator.

speculazione *sf.* speculation.

spedire *vt.* **1.** to send (*v. irr.*) **2.** (*via mare*) to ship **3.** (*via terra*) to forward.

speditamente *avv.* **1.** quickly **2.** (*correntemente*) fluently.

speditezza *sf.* **1.** quickness **2.** (*nel parlare*) fluency.

spedito *agg.* **1.** (*svelto*) quick **2.** (*nel parlare*) fluent.

speditore *sm.* sender.

spedizione *sf.* **1.** forwarding **2.** (*per mare*) shipment **3.** (*di lettere, pacchi*) dispatch **4.** (*scientifico; mil.*) expedition || — *per via aerea,* air-freight.

spedizioniere *sm.* forwarding agent.

spègnere *vt.* **1.** (*un fuoco*) to put (*v. irr.*) out **2.** (*gas, luce ecc.*) to turn off **3.** (*fig.*) to stifle || — *la sete,* to quench one's thirst. ◆ **spègnersi** *vr.* **1.** to go (*v. irr.*) out **2.** (*fig.*) to fade **3.** (*morire*) to pass away.

spegnimento *sm.* extinction.

spegnitoio *sm.* snuffer.

spelacchiare *vt.* to tear (*v. irr.*) out the hair of. ◆ **spelacchiarsi** *vr.* to lose (*v. irr.*) one's hair.

spelacchiato *agg.* **1.** scanty-haired **2.** (*di stoffe, pellicce*) worn-out.

spelare *vt.* to balden. ◆ **spelarsi** *vr.* V. *spelacchiarsi.*

spelato *agg.* **1.** hairless **2.** (*di indumento*) worn.

spelatura *sf.* **1.** hairless patch **2.** (*di indumento*) worn patch.

speleologìa *sf.* speleology.

speleològico *agg.* speleological.

speleòlogo *sm.* speleologist.

spellare *vt.* to skin. ◆ **spellarsi** *vr.* to peel.

spellatura *sf.* **1.** skinning **2.** (*parte spellata*) graze.

spelonca *sf.* den.

spendaccione *sm.* spendthrift.

spèndere *vt.* to spend (*v. irr.*) (*anche fig.*).

spennacchiare *vt.* to pluck. ◆ **spennacchiarsi** *vr.* to lose (*v. irr.*) one's feathers.

spennare *vt.* to pluck.

spennellare *vt.* **1.** to brush **2.** (*med.*) to paint.

spennellata *sf.* touch of the brush.

spennellatura *sf.* (*med.*) painting.

spensieratamente *avv.* thoughtlessly.

spensieratezza *sf.* thoughtlessness.

spensierato *agg.* thoughtless.

spento *agg.* **1.** extinguished, out (*pred.*) **2.** (*estinto*) extinct **3.** (*smorto*) duli.

speràbile *agg.* to be hoped (for).

speranza *sf.* hope.

speranzoso *agg.* hopeful.

sperare *vt. e vi.* to hope (for sthg., in so.).

spèrdersi *vr.* **1.** to get (*v. irr.*) lost **2.** (*dileguare*) to vanish.

sperduto *agg.* **1.** scattered **2.** (*isolato*) secluded **3.** (*smarrito*) lost.

sperequazione *sf.* inequality.

spergiurare *vi.* to swear (*v. irr.*) falsely: *giurare e —,* to swear again and again.

spergiuro *sm.* **1.** perjury **2.** (*di persona*) perjurer.

spericolato *agg.* reckless. ◆ **spericolato** *sm.* daredevil.

sperimentale *agg.* experimental.

sperimentalismo *sm.* experimentalism.

sperimentalmente *avv.* experimentally.

sperimentare *vt.* **1.** to experiment (with) **2.** (*mettere alla prova*) to test.

sperimentato *agg.* **1.** (*provato*) tried **2.** (*esperto*) experienced.

sperimentatore *sm.* experimenter.

sperimentazione *sf.* experimentation.

sperma *sm.* sperm.

spermatozoo *sm.* spermatozoon (*pl.* -zoa).

speronare *vt.* **1.** (*mar.*) to ram **2.** (*un cavallo*) to spur.

speronata *sf.* **1.** (*mar.*) ramming **2.** (*colpo di sperone*) spur.

sperone *sm.* V. *sprone.*

sperperamento *sm.* squandering.

sperperare *vt.* to squander.

sperperatore *sm.* squanderer.

spèrpero *sm.* dissipation.

sperticato *agg.* excessive.

spesa *sf.* **1.** expense: *far fronte a una —,* to meet (*v. irr.*) an expense **2.** (*compera*) shopping: *andare a far spese,* to go (*v. irr.*) shopping.

spesare vt. to maintain.

spesato agg. essere —, to have all expenses paid.

spessire vt. to thicken. ♦ **spessirsi** vr. to thicken.

spesso[1] agg. **1.** thick **2.** (frequente) frequent.

spesso[2] avv. often.

spessore sm. thickness.

spettàbile agg. respectable.

spettàcolo sm. **1.** spectacle **2.** (teat.) performance.

spettacoloso agg. spectacular.

spettante agg. due.

spettanze sf. pl. dues.

spettare vi. **1.** to be (for so.) **2.** (essere dovuto) to be due.

spettatore sm. **1.** spectator **2.** (testimone) witness || gli spettatori, the audience.

spettegolare vi. to gossip.

spettinare vt. to ruffle so.'s hair. ♦ **spettinarsi** vr. to ruffle one's hair.

spettinato agg. uncombed.

spettrale agg. spectral.

spettro sm. **1.** ghost **2.** (fis.) spectrum (pl. -ra).

spettroscopìa sf. spectroscopy.

spettroscòpico agg. spectroscopic(al).

spettroscopio sm. spectroscope.

speziale sm. (farmacista) chemist.

spezie sf. pl. spices.

spezzàbile agg. breakable.

spezzare vt. to break (v. irr.). ♦ **spezzarsi** vr. to break.

spezzatino sm. stew.

spezzato agg. broken.

spezzettamento sm. chopping.

spezzettare vt. to chop.

spezzone sm. **1.** (mil.) incendiary bomb **2.** (metal.) cut-down size.

spia sf. **1.** spy **2.** (indizio) evidence **3.** (di porta) peep-hole || — luminosa, warning light; fare la —, to play the spy.

spiaccicare vt. to squash. ♦ **spiaccicarsi** vr. to get (v. irr.) squashed.

spiacente agg. sorry.

spiacere vi. V. dispiacere.

spiacévole agg. unpleasant.

spiacevolmente avv. unpleasantly.

spiaggia sf. **1.** beach **2.** (riva) (sea)shore.

spianamento sm. **1.** levelling **2.** (il radere al suolo) razing.

spianare vt. **1.** to level **2.** (radere al suolo) to raze **3.** (appianare, lisciare) to smooth. ♦ **spianarsi** vr. to become (v. irr.) smooth.

spianata sf. **1.** levelling **2.** (luogo spianato) open space **3.** (arch.) esplanade **4.** (in un bosco) clearing.

spianato agg. **1.** levelled **2.** (liscio) smooth.

spiano (nella loc. avv.) a tutto —, profusely; (sodo) hard.

spiantare vt. **1.** to pull out **2.** (rovinare) to ruin. ♦ **spiantarsi** vr. (rovinarsi) to go (v. irr.) to ruin.

spiantato agg. (fig.) penniless. ♦ **spiantato** sm. (fig.) pauper.

spiare vt. **1.** to spy (upon) **2.** (aspettare) to watch (for).

spiattellare vt. to blab (out).

spiazzo sm. **1.** open space **2.** (nel bosco) clearing.

spiccare vt. **1.** to pick **2.** (tagliare) to cut (v. irr.) off **3.** (pronunciare) to enunciate distinctly **4.** (emettere) to issue || — un salto, to take (v. irr.) a leap; — il volo, to fly (v. irr.) up; — una tratta, to draw (v. irr.) a bill. ♦ **spiccare** vi. to stand (v. irr.) out.

spiccatamente avv. distinctly.

spiccato agg. **1.** (marcato) marked **2.** (nitido) clear.

spicchio sm. **1.** slice **2.** (di agrumi) segment **3.** (di aglio) clove **4.** (geom.) sector || a spicchi, sliced.

spicciare vt. to dispatch. ♦ **spicciarsi** vr. to hurry up.

spicciativo agg. V. spiccio.

spiccicare vt. **1.** to detach **2.** (pronunciare) to utter.

spiccio agg. **1.** quick **2.** (franco) straightforward || andar per le spicce, to go (v. irr.) straight to the point; moneta spiccia, small change.

spicciolata (nella loc. avv.) alla —, few at a time.

spìccioli sm. pl. change (solo sing.).

spicco sm. far —, to stand (v. irr.) out.

spidocchiare vt. to delouse.

spiedo sm. spit.

spiegàbile agg. explainable.

spiegamento sm. **1.** spreading out **2.** (mil.) deployment.

spiegare vt. **1.** to explain **2.** (stendere) to spread (v. irr.) out **3.** (di vele) to unfurl **4.** (mil.) to deploy. ♦ **spiegarsi** vr. **1.** (farsi *capire*) to make (*v. irr.*) oneself understood 2. (*stendersi*) to spread out.

spiegazione *sf.* explanation.

spiegazzare *vt.* to crumple.

spietatamente *avv.* ruthlessly.

spietatezza *sf.* ruthlessness.

spietato *agg.* ruthless.

spifferare *vt.* to blurt out.

spiffero *sm.* draught.

spiga *sf.* 1. spike 2. (*di cereali*) ear.

spigare *vi.* to ear.

spighetta *sf.* braid.

spigliatamente *avv.* easily.

spigliatezza *sf.* ease.

spigliato *agg.* easy.

spigo *sm.* lavender.

spigolare *vt.* to glean (*anche fig.*).

spigolatore *sm.* gleaner.

spigolatrice *sf.* gleaner.

spigolatura *sf.* gleaning.

spigolo *sm.* edge.

spigoloso *agg.* edgy.

spilla *sf.* 1. pin 2. (*gioiello*) brooch.

spillare *vt.* 1. to draw (*v. irr.*) 2. (*fig.*) to worm.

spillo *sm.* pin: — *da balia*, safety-pin.

spillone *sm.* (*per cappello*) hat-pin.

spilorceria *sf.* stinginess.

spilorcio *agg.* stingy. ♦ **spilorcio** *sm.* miser.

spilungona *sf.* lanky woman.

spilungone *sm.* lanky man.

spina *sf.* 1. thorn 2. (*lisca*) fishbone 3. (*elettr.*) plug 4. (*mecc.*) pin 5. (*di botte*) bung 6. (*fig.*) sorrow, grief || — *dorsale*, backbone; *a — di pesce*, herring-bone.

spinacio *sm.* spinach (*solo sing.*).

spinale *agg.* spinal.

spinare *vt.* (*pesce*) to bone.

spinato *agg.* (*a spina di pesce*) herring-bone || *filo* —, barbed wire.

spinetta *sf.* spinet.

spingere *vt.* 1. to push 2. (*condurre*) to drive (*v. irr.*) 3. (*stimolare*) to urge 4. (*portare*) to carry. ♦ **spingersi** *vr.* to push.

spino *sm.* thorn.

spinone *sm.* (*cane*) griffon.

spinosità *sf.* thorniness.

spinoso *agg.* thorny.

spinta *sf.* 1. push 2. (*stimolo*) incentive 3. (*mecc.; edil.*) thrust.

spinterogeno *sm.* (battery) coil ignition.

spinto *agg.* 1. (*eccessivo*) excessive 2. (*audace*) risky.

spintone *sm.* shove || *farsi avanti a spintoni*, to elbow one's way forward.

spiombare *vt.* to unseal.

spionaggio *sm.* espionage.

spioncino *sm.* peep-hole.

spione *sm.* spy.

spiovente *agg.* 1. drooping 2. (*inclinato*) sloping. ♦ **spiovente** *sm.* 1. slope 2. (*sport*) high kick.

spiovere *vi.* 1. to stop raining 2. (*ricadere*) to come (*v. irr.*) down.

spira *sf.* coil.

spiraglio *sm.* 1. small hole 2. (*barlume*) gleam.

spirale *sf.* 1. spiral 2. (*molla*) spring.

spirante *agg.* 1. (*soffiante*) blowing 2. (*morente*) passing away 3. (*esalante*) exhaling.

spirare *vi.* 1. (*soffiare*) to blow (*v. irr.*) 2. (*morire*) to pass away 3. (*scadere*) to expire 4. (*emanare*) to emanate. ♦ **spirare** *vt.* to exhale.

spiritato *agg.* 1. possessed 2. (*spaventato*) frightened.

spiritico *agg.* spiritualistic.

spiritismo *sm.* spiritualism.

spiritista *s.* spiritualist.

spiritistico *agg.* V. *spiritico*.

spirito *sm.* 1. spirit 2. (*fantasma*) ghost 3. (*arguzia*) wit 4. (*alcool*) alcohol || *far dello* —, to be witty.

spiritosaggine *sf.* witticism.

spiritosamente *avv.* wittily.

spiritoso *agg.* 1. witty 2. (*alcoolico*) alcoholic.

spirituale *agg.* spiritual.

spiritualismo *sm.* spiritualism.

spiritualista *agg.* spiritualistic. ♦ **spiritualista** *s.* spiritualist.

spiritualità *sf.* spirituality.

spiritualizzare *vt.* to spiritualize.

spiritualmente *avv.* spiritually.

spizzicare *vt.* to nibble.

spizzico (*nella loc. avv.*) *a* —, little by little.

splendente *agg.* bright.

splendere *vi.* to shine (*v. irr.*).

splendido *agg.* splendid.

splendore *sm.* splendour.

spocchia *sf.* haughtiness.

spocchioso *agg.* haughty.

spodestamento *sm.* 1. dispossession 2. (*da posizione autorevole*) dethronement.

spodestare *vt.* 1. to dispossess 2. (*detronizzare*) to dethrone.

spoetizzare *vt.* to disenchant.

spoglia *sf.* **1.** (*di animale*) skin **2.** (*veste*) dress **3.** (*bottino*) spoils (*pl.*) || spoglie mortali, mortal remains.

spogliare *vt.* **1.** to strip **2.** (*derubare*) to rob **3.** (*saccheggiare*) to plunder. ♦ **spogliarsi** *vr.* **1.** to strip **2.** (*di alberi*) to shed (*v. irr.*) **3.** (*privarsi*) to strip oneself (of).

spogliarello *sm.* strip-tease.

spogliatoio *sm.* **1.** dressing-room **2.** (*teat. ecc.*) cloak-room.

spoglio *agg.* bare. ♦ **spoglio** *sm.* **1.** (*computo*) counting **2.** (*esame*) examination **3.** (*vestito smesso*) cast-off || fare lo —, to go (*v. irr.*) through.

spola *sf.* shuttle.

spoletta *sf.* **1.** spool **2.** (*di arma*) fuse.

spoliazione *sf.* spoliation.

spolmonarsi *vr.* to talk oneself hoarse.

spolpare *vt.* **1.** to take (*v. irr.*) the flesh off **2.** (*fig.*) to skin.

spolpato *agg.* **1.** stripped of the flesh **2.** (*fig.*) skinned.

spolverare *vt.* to dust.

spolveratura *sf.* **1.** dusting **2.** (*fig.*) smattering.

spolverino *sm.* dust-coat.

spolverizzare *vt.* to dust.

spòlvero *sm.* **1.** dusting **2.** (*disegno*) perforated pattern.

sponda *sf.* **1.** edge **2.** (*di fiume*) bank **3.** (*di mare*) shore **4.** (*parapetto*) parapet.

sponsali *sm. pl.* nuptials.

spontaneamente *avv.* spontaneously.

spontaneità *sf.* spontaneity.

spontàneo *agg.* spontaneous.

spopolamento *sm.* depopulation.

spopolare *vt.* to depopulate. ♦ **spopolarsi** *vr.* to become (*v. irr.*) depopulated.

spopolato *agg.* (*deserto*) deserted.

spora *sf.* spore.

sporàdico *agg.* sporadic.

sporcaccione *sm.* dirty man.

sporcare *vt.* to dirty.

sporcizia *sf.* dirt.

sporco *agg.* dirty.

sporgente *agg.* protruding.

sporgenza *sf.* protrusion.

spòrgere *vi.* to put (*v. irr.*) out. ♦ **spòrgere** *vt.* to put (*v. irr.*) out. ♦ **spòrgersi** *vr.* to lean (*v. irr.*) out.

sport *sm.* sport.

sporta *sf.* basket.

sportello *sm.* **1.** door **2.** (*di biglietteria*) ticket-window **3.** (*di ufficio postale ecc.*) counter.

sportivamente *avv.* sportingly.

sportivo *agg.* sporting. ♦ **sportivo** *sm.* sportsman (*pl.* -men).

sporto *agg.* **1.** leaning out **2.** (*proteso*) outstretched.

sposa *sf.* bride.

sposalizio *sm.* wedding.

sposare *vt.* to marry. ♦ **sposarsi** *vr.* to get (*v. irr.*) married.

sposo *sm.* bridegroom.

spossamento *sm.* exhaustion.

spossante *agg.* exhausting.

spossare *vt.* to exhaust.

spossatezza *sf.* V. spossamento.

spossato *agg.* weary.

spossessare *vt.* to dispossess.

spostàbile *agg.* shiftable.

spostamento *sm.* **1.** shifting **2.** (*cambiamento*) change.

spostare *vt.* **1.** to shift, to move **2.** (*cambiare*) to change. ♦ **spostarsi** *vr.* to shift.

spostato *agg.* out of one's place (*pred.*). ♦ **spostato** *sm.* misfit.

spranga *sf.* bar.

sprangare *vt.* to bar.

sprazzo *sm.* flash: — d'ingegno, brain-wave.

sprecare *vt.* to waste.

spreco *sm.* waste.

sprecone *sm.* waster.

spregévole *agg.* despicable.

spregiare *vt.* to scorn.

spregiativo *agg.* **1.** scornful **2.** (*gramm.*) pejorative. ♦ **spregiativo** *sm.* (*gramm.*) pejorative.

spregio *sm.* contempt.

spregiudicatamente *avv.* open-mindedly.

spregiudicatezza *sf.* open-mindedness.

spregiudicato *agg.* open-minded.

sprèmere *vt.* **1.** to squeeze **2.** (*torcere*) to wring (*v. irr.*) out. ♦ **spremersi** *vr.* to rack oneself.

spremilimoni *sm.* lemon-squeezer.

spremitura *sf.* **1.** squeezing **2.** (*di panni bagnati*) wringing.

spremuta *sf.* squash.

spremuto *agg.* **1.** squeezed **2.** (*di panni*) wrung.

spretare *vt.* to unfrock. ♦ **spretarsi** *vr.* to renounce one's priesthood.

spretato *agg.* unfrocked. ♦ **spretato** *sm.* unfrocked priest.

sprezzante *agg.* scornful.

sprezzare *vt.* V. *disprezzare.*

sprezzo *sm.* scorn.

sprigionamento *sm.* 1. exhalation 2. (*violento*) bursting out.

sprigionare *vt.* to emit. ♦ **sprigionarsi** *vr.* 1. to be emitted 2. (*con violenza*) to burst (*v. irr.*) out.

sprimacciare *vt.* to shake (*v. irr.*) up.

sprizzare *vt. e vi.* to spurt: — *scintille*, to spit (*v. irr.*) sparks; — *gioia*, to burst (*v. irr.*) with joy.

sprizzo *sm.* spurt.

sprofondamento *sm.* 1. sinking 2. (*crollo*) collapse.

sprofondare *vt.* (*far cadere*) to cause tò collapse. ♦ **sprofondare** *vi.* 1. to sink (*v. irr.*) 2. (*crollare*) to collapse 3. (*fig.*) to be absorbed. ♦ **sprofondarsi** *vr.* 1. to sink 2. (*crollare*) to collapse 3. (*fig.*) to be absorbed.

sproloquio *sm.* long rigmarole.

spronare *vt.* to spur.

spronata *sf.* spurring.

sprone *sm.* 1. spur 2. (*mar.*) ram || *a spron battuto*, at full speed.

sproporzionato *agg.* disproportionate, out of proportion (*pred.*).

sproporzione *sf.* disproportion.

spropositato *agg.* 1. full of blunders 2. (*fig.*) enormous.

spropòsito *sm.* 1. blunder 2. (*eccesso*) excess || *a* —, off the point.

sprovveduto *agg.* 1. (*incauto*) unwary 2. (*sprovvisto*) devoid 3. (*impreparato*) unprepared.

sprovvisto *agg.* devoid || *alla sprovvista*, unawares.

spruzzare *vt.* 1. to spray 2. (*inzaccherare*) to splash.

spruzzata *sf.* spray.

spruzzatore *sm.* sprayer.

spruzzatura *sf.* spraying.

spruzzo *sm.* 1. spray 2. (*di liquido sporco*) splash.

spudoratezza *sf.* shamelessness.

spudorato *agg.* shameless.

spugna *sf.* 1. sponge 2. (*tessuto*) sponge-cloth || *cancellare con la* —, to sponge; *bere come una* —, to drink (*v. irr.*) like a fish.

spugnatura *sf.* sponge down.

spugnosità *sf.* sponginess.

spugnoso *agg.* spongy.

spulciare *vt.* 1. to look for fleas (on) 2. (*esaminare; fig.*) to peruse 3. (*raccogliere; fig.*) to gather here and there.

spuma *sf.* foam.

spumante *agg.* foaming. ♦ **spumante** *sm.* sparkling wine.

spumare *vi.* to foam.

spumeggiante *agg.* foaming.

spumeggiare *vi.* to foam.

spumoso *agg.* foamy.

spuntare¹ *vt.* 1. (*smussare*) to blunt 2. (*tagliare*) to trim 3. (*staccare*) to unpin || *spuntarla*, to succeed. ♦ **spuntarsi** *vr.* 1. (*smussarsi*) to get (*v. irr.*) blunt 2. (*staccarsi*) to become (*v. irr.*) unpinned.

spuntare² *vi.* 1. (*sorgere*) to rise (*v. irr.*) 2. (*germogliare*) to sprout 3. (*di capelli*) to begin (*v. irr.*) to grow 4. (*apparire*) to appear.

spuntato *agg.* pointless.

spuntatura *sf.* 1. (*lo smussare*) blunting 2. (*il tagliare*) trimming.

spuntino *sm.* snack.

spunto *sm.* 1. cue 2. (*punto di partenza*) starting point.

spuntone *sm.* spike.

spurgare *vt.* 1. to clean 2. (*med.*) to discharge. ♦ **spurgarsi** *vr.* (*espettorare*) to expectorate.

spurgo *sm.* 1. (*lo spurgare*) discharging 2. (*l'espettorare*) expectorating 3. (*ciò che viene espulso*) discharge.

spurio *agg.* spurious.

sputacchiare *vi.* V. *sputare.*

sputacchiera *sf.* spittoon.

sputacchio *sm.* spittle.

sputare *vt.* to spit (*v. irr.*).

sputasentenze *sm.* wiseacre.

sputo *sm.* spit.

squadra *sf.* 1. (*da disegno*) square 2. (*gruppo; sport*) team 3. (*di operai*) gang 4. (*mil.*) squad 5. (*mar.*) squadron || — *mobile*, flying squad.

squadrare *vt.* 1. to square 2. (*guardare*) to look (so.) up and down.

squadratura *sf.* squaring.

squadriglia *sf.* squadron.

squadro *sm.* squaring.

squadrone *sm.* squadron.

squagliamento *sm.* melting.

squagliare *vt.* to melt. ♦ **squagliarsi** *vr.* 1. to melt 2. (*andar via*) to steal (*v. irr.*) away.

squalìfica *sf.* disqualification.

squalificare vt. to disqualify.
squàllido agg. dreary.
squallore sm. dreariness.
squalo sm. shark.
squama sf. scale.
squamare vt. to scale. ◆ **squamarsi** vr. to scale.
squamoso agg. scaly.
squarciagola (nella loc. avv.) a —, at the top of one's voice.
squarciamento sm. tearing.
squarciare vt. 1. to tear (v. irr.) 2. (fig.) to dispel. ◆ **squarciarsi** vr. to be torn.
squarcio sm. gash.
squartare vt. to mangle.
squartatore sm. mangler.
squassare vt. to jolt.
squasso sm. jolt.
squattrinato agg. penniless.
squilibrare vt. to unbalance. ◆ **squilibrarsi** vr. to lose (v. irr.) one's balance.
squilibrato agg. unbalanced. ◆ **squilibrato** sm. lunatic.
squilibrio sm. 1. lack of balance 2. (mentale) derangement.
squillante agg. 1. shrill 2. (di trombe) blaring 3. (di campane) pealing.
squillare vi. 1. to ring (v. irr.) 2. (di trombe) to blare.
squillo sm. 1. ring 2. (di tromba) blare.
squinternare vt. 1. to ruin 2. (fig.) to upset (v. irr.).
squisitezza sf. exquisiteness.
squisito agg. exquisite.
squittìo sm. squeak.
squittire vi. to squeak.
sradicare vt. to uproot.
sragionare vi. to talk nonsense.
sregolatezza sf. disorderliness.
sregolato agg. disorderly.
stabbio sm. 1. sty 2. (letame) manure.
stàbile sm. building. ◆ **stàbile** agg. 1. stable 2. (permanente) permanent: in pianta —, on the permanent staff.
stabilimento sm. 1. (fabbrica) factory 2. (edificio, lo stabilire) establishment.
stabilire vt. 1. to establish 2. (decidere) to decide. ◆ **stabilirsi** vr. to settle.
stabilità sf. stability.
stabilizzare vt. to stabilize.
stabilizzatore sm. stabilizer.

stabilizzazione sf. stabilization.
stabilmente avv. firmly.
stacanovismo sm. Stakhanovism.
staccàbile agg. detachable.
staccare vt. 1. to take (v. irr.) off 2. (tagliare) to cut (v. irr.) off 3. (separare) to separate 4. (slegare) to unfasten || — un assegno, to issue a cheque. ◆ **staccarsi** vr. 1. to come (v. irr.) off 2. (sciogliersi) to break (v. irr.) loose 3. (scostarsi) to move away 4. (separarsi) to part 5. (distaccarsi) to pull ahead (of) 6. (esser diverso) to differ.
stacciare vt. to sieve.
staccio sm. sieve.
staccionata sf. fence.
stacco sm. detachment.
stadera sf. steelyard.
stadio sm. 1. stadium (pl. -ia), sports ground 2. (fase) stage.
staffa sf. stirrup || perder le staffe (fig.), to lose (v. irr.) one's self-control.
staffetta sf. 1. courier 2. (sport) relay race.
staffilare vt. to lash.
staffilata sf. lash.
staffile sm. whip.
stafilococco sm. staphylococcus (pl. -ci).
staggio sm. 1. (di scala) shaft 2. (di sedia) back leg.
stagionale agg. seasonal.
stagionare vt. to season.
stagionato agg. 1. seasoned 2. (fig.) oldish.
stagionatura sf. seasoning.
stagione sf. season.
stagnaio sm. tinsmith.
stagnante agg. stagnant.
stagnare[1] vi. to stagnate.
stagnare[2] vt. 1. to tin 2. (saldare) to solder 3. (impermeabilizzare) to waterproof 4. (fermare) to staunch.
stagnatura sf. tinning.
stagnino sm. tinker.
stagno[1] sm. tin.
stagno[2] sm. (bacino d'acqua) pond.
stagno[3] agg. water-tight.
stagnola sf. tin-foil.
staio sm. bushel.
stalagmite sf. stalagmite.
stalattite sf. stalactite.
stalla sf. stable.
stalliere sm. stable-boy.
stallo sm. stall.
stallone sm. stallion.

stamattina *avv.* this morning.

stambecco *sm.* ibex.

stamberga *sf.* hovel.

stambugio *sm.* hole.

stame *sm.* (*bot.*) stamen.

stamigna *sf.* bunting.

stampa *sf.* 1. print 2. (*atto di stampare*) printing 3. (*periodici, giornali*) press 4. (*genere*) stamp || *agenzia di —*, news-agency; *errore di —*, misprint.

stampare *vt.* 1. to print 2. (*mecc.*) to press 3. (*coniare*) to coin. ♦ **stamparsi** *vr. — in mente*, to impress (sthg.) firmly on one's mind.

stampatello *sm.* block letters (*pl.*).

stampato *sm.* 1. printed matter 2. (*modulo*) form.

stampatore *sm.* printer.

stampatrice *sf.* printing-press.

stampella *sf.* crutch.

stamperia *sf.* printing-office.

stampigliare *vt.* to stamp.

stampo *sm.* 1. die, mould 2. (*genere*) stamp.

stanare *vt.* to drive (*v. irr.*) out.

stancare *vt.* 1. to tire 2. (*infastidire*) to annoy. ♦ **stancarsi** *vr.* 1. to get (*v. irr.*) tired 2. (*annoiarsi*) to get bored.

stanchezza *sf.* tiredness.

stanco *agg.* tired.

standardizzare *vt.* to standardize.

stanga *sf.* 1. bar 2. (*di carro*) shaft 3. (*di passaggio a livello*) barrier.

stangare *vt.* 1. to bar 2. (*percuotere*) to thrash.

stanghetta *sf.* 1. (*degli occhiali*) bar 2. (*di serratura*) bolt.

stanotte *avv.* tonight.

stantio *agg.* stale.

stantuffo *sm.* 1. piston 2. (*di pompa ecc.*) plunger.

stanza *sf.* 1. room 2. (*strofa*) stanza || *prendere, avere —*, to settle.

stanziamento *sm.* appropriation.

stanziare *vt.* to appropriate. ♦ **stanziarsi** *vr.* to settle.

stappare *vt.* to uncork.

stare *vi.* 1. to stay 2. (*abitare*) to live 3. (*di salute, essere*) to be 4. (*in piedi*) to stand (*v. irr.*) 5. (*dipendere*) to depend (on) 6. (*spettare*) to be up 7. (*andare*) to go (*v. irr.*) 8. (*di abito*) to suit || *— per*, to be going (to); *lasciar —*, to leave (*v. irr.*) alone; *sta' a sentire!*, listen!; *ben ti sta!*, it

serves you right!

starnazzare *vi.* to flutter.

starnutire *vi.* to sneeze.

starnuto *sm.* sneeze.

stasare *vt.* to unclog.

stasera *avv.* this evening.

stasi *sf.* 1. standstill 2. (*med.*) stasis (*pl.* -ses).

statale *agg.* State (*attr.*), of the State. ♦ **statale** *s.* State employee.

statica *sf.* statics.

statico *agg.* static.

statista *sm.* statesman (*pl.* -men).

statistica *sf.* statistics.

statizzare *vt.* to nationalize.

statizzazione *sf.* nationalization.

stato *sm.* 1. state, condition (*anche posizione sociale*) 2. (*giur.*) status 3. (*pol.*) State || *ufficio di — civile*, registry office; *ufficiale di — civile*, registrar.

statua *sf.* statue.

statuaria *sf.* statuary.

statuario *agg.* statuesque.

statuire *vt.* to decree.

statunitense *agg.* United States (*attr.*). ♦ **statunitense** *sm.* United States citizen.

statura *sf.* stature.

statuto *sm.* statute.

stazionamento *sm.* standing.

stazionare *vi.* 1. to stay 2. (*di vetture*) to be parked.

stazionario *agg.* stationary.

stazione *sf.* station.

stazza *sf.* tonnage.

stazzare *vt.* to have the tonnage of.

stecca *sf.* 1. (*di ombrello, ventaglio*) rib 2. (*da biliardo*) cue 3. (*di persiana*) slat 4. (*di busto*) whalebone 5. (*stonatura*) false note.

steccare *vt.* 1. (*chiudere con steccato*) to fence in 2. (*mus.*) to fluff. ♦ **steccare** *vi.* 1. (*cantando*) to sing (*v. irr.*) a false note 2. (*suonando*) to play a false note.

steccato *sm.* fence.

stecchito *agg.* 1. (*secco*) dried up 2. (*magro*) skinny 3. (*morto*) stone dead.

stecco *sm.* 1. stick 2. (*persona magra*) bag of bones.

stecconata *sf.* paling.

stele *sf.* stele (*pl.* -lae).

stella *sf.* star: *— marina*, starfish; *a forma di —*, starlike.

stellare *agg.* 1. stellar 2. (*a forma di stella*) star-shaped.

stellato *agg.* starry.

stelletta *sf.* **1.** (*tip.*) asterisk **2.** (*mil.*) star.

stelloncino *sm.* short paragraph.

stelo *sm.* stem.

stemma *sm.* coat-of-arms.

stemperare *vt.* **1.** to mix **2.** (*diluire*) to spin out. ♦ **stemperarsi** *vr.* to dissolve.

stempiarsi *vr.* to go (*v. irr.*) bald.

stendardo *sm.* standard.

stèndere *vt.* **1.** to spread (*v. irr.*) **2.** (*allungare*) to stretch **3.** (*scrivere*) to draw (*v. irr.*) up **4.** (*rilassare*) to relax || — *il bucato*, to hang (*v. irr.*) out the washing. ♦ **stèndersi** *vr.* **1.** to stretch **2.** (*adagiarsi*) to lie (*v. irr.*) down.

stenodattilografia *sf.* shorthand and typewriting.

stenografare *vt.* to write (*v. irr.*) down in shorthand.

stenografia *sf.* shorthand.

stenògrafo *sm.* shorthand-writer.

stentare *vi.* **1.** to have difficulty (in) **2.** (*mancare del necessario*) to be in need.

stentato *agg.* **1.** hard **2.** (*cresciuto a stento*) stunted.

stento *sm.* privation: *a* —, hardly, with difficulty.

stentòreo *agg.* stentorian.

steppa *sf.* steppe.

sterco *sm.* dung.

stereofonìa *sf.* stereophony.

stereofònico *agg.* stereophonic.

stereografìa *sf.* stereography.

stereogràfico *agg.* stereographic(al).

stereoscopìa *sf.* stereoscopy.

stereoscopio *sm.* stereoscope.

stereotipato *agg.* stereotyped.

stereotipìa *sf.* stereotyping.

stèrile *agg.* barren.

sterilità *sf.* barrenness.

sterilizzare *vt.* to sterilize.

sterilizzatore *agg.* sterilizing. ♦ **sterilizzatore** *sm.* sterilizer.

sterilizzazione *sf.* sterilization.

sterlina *sf.* pound.

sterminare *vt.* to exterminate.

sterminatezza *sf.* immensity.

sterminato *agg.* (*smisurato*) immense.

sterminatore *sm.* exterminator.

sterminio *sm.* extermination.

sterno *sm.* breast-bone.

sterpaglia *sf.* brushwood.

sterpo *sm.* dry twig.

sterrare *vt.* to dig (*v. irr.*) up.

sterratore *sm.* navvy.

sterzare *vt.* to steer.

sterzata *sf.* sudden turn.

sterzo *sm.* (*auto*) steering-gear.

stesso *agg.* **1.** (*medesimo*) same **2.** (*intensivo*) *se* —, oneself; *io*, *me* —, myself; *tu*, *te* —, yourself; *egli*, *lui* —, himself; *ella*, *lei stessa*, herself; *esso* —, itself; *noi stessi*, ourselves; *voi stessi*, yourselves; *loro stessi*, themselves **3.** (*proprio*) very. ♦ **stesso** *sm.* same, ♦ **stesso** *avv.* all the same

stesura *sf.* **1.** (*redazione*) draft **2.** (*di contratto*) drawing up.

stetoscopio *sm.* stethoscope.

stìgmate *sf. pl.* **1.** stigmata (*pl.*) **2.** (*marchio*) brand (*sing.*).

stigmatizzare *vt.* to stigmatize.

stilare *vt.* to draw (*v. irr.*) up.

stile *sm.* style: *aver* —, to be stylish; *con* —, stylishly.

stilettata *sf.* stab.

stilista *s.* stylist.

stilìstica *sf.* stylistics.

stilizzare *vt.* to stylize.

stilizzazione *sf.* stylization.

stilla *sf.* drop.

stillare *vi.* e *vt.* to ooze. ♦ **stillarsi** *vr.* — *il cervello*, to rack one's brain.

stiliicidio *sm.* dripping.

stilo *sm.* stylus.

stilogràfica *sf.* fountainpen.

stilogràfico *agg.* stylographic(al).

stima *sf.* **1.** (*valutazione*) estimate **2.** (*buona opinione*) esteem.

stimàbile *agg.* estimable.

stimare *vt.* **1.** (*valutare*) to estimate **2.** (*tenere in considerazione*) to esteem **3.** (*ritenere*) to consider.

stimatore *sm.* estimator.

stimolante *agg.* stimulating. ♦ **stimolante** *sm.* stimulant.

stimolare *vt.* to stimulate.

stìmolo *sm.* **1.** stimulus (*pl.* -li) **2.** (*pungolo*) goad.

stinco *sm.* shin.

stìngere *vt.* to fade. ♦ **stìngersi** *vr.* to fade.

stinto *agg.* faded.

stipare *vt.* to cram.

stipato *agg.* crammed (with).

stipendiare *vt.* to pay (*v. irr.*) a salary (to so.).

stipendio *sm.* salary.

stìpite *sm.* jamb.

stipulante *agg.* stipulating. ♦ **stipulante** *s.* stipulator.

stipulare *vt.* to stipulate.

stipulazione *sf.* stipulation.

stiracchiare *vt.* **1.** to stretch **2.** (*distorcere*) to twist.

stiracchiato *agg.* (*fig.*) forced.

stiramento *sm.* **1.** stretching **2.** (*muscolare*) strain.

stirare *vt.* **1.** to stretch **2.** (*col ferro da stiro*) to iron.

stiratura *sf.* ironing.

stireria *sf.* (*e tintoria*) laundry shop.

stirpe *sf.* **1.** stock **2.** (*progenie*) issue.

stitichezza *sf.* constipation.

stitico *agg.* constipated.

stiva *sf.* hold.

stivale *sm.* boot.

stivaletto *sm.* ankle-boot.

stizza *sf.* anger.

stizzire *vt.* to vex. ♦ **stizzirsi** *vr.* to get (*v. irr.*) cross.

stizzito *agg.* cross.

stizzoso *agg.* peevish.

stoccata *sf.* thrust: *lanciare una —* (*fig.*), to gibe (at).

stoffa *sf.* **1.** cloth **2.** (*fig.*) stuff.

stoicismo *sm.* stoicism.

stòico *agg. e sm.* stoic.

stoino *sm.* door-mat.

stola *sf.* stole.

stolidità *sf.* stolidity.

stòlido *agg.* stolid.

stoltezza *sf.* foolishness.

stolto *agg.* foolish. ♦ **stolto** *sm.* fool.

stomacare *vt.* to sicken. ♦ **stomacarsi** *vr.* to sicken.

stomachévole *agg.* sickening.

stòmaco *sm.* stomach: *dare di —,* to vomit; *restare sullo —,* to lie (*v. irr.*) on one's stomach.

stomatite *sf.* stomatitis.

stomatologìa *sf.* stomatology.

stonare *vi.* **1.** to be out of tune **2.** (*fig.*) to be out of place **3.** (*di colori*) to clash. ♦ **stonare** *vt.* to upset (*v. irr.*).

stonato *agg.* **1.** out of tune **2.** (*fig.*) out of place **3.** (*turbato*) upset **4.** (*di nota*) false.

stonatura *sf.* false note.

stoppa *sf.* tow.

stoppaccio *sm.* wad.

stoppare *vt.* **1.** to plug **2.** (*sport*) to stop.

stoppia *sf.* stubble.

stoppino *sm.* wick.

stopposo *agg.* **1.** towy **2.** (*di carne*) stringy.

stòrcere *vt.* **1.** to twist **2.** (*un'articolazione*) to sprain || *— gli occhi,* to roll one's eyes. ♦ **stòrcersi** *vr.* **1.** to twist **2.** (*lussarsi, slogarsi*) to wrench.

stordimento *sm.* **1.** dizziness **2.** (*meraviglia*) bewilderment.

stordire *vt.* **1.** to stun **2.** (*di alcoolici*) to dull **3.** (*assordare*) to deafen **4.** (*innervosire*) to drive (*v. irr.*) crazy. ♦ **stordirsi** *vr.* to dull one's senses.

stordito *agg.* **1.** (*sbalordito*) bewildered **2.** (*sbadato*) heedless **3.** (*sciocco*) foolish.

storia *sf.* **1.** history **2.** (*racconto*) story.

storicismo *sm.* historical method.

storicità *sf.* historicity.

stòrico *agg.* historical. ♦ **stòrico** *sm.* historian.

storiografìa *sf.* historiography.

storiògrafo *sm.* historiographer.

stormire *vi.* to rustle.

stormo *sm.* **1.** flight **2.** (*folla*) crowd || *suonare a —,* to ring (*v. irr.*) the tocsin.

stornare *vt.* to divert.

stornello[1] *sm.* ditty.

stornello[2] *sm.* (*zool.*) starling.

storno[1] *agg.* dapple-grey.

storno[2] *sm.* (*zool.*) starling.

storno[3] *sm.* (*comm.*) transfer.

storpiare *vt.* **1.** to cripple **2.** (*rovinare*) to mangle.

storpiatura *sf.* **1.** crippling **2.** (*fig.*) mangling **3.** (*cosa malfatta*) botch.

storpio *sm.* cripple.

storta *sf.* **1.** twist **2.** (*in una articolazione*) sprain **3.** (*chim.*) retort.

storto *agg.* **1.** twisted **2.** (*piegato*) crooked **3.** (*di occhi*) squinting **4.** (*sbagliato*) wrong.

stortura *sf.* **1.** deformity **2.** (*errore*) mistake.

stoviglie *sf. pl.* kitchenware (*sing.*).

stràbico *agg.* squinting. ♦ **stràbico** *sm.* squinter.

strabiliante *agg.* amazing.

strabiliare *vt.* to amaze (*anche far strabiliare*). ♦ **strabiliare** *vi.* to be amazed. ♦ **strabiliarsi** *vr.* to be amazed.

strabismo *sm.* squint.

straboccare *vi.* **1.** to overflow **2.** (*fig.*) to abound (in).

strabocchévole *agg.* overflowing.

strabuzzare *vt.* *— gli occhi,* to roll one's eyes.

stracàrico agg. overloaded (with).

stracciare vt. to tear (v. irr.). ◆
stracciarsi vr. to tear.

stracciato agg. 1. torn 2. (di persona) in rags.

straccio agg. torn, in rags || carta straccia, waste paper. ◆ **straccio** sm. rag: — per la polvere, duster.

straccione sm. ragamuffin.

straccivéndolo sm. rag-and-bone--man (pl. -men).

stracotto agg. overdone. ◆ **stracotto** sm. stew.

strada sf. 1. road 2. (di città) street 3. (percorso; fig.) way || — a senso unico, one-way street; — ferrata, railway; — maestra, main road.

stradale agg. road (attr.), of the road: fondo —, road-bed.

stradino sm. roadman (pl. -men).

strafalcione sm. blunder.

strafare vi. to overdo (v. irr.).

strafottente agg. 1. (noncurante) unconcerned 2. (arrogante) arrogant.

strage sf. 1. slaughter 2. (distruzione) destruction || fare una —, to slaughter.

stragrande agg. enormous.

stralciare vt. 1. (comm.) to remove 2. (fig.) to take (v. irr.) off.

stralcio sm. 1. removal 2. (estratto) extract.

strale sm. dart.

stralunare vt. — gli occhi, to roll one's eyes, to open one's eyes wide.

stralunato agg. 1. (di occhi) rolling, wild-eyed 2. (di persona) upset.

stramazzare vi. to fall (v. irr.) heavily.

stramberìa sf. oddity.

strambo agg. odd.

strame sm. litter.

strampalato agg. queer.

stranezza sf. oddity.

strangolamento sm. strangling.

strangolare vt. to strangle.

strangolatore sm. strangler.

straniero agg. foreign. ◆ **straniero** sm. foreigner.

strano agg. strange.

straordinario agg. extraordinary.

strapazzare vt. 1. to ill-use 2. (sgridare) to scold 3. (far lavorare troppo) to overwork 4. (di uova) to scramble. ◆ **strapazzarsi** vr. to overwork oneself.

strapazzata sf. 1. scolding 2. (fatica) overwork.

strapazzo sm. overwork: abiti da —, working-clothes; scrittore da —, hack.

strapieno agg. full up.

strapiombare vi. 1. to lean (v. irr.) 2. (scendere a precipizio) to fall (v. irr.) perpendicularly.

strapiombo sm. precipice: a —, sheer.

strapotente agg. very powerful.

strappare vt. 1. (lacerare) to tear (v. irr.) 2. (togliere) to snatch 3. (estirpare) to pull up 4. (un dente) to pull out 5. (estorcere) to wring (v. irr.). ◆ **strapparsi** vr. (lacerarsi) to tear.

strappo sm. 1. tear 2. (strappata) pull 3. (infrazione) breach || — muscolare, sprain.

strapuntino sm. folding seat.

straricco agg. immensely rich.

straripamento sm. overflowing.

straripare vi. to overflow.

strascicare vt. 1. to drag 2. (i piedi) to shuffle 3. (le parole) to drawl.

stràscico sm. 1. train 2. (residuo) after-effect 3. (rete) trawl.

strascinare vt. V. trascinare.

stratagemma sm. stratagem.

stratega sm. strategist.

strategìa sf. strategy.

stratègico agg. strategic(al).

stratificare vt. to stratify.

stratificazione sf. stratification.

strato sm. 1. layer 2. (di rivestimento) coat 3. (della società) class.

stratosfera sf. stratosphere.

stratosfèrico agg. stratospheric(al).

strattone sm. 1. pull 2. (sobbalzo) jerk || a strattoni, jerkily; (a intervalli) by fits and starts.

stravagante agg. odd, queer.

stravaganza sf. oddity.

stravecchio agg. very old.

stravedere vi. to see (v. irr.) badly: — per qu., to be crazy about so.

stravincere vt. to crush. ◆ **stravincere** vi. to win (v. irr.) all along the line.

stravizio sm. excess.

stravòlgere vt. 1. to twist 2. (gli occhi) to roll.

stravolto agg. 1. (turbato) upset 2. (di occhi) rolling.

straziante agg. tormenting, heartrending (solo fig.).

straziare *vt.* to tear (*v. irr.*).

strazio *sm.* torment: *far — di*, to play havoc with.

strega *sf.* witch.

stregare *vt.* to bewitch.

stregone *sm.* wizard.

stregonerìa *sf.* witchcraft.

stremare *vt.* to exhaust.

stremo *sm.* extreme.

strenna *sf.* gift.

strenuo *agg.* brave.

strepitare *vi.* to shout.

strèpito *sm.* din, uproar.

strepitoso *agg.* uproarious: *successo —*, striking success.

streptococco *sm.* streptococcus (*pl.* -ci).

streptomicina *sf.* streptomycin.

stretta *sf.* 1. grasp 2. (*calca*) press 3. (*gola*) gorge || *— di mano*, handshake; *essere alle strette*, to be in dire straits; *mettere alle strette qu.*, to put (*v. irr.*) so. with his back against the wall.

strettezza *sf.* 1. narrowness 2. (*povertà*) financial difficulty.

stretto *agg.* 1. narrow 2. (*serrato, piccolo*) tight 3. (*rigoroso*) strict 4. (*pigiato*) packed. ♦ **stretto** *sm.* strait.

strettoia *sf.* narrow passage.

stria *sf.* streak.

striare *vt.* to streak.

stricnina *sf.* strychnine.

stridente *agg.* 1. shrill 2. (*discordante*) jarring.

stridere *vi.* 1. to creak 2. (*di insetti*) to chirp 3. (*contrastare*) to jar.

stridìo *sm.* 1. creaking 2. (*di insetti*) chirping.

strido *sm.* 1. scream 2. (*di animale*) screech.

strìdulo *agg.* shrill.

striglia *sf.* curry-comb.

strigliare *vt.* 1. to curry 2. (*fig.*) to rebuke.

strillare *vi.* to scream.

strillo *sm.* scream.

strillone *sm.* newsboy.

striminzito *agg.* 1. stunted 2. (*di persona*) thin.

strimpellare *vt.* 1. (*di violino*) to scrape 2. (*di pianoforte*) to strum.

strinare *vt.* to singe.

stringa *sf.* lace.

stringare *vt.* 1. to lace tightly 2. (*fig.*) to condense.

stringato *agg.* 1. laced 2. (*fig.*) concise.

stringente *agg.* 1. (*urgente*) urgent 2. (*convincente*) persuasive.

stringere *vt.* 1. to press 2. (*restringere, avvitare*) to tighten 3. (*abbracciare*) to clasp 4. (*impugnare*) to grasp 5. (*fare*) to make (*v. irr.*) || *— la mano a*, to shake (*v. irr.*) hands with; *— i pugni*, to clench one's fists; *stringi stringi*, in conclusion. ♦ **stringere** *vi.* to be tight. ♦ **strìngersi** *vr.* 1. to press (against) 2. (*far spazio*) to squeeze up || *— nelle spalle*, to shrug one's shoulders.

stringimento *sm.* 1. pressing 2. (*restringimento, legamento, avvitamento*) tightening 3. (*l'impugnare*) clasp 4. (*fitta*) pang.

striscia *sf.* 1. strip 2. (*riga*) stripe 3. (*scia*) trail || *a strisce*, striped.

strisciante *agg.* 1. creeping 2. (*servile*) fawning.

strisciare *vi.* 1. to creep (*v. irr.*) 2. (*fig.*) to grovel. ♦ **strisciare** *vt.* 1. to drag 2. (*i piedi*) to shuffle 3. (*radere*) to graze 4. (*fig.*) to fawn (on).

stritolamento *sm.* crushing.

stritolare *vt.* to crush.

strizzare *vt.* 1. to squeeze 2. (*torcere*) to wring (*v. irr.*) || *— l'occhio*, to wink (at so.).

strizzata *sf.* 1. squeeze 2. (*il torcere*) wring.

strofa *sf.* stanza.

strofinaccio *sm.* 1. duster 2. (*per asciugare*) towel.

strofinamento *sm.* rubbing.

strofinare *vt.* to rub.

strombatura *sf.* splay.

strombazzare *vt.* e *vi.* to trumpet.

strombettare *vi.* 1. to blow (*v. irr.*) a trumpet 2. (*auto*) to honk.

stroncare *vt.* 1. to break (*v. irr.*) off 2. (*fig.*) to demolish.

stroncatura *sf.* harsh criticism.

stronzio *sm.* strontium.

stropicciare *vt.* 1. to rub 2. (*i piedi*) to shuffle 3. (*sgualcire*) to crease. ♦ **stropicciarsi** *vr.* 1. (*gli occhi*) to rub oneself 2. (*sgualcirsi*) to crease.

stropiccio *sm. — di piedi*, shuffling.

strozzare *vt.* 1. to strangle 2. (*ostruire*) to obstruct 3. (*fig.*) to choke.

strozzato *agg.* 1. strangled 2. (*soffocato*) choked 3. (*con strozzature*) with narrow passages 4. (*med.*)

strangulated **5.** (*ostruito*) obstructed.

strozzatura *sf.* **1.** strangling **2.** (*il soffocare*) choking **3.** (*ostruzione*) obstruction **4.** (*restringimento*) narrow passage **5.** (*med.*) strangulation.

strozzinaggio *sm.* usury.

strozzino *sm.* usurer.

struggente *agg.* pining.

strùggere *vt.* **1.** to melt **2.** (*fig.*) to wear (*v. irr.*) out. ♦ **strùggersi** *vr.* **1.** to melt **2.** (*affliggersi*) to be distressed **3.** (*languire*) to be consumed (with), to pine (for).

struggimento *sm.* longing.

strumentale *agg.* instrumental.

strumentalismo *sm.* instrumentalism.

strumentare *vt.* to instrument.

strumentazione *sf.* instrumentation.

strumento *sm.* instrument.

strusciare *vt.* **1.** to rub **2.** (*adulare*) to fawn (on). ♦ **strusciarsi** *vr.* to rub (oneself).

strutto *sm.* lard.

struttura *sf.* structure.

strutturale *agg.* structural.

strutturare *vt.* to structure.

strutturazione *sf.* structure.

struzzo *sm.* ostrich.

stuccare[1] *vt.* **1.** to stucco **2.** (*turare*) to fill.

stuccare[2] *vt.* **1.** (*nauseare*) to sicken **2.** (*annoiare*) to bore. ♦ **stuccarsi** *vr.* **1.** to get (*v. irr.*) sick **2.** (*annoiarsi*) to get bored.

stuccatura *sf.* **1.** plastering **2.** (*di dente*) filling.

stucchévole *agg.* **1.** filling **2.** (*nauseante*) sickening **3.** (*noioso*) boring.

stucco *sm.* **1.** stucco **2.** (*per vetri*) putty || *restare di* —, to be nonplussed.

studente *sm.* student.

studentesco *agg.* student (*attr.*).

studiacchiare *vt.* to study fitfully.

studiare *vt.* to study. ♦ **studiarsi** *vr.* to try.

studiato *agg.* (*affettato*) affected.

studio *sm.* **1.** study **2.** (*progetto*) plan **3.** (*cine*) studio || *programma di studi*, curriculum; *essere allo* —, to be under consideration.

studioso *agg.* studious. ♦ **studioso** *sm.* scholar.

stufa *sf.* stove.

stufare *vt.* **1.** to stew **2.** (*fig.*) to bore. ♦ **stufarsi** *vr.* to get (*v. irr.*) bored.

stufato *sm.* stew.

stufo *agg.* fed up (with).

stuoia *sf.* mat.

stuolo *sm.* crowd.

stupefacente *agg.* stupefying. ♦ **stupefacente** *sm.* drug.

stupefare *vt.* to stupefy. ♦ **stupefarsi** *vr.* to be stupefied.

stupefazione *sf.* stupefaction.

stupendamente *avv.* wonderfully.

stupendo *agg.* wonderful.

stupidàggine *sf.* stupidity.

stupidità *sf.* stupidity.

stùpido *agg.* e *sm.* stupid.

stupire *vt.* to astonish. ♦ **stupirsi** *vr.* to be astonished.

stupito *agg.* astonished.

stupore *sm.* astonishment.

stupro *sm.* rape.

sturare *vt.* **1.** to uncork **2.** (*botti*) to unbung.

stuzzicadenti *sm.* tooth-pick.

stuzzicare *vt.* **1.** to prod **2.** (*frugare*) to pick **3.** (*molestare*) to tease **4.** (*stimolare*) to whet.

su *prep.* **1.** on **2.** (*senza contatto; rivestimento*) over **3.** (*al di sopra di*) above **4.** (*circa*) about || *nove volte* — *dieci*, nine times out of ten. ♦ **su** *avv.* **1.** up **2.** (*al piano superiore*) upstairs **3.** (*indosso*) on || — *per giù*, more or less; *in* — (*in avanti*), onwards; *più* —, further up; —, *andiamo!*, come on!

sua *agg.* e *pron.* V. *suo*.

suadente *agg.* persuasive.

subàcqueo *agg.* underwater (*attr.*). ♦ **subàcqueo** *sm.* frogman (*pl.* -men).

subaffittare *vt.* to sublease.

subaffitto *sm.* sublease.

subalpino *agg.* subalpine.

subalterno *agg.* e *sm.* subaltern.

subbuglio *sm.* **1.** turmoil **2.** (*disordine*) mess.

subconscio *sm.* subconscious.

subcosciente *agg.* e *sm.* subconscious.

subdolamente *avv.* underhand.

sùbdolo *agg.* sly.

subentrare *vi.* to take (*v. irr.*) the place (of).

subire *vt.* to undergo (*v. irr.*).

subissare *vt.* **1.** (*sprofondare*) to sink (*v. irr.*) **2.** (*fig.*) to overwhelm.

subisso *sm.* (*gran quantità*) shower.
subitaneità *sf.* suddenness.
subitàneo *agg.* sudden.
sùbito *avv.* **1.** at once **2.** (*presto*) soon || — *prima*, just before; — *dopo*, just after.
sublimare *vt.* to sublimate.
sublimato *sm.* sublimate.
sublimazione *sf.* sublimation.
sublime *agg.* e *sm.* sublime.
sublimità *sf.* sublimity.
sublocazione *sf.* subletting.
sublunare *agg.* sublunar.
subodorare *vt.* to suspect.
subordinare *vt.* to subordinate.
subordinata *sf.* subordinate clause.
subordinato *agg.* e *sm.* subordinate.
subordinazione *sf.* subordination.
subornare *vt.* to suborn.
subornazione *sf.* subornation.
substrato *sm.* substratum (*pl.* -ta).
suburbano *agg.* suburban.
suburbio *sm.* suburb.
succèdere *vi.* **1.** to succeed **2.** (*capitare*) to happen. ◆ **succèdersi** *vr.* to follow one another.
successione *sf.* succession.
successivamente *avv.* afterwards.
successo *sm.* **1.** success **2.** (*esito*) outcome || *aver* —, to be successful.
successore *sm.* successor.
succhiare *vt.* to suck.
succhiata *sf.* suck.
succhiello *sm.* gimlet.
succinto *agg.* **1.** (*di abiti*) scanty **2.** (*conciso*) concise.
succo *sm.* **1.** juice **2.** (*fig.*) pith.
succosità *sf.* **1.** juiciness **2.** (*fig.*) pithiness.
succoso *agg.* **1.** juicy **2.** (*fig.*) pithy.
sùccubo *agg.* entirely dominated (by).
succulento *agg.* **1.** juicy **2.** (*gustoso*) rich.
succursale *sf.* branch.
sud *sm.* south: *del* —, southern, south (*attr.*); *verso* —, southwards.
sudare *vi.* to sweat: — *sette camicie*, to toil hard; — *freddo*, to be in a cold sweat.
sudario *sm.* shroud.
sudata *sf.* sweat.
sudaticcio *agg.* clammy.
sudato *agg.* **1.** sweaty **2.** (*fig.*) hard-earned.
suddetto *agg.* above-mentioned.

suddiàcono *sm.* subdeacon.
sudditanza *sf.* subjection.
sùddito *sm.* subject.
suddividere *vt.* to subdivide.
suddivisione *sf.* subdivision.
sùdicio *agg.* dirty.
sudicione *sm.* dirty fellow.
sudiciume *sm.* dirt.
sudore *sm.* **1.** sweat **2.** (*fig.*) toil.
sudorìfero *agg.* **1.** (*che secerne sudore*) sudoriferous **2.** (*che produce sudore*) sudorific.
sue *agg.* e *pron.* V. *suo.*
sufficiente *agg.* **1.** sufficient **2.** (*altezzoso*) conceited **2.** (*voto sufficiente*) pass mark.
sufficienza *sf.* **1.** sufficiency **2.** (*alterigia*) conceit **3.** (*voto sufficiente*) pass mark || *aria di* —, superior air; *a* —, enough.
suffisso *sm.* suffix.
suffragare *vt.* **1.** to support **2.** (*eccl.*) to pray for.
suffragio *sm.* **1.** suffrage **2.** (*approvazione*) approval.
suggellare *vt.* to seal.
suggello *sm.* seal.
suggerimento *sm.* **1.** suggestion **2.** (*teat.*) prompting.
suggerire *vt.* **1.** to suggest **2.** (*dar l'imbeccata; teat.*) to prompt.
suggeritore *sm.* prompter.
suggestionàbile *agg.* impressionable.
suggestionabilità *sf.* impressionability.
suggestionare *vt.* to influence. ◆ **suggestionarsi** *vr.* to will oneself (to do sthg.), to be influenced.
suggestione *sf.* suggestion.
suggestività *sf.* suggestiveness.
suggestivamente *avv.* evocatively.
suggestivo *agg.* evocative.
sùghero *sm.* **1.** cork **2.** (*albero*) cork-tree.
sugna *sf.* pork fat.
sugo *sm.* **1.** juice **2.** (*di carne*) gravy **3.** (*di pomodoro*) sauce **4.** (*fig.*) gist.
sugosità *sf.* V. *succosità.*
sugoso *agg.* V. *succoso.*
suicida *agg.* suicidal. ◆ **suicida** *s.* suicide.
suicidarsi *vr.* to commit suicide.
suicidio *sm.* suicide.
suino *agg.* swine (*attr.*) || *carne suina*, pork. ◆ **suino** *sm.* swine (*pl. invariato*).
sulfamìdico *sm.* sulphonamide.

sulfùreo *agg.* sulphureous.

sultanato *sm.* sultanate.

sultanina *sf.* sultana.

sultano *sm.* sultan.

summenzionato *agg.* aforesaid.

sunto *sm.* summary.

suo *agg.* 1. (*di lui*) his 2. (*di lei*) her 3. (*di esso*) its 4. (*formula di cortesia*) your. ♦ **suo** *pron.* 1. (*di lui*) his 2. (*di lei*) hers 3. (*di esso*) its 4. (*formula di cortesia*) yours || **i suoi** (*famigliari*), his, her family.

suòcera *sf.* mother-in-law.

suòcero *sm.* father-in-law.

suoi *agg. e pron.* V. *suo.*

suola *sf.* sole.

suolo *sm.* soil, ground.

suonare *vt.* V. *sonare.*

suono *sm.* sound.

suora *sf.* nun, sister.

superàbile *agg.* surmountable.

superaffollato *agg.* overcrowded.

superalimentare *vt.* 1. to overrish 2. (*mecc.*) to overcharge.

superalimentazione *sf.* 1. overfeeding 2. (*mecc.*) overcharging.

superamento *sm.* 1. overcoming 2. (*auto*) overtaking.

superare *vt.* 1. (*oltrepassare*) to exceed 2. (*auto*) to overtake (*v. irr.*) 3. (*attraversare*) to cross 4. (*vincere*) to overcome (*v. irr.*) 5. (*una persona*) to surpass 6. (*un esame, una prova*) to pass.

superbia *sf.* pride.

superbo *agg.* 1. proud 2. (*magnifico*) superb.

superdotato *agg.* highly gifted.

superficiale *agg.* superficial.

superficialità *sf.* superficiality.

superficie *sf.* 1. surface 2. (*area*) area.

superfluo *agg.* superfluous. ♦ **superfluo** *sm.* surplus.

superiora *sf.* Mother Superior.

superiore *agg.* 1. superior 2. (*sovrastante*) upper 3. (*più avanzato*) advanced. ♦ **superiore** *sm.* superior.

superiorità *sf.* superiority.

superlativo *agg. e sm.* superlative.

supermercato *sm.* supermarket.

supernutrizione *sf.* overfeeding.

supersònico *agg.* supersonic.

supèrstite *agg.* surviving. ♦ **supèrstite** *s.* survivor.

superstizione *sf.* superstition.

superstizioso *agg.* superstitious.

superuomo *sm.* superman (*pl.* -men).

supervisione *sf.* supervision.

supervisore *sm.* supervisor.

supinamente *avv.* supinely.

supino *agg.* supine.

suppellèttile *sf.* furnishings (*pl.*).

supplementare *agg.* supplementary.

supplemento *sm.* 1. supplement 2. (*spesa supplementare*) additional charge 3. (*di biglietto ferroviario*) excess fare.

supplente *agg.* temporary. ♦ **supplente** *s.* temporary teacher.

supplenza *sf.* temporary post.

suppletivo *agg.* supplementary.

sùpplica *sf.* 1. entreaty 2. (*petizione*) petition.

supplicante *agg. e s.* suppliant.

supplicare *vt.* to entreat.

supplichévole *agg.* entreating.

supplire *vi.* 1. (*compensare*) to make (*v. irr.*) up (for) 2. (*sostituire*) to substitute (for). ♦ **supplire** *vt.* to take (*v. irr.*) the place of.

supplizio *sm.* torment: *andare al —,* to go (*v. irr.*) to the scaffold.

supporre *vt.* to suppose.

supporto *sm.* support.

supposizione *sf.* supposition.

supposta *sf.* suppository.

supposto che *cong.* suppose (that).

suppurare *vi.* to suppurate.

suppurazione *sf.* suppuration.

supremazìa *sf.* supremacy.

supremo *agg.* supreme: *Comando — (mil.),* headquarters (*pl.*).

surclassare *vt.* to outclass.

surgelare *vt.* to deep-freeze (*v. irr.*).

surrealismo *sm.* surrealism.

surrealista *agg. e s.* surrealist.

surrealìstico *agg.* surrealistic.

surrenale *agg.* suprarenal.

surrettizio *agg.* surreptitious.

surriscaldamento *sm.* overheating.

surriscaldare *vt.* to overheat. ♦ **surriscaldarsi** *vr.* to get (*v. irr.*) overheated.

surrogàbile *agg.* replaceable.

surrogare *vt.* to replace.

surrogato *sm.* substitute.

surrogazione *sf.* (*giur.*) surrogation.

suscettìbile *agg.* 1. susceptible 2. (*permaloso*) touchy.

suscettibilità *sf.* 1. susceptibility 2. (*permalosità*) touchiness || *urtare la — di qu.,* to hurt (*v. irr.*) so.'s feelings.

suscitare vt. **1.** to provoke **2.** (eccitare) to stir up.
suscitatore sm. provoker.
susina sf. plum.
susino sm. plum-tree.
susseguente agg. following.
susseguire vi. to follow.
sussidiare vt. **1.** to support **2.** (di governo) to subsidize.
sussidiario agg. subsidiary.
sussidio sm. subsidy.
sussiego sm. haughtiness.
sussistenza sf. **1.** existence **2.** (sostentamento) subsistence **3.** (mil.) Catering Corps.
sussistere vi. **1.** to subsist **2.** (reggere) to hold (v. irr.) water.
sussultare vi. **1.** to start **2.** (di cose) to shake (v. irr.).
sussulto sm. start.
sussurrare vt. e vi. **1.** to whisper **2.** (criticare) to murmur.
sussurro sm. whisper.
sutura sf. suture.
suturare vt. to suture.
svagare vt. **1.** to divert **2.** (divertire) to amuse. ♦ **svagarsi** vr. **1.** to divert one's mind **2.** (divertirsi) to amuse oneself.
svagatezza sf. absent-mindedness.
svagato agg. absent-minded.
svago sm. amusement.
svaligiamento sm. **1.** robbery **2.** (di una casa) burglary.
svaligiare vt. **1.** to rob **2.** (una casa) to burgle.
svaligiatore sm. **1.** robber **2.** (di case) burglar.
svalutare vt. **1.** to devaluate **2.** (sottovalutare) to undervalue.
svalutazione sf. devaluation.
svanire vi. **1.** to disappear **2.** (dileguarsi, di luce ecc.) to fade.
svanito agg. **1.** (dileguato) vanished **2.** (di mente) feeble-minded.
svantaggio sm. disadvantage.
svantaggioso agg. disadvantageous.
svaporamento sm. evaporation.
svaporare vi. to evaporate.
svariare vt. to vary.
svariato agg. various.
svarione sm. blunder.
svasare vt. (mecc.) to flare.
svasato agg. (di abito) bell-shaped.
svasatura sf. **1.** (di abito) bell-shaping **2.** (mecc.; lo svasare) flaring **3.** (apertura) countersink.
svàstica sf. swastika.
svecchiamento sm. renewal.

svecchiare vt. to renew.
svedese agg. Swedish. ♦ **svedese** sm. Swede.
sveglia sf. **1.** early call **2.** (orologio) alarm clock **3.** (mil.) reveille.
svegliare vt. to wake (v. irr.) (up). ♦ **svegliarsi** vr. to wake (up).
sveglio agg. **1.** awake (pred.) **2.** (fig.) quick-witted.
svelare vt. **1.** to reveal, to disclose **2.** (togliere il velo) to unveil.
svelenire vt. (fig.) to remove the sting from.
svèllere vt. to extirpate.
sveltezza sf. quickness.
sveltire vt. **1.** to quicken **2.** (scaltrire) to wake (v. irr.) up ‖ — la figura, to slim. ♦ **sveltirsi** vr. **1.** to become (v. irr.) quick(er) **2.** (scaltrirsi) to wake up.
svelto agg. **1.** quick **2.** (slanciato) slender **3.** (intelligente) smart. ♦ **svelto** avv. fast ‖ —!, hurry up!
svenare vt. to open so.'s veins. ♦ **svenarsi** vr. to cut (v. irr.) one's veins.
svéndere vt. to undersell (v. irr.).
svéndita sf. (clearance) sale.
svenévole agg. maudlin.
svenimento sm. faint.
svenire vi. to faint.
sventagliare vt. to fan.
sventare vt. to baffle.
sventatezza sf. **1.** thoughtlessness **2.** (atto sventato) thoughtless action.
sventato agg. (sbadato) thoughtless. ♦ **sventato** sm. scatter-brain.
svèntola sf. (schiaffo) slap.
sventolare vt. e vi. to wave. ♦ **sventolarsi** vr. to fan oneself.
sventolìo sm. waving.
sventramento sm. **1.** disembowelment **2.** (demolizione) demolition.
sventrare vt. **1.** to disembowel **2.** (demolire) to demolish.
sventura sf. misfortune: per —, unluckily; per colmo di —, to crown it all.
sventuratamente avv. unfortunately.
sventurato agg. unfortunate.
svenuto agg. unconscious.
svergognare vt. to shame.
svergognatamente avv. shamelessly.
svergognato agg. shameless.
svernamento sm. wintering.
svernare vi. to winter.

svestire *vt.* to undress. ♦ svestirsi *vr.* to undress.

svettare *vt.* to lop. ♦ svettare *vi.* to stand (*v. irr.*) out.

svezzamento *sm.* weaning.

svezzare *vt.* to wean.

sviamento *sm.* 1. diversion 2. (*il traviare*) leading astray 3. (*il traviarsi*) going astray.

sviare *vt.* 1. to divert 2. (*traviare*) to lead (*v. irr.*) astray. ♦ sviarsi *vr.* 1. to be diverted 2. (*traviarsi*) to go (*v. irr.*) astray.

sviato *agg.* led astray (*pred.*).

svignàrsela *vr.* to slink (*v. irr.*) away.

svigorire *vt.* to weaken. ♦ svigorirsi *vr.* to grow (*v. irr.*) weak.

svilimento *sm.* depreciation.

svilire *vt.* to depreciate.

sviluppare *vt.* 1. to develop 2. (*sciogliere*) to loosen 3. (*sprigionare*) to generate. ♦ svilupparsi *vr.* to develop.

sviluppatore *sm.* (*foto*) developer.

sviluppo *sm.* 1. development 2. (*sprigionamento*) generation.

svincolamento *sm.* 1. release 2. (*doganale*) clearance 3. (*riscatto*) redemption.

svincolare *vt.* 1. to release 2. (*sdoganare*) to clear 3. (*riscattare*) to redeem. ♦ svincolarsi *vr.* to get (*v. irr.*) free.

svisare *vt.* (*travisare*) to twist.

sviscerare *vt.* 1. to disembowel 2. (*fig.*) to dissect.

sviscerato *agg.* passionate.

svista *sf.* oversight.

svitare *vt.* to unscrew.

svìzzero *agg.* e *sm.* Swiss.

svogliatezza *sf.* 1. unwillingness 2. (*pigrizia*) laziness.

svogliato *agg.* 1. unwilling 2. (*pigro*) lazy. ♦ svogliato *sm.* lazy-bones.

svolazzare *vi.* to flutter.

svolazzo *sm.* 1. fluttering 2. (*tratto di penna*) flourish.

svòlgere *vt.* 1. to unwind (*v. irr.*) 2. (*trattare*) to develop 3. (*mettere in opera*) to carry out. ♦ svòlgersi *vr.* 1. to unwind 2. (*svilupparsi*) to develop 3. (*accadere*) to take (*v. irr.*) place.

svolgimento *sm.* 1. unwinding 2. (*trattazione*) treatment 3. (*corso*) course 4. (*sviluppo*) development.

svolta *sf.* 1. turn 2. (*fig.*) turning point ‖ *fare una* —, to turn.

svoltare *vi.* to turn.

svuotamento *sm.* emptying.

svuotare *vt.* 1. to empty 2. (*fig.*) to deprive.

T

tabaccaio *sm.* tobacconist.

tabaccare *vt.* to snuff.

tabaccherìa *sf.* tobacconist's.

tabacchiera *sf.* snuff-box.

tabacco *sm.* tobacco.

tabella *sf.* 1. (*lista*) list 2. (*quadro*) board.

tabellone *sm.* notice board.

tabernàcolo *sm.* tabernacle.

tabù *sm.* taboo.

tabulatore *sm.* tabulator.

tacca *sf.* 1. notch 2. (*fig.*) condition.

taccagnerìa *sf.* stinginess.

taccagno *agg.* stingy. ♦ taccagno *sm.* miser.

tacchino *sm.* turkey.

taccia *sf.* 1. reputation 2. (*accusa*) charge.

tacciare *vt.* to charge (with).

tacco *sm.* heel.

taccuino *sm.* note-book.

tacere *vi.* to be silent: *far* —, to silence.

tachicardìa *sf.* tachycardia.

tachìmetro *sm.* tachometer.

tacitare *vt.* 1. to hush up 2. (*un creditore*) to pay (*v. irr.*) off.

tàcito *agg.* 1. silent 2. (*non espresso*) tacit.

taciturno *agg.* silent.

tafano *sm.* gad-fly.

tafferuglio *sm.* brawl.

taglia *sf.* 1. (*riscatto*) ransom 2. (*ricompensa*) reward 3. (*misura*) size.

tagliacarte *sm.* paper-knife (*pl.* -knives).

taglialegna *sm.* wood-cutter.

tagliando *sm.* coupon.

tagliapietre *sm.* stone-cutter.

tagliare *vt.* 1. to cut (*v. irr.*) 2. (*attraversare*) to cut across: — *via*, to cut off ‖ — *a pezzi*, to cut into pieces; — *la corda* (*fig.*), to run (*v. irr.*) away; — *la strada a qu.*, to bar so.'s way. ♦ tagliarsi *vr.* to cut.

tagliatelle *sf. pl.* noodles.
tagliato *agg.* **1.** cut **2.** (*inclinato, disposto*) cut out, fit: *essere — fuori*, to be cut off.
tagliatore *sm.* cutter.
taglieggiare *vt.* to ransom.
tagliente *agg.* sharp.
tagliere *sm.* trencher.
taglio *sm.* **1.** cut **2.** (*il tagliare*) cutting **3.** (*parte tagliente, orlo*) edge **4.** (*dimensione*) size **5.** (*raccolto*) harvest.
tagliola *sf.* snare.
taglione *sm.* retaliation.
tagliuzzare *vt.* to mince.
talare *agg.* talaric: *veste —*, cassock.
talco *sm.* talc: *— borato*, talcum powder.
tale *agg.* **1.** such **2.** (*per tralasciare i dati determinati*) such and such: *il — giorno*, on such and such day **3.** (*suddetto*) above-mentioned || *— e quale*, exactly like, exactly as. ♦ **tale** *pron. indef.* someone.
talea *sf.* scion.
talento *sm.* talent.
talismano *sm.* talisman.
tallonare *vi.* to follow.
talloncino *sm.* slip.
tallone *sm.* heel.
talora *avv.* sometimes.
talpa *sf.* mole.
taluno *agg.* some. ♦ **taluno** *pron.* someone (*pl.* some people).
talvolta *avv.* V. *talora*.
tamarindo *sm.* tamarind.
tamburéggiare *vi.* to drum.
tamburellare *vi.* to drum one's fingers on.
tamburino *sm.* drummer.
tamburo *sm.* **1.** drum **2.** (*mecc.*) cylinder.
tamponamento *sm.* **1.** plugging **2.** (*med.*) tamponage **3.** (*auto*) bumping.
tamponare *vt.* **1.** to plug **2.** (*med.*) to tampon **3.** (*auto*) to bump (against).
tampone *sm.* **1.** plug **2.** (*med.*) tampon **3.** (*di carta asciugante*) blotter.
tana *sf.* den.
tanfo *sm.* stench.
tangente *agg. e sf.* tangent.
tangenza *sf.* tangency: *punto di —*, tangential point.
tangenziale *agg.* tangential.
tànghero *sm.* boor.
tangìbile *agg.* tangible.
tangibilità *sf.* tangibility.

tànnico *agg.* (*chim.*) tannic.
tannino *sm.* tannin.
tanto *avv.* **1.** so **2.** (*coi verbi*) so much **3.** (*di tempo*) so long **4.** (*ad ogni modo*) anyhow || *— quanto*, as much as; *— ... quanto*, as... as (*sia... sia*) both ... and; *— meglio*, so much the better; *— per cambiare*, just for a change. ♦ **tanto** *agg.* so much (*pl.* so many): *— ... quanto*, as much... as (*pl.* as many... as). ♦ **tanto che** *cong.* so (that).
tapiro *sm.* tapir.
tappa *sf.* **1.** (*luogo*) halting-place **2.** (*parte di viaggio*) stage **3.** (*sport*) lap.
tappare *vt.* **1.** to stop **2.** (*con tappo*) to cork.
tapparella *sf.* rolling shutter.
tappeto *sm.* carpet.
tappezzare *vt.* **1.** (*con carta*) to paper **2.** (*coprire*) to cover **3.** (*foderare*) to upholster.
tappezzerìa *sf.* **1.** (*di carta*) paper **2.** (*di stoffa*) tapestry.
tappezziere *sm.* **1.** (*per pareti*) paper hanger **2.** (*per divani ecc.*) upholsterer.
tappo *sm.* **1.** plug **2.** (*per bottiglia*) cap.
tara *sf.* **1.** tare **2.** (*med.; difetto*) taint.
taràntola *sf.* tarantula.
tarare *vt.* **1.** (*mecc.*) to set (*v. irr.*) **2.** (*calibrare*) to calibrate **3.** (*comm.*) to tare.
tarato *agg.* **1.** (*comm.*) tared **2.** (*mecc.*) set **3.** (*med.*) with a taint **4.** (*fig.*) corrupted.
tarchiato *agg.* sturdy.
tardare *vi.* to be late. ♦ **tardare** *vt.* to delay.
tardi *avv.* late: *far —*, to be late.
tardivo *agg.* **1.** (*arretrato*) backward **2.** (*che viene tardi*) tardy.
tardo *agg.* **1.** tardy **2.** (*ottuso*) dull **3.** (*di tempo*) late || *a tarda notte*, late in the night; *tarda età*, old age.
targa *sf.* **1.** (*di metallo*) plate **2.** (*di marmo*) slab **3.** (*auto*) number-plate.
targare *vt.* (*auto*) to give (*v. irr.*) a number-plate (to a car).
tariffa *sf.* tariff.
tarlarsi *vr.* to get (*v. irr.*) worm-eaten.
tarlatura *sf.* worm-hole.

tarlo sm. 1. woodworm 2. (fig.) gnawings (pl.).
tarma sf. moth.
tarmarsi vr. to get (v. irr.) moth-eaten.
tarpare vt. to clip.
tartagliare vi. to stammer.
tartàrico agg. tartaric.
tàrtaro sm. tartar.
tartaruga sf. tortoise.
tartassare vt. to harass.
tartina sf. canapé.
tartufo sm. truffle.
tasca sf. pocket.
tascàbile agg. pocket (attributivo).
tassa sf. 1. tax 2. (d'iscrizione) fee.
tassàbile agg. taxable.
tassàmetro sm. taximeter: — di parcheggio, parking meter.
tassare vt. to tax.
tassativo agg. peremptory.
tassazione sf. taxation.
tassello sm. dowel.
tassì sm. taxi.
tassista sm. taxi-driver.
tasso[1] sm. (comm.) rate.
tasso[2] sm. (bot.) yew.
tasso[3] sm. (zool.) badger.
tastare vt. to feel (v. irr.): — il terreno (fig.), to feel one's way.
tastiera sf. keyboard.
tasto sm. 1. key 2. (tatto) feel 3. (argomento) subject.
tastoni avv. a —, gropingly; andare a —, to grope.
tàttica sf. tactics.
tàttico agg. tactical. ♦ **tàttico** sm. tactician.
tàttile agg. tactile.
tatto sm. 1. touch 2. (fig.) tact || con —, tactfully.
tatuaggio sm. tattoo.
tatuare vt. to tattoo.
taumatùrgico agg. thaumaturgic(al).
taumaturgo sm. thaumaturge.
taurino agg. bull-like (attr.): dal collo —, bull-necked.
tauromachìa sf. bullfight.
tautologìa sf. tautology.
taverna sf. tavern.
taverniere sm. tavern-keeper.
tàvola sf. 1. table 2. (asse) board 3. (di marmo) slab 4. (illustrazione) plate.
tavolaccio sm. plank-bed.
tavolata sf. table.
tavolato sm. 1. (di pavimento) plank floor 2. (mar.) planking 3.

(geogr.) plateau.
tavolozza sf. palette.
tazza sf. cup: — da tè, tea-cup.
te pron. you.
tè sm. tea.
teatrale agg. theatrical.
teatro sm. theatre: — di posa, studio.
tècnica sf. technique.
tecnicismo sm. technicality.
tècnico agg. technical. ♦ **tècnico** sm. technician.
tecnologìa sf. technology.
tecnològico agg. technological.
tedesco agg. e sm. German.
tediare vt. to bore.
tedio sm. boredom.
tedioso agg. boring.
tegame sm. saucepan.
teglia sf. bakepan.
tégola sf. tile: coprire di tegole, to tile.
teiera sf. tea-pot.
teismo sm. theism.
tela sf. 1. cloth 2. (teat.) curtain 3. (dipinto) painting 4. (per dipingere) canvas || — cerata, oilcloth; — di sacco, sackcloth; — di lino, linen; — di ragno, cobweb.
telaio sm. 1. loom 2. (ossatura, cornice) frame.
telecàmera sf. camera.
telecomandare vt. to radiocontrol.
telecomunicazione sf. telecommunication.
telefèrica sf. cableway.
telefonare vt. to (tele)phone.
telefonata sf. (telephone) call.
telefonìa sf. telephony.
telefònico agg. telephone (attr.): cabina telefonica, telephone booth.
telefonista sm. (telephone) operator. ♦ **telefonista** sf. switchboard girl.
telèfono sm. (tele)phone: dare un colpo di —, to ring (v. irr.) up.
telefoto sf. telephotograph.
telegiornale sm. (television) news (-reel).
telegrafare vt. to telegraph.
telegrafìa sf. telegraphy.
telegràfico agg. telegraphic(al).
telegrafista sm. telegraphist.
telègrafo sm. 1. telegraph 2. (ufficio) telegraph-office.
telegramma sm. telegram, wire: fare un — a qu., to wire so.
telèmetro sm. 1. telemeter 2. (in arma da fuoco; foto) rangefinder.

teleobbiettivo *sm.* telephoto lens.
teleologìa *sf.* teleology.
telepatìa *sf.* telepathy.
telerìe *sf. pl.* linen (*sing.*): *commerciante in* —, linen-draper.
teleschermo *sm.* television screen.
telescopio *sm.* telescope.
telescrivente *sf.* teletypewriter.
teleselezione *sf.* long distance dialing.
telespettatore *sm.* televiewer.
teletipìa *sf.* teletype.
teletrasméttere *vt.* to telecast (*v. irr.*).
televisione *sf.* television: *guardare la* —, to watch television; *alla* —, on television; *trasmettere per* —, to telecast.
televisivo *agg.* televisional, television (*attr.*): *trasmissione televisiva*, telecast.
televisore *sm.* television set.
tellùrico *agg.* telluric.
telo *sm.* sheet.
telone *sm.* **1.** (*teat.*) curtain **2.** (*cine*) screen.
tema[1] *sf.* (*paura*) fear: *per* — *che*, lest.
tema[2] *sm.* **1.** theme **2.** (*scolastico*) composition.
temàtica *sf.* themes (*pl.*).
temàtico *agg.* thematic(al).
temerarietà *sf.* rashness.
temerario *agg.* rash.
temere *vt. e vi.* **1.** to fear **2.** (*patire*) not to stand (*v. irr.*) || *temo di sì*, I fear so; *temo di no*, I fear not.
temìbile *agg.* dreadful.
tèmpera *sf.* **1.** (*metal.*) hardening **2.** (*pitt.*) distemper || *dipingere a* —, to distemper.
temperamatite *sm.* pencil-sharpener.
temperamento *sm.* **1.** temperament **2.** (*alleviamento*) mitigation.
temperante *agg.* temperate.
temperanza *sf.* temperance.
temperare *vt.* **1.** to temper **2.** (*matite*) to sharpen.
temperato *agg.* **1.** temperate **2.** (*di matita*) sharpened.
temperatura *sf.* temperature.
temperino *sm.* penknife (*pl.* -knives).
tempesta *sf.* tempest, storm.
tempestare *vt.* **1.** (*assalire*) to assail **2.** (*importunare*) to harass **3.** (*cospargere*) to strew (*v. irr.*) (sthg.

with). ♦ **tempestare** *vi.* **1.** to storm **2.** (*grandinare*) to hail.
tempestività *sf.* timeliness.
tempestivo *agg.* timely.
tempestoso *agg.* stormy.
tempia *sf.* temple.
tempio *sm.* temple.
tempo *sm.* **1.** time **2.** (*atmosferico*) weather **3.** (*gramm.*) tense **4.** (*fase*) stage **5.** (*cine*) part || *un* —, once; *col passare del* —, in the long run; *molto* — *prima, dopo*, long before, after; *a* — *perso*, in one's spare time; *per* —, early.
temporale[1] *agg.* temporal.
temporale[2] *agg.* (*anat.*) temporal.
temporale[3] *sm.* storm.
temporalesco *agg.* stormy.
temporaneità *sf.* temporariness.
temporàneo *agg.* temporary.
temporeggiare *vi.* to temporize.
tempra *sf.* **1.** temper **2.** (*metal.*) hardening **3.** (*fig.*) character.
temprare *vt.* **1.** to temper **2.** (*fig.*) to strengthen **3.** (*plasmare*) to form.
temprato *agg.* (*abituato*) inured.
tenace *agg.* tenacious.
tenacia *sf.* tenacity.
tenaglia *sf.* pincers (*pl.*).
tenda *sf.* **1.** curtain **2.** (*da campo*) tent.
tendaggio *sm.* curtain.
tendente *agg.* tending.
tendenza *sf.* **1.** tendency **2.** inclination.
tendenziale *agg.* tendential.
tendenziosità *sf.* tendentiousness.
tendenzioso *agg.* tendentious.
tèndere *vt.* **1.** (*protendere*) to stretch (out) **2.** (*mettere in tensione*) to tighten. ♦ **tèndere** *vi.* **1.** to tend **2.** (*mirare*) to aim (at).
tendina *sf.* curtain.
tèndine *sm.* tendon.
tenditore *sm.* turnbuckle.
tènebra *sf.* darkness.
tenebroso *agg.* **1.** dark **2.** (*sinistro*) sinister.
tenente *sm.* lieutenant.
tenere *vt.* **1.** to keep (*v. irr.*) **2.** (*sostenere, considerare, contenere*) to hold (*v. irr.*) || — *una lezione*, to give (*v. irr.*) a lesson. ♦ **tenersi** *vr.* (*seguire*) to follow: — *al corrente*, to keep tabs on.
tenerezza *sf.* tenderness.
tènero *agg.* tender. ♦ **tènero** *sm.* **1.** (*parte tenera*) tender part **2.** (*affetto*) sympathy.

tenia *sf.* tapeworm.
tennis *sm.* tennis.
tennista *s.* tennis-player.
tenore *sm.* tenor.
tenorile *agg.* tenor (*attr.*).
tensione *sf.* tension.
tentacolare *agg.* tentacular.
tentàcolo *sm.* tentacle.
tentare *vt.* **1.** to tempt **2.** (*provare*) to try.
tentativo *sm.* attempt.
tentatore *agg.* tempting. ♦ **tentatore** *sm.* tempter.
tentazione *sf.* temptation.
tentennamento *sm.* **1.** shaking **2.** (*traballamento*) tottering **3.** (*esitazione*) hesitation.
tentennare *vt.* to shake (*v. irr.*). ♦ **tentennare** *vi.* **1.** to totter **2.** (*esitare*) to waver.
tentoni *agg.* gropingly.
tenue *agg.* **1.** small **2.** (*leggero*) soft.
tenuità *sf.* **1.** smallness **2.** (*levità*) slightness.
tenuta *sf.* **1.** (*proprietà*) estate **2.** (*capacità*) capacity **3.** (*abiti*) clothes (*pl.*) **4.** (*tec.*) seal || — *di strada*, roadability; *a* — *d'acqua*, watertight.
teocràtico *agg.* theocratic(al).
teocrazìa *sf.* theocracy.
teologale *agg.* theological.
teologìa *sf.* theology.
teològico *agg.* theologic(al).
teòlogo *sm.* theologian.
teorema *sm.* theorem.
teorìa *sf.* **1.** theory **2.** (*fila*) string.
teòrico *agg.* theoretic(al).
teorizzare *vi.* to theorize.
tepore *sm.* lukewarmness.
teppa *sf.* rabble.
teppista *sm.* teddy-boy.
terapèutico *agg.* therapeutic(al).
terapìa *sf.* therapy.
terebinto *sm.* terebinth.
tèrgere *vt.* to wipe (off).
tergicristallo *sm.* windscreen wiper.
tergiversare *vi.* to hesitate.
tergiversazione *sf.* hesitation.
tergo *sm.* back: *segue a* —, please turn over.
termale *agg.* thermal: *stazione* —, spa.
terme *sf. pl.* thermal springs.
tèrmico *agg.* thermic.
terminale *agg.* terminal.
terminare *vt. e vi.* to end.

tèrmine *sm.* **1.** term **2.** (*limite*) limit **3.** (*fine*) end || *contratto a* —, time-contract; *portare a* —, to carry out.
terminologìa *sf.* terminology.
tèrmite *sf.* termite.
termocoperta *sf.* thermal blanket.
termodinàmica *sf.* thermodynamics.
termoelèttrico *agg.* thermoelectric(al).
termòforo *sm.* warming pad.
termògeno *agg.* thermogenetic.
termoiònico *agg.* thermionic.
termòmetro *sm.* thermometer: *il* — *segna...*, the thermometer stands at...
termonucleare *agg.* thermonuclear.
termos *sm.* vacuum bottle.
termosifone *sm.* (*radiatore*) radiator.
termòstato *sm.* thermostat.
ternario *agg.* ternary.
terno *sm.* tern. ♦ **terno** *agg.* triple.
terra *sf.* **1.** (*globo terracqueo*) earth **2.** (*paese; l'opposto del mare*) land **3.** (*terreno*) ground || — —, earth bound; *raso* —, to the ground.
terracotta *sf.* terracotta: *vasellame di* —, earthenware.
terraferma *sf.* dry land.
terraglia *sf.* pottery.
terranova *sm.* (*cane*) Newfoundland dog.
terrapieno *sm.* **1.** bank **2.** (*di fiume*) embankment.
terràqueo *agg.* terraqueous.
terrazza *sf.* **1.** terrace **2.** (*balcone*) balcony.
terrazziere *sm.* digger.
terrazzo *sm.* V. *terrazza*.
terremoto *sm.* earthquake.
terreno[1] *agg.* earthly.
terreno[2] *sm.* ground.
tèrreo *agg.* **1.** earthy **2.** (*di colorito*) wan, sallow.
terrestre *agg.* terrestrial, earthly.
terrìbile *agg.* terrible.
terriccio *sm.* mould.
terriero *agg.* land (*attr.*).
terrificante *agg.* terrifying.
terrificare *vt.* to terrify.
terrina *sf.* tureen.
territoriale *agg.* territorial.
territorio *sm.* territory.
terrore *sm.* terror: *incutere* — *a qu.*, to strike (*v. irr.*) so. with terror.
terrorismo *sm.* terrorism.

terrorista *s.* terrorist.
terrorìstico *agg.* terroristic.
terrorizzare *vt.* to terrorize.
terroso *agg.* earthy.
terso *agg.* clear.
terza *sf.* **1.** (*di scuola, treno*) third class **2.** (*di auto*) third gear.
terzetto *sm.* trio.
terziario *agg. e sm.* tertiary.
terzina *sf.* tercet.
terzino *sm.* (*sport*) full back.
terzo *agg.* third. ♦ **terzo** *sm.* **1.** third **2.** (*terza persona*) third person || *terzi*, third party.
terzùltimo *agg. e sm.* last but two.
tesa *sf.* brim.
tesaurizzare *vt.* to treasure.
teschio *sm.* skull.
tesi *sf.* thesis (*pl.* -ses).
teso *agg.* taut.
tesorerìa *sf.* treasury.
tesoriere *sm.* treasurer.
tesoro *sm.* **1.** treasure **2.** (*pol.*) treasury.
tèssera *sf.* **1.** card **2.** (*di mosaico*) tessera (*pl.* -rae).
tesseramento *sm.* **1.** rationing **2.** (*reclutamento*) enrolment.
tesserare *vt.* **1.** to ration **2.** (*arruolare*) to enrol.
tèssere *vt.* to weave (*v. irr.*).
tèssile *agg.* textile. ♦ **tèssile** *sm.* weaver.
tessitore *sm.* weaver.
tessitura *sf.* **1.** weaving **2.** (*disposizione dei fili*) texture.
tessuto *sm.* **1.** fabric **2.** (*med.; fig.*) tissue || *negozio di tessuti*, draper's shop.
testa *sf.* head: *colpo di —*, rash act; *essere in — a tutti*, to be ahead of everybody.
testamentario *agg.* testamentary.
testamento *sm.* will.
testardàggine *sf.* stubbornness.
testardo *agg.* stubborn.
testata *sf.* **1.** head **2.** (*colpo*) butt **3.** (*di giornale*) heading.
teste *s.* witness: *— d'accusa, di difesa*, witness for the prosecution, the defence.
testìcolo *sm.* testicle.
testimonianza *sf.* **1.** witness **2.** (*prova*) evidence || *far —*, to bear (*v. irr.*) witness.
testimoniare *vt. e vi.* **1.** to witness **2.** (*attestare*) to testify.
testimonio *sm.* witness.
testo *sm.* text.

testuale *agg.* **1.** textual **2.** (*esatto*) exact.
tetànico *agg.* tetanic.
tètano *sm.* tetanus.
tetraedro *sm.* tetrahedron.
tetràggine *sf.* gloom.
tetràgono *agg.* (*fig.*) steadfast.
tetralogìa *sf.* tetralogy.
tetro *agg.* gloomy.
tettarella *sf.* dummy.
tetto *sm.* roof: *— a capanna*, saddle roof.
tettoia *sf.* shed.
tettònica *sf.* tectonics.
teutònico *agg.* Teutonic. ♦ **teutònico** *sm.* Teuton.
ti *pron.* **1.** you, to you **2.** (*r.*) yourself.
tiara *sf.* tiara.
tibia *sf.* tibia.
tic *sm.* tic.
ticchettare *vi.* to tick.
ticchettìo *sm.* ticking.
ticchio *sm.* fancy.
tièpido *agg.* tepid.
tifo *sm.* **1.** typhus **2.** (*fig.*) fanaticism.
tifone *sm.* typhoon.
tifoso *sm.* **1.** typhus patient **2.** (*fig.*) fan.
tiglio *sm.* lime.
tigna *sf.* ringworm.
tignola *sf.* moth.
tigrato *agg.* striped.
tigre *sf.* tiger.
timbrare *vt.* **1.** to stamp **2.** (*lettere*) to postmark || *— a secco*, to emboss.
timbratura *sf.* **1.** stamping **2.** (*postale*) postmarking.
timbro *sm.* **1.** stamp **2.** (*di suono*) timbre **3.** (*postale*) postmark || *— a secco*, embossed stamp.
timidezza *sf.* shyness.
tìmido *agg.* shy.
timo *sm.* thyme.
timone *sm.* helm.
timoniere *sm.* helmsman (*pl.* -men).
timorato *agg.* **1.** respectful **2.** (*scrupoloso*) scrupulous.
timore *sm.* fear: *aver —*, to fear, to be afraid.
timoroso *agg.* fearful.
tìmpano *sm.* **1.** eardrum **2.** (*mus.*) kettle-drum **3.** (*arch.*) gable.
tinca *sf.* tench.
tinello *sm.* living-room.
tingere *vt.* to dye (*v. irr.*). ♦ **tìngersi** *vr.* to dye oneself.

tino sm. vat.

tinozza sf. tub.

tinta sf. 1. (colore) hue 2. (materia colorante) dye 3. (tintura) dyeing.

tinteggiare vt. to paint.

tintinnare vi. to tinkle.

tintinnio sm. tinkling.

tintore sm. 1. dyer 2. (anche per lavature a secco) cleaner.

tintoria sf. 1. dyeworks (pl.) 2. (negozio anche per lavature a secco) dry cleaners' shop.

tintura sf. V. tinta.

tipico agg. typical.

tipo sm. 1. type 2. (modello) pattern 3. (individuo) fellow.

tipografia sf. 1. typography 2. (mecc.) letterpress printing.

tipografico agg. typographic(al).

tipografo sm. typographer.

tiraggio sm. draught.

tiralinee sm. drawing-pen.

tiranneggiare vt. to tyrannize.

tirannia sf. tyranny.

tirannico agg. tyrannical.

tirannide sf. tyranny.

tiranno sm. tyrant.

tirante sm. 1. (mecc.) connecting rod 2. (arch.) tie-beam.

tirapiedi sm. drudge.

tirare vt. 1. to draw (v. irr.), to pull 2. (scagliare) to throw (v. irr.). ♦ **tirare** vi. 1. (sparare) to shoot (v. irr.) 2. (di tiraggio) to draw 3. (di vestito) to be tight. ♦ **tirarsi** vr. to draw.

tirata sf. 1. pull 2. (invettiva) tirade.

tiratore sm. shooter.

tiratura sf. 1. (tip.) printing 2. (numero di copie stampate) circulation.

tirchieria sf. niggardliness.

tirchio agg. niggardly.

tiritera sf. rigmarole.

tiro sm. 1. (trazione) draught 2. (lancio) throw 3. (sparo) shot 4. (scherzo) trick.

tirocinio sm. apprenticeship.

tiroide sf. thyroid.

tisana sf. ptisan.

tisi sf. consumption.

tisico agg. e sm. consumptive.

tisiologia sf. phthisiology.

tisiologo sm. phthisiologist.

titanico agg. titanic.

titillare vt. to tickle.

titolare agg. 1. regular 2. (nominale) titular. ♦ **titolare** s. 1. regular holder 2. (proprietario) owner 3. (capo) principal.

titolato agg. titled.

titolo sm. 1. title 2. (qualifica) qualification 3. (documento) document 4. (comm.) security.

titubante agg. hesitating.

titubanza sf. hesitation.

titubare vi. to hesitate.

tizianesco agg. 1. Titianesque 2. (di capelli) titian.

tizio sm. fellow.

tizzone sm. brand.

toccare vt. to touch || — un porto, to call at. ♦ **toccare** vi. 1. (capitare) to happen 2. (spettare) to fall (v. irr.).

toccasana sm. cure-all.

tocco[1] agg. (pazzoide) touched.

tocco[2] sm. 1. touch 2. (battito) knock 3. (rintocco) toll || al —, at one o'clock.

tocco[3] sm. (berretto) toque.

toga sf. gown.

togato agg. gowned.

togliere vt. 1. to take (v. irr.) 2. (liberare) to relieve. ♦ **togliersi** vr. 1. to get (v. irr.) off 2. (un indumento) to take off || — la vita, to commit suicide.

toletta sf. toilet.

tollerabile agg. tolerable.

tollerante agg. tolerant.

tolleranza sf. tolerance.

tollerare vt. 1. to tolerate 2. (sopportare) to bear (v. irr.).

tomaia sf. vamp.

tomba sf. grave.

tombale agg. grave (attr.).

tombino sm. manhole.

tombola sf. 1. (gioco) "tomboia" 2. (caduta) tumble.

tombolare vi. to tumble down.

tomismo sm. Thomism.

tomista agg. e sm. Thomist.

tomo sm. 1. tome 2. (persona) chap.

tonaca sf. frock: gettare la —, to give (v. irr.) up the frock.

tonalità sf. tonality.

tonante agg. thundering.

tondeggiante agg. roundish.

tondeggiare vi. to be roundish.

tondello sm. round.

tondo agg. e sm. round || chiaro e —, clearly.

tonfo sm. splash.

tonico agg. e sm. tonic.

tonificare vt. to brace.

tonnellaggio sm. tonnage.

tonnellata sf. ton.

tonno sm. tunny.

tono *sm.* 1. tone 2. (*accordo*) tune 3. (*mus.*) strain.

tonsilla *sf.* tonsil.

tonsillectomìa *sf.* tonsillectomy.

tonsillite *sf.* tonsillitis.

tonsura *sf.* tonsure.

tonsurare *vt.* to tonsure.

tonto *agg.* dull. ♦ **tonto** *sm.* dunce.

topaia *sf.* (*fig.*) hovel.

topazio *sm.* topaz.

tòpica *sf.* 1. topic 2. (*errore*) blunder.

tòpico *agg.* topical.

topo *sm.* mouse (*pl.* mice), rat || — *di biblioteca* (*fig.*), bookworm; — *di albergo* (*fig.*), hotel thief.

topografia *sf.* topography.

topogràfico *agg.* topographic(al).

topologìa *sf.* topology.

toponomàstica *sf.* toponymy.

toppa *sf.* 1. (*pezza*) patch 2. (*di serratura*) keyhole || *mettere una* —, to patch up.

torace *sm.* thorax, chest.

torba *sf.* peat.

torbidezza *sf.* 1. turbidity 2. (*esser fosco*) gloominess.

tòrbido *agg.* 1. turbid 2. (*fosco*) gloomy 3. (*inquieto*) troubled. ♦ **tòrbido** *sm.* (*disordine*) disorder: *pescare nel* —, to fish in troubled water.

torbiera *sf.* peat-bog.

tòrcere *vt.* 1. to wring (*v. irr.*) 2. (*attorcigliare*) to twist || *dare del filo da* —, to give (*v. irr.*) a lot of trouble; — *il naso* (*fig.*), to turn up one's nose (at). ♦ **tòrcersi** *vr.* to twist.

torchiare *vt.* to press.

torchiatura *sf.* pressing.

torchio *sm.* press.

torcia *sf.* torch.

torcicollo *sm.* stiff neck.

torcitore *sm.* twister.

torcitura *sf.* twist.

tordo *sm.* thrush.

torero *sm.* bullfighter.

torma *sf.* swarm.

tormalina *sf.* tourmaline.

tormenta *sf.* blizzard.

tormentare *vt.* to torment. ♦ **tormentarsi** *vr.* to worry.

tormentato *agg.* (*inquieto*) restless.

tormento *sm.* torment.

tormentoso *agg.* tormenting.

tornaconto *sm.* profit.

tornado *sm.* tornado.

tornante *sm.* bend.

tornare *vi.* 1. to return 2. (*di conti*) to be correct.

tornasole *sm.* litmus.

torneo *sm.* tournament.

tornio *sm.* lathe.

tornire *vt.* 1. (*mecc.*) to turn 2. (*fig.*) to polish.

tornito *agg.* 1. (*rotondo*) round 2. (*ben fatto*) well-shaped.

tornitore *sm.* turner.

toro *sm.* bull.

torpediniera *sf.* torpedo-boat.

torpedo *sf.* torpedo.

torpedone *sm.* (motor-)coach.

tòrpido *agg.* torpid.

torpore *sm.* torpor.

torre *sf.* tower.

torrefare *vt.* 1. to torrefy 2. (*caffè*) to roast.

torrefazione *sf.* 1. torrefaction 2. (*di caffè*) roasting 3. (*negozio*) coffee store.

torreggiare *vi.* to tower.

torrente *sm.* torrent.

torrentizio *agg.* torrent-like.

torrenziale *agg.* torrential.

torretta *sf.* (*mil.; mar.*) turret.

tòrrido *agg.* torrid.

torrione *sm.* donjon.

torrone *sm.* nougat.

torsione *sf.* torsion.

torso *sm.* 1. trunk 2. (*di statua*) torso.

tòrsolo *sm.* 1. (*di verdura*) stump 2. (*di frutta*) core.

torta *sf.* cake.

tortiera *sf.* bakepan.

torto *agg.* 1. (*piegato*) bent 2. (*contorto*) twisted.

torto *sm.* 1. wrong 2. (*colpa*) fault || *aver* —, to be wrong; *far* — *a qu.*, to wrong so.; *a* —, wrongly.

tòrtora *sf.* turtle-dove.

tortuosità *sf.* tortuosity.

tortuoso *agg.* tortuous.

tortura *sf.* torture.

torturare *vt.* to torture. ♦ **torturarsi** *vr.* to worry.

torvo *agg.* grim.

tosare *vt.* to shear (*v. irr.*).

tosatrice *sf.* clippers (*pl.*).

tosatura *sf.* shearing.

toscano *agg.* e *sm.* Tuscan.

tosse *sf.* cough.

tossicchiare *vi.* to keep (*v. irr.*) on coughing.

tossicità *sf.* toxicity.

tòssico *agg.* toxic. ♦ **tòssico** *sm.* toxicant.

tossicologìa *sf.* toxicology.
tossicòlogo *sm.* toxicologist.
tossicomanìa *sf.* toxicomania.
tossina *sf.* toxin.
tossire *vi.* to cough.
tostapane *sm.* toaster.
tostare *vt.* **1.** to toast **2.** (*caffè*) to roast.
tosto¹ *avv.* at once.
tosto² *agg.* hard || *faccia tosta,* cheek.
tosto³ *sm.* toast.
totale *agg. e sm.* total: *in —,* in all.
totalità *sf.* **1.** totality **2.** (*numero complessivo*) mass.
totalitario *agg.* totalitarian.
totalitarismo *sm.* totalitarianism.
totalizzare *vt.* **1.** to totalize **2.** (*sport*) to score.
totalizzatore *sm.* totalizer.
tovaglia *sf.* (table-)cloth.
tovagliolo *sm.* napkin.
tozzo¹ *agg.* squat, stocky.
tozzo² *sm.* piece: *un — di pane,* a crust of bread.
tra *prep.* **1.** (*fra due persone, cose, gruppi*) between **2.** (*fra più di due*) among **3.** (*nel mezzo di*) amid **4.** (*di tempo*) (with)in.
traballare *vi.* **1.** to stagger **2.** (*di vettura*) to jolt || *entrare, uscire traballando,* to stagger in, out.
trabeazione *sf.* trabeation.
trabìccolo *sm.* ramshackle vehicle.
traboccare *vi.* to overflow.
trabocchetto *sm.* trap.
tracagnotto *agg.* squat.
tracannare *vt.* to gulp down.
traccia *sf.* **1.** trace **2.** (*segno*) mark **3.** (*orme*) footsteps (*pl.*) **4.** (*schema*) outline.
tracciare *vt.* to trace (out): *— a grandi linee,* to outline.
tracciato *sm.* layout.
tracciatore *sm.* tracer.
trachea *sf.* windpipe.
tracheale *agg.* tracheal.
tracheite *sf.* tracheitis.
tracolla *sf.* baldric: *portare qc. a —,* to carry sthg. across one's back.
tracollare *vi.* **1.** to lose (*v. irr.*) one's balance **2.** (*cadere*) to collapse.
tracollo *sm.* collapse: *portare al —,* to bring (*v. irr.*) to ruin.
tracoma *sm.* trachoma.
tracotante *agg.* haughty.
tracotanza *sf.* haughtiness.

tradimento *sm.* **1.** treason **2.** (*infedeltà*) betrayal || *a —* (*agg.*), treacherous, (*avv.*) treacherously.
tradire *vt.* **1.** to betray **2.** (*di coniuge*) to be unfaithful (to).
traditore *agg.* treacherous. ♦ **traditore** *sm.* traitor.
tradizionale *agg.* traditional.
tradizionalismo *sm.* traditionalism.
tradizionalista *s.* traditionalist.
tradizione *sf.* tradition: *per —,* traditionally.
tradotta *sf.* troop-train.
traducìbile *agg.* translatable.
tradurre *vt.* to translate: *— in atto,* to carry out; *— in carcere,* to take (*v. irr.*) to prison.
traduttore *sm.* translator.
traduzione *sf.* translation.
traente *s.* (*comm.*) drawer.
trafelato *agg.* breathless.
trafficante *sm.* dealer.
trafficare *vi.* **1.** to deal (*v. irr.*) **2.** (*affaccendarsi*) to bustle about.
tràffico *sm.* **1.** traffic **2.** (*comm.*) trade.
trafìggere *vt.* to pierce (through).
trafila *sf.* **1.** procedure **2.** (*mecc.*) draw-plate.
trafilare *vt.* to draw (*v. irr.*).
trafiletto *sm.* paragraph.
traforare *vt.* **1.** to perforate **2.** (*ricamare*) to embroider with open-work.
traforato *agg.* **1.** perforated **2.** (*ricamato a traforo*) open-work (*attr.*).
traforatrice *sf.* fret-sawing machine.
traforo *sm.* **1.** perforation **2.** (*galleria*) tunnel **3.** (*falegnameria*) fretwork **4.** (*ricamo*) open-work.
trafugamento *sm.* stealing.
trafugare *vt.* to steal (*v. irr.*).
tragedia *sf.* tragedy.
tragediògrafo *sm.* tragedian.
traghettare *vt.* to ferry.
traghetto *sm.* ferry-boat.
tragicità *sf.* tragicalness.
tràgico *agg.* tragical. ♦ **tràgico** *sm.* tragedian.
tragicòmico *agg.* tragicomic(al).
tragicommedia *sf.* tragicomedy.
tragitto *sm.* **1.** way **2.** (*viaggio*) journey.
traguardo *sm.* goal.
traiettoria *sf.* trajectory.
trainare *vt.* to haul.
tràino *sm.* **1.** haulage **2.** (*carro*) truck.

tralasciare vt. to leave (v. irr.) out, to omit.

tralcio sm. shoot.

traliccio sm. 1. (tela) ticking 2. (per costruzioni) trellis || — di ferro, iron framework.

tralice (nella loc. avv.) in —, askance.

tralignamento sm. degeneration.

tralignare vi. to degenerate.

tralùcere vi. to shine (v. irr.) (through).

tram sm. tramcar.

trama sf. 1. weft 2. (fig.) plot.

tramaglio sm. trammel.

tramandare vt. to hand down.

tramare vt. 1. to weave (v. irr.) 2. (fig.) to plot.

trambusto sm. bustle.

tramenare vt. e vi. to move about.

tramenìo sm. bustle.

tramestare vt. to rummage.

tramestìo sm. 1. rummaging 2. (trepestio) stamping.

tramezzare vt. to partition.

tramezzino sm. sandwich.

tramezzo sm. partition.

tràmite sm. path: — qu., through so.

tramoggia sf. hopper.

tramontana sf. 1. north 2. (vento) north wind || perder la —, to lose (v. irr.) one's head.

tramontare vi. 1. to set (v. irr.) 2. (svanire) to fade.

tramonto sm. 1. setting 2. (del sole) sunset 3. (declino) decline.

tramortimento sm. swoon.

tramortire vt. to stun.

trampoliere sm. wader.

trampolino sm. spring-board.

tràmpolo sm. stilt.

tramutare vt. to change. ♦ **tramutarsi** vr. to change.

trancia sf. 1. shears (pl.) 2. (fetta) slice.

tranciare vt. to shear.

tranello sm. snare.

trangugiare vt. to swallow.

tranne prep. but.

tranquillante agg. tranquillizing. ♦ **tranquillante** sm. tranquillizer.

tranquillità sf. calmness.

tranquillizzare vt. 1. to calm 2. (rassicurare) to reassure.

tranquillo agg. calm: star —, to keep (v. irr.) quiet; sta' —!, do not worry!

transalpino agg. transalpine.

transatlàntico agg. transatlantic. ♦ **transatlàntico** sm. liner.

transazione sf. 1. transaction 2. (accomodamento) arrangement 3. (compromesso) compromise.

transcontinentale agg. transcontinental.

transetto sm. transept.

trànsfuga s. runaway.

transìgere vt. e vi. to compromise.

transistore sm. transistor.

transitàbile agg. practicable.

transitabilità sf. practicability.

transitare vi. to pass through.

transitivo agg. e sm. transitive.

trànsito sm. transit.

transitorio agg. transitory.

transizione sf. transition.

transoceànico agg. transoceanic.

transustanziazióne sf. transubstantiation.

tranvìa sf. tramway.

tranviario agg. tramcar (attr.).

tranviere sm. 1. tram-driver 2. (bigliettario) tram-conductor.

trapanare vt. 1. to drill 2. (med.) to trepan.

trapanazione sf. 1. drilling 2. (med.) trepanation.

tràpano sm. 1. drill 2. (med.) trepan.

trapassare vt. to pierce through. ♦ **trapassare** vi. (morire) to die.

trapasso sm. 1. (morte) death 2. (giur.; comm.) transfer.

trapelare vi. to leak out.

trapezio sm. 1. trapezium 2. (da ginnastica) trapeze.

trapiantare vt. to transplant. ♦ **trapiantarsi** vr. (stabilirsi) to settle.

trapianto sm. 1. transplantation 2. (tessuto trapiantato) graft.

trappista sm. Trappist.

tràppola sf. trap: prendere in —, to trap.

trapunta sf. quilt.

trapuntare vt. 1. to quilt 2. (ricamare) to embroider.

trapunto agg. 1. quilted 2. (ricamato) embroidered || — di stelle, starry.

trarre vt. 1. to draw (v. irr.) 2. (ottenere) to get (v. irr.). ♦ **trarsi** vr. to draw.

trasalire vi. to startle: far —, to startle.

trasandato agg. shabby.

trasbordare *vt.* **1.** to transfer **2.** (*traghettare*) to ferry.

trasbordo *sm.* **1.** transfer **2.** (*traghetto*) ferrying across.

trascendentale *agg.* transcendental.

trascendentalismo *sm.* transcendentalism.

trascendente *agg.* transcendent.

trascendenza *sf.* transcendence.

trascéndere *vt.* to transcend. ◆ **trascéndere** *vi.* to let (*v. irr.*) oneself go.

trascinare *vt.* **1.** to drag **2.** (*affascinare*) to fascinate.

trascòrrere *vt.* (*il tempo*) to spend (*v. irr.*). ◆ **trascòrrere** *vi.* **1.** (*di tempo*) to pass **2.** (*lasciar correre*) to pass over.

trascorso *agg.* past. ◆ **trascorso** *sm.* (*errore*) slip.

trascrittore *sm.* transcriber.

trascrìvere *vt.* **1.** to transcribe **2.** (*giur.*) to register.

trascrizione *sf.* **1.** transcription **2.** (*giur.*) registration **3.** (*trapasso*) transfer.

trascuràbile *agg.* negligible.

trascurare *vt.* to neglect. ◆ **trascurarsi** *vr.* not to care of oneself.

trascuratezza *sf.* **1.** negligence **2.** (*sciatteria*) slovenliness.

trascurato *agg.* **1.** (*negligente*) careless **2.** (*sciatto*) sloven.

trasecolare *vi.* to be amazed.

trasecolato *agg.* amazed.

trasferìbile *agg.* transferable.

trasferimento *sm.* transfer.

trasferire *vt.* to transfer. ◆ **trasferirsi** *vr.* to (re)move.

trasferta *sf.* **1.** transfer **2.** (*indennità*) travelling allowance || *in* —, on transfer; *partita in* — (*sport*), out match.

trasfigurare *vt.* to transfigure. ◆ **trasfigurarsi** *vr.* to become (*v. irr.*) transfigured.

trasfigurazione *sf.* transfiguration.

trasfóndere *vt.* **1.** to transfuse **2.** (*fig.*) to instil.

trasformàbile *agg.* convertible.

trasformare *vt.* to change, to turn. ◆ **trasformarsi** *vr.* to change.

trasformatore *sm.* transformer.

trasformazione *sf.* transformation.

trasformismo *sm.* transformism.

trasfusione *sf.* transfusion.

trasgredire *vt. e vi.* to infringe.

trasgressione *sf.* infringement.

trasgressore *sm.* infringer.

traslazione *sf.* **1.** transfer **2.** (*fis.; eccl.*) translation.

traslocare *vt. e vi.* to move.

trasloco *sm.* removal.

traslùcido *agg.* translucent.

trasméttere *vt.* to transmit.

trasmettitore *sm.* transmitter.

trasmigrare *vi.* to transmigrate.

trasmigrazione *sf.* transmigration.

trasmissìbile *agg.* transmissible.

trasmissione *sf.* **1.** transmission **2.** (*giur.*) transfer **3.** (*mecc.*) drive || — *radio*, broadcast; — *televisiva*, telecast.

trasmittente *agg.* transmitting.

trasognato *agg.* dreamy.

trasparente *agg.* transparent.

trasparenza *sf.* transparence.

trasparire *vi.* **1.** to shine (*v. irr.*) through **2.** (*esser trasparente*) to be transparent || *lasciar* —, to betray.

traspirare *vi.* to transpire.

traspirazione *sf.* transpiration.

trasporre *vt.* to transpose.

trasportàbile *agg.* transportable.

trasportare *vt.* **1.** to carry **2.** (*fig.*) to carry away. ◆ **trasportarsi** *vr.* to go (*v. irr.*).

trasportatore *sm.* conveyer: — *a nastro*, belt-conveyer.

trasporto *sm.* transport: *nave da* —, cargo; *spese di* —, carriage.

trasposizione *sf.* transposition.

trastullare *vt.* to amuse. ◆ **trastullarsi** *vr.* **1.** (*giocare*) to play **2.** (*scherzare*) to trifle.

trastullo *sm.* **1.** plaything **2.** (*divertimento*) amusement.

trasudamento *sm.* sweating.

trasudare *vt. e vi.* to sweat.

trasversale *agg.* transversal, cross (*attr.*). ◆ **trasversale** *sf.* **1.** transversal **2.** (*strada*) cross-road.

trasvolare *vt.* to fly (*v. irr.*) across.

trasvolata *sf.* flight (across).

tratta *sf.* **1.** (*traffico*) trade **2.** (*comm.*) draft || — *a vista*, sight draft; *spiccare una* — *su qu.*, to draw (*v. irr.*) upon so.

trattàbile *agg.* **1.** tractable **2.** (*di argomento*) that can be dealt with.

trattabilità *sf.* tractability.

trattamento *sm.* **1.** treatment **2.** (*paga*) salary.

trattare *vt.* **1.** to treat **2.** (*maneggiare*) to handle **3.** (*commerciare*) to deal (*v. irr.*) (in) **4.** (*negoziare*) to negotiate **5.** (*un argomento*) to deal (with). ◆ **trattarsi** *v. imp.* to be a question of, to be involved.

trattativa *sf.* negotiation.

trattato *sm.* **1.** (*patto*) treaty **2.** (*libro*) treatise.

trattazione *sf.* treatment.

tratteggiare *vt.* **1.** to outline **2.** (*ombreggiare*) to hatch.

tratteggio *sm.* **1.** (*abbozzo*) outline **2.** (*ombreggiatura*) hatching.

trattenere *vt.* **1.** to keep (*v. irr.*) **2.** (*dedurre*) to deduct **3.** (*frenare*) to refrain || — *il respiro*, to hold (*v. irr.*) one's breath. ♦ **trattenersi** *vr.* (*fermarsi*) to stay || *non posso trattenermi dal fare*, I cannot help doing.

trattenimento *sm.* (*festa*) party.

trattenuta *sf.* deduction.

trattino *sm.* **1.** dash **2.** (*di unione*) hyphen.

tratto *sm.* **1.** (*tirata*) pull **2.** (*colpo*) stroke **3.** (*linea*) line **4.** (*brano*) passage **5.** (*estensione di spazio*) way **6.** (*lineamento*) feature **7.** (*comportamento*) manners (*pl.*) || *d'un* —, suddenly; *di* — *in* —, now and then.

trattore[1] *sm.* (*mecc.*) tractor.

trattore[2] *sm.* (*oste*) inn-keeper.

trattoria *sf.* inn.

tratturo *sm.* cattle-track.

trauma *sm.* trauma.

traumatico *agg.* traumatic.

traumatologia *sf.* traumatology.

travagliare *vt.* V. *tormentare*.

travaglio *sm.* **1.** (*fatica*) labour **2.** (*cruccio*) trouble.

travasare *vt.* to pour off.

travaso *sm.* **1.** pouring off **2.** (*med.*) effusion.

travatura *sf.* truss.

trave *sf.* beam.

traveggole *sf. pl. avere le* —, to mistake (*v. irr.*) one thing for another.

traversa *sf.* **1.** (*sbarra*) cross-bar **2.** (*via*) side-road.

traversata *sf.* crossing.

traversia *sf.* misfortune.

traversina *sf.* sleeper.

traverso *agg.* **1.** transverse, cross (*attr.*) **2.** (*obliquo*) slanting || *di* —, askance; *andare per* — (*fig.*), to go (*v. irr.*) wrong with.

travestimento *sm.* disguise.

travestire *vt.* to disguise (as).

traviamento *sm.* corruption.

traviare *vt.* to mislead (*v. irr.*). ♦ **traviarsi** *vr.* to go (*v. irr.*) astray.

travisamento *sm.* alteration.

travisare *vt.* to alter.

travolgente *agg.* sweeping.

travolgere *vt.* **1.** to sweep (*v. irr.*) away **2.** (*investire*) to run (*v. irr.*) over.

trazione *sf.* traction.

tre *agg.* three.

trebbiare *vt.* to thrash.

trebbiatrice *sf.* thrasher.

trebbiatura *sf.* thrashing.

treccia *sf.* plait: *farsi le trecce*, to plait one's hair.

trecento *agg.* three hundred || *il* — (*secolo*), the fourteenth century.

tredicenne *agg.* thirteen years old, thirteen-year-old (*attr.*).

tredicesimo *agg.* thirteenth.

tredici *agg.* thirteen.

tregua *sf.* **1.** truce **2.** (*riposo*) rest.

tremante *agg.* **1.** trembling **2.** (*di freddo*) shivering.

tremare *vi.* **1.** to tremble **2.** (*di freddo*) to shiver.

tremendo *agg.* awful.

trementina *sf.* turpentine.

tremila *agg.* three thousand.

tremito *sm.* **1.** tremble **2.** (*di freddo*) shiver.

tremolante *agg.* **1.** trembling **2.** (*di luce*) flickering **3.** (*di stelle*) twinkling.

tremolare *vi.* **1.** to tremble **2.** (*di luce*) to flicker **3.** (*di stelle*) to twinkle.

tremolio *sm.* **1.** tremble **2.** (*di luce*) flickering **3.** (*di stelle*) twinkle.

tremore *sm.* V. *tremito*.

treno *sm.* **1.** train: — *accelerato*, slow train; — *direttissimo*, fast train; — *rapido*, express train **2.** (*tenore*) way of living, routine.

trenta *agg.* thirty.

trentenne *agg.* thirty years old, thirty-year-old (*attr.*).

trentennio *sm.* period of thirty years.

trentesimo *agg.* thirtieth.

trentina *sf.* about thirty.

trepestio *sm.* stamping.

trepidante *agg.* anxious.

trepidare *vi.* to be anxious.

trepidazione *sf.* anxiety.

treppiede *sm.* tripod.

tresca *sf.* intrigue.

trespolo *sm.* trestle.

triade *sf.* triad.

triangolare *agg.* triangular.

triangolazione *sf.* triangulation.

triàngolo *sm.* triangle.
tribale *agg.* tribal.
tribolare *vi.* 1. to toil 2. (*soffrire*) to suffer. ♦ **tribolare** *vt.* to vex.
tribolazione *sf.* suffering.
tribordo *sm.* starboard.
tribù *sf.* tribe.
tribuna *sf.* 1. (*per oratori*) platform 2. (*sport*) stand.
tribunale *sm.* court.
tribuno *sm.* tribune.
tributare *vt.* to bestow.
tributario *agg.* 1. tributary 2. (*fiscale*) fiscal. ♦ **tributario** *sm.* tributary.
tributo *sm.* tribute.
tricheco *sm.* walrus.
triciclo *sm.* tricycle.
triclinio *sm.* triclinium (*pl.* -nia).
tricolore *agg. e sm.* tricolour.
tricorno *sm.* tricorn.
tricromìa *sf.* 1. trichromatism 2. (*pezzo singolo*) trichromatic print.
tridente *sm.* 1. trident 2. (*per fieno*) hayfork.
tridimensionale *agg.* tridimensional.
triedro *sm.* trihedron.
triennale *agg. e sm.* triennial.
triennio *sm.* period of three years.
trifase *agg.* three-phase (*attr.*).
trifoglio *sm.* clover.
trigèmino *agg. e sm.* trigeminal: *parto* —, birth of triplets.
trigèsimo *agg.* thirtieth: *nel* — *della sua morte*, on the thirtieth day after his death.
trigonometrìa *sf.* trigonometry.
trilione *sm.* 1. (*in sistema italiano, francese e americano* = 1000⁴) billion; (*amer.*) trillion 2. (*in sistema inglese e tedesco* = 1000⁶) trillion; (*amer.*) quintillion.
trillare *vi.* 1. to trill 2. (*squillare*) to ring (*v. irr.*).
trillo *sm.* 1. trill 2. (*di sveglia, telefono*) ring.
trilogìa *sf.* trilogy.
trimestrale *agg.* quarterly.
trimestre *sm.* 1. quarter 2. (*scol.*) term 3. (*paga trimestrale*) quarterage.
trimotore *agg.* three-engined aeroplane.
trina *sf.* lace.
trincare *vt.* to gulp. ♦ **trincare** *vi.* to drink (*v. irr.*).
trincea *sf.* trench.
trincerare *vt.* to entrench.

trincetto *sm.* shoemaker's knife (*pl.* knives).
trinchetto *sm. albero di* —, foremast; *vela di* —, foresail.
trinciante *agg.* sharp. ♦ **trinciante** *sm.* carver.
trinciare *vt.* 1. to cut (*v. irr.*) (up) 2. (*carne*) to carve || — *giudizi*, to judge rashly.
trinciato *sm.* cut-tobacco.
trinità *sf.* trinity.
trinomio *sm.* trinomial.
trionfante *agg.* triumphant.
trionfare *vt.* to triumph.
trionfatore *sm.* triumpher.
trionfo *sm.* triumph.
tripartito *agg.* tripartite.
tripartizione *sf.* tripartition.
triplicare *vt.* to treble.
triplo *agg.* triple. ♦ **triplo** *sm.* 1. triple 2. (*tre volte tanto*) three times as much.
trippa *sf.* (*cuc.*) tripe.
tripudiare *vi.* to exult.
tripudio *sm.* exultation.
trisàvolo *sm.* great-great-grand-father.
trisìllabo *agg.* trisyllabic. ♦ **trisìllabo** *sm.* trisyllable.
triste *agg.* sad.
tristezza *sf.* 1. sadness 2. (*dolore*) grief.
tristo *agg.* wicked.
tritacarne *sm.* mincer.
tritare *vt.* to mince.
tritatutto *sm.* mincer.
trito *agg.* (*fig.*) trite.
tritolo *sm.* trinitrotoluene.
trìttico *sm.* triptych.
trittongo *sm.* triphthong.
tritume *sm.* crumbs (*pl.*).
triturare *vt.* to triturate.
triumvirato *sm.* triumvirate.
triùmviro *sm.* triumvir.
trivalente *agg.* trivalent.
trivella *sf.* 1. (*min.*) drill 2. (*falegnameria*) auger.
trivellare *vt.* to drill.
trivellazione *sf.* drilling: *torre di* —, derrick.
triviale *agg.* coarse.
trivialità *sf.* 1. coarseness 2. (*detto triviale*) coarse expression.
trofeo *sm.* trophy.
troglodita *sm.* troglodyte.
troglodìtico *agg.* troglodytic(al).
trògolo *sm.* trough.
troia *sf.* (*zool.*) sow.
tromba *sf.* 1. trumpet 2. (*di scale*)

well || — d'aria, tornado; — d'acqua, water-spout.

trombettiere sm. trumpeter.

trombone sm. 1. (mus.) trombone 2. (schioppo) blunderbuss || suonatore di —, trombonist.

trombosi sf. thrombosis.

troncare vt. 1. to cut (v. irr.) off 2. (fig.) to break (v. irr.) off.

tronco[1] agg. 1. cut off 2. (fig.) broken.

tronco[2] sm. 1. trunk 2. (d'albero abbattuto) log 3. (geom.) frustum || — ferroviario, railway section; licenziare in —, to sack on the spot.

troncone sm. stump.

troneggiare vi. to dominate (sthg.).

tronfio agg. 1. conceited 2. (di stile) bombastic.

trono sm. throne.

tropicale agg. tropical.

tròpico sm. tropic.

tropismo sm. tropism.

troposfera sf. troposphere.

troppo avv. 1. (con agg. e avv.) too 2. (con v.) too much 3. (di tempo) too long. ♦ **troppo** agg. e pron. too much (pl. too many): anche —, only too; essere di —, to be unwelcome.

trota sf. trout (pl. invariato).

trottare vi. to trot: far — qu. (fig.) to make (v. irr.) so. run.

trottata sf. trot.

trottatore sm. trotter.

trotterellare vi. 1. to trot along 2. (di bambini) to toddle.

trotto sm. trot: mettere un cavallo al —, to trot a horse.

tròttola sf. top.

trovare vt. 1. to find (v. irr.) 2. (far visita) to see (v. irr.) 3. (pensare) to think (v. irr.). ♦ **trovarsi** vr. 1. (essere) to be 2. (sentirsi) to feel (v. irr.).

trovata sf. trick.

trovatello sm. foundling.

trovatore sm. troubadour.

truccare vi. 1. to make (v. irr.) up 2. (sport) to fix.

truccatore sm. maker-up.

truccatura sf. make-up.

trucco sm. 1. trick 2. (cosmetici) make-up 3. (inganno) deceit.

truce agg. grim.

trucidare vt. to slay (v. irr.).

trùciolo sm. shaving.

truculento agg. truculent.

truffa sf. cheat.

truffaldino agg. cheating.

truffare vt. to cheat.

truffatore sm. cheat.

truismo sm. truism.

truppa sf. troop.

tu pron. you.

tua agg. e pron. V. tuo.

tuba sf. 1. tuba 2. (cappello) top-hat.

tubare vi. to coo.

tubatura sf. piping.

tubercolare agg. tubercular.

tubercolina sf. tuberculin.

tubercolosario sm. sanatorium.

tubercolosi sf. tuberculosis: — polmonare, consumption.

tubercoloso agg. tuberculous. ♦ **tubercoloso** sm. consumptive.

tùbero sm. tuber.

tuberosa sf. tuberose.

tubino sm. bowler-hat.

tubo sm. 1. tube 2. (di conduttura) pipe 3. (anat.) canal.

tubolare agg. tubular.

tue agg. e pron. V. tuo.

tuffare vt. to plunge, to dip. ♦ **tuffarsi** vr. to plunge, to dive.

tuffatore sm. diver.

tuffo sm. plunge, dive.

tufo sm. tuff.

tugurio sm. hovel.

tulipano sm. tulip.

tumefare vt. to swell (v. irr.). ♦ **tumefarsi** vr. to swell.

tumefatto agg. swollen.

tumefazione sf. swelling.

tùmido agg. tumid: labbra tumide, thick lips.

tumore sm. tumour.

tumulare vt. to bury.

tumulazione sf. burial.

tùmulo sm. 1. tumulus (pl. -li) 2. (tomba) grave.

tumulto sm. tumult.

tumultuante agg. riotous.

tumultuare vi. to riot.

tumultuoso agg. tumultuous.

tundra sf. tundra.

tungsteno sm. tungsten.

tùnica sf. tunic.

tunnel sm. tunnel.

tuo agg. your. ♦ **tuo** pron. yours.

tuoi agg. e pron. V. tuo || i —, your family.

tuonare vi. to thunder.

tuono sm. thunder.

tuorlo sm. yolk.

turàcciolo sm. 1. stopper 2. (di su-

ghero) cork || _mettere il — a una bottiglia_, to cork a bottle.

turare _vt._ to stop, to fill up. ♦ **turarsi** _vr._ **1.** to stop **2.** (_chiudersi_) to shut oneself up.

turba¹ _sf._ crowd.

turba² _sf._ (_med._) trouble.

turbamento _sm._ **1.** perturbation **2.** (_eccitazione_) excitement **3.** (_sconvolgimento_) upsetting.

turbante _sm._ turban.

turbare _vt._ **1.** to upset (_v. irr._) **2.** (_agitare intorbidando_) to muddy. ♦ **turbarsi** _vr._ to get (_v. irr._) upset.

turbina _sf._ turbine.

turbinare _vi._ to whirl.

tùrbine _sm._ **1.** whirl **2.** (_uragano_) hurricane.

turbinìo _sm._ whirling.

turbinoso _agg._ **1.** whirling **2.** (_tumultuoso_) tumultuous.

turbolento _agg._ boisterous.

turbolenza _sf._ boisterousness.

turbomotore _sm._ turbojet engine.

turbonave _sf._ turboship.

turboreattore _sm._ (_aer._) turbojet.

turcasso _sm._ quiver.

turchese _sm._ turquoise.

turchino _agg._ deep blue.

turco _agg._ Turkish. ♦ **turco** _sm._ Turk.

turgidezza _sf._ turgidity.

tùrgido _agg._ turgid.

turìbolo _sm._ censer.

turismo _sm._ tourism.

turista _s._ tourist.

turìstico _agg._ tourist (_attr._).

turlupinare _vt._ to swindle.

turlupinatura _sf._ swindle.

turno _sm._ **1.** turn **2.** (_servizio_) duty || _di —_, on duty; _a —_, on turn.

turpe _agg._ filthy.

turpiloquio _sm._ coarse language.

turpitùdine _sf._ baseness.

turrito _agg._ turreted.

tuta _sf._ overalls (_pl._): _— spaziale_, spacesuit.

tutela _sf._ **1.** guardianship **2.** (_protezione_) protection.

tutelare _vt._ to guard.

tutelare _agg._ tutelary.

tutore _sm._ guardian.

tuttavìa _cong._ yet.

tutto _agg._ all, whole (_pl._ all); (_ogni_) every || _tutt'e due_, both; _tutt'al più_, at the most; _tutt'altro che_, anything but; _tutt'altro!_, on the contrary! ♦ **tutto** _pron._ all,

everything (_pl._ ali); (_ognuno_) everybody. ♦ **tutto** _s.n._ whole: _del —_, quite.

tuttofare _agg._ _cameriera —_, maid-of-all-work.

tuttora _avv._ still.

U

ubbìa _sf._ whim.

ubbidiente _agg._ obedient.

ubbidienza _sf._ obedience.

ubbidire _vi._ to obey (so., sthg.).

ubicare _vt._ to locate.

ubicato _agg._ situated.

ubicazione _sf._ location.

ubiquità _sf._ ubiquity.

ubriacare _vt._ to make (_v. irr._) drunk. ♦ **ubriacarsi** _vr._ to get (_v. irr._) drunk.

ubriacatura _sf._ intoxication.

ubriachezza _sf._ drunkenness.

ubriaco _agg._ drunk. ♦ **ubriaco** _sm._ drunken man (_pl._ men).

ubriacone _sm._ drunkard.

uccellagione _sf._ feathered game.

uccellare _vi._ to fowl.

uccelliera _sf._ aviary.

uccello _sm._ bird.

uccìdere _vt._ **1.** to kill **2.** (_assassinare_) to murder **3.** (_con pugnale_) to stab to death **4.** (_con arma da fuoco_) to shoot (_v. irr._). ♦ **uccìdersi** _vr._ **1.** to get (_v. irr._) killed **2.** (_suicidarsi_) to commit suicide, to kill oneself.

uccisione _sf._ killing.

uccisore _sm._ killer.

udìbile _agg._ audible.

udienza _sf._ hearing.

udire _vt._ to hear (_v. irr._).

uditivo _agg._ auditory.

udito _sm._ hearing.

uditore _sm._ **1.** listener **2.** (_nella scuola_) auditor.

uditorio _sm._ audience.

ufficiale _agg._ official. ♦ **ufficiale** _sm._ **1.** officer **2.** (_governativo, postale_) official.

ufficialità _sf._ official character.

ufficialmente _avv._ officially.

ufficiare _vi._ to officiate.

ufficio _sm._ office: _capo —_, head clerk; _d'—_, officially; _— informazioni_, information bureau.

ufficiosamente *avv.* unofficially.

ufficioso *agg.* unofficial.

ufo (*nella loc. avv.*) *a —*, without paying.

ugello *sm.* nozzle.

uggia *sf.* boredom: *questo libro mi è venuto in —*, I have grown tired of this book.

uggiolare *vi.* to whine.

uggioso *agg.* dull.

ùgola *sf.* 1. uvula 2. (*voce*) voice.

uguaglianza *sf.* equality.

uguagliare *vt.* 1. to be equal (to) 2. (*rendere uguale*) to make (*v. irr.*) equal.

uguale *agg.* 1. equal 2. (*simile*) like, alike (*pred.*) 3. (*stesso*) same.

ugualitario *agg.* equalitarian.

ugualmente *avv.* 1. equally 2. (*lo stesso*) all the same.

ùlcera *sf.* ulcer.

ulcerare *vt.* to ulcerate. ♦ **ulcerarsi** *vr.* to ulcerate.

ulcerato *agg.* ulcerated.

ulcerazione *sf.* ulceration.

ulceroso *agg.* ulcerous.

ulteriore *agg.* further.

ulteriormente *avv.* further on.

ultimamente *avv.* 1. recently 2. (*da ultimo*) finally.

ultimare *vt.* to finish.

ultimazione *sf.* conclusion.

ùltimo *agg.* 1. last 2. (*il più recente*) latest 3. (*estremo*) utmost.

ultramicroscòpico *agg.* ultramicroscopic(al).

ultramoderno *agg.* ultramodern.

ultrasensibile *agg.* ultrasensitive.

ultrasònico *agg.* ultrasonic.

ultrasuono *sm.* ultrasound.

ultraterreno *agg.* supernatural.

ultravioletto *agg.* ultraviolet.

ululare *vi.* 1. to howl 2. (*di sirena*) to hoot.

ululato *sm.* 1. howl 2. (*di sirena*) hoot.

umanésimo *sm.* Humanism.

umanista *sm.* humanist.

umanìstico *agg.* humanistic.

umanità *sf.* humanity.

umanitario *agg.* humanitarian.

umanitarismo *sm.* humanitarianism.

umanizzare *vt.* to humanize.

umano *agg.* 1. human 2. (*comprensivo*) humane.

umerale *agg.* humeral.

umettare *vt.* to moisten.

umidità *sf.* humidity, dampness.

ùmido *agg.* damp.

ùmile *agg.* humble.

umiliante *agg.* humiliating.

umiliare *vt.* to humble.

umiliazione *sf.* humiliation.

umiltà *sf.* 1. humbleness 2. (*virtù dell'umile*) humility.

umore *sm.* humour: *essere di buon —*, to be in a good humour.

umorismo *sm.* humour.

umorista *s.* humorist.

umoristico *agg.* humorous.

una *art.* e *agg.* V. **uno**.

unànime *agg.* unanimous.

unanimità *sf.* unanimity: *all'—*, unanimously.

uncinare *vt.* to hook.

uncinato *agg.* hooked || *croce uncinata*, swastika.

uncinetto *sm.* crochet-hook: *lavorare all'—*, to crochet.

uncino *sm.* hook.

undicèsimo *agg.* eleventh.

ùndici *agg.* eleven.

ùngere *vt.* to grease.

unghia *sf.* 1. nail 2. (*di equino*) hoof 3. (*fig.*) clutch.

unghiata *sf.* scratch: *dare un'—*, to scratch.

unguento *sm.* ointment.

ungulato *agg.* hoofed.

unicamente *avv.* only.

unicellulare *agg.* unicellular.

unicità *sf.* uniqueness.

ùnico *agg.* 1. only 2. (*senza uguale*) unique.

unificare *vt.* 1. to unify 2. (*uniformare*) to standardize.

unificatore *agg.* unifying. ♦ **unificatore** *sm.* unifier.

unificazione *sf.* 1. unification 2. (*uniformazione*) standardization.

uniformare *vt.* 1. to conform 2. (*rendere conforme*) to standardize. ♦ **uniformarsi** *vr.* to conform (to).

uniforme¹ *agg.* uniform.

uniforme² *sf.* uniform.

uniformemente *avv.* uniformly.

uniformità *sf.* uniformity.

unigènito *sm.* only child.

unilaterale *agg.* unilateral.

unilateralmente *avv.* unilaterally.

uninominale *agg.* uninominal.

unione *sf.* union.

unionista *sm.* unionist.

unipolare *agg.* unipolar.

unire *vt.* to unite, to join. ♦ **unirsi** *vr.* to unite, to join.

unìsono *sm.* unison.

unità *sf.* 1. unity 2. (*fis.; mat.; mil.*) unit.

unitamente *avv.* unitedly: — *a*, together with.

unitario *agg.* unitary.

unito *agg.* 1. united 2. (*accluso*) enclosed.

universale *agg.* universal.

universalità *sf.* universality.

universalizzare *vt.* to universalize.

università *sf.* university.

universitario *agg.* university (*attr.*). ♦ **universitario** *sm.* university student.

universo *agg.* whole. ♦ **universo** *sm.* universe.

univoco *agg.* univocal.

uno, un, una *art.* a, an (*davanti a vocale e h muta*). ♦ **uno, un, una** *agg.* one. ♦ **uno, una** *pron.* 1. one 2. (*un tale*) a man; (*una tale*) a woman || — *a* —, one by one; *l' — e l'altro*, both; *l' — o l'altro*, either; *né l' — né l'altro*, neither; *l' — l'altro*, each other; *un po' per* —, a part each; *costano 5 sterline l'*—, they cost 5 pounds each.

unto *agg.* greasy.

untume *sm.* grease.

untuosamente *avv.* (*fig.*) unctuously.

untuosità *sf.* 1. greasiness 2. (*fig.*) unctuousness.

untuoso *agg.* 1. greasy 2. (*fig.*) unctuous.

unzione *sf.* unction.

uomo *sm.* man (*pl.* men): *un — da nulla*, a nobody.

uopo *sm.* esser d'—, to be necessary; *all'*—, if necessary.

uovo *sm.* egg: *rosso d'*—, yolk; *cercare il pelo nell'*—, to split (*v. irr.*) hairs.

uragano *sm.* hurricane.

uranìfero *agg.* uranic.

uranio *sm.* uranium.

uranite *sf.* uranite.

uranografia *sf.* uranography.

urbanésimo *sm.* urbanization.

urbanista *s.* town planner.

urbanìstica *sf.* town-planning.

urbanìstico *agg.* town-planning.

urbanità *sf.* urbanity.

urbanizzare *vt.* to urbanize.

urbanizzazione *sf.* urbanization.

urbano *agg.* 1. urban 2. (*cortese*) urbane.

ùrea *sf.* urea.

uremìa *sf.* uraemia.

urèmico *agg.* uraemic.

uretra *sf.* urethra.

urgente *agg.* urgent.

urgentemente *avv.* urgently.

urgenza *sf.* urgency.

ùrgere *vt.* to urge. ♦ **ùrgere** *vi.* to be urgent.

uricemìa *sf.* uricaemia.

ùrico *agg.* uric.

urina *sf.* V. *orina*.

urinare *vi.* V. *orinare*.

urlare *vt. e vi.* 1. to shout, to scream 2. (*di vento, animale; per il dolore*) to howl.

urlatore *agg.* shouting. ♦ **urlatore** *sm.* shouter.

urlo *sm.* 1. shout 2. (*di vento, animale; per il dolore*) howl.

urna *sf.* 1. urn 2. (*per i voti*) ballot-box || *andare alle urne*, to go (*v. irr.*) to the polls.

urogallo *sm.* grouse.

urologìa *sf.* urology.

uròlogo *sm.* urologist.

urtante *agg.* irritating.

urtare *vt.* 1. to knock 2. (*infastidire*) to irritate 3. (*offendere*) to hurt (*v. irr.*). ♦ **urtarsi** *vr.* to get (*v. irr.*) cross. ♦ **urtarsi** *vr. rec.* to collide.

urticante *agg.* urticating.

urticaria *sf.* nettle rash.

urto *sm.* 1. push 2. (*scontro, contrasto*) collision || *essere in* —, to be at variance.

urtone *sm.* shove.

usanza *sf.* 1. custom 2. (*abitudine personale*) habit.

usare *vt.* to use: — *una cortesia*, to do (*v. irr.*) a favour. ♦ **usare** *vi.* 1. to be accustomed; (*solo al passato*) to use 2. (*essere di moda*) to be fashionable.

usato *agg.* 1. used 2. (*in uso*) in use 3. (*abituale*) usual 4. (*non nuovo*) second-hand.

uscente *agg.* 1. retiring 2. (*con espressioni di tempo*) closing.

usciere *sm.* 1. usher 2. (*ufficiale giudiziario*) bailiff.

uscio *sm.* door: *abitare* — *a* — (*con*), to live next door (to).

uscire *vi.* 1. to go (*v. irr.*) out, to come (*v. irr.*) out 2. (*sboccare*) to lead (*v. irr.*) 3. (*uscire di strada*) to go off || *uscirne bene, male*, to come off well, badly.

uscita *sf.* 1. way out 2. (*atto di uscire*) going out, coming out 3. (*spese*) expense || *strada senza —*, blind-alley.

usignolo *sm.* nightingale.

uso¹ *agg.* accustomed.

uso² *sm.* use: *d'—*, usual; *all'— di*, after the fashion of.

ùssaro *sm.* hussar.

ustionare *vt.* to scald.

ustionato *agg.* scalded.

ustione *sf.* scald.

usuale *agg.* usual.

usufruire *vi.* to benefit (by).

usufrutto *sm.* usufruct.

usufruttuario *agg. e sm.* usufructuary.

usura *sf.* 1. usury 2. (*logorio*) wear and tear.

usuraio *sm.* usurer.

usurpare *vt.* to usurp.

usurpatore *agg.* usurping. ♦ **usurpatore** *sm.* usurper.

usurpazione *sf.* usurpation.

utènsile *sm.* utensil.

utente *s.* user.

uterino *agg.* uterine.

ùtero *sm.* uterus (*pl.* -ri).

ùtile *agg.* useful. ♦ **ùtile** *sm.* profit.

utilità *sf.* 1. usefulness 2. (*vantaggio*) profit || *non ne vedo l'—*, I do not see the use of it.

utilitaria *sf.* (*auto*) utility car.

utilitario *agg. e sm.* utilitarian.

utilitarismo *sm.* utilitarianism.

utilitarìstico *agg.* V. *utilitario.*

utilizzàbile *agg.* utilizable.

utilizzare *vt.* to utilize.

utilizzatore *agg.* utilizing. ♦ **utilizzatore** *sm.* utilizer.

utilizzazione *sf.* utilization.

utopìa *sf.* utopia.

utopista *s.* utopian.

utopìstico *agg.* utopian.

uva *sf.* grapes (*pl.*): *— passa*, raisin.

uxoricida *sm.* uxoricide.

uxoricidio *sm.* uxoricide.

V

vacante *agg.* vacant.

vacanza *sf.* 1. holiday 2. (*posto vacante*) vacancy.

vacca *sf.* cow.

vaccaro *sm.* cowherd.

vaccherìa *sf.* cowhouse.

vacchetta *sf.* cowhide.

vaccinàbile *agg.* that can be vaccinated.

vaccinare *vt.* to vaccinate.

vaccinazione *sf.* vaccination.

vaccino *sm.* vaccine.

vaccinògeno *agg.* vaccinogenous.

vaccinoterapìa *sf.* vaccinotherapy.

vacillamento *sm.* 1. unsteadiness 2. (*di luce*) flickering 3. (*fig.*) wavering.

vacillante *agg.* 1. unsteady 2. (*di luce*) flickering 3. (*fig.*) uncertain.

vacillare *vi.* 1. to be unsteady 2. (*di luce*) to flicker 3. (*fig.*) to waver.

vacuità *sf.* vacuity.

vacuo *agg.* vacuous.

vademecum *sm.* vade-mecum.

vagabondaggio *sm.* vagrancy.

vagabondare *vi.* to wander.

vagabondo *agg.* vagabond. ♦ **vagabondo** *sm.* vagrant.

vagamente *avv.* vaguely.

vagante *agg.* wandering.

vagare *vi.* to wander.

vagheggiamento *sm.* longing (for).

vagheggiare *vt.* to long (for).

vagheggino *sm.* gallant.

vaghezza *sf.* 1. charm 2. (*indeterminatezza*) vagueness.

vagina *sf.* vagina (*pl.* -nae).

vagire *vi.* to wail.

vagito *sm.* wail.

vaglia¹ *sf.* (*valore*) worth.

vaglia² *sm.* money order: *— postale*, postal order.

vagliare *vt.* to sieve 2. (*fig.*) to weigh.

vagliatura *sf.* screening.

vaglio *sm.* 1. sieve 2. (*fig.*) sifting.

vago *agg.* 1. vague 2. (*leggiadro*) pretty.

vagoncino *sm.* wag(g)on.

vagolare *vi.* to rove.

vagone *sm.* carriage, coach.

vaio¹ *agg.* dark grey.

vaio² *sm.* vair.

vaiolo *sm.* smallpox.

valanga *sf.* avalanche.

valchiria *sf.* Walkyrie.

valente *agg.* 1. skilful 2. (*valoroso*) brave.

valentemente *avv.* 1. skilfully 2. (*valorosamente*) bravely.

valentìa *sf.* 1. skill 2. (*valore*) worth.

valentuomo *sm.* worthy man.

valenza *sf.* valence.

valere *vi.* 1. to be worth: — *la pena*, to be worth while; *far — i propri diritti*, to assert one's rights; *farsi —*, to make (*v. irr.*) oneself appreciated 2. (*contare*) to count 3. (*servire*) to be of use 4. (*essere valido*) to be valid. ♦ **valersi** *vr.* to avail oneself (of).

valeriana *sf.* valerian.

valévole *agg.* valid.

valicàbile *agg.* that can be crossed.

valicare *vt.* to cross.

vàlico *sm.* pass.

validamente *avv.* validly.

validità *sf.* validity.

vàlido *agg.* 1. valid 2. (*fondato*) well-grounded 3. (*forte*) strong.

valigerìa *sf.* leatherware shop.

valigia *sf.* suit-case; *fare le valigie*, to pack up.

vallata *sf.* valley.

valle *sf.* valley.

valletto *sm.* valet.

vallo *sm.* rampart.

vallone *agg. e sm.* Walloon.

valore *sm.* 1. value 2. (*coraggio*) bravery.

valorizzare *vt.* 1. to turn to account 2. (*accentuare*) to emphasize.

valorizzazione *sf.* 1. turning to account 2. (*comm.*) valorization.

valorosamente *avv.* bravely.

valoroso *agg.* brave.

valsente *sm.* commercial value.

valuta *sf.* 1. value 2. (*moneta*) currency: — *estera*, foreign currency.

valutàbile *agg.* valuable.

valutare *vt.* 1. to value 2. (*considerare*) to consider.

valutazione *sf.* 1. evaluation 2. (*considerazione*) careful consideration.

valva *sf.* valve.

vàlvola *sf.* 1. valve 2. (*elettr.*) fuse 3. (*radio*) valve, tube.

valvolare *agg.* valvular.

valzer *sm.* waltz: *ballare il —*, to waltz.

vampa *sf.* 1. blaze 2. (*al viso*) flush.

vampata *sf.* 1. blaze 2. (*folata*) blast 3. (*al viso*) flush.

vampeggiante *agg.* blazing.

vampeggiare *vi.* to blaze.

vampiro *sm.* vampire.

vanagloria *sf.* vainglory.

vanagloriarsi *vr.* to boast.

vanaglorioso *agg.* boastful.

vanamente *avv.* vainly.

vandàlico *agg.* vandalic.

vandalismo *sm.* vandalism.

vàndalo *agg. e sm.* vandal.

vaneggiamento *sm.* raving.

vaneggiare *vi.* to rave.

vanesio *agg.* foppish. ♦ **vanesio** *sm.* fop.

vanga *sf.* spade.

vangare *vt.* to spade.

vangata *sf.* blow with a spade.

vangatore *sm.* spademan.

vangatura *sf.* spading.

vangelo *sm.* Gospel.

vaniglia *sf.* vanilla.

vanigliato *agg.* vanilla-flavoured.

vaniloquio *sm.* empty talk.

vanità *sf.* vanity.

vanitoso *agg.* conceited.

vano[1] *agg.* vain.

vano[2] *sm.* space, room.

vantaggio *sm.* 1. advantage 2. (*sport*) lead.

vantaggiosamente *avv.* advantageously.

vantaggioso *agg.* advantageous.

vantare *vt.* 1. to boast (of) 2. (*lodare*) to praise 3. (*millantare*) to brag. ♦ **vantarsi** *vr.* to boast (of).

vanterìa *sf.* boast.

vanto *sm.* boast.

vànvera (*nella loc. avv.*) *a —*, at random.

vapore *sm.* 1. steam 2. (*mar.*) steamer.

vaporetto *sm.* steamboat.

vaporiera *sf.* steam-engine.

vaporizzare *vt.* to vaporize.

vaporizzatore *sm.* vaporizer.

vaporizzazione *sf.* vaporization.

vaporosità *sf.* 1. haziness 2. (*di abito*) gauziness.

vaporoso *agg.* 1. hazy 2. (*di abito*) gauzy.

varare *vt.* to launch (*anche fig.*).

varcare *vt.* to cross, to pass.

varco *sm.* passage, opening: *aprirsi un — fra la folla;* to force one's way through the crowd.

variàbile *agg.* variable, unsteady.

variabilità *sf.* variability, unsteadiness.

variante *sf.* variant.

variare *vt.* 1. to vary 2. (*di mercato*) to fluctuate.

variato *agg.* V. *vario*.

variazione *sf.* variation, change.

varice *sf.* varix (*pl.* varices).
varicella *sf.* chicken-pox.
varicoso *agg.* varicose.
variegato *agg.* variegated.
varietà *sf.* variety.
vario *agg.* **1.** varied **2.** (*differente*) various **3.** (*parecchi*) several.
variopinto *agg.* many-coloured.
varo *sm.* launch.
vasaio *sm.* potter.
vasca *sf.* basin: — *da bagno*, bath (tub).
vascello *sm.* vessel.
vascolare *agg.* vascular.
vaselina *sf.* vaseline.
vasellame *sm.* **1.** (*di terracotta*) earthenware **2.** (*di porcellana*) china **3.** (*d'argento, d'oro*) silver, gold plate.
vaso *sm.* **1.** vase **2.** (*rotondo*) pot **3.** (*recipiente; anat.*) vessel.
vasocostrittore *agg.* e *sm.* vasoconstrictor.
vasodilatatore *agg.* e *sm.* vasodilator.
vasomotore *agg.* vasomotor.
vasomotorio *agg.* vasomotor.
vassallaggio *sm.* **1.** (*stor.*) vassalage **2.** subjection.
vassallo *agg.* e *sm.* **1.** (*stor.*) vassal **2.** subject.
vassoio *sm.* tray.
vastità *sf.* **1.** vastness **2.** (*estensione*) expanse.
vasto *agg.* wide, large.
vate *sm.* **1.** prophet **2.** (*poeta*) poet.
Vaticano *agg.* Vatican.
vaticinare *vt.* to prophesy.
vaticinio *sm.* prophecy.
vattelappesca *inter.* who knows!
ve *pron:* you: — *lo scrissi*, I wrote it to you. ♦ **ve** *avv.* there: — *ne sono due*, there are two.
ve' *inter.* look, see.
vecchiaia *sf.* old age.
vecchiezza *sf.* great age.
vecchio *agg.* **1.** old **2.** (*antico*) ancient **3.** (*stantio*) stale. ♦ **vecchio** *sm.* old man.
veccia *sf.* vetch.
vece *sf.* stead, place.
vedere *vt.* to see (*v. irr.*): — *la luce* (*nascere*), to be born; *far* —, to show (*v. irr.*); *farsi* —, to show oneself; *non* — *l'ora di*, to look forward to (*con gerundio*). ♦ **vedersi** *vr.* **1.** to see oneself **2.** (*vedersela*) to deal (*v. irr.*) with.
vedetta *sf.* **1.** (*sentinella*) watchman

(*pl.* -men) **2.** (*posto di osservazione*) look-out.
vedova *sf.* widow.
vedovanza *sf.* widowhood.
vedovile *agg.* **1.** (*di vedova*) of a widow **2.** (*di vedovo*) of a widower.
vedovo *sm.* widower.
vedretta *sf.* small steep glacier.
veduta *sf.* **1.** sight, view **2.** (*opinione*) view, idea.
veemente *agg.* vehement.
veemenza *sf.* vehemence.
vegetale *agg.* e *sm.* vegetable.
vegetare *vi.* to vegetate.
vegetariano *agg.* e *sm.* vegetarian.
vegetativo *agg.* vegetative.
vegetazione *sf.* vegetation.
vègeto *agg.* **1.** (*di pianta*) thriving **2.** (*di persona*) vigorous, strong ‖ *vivo e* —, hale and hearty
veggente *sm.* seer.
veglia *sf.* **1.** waking **2.** (*il vegliare*) watch.
vegliardo *sm.* old man.
vegliare *vi.* **1.** to be awake **2.** (*far la veglia*) to watch.
veglione *sm.* masked ball.
veicolo *sm.* vehicle.
vela *sf.* sail.
velame *sm.* **1.** veil **2.** (*mar.*) sails (*pl.*).
velare *vt.* to veil.
velario *sm.* curtain.
velatura *sf.* sails (*pl.*).
veleggiare *vi.* to sail.
veleno *sm.* poison.
velenoso *agg.* poisonous, venomous.
veletta *sf.* **1.** (*mar.*) topsail **2.** (*di cappello*) veil.
veliero *sm.* sailing-ship.
velina *sf.* tissue-paper.
velismo *sm.* sailing.
velìvolo *sm.* aeroplane.
velleità *sf.* foolish ambition, fancy.
vellicare *vt.* to tickle.
vello *sm.* fleece.
vellutato *agg.* velvety: *pelle vellutata*, downy skin.
velluto *sm.* velvet.
velo *sm.* veil.
veloce *agg.* fast, quick, swift.
velocìpede *sm.* velocipede.
velocità *sf.* speed, velocity: *a tutta* —, at full speed; *limite di* —, speed limit; *cambio di* — (*auto*), gearbox; *indicatore di* —, speedometer.
velòdromo *sm.* cycle-racing track.

veltro sm. greyhound.
vena sf. vein.
venale agg. venal.
venalità sf. venality.
venare vt. 1. to vein 2. (di legno) to grain.
venato agg. 1. veined 2. (di legno) grained.
venatorio agg. venatorial.
venatura sf. 1. vein 2. (di legno) grain.
vendemmia sf. vintage.
vendemmiare vi. to gather grapes.
vendemmiatore sm. vintager.
véndere vt. to sell (v. irr.): — a bu: mercato, to sell cheaply; — a credito, to sell on credit; — all'ingrosso, al minuto, to sell wholesale, by retail; — a rate, to sell by instalments.
vendetta sf. revenge.
vendìbile agg. salable.
vendicare vt. to revenge.
vendicativo agg. revengeful.
vendicatore sm. revenger.
véndita sf. sale: — all'asta, auction.
venditore sm. seller.
venduto agg. 1. sold 2. (fig.) corrupted.
veneficio sm. poisoning.
venèfico agg. poisonous.
veneràbile agg. venerable.
venerando agg. venerable.
venerare vt. to worship.
venerazione sf. worship.
venerdì sm. Friday: — Santo, Good Friday.
vènere sf. 1. Venus 2. (fig.) beauty.
venèreo agg. venereal.
veneziana sf. Venetian-blind.
veniale agg. venial.
venire vi. 1. to come (v. irr.): — al sodo, to come to the point; — in mente, to come into one's head; — meno, to faint; — alla luce, to come to light 2. (riuscire) to turn out 3. (derivare) to derive.
venoso agg. venous.
ventaglio sm. fan.
ventata sf. gust of wind.
ventèsimo agg. twentieth.
venti agg. twenty.
ventilare vt. to ventilate.
ventilato agg. airy, windy.
ventilatore sm. fan.
ventilazione sf. ventilation.
ventina sf. score: essere sulla — (di anni), to be about twenty.

vento sm. wind.
ventosa sf. sucker.
ventosità sf. flatulence.
ventoso agg. windy.
ventrale agg. ventral.
ventre sm. 1. abdomen 2. (fam.) tummy.
ventrìcolo sm. ventricle.
ventriera sf. body-belt.
ventriglio sm. gizzard.
ventriloquio sm. ventriloquism.
ventrìloquo sm. ventriloquist.
ventura sf. chance, fortune.
venturo agg. next, coming.
venustà sf. beauty.
venusto agg. beautiful.
venuta sf. coming, arrival.
vera sf. wedding-ring.
verace agg. true.
veracità sf. veracity, truth.
veramente avv. really, truly, indeed.
veranda sf. verandah.
verbale agg. verbal. ♦ verbale sm. minutes (pl.).
verbalizzare vt. to record.
verbo sm. 1. verb 2. (parola) word.
verbosità sf. verbosity.
verboso agg. verbose.
verdastro agg. greenish.
verde agg. green.
verdeggiante agg. verdant.
verdeggiare vi. to be verdant.
verdemare sm. sea-green.
verderame sm. verdigris.
verdetto sm. verdict.
verdògnolo agg. greenish.
verdura sf. vegetables (pl.).
verecondia sf. modesty.
verecondo agg. modest.
verga sf. 1. twig 2. (bacchetta) rod.
vergare vt. (scrivere) to write (v. irr.).
vergata sf. blow with a rod.
vergato agg. 1. striped 2. (scritto) written || carta vergata, laid paper.
verginale agg. virginal.
vérgine agg. e sf. virgin.
vergineo agg. virginal.
verginità sf. virginity.
vergogna sf. shame: aver —, to be ashamed.
vergognarsi vr. to be, to feel (v. irr.) shamed.
vergognosamente avv. shamefully.
vergognoso agg. 1. shameful 2. (timido) shy.
veridicamente avv. veraciously.
veridicità sf. veracity.

verìdico *agg.* veracious.

verìfica *sf.* verification.

verificàbile *agg.* verifiable.

verificare *vt.* to verify, to check.

verificatore *sm.* verifier.

verificazione *sf.* V. *verifica.*

verismo *sm.* realism.

verista *sm.* realist.

verìstico *agg.* realistic.

verità *sf.* truth: *dire la —,* to tell (*v. irr.*) the truth.

veritiero *agg.* truthful.

verme *sm.* worm.

vermìfugo *agg. e sm.* vermifuge.

vermiglio *agg.* bright red.

verminoso *agg.* verminous.

vernàcolo *agg.* vernacular.

vernice *sf.* 1. paint 2. (*apparenza*) varnish.

verniciare *vt.* to paint, to varnish.

verniciatura *sf.* painting, varnishing.

vero *agg.* true, real.

verosimigliante *agg.* likely.

verosimiglianza *sf.* iikelihood.

verosìmile *agg.* likely, probable.

verricello *sm.* windlass.

verro *sm.* boar.

verruca *sf.* wart.

versamento *sm.* 1. pouring 2. (*comm.*) payment, deposit.

versante *sm.* side, slope.

versare *vt.* 1. to pour 2. (*rovesciare*) to spill (*v. irr.*) 3. (*comm.*) to pay (*v. irr.*).

versàtile *agg.* versatile.

versatilità *sf.* versatility.

versato *agg.* 1. poured out 2. (*esperto*) versed.

verseggiare *vt.* to versify.

verseggiatore *sm.* versifier.

versetto *sm.* 1. short line 2. (*della Bibbia*) verse.

versificare *vt.* to versify.

versificatore *sm.* versifier.

versificazione *sf.* versification.

versione *sf.* version, translation.

verso[1] *sm.* 1. verse, line 2. (*suono*) sound 3. (*direzione*) way.

verso[2] *prep.* 1. towards, to 2. (*contro*) against 3. (*circa*) about.

vèrtebra *sf.* vertebra (*pl.* -rae).

vertebrale *agg.* vertebral.

vertebrato *agg. e sm.* vertebrate.

vertenza *sf.* 1. dispute 2. (*giur.*) litigation.

vèrtere *vi.* to be about, to concern.

verticale *agg.* vertical.

verticalità *sf.* verticality.

vèrtice *sm.* 1. vertex (*pl.* vertices) 2. (*fig.*) height, top.

vertìgine *sf.* dizziness (*solo sing.*).

vertiginoso *agg.* dizzy.

verza *sf.* cabbage.

vescica *sf.* bladder.

vescovado *sm.* bishop's residence.

vescovile *agg.* episcopal.

véscovo *sm.* bishop.

vespa *sf.* wasp.

vespaio *sm.* 1. wasps' nest 2. (*fig.*) hornets' nest.

vespro *sm.* 1. evening 2. (*relig.*) evensong.

vessare *vt.* to vex.

vessatorio *agg.* vexatious.

vessazione *sf.* vexation.

vessillo *sm.* flag.

vestaglia *sf.* dressing-gown.

vestale *sf.* vestal.

veste *sf.* 1. dress 2. (*eccl.*) vestment 3. (*qualità*) capacity.

vestiario *sm.* clothes (*pl.*).

vestìbolo *sm.* hall.

vestigio *sm.* vestige.

vestimento *sm.* V. *veste.*

vestire *vt.* 1. to dress 2. (*fig.*) to clothe 3. (*indossare*) to wear (*v. irr.*). ♦ vestirsi *vr.* to dress oneself.

vestito *sm.* 1. (*da uomo*) suit 2. (*da donna*) frock, dress.

vestizione *sf.* 1. (*eccl.*) ceremony of taking the habit 2. (*di monaca*) ceremony of taking the veil.

veterano *sm.* veteran.

veterinaria *sf.* veterinary science.

veterinario *sm.* veterinary.

veto *sm.* veto.

vetraio *sm.* glazier.

vetrame *sm.* glassware.

vetrata *sf.* glass partition: *— a colori,* stained glass window.

vetrato *agg.* glazed: *carta vetrata,* glass-paper.

vetreria *sf.* glass-work.

vetrificàbile *agg.* vitrifiable.

vetrificare *vt.* to vitrify.

vetrificazione *sf.* vitrification.

vetrina *sf.* shop-window.

vetrioleggiare *vt.* to vitriolize.

vetriolo *sm.* vitriol.

vetro *sm.* 1. glass 2. (*di finestra*) window-pane.

vetrocromia *sf.* glass-painting.

vetroso *agg.* glassy.

vetta *sf.* top, summit.

vettore *sm.* vector.

vettoriale *agg.* vectorial.

vettovagliamento *sm.* provisi-n-ing.

vettovagliare *vt.* to provision.

vettura *sf.* 1. coach 2. (*automobile*) car || — *di piazza*, taxi-cab.

vetturino *sm.* cabman (*pl.* -men).

vetustà *sf.* antiquity.

vetusto *agg.* ancient.

vezzeggiare *vt.* to fondle.

vezzeggiativo *sm.* petname.

vezzo *sm.* 1. habit 2. (*collana*) necklace.

vezzosamente *avv.* charmingly.

vezzoso *agg.* charming.

vi[1] *pron.* you, to you.

vi[2] *avv.* 1. (*qui*) here 2. (*là*) there.

via[1] *sf.* 1. street 2. (*strada di comunicazione*) road 3. (*cammino*) way (*anche fig.*) 4. (*linea di condotta*) course. ♦ **via** *sm. dare il* —, to give (*v. irr.*) the starting.

via[2] *avv.* away: *andar* —, to go (*v. irr.*) away.

viabilità *sf.* state of a road.

viadotto *sm.* viaduct.

viaggiante *agg.* travelling.

viaggiare *vi.* to travel: — *in treno, automobile, aereo*, to travel by train, by car, by air.

viaggiatore *sm.* traveller: — *di commercio*, commercial traveller.

viaggio *sm.* 1. journey, trip 2. (*per mare*) voyage 3. (*in aereo*) flight.

viale *sm.* avenue; (*di giardino*) alley.

viandante *sm.* wayfarer.

viàtico *sm.* viaticum (*pl.* -ca).

viavai *sm.* coming-and-going.

vibrante *agg.* vibrating (with).

vibrare *vi.* 1. to vibrate 2. (*colpi*) to strike (*v. irr.*).

vibràtile *agg.* vibratile.

vibrato *agg.* energetic.

vibratore *sm.* vibrator.

vibrazione *sf.* vibration.

vicariato *sm.* vicariate.

vicario *sm.* vicar.

vicecònsole *sm.* vice-consul.

vicedirettore *sm.* assistant-director.

vicegovernatore *sm.* vice-governor.

vicenda *sf.* vicissitude 2. (*evento*) event 3. (*successione*) succession.

vicendévole *agg.* mutual.

vicendevolmente *avv.* mutually.

vicepresidente *sm.* vice-president.

viceré *sm.* viceroy.

vicesegretario *sm.* vice-secretary.

viceversa *avv.* vice versa. ♦ **viceversa** *cong.* whereas.

vicinale *sf.* local road.

vicinanza *sf.* 1. vicinity: *in* — *di*, close to 2. (*adiacenze*) neighbourhood: *nelle vicinanze*, in the neighbourhood.

vicinato *sm.* 1. neighbourhood 2. (*i vicini*) neighbours (*pl.*).

vicino[1] *agg.* near, close. ♦ **vicino** *sm.* neighbour.

vicino[2] *avv.* near, near by. ♦ **vicino** *prep.* near, close to.

vicissitùdine *sf.* vicissitude.

vìcolo *sm.* lane, alley.

vìdeo *sm.* video.

vidimare *vt.* 1. (*firmare*) to sign 2. (*autenticare*) to authenticate.

vidimazione *sf.* 1. (*firma*) signature 2. (*autenticazione*) authentication.

vietare *vt.* to forbid (*v. irr.*).

vietato *agg.* forbidden: — *fumare*, no smoking; — *entrare*, no admittance.

vieto *agg.* antiquated.

vigente *agg.* in force.

vigere *vi.* to be in force.

vigilante *agg.* watchful.

vigilanza *sf.* watch.

vigilare *vt.* to watch over.

vigilato *agg.* watched.

vigile *agg.* watchful. ♦ **vigile** *sm.* policeman (*pl.* -men).

vigilia *sf.* 1. eve 2. (*relig.*) fast.

vigliaccamente *avv.* in a cowardly way.

vigliaccheria *sf.* 1. cowardice 2. (*azione vigliacca*) cowardly action.

vigliacco *agg.* cowardly.

vigna *sf.* vineyard.

vigneto *sm.* vineyard.

vignetta *sf.* cartoon.

vigore *sm.* vigour: *in* —, in force.

vigoroso *agg.* vigorous.

vile *agg.* 1. cowardly 2. (*meschino*) mean 3. (*basso*) low.

vilipèndere *vt.* to despise.

vilipendio *sm.* contempt.

villa *sf.* villa.

villaggio *sm.* village.

villanìa *sf.* 1. rudeness 2. (*azione villana*) rude action.

villano *agg.* rude. ♦ **villano** *sm.* peasant, countryman (*pl.* -men).

villeggiante *s.* holiday-maker.

villeggiatura *sf.* holiday: *luogo di* —, (holiday) resort.

villino *sm.* cottage.

villoso *agg.* hairy.

viltà *sf.* 1. cowardice 2. (*azione vile*) cowardly action.

vilucchio *sm.* bearbind.

viluppo *sm.* tangle.

vìmine *sm.* withe: *paniere di vimini*, wicker basket.

vinaccia *sf.* dregs of pressed grapes (*pl.*).

vinaio *sm.* wine-merchant.

vinario *agg.* wine (*attr.*).

vincente *agg.* winning. ♦ **vincente** *sm.* winner.

vincere *vt.* 1. to win (*v. irr.*) 2. (*battere*) to beat (*v. irr.*) 3. (*sopraffare*) to overcome (*v. irr.*) 4. (*superare*) to outdo (*v. irr.*).

vincìbile *agg.* conquerable.

vìncita *sf.* 1. win 2. (*denaro vinto*) winnings (*pl.*).

vincitore *agg.* winning. ♦ **vincitore** *sm.* winner.

vinco *sm.* withe.

vincolare *vt.* 1. to bind (*v. irr.*) 2. (*comm.*) to lock up.

vincolato *agg.* 1. bound 2. (*comm.*) locked up.

vìncolo *sm.* tie, bond.

vinello *sm.* light wine.

vinìcolo *agg.* wine (*attr.*).

vinificazione *sf.* wine-making.

vino *sm.* wine.

vinto *agg.* 1. that has been won 2. (*sconfitto*) beaten 3. (*sopraffatto*) overcome || *darsi —*, to give (*v. irr.*) in. ♦ **vinto** *sm.* 1. (*al giuoco o in qualsiasi contesa*) loser 2. (*in battaglia*) vanquished man.

viola[1] *sf.* 1. violet: *— del pensiero*, pansy. ♦ **viola** *agg. e sm.* violet.

viola[2] *sf.* (*mus.*) viola.

violàcee *sf. pl.* violaceae.

violàceo *agg.* violet.

violare *vt.* to violate.

violatore *sm.* violator.

violazione *sf.* violation: *— di domicilio*, house-breaking.

violentare *vt.* 1. to violate, to rape 2. (*fig.*) to do (*v. irr.*) violence to.

violento *agg.* violent.

violenza *sf.* violence, rape.

violetto *agg.* violet.

violinista *s.* violin-player.

violino *sm.* violin.

violoncellista *s.* violoncellist.

violoncello *sm.* violoncello.

viòttola *sf.* path, lane.

viòttolo *sm.* path, lane.

vìpera *sf.* 1. adder 2. (*fig.*) viper.

viperino *agg.* viperous.

viraggio *sm.* (*foto*) toning.

virago *sf.* virago.

virare *vt. e vi.* 1. to veer: *— di bordo*, to veer round 2. (*fig.*) to turn about.

virata *sf.* veer.

virginale *agg.* virginal.

virginia *sm.* Virginia.

vìrgola *sf.* 1. (*gramm.*) comma 2. (*mat.*) point.

virgolette *sf. pl.* inverted commas: *tra —*, in inverted commas.

virgulto *sm.* shoot.

virile *agg.* manly.

virilità *sf.* 1. manliness 2. (*età virile*) manhood.

virilmente *avv.* manfully.

virologia *sf.* virology.

virosi *sf.* virosis (*pl.* -ses).

virtù *sf.* virtue.

virtuale *agg.* virtual.

virtualità *sf.* virtuality.

virtuosismo *sm.* virtuosity.

virtuoso *agg.* virtuous.

virulento *agg.* virulent.

virulenza *sf.* virulence.

virus *sm.* virus.

viscerale *agg.* visceral.

vìscere *sm.* 1. vital organ 2. (*f. pl.*) *le viscere*, viscera.

vischio *sm.* 1. mistletoe 2. (*pania*) bird-lime.

vischiosità *sf.* stickiness.

vischioso *agg.* sticky.

viscidità *sf.* viscidity.

vìscido *agg.* 1. sticky 2. (*scivoloso*) slippery.

vìsciola *sf.* wild cherry.

visconte *sm.* viscount.

viscontessa *sf.* viscountess.

viscosità *sf.* viscosity.

viscoso *agg.* viscous.

visìbile *agg.* visible, clear.

visibilio *sm.* great number: *andare in —*, to go (*v. irr.*) into raptures.

visibilità *sf.* visibility.

visiera *sf.* 1. (*di elmo*) visor 2. (*di berretto*) peak.

visionario *agg. e sm.* visionary.

visione *sf.* vision: *prendere — di*, to look over; *prima — (cine)*, first screening.

vìsita *sf.* 1. visit, call: *fare una —*, to pay (*v. irr.*) a visit 2. (*persona che visita*) visitor 3. (*med.*) examination.

visitare *vt.* to visit.

visitatore *sm.* visitor.

visivo *agg.* visual.

viso *sm.* face: *— a —*, face to face.

visone *sm.* mink.

vispo *agg.* lively, brisk.
vista *sf.* 1. sight 2. (*occhi*) eyes (*pl.*).
vistare *vt.* to visa.
visto[1] *sm.* visa.
visto[2] *agg.* seen || — *che*, since as.
vistoso *agg.* 1. showy 2. (*fig.*) considerable.
visuale *agg.* visual. ♦ **visuale** *sf.* sight.
vita[1] *sf.* 1. life (*pl.* lives): *a* —, for life; *in* —, during one's life 2. (*necessario per vivere*) living: *costo della* —, cost of living.
vita[2] *sf.* (*anat.*) waist.
vitaiolo *sm.* bon viveur.
vitalba *sf.* clematis.
vitale *agg.* vital.
vitalità *sf.* vitality.
vitalizio *agg.* for life. ♦ **vitalizio** *sm.* annuity.
vitamina *sf.* vitamin.
vitamìnico *agg.* vitaminic.
vite[1] *sf.* vine.
vite[2] *sf.* (*mecc.*) screw.
vitello *sm.* calf (*pl.* calves).
viticcio *sm.* vine-tendril.
vitìcolo *agg.* viticultural.
viticoltore *sm.* viticulturist.
viticoltura *sf.* grape-growing.
vìtreo *agg.* vitreous.
vìttima *sf.* victim.
vittimismo *sm.* victimization.
vitto *sm.* 1. food 2. (*pasti in pensione o albergo*) board: — *e alloggio*, board and lodging.
vittoria *sf.* victory.
vittorioso *agg.* victorious.
vituperare *vt.* to vituperate.
vituperio *sm.* insult.
viuzza *sf.* lane.
viva *inter.* hurrah!
vivacchiare *vi.* to live poorly.
vivace *agg.* 1. lively, sprightly 2. (*pronto, sveglio*) quick 3. (*di colori*) bright.
vivacemente *avv.* 1. lively 2. (*prontamente*) quickly 3. (*vivamente*) brightly.
vivacità *sf.* 1. liveliness 2. (*di colori*) brightness.
vivaio *sm.* 1. (*di pesci*) fish-pond 2. (*di piante*) nursery.
vivamente *avv.* deeply, keenly.
vivanda *sf.* food.
vivandiere *sm.* sutler.
vivente *agg.* alive (*pred.*), living. ♦ **vivente** *sm.* living being.
vìvere *vt.* e *vi.* to live: *cessare di*

—, to die; *insegnare a* — *a qu.*, to teach (*v. irr.*) so. good manners; — *alle spalle di qu.*, to sponge on so.
vìveri *sm. pl.* victuals.
vìvido *agg.* vivid.
vivificare *vt.* to enliven.
vivificatore *agg.* vivifying. ♦ **vivificatore** *sm.* vivifier.
vivìparo *agg.* e *sm.* viviparous.
vivisezione *sf.* vivisection.
vivo *agg.* 1. living, alive (*pred.*) || *a viva forza*, by main force; *argento* —, quicksilver; *calce viva*, quicklime; *farsi* —, to turn up 2. (*vivace*) lively 3. (*profondo, acuto*) deep, sharp 4. (*vivido*) vivid 5. (*di colori*) bright.
viziare *vt.* 1. to spoil (*v. irr.*) 2. (*guastare*) to vitiate.
viziato *agg.* 1. spoilt 2. (*guasto*) vitiated.
vizio *sm.* 1. vice 2. (*cattiva abitudine*) bad habit.
vizioso *agg.* vicious. ♦ **vizioso** *sm.* vicious man.
vocabolario *sm.* 1. vocabulary 2. (*dizionario*) dictionary.
vocàbolo *sm.* word.
vocale[1] *agg.* vocal.
vocale[2] *sf.* vowel.
vocalizzare *vt.* e *vi.* to vocalize.
vocalizzo *sm.* vocalization.
vocativo *agg.* e *sm.* vocative.
vocazione *sf.* vocation, bent.
voce *sf.* 1. voice: *a* — *alta, bassa*, in a loud, low voice; *parlare sotto* —, to whisper 2. (*diceria*) rumour 3. (*articolo di elenco*) item.
vociare *vi.* to shout.
vociferare *vi.* 1. to shout 2. (*spargere una voce*) to rumour.
vocìo *sm.* shouting.
voga[1] *sf.* (*mar.*) rowing.
voga[2] *sf.* 1. (*moda*) fashion 2. (*energia*) energy.
vogare *vi.* (*mar.*) to row.
vogata *sf.* row.
vogatore *sm.* rower.
voglia *sf.* 1. wish: *aver* —, to feel (*v. irr.*) like 2. (*volontà*) will.
voglioso *agg.* desirous, willing.
voi *pron.* you: — *stessi*, you yourselves.
volano *sm.* battledore and shuttlecock.
volante[1] *agg.* flying: *cervo* —, kite; *foglio* —, loose sheet. ♦ **volante** *sf.* (*di polizia*) flying squad.

volante² *sm.* steering-wheel.

volantino *sm.* leaflet.

volare *vi.* to fly (*v. irr.*): *far* —, to blow (*v. irr.*).

volata *sf.* 1. flight 2. (*corsa*) rush 3. (*sport*) final sprint.

volàtile¹ *agg.* (*chim.*) volatile.

volàtile² *sm.* bird.

volatilizzare *vt.* to volatilize. ♦ **volatilizzarsi** *vr.* to volatilize.

volente *agg.* — *o nolente*, willy-nilly.

volenterosamente *avv.* willingly.

volenteroso *agg.* V. *volonteroso*.

volentieri *avv.* willingly.

volere¹ *vt.* 1. (*forte volontà*) (*pres. indicativo e congiuntivo*) will; (*passato indicativo e congiuntivo, condizionale*) would 2. (*desiderio*) to want, to wish: *voglio che egli venga*, I want him to come 3. (*gradire*) to like (*costr. pers.*): *vorrei, avrei voluto*, I should like, I should have liked 4. (*desiderio intenso*) to wish: *vorrei essere ricco!*, I wish I were rich! 5. (*aver bisogno di*) to need, to require 6. (*con espressioni di tempo*) to take (*v. irr.*): *ci vogliono due ore per andare alla stazione*, it takes two hours to go to the station 7. (*cercare*) to ask for: *c'è qualcuno che ti cerca*, there is somebody asking for you 8. (*essere disposti*) to be willing || *che tu voglia o no*, whether you like it or not; *vuoi ... vuoi* (*sia ... sia*), both ... and; *Dio lo voglia, Dio non voglia!*, God grant it, God forbid!

volere² *sm.* will, wish.

volgare *agg.* vulgar, common.

volgarità *sf.* vulgarity.

volgarizzare *vt.* to divulge.

volgarizzatore *sm.* popularizer.

volgarizzazione *sf.* popularization.

volgarmente *avv.* vulgarly, commonly.

vòlgere *vt.* to turn.

vòlgere *sm.* course.

volgo *sm.* common people.

voliera *sf.* aviary.

volitivo *agg.* 1. strong-willed 2. (*gramm.*) volitive.

volo *sm.* flight: *prendere il* —, to run (*v. irr.*) away; *capire qc. al* —, to grasp sthg. immediately.

volontà *sf.* will: *di sua spontanea* —, of his own free-will.

volontariamente *avv.* voluntarily.

volontario *agg.* voluntary. ♦ **volontario** *sm.* volunteer.

volontarismo *sm.* voluntarism.

volonteroso *agg.* willing.

volontieri *avv.* V. *volentieri*.

volpe *sf.* fox.

volpino *agg.* foxy: *cane* —, Pomeranian.

volpone *sm.* old fox.

volta¹ *sf.* 1. time: *una* —, once; *due, tre volte*, twice, three times; *ancora una* —, once again; *una* — *e mezzo*, half as much; *una* — *o l'altra*, sooner or later; *rare volte*, seldom; *una* — *tanto*, once in a while; *c'era una* —, once upon a time there was 2. (*turno*) turn: *a mia* —, in my turn.

volta² *sf.* 1. (*curva*) bend 2. (*arch.*) vault.

voltafaccia *sm.* volte-face.

voltaggio *sm.* voltage.

voltàmetro *sm.* voltameter.

voltare *vt.* to turn.

voltastòmaco *sm.* sickness.

voltata *sf.* bend, turning, curve.

volteggiare *vi.* 1. to whirl 2. (*svolazzare*) to fly (*v. irr.*) about.

volteggio *sm.* vaulting.

volto¹ *sm.* 1. face 2. (*aspetto*) aspect.

volto² *agg.* 1. turned 2. (*rivolto*) directed.

volùbile *agg.* changeable.

volubilità *sf.* inconstancy.

volume *sm.* volume.

volumètrico *agg.* volumetric.

voluminoso *agg.* voluminous, bulky.

voluta *sf.* volute.

volutamente *avv.* intentionally.

voluttà *sf.* 1. delight 2. (*dei sensi*) voluptuousness.

voluttuario *agg.* voluptuary.

voluttuosamente *avv.* voluptuously.

voluttuoso *agg.* voluptuous.

vòmere *sm.* 1. ploughshare 2. (*anat.*) vomer.

vomitare *vt.* to vomit, to be sick.

vòmito *sm.* vomiting: *conato di* —, retch.

vòngola *sf.* mussel.

vorace *agg.* voracious, greedy.

voracità *sf.* voracity, greed.

voràgine *sf.* chasm.

vorticare *vi.* to whirl.

vòrtice *sm.* whirl: — *di vento*, whirlwind.

vorticosamente *avv.* in whirls.

vorticoso *agg.* whirling.

vostro *agg. poss.* your ‖ *in vece vostra*, instead of you. ♦ **vostro** *pron. poss.* yours ‖ *rispondiamo alla vostra del 3 giugno* (*comm.*), in reply to your letter of June 3rd; *sono dalla vostra*, I am on your side.

votante *agg.* voting. ♦ **votante** *sm.* voter.

votare *vt.* to vote. ♦ **votarsi** *vr.* to devote oneself.

votato *agg.* **1.** passed **2.** (*dedicato*) devoted.

votazione *sf.* voting.

votivo *agg.* votive.

voto *sm.* **1.** (*promessa solenne*) vow **2.** (*augurio*) wish **3.** (*per elezioni*) vote **4.** (*scolastico*) mark: *prendere un bel, brutto* —, to get (*v. irr.*) a good, bad mark.

vulcànico *agg.* volcanic.

vulcanismo *sm.* vulcanism.

vulcanizzare *vt.* to vulcanize.

vulcanizzato *agg.* vulcanized.

vulcanizzazione *sf.* vulcanization.

vulcano *sm.* volcano.

vulneràbile *agg.* vulnerable.

vulnerabilità *sf.* vulnerability.

vuotare *vt.* to empty: — *il sacco*, to speak (*v. irr.*) out one's mind.

vuoto *agg.* **1.** empty **2.** (*sprovvisto*) devoid. ♦ **vuoto** *sm.* **1.** empty space **2.** (*recipiente vuoto*) empty **3.** (*vacuità*) emptiness.

X

xenofobìa *sf.* xenophobia.

xenòfobo *sm.* xenophobe.

xilòfono *sm.* xylophone.

xilografìa *sf.* **1.** (*incisione*) xylograph **2.** (*arte*) xylography.

Z

zaffata *sf.* whiff.

zafferano *sm.* saffron.

zaffiro *sm.* sapphire.

zàino *sm.* knapsack.

zampa *sf.* **1.** paw **2.** (*con zoccolo*) hoof **3.** (*di uccello*) claw **4.** (*di insetto*) leg ‖ *zampe di gallina* (*scrittura*), scrawl; (*rughe*) crow's feet.

zampata *sf.* blow with a paw.

zampettare *vt.* to toddle.

zampillante *agg.* gushing.

zampillare *vi.* to gush.

zampillo *sm.* gush.

zampino *sm.* little paw ‖ *mettere lo — in una faccenda*, to have a hand in the matter.

zampogna *sf.* **1.** reed-pipe **2.** (*cornamusa*) bag-pipe.

zampognaro *sm.* piper.

zanna *sf.* **1.** fang **2.** (*di elefante*) tusk.

zanzara *sf.* mosquito.

zanzariera *sf.* mosquito-net.

zappa *sf.* hoe.

zappare *vt.* to hoe.

zappata *sf.* blow with a hoe.

zappatore *sm.* **1.** hoer **2.** (*mil.*) pioneer.

zappatura *sf.* hoeing.

zar *sm.* czar.

zarina *sf.* czarina.

zarista *s.* czarist.

zàttera *sf.* raft.

zavorra *sf.* **1.** ballast **2.** (*fig.*) rubbish.

zavorrare *vt.* to ballast.

zàzzera *sf.* mane.

zazzeruto *agg.* shockheaded.

zebra *sf.* zebra.

zebrato *agg.* striped.

zebratura *sf.* stripes (*pl.*).

zebù *sm.* zebu.

zecca[1] *sf.* mint: *nuovo di* —, brand-new.

zecca[2] *sf.* (*zool.*) tick.

zecchino *sm.* sequin: *oro* —, first-quality-gold.

zèfiro *sm.* zephyr.

zelante *agg.* zealous.

zelantemente *avv.* zealously.

zelo *sm.* zeal.

zenit *sm.* zenith.

zénzero *sm.* ginger.

zeppo *agg.* crammed (with).

zerbino *sm.* door-mat.

zerbinotto *sm.* dandy.

zero *sm.* **1.** nought **2.** (*in gradazioni*) zero **3.** (*tel.*) 0 ‖ *ridursi a* —, to come (*v. irr.*) to nought.

zia *sf.* aunt.

zibaldone *sm.* miscellany.

zibellino *sm.* sable.

zigano *agg. e sm.* tzigane.

zìgomo *sm.* cheek-bone.

zigrinare *vt.* to knurl.
zigrinato *agg.* knurled.
zig-zag (*nella loc. avv.*) *a* —, zigzag.
zigzagare *vi.* to zigzag.
zimbello *sm.* 1. decoy 2. (*fig.*) laughing-stock.
zincare *vt.* to zinc.
zincatura *sf.* zinc-plating.
zinco *sm.* zinc.
zincografia *sf.* zincography.
zingaresco *agg.* gipsy (*attr.*).
zìngaro *sm.* gipsy.
zio *sm.* uncle.
zircone *sm.* zircon.
zirconio *sm.* zirconium.
zitella *sf.* spinster.
zittire *vt.* to hiss.
zitto *agg.* silent: *star* —, to be silent.
zizzania *sf.* 1. darnel 2. (*fig.*) discord.
zoccolaio *sm.* clog-maker.
zoccolare *vi.* to clatter about with one's clogs.
zòccolo *sm.* 1. clog 2. (*di animale*) hoof 3. (*piedistallo*) base.
zodiacale *agg.* zodiacal.
zodìaco *sm.* zodiac.
zolfanello *sm.* match.
zolfatara *sf.* V. *solfatara*.
zolfatura *sf.* sulfurization.
zolfo *sm.* sulphur.
zolla *sf.* clod.
zolletta *sf.* lump.
zona *sf.* zone, area.
zonzo (*nella loc. avv.*) *andare a* —, to loaf.
zoo *sm.* zoo.
zoofilìa *sf.* zoophilia.
zoòfilo *agg.* zoophilous. ♦ **zoòfilo** *sm.* animal-lover.

zoofobìa *sf.* zoophobia.
zoologìa *sf.* zoology.
zoològico *agg.* zoological.
zoòlogo *sm.* zoologist.
zootecnìa *sf.* zootechny.
zootècnico *agg.* zootechnic: *patrimonio* —, live-stock. ♦ **zootècnico** *sm.* animal expert.
zoppicamento *sm.* limping.
zoppicante *agg.* lame.
zoppicare *vi.* 1. to limp 2. (*di mobile*) to be shaky.
zoppo *agg.* 1. lame 2. (*di mobile*) shaky. ♦ **zoppo** *sm.* lame person.
zoticàggine *sf.* boorishness.
zòtico *agg.* boorish. ♦ **zòtico** *sm.* boor.
zuavo *sm.* zouave ‖ *calzoni alla zuava*, knickerbockers.
zucca *sf.* 1. pumpkin 2. (*testa*) pate.
zuccherare *vt.* to sugar.
zuccherato *agg.* sugared.
zuccheriera *sf.* sugar-basin.
zuccherificio *sm.* sugar-refinery.
zuccherino *sm.* 1. sweet 2. (*fig.*) sugar-plum.
zùcchero *sm.* sugar.
zucchina *sf.* vegetable marrow.
zucconàggine *sf.* 1. (*ottusità*) dullness 2. (*ostinatezza*) stubbornness.
zuccone *sm.* 1. (*ottuso*) blockhead 2. (*testardo*) donkey.
zuffa *sf.* brawl.
zufolare *vt.* e *vi.* to whistle.
zufolìo *sm.* whistle.
zùfolo *sm.* 1. whistle 2. (*mus.*) pipe.
zuppa *sf.* soup.
zuppiera *sf.* tureen.
zuppo *agg.* soaked.
zuzzurellone *sm.* skittish boy.

NOMI PROPRI, STORICI E GEOGRAFICI

Abele Abel.
Abissinia Abyssinia.
Abramo Abraham.
Achille Achilles.
Ada Ada.
Adamo Adam.
Adolfo Adolph.
Adone Adonis.
Adriano Hadrian.
Adriatico (Mar) Adriatic Sea.
Afganistan Afghanistan.
Africa Africa.
Afrodite Aphrodite.
Agamennone Agamemnon
Agata Agatha.
Agnese Agnes.
Agostino Augustin.
Aia (L') The Hague.
Aiace Ajax.
Albania Albania.
Alberto Albert.
Aldo Aldous.
Alessandra Alexandra.
Alessandro Alexander.
Alessio Alexis.
Alfredo Alfred.
Algeri Algiers.
Algeria Algeria.
Alice Alice.
Alpi Alps pl.
Alsazia Alsace.
Amazzoni (Rio delle) Amazon.
Ambrogio Ambrose.
Amburgo Hamburg.
Amelia Amelia.
America America.
Amleto Hamlet.
Andalusia Andalusia.
Ande Andes pl.
Andrea Andrew.
Angelo Angel.
Anna Ann(e).
Annibale Hannibal.
Antartide Antarctica.
Antonino Antoninus.
Antonio Ant(h)ony.
Apollo Apollo.
Appennini Apennines pl.
Arabia Arabia.
Aragona Aragon.
Arcadia Arcadia.
Archimede Archimedes.

Argentina Argentina.
Arianna Ariadne.
Aristofane Aristophanes.
Aristotele Aristotle.
Armando Armand.
Arnaldo Arnold.
Aroldo Harold.
Arrigo Henry.
Arturo Arthur.
Asia Asia.
Atene Athens.
Atlantico Atlantic.
Augusta Augusta.
Augusto Augustus.
Australia Australia.
Austria Austria.
Azzorre Azores pl.

Babele Babel.
Babilonia Babylon.
Bacco Bacchus.
Balcani Balkans pl.
Baldassarre Balthazar.
Baleari Balearic Islands pl.
Baltico (Mar) Baltic Sea.
Baltimora Baltimore.
Barbara Barbara.
Barcellona Barcelona.
Barnaba Barnaby, Barnabas.
Bartolomeo Bartholomew.
Basilea Basel.
Basilio Basil.
Battista Baptist.
Beatrice Beatrix.
Belgio Belgium.
Belgrado Belgrade.
Benedetto Benedict.
Bengala Bengal.
Beniamino Benjamin.
Berenice Berenice.
Berlino Berlin.
Bermude Bermudas pl.
Bernardo Bernard.
Berta Bertha.
Betlemme Bethlehem.
Bianca Blanche.
Birmania Burma.
Boemia Bohemia.
Bolivia Bolivia.
Bonifacio Boniface.
Bosforo Bosporus.

Brandeburgo Brandenburg.
Brasile Brazil.
Bretagna Brittany.
Bruto Brutus.
Bulgaria Bulgaria.

Cadice Cadiz.
Caino Cain.
Caio Caius.
Cairo Cairo.
California California.
Calvino Calvin.
Cambogia Cambodia.
Campidoglio Capitol.
Canadà Canada.
Caraibi (Mar dei) Caribbean Sea.
Carlo Charles.
Carlomagno Charlemagne.
Carlotta Charlotte.
Carolina Caroline.
Carpazi Carpathian Mountains *pl.*
Cartagine Carthage.
Cascemir Cashmere, Kashmir.
Caspio (Mar) Caspian Sea.
Cassio Cassius.
Cassiopea Cassiopeia.
Castiglia Castile.
Caterina Catherine.
Catone Cato.
Caucaso Caucasus.
Cecilia Cecily.
Cecilio Cecil.
Cecoslovacchia Czechoslovakia.
Cenerentola Cinderella.
Cesare Caesar.
Chiara Clara.
Cicerone Cicero.
Cile Chile.
Cina China.
Cinzia Cynthia.
Cipro Cyprus.
Cirillo Cyril.
Ciro Cyrus.
Clara Clara.
Claudio Claudius, Claude.
Clemente Clement.
Clementina Clementine.
Cleopatra Cleopatra.
Clitennestra Clytemnestra.
Colombia Colombia.
Colonia Cologne.
Congo Congo.
Corea Korea.
Corfù Corfu.
Corinto Corinth.
Cornelio Cornelius.
Cornovaglia Cornwall.
Corrado Conrad.

Corsica Corsica.
Costantino Constantine.
Costantinopoli Constantinople.
Costanza Constance.
Creta Crete.
Crimea Crimea.
Cristina Christine.
Cristo Christ.
Cristoforo Christopher.
Cuba Cuba.

Dafne Daphne.
Damasco Damascus.
Damocle Damocles.
Daniele Daniel.
Danimarca Denmark.
Danubio Danube.
Danzica Danzig.
Dardanelli Dardanelles *pl.*
Dario Darius.
Davide David.
Debora Deborah.
Delfo Delphi.
Democrito Democritus.
Demostene Demosthenes.
Desdemona Desdemona.
Diana Diana.
Didone Dido.
Diocleziano Diocletian.
Diogene Diogenes.
Dionigi, Dionisio Dionysius.
Domenico Dominic.
Domiziano Domitian.
Dorotea Dorothy.
Dublino Dublin.

Ebridi Hebrides *pl.*
Edgardo Edgar.
Edimburgo Edinburgh.
Edipo Oedipus.
Edmondo Edmund.
Edoardo Edward.
Egeo (Mar) Aegean Sea.
Egitto Egypt.
Elena Helen.
Eleonora Eleanor.
Elettra Electra.
Elia Elias, Elijah.
Elisa Eliza.
Elisabetta Elizabeth.
Ellade Hellas.
Emanuele Emanuel.
Emilia Emily.
Enea Aeneas.
Enrichetta Henrietta, Harriet.
Enrico Henry, Harry.
Epaminonda Epaminondas.

Epicuro Epicurus.
Eraclito Heraclitus.
Erasmo Erasmus.
Erberto Herbert.
Ercole Hercules.
Eritrea Eritrea.
Ermete Hermes.
Ernesto Ernest.
Erode Herod.
Erodoto Herodotus.
Esaù Esau.
Eschilo Aeschylus.
Esiodo Hesiod.
Esopo Aesop.
Ester Esther.
Etiopia Ethiopia.
Ettore Hector.
Euclide Euclid.
Eufrate Euphrates.
Eugenio Eugene.
Euripide Euripides
Europa Europe.
Eva Eve.
Evelina Evelyn.
Ezechiele Ezekiel.

Farsalo Pharsalus.
Fausto Faust(us).
Federico Frederic.
Fedra Phaedra.
Felice Felix.
Ferdinando Ferdinand.
Filadelfia Philadelphia.
Filippi Philippi.
Filippine Philippines *pl.*
Filippo Philip.
Finlandia Finland.
Firenze Florence.
Formosa Formosa.
Francesca Frances.
Francesco Francis.
Francia France.
Franco Frank.
Francoforte Frankfurt.

Gabriele Gabriel.
Galilea Galilee.
Galles Wales.
Gallia Gaule.
Genova Genoa.
Geova Jehovah.
Gerardo Gerard.
Geremia Jeremiah.
Gerico Jericho.
Germania Germany.
Gerolamo Jerome.
Gerusalemme Jerusalem.

Gesù Jesus.
Giacobbe Jacob.
Giacomo James.
Giamaica Jamaica.
Giappone Japan.
Giasone Jason.
Giava Java.
Gibilterra Gibraltar.
Gilberto Gilbert.
Ginevra Geneva.
Giobbe Job.
Giona Jonah, Jonas.
Gionata Jonathan.
Giordano Jordan.
Giorgio George.
Giosuè Joshua.
Giovanna Jane, Jean, Joan.
Giovanni John.
Giove Jove, Jupiter.
Giovenale Juvenal.
Giuda Judas, Jude.
Giudea Judea.
Giuditta Judith.
Giulia Julia, Julie.
Giuliana Juliana.
Giuliano Julian.
Giulietta Juliet.
Giulio Julius.
Giunone Juno.
Giuseppe Joseph.
Giuseppina Josephine.
Goffredo Geoffrey, Jeffrey.
Golgota Golgotha.
Golia Goliath.
Gran Bretagna Great Britain.
Grazia Grace.
Grecia Greece.
Gregorio Gregory.
Groenlandia Greenland.
Guaiana Guiana.
Gualtiero Walter.
Guascogna Gascony.
Guglielmo William.
Guido Guy.
Guinea Guinea.
Gustavo Gustavus.

Iacopo James.
Iberia Iberia.
Icaro Icarus.
Ignazio Ignatius.
Ilario Hilary.
Imalaia Himalaya.
India India.
Indostan Hindustan.
Inghilterra England.
Innocenzo Innocent.
Ionio (Mar) Ionian Sea.

Ippolito Hippolytus.
Irene Irene.
Iride Iris.
Irlanda Ireland.
Irlanda (Stato Libero di) Eire.
Isabella Isabel.
Isacco Isaac.
Isaia Isaiah.
Iside Isis.
Islanda Iceland.
Ismaele Ishmael.
Israele Israel.
Italia Italy.
Iugoslavia Yugoslavia.

Lamberto Lambert.
Lancillotto Launcelot.
Laocoonte Laocoon.
Lapponia Lapland.
Laura Laura.
Lazio Latium.
Lazzaro Lazarus.
Leandro Leander.
Leonardo Leonard.
Leone Leo(n).
Leonida Leonidas.
Leopoldo Leopold.
Lete Lethe.
Letizia Letitia.
Libano Lebanon.
Libia Libya.
Licurgo Lycurgus
Lidia Lydia.
Liegi Liege.
Lione Lyons.
Lisbona Lisbon.
Livio Livy.
Livorno Leghorn.
Lodovico Ludwig.
Lombardia Lombardy.
Londra London.
Lorena Lorraine.
Lorenzo Lawrence.
Losanna Lausanne.
Lotario Lothar.
Lovanio Louvain.
Luca Luke.
Lucerna Lucerne.
Lucia Lucy.
Luciano Lucian.
Lucifero Lucifer.
Lucio Lucius.
Lucrezio Lucretius.
Luigi Louis, Lewis.
Luigia, Luisa Louise.
Lussemburgo Luxemburg.
Lutero Luther.

Maddalena Magdalene.
Maiorca Majorca.
Malesia Malaya.
Malta Malta.
Manciuria Manchuria.
Manfredi Manfred.
Manica (La) The Channel.
Mantova Mantua.
Maometto Mohammed.
Maratona Marathon.
Marcello Marcellus.
Marco Mark.
Margherita Margaret.
Maria Mary.
Marianna Marianne.
Mario Marius.
Marocco Morocco.
Marta Martha.
Marte Mars.
Martino Martin.
Marziale Martial.
Massimiliano Maximilian.
Matilde Matilda.
Matteo Matthew.
Matusalemme Methuselah.
Maurizio Maurice.
Mecca, La Mecca.
Mecenate Maecenas.
Mediterraneo Mediterranean.
Medusa Medusa.
Mefistofele Mephistopheles.
Melanesia Melanesia.
Menelao Menelaus.
Mercurio Mercury.
Merlino Merlin.
Mesopotamia Mesopotamia.
Messalina Messalina.
Messico Mexico.
Micene Mycenae.
Michele Michael.
Mida Midas.
Milano Milan.
Minerva Minerva.
Minosse Minos.
Minotauro Minotaur.
Mitridate Mithridates.
Molucche Moluccas *pl.*
Monaco (Principato di) Monaco.
Monaco di Baviera Munich.
Mongolia Mongolia.
Mosa Meuse.
Mosca Moscow.
Mosè Moses.
Mozambico Mozambique.

Napoleone Napoleon.
Napoli Naples.
Narciso Narcissus.

Nerone Nero.
Nettuno Neptune.
Nicola, Niccolò Nicholas.
Nilo Nile.
Nizza Nice.
Noè Noah.
Normandia Normandy.
Norvegia Norway.
Nuova Zelanda New Zealand.

Oceania Oceania.
Ofelia Ophelia.
Olanda Holland.
Olimpo Olympus.
Oliviero Oliver.
Omero Homer.
Orazio Horace, Horatio.
Orcadi Orkneys *pl.*
Oreste Orestes.
Orfeo Orpheus.
Orione Orion.
Orlando Roland.
Orsola Ursula.
Osiride Osiris.
Osvaldo Oswald.
Otello Othello.
Ovidio Ovid.

Pacifico Pacific.
Padova Padua.
Paesi Bassi Netherlands *p.*.
Palestina Palestine.
Pancrazio Pancras.
Paola Paula.
Paolina Pauline.
Paolo Paul.
Papuasia Papua.
Paride Paris.
Parigi Paris.
Parnaso Parnassus.
Partenone Parthenon.
Patagonia Patagonia.
Patrizia Patricia.
Patrizio Patrick.
Pechino Peking.
Peloponneso Peloponnesus.
Penelope Penelope.
Pensilvania Pennsylvania.
Pericle Pericles.
Perseo Perseus.
Persia Persia.
Perù Peru.
Piemonte Piedmont.
Pietro, Piero Peter.
Pigmalione Pigmalion.
Pindaro Pindar.
Pio Pius.

Pirenei Pyrenees *pl.*
Pireo Piraeus.
Pitagora Pythagoras.
Platone Plato.
Plinio Pliny.
Plutarco Plutarch.
Polinesia Polynesia.
Polonia Poland.
Pompeo Pompey.
Portogallo Portugal.
Praga Prague.
Prometeo Prometheus.
Prussia Prussia.
Puglia Apulia.

Quintino Quentin.

Rachele Rachel.
Raffaele, Raffaello Raphael.
Raimondo Raymond.
Ramsete Ramses.
Rebecca Rebecca.
Remo Remus.
Reno Rhine.
Riccardo Richard.
Roberto Robert.
Rodano Rhone.
Rodi Rhodes.
Rodolfo Rudolph.
Rodrigo Roderick.
Rolando Roland.
Roma Rome.
Romania Ro(u)mania.
Romeo Romeo.
Romolo Romulus.
Rosa Rose.
Rosalia Rosalie.
Rosalinda Rosalind.
Rossana Roxana.
Rubicone Rubicon.
Ruggero Roger.
Russia Russia.

Saffo Sappho.
Salomone Solomon.
Samuele Samuel.
Sansone Samson.
Sara Sarah.
Sardegna Sardinia.
Sassonia Saxony.
Satana Satan.
Saturno Saturn.
Saul Saul.
Savoia Savoy.
Scandinavia Scandinavia.
Scipione Scipion.

Scozia Scotland.
Sebastiano Sebastian.
Sempione Simplon.
Serse Xerxes.
Siam Siam.
Siberia Siberia.
Sibilla Sibyl.
Sicilia Sicily.
Silla Sulla.
Silvestro Silvester.
Silvia Sylvia.
Simeone Simeon.
Simone Simon.
Siracusa Syracuse.
Siria Syria.
Smirne Smyrna.
Socrate Socrates.
Sodoma Sodom.
Sofia Sophia.
Sofocle Sophocles.
Somalia Somaliland.
Spagna Spain.
Sparta Sparta.
Stati Uniti United States (of America - U.S.A.).
Stefano Stephen.
Stoccolma Stockholm.
Strasburgo Strasbourg.
Sudan S(o)udan.
Susanna Susan(nah).
Svezia Sweden.
Svizzera Switzerland.

Tacito Tacitus.
Tailandia Thailand.
Tamigi Thames.
Tangeri Tangier(s).
Tasmania Tasmania.
Tebe Thebes.
Telemaco Telemachus.
Temistocle Themistocles.
Teodorico Theodoric.
Terenzio Terence.
Teresa Theresa.
Termopili Thermopylae pl.
Terranova Newfoundland.
Teseo Theseus.
Tevere Tiber.
Tiberio Tiberius.
Tirolo Tirol, Tyrol.

Tirreno (Mar) Tyrrhenian Sea.
Tito Titus.
Tiziano Titian.
Tobia Tobias.
Tolomeo Ptolemy.
Tommaso Thomas.
Tonchino Tonkin, Tongking.
Torino Turin.
Toscana Tuscany.
Traiano Trajan.
Tristano Tristan, Tristram.
Troia Troy.
Tullio Tully.
Tunisi Tunis.
Tunisia Tunisia.
Turchia Turkey.

Uberto Hubert.
Ucraina Ukraine.
Ugo Hugh.
Ulisse Ulysses.
Umberto Humbert.
Ungheria Hungary.
Urbano Urban.
URSS USSR (Union of Socialist Soviet Republics).

Valentino Valentine.
Valeria Valeria.
Valerio Valerius.
Varsavia Warsaw.
Vaticano Vatican.
Venere Venus.
Veneto Venetia.
Venezia Venice.
Vesuvio Vesuvius.
Vienna Vienna.
Vincenzo Vincent.
Virgilio Virgil.
Virginia Virginia.
Vittoria Victoria.
Vittorio Victor.
Viviana, Viviano Vivian.
Vulcano Vulcan.

Zaccaria Zachary.
Zurigo Zurich.

SIGLE E ABBREVIAZIONI USATE IN ITALIA

A., *alto:* H., high.
A.C., *Automobile Club:* A.A., Automobile Association.
a.C., *avanti Cristo:* B.C. Before Christ.
A.D., *Anno Domini, nell'anno del Signore:* A.D., Anno Domini, (After Christ).
ago., *Agosto:* Aug., August.
A.M., *Aeronautica Militare:* A.F., Air Force.
am., amer., *americano:* Am., American.
anon., *anonimo:* anon., anonymous.
app., *appendice:* app., appendix.
appross., *approssimativo:* approx., approximate.
apr., *aprile:* Apr., April.
A.R., *altezza reale:* R.H., Royal Highness.
ar., *arrivo:* arr., arrival.
ass., *associazione:* ass., association.

b.f., *bassa frequenza:* L.F., low frequency.
boll., *bollettino:* bull., bulletin.
brev., *brevetto:* pat., patent.

C., *centigradi:* cent., centigrade.
c., **1.** *conto:* acc., account **2.** *cubico:* cu., cubic.
ca., **1.** *circa:* a., about **2.** *corrente alternata:* a.c., alternating current.
cad., *cadauno:* ea., each.
Cap., *Capitano:* Capt., captain.
cap., *capitolo:* c., chapter.
capit., *capitolo:* c., chapter.
Capp., *capitoli:* cc., chapters.
Card., *Cardinale:* Card., cardinal.
C/c, *conto corrente:* c/a, current account.
cc., *corrente continua:* dc., direct current.
C.D., *Corpo Diplomatico:* C.D., Corps Diplomatique.
C.E.E.A., *Comunità europea per l'energia atomica:* A.E.C., Atomic Energy Commission.
cent., centg., *centigrado:* cent., centigrade.
Cf., *confronta:* cp., compare.

cm., *centimetro:* cent., centimetre.
c.m., *corrente mese:* inst., instant.
cm.c., *centimetro cubo:* c.c., cubic centimetre.
Col., *colonnello:* col., colonel.
coll., *collegio:* coll., college.
coop., *cooperativa:* coop., co-operative.
C.P., *Casella Postale:* P.O.B., Post Office Box.
C.S., *Corte Suprema:* Sup. Ct., Supreme Court.

D., *dottore:* dr., doctor.
d.C., *dopo Cristo:* A.D., Anno Domini.
dic., *dicembre:* Dec., December.
Dirett., *direttore:* dir., director.
dom., *domenica:* Sun., Sunday.
dott., *dottore:* dr., doctor.
dozz., *dozzina:* doz., dozen.

E, *est:* E, East.
ecc., *eccetera:* etc., and so on.
ed., **1.** *edito:* ed., edited **2.** *edizione:* ed., edition.
Egr., *egregio:* Esq., Esquire.
es., *esempio:* ex., example.

feb., *febbraio:* Feb., February.
fed., *federazione:* fed., federation.
F.lli, *fratelli:* br., bros., brothers.

g., *grammo:* g., gram.
Gen., *generale:* Gen., General.
gen., **1.** *generale:* gen., general **2.** *gennaio:* Jan., January.
giov., *giovedì:* Thur., Thursday.

h., *ora:* h., hour.
H.P., *cavallo vapore:* H.P., horse power.

ibid., *ibidem, nello stesso luogo:* ibid., in the same place.
id., *idem, come sopra:* id., the same.
iun., *iunior, giovane:* jr., junior.

kg., *chilogrammo*: kg., kilogram.
km., *chilometro*: km., kilometre.
kw., *chilowatt*: kw., kilowatt.

l., 1. *latino*: Lat., Latin **2.** *litro*: l., litre.
lat., *latitudine*: lat., latitude.
lib., *libro*: b., book.
long., *longitudine*: long., longitude.
L.st., *Lira sterlina*: L., pound.
lun., *lunedì*: Mon., Monday.

M., *monte*: Mt., mount.
m., 1. *morto*: d., dead **2.** *mese*: m., month **3.** *metro*: m., metre **4.** *minuto*: m., minute.
M.AA.EE., *Ministero degli Affari Esteri*: F.O., Foreign Office.
Magg., *Maggiore*: Maj., Major.
mar., *marzo*: Mar., March.
mart., *martedì*: Tues., Tuesday.
mass., *massimo*: max., maximum.
m.c.d. *minimo comun denominatore*: L.C.D., Lowest Common Denominator.
m.c.m., *minimo comune multiplo*: L.C.M., Least Common Multiple.
M.E.C., *Mercato Comune Europeo*: E.C.M., European Common Market.
mer(c)., *mercoledì*: Wed., Wednesday.
mg., *milligrammo*: mg., milligram.
mm., *millimetro*: mm., millimetre.
M/n., *motonave*: Ms., motorship.
ms., *manoscritto*: ms., manuscript.
mss., *manoscritti*: mss., manuscripts.
Mus., *museo*: mus., museum.

N., 1. *nato*: b., born **2.** *Nord*: N., North **3.** *numero*: N., Number.
nov., *novembre*: Nov., November.
N.U., *Nazioni Unite*: U.N., United Nations.

O., *ovest*: W., West.
on., *onorevole*: hon., honourable.
O.N.U., *Organizzazione Nazioni Unite*: U.N.O., United Nations Organization.
ott., *ottobre*: Oct., October.

P., *padre*: fr., father.
p., *pagina*: p., page.
P.A., *Patto Atlantico*: N.A.T.O.,

North Atlantic Treaty Organization.
paragr., *paragrafo*: par., paragraph.
p.at., *peso atomico*: a.w., atomic weight.
P.C., *Partito Comunista*: C.P., Communist Party.
p.e., *per esempio*: e.g., for example (exempli gratia).
pres., *presidente*: pres., president.
proc., *procuratore*: att., attorney.
prof., *professore*: prof., professor.
P.S., *poscritto*: P.S., postscript.
p.za, *piazza*: sq., square.

Q.G., *Quartier Generale*: G.H., General Headquarters.

ref., *referenze*: ref., reference.
reg., *registro*: reg., register.
Rev., *Reverendo*: rev., Reverend.
R.M., *ricchezza mobile*: PAYE, Pay As You Earn.
R.U., *Regno Unito*: U.K., United Kingdom.

S., 1. *Santo*: St., Saint **2.** *secolo*: cen., century **3.** *società*: co., Company **4.** *Sud*: S., South.
sab., *sabato*: Sat., Saturday.
S.A.R., *Sua Altezza Reale*: H.R.H., His (Her) Royal Highness.
Sc., *scuola*: sch., school.
S.E., *Sua Eccellenza*: H.E., His Excellency.
segg., *seguenti*: fol., following.
segr., *segretario*: sec., secretary.
serg., *sergente*: sergt., sergeant.
sett., *settembre*: Sept., September.
sig., *signore*: Mr., Mister.
sig.na, *signorina*: Miss.
sig.ra, *signora*: Mrs., Mistress.
S.M.B., *Sua Maestà Britannica*: H.B.M., His (Her) Britannic Majesty.
S.O., *Sud Ovest*: S.W., South West.
s.p.a., *società per azioni*: inc., incorporated.
spec., 1. *speciale*: spec., special **2.** *specialmente*: spec., specially.
s.r.l., *società a responsabilità limitata*: ltd., limited (in inglese); corp., corporation (in americano).
S.S., *Sua Santità*: H.H., His Holiness.
S.U., *Stati Uniti*: U.S., United States.

S.U.A., *Stati Uniti d'America*: U.S.A., United States of America.

T., *tonnellata*: t., ton.
T.B.C., *tubercolosi*: T.B., Tuberculosis.
tel., *telefono*: tel. telephone.

U., *unione*: U., Union.
U.P., *Unione postale*: P.U., Postal Union.
U.R.S.S., *Unione Repubbliche So-cialiste Sovietiche*: U.S.S.R., Union of Socialist Soviet Republics.

V., 1. *vaglia*: P.O., Postal Order
    2. *volume*: vol., volume.
v., *verso*: v., verse.
Ven., *Venerabile*: Ven., Venerable.
ven., *venerdì*: Fr., Friday.
vesc., *vescovo*: Bp., Bishop.
v.le, *viale*: Ave., Avenue.
vol., *volume*: vol., volume.
voll., *volumi*: voll., volumes.
vv., *versi*: vv., verses.

Dellone Noote
BALB 3.
Wolverhampton
University